New York State in Fiction (1751-1999)

& New York City in Fiction (1751-1930)

An Annotated Bibliography

by Robert B. Slocum

North Country Books, Inc.
Utica, New York

ISBN-10 1-59531-019-3
ISBN-13 978-1-59531-019-4

Library of Congress Cataloging-in-Publication Data

Slocum, Robert B.
  New York state in fiction (1751-1999) & New York City in fiction (1751-1930) : an
annotated bibliography / by Robert B. Slocum.
      p. cm.
  Includes bibliographical references and index.
  ISBN 978-1-59531-019-4 (alk. paper)
  1. American fiction--Bibliography. 2. New York (State)--In literature--Bibliography. 3.
New York City (N.Y.)--In literature--Bibliography. I. Title.
  Z1231.F4S585 2008
  [PS374.N435]
  016.813009'358747--dc22

                                          2008033123

Published by:

North Country Books, Inc.
220 Lafayette Street
Utica, New York 13502
www.northcountrybooks.com

With assistance from:

Furthermore: a program of the J. M. Kaplan Fund
www.furthermore.org

The Tioga County Historical Society
www.tiogahistory.org

PREFACE

The late Thomas F. O'Donnell had planned to write a comprehensive literary history of New York State but his untimely death in 1980 ended that hope. However, O'Donnell did complete two essays: Literary history of New York, 1650-1958, and Oneida County: Literary highlights, which were published in Upstate Literature; Essays in Memory of Thomas F. O'Donnell (Syracuse University Press, 1985); and O'Donnell's doctoral dissertation at Syracuse University in 1957: The Regional Fiction of Upstate New York. O'Donnell further contributed various pieces on such New York State authors as James Kirke Paulding, Frances Miriam Whitcher and Harold Frederic (also co-authoring with Hoyt C. Franchere a critical monograph on Frederic's work). No other scholar, as far as one can discern, has taken on or contemplated a full-scale history of the State's creative literature. Perhaps the present annotated bibliography, confined though it is to fiction, can serve as a starting point and incidentally serve as a contribution to New York State's cultural history.

The role of place in literature has been commented upon by a number of observers. In his classical American Studies D.H. Lawrence stated that "every people is polarized in some particular locality which is home, the homeland. ...The spirit of place is a great reality." Leonard Lutwack said: "The most elementary orientation of a reader to a narrative text is through the evocation of place. Setting is immediately positive and reassuring until action and characters are gradually unfolded." (The Role of Place in Literature. Syracuse University Press, 1984). Some critics insist that placelessness has been more prominent, especially in 20th century fiction, which often features protagonists who are misplaced or desperate people with little affinity for the place in which they happen to be or from whence they came. The characters in the novels, plays and narrative poetry of the 19th century seem more generally aware of their roots and environment.

Whatever one's 'take' on the above, it is the contention in the work at hand that setting or place is still important to the framework of most novels, short stories, etc. Regional writing has not vanished; local manners and customs, social perceptions, speech patterns, folklore and history continue to be used very effectively by many creative writers. Those who work in the mystery/detective genre often utilize backdrops of actual places because the latter impart a sense of reality for the reader familiar with those locales.

New York State and its major city have been fertile fields for the imaginations of a host of writers of fiction, both those native to the region and 'foreigners.' Consider the many important historical events and movements that originated in the 'Empire State': the Iroquois Confederacy, major campaigns of the French and Indian War and the American Revolution, the Anti-rent 'Wars' and the Dutch patroons, the Erie Canal, the Seneca Falls Convention on Women's Rights, the Chautauqua movement, the Oneida Community, the beginnings of Mormonism, the Millerites, spiritualism, the 'Burned-over District', Black Friday, etc. The importance of New York City as a particular place in fiction "is underscored by the large number of works about young men and women who come there in search of wealth or fame, by the many novels written about particular groups of New Yorkers whose lifestyles are shaped by the environment in which they have been born and raised." (Zlotnick, Joan. Portrait of an American City; the Novelists' New York. Port Washington, N.Y., 1982).

Then consider New York State's landscape, its physical features; they have long stirred the artistry of painters and writers: the Hudson River and Valley; the Catskills; the Adirondacks; Niagara Falls and the Frontier; the Finger Lakes; the Thousand Islands and the St. Lawrence Seaway; Chautauqua and the Allegheny Plateau; the Mohawk, Susquehanna, Chenango and Genesee Valleys; Lakes George, Champlain, Oneida, Ontario and Erie, etc.

The use of the terms 'Upstate' and 'Downstate' New York in the title requires an explanation. 'Upstate' to historian David M. Ellis and writer Carl Carmer denoted any area of the State outside the boundaries of New York City. There is no room for 'Downstate' if you accept this nearly all-inclusive definition. Nevertheless in this annotated bibliography 'Downstate' is a category that includes Long Island and New York City as well as several southeastern counties: Westchester, Putnam, Rockland, and Orange.

The survey of fiction in the Introduction is broken down by the following 'regions'—Long Island, New York City, Hudson Valley, Capital-Saratoga region, the Adirondacks (and the adjoining North Country, Thousand Islands and St. Lawrence Seaway), the Catskills and southeastern New York counties, Leatherstocking country, the Finger Lakes and the Genesee Valley, and Western New York (including the Niagara Frontier and the Chautauqua-Allegheny region).

The main body of the bibliography contains ca. 3,820 annotated entries arranged alphabetically by author or by title in the case of anonymous works—a fairly comprehensive listing to be sure, but admittedly an incomplete one. Since the numeration ends at 3,780 an explanation is in order. Originally 1998 was the closing date for the bibliography, but as time went by the opportunity to add works published in 1999 presented itself, thus closing out the 20th century. This was done by inserting those works using an 'a' after the numerals—e.g., 240a, 1050a, 2012a, 3231a, etc. Cross references are interfiled; authors are entered under the name with which they most often sign their works. Surnames beginning with 'Mac' or Mc' are separated alphabetically, while surnames like 'De Koven' and 'De Leon' precede 'Dean' or 'DeAndrea.' The entries are indexed by place, subject and title. The annotations are derived from the compiler's own notes, contemporary reviews in periodicals and critical monographs on individual authors.

Adult novels, collections of short stories and long narrative poems are the main components of the bibliography. Fiction for 'young adults' (i.e. young people in their early or later 'teens') by such writers as: Horatio Alger, Jr., Joseph Altsheler, Erick Berry, Herbert Best, Amy Ella Blanchard, John Brick, Alice Turner Curtis, M.E. Kerr, Thomas M. Longstreth, James Otis, William O. Stoddard, Everett Tomlinson and Susan Warner—are included (especially when they have historical backgrounds). Fiction with a New York City setting is covered only up to 1930; that cut-off date was selected because it was decided that the inclusion of the hundreds of fiction titles about the City published after 1930 would have made for too voluminous a work that is already quite extensive.

One has to turn to two novels published in England for very early (if not the earliest) appearances in fiction of references to New York (State and City). In 1751 The Life of Harriot Stuart, by Charlotte Lennox, included descriptions of the Hudson River, Albany, the Mohawk Valley and New York City (see also her Euphemia [London,1790]). John Shebbeare's Lydia; or, Filial Piety (1755) in its first forty pages portrays the Onondaga and Cayuga Indians and two of their chiefs. Michel René Hilliard d'Auberteuil's Mis McRae (1784) was an historical novel based on the murder of Jane McRae by Indian allies of General Burgoyne. The Liberal American (1785) was an epistolary novel published in London that was in part laid in New York City. It was not until 1789 that the first genuinely American novel appeared, William Hill Brown's The Power of Sympathy. The reading of novels was shunned by many of our colonial and post-Revolutionary ancestors as trivial and even dangerous. A pious pamphleteer of the early 19th century declared: "Avoid the perusal of novels. It is impossible to read them without injury." British and French fiction was the recourse of those who sought the pleasures to be derived from the reading of novels.

Susanna Rowson's Charlotte; a Tale of Truth (1791) went through many American editions under the title: Charlotte Temple, and is one of the first novels to have a New York City setting (in part) during the American Revolution. Two American imprints: The History of Maria Kittle (Hartford, 1797) by Ann Eliza Schuyler Bleecker, and The Fortunate Discovery; or, The History of Henry Villars (New York, 1798), are the last of their kind published in the 18th century that have New York State settings.

Although not listed in the present bibliography two novels published in London bear mention: The School for Fathers; or, The Victim of a Curse...(1788) and Charlotte Turner Smith's The Wanderings of Warwick (1794). In the first-named work the Dennison family flee for their lives from Maine's Penobscot region to colonial Albany and New York City and thence to England; in the second the hero is a British soldier in the American Revolution who serves in Philadelphia, New York City, Stony Point and the West Indies.

In 1807 Mrs. P.D. Manvill (a pseudonym?) authored Lucinda; or, The Mountain Mourner, an epistolary novel of seduction and betrayal with scenes in a number of towns of central and eastern New York State. It was closely followed in 1809 by Washington Irving's A History of New York, a satirical account of the Dutch and British rulers of the colonial city as told by a fictional character, Diedrich Knickerbocker. A leap forward to 1819 and Irving's two classic tales of Rip Van Winkle and Ichabod Crane (The Legend of Sleepy Hollow) appeared in his Sketch Book of Geoffrey Crayon, gent. A glance at the chronology that follows the survey will show a steady progression of titles published from 1821, with James Fenimore Cooper's The Spy, to the end of the century.

In an earlier work: New England in Fiction, 1787-1990; an Annotated Bibliography (West Cornwall, CT, Locust Hill Press, 1994) it was stated that "creative writers, especially novelists, have as much [if not more] to tell us about the way we were and the way we are as the historian, the social scientist, the anthropologist and others who research statistical records and contemporary documents" (v. 1, p. ix). Adam Garfinkle in his review of Robert D. Kaplan's The Coming Anarchy; Shattering the Dreams of the Post Cold War (New York times book review, March 19, 2000) says: "Kaplan realizes that much of the wisdom lies not in books of philosophy, history and memoirs, but in fiction." Kaplan writes in his essay in the above publication entitled 'Conrad's Nostromo and the Third World': "Literature may be the only salvation of the policy elite, because in the guise of fiction a writer can more easily tell the truth."

One may be unable to claim any lasting literary significance for most of the works mentioned in this bibliography, but social and cultural historians (especially those concerned with New York State and City) will likely find them an invaluable resource.

INTRODUCTION

A Brief Survey of New York State in Fiction by Region

LONG ISLAND

The fiction about this 'appendage' to the great city west of it is sizable, ca. 350 titles in the present bibliography;over half thesetitles fall into the category of crime/ mystery/detective novels. If that seems unusual perhaps Long Island's proximity to and close association with New York City and its denizens as well as a certain, sometimes morbid, fascination with the Island's wealthy, part-time and permanent residents and their lifestyles, the country-club culture, fashionable and not-so-fashionable beaches and resorts, the sporting life (horseracing, polo, etc.) and the rapid urbanization of the western end of the Island may offer a partial explanation. Generally 'Long Island fiction' with certain exceptions (Fitzgerald's The Great Gatsby for one) is not too memorable. If it often 'embroiders the commonplace' (Nabokov) that holds true for most fiction.

Garrett Furman's Redfield; a Long Island Tale of the Seventeenth Century (1825) has for its hero a shipwrecked sailor (Redfield) rescued by Long Island Indians (the 'Mattowacs'); whatever the sources the author draws upon, he does yield us a picture of the way of life of these little-known natives. Rockaway Beach is the primary setting for Eliza Leslie's Althea Vernon, one of two novellas (the other is Henrietta Harrison) published in one volume in 1838. Two stories ('potboilers') of the American Revolution on Long Island and Long Island Sound issued respectively in 1843 and 1847 are: John Henry Mancur's Christina and Charles F. Sterling's Buff and Blue. The Legends of Montauk (1849) by Jared Augustus Ayres is in part a narrative poem; the Indians of the region and the spirits that inhabit its ocean waters are the subjects of the work. Sea-Spray, a Long Island Village (1857) by Cornelia Huntington is a good-sized novel whose main characters are survivors of a shipwreck and an English clergyman and his daughter settling in the peculiarly-named village. Nearly 25 years elapsed before further fiction with a Long Island setting emerged; the last two decades of the 19th century produced some 17 works, from William Osborn Stoddard's Juvenile, Deb Kinzer (1881) to Mary Breck Sleight's An Island Heroine (1898). In between appeared Helen Stuart

Campbell's Under Green Apple Boughs (1882); Louise Clarkson's The Shadow of John Wallace (1884); Julian Warth's The Full Stature of a Man (1886) and Dorothy Thorn of Thornton (1887); John Treat Irving's The Van Gelder Papers (1887); John Elliott Curran's Miss Frances Merley (1888); Edward Richard Shaw's The Pot of Gold (1888) and Legends of Fire Island and the South Side (1895); Anne Reeve Aldrich's The Feet of Love (1890); Elizabeth Williams Champney's Witch Winnie at Shinnecock (1894); Julien Gordon's Eat Not Thy Heart (1897); etc.

The early years of the 20th century saw the publication of several novels that pique one's interest. The heroine of Louis Forsslund's The Story of Sarah (1901) is a young woman who clings to many of the customs of the original Dutch and English settlers of the Great South Bay region; Forsslund's the Ship of Dreams (1902) is a romantic, rural idyl that takes place in the hamlet of 'Meadowneck.' Two novels: Ferdinand Wiechmann's Maid of Montauk (1902) and Lydia A. Jocelyn's Lords of the Soil (1905) hark back to Long Island's colonial years with the Island's Montauk Indians playing a major role in the lives of the English and Dutch settlers. Crow-Step (1910) by Georgia Fraser, is the name given to an old stone house on Long Island inhabited by the master and his two daughters; he still holds fierce resentment against the British who used his house as a military redoubt during the Revolution. Chauncey Crafts Hotchkiss's Maude Baxter (1911) transpires during the American Revolution; the hero tries to reclaim his Long Island home from a possessive cousin and prevent the marriage of his fiancée to an Englishman. A Long Island fishing village is the scene of a story (Red of Surley [1919]) by Clarence Aaron Robbins about two friends, one a wealthy cripple who turns to philanthropy when he fails as a writer, the other a fisherman's son who follows in his father's footsteps when he too finds no appreciative audience for the poems he has composed. Under the pseudonym Warner Fabian, Samuel Hopkins Adams in Flaming Youth (1923) and Sailors' Wives (1924) created social life in a seaside resort town, 'Dorrisdale'. Charles Hanson Towne served on the staff of the magazine Smart Set, and also penned a novel about Long Island's 'smart set'—The Gay Ones (1924). Screenwriter Charles Brackett in his Week-end (1925) throws a neophytic writer into the company of intellectuals or pseudo-intellectuals partying on Long Island. The major work of the period is F. Scott Fitzgerald's The Great Gatsby (1925), a rather grim picture of wealthy society on Long Island and New York City. Arthur Stringer's The Wolf Woman (1928) is a diverting piece of fluff about a backwoods girl who upsets in a constructive way a wealthy Long Island family. Love affairs and martial problems among the upper echelons of Long Island society are featured in four novels: Margaret Culkin Bannings' Prelude to Love (1930); Laura Lou Brookman's Rash Romance (1930); Wallace Irwin's North Shore (1932); and Elizabeth Daly's High Goal (1934). The effects of the Great Depression on families and individuals are set forth in Dorothy Blake's The Diary of a Suburban Housewife (1936), Gerald Breckenridge's The Besieged (1937) and screenwriter Frances Marion's Molly, Bless Her (1937). Two consecutive, connected novels by George Frederick Hummel—Heritage (1935) and Tradition (1936)—form a family chronicle with the fictional village of 'Norwold' at its center.

A suburban Long Island family, the middle-class Crocketts, faces the problems brought on by World War II in Ward Green's What They Don't Know (1944) and the strains of a marriage between the Irish Catholic Reardons—their daughter Veronica— and the scion of the Protestant upper class Stairs, are treated by Ellen Mackay Berlin (Mrs. Irving Berlin) in Lace Curtain (1948). In Esther Penny Butchers' Manowen (1951), an orphan, Owen Gwynedd, shortly after the Civil War ends, leaves Tidewater Virginia for his uncle's home on an island off the coast of Long Island, establishing friendships with a half-breed Montauk Indian and a girl named Ysel. Lady Caroline Brace, an American-born widow, comes back to the Long Island of her youth to sort out her problems in Nancy Wilson Ross's The Return of Lady Brace (1957).

The pre-colonial history of Long Island is fictionalized in Robert Carse's Winter of the Whale (1961); in their search for food the Manhanset Indians collide with their deadly enemies, the Pequots. The Battle of Long Island (1776) is the defining element of James Forman's The Cow Neck Rebels (1969). Geraldine Trotta's Dune House, Ann Aikman's The Other, William Murray's The Self-starting Wheel, and Mary Natalie Tabak's But Not for Love, are a quartet of novels dealing with summer visitors, resorts and art colonies on Long Island, all published in 1960. Two families, one Jewish, the other Unitarian-Anglo/American, are persecuted by a Long Island community for their liberal beliefs in Laura Z. Hobson's First Papers (1964). William McGivern's novel, Savage Streets (1961), depicts juvenile delinquency in 'Riverdale', a Long Island suburb.

Fire Island is the setting of two novels by Burt Hirschfeld—Fire Island (1970) and Return to Fire Island (1984). The same characters appear in both stories; they are on the whole an unhappy group of people, cynical and insecure, with a veneer of sophistication. Peter Benchley's Jaws (1974), about a fearsome shark off the Island's beaches, became a sensational best seller. The manifold dilemmas of adolescence are treated in Don Bredes' Hard Feelings (1977) and M.E. Kerr's Gentlehands (1978), What I Really Think of You (1982) and Him She Loves? (1984). Many of the components of gothic fiction—haunted houses, family secrets, old curses, traumatized heroines, ghosts––are embedded in the stories of Velda Johnston (five novels issued from 1970 to 1991), Robert Marasco's Burnt Offerings (1973), and the popular, widely-read Phyllis Whitney's The Golden Unicorn (1976) and Rainsong (1984). Perhaps the mantle as prime recorder of the lives of lower middle class life on Long Island should be awarded to Alice Hoffman with her The Drowning Season (1979), Angel Landing (1980) and Seventh Heaven (1990).

Wilfrid Sheed's The Boys of Winter (1987) analyzes the writing and editing 'fraternity' that has taken up permanent residence in Long Island's Hamptons; its members have little respect for summer sojourners but themselves are barely tolerated by the natives. In Cold Spring Harbor (1986) Richard Yates concentrates on longtime residents of a town on the North Shore whose lives take disappointing turns. In four novels published from 1982 to 1998 Eric Kraft records the amusing experiences and recollections of Peter Leroy, owner with his wife of an unprosperous hotel on 'Small's Island', close by Peter's hometown of 'Babington.' The daughter of controversial Anne Hutchinson is taken captive by the Lenape Indians in 1643 after the rest of the family is massacred in Katherine Kilpatrick's Trouble's Daughter (1998). Going to Patchogue (1992) is a stream-of-consciousness novel by Thomas McGonigle in which the writer himself returns to the scenes of his youth. The teenage culture of Long Island has received increasing attention from various writers in recent years as these novels from the 1990s indicate: Shelter for a Seabird (1990) by Terry Farish; Soul Catcher (1990) by Katie Spiegelman; Love Invents Us (1996) by Amy Bloom; and Tomorrow Wendy (1998) by Shelley Stoehr.

The large category of crime/mystery/detective fiction with Long Island settings mentioned earlier begins with the pioneer female detective story writer Anna Katharine Green's Cynthia Wakeham's Money (1892) in which a New York lawyer goes to 'Flatbush' on the Island to make the will of Cynthia Wakeham and incidentally search for her heirs. Arthur Benjamin Reeves invented 'scientific detective' Craig Kennedy, and one of Kennedy's destinations is 'Hampton Hall', Southampton, where he actually tries to solve a murder by using horoscopes (X-rays prove much more useful) in Reeves' The Stars Scream Murder (1915). Beginning with The Curved Blade (1916) and concluding with Crime Tears On (1939) the glib but astonishingly productive Carolyn Wells (over 20 mystery novels among her 170 works) is responsible for ten stories (half of them starring the detective Fleming Stone) with posh Long Island estates as the scenes of lethal goings-on. In 1922 Isabel Egenton Ostrander published two novels— Above Suspicion and The Tattooed Arm—in the first a local carpenter and mason is the person who solves a murder in a little Long Island town; in the second professional detectives are called to the town of 'Brooklea' to fathom the odd behavior of three elderly gentlemen. Frances Noyes Hart's The Bellamy Trial (1927) found many readers who were intrigued by the legal proceedings of the trial and the surprising ending of the story after the trial's conclusion. Lee Thayer, Cortland Fitzsimmons and Elizabeth Sanxay Holding, writers of the 1930s and 1940s, are as likely to leave the solution of mayhem in the hands of amateurs as they are in those of private investigators. Lionel White's 1950s novels deal with such topics as a racetrack robbery in Jamaica, Long Island, a kidnapping, a harried insurance actuary, and a man too much in his cups accused of a suburban homicide. Shooting the gap of the 1960s to the 1970s through the 1990s one comes across the well-plotted mystery and crime fiction of Berton Roueché, David Delman, Clarissa Watson, Susan Isaacs, Michael T. Hinkemeyer, John Westermann, Nelson DeMille and James Brady. Isaacs is especially mordant and amusing as she catalogs the pretensions and quirks of Long Island's mixed population and its encounters with homicide.

NEW YORK CITY

1751-1830—Charlotte Lennox's The Life of Harriot Stuart (1751) and Euphemia (1790), both published in London, have heroines who spend some time in New York City, but also in the Upper Hudson region and the Mohawk Valley. The anonymous The Liberal American (an epistolary novel published in London in 1785) removes a young Englishwoman from her native land to marriage in New York City. Susanna Rowson's residency in America from 1767 to 1778 resulted in her Charlotte; a Tale of the Truth (1791), better known by another title: Charlotte Temple. The heroine of this extremely popular novel is seduced and impregnated and abandoned in New York City during the American Revolution. The scene of another anonymous novel, The Fortunate Discovery; or, The History of Henry Villars (1798) is only in part New York City. It is 1809 before the City becomes the sole center of attention with descriptions of some of its major landmarks in Washington Irving's A History of New York, a satirical fictional narrative. In 1825 James Ahearn Jones, under the pseudonym, Captain Matthew Murgatroyd, released The Refugee, a novel that has been deemed the first fictional account of New York City during the early years of the American Revolution. In the same year John Neal's discursive three-volume Brother Jonathan appeared; its hero, New Englander Walter Harwood, experiences the underside of life in New York as the Revolution rumbles on.

1831-1865—Among the novels that appeared in the 1830s are: Oran, the Outcast; or, A Season in New York (1833), an anonymous work in which the hero is saved from a murder conviction by the strange Oran, son of the slave mistress of General Hezekiah Olmsted; The Kentuckian in New York; or, The Adventures of Three Southerners (1834) by William Alexander Caruthers; Asa Greene's The Perils of Pearl Street (1834), wherein an honest young man from Upstate New York discovers he is no match for the conniving businessmen of the big city; Thirty Years Ago (1836) by the dramatist and theater historian William Dunlap, a 'temperance novel'; Catharine Maria Sedgwick's The Linwoods (1836), a story of tensions engendered by the American Revolution, and her The Poor Rich Man and the Rich Poor Man (1836), contrasting the charitable but poor and the selfish rich in New York; James Fenimore Cooper's Home as Found (1838), critical of American manners; and Theodore Sedgwick Fay's Norman Leslie (1835) and Sidney Clifton (1839), both of which are divided between New York and Europe.

From 1840 to the end of the Civil War novels that vied for the reading public's attention, many of which the modern reader would find hard to digest, were: three short works by Thomas Low Nichols—Ellen Ramsay (1843) in which a country boy is fleeced by the confidence men and women, gamblers, et al. of New York and finally goes back to his New Hampshire girl, Ellen Ramsay; The Lady in Black; a Study of New York Life, Morals and Manners (1844); and Raffle for a Wife (1845) wherein five men-about-New York Town gamble for the favor of a beautiful young woman but lose her to a farmer/artist; John Treat Irving's The Quod Correspondence (1842), a story of murder and forgery; Cornelius Mathews' The Career of Puffer Hopkins (1842), the course of an ambitious young politician (supposedly an orphan) in New York City; Epes Sargent's only novel, Fleetwood (1845), an overly sentimental work that has the hero befriending a young woman who carries the burden of illegitimacy; The Cousins (1845) and Two Lives (1846), two maudlin, didactic novels by Maria Jane McIntosh whose young heroines, educated in New York City private schools, cope with economic, marital and physical health issues. Anna Cora Mowatt who had a triumph with the play Fashion, or Life in New York (1845), preceded and followed it with two novels, The Fortune Hunter (1844) and Evelyn; or, A Heart Unmasked (1845), both about the rich, the struggling poor and the would-be-rich of New York. Rambleton; a Romance of Fashionable Life in New York During the Great Speculation of 1836 (1844) by Charles Sealsfield, is possibly an abridged translation of his Deutsch-amerikanischen Wahlverwandschaften (1839/40). A triad of melodramatic works by George Lippard, are about people, in the main New Yorkers, vying, sometimes viciously, for inheritances or particular advantages——The Empire City (1850), The Midnight Queen (1853) and New York, Its Upper Ten and Lower Million (1853). An obscure writer, George Thompson, was the author (sometimes under the pseudonym 'Greenhorn') of five novels that scrutinized aspects of criminality in the expanding metropolis——The House Breaker (1848), City Crimes (1849), The Brazen Star (1853), The Locket (1855) and The Gay Girls of New York (1858). Robert Hare's Standish the Puritan (1850) is a tale of the American Revolution with British-occupied New York City the place where much of the action occurs; The Potiphar Papers (1853) by George William Curtis were satirical pieces on New York's high society as exemplified in social leader Mrs. Potiphar; Curtis's novel Trumps (1861) is in much the same vein. Herman Melville's Pierre (1852) is set in large part in the Berkshires of western Massachusetts, but the novel's most striking episodes and its climax occur in New York City. The Newsboy (1854) of Elizabeth Oakes Smith paints a shocking picture of the harsh conditions endured by these often orphaned boys selling newspapers on the streets of the city. Solon Robinson's Hot Corn (1854) proffers fictional vignettes of female vendors of hot corn and dressmakers in uncaring mid-19th century New York. The best-selling Ann Sophia Stephens' Fashion and Famine (1854)——the title refers to the fashionable rich and the desperately poor of the City——is intrinsically the story of a manipulative and brutish husband and his estranged, selfish wife. Under the pseudonym, Jonathan Slick, Ms. Stephens created a character (Slick) in High Life in New York (1854), a country bumpkin who conquers the sohisticates of New York despite his frequently voiced criticisms of the pretensions and hypocrisies of the City's social arbiters, yet he is finally forced to leave the City after being 'conned' out of his worldly goods by a slippery couple. Identified in the National Union Catalog by the appellation 'novelist', Henry Edwards in four works portrays young women faced with the prospect of prostitution (they either reject, are forced into it or choose it for purposes of revenge)——Annie; a New York Life (186-?), Fashion and Famine (186-?), not to be confused with Ann Sophia Stephen's' novel with the same title, The Poor of New York (1865) and The Belle of Central Park (1866?). The chief character in Theodore Winthrop's Cecil Dreame (1861) is a much put-upon artist in New York whose real identity comes as a surprise. Allibone's A Critical Dictionary of English Literature ... is one of the few reference works that gives any space to Azel Stevens Roe, citing him as "one of the most popular of modern novelists." The Boston-born New York critic H.T. Tuckerman called Roe "a sort of Long Island Goldsmith... the author of so many unexceptional and detailed stories of domestic life." According to The Critic (London) "Mr. Roe is one of the most successful American writers. He has originality of thought and natural powers of invention." Three of his novels——How Could He Help It? (1860), Like and Unlike (1862) and Looking Around (1865)—— exhibit a penchant for young men of unsullied character who rise in business and love despite obstacles that circumstances or jealous rivals throw in their way. Out in the World (1864) by Timothy Shay Arthur is one of his four novels here that has New York at its center, a rather disarming story different from his usual moralistic, didactic tales, recounting the tragedy of a 'New York marriage' where neither husband nor wife is willing to compromise. Richard Burleigh Kimball, ready for matriculation at Dartmouth when he was only eleven (he entered at thirteen) became a lawyer and banker/financier; from 1850 to 1892 he turned out a number of novels; four of them——Undercurrents of Wall Street (1862), Was He Successful? (1864), Henry Powers (Banker) [1868] and To-day, a Romance (1870)——deal with the search for financial security in New York City from the 1840s to the 1850s. In John Godfrey's Fortune (1865) Bayard Taylor delivered a credible account of New York's literary life in the 1850s as the novel traces its protagonist's efforts to find success as a litterateur.

These years also saw the proliferation of sensational fiction that foreshadowed the dime novels of Beadle and Adams. Three practitioners of such stories and tales were the three B's: the 'rascal' Ned Buntline, Charles Burdett and Osgood Bradbury. They purported to expose the evils of New York City in a manner calculated to excite their readers. Buntline's the Mysteries and Miseries of New York (1848), The B'hoys of New York (1850) and the G'hals of New York (1850) were in a sense, interconnected sociological if trashy tracts that were widely read. Burdett and Bradbury, of whom we know very little, wrote, respectively, nine and eight novels (from ca. 1840 to 1865) that most often depicted the dangers young women sucked into the metropolitan maelstrom faced. Joseph Holt Ingraham, a clergyman among other occupations, and probably a cut above the preceding, is represented by seven historical novels (published from 1839 to 1855) encompassing New York's past and 'present.'

1866-1900——Robert Henry Newell ('Orpheus C. Kerr') in his novel, Avery Glibun (1867), fused several fictional genera: the picaresque, gothic, satirical, etc. with a hero adventuring in New York's underworld, commercial offices and literary and bohemian circles as he strives to reach manhood; Newell's hero in The Walking Doll (1872) is on his own in New York, being told by his stepmother to leave his father's house. Horatio Alger, Jr. has dubious status in the history of American literature; he is not mentioned in Vernon Louis Parrington's Main Currents in American Thought (1927-1930). Still one cannot ignore the influence of his books about the rise to material success of New York newsboys, bootblacks, store clerks, et al. With his Helen Ford (1866) and Ragged Dick (1867) Alger was well on his way for the next thirty-odd years to phenomenal sales of his books (ca. 199 titles); twenty-five novels set in New York City are listed in the present bibliography. Julia McNair Wright penned 'sociological fiction' in which "fallen women survive, widows become independent, spoiled melancholic women are treated with psychological sensitivity and perception" (American Women Writers) as evidenced in The New York Needle-Woman (1868), The New York Bible-Woman (1869), Mr. Grosvenor's Daughter (1893), A New Samaritan (1895) and other works. Margaret Lee's male characters run the gamut from sensitive, concerned individuals to wasteful, conceited and occasionally brutal fellows in her Dr. Wilmer's Love (1868), Lorimer and Wife (1881), Divorce (1882) and A Brooklyn Bachelor (1890). Long forgotten "Edgar Fawcett, though not a very great writer, was the multiple man of his time, the representative man in the twilight of the century. He was a writer of romance during the decline of the romantic novel and a realistic writer upon the emergence of literary realism; he was a naturalist when novels were shaped by a current of deterministic thought and an agnostic in an age of skepticism" (Harrison, S.R. Edgar Fawcett).

The twenty-one novels listed in this bibliography begin with Fawcett's Purple and Fine Linen (1873) and end with The Vulgarian (1903); they examine in a mildly critical way upscale New York society. What Can She Do? (1873) was E.P. Roe's second novel, following upon the best-selling Barriers Burned Away (1872), but it was Roe's third novel, Opening a Chestnut Burr (1874) that impelled him to leave the ministry and become a full-time novelist when that book received good notices. The novel charts the journey of embittered, swindled New York businessman Walter Gregory from deep depression to renewed faith and love. Roe presages our concern with drug addiction in Without a Home (1881)——a wealthy New York merchant loses his money and his daughters are exploited by uncaring employers when he turns to opium to relieve physical pain.

The poet Joaquin Miller's strange polemic novel, The Destruction of Gotham (1886) paints a dire picture of the gutting of New York City by fire and the mobs of the ignored, revenge-seeking poor. Anna Katharine Green's The Leavenworth Case (1878) has been adduced as the first detective novel written by an American woman; in it the millionaire Horatio Leavenworth is murdered in his Fifth Avenue residence and Ebenezer Gryce of the New York Police Department is assigned to the case——Gryce appears in several of Green's novels. She completed ten mysteries with New York City as the arena of action from 1878 to 1900, and from 1901 to 1917 nine more with the same setting. In Ellen Warner, Olney Kirk's early promise was not lived up to; she did have a clever style and definitive ability to capture characters through their conversations" but ultimately she "became less controlled, the repetition of plots more tedious, and powers of observation less acute" (American Women Writers). Of the eight novels by Kirk that appeared between 1878 and 1907 the best are: The Story of Margaret Kent (1886)——a woman with a long absent husband and one child finds a niche for herself in certain social and literary coteries; and Queen Money (1888), a jaundiced look at the demeaning influence of the frantic quest for financial security on the city's artistic, literary and social 'lions.' Robert Grant's 'Boston' novels are perhaps superior to the four he wrote with a New York City and upper class milieu: The Confessions of a Frivolous Girl (1880), An Average Man (1884), Mrs. Harold Stagg (1890) and Unleavened Bread (1900). Much of Constance Cary Harrison's writing is superficial and 'soapy', but several of the novels she completed from 1881 to 1911 do have a satiric bite, poking fun, e.g., at the Anglophilism and other enthusiasms of New

York society. Henry James's Washington Square (1881) requires little comment here; this work by the 'master' has become even better known through the dramatization, The Heiress (1947), by Ruth and Augustus Goetz. Although he was a better short story writer than a novelist, Henry Cuyler Bunner did try his hand at the long form with A Woman of Honor (1883), The Midge (1886) and The Story of a New York House (1887). Three short story collections by Bunner——Short Sixes (1891), Jersey Street and Jersey Lane (1896) and Love in Old Clothes and Other Stories (1896) have settings in New York City, its suburbs and Long Island.

Scholarly Hjalmar Boyesen turned to the writing of fiction late in his brief life. His A Daughter of the Philistines (1883), The Mammon of Unrighteousness (1891), The Golden Calf (1892) and Social Struggles (1893) are dominated by outsiders coming to New York in search of social, literary or financial success. Henry Adams' Esther (1884), the second of his two novels (Democracy [1880] was the first), drew a heroine as artist in New York with a wide range of opinions who cannot accept her fiancé's views——he is an Episcopal pastor.

Nathaniel Hawthorne's son Julian had a long career as an 'adequate' writer of fiction, biography, juvenilia, etc., yet he received little critical attention. From 1884 to 1893 he dashed off eleven novels, serious pictures of New York society, finance and politics, a large share of them, however, being detective stories featuring the policeman Inspector Byrnes. Jewish-American life in New York City was the province of Henry Henry Harland ('Sidney Luska'). When he resided in America the phrase 'dated sensationalism' has been applied to Harland, perhaps unfairly, for As It Was Written (1885), Mrs. Peixada (1886), The Yoke of the Thorah (1887), My Uncle Florimond (1888) and Grandison Mather (1889) can still sustain the interest of the venturesome modern reader.

Besides writing a number of books on drama and the theater and then accepting a professorship at Columbia University Brander Matthews began writing novels and short stories with New York City as their stage, e.g.: The Last Meeting (1885), Tom Paulding (1892), Vignettes of Manhattan (1894), A Confident Tomorrow (1900), a highlight, and Vistas of New York (1900). Amelia E.H. Barr's nine historical novels of New York City (published 1886 to 1911) from the colonial period to Andrew Jackson's second presidential term are sentimental, romantic, of little depth, yet the author researched their backgrounds quite thoroughly and they retain a high degree of historical accuracy.

The upper strata of New York Society is the target of nine of Edgar Saltus's sophisticated and erotic (for their time) novels; six of them (beginning with Mr. Incoul's Misadventure [1887]) were issued before the turn of the century and three of them from 1905 to The Paliser Case in 1919. William Cadwalader Hudson's metier was murder and mystery in the metropolis and he constructed seven novels around them, Vivier, of Vivier, Longman and Company (1890) the most complex.One of his last works, J.F. Dunbar; a Story of Wall Street (1906) diverged, taking on the problems accompanying stock manipulation and speculation. Catholic Christianity and its practice as they relate to the social and economic tensions among the Irish in the State's major city are the keys to the little known novels of Maurice Francis Egan.

Julien Gordon is the pen name of Julie Grinnell Chance (she died in 1920); her novels——A Puritan Pagan (1891), Vampires (1891), Marionettes (1892), Poppaea (1894), Eat Not Thy Heart (1897)——portray women, some sophisticated, some clueless, navigating the shoals of New York society. And young women face various moral choices and the need to find suitable employment in the colorless stories of Lucy Cecil White Lilllie. The orator and controversialist Ignatius Donnelly's Caesar's Column (1890), a semi-utopian, futuristic novel, reports on the state of civilization in 1988/89; New York City has increased in population to ten million souls and technology and science have outstripped social and ethical development.

The expatriate Francis Marion Crawford used the wide world (especially Italy) as the canvas for his fiction. In one spurt, from 1892 to 1895, he delineated the upper class social scene of New York City in the four novels: The Three Fates, Marion Darche, Katharine Lauderdale and The Halstons. Bernardino Giambelli wrote in his native tongue of Italian emigrants in the lower depths of New York City, notably in I Misteri di Mulberry (1893). Women who are able to see their way through difficult social situations are the heroines of Mary Harriott Norris's Afterward (1892), John Applegate, Surgeon (1893) and The Grey House of the Quarries (1898). Slum conditions leading to the prevalence of crippling childhood diseases, the crowded illness-breeding tenements of the working poor, addiction to alcohol and other drugs and the accompanying violence——these were most effectively addressed by the reformer Jacob Riis in his non-fiction writings but also in his sketches and stories, Out of Mulberry Street (1898) and Children of the Tenements (1903).

The protagonists in Richard Henry Savage's melodramatic novels——Delilah of Harlem (1893), A Daughter of Judas (1894), Checked Through, Missing Trunk no. 17580 (1890), In the Swim (1898) and The Midnight Passenger (1900)——range from women at risk to 'con' artists and men climbing politically and financially regardless of consequences. Charles Dudley Warner's trilogy——A Little Journey in the World (1889), The Golden House (1895) and That Fortune (1899)——"satirized the era to which The Gilded Age had given popular name" (Benet's Encyclopedia of American Literature). Ella Wheeler Wilcox's two novels, A Double Life (1891) and Sweet Danger (1892) reflect her interest in marital problems, although the main plot of the first work concerns a man living in New York City under a pseudonym who eventually has to pay for an indiscretion he committed in another city. Newspaperman and war correspondent Richard Harding Davis was an accomplished storyteller; two of his collections of short stories are New York City oriented: Gallegher and other Stories (1891) and Van Bibber and Others (1892).

The Honorable Peter Stirling ... (1894) of Paul Leicester Ford presents a politician determined to right the many wrongs visited upon the citizens of New York in an age when corruption was so pervasive. Ford's other works with a New York setting are generally minor pieces with the exception of The Story of an Untold Love (1897) in which the hero, Donald Maitland, records in a journal from Feb. 20, 1890 to Jan. 10,

1895 his efforts to pay off a debt of honor and gain the love of Maizie Walton, a young woman reputedly wronged by the Maitland family. Julian Ralph's People We Pass (1896) is a collection of short stories about the 'little' people of New York, e.g., tenement dwellers, that he 'studied' as a reporter on the New York Sun. Ralph's The Millionairess (1902) has a beautiful, talented heroine, a leader in New York society, who proposes to make worthwhile use of her fortune. A socially well-connected and well-educated young man supports his luxurious style of living by stealing valuables from his 'friends' in Elizabeth Phipps Train's A Social Highwayman (1896); in her A Marital Liability (1897) Train's hero is a recently released felon who, with the help of two women, proves his wife committed the crime that sent him to prison. In Train's A Queen of Hearts (1898) the heroine skips out on her husband, a sternly orthodox clergyman, and her child, joins a variety company in New York and eventually takes her abandoned daughter in hand and marries her off to the scion of a wealthy New York family.

1900 was the fateful year in which Theodore Dreiser's masterpiece, Sister Carrie, was published in a thousand cheap copies (Doubleday, Page, & Company was more than a little uncomfortable at having to issue this 'scandalous' novel).

1901-1930——Eleven of the writers who have been placed in this timeframe actually issued their early works in the 1880s or 1890s——James Lauren Ford, Kate Jordan, F. Hopkinson Smith, Alexander Black, Edward W. Townsend, Abraham Cahan, Archibald Clavering Gunter, Ellen Glasgow, Robert Chambers, Anna Chapin Ray and Elizabeth Jordan. Ford's novels and short stories treat several levels of society, from the upper classes or those seeking to climb upward (The Brazen Calf [1903], The Wooing of Folly [1906] to working journalists (The Great Mirage [1915], politicians (Hot Corn Ike [1923]) and actors (Dolly Dillenbeck [1895]). World-weary women are the 'heroines' of Kate Jordan's threesome——The Other House (1892), Time the Comedian (1905) and The Creeping Tides (1913). In The Fortunes of Oliver Horn (1902), Peter (1907), Felix O'Day (1915) and Enoch Crane (1916) F. Hopkinson Smith peers into the lives of four very different male New Yorkers whereas Tom Grogan (1896) is the name of a sturdy woman who runs a Staten Island hauling firm.

Alexander Black's novels leave little impression with the exception of Miss Jerry (1895)——the author calls it a 'picture play', combining photographs and spoken dialogue, perhaps the first of its kind. Edward Waterman Townsend is remembered for his stories of Chimmie Fadden, a Bowery newsboy. Abraham Cahan, who wrote in both English and Yiddish, is the author of fiction dealing with Eastern European Jewish emigrants in New York. His The Rise of David Levinsky (1917) is a pioneering 'immigrant' novel. Archibald Clavering Gunter, a former engineer, was undoubtedly a very productive writer of novels (39 in all); those (five) with New York City settings have an overlay of crime and mystery.

Before she started on her series of novels about Virginia, Ellen Glasgow finished The Descendant (1897) whose hero is Michael Akershem, a socialist, and his lover, the painter Rachel Garvin, and Phases of an Inferior Planet (1898) whose protagonist is a wavering Episcopal priest filled with doubts about the church's dogmas. In 1906 The Wheel of Life observed New York society through the eyes of Laura Wilde, a poet of Virginian ancestry; this was followed in 1916 by Glasgow's Life and Gabriella——the heroine leaves her alcoholic, unreliable husband, settles in New York with her children, and becomes a successful milliner. The historical novelist Robert Chambers used New York City as the setting for some sixteen works of fiction, some of them with historical backgrounds (colonial New York, Revolutionary New York, New York during the Civil War). Anna Chapin Ray's novels are generally light pieces, although two of them—— Each Life Unfulfilled (1899) and The Dominant Strain (1903)——do have serious musical themes.

Among novels which carry an air of mystery surrounding her main characters Elizabeth Jordan issued two works that utilized her newspaper background: Tales of the City Room (1898) and May Iverson's Career (1914). Henry George, Jr., son of the noted economist and editor, is the author of The Romance of John Bainbridge (1906), a novel about political reform; the hero, Bainbridge, a lawyer, becomes a New York City alderman, a position he hopes will help him smoke out corruption.

Writers whose works pertinent to this bibliography were published within the first two decades of the 20th century are: Marie Van Vorst, Thomas Dixon, Alfred Henry Lewis, Frances Aymar Mathews, Myra Kelly, Frederic Stewart Isham, Weymer Jay Mills, Charles Belmont Davis, David Graham Phillips, Harry Jerrold O'Higgins, O. Henry, Helen Huntington, James Oppenheim, Edna Ferber, Charles Klein, Upton Sinclair and Arthur Hodges.

Marie Van Vorst's three novels——The Sin of George Warrener (1906), The Sentimental Adventures of Jimmy Bulstrode (1908) and Mary Moreland (1915)—— concern, respectively, a brokerage firm clerk who, spurred by his wife's extravagance, speculates unluckily on the New York Stock Exchange; a wealthy bachelor in Washington Square who is the soul of honor in his deep love for a married woman; and a private secretary who rejects the proposition of the unhappily married man she loves. Adamant Southerner Thomas Dixon set four of his novels in New York City; one of them, The One Woman (1903), appeared two years before Dixon's The Clansman, the source of D. W. Griffith's controversial film, The Birth of a Nation. The other three—— The Root of Evil (1911), The Foolish Virgin (1915) and The Way of a Man (1919)—— had mild success; Dixon's women have varied motivations: greed, feminism, absurdly romantic notions of love and marriage. Best known for his Wolfville stories Alfred Henry Lewis also wrote four books that dealt with the seamier side of life in New York City——Sandburrs (1900), The Boss and How He Came to Rule New York (1903), Confessions of a Detective (1906) and The Apaches of New York (1912). The second title (The Boss) leaves the reader with insight, however crude, into the machine politics (Tammany Hall) of New York City at the turn of the century.

Frances Aymar Mathews wrote about "courtship and marriage in an elegant social milieu... however, her plots are contrived, and she provided little depth of characterization" (American Women Writers)——see her Billy Duane (1905), The

Undefiled (1906) and A Christmas Honeymoon (1912). Stories of recent immigrants to New York's East Side——Little Citizens (1904), Wards of Liberty (1907) and Little Aliens (1910)——were the work of Myra Kelly; she died at age 23 or 24. Frederic Stewart Isham's Black Friday (1904) was built around that infamous day, September 24, 1869, when Jim Fiske and Jay Gould attempted to corner the domestic gold supply. The 'hero' of Isham's The Social Buccaneer (1910) is a modern Robin Hood, a clerk by day and a robber by night, handing the fruits of his thefts to new York City's charitable institutions. The impecunious hero of Isham's A Man and His Money (1912) hires out as a dog's valet; when his employer's daughter vanishes, he picks up her trail and rescues her.

Weymer Jay Mills' four historical novels of New York City——Caroline of Courtlandt Street (1905), The Ghosts of Their Ancestors (1906), The Van Rensselaers of Old Manhattan (1907) and The Girl I Left Behind Me (1910)——cover the years from the American Revolution to the 1830s. Two of Charles Belmont Davis's writings——The Stage Door (1908) a collection of short stories, and In Another Moment (1913), a novel–cast an eye on the New York theater and its people. Two other works——Tales of the Town (1911) and Nothing a Year (1916)——take an occasional glance at characters who have exchanged rural ways for those of the restless city. Ten of David Graham Phillips' 23 novels treat problems of law, journalism, finance and marriage in New York City, with Susan Lenox: Her Fall and Rise (1917), posthumously published, the story of the 'redemption' of a prostitute and 'kept woman', considered his masterpiece. Of Harvey Jerrold O'Higgins' four novels of New York, The Smoke-Eaters (1905) and Old Clinkers (1909), concentrating on the activities of firefighters, are worthy of note. Unlike most of the fiction included in this survey O. Henry's short stories, absorbing the sights and sounds of New York in the early years of the 20th century, still reach a wide audience.

The women in Helen Huntington's novels face a variety of quandaries: e.g. should a wealthy, socially well-connected woman marry the poor, much younger man of indifferent family background she loves? (The Sovereign Good [1908]); how should the girl from Vermont resound to the scandalous, malevolent behavior of the cousin in New York she has endured for three years as 'hired' companion? (An Apprentice to Truth [1910]); Mrs. Wilde, novelist and sparkling lady, is inclined to drink too much to her son's dismay; his efforts to prevent her descent into alcoholism are misinterpreted by his fiancee (The Moon Lady [1911]). As a social worker James Oppenheim's early works observed the lives of the poor working-class of New York's East Side——Doctor Rast (1909), Wild Oats (1910), The Nine-Tenths (1911) and Pay Envelopes (1911). Emma McChesney, a New York businesswoman, was the heroine of two early novels by Edna Ferber (Emma McChesney & Co. [1915] and Personality Plus [1914]); a woman journalist plies her trade in New York and Milwaukee in Ferber's Dawn O'Hara, the Girl Who Laughed (1911).

He was a playwright yet Charles Klein, usually in collaboration with Arthur Hornblow, also novelized his dramas, e.g., The Third Degree (1909), The Gamblers (1911), Maggie Pepper (1911) and The Money Makers (1914). Upton Sinclair was well into his muckraking phase with such novels as Price Hagen (1903), The Metropolis (1908) and The Money Changers (1908). The Essential Thing (1912), Pincus Hook (1916) and The Bounder (1919) by Arthur Hodges take note of the connection between money and high society, portray an art dealer (Hook) who encourages artists and tries matchmaking, and a boorish journalist and novelist who nevertheless appeals to a mysterious girl who lives in an apartment house with other semi-bohemians.

Novelists who began writing in the first decade of the 20th century and continued on into the 1920s include: George Barr McCutcheon, Arthur Stringer, Rupert Hughes, Arthur Train, Leroy Scott, Edith Wharton, Sewell Ford, Owen Johnson, Ernest Poole, Louis Joseph Vance, Ludwig Lewisohn, Basil King, Alice Duer Miller and Edwin Lefevre.

George Barr McCutcheon reached fame with his swashbuckling Graustark novels; nevertheless he did utilize New York City as the main scene of seven novels, Brewster's Millions (1903) being the most familiar. Included in the more than fifty novels written by the Canadian-born Arthur Stringer are five with a New York City background, three of them mysteries; the other two, The Silver Poppy (1903) and The Wine of Life (1921) have, respectively, a young lady from the West 'on the make' in the big city and a man who loses touch with his art when he falls for and marries a flighty, second-rate actress. Eclectic writer Rupert Hughes cast his net to gather in a wide variety of New Yorkers in fourteen novels, novellas and short story collections published from 1904 to 1934. The creator of Ephraim Tutt, lawyer extraordinary, was Arthur Train; his 'non-Tutt' novels portrayed, as might be expected, other lawyers as well as businessmen reaching for success in New York. Most of Leroy Scott's novels (there are eleven annotated here) afford us a glimpse into several areas of illegal activity with New York's underworld playing its part.

Edith Wharton needs little introduction; she is, of course, the foremost observer of upper class New York society in the latter years of the 19th century and early years of the 20th century in such works as: The House of Mirth (1905), The Custom of the Country (1913), The Age of Innocence (1920), The Mother's Recompense (1924) and Twilight Sleep (1927). Two comic characters, Shorty McCabe, physical culturist and commentator on the idiosyncrasies of New York's denizens, and Torchy, New York messenger and office boy, are the inventions of Sewell Ford and appear in six of his writings. Owen Johnson of the Lawrenceville School stories (1910-1923) and Stover at Yale (1911) also wrote novels for adults, seven of which, in a New York milieu, delved into situations driven by the quest for money and the efforts of young women to improve their own lot and that of others. A substantial number (seven) of Ernest Poole's novels were laid in New York; the two that attracted the most attention were The Harbor (1915) and His Family (1917); the latter's protagonist is an elderly man trying to make sense out of bewildering modern life as represented in his three daughters.

If Louis Joseph Vance is remembered at all, it is for his suave Michael Lanyard, the 'Lone Wolf'; beyond that he wrote several other mystery/detective novels and two stories of young women seeking their version of achievement in New York. In The

Broken Snare (1908), Don Juan (1923) and The Island Within (1928) Ludwig Lewisohn considers the problems of marriage, divorce and personal freedom. A clergyman, Basil King, wrote novels in which the protagonists have to wrestle with questions of conscience and faith or lack thereof; The Inner Shrine (1909) was King's only best seller. Alice Duer Miller's small-scale novels may be 'simplistic and sentimental'; but they are also 'solid and clever narratives' (American Women Writers)——viz., Less than Kin (1909), Ladies Must Live (1917), The Beauty and the Bolshevist (1920) and The Reluctant Duchess (1925). From his Wall St. Stories (1901) to The Making of a Stockbroker (1925) Edwin Lefevre's novels and short stories are centered on financiers, brokers and speculators and the money markets of New York City.

Authors whose writings about New York City fall within the second and third decades (up to and including 1930) of the 20th century include the following:
The comic short stories and novels of Montague Glass claim Jewish businessmen as well as ordinary citizens as the butts of his humor; Abe Potash and Morris ("Mawrus") Perlmutter, cloak and suit outfitters, appear as leading or secondary characters in several of Glass's works. George Gibbs, artist, illustrator and matriculant at the U.S. Naval Academy, turned to writing fiction in his middle years (1911 to ca. 1925) churning out novels whose heroines are women of spirit with their eyes on upward mobility in New York. Data about Maximilian Foster is hard to come by; however, we have in view five of his novels written between 1913 and 1928; they seem rather 'run of the mill' with, on the one hand protagonists, who have money or fall into it, and on the other hand, those who will never acquire it honestly no matter how diligently they strive. A Man's World (1912) Comrade Yetta (1913) and the Stranger (1920) by Arthur Ballard, are particularly provocative in their criticism of aspects of Western culture as played out in New York City. Bullard's protagonists are a young man seeking escape from forced religious (Christian) orthodoxy, a Jewish girl enduring sweatshop conditions and helping organize garment workers, and a convert to Islam who joins a circle of New York intellectuals.

Among Mary Stanberry Watts' numerous novels are three——The Rise of Jennie Cushing (1914), The Boardman Family (1918) and the House of Rimmon (1922)——in which her characters respond in quite different ways to their New York environment: Jennie, forsaken by society, survives reform school, and after a number of dissimilar jobs attains enough financial security to become an advocate for unloved children; Alexandra Boardman, a small town Ohioan, tackles New York City and wins renown and a big salary as a dancer; Cleve Harrod, lacking any encouragement from his family, persists with his literary ambitions despite a succession of humdrum jobs, and is finally recognized as a rising dramatist. Josephine Dodge Daskam Bacon's writings about young American women with status in the upper branches of New York society tend to be somewhat satirical (see Square Peggy [1919], a collection of ten short stories). Fannie Hurst has been called "an accurate gauge of her contemporary audience's beliefs" (American Women Writers). Her collections of short stories——Just Around the Corner, (1914) , Every Soul Hath its Song (1916), Gaslight Sonatas (1918). Humoresque (1918) and The Vertical City (1922)——spoke of and to shop girls, immigrants, Jewish-Americans, middle and laboring class New Yorkers; her novels: Lummox, (1912), Mannequin (1926) and Appassionata (1926) verge on sensationalism with their heroines enmeshed in unusual situations and searching for ways to extricate themselves.

Charles G. Norris, the less-talented brother of Frank and husband of Kathleen Norris, was the author of three novels—The Amateur (1916), Pig Iron (1925) and Seed (1930)– that are "workmanlike in the best sense and always intelligently rendered and readable" (Davison, R.A. Charles G. Norris). In The Amateur and Seed Norris's protagonists are an artist and a writer, both of whom seek fulfilment in a New York crowded with like-minded peers. Emilie Benson Knipe in tandem with her husband Alden Arthur Knipe wrote historical fiction with young adults in mind. Three of their works——A Maid of Old Manhattan (1917), The Flower of Fortune (1922) and The Shadow Captain (1925)–– dealt with colonial New York under Dutch and English rule. A fourth novel, The Lost Little Lady (1917), has the Civil War Draft Riots of 1863 in its background.

Sinclair Lewis's third novel, The Trail of the Hawk (1915) introduced a college dropout from Minnesota drifting in New York who briefly pilots airplanes before entering the automobile business; married to an upper class girl he suffers the boredom of office work and the pressure and claustrophobia of the city before fleeing to Buenos Aires with his wife. Lewis's fourth novel, The Job (1917), depicts a working girl who fails at marriage, returns to her old job and rapidly ascends to prominence in the business world of the metropolis. Four of Frank L. Packard's novels of illegal goings-on in New York City enumerate the adventures of Jimmie Dale, society figure and incidental crime fighter masquerading as the Gray Seal, while the stories of Arthur Somers Roche frequently record the missteps of New York's upper classes. The leftist social critic Waldo Frank's early novels, The Unwelcome Man (1917) and The Dark Mother (1920) take a dim view of the bloodless world of business and law, prone as it is to corruption. City Block (1922) is called a 'lyric novel' by Frank, although it is really "a series of episodes in the lives of people who live in the same block, showing something of the currents and counter-currents in their lives" (Bittner, V. The novels of Waldo Frank). In Frank's Rahab (1922), Fannie Luve, stranded in New York, abandoned by her husband, sinks lower and lower to kept woman and the associate of prostitutes. Konrad Bercovici's short stories, collected in Dust of New York (1919), and his novel, The Guest (1925), draw on the encounters of recent European arrivals with teeming New York City.

Hulbert Footner, Canadian-born actor and journalist, was essentially a writer of crime novels, although Antennae (1926) diverges as its two main characters, Joe Kaplan, a mean, vicious graduate of slums, and respectable, timid Wilfred Pell confront one another on several levels from youth to maturity. George Agnew Chamberlain's novels usually have a breezy, light-hearted air about them; one exception is The Great Van Suttart Mystery (1925) in which Cornelius of the now penniless Van Suttarts bonds with the poor but determined Miad Blake——"New York in the period immediately following the close of the Civil War is interestingly depicted" (Literary Digest International Book Review). James Gibbon Huneker's only novel, Painted Veils (1920), pries into the contemporary art world of New York City with a cast of real and fictional characters; the sexual mores of the latter are free of any restraints. Two short story collections——

Hungry Hearts (1920) and Children of Loneliness (1923)——and three novels: Salome of the Tenements (1922), Bread Givers (1925) and Arrogant Beggar (1927)——comprise Anzia Yezierska's major output. They are evocations, realistic and sympathetic, of Jewish life on New York's Lower East Side.

Aside from A Yankee Passional (1927), Samuel Badisch Ornitz (later a screenwriter) published one other novel, Haunch, Paunch and Jowl (1923), a brutally frank portrait of the slums of New York City in the late 19th and early 20th century and the struggle of Eastern European Jews to achieve success on American terms; the 'hero' is Meyer Hirsch, who bribes and connives his way upward to a judgeship on the Supreme Criminal Court of New York. News analyst Elmer Davis found time between his journalistic activities to write short stories and novels, three of the latter: Times Have Changed (1923), I'll Show You the Town (1924) and Friends of Sweeney (1925), have three male protagonists——a high school principal, a Latin professor and a journalist—— falling into predicaments in their New York habitat from which only two are able to extricate themselves. Christopher Morley's The Haunted Bookshop (1919) and Tales from a Rolltop Desk (1921) indulge the author's fascination with the world of booksellers, publishers, and writers in Brooklyn and Manhattan. Nigger Heaven (1926) was Carl Van Vechten's fifth (?) novel; two earlier works, The Blind Bow-Boy (1923) and Firecrackers (1925) scrutinized New York sophisticates, the so-called 'smart set'. Nigger Heaven was one of the first novels to look closely at the well-off, educated African-Americans of Harlem. Van Vechten's last novel was Parties; Scenes from Contemporary New York Life (1930) which documented the boredom and need for stimulation of New York's latest affluent generation. Maxwell Bodenheim's novels—— Crazy Man (1924), Ninth Avenue (1926) and Naked on Roller Skates (1930)——are reflections of his lifestyle which ended in alcoholism and indigence.

Two of the three novels that Thomas Beer wrote——Sandoval (1924) and The Road to Heaven (1928)——are dubbed respectively 'a romance of bad manners' and 'a romance of morals.' The New York of 1870 is the arena of action of the first-named work; Sandoval is a charming Southern scoundrel who thoroughly disillusions the brothers Thorold and Christian. The second novel has a dubious hero in Lamon Coe, village philosopher, who takes the suggestion to remove himself to New York; his experiences there only convince him that his former country life is far to be preferred. In two of her four novels about middle class African-Americans——There is Confusion (1924) and Plum Bun (1929)——Jessie Redmon Fauset has her two heroines striving for different goals; one wants acceptance as an artist; the other is trying to pass for white. John Dos Passos's Manhattan Transfer (1925) is 'kaleidoscopic' in its description of New York City and the course of its inhabitants' lives. S.S. Van Dine's very popular detective stories starring the dapper, worldly Philo Vance broke all existing records for the sale of crime fiction. A rival to Van Dine in prolificity if not in book sales could be Isabel Egenton Ostrander who, from 1916 to 1930 (often under various pseudonyms: Robert Chipperfield, David Fox, Douglas Grant), wrote detective/mystery stories (at least ten) set in several locales, but chiefly New York City and Long Island.

The Cubical City (1926), Paris-based Janet Flanner's single novel, paints a vibrant picture of New York City and its inhabitants as it pursues the fortunes and love-life of scene designer Delia Poole. With two of her novels, Little Sins (1927) and Young Man of Manhattan (1930) and a short story collection, Night Club (1929), Katharine Brush gained a substantial reputation as chronicler of the 'Jazz Age.' Joseph Moncure March's two verse-narratives, The Set-Up and The Wild Party, were published in 1928. The Set-Up recounts the life and death of a black prizefighter from Harlem; The Wild Party describes a reckless get-together of bohemians and theatrical figures that ends in tragedy. Claude McKay's Home to Harlem (1928), one of the first novels by an African-American to attract a large audience, tells the story of a World War I veteran, Jake Brown, who returns to a Harlem of pleasant memories; by the novels conclusion Jake, after work as a railroad porter, etc., is once again back in Harlem which is now crowded and pushed against by white society. The Blacker the Berry (1929) was short-lived Wallace Thurman's first novel; it played on the prejudice its dark-skinned heroine encountered from lighter-skinned peers.

Vina Delmar's Bad Girl (1928), Kept Woman (1929) and Loose Ladies (1929), all of them focusing on working-class woman, were deemed reprehensible, too provocative in their day. Whatever interest one attaches to I Thought of Daisy (1929), a novel by the young Edmund Wilson, is largely owing to his later, much-deserved reputation as a critic and scholar; the story is set in a post-World War I New York with its hero a young man tasting bohemian life via Daisy, a chorus girl, and Rita, a poet. Jews Without Money (1930) by Michael Gold, with its autobiographical overtones, was 'the proletarian novel', depicting the impoverished Lower East Side experiences of its young narrator and eventually influencing other radical writers. Flamboyant Mae West had already scandalized the proper citizens of New York with her play Diamond Lil (1928) when she wrote Babe Gordon (1930): Babe is an amoral woman who takes her pleasure whenever and wherever she finds it (in New York and elsewhere). The novel was reprinted in 1931 under the title: The Constant Sinner.

Additional Notes on New York City in Fiction (To 1930)

Achmed Abdullah's The Honourable Gentleman and Others (1919) is a collection of short stories about the tensions between the older and younger generations in New York City's Chinatown. Broadway Interlude (1929) by Abdullah and Faith Baldwin charts the struggle of a young actress and a novice playwright to 'make it' on the New York stage.

Samuel Hopkins Adams, in addition to his fiction about the Erie Canal and Long Island, used New York City as the locale for Average Jones (1911), Our Square and the People in It (1917), From a Bench in Our Square (1922), The Piper's Fee (1926) and The Flagrant Years (1929).

The Blue Grass region of Kentucky inspired James Lane Allen's most-read fiction, yet he did turn to New York City in a novella, A Cathedral Singer (1916), and a novel, The Heroine in Bronze (1912); in the latter a Kentuckian woos and wins a shy, beautiful girl in the heart of the city.

Of her three 'New York' novels Black Oxen (1922) with its 'erotic' content (at least in the minds of the 'pure souls' of the day) gained notoriety for the Californian Gertrude Atherton.

The protagonists of Anna Robeson Brown's three novels——The Black Lamb (1896), The Immortal Garland (1900) and Truth and a Woman (1903)——search for artistic, religious and romantic fulfillment in New York City.

The humorist Gelett Burgess was not averse to trying his hand at the writing of novels; his efforts are superficially entertaining and include three that are imbued with a New York City flavor——A Little Sister of Destiny (1906), Find the Woman (1911) and The Master of Mysteries (1912). 'Astro', the 'Master' of the last work, uses both occultism and modern science to solve human puzzles.

Who is Laura Daintrey? Is 'Laura' male of female? An extended search has drawn a blank insofar as obtaining any biographical or critical data concerning this author. Nevertheless the following novels——Miss Varian of New York (1887), Eros (1888), Actaeon (1892) and Gold (1893)——attest to the actuality of this writer. Daintrey's fiction is focused on the upper classes of New York City, their misdemeanors and occasional lapses into criminal behavior.

Let it be noted that G.W. Dillingham and Belford, Clarke were publishers of Daintrey's novels. These firms, along with G.W. Carleton, C.T. Dillingham, Street & Smith, et al., were very active from the 1860s to the end of the century, issuing popular fiction that was quite often ignored by reviewing organs.

Alan Dale (the pseudonym of Alfred J. Cohen) glanced at an unhappy stage couple in My Footlight Husband (1893), a female reporter/hack novelist in A Girl Who Wrote (1902) and a married couple with odd notions about the 'New York style' of living in their undersized apartment (Wanted: a Cook [1904]).

Between 1908 and 1923 Louise Maunsell Field (another little-known author) wrote four novels whose heroines, brushing against New York 'society', voluntarily or out of necessity left it to pursue other goals.

Oscar Graeve's novels are laid solidly in New York City (The Keys of the City [1916], Youth Goes Seeking [1919] and the Brown Moth [1921]). His protagonists could not be imagined in any other setting than that city which they hoped to 'conquer' or at least live with.

Two of Helen Green's books—At the Actors' Boarding House... (1906) and The Maison De Shine (1908)——are primarily collections of short stories and sketches of show business people whose non-stage lives are passed at a boarding-house on Irving Place. Green's Mr. Jackson (1908) records the (mis)fortunes of a couple from Iowa visiting New York City.

In two of his many novels——The House of Bondage (1910) and The Spider's Web (1913)——Reginald Wright Kauffman confronts corruption and prostitution in New York City while Ethel May Kelley in her four lighter novels probes the lives of her youthful protagonists——society belles (Over Here [1918], Home, James [1927]), a middle-class girl searching for 'beauty' (Beauty and Mary Blair [1921]) and a young man in search of love at several stages in his life (Wings [1924]).

The Bowery and the slums/streets of the city and its denizens are the realms of Owen Kildare's The Good of the Wicked (1904), The Wisdom of the Simple (1905) and Such a Woman (1911).

Clara Hammond Lanza and Julia Magruder were contemporaries; each of them completed three novels of New York featuring characters seeking careers, new starts in life, entry into high society, or the repair of a once happy marriage.

The novelization of two plays comprises two of the three pieces that Edward Marshall put together; they are The Writing on the Wall (1909) from a play by William J. Hurlbut and Broadway Jones (1913) from the play by George M. Cohan.

Roy L. McCardell's Conversations of a Chorus Girl (1903) and Jimmy Jones; the Autobiography of an Office Boy (1907) have self-explanatory titles; his The Wage Slaves of New York (1899) is a weak, muddled attempt to portray an enlightened mill owner and profit-sharing.

The Philadelphia-born journalist/novelist John T. McIntyre used his native city and New York as settings for a number of his mystery/crime novels. New York is the scene of action of: In the Dead of Night (1908), Ashton-Kirk, Investigator (1910), Slag (1927) and The Museum Murder (1929).

Miscarriages of justice are the themes of John Antonio Moroso's The Quarry (1913) and The People against Nancy Preston (1921). Two orphans, Rosie Rosetti and Danny Lewis, raised on New York's East Side by the same foster parents, are at the center of Moroso's The Stumbling Herd (1923).

William Hamilton Osborne penned two mysteries: The Red Mouse (1909) and The Catspaw (1911); his The Running Fight (1910) however is built around the Panic of 1907 when the stock market plunged downward because of runs on several large New York financial firms.

The arbiter of etiquette in America, Emily Post, wrote, among other novels, Purple and Fine Linen (1905), a title also used by Edgar Fawcett, and Parade (1925); both are stories of New York's upper class society, as one might expect.

Robert Shackleton's two works—Toomey and Others (1900) and Many Waters; a Story of New York (1902)—immerse the reader in such city settings as the Lower East Side, Blackwell's Island, Cherry Hill, Wall Street, plush hotels, etc.

Best know as a compiler of reference works (e.g., The Home Book of Quotations) Burton E. Stevenson was also a writer of mystery/detective stories and light fiction. The Marathon Mystery (1904), The Mystery of the Boule Cabinet (1912) and The Gloved Hand (1913) were firmly placed in New York City settings.

My Wife and I (1871) by Harriet Beecher Stowe was what she called 'a society novel.' The young married Hendersons live happily if frugally in New York City as he pursues careers in journalism and writing, while she, despite a background of wealth and fashion, capably manages their household.

Katrina Trask's heroes are Morton Hunnewell (White Satin and Homespun [1896]), a lecturing reformer living in Delancey Street, who has great influence on Katharine Van Santlandt, a wealthy young woman; John Leighton, Jr. (Trask's 1898 novel has the same 'name') who breaks away from the strict Calvinism of his father and achieves success as a New York lawyer; and John Wright (The Invisible Balance Sheet [1917]), afloat in the social world of the city but committed by terms of his uncle's will to remain a bachelor.

A successful businesswoman who had earlier left her husband and daughters (Nora Pays [1925]) reconciles with her children years later, but is unable to do much to assure their future happiness; Felicia Day (Little Miss-By-The -Day [1919]), returns to the old house in Brooklyn where she was reared by her grandfather, and with imagination, talent and the help of friends restores it to its former grandeur. These strong women are the creations of Lucille Baldwin Van Slyke. A third work by her, Eve's Other Children (1912), is a collection of tales about Brooklyn's poor but vibrant Syrian lace-makers.

Carolyn Wells and her prolificacy (she wrote easily, rapidly, with little reflectiveness) have already been mentioned in the Long Island section of this survey. Eight of her many mystery/detective novels have New York City (and murder among the rich and socially well-connected) as their scene; her favorite sleuth, Fleming Stone, and several other detectives are called in to solve the crimes committed.

The Toltec Cup (1890) by Andrew Carpenter Wheeler gives a detailed picture of life and places of interest in the New York City of 1861/63; the Civil War Draft Riots of 1863 and the less affluent (the 'lower') classes of the city are sharply drawn, although the mystery of a vanished and valuable Toltec artifact is the heart of the story. The Primrose Path of Dalliance (1892) finds a journalist in a bitter love affair with an opera comique actress.

The sports world and the movies touch one another in two of the three humorous stories by Harry C. Witwer—There's No Base Like Home (1920) and Bill Grimm's Progress (1926). The baseball hero of the first novel and the prize-fighting taxi-driver of the second move of their own volition or are inveigled into moviedom with the expected results. Alexander Hanley of Alex the Great (192) is a self-confident country bumpkin who does quite well (he's quite lucky) in the big city.

In between his 'Jeeves' stories the inimitable P.G. Wodehouse stretches to include New York and New Yorkers in three of his amusing novels——Psmith, Journalist (1915), Piccadilly Jim (1917) and The Small Bachelor (1927).

HUDSON VALLEY (Including WESTCHESTER, PUTNAM, DUTCHESS and COLUMBIA COUNTIES)

An early work that has the Hudson Highlands as its setting is Ambrose Walker's The Highlands; a Tale of the Hudson (1826), a melodramatic story of murder and revenge occurring a year after the close of the American Revolution. James Kirke Paulding's The Book of St. Nicholas contains tales based largely on the folklore of the Dutch settlers of the Hudson Valley and New Amsterdam; 'Cobus Yerks', the second tale, bears a resemblance to Washington Irving's Legend of Sleepy Hollow. There are three stories in Emma Catherine Embury's Constance Latimer (1838) with varied locales (Hudson Valley, Long Island and New York City). Two other women writers published short novels in the 1840s: Love's Progress (1840) by Caroline Howard Gilman, and the Hermit of the Hudson (1848) by the pseudonymous Emma Carra. 'Queechy', the village in which much of the novel of the same name (1852) by Susan Warner takes place, is 'clearly based on Canaan [Columbia County] New York' (Foster, Edward H. Susan and Anna Warner). Later, Susan Warner's novel Pine Needles (1877) is set on Constitution Island in the Hudson River, the home of the author and her sister, Anna, for many years. Exchanging urban life for a permanent home in the Hudson Valley countryside even though the husband's business activities are still based in New York City is a move agreed upon by both parties in Alice Bradley Haven's The Coopers (1858). The anonymous 'Brook Farm' (1860) celebrates rural life in southeastern New York State not far from the Connecticut border. Theodore Winthrop's Edwin Brothertoft (1862) pits the honorable hero, an officer in the Continental Army, against his ambitious, unscrupulous wife who entertains British soldiers in the Brothertoft mansion. Stormcliff, a Tale of the Highlands (1866) by Mansfield Tracy Walworth follows its protagonist from despair and thoughts of self-destruction (he has no inkling of his origins) to a life of promise in law and politics. A woman's jealousy keeps two lovers apart in Juliette Kinsie's Walter Ogilby (1869); the novel is of interest as a description of social affairs in Dutchess County in the 1830s. A fictitious town, 'Stemwell', in Dutchess County, is the primary scene of Theodore Davies' Losing to Win (1874), although the leading character, long presumed dead, resurfaces in New York City. The clergyman E.F. Roe achieved so much success with his first two novels (Barriers Burned Away——1872, and Opening a Chestnut Burr——1874) that he gave up his ministry to devote himself to writing, publishing three more novels in the 1870s, all with Hudson Highland settings: From Jest to Earnest (1875), Near to Nature's Heart (1876) and A Face Illumined (1878). Nathan J. Bailey's Johnsville in the Olden Time (1884) is a collection of stories about people living in a fictional village in the Hudson Valley (in Dutchess County?). An Englishwoman inherits mills in the Hudson Valley and endeavors to mange them for her workers' benefit; nevertheless, the employees go on strike; things get out of hand and the heroine decides that marriage is her best recourse––all this occurs in Robert Grant's Face to Face (1886).

The first decade of the 20th century produced six pertinent novels: Stephen Henry Thayer's Daughters of the Revolution (1901); Julian Ralph's The Millionairess (1902), many scenes of which are laid in a country home on the Hudson and in the Beaux Arts Club of New York City; Frances Powell's gothic The House on the Hudson (1903) and The By-ways of Braithe (1904); Paul Leicester Ford's light and amusing A Checked Love Affair and The Cortelyou Feud (1903); and Elma Allen Travis's The Cobbler (1908), the story of a cobbler's son who marries above his class, refuses to accept help from his father-in-law and discovers a talent for writing. Mary Hallock Foote's The Royal Americans (1910) takes place before and during the American Revolution and has two heroines, an American girl brought up in a Dutch village on the Hudson and a French girl rescued from Indian captivity by the American girl's father. Hard Wood (1925) by Arthur Olney Friel is a book title and the hero's name; the upper Hudson Valley during New York State's thriving canal period is the setting. Edith Wharton's Hudson River Bracketed (1929) places the protagonist, aspiring writer Vance Weston, for part of the novel, in 'The Willows', an example of an American architectural style known as Hudson River Bracketed. Alice Beal Parson's three novels: John Merrill's Pleasant Life (1930), A Lady Who Lost (1932) and I Knew What I'd Do (1946) create a town on the Hudson called 'Pawlet'. A Quaker community in early 19th century Dutchess County is shaken when one of its members falls in love with a non-member in Crum Elbow Folks (1938) by Percy Raymond Barnes. Eleven novels appeared in each of the two decades, the 1940s and 1950s. The names of some of the authors may be rather familiar: Stephen Longstreet contributed 'Decade, 1929-1939' (1940) and later Eagles Where I Walk (1960) which has the American Revolution in focus; Anya Seton's Dragonwyck (1944)––patroons in the Hudson Valley in the 1840s; Henry Morton Robinson's The Perfect Round (1945) wherein a World War II veteran returns to the Hudson Valley and Catskill country for the quiet life only to find himself locking horns with crooked politicians and noxious natives; Katharine Newlin Burt's Lady in the Tower (1946), said tower and the house on the Hudson attached to it holding secrets the heroine must unlock, and Burt's Escape from Paradise (1952), 'Paradise' being a large estate on the Hudson presided over by capable, plump Aunt Kinny; Manuel Komroff's Echo of Evil (1948) assesses the effect that a released murderess has on family and community in the Hudson Valley; Carl Carmer's Rebellion at Quaker Hill (1954) fictionalizes the rent 'wars' sparked by tenant farmers in the Valley during the 1760s.

Among the lesser-known novelists are: Alexandra Philips with her historical novel of the Hudson Valley and New York City in the last two decades of the 17th century, 'Forever Possess' (1946); John Brick with Troubled Spring (1950)––a Union soldier comes back from the Confederate prison at Andersonville to his Hudson River hometown; Howard Breslin's Shad Run (1955)––the time is 1788 with ratification of the Federal Constitution in abeyance and, more importantly, to fishermen at least, the run of shad in the Hudson; William Brown Meloney's Rush to the Sun (1937). Mooney (1950) and Many Are the Travelers (1954), are all laid in the small town of 'Haviland' (near Poughkeepsie) which has a full array of human foibles and deficiencies; and Ivan Obolensky's Rogues' March (1956) which headlines another fictional town, 'Red Bank', also close by Poughkeepsie, as it journeys from 1884 to 1945.

Looking at the 1960s to the present the gothic element rules again in Phyllis Whitney's Mystery of the Haunted Pool (1960) and Thunder Heights (1960), Margaret Widdemer's Red Castle Women (1968), Sharon Anne Salvato's Briarcliff Manor (1974) and Catherine Morland's The Legacy of Winterwyck (1976). Jack Pearl's 'Callie Knight' (1974) rises to wealth and influence in the Hudson Valley on the backs of men she bedded down and then loses it all. From the Shamrock Shore (1982) by Jean Francois Webb traces an Irish family in the Hudson Valley from 1848 (The date of their arrival in America) to the beginning of the 20th century. Jean Clark's The Marriage Bed (1983) is an historical romance with its two protagonists, orphan Margretta Van Dyke and tenant farmer Stephen Warner marrying and enduring the hardships of the colonial and Revolutionary Hudson Valley before they can reclaim the happiness of their early married life. World's End (1987) by T. Coraghessan Boyle is a chronicle of three interlocked families, Dutch and Mohawk, in the Hudson Valley covering a period from the 17th to the mid-20th century. Of the ten 1990s 'Hudson Valley novels' in this bibliography six deal with homicide and the occult, e.g., George C. Chesbro's The Language of the Cannibals (1990); Brian Johnson's The Gift Horse Murders (1993); Graham Masterton's The House That Jack Built (1996); etc. Two of the four remaining pieces of general fiction should be noted: Sallie Bingham's Upstate (1993), a depiction of adultery and exclusiveness among urban 'exiles' choosing to live in a Hudson Valley town and Thomas J. Fleming's The Wages of Fame (1998)——the chief characters in a story that begins in 1827 and concludes as the Civil War opens in 1861 are politician and landowner George Stapleton, his capricious wife Caroline and John Sladen, supposedly George's friend but also Caroline's lover.

The number and variety of situations in which Westchester County is a factor in American fiction certainly justify a separate treatment here. Two well-known authors——James Fenimore Cooper and James Kirke Paulding——chose the 'Neutral Ground' of the American Revolution, i.e. Westchester County, as the setting for one of Cooper's earliest novels and one of Paulding's latest works. In Cooper's The Spy (1821) nettlesome Harvey Birch, a peddler and inferentially a British agent, is the purveyor of valuable information forwarded to General Washington. Paulding's The Old Continental (1846) is based on the role of Paulding's own cousin as a patriot warrior in the Revolution; the effect the conflict had on Westchester people receives close scrutiny. Cooper's Littlepage Manuscripts trilogy——Satanstoe (1845), The Chainbearer (1845) and The Redskins (1846)——covers nearly a century (from the French and Indian War to the anti-rent protests which ended in 1846). The Littlepage and Mordaunt families, prime movers in the narratives, own landed estates in Westchester County and contiguous areas. The anonymous Spuytenduyvel Chronicle (1856) marks the vicissitudes of the Page family of 'Aiglemont' (a country estate in Westchester) and New York City. Reminiscences of an Old Westchester Homestead (1897) by Charles Pryer is a medley of tales featuring ghosts and a certain cloven-footed individual as well as stories based on incidents occurring during the American Revolution. The Philipse

Manor House in Yonkers is a focal point in Robert Neilson Stephens' novel of the American Revolution, The Continental Dragoon (1898). Westchester; a Tale of the Revolution (1899) by Henry Austin Adams is a complex and tragic story of the mixed motives of Tories and patriots as narrated by Nathaniel Broadbent, a neutralist. A man who feels compelled to manage the way in which other people live, including his wife and especially the residents of a Westchester community, the 'Westminster Estates', is the dominant figure in Henry Albert Phillips's Other People's Lives (1924). Carolyn Wells' peripatetic detective Fleming Stone solves murders among Westchester's wealthy in The Daughter of the House (1925), The Ghosts' High Noon (1930) and Murder at the Casino (1941). Val Lewton, best know as the producer of several classic horror films, was also a novelist; his Yearly Lease (1932) appraises the mix of characters who have living quarters in an apartment house in 'Sawpits/Chester Manor', Westchester County.   The mystery motif is very much present in some 29 novels published between 1930 and 1995; Ellery Queen, Mary Roberts Rinehart and Charles Jackson, each with one work, are among the dozen writers of this genre, but Frances and Richard Lockridge in collaboration (she died in 1963) and singly were responsible for 19 of them. The Lockridges were active as authors from about 1930 to ca. 1975; their Westchester and Putnam County mysteries invariably star Captain Merton L. Heimrich of the New York State Police and often convey much of the life styles of the residents and their physical surroundings. The American Revolution and its sometimes devastating consequences as it played in Westchester County again appear in Frank Olney Hough's If Not Victory (1939) and The Neutral Ground (1947), Edward Stanley's Thomas Forty (1947), Mildred B. Davis's Lucifer Land (1977) and Maryhelen Clague's So Wondrous Free (1978) and Beyond the Shining River (1980). Among the 14 works of general fiction that appeared between 1940 and 1988 Hilda Morris's The Vantage Point (1940) tells of a widow and former teacher of 46 turning her Westchester home into a boarding-house; Alethia Shelton's The Butterfly Net (1957) covers a single June day on a huge estate in which the Stanton heirs resolve their problems; in Margaret Halsey's The Demi-Paradise; a Westchester Diary (1960) a matron takes issue with an American Legion blacklist; Judith Rossner's Nine Months in the Life of an Old Maid (1969) records the sad existence of the less stable of two sisters on a shrinking Westchester estate; J.P. Donleavy's The Lady Who Liked Clean Rest Rooms (1997) is a conceit limning the frustration of Joceyln Guenevere Merchantière Jones of Scarsdale as her husband leaves her for a younger woman; and Preston Falls (1998) by David Gates portrays a Westchester couple in marital difficulty; the husband displays some bizarre behavior patterns and disappears from their vacation home in Upstate 'Preston Falls' only to reappear in the couple's Westchester home unable to explain his irrational conduct.

Half the fiction about the U. S. Military Academy at West Point in this bibliography is chiefly of interest to boys approaching young adulthood. Upton Sinclair in the late 1890s began writing for the pulps of Street & Smith a series of stories about a West Point cadet, Mark Mallory, that was eventually collated in five volumes in 1903. In the same year Anna Bartlett Warner wrote West Point Colors which traced a cadet from his nomination to the Academy to the graduation parade. Other early 20th century writers of this type of fiction were Paul Bernard Malone, Florence Kimball Russel, Harris Irving

Hancock, Paschal Neilson Strong and Russell Guy Emery. In each of the years 1955 through 1958 Russell 'Red' Reeder put out a novel whose protagonist, Clint Lane, passed from West Point plebe to graduation. The love affairs of cadets seemed to be a fertile topic for a number of 19th century women writers, e.g.: Tactics... a West Point Love Story (1863) by Jeannie H. Grey; Mildred's Cadet (1881) by Alice King Hamilton; Clara Louise Root Burnham's A West Point Wooing ... (1899). Unfortunately these are almost uniformly dull, a chore to read. On a more serious level we have: Cut; a Story of West Point (1886) by G.I. Cervus which provides a well-defined picture of pre-Civil War cadet life; Charles King's Cadet Days (1894) amplifies the details of a cadet's progress through the Academy; Tin Soldiers (1934) by Robert Wohlforth tells how several young men fare in their military training at the Point; Norman Robert Ford's The Black, the Grey and the Gold (1961) examines the West Point honor system; The Academy (1997) by Ed Ruggero looks closely at scandals, largely sex-driven, that have seeped into West Point; Lucian K. Truscott's Full Dress Gray (1998) takes on the pressures that have come with the increasing presence of women cadets.

CAPITAL-SARATOGA REGION

New York State's capital, Albany, is best represented in fiction by the novels of William Kennedy, seven in all, beginning with The Ink Truck (1969), followed by Legs (1975), Billy Phelan's Greatest Game (1978), Ironweed (1983), Quinn's Book (1988), Very Old Bones (1992), and The Flaming Corsage (1996). Kennedy covers the modern city's Democratic machine politics, its journalists and especially the dysfunctional Phelan family. 'Quinn's Book' is a departure, an historical novel ranging from 1849 to 1864 and using Albany and other Upstate New York locations. Two 19th century novels, Sarah E. Coolidge's Ambition (1856) and Florence Wilford's Dominie Freylinghausen (1875) deal respectively with a high-reaching but amoral politician and a bigoted Calvinist pastor who witnesses the decline of his influence. Ruth Hall's historical novel, The Black Gown (1900), offers a knowledgeable picture of the manners and customs of colonial Albany's inhabitants. Frederick L. Hackenburg's This Best Possible World (1934) portrays State Assemblymen and other politicians in Albany with Tammany's influence ever present. A futuristic tale in which electronic devices have displaced human workers in the production of consumer goods, Player Piano (1952) by Kurt Vonnegut moves between Albany-Troy-Schenectady. Most recently Richard Stevenson has taken a close look at the homosexual and criminal scene in four novels published from 1984 to 1995; Don Strachey, a gay P.I. (private investigator) demonstrates his expertise in cracking cases that come his way.

The Mysteries of Troy (1847) by Frank Hazleton is a short piece of fiction of little merit, mentioned only because it is perchance the earliest tale in which that city plays a role. Troy and vicinity are the setting for two mystery novels by Ione Shriber—The Dark Arbor (1940) and Family Affair (1941). The heroine of Samuel Hopkins Adams' Sunrise to Sunset (1950) works in Troy's cotton mills in the early 1800s. In 1994 two novels made Troy the scene of their action—Jack Casey's The Trial of Bat Shea (for a murder committed in 1894) and The Irish Princess, by Mickey Clement, which takes an Irish Catholic family, the Malloys, through the years 1964 to 1982.

John L.E.W. Shecut's Ish-Noo-Ju-Lut-Sche; or, The Eagle of the Mohawks (1841) has Schenectady with its large contingent of Dutch settlers threatened by French and Indian encroachments in the latter part of the 17th century. The same theme is at the center of John J. Vrooman's novel, The Massacre (1954); the 'massacre' of the title occurred in 1690 when Schenectady was sacked and burned by the French and their Indian allies. In A Story or Two from an Old Dutch Town (1878) Robert Traill Spence Lowell (brother of James Russell Lowell) placed his three novellas in the town of 'Westenvliet' (i.e. Schenectady) from colonial times to the 1820s.

There is no dearth of fiction about Saratoga Springs and the Battle of Saratoga (1777). Historical novels centered on the famous battle itself begin with Eliza Cushing's Saratoga; a Tale of the Revolution (1824). Delia Bacon, famous for questioning the authorship of 'Shakespeare's' plays, based The Bride of Fort Edward (1839), a story in play-like dialogue, on the murder of Jane McCrae by Indian allies of General Burgoyne (see also: Michel René Hilliard-d'Auberteuil's Mis MacRae [1784]). From 1848 to 1852 three relatively brief stories appealed to readers' appetites for the romantic aura surrounding the critical fray: Saratoga; a Dramatic Historical Romance of the Revolution, by W.B. Dailey; Grace Dudley; or, Arnold at Saratoga, by Charles Jacobs Peterson; and The Rebel Scout, by Aria Ashland. Joseph Marion Baker's Meladore; a Tale of the Battle of Saratoga (1877), is actually a narrative poem with the heroine beloved by two soldiers, an American and a British officer. Two Young Patriots; or, Boys of the Frontier (1898) by Everett Tomlinson offers young readers a detailed history of Burgoyne's Invasion and subsequent surrender at Saratoga. John Murray Reynold's Men of Morgan (1933) focuses on the vital participation of Morgan's Rifles in the defeat of Burgoyne's army. Benedict Arnold is the real hero of Kenneth Roberts's Rabble in Arms (1933).

The protagonist of Robert Chambers' Love and the Lieutenant (1935) is a British officer who recruits Hessian mercenaries and falls in love with two women who are trying to abort his mission. Bruce Lancaster's Guns of Burgoyne (1939) has a Hessian officer as its narrator. Sergeant Lamb's America (1940) by the English poet and novelist, Robert Graves, ends shortly after Burgoyne's surrender; its narrator is a British non-commissioned officer. John Brick's The Rifleman (1953) is a fictionalized biography of Timothy Murphy, a marksman in Morgan's Rifles credited with the shot that killed the gallant British general, Simon Fraser.

Saratoga (i.e. Saratoga Springs) and New York City on the eve of the presidential election of 1840 are the backgrounds of the anonymous novel, Florence De Lacey; or, The Coquette (1845). J.N.T. Tucker's The Two Brides; or, Romance at Saratoga (1846) and Daniel Shepherd's Saratoga; a Story of 1787 (1856), the latter a small-scale tale, are two other works from the pre-Civil War period. The unending quest for eligible bachelors propels A Brown Stone Front; a Story of New York and Saratoga (1873) by Chandos Fulton, and the pseudonymous Sophie Sparkle's Sparkles from Saratoga

(1873). Closing out the 19th century are two novels by Lucy Randall Comfort: The Belle of Saratoga (1876) and Love at Saratoga (1879); Edgar Van Zile's Wanted——a Sensation; a Saratoga Incident (1886); Marietta Holley's Samantha at Saratoga (1887); Caroline Washburn Rockwood's two novella in one volume——A Masque of Honor and A Saratoga Romance (1889); Sweet-brier (1889) by Mary Sherwood; and William Dean Howells' The Day of Their Wedding (1896) in which a Shaker couple about to leave their order and marry, experience the 'world outside' in the form of sophisticated Saratoga, and An Open-eyed Conspiracy; an Idyll of Saratoga (1897).

Edna Ferber's flamboyant Saratoga Trunk (1941) moves back and forth between Saratoga and New Orleans in the 1880s. The 1880s are also the time frame of James Sherburne's Death's Pale Horse; a Novel of Murder ... (1980). Nine of Stephen Dobyns' mystery/detective novels, all beginning with the key word 'Saratoga ...', often draw upon the atmosphere of Saratoga Springs' famous horse racing tradition. It may be something of a stretch to place the talented Richard Russo's novels in the Capital-Saratoga Region. However, he was born in Johnstown, Fulton County, which falls within that region and his Mohawk (1986) and The Risk Pool (1988) are laid in a fictional town, 'Mohawk' (presumably not to be equated with the actual town of Mohawk in Herkimer County) which suffers from a precipitous economic downturn; workers there with low-paying jobs or without jobs drink and gamble a lot and congregate at such spots as Harry's Mohawk Grill. In Russo's Nobody's Fool (1993) arthritic Sully is 60 and faced with employment, financial and familial problems as he makes the rounds in 'North Bath' (Schuylerville, Saratoga County).

ADIRONDACKS, THE NORTH COUNTRY AND THE THOUSAND ISLANDS-ST. LAWRENCE SEAWAY REGION

Philander Deming, in his Adirondack Tales (1880), was one of the earliest writers to describe in realistic terms the hardships faced by permanent residents of the Adirondacks. Thirty-seven years earlier, to be sure, Newton Mallory Curtis had written a bloody narrative of warfare between French and Indian invaders of the Adirondacks in the 1740s and their colonial American and Mohawk opponents, The Bride the Northern Wilds. The obscure Jean Kate Ludllum's At Brown's and Under Oath, both published in 1890, bore the subtitle: "An Adirondack Story." Elinor Fenton (1893) by David Skaats Foster was laid in a lumber settlement, 'Fentondale' (i.e. Lyons Falls?). The pseudonymous Walter Lecky with his two novels, Mr. Billy Buttons (1896) and Pere Monnier's Ward (1898) profiled life in Adirondack villages that contained a fairly large number of French-Canadians. The Adirondack Tales (1897/98) of William Henry Harrison Murray, former clergyman, public speaker and traveler, in some measure complemented the earlier work of Philander Deming. 1899 saw the advent of Frank Stockton's The Associate Hermits, the misadventures of a middle-aged urban couple in an Adirondack camp, and Gertrude Atherton's The Aristocrats, "being the impressions of Lady Henry Pole during her sojourn in the Great North Woods."

The first two decades of the twentieth century saw an increasing amount of fiction that chose the Adirondacks as the main focus of attention. From a baker's dozen the following warrant mention: Florence Wilkinson's The Strength of the Hills (1901) with a background of lumbering in the Saranac region; Samuel Page Johnson's Zebediah Sartwell (1903), whose protagonist is a wit and homespun philosopher resident in "Whallonsburgh", Essex County; Jacob Van der Veer Shurts' Kedar Kross (1908) in which a wealthy but distraught landowner searches for an abducted son and a wandering, mentally ill wife; Ernest Thompson's Seton's Rolf in the Woods (1911)—the hero, Rolf Kettering, comes to maturity in the forests of the Adirondacks in the early 1800s with the help of an Indian mentor; Della Trombly's The Hermit of the Adirondacks (1915)—the "Hermit" is only one of several "Adirondack" characters who must find ways to brush off afflictions visited upon them, particularly by "Sharky Dandy"; Richard Aumerle Maher's The Heart of a Man (1915), with its conflict between capital, the mill owner, and labor, the mill workers, in a manufacturing town in the lower Adirondacks.

From the 1920s through the 1990s the Adirondacks were a popular setting for the writers of mysteries and detective fiction. However the rugged forests, hills, lakes, streams and villages of the Adirondacks continued to attract writers of general fiction. In William Lindsey's The Backsliders (1922) a young, bookish Methodist pastor grows spiritually and absorbs valuable lessons in living from the Adirondack villagers in his parish. The climax of a major work of American fiction, Theodore Dreiser's An American Tragedy (1926), occurs at Big Moose Lake where pregnant Roberta Alden drowns while her lover, Clyde Griffiths, looks on. John B. Sanford's impressive short novel, Seventy Times Seven (1939), about the hardscrabble life of a Warrensburg farmer, was followed in 1976 by his Adirondack Stories. William Merrian Rouse's Bildad Road (1940) is made up of seventeen stories that introduce us to a gallery of "Adirondackers." The Touch of Human Hands (1947) by Joseph R. Linney draws on the author's own experiences in its portrayal of the operation of an iron mine and an ore-dressing mill in the Adirondacks. Aya Heald's Shadows Under Whiteface (1956) studies the relationships between the mountain and village people of the region and a very wealthy but arrogant man in their midst whom they intensely resent. In Buttes Landing (1978) Jean Rikhoff takes us from Jeffersonian America to the post-Civil War Adirondacks and proceeds through several more generations of the Buttes family.

The leading character in Sloan Wilson's Small Town (1978) is a former photographer and reporter who starts a newspaper in his Adirondack hometown—"memorable chiefly for its lovingly detailed descriptions of the Adirondack countryside" (Library Journal). In the 1979 novel of the same name by E.L. Doctorow, "Loon Lake" is the Adirondack estate of a steel magnate. The Adirondacks may seem a rather odd setting for two "gothics" by Joyce Carol Oates: Bellefleur (1980) and the Mysteries of Winterthurn (1984). Paul Zindel's The Amazing and Death-defying Diary of Eugene Dingman (1987) has its hero record in a diary his experiences as a waiter in an Adirondacks resort. The Sweet Hereafter (1991) by Russel Banks tells what occurred after a tragic school bus accident in a small Adirondack town. The Pinny Family of 'York Ferry' (1992), by Annie David, is deeply involved in the Adirondack town's steady decline. "Blackberry Mountain" in the Adirondacks, founded in the 1950s by charismatic "Doc" Holliday as a retreat from the age's rampant materialism and conservatism, is the scene of Geoffrey Wolff's The Age of Consent (1994).

Fiction about the Lake George and Lake Champlain regions is largely historical in nature. E.g., the French and Indian War (1754-1763) is the subject of novels, juvenile and adult, by Joseph Altsheler, Everett Tomlinson, Howard Breslin, Robert Chambers, Charles Dunning Clark, Sir Arthur Quiller-Couch, George P. R. James, Newton Mallory Curtis, and others. Of course, James Fenimore Cooper's The Last of the Mohicans (1826) is the most easily recognized novel of that period of conflict. A work that has a second title: A Romance of Lake George, is Fernand Claiborne's The Unfinished Tale; or, The Daughter of the Mill (1881); it is a story within a story of two unrequited loves and the possible suicide or murder of one of two heroines.

Two early works that relate (barely) to the history of northern New York are: Newton Mallory Curtis's The Maid of the Saranac (1848) which, despite its title, is concerned with military events in and around Plattsburgh during the War of 1812; and Albert B. Street's Frontenac; or, The Atotarho of the Iroquois, a Metrical Romance (1849), an account of the Governor-General of Canada's expedition against the Iroquois in 1694. John Townsend Trowbridge's Lucy Arlyn (1860) is a long novel that records the travails and ultimate tragedy of a young woman's failed marriage. Abner Beech spells out to his neighbors in a "little farmland township of northern New York" his opposition to Lincoln's war against the Southern separatists in Harold Frederic's The Copperhead (1893).

Irving Bacheller is by far the most prolific author of novels (at least eight) that cover the North Country (and the Adirondacks). Best known of his writings are Eben Holden (1900), a best seller in its day, that explores the relationship between a kind, wise hired man (Eben) and an orphan boy, and D'ri and I (1901), a novel of the War of 1812. Bacheller's contemporary, Everett Tomlinson, came out with three novels: (1) a juvenile, The Boy Soldiers of 1812 (1895), which traces the conflict from Sackett's Harbor to Ogdensburg, then westward to Queenston, Ontario; (2) Exiled from Two Lands (1898), the tragic tale of a French girl banished from her home in Canada to northern New York at the end of the 18th century; (3) The Self-Effacement of Malachi Joseph (1906), the story of a seminary graduate whose first ministry is in a little town of northern New York.

The Thousand Island-St. Lawrence Seaway region (including Jefferson, St. Lawrence and Oswego Counties) has appeared in fiction in a relatively few works, a number of them intended for juvenile readers and chiefly about camping and boating. A narrative poem by John Hugh McNaughton entitled Onnalinda (1884) is based on a battle near Irondequoit Bay in 1687 between the Seneca Indians and soldiers from New France. In 1973 Gardner B. Chapin's Tales of the St. Lawrence was a mix of fiction and historical sketches. Herbert John Sugden's Siege of the St. Lawrence (1948) is a French and Indian War tale much of whose action occurs at La Galette (Oswegatchie, in present-day St. Lawrence County). Of several mystery stories two, Harold MacGrath's Pidgin

Island (1914) and Stephen F. Wilcox's The St. Lawrence Run (1990) are entertaining and atmospheric.

Marietta Holley, 'the female Mark Twain' to some, a native and lifelong resident of Jefferson County, made skillful use of North Country dialect in her 'Samantha' sketches and tales. Samantha Allen is a firm believer in women's rights, suffrage and temperance who travels beyond Jonesville (not to be confused with the Saratoga County village) to New York City, Washington, D.C., Saratoga Springs, etc. Holley's writings more closely keyed to her native grounds include Miss Richards Boy and Other Stories (1883) and The Widow Doodle's Courtship and Other Sketches (1890).

THE CATSKILLS AND SOUTHEASTERN NEW YORK COUNTIES
(ORANGE, ROCKLAND, ULSTER)

If one contemplates the Catskill Mountains as the background for fictional narratives one writer immediately springs to mind: Washington Irving with two stories that appeared his The Sketches of Geoffrey Crayon, Gent. (1819/1820): Rip Van Winkle and The Legend of Sleepy Hollow, which is closely linked with 'Rip' but is primarily set in Tarrytown on the east bank of the Hudson. The Rip Van Van Winkle motif appears in two novels: Henry Llewellyn Williams's Rip Van Winkle (1866) and Sanford Friedman's Rip Van Winkle (1880). Old Cro' Nest (1846) by Robert F. Greeley tells of outlaws whose hideouts are in the forest outside the village of 'Kaaterskill'——the time, the mid-17th century. David Murdoch places his The Dutch Dominie of the Catskills (1861) during the American Revolution; the Reverend Schuneman, the dominie of the title, is a fiery patriot respected by friend and foe. Ann Sophia Stephens's Malaeska (1863) is noteworthy for being the first dime novel published by the firm of Beadle. The Catskill region and New York share the story's scenes. Malaeska, her white husband slain, takes her infant son to the Danforths in the City where he is raised as a white man; the revelation at the end of the novel that his mother is an Indian crushes young Danforth's pride. The Leech Club (1874) by George Washington Owen emphasizes political chicanery accompanied by manifestations of ghostly apparitions, "the mysteries of the Catskills." Henrietta H. Hammond's A Fair Philosopher (1882) by Henri Duage [pseud.] removes the three Alwyns (father John and his daughters, Drosee and Josephine) from New York City to a resort town in the Catskills where intellectual Drosee and beauteous 'Jo' pursue different paths to marriage.

In 1905 Arthur Henry wrote two novels: Lodgings in Town and The Unwritten Law; they are about New York City natives and their varying reactions to rural existence in the Catskills in the early years of the twentieth century. In The Spring Lady (1914) by Mary Brecht Pulver a New York society woman leaves husband and city for the values to be found in living close to nature in the Catskills. Strayed Revelers (1918) by Allan Updegraff portrays artists and philosophers from New York's Bohemia who have repaired to the Catskills just before and during America's entry into World War I. Nat Ferber's Spawn (1930) studies the effects of inbreeding and illegitimacy in 'Pike

Hollow'; the heroine is unable to escape her environment and the traditions of the isolated farming community in which she lives. Some of the atmosphere of the Rip Van Winkle legend can be found in Edmund Gilligan's Stranger in the Vly (1941). From 1949 to 1953 Oriana Atkinson, Russian-born wife of the drama critic Brooks Atkinson, completed three novels that mirror the lives of ordinary people in the valleys of the Catskills: Big Eyes, The Golden Season and The Twin Cousins. Former college teacher and poet and native of Margaretville, Mary Elizabeth Osborn's three well-crafted short novels: Another Pasture (1938), Days Beyond Recall (1942), and Listen for the Thrush (1955), have heroines native to the Catskills who are trying to cope with the slowly or suddenly realized isolation of their surroundings. 'Plutarchus', a small Catskill village in decline when a new highway bypasses it, is briefly enlivened through the efforts of one concerned individual in Victor Wolfson's The Eagles on the Plain (1947). Dusk in the Catskills (1957) by Reuben Wallenrod, translated from Yiddish, 'stars' Leo Halper and his wife, proprietors of the Hotel Brookville. Summer visitors and natives are drawn into the story while Leo unhappily reflects on the fate of victims of Nazi persecution and his own struggle to hold onto the hotel. The protagonists of the late John Gardner's Nickel Mountain (1973) are Henry Soames, overweight owner of a truck stop diner in the Catskills, and his wife Callie whom he married despite her pregnancy by an irresponsible wealthy man's son.

Crisis in the Catskills (1976) by Mary Bogardus is an effective historical novel whose theme is the anti-rent troubles of 1844-1846 in Delaware County in particular. The Cinderella theme is quite obvious in Carolyn Knight's The House in the Shadows (1979)—an orphan is treated shabbily by her guardian and his daughters but finds sympathy from neighbors; murder and puzzles from the orphan's past are revealed— the time, the 1830s. The novel Woodridge, 1946 (1980) by Martin Boris, revolves around a triangular affair in a well-evoked Catskill town. Richard Perry's 'Montgomery' in the Catskills is the home of several Afro-Americans from 1948-1980; they are buffeted by various shades of human debasement even as they search for redeeming love—the novel is entitled Montgomery's Children (1983). More recently David W. McCullough's Think on Death (1990) takes place in a Catskill town, once a 19th century Utopian community, which is now the hub of a successful industry; Allegra Goodman's Kaaterskill Falls (1998) visits the apprehensions aroused in the non-Jewish residents of the town and upscale Jewish summer dwellers as an Orthodox Jewish sect becomes a stronger presence in the community; and Eileen Pollack's Paradise, New York (1998) has as heroine, Lucy Appelbaum, 19, who has taken on management of her parents' Catskill Eden Hotel.

Stephen Crane's Sullivan County Tales and Sketches appeared in book format in 1948; his Whilomville Stories (1900), published posthumously, touch upon boyhood in Port Jervis. The Ramapo Valley and Orange and Rockland Counties are the scene of Elizabeth Oakes Smith's The Salamander (1848), Susan Warner's The Little Camp on Eagle Hill (1873), P. Demarest Johnson's Claudius, the Cowboy of Ramapo Valley (1854), and Marjorie Sherman Green's Cowboy of the Ramapos (1956). The plot of King Washington (1898) by Adelaide Skeel and William H. Brearley hinges on a hypothetical British conspiracy to kidnap General George Washington in 1782 from his headquarters in Newburgh and New Windsor; the title itself refers to an attempt by Colonel Lewis Nicola to persuade the General to be monarch of the new nation. Kate Seredy's Listening (1936) has an 'ancient' colonial house of Dutch ancestry in the Ramapo Mountains of southeastern New York and northwestern New Jersey as its dominating 'character.' The Hermit of the Catskills (1900) by De Witt Clinton Overbaugh is based on events in the American Revolution that took place around Hardenburgh Hall in Rosendale, Ulster County.

LEATHERSTOCKING COUNTRY (MOHAWK, CHENANGO AND SUSQUEHANNA VALLEYS, ONEIDA COUNTY)

Early works of fiction that encompass the Mohawk Valley include: Charles Fenno Hoffman's Greyslaer (1840) with the American Revolution as its background; Newton Mallory Curtis's The Doom of the Tory's Guard (1843), again with the American Revolution influencing the story's characters; Rebels and Tories (1851) by Lawrence Labree, a 'blood and thunder' piece that features the Battle of Oriskany, the massacre at Cherry Valley and various other Tory/Indian raids in the Mohawk Valley; and an anonymous work, The Frontiersman (1854), a post-American Revolution tale in which revenge-seeking Seneca Indians have a major role. James Kent's The Johnson Manor (1877), another post-Revolution story, follows the fortunes and misfortunes of Colonel James Johnson's family (no relation to Sir William Johnson). Mary Elizabeth Quackenbush Brush wrote three novels, primarily for juvenile readers——Paul and Persis (1883), Sarah Dakota (1894) and The Scarlet Patch (1905)——the first and third titles based on the Revolutionary War in the Mohawk Valley. In the Valley (1890) by Harold Frederic is a romance that unites an adopted daughter and the 'brother' who loves her after they pass through the maelstrom of the American Revolution. The heroine of Friedrich Spielhagen's The German Pioneers [Deutsche Pioniere] (1891) is Catherine Weise, an indentured servant, fought over by two brothers as the French and Indians attack their farm. A young Tory switches sides in 1777 just before the Saratoga campaign in Clinton Scollard's excellent The Son of a Tory (1901). As should be clear by now the American Revolution and the French and Indian War play a major role in fiction about the Mohawk Valley and this trend continues with Robert Chambers' The Maid-at-Arms (1902), The Backwoodsman (1904) by Hiram Alonso Stanley, and Frederick Augustus Ray's Maid of the Mohawk (1906). Elsie Singmaster's The Long Journey (1917) fictionalizes the youth of Conrad Weiser, future friend of and translator for the Mohawk Indians. In Alison Blair (1927) by Gertrude Crowninshield a young English girl migrates to the Mohawk Valley during the French and Indian War. The most widely read of all historical novels about the Mohawk Valley is very likely Drums along the Mohawk (1936) by Walter D. Edmonds; it was followed in 1949 by his Wilderness Clearing. Donald Cameron Shafer's Smokefires in Schoharie (1938) traces the fortunes of three generations of Palatine Germans who first settled in the Schoharie Valley in 1713. The Eagle's Song (1949) is a novel by Anne Miller Downes set in a town on the Mohawk River and covers several generations of two families from colonial times to the end of World War I.

Sir William Johnson (1715-1774), superintendent of Indian affairs, and Joseph Brant, Mohawk Indian leader, related to and allied with Johnson, were outstanding personalities in Mohawk Valley history; some of the fiction in which they played prominent roles include: The Trail of the Mohawk Chief (1916) by Everett Tomlinson; West to the Setting Sun (1944) by Harvey Chalmers; Clarissa Putnam of Tribe's Hill (1950) by John J. Vrooman; Margaret Widdemer's Red Cloak Flying (1950), Prince in Buckskin (1952), and The Golden Wildcat (1954); Brother Owl (1980) by Al Hine; Robert Moss's Fire along the Sky (1992) and The Firekeeper (1995); and Keeper of the Dawn (1995) by Alfred Silver. Historical novelist John Brick has the much-maligned Tory, Walter Butler, as a conspicuous character in two novels: The Raid (1951) and The King's Rangers (1954). The latter work emphasizes the Tory assessment of the American rebellion against the mother country. Orlo Miller traverses the same ground with his Raiders of the Mohawk (1958); Daniel Springer, a central figure in the story, is a Tory who joins Walter Butler's Rangers. Two novels that depart from historical themes are Bonnie Jones Reynolds' The Truth about Unicorns (1972) and James Buechler's In That Heaven There Should Be a Place for Me (1994). Reynolds' novel images small town life in the late 1920s and early 1930s; her model is Oriskany Falls in Oneida County. In his short stories centered around the Mohawk Valley Buechler's people are a mix of the children of recent European immigrants and the descendants of the original Dutch and English settlers. The Tory and Indian raid on Cherry Valley and the subsequent massacre (1778) led to Sullivan's campaign against the Iroquois. Four novels about the Cherry Valley incident that have been issued are: Edward Sylvester Ellis's The Rangers of the Mohawk (1862); Everett Tomlinson's The Red Chief (1905); Edward Eastman's The Destroyers (1947); and James Horan's King's Rebel (1953).

****

The Erie Canal has very close associations with the Mohawk Valley (the 15-mile section between Utica and Rome was opened in 1819) and it is fitting that mention should be made of the 24 (at the least) novels and story collections in which it plays a distinctive role. Walter D. Edmonds and Samuel Hopkins Adams are the outstanding chroniclers (fictional) of the Canal——Edmonds contributed Rome Haul (1929), Erie Water (1933), Mostly Canallers (1934), The Wedding Journey (1947), and two stories in The Night Raiders and Other Stories (1980); Adams wrote: Canal Town (1944), Banner by the Wayside (1947), Grandfather Stories (1955), and Chingo Smith of the Erie Canal (1958). Other works that warrant attention are: Jane Ludlow Abbot's Low Bridge (1935), Erick Berry's Lock Her Through (1940), James M. Fitch's The Ring Buster (1940), Zillah Katherine Macdonald's Two on a Tow (1942), Herbert Best's Watergate, a story of the Irish on the Erie Canal (1951), Harvey Chalmers' How the Irish Built the Erie (1965), Marvin A. Rapp's Canal Water and Whiskey (1965), and Patricia Matthew's Gambler in Love (1984).

****

Walter D. Edmonds has taken Upstate New York as his literary domain; four of his works are laid in Boonville, Oneida County and environs: The Big Barn (1930), The Boyds of Black River (1953), Bert Breen's Barn (1975), and, in part, the above-mentioned Night Raiders and Other Stories (1980). Harold Frederic's The Damnation of Theron Ware (1896) is a classic (albeit a minor one) of American literature that Joyce Carol Oates mourns 'is now virtually forgotten.' The novel's theme is the erosion of rigid Christian orthodoxy in the late 19th century. Theron Ware, a Methodist clergyman, is disappointed when he is assigned to 'Octavius' (believed to be Utica) with its strongly fundamentalist parishioners; exposed to enlightened ideas, secular and religious, he loses his way and finally leaves the ministry. In Marsena and Other Stories of the Wartime (1894) Frederic uses the same setting with the Civil War impinging on his character's lives. The growing of hops, once a thriving source of income in Oneida County, is the topic of Clinton Scollard's novel, A Knight of the Highway (1908). Man's Courage (1938) by Joseph Vogel tells of a Polish immigrant living in 'Genesee' (a fictional name for Utica) who is tragically frustrated in his attempt to acquire citizenship. Welsh settlers in the Steuben Hills north of Utica in the 1840s to ca. 1894 are the subject of two novels by Howard Thomas——The Singing Hills (1964) and The Road to Sixty (1966). Umbertina (1979) by Helen Barolini looks at three generations of Italian American women in 'Cato' (i.e. Utica). In 1994 Frank Lentricchia published two novelettes in one volume: Johnny Critelli and The Knifeman; both stories take place in Utica and the two protagonists are Italian Americans, one a rather mythical character, the other a doctor who is also a serial killer.

Venturing into the fiction keyed to the Chenango and Susquehanna Valleys one quite early encounters two novels by James Fenimore Cooper——The Pioneers; or, The Sources of the Susquehanna (1823) and The Deerslayer; or, The First Warpath (1841). Otsego Lake ('Glimmerglass') and Cooperstown provide the setting; the Deerslayer (or Natty Bumppo) is a young hunter living with the Delaware Indians in the first half of the 18th century. 'The Pioneers' finds Natty Bumppo disquieted by the environmental destruction practised by post-Revolution settlers (ca. 1793-1794). Ambition (1856), written by Sarah E. Coolidge under a pseudonym (Kate Willis), laid in Hamilton, Madison County and Albany, has a protagonist, Herbert Wells, who is driven by political ambition and in the end cannot elude the consequences of a sordid past. John Hilton Jones' The Dominie's Son (1874) plays largely in New York City, yet does return occasionally to 'Keesleyville' in the Chenango Valley, the chief character's hometown, Illma is the heroine in an anonymous novel with that title (1881) who is duped into a mock wedding, gives birth to an illegitimate baby girl, and is succored by a doctor and his sister; years later Illma returns to her parents' farm near Cooperstown after a successful opera career in Europe with surprising consequences for the novel's main characters. Although primarily interested in the march of technology in America, Roger Burlingame wrote several novels; his Three Bags Full (1936) takes the Van Huyten family through several generations in Cazenovia (disguised as 'Glenvil'). Harriet McDougal Daniels's Muller Hill (1943) and Nine-Mile Swamp (1941) are fictional evocations of two incidents in the history of the Chenango Valley. In 'Muller Hill' a mysterious French aristocrat builds a mansion for his Dutch American wife and their children and then suddenly abandons them, returning to France after Napoleon's temporary ouster to position himself among the claimants for the French throne; 'Nine-Mile Swamp' recounts the criminal exploits of the notorious Loomis Gang of horse and cattle thieves and counterfeiters in 1850s Madison County. The Covered Bridge (1950) and The Road (1952) by Herman Petersen concern a strong-willed farm woman in the Chenango Valley and, once again, the Loomis Gang (under the pseudonym, the Hugginses). Four of the novels of Frederick Busch who has taught at Colgate University have the aura of Upstate New York; one, Harry and Catherine (1990), involves a local squabble in a Chenango Valley town over a construction project that could disturb a slave burial ground.

FINGER LAKES AND GENESEE VALLEY

William Hosmer's Yonnondio (1844), a flowery narrative poem, renders an account of the French invasion of Seneca Indian country (in the Finger Lakes region) in 1687. Summerfield; or, Life on a Farm (1852) by Day Kellogg Lee is an early novel (perhaps the earliest) that deals at some length with rural life in the Finger Lakes (Cayuga Lake area). Almost fifty years later William Elliot Griffis's novel, The Pathfinders of the Revolution 1900) utilized "the local traditions of New York's [Finger] Lakes region [and] many old letters" as it gives an account of the Sullivan expedition against the Iroquois during the American Revolution. Two of the thirty-nine novels by Mary Jane Holmes (her popularity can be gauged by the sale of her books exceeding the two million mark) are Cousin Maude (1864), with its locale at 'Laurel Hill', just south of Canandaigua, the home of penurious Dr. Kennedy, his second wife, Matilda, two daughters, Nellie and Maude, and a son, crippled Louis; and Edna Browning (1872), whose heroine is ubiquitous, going from the Finger Lakes region to Chicago and western Massachusetts and finally marrying and settling down at the Leighton homestead on the Hudson.

A series of novels known as the Lake Shore series (five in all) published by Oliver Optic (the pen name of William Taylor Adams) were laid in the Finger Lakes region; representative of them is Brake Up; or, The Young Peacemakers (1872), the story of a rivalry between a steamship line (on 'Lake Ucayga'——i.e. Cayuga) and a railroad. With the exception of Tess of the Storm Country (1909) Grace Miller White's eight novels of heroines in the Cayuga Lake region (and Ithaca) battling prejudice, illiteracy and other ills drew little national attention, but they provided natives and residents many recognizable details of their settings, however lurid and melodramatic the stories. The 'Publick Universal Friend', Jemima Wilkinson, is a major figure in Robert St. John's novel, Jerusalem the Golden (1926); Jemima's peculiar blend of Shakerism and elements of Quakerism took root in the Seneca/Keuka Lake regions in the last decade of the 18th century, but faded into obscurity in the second decade of the 19th century.

Edward Havill's two novels set around Keuka Lake——Tell It to the Laughing Stars (1942) and The Low Road (1944)——celebrate a simple, rustic way of life, a retreat from the quickening pulse of early and mid-20th century urban existence. A direct descendant of John Humphrey Noyes, founder of the Oneida Community, wrote Seek-No-Further

(1938), a work of fiction that mixes communal life and spiritualism in the 1860s and 1870s; Grace Noyes Robertson was also the author of other novels that used Troy, Syracuse and several fictional towns somewhere in Upstate (or central) New York as their settings. Two novels that present accounts of the Oneida Community and its concepts of 'complex marriage' and free love are: Worth Tuttle Hedden's Wives of High Pasture (1944) and Blossom Elfman's The Strawberry Fields of Heaven (1983). The Misses Elliot of Geneva (1939) by Warren Hunting Smith is a witty tale of two conservative spinsters of the Seneca Lake town who fight any change or 'improvements' in their beloved Geneva. Included in fifteen entertaining mystery stories by Amber Dean—all with Upstate locales—are at least three with such settings as a 'summer colony in the Finger Lakes' and an 'old house on U.S. Route 15 in the Finger Lakes.'

In 'The Burning Spring' (1947) by Fayette Rowe, a farmer and his two sons scrabble to extract a living from their stunted Finger Lakes farm. In 'There Comes a Time' (1955) by Charles E. Mercer, a 'burned-out' pastor from a fashionable New York City parish comes back at age sixty-three to his native Finger Lakes and renews his faith as he reopens a long-dormant church. Mary Whitby, a schoolteacher, attends the Women's Rights Convention (1848) at Seneca Falls in Dorothea Malm's The Woman Question (1957). The Finger Lakes region as the nurturing ground for strong, independent women is implied in Haniel Long's Spring Returns (1958), although its 'hero' is Roger Wake, an orphan of nineteen, who possesses healing powers for those in mental stress. Maurice E. Miller's Seneca Drums (1969) relates how, with the American Revolution at an end, the sons of a Delaware Basin farmer migrate to a military tract on the shores of Seneca Lake and carve out a living, hampered though they be by inclement weather, vengeful Indians and wild animals. Closer to our own time is Brennan's Point (1988) by Daniel Lynch, the story of a wine-making family based in the Finger Lakes. Miriam Grace Monfredo of Rochester has written five mystery/historical novels whose chief character is a mid-19th century librarian in Seneca Falls, a witness to stirring events in that significant town——the beginnings of the women's rights movement, abolition and the Underground Railroad, and controversies surrounding spiritualism and temperance, etc.

Ithaca may be 'tiny town' population-wise, but it is large in matters educational and cultural, and it provides the background for a number of novels. Clara Loring Bogart's Emily; a Tale of the Empire State (1894) has for its heroine a farm girl who loses one lover to alcoholism, then turns to the nursing profession and eventually marries a merchant, a former clergyman dissatisfied with his church's excessive orthodoxy; Ithaca is the scene of part of this story. Florence Hyde's The Unfinished Symphony (1934) identifies many landmarks in the city of Ithaca, although she dubs the town 'Laconia.' Jane O'Daniel's The Cliff-Hangers (1961) portrays movie-making in Ithaca in the World War I era. Dan McCall's Triphammer (1990) follows an Irish-American policeman on his rounds in Ithaca. In 'The Names of the Dead' (1996) Stewart O'Nan traces the trials and tribulations of a Vietnam War veteran who is currently delivering cakes to Ithaca's food stores.

Since Ithaca is the main seat of Cornell University, the latter has figured in several 'college novels'. Cornell has appeared in disguise in the following: the short-lived

Richard Farina's Been Down So Long It Seems Like Up to Me (1966); The Widening Stain (1942) by W. Bolingbroke Johnson (pseudonym of Morris Bishop, late professor of Romance Languages at Cornell)——it's a tongue-in-cheek mystery involving the murders of two faculty members with the University Library in prominent display; Charles Thompson's Halfway Down the Stairs (1957); Matt Ruff's Fool on the Hill (1988); Katherine Ann Davis Roome's The Letter of the Law (1979); and the temporarily notorious Clifford Irving's On a Darkling Plain (1956). Alison Lurie's The War Between the Tates (1974) is set in a college in 'Corinth', New York; there has been speculation that Cornell University, where she teaches, and the city of Ithaca resemble the author's fictional locales. Nabokov's Pim (1957) has his protagonist, a Russian exile like himself, teaching at an Upstate New York college (Cornell——where Nabokov taught, as the model?).

Edward Noyes Westcott's only novel (he did write a short story, The Teller) was the instantaneous best seller David Harum (1898). Westcott was a Syracusan, but his character, Harum, the homespun philosopher and banker, has most often been linked to the village of Homer, Cortland County.

The city of Syracuse and the role of some of its citizens in the Underground Railroad are the theme of Constance Noyes Robertson's Fire Bell in the Night (1944). Clarence Buddington Kelland's The Lady and the Giant (1959) uses Syracuse at the setting as he novelizes the spurious Cardiff Giant, a traveling medicine show and Erie 'canawlers.' A Syracuse pet shop owner and part-time female detective, Robin Light, is the protagonist of a series of mysteries by Barbara Block (four of them as of 1998).

Perhaps the first substantial appearance in fiction of Rochester, New York State's third largest city, is in a work with the title: Life in Rochester; or, Sketches from Life (1848) 'by a resident citizen' (i.e. John Chamberlain Chumasero). This publication is a short novel (100 p.) which purports to disclose 'scenes of misery, vice, shame, and oppression in the city of the Genesee.' A sunnier view of life in Rochester is to be found in Rossiter Johnson's Phaeton Rogers; a Novel of Boy Life (1881). Paul Horgan's The Fault of Angels (1933) describes a city (he calls it 'Dorchester') endowed by a millionaire with excellent musical institutions; Nina Arenkoff, wife an opera conductor, tries to imbue the community with a zest for living spontaneously, directly and more realistically but fails. Mount Allegro (1943) by Jerre Mangione fictionalizes life in a 'colony' of Sicilian and Italian immigrants and newly naturalized citizens. Henry W. Clune's By His Own Hand (1952) records the rise to power of an industrialist in 'Minerva' (i.e. Rochester). Rochester reporter Jessica ('Jesse') James is the creation of Meg O'Brien who has thus far written four novels about the feisty Jessica as she snoops around the city and nearby towns. David Dorsey's The Cost of Living (1997) tracks the losing rat race of its 'hero'/narrator, employee of a Rochester advertising firm. East of Rochester the town of Newark ('Arcadia') may well be the locale of Charles Jackson's The Sunnier Side; Twelve Arcadian Tales (1950), that dwell on a boyhood and adolescence in Upstate New York.

The Scottish John Galt gathered material for his novel, Lawrie Todd (1830) while working for the Canada Company in Ontario, Canada. The story's hero, after several years in New York City, participates in a commercial venture in the Genesee Valley, but eventually goes back to Scotland. In 1860 Jane Marsh Parker published Barley Wood which draws a picture of the religious revival that swept central New York ('Litchfield' in the Genesee Valley is the chief locale of the novel); in 1886 Parker returned to the scenes of her earlier novel with The Midnight Cry——the time is the 1830s and 1840s and the Millerites with their prediction of the world's end play a prominent role. A curious piece of fiction with the title, Down the Banks; a Romance of the Genesee, by Iron Point (pseudonym of obscure Sireno French), appeared in 1877; the protagonist is 'Doctor' Raatsbein whose mission is to 'civilize' the Indians and the rough-hewn settlers in the Genesee Valley ca. 1787. The popular writer of books for boys, John Townsend Trowbridge, described Genesee Country in A Start in Life (1889). William Wilfrid Whalen's The Golden Squaw (1926) fictionalized the life of the White Woman of the Genesee, Indian captive Mary Jemison. Edward Roe Eastman, editor of the American Agriculturist, was the author of historical novels that were set in various regions of central New York. The Settlers (1950) is the story of several families that migrated from the patroon-dominated Hudson Valley to the Genesee Valley in the 30 years following the American Revolution. Genesee Fever (1943) by the late Carl Carmer is an historical novel of the Valley in the 1790s. Janet O'Daniel's O Genesee (1957) depicts the relationship from 1799 to the War of 1812 between Cyrus Fairchild, a prosperous farmer, and the restless frontiersman, Marcus Hook.

Frances Whitcher's The Widow Bedott Papers (1856) has Elmira as the locale of some its sketches——Whitesboro in Oneida County, the author's birthplace, is another locale. Edward Roe Eastman's No Drums (1951) limns the struggle of farmers in Tioga County to survive the changing weather and illness while supporting the Union cause in the Civil War. Jack Kelly's novel Apalachin (1987) refers to the meeting in that Tioga village of the American 'Mafia' in 1957, but the story itself hones in on the activities of mobsters in a place (possibly Buffalo) far from Apalachin.

For the purpose of this bibliography the designation 'central New York' encompasses the Finger Lakes region, the Genesee Valley, the Chenango and Susquehanna Valleys and perhaps the westernmost portion of the Mohawk Valley. In the works listed below the authors have set their novels in 'central New York' and that is as specific as most of them will be.

Mary Jane Hoffman's Felix Kent (1871) starts out in 'Tasso … a pleasant little village in the central part of New York.' The town nearest it is 'Livy'——such Italianate/classical place names are common coin in the Finger Lakes. 'Mapleville' in north central New York is a village that serves the author, Walter N. Hinman, in his Under the Maples (1888) as the home of a bevy of originals and two straightforward young men determined to succeed in their hometown and even outside its borders. The overplotted and dragged-out Marguerite's Mistake (1899) by Marion C. Donaldson is laid in a suburban college town and its neighboring city, 'H———', in central New York and later in the Adirondacks. Charles Reginald Sherlock's Your Uncle Lew (1901) is very close in conception to Edward Noyes Westcott's David Harum (1899); Uncle Lew, a central New Yorker, is proprietor of a railroad restaurant, but he is also a horse trader and a leading conversationalist at the local men's club. The deacon of Edgar G. Blankman's Deacon Babbitt (1906) is the mentor of the novel's hero; the latter is on a prolonged search for his missing parents whom he finally finds on a small farm in central New York and where he also meets his future wife. By naming the town 'Otsego' in her novel, The Tollivers (1944) Mateel Howe Farnham causes one to ask whether she intended the countryside around Otsego Lake to be the actual setting of this story of the three charming daughters of the flamboyant Tollivers and their escapades. A wholesale grocery business which owes its prosperity to commercial developments in central New York wrought by the Erie Canal is the base of the Quimby family's wealth until the 1930s and the retail trade revolution——Marian Champagne looks at this in her Quimby and Son (1962). Genesee Castle (1970), a short novel by Paul Bernard, records the progress of General Sullivan's troops from the Wyoming Valley of Pennsylvania to 'central' New York and the culminating Battle of Newtown (an Indian village near present-day Elmira) and finally to another Indian village, Genesee Castle.

The Cardiff Giant is the center piece of Harvey Jacobs's American Goliath (1997); the prehistoric hoax is displayed around Onondaga County and other central and eastern New York locales in the latter part of the 19th century——its final resting place is the Farmers' Museum in Cooperstown. Ann Mohin's The Farm She Was (1998) concentrates on the life of spinster 'Reeni' Leahy; it is a solitary and sometimes bitter existence for Reeni who from the age of eighteen to crippled old age manages her 20th century sheep farm in 'Donohue Flats', a town in central New York.

WESTERN NEW YORK STATE (INCLUDING THE NIAGARA FRONTIER AND THE CHAUTAUQUA REGION)

A portion of a little known work published in 1824/25, Tonnewonte; or, The Adopted Son of America, by Julia Catharine Beckwith, is laid in western New York, although it opens in New York City during the yellow fever epidemic of 1796 and pauses briefly in France. Other 19th century novels that are also set in no specifically identifiable place in western New York are: Julia MacNair Wright's temperance tale, Firebrands (1879); Farnell's Folly (185) by John Townsend Trowbridge; and Henry Francis Keenan's The Aliens (1886).

At the dawn of the 20th century Mark Lee Luther issued The Henchman (1900), a novel of local and state politics. Robert Edward Knowles's The Dawn at Shanty Bay (1907), places the main character in a Scottish settlement in western New York——he is a religious conservative who ultimately moderates his views. Canaway and the Lustigs (1909) by Joseph Leiser, is a story of Jewish life in a small western New York town seen through the eyes of two boys. Cecile Hulse Matschat's Preacher on Horseback (1940) portrays an immigrant from Hungary in the mid-19th century who studies medicine and then turns to theology, marries the daughter of a wealthy Long Island family, and carries on a ministry in western New York and Michigan. The grape growing region of western New York is the setting for Edward Havill's The Pinnacle (1951). Stowaway to America (1959) by Borghild Dahl walks in the steps of a Norwegian orphan who joins a group of dissenters in its voyage to America; these venturesome people establish in western the first permanent Norwegian settlement in America. Sally Daniels' The Inconstant Season (1941) has Peggy Dillon, the story's narrator reminiscing about growing up in western New York's wine country.

Richard Dougherty's We Dance and Sing (1971) fabricates the town of 'Jason Corners' where life from the 1920s to the late 1960s has its share of scandals as well as quiet moments. Batavia is the setting for the late John Gardner's The Sunlight Dialogues (1972) in which the town's police chief and a seasoned hippie, 'the Sunlight Man' (actually the son of a once-prominent Batavian family) discuss their opinions of society and morality. Foxfire (1993) by Joyce Carroll Oates, features a group of girls in Hammond (Lockport) rebelling against the hypocrisies of class society. The prolific Oates, born in Millersport, a few miles south of Lockport, frequently uses Upstate New York as a setting for her novels. Stephen F. Wilcox's three mystery novels——The Twenty Acre Plot (1991), The Nimby Factor (1992), The Painted Lady (1993)—— proffer interesting material about the western New York scene that he has selected as the stamping ground of his newspaper editor, Elias 'Hack' Hawkshaw, who enjoys rummaging through 19th century Victorian mansions.

The Niagara Frontier's treatment in fiction early appeared in Jesse Walker's Fort Niagara and Queenston, both published in 1845. In 1870 Charles R. Edward issued A Story of Niagara, an account of smuggling activities on the New York/Canadian border. Julia Evelyn Ditto Young in Adrift; a Story of Niagara (1889) related a story tinged with tragedy——the death of a bored married woman pursued by a New Yorker who in turn is killed when his boat overturns in the Niagara River. Amy Ella Blanchard's A Loyal Lass (1902) follows the War of 1812 to its final year, 1814. Folly Farm (1935) and River's Run (1950) by Jane Ludlow Drake Abbot explore the rigors of life on the Frontier just before and during the War of 1812. An impressionistic portrait of Niagara Falls is drawn by the French writer Michael Butor in Niagara; a Stereoscopic Novel (1969). Robert Lewis Taylor is in his familiar picaresque vein when he narrates the adventures of a wealthy young journalist hired by James Gordon Bennett to report on the fast-growing town of Niagara Falls——his novel's title: Niagara (1980). Niagara; a Novel (1993) by Richard A. Watson, throws together two unlikely associates——'The Great Gravelet', a French high-wire performer, and Anna Taylor, a widowed ex-teacher from Nebraska.

Roger Burke Dooley's trilogy——Days Beyond Recall (1949), The House of Shanahan (1952), Gone Tomorrow (1961)——takes the Irish Catholic Shanahan family of Buffalo from 1901 through the early years of the Great Depression. A.R. Gurney, the playwright, ventures into the field of fiction (a third time?) with The Snow Ball (1984) in which middle-aged Cooper Jones seeks to revive a social event that once attracted the younger members of Buffalo's exclusive families. Anthony Caputi in Loving Evie (1974) places his two main characters on a SUNY Buffalo campus——Merrick Baines, assistant professor of English, impregnates Evie Holman, a giddybrained student; he marries her, runs off searching for a new career start, but eventually returns to his wife and daughter. The decline of the steel industry in Buffalo is at the heart of Connie Rose Porter's All-Bright Court (1991) where a large number of black families reside in the 1960s and early 1970s.

The early years of what was to become the Chautauqua Institution fueled several novels including Isabella Macdonald Alden's (the 'Pansy' of children's literature) Four Girls at Chautauqua (1876), The Hall in the Grove (1881) and Four Mothers at Chautauqua (1913); the clergyman H.H. Moore's Ida Norton; or, Life at Chautauqua (1878); The Chautauquans, by John Habberton (1891); Grace Livingston Hill's A Chautauqua Idyl (1887); Tent V, Chautauqua (1885) by Mariana Tallman; and Cornelia A. Teal's Counting the Cost; or, A Summer at Chautauqua (1889).

Albion W. Tourgée's best-known novels deal with the South in the Reconstruction era, but he also penned three works——Button's Inn (1887), Black Ice (1888) and The Mortgage on the Hip-roof House (1896)——which describe a relatively placid way of life around Maysville, Chautauqua County. There is a face-off between an honest Chautauqua County police chief and gamblers who try to bribe him in Ellery Queen's The Copper Frame (1965). Joyce Carol Oates sets her novel Man Crazy (1997) in Chautauqua County (on the banks of the Chautauqua River——or Creek?); it is about a young girl with an alcoholic mother and a violent father (a Vietnam veteran) who is gang-raped by motorcyclers, but may have a future when she is hospitalized and is loved by an elderly psychiatrist.

'UPSTATE' NEW YORK

The following notes focus on selected works that claim to be laid in Upstate New York or several areas thereof, unspecified designations that could cover a number of places from eastern and central New York and minimally western New York to the Canadian border.

Taylor Caldwell specialized in dynastic, family chronicles. Included in that category are three of her novels laid in Upstate New York——The Wide House (1945), This Side of Innocence (1946) and The Sound of Thunder (1957). The chief characters in The Wide House are Stuart Coleman, a businessman, Janie Cauder (his widowed cousin), the bigot Joshua Allstairs and his daughter Marvina (whom Stuart marries to the undying displeasure of Janie), Sam Berkowitz, a German Jew, Father Houlihan, a Catholic priest; all have established roots in the prospering town of 'Grandeville.' In 'This Side of Innocence' the Upstate town of 'Riversend' is the home of the prominent Lindsey family; the tangled marital affairs of Jerome Lindsey, the adopted Alfred Lindsey, and the beautiful Amalie Maxwell, whom both men love at various intervals, are the main thread of the novel. Portrayed in The Sound of Thunder (1957) is a German-American family, the Engers, living in Upstate New York from 1904 to 1937, which is dependent on stolid, hard-working Ed Enger for its support, a situation that breeds hatred between Ed and his relatives.

A.J. Cline's Henry Courtland; or, What a Farmer Can Do (1870) has a protagonist, an Upstate agriculturist, who firmly believes that the farmer can be just as knowledgeable of human affairs as the sophisticated city-dweller. Yet Henry Courtland does not force his opinion on his sons, letting them chart their own courses.

Mystery writer Elizabeth Daly's Nothing Can Rescue Me (1943) and Night Walk (1947) feature a bibliophile, Henry Gamadge, who investigates murders occurring on a country estate, 'Underhill', and a somewhat gone-to-seed village, both in Upstate New York.

Nebraskan Clyde Brion Davis's Thudbury (1952) is rather far removed in place if not in time from his The Great American Novel (1938). Otis Paul Thudbury is a seeker after political and fiscal power; his 65 years (1880-1945) are largely spent in 'Tolland', an Upstate town, and he epitomizes (for Davis) the right-wing Republican who stretches business ethics to the breaking point.

Justin Stokes, the heroine of Gail Godwin's The Finishing School (1983), is an adolescent Southerner 'displaced' to Upstate New York where she learns much from a sophisticated middle-aged next-door neighbor, Ursula De Vane. The 'finishing school' is a cabin in the nearby forest to which Justin often retreats.

Corruption (1994) by Andrew Klavan deals with political chicanery in an Upstate New York city; the local sheriff, Cyrus Doolittle, the town's political boss, is opposed by

Sally Dawes of the Daily Champion; she is abetted by a Harvard-trained cub reporter and a veteran newsman.

Bernard Malamud's protagonist in Dubin's Lives (1979) is an eminent biographer, William B. Dubin, 56, a resident for 25 years of an aged house in Upstate New York near the town of 'Center Campobello', not far from the Vermont border. The married Dubin is currently at work on a biography of D.H. Lawrence; he is also entangled in a love affair with young Fanny Bick, 22, whom his wife, Kitty, had employed as housekeeper.

The Hammertown Tales (1986) of Hilary Masters, son of Edgar Lee Masters, is a small collection (128 p.) of stories about the inhabitants of an Upstate village bypassed by a freeway and thus in decline since the 1950s.

Peter Hamilton Myers was a lawyer who wrote poetry and five historical novels that are set in several areas of Upstate New York (the Mohawk Valley——Ellen Welles; or, The Siege of Fort Stanwix [1848]; the Hudson River and Valley, Lakes George and Champlain——The King of the Hurons [1850] and New York City and nearby Hudson towns (The First of the Knickerbockers [1848]; The Young Patroon [1849]; The Miser's Heir [1854]).

The playwright David Rabe's novel, Recital of the Dog (1993) is a semi-fantasy about an artist ensconced in Upstate New York, and his quarrel with a neighbor, the Old Man, and the latter's dog. In time the artist abuses his wife and son and is transformed into a dog himself.

The Linden family farm in Upstate New York, from the end of the Civil War to World War II, is the primary scene of Marjorie Kinnan Rawlings's The Sojourner (1953). The farm passes to a Polish family when Asahel, the last of the Lindens to care about the land, dies of a heart attack.

John Howard Spyker's Little Lives (1978) consists of sharply drawn vignettes of fictional characters who live or have died in a township of Upstate New York. The author considers his 'originals' representative of 'the human condition north of Albany.'

Edward Noyes Westcott's brother Frank was the author of a novel, Hepsey Burke (1915) whose main character (Hepsey) is a widow (in another Upstate town somewhat comparable to Edward's) who helps a young Episcopal priest and his wife adjust to their small parish.

BIBLIOGRAPHY

Adirondack bibliography; a list of books, pamphlets and periodical articles ... Compiled by The Bibliography Committee of the Adirondack Mountain Club. Gabriels, N.Y.: Adirondack Mountain Club, 1958-1973. 2v. (1958 vol. goes thru 1955; 1973 vol.—supplement, 1956-1965—published by Adirondack Museum, Blue Mountain Lake, N.Y.).

Allibone, Samuel Austin. *A critical dictionary of English literature and British and American authors, living and deceased, from the earliest accounts to the latter half of the 19th century...* Philadelphia: J.B. Lippincott, 1881. 3v.

American authors, 1600-1900; a biographical dictionary of American literature. Edited by Stanley J. Kunitz and Howard Haycraft. Complete in one volume with 1,300 biographies and 400 portraits. New York: H.W. Wilson Co., 1938.

The American bookseller; a semi-monthly journal, v. 1-32; Jan. 1, 1876–June 17, 1893. New York: American News Co.

American fiction, 1901-1910; cumulative author index to the microfilm collection. Woodbridge, CT.: Reading, Eng., Research Publications, 1984.

American women writers; a critical reference guide. Editor: Lina Mainiero. Associate editor: Langdon Lynne Faust. New York: F. Ungar, 1979-94. 5v.

Austen, Roger. *Playing the game*; the homosexual novel in America. Indianapolis: Bobbs-Merrill, 1977.

Author biographies master index; a consolidated index to more than 658,000 biographical sketches concerning authors living and dead as they appear in a selection of the principal biographical dictionaries devoted to authors, poets, journalists and other literary figures. 2d ed. Edited by Barbara McNeil and Miranda C. Herbert. Detroit: Gale Research Co., 1984. 2v.

Baker, Ernest A. *A guide to historical fiction.* New York: Argosy-Antiquarian, 1968. ("First printing, 1914").

Bassan, Maurice. *Hawthorne's son*; the life and literary career of Julian Hawthorne. Columbus: Ohio State University Press, 1970.

Baym, Nina. *Woman's fiction*; a guide to novels by and about women in America, 1820-70. 2d ed., with new introd. And supplementary bibliography. Urbana: University of Illinois Press, 1993.

Beatty, Richmond Croom. *Bayard Taylor, laureate of the Gilded Age*. Norman: University of Oklahoma Press, 1936.

Beckson, Karl. *Henry Harland, his life and work*. London: Eighteen Nineties Society, 1978.

Bellman, Samuel Irving. *Marjorie Kinnan Rawlings*. New York: Twayne, 1974.

Benet, William Rose. *The reader's encyclopedia*; an encyclopedia of world literature and the arts, with supplement. 2d ed. New York: T.Y. Crowell, 1965.

Benet's reader's encyclopedia of American literature. Edited by George Perkins, Barbara Perkins and Philip Leininger. New York: HarperCollins, c1991.

Bennett, Bob. *Horatio Alger*; a comprehensive bibliography. Mt. Pleasant, Mich.: Flying Eagle Pub. Co., 1980.

Bennett, George N. *The realism of William Dean Howells*. Nashville: Vanderbilt University Press, 1973.

Bergmann, Frank. *Robert Grant*. Boston: Twayne Publishers, 1982.

Bergmann, Hans. *God in the street*; New York writing from the penny press to Melville. Philadelphia: Temple University Press, 1995.

Biography and genealogy master index. 1981-85 cumulation; a consolidated index to more than 2,250,000 biographical sketches in 215 current and retrospective biograhical dictionaries. Barbara McNeil, editor. Detroit: Gale Research Co., 1985. 3v. In 1990 a 1986-1990 cumulation in 3v. was published, covering 1,895,000 biographical sketches in 250 current and retrospective biograhical dictionaries.

Bittner, William. *The novels of Waldo Frank*. Philadelphia: University of Pennsylvania Press, 1958.

Blake, Fay M. *The strike in the American novel*. Metuchen, N.J.: Scarecrow Press, 1972.

Bloodworth, William A. *Upton Sinclair*. Boston: Twayne Publishers, 1977.

Bloom, James D. *Left letters*; the culture wars of Mike Gold and Joseph Freeman. New York: Columbia University Press, 1992.

Blotner, Joseph. *The modern American political novel, 1900-1960*. Austin: University of Texas Press, 1966.

Bolger, Stephen Garrett. *The Irish character in American fiction, 1830-1860*. New York: Arno Press, 1976.

The book news monthly, v. 1-36; Sept. 1882–Aug. 1918. Philadelphia: Wanamaker. (Title varies slightly: *Book news*; a monthly journal [etc.]).

Book review digest, v.1- ; 1905- . New York: H.W. Wilson Co.

Book review index, v. 1- ; Jan. 1965- . Detroit: Gale Research Co.

Book week, v. 1-4; Sept. 15, 1963–July 16, 1967. New York: World Journal Tribune. (Superseded New York herald tribune Books).

The booklist, v. 1-52; Jan. 1905–Aug. 1956. Chicago: American Library Association. Resumed, v. 66- ; Sept. 1969- . (Known under the title: *The booklist and subscrption books bulletin.*—v. 53-65; Sept. 1956–Aug. 1969).

Bookman; a review of books and life, v.1-76, no. 3; Feb. 1895–Mar. 1933. New York: Dodd, Mead.

Breen, John L. *Novel verdicts*; a guide to courtroom fiction. Metuchen, N.J.: Scarecrow Press, 1984.

Briggs, Austin. *The novels of Harold Frederic*. Ithaca, N.Y.: Cornell University Press, 1969.

Brown, Herbert R. *The sentimental novel in America, 1789-1860*. Durham, N.C.: Duke University Press, 1940.

Cady, Edwin H. *Stephen Crane*. Rev. ed., Boston: Twayne Publishers, 1980.

Callow, James T. *Kindred spirits*; Knickerbocker writers and American artists, 1807-1855. Chapel Hill: University of North Carolina Press, 1967.

Canary, Robert H. *William Dunlap*. New York: Twayne Publishers, 1970.

Carey, Glenn O. *Edward Payson Roe*. Boston: Twayne Publishers, 1985.

Chametzky, Jules. *From the ghetto*; the fiction of Abraham Cahan. Amherst: University of Massachusetts Press, 1977.

The Chautauquan, [v.] 1-72; Oct. 1880–May 23, 1914. Meadville, Pa.: [etc.] Chautauqua Press. (Merged into The Independent).

Choice, v. 1- ; March 1964- . Chicago: Association of College and Research Libraries.

Coan, Otis W. *America in fiction*; an annotated list of novels that interpret aspects of life in the United States, Canada and Mexico [by] Otis W. Coan [and] Richard G. Lillard. 5th ed. Palo Alto, Calif.: Pacific Books, 1967.

Colby, Elbridge. *Theodore Winthrop*. New York: Twayne Publishers, 1965.

Contemporary authors; a bio-bibliographical guide to current writers in fiction, general non-fiction, poetry, journalism, drama, motion pictures, television and other fields. v. 1- ; 1962- . Detroit: Gale Research Co.

Cook, Raymond A. *Thomas Dixon*. New York: Twayne Publishers, 1974.

Cooke, Delmar Gross. *William Dean Howells*; a critical study. New York: Dutton, 1922.

Cotton, Gerald Brooks. *Fiction Index*; a guide to over 10,000 works of fiction … Compiled by G.B. Cotton and Alan Glencross. London: Association of Assistant Librarians, 1953.

The Critic, v. 1-49, no. 3; Jan. 15, 1881–Sept. 1906. New York: Critic Print. and Pub. Co.

Current-Garcia, Eugene. *O.Henry* (William Sidney Porter), New York: Twayne Publishers, 1965.

Curry, Jane. *Marietta Holley*. New York: Twayne Publishers, 1996.

Davis, David Brion. *Homicide in American fiction, 1798-1860*; a study in social values. Ithaca, N.Y.: Cornell University Press, 1957.

Davison, Richard Allan. *Charles G. Norris*. Boston: Twayne Publishers, 1983.

Denning, Michael. *Mechanic accents*; dime novels and working-class culture in America. London, New York: Verso, 1987.

The Dial, v. 1, no. 1 (May 1880)–v. 86, no. 7 (July 1929), Chicago: Jansen, McClurg.

Dickinson, A.T. *American historical fiction*. 3d ed. Metuchen, N.J.: Scarecrow Press, 1971.

Dictionary of literary biography., v. 1- . Detroit: Gale Research Co., 1978- .

Dixson, Zella Allen. *The comprehensive subject index to universal prose fiction*. New York: Dodd, Mead, 1897.

DuBois, Paul Z. *Paul Leicester Ford, an American man of letters, 1865-1902*. Introd. by L.H. Butterfield. New York: B. Franklin, 1977.

Dunlap, George Arthur. *The city in the American novel, 1789-1900*; a study of American novels portraying contemporary conditions in New York, Philadelphia, and Boston. New York: Russell & Russell, 1965.

Duyckinck, Evert Augustus. *The cyclopedia of American literature* ... by Evert A. and George L. Duyckinck. Edited to date by M. Laird Simons. Philadelphia: W. Rutter, 1875. 2v.

Echeverria, Durand. *The French image of America*, by Durand Echeverria and Everett C. Wilkie, Jr. Metuchen, N.J.: Scarecrow Press, 1994. 2v.

Edmiston, Susan. *Literary New York*; a history and guide, by Susan Edmiston and Linda D. Cirino. Introd. by Robert Phillips. Neighborhood walking tours rev. by Philip Lyman. Salt Lake City: Peregrine Smith Books, c1991.

Eichelberger, Clayton L. *A guide to critical reviews of United States fiction, 1870-1910*. Compiled by Clayton L. Eichelberger, assisted by Karen L. Bickley [and others] Metuchen, N.J.: Scarecrow Press, 1971-74. 2v.

Fiction catalog., 1st ed.; 1908- . New York: H.W. Wilson Co.

Fine, David N. *The city, the immigrant and American fiction, 1880-1920*. Metuchen, N.J.: Scarecrow Press, 1977.

Firkins, Oscar W. *William Dean Howells*; a study. Cambridge, Mass.: Harvard University Press, 1924.

Foster, Edward Halsey. *Catharine Maria Sedgwick*. New York: Twayne Publishers, 1974.

Foster, Edward Halsy. *Susan and Anna Warner*. Boston: Twayne Publishers, c1978.

Fredrickson, Robert S. *Hjalmar Hjorth Boyesen*. Boston: Twayne Publishers, 1980.

The galaxy, v. 1-25, no. 1; May 1866-Jan. 1878. New York: W.C. and F.P. Church, 1866-68; New York: Sheldon, 1868-78.

Gardner, Ralph D. *Horatio Alger*; or, *The American hero era*. Mendota, Ill.: Wayside Press, 1964.

Gilbert, Julie Goldsmith. *Ferber*; a biography. Garden City, N.Y.: Doubleday, 1978.

Giles, James R. *Claude McKay*. Boston: Twayne Publishers, 1976.

Glasrud, Clarence A. *Hjalmar Hjorth Boyesen*. Northfield, Minn.: Norwegian-American Historical Association, 1963.

Green, Rose Basile. *The Italian-American novel*; a document of the interaction of two cultures. Rutherford, N.J.: Fairleigh Dickinson University Press, 1974.

Griswold, William McCrillis. *Descriptive lists of American, international, romantic and British novels*. New York: Burt Franklin, 1968. ("Originally published Cambridge, Mass., 1891").

Gross, Theodore L. *Albion W. Tourgée*. New York: Twayne Publishers, 1963.

Gruber, Frank. *Horatio Alger, Jr.*; a biography and bibliography. West Los Angeles: Grover Jones Press, 1961.

Grunzweig, Walter. *Charles Sealsfield*. Boise, Idaho: Boise State University, 1985.

Handbook of American-Jewish literature; an analytical guide to topics, themes and sources. Lewis Fried, editor-in-chief. New York: Greenwood Press, 1988.

Hanna, Alfred J. *A bibliography of the writings of Irving Bacheller*. Winter Park, Fla.: Rollins College, 1939. (Rollins College bulletin, v. 35, no. 1, Sept. 1939).

Hanna, Archibald. *A mirror for the nation*; an annotated bibliography of American social fiction, 1901-1950. New York: Garland Pub., 1985.

Hapke, Laura. *Tales of the working girl*; wage-earning women in American literature, 1890-1925. New York: Twayne Publishers, 1992.

Harap. Louis. *The image of the Jew in American literature: from early republic to mass immigration*. Philadelphia: Jewish Publication Society of America, 1974.

Harper's lost reviews; the literary notes by Laurence Hutton, John Kendrick Bangs, and others. Compiled by Clayton L. Eichelberger. Millwood, N.Y.: KTO Press, 1976.

Harris, Susan K. *Nineteenth century American women's novels: interpretive strategies*. Cambridge [Eng.], New York: Cambridge University Press, 1990.

Harrison, Stanley R. *Edgar Fawcett*. New York: Twayne Publishers, 1972.

Hart, James D. *The Oxford companion to American literature, 5ᵗʰ ed*. New York: Oxford University Press, 1983.

Hart, John E. *Floyd Dell*. New York: Twayne Publishers, 1971.

Hart, John Seely. *The female prose writers of America*; 5th ed. Philadelphia: E.H. Butler, 1866 [c1851].

Heilman, Robert Bechtold. *America in English fiction, 1760-1800*; the influences of the American Revolution. Baton Rouge: Louisiana State University Press, 1937.

Hemstreet, Charles. *Literary New York*; its landmarks and associations. New York: G.P. Putnam, 1903.

Herron, Ima Honaker. *The small town in American literture*. Durham, N.C.: Duke University Press, 1930.

Hillway, Tyrus. *Herman Melville*. Rev. ed. Boston: Twayne Publishers, 1979.

Hubin, Allen J. *Crime fiction*; a comprehensive bibliography, 1749-1990. A completely rev. and updated ed. New York: Garland Pub., 1994.

The Independent, v. 1-106; Dec. 7, 1848–Sept. 24, 1921. New York: Independent Corp. [etc.].

Inglehart, Babette F. *The image of pluralism in American literature*; an annotated bibliography on the American experience of European ethnic groups, by Babette F. Inglehart and Anthony R. Mangione. New York: Institute of Pluralism and Group Identity of the American Jewish Committee, 1974.

Irwin, Leonard Bertram. *A guide to historical fiction*. For the use of schools and the general reader. 10th ed., new and rev. Brooklawn, N.J.: McKinley Pub. Co., 1971.

Jensen, Gerald E. *The life and letters of Henry Cuyler Bunner*. Durham, N.C.: Duke University Press, 1939.

Keiser, Albert. *The Indian in American literature*. New York: Oxford University Press, 1933.

Kelley, Mary. *Private women, public stage; literary domesticity in nineteenth-century America*. New York: Oxford University Press, 1984.

Killoran, Helen. *Edith Wharton: art and illusion*. Tuscaloosa: University of Alabama Press, 1996.

Kirk, Clara M. *William Dean Howells*, by Clara M. Kirk and Rudolf Kirk. New York: Twayne Publishers, 1962.

Kirk, John Foster. *A supplement to Allibone's Critical dictionary of English literature and British and American authors …* Philadelphia: J.B. Lippincott, 1891.

Kirkus reviews, Jan. 1933- New York: Kirkus Service. (Title varies).

Klein, Milton M. *New York in the American Revolution*; a bibliography. Albany: New York State American Revolution Bicentennial Commission, 1974.

Knapp, Bettina L. *Stephen Crane*. New York: Ungar, 1987.

Kramer, John E., Jr. *The American college novel*; an annotated bibliography. New York: Garland Pub., 1981.

Kramer, John E., Jr. *College mystery novels*; an annotated bibliography including a guide to professorial series-character sleuths [by] John E. Kramer, Jr. [and] John E. Kramer, III. New York: Garland Pub., 1983.

Lazarus, A.L. *Beyond Graustark*; George Barr McCutcheon, playwright discovered [by] A.L. Lazarus and Victor H. Jones. Port Washington, N.Y.: Kennikat Press, 1981.

Lease, Benjamin. *That wild fellow John Neal and the American literary revolution*. Chicago: University of Chicago Press, 1972.

Leider, Emily Wortis. *California's daughter*; Gertrude Atherton and her times. Stanford, Calif.: Stanford University Press, 1991.

Leisy, Ernest E. *The American historical novel*. Norman: University of Oklahoma Press, 1950.

Library journal, v. 1- ; Sept. 1876- . New York: R.R. Bowker [etc.].

The library journal book review, 1967-1980. New York: R.R. Bowker. 14v.

Liptzin, Solomon. *The Jew in American literature*. New York: 1966.

The literary world, v. 1, no. 1 (June 1878)–v. 35, no. 12 (Dec. 1904)–whole no. 11– whole no. 714. Boston, Mass.: S.R. Crocker.

Logasa, Hannah. *Historical fiction guide for junior and senior high schools and college*, also for general readers, 9th rev. and enl. ed. Brooklawn, N.J.: McKinley Pub. Co., 1968.

Loshe, Lillie Deming. *The early American novel*. New York: F. Ungar Pub. Co., 1958. (First published 1907 by Columbia University Press; reprinted 1930).

Lueders, Edward. *Carl Van Vechten*. New York: Twayne Publishers, 1965.

Lutwack, Leonard. *The role of place in literature.* Syracuse, N.Y.: Syracuse University Press, 1984.

Maida, Patricia M. *Mother of detective fiction*; the life and works of Anna Katharine Green. Bowling Green, Ohio, Bowling Green State University Popular Press, 1989.

Maurice, Arthur Bartlett. *New York in fiction.* New York: Dodd, Mead, 1901. [c1899/1900].

Maurice, Arthur Bartlett. *The New York of the novelists.* New York: Dodd, Mead, 1916.

McClure, Charlotte S. *Gertrude Atherton.* Boston: Twayne Publishers, 1979.

McDowell, Frederick P.W. *Ellen Glasgow and the ironic art of fiction.* Madison: University of Wisconsin Press, 1960.

McDowell, Margaret B. *Edith Wharton.* Boston: Twayne Publishers, 1976.

McGarry, Daniel B. *Historical fiction guide*; annotated chronological, geographical and topical list of five thousand selected historical novels, by Daniel D. McGarry and Sarah Harriman White. New York: Scarecrow Press, 1963.

Menendez, Albert J. *The Catholic novel*; an annotated bibliography. New York: Garland Pub., 1988.

Milne, Gordon. *The American political novel.* Norman: University of Oklahoma Press, 1966.

Milne, Gordon. *George William Curtis: the genteel tradition.* Bloomington: Indiana University Press, 1956.

Minor Knickerbockers. *Representative selections*, with introd., bibliography, and notes by Kendall B. Taft. New York: American Book Co., 1947.

Monaghan, Jay. *The Great Rascal*; the life and adventures of Ned Buntline. Boston: Little, Brown, 1952.

Moore, Jack B. *Maxwell Bodenheim.* New York: Twayne Publishers, c1970.

Morris, Linda A. *Women vernacular humorists in nineteenth-century America.* Ann Stephens, Frances Whitcher and Marietta Holley. New York: Garland Pub., 1988.

Morris, Linda A. *Women's humor in the age of gentility*; the life and works of Frances Miriam Whitcher. Syracuse, N.Y.: Syracuse University Press, 1992.

Nevius, Blake. *Edith Wharton*; a study of her fiction. Berkeley: University of California Press, 1953.

New York herald tribune. *Weekly book review*. v. [1]-40, no. 6; Sept. 21, 1924–Sept. 8, 1963. New York. (Title varies, e.g.: *New York herald tribune books*).

The New York times book review. Oct. 18, 1896- . New York: New York Times Co.

Nield, Jonathan. *A guide to the best historical novels and tales*. New York: Putnam, 1902.

Nineteenth-century American women writers; a bio-bibliographical critical sourcebook. Edited by Denise D. Knight. Emmanuel S. Nelson, advisory editor. Westport, Conn.: Greenwood Press, 1997.

North American review. v.1- .; May 1815- . [Cedar Falls, Iowa etc.] University of Northern Iowa [etc.].

O'Connell, Shaun. *Remarkable, unspeakable New York*; a literary history. Boston: Beacon Press, 1995.

O'Donnell, Thomas F. *Harold Frederic*, by Thomas F. O'Donnell and Hoyt C. Franchere. New York: Twayne Publishers, 1961.

O'Donnell, Thomas F. *The regional fiction of Upstate New York*. [Syracuse, N.Y.: 1957] (Ph.D. dissertation, Syracuse University).

Oliver, Lawrence J. *Brander Matthews, Theodore Roosevelt, and the politics of American literature, 1880-1920*. Knoxville: University of Tennessee Press, 1992.

Osborn, Scott Compton. *Richard Harding Davis* [by] Scott Compton Osborn and Robert L. Phillips, Jr. Boston: Twayne Publishers, 1978.

Overland monthly and Out West magazine. v. 1-15 (1868-1875); new ser., v. 1-47 (1883-1906); new ser., v. 49-64 (1907-1914). San Francisco: A. Roman, 1868-75; San Francisco Overland Pub. Co., 1876-1914.

Papashvily, Helen Waite. *All the happy endings*; the domestic novel in America, the women who wrote it, the women who read it, in the nineteenth century. New York: Harper, 1950.

Parrington, Vernon Louis, Jr. *American dreams*; a study of American utopias. 2nd ed., enl., with a postscript. New York: Russell & Russell, 1964.

Patrick, Walton R. *Ring Lardner*. New York: Twayne Publishers, 1963.

Pattee, Fred Lewis. *The first century of American literature, 1770-1870*. New York: D. Appleton, 1935.

Petter, Henri. *The early American novel*. Columbus: Ohio State Univerity Press, 1971.

Pilkington, John, Jr. *Francis Marion Crawford*. New York: Twayne Publishers, 1964.

Prestridge, Virginia Williamson. *The worker in American fiction*; an annotated bibliography. Campaign [Ill.] Institute of Labor & Industrial Relations, 1954.

Publishers weekly. v. 1- . ; Jan. 18, 1872- . New York: H.W. Wilson Co.

Quinn, Arthur Hobson. *American fiction*; an historical and critical survey. New York: Appleton-Century, 1936.

Ravitz, Abe C. *Alfred Henry Lewis*. Boise, Idaho: Boise State University, c1978.

Ravitz, Abe C. *David Graham Phillips*. New York: Twayne Publishers, 1966.

Rayback, Robert J. *Richards Atlas of New York State*. Robert J. Rayback, editor-in-chief. Contributors: Eleanor E. Hanlon [and others] Phoenix, N.Y.: F.E. Richards, 1959 [c1957-59]. (See Thomas F. O'Donnell's articles & literary maps on New York literature, p. 55-60).

The reader's encyclopedia of American literature, by Max J. Herzberg and the staff of the Thomas Y. Crowell Co. New York: Crowell, 1962.

Reynolds, Larry J. *James Kirke Paulding*. Boston: Twayne Publishers, 1984.

Rideout, Walter Bates. *The radical novel in the United States, 1900-1954*; some interrelations of literature and society. Cambridge, Mass.: Harvard University Press, 1956.

Ringe, Donald A. *James Fenimore Cooper*. Updated ed. Boston: Twayne Publishers, 1988.

Rouse, Blair. *Ellen Glasgow*. New York: Twayne Publishers, 1962.

Saturday review of literature. v. 1-35, no. 2; Aug. 2, 1924–Jan. 1952. New York: Saturday Review Associates [etc.].

Saturday review of politics, literature, science and art. v. 1, no. 1 (Nov. 3, 1855)–v. 124, no. 3236 (Nov. 3, 1917) London: J.W. Parker, 1856-1917.

Scharnhorst, Gary. *The lost life of Horatio Alger, Jr.*, by Gary Scharnhorst and Jack Bales. Bloomington: Indiana University Press, 1985.

Scribner Book Store. *American historical novels, fifteenth to nineteenth century.* A collection of first editions. New York [1937].

Sears, Donald A. *John Neal.* Boston: Twayne Publishers, 1978.

Sejourné, Philippe. *The mystery of Charlotte Lennox, first novelist of colonial America (1727?-1804).* Aix-en-Provence: Faculté des lettres d'Aix-en-Provence, Editions Ophrys, 1967.

Smith, Herbert F. *The popular American novel, 1865-1920.* Boston: Twayne Publishers, 1980.

Smith, Myron J., Jr. *Sea fiction guide*, by Myron J. Smith, Jr. and Robert C. Weller. With foreword by Rear Admiral Ernest M. Eller and craft notes by Edward L Beach [and others] Metuchen, N.J.: Scarecrow Press, 1976.

Smith, Myron J. *War story guide*; an annotated bibliography of military fiction. Metuchen, N.J.: Scarecrow Press, 1980.

Sprague, Claire. *Edgar Saltus.* New York: Twayne Publishers, 1968.

Tebbel, John. *From rags to riches*; Horatio Alger, Jr. and the American dream. New York: Macmillan, 1963.

Turco, Lewis. *The literature of New York*; a selective bibliography of colonial and native New York State authors. [Albany?] New York State English Council, 1970.

Uhlendorf, Bernard Alexander. *Charles Sealsfield*; ethnic elements and national problems in his works. Chicago: 1922.

Upstate literature; essays in memory of Thomas F. O'Donnell. Edited by Frank Bergmann. Syracuse, N.Y.: Syracuse University Press, 1985,

VanDerhoof, Jack Warner. *A bibliography of novels related to American frontier and colonial history.* Troy, N.Y.: Whitston Pub. Co., 1971.

Weathersby, Robert W., II. *J.H. Ingraham.* Boston: Twayne Publishers, c1980.

Weber, Paul C. *America in imaginative German literature in the first half of the nineteenth century.* New York: Columbia University Press, 1926,

Wegelin, Oscar. *Early American fiction, 1774-1830*; a compilation of the titles of works of fiction by writers born or residing in North America, north of the Mexican border and printed previous to 1831. 3d ed., corr. and enl. New York: Peter Smith, 1929.

Wermuth, Paul C. *Bayard Taylor*. New York: Twayne Publishers, 1973.

Who was who among North American authors, 1912-1939. Detroit: Gale Research Co,m 1976, 2v. (Reprint of the 7-vol. work edited by Alberta Lawrence—Los Angeles: Golden Syndicate Pub. Co., 1921-39).

Wilson, Rufus Rockwell. *New York in literature*; the story told in the landmarks of town and country, by Rufus Rockwell Wilson … in collaboration with Otilie Erickson Wilson. Elmira: Primavera Press, 1947.

Wilson library bulletin. v. 1- . ; Nov. 1914- . New York: H.W. Wilson Co. (Title varies: *Wilson bulletin*—to ca. 1936).

Winter, Kate H. *Marietta Holley*; life with 'Josiah Allen's wife'. Syracuse, N.Y.: Syracuse University Press, 1984.

Winter, Kate H. *The woman in the mountain*; reconstruction of self and land by Adirondack women writers. Albany: State University of New York Press, 1989.

Witham, W. Tasker. *The adolescent in the American novel, 1920-1960*. New York: F. Ungar Pub. Co., 1964.

Wright, Robert Glenn. *The social Christian novel*. New York: Greenwood Press, 1989.

Wyld, Lionel D. *Walter D. Edmonds, storyteller*. Syracuse, N.Y.: Syracuse University Press, 1982.

Wyman, Mary Alice. *Two American pioneers—Seba Smith and Elizabeth Oakes Smith*. New York: Columbia University Press, 1927.

Ziff, Larzer. *The American 1880s*; life and times of a lost generation. New York: Viking Press, 1966.

Zlotnick, Joan. *Portrait of an American city*: the novelists' New York. Port Washington, N.Y.: Kennikat Press, 1982.

CHRONOLOGY OF NEW YORK STATE IN FICTION,
1751 TO 1900

1751
Lennox, Charlotte Ramsay. *The life of Harriot Stuart.*

1755
Shebbeare, John. *Lydia; or, Filial piety.*

1784
Hilliard-d'Auberteuil, Michel René. *Mis MacRae.*

1785
The Liberal American

1790
Lennox, Charlotte Ramsay. *Euphemia.*

1791
Rowson, Susanna Haswell. *Charlotte* [Temple]

1797
Bleecker, Ann Eliza Schuyler. *The history of Maria Kittle.*

1798
The Fortunate discovery; or, *The history of Henry Villars.*

1807
Manvill, Mrs. P.D. *Lucinda.*

1809
Irving, Washington. *A history of New York.*

1819
Irving, Washington. *The sketch book of Geoffrey Crayon, gent.*

1821
Cooper, James Fenimore. *The spy.*

1823
Cooper, James Fenimore. *The pioneers.*

1824
Adsonville; or, *Marrying out.*

Cushing, Eliza Lanesford Foster. *Saratoga.*
Harte, Julia Catharine Beckwith. *Tonnewonte.*

1825
Changing scenes.
Furman, Garrit. *Redfield.*
Jones, James Athearn. *The refugee.*
Neal, John. *Brother Jonathan.*

1826
Cooper, James Fenimore. *The last of the Mohicans.*
Walker, Ambrose. *The Highlands.*

1827
Judah, Samuel Benjamin Helbert. *The buccaneers.*

1830
Galt, John. *Lawrie Todd.*
Sedgwick, Catharine Maria. *Clarence.*

1831
Paulding, James Kirke. *The Dutchman's fireside.*

1833
Oran, the outcast.

1834
Caruthers, William Alexander. *The Kentuckian in New York.*
Greene, Asa. *The perils of Pearl Street.*

1835
Fay, Theodore Sedgwick. *Norman Leslie.*
Sedgwick, Catharine Maria. *The Linwods.*
Thomas, Frederick William. *Clinton Bradshaw.*

1836
Crazy Luce
Dunlap, William. *Thirty years ago.*
Paulding, James Kirke. *The book of Saint Nicholas.*
Sedgwick, Catharine Maria. *The poor rich man and the rich poor man.*

1838
Cooper, James Fenimore. *Home as found.*
Embury, Emma Catherine. *Constance Latimer.*
Ingraham, Joseph Holt. *Burton.*
Leslie, Eliza. *Althea Vernon.*

1839

Bacon, Delia. *The bride of Fort Edward.*
The Brigantine or, *Admiral Lowe.*
Briggs, Charles Frederick. *The adventures of Harry Franco.*
Fay, Theodore Sedgwick. *Sidney Clifton.*
Ingraham, Joseph Holt. *Captain Kyd.*
Willet, W.N. *Charles Vincent.*

1840

Bradbury, Osgood. *Ellen Grant.*
Cooper, James Fenimore. *The pathfinder.*
Gilman, Caroline Howard. *Love's progress.*
Hoffman, Charles Fenno. *Greyslaer.*

1841

Brown, John Walker. *Constance*; or, *The merchant's daughter.*
Cooper, James Fenimore. *The deerslayer.*
Jackson, Frederick. *The victim of Chancery.*
Johnson, Aexander Bryan. *The philosophical emperor.*
Shecut, John Lewis Edward Whitridge. *Ish-Noo-Ju-Lut-Sche.*
Willis, John R. *Carleton.*

1842

Ingraham, Joseph Holt. *The dancing feather.*
Irving, John Treat. *The Quod correspondence.*
Mathews, Cornelius. *The career of Puffer Hopkins.*

1843

Abbott, Jacob. *Marco Polo's travels and adventures in the pursuit of knowledge: the Erie Canal.*
Boynton. Charles Brandon. *Isobel Wilton.*
Cooper, James Fenimore. *Wyandotté.*
Curtis, Newton Mallory. *The bride of the northernwilds. The doom of the Tory's Guard.*
Fay, Theodore Sedgwick. *Hoboken.*
Ingraham, Joseph Holt. *Frank Rivers.*
Mancur, John Henry. *Christine. The deserter. Wilfred Lovel.*
Nichols, Thomas Low. *Ellen Ramsay.*

1844

Arthur, Timothy Shay. *Hiram Elwood, the banker.*
Bradbury, Osgood. *Louise Kempton.*
The Family of the Seisers.
Hosmer, William Howe Cuyler. *Yonnondio.*
Ingraham, Joseph Holt. *The miseries of New York.*
Mowatt, Anna Cora. *The fortune hunter.*

Nichols, Thomas Low. *The lady in black.*
Sealsfield, Charles. *Rambleton.*
Shecut, John Lewis Edward Whitridge. *The scout.*

1845
Bradbury, Osgood. *Lucelle.*
Broughton, Joseph. *Solon Grind.*
Burdett, Charles. *The Elliott family. Never too late.*
Cooper, James Fenimore. *The chainbearers. Satanstoe.*
  Florence De Lacey; or, *The coquette.*
Mathews, Cornelius. *Big Abel, and the Little Manhattan.*
McIntosh, Maria Jane. *The cousins.*
Mowatt, Anna Cora. *Evelyn.*
Nichols, Thomas Low. *Raffle for a wife.*
Sargent, Epes. *Fleetwood.*
Shortfellow, Tom, pseud. *Mary Kale.*
Smith, Seba. *May-Day in New York.*
Trumble, Alfred. *Mysteries of New York.*
Walker, Jesse. *Fort Niagara. Queenston.*
Warren, Grenliffe. *The flying cloud.*

1846
Barker, Benjamin. *Clarilda.*
Burdett, Charles. *Chances and changes. The convict's child. Lilla Hart.*
Campbell, Jane C. *Catharine Clayton.*
Cooper, James Fenimore. *The redskins.*
Curtis, Newton Mallory. *The black-plumed rifleman.*
Greeley, Robert F. *Old Cro' Nest.*
Henry Russell.
Ingraham, Joseph Holt. *Leisler.*
Ingram, J.K. *Amelia Somers, the orphan.*
Kringle, Kris, pseud. *The beautiful girl.*
Law and laziness.
McIntosh, Maria Jane. *Two lives.*
Paulding, James Kirke. *The old continental.*
Penfeather, Amabel, pseud. *Elinor Wyllys.*
Smith, I. Anderson. *Blanche Vernon, the actress.*
Tucker, J.N.T. *Theresa. The two brides.*

1847
Burdett, Charles. *Arthur Martin.*
Curtis, Newton Mallory. *The patrol of the mountain. The ranger of Ravenstream.*
Hazelton, Frank. *The mysteries of Troy.*
Ingraham, Joseph Holt. *The treason of Arnold.*
Stephens, Ann Sophia. *Henry Longford.*
Sterling, Charles F. *Buff and blue.*

1848

Buchanan, Harrison Gray. *Asmodeus.*
Buntline, Ned. *The mysteries and miseries of New York.*
Burdett, Charles. *The gambler.*
Carra, Emma, pseud. *The hermit of the Hudson.*
Chumasero, John Chamberlain. *Life in Rochester.*
Curtis, Newton Mallory. *The foundling of the Mohawk.* *The maid of the Saranac.*
Dailey, W.B. *Saratoga.*
Myers, Peter Hamilton. *Ellen Welles.* *The first of the Knickerbockers.*
Oakley, E. *Eliza Atwood.*
Prime, William Cowper. *The Owl Creek letters.*
Smith, Elizabeth Oakes. *The salamander.*
Thompson, George. *The house breaker.*
Wilfred Montressor.

1849

Arthur, Timothy Shay. *Love in high life.*
Ayres, Jared Augustus. *The legends of Montauk.*
Buntline, Ned. *Three years after.*
Caroline Tracy, the Spring Street milliner's apprentice.
Duty versus will.
Hunter, Frederick. *The Spaniard.*
Ingraham, Joseph Holt. *The beautiful cigar vender.*
Mary Beach; or, *The Fulton Street cap maker.*
Myers, Peter Hamilton. *The young patroon.*
Peterson, Charles Jacobs. *Grace Dudley.*
Street, Alfred B. *Frontenac.*
Thompson, George. *City crimes.*
The three widows; or, *Various aspects of city life.*

1850

Buntline, Ned. *The b'hoys of New York.* *The g'hals of New York.*
Cooper, James Fenimore. *The ways of the hour.*
Foster, George G. *Celio.*
Foster, Henrie. *Ellen Grafton.*
Hare, Robert. *Standish the Puritan.*
Lippard, George. *The Empire City.*
Myers, Peter Hamilton. *The king of the Hurons.*

1851

Barlow, David Hatch. *The Howards.*
Bennett, Emerson. *The female spy.* *Rosalie DuPont.* *The unknown countess.*
Labree, Lawrence. *Rebels and Tories.*
Roe, Azel Stevens. *To love and be loved.*

Warner, Susan. *The wide, wide world.*

1852

Annals of the Empire City.
Ashland, Aria. *The rebel scout.*
Bowline, Charley. *The iron tomb.*
Bradbury, Osgood. *Therese.*
Bristed, Charles Astor. *The upper ten thousand.*
Clinton, Park. *Glanmore.*
Huet, M.M. *Silver and pewter.*
Huntington, Jedediah Vincent. *The forest.*
Lee, Day Kellogg. *Summerfield.*
Melville, Herman. *Pierre.*
Scoville, Joseph Alfred. *Clarence Bolton.*
Vose, John Denison. *Fresh leaves from the diary of a Broadway dandy.*
Warner, Susan. *Queechy.*

1853

The beautiful Jewess, Rachel Mendoza.
Bradbury, Osgood. *Emily, the beautiful seamstress.*
Buntline, Ned. *The wheel of misfortune.*
Curtis, George William. *The Potiphar papers.*
Huet, M.M. *Eva May, the foundling.*
Irving, John Treat. *Harry Harson.*
Lippard, George. *The Midnight Queen. New York: its upper ten and lower million.*
The river pirates; a tale of New York.
Thompson, George. *The brazen star.*
Walworth, Mansfield Tracy. *The mission of death.*
White, Rhoda Elizabeth Waterman. *Jane Arlington.*

1854

The Frontiersman; a narrative of 1783.
Greeley, Robert F. *Violet: the child of the city.*
James, George Payne Rainsford. *Ticonderoga.*
Myers, Peter Hamilton. *The miser's heir.*
Robinson, Solon. *Hot corn.*
Smith, Elizabeth Oakes. *The newsboy.*
Stephens, Ann Sophia. *Fashion and famine. High life in New York.*
Stimson, Alexander Lovett. *A tale of Easy Nat.*

1855

Bradbury, Osgood. *Jane Clark. The modern Othello.*
Estelle Grant; or, *The lost wife.*
Helen Leeson; a peep at New York society.
Ingraham, Joseph Holt. *Rivingstone.*
Maxwell, Maria. *Ernest Grey.*

Orton, Jason Rockwood. *Campfires of the Red Men.*
Phelps, Almira Hart. *Ida Norman.*
Stephens, Ann Sophia. *The old homestead.*
Thompson, George. *The locket.*
Thomson, Mortimer. *Doesticks, what he says.*
Warner, Anna Bartlett. *My brother's keeper.*

1856

Buckley, Maria L. *Amanda Willson.*
Burdett, Charles. *The second marriage.*
Coolidge, Sarah E. *Ambition.*
Capron, Carrie. *Helen Lincoln.*
Hazel, Harry, pseud. *Jack Waid, the cobbler of Gotham.*
Shepherd, Daniel. *Saratoga.*
The Spuytenduyvel chronicle.
Warner, Susan. *The hills of Shatemuc.*
Whitcher, Frances Miriam Berry. *The Widow Bedott papers.*

1857

Bradbury, Osgood. *The gambler's league.*
Cummings, Maria Susanna. *Mabel Vaughan.*
Duganne, Augustus Joseph Hickey. *The tenant house.*
Garangula, the Ongua-Honwa chief.
Higgins, Thomas W. *The Crooked Elm.*
Huntington, Cornelia. *Sea-Spray, a Long Island village.*
Old Haun, the pawnbroker.
Sedgwick, Catharine Maria. *Married or single?*

1858

Buntline, Ned. *Thayendanagea.*
Haven, Alice Bradley. *The Coopers.*
Huntington, Jedediah Vincent. *Blondes and brunettes.*
Smith, Charles Hatch. *George Melville.*
St. George De Lisle; or, *The serpent's sting.*
Thompson, George. *The gay girls of New York.*

1859

Howe, William Wirt. *The Pasha papers.*
Neal, John. *True womanhood.*
Two ways to wedlock.

1860

Brook Farm
Burdett, Charles. *Dora Barton.*
Edwards, Henry, novelist. *Annie; a New York life. Fashion and famine.*
Ellis, Edward Sylvester. *Seth Jones.*
Grainger, Arthur M. *Golden Feather.*
Huntington, Jedediah Vincent. *Rosemary.*
Lizzie Lee's daughter.
Parker, Jane Marsh. *Barley Wood.*

1861

Curtis, George William. *Trumps.*
Hankins, Marie Louise. *Women of New York.*
Minster, Annie Marie, pseud. *Glenelvan.*
Murdoch, David. *The Dutch dominie of the Catskills.*
Winthrop, Theodore. *Cecil Dreeme.*

1862

Buntline, Ned. *The Grossbeak mansion.*
Ellis, Edward Sylvester. *The rangers of the Mohawk.*
Gould, Edward Sherman. *John Doe and Richard Roe.*
Kimball, Richard Burleigh. *Undercurrents of Wall Street.*
Roe, Azel Stevens. *Like and unlike.*
Winthrop, Theodore. *Edwin Brothertoft.*

1863

Buntline, Ned. *The convict.*
Grey, Jeannie H. *Tactics.*
Morford, Henry. *Shoulderstraps.*
Sauzade, John S. *Garret Van Horn.*
Stephens, Ann Sophia. *Malaeska, the Indian wife of the White Hunter.*
Taylor, Bayard. *Hannah Thurston.*

1864

Arthur, Timothy Shay. *Out in the world.*
Bouton, John Bell. *Round the block.*
Holmes, Mary Jane Hawes. *Cousin Maude.*
Kimball, Richard Burleigh. *Was he successful?*
Scoville, Joseph Alfred. *Vigor.*
St. Clar, Robert. *The metropolites.*
Stephens, Ann Sophia. *The Indian queen.*
Walworth, Mansfield Tracy. *Hotspur.*

1865

Bradbury, Osgood. *Ellen: the pride of Broadway.*
Buntline, Ned. *Rose Seymour.*
Edwards, Henry, novelist. *The poor of New York.*
Roe, Azel Stevens. *Looking around.*
Taylor, Bayard. *John Godfrey's fortune.*

1866

Alger, Horatio. *Helen Ford. Timothy Crump's ward.*
Buntline, Ned. *Magdalena.*
Edwards, Henry, novelist. *The belle of Central Park.*
John Norton's conflict.
Mr. Winkfield.
Picton, Thomas. *The bootmaker of Fifth Avenue.*
Sadlier, Mary Anne Madden. *Aunt Honor's keepsake.*
Trowbridge, John Townsend. *Lucy Arlyn.*
Walworth, Mansfield Tracy. *Stormcliff.*
Williams, Henry Llewellyn. *Gay life in New York. Rip Van Winkle.*

1867

Alger, Horatio. *Fame and fortune. Ragged Dick.*
Griswold, V.M. *Hugo Blanc, the artist.*
Hammond, William Alexander. *Robert Severne.*
Mayer, Nathan. *Differences.*
Newell, Robert Henry. *Avery Glibun.*
Whitcher, Frances Miriam Berry. *Widow Spriggins.*
Wright, Julia McNair. *The shoe binders of New York.*

1868

Adams, Francis Colburn. *The Van Toodleburgs.*
Baer, Warren. *Champagne Charlie!*
Clark, Charles Dunning. *The lake rangers.*
Elliott, Charles Wyllys. *Wind and whirlwind.*
Kimball, Richard Burleigh. *Henry Powers (banker).*
Lee, Margaret. *Dr. Wilmer's love.*
St. Remy, Dirck. *Seven stories of the river counties.*
Stephens. Ann Sophia. *Mabel's mistake.*
Williams, Henry Llewellyn. *The steel safe.*
Wright, Julia McNair. *The New York needle-woman.*

1869

Alger, Horatio. *Rough and ready.*
Benedict, Frank Lee. *My daughter Elinor.*
Berriedale. *Unforgiven.*
Kinzie, Juliette Augusta McGill. *Walter Ogilby.*
Parker, Helen Eliza Fitch. *Constance Aylmer.*

Wright, Julia McNair. *The New York bible-woman.*

1870
Ames, Eleanor Marie Esterbrook. *Up Broadway.*
Buntline, Ned. *Charlie Bray.*
Cline, A.J. *Henry Courtland.*
Edwards, Charles R. *A story of Niagara.*
'Guilty or not guilty'!
Kimball, Richard Burleigh. *Today.*

1871
Aiken, Albert W. *The white witch.*
Alger, Horatio. *Paul the peddler.*
Crouch, Julia. *Three successful girls.*
Guernsey, Clara Florida. *The silver rifle.*
Harris, Miriam Coles. *Richard Vandermarck.*
Hoffman, Mary Jane. *Felix Kent.*
Howells, William Dean. *Their wedding journey.*
Smith, Miss M.E. *Emma Parker.*
Stowe, Harriet Beecher. *My wife and I.*

1872
Abbot, Lyman. *Laicus.*
Alger, Horatio. Phil the fiddler. *Slow and sure.*
Holmes, Mary Jane Hawes. *Edna Browning.*
Hume, John Ferguson. *Five hundred majority.*
Newell, Robert Henry. *The walking doll.*
Optic, Oliver. *Brake up.*
Searching for the white elephant in New York.
Story, James P. *Choisy.*
Warner, Susan. *The house in town.*

1873
Arthur, Timothy Shay. *Cast adrift.*
Chapin, Gardner B. *Tales of the St. Lawrence.*
Clark, Charles Dunning. *Mossfoot, the brave.*
Fawcett, Edgar. *Purple and fine linen.*
Fulton, Chandos. *A brown stone front.*
Holley, Marietta. *My opinions and Betsy Bobbet's.*
Roe, Edward Payson. *What can she do?*
Sparkles, Sophie. *Sparkles from Saratoga.*
Warner, Susan. *The little camp on Eagle Hill Trading.*

1874

Alger, Horatio. *Brave and bold.*
Blake, Lillie Devereux. *Fettered for life.*
Bricktop, pseud. *The trip of the Porgie.*
Davies, Theodore. *Losing to win.*
Jones, John Hilton. *The dominie's son.*
Kip, Leonard. *In three heads.*
Owen, George Washington. *The Leech Club.*
Perkins, Frederic Beecher. *Scrope.*
Roe, Edward Payson. *Opening a chestnut burr.*

1875

Burns, William. *Female life in New York City.*
Roe, Edward Payson. *From jest to earnest.*
Wilford, Florence. *Dominie Freylinghausen.*

1876

Alden, Isabella Macdonald. *Four girls at Chautauqua.*
Alger, Horatio. *Shifting for himself.*
Bricktop, pseud. *Smith in search of a wife. A trip to Niagara Falls.*
Comfort, Lucy Randall. *The belle of Saratoga.*
Cox, Palmer. *Hans Von Pelter's trip to Gotham.*
Derby, Aleck. *Ida Goldwin.*
Gayler, Charles. *Fritz, the emigrant.*
Reed, Isaac George. *From heaven to New York.*
Roe, Edward Payson. *Near to nature's heart.*

1877

Aiken, Albert W. *The phantom hand. The two detectives.*
Alden, Isabella Macdonald. *The Chautauqua girls at home.*
All for her.
All for him.
French, Sireno. *Down the banks.*
Holland, Josiah Gilbert. *Nicholas Minturn.*
Kent, James. *The Johnson manor.*
Roe, Edward Payson. *A knight of the nineteenth century.*
Ruppius, Otto. *The pedlar.*
Warner, Susan. *Pine needles.*

1878

Aiken, Albert W. *The California detective. The spotter detective.*
Baker, Joseph Marion. *Meladore.*
Bardeen, Charles William. *Roderick Hume.*
Bynner, Edwin Lassetter. *Tritons.*
De Cordova, Robert J. *Miss Fizzlebury's new girl.*
De Kay, Charles. *The Bohemian.*

For each other.
Green, Anna Katharine. *The Leavenworth case.*
Green, Mason Arnold. *Bitterwood.*
Harbaugh, Thomas Chalmers. *The hidden lodge.*
Keyes, Hervey. *The forest king.*
Lowell, Robert Traill Spence. *A story or two from an old Dutch town.*
Moore, H.H. *Ida Norton.*
Oliphant, Lawrence. *The tender recollections of Irene McGillicuddy.*
Roe, Edward Payson. *A face illumined.*

1879

Brown, L. Melyzia. *My Solomon.*
Comfort, Lucy Randall. *Corisande.*
Deming, Philander. *Adirondack stories.*
Fawcett, Edgar. *A hopeless case.*
Grant, Robert. *The confessions of a frivolous girl.*
Holley, Marietta. *My wayward partner.*
Noble, Annette Lucile. *"Out of the way."*
Oldboy, Oliver. *George Bailey.*
Roe, Azel Stevens. *How could he help it?*
Roe, Edward Payson. *A day of fate.*
Thompson, Ray. *A respectable family.*
Verdendorp, Basil. *The Verdendorps.*

1881

Aiken, Albert W. *The wolves of New York.*
Alden, Isabella Macdonald. *The hall in the grove.*
Alden, William Livingston. *The moral pirates.*
Anderson, C.H. *Armour.*
Claiborne, Fernand. *The unfinished tale.*
Douglas, Amanda Minnie. *Lost in a great city.*
Dunn, Julia E. *The bewildering widow.*
Fawcett, Edgar. *A gentleman of leisure.*
Green, Anna Katharine. *The sword of Damocles.*
Harrison, Constance Cary. *The story of Helen Troy.*
Ilma; or, *Which was wife?*
James, Henry. *Washington Square.*
Johnson, Rossiter. *Phaeton Rogers.*
Lee, Margaret. *Lorimer and wife.*
Lute, Uncle. *Paul Hart.*
Markham, Richard. *On the edge of winter.*
Roe, Edward Payson. *Without a home.*
Stoddard, William Osborn. *Dab Kinzer.*
Toland, Mary M.B. *Onti-Ora.*

1882

Alden, William Livingston. *The cruise of the 'Ghost.'*
Campbell, Helen. *Under green apple boughs.*
Hammond, Henrietta Hardy. *A fair philosopher.*
Hartshorn, Nancy, pseud. *Nancy Hartshorn at Chau-Tauqua.*
Lee, Margaret. *Divorce.*
Leslie, Madeline. *Rawlin's Mills.*
Sherwood, Mary Elizabeth Wilson. *A transplanted rose.*
Urner, Nathan D. *Naughty New York.*
Warner, Susan. The letter of credit.
Wilkins, W.A. *The Cleverdale mystery.*
The Witch-woman's revenge.

1883

Bishop, William Henry. *The house of a merchant prince.*
Boyesen, Hjalmar Hjorth. *A daughter of the philistines.*
Brush, Mary Elizabeth Quackenbush. *Paul and Persis.*
Bunner, Henry Cuyler. *A woman of honor.*
Davis, John A. *Tom Bard.*
Green, Anna Katharine. *Hand and ring.*
Holley, Marietta. *Miss Richard's boy.*
Hoppus, Mary A.M. *A great treason.*
Litchfield, Grace Denio. *Only an incident.*
Thiusen, Ismar. *The Diothas.*
Tourgée, Albion W. *Hot plowshares.*

1884

Adams, Henry. *Esther.*
Aiken, Albert W. *The genteel spotter.*
Alger, Horatio. *Dan the detective.*
Bailey, Nathan J. *Johnsville in the olden time.*
Belt, Harriett Pennawell. *Marjorie Huntingdon.*
Chambers, Julius. *On a margin.*
Clarkson, Louise. *The shadow of John Wallace.*
Fawcett, Edgar. *The adventures of a widow. An ambitious woman. Rutherford.*
Gardiner, Cecilia A. *Light ahead.*
Grant, Robert. *An average man.*
Hawthorne, Julian. *Beatrix Randolph. Love–or a name.*
Keyser, Harriette A. *Thorns in your sides.*
Leonie; or, The sweet street singer of New York.
Married above her.
McNaughton, John Hugh. *Onnalinda.*
Noble, Annette Lucile. *Miss Janet's old house.*
Roe, Edward Payson. *Nature's serial story.*
Stimson, Frederic Jesup. *The crime of Henry Vane.*
Victor, Metta Victoria Fuller. *Abijah Beanpole in New York.*

1885

Bayne, George Middleton. *Galaski.*

Campbell, Helen. *Mrs. Herndon's income.*

Cervus, G.I. *A model wife.*

Deming, Philander. *Tompkins and other folks.*

Dunning, Charlotte. *Upon a cast.*

Elmore, Mrs. A. *Billy's mother.*

Fawcett, Edgar. *Social silhouettes.*

Hammond, William Alexander. *Doctor Grattan. Mr. Oldmixon. A strong-minded woman.*

Harland, Henry. *As it was written.*

Hemyng, Bracebridge. *Jack Harkaway in New York.*

Holley, Marietta. *Sweet Cicely.*

Janvier, Thomas Allibone. *Color studies.*

Keenan, Henry Francis. *The money makers.*

Otis, James. *Left behind.*

Roe, Edward Payson. *An original belle.*

Schereschewsky, Mrs. Samuel Isaac Joseph. *Miss Ruby's novel.*

Searing, Annie Eliza Pidgeon. *A social experiment.*

Tallman, Mariana M. Bisbee. *Tent V, Chautauqua.*

Trowbridge, John Townsend. *Farnell's folly.*

Van Vorst, Frederick B. *Without a compass.*

1886

Alger, Horatio. *Helping himself.*

Barr, Amelia Edith Huddleston. *The bow of orange ribbon.*

Brooks, Elbridge Streeter. *In Leisler's time.*

Bunner, Henry Cuyler. *The midge.*

Burke, William Talbot. *Pingleton.*

Campbell, Helen. *Miss Melinda's opportunity.*

Cervus, G.I. *Cut.*

Dunning, Charlotte. *A step aside.*

Grant, Robert. *Face to face.*

The great wrongs of the shop girls.

Hamlin, Myra Louise Sawyer. *A politician's daughter.*

Harland, Henry. *Mrs. Peixada.*

Harper, Harry. *File no. 115.*

Hawthorne, Julian. *John Parmelee's curse.*

Hern, Henry. *A stepmother's victim.*

Johnson, Virginia Wales. *Tulip Place.*

Keenan, Henry Francis. *The aliens.*

Kirk, Ellen Warner Olney. *The story of Margaret Kent.*

Miller, Joaquin. *The destruction of Gotham.*

Montague, Charles Howard. *Two strokes of the bell.*

Morris, Charles. *Handsome Harry.*

Parker, Jane Marsh. *The midnght cry.*
Roosevelt, Robert Barnwell. *Love and luck.*
Valentine, Ferdinand Charles. *Gotham and the Gothamites.*
Van Zile, Edgar Sims. *Wanted—a sensation.*
Walworth, Jeannette Ritchie Halderman. *Old Fulkerson's clerk.*
Warth, Julian. *The full stature of a man.*
Wharton, Thomas Isaac. *Hannibal of New York.*
Wright, Julia McNair. *The story of Rasmus.*

1887

Alger, Horatio. Frank Fowler. *Number 91. The store boy.*
Bunner, Henry Cuyler. *The story of a New York house.*
Cabot, Arthur Winslow. *Two gentlemen of Gotham.*
Call, William T. *Josh Hayseed in New York.*
Coombs, Anne Sheldon. *A game of chance.*
Daintrey, Laura. *Miss Varian of New York.*
Dodd, Anna Bowman Blake. *The republic of the future.*
Eliot, Henry Rutherford. *The common chord.*
Fawcett, Edgar. *The confessions of Claud. The house at High Bridge.*
Gilder, Jeannette Leonard. *Taken by siege.*
Habberton, John. *Country luck.*
Harland, Henry. *The yoke of the Torah.*
Hawthorne, Julian. *An American penman. The great bank robbery. A tragic mystery.*
Hill, Grace Livingston. *A Chautauqua idyl.*
Holley, Marietta. *Samantha at Saratoga.*
Irving, John Trent. *The Van Gelder papers.*
McCray, Florine Thayer. *Environment.*
Munsey, Frank Andrew. *Afloat in a great city.*
Musick, John Roy. *Calamity Row.*
Post, Mary A. *Poverty Hollow.*
Ruben, Edward. *The path to fame.*
Saltus, Edgar. *Mr. Incoul's adventure.*
Savidge, Eugene Coleman. *Wallingford.*
Schaefer, Edward P. *The hidden voice.*
Sleight, Mary Breck. *The flag on the mill.*
Stockton, Frank Richard. *The hundredth man.*
Tourgée, Albion W. *Button's Inn.*
Warth, Julian. *Dorothy Thorn of Thornton.*
Willson, Thomas Edgar. *It is the law.*

1888

Adee, David Graham. *No. 19 State Street.*

Alger, Horatio. Tom Thatcher's fortune. *Tom Tracy.*

Carleton, Henry Guy. *The South Fifth Avenue Poker Club.*

Curran, John Elliott. *Miss Frances Merley.*

Daintrey, Laura. *Eros.*

Dickinson, Ellen E. *The King's Daughters.*

Ewing, Hugh Boyle. *A castle in the air.*

Fawcett, Edgar. *Divided lives. The evil that men do. A man's will. Miriam Balestier. Olivia Delaplaine.*

Green, Anna Katharine. *Behind closed doors.*

Harland, Henry. *My Uncle Florimond.*

Hawthorne, Julian. *An American Monte Cristo. Another's crime. A dream and a forgetting. Section 558.*

Hinman, Walter N. *Under the maples.*

Kirk, Ellen Warner Olney. *Queen Money.*

Litchfield, Grace Denio. *A hard-won victory.*

Longstreet, Abby Buchanan. *A debutante in New York society.*

Lull, De Los. *Father Solon.*

Munsey, Frank Andrew. *The boy broker.*

Owen, Catherine. *Gentle breadwinners.*

Pendleton, Edmund. *A Virginia inheritance.*

Pierson, Ernest De Lancey. *A slave of circumstances.*

Rollins, Alice Wellington. *Uncle Tom's tenement.*

Rouse, Lydia L. *Kezia and the doctor.*

Saltus, Edgar. *Eden.*

Shaw, Edward Richard. *The pot of gold.*

Stimson, Frederic Jesup. *First harvests.*

Tourgée, Albion W. *Black ice.*

Yardley, Jane Woolsey. *A superior woman.*

1889

Barns, Charles Edward. *Digby, chess professor. A portrait in crimson.*

Crowninshield, Mary Bradford. *Plucky Smalls.*

Dick, Herbert. *Sounding brass.*

Fawcett, Edgar. *A demoralizing marriage.*

Harland, Henry. *Grandison Mather.*

Hudson, William Cadwalader. *The diamond button.*

Johnson, Evelyn Kimball. *An errand girl.*

Kirk, Ellen Warner Olney. *A daughter of Eve.*

Lathrop, George Parsons. *Would you kill him?*

Libbey, Laura Jean. *Leonie Locke.*

McCarthy, Emma W. *Assemblyman John.*

McCornick, Joanna. By Hudson's banks.

Murray, William Henry Harrison. *The story that the keg told me.*

Pearson, Henry Clemens. *Her opportunity.*

Powell, Ella May. *Clio, a child of fate.*
Proudfit, David Law. *The man from the West.*
Rockwood, Caroline Washburn. *A Saratoga romance.*
Saltus, Edgar. *A transaction in hearts.   The pace that kills.*
Sheridan, Eugene. *A false couple.*
Sherwood, Mary Elizabeth Wilson. *Sweet-brier.*
Trowbridge, John Townsend. *A start in life.*
Trumble, Alfred. *The Mott Street Poker Club.*
Ulmann, Albert. *Frederick Struthers' romance.*
Warner, Charles Dudley. *A little journey in the world.*
Young, Julia Evelyn Ditto. *Adrift.*

1890

Aldrich, Anne Reeve. *The feet of love.*
Alger, Horatio. *A New York boy.   Struggling upward.*
Blake, E. Vinton. *The Dalzells of Daisydown.*
Bynner, Edwin Lassetter. *The begum's daughter.*
De Leon, Thomas Cooper. *Juny.*
Donnelly, Ignatius. *Caesar's Column.*
Egan, Maurice Francis. *The disappearance of John Longworthy.*
Ellsworth, Louise C. *A little worldling.*
Fawcett, Edgar. *A daughter of silence.   Fabian Dimitry.   How a husband forgave.*
Frederic, Harold. *In the valley.   The Lawton girl.*
Grant, Robert. *Mrs. Harold Stagg.*
Green, Anna Katharine. *A matter of millions.   A strange disappearance.*
Habberton, John. *Couldn't say no.*
Harrison, Constance Cary,. *The Anglomaniacs.*
Harrison, Lewis. *A strange infatuation.*
Holley, Marietta. *Samantha among the Brethren.   The Widow Doodle's courtship.*
Howe, Frank Howard. *A college widow.*
Howells, William Dean. *A hazard of new fortunes.*
Hudson, William Cadwalader. *Jack Gordon, knight errant.   Vivier.*
Kelly, Florence Finch. *On the inside.*
Lanza, Clara Hammond. *A modern marriage.*
Lee, Margaret. *A Brooklyn bachelor.*
Lincoln, Jeanie Thomas Gould. *An unwilling maid.*
Ludlum, Jean Kate. *At Brown's.   Under oath.*
Lynch, Lawrence L. *The lost witness.*
Meredith, William T. *Not of her father's race.*
Munroe, Kirk. Under orders.
Ogden, Ruth. *A loyal little Redcoat.*
Phillips, Ephraim. *Lost in the Adirondacks.*
Pierson, Ernest De Lancey. *A vagabond's honor.*
Quigg, Lemuel Ely. *Tintypes taken in the streets of New York.*
Sidney, Margaret. *An Adirondack cabin.*
Stoddard, William Osborn. *Chuck Purdy. Crowded out o' Crofield.*

Walworth, Mansfield Tracy. *Married in mask*.
Washburn, William Tucker. *The unknown city*.
Wheeler, Andrew Carpenter. *The Toltec cup*.

1891

Allen, Linda Marguerite Sangree. *Florine*.
Atherton, Gertrude Franklin. *A question of time*.
Barr, Amelia Edith Huddleston. *She loved a sailor*.
Bascom, Lee. *A god of Gotham*.
Bouton, John Bell. *The enchanted*.
Boyesen, Hjalmar Hjorth. *The manooth of unrighteousness*.
Bunner, Henry Cuyler. *"Short sixes."* *Zadoc Pine*.
Davis, Richard Harding. *Gallagher and other stories*.
Eggleston, Edward. *The faith doctor*.
Fawcett, Edgar. *A New York family*.
Gilman, Wenona. *A wandering beauty*.
Gordon, Julien. *A Puritan pagan*. *Vampires*
Habberton, John. *The Chautauquan*. *Out at Twinnett's*.
Hale, Edward Everett. *Four and five*.
Hamilton, Alice King. *Mildred's cadet*.
Harrison, Lewis. *Not to the swift*.
Hudson, William Cadwalader. *The Dugdale millions*. *The man with a thumb*.
Kirk, Ellen Warner Olney. *Ciphers*.
Leigh, Oliver Herbrand Gordon. *Dollarocracy*.
Libbey, Laura Jean. *Little Leafy ...*
Lillie, Lucy Cecil White. *For honor's sake*. *The squire's daughter*.
Ludlum, Jean Kate. *John Winthrop's defeat*.
Martel, Henry. *The social revolution*.
Moore, Susan Teackle Smith. *Ryle's open gate*.
Salisbury, Henry Barnard. *Miss Worden's hero*.
Smith, Francis Hopkinson. *Colonel Carter of Cartersville*.
Spielhagen, Friedrich. *The German pioneers*.
Wilcox, Ella Wheeler. *A double life*.

1892

Adee, David Graham. *The blue scarab*.
Aylesworth, Barton Orville. *"Thirteen."*
Bacheller, Irving. *The master of silence*.
Balestier, Josephine. *Life and Sylvia*.
Boyesen, Hjalmar Hjorth. *The golden calf*.
Burnham, Clara Louise Root. *Miss Bagg's secretary*.
Crawford, Francis Marion. *The three fates*.
Cumings, Elizabeth. *Miss Matilda Archambeau Van Dorn*.
Daintrey, Laura. *Actaeon*.
Dare, Arline. *Both were mistaken*.
Daving, Richard Harding. *Van Bibber, and others*.

Deene, Harley. *Cortlandt Laster, capitalist.*
Fawcett, Edgar. *The adopted daughter. An heir to millions. Women must weep.*
Gilliat, John R. W. *The loyalty of Longstreth. Mrs. Leslie and Mrs. Lennox.*
Gordon, Julien. *Marionettes.*
Green, Anna Katharine. *Cynthia Wakeham's money.*
Greene, Homer. *The Riverpark rebellion.*
Holt, Henry. *Calmire.*
Howell, Jeanne M. *A common mistake.*
Hudson, William Cadwalader. *On the rack.*
Jordan, Kate. *The other house.*
Leigh, Oliver Herbrand Gordon. *The family physician.*
Ludlow, James Meeker. *That angelic woman.*
Manley, R.M. *Some children of Adam.*
Mason, Louis Bond. *A survival of the fittest.*
Matthews, Brander. *A tale of twenty-five hours. Tom Paulding.*
Nella, Milton. *His one desire.*
Norris, Mary Harriott. *Afterward.*
O'Donnell, Jessie Fremont. *A soul from Pudge's Corners.*
Payne, Harold. *The Gilded Fly.*
Peeke, Margaret Bloodgood. *Born of flame.*
Scott, Milton Robinson. *Henry Elwood.*
Smith, John Talbot. *Saranac.*
Stoddard, William Osborn. *The battle of New York.*
Tippetts, Katherine Bell. *Prince Arengzeba.*
Wheeler, Andrew Carpenter. *The primrose path of dalliance.*
Wilcox, Ella Wheeler. *Sweet danger.*
Wood, John Seymour. *Gramercy Park.*

1893

Barr, Amelia Edith Huddleston. *Girls of a feather.*
Berry, Edward Payson. *Where the tides meet.*
Boyesen, Hjalmar Hjorth. *Social struggles.*
Ciambelli, Bernardino. *I misteri di Mulberry.*
Commelin, Anna Olcott. *Jerushy in Brooklyn.*
Crane, Stephen. *Maggie, a girl of the streets.*
Crawford, Francis Marion. *Marion Darche.*
Dale, Alan. *My footlight husband.*
De Witt, Julian A. *Life's battle won.*
Donaldson, Alfred Lee. *A Millbrook romance.*
Douglas, Julia. *Deerhurst.*
Ellsworth, Louise C. *Furono amati.*
Foster, David Skaats. *Elinor Fenton.*
Frederic, Harold. *The Copperhead.*
Green, Anna Katharine. *Marked 'personal.'*
Griswold, Hattie Tyng. *Fencing with shadows.*
Harrison, Constance Cary. *Sweet bells out of tune.*

Hawthorne, Julian. *Six Cent Sam's.*

Howells, William Dean. *The coast of Bohemia. The world of chance.*

Hurlbut, Ella Childs. *Mrs. Clift-Crosby's niece.*

Jeanne; the story of a Fresh Air child.

King, Edward. *Joseph Zalmonah.*

Kirke, Genevieve. *An unwedded wife.*

Minton, Maurice Meyer. *The road of the rough.*

Morse, Lucy Gibbons. *Rachel Stanwood.*

Norris, Mary Harriott. *John Applegate, surgeon.*

Otis, James. *Jenny Wren's boarding house. Josiah in New York.*

Piatt, Donn. *The Reverend Melancthon Poundex.*

Riis, Jacob August. *Nisby's Christmas.*

Saltus, Edgar. *Madam Sapphire.*

Savage, Richard Henry. *Delilah of Harlem.*

Stoddard, William Osborn. *Guert Ten Eyck. On the old frontier. Tom and the Money King.*

Stories of New York.

Vanamee, Lida Ostrom. *An Adirondack idyl.*

Way-way-seek-a-hook-ah.

Wright, Julia McNair. *Mr. Grosvenor's daughter.*

1894

Bacheller, Irving. *The still house of O'Darrow.*

Bogart, Clara Loring. *Emily.*

Bradley, Mary Emily Neely. *Martha's mistake.*

Brooks, Byron Alden. *Earth revisited.*

Brush, Mary Elizabeth Quackenbush. *Sarah Dakota.*

Castleman, Virginia Carter. *A child of the Covenant.*

Champney, Elizabeth Williams. *Witch Winnie at Shinnecock.*

Cheever, Harriet Anna. *St. Rockwell's little brother.*

Crawford, Francis Marion. *Katharine Lauderdale.*

Crawford, Marian. *Mam'zelle Beauty.*

Dodd, Anna Bowman Blake. *Struthers.*

Doubleday, E, Stillman. *Just plain folks.*

Downs, Sarah Elizabeth Forbush. *A true aristocrat.*

Edwards, C. *The rejected symbol.*

Ellis, Edward Sylvester. *Brave Tom. Honest Ned. Righting the wrong.*

Fawcett, Edgar. *A mild barbarian. Outrageous fortune.*

Ford, Paul Leicester. *The honorable Peter Stirling.*

Frederic, Harold. *Marsena.*

Giles, Fayette Stratton. *Shadows before.*

Gordon, Julien. *Poppaea.*

Harrison, Constance Cary. *A bachelor maid.*

Hudson, William Cadwalader. *Should she have left him?*

Hull, Charles. *Redeemed.*

Johnes, Winifred. *Miss Gwynne, bachelor.*

Johnson, P. Demarest. *Claudius, the cowboy of Ramapo Valley.*
Justice, Maibelle. *Love affairs of a worldly man.*
King, Charles. *Cadet days.*
Kirk, Ellen Warner Olney. *The story of Lawrence Garthe.*
Matthews, Brander. *Vignettes of Manhattan.*
McVickar, Henry Goelet. *The purple light of love.*
Nicholls, Charles Wilbur de Lyon. *The Greek madonna.*
Otis, James. The boys' revolt. *Jinny and his partners.*
Ottolengui, Rodrigues. *A modern wizard.*
Ross, Albert. *Love at seventy.*
Saltus, Edgar. *When dreams come true.*
Savage, Richard Henry. *A daughter of Judas.*
Stockton, John P. *Zephra.*
Stoddard, William Osborn. *The captain's boat. Chris the model-maker.*
Stratemeyer, Edward. *Richard Dare's venture.*
Sutro-Schucking, Kathinka. *Doctor Zernowitz.*
Warner, Charles Dudley. *The golden house.*
Webster, Leigh. *Another girl's experience.*
Willmott, Nellie Lowe. *A dash of red paint.*

1895

Alger, Horatio. *Adrift in the city.*
Appleton, Robert. *The rise of Mrs. Simpson.*
Baker, Josephine R. *Gee's trap.*
Belden, Jessie Perry Van Zile. *Fate at the door.*
Black, Alexander. *Miss Jerry.*
Buck, Francis Tillou. *A man of two minds.*
Conklin, Jennie Maria Drinkwater. *Three-and-twenty.*
Crawford, Francis Marion. *The Ralstons.*
Dallas, Mary Kyle. *Billtry.*
Davis, Harold McGill. *The city of endeavor.*
De Brose, Edward. *A modern pharisee.*
De Koven, Anna Farwell. *A sawdust doll.*
Drysdale, William. *The young reporter.*
Falkner, William C. *Lady Olivia.*
Ford, James Lauren. *Bohemia invaded. Dolly Dillenbeck.*
Gill, William. *The woman who didn't.*
Green, Anna Katharine. *The doctor, his wife and the clock.*
Hepworth, George Hughes. *Brown studies.,*
Hillhouse, Mansfield Lowell. *Storm King.*
Hyde, Mary Caroline. *Yan and Nochie of Tappan Sea.*
Jarvis, Stimson. *She lived in New York.*
Mason, Caroline Atwater. *A minister of the world.*
Matthews, Brander. *His father's son. The last meeting.*
New, Clarence Herbert. *Franc Elliott.*
Otis, James. *Jerry's family.*

Rives, Hallis Erminie. *A fool in spots.*
Ross, Albert. *A black Adonis.*
Seawell, Molly Elliot. *Midshipman Paulding.*
Shaw, Edward Richard. *Legends of Fire Island Beach.*
Smith, Edgar Maurice. *A daughter of humanity.*
Sullivan, James William. *Tenement tales of New York.*
Tomlinson, Everett Titsworth. *The boy soldiers of 1812. Three colonial boys.*
Townsend, Edward Waterman. *Chimmie Fadden explains ... Chimmie Fadden, Major Max ... A daughter of the tenements.*
Van Zile, Edgar Sims. *The Manhattaneers.*
Walworth, Jeannette Ritchie Hadermann. *An old fogy.*
Wright, Julia McNair. *A new Samaritan.*

1896

Alger, Horatio. *The young salesman.*
Anderson, Mrs. Finley. *A woman with a record.*
Barnes, James. *For king or country.*
Barnes, Willis. *Dame Fortune smiled.*
Blanchard, Amy Ella. *Girls together.*
Brooks, Elbridge Streeter. *Under the Tamaracks.*
Brown, Anna Robeson. *The black lamb.*
Buck, Francis Tillou. *A fiance on trial.*
Bunner, Henry Cuyler. *Jersey Street and Jersey Lane. Love in old clothes.*
Busch, Franc. *The Jewess, Leonora.*
Cahan, Abraham. *Yekl.*
Clingham, Clarice Irene. *That girl from Bogota.*
Craddock, Florence Nightingale. *Edgar Fairfax.*
Crane, Stephen. *George's mother.*
Douglas, Amanda Minnie. *A little girl in old New York.*
Drake, Jeanie. *The Metropolitans.*
Egan, Maurice Francis. *The vocation of Edward Conway.*
Frederic, Harold. *The damnation of Theron Ware.*
Gunter, Archibald Clavering. *Her senator.*
Howells, William Dean. *The day of their wedding.*
King, Pauline. *Alida Craig.*
Lecky, Walter. *Mr. Billy Buttons.*
Lillie, Lucy Cecil White. *Elinor Belden. Ruth Endicott's way.*
Ludlow, James Meeker. *The baritone's parish.*
Magruder, Julia. *The Violet.*
Maynard, Cora. *Some modern heretics.*
Meredith, Katharine Mary Cheever. *Green Gates.*
Merrilies, Meg. *The woman with good intentions.*
Moffat, William David. *Not without honor.*
Otis, James. *Teddy and Carrots.*
Ottolengui, Rodrigues. *The crime of the century.*
Post, Melville Davisson. *The strange schemes of Randoph Mason.*

Ralph, Julian. *People we pass.*
Rand, Edward Augustus. *Behind Manhattan gables.*
Ross, Albert. *His foster sister.*
Savage, Richard Henry. *Checked through, missing trunk no. 17580.*
Tourgée, Albion W. *The mortgage on the hip-roof house.*
Train, Elizabeth Phipps. *A social highwayman.*
Trask, Katrina. *White satin and homespun.*
Yechton, Barbara. *We ten.*

1897

Atherton, Gertrude Franklin. *Patience Sparhawk.*
Barr, Amelia Edith Huddleston. *The king's highway.*
Bickford, Luther H. *Phyllis in Bohemia.*
Clouston, Adella Octavia. *What would the world think?*
Crane, Stephen. *The third violet.*
Davies, Helen. *The reveries of a spinster.*
Denison, Mary Andrews. *Captain Molly.*
Egan, Maurice Francis. *The boys in the block. Jasper Thorn.*
Facilis. Two women who posed.
Fawcett, Edgar. *A romance of old New York.*
Ford, Paul Leicester. *The story of an untold love.*
Frederic, Harold. *Seth's brother's wife.*
Giles, Marie Florence. *The end of the journey.*
Glasgow, Ellen. *The descendant.*
Goodwin, Maud Wilder. *Flint, his faults.*
Gordeon, Julien. *Eat not thy heart.*
Green, Anna Katharine. *That affair next door.*
Greene, Waverly. *George Forest.*
Hamlin, Myra Louise Sawyer. *Nan in the city.*
Hotchkiss, Chauncey Crafts. *A colonial freelance.*
Howells, William Dean. *An open-eyed conspiracy.*
Lanza, Clara Hammond. *Horace Everett.*
Lillie, Lucy Cecil White. *A girl's ordeal.*
Martin, Mrs. George Madden. *The angel of the tenement.*
Mitchell, John Ames. *Gloria victis.*
Murray, William Henry Harrison. *The Adirondack tales.*
Otis, James. *The boys of Fort Schuyler.*
Payson, William Farquhar. *The copy-maker.*
Pryer, Charles. *Reminiscences of an old Westchester farmstead.*
Rayner, Emma. *Free to serve.*
Rockwood, Caroline Washburn. *An Adirondack romance.*
Sellingham, Ella J.H. *The hero of Carillon.*
Slater, Charles William. *A modern Babylon.*
Sparks, Alice Wilkinson. *My wife's husband.*
Stoddard, William Osborn. *Walled in.*
Stratemeyer, Edward. *Shorthand Tom.*

Taggart, Marion Ames. *Three girls and especially one.*
Terhune, Albert Payson. *Columbia stories.*
Townsend, Edwin Waterman. *Near a whole city full. The Yellow Kid in McFadden's Flats.*
Train, Elizabeth Phipps. *A marital liability.*
Trowbridge, John Townsend. *A question of damages.*
Watson, Augusta Campbell. *Beyond the city gates.*
White, Matthew. *The affair at Islington.*
Yechton, Barbara. *Derick.*
Yorke, Anthony. *Passing shadows.*

1898

Ayr, Mrs. Landis. *The Brown-Laurel marriage.*
Cahan, Abraham. *The imported bridegroom.*
Clews, James Blanchard. *Fortuna.*
Coxe, Virginia Rosalie. *The embassy ball.*
Didier, Charles Peale. *Would any man?*
Fawcett, Edgar. *New York.*
Frankel, A.H. *In gold we trust.*
Fuller, Anna. *One of the pilgrims.*
Giles, Marie Florence. *Though your sins be as scarlet.*
Glasgow, Ellen. *Phases of an inferior planet.*
Green, Anna Katharine. *Lost Man's Lane.*
Hale, F. Cameron. *A country tragedy.*
Harrison, Constance Cary. *Good Americans.*
Johnston, James Wesley. *Dwellers in Gotham.*
Jordan, Elizabeth Garver. *Tales of the city room.*
Lecky, Walter. *Pere Monnier's secret.*
Logan, Algernon Sidney. *Not on the chart.*
Magruder, Julia. *Labor of love.*
Maynard, Cora. *The letter and the spirit.*
Norris, Mary Harriott. *The gray house of the quarries.*
Oakley, Hester Caldwell. *As having nothing.*
Otis, James. *An amateur fireman. Corporal 'Lige's recruit. Joel Harford. The princess and Joe Potter. A traitor's escape.*
Peters, John A. *Two odd girls.*
Raymond, Evelyn Hunt. *Among the lindens.*
Riis, Jacob August. *Out of Mulberry Street.*
Rogers, Robert Cameron. *Old Dorset.*
Rouse, Adelaide Louise. *Annice Wynkoop.*
Sanderson, James Gardner. *Cornell stories.*
Savage, Richard Henry. *In the swim.*
Sayre, Theodore Burt. *Two summer girls and I.*
Skeel, Adelaide. *King Washington.*
Sleight, Mary Breck. *An island heroine.*
Stephens, Robert Neilson. *The Continental dragoon.*

Stoddard, William Osborn. *Success against odds.*
Tomlinson, Everett Titsworth. *Exiled from two lands. Two young patriots.*
Tourgée, Albion W. *The man who outlived himself.*
Train, Elizabeth Phipps. *A queen of hearts.*
Trask, Katrina. *John Leighton, Jr.*
Westcott, Edward Noyes. *David Harum.*
White, Matthew. *A born aristocrat.*
Wilson, David. *Life in Whitehall during the ship fever times.*
Yechton, Barbara. *A little turning aside.*

1899

Adams, Henry Austin. *Westchester.*
Alger, Horatio. *Rupert's ambition. Silas Sanderson's office boy.*
Bardeen, Charles William. *Commissioner Hume.*
Barr, Amelia Edith Huddleston. *Trinity bells.*
Behind the veil.
Blanchard, Amy Ella. *A Revolutionary maid.*
Burnham, Clara Louise Root. *A West Point wooing.*
Castlemon, Harry. *The white beaver.*
Chambers, Robert William. *Outsiders.*
Daniels, Cora Linn Morrison. *The bronze Buddha.*
Devoore, Ann. *Oliver Iverson.*
Donaldson, Marion C. *Marguerite's mistake.*
Ellis, Edward Sylvester. *Iron Heart.*
Fish, G. Williston. *Short rations.*
Gale, Sarah Helen. *The Grail brothers.*
Griffith, Susan M. *The ladder of promise.*
Harrison, Constance Cary. *The circle of a century.*
Jarrold, Ernest. *Mickey Finn idyls.*
King, Charles. *From school to battlefield.*
Magruder, Julia. *Struan.*
McCardell, Roy Larsen. *The wage slaves of New York.*
Morette, Edgar. *The Sturgis wager.*
Nicholls, Charles Wilbur de Lyon. *The decadents.*
Norton, Charles Ledyard. *The Queen's Rangers.*
Ogden, Ruth. *Loyal hearts and true.*
Otis, James. *The boy spies of old New York.*
Ralph, Julian. *An angel in a web.*
Schwartz, Julia Augusta. *Vassar studies.*
Sewell, Cornelius Van Vorst. *A gentleman in waiting.*
Stockton, Frank Richard. *The associate hermits.*
Stuart, Eleanor. *Averages.*
Taggart, Marion Ames. *Loyal blue and royal scarlet.*
Teal, Cornelia Adele. *Counting the cost.*
Tomlinson, Everett Titsworth. *Camping on the St. Lawrence.*
Tomlinson, Lena. *The triangle.*

Tyler, Randall Irving. *The blind goddess.*
Veysey, Arthur Henry. *Hats off!*
Warner, Charles Dudley. *That fortune.*
Wheelock, Julia Flander. *Annie Warden.*
Young, Albert A. *Stories from the Adirondacks.*

1900

Alger, Horatio. *Adrift in New York.*
Bacheller, Irving. *Eben Holden.*
Barr, Amelia Edith Huddleston. *The maid of Maiden Lane.*
Barrett, Wilson. *In old New York.*
Bennett, John. *Barnaby Lee.*
Brown, Anna Robeson. *The immortal garland.*
Campbell, Floy. *Camp Arcady.*
Crane, Stephen. *Whilomville stories.*
Dreiser, Theodore. *Sister Carrie.*
Duncan, Norman. *The soul of the street.*
Ellis, Edward Sylvester. *Red Jacket.*
Ford, Paul Leicester. *Wanted—a matchmaker.*
Gard, Anson Albert. *My friend Bill.*
Gilman, Nathaniel Isaiah. *Circumstantial affection.*
Grant, Robert. *Unleavened bread.*
Green, Anna Katharine. *The circular study. A difficult problem.*
Griffin, William Elliot. *The pathfinders of the Revolution.*
Hall, Ruth. *The black gown.*
Hardy, Francis H. *To the healing of the sea.*
Hurd, Grace Marguerite. *The Bennett twins.*
Kane, Edward Charles. *A gentleman born.*
Lewis, Alfred Henry. *Sandburrs.*
Lubin, David. *Let there be light.*
Mathews, Frances Aylmar. *The New Yorkers.*
Matthews, Brander. *The action and the word. A confident tomorrow.*
Meeker, Nellie J. *Beverly Osgood.*
Murphy, David. *Old Monypenny's.*
Myers, Cortland. *Would Christ belong to a labor union?*
Overbaugh, De Witt Clinton. *The Hermit of the Catskills.*
Paine, Albert Bigelow. *The bread line.*
Palier, Emile. *Social sinners.*
Ray, Anna Chapin. *Each life unfulfilled.*
Robinson, Margaret Blake. *Souls in pawn.*
Sadlier, Anna Theresa. *The true story of Master Gerard.*
Savage, Richard Henry. *The midnight passenger.*
Shackleton, Robert. *Toomey and others.*
Stark, Harriet. *The bacillus of beauty.*
Stephens, Robert Neilson. *Philip Winwood.*
Stephenson, Henry Thew. *Patroon Van VolkenBerg.*

Stoddard, William Osborn. *The young financier.*
Thomas, Henry Wilton. *The last lady of Mulberry.*
Tomlinson, Everett Titsworth. *The houseboat on the St. Lawrence.*
Wellington, Courtney. *Congressman Hardie.*

AN

ANNOTATED

BIBLIOGRAPHY

Aaron, Edward Sidney, 1916-1975. See under his pseudonym: Ronns, Edward, 1916-1975.

Abbott, Anthony, pseudonym. See: Oursler, Fulton, 1893-1952.

Abbott, George, 1887-1995, joint author. *Broadway.* See Item #969.

1. [Abbott, Jacob] 1803-1879. *Marco Paul's travels and adventures in the pursuit of knowledge. On the Erie Canal.* By the author of *Rollo*, Jonas and Lucy books. Boston: T.H. Carter, 1843. 140p.

    Marco's tutor, Forester, takes him on a field trip on the Erie Canal as a way of educating the boy. They start out from Albany on a packet and in the course of their journey acquire much knowledge about the technical aspects of canal travel and its boats.

2. Abbott, Jane Ludlow Drake, 1881-1962. *Folly Farm.* Philadelphia: J.B. Lippincott, 1935. 314p.

    The rigors of life on the Niagara frontier (the settlement of Buffalo was not too far away) were in sharp contrast to the comfortable one 13-year-old Jeremy Haverhill had left behind in the Philadelphia area. She was supportive of her father and mother, however, and adapted so well that she was able to play a responsible role when war came. The time frame of the novel is 1809 to 1812.

3. ————. *Heyday.* Philadelphia: J. B. Lippincott, 1928. 313p.

    Bequeathed a boarding house in New York City by her deceased aunt, Jay sets out from her hometown for the metropolis. In the course of establishing herself as proprietor of her legacy Jay falls in love but maintains her own simple, solid life style despite the lures of New York.

4. ————. *Janny.* With illus. by Emlen McConnell. Philadelphia: J.B. Lippincott, 1927. 288p.

    Finding herself in New York City after previous existence in a Canadian mining camp, Janny comes upon a piece of paper that could be the means of bestowing a fortune on the city cousins who have treated her with barely concealed disdain.

5. ————. *Lowbridge.* Illus. by Walter Pyle. Philadelphia: J.B. Lippincott, 1935. 317p.

    The young heroine, Decy, and her father cruise the Erie Canal at the height of its prosperity, touching such canal towns as Utica, Rome, Rochester, and Lockport. Later Decy is turned into a fashionable young lady by wealthy relatives. A subplot deals with some dissatisfied Canadians in a stronghold on a Niagara River island who try to create new dissension between the United States and Great Britain.

6. —————. *Minglestreams*. **With a front. in color by H. Weston Taylor. Philadelphia: J.B. Lippincott, 1923. 320p.**

Hester Browning and Jill Gerard take over the management of the Apple Tree Inn in New York State's Adirondacks. While walking in the woods near the inn they come across a young man (John) suffering from amnesia, the result of shell shock. As his memory slowly returns, John (he is in the diplomatic service) and Jill fall in love. Hester, who has been the chief promoter of the inn project, seems destined to slide back into the baneful middle class life that she had hoped to put behind her.

7. —————. *River's rim*; **a novel. Philadelphia: J.B. Lippincott, 1950. 254p.**

Quint Darby, a patriotic young American on the Niagara frontier during the War of 1912, is an object of suspicion because of the British sympathies of his father and brother. This makes him doubly anxious to prove his loyalty to the new nation.

8. **Abbott, Lyman, 1835-1922.** *Laicus*; **or,** *The experiences of a layman in a country parish.* **New York: Dodd, Mead, 1872. 358p.**

'Wheathedge', the 'country parish' is ca. 60 miles north of New York City. In 1866 John 'Laicus', a lawyer, and his wife Jemmie mutually agree to take semi-permanent residence there, although John continues to transact his legal business from a New York City office. Gradually John is drawn into virtually all aspects of the Calvary Presbyterian Church's affairs (he claims to prefer Congregationalism) reluctantly, at first, teaching a Bible class. The story serves as a vehicle for the author, a Congregational minister, to promote his version of progressive and practical Christianity. In 1873 the novel was reissued under the title: *Layman's story*; or, *Experiences of John Laicus in a country parish*.

9. **Abdullah, Achmed, 1881-1945.** *Broadway interlude*, **by Achmed Abdullah and Faith Baldwin Cuthrell. New York: Payson & Clarke, 1929. 306p.**

'Bedrock', the title of Bob Foster's initial play-writing venture, stars a young actress, Sally Cameron, and is produced by Leo Cardozo. The latter is a preeminent force in the theatrical world of New York City; he develops a more than professional interest in Sally—it is within his power to foster her career as he had with other actresses. However, Sally artfully brushes aside his overtures because she is in love with Bob. 'Bedrock' does not make any impact on Broadway. Yet Sally and Bob marry and, undiscouraged, will continue to strive for success in their chosen profession.

10. —————. *The honourable gentlemen, and others.* **New York: Putnam 1919. 262p.**

Short stories of New York City's Chinatown illustrative in part of the contrast between the older generation of Chinese, retentive of the culture and customs of the old country, and the younger generation, adapting to the language and attitudes of its American peers. There is also drawn a somewhat ugly picture of the dislike, and even contempt, of certain White men for Yellow men and vice versa. Contents: The honourable gentlemen.—The hatchetman.—Pell Street spring song.—Cobbler's Wax.—After his kind.—A simple act of pity.—Himself, to himself enough.

11. **Abel, Hilda.** *The guests of summer.* **Indianapolis: Bobbs-Merrill, 1951. 271p.**
   "A summer hotel in the Adirondacks in 1939 is the scene of the story. The story itself concerns chiefly the thoughts and emotions of a young Jewish girl, daughter of a refugee woman doctor, and her gradual growth to understanding of herself and her mother"—Book review digest.

12. **Abu-Jaber, Diana, 1959-.** *Arabian jazz.* **New York: Harcourt, Brace, 1993. 374p.**
   A Jordanian family in Upstate New York—Matussem, the father, a widower; two daughters, Melvina and Jemorah; and Matussem's sister, Fatima—are struggling to adjust to American manners and customs. Matussem has a gig as a jazz drummer, and his daughters join fellow workers at a bar with the odd name, Won Ton a Go-Go. Jemorah has flings with a gas station attendant and a loud-mouthed pool hustler. Fatima, clinging to the traditional Jordanian/Muslim ways, persistently urges marriage for Melvina and Jemorah.

13. **Adams. Francis Colburn, 1850-1891?** *The Von Toodleburgs; or, The history of a very distinguished family.* **Illustrated from original drawings by A.R. Waud. Philadelphia: Claxton, Remsen & Haffelfinger, 1868. p290.**
   The fortunes of the well respected Von Toodleburgs of Nyack, N.Y., Hanz and Angeline, are intertwined with those of the Chapmans, Bigelow and Dolly, new arrivals in town. Chapman, a 'reformer' but also a seeker of wealth, persuades Von Toodleburg to participate in the Kidd Discovery Company (formed by Philo Gusher, a 'con' man and a Mr. Topman, to search for Captain Kidd's treasure). The company is a disaster; Chapman loses his money and Von Toodleburg loses respect. Fortunately the Von Toodleburgs' son, Titus ('Tite'), a seaman, returns to Nyack with a bonanza. Chapman had never liked Tite, but he has to start all over again and gives his consent to the marriage of Mattie, his daughter, and Tite. Hanz Von Toodleburg is cleared of any blame for the Kidd Discovery Company's collapse and resumes his placid pattern of life.

14. **Adams, Frederick Upham, 1859-1921.** *John Burt,* **Philadelphia: Drexel Biddle, 1903. 473p.**
   John Burt is a successful, honest businessman whose chief antagonist, a wealthy, high-powered New York broker is confronted by a strategic financial operation engineered by Burt. The heroine, the object of Burt's romantic inclinations, is the beauteous socialite, Jessie Carden, the daughter of an affluent banker.

15. **————.** *The kidnapped millionaires; a tale of Wall Street and the tropics.*

Boston: Lothrop Pub. Co., 1901. 504p.

A rather improbable story that opens in a New York City newspaper office where a plan is originated to abduct six millionaires. After the plot is carried out, a panic ensues on Wall Street. The captured tycoons are taken on board the vessel, the Shark; from there they are transferred to 'Social Island' and meet with a bewildering series of adventures before their release.

16. **Adams, Henry, 1838-1918.** *Esther*; a novel, by Frances Snow Compton **[pseud.]. New York: H. Holt, 1884. 302p.**

Esther, a talented New York artist, comes from a fairly prominent family; her education has been humanistic, one with a significant omission—traditional religious studies. She is an independent person quite capable of channeling her particular interests and selecting her friends, among whom are several eminent men. From the latter group comes an Episcopal pastor who falls in love with Esther. They are engaged although Esther shows a good deal of reluctance to move to that stage. Almost predictably the two are unable to reconcile or compromise their opinions and beliefs and they drift apart.

17. **Adams, Henry Austin, 1861-1931.** *Westchester*; a tale of the Revolution. **St. Louis: B. Herder, 1899. 264p.**

The narrator, Nathaniel Broadbent, gentleman, of Waverly Grange in the County of Westchester, Colony of New York, spins a tragic tale. Broadbent takes a neutral stance when the American Revolution breaks out. Broadbent's daughter, Madeleine, supports the patriots; her lover, Victor Weston, is a major in the American army. Sergeant Matthew Darlington, once a friendly acquaintance of Weston, leads a troop of irregulars who generally espouse the rebel cause. The well-liked Weston is exposed as a British agent. He and Darlington play a cat-and-mouse game until they come face to face and wound one another. Meanwhile Nathaniel Broadbent and his friends, Tom MacIntyre and Caleb Wilberforce, are stripped of their holdings and sentenced to banishment from America by the Americans. Madeleine slips into insanity shortly before giving birth to twin sons, and after Major Weston is hanged for treason by patriots. When Darlington cuts down his forgiven enemy, Weston, his motive is mistaken by MacIntyre who shoots and kills him. After the war's end Squire Broadbent and friends come back to Waverly Grange. Madeleine dies shortly thereafter.

18. **Adams, Samuel Hopkins, 1871-1958.** *Average Jones.* **Illus. by M. Leone Bracker. Indianapolis: Bobbs-Merrill, 1911. 345p.**

A comfortably well off New Yorker by the name of Average Jones decides to find out just how authentic some of the personals that appear in the city's newspapers are, so he opens an office from which he randomly investigates them. In his new role as a species of detective Average gets into situations that test his newfound talent.

19. ——————. *Banner by the wayside.* **New York: Random House, 1947. 442p.**

Jans Quintard, former Harvard student (dismissed from that institution because of his penchant for foolhardy escapades) joins a theatrical troupe in the 1840s traveling the route of the Erie Canal. He becomes romantically involved with Endurance (Durie) Andrews, an orphan who is fascinated by the stage, but who is naïve in her approach to the twist and turns of her worldly surroundings.

20. ——————. *Canal town*; a novel. **New York: Random House, 1944. vii, 465p.**
In 1829 Dr. Horace Amlie comes to Palmyra, N.Y. to practice medicine. He has a mission: to improve the health and sanitary conditions of the inhabitants (canallers, ordinary citizens) of the roisterous canal town. His brusque, no-nonsense manner arouses the enmity of several of the town's leading citizens, especially the incompetent Dr. Murchison and above all, the banker Genter Latham. Amlie suspects that Wealthia, Latham's beloved daughter, is pregnant and his efforts to treat her stirs Genter Latham's fury. The doctor marries very young (and supportive) Araminta ('Dinty') Jerrold, Wealthia's best friend. His right to practice medicine is taken away thanks to the efforts of Latham, Murchison, et al. When typhus breaks out (Dr. Murchison says it's measles) in Palmyra, Horace works alongside the eminent Dr. Vought of Rochester to suppress the disease's ravages. Wealthia dies and Amlie does an illegal autopsy to convince her bereaved father of his earlier, correct diagnosis. Latham finally lends his support to Dr. Horace Amlie; when the banker dies he leaves his mansion to Dinty and Horace's renewed medical practice flourishes.

21. ——————. *Chingo Smith of the Erie Canal.* **Illustrated by Leonard Vosburgh. New York: Random House, 1958. 275p.**
"We meet Chingo in 1916—Eighteen-Hundred-and-Froze-to-Death. It snowed in August; that was the month Chingo left his traveling companions. Or rather they broke jail and escaped town without him, and he was just as glad. He set out on his own, a Huck Finn sort of boy who never courted adventure, but could cope with it if it thrust itself on him. The Erie Canal is an important locale, but by no means the only one, for Chingo traveled South to Georgia and worked on dozens of jobs"—Horn book.

22. ——————. *The flagrant years*; a novel of the beauty market. **New York: Liveright, 1929. 304p.**
Consuelo (Connie) Bartlett ventures from her western home to the bustling metropolis of New York where she is able, through the auspices of James (or Ipsy) Smith, to get a job in a beauty parlor. Not only does she learn the tools of her trade—she is also an astute observer of the peculiarly American passion for the retention of the look of youth. Ipsy is a constant presence in the novel and he eventually involves himself and Connie in an adventure that includes an unsolved murder.

23. ——————. *Flaming youth,* **by Warner Fabian [pseud.]. New York: Boni &**

Liveright, 1923. 336p.

The Fentrisses—Mr. and Mrs. Ralph Fentriss and their three daughters, Constance, Dee and Patricia—are a leading family in the social life of 'Dorrisdale', Long Island, a seaside resort town and suburb of New York City. The daughters' freedom from parental authority or guidance draws them into situations fraught with emotional and sexual excess. Pat is especially curious and restless but has an instinctive honesty that shields her from sinking too deeply into the frenzied activities of her peers. However, she does become involved with an older, married man who acts as mentor and friend, a relationship that evolves into a love affair. When Pat is in danger, he is there to extricate her.

24. ————. *The flying death.* **Illustrated by C.R. Macauley. New York: McClure Co., 1908. 239p.**

A boarding house with winter guests in a fishing village on Long Island is the locale of this mystery. Among the boarders are a young doctor seeking improvement in his health, an archaeologist and a science professor. They and others observe and go to the aid of a wrecked ship; one of the 'rescued' crew members is found dead with a horrible gash in his back. In succeeding weeks people in the village keep hearing odd noises in the air and more bodies are found for which the 'flying death' is deemed responsible. The reader will be enlightened only when he peruses the novel's final page.

25. ————. *From a bench in our square.* **Boston: Houghton, Mifflin, 1922. 307p.**

"The eight short stories in this volume are scened in that same 'Our square' which gave Mr. Adams the locality and the characters for a previous volume. 'Our square and the people in it'—an ancient bit of greenery far over on the East Side of New York, the slums round about it, relics of former greatness still watching over it and, take it from Mr. Adams, some very interesting people still frequenting it. The same benignant old dominie who figured in the previous stories is the narrator of these, reporting what he has seen and learned from his particular bench in a select corner of Our Square. Cyrus the Gaunt appears also, although infrequently, and the Bonnie Lassie, now the wife of Cyrus. MacLachan, Terry the Cop, Polyglot Elsa and others who helped to make the human comedy of the previous book contribute their share to these stories also, although these little dramas are, for the most part, worked out by different characters, the older and more familiar ones merely lending a hand now and then"—Book review digest.

26. ————. *Grandfather stories.* **New York: Random House, 1955. 312p.**

The author weaves a series of stories from tales told him in his childhood by Grandfather Myron Adams. Some of the incidents and activities include: the Erie Canal, its construction and the people who operated it; George Eastman and the early days of his photographic innovations; the terrible winter of 1826 in New York State and the great gale of 1829; the cholera epidemic of the 1830s; horse-trading; the traveling circuses; the Underground Railroad.

27. ————. *Our square and the people in it.* **Illustrated by J. Scott Williams. Boston: Houghton, Mifflin, 1917. 423p.**

A collection of stories about an 'oasis' in New York surrounded by slums. The tales, narrated by an individual who has the perception of a romantic and dreamer, are about various denizens of the 'square'—a sculptor, a doctor, a Scotch tailor, et al. Contents: Our square.—The chair that whispered.—MacLachan of our square.—The great peacemaker.—Orpheus, who made music in our square.—'Tazmun'.—The meanest man in our square.—Paula of the housetop.—The little red doctor of our square.

28. ————. *The piper's fee.* **New York: Liveright, 1926. 302p.**

"An accident brings Dorothea Selover, child of the gully in the mill town where the Ruyland dynasty reigned, to the attention of Aunt Augusta, matriarch of all the Ruylands, who makes Dorothea her protégée. In New York where she is sent to an art school, Dorothea rapidly ripens into beauty and worldly wisdom while remaining true to the code of ethics taught by her grandfather. Young and inexperienced [Evelyn] Ruyland finds her way to New York and is inducted by Dorothea into some of its mysteries. Evelyn's ignorance of life leads to disastrous consequences for which Dorothea, as her mentor, assumes the responsibility and pays the piper. But the cloud of shame which for a time rests upon Dorothea is finally lifted and she becomes the favorite of Aunt Augusta and the wife of … [Aunt Augusta's] grand-nephew Laurens"—Book review digest.

29. ————. *Sailors' wives* [by] **Warner Fabian [pseud.]. New York: Boni and Liveright, 1924. 316p.**

A seaside village on Long Island, 'Dorrisdale', is the home of businessmen who commute to the big city while their wives stay at home to fill out their often boring daytimes. A lively young woman, Rollo Trent, who has one more year of sight before blindness overtakes her, comes to town to make the most of that year. She becomes romantically involved with two men, only one of whom she really loves. Blindness arrives, an accident happens, and there is an abrupt change in Rollo's present and foreseeable future.

30. ————. *Success;* a novel. **Boston: Houghton, Mifflin, 1921. 553p.**

"The romance of a young society girl from New York and a lonely station agent in the Southwest furnishes the framework around which the entire story of modern journalism is told. The love episode with Io Welland has left young Banneker restless and he goes to New York to start his career as a reporter. Unusually gifted, he rises rapidly but refuses to 'eat his peck of journalistic dirt.' His frequent changes are always advancements and he reaches the highest rung as editor-in-chief of a daily. Here at last he can honestly express himself, but all he achieves is courageous editorials in the yellowest of yellow sheets. When the dictatorship of the advertiser invades even his domain, success has lost its glamour and he returns to the desert. Io has likewise entered upon a new phase and romance takes the place of success"—Book review digest.

31. ————. *Summer bachelors* [by] **Warner Fabian** [pseud.]. **New York: Boni and Liveright, 1926. 363p.**

   The novel records the pleasure-seeking life of Derry Thomas, a vivacious stenographer, in the company of some of New York City's affluent young men—married and single. Nevertheless, even as she hits the city's nightspots with them she does not lose her sense of balance, meeting their declarations of affection cool-headedly and with an almost detached air.

32. ————. *Sunrise to sunset.* **New York: Random House, 1950. 373p.**

   The protagonist in this novel is a working-class girl, Obedience Webb, who is employed in the cotton mills of Troy, N.Y. in the early 1800s. Her boss, Gurdon Stockwell, woos and weds Obedience, but he is a bad lot who is whisked off the stage and out of Obedience's life in time for her to fall into the arms of Gurdon's cousin, a reformer who is trying to better the workers' conditions.

33. **Adamson, Lydia.** *A cat on a beach blanket*; an Alice Nestleton mystery. **New York: Dutton, 1997. 183p.**

   While housesitting on Long Island, Alice Nestleton, idle New York actress and amateur sleuth, takes time out to appear at a nearby poetry reading. When one of the poets is killed by a car bomb after the meeting, Alice 'abets' the local police with some unsought detecting of her own. The community in which the murder occurred yields several suspicious characters including a would-be cookbook author, a libidinous artist, a news-mongering writer and several peculiar permanent residents. After the house Alice is guarding is gutted and the cookbook author is gunned down, Alice begins looking for the source of tinkling bell sounds that she had heard before the first murder and after the second. Alice has no difficulty tracking down a bell-wearing cat and the murderer.

34. **Addison, Thomas, b. 1861.** *Come-on Charley.* **New York: Dillingham, c1915. 342p.**

   Charley Carter is given a challenge. The $10,000 he receives as a bequest may be followed by an additional $2,000,000 if he can turn the original bequest into $1,000,000. With a friend, Percival Teeters, Charley comes to New York City to survey opportunities for expansion of his $10,000. He receives little encouragement from the higher circles of New York society and finance. But his small legacy does draw confidence men to his door. Charley proves to be smart enough to outplay these slick operators and succeeds in attaining the goal set out for himself.

35. **Adee, David Graham.** *The blue scarab.* **Chicago: Laird & Lee, 1892. 348p.**
"An exciting search for a lost jewel, made to imitate a scarabaeus or Egyptian beetle, involves a character cast in which there is a strange admixture of the honest man and knave, aristocrat and plebeian, with various representatives of Bohemianism. The mystery of the jewel, the several motives of those who participated in the mad hunt, and the chicanery of successive owners of the coveted pin, is revealed in the personal reminiscences of an ex-professional boxer. The scenes are well-known New York localities"—Annual American catalogue. Also published under the title: *The lost diamond* (1899).

36. ————. *No. 19 State Street.* **New York: Cassell, 1888. 339p.**
"This weird story purports to have been found in a manuscript left in the chambers of a New York lawyer. The writer was also a lawyer who, during the years 1843-1845, occupied these offices while employed upon the case he describes. The author shows an intimate acquaintance with the political, social, and everyday life in New York City fifty years ago. The story is full of mystery, horror, and supernatural events. All hinges upon the faith of the inhabitants of 19 State Street in the Hindu religion and their importation of a large snake into their modern home. Almost all the characters smoke hashish"—Annual American catalogue.

Adirondack, Al. **See: Young, Albert A.**

37. *Adsonville*; or, *Marrying out.* **A narrative tale … Albany, N.Y.: S. Shaw, 1824. viii, 280 (or 285)p.**
Two young lovers, Edgar F_____, a Quaker, and Caroline Adson, whose father, a former army officer, looks with disdain on Edgar's peace-loving proclivities, are caught in a violent storm on a central New York lake. However they land safely on an island in the lake and meet an elderly man and his wife. Caroline is sent to school in eastern New York (Dutchess County?). When Edgar travels eastward to relatives in the same area he meets Penelope Smith who bears a remarkable resemblance to Caroline. The aforementioned elderly island man reveals that Penelope is actually Caroline's twin sister. After a near-fatal adventure in the Catskills, Edgar, finally accepted by Mr. Adson, marries Caroline (he leaves, without rancor, the Society of Friends, since he has broken its rule of not marrying outside the sect). Penelope finds love with a Captain W_____. This work is sometimes attributed to an Edward Hull.

38. **Aiken, Albert W., 1846-1894.**
Very little is known about Aiken other than his talent for producing dime novels for Beadle & Adams at the rate of one a week. Listed below are six of his works that have New York City as their scene of action and which occasionally reveal Aiken's anti-Semitic bias:

The California detective; or, *The witches of New York*. **New York: Beadle & Adams, 1878. 31p.** (A leading character is Isaac Abrams, diamond broker, forger, high-living woman chaser and manipulator of documents.)

The genteel spotter; or, *The nighthawks of New York*. **New York: Beadle & Adams, 1884. 22p.** (Two of the reprehensible characters in this story are: 'Sheeny Lew', burglar and pugilist, companion in crime with Red Barry; and Moses Cohenson, fence for stolen goods.)

The phantom hand; or, *The heiress of Fifth Avenue*. **A story of New York hearths and homes. New York: Beadle & Adams, 1877. 44p.** (An impoverished actor pawns all his belongings at the shop of Abel Hameleck.)

The spotter-detective; or, *The girls of New York*. **New York: Beadle & Adams, 1878. 27p.** (The detective, Campbell 'the Virginian', uses a disguise as a Jewish peddler in order to gain entrance to the villain's living quarters.)

The white witch; or, *The League of three*. **New York: Beadle & Adams, 1871. 100p.** (The villain is Herman Stoll, a wealthy German Jew of New York and Newport, who plots to wrest from the hero his money and the woman he loves.

The wolves of New York; or, *Joe Phoenix's great man hunt*. **New York: Beadle & Adams, 1881. 24p.** strange story of the inner life of the great metropolis by day and by night; a tale of the wiles of the human wild beasts who have their lairs in the heart of the great city, and of the honest watch-dogs who guard society against them. (Joe Phoenix, the detective, disguises himself as Moses Solomon, Wall Street broker, and is thus able to get an authentic will into the hands of the rightful heir.)

39. **Aikman, Ann, 1928- .** *The others*; a novel. **New York: Simon and Schuster, 1960. 185p.**
    Two couples, the Alexanders and the Mooneys, meet haphazardly at a little-frequented spot on the shores of Long Island. Through a long summer vacation they share life on the beach and come together for various leisurely activities. When the summer draws to a close, the couples part amicably, but with no desire to continue any further relationship. Both sense that they are 'different', that their brief 'moment in the sun' may not bear repeating.

    Aitken, Robert, b. 1872. See under his pseudonym: Douglas, Hudson.

40. **Albrand, Martha, 1914-1981.** *A taste of terror*. **New York: Putnam, c1976. 192p.**
    "Recuperating on Long Island after an airplane wreck that killed twenty, pilot Tom Kent receives an anonymous ultimatum: kill yourself (out of guilt), or your daughter Kate will suffer. Kent seeks to unmask the psycho … while

wife Kitty and teen-aged Kate overreact in various—adultery, bravery, and idiocy—ways"—Kirkus reviews.

Alden, Mrs. G.R., 1841-1930. See: Alden, Isabella Macdonald, 1841-1930.

41. **Alden, Isabella Macdonald, 1841-1930.** *The Chautauqua girls at home*, **by Pansy [pseud.]. Boston: Lothrop Pub. Co., c1877. 466p.**

Also published in 1878 (Glasgow, Marr) under the title: *Obeying the call*. In her second 'Chautauqua' novel the author describes the lives of her four heroines—Eurie Mitchell, Ruth Erskine, Marion Wilbur and Flossy Shipley—after they return to their homes in New York City and eastern New York State. Still fresh in their minds, however, are the experiences they had during their two weeks at the newly founded institution at Lake Chautauqua the previous summer.

42. ————. *Four girls at Chautauqua*, **by Pansy [pseud.]. Illustrated by Elizabeth Withington. Boston: Lothrop Pub. Co., 1876. 474p.**

Four young women—Eurie Mitchell, Ruth Erskine, Marion Wilbur and Flossy Shipley—decide to spend two weeks tenting at the fairly new lyceum at Fair Point (now Chautauqua), New York, presuming it will be a relaxing, entertaining vacation. At the time of the story, study of the Bible and Sunday school methods were the main order of business at Chautauqua. Eurie, the daughter of a hard-working physician, has intellectual reservations anent the 'simplicities of Christianity'; Ruth, from a comfortably well-off background, is barely a 'Christian', rather bored by sermons and more interested in the social amenities of Saratoga; Marion, a schoolteacher, is the 'infidel' of the four, a skeptic and agnostic who is also reporting on the activities at the lyceum; Flossy, rather selfish and light-headed, is the "petted darling of a wealthy home." All four, willingly or unwillingly attend the many meetings at which inspired preachers, theologians, educators and laymen intriguingly spell out the Christian message, and become, to their surprise, 'converted'.

43. ————. *Four mothers at Chautauqua*, **by Pansy [pseud.]. Boston: Lothrop, Lee & Shepard, 1913. 408, [10]p.**

This sequel to the author's, *Four girls at Chautauqua,* places the quartet back to the place they had visited 24 years before. With their husbands and children in tow, they have an opportunity to see just how Chautauqua affects the second generation. "The most interesting turn of the plot is a Cinderella-like episode in which figures a poor relation of a poor family which is trying to keep up appearances"—Book review digest.

44. ————. *The hall in the grove*, **by Pansy [pseud.]. Boston: D. Lothrop, [1881]. 431p.**

A novel about the Chautauqua Institution, recounting the experiences there of several members of a branch of the Chautauqua Literary and Scientific Circle, said branch being started in her hometown by a modest but enthusiastic lady.

45. **Alden, William Livingston, 1837-1908.** *The cruise of the 'Ghost'.* **New York: Harper, 1882. 210p.**

A spin-off from the author's earlier *The moral pirates'* (q.v.). Here we have the record of a cruise by the sailboat 'Ghost' that started in Harlem, went down the Hudson, then turned towards the southern shore of Long Island and into the Great South Bay. The sailors on this trip were: Tom Schuyler, Jim and Joe Sharpe and Harry Wilson; their commander was Charly Smith, an Annapolis cadet, older and more experienced than the others.

46. —————. *The moral pirates.* **New York: Harper, 1881. 148p.**

Tom Schuyler, Jim and Joe Sharpe, and Harry Wilson have romantic daydream-like notions about freebooting in the river and seawaters around New York City. Treated to a cruise up and down the Hudson River by an uncle of one of the boys, they put such illogical notions aside as they learn the intricacies of handling 'their' boat.

47. **Alden, Winthrop, pseud.** *The lost million.* **New York: Dodd, Mead, 1913. 378p.**

On shipboard Lionel Kemball befriends a fellow passenger, an elderly man who dies when they arrive in New York. Before he passed away he made Lionel agree to the destruction of a huge pile of banknotes, gave him instructions to deliver a letter, and presented him with a sealed Egyptian cylinder that Lionel was to eventually hand over on a specific day to the first individual who asked for it—as it happened, a stranger who would be wearing a red tie with a carnation in one of his buttonholes. Obviously there remained much to be explained.

48. **Alderman, Clifford Lindsey, 1902- .** *Joseph Brant, chief of the Six Nations.* **New York: J. Messener, 1958. 192p.**

Fictionalized biography for young adults of the Mohawk chief who fought on the British side in the French and Indian War and the American Revolution and was noted for his leadership and diplomatic skills.

49. **Aldrich, Anne Reeve, 1866-1892.** *The feet of love.* **New York: Worthington Co., 1890. 290p.**

An Episcopal clergyman is wooing an heiress while the two are vacationing at a summer resort, 'Gilead', located somewhere on Long Island. The heiress's companion, a pretty young woman, was shamefully involved with the same clergyman in the recent past. Of course, that fact has a significant impact on the heiress, the suitor and his current relationship with the two women.

50. **Aldrich, Darragh.** *Enchanted hearts.* **Front. by Frances Rogers. Garden City, N.Y.: Doubleday, Page, 1917. 406p.**

Mrs. Prouty's boardinghouse on West 6 Street and a town house in Manhattan are the scenes of most of the novel's 'action.' 'Little Comfort', an orphan girl given a home by Mrs. Prouty, fancies herself as a fairy godmother; she does odd jobs around the boarding house and chooses Katherine Woods, a struggling writer, as her 'Princess.' Little Comfort is the catalyst who brings together Katherine and Charles Edward Martin, a rich yet bored bachelor. A hurdle in the burgeoning romance is the resentment Katherine feels when she learns that Charles was strongly opposed to his brother Robert's marriage to Katherine's sister Mollie—Robert died in the 'Titanic' disaster and Mollie committed suicide. The story ends happily, however, and Charles adopts Little Comfort.

51. **Alexander, Elizabeth.** *Rôles*. **With illus. by Charles D. Mitchell. Boston: Little, Brown, 1924. 310p.**

Dissatisfied with her Mid-western environment, an affluent young wife, Gwynne Sheldon, comes to New York with the hope of a theatrical career. She gets to know Eva Grahame, an actress who possesses little real talent. Gwynne persuades Eva to change places and Gwynne makes a successs in a role originally slated for Eva. There are more than a few repercussions when Mr. Sheldon and Miss Grahame's lover appear on the scene.

52. **Alger, Horatio, 1832-1899.** *Adrift in New York*; **or,** *Tom and Florence braving the world*. **New York: Federal Book Co. [1900?] 221p.**

Wealthy but sickly John Linden has his niece, Florence Linden, and his nephew, Curtis Waring, to keep him company while he yearns for a son who years ago was abducted by a servant. He retains some hope that the lad is still living, but a present concern is to have Florence and Curtis wed one another before he passes on. Florence refuses to marry Curtis; her angry uncle forces her to leave his house. Fortunately Florence finds a friend in a street boy, the 'Dodger', who is a year older than she. We learn that Curtis Waring is the person who planned the abduction of John Linden's son, hoping to gain possession of the wealth his uncle will leave. The Dodger and several Bowery acquaintances frustrate Curtis's plans and restore Florence to her uncle's hearth after she has struggled to survive in a Bowery tenement. Of course the Dodger turns out to be John Linden's long-lost son Tom and all the loose ends are neatly bundled up.

53. ————. *Adrift in the city; or, Oliver Conrad's plucky fight*. **Philadelphia: H.T. Coates, 1895. 325p.**

The stepfather of Oliver Conrad is a conniving rascal. He incarcerated Oliver's mother in a hospital for the insane and forged a will that made him the sole inheritor of her money. The stepfather's son and Oliver are continually at loggerheads. When Oliver finally leaves home, he makes his way to New York City where he has many enlightening experiences before he unseats his stepfather and regains his mother's freedom.

54. ————. *Brave and bold; or, The fortunes of a factory boy*. **Boston: Loring, 1874. 342p.**

Subtitle varies on some later editions: The fortunes of Robert Rushton. Although 'Millville', a village not far from New York City, is the chief seat of the story, the hero also has adventures in that city, on ocean-going vessels, in Pacific waters and in India. Despite the animosity of the affluent Davis family, Robert Rushton, through hard work, perseverance, good luck, and the interest of men of good will, is just barely able to support his mother and himself. Captain Rushton, his father, presumed lost at sea, finally turns up with a receipt for the $5,000 he had placed trustingly in Mr. Davis' hands. Davis is forced to cough up the money (plus interest) that he had been using for his own purposes. Robert is left a tidy sum by the reclusive, miserly Paul Nichols whom he had protected from an evil nephew.

55. ————. *Dan the detective.* **New York: Street & Smith, 1884. 296p.**
Reissued in 1898 (New York, A.L. Burt) under the title: *Dan, the newsboy.* After Mr. Mordaunt's financial collapse and death Mr. Mordaunt and her son Dan are forced into cramped quarters at Five Points, a far cry from their previous Madison Avenue home. Dan sells newspapers in front of the Astor House. A typical Alger hero, Dan is presented with a number of favorable circumstances that quickly elevate him to a position of responsibility. His flair for detective work results in his rescuing a kidnapped child; the gratitude of the child's aunt leads to Dan's 'adoption' by her, an opportunity to further his education and his recovery of funds stolen by his father's business associate.

56. ————. *Fame and fortune*; or, *The progress of Richard Hunter.* **Boston: A.K. Loring, 1867. 279p.**
'Ragged Dick's story continues, although Dick (Richard Hunter) is well on his way to some worldly success in the metropolis (New York City). This is the second volume of the 'Ragged Dick' series. Other volumes in the series are: Mark the match boy; Rough and ready; Rufus and Rose; Ben the luggage boy.

————. *The cash boy.* **See note under Item #57.**

57. ————. *Frank Fowler, the cash boy.* **New York: A.L. Burt, 1887. 262p.**
Told by the widow Mrs. Fowler just before she dies that she is not his biological mother, penniless Frank Fowler heads for New York City to earn his living. A department store hires him as a 'cash boy' at wages of three dollars per week. One night Frank prevents elderly Mr. Wharton from having a bad fall. The wealthy gentleman pays Frank to read to him in the evenings. Wharton's nephew, John Wade, plots to wean Frank from the old man's favor. Several adventures and some investigative work later, Frank is able to tell Mr. Wharton that Wade had lied to him about the 'death' of the male infant left by Mr. Wharton's deceased son. It was John Wade who had dropped the infant Frank on the Fowler doorstep: the Fowlers had raised the boy as their own. And, of course, Mr. Wharton is Frank's grandfather. This novel was later published under the title: *The cash boy* (New York, Hurst, 189-?).

58. ————. *Helen Ford.* **Boston: A.K. Loring, 1866. 297.**

A fairly complex tale that gives Alger the opportunity to intersperse descriptions of life in a New York City boarding house and life on the streets of the city itself. Helen and her father—the latter is an impractical inventor of flying machines—struggle for mere existence on her wages as a seamstress. Mr. Ford turns out to be the long-lost son of wealthy Lewis Rand, while Helen is discovered as having an excellent singing voice. A bevy of characters are involved in the fortunes of Ford (a.k.a. Robert Rand) and Helen, some of them with villainous intentions. In the end, however, Ford/Rand inherits a large portion of his father's estate while Helen is left in limbo: "What remains in store for Helen Ford," says Alger, "whether of joy or of sorrow, it is not mine to read."

59. ————. *Helping himself*; or, *Grant Thornton's ambition.* **Philadelphia: Porter & Coates, 1886. 320p.**

Grant Thornton is the 15-year-old son of a rural parson who becomes aware of his father's accumulating debts and their lack of many of the basic necessities. Leaving behind his home, Grant arrives in New York City and takes a job with a Wall Street financier. He gradually scales the heights of success; in his upward journey, he acquires a lot of friends and extends his help to others less fortunate.

————. *Jack's ward.* **See note under Item #72.**

60. ————. *A New York boy*, **by Arthur Lee Putnam [pseud.]. New York: United States Book Co., 1890. 307p.**

The hero of this tale is Rufe Rodman whom we follow through his many 'haps and mishaps.' The author observes that the law tends to favor private interests and too often convicts the innocent or disadvantaged. And "while it is a good thing to save money, it is still better to use it judiciously to aid those who stand in need of a helping hand" (p. 260).

61. ————. *Number 91*; or, *The adventures of a New York telegraph boy*, **by Arthur Lee Putnam [pseud.]. New York: J.W. Lovell [ca. 1887]. 205p.**

Paul Parton works out of the office of the American District Telegraph 'on Broadway, not far from the St. Nicholas Hotel.' Paul is an orphan; he shares a room in a poor district of the city with a miserly old man, Jeremiah (Jerry) Barclay. Barclay's son, James, is a ne'er-do-well, neglectful of his wife and two children, using all available means to wean money from his father. Paul stands in his way and gradually succeeds in connecting old Jerry with his daughter-in-law and grandchildren. And Paul, with typical Alger heroics, is able to ingratiate himself with very influential people; by the end of the novel Paul is no longer a telegraph boy but has graduated to a responsible clerkship in a flourishing retain clothing store on Broadway.

62. ————. *Paul the peddler*; or, *The adventures of a young street merchant.*

Boston: Loring, 1871. 281p.

The story opens with Paul Hoffman, the main support of his widowed mother and crippled brother Jim, selling prize packages in front of the New York Post Office on Nassau Street. When competition and thievery make hawking prize packages unprofitable, Paul substitutes as a necktie salesman for an ill friend, George Barry. Paul also finds a friend in Mr. Preston, a businessman, who hires Mrs. Hoffman to make shirts for him. When Paul is offered a chance to buy out Barry's necktie operation he attempts to raise money by offering a diamond ring in Mrs. Hoffman's possession for purchase by Tiffany jewelers. Before he can conclude the sale, he shows the ring to a con artist who absconds with the prized object (question: would a supposedly street-wise kid of the 1870s be so easily taken in?). However, Paul tracks down the thief, receives an ample sum from Tiffany's for the recovered ring and when last heard from is about to set up his own retail necktie business on New York's streets.

63. ————. *Phil the fiddler*; or, *The story of a young street musician.* Boston: Loring, 1872. 265p.

Phil (Filippo) is a victim of the padrone system. Sold by his Italian father to an exploitative employer (a padrone) in New York City, Phil plays his violin on the streets of the metropolis; the few coins he earns go into the pockets of the padrone. Tired of his virtual slavery and the beatings he must undergo when his earnings fail to satisfy his master, Phil finally runs away to New Jersey where he is found half-frozen by a kind doctor and is adopted by the physician and his wife. Alger had a purpose in penning this story: to call attention of the reading public to the sad plight of Italian street boy musicians and thus to induce reforms.

64. ————. *Ragged Dick*; or, *Street life in New York City with the bootblacks.* Boston: A.K. Loring, 1867. 295p.

"Nearly half the volume is devoted to a tour of New York City, conveying something of Alger's excitement about his new home"—Tebbel, J. *From rags to riches.* Dick (full name: Richard Hunter) is a mixture of good intentions and careless behavior (addiction to smoking, swearing and the theater). He is fortunate enough to go from selling newspapers and shining shoes to finding a 'patron' or two who eventually turn Dick into an honest, well-groomed clerk.

65. ————. *Rough and Ready*; or, *Life among the New York newsboys.* Boston: Loring, 1869. 300p.

In this novel Alger muses on a favorite place of his—the Newsboys' Lodging House in New York City, which was founded in March 1854. The hero of the story is a newsboy with an alcoholic stepfather and it "reads like a temperance tract draped over a flimsy story line." (Scharnhorse, Gary & Bales, Jack. *The lost life of Horatio Alger, Jr.,* Indiana University Press, 1985.) The protagonist is noteworthy in that he is always scrupulously clean, in contrast to the average newsboy, despite the coarseness of his clothing. Alger judges most unfavorably a childless millionaire who contributes nothing from his wealth to help the poor of the city.

66. ————. *Rupert's ambition*. **Philadelphia: H.T. Coates, 1899. 366p.**
Forced to give up his job in a dry goods store in New York City because of slack times, Rupert Rollins, a lad of sixteen who has provided his mother and sister with life's necessities, is understandably very downcast. In typical Alger fashion, to be sure, help for him arrives in unexpected and coincidental ways; he finds work as a hotel bellboy and a short while later becomes a wealthy man's clerk and confidante. Rupert's bright outlook, his honesty and his concern for others pave the way for the realization of his ambitions.

67. ————. *Shifting for himself*; or, *Gilbert Greyson's fortunes*. **Boston: Loring, 1876. vi, 356p.**
Departing Dr. Burton's boarding school in 'Westville', some 40 miles from New York City, because of the drying up of funds left him by his deceased father, Gilbert Greyson heads for New York City in search of employment. In actuality Gilbert's guardian, Richard Briggs, is holding for his own use a small fortune that is rightfully Gilbert's. Gilbert endures the usual privations of an Alger hero, but his strict honesty and sense of humor see him through. He impresses several prominent businessmen and finally, through one of those coincidences so prominent in Alger fiction, Gilbert comes across a Mr. Talbot, his father's former accountant. Talbot possesses documentation of Gilbert's inheritance; it remains for the hero to confront Briggs and receive his full due.

68. ————. *Silas Snobden's office boy*. **New York: J.S. Ogilvie, 1899. 240p.**
Frank Manton lives with his mother in a crowded New York tenement. Employed by the penurious Snobden he is hard-pressed to keep himself and his mother (a seamstress) from dire poverty. But Frank has the virtues of an Alger hero; he breaks up a robbery, restores a wallet to its rightful owner and rescues a kidnapped child. His reward is $10,000 and a bright future. Along the way he encounters several interesting characters: his helpmates: the generous and gentlemanly Allen Palmer; elderly eccentric Samuel Graham; Stacia Jane, a useful drudge; and Seth Hastings, a milkman; and villains: intemperate John Carter; Snobden's devious nephew, Luke Gerrish; Mrs. Manton's secret, brutish, alcoholic husband;and Gideon Chapin, who has the qualities of Dickens' Uriah Heep.

69. ————. *Slow and sure*; or, *From the street to the shop*. **Boston: Loring, 1872. 280p.**
A sequel to *Paul the peddler* (q.v.). Paul Hoffman now has a necktie stand just below the Astor House, which is fairly successful. When fire destroys the tenement in which Paul, his mother and brother Jimmy rent rooms, they have to find new living quarters. Fortunately the friendly businessman, Mr. Burton, tells Paul of a Mr. Talbot who wants a responsible family to take care of his residence on Madison Avenue while he and his wife are in Europe. Paul, with

the help of Julius, a street-boy living with two criminals, foils the attempt of the latter to burglarize the Talbot home. Julius survives the designs of the more dangerous of the two criminals to pay him back for his betrayal and goes west to start a new life. Paul, again helped by Mr. Preston, purchases a small clothing store and seems to be on his way to relative prosperity.

70. ————. *The store boy*; or, *The fortunes of Ben Barclay*. **Philadelphia: Porter & Coates, 1887. 314p.**

'Pentonville' in Upstate New York is the place where Ben Barclay sets out on his career in retailing. He is employed in a store there; his chief rival is Tom Davenport, son of the grasping Squire Davenport. Ben finds a fast friend in Rose Gardiner, however. He takes a short trip to New York City and has a run-in with two of that city's shady characters; he captures a pickpocket and is given a reward for his efforts. His eventual besting of Squire Davenport, the reclamation of his mother's stolen property and the launching of his own successful business marks Ben's return to Pentonville.

71. ————. *Struggling upward*; or, *Luke Larkin's luck*. **Philadelphia: H.T. Coates, 1890. 333p.**

The primary setting is a village north of New York City—'Groveton'—although New York City itself and the West of the period (Chicago, Minnesota, and the Black Hills) are also in the picture. The incredibly snobbish Randolph Duncan, son of the village banker, Prince Duncan, hampers Luke, struggling to earn enough to help his mother. Falsely accused of bank theft, Luke is cleared with the timely help of the mysterious Roland Reed and also earns the respect of businessman John Armstrong. These two men entrust Luke, only 16, with an important mission out West. After several adventures Luke returns to New York City, mission accomplished. In Groveton the Duncans get their comeuppance; Prince Duncan has to make restitution to Mr. Armstrong whose bonds he has been using to pay off his debts and Randolph is reduced to working as an office boy. Luke is rewarded with money and a responsible position in Mr. Armstrong's New York office.

72. ————. *Timothy Crump's ward*; or, *The New Year's loan, and what came of it*. **Boston: A.K. Loring, 1866. 188p.**

The poor but honest Crump family, occupants of a tenement on the outskirts of New York City, are 'blessed' with a basket bearing a female infant and $300 left on their doorstep. Some years later Peg Hardwicke kidnaps the infant, now a child with the name of Ida Crump, at the behest of John Somerville (the child's real father). Enter the rich Mrs. Clifton of Philadelphia who takes Ida in hand, reforms Peg and sets the worthy Timothy Crump and his son Jack up in business. The coincidences that multiply throughout the tale seem over many even for an Alger story. The novel was later rewritten under the title: *Jack's ward* (1875).

73. ————. *Tom Thatcher's fortune*. **New York: A.L. Burt, 1888. 258p.**

This novel has a fairly close resemblance to a later Alger work, Struggling upward (q.v.); one might conclude that the author was running low on plots. A little over half the story is set in 'Wilton', a New York State town 30 miles from New York City, and in the big city itself. The hero, Tom Thatcher, and his mother are ill-treated by Wilton's wealthiest man, John Simpson, who was once an associate of Mr. Thatcher (Tom's father). Simpson and Thatcher had left Wilton together to seek gold in California. Simpson returned with a fortune; Thatcher had disappeared and was presumed dead. With the help of sudden friends Tom is sent westward to look into the circumstances surrounding the mystery of his father's disappearance. After some harrowing adventures Tom comes back to Wilton accompanied by the long-missing Mr. Thatcher and a great deal of money. John Simpson's past catches up with him and he is forced to leave Wilton after turning over much of his ill-gotten wealth to the Thatchers.

74. ————. *Tom Tracy*; or *The trials of a New York newsboy*, **by Arthur Lee Putnam [pseud.]. New York: F.A. Munsey, 1888. 205p.**

"Tom Tracy, who sold the Telegram, Mail and Commercial and 'all the evening papers' along Lower Broadway is, as his story opens, telling a customer that he pays five dollars a month rent for a flat on Bleecker Street. While Tom is engrossed in conversation, his friend, Jimmy O'Hara, has sold six newspapers, netting a six-cents profit. Fortunately, Tom's customer buys three papers, generously giving him a silver dollar, so he is not the loser for having tarried"—Gardner, Ralph D., Horatio Alger... (Mendota, Ill., Wayside Press, 1964). From this point on Tom pays stricter attention to his job and rises in the world, as do most of Alger's protagonists.

75. ————. *Tony the tramp.* **New York: J.S. Ogilvie, 1880. 251p.**

The scene of the story wanders from the countryside of eastern New York State to New York City and thence to rural England and London. The hero is Tony Rugg, an orphan, whose guardian is Rudolph Rugg, a sinister tramp who lives by his wits and talent for thievery. The novel relates the tug of war between Tony and Rudolph as the former tries every means possible to escape Rudolph's presence. Tony has the usual good luck of Alger heroes; a wealthy young New Yorker adopts him. On a trip to England Tony learns that he is the true heir of an estate left by his deceased parents. Rudolph Rugg and Mrs. Henry Middleton, both fairly distant relatives of Tony (his real name is Robert Middleton), had earlier conspired and failed to do away with Tony so that they could share in the revenues from the estate. Tony confronts the guilty pair and reclaims his inheritance. The novel was also published in 1890 under the title: *Tony, the hero; a brave boy's adventures with a tramp* (New York: A.L. Burt).

76. ————. *The young salesman.* **Philadelphia: H.T. Coates, 1896. 352p.**

A boy of sixteen fresh from England finds himself in teeming New York City with few prospects. Victimized by one of the city's denizens, he loses half the money he came to New York with. Good fortune comes to him when he is given a job by an uncle in the latter's clothing business, although he is treated quite badly by his relative. Cleared of an accusation of theft he makes several friends who help him improve his circumstances. Within an eventful year he is a traveling salesman with a comfortable salary.

77. *All for her*; or, *St. Jude's assistant.* **A novel by? New York: G.W. Carleton, 1877. 429p.**

Olive Gray breaks off her engagement to Paul Ogden and transfers her affections to the Rev. George Brand, assistant rector at St. Jude's On-the-Avenue. The infuriated Paul kills Brand and Olive loses her sanity. Detective John Strasburger gathers information to fix Paul's presence at the scene of the crime. Ogden returns from Europe to New York and is indicted for murder. He flees with Mara, the adopted daughter of his aunt and uncle (Ogdens), and is tracked down in Nova Scotia. Paul Ogden uses a slow-working poison to commit suicide. Strasburger is killed by an old enemy, Job Price, after he has informed the Ogdens that Mara is his natural daughter by Price's estranged wife. Olive Gray shows signs of recovering from her dementia.

78. *All for him*; **a novel by?, the author of** *All for her.* **New York: G.W. Carelton, 1877. 376p.**

Also published under the title: *Sweetheart and wife.* In 1872 a short while after a woman's body parts are found in two trunks, one shipped to the Congress Hotel in Saratoga Springs, the other to a resort at the Delaware Water Gap, detective John Strasburger discovers the trunks were shipped from Apt. No. 40 on West 44th Street, New York City. Strasburger picks up two letters addressed to that apartment at the dead letter office; their contents indicate that the murdered woman was very likely the victim of a man who wanted to get rid of his mistress. The chief suspect is Charles, one of three Barton siblings. There is a match between his handwriting and that of some letters. Barton had previously tried to focus suspicion on one, Reynart Rensselaer, by slipping the check for the Saratoga trunk into Rensselaer's possession. At Barton's trial the murdered woman is identified as the runaway daughter of a clergyman; she had been the mistress of Dexter Shove, a soldier of fortune, before she met Charles Barton. The latter suffers a fatal heart attack during his trial.

79. **Allan, Francis K.** *First come, first kill.* **New York: Reynal & Hitchcock, 1945. 188p.**

The interior of a millionaire's mansion in Westchester County is the scene of two murders: that of a mysterious woman who had insisted on drawing $5,000 from the owner and then the sudden demise of the millionaire himself. He left behind a daughter who did not hesitate to take marriage vows. Private investigator John Storm sets about unlocking the riddle with the help of several useful clues.

80. **Allen, Alice E. Little.** *Aunt Emmie.* **With illus. by Frances Brundage. Philadelphia: Lippincott, 1925. 286p.**

The young heroine of this Adirondack tale, Emmie Grant, is aunt to the older David Grant Gordon, son of Emmie's sister Dora. Emmie's father, the guide David Grant, and her Aunt Sally Lane take in David when his mother dies. David Gordon, a city boy from New York, gradually acclimates himself to life in the Adirondacks; at one juncture in the story he rescues his guardian, Mr. Grant, when the latter suffers amnesia following an accident in the forest and believes himself to be an Indian. The mystery of a notice from a New York City law firm, requesting information as to the whereabouts of a David Grant, is solved when the boy's grandfather, Ross Gordon, Sr., an amateur ornithologist, comes to the Adirondacks and meets the Grant family. Emmie discovers she is also aunt to David Gordon's sister, Dorothy, who has been living with Ross Gordon, Sr., her grandfather.

81. **Allen, Anne Story.** *Merry hearts; the adventures of two bachelor maids.* **With front. by Eliot Keen. New York: H. Holt, 1903. viii, 277p.**

A harmless little tale wherein the two women of the title come to New York City to earn their living. They achieve marginal success, one as a painter of miniatures, the other as a storywriter. Despite several embarrassing situations they are satisfied with their lives. Eventually they are drawn into romantic attachments involving a playwright and a philosopher and the story winds down to a happy end.

82. **Allen, Billie.** *Explanation, please.* **Elizabethtown, N.Y.: 1967. 96p.**

Cover title: *E.S.P. stories.* Ghost stories reprinted from the author's column in Valley News. "They were related to her by her guests at Roaring Brook Lodge or by neighbors and friends whom she interviewed. Almost all of them are anecdotes, tales or legends of the Essex County countryside"—New State tradition.

83. **Allen, James Lane, 1849-1923.** *A cathedral singer.* **With front. by Sigismond de Ivanowski. New York: Century Co., 1916. 142p.**

Allen sets his novelette in Morningside Heights in 1916 with the Cathedral of St. John the Divine having special significance. The widow Rachel Truesdale, a dignified though poverty-stricken lady, is proud of her only son, Ashby, a 10-year-old newsboy who occasionally sings in Central Park. The choirmaster at St. John accepts Ashby as a choirboy, but Ashby is killed when struck by one of the city's trucks. Despite Ashby's death Rachel gains strength by reaffirmation of her Christian faith. To her Ashby is a symbol of hope who has attained immortality through his voice and his story.

84. ————. *The heroine in bronze*; or, *A portrait of a girl.* **A pastoral of the city. New York: Macmillan, 1912. 281p.**

"To be wooed and won in the shaded corner of an old garden in the heart of the City of New York—this is the happy lot of Muriel Dunstan. Through the book moves Muriel, frank in the helpful impulse of dawning womanhood, elusive in her shy maidenhood, beautiful among her roses. Through them also advances Muriel's lover, [Donald Clough] a budding author from the Blue Grass State, chivalrous, yet determined, paying every deference to love and his lady, yet faithful to his own convictions of a man's right way with his own works"—Publisher's weekly. And Donald toils away in New York while Muriel is in Europe, his only 'companion', the 'heroine in bronze', and a lamp/statue that he had purchased at an auction. His completed novel, In Years Gone By, 'to the amazement of both my publisher and myself', does very well. And Muriel is at last ready to entrust herself to him and his future.

Allen, Mrs. Josiah, pseud. See: Holley, Marietta, 1836-1926.

85. **[Allen, Linda Marguerite Sangree]** *Florine*; or, *The inner life of one of the 'Four Hundred.'* **By the author of** *Mignonette, The Devil and I,* **etc., etc. New York: G.W. Dillingham, 1891. 326p.**

The novel takes the form of a journal kept by Florine Dwight for the ultimate perusal of her daughter only. "These confessions … were never written to be seen; that nothing ever was further from the mind of the writer of them than the desire or intention to have them seen" ('Compiler's' preface, p. vi). The first entry is dated May 6, 1867 when Florine is nine; the last entry bears the date Dec. 27, 1888. Florine frequently attends the New York theater, opera and ballet and she becomes acquainted with such personalities as the actress Charlotte Cushman and the poet/editor William Cullen Bryant. She discovers her power to attract male admirers, but marries wealthy Aubrey Willis, twice her age when her father's death leaves her and Mrs. Dwight a little tight financially. Aubrey's death is followed by Florine's very brief marriage to Nono, her childhood sweetheart, yet he too expires and the young widow has two futures to think about—hers and her daughter's.

86. **Allen, Merritt Parmelee, 1892-1954.** *Red heritage.* **Decorations by Ralph Ray. New York: Longmans, Green, 1946. 314p.**

The young hero of the novel is the patriot Cobus Derrick, a seventeen-year-old who is present at the Battle of Oriskany and other skirmishes in Revolutionary Upstate New York.

87. **Alpert, Hollis, 1916- .** *The summer lovers.* **New York: Knopf, 1958. 307p.**

"Set in a transparently disguised town near the tip of Long Island that Hollis Alpert calls 'East Nines'. His story focuses on a nineteen-year-old charmer named Sally, whose divorced mother has reared her to look the facts of life serenely in the face. But Sally is neither so knowing nor so invulnerable as she believes; and when she decides that she isn't in love with Chris, an agreeable youth waiting around to be drafted, but that she is very much in love with her mother's new husband, she runs headlong into trouble"—New York herald tribune book review.

88. **Altman, Thomas, 1944-.** *Dark places.* **New York: Bantam Books, 1984. 243p.**

Although the New York suburb of 'Bristol' has all the features of a snug, peaceful residential village, a soothing oasis in a turbulent world, the McNairs, Christie and Zachary, suddenly face disquieting events of their present and past. Christie, writer of a column for the local 'Chronicle', finds several weird paintings in the McNair attic and wards off the seduction attempt of a beguiling stranger; Zachary is a New York publisher bothered recently by odd phone calls. Further, through newspaper research, Christie reads about the suicide of her husband's first wife, and meets Leonora, a sister of Zachary that he had never mentioned. Despite all of these and other revelations Christine and Zachary, at the novel's end, step unconcernedly (or so it seems) into the future.

89. **Altsheler, Joseph Alexander, 1862-1919.** *The hunters of the hills: a story of the great French and Indian War.* **New York: D. Appleton, 1916. 359p.**

The first of novels by Altsheler (see infra) revolving around the French and Indian War in New York State and its neighbors as experienced by three woodsmen: young Robert Lennox, his mentor David Willet, and the Onondagan Indian Tayoga. The three are on a mission to deliver an urgent message from the Governor of New York Colony to the Governor General of French Canada. Even though war has not yet broken out the three couriers must travel through the dangerous northern New York wilderness, tracked by hostile Indians, until they finally deliver the letter. After several exciting incidents in Montreal and Quebec, Lennox, Willet, and Tayoga move down Lake Champlain and then westward to the Vale of Onondaga and a council attended by the Iroquois chiefs and a representative from Canada. It is there that Robert Lennox debates his talented French opponent and keeps the Iroquois faithful to their English alliance.

90. ————. *The lords of the wild; a story of the old New York border.* **Illustrated by Charles L. Wrenn. New York: Appleton, 1919. 297p.**

The French and Indian War in Upstate New York (primarily in the Lake George region) is the setting for an attention-holding novel about Robert Lennox and his associates who are constantly on the run from pursuing hostile Indians and their French allies. Their expertise in woodcraft is vital to the young men's survival. The story's climax is the capture of Fort Ticonderoga by British colonial troops under Lord Amherst.

91. ————. *The masters of the peaks; a story of the Great North Woods.* **New York: Appleton, 1918. 310p.**

A sequel to The Rulers of the lakes (q.v.) the story takes the young hero Robert Lennox and his friends, the Indian Tayoga and David Willet, through that period of the French and Indian War between William Johnson's repulse of French forces near Lake George and the capture of Fort William Henry by General Louis Montcalm (ca. 1755-1757). While scouting in the forests of the

Lake George and Lake Champlain regions the three young warriors get the better of a French spy.

92. —————. *The rulers of the lakes; a story of George and Champlain.* **Illustrated by Charles L. Wrenn. New York: Appleton, 1917. 332p.**

Not long after Braddock's defeat by the French and Indian forces in 1755, the young colonial Robert Lennox and his Indian friend Tayoga set out on a perilous wilderness journey to warn the soldiers at Fort Refuge of impending attack. Afterwards the two serve as scouts and participate in hard fighting around Lakes George and Champlain.

93. —————. *The shadow of the North; a story of New York and a lost campaign.* **New York: D. Appleton-Century, 1917. 357p.**

The second volume of the author's Great French and Indian War series. Robert Lennox, of unknown origin, is the chief character; he and his friends, the woodsman David Willet and the noble Onondagan Tayoga, are among the first to recognize the dangers to New York and the other colonies of the sudden, systematic incursions of the French and their Indian allies. They save inexperienced colonial troops from annihilation and are present at the construction of Fort Refuge in western New York. Later they meet with William Johnson and his Mohawks and then move on to Albany and New York City, observing British and colonial preparations for resistance to their enemies from French Canada. The final few pages describe the ignominious and devastating defeat of General Braddock in the forests near Fort Duquesne.

94. —————. *A soldier of Manhattan and his adventures at Ticonderoga and Quebec.* **New York: Appleton, 1897. 316p.**

"A young soldier of the Royal American troops tells his experiences during the French and Indian War. The descriptions of New York and Albany in that day are full of interest. The great battle in which Wolfe and Montcalm fell is vividly described. A character somewhat on the order of Cooper's 'Spy' early on takes a fancy to the hero and befriends him throughout in the most dangerous moments of his career. Love for a French maiden plays an important part in the young man's career, and when the French are beaten, she remains a willing captive to the young American officer"—Annual American catalogue.

95. —————. *The sun of Saratoga; a romance of Burgoyne's surrender.* **New York: D. Appleton, 1897. 313p.**

American soldier Dick Shelby is the narrator of this story of personal adventure, which is built around Burgoyne's invasion and his final defeat at Saratoga. Shelby's ladylove is Kate Van Auken, a young woman with pronounced 'rebel' sympathies, despite the strong Loyalist stance of the rest of her family. Shelby's chief rival for Kate's attention is the British officer Captain Roger Chudleigh, the man Kate's mother had expected her to marry.

96. **Alverson, Charles E., 1935- .** *Fighting back*. **Indianapolis: Bobbs-Merrill, 1973. 177p.**

Rizzo, a small-time hood from New York City tries to move in on and extort money from Harry, owner of a thriving bar in a suburb of the city. Henry gets help from a private detective who is willing to use strong-arm tactics, even murder, in the interest of his client. There is no satisfactory conclusion to the situation—several people, innocent and guilty, end up dead or badly hurt.

American, An. The Brigantine; **or**, *Admiral Lowe*. **See:** *The Brigantine*; **or**, *Admiral Lowe*.

97. **Ames, Eleanor Marie Easterbrook, 1831-1908.** *Up Broadway,* **and its sequel,** *A life story*, **by Eleanor Kirk (Nellie Ames). New York: Carleton, 1870. 271p.**

'Eleanor Kirk' is the go-between who is responsible for uniting Mary Montgomery—she had been forced into prostitution to support herself and her daughter—and the businessman who had married her under false pretenses (he already had a wife). Ten years passed, years of hardship and shame for Mary, while her lover, after shedding his incompatible wife, finds Mary with Mrs. Kirk's aid, sets aside Mary's recent past, and marries her, this time in compliance with the law. A Sequel to *Up Broadway* (p.[163]-271 is a vehicle for the author's ruminations about the inequalities that hamper women in marriage and at work. She tells the story of 'Nellie' whose husband turns out to be alcoholic and totally irresponsible. His attempt to reform is an utter failure and Nellie is left with a sister and her own children to provide for. She receives moral support from the likes of Susan B. Anthony and achieves some success as a writer. Her husband returns and seeks to lean on her, but Nellie rejects him despite the entreaties of the male establishment, which states that a woman must abide by her marital commitment.

Ames, Nellie, 1831-1908. See: Ames, Eleanor Marie Easterbrook, 1831-1908.

98. **Ames, Warren W.** *The mystery of Muller Hill*; **an entertaining love story of pioneer days. A history of the mysterious settler of the Georgetown hills, and an interesting article disclosing the identity of the wealthy refugee, who was, afterwards, Charles X, King of France. 3rd ed. De Ruyter, New York: Gleanor Press, 1930, c1899. 98p.**

The author, in part, fictionalizes an incident in central New York history—the construction and temporary occupation of an estate house, Muller Hill, in Georgetown, Madison County, New York, by the mysterious Frenchman, Louis Anathe Muller and his Dutch-American wife, Adaline Stuyvesant (p. 3–47). 'The History' (p. 48–98 provides some documentary data. Included in the fictional half is the story of an American, William Brent, and his marriage to Lois d'Orsay Vaudere, friend and companion to Adaline Stuyvesant Muller.

99. **Amrein, Vera R.** *A cabin for Mary Christmas*. **Illustrated by Peter Spier. New York: Harcourt, Brace, 1955. 183p.**

Three young people spend a longer than usual Christmas holiday on Long Island so that they can construct a cabin on the vessel of a friend suffering from polio. It will serve as a shelter for him when he takes cruises on his boat during the summer months.

100. Anderson, C.H. *Armour*; or, *What are you going to do about it?* **New York: W. B. Smith, 1881. 272p.**

'Armour' is a town whose location (whether in Upstate New York, or, perhaps more likely, in northeastern Pennsylvania) is never really made clear. It also happens to be the locale where much of the story takes place, although New York, Washington, D.C., and Philadelphia are also scenes of important events in the novel. The two chief characters are Lawrence Hamilton, a man of honor and integrity living on inherited wealth, and Malcolm Conyngham, greedy and unconscionable and presumably a good friend to Hamilton. When the Civil War begins, Hamilton serves as a Union Army officer and is severally wounded. Conyngham and his father use the war as an occasion to enrich themselves. After the conflict, 'friendly' Conyngham is the primary factor in the financial ruin of Hamilton and the thwarting of the latter's political ambitions. The author savages the hypocrisy and unchristian disposition of Conyngham and his ilk. At a ball attended by the impoverished Hamilton and his wife Fanny, Hamilton snubs Conyngham, then falls to his death after too much drinking. Conyngham's 'kingdom' begins to unravel and his un-worthiness is laid bare for all to see.

101. Anderson, Douglas, 1949- . *First and ten.* **New York: Crown Publishers, 1993. 218p.**

The National Football League players are on strike and Buffalo Bills' defensive back Santa Arkwright is sitting quietly by when he receives a letter that states 10 of his teammates will be in mortal danger if the strike isn't settled soon. The police don't have a handle on the situation and Arkwright springs into action as several of the Bills are actually murdered. His quest for evidence brings him in touch with some eccentric and suspicious characters, but he also meets a nice young woman, owner of an art gallery. With input and assistance from friends, Santa outdoes the incompetent police to unmask the killer, narrowly escaping death himself.

102. Mrs. Finley. *A woman with a record.* **New York: G.W. Dillingham, 1896 223p.**

The narrator and heroine of this novel set in New York City is the venturesome Lenoir Vaillant, a woman who plays at love. A gambler, a pleasure-seeker, she has style tinged with distrust. Lenoir indulges herself with a never-ending round of theater going, wine consumption, selective dining and flyers in the stock market. One of her paramours, Solon Maurel, a gamester too, is dependent on her when his luck turns sour; ill chance attends him when a vengeful lover knifes him in his apartment.

103. Anderson, Frederick Irving, b. 1877. *Adventures of the infallible Godahl.*

New York: Crowell, 1914. 241p.

The adventure-seeking New Yorker, Mr. Godahl, knows how to handle himself in the tightest situations; he is not averse to exercising his skills in shady and even blatantly criminal activities. At one point he even tries to burgle the United States Assay Office. On another occasion, while trying to get at a cache of jewels, he is surprised when a huge number of burglar alarms go off—this happens in New York City's Maiden Lane neighborhood.

104. **Andrews, Annulet, b. 1866.** *The wife of Narcissus.* **New York: Moffat, Yard, 1908. 250p.**

The heroine of the story is a young woman artist who resides in New York City yet is still watched over by a vigilant old nurse. Our protagonist, accompanied by a friend, goes to a meeting of a group called the New Hedonists. The men and women of this society flout the 'accepted' practices concerning love and marriage. There the heroine meets 'Narcissus', a Welsh poet, and marries him. The union of these two, an unhappy one, is rife with misunderstanding, self-seeking, and negligence.

Andrews, Eliza Frances, b. 1840. See under her pseudonym: Hay, Elzey.

Andrews, Fanny, b. 1840. See under her pseudonym: Hay, Elzey.

105. **Andrus, Dyckman, 1942- .** *Days when the house was too small.* **New York: Scribner, 1974.**

"A short novel and a handful of stories or rather conversations set in the remote, wintry Adirondacks, and they're as lifelike, and sad to say, lifeless as those days when the house becomes too small. Particularly for Mory, the seventeen-year-old son of Hilda and Fred Macken—caretakers of a summer camp—who had been badly burned and lost almost all of his sight due to the carelessness of his stepfather. With the messy clutter of neglect and shiftlessness all around him, Mory is 'alive' to many other places and quite dead to where he is—until the second deliberate tragedy when he picks up a gun. The stories, some reducing to only a page or two, are random, flat discussions re sex or giving up cigarettes or old age—taking place in bars or cars"—Kirkus reviews.

106. *Annals of the Empire City, from its colonial days to the present.* **By a New Yorker. Tale 1, The quadroon; or, New York under the English. New York: J.F. Trow, Printer, 1852. 238p.**

The time of the story is 1721-1723, years in which Catholics were persecuted in the Colony of New York. Father Bernard Ury marries Albert Farquhar and Isadora, a quadroon. Albert soon tires of Isadora and falls in love with Clare Walton. His dependent brother, James, hoping to gain a major share of Albert's wealth, creates mischief by telling Isadora of Albert's duplicity. The unfortunate Isadora is summarily rejected by Albert and she dies of fever. Albert marries Clare; the union is an unhappy one and is especially ruptured when Albert kills Clare's brother in the mistaken notion that this 'stranger' is his wife's lover. In a subplot the tale takes Father Ury to Schenectady where he witnesses a raid on the settlement by French and Indians and resists the amorous overtures of a Dutch lady, Emma Vrooman.

107. Anthony, Geraldine, d. 1912. *Four-in-Hand*; **a story of smart life in New York and at a country club. New York: D. Appleton, 1903. vi, 377p.**

The 'Four-in-Hand' are the four orphaned Fenwick children, Archie, Robin, Henry and Effie, who are being raised in New York City by George Fenwick, their grandfather, and his formidable sister, Katherine Foster. Upon Mr. Fenwick's death the four are, at his insistence, placed under the guardianship of members of the Fort Mounthouse Country Club, effectively shutting off much further influence over them by Mrs. Foster. They boys are an innocuous trio, although Archie does get mixed up in a foolish affair, and they fade into the background. Effie takes center stage. Surprisingly strong-minded Effie marries Sidney Percival, one of her guardians; he is a haughty, world-weary, blasé individual who had hitherto lavished his amorous attentions on 'Clip' Trevor, wife of a close friend. Effie at first dislikes her spouse, but she and Sidney do eventually arrive at a state, if not of connubial bliss, at least of 'comfortable' affection. The novel does not wander outside the confines of Fifth Avenue and Washington Square.

108. ————. *A victim of circumstances*; **a novel. New York: Harper, 1901. iii, 368p.**

The heroines are two girls in the New York City social swim with the unlikely nicknames of 'Spriggy' and 'Clip'; they are the grandchildren of the stern, sturdy Madame Trevor. Spriggy's marriage is disastrous while Clip fails to marry the man who seems to be an ideal choice. Each remains a 'victim of circumstances'—their lives seem governed by forces beyond their control or choice.

109. Anthony, Joseph, 1897- . *The gang.* **New York: Holt, 1921. 276p.**

Harlem and Manhattan's East Side in the early part of the 20th century—the people, the streets, the conversations (a mixture of substandard English, Yiddish, self-taught English, and the idioms of the swollen district)—is the scene. Harold Diamond, a 12-year-old, is an observer of the milling life around him.

110. Appleton, Robert, pseud. *The rise of Mrs. Simpson*; **a true story. New York: G.W. Dillingham, 1895. 364p.**

The author looks askance at the motives of those who make concerted efforts to establish themselves in 'proper society.' Mrs. Simpson uses money and hard work to do just that—not only in New York City but also in Boston and Chicago. Two characters from Appleton's earlier novels—'Mrs. Harry St. John' and 'Violet, the American Sappho' –make their appearance in this work too.

111.	**Archibald, Joseph, 1898-1986.** *West Point wingback.* **Philadelphia: Macrae, 1965. 189p.**

Ron Burritt, pampered by his mother, is now at West Point complaining in his first year and reluctant to perform any hard tasks; that plus his unsportsmanlike attitudes have pegged him as a lout. Kicked off the football team he still gets good grades academically and so he sticks around. Blamed for an injury to the football team's star fullback, Ron is nevertheless accepted as a volunteer for the B-squad in his third year at the Point and eventually works his way back to the A-team. He becomes a vital factor in a victory over Navy.

112.	**Ard, William, 1922-1962?** *A girl for Danny.* **New York: Popular Library, 1953. 159p.**

Danny, cashier on a Hudson River excursion boat, is caught up in a plot that leads to violence and three sudden deaths, all occurring on just a one-day trip on the river, but he also finds an interesting girl.

113.	**Arkin, Frieda, 1917- .** *The Dorp.* **New York: Dial Press, 1969. 360p.**

The inhabitants of 'Kuyper's Dorf', a small town in Upstate New York, are a most varied lot, many with dreams that never have a chance of becoming realities. e.g., a clergyman with a flock whose doubts and hypocrisies he is unable to redirect; Vebber Stevens, who has an idea for a book listing all the human sicknesses, a reference work for the medical establishment; Eunice Dewsnap, a hopeless romantic; Evelyn Clancy, an alcoholic who gained five months of fame via a television appearance; and Justin Barrows, journalist, furnishing in his newspaper the facts he deems most important for his readership.

Arling, Emanie Nahm. See: Sachs, Emanie Louise Nahm.

114.	**Armstrong, Charlotte, 1905-1969.** *The innocent flower.* **New York: Coward-McCann, 1945. 185p.**

"Mrs. Mary Moriarty, a New Rochelle divorcée, is distressed by the notion that one of her six children might have dropped nicotine sulphate into the sherry that finished off Miss Emily Brown who was visiting the family. MacDougall Duff, a private detective happens along, is entranced by the Moriarties, becomes part of the household and works out an explanation after encountering a number of red herrings"—New Yorker.

115.	**Aronson, Harvey, 1929- .** *Establishment of innocence,* **by Harvey Aronson and Mike McGrady. New York: Putnam, c1976. 347p.**

"Chapin Hope, New York State Senator from Suffolk County [Long Island], finds himself on the spot when his cocktail waitress paramour Ginny is brutally hacked to death right after one of their nocturnal Mineola trysts. It happens that the not-so-Honorable conservative Republican will get away with the indiscretion—until a boozing has-been of a reporter catches wind of his involvement as well as some political hanky-panky"—Kirkus reviews.

116. Arrick, Fran, 1937- . *Where'd you get the gun, Billy?* **New York: Bantam Books, 1991. 104p.**

A small Upstate New York town is the stage for the puzzling murder of his girlfriend by Billy, a 16-year-old. How did Billy get his hands on a gun in the first place is a question that springs to the minds of Liz and David, Billy's classmates. Police Lieutenant Wisnewski talks with the two youngsters and frames a scenario on the passage of the handgun. Gun control is obviously on the author's mind. The cast includes abused wives, overbearing men and restless students.

117. Arthur, Timothy Shay, 1809-1885. *Cast adrift.* **Philadelphia: J.M. Stoddart, 1873. 364p.**

The heroine, Edith Dinneford, against her mother's plans, marries George Granger, a poor but enterprising young man who forms a business partnership in New York City with Lloyd Freeling. Through the unscrupulous Freeling's machinations George is accused of forgery and imprisoned. The son of Edith and George is born; Mrs. Dinneford conspires with Nurse Bray to dispose of the infant, handing it over to a stranger, an unfit woman. Edith told by her mother that the child is dead, gradually becomes certain that Mrs. Dinneford is lying. Several years pass; the child, with the name Andy, is raised in the slums of the city by various dubious characters. He is finally located by Edith in a children's hospital—Andy bears a telling red birthmark on one of his arms. Freeling writes a letter confessing to his wrongdoing that falls into the hands of Edith and Mr. Dinneford. Mrs. Dinneford dies, George is released, and he, Edith and Andy are reunited.

118. ————. *Hiram Elwood, the banker*; or, *Like father, like son.* **New York: J. Allen, 1844. 93p.**

Among honest brokers in New York financial circles, the Elwoods, father and son, had dubious reputations. Both were stock manipulators, but to the general public they presented a façade of respectability that allowed them to succeed in amassing comfortable fortunes. The story focuses on Hiram Elwood, Jr. and his wife Theresa Berenger Elwood whose love for her husband endures through his fall from fiscal grace and prison (seven years). Upon his release and at the urging of his father young Hiram abandons faithful Theresa and his 10-year-old son and goes south to resume his business operations. Years after Theresa's sudden death, rumor has it that Hiram, Jr., under the name of P—— —— has prospered.

119. ————. *Love in high life*; a story of the 'Upper Ten.' **Philadellphia: T.B. Peterson, 1849. 100p.**

At the insistence of his father Percy Edwards agrees to marry Kate Harrison whom he finds personally unattractive but whose dowry and likely future inheritance are strong inducements. Kate herself is reluctant to enter into marriage with Percy, but she too is influenced by her father's wish for the union. The marriage is an unhappy one; Percy's coldness toward Kate is made somewhat endurable when she gives birth to her child. Percy has a brief fling with the beautiful Mrs. S——; Kate's health deteriorates. In the course of preparations for a pistol duel with the offended Mr. S—— (really looking for a way to rid himself of his wife) Percy comes to the sudden realization that he does have a wife he loves. The scene of Arthur's tale of a 'New York' marriage is that city and Newport.

120. ————. *Out in the world*; a novel. New York: Carleton, 1864. 312p.
A chronicle of misunderstanding, stubbornness and the failure of compromise between Carl Jansen and his wife Madeline Spencer Jansen. Both are New Yorkers—Carl is a wealthy businessman and Madeline has absorbed the new ideas of women's equality. They clash when Carl insists on his authority and Madeline demands equal rights. Though still in love they separate and eventually divorce. Carl's second marriage is an unhappy one. Madeline searches unsuccessfully for a livelihood. More than 15 years pass and Madeline is ill and poor, alone in a cold room. Her best friend, Mrs. Lawrence, and Carl find Madeline who is deathly sick. Carl, regretting his past mistakes and burdened with a frivolous wife and daughter, loses his will to live. At the bedside of the only woman he ever loved Carl and Madeline almost simultaneously 'pass to God'.

121. Asbury, Herbert, 1891-1963. *The tick of the clock.* New York: Macy-Masius, 1928. 206p.
Mrs. Hannah Johnson discovers the body of her employer, James B. Walton, in his New York City home. Two other people are in the house—Helen Walton, Mr. Walton's stepdaughter, and Lee Sing, his servant—both had been unconscious but were awakened by Mrs. Johnson, the housekeeper, and the policeman she had summoned. Inspector Conway takes on the case; there are thirteen suspects—he assembles them in one room and baits the individual responsible for the homicide into giving a confession.

122. Asch, Nathan, 1902-1964. *The office.* New York: Harcourt Brace, 1925. 265p.
In its first few pages the novel evokes the high-strung atmosphere of a Wall Street bucket shop, a brokerage house that aggressively sells speculative stocks of questionable worth. When the operation fails, the author traces the steps of twenty people from the office staff as they wend their way homeward or step off to amuse themselves as best they can considering their present circumstances.

123. ————. *Pay day.* New York: Brewer and Warren; Payson and Clarke, 1930. 265p.
"Jim is a clerk in downtown New York. His light loves and rather pitiful pleasures are focused into that brief interval when he spends his week's

earnings. … The author has etched Jim's night of tawdry pleasures against the ghastly background of the Sacco-Vanzetti execution. The newsboys call the extras; the patrons of speakeasies and dance halls discuss the case, reeling with bad liquor and jazz. The horror and roar of that well-remembered night provide the undertow in the current of Jim's trivial preoccupations"—Outlook and Independent.

124. Asch, Sholem, 1880-1957. *The mother.* Translated by Nathan Ausubel. Pref. by Ludwig Lewisohn. New York: H. Liveright, 1930. 350p.

A novel depicting the life of a family of Jewish immigrants in New York City at the beginning of the 20th century."The Zlotniks migrate to America following the success of their eldest son in the new country. Here as in Poland, Suré, the mother finds she must fight against poverty, and works herself to death. Droyrelè, the eldest daughter, gives her love and encouragement to a dependent young sculptor until he achieves success; then she returns to her own family to care for the younger brothers and sisters, left motherless"—Book review digest.

125. Ashbrook, Harriette, 1898-1946. *Lady in danger*, by Susannah Shane [pseud.]. New York: Dodd, Mead, 1942. 274p.

"Christopher Saxe, the most exasperating and unpredictable man Inspector Redfern has ever met, solves the riddle of the poisoned pancakes served at a supper party on a yacht off Long Island. A mixed lot, all of whom are involved in an earlier crime, attend the party"—New Yorker.

126. ————. *The murder of Steven Kester.* New York: Coward-McCann, 1931. 312p.

"For … [the] necessary corpse we have a retired millionaire and horticulturist stabbed during a fancy dress party at 'Long Hills' [Long Island, and] bounded on all four sides by suspicious relatives, servants, neighbors and guests, among them beauteous granddaughter, Jennifer Vinton; her sweetheart, Cliff Millard, who apparently tried to get away in the green roadster; Roger Herries, a mystery man from the past; and Lenox, the butler. Enter Spike Tracy, the handsome but cheerful amateur detective, who wrings truly surprising things from the ensanguined handkerchief, the little black notebook, the Arco mining bonds [etc.]"—New York herald tribune book review.

127. Ashland, Aria. *The rebel scout*; a romance of the Revolution. New York: Stringer & Townsend [1852]. 109p.

Gilbert Wolcott, a scout and spy for the Americans, abducts Margaret Graham, daughter of British officer Colonel Graham of Burgoyne's invading army. In her captivity Margaret comes to know and become deeply attached to Ruth Wolcott, Gilbert's physically deformed 'daughter'. Margaret learns that her father had seduced Gilbert's wife (now deceased) years ago and that Ruth was the child of the seduction. The Colonel, mortally wounded during the Battle of Saratoga, asks for and receives forgiveness from Margaret and

Gilbert Wolcott. Margaret marries Duncan Gleig, a British soldier and sails for Scotland. Ruth lives with Gilbert, the man who adopted her, and never marries.

128. Ashmun, Margaret Eliza, 1875-1940. *Topless towers*; a romance of Morningside Heights. New York: Macmillan, 1921. 307p.

"The 'romance' of Morningside Heights … is the story of two young women and their life together in a New York City apartment. The spirit of the city, the moods and problems of the two girls, their difficulties in adjusting themselves to the habits and temperaments of each other, their jealousies, their love affairs, their friendships, their differing interests, are described with truthfulness and simplicity. One of the two is shown steadily developing throughout the story, learning her values, daring to be her real self, till at the end she is ready for the choice which is asked of her"—Book review digest.

Aspinwall, Marguerite, joint author. *Counter currents*. See Item #1802.

129. Atherton, Gertrude Franklin 1857-1948. *The aristocrats being the impressions of the Lady Helen Pole during her sojourn in the Great North Woods as spontaneously recorded in her letters to her friend in North Britain, the Countess of Edge and Ross*. London: New York: J. Lane, 1901. 308p.

Lady Helen is much taken with the beauty and ruggedness of the Adirondacks and their inhabitants. She frequently walks in the forests, boats on the lakes and rivers and joins a particularly adventuresome 'open' camping expedition into the wilderness. However this anonymously published novel is bent on exposing "the pretensions of some American literary and fashionable types from the point of view of an intelligent young English noblewoman" (McClure, C. Gertrude Atherton). Miss Pole also has to deal with ardent suitors (three of them). She avoids any decision on this score when the novel concludes.

130. ———. *Black oxen.* New York: Boni & Liveright, 1922. 346p.

"Mary Ogden, the beauty and belle of her day in New York, had married a Hungarian diplomat, Count Zattiany, left America and passed out of the knowledge of her friends except as an occasional report of her was brought home by some returning traveler. Then after an interval of thirty-four years there appears in a fashionable New York first-night audience a beautiful young woman who is a replica of the Mary Ogden of memory, yet who cannot be her daughter since the Countess Zattiany was known to be childless. Seen repeatedly and always alone, she becomes the center of mystery and conjecture. Men are fascinated by her. Lee Clavering, a brilliant young journalist, bolder than the rest, finds a way to meet her. She offers an explanation of her identify, which is accepted but hardly believed. Then one day she tells the truth about herself and the mystery develops into a miracle story. She is on the point of marrying Lee Clavering when, as suddenly as she appeared, she takes herself back to Europe and out of his life"—Book review digest.

131. ————. *Mrs. Balfame*; a novel. **New York: F.A. Stokes, 1916. 335p.**

A mystery novel. Mrs. Balfame had already concocted an elaborate plan to dispose of her husband David, but he was shot and killed by someone outside of her ken. However, Mrs. Balfame was still the chief suspect and she was put on trial. Her acquittal and the unmasking of the real culprit are largely owing to the sharp investigative work of reporters from New York City newspapers.

132. ————. *Patience Sparhawk and her times*; a novel. **London: New York: J. Lane, 1897. 488p.**

Patience Sparhawk, daughter of a notorious mother and a well-educated Yankee father, comes to New York City after her parents' deaths. Married to wealth and affluence Patience has no qualms about leaving her husband when her love for him fades. For a while she is a newspaper employee but gives that up to see her husband through a grave illness; an overdose of morphine causes his death. Wrongly accused of poisoning him, Patience goes to trial, is convicted and condemned to be electrocuted. Her lawyer has fallen in love with Patience and tries desperately to effect her release. Patience is in the death chamber when a last second confession by another woman saves her.

133. ————. *A question of time. Mrs. Pendleton's four-in-hand.* **New York: J.W. Lovell Co. [United States Book Co.] 1891. 250p.**

The first novella '*A question of time*', takes place in the serene village of 'Danforth', Long Island. A beautiful widow, Boradil Trevor, 46, quite talented artistically, is drawn to a remarkable young man of 22, Mark Saltonstall. The attraction is mutual despite the differences in ages; these two ignore the conventions of the place and time as they allow their natural affinities to govern their relationship. There are no horses pertinent to '*Mrs. Pendleton's four-in-hand.*' The four are suitors, all known to one another, who ask for the young widow, Mrs. Pendleton's hand in marriage simultaneously by letters.

134. Atkin, George Murray, b.1891. *The captive herd.* **New York: Crowell, 1922. 311p.**

A selfish, ambitious young Canadian embraces New York City with the goal of ultimate wealth and power. "Employed by two wealthy Jewish bankers in a position of trust, he uses his confidential knowledge to enrich himself at their expense. While still in Canada he had had an affair with an engaging young girl that had been serious for her part, but a pastime for him. After his double-dealing is exposed and he loses his position, he returns to Canada, bethinks himself of Natalie and for the first time in his life sees himself as an integral part of the human race. He learns to fit himself socially and ethically into the herd, marries and founds a family"—Book review digest.

135. Atkinson, Eleanor Stackhouse, 1863-1942. *Hearts undaunted*; a romance of

four frontiers. New York: Harper, 1917. 348p.

An historical novel that describes frontier life as it moves from northern New York State westward to Illinois. The heroine, Eleanor Lytle, a child of the frontier, is taken captive by the Iroquois and adopted by Chief Cornplanter. Her life for many years is that of her captors. When she finally returns to the white settlements she marries a Scots trader and silversmith, reportedly one of the founders of the modern city of Chicago.

136. **Atkinson, Oriana Torrey, 1894-1989.** *Big Eyes*; **a story of the Catskill Mountains.** New York: Appleton-Century-Cofts, 1949. 294p.

The small village in the Catskill Mountains in which the story takes place (in the early years of the 20th century) is the home of Eyzie Miles, of half-Indian stock, whose ambition encompasses a fine house, once the center of the prominent Wall family, and a young man, Bo Bedell; her behavior is often deemed scandalous, but in the long run she gets what she wants.

137. —————. *The golden season: a romance of early America.* **Indianapolis: Bobbs-Merrill, 1953. 309p.**

A sequel to the author's *The twin cousins* (q.v.); continuing characters from that novel, set in Catskill, New York, are Content and Luther Ware, but the Ware daughter, Freedom, takes center stage here, along with Gretchen, Luther's wife following Content's death, and Freedom's choice of a husband, Pup Van Loo.

138. —————. *The twin cousins*; **a novel. Indianapolis: Bobbs-Merrill, 1951. 320p.**

"A romance of life in and around Catskill, New York after the Revolution. It is the story of Luther Ware and his wife Content, and the widowed Dutch wife of Luther's cousin, and the inn they built on the Susquehanna Turnpike"— Book review digest.

139. **Atwell, Lester, 1908- .** *Life with its sorrow, life with its fear*; **a novel. New York: Simon and Schuster, 1971. 414p.**

"Paul [an orphan] is sent by his stepmother to visit his father's family in a New York suburb [the time is the 1930s]. Living there are widowed Aunt Dottie and her two obstreperous small sons, an acid and sensible great-aunt who runs the busy household, and above all, Uncle Reggie, fat, pompous, generous, and a little pathetic. They [this family] are so full of life and affection that Paul blooms and prospers, and even when Uncle Reggie proves to have provided for his family by using their private savings Paul—whose educational plans are thereby curtained—loves him"—Saturday review of literature.

140. **Austin, Hugh.** *Drink the green water*; **or,** *Young Caldwell's toe.* **A Sultan's harem mystery. New York: Scribner, 1948. 212p.**

"Dessicated New York law firms get a good deal of kidding in this one. A young lawyer named Sultan, who has all the stuffy mannerisms of his grandfather, undertakes to find the solution to a murder that occurred in the eighteen-nineties; he is aided in his researches (which take place on Long Island) by his file clerk, his secretary, and his receptionist, all of them good looking young ladies with a healthy distaste for codicils. Very funny in spots, but the plot at times is overwhelmingly complex"—New Yorker.

141. ————. *It couldn't be murder.* **Garden City, N.Y.: Published for the Crime Club by Doubleday, Doran, 1935. viii, 301p.**

"No less than fifty-four sections, or shortest chapters, are listed in the table of contents, all times to the minute, from 2:25 A.M. of one day to 2:30 A.M. of the next. ... First, Mrs. Charles Haughton, of the Hudson Bank and Trust Haughtons, an invalid, dies in her room while Nurse O'Toole is doped. Mr. Haughton gets his later, and there's also a third corpse. In an initialed testimonial the author alleges: 'There are no hidden rooms, secret passages. ... The murderer had no outside assistants or accomplices. ... In short, this mystery can be solved on the basis of the clues that are given, and the solution is the one and only possible solution"—New York herald tribune books.

142. **Austin, Mary Hunter, 1868-1934.** *No. 26 Jayne Street.* **Boston: Houghton, Mifflin, 1920. 353p.**

"The action of the story takes place in the year after America's entrance into the [First World] War. Neith Schuyler, the heroine, has lived abroad with an invalid father for a number of years, and following his death has done relief work in France. She returns home hoping to learn to understand America. To come nearer to the problem she leaves the luxurious home of her two great aunts and takes a modest apartment on Jayne Street, just off Washington Square. Here she comes into contact with many shades of radical opinion and contrasts it with the 'capitalistic' attitude of her own family and friends. Two men fall in love with Neith, Eustace Rittenhouse, an aviator, and Adam Frear, a labor leader. She becomes engaged to Adam and then learns that there has been another woman in his life, Rose Matlock, one of the radical group. The attitude of the two women, who represent the new feminism, puzzles Adam and he leaves for Russia. Eustace is killed in France and Neith is left to grope her way into the future alone"—Book review digest.

143. **Aylesworth, Barton Orville, 1860-1933.** *"Thirteen" and twelve others from the Adirondacks and elsewhere.* **St. Louis: Christian Pub. Co., 1892 [c1893]. 259p.**

Mirror Lake, Maiden Rock, Ausable Chasm and other Adirondack points of interest are featured in seven of the author's short stories (the first six and 'A double revelation'). Contents: "Thirteen" and twelve others.—The fairies at Au Sable Chasm.—Maiden Rock.—A woman?—A dream.—Jim's vict'try.—Aunt Modgie.—John Brown (a poem read at John Brown's grave in the Adirondacks, July 11th, 1982).—A double revelation.—A Christmas story.—Oduna.—Where there is life there is hope (?).—A soul's resurrection.

144. **Ayr, Mrs. Landis.** *The Brown-Laurel marriage.* **London, New York: F.**

Tennyson Neely, 1898. 219p.

New York City is the stage upon which this social drama is played. Returning from Europe Eldris Laurel, a young widow, resumes her friendly relationship with Barry Brown, a dashing bachelor. Despite a growing sexual attraction convention dictates that Eldris and Barry avoid matrimony, until a mutual friend suggests that they enter into a 'conditional' marriage. With that stipulation the pair are joined: the story follows closely the consequences of complying with the contract.

145. **Ayres, Jared Augustus, 1814-1886.** *The legends of Montauk.* **With an historical appendix. Hartford [Conn.]: E. Hunt; New York: Putnam, 1849. 127p.**

A long descriptive, and, in part, narrative poem in the first person. The narrator expatiates upon the Montauk Point region on the easternmost tip of Long Island, weaving in two Indian Legends about the Montauk warriors, Wyandannee and Weeoncombone. In the last section of the poem the narrator listens as the spirits of the surrounding ocean waters, 'the ghosts that mariners fear', speak singly and in chorus.

B., C.R. Redeemed. See: [Hull, Charles] Redeemed.

B.H.L. *Chevrons*; a story of West Point. See: Lippincott, Bertha Hartmann, 1880-1963. *Chevrons*; a story of West Point.

146. **Bacheller, Irving, 1859-1950.** *'Charge it'*; or, *Keeping up with Harry.* **A story of fashionable extravagance and of the successful efforts to restrain it made by the Honorable Socrates Potter, the genial friend of Lizzie. New York: Harper, 1912. 191p.**

In this humorous account of wealthy New Yorkers "the Honorable Socrates Potter again discourses genially on certain modern economic tendencies. Having successfully disposed of Lizzie, he undertakes this time the reform of Harry, the young man who had had every advantage in life except poverty, who habitually exceeded the speed limit and who, whenever he wanted a thing, picked it up and said 'charge it.' The Honorable Socrates checks Harry's fool progress and starts him on the road to honest self-respecting manhood, incidentally effecting other reforms in the social life of 'Pointview'"—Book review digest.

147. ———. *Darrel of the Blessed Isles.* **Illustrated by Arthur I. Keller. Boston: Lothrop, 1903. 410p.**

The tale begins in 1835 in 'Bacheller country' (i.e. Upstate New York) when a baby boy is left on the doorstep of Theron Allen and his wife. They rear the boy who comes to be known as Sidney Trove. As the years pass and Sidney acquires knowledge, his best friend and counselor is the benign, scholarly Roderick Darrel, tinker, clock repairer. The mystery of Sidney's birth, the ups and downs of his love affair with Polly Vaughn, Sidney's facing an accusation of bank robbery, etc.—these and other incidents are resolved as the story concludes. The novel is enhanced by the presence of a number of characters with their peculiar way of life and distinctive speech.

148. ————. *D'ri and I*; a tale of daring deeds in the second war with the British. Being the memoirs of Col. Ramon Bell, U.S.A. Illustrated by F.C. Yohn. Boston: Lothrop Pub. Co., 1901. 362p.

D'ri is Darius Olin, 'a pure-bred Yankee, quaint, rugged, wise, truthful', employed by Ramon's father; he is ever watchful over Ramon as the two take part in many military adventures during the War of 1812 on the northern New York and the Canadian borders. 'Ramon had the hardy traits of a Puritan father, softened by the more romantic temperament of a French mother' (Preface).

149. ————. *Eben Holden*; a tale of the North Country. Boston: Lothrop Pub. Co., 1900. viii, 432p.

This novel was one of the most popular of its time and was praised by W.D. Howells and E.C. Stedman. Laid in the middle of the 19th century its main characters are Eben Holden ('Uncle Eb'), a kind-hearted, wise, honest hired farm hand who serves as mentor and guardian of an orphan boy. The two come to St. Lawrence County in Upstate New York where they find a home with the farmer David Brower. The orphan, given the name William Brower, evolves successively into a college student (St. Lawrence University), a journalist in New York City under Horace Greeley, and a soldier in the Civil War. Hope, the daughter of David and Elizabeth Brower, and William are the principals in a love affair that develops through the years.

150. ————. *Eben Holden's last day a-fishing*. New York: Harper, 1907. 60p.

Eben Holden in his latter years remains the gentle, humorous, wise and unassuming character that one met with in Bacheller's best-known work, *Eben Holden*. Still living in Upstate New York's St. Lawrence County, Eben is limned as he spends a day in June fishing and then opens his humble country home for the Christmas holidays.

151. ————. *The hand-made gentleman*; a tale of the battle of peace. New York: Harper, 1909. 331p.

The hero, James Henry McCarthy, his mother a washwoman, is determined to acquire the trappings of good breeding, in other words to become a 'gentleman'. He has a knack for business and with a plan for organizing the railroads goes to Commodore Vanderbilt. Approval is given and McCarthy's rise begins. He meets with Andrew Carnegie and other railway and business leaders in New York City; McCarthy does succeed in his original mission and, more importantly, becomes a valued figure in the drive towards railroad consolidation in the latter part of the 19th century.

152. ————. *The harvesting*. New York: F.A. Stokes, 1934. xi, 303p.

New York State's 'North Woods' is the locale of this novel, which "begins by reversing the father and son roles in the parable of the prodigal. Back in the middle [eighteen] seventies Cyril Barrett, blonde, handsome, blue-eyed, with a tenor voice and noble instincts, fell in love with Ruth, but his father told him he was too young to marry. Elihu Barrett, respected widower and father of three children, succumbed to a temptation, 'like a mighty wind that fells the oak.' He confessed to his son that Ruth was going to have a child. 'I got into the current and went over the dam', he said 'I am terribly bruised.' Cyril said, 'My soul has been hit with the ax.' Ruth said, 'I'm crushed.' So the noble son assumes the guilt of the fallen oak"—New York herald tribune book review.

153. ————. *The house of the three ganders.* **Indianapolis: Bobbs-Merrill, 1928. 315p.**

A rural community in the Adirondacks is the setting of a novel that includes a murder case and a plethora of vivid characters, e.g., a homeless boy named Shad who sauntered into town and settled down; Miss Betty Spenlow, a maiden lady composed of equal parts of benevolence and severity; the lad 'Bony' to whom the village's meeting-house is known as 'the Sob Works'; the elderly, eccentric town character; a kind, honest tinker who is falsely accused of murdering a woman and her father and almost pays with his life. Dry Yorker wit and humor is much in evidence in Bacheller's country folk.

154. ————. *The light in the clearing*; a tale of the North Country in the time of Silas Wright. **Illustrated by Arthur I. Keller. Indianapolis: Bobbs-Merrill, 1917. 414p.**

Barton (Bart) Baynes, an orphan, and the narrator of the story is brought up in northern New York State on the farm of Aunt Deel and Uncle Peabody Baynes. Bart's hero, the man after whom he wishes to model his own life, is Silas Wright, U.S. Senator and later Governor of the State of New York. Bart is the only witness of a murder and later must identify the culprit, Amos Grimshaw, son of the hard-bitten moneylender, Benjamin Grimshaw. Grimshaw's threats to make things difficult for Uncle Peabody do not sway Bart from his duty as State's witness in the trial of Amos Grimshaw. Near the conclusion of the tale Bart learns much about the true identify of 'Roving Kate' who follows the elder Grimshaw's every move. Bart also pledges his love to Sally Dunkelberg and spends time in the nation's capital as secretary to Senator Wright. The novel encompasses the 1830s and 1840s.

155. ————.*The master of silence*; a novel. **New York: C.L.Webster, 1892. 176p.**
"Rayel Lane, the hero of this strange romance, lives for eighteen years shut up in an isolated house in the northern part of New York State, his only companions being his father, a deaf-mute and a tame lion. He has never been taught to speak, with the exception of a few worlds of Sanskrit, and has a strange power of reading other men's minds. Add to this fact that he has never seen a woman, and some conception may be formed of the strange part he plays in the world after this father's death. An English cousin, escaping a

conspiracy against his life, finds Rayel in his retreat, teaches him language and takes him to New York City. Love for the same woman tests the character of both men"—Annual American catalogue.

156. ————. *Silas Strong, emperor of the woods.* **New York: Harper, 1906. vii, 339p.**

The author says: 'it pretends to be nothing more than a simple account of one summer life, pretty much as it was lived, in a part of the Adirondacks.' Dryly humorous, philosophical Silas Strong is at war with the lumber barons who look upon 'his' forests as a source of great wealth. Silas also oversees a love affair between a wealthy young politician from New York City and a girl whose life has been circumscribed by the woods she cherishes. When a forest fire set by his enemies threatens his sister's life, Silas tries to save her, with tragic results for himself.

157. ————. *The still house of O'Darrow.* **London: Cassell, 1894. 143p.**

Sir George O'Darrow resides solitarily in a huge mansion in New York City. He invites Burton Fanning, a newspaper reporter, to share some of his secrets and work for him. His past excesses have led O'Darrow to believe that a particular enemy lies in wait to secure revenge for the wrongs O'Darrow has committed towards him and many others. When O'Darrow's body is discovered in his library, an inquest comes to the conclusion that O'Darrow, verging on insanity and possessed of a dual personality, is a suicide. Fanning is O'Darrow's chief heir. The young man opens up O'Darrow's 'still house' to the poor and homeless of New York and also wins the hand of the woman both he and O'Darrow had hitherto pursued unsuccessfully.

158. ————. *The winds of God*; a tale of the North Country. **Illustrated by John Rae. New York: Farrar & Rinehart, 1941. xiv, 318p.**

"The story of a Vermont boy's experiences many years ago in his own state and upper New York State. After his mother's death the boy had to make his way, so he started out with only a faithful dog companion, and tried to make a living singing at country fairs. It ends with his days at St. Lawrence College [Canton, N.Y.]"—Book review digest.

159. [Bacon, Delia] 1811-1859. *The bride of Fort Edward.* **Founded on an incident of the Revolution. New York: S. Colman, 1839. 174p.**

Although the work has the format of a play, the author insists, "It is not a play. It was not intended for the stage. ... I have chosen the form of the dialogue as best suited to my purpose." The incident referred to is the murder of Jane McCrea by Indian allies of General Burgoyne. Helen Grey is the ill-fated 'heroine' in Bacon's story; she is the bride of the Tory officer, Everard Maitland. When her patriotic mother and sister make haste to retire to Albany, Helen insists on staying behind, hoping to be reunited with her lover. Treacherous Indians, ignoring orders to conduct Helen safely through British lines, vengefully kill her. Her murder shocks and angers both the British and especially the Americans who use the slaying as a rallying point.

160. **Bacon, Dolores, b. 1870.** *In high places.* **Illustrated by George L. Tobin. New York: Doubleday, Page, 1907. 347p.**

New York City is the scene of a novel about the never-ending pressures to make more money to satisfy an acquisitive, jealous wife that almost drive a financier to ruin. Jean Meredith of his office staff is of immeasurable value to the businessman, but his wife forces him to fire Jean. Clandestinely, Jean continues to look after his interests and is a key in saving him from bankruptcy. The author presents contrasts by pointing to the happy home life of the financier's Jewish partner and the placid domesticity of two violinists who are employed by a second-rate restaurant.

161. **Bacon, Josephine Dodge Daskam, 1876-1961.** *Kathy.* **Illustrated by Joan Esley. New York: Longmans, Green, 1934. ix, 335p.**

"Kathy, the heroine, helps out during her vacations in a tea-room in a little Catskill village, which is the background. The story takes her through her years at Smith College and ends with her engagement. There is a note of mystery"—Book review digest.

162. ————. *Medusa's head.* **New York: D. Appleton, 1926. 120p.**

The mystery posed by this brief novel is the strange disappearance of a beautiful belle of New York society and the unanswered reason for her vanishing into 'thin air.'

163. ————. *On our hill.* **With illus. by T.M. and M.T. Bevans. New York: Scriber, 1918. xii, 336p.**

"Our hill is Beech Hill, Pleasantville, N.Y. and the three children, Prima, Secunda and Tertius, whose sayings and doings fill these pages, are apparently Anne, Deborah and Selden Bacon, to whom the book is dedicated by their loving mother. It is written for adults, from the adult point of view, and tells of the 'solemn little joys and funny sorrows' of the children—their lessons, the theater, the books they like and the books their mother wishes they would like, etc. 'Our governess' and 'our mother' come into the story, but there is no sign of a father"—Book review digest.

164. ————. *Open market.* **Illus. by A.I. Keller. New York: Appleton, 1915. 333p.**

Evelyn Jaffray, formerly a member of the highest circles of New York City society, is reduced to penury by the death of a wealthy aunt who left Evelyn out of her will. Evelyn happens to be in the Adirondacks when she meets a lame young man, Gard, the son of a French guide who leaves the cripple a substantial inheritance. Seizing her opportunity Evelyn offers Gard her hand in marriage. The inexperienced Gard, who has had virtually no contact with women, eagerly accepts. Strangely enough, Evelyn, the fortune seeker in this case, finds happiness with her unusual spouse.

165. ————. *Square Peggy.* **New York: D. Appleton, 1919. 339p.**
"Square Peggy of the title story was not the only of the ten heroines of these ten short stories who was a square peg in a round hole. Indeed the stories are based on the efforts of certain young American girls to adjust themselves to their individual environments. The girls in general are of that class of [New York] society where money is no object or obstacle and the [1st World War] activities of the wealthy enter largely into the setting. True to fiction their problems inevitably find their solution in matrimony"—Book review digest. Contents: Square Peggy.—Comrades in arms.—The ghost of Rosy Taylor.—Alice of the Red Tape.—The fruits of the earth.—The file of fate.—Stepping stones.—Merry-Go-Round.—Quartermastery.—Ru of the Reserves.

166. ————. *Today's daughter.* **Illustrated by C.D. Williams. New York: D. Appleton, 1914. 348p.**
On the surface Lucia Stanchon seems to be a young woman who, despite the advantages of a comfortably well-off family and solid status in New York society, has enough of an independent streak to strike out on her own, to make her own economic mark. Nevertheless, she accedes to a trial marriage to one of her father's professional associates. The 'venture' is about to end calamitously until Lucia does an about face, tossing aside her 'modern up-to-date' attitudes and going along with the dutiful wife and perhaps mother-to-be theme.

Bacon, Mary Schell Hoke, b. 1870. See: Bacon, Dolores, b. 1870.

167. **Baer, Warren.** *Champagne Charlie*; or, *The 'Sports of New-York.'* **Exhibiting in lively colors all the 'ins and outs, and ups and downs' of every class of fast Gothamites! Including scenes of drawing rooms, billiard saloons, free and easy's, gambling houses, private supper rooms! Every phase of fashionable and unfashionable life in the Empire City. New York: R.M. De Witt, c1868. 144p (in couble columns).**
'Champagne Charlie' is the leader of a bevy of revelers, male and female, who too often partake of sparkling wines and frequent saloons and houses of carefree pleasure and dissipation. Charlie pays dearly for his excesses, but several of his companions are more fortunate, settling down to relatively placid existences in town and country.

168. **Bagby, Albert Morris, 1859-1941.** *"Mammy Rosie."* **New York: A.M. Bagby, 1904. 333p.**
The title refers to a Black lady, a former slave, who takes over the care and feeding of a single White male, a paragon of fashion among the elite of New York City society. Mammy Rosie is not above listening in on conversations

that do not concern her. The information she gathers is helpful when her young employer falls in love while vacationing in Newport.

169. **Bailey, Anthony, 1933- .** *Major André.* **New York: Farrar, Straus, Giroux, 1987. 200p.**

A fictionalized version of British Major John André's dealings with General Benedict Arnold who had apprised André that he was to obtain command of West Point. The novel (narrated by André) focuses on the several days in late September of 1780 when André met Arnold on the Hudson, arranged terms for the surrender of the American stronghold, and then tried to pass through the American lines in civilian dress. André's interception by suspicious American militia led, of course, to his being hanged as a spy on October 2, 1780 at Tappan, N.Y.

170. **Bailey, Nathan J.** *Johnsville in the olden time, and other stories.* **New York: Printed by E.O. Jenkins, 1884. 255p.**

'Johnsville' is very likely a village in the Hudson Valley (very probably in Dutchess County); in any event the author in his first piece gives a detailed description of the people and activities of Johnsville. In other stories in his collection Dutchess County, with an emphasis on Fishkill, East Fishkill and the Fishkill Creek area, is most often the scene. Partial contents: The early settlers of the Valley of the Sprout.—The robbers of Windam Peak: a tale of Fishkill Hook.—The fight at Stebbins' Corners.—The gold-diggers of Moccasin Hill.—The ghost of Brinckerhoff's Pond.—An abstract from the minutes of the Spankers Club of Peekskill.—The buried treasure: a tale of Dobbs Ferry.—A legend of Adrian Pond.—The big turtle of the Benny Pond.—The legend of Manitou Hill.—The black cat of Wall Street [of Fishkill Hook].

171. **Baird, Thomas, 1923- .** *Where time ends*; **a novel. New York: Harper & Row, 1988. 230p.**

"Teenagers hiking in the Adirondacks learn that the U.S. and the Soviets are at war. At first the story focuses on the personal bonds and conflicts in the group as they struggle to get home. Ernie is trying to support her brother Orin who is angry and humiliated about his disability from a motorcycle accident. They are joined by two friends, Loop and Doug, both of whom are attracted to Ernie. Macho Doug has been in trouble for manslaughter and now he kills again, attacking a man who tries to molest Ernie. Gradually, survival becomes hopeless as they learn that the two world powers have loosed biological weapons. … The message is heavy-handed, both in Doug's quotes from his wise grandfather and the lyrics of an adult folk singer who joins them for a while. But the action and the [Adirondack] wilderness lore are exciting"—Booklist.

172. **Baker, Carlos Heard, 1909-1987.** *A friend in power.* **New York: Scribner, 1958. 312p.**

Enfield University, a New York State school, a short distance from New York City, is looking for a new president. The trustees gradually view the chairman of the faculty search committee, modest Ed Tyler, as the best possible choice for the position. And Ed, professor of modern languages, receives the appointment.

173. Baker, Elliott, 1922- . *The Penny wars.* **New York: G.P. Putnam, 1968. 255p.**

"The setting is the small-town lower middle class of the 1930s [in Upper New York State] with everyone listening to the Major Bowes Amateur Hour on this side of the Atlantic, while Hitler is marching into Poland on the other. Tyler [aged sixteen and a half] feels that he ought to be fighting for democracy at the head of a squadron of Spitfires, but first there are battles to win at home—his endless struggle to unburden himself of his aching virginity; his ignominious attempt to get the best of an anti-British professionally Irish teacher-bully; and his guerrilla war with the only person who is even more of a misfit than he, a German refugee dentist named Axelrod"—Saturday review.

174. Baker, Etta Iva Anthony. *The captain of the S.I.G.'s.* **With illus. by H. Burgess. Boston: Little, Brown, 1911. 323p.**

The Staten Island Giants (S.I.G.'s) comprise a group of boys interested primarily in baseball and other sports. However, other activities also warrant their attention: e.g., organizing a fundraising tent circus, forming a boys' brigade, taking on the dress and mannerism of the native Indians, etc.

175. Baker, Joseph Marion. *Meladore; a tale of the Battle of Saratoga.* **Grand Rapids, Mich.: Eaton, Lyon, c1877. 69p.**

A narrative poem in which the young heroine, Meladore Weldon, is beloved by two soldiers, the American Henry Johnson and the British officer Herford. The story follows Meladore as she moves towards the site of the Battle of Saratoga. Meladore is given permission by the British to be at the side of her dying brother Hiram. The two opposing armies clash; after the battle Herford, Meladore and several non-combatants (including Lady Acland whose wounded husband is held by the Americans) try to enter the American lines peacefully, but a startled sentry inadvertently fires on their boat. Meladore is hit and falls overboard. Herford jumps in after her but both are swallowed by the waters of the Hudson. Joseph Brant appears in these pages as a noble, benign figure generous to his enemies, lacking the cruelty or vindictiveness attributed to his warriors.

176. Baker, Josephine R., d. 1942. *Gee's trap*; or, *The Lambs and Field Street.* **Boston: Congregational Sunday-School and Pub. Society, 1895. 286p.**

"The Lambs lived in palatial residences, with large grounds in the rear. Field Street was a dingy neighborhood at the foot of the Lambs' grounds. The contrast between Aster Lamb and 'Lize Closson, of Field Street, is described, and the influence which they had on each other's lives is shown"—Annual

45

American catalogue. These two women are eventually responsible for the interest in the clearing of the slum assumed by the Lamb family.

177. Baldwin, Faith, 1893-1978. *Betty.* **New York: Clode, 1928. 320p.**
Betty Warren, a typist in a New York City authors' agency, must delay her marriage to Bob Stevenson, an auto mechanic, because of her family's economic problems. Predatory playboy and author, Anson Lorrimer believes Betty is ripe for sexual conquest, but his attempt to seduce her backfires. Betty takes a better-paying job in an advertising agency and meets helpful Harry Martin. Martin knows Lorrimer and distrusts him, as does Lorrimer's cousin, Peter Lessways, an athletic, wealthy young man. Martin falls in love with Betty's sister, Gladys, and another sister, Helen, fascinates Lessways. Lorrimer finally offers marriage to Betty and is quickly rejected. By the novel's end the Warren sisters (including Virginia, the eldest, the wife of a gassed World War I veteran) have brighter futures before them.

Baldwin, Faith, joint author. *Broadway interlude.* **See Item #9**

178. ————. *The incredible year.* **New York: Dodd, Mead, 1929. 298p.**
"Julie Montgomery, brought up by her father in the North Woods, is suddenly transported at twenty to a year in New York society among the younger generation. She tries to re-make herself to conform to the flapper type that she meets, thereby thinking to win Bruce Stepney, the man with whom she has fallen in love. But Bruce prefers her original North Woods self"—Book review digest.

179. ————. *Judy, a story of Divine Corners.* **Illustrated by Robb Beebe. New York: Dodd, Mead, 1930. 255p.**
'Divine Corners', a town in northern New York State overlooking the St. Lawrence River, is the home of Judy Edwards, the novel's heroine. She and her high school girl friends are given a camp with a sturdy lodge by the wealthiest man in town. The story relates several of their summertime adventures—boating on the sometimes treacherous St. Lawrence, sharing activities with their male counterparts, exploring islands in the river, etc. The latter leads to the discovery of a cave that turns out to be the hiding place of booty taken by a gang of thieves. Customs officials round up the outlaws and Judy and her friends—tomboy Baba Howard, British visitor Richard Kirby, and schoolteacher, Mr. Willing—share a cash reward.

180. ————. *The juniper tree.* **New York: Rinehart, 1952. 303p.**
Inconsolable because of the premature death of his son, Dave Barton tries to drown his sorrows in alcoholic drinks. Liquor is not the answer; neither do psychiatric sessions draw him out of his despondency. It is only when he is left alone with his thoughts in a distant Adirondack cabin that he begins to work his way out of his depression.

181. ————. *White-collar girl.* **New York: Farrar & Rinehart, 1933. 306p.**

Linda Anthony was left without much in the way of financial resources when her father died suddenly. The Upstate New York town where she was born and raised seemed a not too likely choice for someone starting out in the business world; however, Linda made a small success in the bond market. Her interests broadened and Linda soon discovered that in her own case love leading into marriage offered her a better choice than just pushing a business career.

182. **Balestier, Josephine.** *Life and Sylvia*; a Christmas journey. **Illustrated by Margaret Wendell Huntingdon. New York: United States Book Co., 1892. 58p.**

Sylvia is dissatisfied with her Uncle Will's reply to her question—"What is 'sperience'?"—And she set out to find her own answers. She has heard that Mulberry Street in New York City may be just the place to go to in order to taste some unique life-enhancing sensations. Perhaps she is really unprepared to deal with the peculiar consequences of her sojourn in that milling neighborhood of the great metropolis.

183. **Ball, Eustace Hale.** *The voice on the wire*; a novel of mystery. **New York: Hearst's International Library Co., 1915. iv, 325p.**

An amateur sleuth, the independently wealthy 'Monty' Shirley, takes on an assignment (given him by a private detective agency) to get to the bottom of several murders in which the victims have been men from the upper strata of New York City society. The partner in his quest is an attractive young lady who goes by the name Helene Marigold. Shirley adopts the guise of an elderly playboy and edges his way into the confidence of several clever and seemingly friendly criminals whom he suspects of complicity in the homicides. Along the way Monty discovers that Helene has some quite fetching qualities beyond her utility as a co-investigator.

184. **Ball, Walter S.** *Carmela commands.* **With illus. by Frederic Dorr Steele. New York: Harper, 1929. vii, 277p.**

"A breezy tale of a girl of the Italian quarter in New York. She is an aggressive, impudent, self-reliant young person who acts as interpreter for her father in his business. Her management of his affairs is somewhat of a strain on our credulity, especially when … she induces a real estate agent to pay twice what her father asks for a bit of land. … The book discusses the problem of the two generations, the children Americanized, and the parents clinging to their native language and customs"—Saturday review of literature.

185. **Bangs, Nickerson.** *The Ormsteads*; a novel of three generations. **New York: H.C. Kinney, 1939. 298p.**

"Three generations of the Ormsteads [in New York State], presided over by Old William, founder of the family fortune, figure in the story. Old William typifies the dignified head of the conservative family. It was his earnest desire to have all his children around him, and to achieve that end he bought estates for the married ones near the family home. Thacher, the youngest son, went west and took up ranching, but when he married he came back to New York State, bringing his Western wife with him. The new wife, with her Western ways, plus the revolt of the third generation, provided Old William with plenty of problems to enliven his declining years"—Book review digest.

186. **Banks, Russell, 1940- .** *Rule of the Bone.* **New York: Harper Collins, 1995. 400p.**

Not at all averse to leaving the trailer home in Au Sable, N.Y. he shared with an abusive stepfather and a vacillating mother, 14-year-old Chappie wanders around Essex County, Plattsburgh & Vermont piecing together the bare-bones of an existence which is punctuated by frequent ingestions of 'pot.' In the last 150 pages of the novel Chappie—who now calls himself 'Bone'—follows the Rastafarian and illegal alien, the 'I-Man', to Jamaica and a series of picturesque episodes there.

187. ⸻. *The sweet hereafter*; **a novel. New York: Harper Collins, 1991. 254p.**

The story "is told by four people: Dolores Driscoll [an experienced] school-bus driver in a small town [in the Adirondacks]; Billy Ansel, father of two of the children on the bus; Mitchell Stephens, a lawyer; and Nichole Burnell, a student. In the accident on which the story is centered, Ansel loses his children and Nichole is paralyzed. Dolores survives the accident—the plunge of the bus through the guardrail and into the water-filled quarry—and then tries to survive survival [she has become something of an outcast in the town]. Mitchell Stephens becomes the attorney for the group of parents who mount a lawsuit"—Christian science monitor.

188. **Banning, Margaret CulkScin, 1891-1982.** *Out in society.* **New York: Harper, 1940. 291p.**

"'Dunster City's' loveliest and wealthiest debutante was the Ferratin girl, Barbara. Barbara was engaged to the town's most promising young lawyer, Judge Slade's son; then into these two well-planned lives come two others, another young lawyer who lacked Wedge Slade's background and a girl just graduated from business college. How and why the affairs of all are shuffled about forms the central theme of this story of society and politics in a city not too far from New York"—Book review digest.

189. ⸻. *Prelude to love.* **New York: Harper, 1930. 278p.**

Thrust into upscale Long Island society when she arrives for her stepbrother's wedding, Janis, an unsophisticated girl from the Midwest, is rudderless for a while, some of her most cherished ideals left flying into an uncaring wind. The marriage that she witnessed soon comes to a bitter, sad end. It takes time, but she learns from that failed marriage, and Janis ends up marrying a man whose proposal she had earlier declined.

190. Barber, Marcin. *Britz, of Headquarters.* **New York: Moffat, Yard, 1910. 394p.**

Detective Britz of the New York City Central Office Force is detailed to locate and return to the owner, Mrs. Missioner, a wealthy widow, the diamond necklace that had been stolen from her. Perhaps Mrs. Missioner would not have been aware of her loss if she had not broken the chain of a 'diamond' necklace she was wearing at the opera. As the presumed gems scattered, her guests bent to the task of retrieving them. When one of the men stepped on a piece, it was ground to powder, proving that the necklace in hand was a paste substitute for the real thing.

191. Barbour, Anna Maynard, 1856-1941. *That Mainwaring affair.* **Illustrated by E. Plaistead Abbott. Philadelphia: J.B. Lippincott, 1901. 362p.**

A mystery story, 'That affair' is the murder of a wealthy New York stockbroker that took place in his luxurious quarters in one of the city's suburbs.

192. Barbour, Ralph Henry, 1870-1944. *Captain Chub.* **With illus. by C.M. Relyea. New York: Century Co., 1909, c1908. ix, 413p.**

This is the fourth in a series of novels about the three boys, Tom, Dick and Roy, and a girl, Harriet (Harry), this time renting a houseboat and cruising up and down the Hudson River. Actually Harry and her father are the boys' guests. When not on the river or fishing, they dock for dances at hotels along the river and even run a store in the owner's absence. Gypsies enter the picture—they are up to their ancestral habits of stealing whatever comes to hand—and the four young people have to deal with that unforeseen problem.

193. —————. *Four afoot, being the adventures of the big four on the highway.* **New York: D. Appleton, 1906. x, 285p.**

"The further adventures of the four boys [Nelson, Bob, Tommy and Dan] who went through so many experiences in 'Four in camp' [in the New Hampshire woods]. The scene in this story is on Long island, where the boys join a baseball team, meet a 'wild man', are refused food by a farmer and are compelled to go hungry, and have many other adventures"—Annual American catalogue.

194. —————. *Harry's island.* **With illus. by C.M. Relyea. New York: Century Co., 1908. 306p.**

Tom, Dick, Harriet (Harry) and Roy have appeared in several of Barbour's juvenile adventure stories. In this tale the four are camping out during the summer on an island in the Hudson River.

195. —————. *Left-end Edwards.* **With illus. by Charles M. Relyea. New York: Dodd, Mead, 1914. 365p.**

Football is the main ingredient in this story of a boy's preparatory school—Brimfield Academy—located not far from New York City. Steve Edwards and Tan Hall are the chief actors; they undergo the tribulations and the moments of triumph that one would expect in one of the many 'prep' school novels that Barbour penned for his young readership.

Barbour, Ralph Henry, 1870-1944, joint author. *Phyllis in Bohemia.* **See Item #296.**

196. ————. *Skate, Glendale! The story of hockey, battles and victory.* **New York: Farrar & Rinehart, 1932. 249p.**

Tom, a student at Glendale Academy on the Hudson River, earns the contumely of his classmates because of his aversion to participation in athletics. When he finally does take up cross-country running, football and hockey, he achieves measurable success and even hero status.

197. **Bard, pseud.** *Ahead of the ticker.* **New York: Serial Book Co., 1901. 51p.**

Listed in Publisher's weekly as 'the first [and most likely the only one] of a collection [White tape series of Wall Street tales, v. 1, no. 1] of stories of Wall Street ways and events.' Not listed in the National Union Catalog.

198. **Bardeen, Charles William, 1847-1924.** *Commissioner Hume*; **a story of New York schools. Syracuse, N.Y.: C.W. Bardeen, 1899. 210p.**

This sequel to the author's 'Roderick Hume' was originally published as a serial in The School bulletin (1879?). Hume, principal of the Norway Free High School and College Preparatory Institute, reluctantly agrees to be a candidate for school commissioner of 'Macedonia County' in Upstate New York on the Republican ticket. He is a man of probity and no-nonsense who refuses to toady to anyone (including politicians and newspaper editors). Duly elected to the office—his Democratic opponent, Tony Tippit, good-natured but too fond of liquor, has little chance in a Republican stronghold—Hume deals equitably with the various problems and characters that come his way. Conditions of New York rural schools in 1875 are well described.

199. ————. *Roderick Hume*; **the story of a New York teacher. Syracuse, N.Y.: Davis, Bardeen & Co., 1878. 295p.**

The novel follows the career of a young schoolteacher in Upstate New York. Fresh from college Roderick applies for and secures a position that is fraught with unforeseen complications. He gains experience by working in a variety of situations and learning to deal with school administrators, women teachers, et al. The story is a mine of information about educational practices in public schools of the last quarter of the 19th century in New York State.

200. **Barker, Benjamin.** *Clarilda*; **or,** *The female pickpocket.* **A romance of New York City. Boston: United States Pub. Co., 1846. 50p.**

In this lurid, melodramatic novelette the Ayres and their children, barely surviving in Five Points, still provide shelter to homeless Clarilda. Mrs. Jayne Ayres is arrested for picking the pocket of heartless William Morgan, her husband Adam's former employer and the man who had seduced her years ago. Morgan is shot by Mrs. Ayres and she then commits suicide. Henry Morgan, the reprobate's son, disowned by his father when he refused the woman selected for him, marries Clarilda who is revealed to be the daughter of William Morgan's brother.

201. Barlow, David Hatch. *The Howards*; **a tale founded on facts. Philadelphia: Getz & Buck, 1851. 45p.**

The two sons of farmer Marmaduke Howard of 'Mapleton', a village in Upstate New York, select differing paths. George marries Maria Grey, a local farmer's daughter, and continues to farm; Edward chooses a business career in New York City, marries flighty Helen May, and living beyond his means loses his mind and dies. His impoverished family moves into the home of George and Maria Howard. Mary, the eldest daughter of Edward and Helen Howard, comes between the Rev. Charles Cameron and his fiancée, Anna, George and Maria Howard's daughter. Mary steps away from this awkward situation and secures employment in New York City as a governess. Her mother dies and Mary returns to Mapleton in a weakened condition. She helps patch up a rift between Charles Cameron and Anna and then leaves this life.

202. Barnard, John Lawrence. 1912-1977. *Revelry by night.* **Garden City, N.Y.: Doubleday, Doran, 1941. 273p.**

In the summer of 1940 a number of young members of the so-called smart set of a town on Long Island's South Shore, fairly close to New York City, whoop it up at a weekend party. Drinking, amorous dalliances, the gamut of sophisticated excess take Park Cushing's wife, Lynne, to the brink of accidental death; from that point the couples back away and take a long step toward responsible adulthood.

203. Barnes, Geoffrey, b. 1891. *Party husband.* **New York: A.H. King, 1930. 242p.**

A young married couple from Maine comes to New York City; both fall into adulterous relationships. The husband's mistress dies in childbirth; her baby is the key to the reconciliation of husband and wife.

204. Barnes, James, 1866-1936. *The clutch of circumstance.* **New York: Appleton, 1908. vii, 385p.**

After the passage of ten years Laurence Kellogg returns to his hometown in western New York State. Kellogg is now a physician and also possesses a small fortune. A longtime friend, a clergyman, had married Laurence's sweetheart. Laurence learns from his lost love that her marriage is an unhappy one and that she still loves him. He also learns that the minister is a drug addict with a severely troubled conscience. The clergyman dies and Dr. Kellogg is charged with murder and goes to trial. Circumstantial evidence seems to clearly point to his guilt, but in the end he is cleared and reunited with the woman he loves.

205. ⸻. *For king or country*; **a story of the American Revolution. New**

York: Harper, 1896. iv, 269p.

Twin brothers George and William Frothingham look so much alike that it is easy to mistake one for the other. With the outbreak of the American Revolution they go their separate ways—George into the Continental Army and William into the King's. Military events that they participate in include: The Battle of Long Island, various skirmishes in the Hudson Valley, and the evacuation of New York City by the British forces in 1783. Of particular interest are an account of clandestine patriotic groups in New York while under British occupation and a word sketch of the 'Sugar-House' prison in that city.

206. ————. *Outside the law*. **New York: Appleton, 1906 [c1905]. 281p.**

Lorrimer is a New Yorker of middle years, a bachelor and a millionaire; he has developed expertise in judging engravings and discovers a method of reproducing antiques so that they can hardly be differentiated from the originals. His servant, an elderly Dutchman, is cognizant of the technique and it is only after he dies abruptly that Lorrimer finds out he had dealings with a band of counterfeiters. Lorrimer is soon enmeshed in several ticklish situations, including a bank robbery. A skillful nurse steps into this picture and proves to be of tremendous help to the beleaguered Lorrimer.

207. **Barnes, Percy Raymond, b. 1880. *Crum Elbow folks*. Philadelphia: Lippincott, 1938. 283p.**

'Crum Elbow', a small Quaker community, which is placed in the early 19th century in Dutchess County, New York, is more or less identical with present-day Hyde Park. Huldah Sheldon, a Quaker, is the central figure in the novel. It is her love for a young man who is not a member of the Society of Friends that causes a stir among the older inhabitants of the village.

208. **Barnes, Willis, b. 1843. *Dame Fortune smiled*. The doctor's story. Boston: Arena Pub. Co., 1896. 335p.**

The unnamed doctor, a German trained in Europe, comes to New York City in 1886 at the behest of Emily Von Hoffman, a patient whom he had treated in Paris. His New York practice brings the doctor in contact with men and women of wealth; not only does he minister to their physical ailments but he also urges them to give freely of their riches to charitable causes while they are still active. The doctor marries Frances Adams and the couple, sharing a windfall from an investment in stocks, donates a large portion of their newfound money to benevolence. The story is retrospective from the year 1900.

209. **Barns, Charles Edward. *Digby, chess professor*. New York: Fracker, 1889. 152p.**

Silas John Digby of Hempstead, Long Island, one of the founders of the Zatrikion [Greek for chess or a similar game] Club ruminates on the present and future of chess in New York City, writes a letter to the New York Courier on the subject, visits the Pickwick Club, Pixley Street, a French café in Gotham's 'Little Paris', Central Park, the Astor Library, the Metropolitan Opera—all in the pursuit of chess and its propagation.

210. ————. *A portrait in crimsons*; a drama-novel. **New York: Welch, Fracker Co., 1889. 195p.**

The setting of this 'drama novel' is New York City and a country residence north of the city on the Hudson River. Dr. Robert Van Tansell meets a disturbed sculptor, Maynard, who is haunted by the portrait of a young man, which he idealizes. The doctor has the support of his sister Marguerite (Peggy) as he attempts to restore Maynard to reality. The mission accomplished, Maynard then announces his engagement to Marguerite.

211. **Barolini, Helen, 1925- .** *Umbertina.* **New York: Seaview Books, 1979. 424p.**

Immigrant Umbertina, pragmatic and ambitious though illiterate, finds business success in 'Cato' (i.e. Utica), New York. Her daughter Marguerite has psychological problems and an introspective turn of mind, while Marguerite's daughter, Tina, studying for her Ph.D., takes pride in her Italian-American roots. Tina falls in love with WASP Jason Towers whom she will eventually marry.

212. **Barr, Amelia Edith Huddleston, 1831-1919.** *The belle of Bowling Green.* **Illustrated by Walter H. Everett. New York: Dodd, Mead, 1904. 342p.**

A love story set in New York City during the War of 1812. The two chief figures are Sapphira Bloomaert and Annette De Vries, the first a model of the 'good woman', the second a waspish, scheming beauty. They are cousins and their lovers are a Scot and a refugee French marquis.

213. ————. *The bow of orange ribbon*; a romance of New York. **New York: Dodd, Mead, 1886. 345p.**

The novel covers the years 1760 (ca.) to the outbreak of the American Revolution. It offers an excellent view of the social life of New York City in that period, concentrating on a Dutch family, the Van Heemskirks. Katharine Van Heemskirk, the youngest daughter, falls in love with Captain Richard Hyde, a British officer quartered in the home of a friendly neighbor of the Van Heemskirks. Despite her father's opposition, Katharine marries Hyde after a near-deadly duel between the mercurial Hyde and a rival for Katharine's hand. The married couple spends over a decade in England at Hyde's manor house but returns to New York City shortly before the Battle of Lexington. Hyde, who has resigned his commission in the British Army, offers his services to the American cause.

214. ————. *Cecilia's lovers.* **New York: Dodd, Mead, 1905. viii, 389p.**

An artistic but improvident father dies and leaves behind a daughter who has no idea of how to support herself in the indifferent atmosphere of New York City. By choice Cecilia strikes up an acquaintance with a young artist who asks her to serve as his secretary. She attracts a number of eligible men who are soon suing for her hand in marriage. Cecilia weighs her options, adds to her own knowledge of life's vagaries and then chooses the person whom she believes will be a most suitable mate.

215. ————. *Girls of a feather*; **a novel. With illus. by J.O. Nugent. New York: R. Bonner, 1893. 366p.**

The cousins Ambrosia (Amber) Shepherd and Bessie Madison, New York society belles are quite similar in many respects but seeds of rivalry can be detected. Amber marries the distinguished Dr. Robert Carter, a physician and medical researcher; it is not long before she feels neglected by her husband, jealous of his close association with a pretty young secretary and envious of Louisa Madison, Bessie's cousin and wife of Will Carter, Robert's brother. Bessie wrongly assumes Amber is entwined with Dr. Carter's research assistant. Misunderstandings of this nature bring much grief to Amber and others, but Robert and Amber reconcile while their friends embark for Europe.

216. ————. *The house on Cherry Street.* **Front. by Z.P. Nikolaki. New York: Dodd, Mead, 1909. 375p.**

Colonial New York during the reign of George II (in the 1730s and 1740s) sets the scene. The chief characters in the novel are a Dutch sea captain, his wife and bright daughter; the latter is in love with an Englishman who is the owner of a splendid house on Cherry Street. The beginnings of a free press are an outstanding element in the story—the journalist John Peter Zenger is placed on trial and defended by Andrew Hamilton. The Dutch captain sees fit to invest a goodly portion of his wealth in a newspaper.

217. ————. *The king's highway.* **New York: Dodd, Mead, 1897. 371p.**

"According to Christian in the 'Pilgrim's Progress' the king's highway is the way of holiness. One of the vexed questions dealt with, in a novel, which introduces the teachings of Christian socialism, is the marrying of wealthy Americans to titled and impecunious foreigners. Nicholas Lloyd, a Wall Street speculator, having been bitterly disappointed at his son's refusal to join him in financial schemes, consoles himself by thinking that his daughter will help in the furtherance of plans for her social future. Other influences are the cause of the girl's acting in a more interesting way. Unorganized labor and theories about labor and capital are incidentally discussed"—Annual American catalogue.

218. ————. *The maid of Maiden Lane*; **a sequel to** *The bow of orange ribbon.* **A love story. New York: Dodd, Mead, 1900. 338p.**

"The year 1791 in the City of New York was a momentous one. The question whether New York or Philadelphia should be the seat of government led to many hot discussions and much ill feeling. The death of Benjamin Franklin, the great influx of French refugees and the division of opinion regarding English rights in the lost colonies [are also touched upon]"—Annual

American catalogue. The plot line of the novel has to do with the love affair of the beautiful Cornelia Moran, New York belle and daughter of a prominent physician, and an Englishman, Joris Hyde.

219. ————. *A maid of old New York*; a romance of Peter Stuyvesant's time. New York: Dodd, Mead, 1911. 377p.

A novel about colonial New York City that is set in those years (ca. 1647-1664) when the autocratic Peter Stuyvesant was the Dutch governor. Briefly stated the story focuses on the love that develops between Agatha Van Ruyven and Lord Gael McIvar, a Scotsman, and the difficulties that arise when in frustration he kidnaps Agatha.

220. ————. *She loved a sailor.* New York: Dodd, Mead, 1891. 459p.

During Andrew Jackson's second presidential term two young New Yorkers, Virginia Mason and Captain Marius Bradford, are involved in an ongoing love affair. The author integrates significant historical events into her novel, including the failure of the United States Bank in Philadelphia, the early abolitionist movement, and the political and financial maneuverings of Andrew Jackson, Nicholas Biddle, the philanthropists Arthur and Lewis Tappan, et al.

221. ————. *A song of a single note*; a love story. New York: Dodd, Mead, 1902. 330.

"The scene is laid in New York, a few years before General Clinton's evacuation, i.e. in 1779. The title has an amatory allusion, but the most interesting characters have ceased pranking with Cupid before the story opens. They are a Wesleyan saddler who heroically accompanies his son while the latter is drummed out of the city for a spy, and a Jewish shopkeeper who renders a great service with the tact of a prince. Both these men touch the imagination, but it is not touched either by the prettiness of Maria or the seriousness of Agnes, the two heroines. An English peer [Lord Medway] exacts from Maria a promise to marry him if he saves the forfeited life of the patriotic American she professes to love. ... Mrs. Barr makes Maria happy in keeping her word. There shall be no mistake about her heroism. Mrs. Barr sends her to a tyrannical father in London who drives her to the altar with a man of his choice, only to hear her repudiate the bridegroom for Medway's sake when the priest asks her the crucial question"—Athenaeum.

222. ————. *The strawberry handkerchief*; a romance of the Stamp Act. New York: Dodd, Mead, 1908. 368p.

This romance takes place in New York City in the turbulent years surrounding the imposition of the Stamp Act (1765). The title refers to a love token given by the Dutch maiden/heroine to her lover—a handkerchief embroidered with strawberry leaves and berries. The novel provides a graphic picture of the time (including a 'Liberty Boys' parade down Broadway) and of New Yorkers of Dutch ancestry.

223. —————. *Trinity bells*; a tale of old New York. Illustrated by C.M. Relyea. **New York: J.F. Taylor, 1899. viii, 278p.**

"A romance of old New York, opening with the return of Catharine Van Clyffe from the Moravian school of Bethlehem [Pennsylvania] to her brother and her handsome home [in New York City]. Their father had been captured by Tripolitan pirates and held in slavery by the Dey of Algiers. The story turns on the courageous efforts of [Paul Van Clyffe] to ransom his father, and the self-denial of his father and sister. The silver Trinity [Church] bells sound messages of hope and joy throughout the story"—Annual American catalogue.

224. **Barrett, Andrea. *The forms of water*. New York: Pocket Books, 1993. 292p.**

About an 82-year-old, Brendon Auberon, who wants to escape the nursing home he has been placed in and return to the abbey in Upstate New York where he had served early years as a monk. Unfortunately the abbey had been flooded to make way for a reservoir some 50 years ago. Brendon persuades his nephew Henry to drive him in the nursing home van (Brendon had swiped the keys) to the abbey site. Wiloma, Brendon's niece, her alienated husband Waldo, and their children, Win and Wendy, apprised of the wild scheme, go after Brendon and Harry. Past family history, a deadly accident and Brendon's arrival at the site of the old abbey—all have a distinct impact on the Auberon family and their perception of responsibility for their own individual lives.

225. **Barrett, Harold James, b. 1885. *Patricia's awakening*. New York: Crowell, 1924. 419p.**

"The love story of a modern [New York society] girl of the jazz type. Patricia Keller, daughter of a wealthy contractor, was twenty-five and still unmarried. She had her own ideas as to the type of man she would marry, but when she first met him as one of her father's superintendents, she did not recognize him. Gordon was of the quiet, intellectual type, but a good superintendent. As time went on Gordon and Patricia each became engaged. Then Gordon was accused of falsifying his accounts and in the troubled days which followed Patricia awoke to the fact that Gordon was the man she loved"—Book review digest.

226. **Barrett, Mary Ellen, 1927- . *Castle Ugly*. New York: Dutton, 1966. 255p.**

At the book's opening Sally, the only child of Sarah and Harry Courtland, is married to a Frenchman and residing at his family's home on the Riviera. When Daniel Relston, an old lover, drops by, Sally's memory is stirred. She recalls her last summer in a big, rambling house on Long Island. Her parents, Sarah and Harry, wealthy New Yorkers, were also there as the summer was winding to an end. Sarah Courtland and her lover were shot and killed. The identity of the individual[s] responsible for the double murder has never been established.

227. Barrett, Richmond Brooks, b. 1895. *The enemy's gates.* **New York: Boni & Liveright, 1926. 351p.**

"Mark Morgenthal [of New York] was an immensely wealthy Jew. Each of his three children sensed the power of the Morgenthal name, though Morton and Jessica denied their heritage and passed when they could for Gentiles. The book tells the story of the three, but centers chiefly on the proud, sensitive figure of George, the eldest, and his marriage to Ann Carter from New England, who though stronger than he, is yet unable to save him from himself. His character is his destiny; stark, unrelieved catastrophe is his end"—Book review digest.

228. ————. *Rapture.* **New York: Boni & Liveright, 1924. 310p.**

"A story of New York and New York society centering about the marriage of Lilla Colby and Townsend Prime. The sensitive, high-strung, keenly critical Lilla had no illusions about Townsend when she married him except her infatuation with his physical perfection. His failings and limitations were apparent and their first few weeks of living together showed her how weak and untrustworthy he was, but his physical spell grew steadily stronger. She bent all her will and energy to keeping him and she succeeded, but she killed herself doing it and all the time she realized how petty her triumph was"—Book review digest.

Barrett, Walter, clerk, pseud. See: Scoville, Joseph Alfred, 1815-1864.

229. Barrett, Wilson, 1848-1904. *In old New York*; **a romance, by Wilson Barrett and Elwyn Barron. Illustrated by H.C. Edwards, Boston: L.C. Page, 1900. 410p.**

Scene: New York City in the 1750s. The love affair of Luya Vanbergen, daughter of a prosperous Dutch merchant, and Wallace Waring, impecunious son of the class-conscious Stephen Waring, hits many snags. Stephen Waring is against any alliance that would make a 'mere tradesman' his brother-in-law, although he is willing to have Vanbergen handle his investments for the present. The rich Sophie Boylston, a conceited schemer, seems to Waring to be the proper wife for his son. When the New York Exchange is shaken by rumors of a Stuart takeover of the English throne, Stephen Waring faces financial ruin. He is saved through the efforts of Luya Vanbergen, her father, and Jacob Wilbruch, a partner of Vanbergen, who is hopelessly in love with Luya. Jealousy prompts Wallace Waring to engage in a duel with Wilbruch in which he wounds the young Dutchman. Made aware of his mistaken jealousy Wallace begs Luya's forgiveness. The novel ends inconclusively with the always honorable, magnanimous Jacob Wilbruch probably bleeding to death with the saddened, troubled Luya by his side.

230. Barretto, Larry, 1890-1971. *Old enchantment.* **New York: J. Day, 1928. 319p.**

"Aunt Ellen, the indomitable old aristocrat of one of New York's old families, rules with arrogance her nephew and his twins, Audrey and Alexander.

Rather than have them earn their own living, they live on the little money she has left and without friends. Suddenly awakened to the modern world, the two young people set aside the old traditions to go to work. Alexander finds work in a missionary office and Audrey [is] dancing at a nightclub. One can not help sympathizing with the old aunt in the end as we see her entering an old lady's home, and the father dying. Alexander goes to a small mining town to marry his childhood sweetheart, and Audrey is now able to marry Jack Harris, the divorced man she met while dining at the club"—Cleveland [Public Library] staff notes.

231. ————. *To Babylon*. **Boston: Little, Brown, 1925. 322p.**

The odyssey of Anthony Thorne, a young man from the western United States, with some of the requisites for success in his chosen profession of architecture—talent, personal charm, ambition, ideals—who arrives in New York City. With a combination of the right business associations, marriage into high society and the dismantling of his idealism, he ascends the ladder of 'success'—at what cost?

Barron, Elwyn Alfred, b. 1855, joint author. *In old New York*. See Item #229.

232. **Barry, Jane, 1925- . *Grass roots*. Garden City, N.Y.: Doubleday, 1968. 327p.**

A rural district in New York State in the throes of a congressional election is the scene of the novel. A member of a distinguished old family is taken under the management of Barney and pushed forward in the Republican primary; his opponent is the governor's nephew who is sponsored by the party machine. Barney's client wins the Republican nomination but is defeated in the general election by the Democratic incumbent. Barney is so tied up with political gamesmanship that he ultimately loses his long-term mistress, Grace, a talented artist.

233. **Barry, Jerome, 1894-1975. *Strange relations*. Garden City, N.Y.: Published for the Crime Club by Doubleday, c1962. 215p.**

A tale of crime with a Long Island setting. "Dennett Marberry, who fears the loss of his wife to another man, and of his best account to the same intruder, is asked to find a valuable watch missing from his wife's horological collection. The search takes him through a murder, the kidnapping of his son, the diversionary tactics of a young relation, and the evil activities of a Long Island dope ring"—Kirkus reviews.

234. **Barry, John Daniel, b. 1866. *A daughter of Thespis*; a novel. Boston: L.C. Page, 1903. 347p.**

The novel outlines the final year or so of Evelyn Johnson's career as an actress. Theatrical life in New York City and on the road shares equal billing with a recuperative summer in the resort town of Cohasset, Mass. Special attention is paid to Evelyn's relationships with her sister actresses (most pointedly with the mercurial Madge Guernsey), and romantic attachments to three men: the actor Harold Seymour, Novelist and critic Oswald Webb and playwright Leonard Thayer.

235. Barry, Richard Hayes, b. 1881. *The bauble*; **a novel. New York: Moffat, Yard, 1911. vi, 342p.**

Constance Rudd evinces her support for women's suffrage by walking away from her husband and baby and getting out on the hustings. It is not an easy task she has set for herself; in fact the strikes and agitation on the street and in the halls of New York City leave her exhausted and rather chagrined. Her final act is to return to husband and child, accepting the age-old platitude—woman's place is in the home.

236. Barth, Richard, 1943- . *Furnished for murder.* **New York: St. Martin's Press, 1990. 202p.**

"Suburban New York furniture salesman Leo Perkins can't find his cuff links. In a middle-aged snit, he suspects his daughter's piano teacher, the snooty Harmon Parrish, of theft. Leo follows Parrish to the homes of his other students. A few phone calls reveal those households have also experienced petty theft. But when Leo calls the police to report his findings, he learns that Parrish was just murdered and had Leo's license number in his pocket. Now a prime suspect, Leo enlists the aid of his favorite chess partner, Jakob Barzeny, a former Soviet cop"—Booklist.

237. Bartlett, Frederick Orin, 1876-1945. *The Wall Street girl.* **With illus. by George Ellis Wolfe. Boston: Houghton Mifflin, 1916. 333p.**

The story of Donald Pendleton and the two women most important in his life. His father left him the family house with funds necessary to maintain it, but Donald has no money of his own. When he takes a job in a New York City bank, Sally Winthroop, a stenographer there, falls in love with Donald, although she gives him no indication thereof. His own fiancée, Miss Stuyvesant, is touring Europe; at Sally's suggestion Donald tries to persuade Miss Stuyvesant to cut short her European venture and return to marry him. Her curt refusal brings Donald to the realization that the right woman for him has been Sally all along.

238. Bartley, Nalbro Isadorah, b. 1888. *The gray angels.* **Boston: Small, Maynard, 1920. 420p.**

"The first notice the world took of Thurley Precore was when she sang for her supper and then continued to sing herself into people's hearts generally. The rich ghost lady heard the voice in her living tomb and came out to take Thurley to New York and give her a musical education. She became a prima donna, lived in an intimate circle of first class artists, and experienced their disappointments, their boredom and the restlessness of fame. She tried to become reckless and flirted with the forbidden, when her singing teacher, also a man of genius whom she secretly loved, set her right by confiding to her his vision of America's supreme mission in art. Winning the violet crown, he called it. Later the [1st World] War with its war madness showed to Thurley that her own particular mission lay in helping to restore a hysterical people to sanity and to become one of the gray angels to the broken ones of the war"—Book review digest.

239. Barton, Bruce, 1886-1967. *The making of George Groton.* **Illustrated by Paul Stahr. Garden City, N.Y.: Doubleday, Page, 1918. cv, 331p.**

For a time George Groton, a native of a small town, has tasted moneymaking success in New York City but further experience and inevitable mistakes force him to reconsider just what he really wants. Obviously money is not the answer, is not a true measure of accomplishment or inner satisfaction. Helping George in his ultimate quest is Betty Wilson, a childhood sweetheart who has never left his thoughts.

240. Bascom, Lee. *A god of Gotham*; **a romance from the life of a well-known actress. New York: G.W. Dillingham, 1891. 277p.**

The celebrated actress, Donita Lorraine, is not only beautiful but also talented (she paints) and witty, inspiring jealously in many women, but securing the adoration of men. Donita falls passionately in love with Gordon Grey, a prominent socialite, and their affair is a prolonged, insecure one since Donita shies away from the notion of marriage. Separation comes when Donita and her faithful companion, Angela Deane, go to the Riviera for Donita's health. A former lover of Donita, Bennett Blanding, surprises her when he marries Angela. Returning to America Donita eventually retires to a house on the Hudson. Both friends and enemies slander her. Gordon Grey comes to her and informs her that his father has threatened him with disinheritance if he continues to see her. Donita's health problems worsen, and just before she dies Gordon and she are married. Four years later Angela and Bennet Blanding have a girl child to whom they have given the name Donita; Gordon is a commanding figure in the social and financial world of New York.

240a. Bat-Ami, Miriam, 1950- . *Two suns in the sky.* **Chicago: Front Street/Cricket Books, 1999. 224p.**

The locale of this rather unusual novel is Oswego, N.Y. during World War II when a refugee camp was set up there to house people fleeing from Nazi persecution and conquests. The hero is Adam Bornstein, a 17-year-old Jew from the Balkans, interned along with his mother and sister. Adam is able to surmount physical barriers to pursue a romantic affair with a Christian girl, Christine Cook, an Oswego native, whose father is exceedingly bigoted towards anyone outside his own narrow circle.

241. Bates, Morgan. *Martin Brook*; **a novel. New York: Harper, 1901. 364p.**

New York State shortly before the outbreak of the Civil War is the canvas on which the scenes of this novel are displayed. Martin Brook, the bondservant of a cruel employer, is released into the service of Judge Northcote and is ultimately adopted by the Judge. When Martin and the Judge develop sharp differences on the remanding of runaway slaves, Martin leaves the Judge. He becomes a crusading preacher, one filled with the mission of abolishing slavery.

242. Bauer, Douglas. *Dexterity*; a novel. **New York: Simon & Schuster, 1989. 317p.**
"An oppressed young woman barely out of her teens struggles to lift herself from extremely bleak experience. The scene is 'Myles', New York, an imagined, going-nowhere 'desolate village' in real Columbia County. The heroine, Ramona King, conceives as a school kid the hope of 'stay(ing) above the common moments' of the place, believes ... that she can realize that hope by marrying her high school sweetheart, suffers ... a swift disillusionment— yet doesn't capitulate. Her first attempt at flight ends with a car accident and the loss of a hand; helpless and wretched, she's returned to her stony husband. After bearing him a son, she strikes out once more as a runaway minus her child, this time for good"—Atlantic.

242a. Bauer, Joan. *Backwater.* **New York: Putnam, 1999. 185p.**
The Adirondacks are the backdrop to his story in which 16-year-old Ivy Breedlove searches for missing pieces of her family's genealogy. She had been expected by her father to eventually take up the study of law, but Ivy was more inclined to pursue the historian's path. It is in the wintry, rugged Adirondacks that Ivy meets her father's long-forgotten sister, her aunt, Josephine, and discovers illuminating facts about the Breedlove heritage.

243. Baumer, Marie, 1905- . *The seeker and the sought.* **New York: Scribner, 1949. 217p.**
Childless Walter Williams and his wife were residents of a New York City suburb. One night a strange, weeping and frightened boy came knocking at their door asking for help and shelter. Mr. Williams quickly turned the lad away, but then he began to feel pricks of conscience and responsibility for his fellow man. After more reflection Williams started to search for the boy to rectify his earlier lack of sympathy. His quest brought a momentous change in his life when he found himself privy to unpleasant aspects of New York juvenile activity.

244. Bayne, George Middleton. *Galaski*; a novel. **New York: J.W. Lovell, 1885. 237p.**
Albany, New York is the scene of this story about an individual, Petros Simonds, who took an alias—Ivan Galaski—after he had seized his late employer's testament and made himself the beneficiary of all the funds therein.

245. Beach, Rex Ellingwood, 1877-1949. *The auction block*; a novel of New York life. **Illustrated by Charles Dana Gibson. New York: Harper, 1914. vii, 440p.**
Her parents recognize Lorelei Knight, daughter of a conniving politician and his wife, as their most prized 'possession'. Lorelei's beauty is used to good

effect on the stage and Peter Knight moves his wife and daughter to New York. The Knights push Lorelei into marriage with Bob Wharton, a drunkard, whose father, a rake himself, disinherits him. Lorelei becomes her husband's sole support, but gradually so improves his character that Bob's family must give her full credit. She asks (or demands) from them funds that allow her to purchase her independence from any further close relationship with her own greedy family.

246. ————. *Padlocked*; a novel. New York: Harper, 1926. 336p.
"Henry Gilbert was one of the ultra prudish to whom all things are suspect. His insinuations about his young daughter's probable mode of life drove his wife to suicide and Edith herself out of the house. For all her surface sophistication Edith was an innocent soul. She went to New York and, wanting to be a singer, accepted the backing of a wealthy promoter. She made the wrong kind of friends and misunderstood the attentions of the one man who really wanted to help her. One dreadful thing after another happened to her with the culminating horror caused by her father. Retribution came to him at the hands of his second wife, while Edith's vindication was complete, and her nobility of character justly rewarded"—Book review digest.

247. Beam, Maurice. *Murder in a shell*, by Maurice Beam & Sumner Britton. New York: Messner, 1939. 242p.
The Poughkeepsie Regatta is thrown into a state of confused terror when the coxswain of a 'Gotham University' crew is felled by cyanide and another athlete imbibes poisoned gin. Lieutenant Whitehall of the police and sports editor Harry Leaman combine to solve the double murder.

248. *The Beautiful Jewess, Rachel Mendoza, her lamentable connection with the dark and eventful career of Charles Bernard, otherwise called 'Prince Charles.'* Philadelphia: E.E. Barclay, 1853. 39p.
"Charles Bernard saves the beautiful Rachel Mendoza from murder in a New York village and kills the attacker. The grateful girl tells Bernard the story of her life. ... Rachel marries Bernard, and then a bewildering, complicated set of adventures follow"—Harap, L. *The image of the Jew in* American literature.

249. Beckley, Zoe, d. 1961. *A chance to live.* With a foreword by Kathleen Norris. Illus. by Charles G. Voight. New York: Macmillan, 1919. 329p.
"The story of one small, ambitious, wistful, life-hungry girl, Annie Hargan, lost in the lower regions of New York like a hundred thousand others, climbing and hoping in spite of the pitfalls and despairs that we leave in the path of such girls, studying life with half-puzzled and half-frightened eyes, holding tight to the miraculous truth of her own soul—as so many girls mysteriously do, in spite of all our civilization does to crush it and them"—Foreword. Annie is a factory girl whose work experience includes employment by the Circle Waist Company (synonymous with the Triangle

Shirtwaist Company, scene of a fire that killed over 100 girls in 1911) and terms as switchboard operator and typist. As a wife (Mrs. Caroll) and mother Annie struggles with poverty; however she is buoyed by the deepening interest both she and her husband find in the young Socialist Party.

250. Beecher, Carolyn. *Maid and wife.* **New York: Britton Pub. Co., 1919. 380p.**

"Story of a girl brought up in luxury in a small town who, because of adverse circumstances, is forced to seek her living in New York. There as shop girl, waitress, typist, and finally private secretary she made her way for several years. She refused several offers of marriage, for her heart was with her first sweetheart whom she had refused. Finally, however, she married him and settled down on his Western ranch. She had one outbreak of rebellion before she was perfectly content with what she fancied was not as full a life as her city existence"—Book review digest.

Beeckman, Ross, pseud. See: Dey, Frederic Van Rensselaer, 1861 or 5-1922.

251. Beer, Thomas, 1889-1940. *The road to heaven*; a romance of morals. **New York: Knopf, 1928. 266p.**

His reputation as village philanderer has more or less led to the suggestion that he, Lamon Coe, take an extended leave. He has a cousin, Abner, in New York City who takes him in and introduces Lamon to his friends. Lamon latches onto a sympathetic, good-hearted dancer named Frankie; despite her often-comforting presence, Lamon still longs for the country scene from whence he came. He meets a girl from his home place who happens to be in the city. Frankie dies tragically and Abner follows shortly thereafter. Lamon, together with the hometown girl, heads back to farm country.

252. ————. *Sandoval*; a romance of bad manners. **New York: Knopf, 1924. 219p.**

"The New York of 1870 is its background. The action covers a few vivid days in the life of Thorold Gaar, a seventeen-year-old boy who tells the story. Though he is the son of a newly rich Civil War profiteer, he has in him the making of a sincere gentleman. In his vague groping for an ideal he finds the embodiment of virile manhood in his reticent brother Christian. A mysterious, fascinating scoundrel from the far South, Christian Coty de Sandoval, comes to agitate the hearts of society for a moment, and to unearth for his own gain a shady business deal of Civil War times in which the boy's father was presumably implicated. Christian is already the victim of an empty love affair and Sandoval's revelations, while working his own destruction, complete the disillusionment of the two brothers. We take leave of them as they are setting sail from New York to seek their escape in fabulous California. The scene shifts from Dobbs Ferry to New York and the gay theatrical whirl, with Clara Morris starring at Daly's Theatre, and again to the haunts of Boss Tweed and his kind and the life of the docks"—Cleveland open shelf.

253. Begley, Louis. *About Schmidt.* **New York: Knopf, 1966. 320p.**

In retirement and living in splendid isolation in Bridgehampton, Suffolk County, Long Island, former lawyer and widower Albert Schmidt sees himself as a faithful adherent to traditional (WASPish) standards. He is dismayed and his latent anti-Semitism is stirred when his daughter Charlotte decides to marry an up-and-coming Jewish lawyer. Schmidt extends his prejudices against another Suffolk County community, Quogue, and its long-time and part-time residents. This paragon of 'correct' behavior who has alienated the affections of his daughter (Charlotte finds solace and comfort in her fiancé's family) then becomes almost inextricably involved with Carrie, a Puerto Rican waitress. Twenty-year-old Carrie traps Schmidt with her sexual allure and brings her boyfriend, Brian, an off-and-on carpenter and drug-pusher, into the equation.

254. *Behind the veil.* **Boston: Little, Brown 1899. 107p.**

The story of an artist native to Virginia who makes his way to New York City. There he marries the daughter of another poverty-stricken artist and must watch his wife struggle with illness and material deprivation. He casts aside his ambitious dreams, and takes work as a street laborer. The story becomes a contemplation of life after death when—frozen into unconsciousness—he drifts into a world far removed from this earthly one.

255. Belden, Jessie Perry Van Zile, 1857-1910. *Antonia.* **Illustrated by Amy M. Sacker. Boston: L.C. Page, 1901. xi, 258p.**

"Love is perhaps more predominant in this story than in most historical novels. The background is the Hudson, with its three cities—Amsterdam, Rensselaerswyck and Schonowe, during the sway of the Dutch West India Company, but the haughty, capricious, yet loving Antonia [she has a drop of Spanish blood] and her brave, humble lover are never subservient to mere historical details"—The Critic.

256. ———. *Fate at the door.* **Philadelphia: J.B. Lippincott, 1895. 240p.**

John Strathmore, after many years in India, returns to New York City. His closest companions there are the couple Ernest and Beatrice Courtlandt, well-to-do members of the so-called 'smart set.' Ernest is a chum from Strathmore's college days. Beatrice begins to feel that her husband is purposely neglecting her and turns to Strathmore for reassurance. But he has fallen in love with her, and when he declares this to Beatrice she realizes that it is best not to go any further with him. They part. Strathmore sails on the 'Paris' on another world trip and probably will take permanent residence in India.

256a. Belfer, Laura. *City of light.* **New York: Dial Press, 1999. 518p.**

The electric power capabilities of Niagara Falls are the source of political wrangling in Buffalo, N.Y. as the 20th century opens. Peripherally involved is Louisa Barrett, principal of a private school for upper class girls. She is the unwed mother of a child conceived after a prominent politician raped her. The child, Grace, is reared by Louisa's close friend, Margaret Sinclair, and Margaret's husband, Tom. After Margaret's death, Tom Sinclair (who is behind the development of a Falls' powerhouse) becomes a suitor for Louisa's hand in marriage—a journalist is also wooing her. The controversy between electric power enthusiasts and cautious citizens of Buffalo concerned with the environment (e.g., the effect of large-scale diversion of the Niagara River and Falls) heats up and two engineers working for a power company are murdered. Louisa wonders about the extent of Tom Sinclair's involvement in these events.

257. Bell, Lilian Lida, 1867-1929. *Hope Loring.* **Illustrated by Frank T. Merrill. Boston: L.C. Page, 1903. 328p.**

Southerner Hope Loring finds the artificialities and structures of upper class social life in New York irritating and decides that she is not required to copy them. Although New York City is the scene of most of the novel, one also visits several Hudson River estates and the Princeton, N.J. area.

258. Bell, Pearl Doles, d. 1968. *His harvest.* **New York: J. Lane, 1915. 319p.**

Jeanne Delaine's stepfather left her nothing when he died, ceding his farm to a millionaire who had a mortgage on it. Jeanne comes under the patronage of a New York bachelor who has her promising voice trained by a demanding teacher. The latter tells Jeanne to get on with a career, but also to remember to be very grateful to her benefactor. However, Jeanne falls in love with another man, Jim Atherton, while in Paris. Back in New York she seems to have lost her zest for singing, although she is successful for a while. Happily her patron is most understanding and he lets her go her own way.

259. Bellamann, Henry, 1882-1945. *Crescendo.* **New York: Harcourt, Brace, 1928. 296p.**

"Robert Ives is an artist approved by fashionable New York. He appeals strongly to women of many types, and at least four women are in love with him. Robert himself is honestly in love with his wife, a noted concert pianist, and Leslie a twenty-year-old society girl. He wishes to keep both; but this solution, which seems so simple to Robert, is acceptable neither to wife nor maid. Extraordinarily sympathetic and unselfish as the two are, they insist on some other solution. Robert finds it, at great cost to all three"—Book review digest.

260. Bellamy, Francis Rufus, 1886-1972. *The balance*; a novel. **Illustrated by Arthur Little. Garden City, N.Y.: Doubleday, Page, 1917. ix, 347p.**

S. Sydney Tappan (Sammy) is a playwright whose works are brilliant and suggestive but shallow. The New York theatrical crowd admires him, but Sammy, who has tasted poverty in the city, is more interested in developing a vision of the 'balance of society.' Carrie Schroeder, a girl he had known in his native town of 'Melchester', comes to New York and faces the reality of life in a tenement. She is in the audience when Sammy's first play, 'Lady in the lion skin', is performed and is rather shocked by it. He achieves greater success with the drama 'Dr. Paulding.' However Sammy comes to see things as Carrie does and in the long run can see using his talents to better purpose.

261. **Belt, Harriett Pennawell.** *Marjorie Huntingdon*; a novel. **Philadelphia: J.B. Lippincott, 1884. 322p.**

'Bowlesborough', the native town of the heroine, Marjorie Huntingdon, lies on the banks of the Hudson within easy access to New York City. Marjorie's plea for further education leads to her matriculation at Madame Gaubert's School in New York City. Louise Raymond, a lady of 42, takes Marjorie into New York social circles. Marjorie piques the interest of three men—Gilbert Woodford, wealthy, well informed; Roger Houghton, socially 'acceptable', but of restricted means, and a Bowlesborough fellow, Ned Bertram, who appears only briefly. Marjorie turns down Roger Houghton's marriage proposal and chooses to make her own way, especially after her mother dies and during her father's fiscal difficulties. Roger marries his cousin Edith even as Marjorie realizes that she does love him. Edith, despite Roger's loyalty, suffers from dementia and finally passes away. Gilbert Woodford is still available, but Marjorie selects the man she loves, Roger Houghton, who is infused with energy and commitment to his new wife.

262. **Benchley, Peter, 1940- .** *Jaws*. **Garden City, N.Y.: Doubleday, 1974. 311p.**

"A young woman makes love on the beach, then takes a midnight swim. As she swims, she is violently struck, chopped in two. The next morning pieces of her body are found at the water's edge. ... [In the] Long Island resort town called 'Amity' ... the town fathers ... decide to cover up the woman's death: news of a killer shark could ruin the summer business. They forbid police chief Martin Brody to close the beaches. The shark has gone, they say. But the shark remains and kills again, and the life of the town becomes governed by the ... almost supernatural presence offshore"—Publisher's note.

263. **[Benedict, Frank Lee] 1834-1910.** *My daughter Elinor*; a novel. **New York: Harper, 1869. 257p. (in double columns)**

A 'society' novel depicting the life of the wealthy upper class of New York City and Washington. The heroine is Elinor Grey, whose father, a former ambassador, prizes her above all else. Clive Farnsworth loves Elinor and she is inclined to love him in return. However, Elinor discovers that Clive has had an indiscrete affair with Ruth Sothern and refuses further serious contact with him. Clive marries Ruth and Elinor stays by her father's side. It is only after the deaths of both Ruth and Mr. Grey that Clive achieves reconciliation with Elinor.

264. **Benefield, Barry, 1877-1956.** *Bugles in the night*. **New York: Century Co., 1927. vii, 309p.**

"The elderly inmate of a soldiers' home rescues a young girl from a house of ill-fame, adopts her and wanders across the country with her till they come to New York. Unable to make his way in the city, he finds lodging in an old scow on the Brooklyn waterfront. There the girl nurses to health a derelict suffering from aphasia and falls in love with him. He recovers suddenly, forgetting his illness completely and is lost to Alice for four years. An advertisement brings them together again just before the good old soldier's death"—Book review digest.

265. **Bennett, Clarence E.** *Vacant niche*; or, *Land of Gold*. **Schenectady, N.Y.: Robson and Adee, 1928. 159p.**

"A secluded valley of Washington County, New York" is the new home of Jim Newcomb, a motherless/fatherless boy now subject to the not so tender mercies of foster father Frank Stonehart. As he edges toward manhood Jim falls in love with Constance Burrow, a neighbor. The death of Mrs. Stonehart softens Frank Stonehart's attitude toward Jim and he gives the lad a deed to the Land of Gold, a prime piece of acreage not far from the Stonehart and Burrow farms. When Constance stumbles into an engagement with a smooth-talking stranger and another rival for Constance's hand is accidentally killed, Jim heads west, completes his engineering education and goes to work for a mining firm. He returns to Upstate New York for a few years; the still unmarried Constance has become a schoolteacher. The 'vacant niche' refers to the empty place within the Battle of Saratoga Monument that would have been occupied by a likeness of Benedict Arnold had he not turned traitor. As a boy Jim had been fascinated by the story behind the monument.

266. **Bennett, Emerson, 1822-1905.** *The female spy*; or, *Treason in the camp*. **A story of the Revolution. Cincinnati: L. Stratton, 1851. 112p. (in double columns).**

The novel is a device for explaining in great detail the Arnold-André affair. The author manifests his contempt for the traitor Benedict Arnold and his admiration for the unfortunate Major André. The heroine is Rosalie Du Pont ('the female spy') who, unsuspected by her British admirers in New York City, has acquired knowledge of the plans of Sir Henry Clinton to move against Washington after Arnold has placed West Point in the British commander's hands. She has no success in apprising Americans of the treasonable goings-on, however. After a clandestine meeting with Arnold, André is intercepted by suspicious American soldiers and papers on his person seal his fate, while Arnold escapes to British headquarters in New York City.

267. ————. *Rosalie Du Pont*; or, *Treason in the camp*. **A sequel to** *The female spy*. **Cincinnati: L. Stratton, 1851. 109p. (in double columns).**

Rosalie Du Pont, 'the female spy', is ensconced in New York and in the good graces of Sir Henry Clinton. The Americans hatch a plot to snatch the traitor Benedict Arnold. Leader in the effort is Captain Edgar Milford, Rosalie's lover, who poses as a deserter in order to get close to Arnold. The effort meets with failure and Milford is captured and condemned to death for spying. Rosalie pleads for his life with Sir Henry, reminding him of the favor he had promised her when she returned Major André's ring to him. Clinton releases Rosalie and Milford who promise to take no further part in the American cause.

268. ————. *The unknown countess.* [and *The outlaws of New York*; or, *The mysterious marksman*]. **Cincinnati: L. Stratton, 1851. 110p. (in double columns).**

In the first story the dying Madame La Roix, separated from her husband, the Count, leaves her daughter Marianne with a former seducer, Dr. Edward Barton of Five Points and vicinity. The evil Barton discovers that Marianne will be the heir to a sizeable fortune. His efforts to drive her to despair and suicide are thwarted by Henry Neville, Marianne's lover, and a La Roix servant, Mary. Barton confesses to his criminality and commits suicide. In the second story, James Clarendon saves Lionel Gilmore from ruin at the hands of his supposed friend, the gambler Samuel Higgs. Clarendon turns out to be Gilmore's father and also the 'mysterious marksman.' Gilmore and Clarendon take arms against Higgs, seducer of Clarendon's daughter Eveline. Higgs tries to ingratiate himself with Colonel Howard and his daughter Florence, all to no avail. Florence recognizes Lionel Gilmore as the lover she had been told was lost at sea.

269. **Bennett, John, 1865-1956.** *Barnaby Lee.* **With illus. by Clyde O. De Land. New York: Century Co., 1900. 459p.**

In New Amsterdam during the governorship of Peter Stuyvesant a young fellow is a fugitive from the tyrannical ministrations of a sea captain. His troubles are ended when the British fleet enters New York Harbor to take over rule of the colony from its former Dutch masters.

270. **Benson, Edward Frederic, 1867-1940.** *The relentless city.* **New York: Harper, 1903. 305p.**

English author Benson takes some pride in his knowledge of the physical aspect of New York City, but he quite obviously disdains certain aspects of American 'social' life. His fictional hero is Lord Keynes (not to be confused with the economist) and the story moves quickly from London to New York, the 'relentless city.' Lord Keynes' hosts on Long Island are Mr. and Mrs. Lewis S. Palmer (their estate is 'Mon Repos'). At one of the Palmers' parties the guests fish for pearl oysters that have been laced at great expense throughout a lagoon fronting the estate. Such vulgarities aside, Lord Keynes marries the Palmers' daughter, and the old cliché of rich American girls marrying European nobility who more likely than not are financially insecure, continues.

271. **Benson, Therese, pseud.** *The unknown daughter.* **New York: Dodd, Mead, 1929. 323p.**

At the age of 18 Claire Bouvier had married the millionaire Griffith ('Grif') Goodhue. When the Goodhue fortune began diminishing Grif bought up real estate on underdeveloped Park Avenue as a business venture. This stirred Claire's displeasure and she divorced Grif to marry Arnold Bassett, another millionaire from the West. Grif takes their 4-year-old daughter, Eve, with him to Africa. Fourteen years later, Eve returns to New York City with Grif, the latter now a Muslim. Eve creates quite a stir in society circles and Claire, a rich widow, moves into her daughter's life. Then a bombshell—Mrs. Lefferts, anxious for Claire to marry her son, declares that Grif and Eve perished at sea long ago—therefore the 'living' Eve is an imposter.

272. **Bentley, John. *Kill me again*. New York: Dodd, Mead, 1947. 234p.**
Published in England under the title: Call off the corpse (London:Hutchinson). When businesswoman and corporation head Ms. Alias Herstel is poisoned and stabbed in her Long Island mansion, it falls to her lawyer, Glen Gibson, to study the situation. Among the possible suspects are: Abbott Dodds, an ungrateful nephew, whose primary interest is turbo-superchargers; Harvey Creel, a close-to-the-vest liquor salesman, and Arno, Ms. Herstel's butler. Gibson's snooping irritates the local police, but it is he who comes up with the solution.

273. **Bercovici, Konrad, 1882-1961. *Dust of New York*. New York: Boni & Liveright, 1919. ix, 239p.**
"New York is an orchestra playing as a 'symphony'" says the author in the first of these stories. "If you hear the part of only one instrument… it is incongruous. To understand the symphony you must hear all the instruments playing together." The stories are sketches of New York life drawn from the various foreign quarters: Hungarian, Russian, Jewish, Spanish, French, Romanian, and so on. Among the titles are: Theresa the vamp.—The troubles of a perfect type.—The little men of Twenty-eighth Street—The newly-rich Goldsteins.—All in one wild Roumanian song.—Expensive property.

274. **————. *The marriage quest*; a novel. New York: Boni & Liveright, 1925. 285p.**
"Against the colorful background of New York's East Side the author draws the vigorous portraits of Anton Zwange, the violin repairer; of his wife, who betrays the Old World in her ambition for the New; of Karl, the diffident musician of great talent and little means; of George, the hustling contractor; and of Greta, who at nineteen has too little patience. Greta marries George, with Karl in her heart. Only by evoking Karl's loved image is she able to bear her husband's caresses. When her child is born, she thinks of it not as her husband's but as Karl's. About this unusual situation the story evolves"—Book review digest.

Berkley, Helen, pseud. See: Mowatt, Anna Cora, 1818-1870.

275. **Berlin, Ellin Mackay, 1903-1988. *Lace curtain*. Garden City, N.Y.:**

Doubleday, 1948. 375p.

Veronica Reardon, a devout Catholic, marries into the high-on-the-social-scale Stair family of Long Island and New York. The 'lace curtain Irish' Reardons are not recognized as equals by the Protestant Stairs. The mixed marriage brings in its wake strains and stresses; at times Veronica's husband is a more sympathetic character than she. The author is well aware that there are prejudices within those who are discriminated against.

276. **Berman, Henry.** *Worshippers*; **a novel. New York: Grafton Press, 1906. 272p.**

The three leading personages in this story about Russian Jews trying to establish themselves in New York and Philadelphia are: a doctor, a writer and an actress just starting out in her craft. They are alternately optimistic and pessimistic, and choose in large part a bohemian way of life, and gather around themselves 'worshippers' sympathetic to their socialistic views.

277. **Berman, James Gabriel.** *Uninvited.* **New York: Warner Books, 1995. 223p.**

Patricia Carver and her two small children are found dead in their spacious home located in an especially up-scale section of Long Island (the so-called 'Gold Coast'). Presumably they were murdered by Patricia's husband who then shot himself. However, a half-year later Tony McMahon, a young man from a village not far from the tragic scene, is held on the charge of murder. Tony comes from a family background of alcoholism and evidently had been obsessed with Patricia (from afar) since adolescence. Ralph Barolo, sophisticated, street-smart lawyer, defends Tony. He has to deal with the facts of Tony's almost pathological worship of Patricia, the prejudice directed at his disheveled, lower class client and a criminal justice system that often does not treat those at the bottom of the social scale too kindly.

278. **Bernard, Paul, 1911- .** *Genesee Castle.* **Philadelphia: Dorrance, 1970. 152p.**

A short novel that describes in almost numbing detail the Sullivan campaign in central (Finger Lakes region) New York against the Iroquois Confederacy. Philip Cochran, a corporal in the Pennsylvania Regiment, is the ostensible 'hero' but he does not have much of a part in the narrative. The expedition starts out from the Wyoming Valley of Pennsylvania and links up with General Clinton's forces coming down from the Mohawk Valley. Various skirmishes and the Battle of Newtown are recounted. Philip is there, to be sure, but he seems more interested in his love life, which veers from Claire Shillington (whom he finds to be too free with her favors) to a widow, Mary Anderson, whose husband had been killed in the Wyoming Valley massacre.

279. **Bernstein, Herman, 1876-1935.** *In the gates of Israel*; **stories of the Jews. New York: J.F. Taylor, 1902. 316p.**

"Sacrifice, renunciation, and the acquiescence to fate are the recurrent themes in ... [a] collection of stories about New York's Lower East Side immigrants . ... The characters by and large are poor ghetto Jews who discover their fate in obedience, duty, and acceptance of their cultural heritage"—Fine, D.M. *The city, the immigrant, and American fiction, 1880-1920.* Contents: Soreh Rivke's vigil.—The messenger or the community.—The awakening.—Alone.—The sinners.—The straight hunchback.—The marriage-broker.—The artist.—A jealousy cure.—The disarmed reformer.—A ghetto romance.

280. Berriedale, pseud. *Unforgiven.* **A novel. New York: T.W. Brown, 1869. 425p.**

The much-put-upon heroine of this drawn-out story is Clarine Rivington, daughter of the Rev. Robert Rivington. While living with her uncle and his wife, the Bells, in New York City, Clarine bears the child of an English adventurer, Segismund Maltby. She refuses to marry the child's father despite the urgings of her disapproving father and Mrs. Bell. Clarine's brother George dies in India and she adopts his two children (one dies en route to New York). Possible suitors shy away from Clarine because of her illegitimate daughter but she is content with spinsterhood. With money left by her deceased brother and $50,000 bequeathed by the late Mr. Maltby, Clarine is accepted by New York and Newport society. In later years she tries unsuccessfully to mend the broken marriage of willful Isabel Holms (Mr. Bell's ward) and mild Edward Radleigh. Clarine and her father take a cottage on the Hudson; she embraces Christian ideals and forgives Maltby, her judgmental father and others who caused her anguish at various stages in her life.

281. Berry, Edward Payson. *Where the tides meet.* **Boston: Arena Pub. Co., 1983. iv, 302p.**

"The story deals largely with certain phases of the life and habits of the 'lower half' in New York City, and portrays in realistic colors the relations which its members not infrequently sustain to the upper classes. The ludicrous side of the deplorable tenement packing system, as seen in 'Mr. Silas Slack' [he is a clerk in the law office of Jeremiah Hardangle and inhabits a tenement with his wife and four children]; the criminal relationships existing between 'Lawyer Hardangle' and 'Shadow', and 'Robert Moreland' and 'Rachel Underwood', and the pitiable destitution of poor 'Mammy', are by no means 'phantoms of the mind'"—Annual American catalogue.

282. Berry, Erick, 1892-1972. *Harvest of the Hudson.* **New York: Macmillan, 1945. xi, 239p.**

The death of their parents leaves Deborah and Sebastien on their own in this novel set in the 18th century. Deborah is taken into the Hudson River home of the kind patroon Van Dieman as companion to his light-hearted, generous daughter Lancy. Sebastien sets sail in his sloop 'Beaver' for Manhattan where he is ordered to carry cargo to the Caribbean; he and an Old Danish friend have many adventures. Deborah and Lancy, suspicious of Van Dieman's ugly, underhanded overseer, are the chief causes of his being brought to justice and dismissal.

283. ————. *Hearthstone in the wilderness.* **Illustrated by the author. New York: Macmillan, 1944. 242p.**

"Pioneer tale for older boys and girls. The scene is laid in northern New York State. Mercie Stark accompanies her father on his trip to their grant in place of her brother who stays in Glens Falls to earn enough money to finish payment on the land. The stories of both Mercie and her brother are told as the two young pioneers struggle to help the family in its new venture"—Book review digest.

284. ———. *Homespun.* **Illustrated by Harold Von Schmidt. Boston: Lothrop, 1937. 308p.**

In the 1820s and 1830s a family copes fairly successfully with the challenge of earning a living in Upstate New York (e.g., Jerusha becomes expert at spinning and weaving), but in the end other members of the family disperse to various regions of the Americas; Luke goes hunting in the Canadian wilds; Mark and his wife head West to New Mexico in their Conestoga wagon; and Stephen enters the cotton trade in New Orleans.

285. ———. *Lock her through.* **Illus. by the author. New York: Oxford University Press, 1940. 246p.**

In the early years of the 19th century Sabrina Parrott, daughter of an innkeeper, lives on the Mohawk Turnpike nearby the Erie Canal. In combination with a young English immigrant, Gideon, and the sheriff's son, 'Trapper', she helps smash a ring of horse thieves.

286. ———. *The road runs both ways.* **New York: Macmillan, 1950. 196p.**

The mail-carrying stagecoach line running from Fishkill, New York to Albany that Rett Apley has taken over from his uncle is faced with stiff competition from another line traveling the same route.

Best, Allena Champlin, 1892-1972. See under her pseudonym: Berry, Erick, 1892-1972.

287. **Best, Herbert, 1894-1980.** *Border iron.* **Illustrated by Erick Berry. New York: Viking Press, 1945. 219p.**

"The scene is the border region between Massachusetts and what was called York Province, about 1740. The hero is a young orphan, Tod Randall, who runs away from an overbearing deputy sheriff who had tried either to work him to death or beat him into submission. Tod finds work in an ironworks and helps to settle a border dispute"—Book review digest.

288. ———. *Gunsmith's boy.* **Illustrated by Erick Berry. Philadelphia: Winston, 1942. ix, 220p.**

The year 1813 in Upper New York State was a freezing one, with frost and snow in every month of the year. During that period Seth Ellis went from Albany to Cold Brook Farm, apprenticed to Gamaliel Reed, the noted gunsmith, and had a heroic part in saving his village from extreme hunger.

289. ————. *The long portage*; a story of Ticonderoga and Lord Howe. Illus. by Erick Berry. **New York: Viking Press, 1948. v, 250p.**

The New York State countryside is the setting for this tale of Philip Dearborn, who signed up with Rogers' Rangers in the French and Indian Wars, and met William Howe, fifth viscount (1729-1814) at Ticonderoga.

290. ————. *Ranger's ransom*; a story of Ticonderoga. **Illustrated by Erick Berry. New York: Aladdin Books, 1953. 192p.**

Although the author's characters seem sketchy, some dramatic situations are underemphasized and the historical background does not encompass enough, there are compensations in this tale for young readers of Cass Purdie who flees the blacksmith shop where he is serving as an apprentice, joins Roger's Rangers and witnesses the fall of Fort Ticonderoga in 1759.

291. ————. *Watergate*; a story of the Irish on the Erie Canal. **Illus. by Erick Berry. Philadelphia: Winston, 1951. xv, 240p.**

Irish laborers who migrated to New York State when the Erie Canal was under construction are the chief characters in Best's novel. There are those who take to the backbreaking work of digging the canal while others find jobs that demand greater skills. e.g., Sean, the hero, is a driver for a canal boat, the 'Annekje': his female interest is Judy, daughter of an Irishman who has an aversion to manual labor but a limitless capacity for high-flying gab.

292. ————. *Whistle, daughter, whistle*. **New York: Macmillan, 1947. 300p.**

"The Lake Champlain country is the background for this novel about [Thirza], a flirtatious young lady from Albany, sent to stay for a while with her lively little grandmother. Gramma Tuttle was a character with a will of her own—[she had spent her own girlhood fighting Indians in the wilderness of northern New York]—and before long her granddaughter had laid aside her foolishness and had fallen in love with the man of Gramma's choice"—Book review digest.

293. ————. *Young 'un*. **New York: Macmillan, 1944. 271p.**

Following the end of the American Revolution the fur trade around Lake Champlain resumed. The children of one family in the region were pushed to the extreme in trying to keep themselves together when a catastrophic fire destroyed their barely livable quarters and killed their mother; their father had left to hunt for more propitious fur trading conditions.

Best, Mrs. Herbert, 1892-1972. See under her pseudonym: Berry, Erick, 1892-1972.

294. **Betts, Lillian Williams.** *The story of an East-Side family.* **New York: Dodd, Mead, 1903. 342p.**

The story of the progress of a young couple who were the principals in a 'marriage of convenience.' Their East Side of New York City beginnings were not promising, but the pair methodically scrimped, worked tirelessly and observed the principles of good management. The reward was the husband's promotion to factory foreman, while the wife took a leading role in the affairs of their community.

295. **Bianchi, Martha Gilbert Dickinson, 1866?-1943.** *The kiss of Apollo*. **New York: Duffield, 1915. 408p.**

Judith, the heroine of the novel, which has New York City as its primary scene, is not interested in being a decorative young woman in the social swim. She will not gain any useful information on living from her sophisticated sister or her unworldly brother. As she starts out she decides that a conventional marriage would serve no useful purpose and she tries to avoid that bond. But gradually persuaded that she may enjoy greater freedom in marriage than she ever suspected, Judith marries Drake Heminway, a rich clubman older than she. Her philanthropic activities and her wifely duties wear thin and Judith falls deeply in love with Julian, a childhood friend and now a lover. Judith herself says: "The kiss of Apollo is just as fatal to overturn any shrine as it ever was. Tell them I love—and therefore I am!"

296. **Bickford, Luther H.** *Phyllis in Bohemia*, **by L.H. Bickford and R. Stillman Powell [pseud.]. Illustrated by Orson Lowell. Chicago: H.S. Stone, 1897. 233p.**

"A country girl named Phyllis, tired of an ideal existence in a rural locality, referred to in the story as Arcadia, and longing to be brought in touch with the life of Bohemia, appeals to her betrothed, who gratifies his sweetheart by settling in a New York house, which is literally filled with aspirants to artistic or literary fame. Through association with the 'poet lariat', the boy poet Vedo Venner, the coming Duse, and other types which are cleverly portrayed, Phyllis learns that in Bohemia hopes are seldom realized, hence a return to Arcadia"—Annual American catalogue.

Biddle, Clement, 1925-1994. See: Wood, Clement Biddle, 1925-1994.

297. **Bingham, Sallie, 1937- .** *Upstate; a novel.* **Sag Harbor, N.Y.: Permanent Press, 1993. 128p.**

Adultery and exclusiveness among urban 'exiles' living in a Hudson Valley town are themes of the novel. Ann, the heroine, is separated from her husband David, but at the moment they are preparing to sell their house and its contents. Ann is the narrator; she recalls the eight years she and David were in this town where they joined other refugees from the city in a little circle headed by Flora Fields and her husband Edwin, a psychoanalyst. The Fields' open marriage 'allowed' Edwin to bed whomever he like, Ann included, while his wife inwardly seethed. Ann seeks revenge when her request that Edwin leave Flora is rejected.

298. **Birmingham, Stephen, 1932- .** *Fast start, fast finish.* **New York: New**

American Library, 1966. 308p.

The Lord family is a paragon of dysfunction. The head of the brood, Charlie, is sadly immature, 39, anxious to quit the advertising game in California and devote himself to 'art'. With his wife and three children he settles in Westchester County and paints; unfortunately the chief subjects of his painting are fallen women. Mrs. Lord is in analysis and spends every dime she can get her hands on. Charlie's teenage son steals from neighbors and robs gay men; his daughter dies after a botched abortion.

Bisbee, Mariana M. See: Tallman, Mariana M. Bisbee

299. **Bishop, Claudia, 1957- .** *A touch of the grape.* **New York: Berkley Prime Crime, 1988. 241p.**

Strapped by the decline of tourism to 'Hemlock Falls', where their Upstate New York inn is located, Sarah ('Quill') and Meg Quilliam play host to the area's Craft Ladies, elderly women who have formed a business to sell their creations. Their president fails to put in an appearance and after one of the ladies dies in a fire at the hotel, Quill is inclined to believe the whole thing was not accidental, especially since the Quilliams had just changed insurance agents. Quill's suspicions fall primarily on the missing Craft Ladies president who runs a diner in Hemlock Falls and is keenly interested in acquiring the inn.

300. **Bishop, Morris, 1893-1973.** *The widening stain,* **by W. Bolingbroke Johnson [pseud.]. New York: Knopf, 1942. 242p.**

The late Morris Bishop, professor of Romance languages at Cornell University and the University's historian, has been accepted by those in the know as the true author of this 'classic' mystery. Certainly the library described as the scene of the murder of two faculty members is a dead ringer for the old Cornell University Library that was later converted into the Undergraduate (Uris) Library. In any case, Gilda Gorham, head cataloger and 30ish (the object of the affections of two male faculty members) is the person who solves the murders and in so doing nearly gets herself murdered. Most amusing is the author's portrait of the jealousies, rivalries and intrigues of those professors whose chief concern is supposedly the advancement of scholarship (but really their own careers).

301. **Bishop, William Henry, 1847-1928.** *The house of a merchant prince*; **a novel of New York. Boston: Houghton, Mifflin, 1883 [c1882]. 420p.**

"Presents a remarkably realistic picture of wealthy, fashionable New York, as seen in the homes of our Vanderbilts, Astors and A.T. Stewarts. The scene sometimes changes to Newport, but never goes outside of the haunts of the wealthy, favored classes. ... The plot... [turns] upon the efforts of Mr. Rodman Harvey, the 'merchant prince', to get into the Cabinet, and the schemes of his enemies to unveil some disgraceful secrets in his past. His daughter is capitally drawn, with her devotion to her toilettes and her conviction that she must marry position. So is his Western niece, who comes to help her aunt keep house, and who has a charming love story, and is one of the few noble characters in the book"—Annual American catalogue.

302. **Black, Alexander, 1859-1940.** *The great desire.* **New York: Harper, 1919. 396p.**

"A novel of New York life as seen through the eyes of two young New Englanders. Anson Grayl, who tells the story in the first person, is a hunchback of keen mind and philosophical temperament. He is seeking to unearth the 'great desire', which he believes is indwelling in the heart of humanity. He has come to the great city to find the answer to his question. It is to be the subject of his book. His sister Sarah, a brilliant, flashing girl, has come to the city to live its life. But the two are not homeless wanderers, socially adrift. They enter at the front door and are under the guarding eye of a delightful person, their aunt, a woman of ample girth, large heart and keen wit. Many phases of the city's life pass under review, including aspects of the city at war. In the end Anson as well as Sarah finds love, and so, in his personal relationships at least, feel that his question is answered"—Book review digest.

303. ———. *Jo Ellen.* **New York: Harper, 1923. 325p.**

Jo Ellen "is a girl living up Inwood way and familiar with all the paths to the riverside and to the Palisades. The fine daughter of a household measurably strange, Jo Ellen grows up through much girlish adventure into young womanhood keenly marked by circumstances of love, pursuit and wrong marriage. Local color, the reign of jazz and the revolt against the straight-laced are strong in Mr. Black's pages. 'Jo Ellen' is a lively story from which readers may draw text and sermon, as they will, with neither aid nor hindrance from the author. When the tale is told, we are a trifle shady as to the future of the heroine who has still her advantages of youth, beauty and appreciation of the joy of life"—New York world.

304. ———. *Miss Jerry.* **With thirty-seven illus. from life photographs by the author. New York: Scribner, 1895. x, 212p.**

The author calls this a 'picture play'; the photographs are arranged like successive pictures on a strip of film. The story (it is not a 'play'), with its scene in New York City in the winter and spring of 1893, has a heroine in Geraldine (Jerry) Holbrook whose father, Richard, is facing a crisis as his mining investments drop sharply in value. The editor of the New York Daly Dynamo, Walter Hamilton, interviews Jerry for a job. Her hires her and is soon declaring his love for the new employee, which is more than pleasing to Jerry.

305. ———. *Richard Gordon.* **Illustrated by Ernest Fuhr. Boston: Lothrop Pub. Co., 1902. 506p.**

"Richard Gordon, a young New Yorker of sound and active principles, is in love with a woman with a past—but also, by the same token, a present and a future. His experiences, which are various and dramatic, carry one with him into the worlds of [New York] politics, art, society, ['Bohemia'] and warfare to the end that one receives some sound instructions as to the 'internal workin's' of each and all, while remaining under the spell of the story itself and absorbed in its plot"—The independent.

306. ———. *The seventh angel.* **New York: Harper, 1921. 360p.**
After World War I there are indications that society's 'old order' is about to give way to a new one. In a novel set primarily in New York City, the heroine, Ann Forrest, is committed to carefully researching all the facets of her life. Her friend, Irma Kane, has more direct experience with life's vagaries than Ann and she looks at the larger picture. The two friends are touchstones for one another's visions.

307. ———. *Stacy.* **Indianapolis: Bobbs-Merrill, 1925. 343p.**
"Ralph Stacey comes to New York City knowing only small-town life in the Middle West, and attempts to succeed in business—for which he has no ability. His dreams are ever large; always he looks for 'big money', but honestly. His dream continues when he meets under extremely questionable circumstances the woman who is to be the one woman in his life for years, though he later learns from herself that she has an ugly record on the Western coast. He loses her in the end, and his dreams go with her. He marries the stolid daughter of his respectable though bourgeois landlady and becomes part owner in the deadly common 'hash house.' His prospect now, like that of most mortals, includes safety and comfort, but no romance"—Springfield Republican.

Black, Campbell, 1944- . See: Campbell, Jeffrey, the joint pseudonym of Campbell Black and Jeffrey Caine.

Black, Ivory, pseud. See: Janvier, Thomas Allibone, 1849-1913.

Black, Mrs. J.D., 1881-1911. See: Potter, Margaret Horton, 1881-1911.

308. **Black, Simon.** *Me and Kev*; **a novel. Dallas, Tex.: Baskerville Publishers, 1993. 263p.**
The narrator of the novel is an 11-year-old, Steven Jones, whose parents run a farm in Upstate New York. His father is an alcoholic who abuses Steven and beats his wife. Mr. Jones knocks Steven when the latter mimics his father by staggering around after imbibing from a bottle of bourbon whiskey. Still reeling from the blows, Steven starts a conversation with an imagined boy inside his body named Kevin. He becomes more and more a loner, tries to commit suicide, loses interest in personal hygiene, gains weight and has a

tragic romance with a disturbed girl; a chimerical Kevin remains his constant companion.

308a. Blaine, Michael. *The desperate season.* **New York: Morrow/Avon, 1999. 304p.**
Schizophrenia impels young Maurice, an escapee from a mental hospital, to commit several murders near his parents' home in the Catskills. Maurice's father, Nathan, a bank president, gives his son unqualified love, but Nathan is an embezzler, stealing bank funds to feed his addiction to gambling. The escapee uses his family (Nathan, mother Moira and sister Chrissie) as a shield against the authorities. Drawn into the situation is Vince, an attorney, who, having a son of his own, has sympathy for Maurice. The Upstate New York countryside has a rather 'menacing' effect on Maurice and those around him.

309. Blaisdell, Elijah Whittier, 1825-1900. *The hidden record*; **or,** *The old sea mystery.* **A novel. Philadelphia: T.B. Peterson, 1882. 466p.**
In this overblown, turgid and ultimately tedious novel Lt. Paul Raymond, U.S. Navy, searches for the real story behind his father's hanging for the crime of piracy. Her serves his country well in the War of 1812 and falls in love with Helen, sister of his friend, Edward Clayton—the Clayton family resides in a Hudson Valley mansion 20 miles from New York City. Paul becomes aware of a cabal that hatches criminal ventures from New York City's Battery and may have knowledge of his father, Captain James Raymond. One of the cabal, the dying Pierre Gauthier, confesses that he was responsible for leading a mutiny that killed Paul's father, turned the brig 'Elizabeth' into a pirate ship and substituted a look-alike for the murdered Captain Raymond. The false captain was captured and hung in London, still using the name James Raymond. Before Helen and Paul are joined she escapes a kidnapping and the elderly Mr. Clayton barely survives the fraudulent financial manipulations of a supposed friend.

310. Blake, Dorothy, pseud. *The diary of a suburban housewife.* **New York: Morrow, 1936. 274p.**
"A day-by-day record of one year in the life of a Long Island family hit hard by the Depression. There are amusing anecdotes concerning the two children, dinner menus featured by roast turkey or black bean soup, gardening hints, Parent-Teacher Association meetings, and other incidents characteristic of suburban life"—Book review digest.

311. Blake, E. Vinton. *The Dalzells of Daisydown.* **Boston: D. Lothrop Co., 1890. 411p.**
Members of the Dalzell family of the seaside village of 'Daisydown' (of uncertain location) are seen enjoying the pleasures of home life and the ordered activities of school. Their vacations take them to New York City, the Hudson River and Newport; they take part in fox hunting, boating, fishing, and other activities that befit a relatively affluent household of the last decades of the 19th century.

312. **Blake, Lillie Devereux, 1835-1913.** *Fettered for life*; or, *Lord and master.* **A story of today. New York: Sheldon, 1874.**

> The tyranny of her father induces Laura Stanley to leave an otherwise comfortable life on a prosperous farm and seek employment and self-support in New York City. It doesn't take long for Laura to learn that a single woman in the metropolis has to face a number of disadvantages. When she does secure a job she is paid less than men who hold similar positions and she suffers the disrespect of the many who look down on working women. She even draws the attention of an unethical judge/politico who attempts to kidnap her. When love comes her way Laura tries to balance her relationship with her lover with the need to retain an adequate measure of her own independence. Republished in 1996 (New York, Feminist Press).

313. **Blakeslee, Mermer.** *In dark water*; a novel. **New York: Ballantine Books, 1998. 292p.**

> In Upstate New York in 1958 Eudora Bell, 11, is deeply bereaved by the death of her only sibling, David Bell. Unfortunately Eudora's unbalanced mother, Florence, in her grief treats Eudora badly while her husband, Michael, tries to calm his wife down. Suffering mental lapses of her own, Eudora comes under the care of Pop and Beulah Tappen until her worsening emotional condition warrants placement in various institutions (schools and hospitals).

314. **Blanchard, Amy Ella, 1856-1926.** *Because of conscience*; being a novel relating to the adventures of certain Huguenots in Old New York. With front. by C. Benson Kennedy. Philadelphia: Lippincott, 1901. 355p.

> The heroine is Alaine Hervieu, a Huguenot maiden, whose conscience dictates that she remain true to Protestant principles. The three men who are much attracted by her charms are François Dupont, a Catholic; Pierre Boutillier, a Huguenot; and Lendert Verplanck, a Dutch Protestant. The story begins in Rouen, France and moves to New Rochelle, New York in the days of Jacob Leisler's rule (1688-1691). The New York Times of Nov. 23, 1901, states that the story is 'unnecessarily long and has neither local color, historical atmosphere, nor the spirit of adventure'—a too harsh indictment. Presumably the leading motif of the novel is a young man's (Dupont's) ill-treatment of the heroine, forcing her to marry him, not that he loves her, but that he wants to hurt a man who has another woman as his wife.

315. ————. *Girls together.* **Illus. by Ida Waugh. Philadelphia: J.B. Lippincott, 1896, c1895. 259p.**

> Two young women with artistic proclivities settle in New York City to further their studies. One is an aspiring painter, the other a hopeful musician. While they room together in modest quarters and adopt a Bohemian life-style, the brother of one of the girls matriculates at a law school in New York; he and a friend play important, even romantic roles in the young women's lives, although the artist eventually winds up in Paris.

316. ———. *A loyal lass*; a story of the Niagara campaign of 1814. Illustrated by Frank T. Merrill. Boston: W.A. Wilde, 1902. 319p.

Actually the novel encompasses almost the entire period of the War, from 1812 through 1814. The 'loyal lass', Marianne Reyburn, is a fiery supporter of the American cause; her father has taken up arms for that cause, but his son, Royal, Marianne's brother, joins the British/Canadian forces. As the conflict on the Niagara frontier deepens, the Reyburns, through Royal, have contacts with the Silverthorns on Canadian soil who support the Crown. The scenes of action move back and forth on both sides of the New York/Canadian border. Jack Silverthorn falls in love with Marianne, but she rebuffs him initially because of his service in the forces of her country's enemy. The marriages of dear friends and the tragic deaths of her brother Royal and Major Silverthorn, Jack's father, eventually convince Marianne that she can no longer deny her love for Jack.

317. ———. *A Revolutionary maid*; a story of the middle period of the War of Independence. Illustrated by Ida Waugh. Boston: W.A. Wilde, 1899. 321p.

New York City just before the outbreak of the American Revolution is the home of Kitty De Witt who must decide whether she should remain loyal to the English crown or give herself over to the American ideal of independence. She observes the so-called 'Liberty Boys' as they strike down King George III's statue and the fires of patriotism flare up within her. She remains true to her choice despite consequences that follow British occupation of the city and the perilous course of events in the middle period of the War of Independence.

318. Blankman, Edgar Gerritt, b. 1861. *Deacon Babbitt*; a tale of fact and fiction. Philadelphia: J.C. Winston, 1906. 334p.

The hero of the novel (which may well be semi-autobiographical) is young Gerry Arnoldus who goes on an odyssey to find his parents from whom he was separated when the dikes broke, and Amsterdam was inundated. From Western Europe Gerry sails for America and finds a home with Deacon Babbitt, a shrewd but straightforward businessman/trader who more or less adopts the boy. 'Marshville', N.Y. is the base of the Deacon's commercial ventures; he allows George to scour central New York for possible news of the Arnoldus family. As Gerry matures the Deacon encourages him to study for the ministry. That failing, the Deacon suggests a career in education for Gerry. However, Gerry's preference is the legal profession and he finally becomes a lawyer with an office in Ogdensburg and later Syracuse. In his sporadic travels through central New York Gerry meets his future wife and finds his parents settled on a small farm. Paul Smith, the famous Adirondack guide and hotelman, is one of the 'real' personages with a role in the novel.

319. Bleecker, Ann Eliza Schuyler, 1752-1783. *The history of Maria Kittle ... In a letter to Miss Ten Eyck*. Hartford: Printed by Elisha Babcock, 1797. 70p.

During the French and Indian War Maria Kittle, born on a farm (in 1721) on the banks of the Hudson, 18 miles from Albany, married at 19, mother of two children, is taken prisoner at Tomhannock, N.Y. by Indians and carried north over Lake Champlain to Canada. Her husband, seeking help in the village of Shochticook, comes home to a scene of desolation, the two children dead and Maria nowhere to be found. He joins the British and colonial troops and eventually tracks down Maria in Montreal. Bleecker's tale is perhaps the first piece of American fiction to portray Indians; in the author's jaundiced view they appear untrustworthy, unmerciful, bloodthirsty. This work was first published in Bleecker's posthumous works (New York, Printed by T. and J. Swords, 1793).

320. Bliss, Tip. *The Broadway butterfly murders.* **New York: Greenberg, 1930. 264p.**

The murder of Broadway 'tart' Tots Harland is quickly followed by the slaying of her friend and cohort Billie Quaid, former wife of unemployed reporter Ole Monahan, of window washer Martini, and of Rhoda Bishop, maid to the two 'Broadway butterflies.' Captain Michael McAn of New York's Homicide Division is placed in charge of the case, but is unofficially 'superseded' by amateur investigator Oliver Oliphant and his assistant, Albert Lavery. The story moves through the speakeasies and upper scale apartments of the city; Ole Monahan is a prime suspect, although he has plenty of company—elderly playboy Walter Humphrey Dexter, young playboy Anthony Proctor, lawyer Charlie Caminetti, showgirl Goldie La Douce, and even Doris Blue, Caminetti's secretary, who has a crush on Ole Monahan. Despite McAn's astute police work and Oliphant's complex theorizing, it remains for Ole to unravel the twisted skeins of the murders and further attempted homicides.

321. Bloch, Bertram, 1892-1987. *The only Nellie Fayle*; a novel. **New York: Doubleday, 1961. 287p.**

The novel studies the interrelationship of a number of people connected with the theater who are sojourning at a well-appointed dwelling on Long Island. Chief among those present are: Desmond Comfort, an English playwright in his middle years; his brother, Emmett, who is both a director and an actor and Nellie Fayle, an actress possessing a little talent but obviously ambitious, willing to do almost anything to get what she wants.

322. Blochman, Lawrence G., 1900-1975. *Rather cool for mayhem.* **Philadelphia: Lippincott, 1951. 208p.**

"Jim Lawrence had barely got back from the war in Europe before he was involved in murder. His old newspaper partner, Grace Boyd, had asked him up to the country [in Upstate New York] for a peaceful weekend. ... But instead of relaxing, he discovered the dead body of Dr. Norman [Grace had been considering him as a partner in marriage] in Grace's living room and from then on he found himself a primary suspect in a particularly puzzling crime. Who, for instance, had sent the invitations to a cocktail party, which had brought Grace's friends flocking to the house just in time for murder? And which of these unwanted guests had committed the crime? The clues are Grace's Leica camera, a broken audition record, and one of Dr. Norman's prescriptions, locked up in a Greenwich Village drugstore"—New York herald tribune books.

323. **Block, Barbara.** *Chutes and adders.* **New York: Kensington Books, 1994. 296p.**

Robin Light's pet store in Syracuse, New York shows little profit and her troubles increase when an employee dies after a poisonous snake strikes from a just opened package; the police find $50,000 stashed away in the store and make the assumption that Robin has been dealing illegally in rare animals. Robin herself comes across an additional bundle of cash ($20,000) in her apartment. Since she is suspect in the killing, Robin decides to do a little sleuthing of her own. Several unpleasant people cross her path and a neighbor falls to his death (pushed off his balcony). The Caribbean religion of Santeria that has found practitioners in cool Upstate New York has a significant role in the story.

324. ————. *The scent of murder.* **New York: Kenington Books, 1997. 323p.**

Robin Light is minding her pet shop in Syracuse, N.Y., when Amy Richmond, a street-wise girl, stumbles in seeking Robin's help. Amy is being pursued by the police and tells Robin that Murphy, Robin's late husband, had directed her to see Robin whenever in trouble. Amy flees and perplexed Robin learns that Amy is actually Murphy's daughter. Robin expects Amy to reappear, but happens on the body of Amy's legal father instead. Searching for Amy, Robin investigates three members of the girl's dysfunctional family: Brad, the deceased Murphy's brother and partner in the Syracuse Casket Company; Brad's son, Frank; and Charles, Murphy's son. Robin starts sorting out relationships and learning the reason why Amy is so far down and out.

325. ————. *Twister.* **New York: Kensington Books: 1995. 307p.**

Block's second novel about Syracuse, New York pet shop owner, Robin Light, finds her in trouble when an old friend, glamorous Lynn, asks Robin to come along as she meets 'this guy.' Lynn disappears for a while; when Robin sees her again Lynn is staring at a corpse. That there is something familiar about the deceased's face to Robin is confirmed when one of her former journalist's business cards is found in his pocket. Robin discovers the dead man had something to do with a murder that took place eight years ago; but why did he still have her card and what is Lynn's connection to him?

326. ————. *Vanishing act.* **New York: Kensington Books, 1998. 313p.**

Melissa Hayes has been missing for four months and her brother Bryan and their terminally ill mother are determined to find her. Bryan employs Syracuse pet shop owner and part-time detective Robin Light. Robin talks to college acquaintances of Melissa on the Syracuse campus; former roommates, boyfriend Tommy West, and professor of psychology Fell. All of them believe the death of Melissa's friend, Jill Evans, a year ago has a connection to Melissa's vanishing. In the course of her investigation Robin has a run-in with Tommy West's affluent father and learns that Tommy and Bryan have concealed some soiled linen.

Block, Rudolph Edgar, 1870-1940. See under his pseudonym: Lessing, Bruno, 1870-1940.

327. **Bloom, Amy, 1953- .** *Love invents us.* **New York: Random House, 1996. 205p.**
In the first two-thirds of the novel Elizabeth Taube of Great Neck, Long Island, is entering adolescence with little support or love from her upscale parents—her mother is an interior decorator; her father is an accountant. She receives instruction in sexuality from an old furrier and then has two love affairs: the first with Max Stone, a junior high English teacher; the second with Huddle Lester, black high school athletic star. Towards the novel's end Elizabeth is pictured as a mother in her middle years.

328. **Blunt, Elizabeth Lee, b. 1839.** *When folks was folks.* **New York: Cochrane Pub. Co., 1910. 174p.**
Life in central New York State ca. the 1850s is the author's focus as she describes in sketches and stories the daily routines of a small town's inhabitants. The training of the village's children ('it takes a whole community to raise a child') is taken very seriously, but there is time for amusements, gossip, readings and other literary pursuits, etc., after life-supporting labors are completed. One draws from the author's work a detailed picture of the manners and customs, the dress, and the furniture and other appurtenances of the various households.

329. *Bobbed hair,* **by twenty authors … New York: Putnam, 1925. vi, 357p.**
Contributors to this novel include George Barr McCutcheon, Alexander Woollcott, Elsie Janis, Carolyn Wells, Louis Bromfield, Edward Streeter, et al. It is a tale of high society, shop girls, bootleggers and others floating around New York City. The heroine is an American girl faced with the dilemma of choosing between two lovers or losing an inheritance. She uses a rather bizarre disguise in order to delay the news of her final choice.

330. **Bodenheim, Maxwell, 1893-1954.** *Crazy man.* **New York: Harcourt, Brace, 1924. 238p.**
"The crazy hero [John Carley] … is very close kin to the 'Blackguard' [Carl Felman of Chicago] who gave the title to Mr. Bodenheim's former novel. Both are absolute idealists and both are, by ordinary standards, criminals. Both, rejecting utterly the ordinary definitions of success, happiness and virtue, test all things by purely internal criteria, and both gain their livelihood by thievery—going on the theory that such a process is not morally wrong in a society where the distinction between legitimate commercial operations and

stealing is merely legal, and that the periods which they are compelled to spend in jail are less irksome and less destructive of their integrity than the hypocrisy and compliance necessary to gain 'an honest living'—Literary review of the New York evening post. John Carley and his girl friend, Selma Thallinger, who works in a dime-a-dance joint, the 'Merry Grotto', experience in full measure 'the ugliness of city life and the bleakness of city hopes' (as represented primarily by New York City)—See Moore, Jack B. Maxwell Bodenheim, New York, c1970.

331.   ————. *Naked on roller-skates*; a novel. New York: H. Liveright, 1930. **279p.**

"A fifty-six-year-old adventurer, Terry Barberlit, who at the opening of the story is peddling snake-oil in a Connecticut village, meets Ruth Riatt, promising widow of twenty-four, who wants to see life in the raw. She makes Terry take her with him to New York City where, in Harlem speakeasies and kindred underworld danger-spots Ruth does some slack-rope experimenting. Finally, somewhat bruised and battered, and having had her fill of wild life, she roller-skates back to the waiting arms of Terry"—Book review digest.

332.   ————. *Ninth Avenue.* New York: Boni & Liveright, 1926. **267p.**

"In spite of occasional lapses into physical intimacy with men who took her out, Blanche Palmer of Hell's Kitchen, Ninth Avenue, New York, keeps her vague dream of a mate finer than they, finer than herself, and refuses to marry either the half-educated Jew or the flashy vaudeville actor who offer themselves. Her family is no help to spiritual progress (or any other), and leaving home Blanche gets in with some Greenwich Villagers, smooths out her grammar and starts to write. At a cabaret in Harlem she meets a young poet and falls in love with him without knowing that he is part Negro. Both Blanche and Eric suffer acutely. When the book closes, their problem, though temporarily settled, is not solved"—Book review digest.

333.   **Bogardus, Mary.** *Crisis in the Catskills.* **Cornwallville, N.Y.: Hope Farm Press, 1976. 287p.**

A well-written historical novel whose theme is the anti-rent troubles of 1844-1846 in Delaware County in particular and eastern New York State in general. The hero is Ed O'Connor, a young farmer, swindled out of 'leased' land he had improved by the devious Judge Hathaway. Nevertheless Ed joins the moderate faction of the tenants fighting the landlords (many of them absentees) and their often-corrupt agents. However the murder of Sheriff Osman Steele at an eviction sale sets off a vengeful outcry against the tenant farmers and Ed and his friend Jon Van Steenburgh are arrested and accused of Steele's murder. The judge presiding at their trial, Amasa Parker, twists the law to suit his pro-landlord/establishment prejudices; Ed and Jon are found guilty and sentenced to be hanged. Governor Silas Wright commutes the sentence to life imprisonment. Shortly thereafter John Young wins the State's governorship and the many hundreds of imprisoned anti-renters, including Ed and Jon, are released.

334. Bogart, Clara Loring. *Emily; a tale of the Empire State*. **Ithaca, N. Y.: Printed by Andrus & Church, 1894. 245p.**

Farm life in central New York of a century ago (part of the story takes place in Ithaca). Emily Allen's parents are hard-pressed to meet mortgage payments on their land and she hires out to relieve them of some of their financial burden. Arthur Benson, a neighbor, has long been in love with Emily, but his alcoholism forms a barrier between the two. In the city where Emily is servant of all work to the Watson family, Arthur finally loses his battle with strong drink and dies. Years later Emily becomes a professional nurse and finds love with Horace Blackman, a young merchant who has left the ministry because of his aversion to certain orthodox doctrines that he would have to accept for ordination.

Bogue, Mrs. A. H., 1867-1929. See: Bell, Lilian Lida, 1867-1929.

Boisgilbert, Edmund, M. D., pseud. See: Donnelly, Ignatius, 1831-1901.

335. Boston, Ivy May, b. 1879. *Rebels in bondage*. **Illustrated by Amy Hogeboom. New York: Longmans, 1938. ix, 234p.**

Rather innocently caught up in the Monmouth Rebellion of 1685 in England, two girls are transported to the American colonies to work as bond servants for a Dutch patroon whose estate is near Albany.

336. Bond, Alexander Russell, 1876. *With the men who do things*. **New York: Munn, 1913. xiii, 275p.**

The observations and experiences of two schoolboys whose summer vacation is spent in and around New York City with the builders of the subways and high-rise structures. The engineering details in this work of fiction are as accurate as the writer's research can make them.

337. Bonnell, James Francis. *Death over Sunday*. **New York: Scribner, 1940. 248p.**

A Greek blackmailer (Damatos) is murdered in a Long Island villa while a weekend party is in progress. One of the guests, lawyer Mike Powel, digs up enough evidence to single out the guilty individual.

338. Bonner, Charles, 1896-. *The Fanatics*. **New York: Mohawk Press, 1932. 309p.**

The Canterbury family of a small town in New York State in the early years of the 20th century has a positive, upbeat approach to life. But when a man named Spooner, a pinched, intolerant preacher appears, his rabid conservatism in matters of morals and religion produces divisions between the Canterburys and the villagers.

339. Bonner, Geraldine, 1870-1930. *The Black Eagle mystery*. **Illustrated by**

Frederic Dorr Steele. New York: Appleton, 1916. 308p.

"Hollings Harland, a wealthy New York corporation lawyer, commits suicide by jumping from the eighteenth story of the Black Eagle building. The act follows his quarrel with Johnston Barker, the copper pool magnate. The pool breaks and Johnston Barker disappears. A suspicion of foul play causes the office of Wilbur Whitney to take up the case. Molly Morgenthau Babbits, 'the girl at the central', is again employed, together with her husband (a reporter), Jack Reddy (Mr. Whitney's assistant), and others. The mystery turns on the relation of the beautiful young Miss Carol Whitehall, manager of the Azalea Woods Estates, to both Harland and Barker, her office being directly below that of the murdered man. There is a plot within plot and sensation after sensation until the final surprise … of finding Harland alive in Canada, the self-confessed murderer of Barker"—Book review digest.

340. **Bonner, Geraldine 1870-1930.** *The book of Evelyn.* **With illus. by Arthur Brown. Indianapolis: Bobbs-Merrill, 1913. 339p.**

The young widow Evelyn Drake comes back to New York City after what has been a brief and unfortunate marriage. She becomes reacquainted with an old friend, Roger Clement of Gramercy Park; their friendship is deepening into something more intimate when Roger suddenly falls in love with Miss Harris, a singer. Oddly enough Evelyn has knowledge of a dark, disturbing secret in Miss Harris' past; her failure to pass it on to Roger is almost devastating in regard to her own future.

341. **Bonney, Joseph L.** *Death by dynamite*; a Simon Rolfe mystery. **New York: Carrick & Evans, 1940. 269p.**

"Simon Rolfe, criminologist, [has a method] based on 'psychological logic'— a system of pure reason buttressed by elementary psychological and behavioristic truths 'instantly comprehensible to the layman.' Now forget it and see if you can figure out who caused the fatal explosion in the Diamond Room, a cavern on the Long Island estate of Arthur Engelsted, a retired chemist, a place full of problem youths and Professor Emilio Delcastro, a spiritualist. Four main suspects, a green elephant, and a startling solution, to put it mildly, by the aforesaid master mind"—New York herald tribune books.

342. **Borden, Mary.** *Flamingo*, a novel. Garden City, N.Y.: Doubleday, Page, 1927. 418p.**

"The story has to do with a 'group of English people who are on their way to America, and with a group of Americans. This dozen or so of men and women are drawing together as the result of some cause that is obscure; some complicated delicate interplay of forces perhaps beyond the stars, some pattern of small accident.' New York is the magnet. The hero, Peter Campbell, is an architect of ideals and imagination who has caught a vision of the city as a modern Babylon of skyscrapers with sharp towers cutting the sky"—Book review digest. The characters undergo various crises and romances, which fade quickly and pass into obscurity.

343. Boris, Martin, 1930- . *Woodridge, 1946.* **New York: Crown Publishers, 1980p. 273p.**

A Catskill resort town is the setting for a tale of three people, Arlene, Phil and Andy, who have difficulty deciding who they love while the people in the village observe the odd triangle that develops. Phil is the servile, henpecked husband of the shrewish Arlene; she latches onto Andy, a war hero, with Phil accepting the situation since he figures Andy will soon tire of the demanding Arlene. Strangely enough it is Arlene who breaks off with Andy, finally appreciating the patient Phil. By this time, however, Phil realizes he doesn't need Arlene anymore. The writer evokes the aura of a Catskill small town and tosses in a teenage love affair to balance the shenanigans of the elders.

344. Bosch, Mrs. Herman. *Bridget.* **New York: B.W. Dodge, 1908. 390p.**

Bridget Burke is a hefty, fetching Irish lass freshly arrived at Ellis Island and seeking employment in the metropolis. The wife of a liquor merchant hires her; after this first experience she is employed as a cook and continues to advance to better paying jobs. Bridget is not always a model of competency or understanding; in fact she gets into some embarrassing if humorous situations, but she has resiliency, does not take herself too seriously, is good-natured, and is able to survive in this strange city.

345. Bosher, Kate Lee Langley, 1865-1932. *The man in Lonely Land.* **New York: Harper, 1912. 181p.**

At the age of forty New Yorker Winthrop Laine is still a bachelor, having searched in vain for a woman he will feel comfortable marrying. This changes when Claudia Keith drops in on his sister. In Claudia, Winthrop joyfully recognizes a lady who can convert his romantic hopes into reality, and then New York will no longer be a lonely place.

346. Boswell, Barbara, 1946- . *Red velvet.* **New York: Jove Books, 1995. 393p.**

The sale of his shares in the Everly Wine Company of Upstate New York by the late Willard Everly stuns the winery's acting president, Sierra Everly, Willard's grandniece. The buyer is Nicholas (Nick) Nicholi of the Security Investment Corporation. Sierra offers to buy back Nick's shares, but he will not budge. Troubles mount: Sierra's teenage sister vanishes; heavy rains may irreparably damage the grapes; the temperature gauges in the wine cellar are altered; and Nick, working with the winery's outdated computer, comes across fiscal chicanery. Brittle tempers flare and the main characters search for solutions to the winery's problems.

347. Botkin, Gleb, 1900- . *The baron's fancy.* **Garden City, N.Y.: Doubleday, Doran, 1930. 308p.**

"How Baron Maximilian Nikolaevich von Waldenscherna escaped from the Bolshevists and came to New York to earn his living as a painter; how he became the confidential adviser to the Duchess Alexandra, claimant to the

Romanoff throne; and how he preferred to marry the charming Nancy of the titian hair rather than the Duchess"—Book review digest.

348. Boutcher, Esther Penny. *Manowen.* **New York: Duell, Sloan & Pearce, 1951. 338p.**

The adventures of a 14-year-old orphan, Owen Gwynedd, who leaves a Virginia Tidewater plantation soon after the Civil War and makes a new home with his Uncle Pel on 'Manocc Island' off the coast of Long Island. Uncle Pel's estate carries the name—Manowen, and here Owen forms friendships with a half-breed Monatuk Indian lad and a girl, Ysel. His rompos with these two companions end when he is enrolled at Sag Harbor Academy and later goes whaling with Captain Penny of the ship 'Alive-O.'

349. Bouton, John Bell, 1830-1909. *The Enchanted*; **an authentic account of the strange origin of the new Psychical Club. New York: Cassell Pub. Co., 1891. 283p.**

"Mr. Gustavus Adolphus Swann was an incorporator of the Hailfellows Club of New York. He had been a member for twenty years when he died. Immediately after his death several of his associates were stricken with fear at the sight of Uncle Gus's ghost in the clubrooms. Out of this incident grew a psychical experiment of Meldrum and Wadlow. By their methods they are enabled to witness the literary phenomena which is told in the story, and to their efforts may be traced the origin of a club whose enrolled members are a select few fitted by nature to belong to the 'Enchanted'"—Annual American catalogue.

350. ———. Round the block. *An American novel.* **New York: D. Appleton, 1864 [c1863]. 468p.**

Three bachelors in New York City of the 1850s share an apartment—bookish Marcus Wilkeson, retired Wall Street broker; Fayette Overtop, lawyer and philosopher; Matthew Maltboy, 'fat and calm', also a lawyer with an eye for any comely female. Their immediate neighbors, old Eliphalet Minford, mechanic and inventor, and his ward Patty ('Pet') are of special interest to Marcus who gives them financial and educational support. An accusatory anonymous letter leads to a quarrel between Marcus and Minford; the latter's sudden death casts suspicion on Marcus. However Minford's death is proved to be accidental. Pet, who had disappeared for a while, turns out to be Marcus's niece, the daughter of his deceased brother Aurelius. The love affairs of Fayette Overtop and Matthew Maltboy form one of the novel's subplots. In the end only Overtop takes a wife—Miss Pillbody whose private school Pet had attended. Marcus is jolted by the discovery of his kinship to Pet, but his beloved books solace the bibliophile.

351. Bowline, Charley. *The iron tomb*; **or,** *The mock count of New York*, **a local** *tale.* **Boston: G.H. Williams, 1852. 100p. (in double columns).**

The story begins at the Astor House in August 1851. 'Count' Norand le Chandau, adventurer and recent escapee from a French prison (a galley), lays plans to woo and marry Carolina, daughter of wealthy merchant Edgar Raymond. He has a rival in Elbert, a struggling doctor. Despite her father's preference for the Count, Carolina accepts Elbert's marriage proposal. The spurned Count vows vengeance. With the assistance of dissipated, ne'er-do-well Conrad Daring he poisons the medicine the doctor has prescribed for ailing Carolina. She 'dies' and is interred in 'the iron tomb'. Body snatchers enter the tomb and take Carolina's body to unsuspecting Elbert and his assistant for dissection. Elbert recognizes his fiancée and she miraculously returns to life. The bogus count, tracked down by his Parisian nemesis, Jean Harra, ends up in a vault where he expires from starvation and the attacks of voracious rats. The repentant, reformed Daring becomes an engineer on one of the Hudson River boats.

352. **Box, Edgar, pseud.** *Death likes it hot.* **New York: Dutton, 1954. 187p.**
P.C. Sargeant III, a public relations man and part-time sleuth from New York City, is at a house party on Long Island, which is also attended by Social Register and artistic types. It falls on Sargeant's shoulders to use whatever deductive skills he possesses to track down the individual responsible for a murder committed during the 'festivities.' The author takes the opportunity to comment sarcastically and bitingly on the foibles of the guests.

353. **Boyce, Burke, 1901- .** *The perilous night*; a novel. **New York: Viking Press, 1942. 560p.**
"Historical novel of New York State during the Revolution. The Hudson Valley of the region across from West Point is the locale, where both patriots and Tories have their prosperous farms. Asa Howell, his two grown sons and his lovely daughter Tempy Ann, with her attendant, swains, are the central characters"—Book review digest.

354. **Boyce, Neith, b. 1872.** *The bond.* **New York: Duffield, 1908. 426p.**
A young couple, members of New York City's artistic, literary and intellectual bohemian clique, decide to marry. However, being bohemians, they make a pact allowing each to do his or her 'thing' without reference to the other. This works to the benefit of both for some years, and then debts and children disrupt their carefree existence. Jealousy too rears its ugly head and tragedy looms on the horizon.

355. **Boyd, Dean [Wallace].** *More than welcome.* **New York: Harcourt Brace & World, 1963. 218p.**
Bee Preminger, a widow, offers her services as a welcome wagon hostess in the Westchester County (N.Y.) village where she lives with her twin teen-age sons. Her duties turn out to be more challenging than she had anticipated when she encounters a womanizing bachelor (more honorable than most), a

trade delegation from Africa, East German refugees, a rich toy manufacturer, and a surprisingly diverse collection of suburban characters.

Boyden, Emma. See under her pseudonym: Dare, Arline.

356. [Boyesen, Hjalmar Hjorth] 1848-1895. *A daughter of the philistines.* Boston: Roberts Bros., 1883. 325p.

Mrs. Hampton has persuaded her rich husband, Zeke, to take the family from its confining Western surroundings to New York City where she hopes to rise to the top echelons of society. The beauty of her daughter Alma, the 'heroine' of this novel, is an enabling factor toward this goal. Alma is a shallow individual who will probably always be one of the 'Philistines', but she surprisingly rejects the most eligible bachelor in New York, marries the decent, idealistic Harold Wellingford, and drops out of 'society.' Her brother Walter is a cad who seduces quiescent Rachel, daughter of Wall Street broker Simon Loewenthal. When Zeke Hampton loses his fortune, Simon is in large part responsible. After Zeke dies Mrs. Hampton decamps to Paris with funds she herself has earned from Wall Street manipulations.

357. ————. *The golden calf*; a novel. Meadville, PA.: Flood & Vincent, Chautauqua Century Press, 1892. 230p.

When Oliver Tappan comes to New York City to fulfill his 'destiny', still retaining the ideals that spring from his New England upbringing and the admonitions of his German mentor, Dr. Habicht, it is not long before he is caught up in the city's vitality and starts on the track of the American measure of success, money/power. Carter, the president of the railway firm that employs Oliver, offers him a position, which eventually leads to lobbying in Washington and Oliver's climb to wealth. Oliver has long since forgotten the girl, Mina, he left behind in New England and marries the railway president's niece, Madeline, a cold, loveless woman, purposeful only in her encouragement of Oliver's worldly achievements. The starkly colorful New York that Boyesian describes has a disturbing impact on the innocent newcomer; it and Washington become the familiar fields of Oliver's corrupting accomplishments.

358. ————. *The mammon of righteousness.* New York: United States Book Co., 1891. x, 386p.

It is not difficult to detect a resemblance between the university at 'Tarryville' in central New York State that the millionaire Obed Larken founds and endows and Cornell University. Obed has two nephews, Alexander (Aleck) and Horace Larkin who have quite different outlooks. Both are lawyers, but Aleck abandons the legal profession to become a writer in New York City after he discovers Horace using the law firm to advance his political ambitions. Horace, of course, is geared for 'success' and marries the wealthy Kate Van Schaak as an ally. Gertrude, adopted daughter of Obed Larkin, leaves the dictatorial Obed and goes to New York City to help, unsuccessfully as it turns out, her drug-addicted real mother. The marriage of Horace and Kate is an unhappy one, although both are still striving to establish Horace in diplomacy and/or politics. Gertrude and Aleck fall in love, marry, and face an uncertain future.

359. ————. *Social strugglers*; a novel. **New York: Scribner, 1893. 299p.**

Mr. Peleg Lemmuel Bulkley, a Westerner with a fortune from his tailoring firm, comes to New York City with his wife and three daughters in search of social affluence. At first ignored by their fashionable neighbors, the Bulkleys gradually secure recognition through chance and the leverage of Mr. Bulkley's wealth. His daughter Maud is the heroine; she is caught up in the superficialities of New York and Long Island society, and is almost at the point of marrying the penniless, irresponsible gentleman, Fanchley, when 'rescued' by a growing interest in the work with the poor that has become the passion of Philip Warburton, the hero a 'former member' of the aristocracy. Like Warburton, Maud casts aside the shallowness of polite society, joins his mission and is proposed to by Warburton.

360. **Boyle, T. Coraghessan, 1948- .** *World's end*; a novel. **New York: Viking Press, 1987. 456.**

This book "chronicles the interlocked destinies of three families in the Hudson Valley of New York. In the 17th century, when the area was still under Dutch rule, the Van Warts were wealthy landowners; the Van Brunts were tenant farmers and the Mohawks indigenous Indians whose claim to the land had been brutally shoved aside. ... By 1949 Depuster Van Wart is a powerful manufacturer; Truman Van Brunt is part of a group of left-wing activists whose attempt to organize a peaceful festival end up in a night of ... anti-communist rioting. ... Amid rumors that he betrayed his comrades to Van Wart, Truman abandons his child, Walter, and disappears in the aftermath of the riot"—New statesman & society.

361. **Boynton, Charles Brandon, 1806-1883.** *Isobel Wilton*; or *The Oswegatchie's captive*. **A tale of the French War. Canton, N.Y.: Northern Cabinet Office, 1843. 25p. (in double columns).**

In 1760, on the east bank of the Hudson some few miles from Albany, Colonel Wilton's daughter Isobel, loved by both John Johnson, Sr. William's son, and Lt. Harry Bradford of the colonial Rangers, is kidnapped by Untekahyo, war chief of the Oswegatchie Indians. The latter intends to make Isobel his wife, but French commandant Montmartre a takes her away from Untekahyo. Harry Bradford, accompanying Lord Jeffrey Amherst's expedition to northern New York, is sent with the vengeful Untekahyo to spy on the French forces. Montmartre and his aide, Antoine St. Martin who have Isobel with them, discover them. Untekahyo slays Colonel Montmartre and is about to kill Isobel when Harry and St. Martin combine to end Untekahyo's life. Captured by the French, Harry (with Isobel) is aided in his escape by Antoine St. Martin. Bradford and Isobel go back to Albany to marry. Harry's real identity is revealed by the 'father', Dick Bradford, who adopted Harry after a shipwreck had left him alone in the world.

362. Brace, Ernest. *Commencement.* **New York: Harper, 1924. 366p.**

"Gregory Thrumn, good-looking and an idealist, graduates from college with scholastic honors, a fiancée, a prospective job and a thousand dollar check. With these assets he starts his business career as a copywriter for the Blooker Advertising Agency [in New York City]. His first ad is so successful that his employer increases his salary. Then comes a slump in his work, which results in his being discharged. Leonora Prail, his fiancée, an attractive and extravagant girl, calmly breaks her engagement with this man of no prospects. Gregory finally opens a bookshop and marries Georgia Rossby, a former stenographer in the Blooker concern. The bookshop is a miserable failure and Gregory, desperate lest he lose the love and respect of Georgia, tries again to write the ad upon which he was working when he left the agency. Upon presenting it to Mr. Blooker he is given his position again—and the future for Gregory and Georgia looks bright"—Book review digest.

363. Brackett, Charles, 1892-1969. *Weekend.* **New York: McBride, 1925. 157p.**

A blossoming author attending a Long Island weekend gathering of intellectuals, or at least would-be intellectuals, is advised by the 'knowledgeable' (?) Mrs. Pendarvis, the hostess, as follows: "About this book of yours. Have it light—if you would have it clutch the heart occasionally it might be wise. Don't have a plot. Just use anecdotes. If you can't think up the right ones, why not go to some Frenchman or Italian?As to style, keep one eye on [Aldous] Huxley, and you might just glance at [Ronald] Firbank. The soupçon of decadence." Is that a palatable formula for his creation?

364. Bradbury, Bianca, 1908 or 9-1982. *Mike's island.* **Illustrated by Charles Geer. New York: Putnam, 1959. 128p.**

An isolated island in Long Island Sound calls forth the adventurous spirits of Mike and Ned, two boys on vacation with their parents. A girl whom they reluctantly allow to join them interrupts the exploration of this piece of land. She proves to be a capable helpmate who can hold her own in just about any task. By vacation's end Mike has assurance from the island's owner that he and his friends can use the island in perpetuity so long as they clear away flotsam that washes up on it.

Bradbury, Osgood, fl. 1844-1865. *The banker's victim*; or, *The betrayed seamstress.* **See Item #369.**

365. [Bradbury; Osgood] fl. 1844-1865. *Ellen Grant*; or, *Fashionable life in New York.* **By the author of Emily Mansfield, Mary Beach, & c., & c. New York: Dick and Fitzgerald [184-?]. 117, [1] p. (in double columns).**

Seduction, illegitimacy, prostitution—this triad is the theme of the author's tale; the subtitle 'fashionable life in New York', is a misnomer. The two primary villains are men of medicine—the licentious Dr. Hooker and the quack Dr. Boyden (alias Francis Dermot when he posed as a Methodist preacher). Ellen Grant is a prostitute seeking vengeance on her seducer Boyden/Dermot. Dr. Hooker has high hopes of seducing and marrying wealthy Catharine Watson, but first he must rid himself of his meek wife (which he accomplishes with a poisoned potion). Honest, good-hearted Tom Turner is the *deus* ex *machina* who unveils the doctors' secrets and malefactions; he also takes under his protection the young women (and their offspring) who have been victimized by the villains. It is, of course, inevitable that the miscreants should suffer the severest penalties for their actions. The last 25 pages of this potboiler are given over to 'Edwin's novel', Edwin Gordon being a rejected suitor for Catharine Watson's hand.

366.   ————. *Ellen: the pride of Broadway.* **New York: F.A. Brady [1865]. 103p. (in couble columns).**

A Maine girl, motherless and illegitimate Ellen Holmes, is persuaded by 'Colonel Beaufort' on the promise of marriage to accompany him to New York City. Lodged in the procuress Mrs. Tetford's boarding house, Ellen is informed of Beaufort's real identity by young Fairchild, a man-about-town. 'Beaufort' is James Turner, Broadway saloon owner with a wife and children. Ellen enters New York's demi-monde, becomes Fairchild's mistress and inherits his apartment and a small amount of money after the dissipated Fairchild's death. She then meets Charles Moreton, a fiftyish bachelor with high moral and religious standards. It soon becomes apparent to both that Moreton is Ellen's biological father. They form a strong bond, tour Europe together, and after Moreton's death Ellen, his heir, the former 'pride of Broadway', now 34, has the wherewithal to embark on a life devoted to helping innocent young women avoid the pitfalls of urban life.

367.   ————. *Emily, the beautiful seamstress*; or, *The danger of the first step.* **A story of life in New York. Boston: G.H. Williams, 1853. 100p. (in double columns).**

Emily is the target of Major Borland, a married roué, who wants to make her his mistress; she is befriended by Charles Colburne, a kindly bachelor, who hopes to adopt and educate her. With his help Emily is able to escape the plot of Borland and his confederate Job Snyder to enmesh her in a life of prostitution. The Major is confronted by Mary Dillingham, a young woman he had seduced and left with child. Shamed before his wife and daughter he begs for forgiveness. Colburne eventually marries Emily despite the wide disparity in their ages.

368.   ————. *The gambler's league*; or, *The trials of a country maid.* **By the author of *The mutineer.* New York: R.M. De Witt [1857?] 99p. (in double columns).**

Mrs. Powell and her daughter Caroline select a servant girl at the New York Intelligence Office. The girl's name is Grace Manton. Grace impresses all who get to know her (especially Caroline Powell) with her Christian virtues;

she also draws the attention of the vile Clarkson Hamilton—an alias for Andrew Rawdon—who hopes to seduce her. But evil Hamilton/Rawdon is won over by Grace's simple faith. Grace is able to convince him to marry Arabella Wheaton, a courtesan still in love with him despite his ill usage of her. Poor Grace loses her position in the Powell household when she is accused of stealing pieces of the family's silverware. Destitute Grace arouses the pity of two 'girls of the town'; she dies before two Methodist missionary ladies can offer more substantial aid. Andrew and Arabella Rawdon are deeply saddened when they hear of Grace's passing as are Caroline Powell and her parents, the latter realizing how mistaken they were setting Grace adrift in a cruel New York City.

369. ————. *Jane Clark*; or, *Scenes in metropolitan life.* **A tale descriptive of New York scenes. Boston: G.H. Williams, 1855. 100p. (in double columns).**

Reissued in 1857 under the title: *The banker's victim*; or, *The betrayed seamstress* (New York: R.M. De Witt). New York City as here represented is a lure for young women who too often fall into the snares set by unprincipled, libidinous men. Jane Clark, a maker of parasol covers, catches the eye of Colonel Mellen, a Wall Street broker who, although already married, promises to wed Jane. She falls in love with the Colonel, is seduced, and only learns of his false promises through Julia Sandford, a prostitute who has murdered her former lover. Mrs. Mellen, her daughter Ida, and an honest mason, George Stedman (once in love with Jane), have also discovered the Colonel's duplicity. The Colonel ultimately dies of brain fever—but not before he has made substantial payments to Jane. George Stedman and Ida Mellen marry, while Jane Clark and Julia Sandford retire to their native New Hampshire to live together as spinsters and as dispensers of good works for the needy.

370. ————. *Louise Kempton*; or, *Vice and virtue contrasted.* **Boston: F. Gleason, 1844. 66p.**

Sequel to Bradbury's *The mysteries of Boston.* Louise Kempton continues her immoral ways in New York City, driving her lover, Charles Raymond, to a drunkard's death after she has freely drawn on his funds, and then living with a young fortune hunter, George Tudor, of whom she soon tires. Louise dispatches Tudor with a quick knife thrust and weathers a jury inquest. The virtuous Alice Jane, Louise's sister, comes to New York and vainly pleads with Louise to reform. In the end Louise, haunted by the murder of George Tudor, bursts into Alice Jane's wedding in Boston and commits suicide before the startled guests. One surmises that Bradbury is painting New York City as a place where 'sin' is a more common occurrence than it is in staid Boston.

371. ————. *Lucelle*; or *The young Iroquois!* **A tale of the Indian wars. Boston: H.L. Williams, 1845. 75p. (in double columns)**

Eighteen-year-old Lucelle de la Motte lives with her father on the shores of Lake Champlain, 'within a cannon shot of Ticonderoga.' Although her father is neutral in the conflict between British and French for control of North America, Lucelle sides with the French who are besieged at Fort Ticonderoga by General Amherst. Lucelle's constant companion is Turok, a young Iroquois who is in love with her. French officer Lieutenant Delano bedazzles Lucelle with his offer of marriage and a life in Paris. But Delano is a proven coward who deserts to the British. After the French abandon Ticonderoga Delano murders Lucelle's father (he is rumored to possess a large fortune) and attempts to ravish Lucelle. Turok appears and kills Delano. Lucelle puts aside her earlier prejudices and marries Turok.

372. ————. *The modern Othello*; or, *The guilty wife: a thrilling romance* of *New York fashionable life.* **By the author of Ellen Grant. New York: R.M. De Witt, 1855. 84p. (in double columns).**

The author displays his disdain for the excesses of "what is called fashionable life" in New York City. In contrast to the licentiousness of Catherine (Catten) Forrsteer and her even more dissolute sister, Margaret Lureies, is the virtuous behavior of beautiful, wealthy Etty Leach who bestows her love on a promising but as yet unproven young lawyer, Charles Armstrong. The two first-named women are followers of Amelia Bloomer, the women's rights advocate; both are married yet feel free to take lovers of their own choosing outside the marriage bond. Mrs. Forrsteer's husband, Irvine, a prominent thespian, divorces her; she receives a generous settlement and enters upon a stage career of her own. Bradbury sporadically makes quite clear his antifeminist opinions; presumably Bloomerism and sexual misconduct are intertwined in his judgment.

373. ————. *Therese*; or, *The Iroquois maiden.* **A tale of New York City and of forest life. Boston: G.H. Williams, 1852. 100p. (in double columns).**

While stationed in the Plattsburgh-Lake Champlain region of northern New York during the War of 1812 three cowardly Americans, Captain Edwin Dashford, scout Job Bellows and Corporal Michael Quin, desert and kidnap half-Indian, half-French Therese, taking her to New York City. In pursuit are Dashford's superior officer, Major Rockwell and the Vermonters Victor Gravel and Hugh Fitzgerald. The three win Therese's release. Mrs. Dashford is grief stricken by her son's behavior although her daughter Emily is not too astonished by her brother's actions. Another surprise in store for Mrs. Dashford is that Therese is the daughter of her sister, Therese Corveille, and the Indian Tomus. Bellows is slain by Tomus, Quin is imprisoned and Emily Dashford and Major Rockwell marry. Edwin Dashford finds redemption in Cuba; Therese marries a French planter there.

374. **Braden, James Andrew, b. 1872.** *Little Brother of the Hudson*; a tale of the **lost Eries. With illus. by Pitt L. Fitzgerald. New York: Harper, 1928. viii, 279p.**

In the mid-1600s Alvin Fairlea, most of whose youthful years have been spent on the banks of the Hudson River, is sent by his parents to Rensselaer[wyck] to pick up supplies. His treacherous Pequot companion, Pokop, suddenly attacks him to gain a lottery ticket that he believes contains magical powers. Alvin manages to overpower Pokop but flees the scene and wanders westward to the land of the Senecas and finally to the Cuyahoga River, the 'Little Brother of the Hudson', and friendship with the Erie Indians who inhabit this area of northern Ohio. War between the Senecas and Eries breaks out. As the conflict rages from the western borders of New York to Erie country Alvin is caught in the middle, but after the decimation of the Eries in 1654 he finds his way back to the Fairlea farm.

375. **Bradley, Mary Emily Neely, 1835-1898.** *Martha's mistake.* **New York: Hunt & Eaton, 1894. 348p.**

Martha is bored with the humdrum quality of her existence in the New York City apartment she shares with her family. The extravagant life style of a girl next door arouses jealousy, but another look confirms Martha's suspicion that this girl, with her dilatory, lackadaisical attitude is not a model to be copied. Then one day Martha picks up a lost pocketbook, uses some of the money found in it and then returns it to the owner anonymously. This was probably not the best way to handle this particular situation; temptation impelled her to spend money that did not belong to her and perhaps she should have identified herself when she did return the purse. But indirectly the affair worked out satisfactorily, ultimately sowing seeds of her satisfaction and peace of mind.

376. **Bradley, Mary Hastings, d. 1976.** *The innocent adventuress.* **New York: Appleton, 1921. 244p.**

"Maria Angelina Santonini, beautiful daughter of an ancient Italian family, is sent to relatives in America to retrieve fallen fortunes by a rich marriage and to leave the field clear for her unattractive sister Julietta. Her inherited notions of propriety and chivalry suffer a rude shock when she is plunged into the freedom of American society life and she feels herself hopelessly compromised when she is lost in the Adirondacks with a millionaire admirer and forced to spend the night with him in a mountain shelter. She is rescued from her plight by a handsome young journalist whom she had met and viewed favorably on the day of her arrival in America and whom a recently acquired fortune enabled [him] to meet her material as well as her emotional needs"—Book review digest.

377. **Brady, Charles Andrew, 1912- .** *Viking summer.* **Milwaukee: Bruce Pub., 1956. ix, 200p.**

The placid life of a professor of English at a college in Buffalo and his family are thrown into jeopardy by a communist kidnapping plot, and into a state of wonder by a Viking legend and an Indian tale.

378. **Brady, Cyrus Townsend, 1861-1920.** *The corner in coffee.* **Illus. by Gordon H. Grant. New York: G.W. Dillingham, 1904. 298p.**

Elijah D. Tillotson, a civil engineer of 50, a rough and ready type that New York society frowns upon, still pursues Constance (Connie) Livingston, 35, a former belle and the owner of 10 million dollars. Against her brother Bertie's wishes and those of other relatives Connie looks upon Elijah favorably. Elijah has at least two rivals: the son of an English baronet and Mr. Cutter, a coffee broker. A corner on the coffee market is threatening Connie's fortune and Bertie is also in trouble as he speculates on the New York Stock Exchange. Will Elijah be the one who sets things aright?

379. ————. *The ring and the man: with some incidental relation to the woman.* **Illustrated by George Gibbs. New York: Moffat, Yard, 1909. vii, 369p.**

Gormley, 'the man', is a successful merchant, owner of one of the largest department stores in New York City. An interest in politics impels him to come forward as candidate for mayor, running as an independent. 'The ring', the political group that has the city's government in its grasp, is unpleasantly surprised by the generally favorable reaction to Gormley's candidacy. After several false starts the ring's detectives, hired to uncover something unsavory in Gormley's past, do latch on to a single event in his youth that might topple him. At the strategic moment an unanticipated declaration clears Gormley.

380. **Brady, James, 1928- .** *Further Lane*; a novel of the Hamptons. **New York: St. Martin's Press, 1997. 259p.**

Mr. Beecher Stowe is back on Long Island at the family hearth preparing an article on Hannah Cutting, local Hampton celebrity, when her corpse is found on the beach impaled by a stake. Stowe initiates his own investigation of the murder aided by book editor Alix Dunraven; Alix has been trying to locate the manuscript of Hannah's revealing autobiography. There are a number of East Hamptonites (the rich, the famous, even the 'working class') who might welcome Hannah's demise and Alix and Beecher study all of them.

381. ————. *Gin Lane*; a novel of Southampton. **New York: St. Martin's Press, 1998. 249p.**

The 'uppity' homeowners of Southampton, Long Island, are furious with disk jockey 'Cowboy' Dils and his innuendos, and he meets with several so-called 'accidents.' It is Memorial Day weekend and journalist Beecher Stowe and his lover, Lady Alix Dunraven, are in the neighborhood and cannot avoid being mixed up in the goings-on as celebrities, industrial executives, and aspiring socialites like Tom and Daisy Buchanan (their daughter is about to marry Viscount Albermarle) fill the scene.

381a. ————. *The house that ate the Hamptons.* **New York: St. Martin's Press//Dunne, 1999. 320p**

The residents of a sophisticated, wealthy Long Island community are not pleased with the lifestyles of some newly rich denizens. Led by their Congressman, Buzzy Portofino, the conservatives are especially 'put off' by a Texas oil baron who is planning a huge, garish house in their 'sacred' precincts. The story is narrated by journalist, Beecher Stowe with his girlfriend, Alix Dunraven. Among the personages who move through the story are the fictional Sammy Glique, a movie director and Dixie Ng, his Asian-

American consort, and several real-life characters, e.g., Ayn Rand, Kurt Vonnegut, George Plimpton, et al.

382. **Brainerd, Eleanor Hoyt, 1868-1942.** *Concerning Belinda.* **Illustrated by Harrison Fisher and Katharine N. Richardson. New York: Doubleday, Page, 1905. 193p.**

Belinda is the youngest and perhaps the least experienced teacher at a private school for girls in New York. However she quickly learns that her pupils represent an odd medley of dreams and wants: the stage-struck, the stickily sentimental, the fatalistic (one girl composes her last will and testament), the homesick (another student wills herself into anorexia in order to be sent home), et al.

383. **Brainerd, Norman, b. 1879.** *Winning his shoulderstraps*; or, *Bob Anderson at Chatham Military School.* **Illustrated by Frank Vining Smith. Boston: Lothrop, Lee & Shepard, 1909. xi, 330p.**

A military school story for boys who might be interested in the structured training offered by such institutions. 'Chatham' is located in northwestern New York State. Bob Anderson, the hero, along with four bosom friends, has a goal: to become an officer/leader in the school—realizing that his quest entails working much harder than most of his classmates.

Branson, Allegra, 1934-, joint author. *Frontiers aflame.* **See Item #2077.**

384. **Branson, H.C., ca. 1905-1981.** *The fearful passage.* **New York: Simon & Schuster, 1945. 249p.**

"John Brent, the private op who has been gaining quite an audience because of his aggressive normality, is summoned to a village not far from New York [City] to investigate the murder of an avant-garde poet and critic who seems to have been lowering the tone of the place considerably. After the customary number of good hot cups of tea, Brent picks out the guilty party, whose motive, by the way, it would be charitable to overlook"—New Yorker.

Brearley, William Henry, 1846-1909, joint author. *King Washington.* **See Item #3091.**

385. **Breckenridge, Gerald.** *The besieged*; a novel of present-day family life. **Garden City, N.Y.: Doubleday, Doran, 1937. 360p.**

The Graveses and the Lawrences are two Long Island families who are trying to weather the Great Depression. The snobbish Lawrences watch helplessly as their fortune melts away in Wall Street. The Graveses tend to remain fairly stable economically and emotionally. Colby Lawrence and Lewis Graves were in college when hard times came. Both took jobs: Lewis as a timekeeper on a construction project, Colby as a hotel night clerk. Colby gets into bootlegging and spends a year in jail—his courageous wife Helen stands by him.

386. Bredes, Don, 1947- . *Hard feelings.* **New York: Atheneum Publications, 1977. 377p.**

As a junior in a Long Island high school Bernie Hergruter is uncertain that he will last out the year. Adolescence is a particularly troubling time for him: he has seen his grade average dip sharply, he has lost his edge in his tennis game, and his family is squabbling interminably. And he is trying to dodge the school tough guy, which disrupts his so-called love life (he has three girlfriends to manipulate). Running away, which he does, is no solution—he must come back to confront his problems. Bernie tells his own story.

387. Breen, Charles P. *Love and the Twentieth Volunteers.* **Garden City, N.Y.: Doubleday, 1961. 259p.**

"George Wicker … has talked his suburban community into buying a new fire engine. It arrives. It is $55,000 worth of every boy's dream, and too good for 'Cus Bay', New York. So George and his friends appropriate it, careen around on back roads, and form a new Volunteer Company which barricades itself, and the new engine, in the firehouse, challenging wives, townspeople and society in general to come and get them. It is a semi-legal, successful revolt of the downtrodden male, full of the delights of hatching it, learning a whole new technical vocabulary, and the excitements of some wildly mismanaged fires"—Kirkus reviews.

388. Brenn, George J. *Voices.* **New York: Century Co., 1923. 317p.**

New York financier Warren Wilmer is so nervously distracted by voices over the telephone that bombard him everywhere day and night that he asks the telephone company to investigate. Its representative, Charles Fenwick, discovers that Wilmer and his two partners, Otis King and Pendleton Kirke, are so secretive that he is unable to garner information that might be useful from any of them. Then Pendleton Kirke dies mysteriously; although Fenwick is aware of how he died, he retains this data until he is prepared to spring it and resolve the mysterious happenings.

389. Breslin, Howard, 1912-1964. *The bright battalions.* **New York: McGraw-Hill, 1953. 325p.**

"The setting is the war between the French and the English that raged up and down Lakes Champlain and George during the years 1756 to 1759. The hero is Kevin O'Connor, an Irishman, fighting on the French side. Apart from the fighting … there are troubles with a corrupt French trader and with some venal French noblemen in Canada who are robbing the King's armies of supplies and building up considerable fortunes. And there is that romance. [The lovers] flounce back and forth, in and out of the battle scenes at tedious length. Finally for no conceivable reason except the approach of the book's end, [O'Connor's lady love] consents to marry him and does, providing the most dubious ending of recent fiction"—Saturday review of literature.

390. ————. *Shad run.* **New York: T.Y. Crowell, 1955. 276p.**

Lancey Quest, a Hudson River fisherman's daughter, is perplexed by the problem of choosing among her three suitors. The time is 1788 and two events are of particular interest to most of Lancey's contemporaries who live around Poughkeepsie, New York—ratification of the newly drawn up Federal Constitution and the run of shad in the Hudson River.

391. **Brick, John, 1922-1973.** *Captives of the Senecas.* **New York: Duell, Sloan & Pearce, 1964. 149p.**

During the American Revolution settlers in Upstate New York and along the Pennsylvania/New York border were in constant danger of Indian attack. Brick's novel intertwines fact and fiction and gives an excellent portrayal of Seneca Indian village life where one of the story's chief characters, a 17-year-old white boy, is taken, along with other captives, after an Indian raid.

392. ———. *Eagle of Niagara*; **the story of David Harper and his Indian captivity. Garden City, N.Y.: Doubleday, 1955. 253p.**

David Harper is a soldier in the Continental Army who is taken prisoner by the Mohawk chieftain, Joseph Brant. Harper develops a good deal of respect and admiration for Brant and his complete loyalty to the British crown. Other than Harper and Brant, two young women represent the female contingent, one a white damsel, the other a beautiful Indian girl.

393. ———. *Homer Crist*; **a novel of Highland County. New York: Farrar, Straus and Young, 1952. 255p.**

Homer Crist is a farm boy in 'Highland County' New York when the novel opens. It takes Crist through the years 1833 to 1872—from his rise in the profession of law to his election to the U.S. Congress. Bitter family quarrels, marital unhappiness and, of course, politics enter into the story.

394. ———. *The King's Rangers.* **Garden City, N.Y.: Doubleday, 1954. 290p.**

The novel gives the Tory viewpoint on the American Revolution. The main characters are soldiers in the King's Rangers, woodsmen of the Tory persuasion under the command of Captain Walter Butler, and the action takes place in the Mohawk Valley and other regions of Upstate New York. Dan Millard, born in the Mohawk Valley, is one of those who remains loyal to the British king, but he finally realizes that his cause is doomed and he must seek a new life for himself in Canada.

395. ———. *Panther Mountain.* **Garden City, N.Y.: Doubleday, 1958. 287p.**

Jim Geraghty lost his brother in the Civil War and Mrs. Geraghty, bemoaning the loss, places part of the responsibility on Jim. He leaves home and hits the road until he gains employment on an Upstate New York farm run by the Linquist family. It is there that he meets and bonds with Clara Linquist and Taylor, her illegitimate, moody son.

396. ———. *The raid.* **New York: Farrar, Straus & Young, 1951. 308p.**

The author takes up the incidents of the American Revolution that involved the forces of the American patriots vs. Captain Walter Butler's Rangers and his Indian allies under Joseph Brant (see also Brick's The King's Rangers). Jessica Currie is taken prisoner by Desmond of the King's Rangers on one of their raids in the Mohawk and Hudson Valleys. She bravely endures the ordeals of captivity while awaiting rescue by her husband.

397. ————. *The rifleman*; a novel. Garden City, N.Y.: Doubleday, 1953. 349p.
A novel based on the exploits of an actual, but little known, historical figure, Timothy Murphy, a marksman with Dan Morgan's Rifles. At the Battle of Saratoga it was his shot that ended the life of the gallant British general, Simon Fraser, who was rallying his troops for a counter-attack. Although illiterate, Timothy gains the attention of two beautiful women, one true to him, one false. When the Revolution is over, Timothy mills flour and is a local hero in the Schoharie Valley.

398. ————. *Tomahawk trail.* New York: Duell, Sloan & Pearce, 1962. 149p.
Matt Finch joins the American Revolutionary army with patriotic fervor; he has another reason for taking this step—to search for a girl the Seneca Indians have kidnapped. The Sullivan expedition into Iroquois country plays a prominent part in the story. Matt does locate the captured girl; the two of them encounter harrowing adventures as they take the long road back to friendly villages.

399. ————. *Troubled spring.* New York: Farrar, Straus, 1950. 279p.
"The story of a soldier's return from the Confederate prison at Andersonville and what he found in his postwar Hudson River town. Sam Bellnap had been reported dead, but came home to find his girl, Martha, married to his older brother and his staid old town blatant with war profits. In some chapters Sam reviews his ordeals in the prison camp, in others he faces his immediate problems, tries to be fair to Martha and his brother, sees that the best chance of happiness for all of them lies in his going away"—Christian science monitor.

400. Bricktop, pseud. *Smith in search of a wife.* Illustrated by Thos. Worth. New York: Collin & Small, 1876. 59p.
Reuben Smith of 'Yaphank', Long Island (a 'town not quite so well known as the name of Smith, but I will try and help Yaphank into prominence before this story is finished') "was a small farmer, poor, tall, homely as a broken gate, and an orphan." His search for a wife in Yaphank is fruitless. When he is unexpectedly left $20,000 by a forgotten aunt, Reuben gives away his decrepit farm to a poor woman and sets out for New York City, certain that his new-found wealth will attract a bevy of eligible young ladies. Feckless Reuben falls victim to various confidence games and a breach of promise suit. Shorn of a substantial portion of his inheritance Reuben returns to Yaphank, perhaps a little wiser; at long last he finds a soulmate in a Yaphank girl, Rebecca

Quilter, and the two are 'spliced' and begin their married life on the tidy little farm Reuben has purchased. "Reuben is all right enough now, but to his dying day he will never forget his experiences in searching for a wife."

401. —————. *The trip of the Porgie*; or, *Tacking up the Hudson*. **The sentiment and humor of events en route. New York: Collin & Small, 1874. 124p.**

The members of the Sardine Club are introduced, viz.: Gasper Finecut, president; Byron Bleat (pronounced Ble-at), vice-president; William Bitters, secretary; Tom Bubble, treasurer; John Stump—five, the total partnership. Their yacht, the Porgie, leaves New York City and proceeds by stages (or 'tacks') up the Hudson River to Albany. The various landmarks on the river's shores are described and pieces of their history related. Two of the 'mariners' fall for the charms of the fair sex when they go ashore hither and yon. On arriving in Albany the Sardine Club is feted at a dinner given by the Stuffed Club of the Capital City. Later the intrepid sailors attend a theatrical performance of the Stuffed Club—the presentation is entitled 'The Original Hudson'; or, Taken in and Done for'. The script of the play is given in full. And so the nautical adventures of the heroic five end, more or less.

402. —————. *A trip to Niagara Falls*. **New York: Collin & Small, 1876. 59p.**

From seaboard to Niagara Falls (400 miles) in a railroad drawing-room car—up the Hudson to Albany and then westward—Bricktop, 40, observes his fellow passengers. He then records the varying impressions the Falls themselves make on his fellow tourists—Yankees, Irishmen, Englishmen, an 'Irish Indian', et al. After his own survey of the American and Canadian sides of the Falls, Bricktop concludes 'that it was high time for me to get back to New York [City] again, the abode of still waters.'

403. *The Brigantine*; or, *Admiral Lowe*. **A tale of the 17th century. By an American. New York: Crowen & Decker, 1839. 201p.**

Scene: New York City (New Amsterdam or New-Orange) under Dutch rule in 1673. The heroine is Elvellynne DeMontford; Alderman Oolen Van Brooter is her guardian. The hero, Captain Charles La Vincent, a British naval officer who is in pursuit of Admiral Lowe, the pirate, secretly visits his ladylove, Elvellynne and is apprehended by Dutch officials (England and Holland are at war). Admiral Lowe frees La Vincent. The latter is allowed to reach his own vessel, the Greyhound, while Lowe, with Elvellynne by his side, rejoins his crew on the brigantine, The Merry-Christmas. After further escapades Admiral Lowe reveals himself to Elvellynne as her father, the banished Edward Hyde, Earl of Claredon. In a scuffle with the Dutch Hyde/Lowe is fatally wounded, but he oversees the marriage of Elvellynne and Charles La Vincent before he dies. Meanwhile the Anglo-Dutch War has ended.

404. [Briggs, Charles Frederick] 1804-1877. *The adventures of Harry Franco*; a **tale of the Great Panic. New York: F. Saunder, 1839. 2v.**

Harry leaves his Hudson Valley village for the big city, New York; he falls victim to the nefarious schemes of several new acquaintances and ships out as a common seaman. Returning to the metropolis after two years of privation he secures employment in the counting house of Marisett & Co. Harry wins the confidence of Mr. Marisett and the latter's niece, the beautiful Georgiana De Lancey. On a mission to New Orleans to corner the cotton market Harry is witness to the financial panic of 1837 and hears of the failure of Marisett & Co. All ends well, however, with Harry and bride-to-be Georgiana and Mr. Marisett who retires from any further commercial activities. Harry's straitened parents realize wealth through the sale of land to the railroads and Harry with his wife Georgiana exchanges city life for the quietude of Harry's home village.

405. **Brinig, Myron, 1901-1991.** *Anthony in the nude.* **New York: Farrar & Rinehart, 1930. 320p.**

Anthony, a young Westerner, goes 'on the make' in New York City. He is a poseur with a taste for expensive things. His job as a reader for a magazine publisher hardly pays enough to purchase the luxuries he covets, so he pursues another desire—marrying a wealthy woman. He finds her in Helen Brale, a middle-aged neurotic with a jealous streak, which she directs at Emiliana, an artist's daughter Anthony had loved. Anthony is shocked when Helen poisons Emiliana's dog and he leaves her. Nevertheless, when his search for employment fizzles, he crawls back to Helen.

406. ——————. *Madonna without child.* **Garden City, N.Y.: Doubleday, Doran, 1929. 352p.**

"The psychological study of a childless old maid who was a born mother. Mary Dunston, 40, works as a stenographer and secretary to Albert Camden [in his New York office]. The first time Camden brought his motherless daughter to the office an unusual relationship sprang up between the yearning woman and the eager little girl. Camden brought them often together and with his new attitude gave Mary hope of marriage and of having Claire always with her. It turned out otherwise, but the relationship had given Mary something she could never lose"—Book review digest.

Britton, Sumner, 1902- , joint author. *Murder in a shell.* **See Item #247.**

407. **Bristed, Charles Astor, 1820-1874.** *The upper ten thousand*; sketches of American society. **New-York: Stringer & Townsend, 1852. 274p.**

The author's stated purpose in this 'novelized' series of sketches is to assure his English cousins that Americans, especially those several hundred of upper New York society, are not 'wild, savage, frightful' stereotypes. The affluent New York gentleman Henry Masters is followed from his marriage to Clara Vanderlyn to his friendship with an Englishman, the Honourable Edward Ashburner, their leisurely sojourn at 'Oldport', a fashionable watering-place and a jaunt to the horse races on Long Island. At the close of the book Henry and Edward are guests at the country home (Ravenswood on the Hudson) of Henry's brother, the quite somber Carl, who had completed his education in England.

408. Britton, Sumner Charles. *Dreamy Hollow*; **a Long Island romance. New York: World Syndicate Co., 1921. 307p.**

Dreamy Hollow, near Patchogue, Long Island, was the magnificent estate of Drury Villard, recently retired businessman; Villard had hoped that the woman he loved, Winifred, would share Dreamy Hollow with him, but she had died before they were to be married. He remained single, yet found a new lease on life when he met Winifred Barbour, an innocent young native of Patchogue. Drury falls in love with her and despite the disparity in their ages resolves to ask for her hand in marriage. William Parkins, the man Villard had named as his successor in the firm, has plans to strip his former employer of his holdings and to seduce Winifred Barbour. Henry Updyke, Villard's friend and owner of the agency that oversees security matters pertaining to Villard's firm, frustrates Parkin's schemes. Winifred Barbour marries young George Carver, also a Patchogue native, and a key figure in running down the now fugitive Parkins. Drury Villard reconciles himself to the loss of Winifred Barbour and heeds the call of his long deceased Winifred to join her.

409. Brody, Catharine. *Babe Evanson*; **a novel. New York: Century Co., 1928. v, 425p.**

"The story reproduces faithfully the drab environment of a Harlem stenographer and the monotonous level of her life. There is nothing fine, or even intelligent in Babe Evanson's home life, in her friendships, or in her commonplace love affairs; yet by her very faithfulness of portraiture the author invests Babe Evanson's story with actuality, if not with interest"—Book review digest.

410. —————. *West of Fifth*. **Garden City, N.Y.: Doubleday, Doran, 1930. 318p.**

The locale of the novel is New York City's Broadway and Fifth Avenue. The protagonist is a press agent, Grace Kline, who takes full advantage of her good looks and personality to gain the job she wants and, if opportunity presents itself, to acquire another woman's spouse.

411. Bromfield, Louis, 1896-1956. *Twenty-four hours*. **New York: F.A. Stokes, 1930. 463p.**

New York City is a brooding, atmospheric presence in this novel that encapsulates 24 dramatic hours in the lives of its principal characters: Jim Towner, 45, sportsman and alcoholic, having an affair with Rosa Dugan (a.k.a. Rosie Healy), night-club singer; Fanny, Jim's wife, involved with David Melbourn, multimillionaire; Hector Champion, 71, bachelor, effete hypochondriac, collector of art objects; Philip Dantry, his beloved nephew, who is on the verge of asking Janie Fagan, an actress, to marry him; Ruby Wintringham, beautiful, intelligent, rather calculating divorcée who catches the eye of Melbourn; Tony Bruzzi, small-time hood, husband to Rosa Dugan and still able to awaken her sexual appetite; Savina Jerrold, 67, an old maid, solicitous of Hector's welfare. Rosa's murder by Tony while Jim Towner is in a drunken stupor in her apartment is a climactic point in the novel. Fanny Towner reconciles with her distraught husband; David Melbourn dismisses Fanny and proposes marriage to Ruby Wintringham; Philip Dantry marries Janie Fagan; and Savina Jerrold, observer and analyst of all that has occurred, decides to propose to Hector and thereby mollify his morbidity.

412. **Bronk, Mitchell, b. 1862.** *Manchester boys.* **Philadelphia: Judson Press, 1937. 128p.**

Fictional sketches very likely based on the author's (the unnamed "I" narrator) memories of a boyhood in the Upstate New York town of Manchester (south of Palmyra) in the 1880s. Activities engaged in by the youngsters were maple sugaring, fishing, ice-skating, snowball battles, and gathering black walnuts. Characters in the town and the surrounding region were: the reprobate, Old Butts, beneficiary of a yard cleanup by the boys; 'Mosquito Bars', the name tacked onto Sadie Young because she wore a sash made from mosquito netting; Dod Brown, the drunkard, who accidentally stumbled into a pond and drowned; Tom Hardwich, the blacksmith, morose because of the loss of his beloved son in the Civil War, but later a great friend of the boys of Manchester.

Bronson-Howard, George Fitzalan, 1883-1922. See: Howard, George Fitzalan Bronson, 1883-1922.

413. *Brook Farm*; **the amusing and memorable of American country life. New York: Carter, 1860. 208p.**

"Brook Farm, the scene of all but two or three of the following sketches, covered some two hundred acres of the State of New York. It lay about seven miles east of Hudson and within an easy drive of the border of Connecticut" (p.[9] … "The River 'Aquehung' formed our western borderline" (p.[1]). The Farm is about three miles from the village of 'Lawrence.' The 'we' narrators are scarcely a year out of England and their neighbors doubt they do much to nurture their farm; the new owners set about to disabuse them of that notion. Daily activities around the farm are depicted; difficulties with a squatting Irish family are related. Also mentioned is a Polish 'exile' with whom they are unable to communicate because of the language barrier; he is dubbed 'Count Flusteryblusterybrowski.'

414. **Brookes, Sally.** *Manhattan fever*; **a girl's story that's true. New York: Sears Pub. Co., 1930. 289p.**

"The confession story of a Middle Western college girl who comes to live in New York. Sally does not remain naïve. She has success at work, followed by failures resulting from dissipation. But you know all along that she is good at heart, she never goes too far; and in the end, after her illness and return home, she once more sets her face toward Manhattan, unbeaten, determined now to reform and 'get somewhere' at last"—New York herald tribune books.

415. **Brookman, Laura Lou, 1898- .** *Rash romance.* **New York: Grosset & Dunlap, 1930. 367p.**

Stenographer Judith Cameron marries Arthur Knight, executive in a New York City publishing house, a man twice her age. Their Bermuda honeymoon is interrupted by the return of Arthur's daughter, Tony, from Europe. The newly married couple settles in Knight's Long Island home and Judith faces her stepdaughter's pernicious resentment; Tony deliberately plants suspicion in her father's mind about Judith's faithfulness to her 'aged' husband. Even after Judith almost collapses because of her loving care during Arthur's nearly fatal bout with pneumonia, Tony continues her attempts to undermine the marriage. Judith leaves the Long Island house and sequesters herself in a cheap New York hotel. Arthur comes to her and they clear away the lingering doubts and situations that have interfered with their love for one another. Restless, mercurial Tony suddenly marries a long-time suitor and departs for a European honeymoon.

416. **Brooks, Byron Alden, 1845-1911.** *Earth revisited.* **Boston: Arena Pub. Co., 1893 [i.e. 1894]. 318p.**

"The story of a man who, long after death, and after a varied experience in other spheres, revisits the earth in 1992, returning to his native city of Brooklyn. The changes, which he witnesses that have been wrought in the way of moral, material and spiritual progress in the course of one hundred years, are minutely described. Churches and creeds have disappeared, and the 'reign of righteousness' is in full bloom and life. [Evidently the author] chiefly aims to delineate the effects of real religion as contrasted with 'ecclesiasticism'"—Annual American catalogue.

417. **Brooks, Elbridge Streeter, 1846-1902.** *In Leisler's times*; **an historical story of Knickerbocker New York. Twenty-four illus. by William T. Smedley. Boston: D. Lothrop, 1886. 299p.**

A tale about "the very first 'people's governor' in America [Jacob Leisler] who was tried and executed for treason; [the novel] also deals with the beginnings of self-government by the people, and republican representation. The action of the story envelops the young folks of several prominent Knickerbocker families and the incidents and scenes are highly dramatic, but yet appertain to the political interests of the time. Careful studies of old New York have been made, and the modes and forms of early Knickerbocker speech and customs seem to have been faithfully reproduced"—Annual American catalogue.

418. **————.** *Under the Tamaracks*; **or,** *A summer with General Grant at the Thousand Islands.* **Philadelphia, PA: Pub. Co., 1896. 336p.**

The 'Tamarack Three' are Penfield (Pen) Arthur, Joey Terhunee and 'The Skipper', a lad of fifteen; they are privileged to spend an interesting summer at a resort, 'Edenshore' (with its commanding Tamarack Tower) in the Thousand Islands of the St. Lawrence River. The boys upset the nefarious plans of young Terry Perhac and Hinchman (?), the 'seedy' law-spouting evil genius of Whiskey Island. These two get their revenge by inadvertently burning down Tamarack Tower and then disappear without a trace. A highlight is the Tamarack Three's getting acquainted with General Ulysses S. Grant, a visitor at Alexandria Bay, and hearing him talk about his experiences in the Civil War and dispense useful advice.

419. **Brooks, Elisabeth W.** *As the world goes by*. **Boston: Little, Brown, 1905. 375 p.**
'Mary Manton has been a leading actress on the New York stage for 20 years. Divorced from a stern, conventional husband who frowned on her bohemian ways, Mary has a daughter—the latter dearly loves her mother, but is curious to know more about her father. She goes to him in his New York home with its luxurious appointments. Participating in the upper class activities of the city she finds a romance of her own. The novel presents a realistic picture of the theatrical and social life of the New York City of the period.

420. **Brooks, Emily.** *Riding high*; a novel. **New York: Poseidon Press, 1989. 400p.**
The Manville and Miles estates are close by one another in 'Edgeville', New York, and both families take pride in their equestrian pastimes. Charles 'Wirelegs' Manville and his best friend Conrad Miles had each received 500 acres of scrubby land as their graduation present from Princeton University in the 1920s. The two resolve that whoever 'jumps the most fences in the next 50 years' may lay claim to all the 1,000 acres. In the 1970s the widower Wirelegs is dying—his daughter Carlin is unhappy and his son Conrad, married to former secretary Peg, is impotent. Traditions are no longer important to this generation, but the money left by Charles 'Wirelegs' Manville is. Carlin has the choice of bearing children or concentrating on her horsemanship. Peg now has enough money so that she can contemplate leaving Conrad.

Brosé, Edward De. See: De Brosé, Edward.

Bross, Edgar Clifton. See under his pseudonym: De Brosé, Edward.

Brossé, Edgar Clifton. See: De Brosé, Edward.

421. **Broughton, Joseph.** *Solon Grind*; or, *The thunderstruck hypocrite*. **New York: Burgess, Stringer, 1845. 120p.**
"The town which gave birth to the principal incidents ... narrated herein, is situated somewhere within the limits of New York [State]." Deacon Solon Grind is a prototype of the greedy Yankee, deemed by his neighbors as the 'sublimation of piety, honesty, wealth, and benevolence.' However, we learn that years ago he conspired with Ezek Smith to bilk the Widow Marston of her

deceased husband's estate. Grind also falsely declares his bankruptcy so that he can keep the funds invested with him by townspeople. The downfall of Grind and Smith comes about in the court at Auburn, N.Y. when papers detailing the schemes of the two malefactors are brought to light. The Widow Marston regains her husband's estate and Grind and Smith reap their just desserts.

422. Broughton, T[homas[Alan, 1936- . *The horsemaster.* **New York: Dutton, 1981. 276p.**

Lewis Beede, horse breeder on a rich man's Upstate New York ranch, faces unexpected changes in his hitherto placid life when he learns his employer plans to sell his ranch, and the daughter he had put up for adoption in New York years ago suddenly arrives in this small New York town. Lewis Beede has to examine his past and plan for a future he had never envisioned.

423. Broun, Heywood Campbell, 1888-1939. *The sun field.* **New York: Putnam, 1923. 204p.**

"Judith Wintrop, a Vassar graduate of Mayflower antecedents, [a New York journalist/writer], and an intellectual, puts to the test her modern theories of life by falling in love with and marrying 'Tiny' Tyler, a [New York Yankee] baseball player to whom she has been attracted by his physical strength and beauty. The story of their marriage and its problems during the inevitable period of adjustment is told by a friend, George Wallace, who had hoped to win Judith for himself"—Book review digest.

424. Brown, Anna Robeson, 1873-1941. *The black lamb.* **Philadelphia: Lippincott, 1896. 322p.**

The 'black lamb' of the novel is Andrew LeBreton (alias Musgrave) who imposes on the good will of Noel Conway, a young man interested in Buddhism and Eastern mysticism, and Conway's friend Jack Sartoris. Noel and Jack are scraping a living in New York City; Jack especially had been accustomed to wealth and leisure, but that disappeared when Colonel Sartoris lost his fortune. LeBreton borrows money from Noel and also resorts to thievery; he is brought to justice only after he tries to get insurance money by planning the sinking of an oceangoing steamer. His stepmother, Lady LeBreton, comes to New York to plead for him; she is also the mother of Noel whom she had more or less abandoned after her first husband's death. Her pleas are unavailing and she returns to England. Noel has never been happy in exciting New York City and he decides on a future in East Asia and the contemplative life of Buddhism. Jack Sartoris marries Marion Forbes, an intelligent, creative young New Yorker. Philippa Axenard, a wealthy socialite, especially regrets Noel's departure, rejecting the marriage proposal of Clement Frey, an eminent littérateur.

425. ————. *The immortal garland*; a story of American life. **New York: Appleton, 1900. vi, 324p.**

"A distinctively American novel, treating entertainingly of personal, artistic, and social evolution. Most of its action takes place in New York, although its earlier scenes are in a New Jersey town, and others occur on the coast of Maine and among the New Hampshire mountains. The story has chiefly to do with three young persons—one who means to win fame as a poet, another who hopes to become a great actor, and another who adopts portrait painting as a profession"—Annual American catalogue.

426. ————. *Truth and a woman.* **Chicago: H.S. Stone, 1903. 206p.**
The heroine, Mary Langland, a rather superficial New York socialite, falls in love with an agnostic. Faithful to the traditions of the 'Church', she breaks off her engagement despite continuing affection for her lover. Then she opts for reconciliation by offering to surrender to his will; he ignores her gesture and the parting is final.

427. **Brown, Beth.** *Applause.* **New York: Liveright, 1928. 312p.**
"The ancient story of a burlesque queen and a baby and a handful of scoundrelly men! Kitty Darling produces an infant girl back-stage, rears it as she tours the sticks, takes it to a cultivated convent on the Hudson, and ends with a sweet, tender, well-bred, loving daughter [April] on her hands, and no place to put this paragon. Eventually of course, the paragon finds a beautiful young man, whereas Kitty, the feted queen, goes from bad to worse and meets her final fate in the shape of a box of mysterious white powders"—New York herald tribune books.

428. **Brown, Estelle Aubrey.** *With trailing banners.* **Boston: Little, Brown, 1930. viii, 295p.**
"The story of a girl, Merry Melton, from a village in northern New York, who, after a sturdy, independent girlhood, gave up her chances of a better education to marry a handsome, brutal village youth. The aftermath was one long session of suffering, until Merry took her secret savings and slipped away Down East"—Book review digest.

429. **[Brown, John Walker], 1814-1849.** *Constance*; or, *The merchant's daughter. A tale of our times.* **New York: Gould, Newman and Saxton, 1841. 160p.**
New York businessman Mr. Barnwell and his children, Constance, Charles and Josephine, face a bleak 'future' when his investments turn sour. The Barnwells move to a small farm 'on the banks of the Hudson, a few miles from the City of New York.' Mr. Barnwell still has 'a yearning for the crowded streets, the Exchange and the counting room.' Constance's romance with Edward Seaman, a law student, is stalled by her deep concern for Edward's rational, doubting stance toward Christianity. A neighbor, George Gregory, evinces interest in Constance. The latter becomes governess to the Gregory children to help her father's finances. When Edward Seaman reappears and announces his full religious conversion, Constance accepts his marriage proposal. Sickly Charles Barnwell dies. George Gregory gracefully

accepts his 'loss' of Constance and begins to study law. More moralizing about the importance of religion in women's lives closes the tale.

430. **Brown, L. Melyzia.** *My Solomon*; **a story of modern New York. New York: W.L. Hyde, 1879. 330p.**

John Remington, protégé of the millionaire Mr. Manning, after army service in the Civil War, learns of his mother's tortured existence. Now occupied in reclaiming 'lost' girls Magdalena (John's mother) had been forcibly separated from her husband and child by an evil acquaintance and pushed into prostitution. In a somewhat parallel situation Mr. Manning's daughter Julia had been lured away from her father by a devious politician, J.W. Devier. Although Devier presumably married Julia, she fled from him to her father's house where she died, leaving behind a female child. This girl, given the name Julia (Judy) Manning Sanborn, is reared by Remington and family retainers. As she matures the question of her legitimacy comes up. Devier had lost the certificate that would prove Julia Manning to be his lawful wife, yet Judy's protectors are quite certain that Devier is her father. They prevent Devier from claiming any portion of the Manning estate that Judy has inherited from Mr. Manning. Finally Devier dies and the lost marriage certificate turns up to everyone's relief.

431. **Brown, Robert Carlton, 1886-1959.** *What happened to Mary*; **a novelization from the play and the stories appearing in the Ladies' World. New York: Clode, 1913. 309p.**

In this formulaic tale, 'Mary Craig' comes to New York when she reaches the age of eighteen; she had been kidnapped while an infant and thus has little recollection of her real parents and relatives. There is a wicked uncle involved in all that has taken place. Mary, on her own, finds success in the theater, has several rather unbelievable adventures and finally forces the villain to cede her rightful inheritance and wins the man she loves.

432. **Browne, Howard, 1908- .** *Thin air.* **New York: Simon & Schuster, 1954. 209p.**
A young Westchester society matron, the wife of Ames Coryell, is kidnapped. Ames, an executive in an advertising agency, uses all the resources of his firm in an effort to find his abducted wife.

Brownell, Gertrude Hall, 1863-1961. See: Hall, Gertrude, 1863-1961.

Broyles, Lester Everett. See under the author's pseudonym: Terreve, Retsel.

433. **Bruce, Caleb.** *Knickerbocker Gardens*; **a pursuit of happiness. New York: Scribner, 1941. 564p.**
From 1927 to 1937 life in 'Knickerbocker Gardens' a 'garden' suburb of New York City, is experienced by a diverse cluster of Americans. They represent a wide spectrum of social classes and standards of living. How representative

this fictional suburban community is of others scattered around the country is perhaps for the reader to decide.

434. **Brudno, Ezra Selig, b. 1877.** *The fugitive*; **being memoirs of a wanderer in search of a home. New York: Doubleday, Page, 1904. xii, 392p.**

After witnessing anti-Semitic persecutions in Lithuania, Israel Rusakoff, young orphaned Jew, migrates to New York City where he rapidly ascends to citizenship and importance. The woman he falls in love with is Katia Bialnik, daughter of a penitent Christian, who had years before accused Rusakoff's father of the ritual slaughter of a Russian girl. However, a happy ending seems to be in view by the end of the novel.

435. **Brunner, Emma Beatrice Kaufman.** *The personal touch*. **New York: Brentano's, 1922. 312p.**

"The 'Justifiables' of this tale [of New York] are a band of criminals, swindlers and thieves who are pretending to operate on the exact lines of any other business corporation, with a board of directors, agents, etc., and even capital stock for sale to outsiders. They consider their proceedings justifiable because all big business—the banks, insurance, railroads, and so on—are, they believe, run upon equally dishonest lines. The plot itself is concerned with the exploits and education of a young emissary of this 'trust', who goes into high society for the purpose of theft, but who is led to reform by the discovery that not all successful business folk are dishonest. There is, of course, also the thread of a love story running through an intricate series of adventures. The story leaves the reformed young hero about to begin a career of honest work, thereby pointing its moral"—Literary review of the New York evening post.

436. **Brush, Katharine, 1902-1952.** *Little sins*. **New York: Minton, Balch, 1927, c1926. vii, 304p.**

"The 'little sins' of deception and self-indulgence are the foxes that spoil the vines of [New Yorker] Gay Leonard's character. She is a spoiled young modern, used to taking her own way, but in the matter of Jerry Davis she does not get it. Dolly Quinn, a virtuous, working girl, preempts him at their first meeting. The society girl's reaction is to marry a devoted lover and make him miserable. As the story progresses Gay goes down the scale, little by little losing all she cared about, while Dolly Quinn comes steadily up the top"—Book review digest.

437. **————.** *Nightclub*. **New York: Minton, Balch, 1929. 298p.**

Nine of the eleven stories are steeped in the lives of New Yorkers (most of whom fall in the category of 'losers'). The tales have an O. Henry flavor, and the cast includes a doting mother who runs a speakeasy to support her son's expensive education; a secretary (the 'maiden aunt') who clings to a last hope for romance; a sophisticated young adult dealing with an unwanted pregnancy; a manicurist and her shipping-clerk boyfriend, both saddled with demanding mothers; a rather bored, plodding maid in the powder room of a nightclub. Contents: The long young dreams.—'The mother has the custody'.—Fumble.—Gaudy lady.—Eye-opener.—Seven blocks apart.—Debutante.—'All the king's horses'.—Silk hat.—Portrait of a maiden aunt.—Nightclub.

438. ————. *Young man of Manhattan.* **New York: Farrar & Rinehart, 1930. 325p.**

"Toby McLean, sports writer of the New York Star and Ann Vaughn, movie columnist, meet and in a space of five days marry. Ann, beautiful and much more clever than Toby, makes more money than her easy-going husband. He doesn't like it when she pays a vast accumulation of debts accrued from nightclubs, speakeasies, and fast life in general. Toby has dates with a sophisticated young flapper, Puff; Ann, who has urged him on, becomes jealous. Things go from bad to worse and a temporary separation follows. Then Ann gets methyl poisoning from drinking bad bootleg whisky. While she is slowly recovering, Toby reforms, swears off drinking, writes three short stories which the editors immediately accept for $500 and more each, and produces a novel which the publishers consider a knockout. The book ends on a note of happy reconciliation between the young couple"—Book review digest.

439. **Brush, Mary Elizabeth Quackenbush, b. 1857.** *Paul and Persis*; or, *The Revolutionary struggle in the Mohawk Valley.* **Boston: Lee & Shepard, 1883. 228p.**

This historical novel opens in a settlement of Germans from the Palatinate in the Mohawk Valley (1775) just before the onset of the American Revolution. Persis, the heroine, is a girl who, as an infant, was left on the doorstep of Paul's father's house. Inevitably Paul and Persis fall in love with one another. Of all the stirring events they observe or take part in as the Revolutionary Conflict spreads, certainly the most personal is the disclosure of Persis' real father.

440. ————. *Sarah Dakota.* **New York: Hunt & Eaton, 1894. 315p.**

"Sarah Dakota—named after her native state—is a motherless hoyden of fourteen, the only child of a careless, good-natured 'cattle-king', Colonel Vandercar. The introduction of a young stepmother into the ranch home results in Sarah's departure for the East, to be educated and trained into propriety by her mother's maiden sister in the old homestead in the Mohawk Valley. Her unconventionalities, shocking the proprieties of Van Dorn Manor, her school life and religious development, the influence of her honest, unselfish nature on her silly, selfish cousin Julie, and her final recognition of her stepmother's love make the story"—Annual American catalogue.

441. ————. *The Scarlet Patch*; the story of a patriot boy in the MohawkValley. **Illus. by George W. Picknell. Boston: Lee and Shepard, 1905. vii, 306p.**

A young patriot, Donald Bastien, a 'bound boy' to his uncle, is apprehensive upon discovering that the latter is clandestinely associated with a Tory organization that uses the 'Scarlet Patch' to identify itself. Donald is caught in a sequence of exciting adventures in which he is joined by a loyal Indian ally. The novel is a useful resource for an understanding of the educational, domestic and political life of the American Revolutionary era.

442. **Brussel, James Arnold, 1905- .** *Just murder, darling.* **New York: Scribner, 1959. 192p.**

Quite certain that his wife is having a clandestine affair, Glenn Gordon works out a plan whereby he will kill his wife's lover, but make it look as if she had committed the murder. He sets up an alibi for himself in Albany, returns to his Long Island home where wife and lover are together, knocks his wife out and kills her inamorato. What ensues—including a trial—seems to be hewing closely to Gordon's plans.

443. **Buchanan, Harrison Gray.** *Asmodeus*; or *Legends of New York.* **Being a complete exposé of the mysteries, vices and doings, as exhibited by the fashionable circles of New York … Facts without fiction. New York: J. D. Munson, 1848. 96p.**

Despite the statement, 'Facts without fiction', the author uses fictional characters—Wall Street brokers, married men of high social position, college students, madams of houses of assignation, gamblers, prostitutes, thieves—to depict illegal activities in the metropolis via his sixteen 'legends'.

Buchanan, Rachel, pseud. See: Longstreet, Abby Buchanan.

444. **Buchanan, Thompson, 1877-1937.** *The second wife.* **Front. by Harrison Fisher. Illus. by W.W. Fawcett. New York: Watt, 1911. 318p.**

Complications abound in this novel of stylish and affluent New Yorkers. Willa, the daughter of John Chase and his first wife, chose to stay with her father after the divorce. Willa falls in love with Jack Hendrix, her mother's stepson. Jack's former fiancée becomes the new wife of John Chase despite the disparity in ages—all of which adds to the confusion.

445. **Buck, Francis Tillou.** *A fiancé on trial.* **New York: Merriam Co. [c1896]. 319p.**

Fashionable New York society is the tableau of this novel in which the 'hero', Malcolm Styrges, who has long since sowed his wild oats, is now ready at 32 to accept the humdrum social nexus. He is in love with Margaret Heslow, a charming young woman of 22 or 23, but reports have been circulating that he is, or is about to be engaged to Sylvia Pelton. Craik Orcutt, extremely wealthy but undereducated, and a not very popular figure, meddles, with little to show for it. A friend of Malcolm, Gerald Anthony, 28, dainty in appearance but quite proficient at rescuing people in life-threatening situations, has a yearning for Sylvia, but she offers him little encouragement. Opportunely Sylvia releases Malcolm from any commitment he may feel he owes her. Margaret is now fully available.

446. ———. *A man of two minds*. **New York: Merriam Co., 1895. 338p.**
Alfred (Fred) Wyborn Sheldon's dilemma is that he is in love with two women simultaneously—one is a married lady, Alice Mills; the other is Bessie Brentworth, the daughter of an Episcopal clergyman. The scenes veer from New York City to a country residence on the Hudson. Fred's friend, Gordon Blake, Jr., a classmate of his at Columbia University, offers his counsel, but it is the sincere and high-minded Bessie who steers Fred Sheldon towards the right choice—herself.

Buckley, Christopher, 1952- ., joint author. *God is my broker*. See Item #3423.

447. **Buckley, Fergus Reid, 1930- . *Eye of the hurricane*. Garden City, N.Y.: Doubleday, 1967. xii, 562p.**
As the novel opens Jonathan Wright, born in 1882, is 14 years of age. His ancestors were early inhabitants of Long Island who had a significant role in establishing South Hampton and had moved to Sag Harbor when whaling was a thriving occupation. After the whaling industry went into decline the family moved to Fair Haven on Great South Bay. As Jonathan matures he tries his hand at fishing and hunting for fowl and eventually parlays his natural shrewdness to the founding of an industrial conglomerate. The story concludes with an account of the 1938 hurricane that laid waste the South Shore of Long Island.

448. **Buckley, Maria L. *Amanda Willson*; or, *The vicissitudes of life*. New York: Published by the author; printed by Urner & Co., 1856. 40p.**
"A sketch of the working classes of New York; or, The sufferings of the sewing girls [and two poems]": p. [31]—40. The story of 'Amanda Willson' is an example of a type of Victorian melodramatic fiction in which virtuous girls are the would-be victims of conscienceless rakes. The two heroines, Amanda Willson and Susan Archer, both orphans and destitute in wicked New York City, are placed in a house of assignation managed by a Mrs. Young. The latter unaccountably becomes the girls' protector and they eventually are rescued from a dire fate. Amanda and Susan find true lovers and the villains suffer violent deaths. The one-time madam, Mrs. Young, gives up her 'trade' and devotes herself to charitable work.

Budlong, Ware, 1905-1967. See under his pseudonym: Crosby, Lee, 1905-1967.

449. **Buechler, James. *In that heaven there should be a place for me*; stories of the Mohawk Valley. Duxbury, Mass.: Cranberry Books, 1994. 250p.**

"The people living in these [Mohawk Valley] houses were a mixture of the children of recent European immigrants and the descendants of the English and Dutch who had settled in the area originally, all brought together by the General Electric and American Locomotive Companies established around the turn of the century. ... Their life involved a movement between county and city, city and county, and the culture ... represented by each, that is reflected in these stories,"—Foreword. Contents: The second best girl.—In that heaven.—The paper boy's last day.—The ambulance driver.—Pepicelli.— John Sobieski runs.—The proud suitor.—On Cuthbert Street.—Magister Pietro.—The washing machine.

450. Bullard, Arthur, 1879-1929. *Comrade Yetta*, by Albert Edwards [pseud.]. New York: Macmillan, 1913. vi, 448p.

The Jewish heroine, Yetta Rayefsky endures work in a dehumanizing sweatshop, rebuffs the enticements of a pimp who tries to recruit her for his stable of prostitutes, and participates in the drive for unionization of New York City garment workers. The novel explores the underworld of the East Side, Tammany Hall corruption, and the grinding poverty of the tenement dwellers. Capitalism, the author contends, is the culprit for the ills that plague the teeming masses of the ghettoes.

451. ————. *A man's world*, by Albert Edwards [pseud.]. New York: Macmillan, 1912. 312p.

The period covered by the novel is 1866 to 1912. Arnold Whitman escapes from an orthodox religious boyhood with its puritanical, if Southern, overtones, and comes to New York City where he gets a job as a probation officer in the 'Tombs' and gradually rises to expert criminologist. He explores and reports on the city's underworld and looks closely at the currents of the time: socialism, anarchism, and social settlements, prison reform and feminism. Despair could engulf him had not the promise of a better world seemed possible of fulfillment by a new generation.

452. ————. *The stranger*. New York: Macmillan, 1920. 332p.

"The story takes the reader into an intellectual circle of lower New York among social workers, literati and artists—America's aspirations at their best. Into this circle is injected a Moslem—son of an American missionary couple in Turkey—born and brought up there, a convinced Mohammedan. This leads to comparisons between Eastern and Western life and religion, not always flattering to our Western civilization. Some flaws are detected in the proud and secure foundations of our science and 'efficiency'. The finest exponent of the latter and of feminism, Helen Cash, meets her Waterloo in the calm, questioning eyes of this stranger. Frank Lockwood, the artist, sees in him the savior of his soul, and to Eunice Bender, the rich girl, he opens up heaven before she dies, through the spirituality of his love"—Book review digest.

453. Bullock, William, b. 1876. *In the current*. New York: W. Rickey, 1911. 274 p.

The differences that the heroine, daughter of a clergyman based in a small Long Island village, has with her father impel her to run off to New York City. Her father had urged her to marry a man she had known all her life, but she had an unfavorable opinion of her prospective mother-in-law and was not at all certain she loved that woman's son. New York City is not kind to her; she almost steps to the altar with a rich but dissolute young man. By the novel's end she has decided that her father's choice is perhaps the right one for her too.

454. Bunner, Henry Cuyler, 1855-1896. *Jersey Street and Jersey Lane*; **urban and suburban sketches. Illustrated by A.B. Frost [and others]. New York: Scribner, 1896.**

Sketches and short stories populated by real and fictional characters alternating in scene between New York City and the country immediately bordering on it. The author looks closely at the varieties of human beings that are the vital part of a great city, especially the tenement dwellers, the ethnic mix, the bohemians, the comfortable middle class, et al., and in his last piece weighs the advantages of suburban vs. urban living. Contents: Jersey and Mulberry.—Tiemann's to Tubby Hook.—The Bowery and Bohemia.—The story of a path.—The lost child.—A letter to town.

455. —————. *Love in old cloathes and other stories.* **Illustrated by W.T. Smedley, Orson Lowell, and Andre Castaigne. New York: Scribner, 1896. 217p.**

The lovesick letter-writer of 'Love in old cloathes' uses obsolete English spellings as he recounts the passage of his obsession with the unapproachable Miss French, even though the letters bear the place and date of New York, 1883. In 'A letter and a paragraph' a bachelor New York journalist, writing to a newspaper colleague two days before his death at age 30 on Nov. 18, 1883, fantasizes about a wife and child he never had. The 'on trial' clergyman of 'French for a fortnight' boards in a Westchester County inn prior to the sermon he is to deliver at an exclusive New York City church. He falls ill, and upon recovering some two weeks later, he uses the French innkeeper's figures for time passed. The upshot is that he uses his 'preaching' Sunday (believing it is Saturday) to attend a picnic with innkeeper Perot and his family. Ambitious Horace Walpole from St. Lawrence County, N.Y. clerks in a New York City law firm in the novella 'The red silk handkerchief'. On an important mission to Sand Hills, Long Island, Horace falls deeply in love with Rosmond Rittenhouse. Taking her reciprocal love for granted, he is in for a surprise after he performs an heroic act that prevents a railroad disaster. Contents: Love in old cloathes.—A letter and a paragraph.—'As one having authority'.—Crazy wife's ship.—French for a fortnight.—The red silk handkerchief.—Our aromatic uncle.

456. —————. *The midge.* **New York: Scribner, 1886. 235p.**

"A witty, humorous and tender story of life in the French quarter of New York City, which extends from Broadway to Sixth Avenue and from Washington

Square south to Prince Street. ... A college-bred physician, whose only practice is for cases of charity; 'the midge', a little girl of twelve, whom he adopts after the death of her mother, under circumstances which the author describes with admirable minuteness; and a young junior officer in the Navy, home on sick leave, who employs his time in making sketches of great merit—[these] are the leading characters. The story is simple in plot, but every word tells of the author's knowledge of human nature, and proves once more now much 'laughter is akin to tears'"—Annual American catalogue.

457. ————. *"Short sixes," stories to be read while the candle burns.* **Illustrated by C. Jay Taylor, F. Opper and S. B. Griffin. New York: Keppler & Schwarzmann, 1891 [c1890]. iv, 232p.**

In six of the thirteen stories in this collection (The tenor; The love-letters of Smith; Mr. Copernicus and the proletariat; Hector; Zozo; An old, old story) Bunner draws humorous and loving portraits of such denizens of New York City, its suburbs and neighboring Long Island as: two very young female students of music who 'worship' the fashionable tenor of the moment; a shy, lonely seamstress who becomes the object of ardent if distant attentions of the shy, lonely Mr. Smith, foreman at an East River lumberyard; rich publisher T. C. Copernicus in semi-retirement who is 'conned' by black sheep Dudley Winthrop Chester (a.k.a. Michael Quinlan); three virginal ladies who acquire a watchdog to shield them from unwanted male intrusions; a half-literate astrologer who uses his 'science' to 'solve' a benefactor's romantic difficulties; and the on-again, off-again affair of the English housekeeper and the butler of the very English Tullingworth-Gordons of Long Island

458. ————. *The story of a New York house.* **Illustrated by A.B. Frost. New York: Scribner, 1887. vii, 152p.**

The 'house' is a 'country' residence on the fringe of New York City ca. 1807 that was built by Jacob Dolph, although he still maintains an 'in-city' dwelling. Dolph's friend, Abram Van Riper, Sr., buys the in-city dwelling when Dolph finds himself in financial straits. The country house becomes the sole residence of Jacob Dolph, Sr., Jacob, Jr., his son Eustace and a daughter Edith who is born when Jacob, Jr. and his wife Aline are well advanced in age. Not long before the Civil War, Eustace Dolph, an employee of Abram Van Riper, Jr., steals funds from his employer to speculate on Wall Street and loses. Eustace flees and his father is forced to sell what little real estate he possesses. From 1863 to 1873 tenements and shops grow up around the 'house.' Edith and her father move from their home and exist on Edith's sewing and a sum given them by Van Riper as an addition to the price his father paid for the aforementioned 'in-city' dwelling. Jacob Dolph, Jr.'s death comes a few years after the Great Panic of 1873 as he watches the 'house' being demolished to make way for new construction.

459. ————. *A woman of honor.* **Boston: J.R. Osgood, 1883. iv, 336p.**

The artist Jack Carnegie, who lost a fortune and his first ladylove, has a studio on Manhattan's Tenth Street, which is visited frequently by his best friend, Cecil Kent, art critic/journalist. Faith Ruthven, daughter of a patron of the arts, is now the object of Jack's romantic ardor. But misunderstandings cloud the present and possibly the future of the two lovers. Mrs. Adelaide Swift suspects that her husband Robert is having an affair with Faith, while Faith looks askance at Adelaide's presence in Jack's studio, Adelaide being the aforementioned first ladylove of Jack. Cecil Kent intervenes and sets things right with all parties involved and a happy conclusion is assured.

460. ————. *Zadoc Pine and other stories*. **New York: Scribner, 1891. 256p.**
Zadoc Pine, unemployed Adirondack native, migrates to South Ridge, New Jersey and carves a niche for himself because of his willingness to tackle any odd job at any time and carry it out to the customer's complete satisfaction. The novella 'Natural Selection' puts at odds the bourgeois Leetes with the upper class, aristocratic Wykoffs. Celia Leete, engaged to Randolph Wykoff, springs a stunning surprise on him during an invitational sojourn at the Long Island home of the Wykoffs. Plain-Jane Mrs. Tom pays a price for her spree with the 'smart set' of Upstate New York resort 'Northoak'. John Gerrit (Squire Five-Fathom) is the heir of his father's exploded dream to build a flourishing town on the southern shore of Lake Ontario to rival Rochester and Oswego. John lives to see the possibility of the dream becoming reality when a final catastrophe strikes. Contents: The Zadoc Pine Labor Union.—Natural selection: a romance of Chelsea Village and East Hampton Town.—Casper.—A second-hand story.—Mrs. Tom's spree.—Squire Five-Fathom.

461. **Buntline, Ned, 1823-1886.** *The b'hoys of New York*; **a sequel to the** *Mysteries & miseries of New York*. **New York: W.F. Burgess, 1850. 194p.**
The author provides the reader with an overall view of the seamier aspects of New York City life: its gambling dens, brothels, and hapless prostitutes. The story hinges on the plot of the libidinous Count Alvorado to acquire the vast fortune held by Captain Harris, the 'Pirate of the Hudson', in a cave along the shore of that river. Alvorado also has plans to kidnap and ravish the beauteous Agnes Morton whose brother George is on his way to Cuba and a new future. Alvorado has a measure of success, but in the end death overtakes most of the chief characters: Agnes, Captain Harris and his wife Alvinda, and George Morton. Alvorado escapes their fate: the author declares that his future will be recounted in a volume yet to come.

462. ————. *Charley Bray*; or, *The fireman's mission*. **The story of a New York fireman. New York: [Published for the trade, 1870?]. 8p. (double columns).**
The author assumes that the fireman's mission includes not only fighting conflagrations but also rescuing young women from the dastardly intentions of idle, rich pleasure-seekers. Charley (or Charlie) Bray and his companion Charlie Johnson protect Ella Crosby and a girl named Fanny from the designs of Clarence Willis and his friend Whitmore. Bray's and Johnson's efforts are

rewarded in part when Willis gradually finds his better self and goes back to Mary Hamilton, the wife (and child) he had deserted. Charlie Johnson pulls Fanny away from a dangerous fire and the two firemen become the lifelong guardians (husbands) of Fanny and Ella.

463. ————. *The convict*; or, *The conspirator's victim*. **A novel written in prison New York: Dick & Fitzgerald, 1863. 297p.**

Ernest Cramer, philosopher and would-be reformer of New York City's many social ailments, exhibits a morbid fear of Jesuitism and Roman Catholicism. He also carries hostility towards Great Britain and its class structure although he is married to Serena Clifford an English beauty. The Jesuit known as 'His Eminence' uses female dupes to seduce Cramer with little success, yet Serena remains suspicious of her husband. When Cramer stumbles upon the Astor Place Riot of 1849 he is arrested as a leading troublemaker. The novel concludes with Cramer languishing in prison and evidently abandoned by his wife. A promised sequel, *The convict returns*, is unavailable if ever it did appear.

464. ————. *Elfrida, the Red Rover's daughter*; or, *A new mystery of New York*. **New York: F.A. Brady, c1860. 103p (in double columns).**

Adelia Mildollar, rejected by her father after becoming pregnant by Captain Gerald Andros, one of Richard Mildollar's shipmasters, dies in childbirth in the humble home of Jonathan and Betsy Birdsall with Dr. Watson the attending physician. Andros, cut off by Mildollar, turns to piracy as the Red Rover; nevertheless he still wants to provide for his child by Adelia. The dying Mildollar relents and has a will drawn up and attested, leaving most of his wealth to the child, Elfrida. Mrs. Mildollar and her worthless son Harry plot to steal the will and get rid of the witnesses. Years later, the chief witness, Dr. Watson, reappears in New York after a long absence and confirms Elfrida as the primary heir to the Mildollar fortune. Elfrida is now the adopted daughter of Sam Latrobe, a fireman who had rescued Elfrida in a fire that claimed the lives of the Birdsalls and his wife.

465. ————. *The g'hals of New York*; a novel. New York: De Witt and **Davenport, 1850. 236p.**

Buntline moralizes that exceedingly low wages and poverty drive seamstresses into prostitution and young men into thievery, pickpocketing, counterfeiting and other criminal careers in the lower depths of New York City. Chris Barton, head of a criminal organization, is just another example of a man born a bastard and brought up as a 'charity boy' who tried to live honestly, but buffeted by society turns to crime and revenge on his persecutors. Barton, in league with two Jesuits (Buntline has definite antipathy toward the Roman Catholic Church), conspires to change the will of dying Frederick Orson, a greedy, wealthy landlord. His plans to remove Orson's granddaughter from the scene are overturned by Constance Lindsay, Barton's former mistress, whom he had betrayed and abandoned. Barton and his cronies sink further into the lower rungs of criminality. Constance retires to her home on the Hudson.

466.   ————. *The Grossbeak mansion*; a mystery of New York. New York: F.A. Brady, c1862. 90p. (in double columns).

Upright Martin Grossbeak is in the midst of a libel suit against miserly Levi Martin when Martin's children by his first wife, differing sharply with their father, leave home. Martin's second wife seeks to relieve him of his wealth with the assistance of her mother, Mrs. Desha (a.k.a. Moll Miller) and deprive Edgar and Ellen Martin of their inheritance following Levi Martin's death. The failure of their plans results in the suicide of mother and daughter. Edgar Martin, secure in the love of Grossbeak's daughter, Eliza, rescues his sister Ellen from bandits in Italy. Ellen is reunited with her husband, Charles Armstrong, who had been presumed lost at sea; their two children, left in their infancy at the Grossbeak Mansion by the then distraught Ellen, have been carefully nurtured by the Grossbeaks.

467.   ————. *Magdalena, the outcast*; or, *The millionaire's daughter*. A story of life in the Empire City. New York: Hilton, 1866. 96p. (in double columns).

Wall Street financier Linden Van Linden, a resident of Fifth Avenue with his naïve daughter Magdalena, is most suspicious of her music teacher, Señor Desmondo—and well he might be. Desmondo is one of a gang of thieves (the N.O.C.) and is concocting a scheme to relieve Van Linden of his millions. Though constantly warned by her father, Magdalena falls in love with Desmondo and refuses to believe ill of him. Buntline here introduces a number of other characters in his story who seem rather superfluous to the main plot. Magdalena eventually runs off with Desmondo and marries him. When the latter suspects that Magdalena's vexed father will cut her out of his will (Van Linden has just passed away) he deserts her and hands her over to several roués. Magdalena, now an 'outcast', embarks on a life of prostitution and thievery. After an especially shocking murder in which one of Magdalena's criminal associates implicates her, she is released by the courts and, with money derived from her father's estate, leaves New York for Cincinnati and a life of 'reform for her past mistakes.'

————. *Miriam*; or, *The Jew's daughter* … See Item #472.

468.   ————. *The mysteries and miseries of New York*; a story of real life. New York: Berford, 1848. 5v. in 1.

Buntline's 'magnum opus' is in five parts. The novel consists of three separate stories: Charlie Meadows, a clerk addicted to gambling, embezzles, sacrifices his sister's virtue and even murders to satisfy his creditors. Francis, a criminal, becomes secretary to a philanthropist in order to set him up for robbery. Angelina, a seamstress suffering from tuberculosis, is in harm's way at the hands of a libidinous man-about-town. In Angelina's case a sometimes softhearted prostitute, Big Lize, assumes the role of her protector. The several young women in the novel generally meet with cruel, sudden deaths or face a life in the lower depths. Buntline's avowed purpose is to expose the iniquities of the metropolis, and thereby incite responsive citizens, clergymen especially, to activate reform movements. Two additional 'parts' were added ca. 1850?

469. ————. *Rose Seymour*; or, *The ballet girl's revenge*. **A tale of the New York drama. New York: Hilton, 1865. 96p. (in double columns).**

Seeking a future in the Broadway theater Rose Seymour suffers the slings and arrows of outrageous fortune in this incredible tale. She is constantly on the run from the infatuated James Briggs (a.k.a. Pierre Duval), a former convict, forger and counterfeiter and presently a member of New York's affluent society. Brigg's/Duval's wife, Clara, is a murderous wench who prizes her jewels above her husband's affection. Bandied about by various criminals Rose is last seen trying to escape from a lecherous band of quarrymen. Clara and a new lover, New York playboy Jesse Dumar, embark for Europe, avoiding death when their ship is destroyed by fire.

470. ————. *Thayendaneaga the Scourge*; or, *The war-eagle of the Mohawks*. **A tale of mystery, ruth and wrong. New York: F.A. Brady, 1858. 77p.**

The novel portrays the role played in the American Revolution by Joseph Brant (Thayendaneaga), the Mohawk chieftain, who stood firmly with the British. It has the usual elements: a hero, heroine and villain, but also brings in Ron Yost, who much of the time is under the influence of liquor he consumes in vast quantities.

471. ————. *Three years after*; a sequel to *The mysteries and miseries of New York*. **New York: W.F. Burgess, 1849. 175p. (in double columns).**

Continued by *The b'hoys of New York*. Harry Whitmore, very much in love with Constance Shirley (and the fortune she is heir to), is most anxious to cut all ties to Isabella Meadows, a courtesan, but previously Whitmore's mistress. Charles Meadows, Isabella's brother, although addicted to alcohol and gambling, vows to avenge the wrongs suffered by Isabella at Whitmore's hands. When Whitmore's true character is made known to Constance she refuses to marry him. With the help of the gambler Henry (or Harry) Carlton, Carlton's crony, Sam Selden, and the pirate Gaspar Alvorado, Whitmore has Constance kidnapped (Isabella Meadows is simultaneously abducted). Charles Meadows, Constance Shirley's father, Mose, an honest young fireman and laborer, and the police appear on the scene and disrupt the villains' plans. Gaspar Alvorado eludes the police net; Carlton and Selden escape punishment because they have knowledge of a dark secret in Mr. Shirley's past. As usual Buntline weaves in a plethora of subplots and characters, ever admonishing young women to avoid the many traps that await them in wicked New York City.

472. ————. *The wheel of misfortune*; or, *The victims of lottery and policy*

dealers. **A yarn from the web of New York life. New York: Garrett [1853]. 100p. (in double columns).**

Two crooked lottery operators, Mr. Grab and his agent Tullius Catlin, are creating havoc among New Yorkers. The seductive Catlin is the more pernicious of the two; one of his victims, Constance Morley, uses her beauty to persuade underworld figures to punish Catlin. Other victims are young Charles Brennon, his wife Mary and her father, Mr. Brent, all ruined by the infamous lottery. Tragedy overwhelms them when Mary strikes her head against a marble fireplace after her angry husband shoves her. Brent kills his son-in-law and commits suicide. Oddly enough this work was also published under the title: *Miriam*; or, *The Jew's daughter*. A tale of city life (New York, Dick & Fitzgerald [185-?]). That title is a misnomer since 'Miriam' is a minor character who has little to do with the story's main themes.

473. **Burdett, Charles, b. 1815. *Arthur Martin*; or, *The mother's trials*. New York: Harper, 1847. 225, 16, [10]p.**

Mrs. Martin and her children, Arthur and Annie, eke out a bare subsistence after her husband, Sam, is crushed under the Brooklyn Ferry. Employed as a clerk in Mr. Gabriel's store Arthur falls under the bad influence of another employee, the extravagant Jenks. The latter seduces Annie and Arthur, faced by debts, steals from the store. He runs off to sea on a whaling vessel and returns with sufficient funds to square himself with Mr. Gabriel and get his old job back. Poor Annie is abandoned by Jenks after a mock marriage and returns to her mother's hearth. Arthur climbs the ladder of success to a partnership in Gabriel & Co. Burdett, a New Yorker, is quick to preach morality and piety and explore the contrast between the fashionable life and poverty.

474. ————. *Chances and changes*; or, *Life as it is illustrated in the history of a straw hat*. **New York: D. Appleton, 1846. 158p.**

The narrator is a special straw hat—"I woke to consciousness in the splendid establishment of Madame B. in Broadway, in the City of New York"—sold to Anna Edson of W. Place, daughter of a wealthy widower. Anna becomes interested in Jane Stevens, whose work at Madam B.'s is the only source of income for Jane and her mother. Taken into the Edson household, Jane finds a permanent home there. The two women are left alone after the deaths of Mrs. Stevens and Mr. Edson. Anna inherits great wealth. Henry Edgerton, a fortune hunter, courts her, but Jane unmasks him. It comes to light that the Edgertons, father and son, defrauded Mrs. Stevens of money left by her husband. Anna dismisses Henry Edgerton and never marries, but goes about her good works with the needy, accompanied by Jane (now Mrs. Adams), wearing her beloved old straw hat.

475. ————. *The convict's child*. **New York: Baker and Scribner, 1846. 288p.**

Alida Thorne and her drunken father, James, live in a tenement on the Bowery. Ill and beaten unmercifully by her father, Alida is placed by a kindly doctor with Mrs. Elliott. After James Thorne is sentenced to prison for a robbery he did not commit, Alida passes to the well-to-do Darntons who adopt her when they lose their son. Released from prison James Thorne takes part in a robbery of the Darnton residence in the course of which he stabs his daughter. Upon her recovery Alida disappears into the city's depths and finds her father near death. She stays with the repentant sinner until he dies and then goes back to the Darntons. The story of Alida's past is inadvertently revealed to her adoptive parents' social circle. Crushed by the swirl of controversy that surrounds her, Alida sinks slowly to her death. Buried in a New York churchyard the headstone next to her marker bears the initials—"J.T."

476. ————. *Dora Barton, the banker's ward.* **A tale of real life in New York. New York: S.A. Rollo, 1860. 355p.**

Bachelor banker Charles Barton adopts an abandoned female child, bypassing the usual legal documents, and gives her the name Dora Barton. Barton's niece, Clara Edson, treats Dora shabbily and when Mr. Barton dies, apparently intestate, his sister, Mrs. Edson and Clara take over his riches. Dr. Thornton, an old friend of Barton, receives Dora into his household. Dora falls in love with the doctor's nephew, Arthur Randolph. The doctor himself is smitten with Miss Arden, a visitor from the West. Astonishing revelations follow closely on one another. An early will executed by Barton and his lawyer is brought to light; it names Dora heir to the major share of Barton's fortune. And Miss Arden and Dora are long-lost mother and daughter—the story behind that is left for the reader to fathom, and all's well that ends well.

477. ————. *The Elliott family*; or, *The trials of New York seamstresses.* **New York: E. Winchester, 1845. 162p.**

The novel is a diatribe against clothing manufacturers who pay their women workers 'starvation wages'. Left in straitened circumstances by Mr. Elliott's sudden death, Mrs. Elliott and her two daughters, Clara and Laura try in vain to scrape a living from piecework given them by shirt and dress manufacturers. Destitution and lingering death are their lot. In contrast, the Simmons family rises from humble circumstances to wealth, but deals ruthlessly with those (including the Elliotts) who are on the lower economic and social scale. They receive a partial comeuppance, but survive.

478. ————. *The gambler*; or, *The police story.* **New York: Baker and Scribner, 1848. 179p.**

Starr, a New York policeman, follows the career of Mr. James Andrews, an inveterate gambler, who embezzles and burglarizes to feed his habit. Andrews leaves his wife in poverty, his daughter Julia disappears, and he himself takes to strong drink. When Starr tracks Andrews down, the latter blames his fall from grace on Robert Pearson, a roué and man-about-town. His victims refuse to prosecute Andrews and he seems to be on his way to reformation. But he suffers a relapse and eventually ends up in the Lunatic Asylum at Blackwell's Island. Mrs. Andrews expires and Julia, inheritor of a tidy sum from Pearson whom she has married near the point of his death, lives out her days peacefully.

479. ————. *Lilla Hart*; a tale of New York. **New York: Baker and Scribner, 1846. 197p.**

Sandford the narrator, takes Lilla Hart and her mother into his home after father and husband Samuel Hart is found dead on the street. A merchant, James Wilson, has a special interest in Lilla; he and a confederate, George Brown, who were involved in Samuel Hart's ruin and death, kidnap Lilla. A much-bruised young girl's body is identified as Lilla's from a cross around the girl's neck. It now comes out that Wilson's daughter Delia is the inheritor of an estate that would have gone to Lilla had she been alive. When Lilla does turn up (a shamed George Brown had not carried out Wilson's orders to dispose of her), Wilson is forced to hand over the inheritance to Lilla. Magnanimously relieved of any penalty for his crimes, Wilson gradually leaves this life fully repentant.

480. ————. *Never too late*. **New York: D. Appleton, 1845. 180p.**

The story opens with teenager George Edgar on Broadway begging for money to help his ill and dying mother. Left alone in the world George finds a berth on Captain Jack Hart's vessel, the Irene. He prospers under Hart's guidance, but disaster strikes when the Irene sinks; the Captain is lost and his family, a wife and three daughters, are left destitute in New York City. George survives the shipwreck and must search for a new berth. He not only achieves that, his mother's long absent uncle also finances him in new ventures. Eventually George finds Irene Hart, the only surviving member of Captain Hart's family and marries her. Parallel to George Edgar's story is that of Eugene Rawson, a spoiled rich man's son, who goes to sea in the United States Navy, and after many false starts proves that it is 'never too late' to turn one's life around.

481. ————. *The second marriage*; or, *A daughter's tale*. **A domestic tale of New York. New York: C. Scribner, 1856. 238p.**

Her father's second wife succeeds in having his daughter, Cora Marvin, banished from his house. Cora's husband is away at sea and Cora and her 18-month-old son are living in dire poverty in a shabby room near the corner of Bleecker and Christopher Streets. The primary aim of Cora's stepmother is, with the help of her daughter Mattie and an accomplice, Robert Barton, to get her hands on Mr. Marvin's wealth. A sympathetic doctor, the story's narrator, comes to Cora's aid, reuniting father and daughter and forcing the scoundrel Barton to flee the city. The death of Cora's long-absent husband opens the door for the doctor to marry Cora, the woman he has come to dearly love.

482. **Burgess, Gelett, 1866-1951.** *Find the woman*. **Illus. by Hanson Booth. Indianapolis: Bobbs-Merrill, 1911. 342p.**

The young hero of this picaresque tale is a man in search of himself. He has fallen in love with the portrait of a girl he has never seen in the flesh. After several fantastic adventures he is in New York one night when confronted with even more peculiar experiences as he traverses the city from Wall Street to Harlem. Yet he finally learns who he really is, identifies the girl in the picture and wins her love, and is the surprised beneficiary of a fortune.

483. ————. *A little sister of destiny.* **Boston: Houghton, Mifflin, 1906. 258p.**
A rather unsophisticated but high-spirited girl who has inherited millions invested in California properties and industries is a center of attention for the arbiters of society in that Pacific Coast State. Weary of it all, she heads for New York City where she uses her money and good will to turn several unhappy or fragmented lives around. She herself has the good fortune to find a husband who shares her concerns, is supportive of her occasionally rash ventures and welcomes the opportunity to manage her finances, a task she abhors.

484. ————. *The master of mysteries*; **being an account of the problems solved by Astro, seer of secrets, and his love affair with Valeska Wynne, his assistant. With illus. by Karl Anderson and George Brehm. Indianapolis: Bobbs-Merrill, 1912. 480p.**
'Astro' may read palms and may be a crystal gazer but he is not a charlatan. His sphere of action is generally the affluent sections of New York City; his clients are often the well-heeled. Astro has a talent for solving human enigmas; his methodology has at times a mystical Eastern flavor, but he is still well-versed in the latest scientific techniques of the Western world. The book contains 24 chapters, each of which represents a case to be solved.

Burke, Talbot. See: Burke, William Talbot.

485. **Burke, William Talbot.** *Pingleton*; or, *Queer people I have met.* **From the notes of a New York cicerone. Edited by Talbot Burke. New York: W.T. Burke, 1856. 156p.**
American Pickwickian, Philander Pingleton, and Mr. Beggs, both of Teaneck, New Jersey are taken around New York City by the narrator and a fellow by the name of 'Ike' (who could serve as Sam Weller's double). They are not only sightseers—Wall Street and its 'bucket' shops and Poe Cottage are of special interest to them—but also show concern for people in need of help: e.g., Ben Losing, a former Pingletonian, and a broker who loses a fortune on Wall Street; Mr. Dillingham, falsely accused of wrong-doing by his evil partner, Mr. Lockman; Jennie Hildebrande, a young woman whose virtue Lockman would steal. 'Aunt Anna' of 'Harborville' draws Pingleton into matrimony; Dillingham marries Jennie after the villainous Lockman is routed; there is the possibility of a brighter future for Ben Losing.

486. **Burlingame, Roger, 1889-1967.** *Three bags full.* **New York: Harcourt, Brace, 1936. 637p.**

"Late in the eighteenth century Hendrik van Huyten and his friend and brother-in-law, Pieter de Groot, pushing into the wilderness of central New York, came upon a lovely little lake and there settled. in time others joined them and the town of 'Glenvil' [Cazenovia] was founded. This long historical novel carries the tale of the Van Huytens and their town to the 1920s"—Book review digest.

487. Burnet, Dana, 1888-1962. *The shining adventure*. New York: Harper, 1916. 266p.

He was only a boy of '8 going on 9', but he was acutely aware of the needy children who gazed longingly through the iron fence as he played in his domain, Gramercy Park. He was called 'the King' and dwelt in a large house on the north side of the Park. With his tin sword and a pocketful of change the 'King' crossed over into a poor section of Manhattan, O'Connor's Alley, where he met lame Maggie O'Connor, had a fight with Mickey Finn, formed an army, made the Park accessible to those 'other children', and had other adventures. Could one doubt that the 'King's' concerns eventually led to a softening of stern Miss Philomena Van Zandt, president of the United Charities of New York, the election of good Mr. Terence O'Connor as alderman and the cure of 'Queen Maggie's' crippled condition?

488. Burnham, Clara Louise Root, 1854-1927. *Miss Bagg's secretary*; a West Point romance. Boston: Houghton, Mifflin, 1892. 424p.

When her wealthy uncle, Jotham Bagg, dies intestate, his fortune goes to spinster Lydia Bagg, 51, from Massachusetts. The intended heir, ex-Army lieutenant Maxwell (Max) Van Kirk, persuades Lydia to move into her uncle's residence in New York City and he agrees to serve as her private secretary. Max refuses the offer when Lydia suggests he take a major portion of Jotham's money. Invited to West Point by a friend, Mrs. Spencer, to attend Ralph Spencer's graduation, Lydia is accompanied by Bertha ('Baby'), Mrs. Spencer's daughter and Olive Carlyle, a cousin of Ida Fuller; Ida is a widow Max has been seeing quite frequently. Before long Max, disenchanted with mercenary Ida, has fallen in love with Olive and Bertha is engaged to a cadet captain. Lydia is a benign presence in all these happenings. She announces that her wedding present to Max's fiancée Olive will be a substantial sum of money "but not … so much as to turn him [Max] into a fortune hunter."

489. ————. *A West Point wooing, and other stories*. Boston: Houghton ,Mifflin, 1899. 305p.

The first five stories (half of the volume) are about cadets and officers at West Point pursuing or being pursued by a variety of young women. Without exception the tales conclude with the couples married or on the verge of marriage. Partial contents: A West Point wooing.—Pursuer or pursued?—A cadet camp episode.—A Franco-American.—The cadet captain's experiment.

490. Burns, William. *Female life in New York City*. Illustrated with forty-four real

portraits from life. Philadelphia: T.B. Peterson [1875?]. 94p. (in double columns).

The 44 sketches (only 43 in this edition) that portray the many occupations women in the city pursue in order to support themselves and/or their dependents are often fictional—e.g., 'The artificial flower maker', Nelly, is pursued by Mr. Vickar who wants her to be his mistress; she refuses. 'The vest maker' is in love with a young cooper, but she is prepared to continue her trade should he not succeed. 'The milliner', Ellen Stanley, becomes a prosperous entrepreneur following her unfortunate father's ruin and death, etc., etc. Contents: The artificial flower maker.—The vest maker.—The choir-singer.—The milliner.—The type rubber.—The shop-woman.—The dress maker.—The tailoress.—The umbrella maker.—The suspender-maker.—The 'school-marm'.—The gimp-weaver.—The actress.—The ballet girl.—The cap-maker.—The book folder.—'Sweets to the sweet'.—The pocket book maker.—The weaver.—The straw braider.—The print colorer.—The embroidress.—The fancy box-maker.—The hat trimmer.—The gold leaf packer.—The bazaar tender.—The chair painter.—The button maker.—The book sewer.—The shoe binder.—The corset maker.—The nurse.—The shirt-maker.—The press feeder.—The bar-maid.—The wool picker.—The fruit vendor.—The market-woman.—The chambermaid.—The apple woman.—The cook.—The washerwomen.—Street minstrels.

Burr, Anna Robeson Brown, 1873-1941. See: Brown, Anna Robeson, 1873-1941.

491. **Burr, Jane, pseud.** *The glorious hope*; a novel. **Croton-on-Hudson, N.Y,: Jane Burr, 1918. 272p.**

Along with a description of artistic life in New York the novel records the constant struggle for success and celebrity and nighttime revels. "The story portrays the adverse psychological effect that the love of two people for each other has on both of them. Evelyn Kerwin marries Stanley Bird in the hope that her mothering will stimulate his delicate genius into activity. As a result he slumps more and more into discouraged apathy and her own ambitions become paralyzed. When she finally breaks away from him her undertakings succeed beyond expectations and he too begins to make a name for himself as a cartoonist. They lose sight of each other and Evelyn secures a divorce and remarries. When they meet again in Paris, he has become a great artist under a French name, with a French wife and French children. Simultaneously with the discovery that their old love is still alive in both of them comes the discovery of its old baneful effect"—Book review digest.

492. **Burt, Katharine Newlin, 1882-1977.** *Escape from Paradise.* **New York: Scribner, 1952. 308p.**

"The 'Paradise' was a large estate on the Hudson presided over by stout lovable Aunt Kinny. Those who lived with her were the children, Luke, Maggie and Selena, with various others dependent on Aunt Kinney's wealth.

127

The novel describes the love of both of the girls for the handsome, undependable Luke, and various 'escapes' from the too loving care of Aunt Kinney"—Book review digest.

493. ————. *Lady in the tower.* **Philadelphia: Macrae-Smith, 1946. 284p.**
Jenny, the heroine, lives in a house on the Hudson whose most prominent feature is an imposing tower. The house holds secrets, one of which relates to Jenny's own mother. If Jenny can unlock that secret, her future might be bright. There is no dearth of romance and adventure for Jenny as she seeks answers.

494. ————. *No surrender*; **a novel. Philadelphia: Macrae-Smith, 1940. 258p.**
The father of Jed and Rufus Galt leaves the Galt estate, 'Faildyke', in Upstate New York, to Cathryn (Cathie) Kiethan. The land is in default, but the two brothers still undertake the management of the property. Jed and Cathie are hateful to one another for a number of years before the mutual antagonism turns to love (Cathie at one time had threatened to marry Perry, a neighbor). Rufus had even looked at Cathie as a possible bride for himself, though he had been half-promised to Cissie, Cathie's friend.

495. **Burt, Maxwell Struthers, 1882-1954.** *The interpreter's house.* **New York: Scribner, 1924. xi, 445p.**
The New York that took shape immediately after the end of World War I is the setting for a novel that concentrates on three generations of the Eyre family—the oldest, which was fully mature in the very early years of the 20th century; the middle, bursting into full bloom just before 1914; and the present, escaping from adolescence into the sophistication of the jazz age. Three of the principal characters are: Philip Eyre, the banker; Drusila, the unhappy wife; and especially Gulian, the youngest, who had served in the war, but was now restless, writing poetry, and contemplating a diplomatic career—he finally readjusts to the family, although he still asks the eternal question: Is there beauty yet to find? And certainty? Philip, the supposedly steady Eyre, shoots and kills himself.

Burt, Struthers, 1882-1954. See: Burt, Maxwell Struthers, 1882-1954.

496. **Burton, Gabrielle, 1939- .** *Heartbreak Hotel.* **New York: Scribner, 1986. x, 303p.**
"Hospitalized and unconscious after a hit-and-run motorcycle accident [Margaret] Valentine conjures up Quasi, a drooling white-haired, pink-eyed hunchback who has been similarly injured and is also comatose. ... In Valentine's dream Quasi's critical condition challenges the six housemates [Quasi, Meg, Rita, Gretchen, Daisy and Pearl] living with her in Heartbreak Hotel. ... All but Quasi are named a diminutive of Margaret. ... They work at the Museum of the Revolution ... a repository ... of female life experiences. ... Valentine dreams that the city fathers of Buffalo try to close the museum

by first launching an attack on the hotel. Quasi's accident and a sudden rush of summonses … appear to be part of a patriarchal plot to destroy the museum. The six Margarets must fight to save their past in the museum and their future possibilities in Quasi"—Ms. magazine.

497. Busch, Franc. *The Jewess, Leonora*; a novel. New York: W. Paulding Caruthers, 1896. 222p.

The novel opens in 1843 in New York City (St. John's Park). Leonora Arnstein (unbeknownst to her, an orphan, the daughter of Karl Sturmer, a Christian, and his Jewish wife), 12, is being reared by the elderly servant Lispeth and her 'father' (actually her grandfather) Enos Arnstein. Enos plans to join his nephew Leon and Leonora in wedlock when Leonora reaches the proper age. But the years pass, and while resting in the Hudson Highlands with the faithful Lispeth, Leonora falls in love with Dr. Richard Leighton; the two plan to marry. The open-minded Leon apprises Enos Arnstein of Leonora's intentions. Arnstein is enraged; he suffers a paralyzing stroke when Lispeth (real name: Marie Elizabeth Rabowski) shows him an Arnstein family casket filled with valuables that he had long sought as Leonora's patrimony. Leonora and Richard marry and Leonora, leaving behind her Jewish faith, converts to Christianity. Enos spends his last years in London with Leon and his family.

498. Busch, Frederick, 1941- . *Closing arguments*. New York: Ticknor & Fields, 1991. 288p.

Mark Brennan, an attorney in a small Upstate New York town, is accorded local hero status (which he is uneasy with) because of his Vietnam War experiences. His family includes his wife, a former anti-war demonstrator, a son in high school always on the verge of real trouble, and a daughter in New York City who may have made a deadly romantic choice. When Brennan accepts a feeless murder case in which he defends a woman charged with murdering her boyfriend while they were having 'rough sex', he finds himself giving in to despondency as past indiscretions, lies and facts are laid bare.

499. ————. *Harry and Catherine*. New York: Knopf, 1990. 290p.

Two former lovers, Harry Miller and Catherine Holland, meet again when he, a journalist but now assistant to a liberal U.S. senator, comes to the Chenango Valley in south central New York State to look at a construction site that could contain the bones of slaves. Catherine, the divorced mother of two boys, has an art gallery not far from the site. Her present lover, Carter Kreuss, runs a paving firm that has a vital stake in the contemplated construction project. Olivia Stoddard, a small-town banker's wife (and quondam lover of Carter Kreuss), is the leader in a movement to head off any activity that would disturb the remains of the dead slaves. Then the matter of wetlands conservation also comes into play. In the end the projected mall is called off: Carter suffers a crippling financial loss, but moves the bones to a location near

Catherine's home. Harry and Catherine decide to get back together on a permanent basis.

500. ————. *Rounds.* **New York: Farrar, Straus & Giroux, 1979. 243p.**

This novel takes place in upper New York State. The central character "is Eli Silver, a pediatrician whose ... child died in an automobile accident ... [Another character is] Phil Sorenson [who] has come to nearby Bailey College to teach English. ... Phil's wife, Annie, after two marriages, longs desperately for a baby. Lizzie Bean, the college psychiatrist, spunky and unstable, is pregnant by one of Phil Sorenson's colleagues, who takes no responsibility for her. Eli Silver, the pediatrician, separated from his wife, loves Lizzie Bean, and wants her unborn child to belong to a family; he arranges for the Sorensons to adopt the child. The 'real' father, growing unbalanced and obsessed, kidnaps the baby. ... The 'rounds' of the title are Eli Silver's visits to his patients"—Harper's magazine.

501. ————. *Sometimes I live in the country.* **Boston: D.R. Godine, 1986. 218p.**

Intelligent adolescent Petey, 13, has moved from Brooklyn to Upstate New York with his single, reticent father, an ex-policeman. Petey has a suicidal impulse that compels him to play Russian roulette with his father's service revolver. Not being able to draw much response from his dad, Petey turns to Lizzie Bean, his father's girlfriend, and the school guidance counselor, but when he becomes friendly with a black senior citizen, Petey draws the ill will of the local Ku Klux Klan. By the close of the novel Petey and his father have worked out a close, more loving relationship.

502. **Butor, Michael, 1926- .** *Niagara***; a stereoscopic novel. Translated from the French by Elinor S. Miller. Chicago: H. Regnery, 1969. 267p.**

Translation of: 6,810,000 [i.e. Six million huit cent dix mille] litres d'eau par seconde. An experimental novel that gives one an impressionistic portrait of Niagara Falls and glances at the people visiting this world famous attraction—old couples recalling their memories of the Falls and newly married couples aware only of one another—all taking in the profusion of flowers, the cataracts, the ambiance.

Butters, Dorothy Gilman, 1923- . See: Gilman, Dorothy, 1923-

503. **Bynner, Edwin Lassetter, 1842-1893.** *The Begum's daughter.* **With illus. by F.T. Merrill. Boston: Little, Brown, 1890. vi, 473p.**

The novel "is in a large measure historical, dealing with a most interesting and picturesque epoch—the old Knickerbocker life in New York, when the present great metropolis was a little Dutch town, surrounded by palisades. Names well known in New York history appear, and a vivid presentation is made of the political conflicts of the period. The Begum is an East Indian married to a prominent New Yorker [a Dutch physician] of the time. She and her daughter are strong factors in the story [which also deals with Leisler's

Rebellion against the supposed accession of Catholic power in New York"]—Annual American catalogue.

504. ———. *Tritons*; a novel. **Boston: Lockwood, Brooks, 1878. 406p.**

It had always been assumed that Ralph Dexter was the son of New York millionaire Sydney Dexter and his wife, but after Sydney Dexter dies intestate Ralph learns that his real mother is Rebecca Hoyt whose burial he had inadvertently witnessed. Refusing to accept money from Mrs. Dexter, Ralph sinks into dissipated ways. Rebecca Hoyt had two other children by Sydney Dexter—Rachel and Baby—who have been reared by the peddler 'True Blue' (Truman Ballou) and his wife 'Lady Pamela' (the 'Tritons'). Changing his lifestyle out of love for Dorothy Dighton, Ralph leaves New York and gradually achieves success out West as an architect. On his return to New York Ralph learns more about his origin and befriends his little brother and sister and the Ballous. The loss of a leg in a fire draws Dorothy to Ralph's side and the two are married. Upon her death Mrs. Dexter leaves Ralph a large bequest; 'True Blue' and 'Lady Pamela' become caretakers of a seaside cottage deeded to Dorothy by an uncle.

505. Byrne, Donn, 1889-1928. *The foolish matrons*. **New York:Harper, 1920. 383p.**

"The heroines of the story are four [women of upper society in New York City]: one wise and three foolish. The wise one was a great actress who married the big, uncouth surgeon whom she loved, gave up her career and became the guardian angel and mother of her children. Georgia, pretty and frivolous, craved the excitement of [the city]. Married, she was a vampire and finally drifted to the underworld. Sheila, the college graduate and newspaperwoman, clever and heartless, dreamt of a career, married a poet for the glamour of it and drove him to drink with her coldness. Sappho, the model, frankly married for money, and posed as a patroness of amateur artists. She became ashamed of her plain millionaire husband and thought to do better for herself, but almost lost in the game"—Book review digest.

Byrnes, Garrett Davis, joint author. *Scoop.* **See Item #1520.**

C. & C. *Two gentlemen of Verona.* **See Item #506.**

C.R.B. Redeemed. See Item #1711.

506. [Cabot, Arthur Winslow]. *Two gentlemen of Gotham*, **by C. & C. New York: Cassell, 1887. 344p.**

The two bachelors, men-about-town and inveterate New Yorkers, Percy Alymer and Sydney Harleston, give little indication that they take anything very seriously, least of all the concept of marriage. Mona Vere, a proper Bostonian—her father had been ambassador at the Court of St. James—changes all that for Percy. He is drawn to her, first meeting Mona at the Metropolitan Opera. Bonnie Maccoume, daughter of a speculator in railroads, has designs on Percy and schemes to keep the two, Percy and Mona, apart. When Percy proposes to Mona while at 'Ennerslie', the Hudson Valley home of the Veres, Mona rebuffs him. Months go by; Percy returns from a Western sojourn, and this time Mona can no longer reject Percy's suit for she is in love with him and he assures her that there has been a more serious turn to his life. Sydney Harleston has in the meantime surrendered to the captivating charms of Gladys Maccoume, Bonnie's warmhearted sister; Bonnie must content herself with her engagement to Prince Orloff who, along with the poet Wilfred Lee, had been in the 'contest' for Mona's affections.

507. **Cahan, Abraham, 1860-1951.** *Fenni's hasanim.* **Di neshome yeseyre. New York: Forward Association [1913?]. 211p.**

In Yiddish. Translation of titles: *Fanny's suitors. The transcendent spirit.* Fanny is, so she tells the unnamed editor, an uneducated woman, a shop worker in New York, who has incidentally written a story about her inability to attract reliable suitors. As he gets to know Fanny better, he perceives that she pleads her own ignorance of other matters to veil her own narrow-mindedness. She is, however, deeply interested in having her writings published. The second piece is about: (1) Cutler, a socialist, who is deeply disturbed when his son, Muzi, a City College of New York graduate, attains wealth, abandons his father's socialism and vocally supports the local Tammany politician; (2) A once honest man who turns into a corrupt saloon owner. Cahan closes with other bits about the decline of the socialist spirit, but with hopes for an improving mankind.

508. —————. *The imported bridegroom and other stories of the New York ghetto.* **Boston: Houghton, Mifflin, 1898. 256p.**

Tales of Russian Jews recently settled in New York City's Lower East Side, many of whom work in sweatshops and attend religious classes at Beth Hamedrash Hagodol on Norfolk Street. In the long title story a learned young Talmudist (Shaya) is brought to America by Asriel Stroon, a New York businessman, as a match for his daughter, Flora. Much to Asriel's chagrin Shaya starts to take on the Western intellectual ways of his new environment. Flora and Shaya marry, but even she, quite Americanized, feels that Shaya is drifting farther away from her as he concentrates on Comte's positivism, etc. Contents: The imported bridegroom.—A providential match.—A sweatshop romance.—Circumstances.—A ghetto wedding.

509. —————. *Rafael Naarizokh*; **an erzaylung vegn a stolyer voz iz gekommen zum saykhl. New York: B. Weinstein, 1907. 206p.**

In Yiddish. Translation of title: Raphael Naarizoch, a story of a carpenter who came to his senses. Revision and expansion of: Rafael Naarizokh iz gevoren a sozialist. Rafael Radetzky, a carpenter, leaves his native village of Kriletz in Eastern Europe for the promise of opportunities in New York City. He is soon disillusioned by the low wages and the machine-driven intensity of factory work. He is converted to socialism and the idea of public ownership of the means of production (an intellectual by the name of Vicker is a major influence). Rafael is now a new man, 'not richer, not more pious, but more of a mensch.'

510.　————. T*he rise of David Levinsky*; a novel. New York: Harper, 1917. **529p.**

A Russian Jew, David Levinsky, leaves the ghettos of Russia in 1895 when he is 20 to migrate to New York City's East Side. At first an unsuccessful street peddler, he goes to work in a clothing factory, hoping to earn enough to enroll at City College of New York. However he is sidetracked by unforeseen circumstances and uses his knowledge to start a clothing operation of his own. By virtue of shady practices he prospers and has affairs with several women, none of whom he is inclined to marry. His search for a more meaningful, pleasant life eludes him despite his money and the trappings of worldly success. Cahan's novel, narrated by his protagonist, David, is perhaps the earliest significant piece of "immigrant fiction," focusing on the garment trade, unionism, and socialistic currents in New York City.

511.　————. *Yekl*; a tale of the New York ghetto. New York: Appleton, 1896. **v, 190p.**

Jake Podgorny (Yekl is his Old World name), a cloak-maker in a sweatshop, in 3 years has become Americanized and is involved with blond Mamie Fein when he decides to bring his wife Gitl from overseas to New York. Gitl arrives and Jake is taken aback by her shapeless garments and Orthodox wig. Gitl makes improvements in her appearance, but jealous Mamie comes back into Jake's life. Jake and Gitl are divorced. She remarries; with a good deal of reluctance Jake finds himself on the way to the City Hall and marriage with Mamie.

Caine, Jeffrey, 1944- . See: Campbell, Jeffrey, the joint pseudonym of Jeffrey Caine and Campbell Black.

512.　**Caldwell, Taylor, 1900-1985.** *The sound of thunder.* **Garden City, N.Y.: Doubleday, 1957. 608p.**

"A family chronicle [1904-1937] about a German-American family, the Engers, living in Upstate New York. [Heinrich, the father, started a profitable food store chain]. Ed, the family drudge builds up his father's delicatessen business until it is worth a fortune. But the rest of the family depends upon him for support, hating him all the time, and Ed returns their hate. A coronary thrombosis, which takes Ed to death's door, brings a better understanding to the whole family and to Ed himself"—Book review digest.

513.　————. *This side of innocence.* **New York: Scribner, 1946. 199p**

The novel follows the fortunes (and misfortunes) of the Lindsey family and the town, 'Riversend', in Upstate New York, that they loom over. Alfred, adopted by William Lindsey, and cousin to Jerome, Mr. Lindsey's son, marries the beautiful Amalie Maxwell. The bride quickly discovers that she has no tolerance for Alfred's sexual advances and turns to the dashing Jerome. The affair results in Amalie's pregnancy; Alfred divorces Amalie and she marries Jerome. After the patriarch's death, Alfred and Jerome jointly manage the Lindsey bank, but Jerome successfully pushes for the industrialization of Riversend; conservative Alfred is lukewarm to Jerome's plans. Jerome, now wealthy, takes an interest in Philip, Alfred's son by his first wife, Martha. When Jerome dies in an accident, Alfred, displaying compassion and a renewed interest in Amalie, comes to her. Amalie is grateful for his presence and she assures him that future visits would be welcomed. The marriage of Philip and Mary, daughter of Jerome and Amalie, meets with the approval of Amalie and Alfred.

514. ————. *The wide house.* **Garden City, N.Y.: Sun Dial Press, 1945. 563p.**
The entrepreneur Stuart Coleman owns several shops in the booming town of 'Grandeville', New York and is ready to expand his business. He borrows $20,000 from his avaricious, homely cousin, the widow Janie Cauder, who has just moved to the town with her four children. When Stuart announces his marriage to Marvina, daughter of the bigoted Joshua Allstairs, he acquires the undying hatred of Janie Cauder (who had expected Stuart to marry her) and Joshua. Intolerance rears its head in Grandeville and Stuart is protective of his good friend, Sam Berkowitz, a German Jew, and Father ("Grundy") Houlihan, but he cannot prevent the murder of Berkowitz. Stuart's commercial interests suffer a sharp decline and Angus, Janie's son, is ready to take them over. Angus has a miraculous change of heart, converts to Catholicism, studies to be a missionary and returns Stuart to solvency. Joshua Allstairs is found guilty of arranging Sam Berkowitz's murder. Marvina leaves Stuart, but he has the comfort of visits by his daughter, Mary Rose, and possible union with Laurie, Janie's daughter and a career-oriented singer.

515. **Call, William T.** *Josh Hayseed in New York.* **Edited by Wm. T. Call (Sprouts). Illustrated by Coultaus. New York: Excelsior Pub. House, c1887. 127p.**
Cover title: *Josh Hayseed's trip to New York.* Enos Tooksbury of Musquash County says goodbye to his cousin Jersusha and starts out for New York City, his great adventure. He adopts the name, Josh Hayseed [of] Squashville as suggested by a fellow rail passenger. Jerusha has requested that Enos (Josh) keep a 'gernul' (journal) of his experiences in the modern Sodom and Gomorrah and Josh complies. Thus the reader is confronted with all the misspellings and malapropisms of Josh's dialect. The author, under his byname, Sprouts, accompanies our country bumpkin hero as he tussles with the peculiar inhabitants and artifacts of the big city—confidence men and women, high society, Bowery toughs, Delmonico's Restaurant, the Astor Library, Cleopatra's Needle, Grant's Tomb, Central Park, Brighton Beach, Niblo's garden, an opium den, Brooklyn Bridge, etc. Josh has a moment of glory when he "sees the Elephant [Hotel on Coney Island] and rides home triumphant."

516. Cameron, Donald Clough, ca. 1909- . Grave without grass. New York: Holt, 1940. 272p.

"A number of the residents of the Long Island village of 'Waldham' are knocked off in this story, which features Abelard Voss, a criminologist. What starts out to be blood red ends up medium rare. A confused plot interferes with some neat writing"—New Yorker.

517. Cameron, Kenneth M., 1931- . *Sky woman*. New York: Popular Library, 1982. 352p.

Catharine's family migrates to colonial America, escaping the slums of London, only to be exposed to the dangers of a primitive frontier. Her father is killed by Seneca Indians and Catharine is abducted. The Indians observe with admiration Catharine's reserves of strength and acceptance of her new status and the tribe's matriarch, Bright Sky, adopts her. Taught the Indian's traditions and customs, Catharine rises to a position of honor. Persuaded by a British officer to go to London as an Indian princess and help prepare an alliance between her people and the British versus the French, Catharine returns to America only to see the Indians decimated and eventually massacred when their presumed allies fail to provide the necessary stipends and protections.

518. Cameron, Peter, 1959- . *The weekend*. New York: Plume, 1994. 241p.

John and Marian, half-brother and sister-in-law of the late Tony, who died of AIDS the year before, have left Manhattan 'forever' for the countryside of Upstate New York. Their friend Lyle, an art critic and Tony's former lover, visits them. His new boyfriend, Robert, whose goal is to be a successful painter, accompanies him. The reunion, hardly a happy one, is burdened with tensions and disagreements. A neighbor, Laura Ponti, invited to dinner by Marian, is also doomed to disappointment as her efforts to strengthen very thin connections with her daughter fail miserably.

519. Campbell, Bruce, 1909- . *The clue of the marked claw*. New York: Grosset & Dunlap, 1950. vii, 211p.

Smuggling operations near a Long Island fishing village catch the attention of Ken Holt and Sandy Allen, two vacationers. Their curiosity is rewarded when a cabal of smugglers is captured, largely because of Ken and Sandy's investigative activities.

520. Campbell, Eugene. *The long whip*. New York: Scribner, 1934. 361p.

The Fortescue family of Long Island's 'fox-hunting class' is wealthy enough to put aside any memories of their obscure beginnings. Yet it was in the 1830s that a blacksmith surnamed Fortescue fled England after being whipped by a nobleman. In the space of 50 years the dying former blacksmith had amassed a fortune and had pictured himself as the descendant of aristocratic forbears.

In the 1930s the Fortescue family is seeking ways to perpetuate his dubious chronicle. Horse racing has an important role in the novel.

521. **Campbell, Floy, b. 1873 or 5.** *Camp Arcady*; **the story of four girls and some others who kept house in a New York flat. Boston: R.G. Badger, 1900 [c1899]. 164p.**

"Four girls who have left country homes to study art, music, etc., in New York City, make their home for one winter on the top floor of an old mansion turned into 'flats.' The details of their efforts, disappointments, and pleasures are given. At the end the girls give up their ambitious plans, all having found that the most satisfactory thing to which a girl can aspire is a home in its true meaning"—Annual American catalogue.

522. **Campbell, Helen Stuart, 1839-1918.** *Miss Melinda's opportunity*; **a story. Boston: Roberts Bros., 1886. 217p.**

"Miss Melinda, after her sister Matilda's death, goes on living in the family mansion, reading history, Scott's Commentaries, and very instructive literature just so many hours a day, as she had been accustomed to do for nearly fifty years with Miss Matilda. She is a descendant of old Dutch New Yorkers, and knows no people outside her set. One Sunday a young clergyman wakes her up by preaching a sermon on 'Spirits in Prison' and the good work that could be done among working girls in New York City. She begins to think and then to help, finding by chance her 'opportunity'"—Annual American catalogue. The founding of a housing and recreation center for the girls follows.

523. ———. *Mrs. Herndon's income*; **a novel. Boston: Roberts Bros., 1885. 534p.**

"The first part of the novel concerns 'Meg', a beautiful gypsy-like girl whom Margaret Wentworth (afterwards Mrs. Herndon) becomes interested in during her sojourn in New England. Mrs. Herndon reappears, a widow with a fortune. … Her one idea is to help others. … The scene is [now] New York City, and the descriptions of its tenement houses, factories, liquor dens, etc., are based on facts. The author is fair, and her socialists, workingmen, theorists, property owners, demagogues, fanatics, aesthetes, etc., have an impartial hearing. The story is not without plot, although this is naturally sacrificed to purpose. The author's theory, put into the mouths of her best characters, is that nothing can be done by force … to 'love his brother as himself' and kill the serpent of selfishness"—Annual American catalogue.

524. ———. *Under green apple boughs.* **New York: Fords, Howard & Hulbert, 1882. 272p.**

"Much ethics and some philosophy, have been expended on the character of Professor Boynton, the great skeptic and chemist from New York, who has come [with his sister] to lead a farmer's life in Long Island to recover from the effects of an explosive experiment, and on that of Sylvia, the little waif-child, whose sympathies are akin to the birds, the beasts, the forest trees and woodland flowers. Professor Boynton is not a Doctor Rameau, nor are the results of Sylvia's influence the same as those brought to bear on the French materialist by Adrienne. The unpleasantness apt to hang about the relations of a man of more than middle age who falls in love with and marries the child he has adopted has not been wholly avoided here. That situation treated sentimentally is never satisfactory. Ms. Campbell has marred her otherwise very clever conceptions by letting them wander into the mazes of sensational bewilderments. Towards the close the various personages engage in a sort of game of blind-man's-bluff across the Atlantic which fatigues the mind to follow"—Saturday review (London). The author describes the Long Island village where Prof. Boynton goes as "A fossil community with an interest attaching to fossils, [where modern influences] make as much real progress as waves against a Holland dyke. The village held its own, looking straight over the heads of these audacious foreigners with their nineteenth-century madness."

525. **Campbell, Jane C.** *Catharine Clayton*; **a tale of New York. Boston: Gleason's Pub. Hall, 1846. 66p.**

William Clayton's untimely death and the failure of his investments a year later left his family—Mrs. Clayton and three children (Catherine, William, Jr. and Amy—in difficult circumstances). After Catherine's one bad experience as a governess in an unstable family, wealthy, kindly Mrs. Clinton hires her as teacher of her two children. Through the interest of Mrs. Clinton the Claytons' situation improves. Edward Lester, a young Englishman teaching classics in a private school in New York, falls in love with Catherine. After a sojourn in England of 5 years duration with his ill grandfather, Lester returns and marries Catherine. A subplot deals with the rise and fall of the Archer family, old acquaintances of the Claytons, who snubbed them when the Claytons fell into near poverty.

526. **Campbell, Jeffrey, pseud.** *The homing.* **New York: Putnam, 1980. 275p.**

"George Kenner drives from New York to Upstate 'Chilton' to stay with his daughter Katherine and her husband of two years, David. But Chilton turns out to be a dream village out of time like Brigadoon, a community of such utter rectitude that humming in the bathtub is practically left of center. Everyone talks in emasculated clichés … and George is appalled by the change in daughter Katherine—she has given up very promising post-graduate work in parapsychology to become an anti-women's-lib housewife. … So, both bored and disturbed by Katherine's household, George moves out to a motel for the balance of his visit. And meanwhile George's dread of this quintessential hick town builds as he experiences endless flashes of déjà vu … till at last he discovers a newspaper microfilm detailing Katherine's death two year earlier during a flu epidemic! Further clues lead him to believe that a web of super-American hick villages is being psychically cultivated by the Federal Government through every known method of subliminal brainwashing. But why is George's every action, no matter how bizarre, known beforehand by the town's fathers?"—Kirkus reviews.

527. **Campbell, Scott, 1858-1933.** *Below the Dead-Line.* **New York: G.W. Dillingham, 1906. 313p.**

A district of New York City known as 'Below the Dead-Line' (south of Fulton Street) is infiltrated by thieves despite the efforts of the police to shut them out. Inspector Byrnes tries to alleviate the situation by issuing orders to his men to sweep the streets of the criminal element day and night; he fears for the safety of the banks and diamond dealers who conduct business there.

528. **Campbell, Thomas Bowyer, b. 887.** *Black Sadie*; **a novel. Boston: Houghton, Mifflin, 1928. 303p.**

A Black girl raised in the South comes North to New York City and gradually gains a bit of fame as a model for artists. Sadie is taken in hand by some prominent Harlemites; a cabaret in which she appears as an entertainer three nights a week bears her name. Sadie is appreciative of the attention she receives from both Black and White admirers, but it eventually palls on her and she is happy to revert to her old ways.

529. **Canfield, William Walker, 1855-1937.** *At Seneca Castle.* **Illustrated by G.A. Harker. New York: Dutton, 1912. 274p.**

Continues the author's *The White Seneca*. Henry Cochrane (Dundiswa or the White Seneca), appalled by the frontier massacres carried out by the Tories and their Indian allies, offers his services to the Continental Army and is asked by General Washington to carry a message to General John Sullivan. Sullivan organizes a punitive expedition against the Iroquois with Henry serving as a scout. With the success of Sullivan's campaign assured, Henry is released from his scouting duties and goes in quest of Constance Leonard, long an honored captive of the Senecas. Aided by his Indian brother Hiokoto and by the intervention of Queen Catherine Montour, the French/Indian, Henry Cochrane is reunited with Constance who, after fleeing from Seneca Castle to Fort Niagara and then to Montreal, is exchanged for American-held prisoners. Henry is always sympathetic towards the Indians with whom he had lived. The author feels bound to present 'Indian life and character … in its true light' and has 'held closely to the real Indian, his life, manners and customs.'

530. ————. *The White Seneca.* **Illustrated by G.A. Harker. New York: Dutton, 1911. vii, 281p.**

An 'Indian' story which depicts faithfully the aboriginal American's life and character. "The hero is a white boy [Henry Cochrane] who has been captured by tribes of the Iroquois, and a large part of the story deals with his life among his captors. So strong a hold does the life have upon him that he adopts the ways and manners of the savages [he is given the name Dundiswa or the White Seneca] and with them allies himself to the cause of the British during the Revolutionary War. There is a conflict of ownership between the warriors of the Senecas and the Cayugas as to which shall possess the boy, and the test of skill that the judges demand for the decision is described with vividness. Inasmuch as Hawk [Hiokoto] of the Senecas is victorious, the White [Seneca] … wins the undying hatred of Beaver [Onontigo] of the Cayugas. From this fact there results many of the exciting incidents of the story"—Literary digest.

Cannon, Charles James, 1880-1860, supposed author. *Oran the outcast.* **See Item #2561.**

531. **Capron, Carrie.** *Helen Lincoln*; **a tale. New York: Harper, 1856. 308p.**
Helen (Nellie) Lincoln (a.k.a. Nellie Burke) and her sister are orphans after the loss at sea of their father, George Lincoln, and the death a year or two later of their frail mother. A widower, Mr. Burke, whose farm is just a few miles outside New York City, gives Helen a home. Her sister is placed in an orphan asylum. The remarriage of Mr. Burke eventuates in Helen's semi-employment by a wealthy couple, the Whites, of New York City. The Whites' adopted daughter, Minnie, and Helen form a close bond. Minnie's fiancé, Harry Lee, a lawyer from the East Indies, recalls his friendship with Helen's father. Simultaneously the mysterious Dr. Duval reveals that Minnie and Helen are true sisters and confesses that their mother had spurned him years ago. Helen in her turn refuses the doctor's offer of marriage and accepts the proposal of the clergyman, Reverend Ashton.

532. **Caputi, Anthony Francis, 1924- .** *Loving Evie.* **New York: Harper & Row, 1974. 259p.**
Evie Holman, a feather-brained student at a SUNY Buffalo campus, is pregnant and Merrick Baines, assistant professor of English, is responsible. Merrick marries Evie; physically their union is satisfactory, but he feels he needs a new career start and takes off. Devastated, Evie tries to commit suicide. Merrick, consumed by guilt, comes back to Evie and their daughter.

533. **[Carleton, Henry Guy], 1856-1910.** *The South Fifth Avenue Poker Club.* **New York: M.J. Ivers, 1888. 107p.**
Playwright and editor Carleton wrote three humorous works about Afro-Americans: The above; *Lectures before the Thompson Street Poker Club* (New York: White and Allen, 1889); and *The Thompson Street Poker Club* (New York: White and Allen, 1888). He portrayed Afro-Americans in New York City in their lighter moments; to the modern reader the dialect and situations he employs seem grossly stereotypical. The chief characters in these short works are the Reverend Thankful Smith, Cyanide Whiffles and Jubilee Anderson, "everyone of them with a 'balmy' conscience and a loud aversion to interloping 'suckahs from Hoboken' [Reverend Thankful Smith is the supposed author of the 'Lectures']"—Kunitz & Haycraft. *American authors, 1600-1900.*

534. Carlisle, Helen Grace, 1898- . _Mothers cry_. New York: Harper, 1930. 267p.
"Telling the story of her life and the lives of her four children in her own words, Mary Knight narrates the events of her naïve girlhood, her engagement, her marriage in nineteen hundred to Frank Williams, her boss in the New York department store where she was employed. At the age of twenty-four her husband was killed in an accident, leaving her practically penniless to bring up her four babies, Danny, Artie, Fanny and Beatty. By every conceivable sacrifice she succeeds. Artie grows up to be a great architect; Fanny, like her mother, marries and settles down happily; Beatty, with advanced but impractical ideas of modern woman and free love, is betrayed by her employer; and Danny, the ever incorrigible black sheep of the family, kills his sister in a final quarrel and dies in the electric chair"—Book review digest.

535. ——— . _See how they run_. New York: J. Cape & H. Smith, 1929. 304p.
Three young women come to New York City in search of new, unusual experiences and lovers or husbands. They share a cramped apartment, join a chorus called the 'Dancing Daisies', become party-goers and party-givers, and are the butts of misadventures. Olivia, brought up by well-meaning parents, hopes for a career on the legitimate stage, but ends up as a show-girl and mistress of a boorish cab-driver; Mary Elizabeth leaves a conventional suburban life-style and attains the goal of securing a (French) husband, if not an ideal one; Rose is a product of the tenements with numerous siblings who wants to walk in beauty and be exalted by love, but finds only imperfection and pain.

536. Carlson, Patricia M., 1940- . _Audition for murder_. New York: Avon Books, 1985. 224p.
"Young actor Nick O'Connor gives up a promising musical comedy role to help his beautiful wife, Lisette, escape to Upstate New York, where she hopes to rid herself of alcohol and cocaine addictions. Lisette, tortured by guilt over a tragic accident in her past, feels that starring in a college production of Hamlet will exorcise her excoriating memories. Alas, the play is beset with prop accidents, cruel practical jokes, and a murderous plot against Lisette herself"—Booklist.

537. ——— . _Murder is academic_. New York: Avon Books, 1985. 174p.
It all takes place on an Upstate New York campus [at 'Laconia'] "that is part Ithaca and part Fredonia"—Armchair detective. Statistician graduate student Maggie Ryan is the amateur detective when a coed is murdered by someone given the name, 'The Freeway Slayer.' Jane Freeman, a professor and psychologist, is asked by the students to help them defend themselves against future attacks. But it is Jackie Edwards, a grad student in French who becomes one of the murderer's victims. "Not only the college residents but the entire area, including Syracuse, is being terrorized by a series of rape-murders, with

the victims usually found near highway ramps, hence 'The Freeway Slayer'"—Armchair detective.

538. ————. *Murder misread.* **New York: Doubleday, 1990. 181p.**

"Protagonist Maggie Ryan is a statistician who returns to her alma mater [at 'Laconia' in Upstate New York] on a contract basis to help Professor Charlie Fielding with his current project on reading theory. … Carlson's premise is that even a skilled detective can misread clues, as virtually everyone, police and amateur detectives, does in this crime novel. Tal Chandler, an immensely popular retired professor, is murdered on campus, and Maggie teams up with his widow Anne, to find the criminal, whom they suspect is a member of the psychology department"—Armchair detective.

Carman, Dorothy Walworth, 1900- . See: Walworth, Dorothy, 1900-

539. **Carmer, Carl Lamson, 1893-1976.** *Genesee fever.* **New York: Farrar & Rinehart, 1943. 360p.**

"Historical novel about the Genesee Valley in the 1790s. The hero, Nathan Hart, was a young schoolteacher from Pennsylvania who had been caught while siding with the farmers in the Whiskey Rebellion and had escaped to the Genesee country [of western New York]. In the valley he met Colonel Williamson, an Englishman of aristocratic ideas, who was selling real estate to wealthy landowners with the idea of establishing in America a replica of European country landed estates. In the struggle between Williamson and the small landowners, Nathan once more sided with the farmers"—Book review digest.

540. ————. *Rebellion at Quaker Hill, a story of the first Rent War.* **Illus. by Harve Stein. Philadelphia: Winston, 1954. 174p.**

A book for young people that fictionalizes the rent 'wars' of Hudson Valley tenant farmers in the mid-1760s protesting the high fees extracted from them by the 'lords of the manors' whose land they cultivated. William Prendergast and his wife Mehitabel were leaders of the rebelling farmers and the story is centered on these two.

541. *Caroline Tracy, the Spring Street milliner's apprentice*; or, *Life in New York in 1847-8.* **Being the narrative of actual occurrences, which came to the knowledge of a young physician of New York City. New York: Stearns [or Garrett] 1849. 91p. (in double columns).**

Includes "The Sister-in-law; a tale of real life" (p. [79]-91). Caroline Tracy and Emma Stirling are just two of the young women whom their employer, Mrs. Randall, tries to use for dubious purposes beyond their millinery chores. Dr. Everts has some knowledge given him by Caroline of the true situation in Mrs. Randall's establishment and investigates further. We learn that Mr. Ritton, one of Mrs. Randall's 'clients', is the father of Caroline (the result of a seduction years ago in a New England town). Ritton has been posing as a pious Christian while simultaneously engaging in shady business practices. In the end, however, Ritton takes the road to repentance and makes efforts to recompense his daughter and Emma for his shabby treatment of them. Caroline and Emma find suitable husbands while Mrs. Randall leaves New York and drifts westward.

Carpenter, Chris, joint author. *Murder at the Baseball Hall of Fame.* See Item #754.

542. **Carr, Harriett Helen, 1899- .** *Valley of defiance.* **New York: Macmillan, 1957. 178p.**

In 1843 fifteen-year-old Walter Platt and his older brother Gerrit sided with the tenant farmers of the Hudson Valley in their struggle to abolish the injustices of the patroon system. The knowledge he gains from the anti-rent fight convinces Walter that he must become a lawyer and strive to promote just laws.

543. **Carr, John Dickson, 1906-1977.** *A graveyard to let*; another adventure of Sir Henry Merrivale, by Carter Dickson [pseud.] New York: Morrow, 1949. 247p.

"Sir Henry Merrivale outdoes himself this time when he accepts an invitation to suburban Westchester to witness a miracle and to explain it if he can. It occurs bright and early the following morning, when his middle-aged host dives, fully clothed, into a swimming pool and disappears … The subsequent chase leads [Merrivale] from a night baseball game, during which Sir Henry electrifies the local boys by whacking a couple over the fence, to an abandoned graveyard, and finally winds up in a studio over Grand Central Station, where, piquantly enough, a mysterious and somewhat sleazy woman happens to live"—New Yorker.

544. **Carra, Emma, pseud.** *The hermit of the Hudson*; or, *The farmer's daughter.* **A tale of the seventeenth century. Boston: F. Gleason, 1848. 100p. (in double columns.)**

Issued with: *The returned prodigal*; or *The reward of merit*, by Lewis Gridley: p. [86]-100.
The 'Hermit' (Edgar Luzerne) befriends the young hunter, Conway Welland. Villainous Herbert Montford, presumed to be a friend of Conway, is involved in robbery and tries to terminate the love affair of Conway and Emily, Squire Verner's daughter. Herbert's mistress, Elvira Willis, with her infant, is left in poverty in New York City. The reality of his misdeeds haunting him, Herbert tries to commit suicide, but is rescued from drowning by a young farmer. He confesses his crimes to Conway and seeks out Elvira in New York. After Herbert, Elvira and their child are placed in harm's way but escape, Herbert and Elvira are fully reconciled. Conway's 'father', Enrie Welland, tells witnesses that Conway is actually the Hermit's son and that Herbert Montford is his son. He, Welland, had changed his surname from Montford, and had

'stolen' the Hermit's (Edgar Luzerne's) wife by informing her that her husband (Luzerne) had died. The young principals of the tale find true happiness.

545. **Carrick, Gertrude, 1914- . *Consider the daisies*. Philadelphia: J.B. Lippincott, 1941. 365p.**

Vassar student Frances Flippen goes through her junior and senior years carrying romantic feelings toward her bachelor English professor, Brooks Creighton. However, Creighton is deep into his research and has little interest in furthering Frances' affections. When Frances continues to exert pressure on the professor, he finally tells her to search for a young man in her own age group. The novel is noteworthy for its accurate portrayal of undergraduate life at Vassar College in the 1930s.

546. **Carrington, Elaine Sterne. *The crimson goddess*. New York: Appleton-Century, 1936. 245p.**

A gathering of upper crust New York society to greet a returning explorer is numbed by his murder, a suicide and another killing by strangulation. Dr. Dominy Faire tries to make sense of these untoward events as he slices through an aura of mental instability, melodramatics and thuggery inspired by the worship of the Hindu goddess Kali.

547. **Carroll, Consolata Sister, 1892- . *Pray love, remember*. Illus. by Theresa Kilham. New York: Farrar, Straus, 1947. xi, 303p.**

"Autobiographical novel based on the author's childhood days in an Upstate New York town at the turn of the century. The daily doings of a Catholic family are set forth in episodic style, recalling the days when brides were known to go to church in black silk, and a seven-pound tenderloin roast cost $1.50"—Book review digest.

548. **Carroll, Jonathan, 1949- . *Kissing the beehive*. New York: N.A. Talese/ Doubleday, 1998. 232p.**

Sam Bayer has just gone through his third marriage; he has writer's block and is currently paying some attention to an enigmatic blonde and fan named Veronica Lake (!). With little forethought Sam suddenly decides to betake himself to his hometown, 'Crane's View', on the Hudson. It was there, when he was an adolescent that he came upon the corpse of Pauline Ostrova, a girl in his high school and an honor student with a sluttish reputation. Sam believes a book could be written about this unsolved murder and he sets about investigating those who knew Pauline: her boyfriend, a prison inmate; the local bigwig gangster; et al. His quest for the true facts takes him across the country.

Carruthers, William Alexander. 1800 (ca.)-1846. See: Caruthers, William Alexander, 1800 (ca.)-1846.

549. Carse, Robert, 1913- . *Hudson River hayride.* **Greenwich, Conn.: New York Graphic Society, 1962. 89p.**

> The time of this novella is 1693 and the chief characters are the adolescents Lise Vernel, Pieter Hulet and Joe Byram; they live in the Dutch village of 'Onderdonckelberg' on the Hudson River. The three build a boat that is surprisingly seaworthy and is the source of several rather unrealistic encounters with whales and pirates.

550. ————. *Winter of the whale;* **a novel. Illus. by Joseph Cellini. New York: Putnam, 1961. 160p.**

> A pre-Colonial narrative about the Manhanset Indians of Long Island. Having survived a severer than usual winter the Indians are in dire need of food. Wequarran, a 15-year-old Manhanset lad, hunts on foot for edibles with two friends. Not being very successful they man their canoes and go after whales in the waters of Long Island Sound. Unfortunately they are seized by the Pequots, their deadly enemies, and are subjected to ordeal by fire.

551. Carson, Norma Bright, b. 1883. *Trueheart Margery.* **New York: Doran, 1917. 274p.**

> Richard Craven is alternately neglectful and caring of his daughter, Jean, whose mother had died in childbirth. She rejects her father's choice of Gerry Gordon as a husband for her and marries Raymond Heath. Craven cuts her out of his will, but Jean and Raymond live happily in New York City until he guns down a man and vanishes. His wife dies after striving for survival of herself and her baby. The child is placed in an orphanage; she acquires the name Trueheart Margery. Meanwhile, in a change of heart Richard Craven searches for the daughter he abandoned, but finds by chance his granddaughter, Trueheart Margery. She becomes the center of his life and his long dormant love. When Margery matures she marries Gerry Gordon, the man her mother had rejected.

552. Carson, William Henry, b. 1859. *Evelyn Van Courtlandt.* **New York: R.F. Fenno, 1907. 373p.**

> The Van Courtlandts are a family closely associated with New York City. The head of the family, wealthy Howard Van Courtlandt, begrudges his business partner's attentiveness to Mrs. Van Courtlandt and her daughter Evelyn, and the latter hears her father's threats. Van Courtlandt's associate is murdered following a party given by the Van Courtlandts, but Malcolm, a young man employed by the two partners—not Howard Van Courtlandt—is the person charged with the homicide. A trial follows; Evelyn discovers her father's guilt and tries to absolve Malcolm by passing incriminating information to the district attorney. Her efforts are of little help to Malcolm. In a melodramatic climax Van Courtlandt owns up to his culpability, collapses and dies.

553. ————. *Tito.* Illus. by Charles H. Stephens. Boston: C.M. Clark, 1903. **363p.**

>Tito, the hero of the story, is the offspring of an Italian mother and an American father. He has never known his father who had left his mother shortly before Tito's birth. Determined to seek him out and wreak some form of revenge on him, Tito migrates to New York's Bowery where his slim resources dictate the use of cheap lodgings and restaurants. When father and son actually meet they hardly recognize one another, but their coming together has its poignant moments. The author is quite familiar with the New York of the laboring classes at the turn of the century.

554. Carter, Noel Vreeland. *The mooncalf murders.* New York: Walker and Co., 1989. **328p.**

>The scene of this mystery is Upstate New York and personalities in this region give the story a special flavor. The narrator, Miranda Fay, comes upon a fetus strangled with its own umbilical chord. Its mother (also dead), she discovers, was a prostitute who was paid to carry the baby. Then Miranda is confronted with two cases of rape and sodomy, a mansion combed with secret passageways, and intimations of a family's degeneracy. Miranda is determined to arrive at the correct explanation of this semi-Gothic mixture.

Carter, Russell Gordon, 1892-1937, joint author. *The giant's house.* See Item #2755.

Carter, Russell Gordon, 1892-1937, joint author. *The glory of Peggy Harrison.* See Item #2756.

555. ————. *A patriot lad of old Long Island.* Illustrated by Charles Hargens, Jr. Philadelphia: Penn Pub. Co., 1928. **238p.**

>Two boys, William Dean and his friend, Paul Coburn, are whisked into adventure when they help a wounded man, Capt. Christopher Blatch, recover from a leg wound in the Widow Dean's tavern, the Sign of the Drum Major. William and Paul go towards New York City in search of Luke, William's brother, who is serving in Washington's army. They carry a pouch containing a chart given to them by Capt. Blatch. The two lads are nearby when Howe's forces drive the Continentals from Long Island and eventually from New York City. Accompanied by Quint, a sailor recommended by Capt. Blatch, William and Paul locate the wounded Luke and head for home. But first they make a detour in Capt. Blatch's ship and find (ahead of the Tory, Festus Bender) buried British gold the Captain had appropriated. Half of the treasure is given to the patriot cause; the other half is divided among all who had taken part in its recovery.

556. Carus, Paul, 1852-1919. *The chief's daughter*; a legend of Niagara. With illus. by E. Biedermann. Chicago: Open Court Pub. Co., 1901. **54p.**

"A story of the emancipation of the tribe of the Oniahgahraha from religious superstition. According to an Indian legend, the Oniahgahrahas were in the habit of sacrificing to Niagara Falls, once a year, a beautiful maiden. Through the preaching of Father Hennepin, Lelawala, daughter of Eagle Eye, chief of the tribe, was persuaded that the custom was debasing and wrong. Accordingly, when she was chosen to sacrifice her life, she pleaded with her people to give up the belief; and, to show that her conversion was true and not founded on personal fear, she unflinchingly gave herself up to the cataract, finally urging that her sacrifice be the last"—The Chautauquan.

557. **[Caruthers, William Alexander] ca. 1800-1846. *The Kentuckian in New York; or, The adventures of three Southerners.* By a Virginian. New York: Harper, 1834. 2v.**

Two Carolinians, Victor Chevillere and Augustus Lamar and a Kentuckian, Montgomery Damon, a politician and Indian-hater, travel to the Yankee metropolis. In a series of letters Victor tells Beverley Randolph, a Southern friend, his impressions of New York and his experiences there. Randolph's replies describe life in the South and his wooing of Virginia Bell, Victor's cousin. All three of the visiting Southerners return to their homes with Northern brides.

Case, Frances Powell. See: Powell, Frances

558. **Case, Josephine Young, 1907- . *At midnight on the 31st of March.* Boston: Houghton, Mifflin, 1938. 131, [1]p.**

"A long narrative fantasy, written entirely in blank verse, describing the manner in which a small New York village of modern times reacts when the rest of civilization suddenly disappears, leaving the village and its people completely alone in a new and silent world"—O'Donnell, T.F., Literary history of New York, 1650-1958—in: *Upstate literature* ... Syracuse University Press, 1985). Several years before the age of atomic energy the village of 'Saugersville' finds itself the only inhabited place in its region and perhaps in the U.S. and the world. No explanation is forthcoming for the disappearance of surrounding civilization—there is no longer a Centerfield, Schuylers Falls, Indiantown, 'the Springs'. Saugersville people, nevertheless, resume the process of living, loving, making do with what supplies they have left, planning the production of food crops, dying, and at the end of the narrative celebrating a double wedding and welcoming a burgeoning spring as midnight on the 31st of March (exactly one year after the onset of outward silence) arrives.

559. **Casey, Jack, 1939- . *Lily of the Mohawks.* New York: Bantam Books, 1984. 308p.**

A novelized version of the short but significant life of Kateri Tekakwitha (1656-1680), the Mohawk Indian girl who converted to Catholicism and tried to bring the message of the Christian Gospels to her people. The story has frightening aspects—especially the Indian custom of torturing their captives and the persecution of Kateri Tekakwitha.

560. ————. *The trial of Bat Shea*; a novel. Troy, N.Y.:Diamond Rock, 1994. 369p.

> A slice of Troy, New York's past—a murder trial in 1894—is the basis of this work of fiction. Political passions flare between poll-watchers and voters who are hoping to cast a second or third ballot. Republican Robert Rose, a complete bigot and member of the American Protective Association, is killed. Bartholomew ('Bat') is indicted for Rose's murder on the flimsiest evidence and the A.P.A.'s lawyer, Frank Black, is able to win a conviction. Bat dies in the electric chair.

Casey, John [Dudley], 1939- . See: Casey, Jack, 1939-

561. **Caspary, Vera, 1904-1987. *Ladies and gents*. New York: Century Co., 1929. 288p.**

> Determined not to be a circus performer like her famous acrobatic parents, Rosina Monticelli carves out a career for herself in vaudeville, advances to musical comedy, then marries for love and becomes the mistress of a home on Park Avenue. Elements of shyness, innocence and perplexity accompany Rosina from childhood through adulthood, but this is part of her appeal.

562. **Castleman, Virginia Carter, b. 1864. *A child of the Covenant*. Milwaukee: Young Churchman Co., 1894. 220p.**

> "In a little home in the northern suburbs of New York City a dying mother has her daughter made a 'child of the Covenant' by baptism. The little girl, left wholly orphaned at four years of age, lives in different homes until she is twenty-four and then marries in a way that is a surprise to the reader. Charities and work of education among the poor figure largely in the story"—Annual American catalogue.

563. **Castlemon, Harry, 1842-1915. *The white beaver*. Philadelphia: H.T. Coates, 1899. iv, 424p.**

> "Paul and Hugh's fathers were partners in the sawmill business up in the Adirondacks. After the boys had left school, they were given positions in the mill. They were treated with a good deal of leniency as they were healthy, active boys unused to confinement, and were given a resting spell whenever they asked for it. So when Hugh asked Paul to go with him on a shooting expedition after an old turkey, for a week or two, there was no objection. The shooting also of a white beaver is only one of many adventures that befall them"—Annual American catalogue.

564. **Catlin, Louise Ensign, b. 1861. *My little lady-in-waiting*. Illustrated by E. Pollak. Boston: Lee and Shepard, 1905. 283p.**

Parentless Nellie Rose escapes for a while from her rather dismal New York City tenement environment by enrollment in a 'vacation school' where she is given lessons in homekeeping. Her aptitude and good manners lead to her being brought into a family that takes the place of her previous caretakers who have left New York. Her benefactors' spoiled children give Nellie many troublesome moments, but a trip abroad brings about a radical change in attitude.

Cattell, Edward James, 1856-1937. See under his pseudonym: Hardy, Frances H.

565. **Cautela, Giuseppe, b. 1883.** *Moon Harvest.* **New York: Dial Press, 1925. 253p.**
Ramualdo Sinisi's hard-earned education has led to a teaching position in his native Italy, when he and his wife decide to pack up and emigrate to New York City. While working at his first job there (in a tin factory), Ramualdo applies himself to mastering the English language. Eventually he is fluent enough to secure a post as teacher of Italian to young Italian-Americans who have little knowledge of the native language of their parents. Ramualdo then stumbles into a triangular love relationship that is most troublesome and frustrating.

566. **Cavanagh, Dermot.** *Tammany boy*; **a romance and a political career. New York: J.H. Sears, 1928. 297p.**
"Thomas Jefferson Gentry, novice at law, loses his first eleven cases … A bit of wire pulling from Tammany Hall wins the twelfth for him and makes him a Tammany man. As he rises to prominence in politics Thomas … finds out how Tammany stands back of its candidates, exacting like loyalty of them, and what happens to a man who tries to buck the machine. The progress of his love affair with Peggy McShane is incidental to the political interest of the story"—Book review digest.

567. **Cervus, G.I., pseud.** *Cut; a story of West Point.* **Philadelphia: J.B. Lippincott, 1886. 286p.**
Robert Thorne, a cadet at West Point, is the narrator, but the most arresting character in the novel is Wirt Kenyon, another cadet, refusing to duel with Burr Hassler who demands satisfaction for a fancied insult and also accuses Kenyon of theft. Kenyon is branded a coward and is 'cut' (given the silent treatment) by most of his classmates. Kenyon does have his defenders (Thorne isn't one). Several years pass and the Civil War begins. Kenyon proves his mettle on the battlefield, ascending to the rank of general. His antagonist, Hassler, joins the Confederate side. After the war has ceased Hassler is killed by his first wife whom he had deserted before marrying again. Before dying Hassler clears Kenyon of any wrongdoing. We learn that it was Kenyon's strong commitment to the Christian principles of his Quaker aunt that led to his refusal to engage in duels. Robert Thorne has two romances, neither of which turns out favorably. Both of the women he pursued married classmates

of his (Kenyon was one). The life of cadets at pre-Civil War West Point is well-drawn.

568. ———. *A model wife*; a novel. **Philadelphia: J.B. Lippincott, 1885, 343p.**

"Vernon Calwyn, after being brought up a rich man's son, loses his father at the age of eighteen. After affairs are settled he is obliged to leave college and go to work. He first idles away his time on a well-to-do uncle's farm, then becomes a village schoolteacher. He engages himself to Cora Lindsay and goes to New York to seek work, is employed in an insurance company and stays until the officers wreck the concern. He has married in the meantime. Now the trouble begins. On one of his trips for work he catches cold and is very ill with pneumonia. His wife parts with all her trinkets, does plain-sewing, tries to sell his paintings, etc.; finally she accepts some wine for her husband from an old acquaintance. Vernon is jealous and the part he plays during his convalescence would have made almost any woman leave him. The 'model wife' loves him in spite of all. Almost at the end they inherit $10,000 and all ends happily. The picture of New York life for 'refined' poor people is truthful"—Annual American catalogue.

568a. **Chace, Rebecca, 1960- .** *Capture the flag.* **New York: Simon & Schuster, 1999. 288p.**

In the late 1960s and early 1970s the affluent Edwards family of Manhattan has taken its annual summer vacation in Upstate New York at a country house owned by the Shanlicks. The latter family is hardly a stable one—drugs and sex are main sources of its recreational pursuits—and it has an impact on the Edwards, especially young Annie Edwards. By 1975 she is desperately seeking order in her life and approval from her father who has just divorced her mother and brought his girlfriend along to share in the summer vacation. In playing the game 'capture the flag', Annie happens upon some unsettling family secrets and everything seems to be falling apart.

569. **Chadwick, Dorothy Lester, 1903- .** *Young April.* **New York: Arcadia House, 1936. 281p.**

A piece of romantic 'fluff' in which a love affair is made difficult because of a family feud and the contrariness of interested parties. The scene is Long Island's South Shore.

570. **Chalmers, Harvey, 1890-1971.** *How the Irish built the Erie.* **New York: Bookman Associates, 1965 [c1964]. 190p.**

The most prominent character in this historical novel about the construction of the Erie Canal is J.J. McShane, a knowledgeable Irishman who is the driving force behind the solution of many of the engineering problems that confront the Canal's planners. He takes his crew of Irish laborers, drawn from the jails of New York City and from recent migrants to America, and makes them a key element in the final success of the tremendous project. The heroine is beautiful Pippa Post, a most capable ally of McShane; her expertise with knives keeps would-be swains at bay. A bundle of historical personages appear throughout the story and a good deal of technical detail [with drawings] accompanies the narrative.

571. ————. *West to the setting sun.* **Toronto: Macmillan Co. of Canada, 1944. xii, 362p.**

A fictionalized biography of the Mohawk leader, Joseph Brant, beginning with his initial experience as a warrior under Sir William Johnson at the Battle of Lake George in 1755 and ending with the surrender of Cornwallis, Brant's leave-taking of his Tory comrade-in-arms, olonel John Butler and his marriage to Catherine Croghan. Chalmers sympathizes with Brant, recognizing his admirable traits—his loyalty to the Johnsons and the British cause during the American Revolution, his skill as a fighting man, his sense of honor and his frequent leniency towards his enemies, the American 'rebels.'

572. **Chalmers, Stephen, b. 1880.** *The crime in Car 13.* **Garden City, N.Y.: Published for the Crime Club by Doubleday, Doran, 1930. 293p.**

The reporter Hamlin Douglas' fishing trip to the Adirondacks is interrupted when he is asked to appear for questioning in the murder of an Englishman, the Honorable Lionel Morepath, that took place on the New York to Montreal train (Douglas was a passenger who had met Morepath). The story veers from the Adirondacks, Montreal, the Hudson Valley to New York City as the U.S. Secret Service gets into the act. The questions that need answering are: what was Morepath's background, was he on some diplomatic mission, and why was he murdered? Douglas is 'deputized' as a Secret Service agent by Chief Macklin and he is the individual who finally provides most of the answers. The time frame of the novel is the period just before the outbreak of World War I, with German spies, President Woodrow Wilson, the British ambassador to Washington, et al. making brief but important appearances.

573. ————. *House of the two green eyes.* **Garden City, N.Y.: Published for the Crime Club by Doubleday, Doran, 1929. viii, 389p.**

"The scene of this murder mystery is the New York City Tenderloin in the early nineteen hundreds. Belle Villiers, elderly wife of a millionaire and formerly a showgirl, is found strangled on a park bench. A newspaper reporter, untangling the crime, finds curious ramifications in the family history of the Villiers which affect certain of the reporter's friends and the girl he loves"—Book review digest. The author's portrayal of the old Tenderloin district has an air of authenticity about it.

574. ————. *The trail of a tenderfoot.* **Illus. by H.T. Dunn, C.F. Peters and J.M. Gleeson. New York: Outing Pub. Co., 1911. 234p.**

"An account of various [fictionalized] experiences in hunting, fishing and other outdoor enjoyment, chiefly in the localities of the Adirondacks and the Bay of Fundy. The author begins as a typical tenderfoot who advances in blissful ignorance of guns, guides and rods, and the weight of whose catch is prone to rise like mercury under a warm imagination"—Catholic World.

575. **Chamberlain, George Agnew, 1879-1966.** *The great Van Suttart mystery.* **New York: Putnam, 1925. iv, 315p.**

"What was the curious bond between Cornelia Van Suttart, child of New York's old family, and Miad Blake, whose home was a musty shop on Cobbled Court? What was the evil purpose so long guarded by Prosper Frete's green eyes? What became of the Van Suttarts? And where did their fortune go? In this unusual story of lower New York when Brooklyn Bridge was building, the reader knows most of the facts from the start. To those most closely concerned the mystery is slowly unveiled after the passage of many years"—Book review digest. "New York in the period immediately following the close of the Civil War is interestingly depicted, and the determined Miad Blake proves a likeable and efficient hero"—Literary digest international book review.

576. —————. *Mr. Trumper Bromleigh presents no ugly duckling.* **New York: Putnam, c1926. 387p.**

Bromleigh's peculiar gift is the ability to take an outwardly drab young woman and turn her into a glamorous one. He plies his 'trade' in New York City, even designing the fashionable clothing his current beauties wear. His final big success, a very personal one, involves the wife who had left him some time ago.

577. —————. *Rackhouse*; a novel. **New York: Harper, 1922. 302p.**

"The story introduces Capt. Roderic Norris, 'darling of [New York] society and the gods, scion of an honored family, clubman, polo player, contented loafer, embryonic financier and … bankrupt.' In the course of the plot he goes through a number of sensational metamorphoses. For a week in his old army uniform, a black mask, faking the loss of an arm, he turns a hurdy-gurdy and with the help of a monkey rakes in pennies to the amount of $6,000. In partnership with a runaway college professor he becomes the king of bootleggers, breaking the law to the tune of a million dollars a year and with adventures that harden his physical and moral fiber out of all recognition. Then, presto, as a millionaire he changes back to the smiling, debonair Roddy Norris, beloved by his friends in prosperity"—Book review digest. The novel does provide fascinating glimpses of various shades of life in New York City.

578. —————. *Taxi*; an adventure romance (in lighter vein). **Illustrated by Lejaren A. Hiller. Indianapolis: Bobbs-Merrill, 1920. 222p.**

The hero, Robert Hervey Randolph (alias Slim Hervey), is a handsome, tall, well-dressed 26-year-old, a magnificent figure of a man who exchanges places with a New York City cab driver. The heroine is Imogene Pamela Thornton (alias Vivienne Vivierre); she and Randolph possess all the graces and form of a rather happy-go-lucky couple. Randolph's taxi-driving, really a kind of experiment, leaves him with the impression that cab companies in New York should have two employees in each cab, one serving as a chaperone.

Chambers, Dana, pseud. See: Leffingwell, Albert, 1895-1966.

579. **[Chambers, Julius] 1850-1920. *On a margin*. New York: Fords, Howard and Hulbert, 1884. 416p.**

'Crumpet', a village on the Hudson; the 'Willows', an estate near Boston; New York City—these are the primary locales of the activities of the Rawson family. Cotton Mather (Rawson) leaves Crumpet and bases himself at the 'Willows', adopts a baby girl with the strange name of 'Mootla' (the daughter of a former love, Alice Dean, who had died in the Crumpet almshouse), and makes occasional forays into the Wall Street stock market. Walter Rawson, the son of Cotton's brother, Crumpet resident Richard, inherits his father's small property, marries Violet Vreeland of the Crumpet Vreelands, and moves to New York City. Investment in a telephone innovation enriches Walter and he speculates on Wall Street, sometimes in alliance with Cotton—they are not hesitant in cutting very shady corners. It all ends with Cotton's accidental death and the unhappy Walter's decision to distribute his millions to charitable causes and retire to a spot on Long Island Sound—Walter's wife had left him and 'his career, with all its success, had been a failure, because it lacked an essential element—happiness.'

580. **Chambers, Robert William, 1865-1933. *Ailsa Page*; a novel. New York: Appleton, 1910. 501p.**

The novel draws a picture of New York City in the troubled days just before and after the fall of Fort Sumter. Leading characters are: Ailsa Page, a widow at a very early age; Philip Berkeley, he discovering from old letters that his birthright and his mother are darkly clouded; Colonel Arran of a prominent New York family. Berkeley is so mortified by his findings that he becomes a lawbreaker and a desperate dissipater. Ailsa steps forward and devotedly regenerates young Berkeley; the Civil War is also a factor in his revival. The story, now concentrating on the first year of the war, shifts to Virginia and the disastrous defeats of an overconfident Union Army.

581. **————. *Athalie*. With illus. by Frank Craig. New York: Appleton, 1915. 404p.**

"Athalie Greensleeve is one of the three daughters of a Long Island roadhouse keeper. When a child she makes friends with Clive Bailey, a New York boy staying with his father … at an inn for duck shooting. Some years later the two again meet. Athalie's father is dead and she and her [two] sisters are supporting themselves as a stenographer, a chorus girl and a model respectively. The friendship is renewed and Clive Bailey installs the sisters in a comfortable apartment and fills Athalie's leisure with theater and restaurant parties. His relation to her is presented as a purely platonic one. Clive's engagement to a girl in his own social circle puts an end to the luxuries for

Athalie. She realizes that she possesses the gift of second sight and becomes a fashionable clairvoyant. The story concludes with the marriage of the two and with Athalie's subsequent death"—Book review digest. The New York the author portrays is a city of hard work in the daylight hours (dowdy offices and stores) and glittery nightclubs in the evening hours.

582. ————. *The better man.* **Illustrated by Henry Hutt. New York: Appleton, 1916. 343p.**

The 15 stories in the collection range in scene from the Adirondacks to the Florida woodlands. Those that concern the North Woods of Upstate New York have a cast of new young foresters and skilled woodsmen whose boss is John Burling, conservation commissioner and opponent of crooked game wardens, timber thieves, et al. The heroines, North and South are invariably beautiful whether drably dressed or finely clothed. Contents: The progress of Janet.—A Lynx Peak pastoral.—Wildrick's dump.—Hell's ashes.—The fire-bird.—The better man.—The germ of madness.—Lucille's legs.—A nursery tale.—Number Seven.—Down and out.—Carondelet.—Owl's Head.—Ole Hawg.—The real thing.

583. ————. *The business of life.* **With illus. by Charles Dana Gibson. New York: D. Appleton, 1913. viii, 517p.**

Jim Desboro, one of New York City's fashionable but idle rich, marries Jacqueline, a young woman of sterling character—she manages the antique store inherited from her father. Jacqueline displays a talent for business, but has to deal with nasty rumors about her husband spread by a woman from his circle. Amid her application of her expertise to the collection of arms and armor, Jacqueline must find time to straighten out her marriage. Fortunately Jim listens to Jacqueline and gives up his wasteful ways for a steady and useful life in business and his home.

584. ————. *Cardigan; a novel.* **New York: Harper, 1901. 512p.**

Michael Cardigan, the hero, is a ward and protégé of Sir William Johnson, along with Felicity Warren ('Silver Heels'), the heroine. The year is 1774 and Cardigan wanders from the Mohawk Valley to Virginia, back to New York State (Albany) and finally to Boston where he is on the side of the patriots when hostilities break out in nearby Concord (1775). Along the way Cardigan has a quarrel with the Earl of Dunmore, former governor of New York and presently governor of Virginia, and is swept up in Lord Dunmore's War. Cardigan's love affair with Silver Heels is climaxed by their marriage.

585. ————. *The common law.* **With illus. by Charles Dana Gibson. New York: Appleton, 1911. viii, 535p.**

The artist Louis Nevill gives employment as his model to Valerie West, a young woman who has spent many hours taking care of an invalid mother. Valerie's innocence, beauty and openness have their effect on Louis and he falls in love with her. Unfortunately Louis' family is one of high social standing that frowns upon allowing Valerie to enter as Louis' wife, viewing such a marriage as an impediment to his artistic and social advancement. The family suggests that Louis take Valerie as his mistress, a condition unacceptable to the lovers. When Valerie does come face-to-face with Nevill opponents, she wins them over with her wonderfully apropos behavior during several family crises.

586. ————. *The crimson tide.* **Illus. by A.I. Keller. New York: Appleton, 1919. xi, 366p.**

Palla Dumont has been an eyewitness to some of the cruelties following the Bolshevik takeover of Russia and she "has no real desire to settle down to the ordinary life of the United States after the signing of the armistice [ending the First World War]. The story is largely concerned [however] with Palla's revolt against the conventional and her endeavor to fight the rising tide of Bolshevism [so she sees it] in New York by preaching her gospel of love and service"—Boston transcript.

587. ————. *The danger mark.* **With illus. by A.B. Wenzell. New York: Appleton, 1909. vii, 495p.**

The orphaned Seagrave twins, brother and sister, are heirs to a large fortune held for them in trust, with an elderly, puritanical Dutchman from Long Island as their guardian. The young widow who acts as their governess does her best to introduce them to good use of their time, but they evince an absence of self-control and a longing for greater companionship. Thrown into a circle of overrich society people—individuals who seek only pleasure, relief from boredom, physical and financial satisfaction—the Seagrave girl tries to cling to her ideals and prove her worth to the man she loves, a man who is also struggling against his own weaknesses of character. Together they resist temptations, back-slide, recover—they are the best of the crazily tilted milieu they inhabit—this milieu 'whose sole intellectual relaxation is pirouetting along the danger mark with overstepping, and in concealing what they do.'

588. ————. *The fighting chance.* **With illus. by A.B. Wenzell. New York: Appleton, 1906. 499p.**

The author again swims in the miasma of fashionable, upper New York City society. The scene shifts from a house party at a luxurious country estate to the city where the 'good times' continue. Chief characters are: Silvia Landis, typically spoiled; Stephen Siward who has an affinity for liquor; Howard Quarier, a multimillionaire and Silvia's fiancé; Leila Mortimer whose marriage is no impediment to her infatuation with the wealthy bachelor Beverly Plank. In progress is a burning love affair between Silvia and Stephen, but she refuses to give up her plan to marry Quarier. Stephen combats his alcoholism and Silvia tries to lose herself in social diversions, but in the end Chambers tacks on a happy (but artificial) solution to the dilemmas of Stephen and Silvia. The author is especially insightful about the sordid aspects of behind-the-scenes New York City.

589. ———. *The flaming jewel.* **New York: G.H. Doran, 1922. 273p.**

"Mike Clinch's camp in the backwoods of the Adirondacks is the meeting place for the dregs of humanity. Clinch, a disreputable villain, has stolen, while in Paris during the [First World] War, the flaming jewel from one Quintana who had in his turn stolen it from the grand duchess of Estonia. James Darragh, a Secret Service agent, arrives at Clinch's on the trail of the stolen jewel and in the disguise of a poacher enjoys his hospitality. Clinch's stepdaughter, Eve, is the one touch of refinement in this motley crowd, and it is because her stepfather loves her and is determined to make a lady of her that he has stolen the jewel. Quintana and his band of ruffians arrive from Europe and track down Clinch. There are desperate doings in which the jewel is stolen and re-stolen and through Darragh's efforts Eve finally returns it to its rightful owner. Eve's love story and that of the grand duchess are woven into the sensational background"—Book review digest.

590. ———. *The gay rebellion.* **Illustrated by Edmund Frederick. New York: Appleton, 1913. 299p.**

This fantasy satirizes the suffragettes and eugenicists of the early years of the 20th century. Incensed by the stubborn denial of their rights by the male of the species a number of women take refuge in the Adirondacks. They organize the New Race University, make their homes in caves and hunt with their butterfly nets for marriageable male exemplars, taking them back to their domiciles for mating purposes. Unfortunately for the experiment certain females fail to follow the guidelines, surrendering themselves to love and the probability of the ancient pattern of male domination.

591. ———. *The girl in golden rags.* **New York: Appleton-Century, 1936. 314p.**

Anne Ardres, a widow, and her daughter, Jacqueline, struggle valiantly to draw subsistence from their farm in Upstate New York. They are cultivating only 30 acres of their land, which totals 20,000 acres—most of which is woodland, thickets and wetlands. It is a losing battle until P.J. Conner, a wealthy businessman on a hunting trip in the area, takes a liking to the Ardres holdings. He decides to buy the acreage while simultaneously courting the widow. Happy, nature-loving Jacqueline has her eye on J. West Halton, a haughty young artist, who needs a push from P.J., plus the transformation of Jacqueline into a beautiful young woman akin to those of his own 'class'— before he discovers that he really loves the girl enough to marry her.

592. ———. *The hidden children.* **With illus. by A.I. Keller. New York: Appleton, 1914. xv, 650p.**

The theme of the novel is "border warfare between American troops and the English and Indian allies in western New York State [more pointedly the Sullivan Expedition of 1779]. The hero is Euan Loskiel of Morgan's Rifles, a young ensign who finds himself interested in a ragged and tattered gypsy girl [Lois] who follows his regiment [and hopes to see the Indian stronghold,

Catherine's Town, to search for her mother]. Although she seems quite alone the girl is found to be under the protection of a mysterious Indian, and in the course of its development, many strange Indian customs are woven into the action of the narrative"—Book review digest.

593. ————. *Iole.* **New York: Appleton, 1903. xvii, 142p.**

Iole was only one of the eight daughters of a poet, a votary of 'l'art nouveau' as applied to literature, painting, the book arts, music, etc. His daughters' names were derived from species of butterflies; all were fluent in Greek and Latin, and they were devotees of the out-of-doors. Because money was in short supply, he and his girls domiciled in rural New York State. Wealthy young lovers romanced several of the girls and the whole family eventually found themselves back in New York City where three of the girls acquired husbands. Chambers' slim novel is a burlesque on the pretentious artists of the turn of the century who seemed more interested in intellectual discussions than in work.

594. ————. *Japonette.* **With illus. by Charles Dana Gibson. New York: Appleton, 1912. 384p.**

James Edgerton III came back to New York City from Europe broke and facing the collapse of the business he worked for. His apartment on 56th Street, he discovers, has been 'infiltrated' by Diana and Silvette Tennant. They too have been victims of the business failure, being granddaughters of his father's partner in the firm. In addition Diana and Silvette are distant cousins of his. Together the three endeavor to work out their fiscal salvation, advertising their services as organizers of parties and the like. The scene shifts to the Berkshires where love makes its kindly presence known. Edgerton experiences a change of fortune and recovers some financial stability.

595. ————. *The little red foot.* **New York: Doran, 1921. 351p.**

"Chambers has returned to the manner of 'Cardigan' and his early historical novels. The story is of the bloody struggle in northern New York, 1774 to 1782, between the Tories, with the Iroquois Indians and the Hessians on their side against the colonists with the Oneidas friendly to them. The historical facts are built about the love story of John Drogue, formerly overseer for Sir William Johnson, now fighting for the colonies, and the winsome Scots girl, Penelope Grant. The horrors of Indian warfare in the Revolutionary era are made very real"—Book review digest.

596. ————. *Love and the lieutenant.* **New York: Appleton-Century, 1935. viii, 402p.**

The first half of this novel of the American Revolution is placed in Germany where Lieutenant Grey Seadrift is recruiting Hessians for British service. Seadrift falls in love with the Baroness Von Lessing who, with her sister, Peggy Wymple—they are both Americans—is secretly attempting to abort Seadrift's mission. The second half of the novel deals with Burgoyne's invasion of northern New York, the battles of Bennington and Saratoga, and activity around Ticonderoga. Seadrift—he was brought up in the Hudson Valley—starts to shift his sympathies towards the American cause and his romantic inclinations towards Peggy Wymple. Unfortunately he falls into American hands and is made a prisoner-of-war.

597. ————. *The maid-at-arms; a novel.* **Illustrated by Howard Chandler Christy. New York: Harper, 1902. vi, 342p.**

The stage of this historical romance is Upstate New York (primarily the Mohawk Valley and Tryon County) during the American Revolution. A young Southerner, George Ormond, comes North to accept the hospitality of his cousins, the Varicks. Dorothy Varick is especially pleasing in his sight and he quickly falls in love with her, although she is engaged to another. Ormond commits himself to the rebel cause and is witness to and participant in the Battle of Oriskany, the relief of the besieged Fort Stanwix, the beginning of the Saratoga campaign, and several bloody encounters with Tories and Indians. His good friend, Sir George Covert, who has also cast his lot with the Americans, frees Dorothy of any commitment to him, for he has a new love, one of the Brants (Magdalen).

598. ————. *The man they hanged.* **New York: Appleton, 1926. 416p.**

"A sympathetic rendering of the story of Captain Kidd, which pictures him a brave and kindly soul, a man of charm no less than force who had made his wealth in commerce, and who lived an honored figure in old New York. The atmosphere of the city in the turbulent last quarter of the seventeenth century is successfully evoked. Dirck Hazlett, youthful friend of Captain Kidd and companion in his misfortunes, tells the story of the British conspiracy against his hero and of its shameful ending, weaving into the narrative the brighter strands of the Captain's happy love affair, and his (Dirck's) own"—Book review digest.

599. ————. *Outsiders; an outline.* **New York: F.A. Stokes, 1899. 301p.**

The 'hero' of the story is Oliver Lock, a young writer of fiction seeking endlessly and almost hopelessly a publisher for his literary creations. As he paces the streets of New York City he is a keen observer of all that goes on in the great metropolis. His first successful novel, 'The Iron City', springs from his observations. Before that, however, Oliver experiences the pangs of hunger and poverty, but is fortunate enough to find friends like Duncan Wayward, Jack Payser, Ivan Lacroix, et al. who provide him support and a lucrative job as a writer for the Zig-Zag magazine. The literary, journalistic and artistic life of the city is an important element in the novel. Oliver very gradually falls in love with Dulcie Wyvern, daughter of his boardinghouse landlady. They live innocently together until Dulcie leaves to take care of her mother. Oliver goes to Dulcie when she is badly crippled in a train wreck, but it seems inevitable that 'she had already drifted far beyond his hail.'

600. ————. *The painted minx.* **New York: Appleton, 1930. xiv, 306p.**
During the British occupation of New York City in the early years of the American Revolution, Marie Guest is a Tory actress who performs at the John Street theatre that is managed by Major John André. Loyalties aside, Marie is in love with Captain Barry Hood of Moylan's Horse, a unit of the American army. When Hood is in danger of gracing the gallows, André and Marie assist in his escape from the British. Later Marie herself is taken prisoner by the rebels and steps on a stage at Valley Forge. At the novel's close, the Continental Army marches into New York and the two lovers are reunited.

601. ————. *The reckoning.* **New York: Appleton, 1905. xv, 386p.**
One of a series of novels that Chambers devoted to the American Revolution. In this story the hero is spying for the patriot cause in New York City, of course risking his life in so doing. A Loyalist anxious to gain access to Sir Henry Clinton's councils unmasks the spy. Faced with execution the young patriot is saved at the last moment by a woman's intervention.

602. ————. *The restless sex.* **Illustrated by W.D. Stevens. New York: Appleton, 1918. 419p.**
"The principal scene of the story is laid near Washington Square in New York's Bohemian quarter. John Cleland, a man of culture and wealth, adopts Stephanie Quest, the heroine, as a child. His only son, Jimmy is a few years Stephanie's senior. When she is nineteen, her foster father dies. Pursuant to his expressed wish, Jimmy goes to Paris to study for a literary career, while Stephanie [briefly joins a New York artists' colony and then] enters a hospital to train as a nurse. Jimmy lingers in Paris for a number of years, but learning that his 'sister' has married a college classmate, suddenly returns home. He finds, however, that Stephanie's marriage [to his best friend, Grismer] is merely an 'arrangement,' although legal enough. Then he makes the disconcerting discovery that his sentiments towards her are different from those of a brother for a sister. The romance of Stephanie and Jimmy follows a devious course to an impasse, from which Mr. Chambers extricates his characters in a violent though logical manner"—Springfield Republican.

603. ————. *Some ladies in haste.* **New York: Appleton, 1908. xiii, 242p.**
After being cured of heavy smoking by mental suggestion "a New York man of leisure discovers that he has hypnotic power and exercises it upon a few of his acquaintances with the hope of turning them from their frivolous society inanities to nature and the open. Most astonishing things happen—whimsical, curious, surprising ones, not the least fantastic of which is the wooing of a society girl by a clubman on a tree-top"—Book review digest.

604. ————. *The streets of Ascalon*; **episodes in the unfinished career of Richard Quarren, Esquire. Illustrated by Charles Dana Gibson. New York: Appleton, 1912. ix, 440p.**

"A story of idle, glittering New York society in which a young woman [Strelsa Leeds], frankly intent on marrying money and a young man [Quarren], without fortune, figure as central characters. Around them circle the usual types of men-about-town, society matrons and fair young girls, and smart conversation and cleverly managed incidents serve to keep afloat a story whose plot is slight. Richard Quarren [with Strelsa's urging], comes in the end to abandon the role of society favorite for more . . . [useful] and lucrative occupations [e.g. he successfully renovates several paintings by old masters owned by a member of the English nobility and Strelsa awakens to the real importance of love in life"—Book review digest.

605. ————. *The talkers.* **New York: Doran, 1923. 291p.**
"Sadoul is a genius of sorts and among his specialties are hypnotism and psychic research. He falls in love with his secretary, Gilda Greenway, and, failing of response, acquires hypnotic power over her, compelling her while under his influence to contract a civil marriage with him. She refuses to live with him. … He kills her instantly by a stab into the nymphalic gland. While a gland specialist is getting ready to revive her by grafting a new, healthy nymphalic in its place, Sadoul … endeavors to inject a new ego into her in place of her slowly departing soul. He succeeds, however only giving her two personalities that alternately fight for control. Thus a gross, sensual Gilda, on occasions, displaces the real spiritual one, and renders the romance between her and young Sutton [the man she truly loves] a stormy and distressing one"—Book review digest. This strange tale is told against the background of New York City in the 1920s.

606. ————. *The tracer of lost persons.* **New York: Appleton, 1906. 293p.**
The 'tracer of lost persons' of the title is Kean & Co., a Fifth Avenue firm comprised of lawyers and detectives whose specialty is locating for their clients people who seem to have disappeared from their customary surroundings. An example of the firm's work is its uncovering, for a distraught young gentleman high in the social swim of New York, the whereabouts of a young woman who has been his ideal and joy.

607. ————. *War paint and rouge.* **New York: Appleton, 1931. 376p.**
John Cardress, a New Yorker of Scottish birth, and an officer in Roger's Rangers, is the narrator. We follow him from New York City to Fort Edward (near Saratoga) whose commanding general is Daniel Webb. Webb has a deadly fear of Indians and their style of warfare; thus, when Fort William Henry comes under attack by French and Indian forces, Webb refuses to send requested relief. After the fall of Fort William Henry, Cardress is sent on a secret mission to Louisbourg which ultimately surrenders to British and colonial forces. New Yorker Cardress does not conceal his dislike for the dour New Englanders. The novel includes a love story, which is rather negligible alongside the main threads of the plot.

608. ————.*The younger set.* **With illustrations by G.C. Wilmshurst. New York: Appleton, 1907. 513p.**

The author's focus is on members of wealthy New York society and its problems, some of which are peculiar to this caste—too much money, divorce, the reckless behavior of footloose Fifth Avenue young men and women, the screening out of a family's heritage of insanity, etc. The hero is an ex-army officer who has been devastated by the desertion of his wife, a woman quite a bit younger than he. The heroine is a finely-bred young lady who has no illusions about the ways of the world, but is imbued with honesty and good faith.

609. Champagne, Marian Mira Grosberg, 1915-. *Quimby and Son.* **Indianapolis: Bobbs-Merrill, 1962. 349p.**

In the 19th and early 20th century the wholesale grocery business built around the commerce generated by the Erie Canal made the Quimby family rich. As wholesaling declined in the late 1920s and the 1930s the retail trade seemed a more likely source for the family's continuing livelihood. Simon Quimby, however, resists the dramatic innovations wrought by the supermarket. The Quimby women become an especial focus of the novel: Victoria, Simon's sister, the spinster who finally agrees to a marriage of convenience and Anita, Simon's daughter, who wants to be a vital cog in the family business. The novel offers a fairly solid study of small town life in Upstate New York.

610. Champney, Elizabeth Williams, 1850-1922. *A daughter of the Huguenots.* **New York: Dodd, Mead, 1901. ix, 315p.**

New Rochelle, New York, settled in 1688 by Huguenots, is the chief scene of this historical novel, although the author does look backward at events in France (La Rochelle especially) that led to the emigration of this persecuted religious minority. Yvonne, 'a daughter of the Huguenots,' is the heroine and we follow her life in the new colony into the early years of the 18th century.

611. ————. *Witch Winnie at Shinnecock*; or, *The king's daughters in a summer art school.* **Illustrated by J. Wells Champney. New York: Dodd, Mead, 1894. vii, 294p.**

An art colony at Shinnecock [Hills], Long Island is presided over by the artist William M. Chase, dispensing criticism and advice to the students who gather there to attend classes and sketch, paint or draw landscapes. 'Witch Winnie' and 'Millie' are just two of the young women who combine vacations and art at Shinnecock. They will eventually go on to even more serious art studies in Paris. Unique talents are discovered in a young coachman who is encouraged by the aforementioned Mr. Chase.

Chance, Julia Grinnell, d. 1920. See under her pseudonym: Gordon, Julien, d. 1920.

612. ————. *Changing scenes*; **containing a description of men and**

manners of the present day with humorous details of the Knickerbockers. By a lady of New York. New York: printed for the author, 1825. 2v.

A potpourri of impressions of a diverse group of characters (several of Dutch ancestry) who relate their stories and their travels in New York City, Hudson River Valley, e.g.) and then to New Jersey, Ohio, etc.

613. Chapin, Gardner B. *Tales of the St. Lawrence.* **Rouse's Point [N.Y.]: J. Lovell, Lake Shore Press, 1873. 382p.**

"A portion of the within sketches are strictly historical—others, and the smaller number, wholly molded from fiction, save in the description given of localities, which are always intended to be strictly accurate"—Introduction. Contents: Isadore.—Maleeta, the river waif.—A country lost for a love.—The triple mistake.—Given to the wolves.—The church bell of Caughnawaga.—A memory of a masquerade.—The tale of Chateau Bigot.—The hidden treasure of the Isle Royal.—The Battle of Wind Mill Point.—William Johnson.—Saved by an earthquake.—The fatal wager.—The captain of Crane's Island.—Down the rapids.—The isle of massacre.—Catching a smuggler.—The phantom of Isle Perce.—Little Mary of Villa Maria.—The Hunter Lodge movement of 1938.

614. Charles, Cecil. *Miss Sylvester's marriage.* **Illustrated by W. Sherman Potts, New York: Smart Set Pub. Co., 1901. 254p.**

This story is of the turbulent marriage of Miss Sylvester, the tempestuous niece of a woman who is an outstanding figure in New York City social circles, to the Count Geraldina. The latter asserts that his interest in a pearl fishery has given him vast wealth; Miss Sylvester has Spanish blood coursing through her veins. The mix gives rise to a strange union whose outcome is unpredictable.

615. Chater, Melville. *The Eternal Rose*; **a story without a beginning or an end. New York, Chicago: Revell, 1910. 288p.**

The novel traces the influence of a legendary ancient chest, the 'Eternal Rose,' has on the characters in the story. The scene is New York City in the first decade of the 20th century. The ordinary activities of everyday urban life on Fourth Avenue to 23rd Street coalesce with mysterious currents that have their source in Eastern monasticism.

616. ————. *Little love stories of Manhattan.* **New York: Grafton Press, 1904. 1904. 225p.**

The 21 sketches of New York City life in the book portray a number of urban types: a ne'er-do-well who courts an Italian girl over the fence that separates them; an elevator boy who is fascinated by the young woman who sells candy in the lobby of 'his' skyscraper; the fellow who announces train destinations from Grand Central Station; the high-stepping dancer in the chorus of the musical comedy, 'The Liberty Girls'; the lunch-counter waitress who gives her customers' orders to the kitchen crew in the odd language of short-order restaurants; et al.

617. Cheever, Harriet Anna. *St. Rockwells' little brother.* **Boston: Congregational Sunday School and Pub. Society, 1894. 359p.**

The story of a New York businessman, St. Rockwells, who reaches out beyond his comfortable bachelor existence and takes responsibility for steering a street urchin toward a richer, more useful way of life.

618. Chesbro, George C., 1940- . *An incident at bloodtide.* **New York: Mysterious Press, 1993. 197p.**

The two themes running concurrently in this novel are the fear of occult, witch-ridden manifestations and environmental concerns for the Hudson River. Garth Frederickson and his wife Mary, a well-known folksinger, are being visited by Mongo Frederickson, Garth's dwarfish brother, a former circus performer now dabbling in criminology. Another arrival in the Hudson Valley village is Sacra, a one-time lover of Mary, who wants her back. Mary is frightened by Sacra's demands and believes he is capable of practicing sorcery. Then close by Garth's and Mary's home, oil is seeping into the Hudson from a ship that is taking on an undefined cargo for export. An environmentalist who looks into this situation dies under the ship's propeller blades. There is only one tangible suspect in what seems to be a murder.

619. ————. *The language of cannibals*; **a Mongo mystery. New York: Mysterious Press, 1990. 200p.**

"With brother Garth, who's unusual in his own right, [Robert] 'Mongo' [Frederickson, dwarf Ph.D., private eye extraordinaire and former circus aerialist] butts heads in this novel with crazed ultra-conservatives running a death squad in an artsy Hudson Valley town. Chesbro's villains, at least those Mongo confronts, are also bizarre—bigger than life, Bondish megalo-maniacs. Often using real social and political concerns as motifs, Chesbro's stands on those issues are passionately held and stated. Here it is the danger of the Far Right's effective manipulation of symbols and Orwellian double-speak and the suggestion that KGB sleeper agents are manipulating the manipulators"—Booklist.

620. Chester, George Randolph, 1869-1924. *The ball of fire,* **by George Randolph and Lillian Chester. New York: Hearst's International Library Co., c1914. 370p.**

The members of the affluent Market Street Church in New York City are more interested in its financial affairs than in more seemly Christian concerns. A young woman from the Midwest, Gail Sargent, niece of a businessman who wields a lot of influence in the church, ingratiates herself with many of its members and the Rev. Boyd Smith. He and Gail begin to question what looks more and more to be the commercialization of the church. Rev. Smith also has reservations about the church's doctrines. Particularly disturbing is the church's ownership of Vedder Court, a pesthole of filthy rented tenements which the church hopes to sell to partially finance the construction of a new cathedral. Supported by Gail, Reverend Smith finally decides to go out into the world preaching a message more commensurate with Christian ethics and social thought.

Chester, Lillian, joint author. *The ball of fire.* **See Item #620.**

621. Child, Richard Washburn, 1881-1935. *The hands of Nara.* **New York: Dutton, 1922. 326p.**

"The purpose of the story is to show that cold scientific facts do not cover the whole of life, that something of miraculous power still remains by which the human mind can transcend the apparent workings of cause and effect. Two [New York City] physicians, father and son, are reluctantly forced to this admission when they see the healing power emanating from the presence of Nara Alexieff, a spiritually sensitive young Russian. Nara herself comes to realize that the power resides within each individual and that circumstances have merely favored her in being the medium to draw it out. The various steps that lead to these discoveries mark the somewhat stormy progress of the romance between Nara and young Dr. Clavelous"—Book review digest.

Childs, Eleanor Stuart Patterson, b. 1876. See: Stuart, Eleanor, b. 1876.

Chipperfield, Robert Orr, pseud. See: Ostrander, Isabel Egenton, 1883-1924.

Chauncey, Shelton, pseud. See: Nicholls, Charles Wilbur de Lyon, 1854-1923.

622. Christie, May. *The gilded rose*; **a novel. New York: Putnam, 1925. iv, 379p**

Left a fortune by her innkeeper father, the heroine ('the gilded rose'), an innocent, virtuous maiden from Long Island, marries the man she deeply loves. He is cultured but has no money and is secretly enamored of a woman of questionable character who is allied with a smuggling bootlegger. The latter and his lady partner try to separate the married couple—the bootlegger would like to have the 'gilded rose' for his own. Yet the young marrieds are able to ward off the villains as the husband finally comes to his senses.

623. ————. *The high speed girl*; **a novel. New York: Grosset & Dunlap, 1931. 261p.**

Lauren, a Long Island social figure, is the 'high speed girl'; her objective is to lay to rest the notion that 'love' matters all that much.

624. [Chumasero, John Chamberlain] 1816-1903. *Life in Rochester*; **or,** *Sketches from life.* **Being scenes of misery, vice, shame and oppression in the City of**

the Genesee. By a resident citizen. Rochester [N.Y.] D.M. Dewey, 1848. 100p.

Lawyer Daniel Grab—'honest according to the law'—enriches himself at the expense of defauded victims, including widow Mary Ashmun. Mrs. Ashmun's son, Oliver, years later is one of the instruments of Grab's downfall as he, with the help of a bank cashier, William Brown, takes Grab to court and reveals Grab's dishonest stratagems. As his world disintegrates Grab dies of apoplexy. The tale is full of heinous characters: Swindlem Skinflint; Mrs. Squab, brothel owner; Jim Pilfer, theif and fortune hunter; Pimento Blister, grasping tradesman, et al.—and a bevy of innocent victims. Another work by Chumasero, *The mysteries of Rochester* (1845) is unavailable for perusal.

625. Ciambelli, Bernardino. *I misteri di Mulberry*; romanzo. New York: Frugone & Balletto, 1893. 320p. (in double columns).

Rinaldo (a.k.a. Renato) Ruiz (or Ruizzi), pursuing a criminal career in New York that had begun in Italy, attacks his wife Vittoria, a recent immigrant who had been searching for him. Alberto Righetti, an admirer of Vittoria, stumbles onto the scene and as Rinaldo flees, is accused of attempted murder. Vittoria recovers while innocent Alberto languishes in Sing-Sing. The New York police step in to investigate further. Ruiz is presumably drowned when he takes passage on a ship that sinks three days out of New York. On release from prison Alberto Righetti marries Vittoria. The possibility that Rinaldo Ruiz actually survived is presented at the story's end. Three other works by Ciambelli that treat the Italian experience in New York City are: *I misteri di Bleecker Street* (1899); *I sotteranei di New York* (1915); and *La trovatella di Mulberry Street* (1919). They are difficult to come by.

Cicchetti, Janet O'Daniel, 1921- . See: O'Daniel, Janet, 1921-.

Citizen of Milwaukee. *Garangula, the Ongua Honwa chief.* See Item #1266.

626. Clague, Maryhelen, 1930- . *Beyond the shining river.* New York: Coward, McCann & Geoghegan, 1980. 432p,

The novel's scenes are ensconced in Westchester County during the American Revolution and shortly thereafter. The leading character, Celia Deveroe, is a member of a family sharply divided politically. Celia herself is facing the dilemma of choosing between two men she loves, one throwing his support to the American cause, the other maintaining his loyalty to the British crown. Perhaps even more central for Celia are her efforts for self-realization.

627. ———. *So wonderous free.* New York: Stein and Day, 1978. 314p.

The American Revolution as it 'played' in Westchester County is the focus of the novel. The heroine is an indentured servant, Nabby Colson, beautiful and neutral in her selection of lovers. Warding off the carnal advances of her master, Nabby becomes mistress of a colonel in the British Army, and then finds solace in the arms of a captain in the Continental Army. All in all she experiences the best and worst of human elements on both sides of the conflict.

628. Claibourne, Fernand. *The unfinished tale*; or, *The daughter of the mill.* **A romance of Lake George. New York: W.L. Allison, 1881. 316p.**

While exploring the Lake George area the story's narrator saves Henry Thurling from drowning and meets his niece, Ethel Thurling. Mr. Thurling spins a tale for his savior; the hero of the tale is an orphan named Harry whose love for Elsie Moore, a miller's daughter, takes wild turns. Harry is held responsible for a stranger's death when he rams a boat on which Elsie is one of the passengers. Harry exiles himself to California and Elsie marries a Mr. De Haven who bears a marked resemblance to Harry. Returning to the Lake George region Harry is arrested; Elsie visits him in prison. After release Harry hears of Elsie's death by drowning—was it suicide or murder at the hands of the vanished De Haven? Should one assume that all this is in part Thurling's own life story? Our traveler/narrator is by now in love with Ethel Thurling but receives no encouragement from her and sadly leaves the area.

629. Clark, Charles Dunning, 1843-1892. *The lake rangers.* **A tale of Ticonderoga, by W.J. Hamilton [pseud.]. New York: Beadle, 1868. 98p.**

Jake Dowdle, Ned Weston, Bill Eagan and other American rangers under the command of Major Charles Seely scout the Lake George region preliminary to the attack of General Abercromby and his colonial and British troops on French-held Fort Ticonderoga in 1758. Dodging attacks by the French and their allies, the St. Regis Indians, the rangers link up with Abercromby's army, but not before Ned Weston is killed and the traitor Bill Eagan deserts to the enemy. Weston's daughter, Nattie, disguised as a boy, tries to warn Abercromby of the futility of a frontal ttack on heavily–fortified Ticonderoga. He ignores all advice and disaster ensues. However, Dowdle kills Eagan and some months after the British retreat, Major Seely and Nattie are married.

630. ————. *Mossfoot, the Brave*; or, *The scout of Oneida Lake*, by W.J. **Hamilton [pseud.]. New York: Beadle and Adams, 1873. 94p.**

The Tory, Captain Walter Butler, appears in this 'thriller' using the alias, 'Ralph Swinton.' Mossfoot is an Oneida Indian who is trying to decide whether to throw in with the British or with the Americans as the Revolutionary War rages in east central New York State. Swinton/Butler poses as a neutral to the Yankee Ichabod Salmon, but is busy hatching plans to further the Loyalist cause. His chief adversaries are Ichabod Salmon, Joseph Seaman, a patriot doctor, and especially the Dutchman Hans Phiffer, Ichabod's hired helper. Butler and his Indians kidnap Ichabod's daughter Bessie and Silver Voice, Mossfoot's wife. The crafty Hans ('the scout of Oneida Lake'?), who has a charmed life, pursues the kidnappers relentlessly. A battle between Mossfoot and his Oneidas (Mossfoot has joined the Americans) and Butler with his Huron (?) allies ensues. Butler meets death at the hands of Mossfoot; the two women escape and are picked up by Hans and

Seaman. In between these happenings the Battle of Oriskany takes place and Arnold relieves Fort Schuyler.

631. Clark, Imogen, d. 1936. *God's puppets*; **a story of old New York. New York: Scribner, 1901. x, 381p.**

New York City in the middle of the eighteenth century is the scene of this novel which treats of a Dutch dominie (minister) and Annetje, his beautiful daughter. There is a triangle of sorts when Annetje falls in love with a British army officer whose affections are directed chiefly towards Peggy Crewek, a girl of his own nationality and class. The novel was also published in London (J. Murray) under the title: *The dominie's daughter*.

632. Clark, Jean. *The marriage bed*; **a novel. New York: Putnam, 1983. 295p.**

The Hudson River Valley of colonial New York is the scene of this historical romance. The heroine of the story is the beautiful but poor orphan Margretta Van Dyke who is governess to the children of the Reverend Hardenbroeck, family chaplain of the Van Badenswycks, owners of a huge estate along the Hudson. Besieged by several suitors Margretta pursues the dictates of her heart and marries a tenant farmer, Stephen Warner. The Warners' marriage is no 'bed of roses'. They are buffeted by scandal mongering, misfortune and the general dislocations of the Revolutionary period in which they live before they reawaken the happiness that once was theirs.

633. Clark, Margaret Goff, 1913- . *Adirondack mountain mystery*. **Illustrated by Ernest Kurt Barth. New York: Funk & Wagnalls, 1966. 158p.**

New York State troopers capture an escaped bank robber, but are unable to locate the money he helped steal—he isn't talking. Andy Scott, 13, and his cousin come upon a roughly sketched map that points to a cave in the Adirondacks where the stolen funds may be cached. Guided by a friendly Adirondack mountaineer the two lads go for the money but are closely followed by the thief's ruthless accomplices.

634. Clark, Valma, 1894- . *Horn of plenty*. **New York: Duell, Sloan and Pearce, 1945. 247p.**

An Upstate New York family, the Rathbones, possess a rather superficial vitality and their antics are fairly amusing, but it is up to Effie, their hired woman of many years standing, who provides the glue that holds this turbulent family together. Not only is she a superb housekeeper; she is also shrewd and wise in the practical aspects of living.

635. —————. *Their own country*. **New York: Putnam, 1934. 315p.**

"Abby Winslow, orphaned at the age of twelve, goes to live with an aunt in a small town in the Finger Lakes region of New York. As the years go by, Abby develops from a sensitive child to a lovely young woman with marked literary talent, but at the same time there grows up between her and her aunt's husband a deep sympathy which at last changes to a tragic love"—Book review digest.

636. Clarke, Donald Henderson, 1887-1958. *Louis Beretti*; **a novel. New York: Vanguard Press, 1929. 285p.**

The novel limns the career of an Italian-American, Louis Beretti, whose parents are proprietors of a Bowery pushcart. Louis muscles his way out of his bleak surroundings and moves up the ladder from chief hoodlum to kingpin of bootleggers and owner of a speakeasy in the slums and a Broadway night club.

637. Clarkson, L[ouise] 1865-1928. *The shadow of John Wallace*; **a novel. New York: White, Stokes & Allen, 1884. 417p.**

The time frame of the novel, which is set in a small village on Long Island, is ca. 1844 to 1884. A man bearing the name 'John Wallace' comes to this place, a complete stranger who has presumably been dealt the loss of his domestic tranquility. However, the mystery surrounding him is never satisfactorily resolved, though the objects named in the title of Robert Browning's 'The Ring and the Book' play a role here too.

638. Clausen, Carl. *The Gloyne murder.* **New York: Dodd, Mead, c1929. 266p.**

Miss Doris Gloyne was murdered in her New York apartment; most of the suspects seemed to conduct themselves as if they had guilty secrets to hide and a few other suspicious individuals had been seen close by the scene of the crime. Upon the shoulders of police Lieutenant Ames rested the burden of uncovering what really took place. His wife fills in the details for the reader.

639. Clement, Mickey. *The Irish princess.* **New York: Putnam, 1994. 254p.**

The novel is about the Malloy family of Troy, N.Y. during the years 1964-1982. Of chief interest are Mike and Clare Malloy and their daughters Marge and Maureen ('Mo'). Mo is the family's star; she is pretty and very bright, but her affair with David Markovitch, a young Jew, leads to an unwanted pregnancy. Mike is a devout Catholic while Clare's faith has been in a downturn since the loss of a baby. Other people moving through the story are: Bridey, Mike's sister, contemptuous of non-Catholic faiths; Paul, a brother with a political career; and Hildy, a sister-in-law of German extraction.

640. Clement, Peter. *Lethal practice.* **New York: Ballantine Pub., 1997. 343.p**

The narrator of the story is Earl Garnet, emergency room doctor and highly skilled cardiac specialist. The personnel of St. Paul's Hospital in Buffalo, N.Y., suffer both confusion and fear when its head administrator, Everett Kingsley, is murdered—the weapon that killed him was a cardiac needle driven into his heart. Garnet's search for the motive behind the murder and a realistic portrayal of how a hospital is run keep the novel moving at a fast pace.

Clements, Colin, joint author. *The Borgia blade.* **See Item #2944.**

641. **Clews, James Blanchard, b. 1869.** *Fortuna*; **a story of Wall Street. New York: J.S. Ogilvie, 1898. 215p.**

Fortuna is a wealthy young woman (worth fifty million!) who decides to manage her own investments; in order to do so she bones up on Wall Street methodology with the teaching assistance of Fred, a young broker of high social standing, who has had proven success on the 'Street.' As he explains to Fortuna the peculiarities of Stock Exchange verbiage, Fred also falls in love with his pupil. One can gather much information on the operations of Wall Street in the early 20th century, especially since the author himself was a prominent Wall Street banker.

642. **Cline, A.J.** *Henry Courtland*; **or,** *What a farmer can do.* **Philadelphia: Lippincott, 1870. 398p.**

Henry Courtland, a farmer in Upstate New York, is convinced that the pastoral life is not only good in itself, but that its adherents can be just as sophisticated politically, socially and intellectually as their urbanites. However, he allows his sons to make their own choices. Harry stays on the farm, Courtland Hall. Percy ventures into the outside world; he retains a warm affection for his childhood friend, Agnes Russell. The latter, convinced that her brother Alfred, long presumed dead, is still alive, follows the conniving Captain Lamberton to the California of the 1849 gold rush in her quest. Lamberton had been a whilom 'friend' of Percy, yet now he devises plans to claim Agnes for himself. Agnes, her faithful maid Maggy and an old confidante, Billy Braxton, outwit the Captain, find the ailing but recovering Alfred Russell, and depart for the calmer climes of Courtland Hall.

643. **Clinghan, Clarice Irene.** *That girl from Bogotá*; **a novel. New York: Home Pub. Co., 1896. 262p.**

"Virginia Lemar, leaving a school in South America on account of an epidemic among the pupils, comes to Cragskill on the Hudson to visit the Maxwells, who are relatives; unfortunately these friends are travelling, and Virginia and her Inca maid force an entrance to the deserted mansion, where they live very uncomfortably until Assunta, the maid, seeks aid of Demetrius Newcastle, rector of Cragskill, who later plays the part of Good Samaritan and hero in a story in which there is a murder and other dramatic and sensational incidents"—Annual American catalogue.

644. **Clinton, Park.** *Glanmore*; **or,** *The bandits of Saratoga.* **A romance of the Revolution. Cincinnati: U.P. James [ca. 1852?]. 102p.**

The Glanmores, father and son (Gordon), feign support for the American cause, but secretly aid the British war effort. Gordon Glanmore and his band of Tories establish headquarters in a dug out cave near Saratoga Lake and Snake Hill. From there, disguised as Indians, they raid and kill those who espouse sympathy for the rebels. The young patriot George Rushwood stands in Glanmore's way when the Tory seeks to win the hand of Caroline Mansfield (Glanmore had pretended that he had been a prisoner of Burgoyne's British forces). Caroline and George wed secretly and George goes off to help stem the advance of Burgoyne's army. An old Indian friend of Rushwood, Kwa-ta-hu, thwarts Glanmore when the latter tries to kill Rushwood, although the Tory does kidnap Caroline. The novel concludes with Caroline's release, an attack by the bandits on Rushwood's home (occupied by Mrs. Rushwood and Caroline's parents)—repulsed by Rushwood and his troops—and the death by drowning in the Mohawk River of the fleeing Glanmore.

645. Clouston, Adella Octavia, b. 1864. *What would the world think?* **A novel. New York: Dodsworth Pub. House, 1897. 283p.**

Helen is only nine when her parents (Gertrude and Robert Channing, the latter a man of small worth who had lured his wife from her former husband, the New York banker Sidney Bryan) die and she has to fend for herself in 'Clydesville,' New York. Mrs. Marvin's husband rejects his wife's hope to provide a place for Helen in their home and Helen ends up with Mrs. Timothy Hopdyke, a hard woman, who offers Helen only drudgery. Helen runs away to shelter with the kind but poor Rudens. Departing Clydesville she has several frightening experiences in New York City before being adopted and educated by Sidney Bryan. As a socially prominent young woman Helen goes back to Clydesville, reacquaints herself with the elderly Mrs. Marvin, provides suitable living quarters for the widowed and poverty-stricken Mrs. Hopdyke and amply rewards the Rudens. The story concludes with Helen's engagement to Billy Marvin, a Yale graduate about to embark on a New York City career.

646. Clune, Henry W., b.1890 or 2. *By his own hand.* **New York: Macmillan, 1952. 586p.**

Alan Wesley had risen from virtual poverty to power as an industrialist in the city of 'Minerva' in upper New York State. He was essentially a lonely man. The only woman who was really important in his life was his mother who had died in 1906 before the story begins. Three other women did have a share in his life: Bernice, daughter of one of Minerva's first families who acted as hostess when Wesley gave a party in his big house; his daughter Judy, one of the few who would not defer to his riches and power; and Ann, a former showgirl, at one time or another Alan's mistress, and wife of a British remittance man and of a Chicago gambler. The lawyer Hillyard was a friend whom Alan had enriched but had then suffered a nervous breakdown. Although respected Wesley was never looked upon with any real affection (with the possible exception of some of the women around him). Rochester, New York and one of its best known citizens is reputed to be the basis for this novel.

647. Cobb, Irvin S., 1876-1944. J. *Poindexter,* **colored. New York: Doran, 1922. 270p.**

"Jeff Poindexter, who had worked for Judge Priest of Paducah, Kentucky, for sixteen years, was out of a job when the Eighteenth Amendment drove the old Judge from the United States. Jeff was lent for a while to young Dallas Fulliam who took him as his body servant on a visit to New York. Jeff tells of his adventures there and how, when his young master fell among sharpers and vamps, Jeff was able, by superior gifts of lying and invention, to rescue him from their toils"—Book review digest.

648. ————. *The life of the party.* **Illustrated by James M. Preston. New York: Doran, 1910. 66p.**

Algernon Leary is a stately lawyer, 37 years of age, who has attended a costume ball in Greenwich Village dressed as a three-year-old boy. After the ball he has a tiff with a besotted taxi driver and is left to roam the streets of the city still attired as a child of three.

649. ————. *Murder day by day.* **Indianapolis: Bobbs-Merrill, 1933. 306p.**

"All about the strange death of Uncas Cresap, an eccentric miser, and Wong Gee, his Chinese butler, in the boathouse at Kettle Pond, way out in Long Island; for that matter, Manuel Sabino, a baleful dwarf, gets his later. All of which is related by Gilbert Redd, a lovable old codger with a gift for getting you hep to the right clues at the right moment. Among the problems: Why is beautiful Florence Dane so frightened? Where is Gregory Thorpe, her fiancé? What about Fitified Jake, an afflicted bystander; Haw Variety, general factotum; and Ole Olsen, chauffeur? ... Flashes of the inimitable Cobb humor lighten the tense developments"—New York herald tribune books.

650. **Coe, Charles Francis, 1890- . *The river pirate.* New York: Putnam, 1928. c1927. 254p.**

A tale of theft along the wharves of Lower Manhattan. The protagonist is a young man just released from a reformatory. He, the narrator, hooks up with Sailor Frink, an old hand at stealing from the docks.

Coffey, Edward Hope, 1896- . See: Hope, Edward, 1896.

Cohan, George M., 1878-1942. *Broadway Jones.* See Item #2248.

Cohen, Alfred J., 1861-1928. See under his pseudonym: Dale, Alan, 1861-1928.

651. **Cohen, Hyman. *Aaron Traum,* by Hyman and Lester Cohen. New York: Liveright, 1930. 413p.**

The odyssey of Aaron Traum begins shortly before 1886. Aaron, a recent immigrant, is only 11 when forced by his family's poverty to work in the sweatshops of Manhattan's Jewish ghetto. With no access to public schooling, Aaron embarks on a program of self-education, along the way imbibing the tenets of socialism, fighting for workers' rights and unionism. His dream of becoming a teacher (with enrollment at Sewanee, University of the South) is dashed by the theft of his savings. Gaining employment in an Upper Midwest lumber camp, Aaron meets and marries Laura. The two end up in New York City. After a half-hearted stab at medical school, Aaron opts for woodworking and gains a good reputation as a wood sculptor. In large part episodic, the novel presents a rather absorbing portrait of the disenchantment and grim poverty that faces many immigrants when they first arrive in America.

Cohen, Lester, 1901— joint author. *Aaron Traum.* **See Item #651.**

652. Colby, Nathalie Sedgwick, 1875-1945. *Black stream.* **New York: Harcourt, Brace, 1927. 314p.**

A novel of New York City in which "the flow of human emotions is the 'black stream.' It reaches a vortex during a period of twenty-four hours in the lives of a group of people—two New York families living opposite each other: the Brazees, rich, socially ambitious; the Farradays, divided in their ideals. Dr. Farraday's wife copies her rich neighbors as far as possible, scorning her husband's devotion to research and prodding him to secure luxurious and social positions for his children. The interplay of these two families creates the drama of the story whose characters stand revealed by the stream of consciousness method—the thoughts that course through their minds, with frequent flashbacks for facts necessary to the story"—Book review digest.

653. ————. *A man can build a house.* **New York: Brace, 1928. 355p.**

New York City's Upper West Side is the setting of this novel concerning the lives of a varied assortment of individuals. "In a net spread for Eisinstein, Ruby catches [Peter] Kaufman, owner of the store. He marries her with a dream in his heart. Ruby knows nothing of the dream, having her mind on an 'artist gentleman' who once noticed her in a cabaret. He, poor fellow, is drinking himself into worthlessness, knowing that Joan is too good for him. To Kaufman and to Joan, love is a searing pain for the unworthiness of their loved ones; but to Maria, Kaufman's maid, it is peace and fulfillment as she and her Carl build their home. The story is unfolded through the thoughts and emotions of the principal characters"—Book review digest.

654. Cole, Donna Rieta Bramhall. *Faith-Hope, child of the slums,* **by D.R.C. Edited by G.O. Tubby. New York: G.O. Tubby, 1909. 300p.**

A child living on the streets of New York after abandonment by the elderly woman who had been entrusted with caring for her, Faith-Hope becomes the constant attendant of Emily Worden ('Dearest-Dear' to Faith-Hope), an ill lady who lives in 'Cat Alley' near Fourth Avenue. Emily tells the story of her past to Mrs. Ann Clancy; the latter has as her mission support of the poverty-beset tenants of Cat Alley. Faith-Hope, too, is always prepared to stand up for the downtrodden and targets of prejudice. The appearance of Theodore Melvin in the neighborhood signals the revelation of Faith-Hope's true identity; she is the daughter of a gentleman and a lady (deceased) well-known to Theodore and she is related to John Hamilton, another acquaintance of Theodore's and the long-absent husband of Emily Worden. Faith-Hope leaves Cat Alley with Theodore Melvin; the two embark for Europe with a vociferous send-off by their friends of Cat Alley.

Cole, Lois Dwight, 1902-1979. See under her pseudonym: Eliot, Anne.

655. Cole, Patience Bevier, b. 1883. *Dave's daughter*; a novel. **New York: Stokes, 1933. 256p.**

Christabel Sayne inherited fabulous wealth from her father Dave (owner of copper mines). She presently resides in New York City, but finds it most convenient to get away from the city occasionally to the home of her maiden aunts, Mattie and Matie, in a Long Island village. The proud young man with whom Christabel is in love is reluctant about asking her to marry him because he is poor and does not wish to be labeled a fortune hunter. Disappointed, Christabel is about to marry an elderly New Yorker when the aunts talk to the younger man and convince him of the error of his point of view.

Coles, Bertha Horstmann Lippincott, 1880-1963. See: Lippincott, Bertha Horstmann, 1880-1963.

656. Collins, Max Allan, 1948- . *Nice Weekend for a murder.* **New York: Walker, 1986. 190p.**

The famous Mohonk Mountain House near New Paltz, N.Y. is well known for its Mohonk Mystery Weekends in which mystery writers and fans are both 'suspects' and detective teams. During this particular session the 'murder victim' is to be an acerbic, hated, but powerful critic. Mallory, a crime writer, watches as the critic walks out in a huff during the first meeting; then later that evening Mallory believes he has seen the critic being murdered. Mallory and Jill, his girlfriend, know there is no hoax involved when they come upon the critic's corpse on a mountain top. Because of an oncoming blizzard Mallory can't get hold of the police, so he does his own detecting.

657. Collins, Michael, pseud. *Walk a black wind.* **New York: Dodd, Mead, 1971. 188p.**

Acquaintance John Andrea puts Danny Fortune, the consummate urbanite, to work searching for the killer of Francesca Crawford, 20, daughter of 'Dresden', New York's mayor. Thus begin extended twists and turns for Danny through the Crawford family history and eventually a long journey to a Comanche Indian reservation in Arizona where many things fall into place.

658. Collins, Michelle, pseud. *Murder at Willow Run.* **New York: Zebra Books, 1979. 207p.**

A murder takes place in an Upstate New York art colony, 'Willow Run.' The room in which the body is finally found has been locked both from the inside and outside—the device is not especially original—but the author has style and flair enough to make the story palatable.

659. Collison, Wilson, 1893-1941. *The murder in the brownstone house, from the records of a young lawyer.* **New York: McBride, 1929. 308p.**
> Robert Caslon, the story's first person narrator, is a civil lawyer with an office in the Knickerbocker Building at Broadway and 42nd Street. He takes on his first criminal case, defending Jerry Belden, scion of a prominent family, who has been accused of killing May Marnes, a gold-digging Broadway show girl. Caslon and Webster Brette, the assistant district attorney, duel on more or less equal terms in the courtroom, each in turn calling eight witnesses for the defense and eight for the prosecution. The impasse is broken when the valet of Jerry's uncle, Roland Belden, presents a deposition to the court.

660. ————. *Shy Cinderella.* **New York: McBride, 1932. 276p.**
> Two chorus girls from the 'Big Town' find jobs as cook and serving-maid in a Long Island home; the wealthy owner, their employer, has just lost his wife— she decided to take off and be entirely on her own.

661. ————. *A woman in purple pajamas,* **by Willis Kent [pseud.]. New York: McBride, 1931.**
> A swinging weekend party in White Plains, N.Y. is abruptly interrupted by the murder of one of the guests, young Jimmie Reed.

662. Colver, Alice Mary Ross, 1892- . *Joan Foster, sophomore.* **New York: Dodd, Mead, 1948. 207p.**
> One of several novels about a young woman's life—academic, social and emotional—at a college located in Upstate New York. Other titles in the series are: *Joan Foster, freshman* (1942); *Joan Foster, junior* (1949); *Joan Foster, senior* (1950); and *Joan Foster, free lance writer* (1948).

663. ————. *The parson; a novel.* **Philadelphia: Macrae, Smith, 1951. 272p.**
> A suburban community near New York City is in turmoil because one of its wealthy citizens is determined to be the most powerful figure in the town. He is behind gossip and slander, much of which is aimed at a new teacher who is an inspiration to the students in the high school. A broad-minded minister, Barth Atwood, supports the teacher despite a groundswell of opposition. Atwood and his allies are able to ensure the retention of the teacher, but the Rev. Atwood himself is left without a pulpit.

664. Colvin, Addison Beacher, b. 1858. *Lumberman 'Lew'; a story of fact, fantasy and fiction,* **by Harvester Hiram [pseud.] Glens Falls, N.Y.: Glens Falls Publishing Co., [1912?]. 117p.**
> Lumberman "Lew', who has devoted his life to politics, serving in various offices, including the U.S. Congress, reflects from his 'Warrensville' (i.e. Warrensburg) home ('at the foothills of the Adirondacks') on his career and

the political health of New York State, his county and the nation. His inquisitive 12-year-old nephew, Albert, draws from the elderly statesman (and 'boss') pointed stories that illustrate the uncertainties that face people who embark on public service. A romance between the beautiful, unsophisticated Elsie Anis of Warrensville and the aristocratic Major Donald Livingston DePuyster is a secondary 'plot' in the short novel. The author takes exception to those who devalue politicians, stating his belief that 'they are for the greater part honorable, trustworthy, self-denying and high minded' (p. 8).

665. ————. *'Stray steps'* **by Harvester Hiram (Addison B. Colvin). Glens Falls, N.Y.: Glens Falls Pub. Co., 1920. 220p.**

The author claims that this work is not fiction, but it surely has the dialogue and situations of a novel. Ephraim, son of Addison and Melissa Adamson (they publish a paper in 'The Glen'—Glens Falls?) explores opportunities in New York City. Hired by his Uncle Orson, a renowned lawyer, Ephraim attracts the not unwelcome attentions of Orson's beautiful young wife, Norma. However he impulsively marries Ina De Forest whom he had accidentally injured on a city sidewalk. Ephraim's business career stalls and he pays little heed to his mother and sister, Annabella, back in The Glen. Ina dies in childbirth and the now distraught Ephraim commits suicide. Norma Addison, her husband recently deceased, plays down the tragedy to ease the pain of Ephraim's parents and Annabella. Odd circumstances surrounding Ephraim's death have the police believing that his demise may have been a homicide.

666. Comfort, Lucy Randall, 1833-1914. *The belle of Saratoga*; or, *The heart of the St. Severns.* **New York: G. Munro, 1876. 93p. (on double leaves).**

Not only Saratoga, but also New York City, Niagara Falls, Albany and 'Wildford' in northern New York are scenes of the novel. Clarita (later Clara) Romayne, the heroine, catches the eye of the already married Wycherly Lennox. He dies in a railroad wreck; his brother Philip is not particularly attracted to Clara but he marries her anyway. Clara runs off and is hired as governess to Florine, the daughter of Eustace St. Severn. It comes as no surprise (19th century women's fiction is rife with such revelations) that Clara is the long lost daughter of St. Severn. With other loose ends neatly tied together Clara's 'suffering' is rewarded by the passionate avowals of a now love-smitten Philip Lennox. Reissued in 1890 287p.

667. ————. *Corisande*; or, *The ladder of gold.* **New York: G. Munro, 1880. 52p.**
A young girl whose early environment is the streets of New York is given a free education; and now that it is time to make her own way in the world of work she clings to one goal—to acquire wealth by whatever means she can, sacrificing everything, if need be, in her quest.

668. ————. *Love at Saratoga*; or, *Married in haste.* **New York: G. Munro, 1879. 50p. (in triple columns).**

Farm-raised Theodora (Dora) Beck, piqued by her own beauty, samples the excitement of the Saratoga racing season. Sir Basil Branchley espies her in the crowd and promptly falls in love with the comely Dora, whom he marries and tries to educate for her new station in life. The couple have twins, a boy and a girl. Sir Basil departs alone for England to settle his father's estate. The displeased, offended Dora returns to her parent's farm. The travails of Dora and Basil from thereon are numerous and frustrating. The two children, left with Dora's stern sister, have, like their parents, been separated and both Dora and Basil institute searches for them. Years later in England Dora, under a pseudonym and serving as a governess, earns the affection of Basil's mother, Lady Branchley. Basil, suffering from brain-fever, is nursed back to health by his concerned wife. The lost children are found—and as one of the characters says: "It's just like a novel."

669. **Commelin, Anna Olcott.** *Jerushy in Brooklyn*, **by Jerushy Smith of Smithville (Anna Olcott Commelin). New York: Fowler & Wells Co., 1893. 84p.**

"An account of a visit to Brooklyn by a lady from the rural districts. It is a dialect story in which there is found a clever comment on some of the fads and follies of fashionable life in our large cities. Jerushy discusses the 'Si Dell Society', Cousin Sarta's days, teas and receptions, charity balls, fairs, etc."— Annual American catalogue.

Compton, Frances Snow, pseud. See: Adams, Henry, 1838-1918.

670. **Comstock, Harriet Theresa Smith, b. 1860.** *Janet of the dunes.* **Illustrated by Carle Michel Boog. Boston: Little, Brown, 1908. vii, 297p.**

The heroine of this tale, set on Long Island, is Janet, adopted daughter of 'Captain Billy' of the Life Saving Service. A pretty, personable, unpretentious girl, she comes in contact with a group of artists from the city who are lodged in summer homes. From these sophisticated people she receives an introduction to the vagaries of love and the onset of adulthood. One elderly man in the coterie turns out to be her father. Through it all Janet retains her naturalness, the warm simplicity that has its origin in her long association with the fishermen, lighthouse keepers and life savers of Long Island.

671. ————. *The mark of Cain.* **Garden City, N.Y.: Doubleday, Doran, 1935. 309p.**

"From a car window in the train carrying him to the North Woods [in the Adirondacks] Malcolm Churchill witnesses a fatal shooting. Later he encounters the woman he believes to be the murderess and she tells him a strange story. Though unconvinced by her tale, he falls in love with and marries her, but it is several years before he finds that she had not lied to him"—Book review digest.

672. **Conklin, Jennie Maria Drinkwater, 1841-1900.***Three-and-twenty.* **Boston: A.I. Bradley, 1895. 354p.**

Leah Ritchie goes from a New England girlhood to the vocation of journalism in New York City. She has arrived at the age of 23 when she is faced with a marriage proposal. How she deals with the situation is the crux of the novel.

673. Conners, Bernard F., 1926- . *Dancehall.* **Indianapolis: Bobbs-Merrill, 1983. 358p.**

The recovery of Ann Conway's body from Lake Placid 20 years after her death has repercussions for Dave Powell. He is in financial trouble; his wife Sue and he are beginning to disagree on a number of things. Their daughter Dana seems to be the one person that Dave has left to cherish. From Lake Placid the scene changes to the Powell estate in Tarrytown where two more bodies are discovered. By the story's end the individual held responsible for these deaths is in Green Haven Prison waiting in the 'Dancehall', the cell nearest the execution room.

674. Conners, William Fuller. *James Lee.* **Chicago: Clinic Pub. Co., c1906. 238p.**

James Lee, from Jamestown, N.Y., studies medicine in New York City. It is he who intervenes and incapacitates Arthur Van Ogden when the latter threatens harm to his wife, Louise. She flees with her child Virginia, and Arthur, infatuated with his secretary Rose Thorne, disappears from the scene until the story's conclusion. After James Lee receives his medical degree, he practices his art in Lincoln, Mass., making occasional trips back to New York to consult with or help his colleagues. Old Mr. (Charles) Van Ogden of New York, Arthur's father, marries Mary Lang, a nurse, after his wife's death. Virginia, grown to a young woman of 18, falls in love with Dr. Lee, and the novel moves to conclusion with all the chief characters in New York. Arthur Van Ogden, fully recovered physically and cured of his passion for Rose Thorne, is reunited with his long absent wife, Louise. James Lee and Virginia Van Ogden are wed; elderly Charles Van Ogden and his young wife Mary share their home with these couples. Rose Thorne confesses past crimes and commits suicide before the court's judgment can be passed on her.

675. Converse, Florence, b. 1871. *The children of light.* **Boston: Houghton, Mifflin, 1912. vii, 308.**

"A naïve plea for socialism centering about a mayorality campaign. A strike of women garment workers serves to differentiate Lucian Emery and Llewellyn Evans, the socialists, from Tristram Lawrence, the reform candidate. Emery and Evans put up an active and determined fight for their beliefs, but the cynical Lawrence caves in when the election fight becomes intense and he is willing to compromise his ideals. The strike escalates into a general strike. When it is broken, Emery goes to prison, but Lawrence has been exposed as a double-dealer, a liar and a tool of reaction"—Blake, F.M. The strike in the American novel. An important character in the story is Clara Emery, a well-educated, upper class heroine; she works in a settlement house in the immigrant quarter of New York and acts as a mediator and interpreter of lower-class life to her 'uptown' friends and family. The climax of the work is the city-wide strike—the Uprising of the 20,000—of immigrant girls in the garment industry.

676. Cook, Karin, 1969- . *What girls learn*; **a novel. New York: Pantheon Books, 1997. x, 304p.**

Tilden and Elizabeth follow their divorced mother, Frances, from Atlanta to the Long Island home of Nick with whom Frances has fallen in love. The transition is at first rather difficult for the girls who carry their Southern accents with them as they enter a 'Northern' public school. But that can be dealt with much more easily than the breast cancer that takes their mother from them.

677. Cook, Metta Horton. *Yennycott folks*; **an historical romance of the pioneer days of Long Island, touching upon well-known families. New York: J.S. Ogilvie, c1909/10. 128p.**

The author uses a mixture of fact and fancy to delineate the beginnings of white settlement in what is now the town of Southold (or Southhold?). The Indians in the story are welcoming and peaceful. There is not the slightest hint of any friction between white man and red man, or between white and white, so it's all very soporific. 'Yennycott' was the name of a wise old Indian and was for a short time applied to the English settlement. Mrs. Horton also wrote *Helen's choice*; a tale of Long Island (New York, J.S. Ogilvie, 1913. 96p.), a work not seen by the compiler.

678. Cook, Thomas H., 1947- . *Instruments of night.* **New York: Bantam Books, 1998. 293p.**

His sister was murdered when crime novel writer Paul Graves was a mere child and the memory still haunts him. Yet he jumps at the chance when asked by Allison Davies to investigate an unsolved murder that took place in 1946. The victim was Faye Harrison and the scene of the crime was 'Riverwood' in the Hudson River Valley, an estate since turned into an artists' colony which is run by Ms. Davies. Fay's mother is still living; she is anxious to finally see justice served.

679. Cooke, Edmund Vance, 1866-1932. *A morning's mail.* **Philadelphia: Pearson Bros., 1907. 47p.**

The individual conducting this monologue is a threadbare poet who occupies an almost unfurnished room in a New York City boarding house. He has just picked up his morning mail; there are letters that prompt humorous rejoinders and there are letters that illuminate his present, semi-desperate situation (rejections and the like). But at the bottom of the sheaf of letters is one that includes a check for work accepted and the poet is rejuvenated.

680. Cooke, Frances. *'My Lady Beatrice.'* **New York, Cincinnati: Benziger Bros., 1908. 244p.**

Exhausted by the constant round of parties and other social diversions that she has participated in as an upper class New Yorker, a young woman with a Catholic upbringing decides to try country living. Settled in a farmhouse she quickly develops friendships with people in the rural community and is influenced by their warmth and directness. No longer engaged to a wealthy New Yorker she marries a young farmer who lives in the farmhouse that has become her home away from home.

681. Cooke, Grace MacGowan, 1863-1944. *The fortunes of John Hawk, a boy of old New York*, **1781. Illustrated by Frank Eltonhead. New York: Century Co., 1928. xi, 355p.**

"New York [State] in the period following the Revolution is the setting. ... The central figure of the story [John Hawk] has various adventures, beginning with his running away from British officers and culminating in a good old-fashioned discovery of hidden treasure"—Saturday review of literature.

682. Cooke, Marjorie Benton, 1876-1920. *Bambi.* **Illustrated by Mary Greene Blumenschein. Garden City, N.Y.: Doubleday, Page, 1914. 366p.**

A fairy tale for adults. Bambi is a charming young woman who, on a whim but primarily because she is a natural helpmate, marries the dramatist Jarvis. The latter walks the streets of New York City trying unsuccessfully to interest agents and producers in his plays. In order to subsist he takes a job as a cab driver. In the meantime Bambi writes a novel and persuades the producer Charles Frohman to commission Jarvis to convert it into a play. Jarvis is unaware that Bambi is the author of the work he is dramatizing and corresponds with the unknown author to the point of falling in love with her. The inevitable disclosure is a complete surprise to the chagrined but happy Jarvis.

683. ————. *Cinderella Jane.* **Garden City, N.Y.: Doubleday, Page, 1917. 307p.**

"By day Jane Judd cleaned studios in the Washington Square neighborhood [of New York]. By night she devoted herself to the art of letters. For, unknown to the 'Studio colony', Jane had not only ambition, but ability of a rare order. Jerry Paxton, for whom she had worked for six years, had never taken any notice of Jane. To him she was a quiet, undemonstrative, domestic woman—the ideal wife for a popular society painter, unhappily beset by the women who fell victim to his charms. Unexpectedly Jerry asked Jane to marry him, and she accepted. Interesting developments follow; Jane's first novel is published, and Jerry, who believes that a woman's one career should be her husband, finds himself married to a woman who is famous. Their adjustment is the substance of the latter half of the story"—Book review digest.

684. [Coolidge, Sarah E.] *Ambition* **[by] Kate Willis [pseud.], Boston: J. French, 1856. 318p.**

The scene of the story moves back and forth from Hamilton in central New York to the State's capital, Albany. The chief character is Herbert Wells, a man of dubious morals and great ambition. Despite his obvious defects Wells awakens deep love in several women, including Laura Wellmont and Fannie Thorne of Hamilton and the widow Mrs. Ashland and Clara Woodville of Albany. To advance his career Herbert marries Clara Woodville, despite his having fathered a child by Fannie Thorne. As the years go by Wells gains fame, yet he must contend with his guilty past. The love of the aforementioned women for him never ceases, but they all have to make adjustments in their lives. Fannie Thorne marries a nephew of the influential Hamiltonian, Joseph Metcalf; Laura Wellmont and Mrs. Ashland marry men they presumably love, although the image of Wells is still fixed in their memories. Herbert's illegitimate son, Orville Metcalf, eventually meets his biological father when the latter is near death. Orville marries Laura Clifford, the daughter of Laura Wellmont and her husband Edgar Clifford.

685. Coombs, Anne Sheldon, 1858-1890. *A game of chance.* **New York: Appleton, 1887. 245p.**

"Nineveh, Long Island, is the home of Mr. and Mrs. Melrose and their only child, Barbara. 'Charley' Melrose is a shiftless, unlucky man who succeeds at nothing he undertakes and finally dies from drink, leaving his family penniless. Barbara's hatred of poverty, and its attending miseries, leads her to think only of money in marrying. She has two chances and takes the one which seems most hopeful of bringing her wealth and position. The story of her sad married life is a picture of a phase of living familiar to old New Yorkers"—Annual American catalogue.

686. Cooney, Caroline B., 1947- . *Flight #116 is down.* **New York: Scholastic Inc. 1992. 201p.**

The crash of a 747 jetliner at night in the small Upstate New York town of 'Nearing Falls' has varying effects on the rescue team that includes paramedics and teenage ambulance drivers. They are under pressure to carry out their duties in an atmosphere of human tragedy, panic, bias, and distrust.

687. Cooper, Courtney Ryley, 1886-1940. *Caged.* **Boston: Little, Brown, 1930. 293p.**

Joe Barry is a country boy hoping to strike gold in New York City with his accordion music; however, he ends up in a dead-end job in a run-down boarding house that barely allows him to survive. He does get to play his accordion in a restaurant patronized by underworld types, but then is led into a trap that results in his being arrested for murder. He escapes from custody, joins the circus, finds love with one of the dancers, and falls into a number of adventuresome situations.

688. Cooper, Elizabeth, 1877-1945. *Living up to Billy.* **New York, Stokes, 1915. 202p.**

Broadway dancer/chorus girl Nancy Lane in letters to her sister Kate tells how she stays on a straight path, largely because of her loving care for her baby nephew, Billy. Kate, Billy's mother, is in prison and his father is a thief as was his grandfather. Nancy does her best and deservedly wins the love of Tom Cassidy of the New York Police. Nan writes: "Can you beat that? Me, Nancy Lane, who has been brought up since a kid to feel that cops is her natural enemy!" Kate is released from prison and she and Billy are last seen on a farm in New Jersey.

689. **Cooper, Francis L. *Captain Pott's minister*. Illustrated by John Goss. Boston: Lothrop, Lee & Shepard, 1922. 392p.**

"Old Captain Pott is not much pleased when the church committee decides that the new minister, Mack McGowan, is to live in his [Long Island] home, but the plan proves to be a good one in the long run. Elder Fox, who has a mysterious dislike for the young minister, tries to influence Captain Pott to drive him from the town, but the trusty Captain will not be persuaded. Instead he uncovers the true cause of the antagonism to McGowan and the mystery of which he is the unconscious center. Fox, confronted with his Australian past, decides to make amends. The story has its love interest in the romance of Fox's daughter, Beth, and the young minister, and its humor in the affair between the Captain and Miss Clemmie Pipkin"—Book review digest.

690. **Cooper, Frank Albert, 1905- . *Mr. Teach goes to war*. New York: Whittlesey House, 1957. 187p.**

During the War of 1812, a youthful schoolteacher in Plattsburgh, New York, known to his students as Mr. Teach, takes up arms for the American cause. Another colorful character in the novel is 'Muskrat Jack', a Canadian half-breed and son of a father known to be a guide for pirates along the Canadian-New York border. Mr. Teach is effective not only in resisting the British forces, but also in scouting the trails of the pirates.

691. **[Cooper, James Fenimore] 1789-1851. *The chainbearers*; or, *The Littlepage manuscripts*. Edited by the author of *Satanstoe, spy* ...New York: Burgess, Stringer, 1845. 2v.**

Following the American Revolution Mordaunt Littlepage, the son of Cornelius Littlepage (see Cooper's 'Satanstoe'), wants to confirm and extend the family's land patent, but has to contend with the squatter, Aaron Timberman (known as Thousandacres). Andries Coejemans, the Chairbearer, humble and respectful toward those socially and intellectually superior to himself, is the natural opponent of Thousandacres; the two come to blows, the Chairbearer is mortally wounded, while Thousandacres is killed by the Indian Susquesus, the Chainbearer's friend. Mordaunt is thus witness to the maintenance of the social order (somewhat democratized) and the rule of law. Incidentally the term 'chainbearer' refers literally to a person who carries a surveyor's chain.

692. ————. *The deerslayer*; or, *The first warpath: a tale*. **By the author of *The**

last of the Mohicans. The pathfinder ... **Philadelphia: Lea and Blanchard, 1841. 2v.**

Otsego Lake (Glimmerglass in the story) is the scene of the action. A young man of twenty, Deerslayer (Natty Bumppo or Hawkeye) joins his Delaware Indian friends (among them the chief Chingachgook) in their fights against the Hurons. He becomes the object of the love of Judith Hutter who is imbued with some of the worst traits of the settlements. Judith's father, Tom Hutter, is an unsavory character, greedy enough to scalp Indians for a bounty. In the end Deerslayer fends off Judith's advances, Tom Hutter is slain by Indians, and the Hutter's younger daughter, Hetty, a simple Christianized girl, is accidentally killed.

Cooper, James Fenimore, 1789-1851, supposed author. *Elinor Wyllys.*
See note under item #2681.

693. —————. *Home as found.* **By the author of** *Homeward bound, The pioneers,* **& c., & c. Philadelphia: Lea & Blanchard, 1838. 2v.**

Published in England under the title: *Eve Effingham*; or, *Home*, a continuation of Cooper's Homeward bound. The plot of the novel, laid in New York City and the countryside, is really secondary to the author's criticism of American manners. Eve Effingham, a descendant of Judge Temple of Cooper's *'The pioneers',* is married to Paul Powis, John Effingham's son via a secret marriage. They and various other characters represent American types—social climbers, the businessman whose only interest is commerce, the scandalmonger, the Anglophile and the Anglophobe, individuals with literary pretensions, et al.

694. —————. *The last of the Mohicans*; **a narrative of 1757. By the author of** *The pioneers* **...Philadelphia: Carey & Lea, 1826. 2v.**

Cooper's most 'action-packed' novel describes incidents before and after the fall of Fort William Henry to Montcalm and his French and Indian forces. Hawkeye (Natty Bumppo or Leatherstocking in other Cooper novels) and his Indian friend Chingachgook along with the latter's son Uncas, Alice and Cora Munro and the soldier Duncan Heyward flee through Upstate New York forests with the Huron Magua in pursuit. Uncas is 'the last of the Mohicans', hopelessly in love with Cora Munro, quadroon daughter of the British commander of Fort William Henry. Both Uncas and Cora die when the former fails in his attempt to wrest Cora from the hands of Magua. Heyward's suit for the hand of Alice Munro had received the paternal blessing of Colonel Munro before the Colonel's death.

695. —————. *The pathfinder*; **or,** *The inland sea.* **By the author of** *The pioneers,* **The last of the Mohicans, Prairie, & c. Philadelphia: Lea and Blanchard, 1840. 2v.**

The scene of the novel is the Lake Ontario region of Upstate New York ca. 1760. The Pathfinder (Natty Bumppo) is the rival of Jasper Western, a Great Lakes sailor, and Lieutenant Muir, a British quartermaster, for the hand of Mabel Dunham, a sergeant's daughter. The Pathfinder finally cedes Mabel to Western, the man she really loves, and returns to his beloved wilderness.

696. ————. *The pioneers*; or, *The sources of the Susquehanna*. **A descriptive tale. By the author of** *Precaution*. **New York: C. Wiley, 1823. 2v.**

The scene is Otsego Lake (Cooperstown in 1793-1794). Judge Marmaduke Temple, a moral, just man, divides his estate with Oliver Edwards, an heir of the Effinghams, who had prior claim from royal grants to that selfsame estate. The judge views himself as the vanguard of civilization and looks with much disquiet on the destructive activities of a number of the settlers. Natty Bumppo, the Leatherstocking, has retired to the vicinity of Otsego Lake and is even more aggrieved and disgusted with the disregard of the natural order by the settlers. When Natty shoots a deer out of season, however, the Judge must apply the law to his action and Leatherstocking is punished in the stocks. Eventually he leaves the settlement for his natural habitat, the unpathed forest; the settlement is destined for human change and continual growth.

697. ————. *The redskins*; or, *Indian and Injin*, **being the conclusion of** *The Littlepage manuscripts*. **By the author of** *The pathfinder, Deerslayer*…**New York: Burgess & Stringer, 1846. 2v.**

The novel deals with a period in Upstate New York history when anti-rent protests were rife (1819-1845). Agitators against the landlords (the patroons) disguised themselves as 'Injins.' Cooper's sympathies were with the land-owners, however, as seen through the eyes of Hugh Littlepage, a principled man who is fearful of demagoguery and the tyranny of the majority. He suffers arson and calumny at the hands of the 'Injins.' Cooper brings into his story's conclusion a group of real Indians who serve to rebuke the white men in general because they fight over land that was originally stolen from the true owners, the Indians.

698. ————. *Satanstoe*; or, *The Littlepage manuscripts*. **A tale of the colony. By the author of** *Miles Willingford, The pathfinder*, **& c. New York: Burgess, Stringer, 1845. 2v.**

"The first novel of a trilogy called *The Littlepage manuscripts*. [It is] autobiographical in form. Cornelius Littlepage is the heir of an aristocratic family of Dutch descent living at Satanstoe, a strip of land in Westchester County, New York. Cornelius is educated at Princeton, makes fun of Yankees, is enthralled by the sights of New York City, comes out in society, saves a girl from a caged lion, rescues her again from the Hudson in flood, and fights the French at Lake George"—Benet's reader's encyclopedia of American literature. The other family in the narrative is the Mordaunts who are above the Littlepages on the social scale. Both the Littlepages and the Mordaunts, however, possess landed estates, and the social order of the time, despite class divisions, presents no particular problems for the characters, with the exception of Jason Newcome, a go-getter determined to rise to high position and who considers wealth the only distinction between one man and another.

699. —————. *The spy*; a tale of the neutral ground. By the author of *Precaution*. New York: Wiley & Halstead, 1821. 2v.

The protagonist, Harvey Birch, a Yankee peddler and, presumably, a British agent is actually feeding vital information to General Washington. The setting is Westchester County, New York, a part of which is neutral ground during the American Revolution. Despite his patriotic sympathies, Birch is also a friend of the Loyalist Wharton family. The novel gives us a striking picture of the moral dilemmas faced by several of the principal characters, whether they are Loyalists or patriots.

700. —————. *The ways of the hour*; a tale. By the author of *The spy*, the red rover, & c., & c., New York: Putnam, 1850. 512p.

This minor work of Cooper's concerns a young woman, the so-called Mary Monson, who is placed on trial in the town of 'Biberry, Duke's County', New York for arson and murder. The home of Peter and Dorothy Goodwin has burned to the ground and two skeletons are found in the ashes. Are they the remains of the Goodwins, or are they of two unknown women? The hero is lawyer Tom Dunscomb who defends the accused. The trial itself is covered in ca. 100 pages of the story wherein the mysterious Mary Monson is found guilty and sentenced; a last-minute revelation brings about a new trial.

701. —————. *Wyandotté*; or, *The hutted knoll*. A tale, by the author of *The pathfinder, Deerslayer* ... etc. Philadelphia: Lea and Blanchard, 1843. 2v.

The honest Captain Hugh Willoughby, formerly a British officer, is undecided whether to support the Crown or join the American rebels. The scene is the Willoughby land patent in Upstate New York. The Tuscarora Indian, Wyandotté, long associated with the Willoughby's, remembers floggings given him at the orders of the Captain, and in the heat of Revolutionary activity kills Willoughby. Hugh's son, Bob, leans towards the British side in the conflict. After the war Bob and his wife Maude return to Upstate New York from their voluntary stay in England, to reclaim the land patent. He is accepted by the Americans who had been antagonistic to his father; he also forgives Wyandotté for slaying his father, whereupon Wyandotté cries 'God forgive' and dies.

Cooper, Jefferson, pseud. See: Fox, Gardner F., 1911- .

Cooper, Susan Fenimore, 1813-1894, supposed author. *Elinor Wyllys.*
See note under item #2681.

702. Copus, John Edwin, b. 1854. *Harry Russell, a Rockland College boy*, by J.E.

Copus (Cuthbert [pseud.]). New York: Benziger Bros., 1903. 229p.

In this novel, cut from the cloth of Horatio Alger, Jr., the newsboy hero, Harry Russell, is peddling his wares on the streets of New York City and taking the side of a crippled girl who is also selling papers. His chivalrous actions commend Harry to a lawyer and a businessman, both prominent New Yorkers. They send Harry to Rockland College, a Roman Catholic institution, where he receives an excellent education. As the story winds down Harry and the aforementioned lame girl prove to be cousins and heirs to a handsome fortune.

703. **Corbett, Elizabeth Frances, 1887-1981.** *Puritan and pagan.* **New York: Holt, 1920. 347p.**

"Nancy Desmond is the Puritan, Mary Allen the pagan. Nancy is a painter with a studio on Washington Square; Mary Ellen is a distinguished actress. Max Meredith, who has married one of Nancy's college friends, comes to New York on business and looks her up. They see much of one another during his stay and find to their dismay that they have fallen in love. True to her instincts and her ideals, Nancy sends Max away. ... In the meantime Roger Greene, Nancy's friend and teacher, has become infatuated with Mary, and between these two there is no question of renunciation. They accept their love as a fact, although Mary refuses marriage. When Nancy learns of their affair, she is crushed and finds how much Roger has meant to her. Later, after a long separation, after she has seen Max again and after the other love has run its course, Nancy and Roger come together"—Book review digest.

704. **Corbin, John, 1870-1959.** *The cave man.* **New York: Appleton, 1907. 365p.**

A plunge into the world of high finance in New York City with a look at trusts, speculation in the stock market and stock promotion, chicanery that includes blackmail, etc. The 'cave man', the hero, has a talent for business and starts out with rather high ideals. The heroine, the daughter of a man ruined by bad investments but still clinging to the old principles, takes the hero in hand and helps infuse him with a modern outlook on the world of commerce and the motor trust he is currently involved with—which results in a lowering of his ethical standards, the author implying (sarcastically) that it's all o.k.

705. —————. *The edge*; a novel. Front. in color by Katherine Gassaway. **New York: Duffield, 1915. 403p.**

"A story of modern life and modern problems [with New York City as the scene]. The central figures are Roger and Mary Jaffray, young married people who face the problem of living on an income [$60 a week] much smaller than that of their social equals. Many other characters enter into the story and there is much discussion of many modern movements and tendencies. Childlessness among the moderately well-to-do absorbs much of the author's attention as do other phases of modern marriage, but he also gives consideration to a wide variety of topics, including immigration, professors' salaries, Christmas giving and housewives' leagues"—Book review digest. Eventually Roger Jaffray, through talent and honesty, achieves success, while Mary proves capable of dealing with some quite onerous enigmas.

706. Corley, Donald. *The fifth son of the shoemaker.* **New York: McBride, 1930. x, 282p.**

"Here is a many-threaded story of the rise of an old Russian family of hereditary shoemakers, Muscovites, from an East Side [of Manhattan] cellar to the achievement of high romance—the romance of exotic slippers." [Old Ivan and his 5th son Pyotr make footwear that becomes the rage of social and theatrical New York. Ivan's other sons are more interested in the commercial aspects of the metropolis's life]. "In a sense it is a Cinderella story in which there is the theme of dreams versus the machine-made; the influence of a settlement house on the sons of Ivan the shoemaker; the career of the 5th son contrasted sharply with the other four"—Book review digest.

Corley, Edwin [Raymond] 1931-1981. See under his pseudonyms: Harper, David and Judson, William.

Corson, Geoffrey, pseud. See: Sholl, Anna McClure.

707. Costantin, M[ary] Mc[Caffrey] 1935- . *God and the others.* **Boston: Houghton, Mifflin, 1972. 296p.**

Rory Mulligan, an organizer for the Congress of Industrial Organizations (CIO) was sent to 'Freshkill', New York because he was in danger in Detroit and because the mill in Freshkill was still non-union. The Mulligan family assumed that it could rest after Rory's first organizing efforts and his talks with the mill's managers (fairly successful). Then Rory was confined to his bed by emphysema, and his daughter, Mary Catherine, had to look to herself if she were to take hold of educational opportunities. She received high grades in school and was admitted to Barnard College in New York City, but her social consciousness was sensitized by all her experiences at this stage of her life.

Cotes, Mrs. Everard, 1862?-1922. See: Cotes, Sara Jeannette Duncan, 1862?-1922.

708. Cotes, Sara Jeannette Duncan, 1862?-1922. *Those delightful Americans,* **by Mrs. Everard Cotes (Sara Jeannette Duncan). New York: Appleton, 1902. 352p.**

In contradistinction to several famous 19th century accounts by English travelers (notably Dickens and Mrs. Frances Trollope) of unpleasant experiences with 'crude' Americans, Mrs. Cotes' novel takes a group of English tourists through New York City and adjoining country-houses in the summertime, resulting in some favorable impressions of America and Americans. On occasion these sojourners from Albion seem rather naïve-their American acquaintances retain the notion that Englishmen in general are highly sophisticated and worldly, but the author paints a picture of American wit, humor and freshness that is most appealing to their foreign guests.

709. Cotler, Gordon, 1923- . *The artist's proof.* **New York: St. Martin's Press, 1997. 263p.**

Retired cop Sis Shale looked forward to a quiet but productive life as a painter of talent when he moved to a small beach house in a Long Island town. However, when a teenager, Cassie Brennan, dies mysteriously in the ostentatious home of restaurateur Misha Sharanov, Sid is sucked into the situation because of the nude drawings he had made of Cassie. Sid's ex-wife Lonnie, his daughter Sarah, Sharanov and his dispirited wife, a conspiratorial Texas couple, and Cassie's boyfriend—all play roles in the narrative.

710. Cox, Palmer, 1840-1924. *Hans Van Pelter's trip to Gotham.* **In pen & pencil by Palmer Cox. New York: Art Print. Establishment, 1876. 64p.**

The Dutchman, Han Von Pelter, is a novice when it comes to deciphering the peculiar ways of a great city like New York. This is his first visit to the metropolis and he has many misadventures despite his close perusal of all the up-to-date guidebooks and directories. In words and pictures the author-illustrator recounts his protagonist's trials and tribulations.

711. Coxe, George Harmon, 1901-1984. *The groom lay dead.* **New York: Knopf, 1944. 227p.**

Marine Captain Alan Wallace is invited, along with a number of other people, to greet the honeymooning Johnny Marshall and Carol Gibson in the Finger Lakes region of New York State. Carol had jilted Wallace for the wealthy but drunken Marshall. When the latter is killed, it looks like a homicide and Captain Wallace is deeply interested in finding out who might be a killer and in winning back the rather puzzling Carol.

712. Coxe, Howard. *Commend the devil.* **New York: Duell, Sloan & Pearce, 1941. 245p.**

Carlotta Farragut, owner of a handsome old property in 'Port Credit' on the Hudson, is also burdened with two headstrong, semi-delinquent, pleasure-seeking children, Joel and Evelyn. These two cavort in some unpleasant ways around Port Credit, a suburb of New York, which has always been known as a hub of quiet, content, gracious living. Carlotta is thwarted at every turn as she essays to give them guidance. They seem determined to 'go off the deep end' in their own time, in their own way.

713. Coxe, Virginia Rosalie. *The embassy ball.* **New York: F. Tennyson Neely, 1898. 377p.**

The narrator, Delancy Courtney, is the hero; he is a member of the fashionable set of New York and its suburb 'Dashwood', "just fifteen miles from New York." The jaunty Courtney boasts of several affairs of the heart, one of which involves Vera, the wife of an acquaintance, Granville Churchill. However, he is drawn to the relatively innocent Doris Aymar—and at the novel's conclusion Courtney and Doris are married. The title refers to a ball in the Russian embassy at which Courtney was a guest. The final pages of the novel find the major figures in St. Pascal on the French Mediterranean coast.

714. Coxhead, Nona. *Though they go wandering.* New York: Scribner, 1945. 271p.
Persuaded by her husband to give up the theater, former actress Marlowe McCann accompanies him to a small community, 'Little Winton', which is reasonably close to New York City. Several years of domesticity and efforts to participate fully in the suburban social activities of Little Winton take their toll on Marlowe, temperamentally unfit for the slow, dull pace of the small town. Roger, her husband, is a stuffy, conventional man with whom Marlow finds she has little in common. Thus the time arrives when Marlowe firmly decides to go back to the city and resume her theatrical career.

715. Coy, Nancy. *Freedom Trail*; the story of two of Morgan's young scouts during the American Revolution. New York: Dodd, Mead, 1957. 252p.
The two young scouts, a white lad and his Indian friend, are engaged in the Revolutionary conflict in the Upper Hudson Valley and Ticonderoga and are present at several of the events leading up to the surrender of Burgoyne at Saratoga. At least one reviewer found this novel poorly conceived and developed.

716. Coyle, Harold, 1952- . *Savage wilderness.* New York: Simon & Schuster, 1997. 519p.
An historical novel about the French and Indian War of 1754 to 1759; it covers such key places of conflict as Fort Duquesne, Ticonderoga, Lake Champlain and Quebec. The protagonists are Ian MacPherson, a Scot banished to the American colonies for his rebellious activities against the English Crown, who then becomes a colonial militiaman; supercilious, ambitious British Army Captain Thomas Shields, ignorant of wilderness warfare; and Anton de Chevalier, a cultured French officer who gradually adopts the barbarisms of his Indian allies.

717. Coyne, John, 1940- . *Hobgoblin.* New York: Putnam, 1981. 307p.
Hobgoblin is another one of those fanciful games (think 'Dungeons and Dragons') that absorb so much of Scott Gardiner's attention. When his father dies suddenly, Scott's mother, Barbara, goes to work at Ballycastle (an old Irish edifice reconstructed stone by stone) on the banks of the Hudson River. Scott drops out of prep school in Connecticut and enrolls at Flat Rock High near his mother's place of work. Barbara, an art historian, researches Ballycastle's lurid past of sexual abuse and murder and becomes romantically involved with her employer. The students at Scott's high school hold a Halloween party at the castle at which pieces of its bloody past are brought back to life via the game of Hobgoblin.

718. ————. *The hunting season.* New York: Macmillan, 1987. 245p.

An anthropologist, April Bernard, is doing research on the natives of a Catskill area who have suffered gross physical deformities after many years of inbreeding. Her husband, Marshall, and their children from earlier marriages accompany April. Marshall starts chasing after women from New York City who are spending summer in the Catskills, while April finds herself in a 'contest' with her teenage stepdaughter for the attention of Luke, the Bernards' handyman. The novel's climax comes after several terrifying incidents, with April trying to survive attacks by incestuous natives.

719. Craddock, Florence Nightingale. *Edgar Fairfax*; a story of West Point. New York: G.W. Dillingham, 1896. 203p.

"A story dealing with the divorce evil. The hero is a Virginian who marries a German actress just as he is entering West Point. Fearing the disapproval of his family he keeps the marriage secret. In a little while, tiring of his wife, he gets a divorce from her. He falls in love with another woman, a rich Baltimore belle, who is visiting West Point, and he becomes engaged to her; as she thinks divorce is wrong he conceals his past life from her. A jealous woman reveals the story [with dramatic consequences for all involved]"—Annual American catalogue.

720. Crane, Caroline, 1930- . *The foretelling.* New York: Dodd, Mead, 1982. 234p.

'Burley's Falls', a Catskill village, is the hometown of Angela Dawn who initiates a palm-reading venture in order to raise money for a new community center. To Angela's amazement her prophecies are given credence and even seem to be fulfilled. Angela's husband is pushed to extremes by a prognosis of great prestige and financial prosperity. Then bad things begin to happen to the inhabitants of Burley's Falls: a prediction of Angela's early death, treachery, homicide, the collapse of a dam and a resulting flood.

721. ————. *Man in the shadows.* New York: Dodd, Mead, 1987. 224p.

"A stunning fashion model is plagued by a psychopath who panics her with a series of sinister anonymous phone calls and messages. After her lawyer is murdered and her children are threatened, Denise Burns flees to the rural sanctuary of her childhood home in Upstate New York. Unfortunately, her illusory security is soon shattered when it becomes apparent that her demented nemesis is still stalking her trail. Isolated on a lonely farm, Denise and her family attempt to match wits with a cunning enemy bent on meting out a horrible brand of revenge"—Booklist.

722. ————. *The people next door*; a novel of suspense. New York: Dodd, Mead, 1988. 213p.

Debra and Kurt Gillis, newcomers to the Long Island resort town of 'Luna Beach', do not get along with their landlady who lives next door. Debra's stepdaughter Gigi is rebellious and latches on to Todd Jorgenson, a drug-pusher; Debra's son Drew, two years old, does not take kindly to instructions. The landlady has her problems too: the infidelity of her husband and the care of a brain-damaged child, Billy. The unsolved murder of a three-year-old boy that occurred one year before the Gillises' arrival preys on Debra's mind, while simultaneously husband Kurt, a professor, connects with a female colleague. What response can Debra make to alleviate some of these tensions?

723. —————. ***Someone at the door.*** **New York: Dodd, Mead, 1985. 152p.**

Cathleen Sardo answers the call for assistance of her pregnant sister, Gwen Faris, who is in labor at her suburban Long Island home. The door is unlocked when Cathleen arrives; the only person to greet her is autistic, mute Derek Faris, a three-year-old, who cannot, of course, provide information about the strange circumstance Cathleen encounters. Paul, Gwen's husband, and Cathleen search in vain for the missing Gwen. Cathleen has only Gwen's final phrase over the phone to go on: "There's someone at the door."

724. —————. ***Summer girl; a novel of suspense.*** **New York: Dodd, Mead, 1979. 201p.**

Mary Shelburne hires 14-year-old Cynthia Ricks as baby-sitter when she rents a Long Island beach house, not knowing that Cynthia is a psychotic thief and nymphet and a killer of the mongoloid baby of her married lover. Cynthia seduces Mary's husband and draws Mary's children into her affections. Realizing at last Cynthia's evil, Mary tries to get help from her friends and neighbors, to no avail. When she fires Cynthia, the latter kidnaps the kids whom she intends to drown when she fails in her plan to become pregnant by Mr. Shelburne. Mary has to perform some super feats in order to reclaim her children and husband.

725. —————. ***The third passenger.*** **New York: Dodd, Mead, 1983. 224p.**

Diane Hastings is one of several passengers on a private plane that will take her to Canada and the hospital room of her gravely injured son. The plane's pilot is Travis Andrews, reputed to be the boy's father. The two other passengers on the aircraft are Travis's daughter Shelley, 12, and Arnold Dearborn, an apparently mild young fellow eager to see his ill wife. When the plane fails to reach its destination there is a presumption that it has crashed during a winter storm. Actually, the armed Dearborn, who turns out to be on the run from killing a policeman, has ordered Travis to crash land in the Adirondacks. Shelley is taken hostage by Arnold while Travis and Diane are left for dead; of course, they have survived and an intensive hunt for the plane by experienced searchers is underway.

726. Crane, Stephen, 1871-1900. *George's mother.* New York: E. Arnold, 1896. 177p.

Set in a vividly described slum of New York (the Bowery) the novel's two protagonists are George Kelcey, a laborer and a dreamer, and his mother, a regular church attendee espousing the tenets of temperance and fighting a nearby brewery. George is turned off by his mother's single-mindedness and in defiance drinks more and more heavily. When he loses his job, Mrs. Kelcey becomes ill and wastes away, no longer recognizing her son and groping for her happier past. She dies; George, his life in ruins, dully receives the insipid words of the pastor: "My poor lad."

727. ————. *Maggie, a girl of the street*s, **(a story of New York), by Johnston Smith [pseud.]. New York: [privately printed, 1893]. 163p.**

This harrowing portrait of tenement life in New York City's Bowery is a masterly work that stands alongside Crane's *Red Badge of Courage*. Maggie Johnson, the title character, is a girl of the slums, scorned by her mother and brother, driven from her home and seduced and abandoned by a Bowery trickster. All those to whom she turns for help shun her. Her only recourse is prostitution if she is to survive. Maggie's desperation leads her finally to the East River where she ends her brief life in a corrupt and hypocritical social environment by drowning.

728. ————. *Sullivan County tales and sketches*. **Edited and with an introd. by R.W. Stallman. Ames, Iowa: Iowa State University Press, 1968.xi, 151p.**

"[Crane's] grotesque and pseudo-spooky Sullivan County [New York] tales hark back to Western tall tales and to the Poe-like horror tales of Ambrose Bierce. … The tales are imaginatively narrated incidents recast with 'tall tale' ingredients not intended to be after the facts"—Introduction. Contents: The last of the Mohicans.–Hunting wild hogs.–The last panther.–Sullivan County bears.–The way in Sullivan County.–Bear and panther. Killing his bear.–Four men in a cave.–Across the covered pit.–The octopush. –A ghoul's accountant. –The black dog. –A tent in agony. –An explosion of seven babies. –The cry of a huckleberry pudding. –The holler tree.–The snake.–The fables.–The mesmeric mountain.–How the donkey lifted the hills.

729. ————. *The third violet*. **New York: Appleton, 1897. 203p.**

Billie Hawker is a struggling artist with a studio in New York City who goes back to Sullivan County, N.Y. to see his parents, hard-working farmers. He meets Miss Grace Fanhall, a lovely young woman of the upper social class, who is staying at a resort hotel in the area. Drawn to Grace, Hawker feels the constraints of his lower station in life, although Grace is free of any notions of superiority. They return to New York, he to his studio and she to her elegant home. Billie is at a loss as to how he should proceed with the sincere and spontaneous young woman, but as she drops the first violet and then offers him the second and third, he loses his despair and glimpses hope for the future. Critics H.G. Wells and Richard Harding Davis were clearlydisappointed with the realist Crane's 'love story.'

730. ————. *Whilomville stories*. **Illus. by Peter Newell. London, New York: Harper, 1900. vi, 198p.**

"Deals exclusively with boyhood. . . The stories are drawn from events and episodes occurring in Port Jervis [New York] where Crane had lived from the age of seven to twelve . . . The stories, with their close-ups of small-town America, focus on the individual and the collective . . . with all of . . . a [town's] righteousness, rigid codes and so-called ethics. The stories open up the child's mysterious world to the reader; the boy countering the domination of his parents, the gender and generation gaps, and the hatreds and loves these conflicts elicit" —Knapp, B.L. Stephen Crane. Contents: –The angel child. –Lynx hunting.–The lover and the telltale.–Showin' off.–Making an orator.–Shame.–The carriage lamps.–The knife.–The stove.–The trial, execution, and burial of Homer Phelps.–The fight.–The city urchin and the chaste villagers.–A little pilgrimage.

Cranston, Ruth. See under her pseudonym: Warwick, Anne.

731. Craven, Thomas, 1889-1969. *Paint*. New York: Harcourt, Brace, 1923. 229p.

"A story—a history—of achievement, of suffering, of soul misery of an artist's ten-year struggle in unaesthetic New York—never beautiful except in its stark power. Carlock is incessantly present, at one with his medium, paint. [He is a genius with an insatiable desire to create who has an unending struggle for recognition. Carlock is] "a figure with the desires of ... [Dreiser's] Cowperwood and the madness of ... [Dostoevsky's] Raskolnikoff, yet precisely reminiscent of neither"—Literary review of the New York evening post.

732. Crawford, Francis Marion, 1854-1909. *Katharine Lauderdale*. With illus. by Alfred Brennan. New York: Macmillan, 1894. 2v.

"The love and jealousy, the strife and intrigue, the romance and commonplace, which enter into . . . [the] lives [of two American families, the Lauderdales and the Ralstons] are graphically pictured . . . The background of this volume is New York City; the characters belong to the '400'. Jack Ralston, the hero, is a 'failure' from a business point of view, and is addicted to drink. A secret marriage he enters into with his cousin Katharine Lauderdale is the motive"—Annual American catalogue.

733. ————. *Marion Darche*; a story without comment. New York: Macmillan, 1893. 309p.

Marion Darche and her husband John, residents of Lexington Avenue in New York City, are not an especially well-matched couple. He is responsible for destroying the financial structure of the manufacturing business of which he is treasurer and must abscond, with his wife's assistance, to elude the law. Marion receives comfort from such friends as Dolly Highlands, a former classmate, Russell Vanbrugh, a criminal lawyer, and Harry Brett, a one-time suitor, who now resumes his wooing of Marion. Rumors that John Darche is still alive are quashed when a sailor who knew Darche turns up in New York bearing Darche's name. The sailor apologizes and tells Harry that John

Darche died on the Patagonian coast. Harry relays the information to a much-relieved Marion who had made up her mind to stay by her felonious husband.

734. ————. *The Ralstons.* **Copyright ed. Leipzig: B. Tauchnitz, 1895. 2v.**
The second of Crawford's 'Ralstons' novels (Katharine Lauderdale was the first; a projected third was never written). Katharine is again the chief character around whom the jealousies and monetary rivalries of the other characters in this novel of New York's high society swirl. Her beauty arouses devotion and love in the young men who are unaware of her secret marriage to Jack Ralston; however, Katharine becomes an object of hatred to a former friend, Hester Crowdie, who suspects Katharine of overtures to her artist-husband, while Katharine's mother is overly envious of her daughter's youthful beauty. The story is much engaged with the controversies surrounding the distribution of old Robert Lauderdale's vast financial and property holdings. Two wills are abrogated and the courts decide as to the disposal of Lauderdale's estate, to the dissatisfaction of several potential heirs. Perhaps unique in American literature is the long scene in which young Katharine excoriates and cows her miserly, hypocritical and control-minded father, Alexander Lauderdale, Jr.

735. ————. *The three fates.* **New York: Macmillan, 1892. 412p.**
"New York City is the scene. George Winton Wood, who occupies the center of interest throughout, was born rich and independent, but before his boyhood is past, his father is ruined financially by an unprincipled relative. George was designed for a business life by his father, but he hates business, and early drifts into literature, first as a writer of reviews and finally as a writer of novels which bring him fame. 'The three fates' are three women whom he loves, or who love him, and who each exercises a strong influence on his career. The relative who had robbed his father makes unexpected reparation to the son"—Annual American catalogue.

736. Crawford, Marian. *Mam'zelle Beauty.* **Chicago: C.H. Sergel, 1894. 254p.**
A girl who was brought up on a farm close by Montreal comes to New York City when she is only seventeen. Her name is Beatrice Standish; she manages to gain an entry into New York's fashionable social circles and becomes known as 'Mam'zelle Beauty.' The novel dwells on what were considered at the time sensational goings-on under the surface of the city's upper class echelons.

737. *Crazy Luce*; **or,** *A correct history of the life and adventures of the wandering woman.* **Cortland Village [N.Y.]: Printed for the Peddlers, 1836. 18p.**
A sentimental little tale told to the 'author' by Harry Martin, erstwhile friend of Eugene Mervyns, the story's 'villain.' Innocent orphan Lucy Denmore lives with her aunt in a cottage close by Cazenovia. She falls deeply in love with romantic Eugene Mervyn and eagerly awaits his return from a sojourn in western New York State. Return he does, but with a bride, Maria Denmore,

Lucy's sister. Profoundly shocked, Lucy loses her mind and wanders off; distraught Maria gradually sickens and expires with remorseful Eugene at her side. Lucy, now know as Crazy Luce, roams aimlessly around the country-side, avoiding all males but gentle with females and nature's creatures. Partial sanity returns to Crazy Luce shortly before she dies.

738. **Crespi, Camilla T.** *The trouble with a hot summer*; a Simona Griffo mystery. **New York: Harper/Collins, 1997. viii, 309p.**

Simona Griffo and her companion, Dmitri K., are on a vacation in Long Island's Hamptons when businessman Bud Warren engages them to look into the death of his ex-wife Polly. It had been declared a suicide, but Bud disagrees. Then fire claims Bud's house and his body turns up in the close-by ocean. Was Bud also a suicide? His daughter Laurie doesn't think so. She hires Simona and Dmitri to track down Bud's presumed killer. Digging into Bud's past, Simona and Dmitri find that in the 1950s Bud and his lover, Rebecca Barnes, were in the Hamptons. So the jilted Rebecca becomes a prime suspect, if one believes that Bud and Polly were murdered. But there are others who had motives for ending the Warrens' lives: Polly's architect lover; heiress Laurie; her beau, a young man whose father had been tricked by the wealthy, land-dealing Polly; and several of Bud's business associates.

Crinkle, Nym, pseud. See: Wheeler, Andrew Carpenter, 1835-1903.

739. **Crosby, Lee, 1905-1967.** *Night attack*; a novel. **New York: Dutton, 1943. 219p.**

During World War II Peter Wayne is sent on a mission to a war plant on the South Shore of Long Island where sabotage has disrupted the production of sorely needed military materiel. He has his share of close calls, but is finally able to pinpoint the source of the plant's troubles.

740. **Cross, Ruth, b. 1887.** *Enchantment;* a novel. **New York: Longmans, Green, 1930. 295p.**

She may have been born and raised in Texas on the wrong side of the tracks, but Rosemary (Rose) Mooney grabs the devotion of Roger Aiken, a New York millionaire, and they are married. Rose is not at all popular with the snobbish, tradition-bound Aikens, although she is admired by several of Roger's friends, among them Wyman Goodhue, a playwright, and Max Lehman, theatrical producer. When, in a fit of jealousy, Roger divorces Rose, she overcomes her unhappiness by embarking on a successful career on the stage with the help of Goodhue and Lehman. A few years later Roger returns to New York from a Tibetan sojourn and realizes he still loves Rose. His plea for a resumption of their love affair receives no definite yes from Rose, but there is room to believe that reconciliation is a future possibility.

741. **Crouch, Julia.** *Three successful girls.* **New York: Hurd and Houghton, 1871. vii, 382p.**

The Windsor girls—Mary, the musician, Kate, the painter, and Hannah, the writer—depart the seclusion of their country home for the challenge and outward glamour of New York City. They soon realize that the city is not going to welcome them with open arms, that whatever success they attain will be hard-won, although Stephen St. Maur and David DeWitt uphold them. The latter two ultimately becomes husbands to Kate and Mary respectively. Religion plays a role in the young women's lives—attending services at the Plymouth Church to hear Henry Ward Beecher preach, discussion of the seriousness of David DeWitt's Catholicism, e.g. Hannah, despite an offer of marriage, chooses to remain single.

742. **Crownfield, Gertrude, 1867-1945.** *Alison Blair.* **Illustrated by George M. Richards. New York: Dutton, 1927. 301p.**

"The story of Alison Blair, a young girl of Kent [England] who came to . . . [the Mohawk Valley] in the days of the French and Indian Wars. Although mistreated by her relatives and captured by the Indians, she found able allies in . . . [Sir William Johnson and his family, and was rather loathe to leave the . . . Valley when it was time to return to England"—Book review digest.

743. —————. *Jocelyn of the forts.* **Decorations by George M. Richards. New New York: Dutton, 1929. 282p.**

"Jocelyn Armstrong was only a girl, but a soldier's daughter every inch. Her father, an officer in the provincial army, was transferred from his post at Albany to the frontier Fort William Henry. On the way the party was attacked by Indians and the Armstrong family was separated, not to be re-united until some time later in Albany. Montcalm, Abercombie," [the Schuylers, Colonel Munro are among historical personages present in the novel]—Book review digest.

744. **Crowinshield, Mary Bradford, d. 1913.** *Plucky Smalls*: **his story. Illus. by Frank T. Merrill. Boston: D. Lothrop, 1889. 203p.**

"Plucky Smalls is a street arab, or 'wharf rat', in New York City, who has never known a home, or parents, or friends. He has a single companion, the Tinker, as he calls him, and the two live by picking up scraps of food anywhere and sleeping in boxes around the wharves. One day Plucky saves the life of a child who has fallen overboard from a vessel lying at the wharf, and its father, who is a naval officer, makes places for the two boys on board his ship. As naval apprentices they visit various parts of the world, and much of the book is taken up with the story of their adventures"—Annual American catalogue.

745. **Croy, Homer, 1883-1965.** *Coney Island.* **New York: Harper, 1929. x, 294p.**
"The sound and color of cheap amusements, the freaks, and the hot dogs of Coney Island intermingle in this story. Chic Cotton, young inventor, has come to New York with an idea for a giant top amusement, which Zimmerman, the

czar of Coney Island, contracts to construct for him. Queenie, the tightrope walker falls in love with Chic. He finds himself engaged to her, and at the same time betrothed to Charmian De Ford, a girl of culture and refinement. But an accident happens at the tryout of the giant top. Chic gives Queenie up to Zimmerman and turns with a free conscience to new inventions and to Charmian"—Book review digest.

746. **Crozier, Alfred Owen, 1863-1939.** *The magnet*; a romance of the battles of modern giants. Illustrated by Wallace Morgan. New York: Funk & Wagnalls, 1908. 497p.

A scrupulously honest United States senator takes on the financial finaglers of Wall Street—his aim is to find ways of regulating their power-driven, often shady practices, to put a stop to marginal speculations and the lending of money at exorbitant interest rates.

Cruger, Julia Grinnell Storrow, d.1920. See under her pseudonym: Gordon, Julien, d. 1920.

Cruger, Mrs. Van Rensselaer, d. 1920. See under her pseudonym: Gordon, Julien, d. 1920.

747. **Cuddeback, Jane, b. 1891.** *Unquiet seed*; a novel. New York: Pellegrine & Cudahy, 1947. 293p.

Tobacco farming in Upstate New York's Wayne County is the author's frame of reference. George and Bella Bennett and their children are joined in their tobacco-raising efforts by Charlie, a homeless hired hand who regularly puts in an appearance when the growing season is at its height, and by Emma Dutcher, a young woman with a scandalous reputation who comes to the farm when Bella is feeling poorly. Adolescent Anna Bennett is a close observer of all that is going on. George Bennett is tempted to have an affair with Emma, but stops when he realizes how important Bella and the success of his crops are. The popular Charlie leaves the Bennett farm, perhaps for the last time, as the novel concludes.

Cuffee, Nathan Jeffrey, b. 1852, joint author. *Lords of the soil.* **See Item #1817.**

748. **Cullen, Clarence Louis, d. 1922.** *The eddy;* a novel of today. Illus. by Ch. Weber Ditzler. New York: G.W. Dillingham, 1910. 352p.

A young girl, after completing her finishing school education, returns to her divorced mother in New York. To her dismay, her mother is enjoying the luxury that her 'position' as mistress to a wealthy lover affords her. The girl resents the slurs and misinterpretations that she suffers because of her mother's way of life. She is able to distance herself from this disagreeable situation; and then her mother, eager to win back her daughter's love and respect, withdraws from the situations that have been so embarrassing to the girl.

749. Cumings, Elizabeth. *Miss Matilda Archambeau Van Dorn.* **Boston: D. Lothrop, 1892. 178p.**

"The story of a little New York girl born in the Mohawk Valley, whose great effort in life was to support with sufficient dignity the imposing name she bore. Being a bright and original child, full of odd ways and quaint sayings, she is a great trial to her Aunt Elizabeth, an elderly spinster with narrow views of life generally, who is her guardian. Presents an excellent character sketch of a girl's real life thirty years ago [around the Civil War period]"—Annual American catalogue.

750. Cummings, Maria Susanna, 1827-1866. *Mabel Vaughan.* **By the author of** *The lamplighter.* **Boston: J.P. Jewett, 1857. 508p,**

Our heroine has the 'right stuff', bolstered by an enduring strain of Christian morality (a 'given' with a large number of 19th century women writers) to resist the debilitating blandishments of New York City's fashionable social life. Her selfish, indulgent sister, Louise, and her beloved but free-spending indolent brother, Harry, are a cross Mabel bears stoically. Two-thirds of the way into the novel, Mr. Vaughan, father of this brood, loses his fortune via bad investments and land speculation. Mabel takes the two young sons of her deceased sister on a trek to Illinois where Mr. Vaughan and Harry are clinging to a cabin and a small piece of land. Her energy and optimism, the help of friends in a frontier environment, and the turnabout of Harry into a productive farmer, provide the base for a bright future for Mabel and her charges.

751. Cunningham, Laura, 1947- . *Third parties.* **New York: Coward, McCann & Georghegan, 1980. 286p.**

"Darton's Wood" is an Upstate New York village facing the threat of unprincipled developers who want to replace the community's splendid old houses and groves with tract housing. Inadvertently, divorcing couples in Darton's Wood are contributing to the developers' plan by putting their houses up for sale. Mr. Katcher and his wife are splitting too, but after he attends a town meeting and notes the unconcern of his neighbors, Katcher arranges a very significant all-night filibuster just before the vote of the town council on the project and the developers are blocked for a long time to come.

752. Curle, Richard, 1883-1968. *Corruption.* **Indianapolis: Bobbs-Merrill, 1968. 316p.**

"Clive Whitman, a born snoop . . . becomes hip to some awful three-cornered murder plans while visiting a former pal in a lustful neighborhood near the [Long Island] Sound, organizes a defense for the nicest lady in the threatened group, overhears things in the woods, witnesses a dreadful tableau through a window, runs across a new-made grave and the like of that, and finally confesses who he really is. Involved in same are a beautiful siren with snake eyes, a couple of ape-men, illicit passion, secrets, unmaskings and plenty of mental kinks. From the first you're sure of murder—but the question is how"—New York herald tribune books.

753. Curran, Henry Hastings, b. 1877. *Van Tassel and Big Bill.* **New York: Scribner, 1923. 311p.**

Stories about Alderman Jimmy Van Tassel and the local politics of New York City. Jimmy is a young aristocrat made an alderman through the influence of his father and a New York saloon owner/political operator. Contents: 'Hey', Toolan's marchin'!—The chanty that settled it.—Callahan of Carmine Street.—Garry's Christmas.—Thomas.—Big Bill speaks his mind.—Flanagan's getaway.—The stolen band.—The imperturbability of Pick.—'Cassidy—is that the name?'—'Uffs'.—'Heads up!'

754. Curran, John Elliott, 1818-1890. *Miss Frances Merley*; a novel. **Boston: Cupples and Hurd, 1888. viii, 406p.**

"The heroine is a remarkable young lady of eighteen, possessing a fortune of over a hundred thousand dollars, who is prey to ennui and at a loss to know what to do with her life. She is living in a small village, 'Marshton', Long Island Sound, with her uncle and guardian, a retired New York merchant. Her first attempt to 'live on the earth', as she calls it—that is, to get away from her stocks and bonds—results in a marriage with the village schoolmaster. They are both too proud to live on her fortune, and a long siege of poverty and suffering is the result. Left a widow, she goes into a convent, which she leaves through love for another man. Miss Merley is certainly a new character in fiction, and well described"—Annual American catalogue.

755. Currie, Barton Wood, b. 1878. *Officer 666*, by Barton W. Currie & Augustin McHugh. **New York: H. K. Fly, 1912. 308p.**

Apprised of a thief's scheme to sneak into his Fifth Avenue home and make off with highly prized art objects, Travers Gladwin borrows Officer 666's uniform and waits for the criminal to appear. Before this odd situation is resolved to Travers' satisfaction, he is involved with a beautiful heiress and her cousin, a very wealthy friend and Officer 666 himself.

756. Curtis, Alice Turner, 1860-1958. *A frontier girl of New York.* **Illustrated by Harold E. Snyder. Philadelphia: Penn Pub. Co., 1931. 275p.**

Annette Milton is the fictional character that leaves behind her home in New York City in 1675 to embark on a dangerous journey to the Mohawk River frontier country.

757. ———. *A little maid of Mohawk Valley.* **Illustrated by Grace Norcross. Philadelphia: Penn Pub. Co., 1924. 203p.**

The story of the reactions of the heroine, Joanne, to the invasion by General John Burgoyne of northeastern New York.

758. ———————. **A little maid of Ticonderoga. Illustrated by Wuanita Smith. Philadelphia: Penn Pub. Co., 1917. 216p.**

On an extended visit to her aunt at Ticonderoga, Faith Carew, whose home is not far from Lake Champlain, has an opportunity to be of help to Ethan Allen and the American cause as Revolutionary currents swirl around Ticonderoga and other important points fronting on Lake Champlain.

759. Curtis, George William, 1824-1892. *The Potiphar papers.* **(Reprinted from Putnam's monthly) Illustrated by A. Hoppin. New York: G.P. Putnam. viii, 251p.**

Satires on the high society of New York City; the chief character, Mrs. Potiphar, is a social climber whose long-suffering husband puts up with her follies as best he can. Other individuals who frolic in New York, Saratoga and Newport (and Paris) are characterized by their names: Minerva Tattle, Caroline Pettitoes, the Rev. Cream Cheese, Mrs. Settum Downe, Mrs. Croesus, et al.

760. ———————. *Trumps*; **a novel. Illustrated by Augustus Hoppin. New York: Harper, 1861. 502p.**

"The vulgarity of wordliness pervades every page of this picture of New York society; it is as though the universe were suddenly changed into one great stock-exchange, where to make money and to spend it upon fine upholstery, fine dinners, and fine dress are the being's end and aim of all human creatures—the chief end of man and his whole duty"—The critic. The chief characters are Abel Newt, who is thoroughly dishonest and dissolute, Fanny, his successful husband-hunting sister, and Hope Wayne, an heiress who has several love affairs but no husband when the novel ends.

761. Curtis, May Belle. *'Kathi' of Skenesborough.* **Glens Falls, N.Y.: Champlain Pub. Co., 1914. 255p.**

An historical novel in two parts. Part one records the activities of the Skene family shortly before the outbreak of the American Revolution. The heroine, Kathi Skene, is the willful, luxury loving but resourceful daughter of Colonel Philip Skene, founder of Skenesborough and loyal to the British Crown. Part two covers the early years of the Revolution in northern New York around Lake Champlain. The Skenes, captured by the rebels, eventually find their way to Canada. Kathi marries British officer Frederic de Piquet, but there is no return to Skenesborough, which is the scene of the confiscation of Colonel Skene's properties by the victorious Americans (Skenesborough's name was changed to Whitehall, N.Y.).

762. Curtis, Newton Mallory, d. 1849. *The black-plumed rifleman*; **a tale of the Revolution. New York: Burgess, Stringer, 1846. 125p. (in double columns).**

Harry Lenoir is dismissed from his foster father's (Judge Maillard's) home after wounding the traitorous Howland (a.k.a. Joseph Betteys), an associate of the judge. Harry and Louise Maillard, the judge's daughter are lovers, a situation he frowns upon (the judge has Tory sympathies). Harry joins the American rebels in New York City and participates in theSchuyler-Montgomery expedition to Montreal. Later he fights in the Saratoga campaign that results in Burgoyne's surrender. Howland/Betteys' forces himself upon Louise who has fled to Canada and northern New York in search of her misled father. The latter dies, realizing Howland/Betteys treachery too late. The villain is sentenced to death by a Revolutionary tribunal in Albany and Harry is finally reunited with Louise.

763. —————. *The bride of the northern wilds*; a tale. New York: Burgess & Stringer, 1843. 64p. (in double columns).

In the 1740s colonial troops and the Mohawks, their Indian allies, met French and Indian incursions on settlements in the Adirondack region with resistance. Herman Peters, his friend the soldier Bancker, and Ben Meredith were key figures in this resistance. The author describes quite vividly the savagery and cruelty of the frontier battles. Indians allied with the French slaughter Ben's father, stepmother and baby stepbrother; the village of Saratoga is leveled, the heroine, Rosalind Malcom, is captured by the French leader, Fieschi. By the story's end, complex relationships between the principal characters are unraveled. Rosalind is freed by her lover Ben, and in a final battle Fieschi and his chief Indian associates are killed. Governor George Clinton is portrayed benignly in this work, although history's assessment of his character is often not so kind.

Curtis Newton Mallory, d. 1849. *Brian Blonday.* **See note under Item #765.**

764. —————. *The doom of the Tory's Guard*; a tale. New York: Burgess and Stringer, and M.Y. Beach, 1843. 48p. (in double columns).

The Van Loan mansion near the present-day site of Canajoharie (then known as The Station) in 1774 was occupied by the squire Teunis Van Loan, a rabid Tory and leader of the Tory's Guard, his deceased wife's sister Josephine, his niece Alice (due to be independently wealthy when she reaches 18 years), and a son Frederick. Van Loan was anxious to marry Alice to Frederick in order to gain access to her future wealth. Van Loan's opponents were the patriotic Americans, Reginald Mervale and Jacob Dash, a soldier. When the American Revolution breaks out, Tory and Whig forces fight for control of the Mohawk Valley. Alice is subjected to successive dangers from her scheming uncle and is even rescued from an insane asylum on the Hudson by Reginald and Jacob. A final Whig-Tory clash at The Station eventuates in a crushing defeat for the Tory's Guard and the deaths of Teunis and Frederick Van Loan. Reginald and Alice marry and take up residence in the still-standing Van Loan mansion.

765. —————. *The foundling of the Mohawk*; a tale of the Revolution. New York: Williams Bros., 1848. 89, 7p. (in double columns).

After Abram Van Kempen's death his nephew Hans, a Tory, takes sole possession of 'Van Kempen's Castle' in Upstate New York. Viola Fordham,

Abram's niece, is a bone of contention between Hans and Bryan Blonday (known as the 'foundling of the Mohawk') for both love her; Viola's preference is for Bryan. Bryan, brought up by Edward Fielding, a farm laborer, favors the patriot cause and joins the Blue Brotherhood, an independent arm of the Continental Army. Captured by Hans Van Kempen, Bryan is imprisoned. Hans tries to force Viola to marry him by threatening to execute Bryan. The American Captain Drake not only rescues Viola from marriage to Hans, but he also releases Bryan from his imprisonment. While all this is going on, Henry Fozzle, an attorney, uncovers proof that Bryan is the son of Abram Van Kempen and Van Kempen's still living, estranged widow. The House of Delegates at Albany confirm's Bryan's rightful ownership of the Van Kempen estate. This work was also issued under the title: *Brian Blonday*; or, *The blue ranger of the Mohawk* (1854).

766. ————. *The maid of the Saranac*; a tale of the War of 1812. New York: Williams Bros., 1848. 79p. (in double columns).

Scene: a mansion near Plattsburgh, the residence of brutish Colonel Harcourt of the American Army and his mistreated wife. When Lt. (later Col.) Maurice Brandon is wounded in a skirmish with British foragers, he is taken to the mansion to recover. Brandon and Mrs. Harcourt fall in love. Colonel Harcourt falls under the spell of John Frazer, a speculator and supplier, and his paramour Madeline who is passed off as his daughter. Frazer fancies Mrs. Harcourt and makes plans to get rid of Brandon. Mrs. Brandon flees from her husband to a cottage in the woods owned by the 'Maid of the Saranac.' Brandon takes part in military actions against the British around Plattsburgh. Again wounded he is taken to the cottage occupied by Mrs. Harcourt. The Colonel, who has turned over much of his fortune to Frazer, commits suicide. Frazer and Madeline have been consorting with the British and are forced to flee Plattsburgh. The 'Maid of the Saranac' is revealed as the abandoned wife of Frazer. Brandon recovers from his wounds and he and Mrs. Harcourt are free to wed on another.

767. ————. *The matricide's daughter*; a tale of life in the great metropolis. New York: Williams Bros. 1847. 102p. (in double columns).

————. *The star of the fallen.* New York: Williams Bros., 1847. 103p. (in double columns).

————. *The victim's revenge* … New York: Williams Bros., 1848. 89p. (in double columns).

The above 3 titles form a continuous narrative. The story opens in 1834 in the residence of Mrs. Sydenham at the upper end of Broadway. She has been ill and has been contemplating reconciling with her estranged son Floyd. Her other son, Seymour, is anxious to ensure that he remains the sole beneficiary in the event of the rich widow's death. He plots endlessly with several crooked denizens of New York—an attorney, a politician, a doctor, a number of criminals—and in the end he himself murders his mother before she can change her will. He accuses Floyd of being the guilty party, but one of his partners in crime convinces the courts that Seymour is solely responsible for the murder. Seymour is convicted and commits suicide while in prison. One of the two subplots has Claude Sydenham, the wayward son of Floyd, and Fanny Hemans, an actress, deeply in love; Fanny, perhaps to her own surprise and ours, is disclosed to be Seymour's daughter by a clandestine marriage. The second subplot follows the hapless Frances Farleigh, daughter of a struggling artist, who innocently finds herself being groomed in a fashionable brothel for a life of prostitution.

768. —————. *The patrol of the mountain*; a tale of the Revolution. New York: Williams Bros., 1847. 112p (in double columns).

Also published in 1883 under the title: *Giant Jack, the patrol of the mountain* (New York, Beadle and Adams). Henry Robinson of Shoreham, Vermont breaks off relations with his Tory father, the Major, when he joins the American armed forces. As a young officer Henry, with his knowledge of Lake Champlain, is invaluable to Benedict Arnold who is leading a small navy against British sloops of war on the lake. The story moves to the New York side of Lake Champlain when Arnold requests Henry to seek out Jacob Dash, known as the Patrol of the Mountain. Robinson and Dash have their share of adventures in the region around Crown Point, New York, but set out on a mission to free Clara Marion, Henry's fiancée, who has fallen into British hands. Henry is taken prisoner; Dash and Indian allies release both Henry and Clara, take over a British schooner and sail down Lake Champlain to Arnold's position at Crown Point.

769. —————. *The ranger of Ravenstream*; a tale of the Revolution. New York, Boston: Williams Bros., 1847. 118p. (in double columns).

Sir William Johnson and his home, the 'Hall', in Johnstown, New York, have leading parts in this tale of adventure. Johnson has a mildly villainous role as he tries to marry off his 'niece', Constance Morton, to his nephew James Johnson, and maneuvers his forces of Tories and Mohawk Indians against the rebel forces of Colonel Marinus Willett and Patrick McArran (the latter a purely fictional character). The hero, Bernard St. Hubert, the 'ranger of Ravenstream', with the assistance of the hunter/trapper 'Old Tiger', rescues Constance from her imprisonment at the 'Hall.' Bernard and Constance are in turn saved from capture by the Tories by Willett and McArran. The latter discloses that Constance is his niece and the daughter of his sister Kathleen and her husband William McBrail, presently employed by the Continental Congress. Sir William chooses to wait out the war in Canada (the author was unaware or conveniently 'forgot' that Sir William died in 1774, before the outbreak of the American Revolution).

770. Curtiss, Philip Everett, b. 1885. *Between two worlds*; a novel. New York: Harper, 1916. 351p.

A young New York architect Sydney Gresham was certain that Ruth Abbot, a complex and sophisticated but still rather conventional woman of his own milieu, was the right choice for him. He had not reckoned with the powerful attraction exerted by Dora Middleman, a professional cabaret singer. Dora was uncomplicated and forthright, intensely human and lovable. Sydney's friend, Hugh Nelson, at one time closely connected to Dora, told him that Dora was not a woman one could play fast and loose with. Despite reservations of 'class' and propriety his heart guides Sydney to the woman who possesses the most human qualities.

771. [Cushing, Eliza Lanesford Foster] b. 1794. *Saratoga*; a tale of the Revolution. Boston: Cummings, Hilliard, 1824. 2v.

Although they occur early in the novel, events surrounding and following the Saratoga campaign, as the title implies, are of great importance to the story, most of which, however, takes place on Major Courtland's estate on the Schuylkill River not far from Philadelphia. The Major's daughter, Catherine, sympathetic to the American cause, is the heroine; her father is loyal to the British crown and unsheathes his sword in its defense. Colonel Grahame, the hero, an officer in the American army, wins the Major's respect by his concern for the welfare of his wounded British foes (the Major included). Grahame and Catherine fall in love. The Major eventually accedes to their wishes despite his own plans for Catherine's future. One of the subplots narrates British officer Captain O'Carroll finding his long-lost love (after losing her in Ireland) in a hidden cottage nearby the Courtland estate. Hyperbole and sentiment, so characteristic of much early American fiction, are present in Ms. Cushing's novel.

772. Cushman, Clarissa Fairchild, 1889-1980. *I wanted to murder*. New York: Farrar and Rinehart, 1940. 306p.

"Sally Richmond, married, forty, amusing and modern in a ladylike way, and the equal of any spinster narrator you're likely to recall." She has an in on suburban secrets "writing a book in which Hal Beveridge, the philosopher found dead at the bottom of a gorge, was the victim, so what could people think? Before the verdict comes in, the customer has accompanied Sally through a readable tangle of intrigue, with numerous clues strewn here and there and suspense mounting to a satisfactory pitch. Sally and Chief Brennan deduce in fairish amounts, leaving the main jolt for that inquest—it has all the zip of a trial for life"—New York herald tribune books.

773. Cussler, Clive, 1931- . *Night probe*. New York: Bantam Books, 1984. 344p.

In 1989 Dirk Pitt is hard at work investigating a ship claimed by the waters of the St. Lawrence River and a train buried deep in the Hudson. The possibility is that a treaty signed by the United States and England in 1914 is in one of those two places. It is to England's interest that the lost treaty be found by one of its agents since its contents could have international repercussions. The

English assign Brian Shaw, an elderly but masterful functionary, to find the document before the American Pitt does.

Cuthbert, pseud. See: Copus, John Edwin, b. 1854.

Cuthrell, Faith Baldwin, 1893-1978. See: Baldwin, Faith, 1893-1978.

774. **Cutting, Mary Stewart Doubleday, 1851-1924.** *Heart of Lynn.* **Illustrated by Helen B. Stowe. Philadelphia: Lippincott, 1904. 264p.**

> The Barry family—consisting of the widowed mother, Lynn, the heroine, and her sisters and a brother—live on the far edge of Brooklyn and have to struggle to survive without a major breadwinner present. Lynn, a comely, energized young woman, takes on the task of stretching their financial resources by making and selling food items, having several stories published, etc. The Barrys have problems with neighbors who turn out to be counterfeiters, but the author is of the 'happy ending school', and sees to it that her heroine has a promising romance entering her full life.

775. ———. *The unforeseen.* **Illustrated by Will Foster. Garden City, N.Y.: Doubleday, Page, 1910. 273p.**

> Evelyn Gaynor, a country-bred young woman, comes to New York City and lands a job editing a children's magazine. After two years she is disappointed by the small salary she receives which is barely adequate to live on. A young author who made her his confidante and from whom she may have expected more ignores her when he becomes heir to a fortune. As she is about to give it all up and leave New York for her native town, the unforeseen happens. Another man, in love with her, but heretofore reluctant to press forward because of his relative poverty, is suddenly enabled by 'unforeseen' circumstances to propose to her.

776. **Dahl, Borghild Margarethe, 1890-1984.** *Stowaway to America.* **New York: Dutton, 1959. 192p.**

> "Based on historical data, the story tells how [Norwegian] orphan Margit escapes from a life of drudgery by joining a small band of dissenters en route to America in 1825. The voyage is a hazardous one and Margit proves a valuable asset to the group. When their ship finally reaches port, Cleng Peerson, one of Norway's great inspirational leaders, guides them to western New York State. Here they establish the first permanent Norwegian settlement in America"—Chicago Sunday tribune.

777. **Dailey. W. B.** *Saratoga; a dramatic historical romance of the Revolution.* **Corning [N.Y.]: T. Messenger, Printer, Journal Office, 1848. 96p.**

> A narrative poem that opens with a discussion by British officers General Simon Frazier (i.e. Fraser), Major-General Philips (i.e. Phillips), and Major John Acland of Burgoyne's campaign—deploring their ravaging Indian allies and admiring the tenacity of their American foes. A short scene finds patriot

George _____ saying goodbye to his sweetheart, Adelia, daughter of Major-General Philip Schuyler; she is captured shortly thereafter by a Tory and four Indians. Burgoyne does not come off well in the author's characterization—he is painted as a rather cold, efficient soldier determined to quell the rebels by any means available. After the Battle of Saratoga Adelia guides Lady Harriet Acland to her husband, a prisoner in American hands. They story-poem concludes with the encirclement of stubborn Burgoyne's troops, their surrender, and Adelia's reunion with George _____.

"*Chippewa and Bridgewater*, an historical romance": p. [49]-64.

"*Tecumseh*; a romance of the Thames": p. [65]-96.

778. Daintrey, Laura. *Actaeon.* **New York: Empire City Pub. Co., 1892. 280p.**

A story of life among the 'upper crust' of New York society. Sylvia Leroyand And Pauline Belmore are good friends. Both are intrigued by Jack Conquest (Actaeon), the novelist and socialite. When it becomes clear to Pauline that Conquest prefers Sylvia, she reviews her rather sordid past—she had been involved with the vengeful financier, Bleecker Falk—and decides that she no longer has any interest in stretching out the years. After her suicide Sylvia and Jack Conquest marry.

779. ————. *Eros.* **Chicago, New York: Belford, Clarke, 1888. 255p.**

"The author divides women into two classes, the very good and the very bad. The scene of this unhealthy story is New York City. Miss Remington, at the age of twenty-five, decides it is time to marry and deliberately lays her plans to secure an offer of marriage from a rich young broker. She is successful, and for a short time makes him miserable. Incidents in her life before marriage entail their natural consequences, and she suffers herself, and makes others suffer. As offset there is a pure young girl who, after many days, is made happy"—Annual America catalogue.

780. ————. *Gold*; a novel. **New York: G.W. Dillingham, 1893. 316p.**

The owner of a dry goods emporium in New York City, a wealthy man worth 20 million dollars, is murdered on Christmas Eve even as the Hotel Royal is being destroyed by fire. The chief suspect's only hope of avoiding a charge of murder is to substantiate his absence from the scene of the crime. Two women, both of whom love him, are the keys to his being cleared. The author obviously holds the women of upper New York society in low esteem in her slice of life in the metropolis.

781. ————. *Miss Varian of New York*. **A Newport and New York Society novel. By ? . New York: G.W. Dillingham, 1887. 372p.**

"A novel that deals with the vices and follies of a certain class of rich men with perfect candor and fidelity. 'Society', as represented here, is a very disreputable affair. … The plot of the story hovers around the courtship and early matrimonial experiences of an innocent and beautiful girl, who weds and unprincipled man of pleasure, deeming him to be truth and virtue personified. The man is not wholly bad, however, and having come very near to being the indirect murderer of his wife, has the grace to repent of his sins and become all that a husband should be. Some very questionable characters are introduced to the reader in the course of the narrative, and a kind of light is thrown upon some of the gayeties of our luxurious metropolis. There is a pretty fair representation of average society men and women, some good, some bad, and some neither one nor the other, making a picture not particularly elevating, but sure to attract attention"—North American review.

782. Dale, Alan, 1861-1928. *A girl who wrote.* **New York: Quail & Warner, 1902. 375p.**

Newspaper Row in New York City and its activities are the principal concerns of the story. Through the influence and friendship of Charlie Covington, Sally Sydenham secures a reporter's job with a rather sensational daily edited by Jack Childers. As the novel progresses Sally's boss, Childers, warms toward his novice reporter, and by the end of the story Sally and Jack share the same romantic feelings for one another. Sally reveals to Jack that she has added substantially to her income by writing successful love stories.

783. ————. *My footlight husband*; **a story of the stage. New York, Cleveland: Cleveland Pub. Co., 1893. 203p.**

"After many conquests and a successful opera bouffe career, Ursula Bickmore marries a young New Yorker of good position. He shows at once his intention to live on her income, and afterwards goes upon the stage himself. The end of a career like Ursula's, her weak love for her utterly worthless husband and her final sacrifice are told by one evidently acquainted behind the footlights" – Annual American catalogue.

784. ————. *Wanted: a cook*; **domestic dialogues. Indianapolis: Merrill, 1904. 382p.**

A comic novel in which a young couple with fanciful ideas about the care and nurture of their home despite the smallness of their New York City apartment, undertake a quest for a cook who meets their specifications. The several ridiculous situations they stumble into are indicative of the follies of 'modern life.'

Dale, Annan, pseud. See: Johnston, James Wesley, b. 1850.

Dale, J.S. of, pseud. See: Stimson, Frederic Jesup, 1855-1943.

785. Dallas, Mary Kyle, 1830-1897. *Billtry.* **New York: Merriam Co., 1895. 133p.**

This short novel is presumably a parody of George Du Maurier's 'Trilby.' The 'Giraffe', Sally Jane Smith (the 'Lady of Shallot') and Rebecca (Beckie) are three unmarried, artistic girls who share an apartment in New York City. They use as a model 'Billtry', he of the magnificent toes. Beckie falls very much in love with Billtry, but he refuses to marry her when her grandfather,

Mr. Amos Bags, will not agree to support them financially. Billtry takes as his wife instead, Miss Snivly, a teacher of the accordion. He becomes a vaudeville headliner because of his ability to play the accordion with his toes while standing on his head. When the girls move to Boston, Billtry will no longer perform. He takes to the bottle; his ultimate fate no one knows. Does Beckie jump off the Brooklyn Bridge? The 'Giraffe' marries a farmer and the 'Lady of Shallot' becomes Mrs. Amos Bags.

786. Dallas, Richard, pseud. *A master hand*; the story of a crime. New York: Putnam, 1903. vi, 257p.

Arthur White is a quiet young bachelor who has a few good friends and presumably no real enemies. When his body (with stab wounds) is discovered in his New York apartment, the detective in charge of investigating the puzzling homicide plods slowly but intelligently towards the solution of the murder.

787. Daly, Conor. *Local knowledge*. New York: Kensington Books, 1995. 258p.

A mystery with its setting the 'Milton Country Club' in Westchester Country. The club's golf professional, Kieran Lenahan, is about to enter a local professional golfers' association tournament when the police tell him that a club co-owner's body was removed from one of the golf course's water hazards. The dead man, named Kieran in his will, and has asked him to evaluate a set of rare 'Blitzklubs', manufactured by the Nazis, and part of the estate. The clubs disappear and Kieran's shop helper, a former juvenile delinquent, is charged with murder. Lenahan looks for the clubs, tries to clear his helper, and prepare for tournament play, while simultaneously deducing motives for the murder and fingering the guilty party.

788. Daly, Elizabeth, 1878-1967. *Arrow pointing nowhere*. New York: Farrar & Rinehart, 1944. 250p.

An aristocratic family whose members are scattered from New York City to 'Rockcliffe on the Hudson' is paralyzed and at a loss to explain why two murders and a suicide should occur within its circle. Henry Gamadge, the private detective, is called in to supply meaning to the matter.

789. —————. *Night walk*. New York: Rinehart, 1947. 196p.

"The bibliophile Henry Gamadge . . . investigates the clubbing to death of old George Carrington, a gentleman of taste who lives on a small annuity in a village in New York [State]. The town, which is somewhat run down, contains an expensive rest home, an inn, a refined rooming house, a library, and an elaborate, moderately plausible array of witnesses, who have been made to believe that the murder is the work of a roaming maniac. Gamadge, of course, knows better"—New Yorker.

790. —————. *Nothing can rescue me*. New York: Farrar & Rinehart, 1943. 281p. 1943. 281p.

"Henry Gamadge goes to Underhill, Florence Mason's Upstate [New York] country estate to find out who is interposing strange quotations in a novel Mrs. Mason is writing there. When Gamadge leaves for home, the score stands at two dead, one partly strangled, and one on the crazy side"—New Yorker.

791. **Daly, Elizabeth Harding.** *High goal*; **a novel. Philadelphia: Macrae, Smith, 1934. 313p.**
"After Denise [Carstairs] has met the fascinating polo player, Ripley Sears, she is willing to end her unhappy marriage with Alan Carstairs and try a second time with Rip. How Rip and Denise finally make a success of their marriage is told against a background of life among the polo and hunting set of Long Island"—Book review digest.

792. *Damned*; **the intimate story of a girl. Anonymous. New York: Macaulay Co., 1923. 352p.**
Dolores Trent suffers the 'slings and arrows of outrageous fortune' as she contends with the vagaries of life on and around New York City's Fifth Avenue, until she is cut off by premature death.

793. **Dane, Joel Y., 1905- .** *The cabana murders*; **a Sergeant Cass Harty detective story. Garden City, N.Y.: Published for the Crime Club by Doubleday, Doran, 1937. xi, 298p.**
Sergeant Harty and his assistant, Barney, are kept on their toes as they try to find the motives and culprit behind four murders that take place on a private island off Long Island Sound where an atmosphere of excessive drinking, dishonest business dealings and flimsy love affairs reign.

794. ————. *Murder cum laude*. **New York: H. Smith and R. Haas, 1935. 352p.**
A suburban New York institution, Cardaff University, is the scene of the murders of two undergraduates, one shot, and the other stabbed. Police sergeant Cass Harty is in charge of the case and is turned off by the students' frivolities, radical politics and secretive associations, but doesn't let that or a stunned faculty and administration deter his persistent and successful search for the murderer.

795. **Daniel, David.** *Murder at the Baseball Hall of Fame*, **by David Daniel and and Chris Carpenter. New York: St. Martin's Press, 1996. 215p.**
Bostonian Frank Branco, a private investigator, is in Cooperstown, New York, courtesy of the winning ticket in a radio contest. The annual induction ceremony at the Baseball Hall of Fame is in place when, at an out-of-doors reception, a car goes out of control; Frank is the first person to reach the cracked-up vehicle, but rescue of the driver is not possible—the car blows up. The casualty is Herb Frawley, a former major leaguer of 30 years ago. Branco feels Frawley's death was not accidental; the local police disagree and

tell him to back off. Frawley's ex-wife hires Branco to dig further; he does and confirms his suspicions.

796. Daniels, Cora Linn Morrison, b. 1852. *The bronze Buddha*; **a mystery. Boston: Little, Brown, 1899. 295p.**

"A strange medley of the theories of theosophy, occultism, telepathy, and the many other seekings that reach into the unknown. The scene is chiefly New York City. A bronze Buddha is seen in the Academy of Design by the rich, idle young hero and the devoted daughter of a man who had spent his best years among the Brahmins of India. It fascinates them both when they return and it is gone. The girl's father makes her promise to devote her life and fortune to finding the lost god. This search brings them [the two young people] together often, and a most remarkable family history is discovered for both of them"—Annual American catalogue.

797. Daniels, Harriet McDoual, b. 1871. *Muller Hill.* **New York: Knopf, 1943. 402p.**

Most of this historical novel takes place in Oneida County, New York, with opening scenes in New York City, when in 1795 a mysterious French aristocrat who goes by the name—Lewis Anathe Muller—appears in the city's highest social circles. Muller marries Adeline Stuyvesant and moves to the Chenango Valley, building a mansion there for his wife and the children she bears him. Adeline's foster brother, John Linden, secretly in love with her, attends school nearby at Hamilton Oneida Academy (predecessor of Hamilton College). When Napoleon is ousted and the monarchy is restored in France, Muller leaves his wife and children never to return. John Linden uncovers some murky data concerning the Frenchman—is he the Comte d'Artois, in line for the French throne, or has he been killed in the tumult surrounding Napoleon's return from exile? In any event, the marriage of Adeline and 'Muller' is adjudged to be null and void, and true lovers, John Linden and Adeline, are free to marry.

798. ————. *Nine-Mile Swamp*; **a story of the Loomis Gang. New York: Penn Pub. Co., 1941. 412p.**

"Story of the Loomis family [horse and cattle thieves], horse traders and passers of counterfeit money, living in Upstate New York before the Civil War. In 1802 the original 'Wash' Loomis bought a frontier farm that included the Nine-Mile Swamp, and proceeded to raise a large family. This tale of his descendants takes place in the 1850s and ends with the murder of the then leader of the Loomis Gang and the near-lynching of the one straight member of the family"—Book review digest.

799. Daniels, Sally, 1931. *The inconstant season.* **New York: Atheneum Publishers, 1962. 244p.**

"Essentially a group of interconnected vignettes, this is a first person narrative . . . of growing up as one of a large comfortable family in the wine and lake region of western New York. Going back some twenty years directly, Peggy Dillon, the narrator, filters the memorable events of school, family, and the coming of war through her own sensibility"—New York herald tribune books.

800. Darby, Ruth. *Beauty sleep.* **Garden City, N.Y.: Published for the Crime Club of Doubleday, Doran, 1941. 274p.**

"Mrs. Nettie Carrington was too fond of men and did she drink? One day, while some of her neighbors were sitting around in mudpacks and things at Emily Bokart's beauty parlor, Nettie staggered into the steam room and never came out alive. Somebody had done her in by a method that struck us as clever but might be hard to use. One of the main suspects is Guy Sherman, the village philanderer. What became of Nettie's diamond and emerald necklace? Soon there's a second fatality, and Janet Barron dashes cheerfully about as sleuth. She solves the fearful crime with the aid of Peter, her husband, after quite a bit of random excitement. This startling picture of life in a Long Island town may be aimed at the feminine trade"—New York herald tribune books.

801. Dare, Arline, pseud. *Both were mistaken*; **a novel. New York: G.W. Dillingham, 1892. 287p.**

Eugene Searle, a wealthy New York man-about-town, falls madly in love with Madeline, wife of an acquaintance, Francis Tabor. The Eugene/Madeline affair continues until Francis Tabor dies in Mexico while his wife is enjoying the social whirl in New York. Madeline goes back to Mexico; her deceased husband left her only a few thousand dollars, so she feels constrained to accept the proposal of marriage of Benitto Rogerio. Searle, after recovering from a stroke brought on by Madeline's request that he no longer seek her company, heads for Mexico. In a moment of insanity he strangles Madeline. Life goes on in New York, marriages in Eugene's milieu take place and his friend Sydney Gray, who had warned him of Madeline's duplicity, bemoans Eugene's downfall.

802. Daring, Hope, pseud. *The appointed way*; **a tale of the Seventh Day Adventists. Philadelphia: Griffith & Rowland Press, 1905. viii, 336p.**

"A preacher of the sect, a man of great personal magnetism, converts the father of a little family living a serene life in a pretty New York town. He [the father] dies shortly thereafter, but [he] has made promises to the Adventist that completely change the future of the household"—Annual American catalogue.

803. Daulton, Agnes McClelland. *Fritzi*; or, *The Princess Perhaps.* **With illus. by Florence E. Storer. New York: Century Co., 1908, c1907. 417p.**

Fritzi is a young German girl whose mother has died in a New York City hospital—Fritzi's father is somewhere in Germany. The semi-orphaned girl, alone in the metropolis, is taken in by a blind musician and his wife. They discover that Fritzi has an affinity for the violin. Along with musical training Fritzi is taught how to take care of herself in daily life. Some time later, falling into the hands of a fortune teller who eventually deserts her, Fritzi has the good luck to spend several years with a kindhearted Staten Island family. Her new friends are instrumental in bringing Fritzi together with the father she scarcely remembered. Then comes the revelation that she actually comes from a long line of aristocratic forebears.

804. Davenport, Diana. *Wild spenders*; **a novel. New York: Macmillan, 1984. 258p.**

Four women in their thirties (or thereabouts) are spending the summer in upscale East Hampton, Long Island, and trying to sort out their lives: Kate has fled from Los Angeles and an 18-year-old marriage to a rambunctious husband definitely out of control; Blair is a playwright who now sells real estate to support herself and is in love with a man who can't stand her; Lu, an airplane pilot with the queasy task of shipping bodies to funeral directors, 'sticks to one-night stands, bar-stool cowboys with the depth of a stick of gum'; and Sybil, a none-too-successful novelist, is presently pursuing a 22-year-old actor.

805. Davenport, Russell Wheeler, 1899-1954. *Through-traffic*. **Garden City, N.Y.: Doubleday, Doran, 1930. 307p.**

"Joe Hurd, scion of a wealthy Park Avenue family, failed at Harvard and had a dislike in general for work, academic or otherwise. And he could not forgive why his father committed suicide—nor forgive his mother who was the direct cause. Then Joe fell in love, reformed morally, suddenly went to work and made a fortune in Wall Street"—Book review digest. "The story reflects New York life in certain surface aspects, and Park Avenue is thrust at the reader with a reiteration which finally ceases to imnpress. The ending is the happy Park Avenue sort"—New York herald tribune books.

806. Davidge, Frances. *The game and the candle*. **New York: Appleton, 1905. xi, 371p.**

"Certainly not worth the candle is the great, rushing, whirling game that is being played in the great city of New York for money, for power, for place, for husbands. Just before his soul was killed by New York, that 'all-devouring demon', Richard Faxon who had drifted in to the idlest, laziest, most unsatisfactory life, was turned [onto] better things by his cousin Emily. He was married; his wife wanted a divorce which he absolutely refused. Emily sent him out West to work as a physician in a mining community and from that dated the events of the plot which shifts between New York, Newport, the West and South Carolina which seems the satisfactory end"—Annual American catalogue.

807. Davidson, George Trimble, b. 1863. *The moderns*; **a tale of New York. New York: F.A. Stokes, 1901. 364p.**

The novel's opening scenes are in Paris where Mildred Hope, the heroine, a wealthy and delightful young woman, is rescued from a fire at the Bazar de Charité in 1897 by her cousin, Kenneth Fairfax, a struggling portrait painter.

The scene changes to New York City where Mildred continues to be pursued by the spurious Duke of Montfort. However, Fairfax is on hand to look after Mildred's best interests and he is, in the end, the logical match for her.

808. Davies, Helen. *The reveries of a spinster.* **New York, Chicago: F. Tennyson Neely, 1897. 216p.**

"The supposed repinings of a New York school teacher, who never having had time or opportunity in her lonely life for love making, satisfies her cravings for sympathy by communing with an imaginary lover. Later her sphere broadens; a real lover enters her life and she becomes a professional musician who ruthlessly rejects love and espouses art. When surfeited with adulation and the attention of many suitors, the heroine comes to the conclusion that her life on this account is a failure"—Annual American catalogue.

809. Davies, Mary Carolyn. *The husband test.* **Front. by Elizabeth Pilsbry. Philadelphia: Penn Pub. Co., 1921. 259p.**

"How Bettina Howard, bored with the ways of convention, postpones her decision to marry by planning to try out Temp, the Greenwich Village poet, and William Clark, the lawyer, for one month each on 'trial marriage', is the plot. . . . Betty's trial with Temp consumes the bulk of the book; yet what happens at the end just when Betty's marriage to William Clark is almost consummated, compensates for the rather one-sided treatment"—Literary review of the New York evening post.

810. Davies, Theodore. *Losing to win.* **A novel. New York: Sheldon. 1874. 407p.**

George Denton, Sr., of 'Stemwell', a town in Dutchess County, N.Y., mourns the loss of George, Jr.; the tattered clothes of a decomposed body in the Hudson River contained a handkerchief with the initials 'G.D.' Paul Allington, a nephew of Denton's, is brought to Stemwell to replace the supposedly deceased George, Jr. Allington is a flawed individual. He falls in love with Lily Vevere, the orphaned niece of Josiah Wharton, a friend of old Denton. Wharton, at the urging of speculator Homer Graynan, makes several bad investments, but is able to recoup his finances with lucky dealings on Wall Street and the revival of his brickyards in Stemwell after a strike is settled. New York journalist Frederick Bayner and 'Frank' Sturdy, a sculptress, shield Lily who is pursued by the obsessed Allington. Bayner falls in love with Lily, reveals his real name, George Denton, and rejoins his overjoyed father. The thwarted Allington makes a last effort to kidnap Lily and dies in the attempt.

811. Davis, Charles Belmont, 1866-1926. *In another moment.* **With illus. by Wallace Morgan. Indianapolis: Bobbs-Merrill, 1913. 372p.**

"The heroine [Fay Clayton] is a young girl from the country who goes to New York to win success as a chorus girl. The men of the story are the broker who meets her in the New Jersey village and who first suggests to her the idea of attempting a stage career; the friend who has been her girlhood lover who comes to New York at the same time she does; and the eccentric young millionaire who takes a philanthropic interest in her. The plot of the story takes an original turn at the end when the girl, instead of choosing the country lover, as one had expected, marries the young millionaire"—Book review digest. The author dwells to some extent on the temptations and degradations that often accompany theatrical careers and the shoddy treatment accorded performers by managers. Fay Clayton sees it all but is able to avoid the uglier aspects.

812. ————. *Nothing a year*; a novel. **New York: Harper, 1916, c1915. 291p.**

"The story of an unscrupulous Southern girl whose ambitions are fixed on a position in New York society. Barbara Clyde is determined to leave at the first opportunity the Virginia village where her mother keeps a boarding house for visitors from the North. And opportunity to her means marriage to Johnny Lister who offers her the way of escape; [he] is a popular youth who owes his position to his personal traits rather than to income. But Barbara is willing to accept him for the position's sake and to trust to the future for the income. Her husband loves her devotedly but her methods lead to a break between them. After the divorce she attempts various doubtful means of holding her footing [even returning to her old home for a spell], but just as she is on the verge of disaster Johnny returns to condone all and, most probably, to be duped again"—Book review digest.

813. ————. *The stage door.* **New York: Scribner, 1908. 360p.**

Ten stories of life on the New York stage which assume that theatrical people are little different from the general run of people, exposing their own failings but exhibiting good qualities under trial. Contents: Everyman's riddle.—'Beauty' Kerrigan.—Coccero the Clown.—'Sedgwick'.—A modern Cleopatra.—The cross roads, New York.—The kidnappers.—The flawless emerald.—Carmichael's Christmas spirit.—The road to glory.

814. ————. *Tales of the town.* **New York: Duffield, 1911. 339p.**

Tales of New York City. They contrast the sights, sounds and smells of country life with those of the city and its wider human dimension. Contents: The gray mouse.—The romance of a rich young girl.—Once to every man.—The conquerors.—The most famous woman in New York.—Where ignorance was bliss.—The extra girl.—The rescue.—Marooned.—The song and the savage.

815. **Davis, Christopher, 1928- .** *Dog, horse, rat.* **New York: Viking Press, 1990. 244p.**

The village of 'Whitehead' in Upstate New York is a case study of a society unaware or uncaring of cultural developments in the outside world. Whitehead has a prison and several saloons and a population that closes ranks whenever any of its members get into trouble. The brothers Van and Royal

West go on a crime spree, robbing a professor's summer home and murdering his talented son; they do their best to escape the consequences by involving themselves in tiffs with their family and the town's citizens. The latter seem willing to put up with the chilling Van, a Vietnam veteran, and the once harmless Royal—after all, they are a part of us.

816. Davis, Clyde Brion, 1894-1962. *Thudbury*; an American comedy. Philadelphia: Lippincott, 1952. 446p.

The novel satirizes the life of the leading businessman of 'Tolland', New York, an Upstate town. His name is Otis Paul Thudbury and the editor of the Tolland Enterprise tells his story. Thudbury's life extends from 1880 to 1945; he is a right-wing Republican who isn't averse to some questionable business practices in order to increase his financial and political power. In his younger years Thudbury had entered a New York to San Francisco motor race, which he won, partly because he rode in a boxcar during one arduous stretch. One can discern in Davis's work informative pieces of the social history of the 65 years covered.

817. Davis, Elmer Holmes, 1890-1958. *Friends of Mr. Sweeney*. New York: McBride, 1925. 282p.

Asaph Holliday had evolved into a routine journalist, writing editorials for the Balance, a New York City newspaper, which reflected the owner's (Mr. Brumbaugh's) ideas more than his own. An old college friend turns up and takes Asaph out for a full night on the town. Asaph was 'recreated'—he became the 'Ace' Holliday of his college years, a real man now ready to get respect from his wife, the attention of Mr. Brumbaugh, a higher salary and an editorial policy all his own. Several reviewers saw the novel as a biting satire of New York City life.

818. ————. *I'll show you the town*. New York: McBride, 1924. 373p.

"A young assistant professor of Latin with a reputation for respectability and the confidant of ladies in distress finds himself charged with showing the town—New York—to three women of widely different types. One is a rich, young, but dowdy widow in whom he awakens the sense of tasteful personal adornment; the second, a nineteen-year-old millionairess with twenty millions and a taste for adventure; the third, his former college sweetheart who has run away from her husband to express her individuality in New York. The time is short but the predicaments that he falls into as a result of his escorting are many and amusing. Though actually innocent, he seems to be continually caught in compromising acts. But after all, his adventures end happily"— Book review digest.

819. ————. *Times have changed*. New York: McBride, 1923. 300p.

"Mark O'Rell [of New York City and environs] departed from the beaten path only a step or two. He meant no harm and did none. But when his wife looked for him in the accustomed place, he was with a chorus lady and a sweet girl graduate of the high school whereof Mark was principal. And they had all been to a masked ball. He was also being followed by a couple of thugs with felonious intent; and he was himself a fugitive from the law, having assaulted and escaped from a police officer. One step at a time did it, and he never meant any harm. It was only that people did not understand; they wanted explanations of everything which, when he was among friends, would have been taken for granted."

Davis, Frederick William, 1858-1933. See under his pseudonym: Campbell, Scott, 1858-1933.

Davis, Katherine, joint author. *Lucifer Land.* **See Item $824.**

820. **Davis, Harold McGill.** *The city of endeavor*; **a religious novel devoted to the interests of good citizenship in the City of Brooklyn, New York.Brooklyn: Collins & Day, 1985. vii, 98p.**

In his preface the author states: "I cannot understand how a man, and especially a follower of Jesus Christ, can countenance the drinking of liquor when he knows that liquor drinking is responsible for 80 per cent of the crimes in this country." The storekeeper, Carl Berg, and his wife attend a prayer meeting at Brooklyn's Plymouth Church sponsored by the Christian Endeavor Society. The Brooklyn Christian Endeavor Union forms a Citizenship Committee, one of whose aims is to close the many saloons that infest the 'City of Churches.' Bert is an enthusiastic supporter and he and his wife are gratified when their two wayward sons are transformed; one of them, Horace, stops drinking, marries, and joins Christian Endeavor. By the story's conclusion most of the goals of the Citizenship Committee are met.

821. **Davis, John A., d. 1897.** *Tom Bard, and other Nortonville boys.* **Philadelphia: Presbyterian Board of Publications, 1883. 408p.**

Tom Bard is one of a company of boys in the village of 'Nortonville' (located near New York City) whose high spirits sometimes create mischief that draws censure from the citizens of the community. The author was a clergyman and his story has didactic overtones.

822. **Davis, Kathryn, 1946- .** *The girl who trod on a loaf*; **a novel. New York: Knopf; distributed by Random House, 1933. 399p.**

The convoluted, rather unlikely friendship of two women living in Upstate New York has an unusual result. Helle Ten Brix is a Danish composer; Frances Thorn, a waitress in an airport diner, has twin 10-year-old daughters, Flo and Ruby. Helle dies as the novel opens; she has left behind an unfinished opera (the title of which, the title of the novel, is derived from a translated Hans Christian Andersen tale), which is willed to Frances. Frances' two girls share most of the residue of Helle's estate. There are flashbacks to early 20th century Denmark and Helle's despondent family life.

214

823. Davis, Mildred B. *The invisible boarder*. New York: Random House, 1974. **214p.**

"None of the residents of a Long Island boardinghouse is safe from suspicion as Norma Garretson returns after a four-year absence to seek out the person who murdered her young child. Under an assumed name and desperately trying to preserve her alias, Norma devotes herself to less than discrete and occasionally off-target sleuthing, but she eventually discovers the culprit and a new romance"—Kirkus reviews.

824. ————. *Lucifer Land*, **by Mildred Davis & Katherine Davis. New York: Random House, 1977. 326.**

The American Revolution had devastating consequences for Westchester County, New York. The British and the rebel armies were both destructive to the countryside and its inhabitants. Families that had lived peacefully together before the war were suddenly on opposite sides when the conflict broke out. The heroine in the novel is Cassie, oldest of the Bewdham daughters; she has a romantic connection with a mysterious character named Gideon. However, the plot of the story is of much less interest than the fairly accurate description of the historical events and locales.

825. Davis, Richard Harding, 1864-1916. *Gallegher and other stories*. **New York: Scribner, 1891. vii, 236p.**

But for 'Gallegher' and 'There were ninety and nine' all the short stories in this collection (ten in all) have the aura of New York City life in the last two decades of the 19th century. The wealthy and elegant Courtlandt Van Bibber of New York's 'Four Hundred' appears in the final three pieces while low-lives and the socially correct appear in the five other 'New York' stories. Contents: Gallegher: a newspaper story.—A walk up the avenue.—My disreputable friend, Mr. Raegen.—The other woman.—The trailer for Room no. 8.—'There were ninety and nine'.—The cynical Miss Catherwaight.—Van Bibber and the swan-boats.—Van Bibber's burglar.—Van Bibber as best man.

826. ————. *Van Bibber*, **and others. New York: Harper, 1892. 249p.**

Courtlandt Van Bibber is an elegant New York man-about-town who roams the city searching for varied experiences. He has the money and leisure to frequent the best restaurants (e.g., Delmonico's), clubs, the theater, and even look in on some of the less desirable aspects of life in New York City. Roughnecks Hefty Burke and Rags Regan are the focus of other tales in the collections. Contents: Her first appearance.—Van Bibber's manservant.—The hungry man was fed.—Van Bibber at the races.—An experiment in economy.—Mr. Traver's first hunt.—Love me, love my dog.—Eleanore Cuyler.—A recruit at Christmas.—A parton of art.—Andy McGee's chorus girl.—a Leander of East River.—How Hefty Burke got even.—Outside the prison.—An unfinished story.

827. ————. *Vera the medium.* **Illustrated by Frederic Dorr Steele. New York: Scribner, 1908. 216p.**

Winthrop, district attorney for New York City, falls for Vera, a medium involved in a criminal conspiracy—the victim, Cyrus Hollowell, is being swindled by Judge Gaylor with Vera's assistance. She discloses the plot to Winthrop, but Hollowell wants her punished anyway. Winthrop refuses to indict Vera since he is aware that Hollowell has used legal trickery to amass his fortune.

Davis, Martha Wirt, 1905-1952. See: Van Arsdale, Wirt, 1905-1952.

828. Dawe, Margaret, 1957- . *Nissequott.* **New York: New Directions, 1992. 300p.**

Sheila Gray, the narrator, tells us that 'this is the story of my face.' The scene is 'Nissequott', Long Island, a suburban community in the late 1960s and early 1970s. Sheila, smart and self-conscious, deals with eccentric parents, school life and her own hangups and the big questions: should she undergo plastic surgery to remove the bags under her eyes?

829. Dawid, Annie, 1960- . *York Ferry.* **New York: Cane Hill Press, 1992. 188p.**

The Adirondack town of 'York Ferry' had once survived fairly well on the money generated by the presence of summer residents, but as more viable cities not too far away expanded, it declined. The Pinny family is involved in the destiny of the town. Vernon Pinny departed in 1960 from his wife and five children to search in Belgium for the burial plot of a Jewish woman he had an affair with during the Second World War (he never gets there.) Two of the Pinny children are out of work when the grocery store that had employed them closes. Another Pinny, an alcoholic, has a brief romance with an Israeli exchange student. The only girl in the family joins the Coast Guard to get away from York Ferry, but finds it just about as confining. The story concludes in the 1970s with the town's small talk and creature comforts surviving despite further misfortunes.

De Andrea, William L[louis] 1952- . See: DeAndrea, William L[ouis] 1952- .

830. Dawson, William James, 1854-1928. *A prophet in Babylon*; **a story of social. New York: Chicago, Revell, 1907. 366p.**

"John Gaunt, the rector of a prosperous New York church, awakens from the preaching which has been along the line of least resistance, [and] 'speaks out', consequently incurring the wrath of his fat flock, and finally [goes] out into the highways according to his Master's bidding—and establishes a great, unselfish League of Universal Service, a new social force, that League of Universal Service, whose emblem is the Cross, whose motto is the union of all who love in the service of all who suffer"—Review of reviews.

831. De Brosé, Edward, pseud. *A modern pharisee.* **New York: G.W. Dillingham, 1895. 266p.**

"The modern pharisee is Egbert Makepeace, a leading member of the village church of 'Redfern' [New York]. He wins the love of Judge Carlyle's daughter [Charlotte] who earlier had been the object of affections of Willard Mitchell, a student at Columbia University. Charlotte, [made aware of the defects of Makepeace's character], prefers social ostracism to marriage with him [despite her father's urging of the union]. Subsequent events reveal Makepeace's real character, [Charlotte and Willard find one another again and marry]. The novel claims to be an exposé of some of the shame in modern life"—Annual American catalogue.

832. [De Cordova, Robert J.] *Miss Fizzlebury's new girl*; a truly domestic story. **With illus. by C.B. Canton. New York: G.W. Carleston, 1878. 160p.**

Those who had worked for the Fizzleburys said they kept the "meanest, stingiest and most miserable [house] in all the City of New York." Fred Parkin, a friend of Otto Potthausen, a baker's son disdained by the elder Fizzleburys, but loved by their daughter Arabella, agrees to apply for a maid's position in the Fizzlebury household. Hired, Fred acts as go-between for Otto and Arabella. A spurious, penniless French count, Monsieur Couac, enters as a suitor for Arabella's hand. The embarrassments suffered by Parkin as Mary Murphy, the new girl, the mix-ups as both Otto and Couac attempt to elope with Arabella, are resolved in the end when Mr. Fizzlebury's wealth evaporates on Black Friday and he and his wife must adopt a more humble lifestyle. Couac attaches himself to a wealthy widow and Otto marries Arabella. Parkin vows that henceforth, he will dress only in male attire.

833. De Kay, Charles, 1848-1935. *The Bohemian*; a tragedy of modern life. **New York: Scribner, 1878. 107p.**

Perhaps the reader should not take this novella too seriously. Its hero is De Courcy Plantagenet Lee, cashier in a dry goods store, and member of the Expressionists, a group of bohemian 'intellectuals' in Washington Square headed by Harpalion Bagger, a would-be writer/poet. De Courcy's improvident father, Major James De Courcy Lee, comes from Lynchburg, Va. to borrow money from his penniless son. The Major has aristocratic pretensions which do not fit well with Bagger's rants against New York City's caste system. De Courcy rescues Adelaide Bryce from an embarrassing situation and this wealthy, carefree woman takes a fancy to the young man. Their love affair is shattered when he finds Adelaide in a compromising position with Seward Peel, Adelaide's former lover. The stricken De Courcy throws himself in front of an oncoming train. Unhappy Adelaide eventually marries the philanderer, Seward Peel.

834. De Koven, Anna Farwell, 1860 or 2-1953. *A sawdust doll.* **Chicago: Stone and Kimball, 1895. 237p.**

"Alexander Rivington, when fifty years old, was called upon to help an old friend in financial difficulties, and this led to his marriage with the friend's daughter, Helen, a young, beautiful, emotional girl of twenty years. The years passed quietly in their New York City home, when Philip Aytoun, a young artist and former lover, comes upon the scene. Mrs. Rivington controls her love, and Aytoun goes out of her life to his own misery"—Annual American catalogue.

De Koven, Mrs. Reginald, b. 1860 or 2-1953. See De Koven, Anna Farwell, 1860 or 2-1953.

835. **De Leon, Thomas Cooper, 1839-1914.** *Juny*; or, *Only one girl's story*. **A romance of the society crust—upper and under. Mobile [Ala.]: Gossip Print Co., 1890. 271p.**
   "Opening in a moonshine's camp, in the oldest mountains of North Carolina, the story shifts to New York, showing various phases of the great city, in the salon, the clubs, and the slums. A beautiful octoroon is a prominent actor in these scenes—her story being sad and tragical. "Juny' is a waif found in the moonshine's camp. The mystery of her birth remains a mystery through many chapters"—Annual American catalogue.

836. **De Montalvo, Marie, d. 1950.** *Burning witches*. **New York: Sears, 1927. 341p.**
   "The heroine, Sedenna Blue, eighteen, comely, high-spirited, ends a family squabble by leaving home to earn her livelihood in New York. A year later we find her among the emancipated fold of Greenwich Village, being wooed by and seducing John Bradley, a bashful, straight-laced young Bostonian. It is the woman who pays when, helpless to avert approaching motherhood, unknown to the missing John, Sedenna bears a baby girl. John, we are sure, would have done the right thing had he known of Sedenna's plight; instead he innocently weds another. That old rogue coincidence here succeeds in bringing to pass customary improbabilities, contriving the death of Sedenna in a railroad wreck, but sparing the child, who is then adopted and reared by John and his unsuspecting wife"—Saturday review of literature.

De Steuch, Harriet Henry, 1897?-1974. See: Henry, Harriet, 1897?-1974.

Deventer, Emma Murdock van. See under her pseudonym: Lynch, Lawrence L.

837. **De Witt, Julia A. Woodhull, d. 1906.** *Life's battle won*. **New York: Hunt & Eaton, 1893. 372p.**
   "The power of Christian influence in moulding characters so that they may stand firm in life's battles is the author's keynote. Describes . . . incidents of the Civil War and introduces [quite briefly] General Grant and President Lincoln. Life in the tenement-house district of New York City receives [a much larger share of] attention"—Annual American catalogue. The heroine is

Elsie, wealthy Judge Peters' daughter; she and the Judge are people of high social position, residents of 'Vertville' near New York. After the Judge dies, Elsie is drawn into social concerns by Margaret Fleming, who lost her child and her husband, Robert, in the Civil War. One result is Elsie's financing of housing (tenements, etc.) for residents of the great city's slums.

838. Deal, Babs H., 1929- . *Waiting to hear from William.* **Garden City, N.Y.: Doubleday, 1975. 181p.**

William McLaughlin died in Ireland, but he left behind a will that enjoins his brother Hank, wife Flora and friend Ted Gordon to wait in the charming McLaughlin country house in Dutchess County, New York for his return. You see, William, an occultist, has no doubt that he will rise from a 'temporary' death to greet them once again. Minnie, McLaughlin's house-keeper, and Deirdre, a beautiful woman whose origins are unknown, are also among those who await their master. A dream-like aura and memories of the past enfold the group.

839. Dean, Amber, 1902-1985. *August incident.* **Garden City, N.Y.: Published for the Crime Club by Doubleday, 1951. 182p.**

"As kidnappers, Tom and Thala Diggs had a superb plan. They enrolled their small victim with a group of Fresh Air children going to upper New York State for a vacation. In this way the child was well hidden from his anxious parents and yet not a burden on the kidnapers themselves. Unfortunately for the Diggs, they picked a vacation spot this year that had also been picked by a convalescent Treasury agent. And it was he who succeeded in blowing the case sky high"—New York herald tribune books.

840. ————. *Be home by eleven.* **New York: Putnam, 1973. 190p.**

"Why does Conrad, a new young man on a summer job, disappear after a first date with Mary, a very nice girl? And why is she so uncomfortable with Ross Muskingum, one of those losers ever since he was abandoned as a child? And won't you be able to guess what has happened long before you find out that Ross once tied up some cats in a cleaner's plastic bags? Even so you won't lose interest since it takes place in one of those Upstate New York towns where people are still folks"—Kirkus reviews.

Dean, Amber, 1902-1985. *The blonde is dead.* **See note under Item #842.**

841. ————. *Bullet proof.* **Garden City, N.Y.: Published for the Crime Club by Doubleday, 1960. 191p.**

The story's "principal concern is a shambling sixteen-year-old with a gun and an animal cunning that (with luck) keep him on the run somewhere in New York State in spite of alerted and alert police. So that when he decides he needs a car and happens on young Hallie Brown's, the situation is more than just scary. . . . The genuine grits in this story stay through a slippery, long night of apprehension"—New York herald tribune books.

842. ————. *Call me Pandora.* Garden City, N.Y.: Published for the Crime Crime Club by Doubleday, 1946. 220p.

Also published under the title: The blonde is dead (Mystery Novel Classics, 1946). Upstate New York's 'Old Village' is the home of Abbie Harris, a widow, who has purchased an apartment house there. She is much disconcerted when she discovers that she has inadvertently also acquired a hairdressing salon. Abbie is even more distraught when the body of the salon's former owner turns up. Max Johnson, Army Intelligence operative and Abbie's friend, calls upon Police Lieutenant York. York and Max uncover a flurry of criminal activities while Abbie does a little independent detection that leads to frightening results.

843. ————. *Canticleer's muffled crow.* Garden City, N.Y.: Published for the Crime Club by Doubleday, 1945. 187p.

"Abbie Harris, plump widow of 'Old Village' [on an Upstate New York lake] works hard and with some success at being an early Rinehart narrator in this rather tangled tale of love, war-time secrets and what-not. She was already worried about a sweet young girl's emotional life when an unknown woman on the bus slipped her a brown envelope—and the woman was found dead the next day. Then Max Johnson, [Army] Intelligence man, came home with some fighting cocks and things took a turn that confused even Sheriff Dunbar"—New York herald tribune books.

844. ————. *Collector's item.* Garden City, N.Y.: Published for the Crime Club by Doubleday, 1953. 192p.

A Columbia University professor engaged in research in New York State's Finger Lakes region is suspected of being the perpetrator when one of his chief competitors, a collector of antiques, is murdered. The Upstate wanderings of Joseph Bonaparte, Napoleon I's brother, form part of the background of the story. The real murderer is a chilling character; two minor villains and a beautiful young woman are also in the cast.

845. ————. *Dead man's float.* Garden City, N.Y.: Published for the Crime Club by Doubleday, 1944. 180p.

"A gorgeous young blonde named Bethine [Colt] who seems to be indifferent toward her husband, a salesman of dental supplies, is found drowned under a float in 'Lake Ogg' [in Upstate New York] rather to the relief of the ladies in the other cottages of the resort. The mystery is cleared up by a middle-aged widow [Abbie Harris], a pillar of the community, after a series of mishaps of the type likely to befall ladies who hunt murderers in empty houses at night. Her family doctor, described as lovable in a grumpy way, helps out too"— New Yorker. Max Johnson, formerly of Army Intelligence, almost gets killed in a boating accident—a friend of Abbie, he lives nearby with his wife and their three little girls.

846. ————. *Deadly contact.* **Garden City, N.Y.: Published for the Crime Club by Doubleday, 1963. 190p.**

"The story is placed in Rochester's main Post Office building and in a soon-to-be-discarded Highway Post Office vehicle" (verso of t.p.). When Jim Filmore, the vehicle driver, is electrocuted as he touches a loose cable, Henry Granger and Jane Lambert, both of whom work for the Post Office, come to the realization that Henry was the intended victim. They suspect that mail theft may be the factor driving the criminal[s] to extreme measures.

847. ————. *The devil threw dice.* **Garden City, N.Y.: Published for the Crime Club by Doubleday, 1954. 187p.**

A large cast of characters marches through this mystery novel set in Upstate New York: Abbie Harris, a bubbly newsmonger, being especially noteworthy. The puzzle posed is: who killed Mrs. Tina Burch with an Indian artifact? The unpleasant Mrs. Burch easily aroused the murderous instincts of any number of people. An unsought confession, surrounded by much commotion, provides the answer.

848. ————. *The Dower chest.* **New York: Putnam, 1970. 187p.**

A mystery, whose scene is a handsome old house on U. S. Route 15 in the Finger Lakes region of New York State: The Millards, Harry and Grace, are owners of an antique business. Harry, a retired wood pattern maker, has gone off to purchase additional items and Grace receives a shipment of furniture. Among these pieces is a Pennsylvania Dutch dower chest. The chest must be an object of deep desire for it keeps disappearing and reappearing. Harry, back from his trip, peers into this dilemma and in so doing gets involved with the local Mafia, arson, abduction and murder—all this in what one had thought was an area of peace and quiet.

849. ————. *No traveller returns.* **Garden City, N.Y.: Published for the Crime Club by Doubleday, 1949. 189p.**

When an ancient country inn in New York State becomes the locale of conspiracy and murder, an in-residence detective with a background in federal intelligence techniques takes charge of the investigation.

850. ————. *Snipe hunt.* **Garden City, N.Y.: Published for the Crime Club by Doubleday, 1949. 219p.**

"Two Treasury men, John Trzeciak and Orville Smith, are chasing a counterfeiting gang and the hunt leads them to a small community in Upstate New York. There's some pretty brutal action before they discover the gang's hideout, and they have to enlist the help of a local government man, Max Johnson. The daughter of the engraver who had mysteriously disappeared has a lot to do with solving the case and provides a romantic interest too"—New York herald tribune book review.

851. ————. *Something for the birds.* **Garden City, N.Y: Published for the**

Crime Club by Doubleday, 1959. 190p.

A trio of thieves gets away with robbing the Iroquois Federal Bank in Buffalo. As they flee with their loot two mix-ups land them in a small Upstate community and into the purview of two bird-watchers, young Mrs. Bryant and her friend Dot Cobb. The police do finally nab the robbers, but the two women offer the law no information relative to the three crooks.

852. ————. *Ticket to Buffalo*. Garden City, N.Y.: Published for the Crime Club of Doubleday, 1951. 219p.

"An atmospheric and feminine mystery in which an old crime is solved by a young couple on their honeymoon. Tammis Ford was a young geologist who had come to Washington to find a job and in five days had fallen in love with and married a fellow-geologist, Scott Wood. On their honeymoon they stop over in Buffalo, Scott's home, where a year before his father had committed suicide. There, for the first time, they begin to suspect that the suicide might have been murder. A letter from Scott's father accidentally starts them on the trail. It leads to a housewife who hits them over the head with a mop; a fortune in cash concealed in a rolled-up map; and a sympathetic policeman who helps Tammis follow a path marked by the turquoise beads from her own necklace"—New York herald tribune books.

853. ————. *Wrap it up*. Garden City, N.Y.: Published for the Crime Club by Doubleday, 1946. 222p.

"More uproar in Harris Cove, a summer colony in the Finger Lakes region, which has been the scene of several mysteries of this series. Abbie Harris, one of the two middle-aged Harris Sisters recounts in her usual voluble way, just how her psychoneurotic nephew, accused of murdering his best friend, is cleared of the charge by Max Johnson, who always does the amateur detection around Harris Cove"—New Yorker.

854. Dean, Leon W., 1889- . *Guns over Champlain*. New York: Rinehart, 1946. 245p.

The young Vermonter, Asa Barnum, is into a cauldron of danger and adventure in 1813. He enlists in the American Navy with Lieutenant (later Commodore) Thomas McDonough as his commanding officer. Captured, Asa and his companion, Carter Wayne, spend time on a British prison ship, escape, go into winter quarters and are in the thick of the Battle of Lake Champlain at Cumberland Head/Bay, New York in Sept. 1814, an American victory.

855. DeAndrea, William L., 1952- . *Killed on the rocks*. New York: Mysterious Press, 1990. 232p.

The possibility that G.B. Dost, corporate raider and recent purchaser of a TV station, may be in harm's way brings former military policeman Matt Cobb to billionaire Dost's estate in the Adirondacks. In the morning following a blizzard that KO's the phone line, Dost's body is discovered on the rocks lining the driveway. There are no footprints near the corpse; Cobb questions houseguests, family members and Dost's insecure son Barry. Another murder occurs; it is connected to G.B. Dost's last message as left on an unplugged TV set. Cobb has no easy task finding answers from the few leads he has to work with.

856. ————. *Killed with a passion*. Garden City, N.Y.: Published for the Crime Club by Doubleday, 1983. 177p.

The story "centers on a domestic murder-mystery unconnected to Matt [Cobo's] job [as a TV-network troubleshooter]. The throat-battered victim [is] Upstate New York heiress Debra Whitney who was about to marry a preppy swain after jilting longtime lover Dan Morris (Matt's old college chum) for the umpteenth time. So karate expert Dan—who was heard to say "I'm going to stop that marriage if I have to strangle her!"—is the prime suspect. And Matt, Upstate for hearings on cable licensing . . . decides to clear his pal's name, with help from lawyer Eve (an old, rekindled flame) and the loyal assistants up from New York City. Unfortunately, there are only one or two other possible culprits—and it's easy to spot the killer. But Matt is a bright, if occasionally smirky narrator [and there] is a strong subplot"—Kirkus reviews.

857. Deaner, Janice. *Where blue begins*. New York: Dutton, 1992. 423p.

Maddie, a 10-year-old, wants to know why her mother, Lana, a semi-invalid, is so overwrought after the family has moved to an Upstate New York village where her father Leo has accepted a position on the music faculty of a small college. Leo has renewed his interest in jazz music while Lana spends most of her time keeping a journal. The precocious Maddie learns a few things about her parents' life in New York City with its charged atmosphere of brothels, jazz clubs in Harlem and vestiges of violence and racism—and Maddie has to deal with the data she has uncovered and face parents whose marriage is tottering on the brink of failure.

858. Debrett, Hal. *Before I wake*. New York: Dodd, Mead, 1949. 211p.

Following the death of her father, April Haddon and Mr. Haddon's second wife, April's stepmother—they heartily dislike one another—have an 11-day confrontation in the Long Island home left by Mr. Haddon. While April's stepmother may be a vicious, dishonest individual, April herself may be just as responsible for the tragedy that ensues.

859. Decker, Malcolm [Grove]. *The rebel and the turncoat*. New York: Whittlesey House, 1949. 250p.

"Historical novel of New York and Philadelphia during the [American] Revolution. The hero is young Henry Prince, nephew of a New York Tory bookseller. For some time Henry could not decide where his loyalty lay, but eventually he chose the side of the colonies. Two girls helped in this decision—one a Tory belle, the other a spy for General Washington"—Book review digest.

860. Dee Jonathan. *The liberty campaign.* **New York: Doubleday, 1993. 272p.**

Gene Trowbridge has spent his working years in the advertising business and is looking forward to a 'quiet life' as a Long Island suburbanite when he meets a new arrival in the community, a Brazilian, Albert Ferdinand. The latter seems to be a most likeable addition to the neighborhood and Trowbridge forms a close relationship with him. Then word leaks out that Ferdinand is an illegal immigrant, a former army officer who terrorized Brazilian 'leftists.' Mrs. Trowbridge and others begin to question Gene's continuing association with Ferdinand and he has to determine just what his future course should be.

861. Deene Harley. *Cortlandt Laster, capitalist.* **Chicago: Laird & Lee, 1892. 326p.**

"Cortlandt Laster, a mature married man and American of wealth, sojourning in Paris, is enamored of Zelia Van Cleet, a beautiful Southern girl. He finally makes it worth Mrs. Van Cleet's while to remove with her daughter to New York. This step results in a social scandal, which involves the millionaire and Zelia. The former, to extricate himself, concocts a scheme in which are seen not only his dastardly act, but some well-known weaknesses and vices of modern society, a just retribution and a tragedy. The story opens in a fashionable New York gambling house"—Annual American catalogue. Republished in 1896 under the title: *The American duchess*; or, *Cortlandt Laster*, capitalist.

862. DeFilippi, Jim, 1943- . *Blood sugar*; a novel. **New York: HarperCollins, 1992. 275p.**

Long Island detective Joe LaLuna persuades the Nassau County coroner, Dr. Sharon Slabb, to reexamine the body of a victim of drug overdose (or so it has been assumed). The body is that of the husband (Milton) of Joe's high school girlfriend Audie. The autopsy reveals that Milton was actually murdered by the injection of insulin into his eye. Joe, trying to prove wayward Audie had nothing to do with Milton's demise, neglects his sick wife, Madeline, who then is killed in the same way as Milton. Joe's partner, Winky Dink Hraska, stands by him as Joe tries to find the motives for the killings and their perpetrator.

862a. ⸻. *Duck Alley*. **Sag Harbor: Permanent Press, 1999. 253p.**

Two buddies whose youthful years were passed in 'Duck Alley', a rough enclave on Long Island, take radically different turns as adults. Italian-American Jay Tasti is now (1973) a high school English teacher while Hungarian-American Albert Niklozak is a pimp and conduit for stolen merchandise. Arlynn Svenson, one of Jay's students, falsely claims she is pregnant by him, and Jay seeks Albert's help. Arlynn is murdered and perhaps Albert is responsible, at least Jay so believes, and he reluctantly bears witness against his erstwhile friend.

863. Deland, Ellen Douglas, 1860-1923. *Miss Betty of New York.* **Illustrated by Rachael Robinson. New York: Harper, 1908. 284p.**

> This novel for young people follows the friendship and adventures of Betty and Chris (both are about twelve years of age). Originally New Yorkers they go to the country and almost immediately meet with a queer accident, extricating themselves by dint of Betty's fertile wits. Country life is portrayed with humor and understanding. At the end of the story Chris, ever loyal to the memory of his father, takes a giant step out into the world dependent only on his own resources.

Delany, Joseph Francis, 1905- . See under his pseudonym: Dane, Joel Y., 1905- .

864. Delavan, Elizabeth Garnsey. *Charlotte Murray.* **Ovid, N.Y., W.E. Morrison, Printers, c1977. 100p.**

> "Mynderse Mills' is the name the author gives the town which is at the center of her novella, but there seems to be little doubt that Seneca Falls, N.Y. is the actual locale of the story. Place names like Montezuma, Moravia, Auburn, Cayuga, et al., familiar to central New Yorkers, receive mention. Charlotte Murray, the chief character, marries Jamie Wilson just as the Civil War is intensifying. When he dies of consumption contracted on the cold, wet battlefields, Charlotte decides not to remarry, even though pursued by David Harris, a young military surgeon, whom she had once fancied as her lover. David goes on a medical mission to Liberia and Charlotte teaches French at a recently opened girls' school. The story concludes with an implied budding romance between Charlotte and a music teacher, Douglas MacIvers.

865. Dell, Floyd, 1887-1969. *Love in Greenwich Village.* **New York: Doran, 1926. 321p.**

> "A collection of short stories and verse about artists, poets, authors and others in love with life and love in Greenwich Village. [Mr. Dell] describes its [the Village's] glorious past with the mellow cheer of an alumnus recalling his undergraduate days"—Book review digest. Contents: The rise of Greenwich Village.—The kitten and the masterpiece.—Phantom adventure.—The button.—The tigress.—April-May.—'Hallelujah, I'm a bum.'—The ballad of Christopher Street.—A piece of slag.—The ex-Villager's confession.—Green houses.—The fall of Greenwich Village.

866. ————. *Souvenir*; **a novel. Garden City, N.Y.: Doubleday, Doran, 1929. viii, 278p.**

> "Felix Fay, the adolescent protagonist of 'Moon-calf', is now a successful playwright, married for the second time and living in a suburban home [outside New York City] with his sensible, charming wife and two small children. The son of his first marriage, [Prentiss], comes to spend a summer with his father, and in the boy's experiments with life and love in Greenwich Village, Felix Fay lives again the torment and ecstasy of his own youthful

experiences. The characters are all real and attractive people, and their rather difficult relations are described with penetration and humor"—Book review digest.

867. Delman, David, 1924- . *The nice murderers.* **New York: Morrow, 1977. 240p.**
Jacob Horowitz of Nassau County [Long Island] Homicide is looking closely at "Long Island's William & Lizzie Winter—professional thieves, amateur but blasé murders. . . .True, their murder victim is foul . . .he's a Machiavellian millionaire, Piggy Ott, who bankrupts William at poker . . . drops hints about diamonds in the Ott family safe, and appears with a gun (Wm. shoots him first) when the Winters sneak in to lift the ice. And Piggy's survivors are chips of the old blech—salacious second wife, filthy son, . . . psychotic son. . . . They manage to frame each other and kill each other off under the . . . complex supervision of the Winters, who are last seen flying from Monte Carlo to London"—Kirkus reviews.

868. ————. *One man's murder.* **New York: D. McKay, 1975. 165p.**
"A neither very pleasant nor consequential case for Nassau County's Jacob Horowitz, dealing with three marriages which seem to dissolve as easily as the ice in the drinks at a large party given in honor of an aging, impotent and rotten advertising tycoon"—Kirkus reviews.

869. Delmar, Viña. *Bad girl.* **New York: Harcourt, Brace, 1928. 275p.**
"A flirtation begun on a Hudson River excursion boat ends shortly in a hasty marriage and a flat in Harlem. Dotty Healey, typist, and Eddie Collins, a radio mechanic, have everything to discover about each other, about being married and about having a baby"—Book review digest.

870. ————. *Kept woman.* **New York: Harcourt, Brace, 1929. 303p.**
"Hubert Scott sold his business, considered himself, with fifteen thousand dollars, a gentleman of leisure, and found a [Manhattan] shop-girl, Lillian Cory, to help him spend it. Lillian soon adapts herself to the position of 'kept woman', and Hubert, having furnished a [New York] apartment for her, goes less frequently to the home of his wife and son. Careless living and spending rapidly exhaust Hubert's capital. Hubert prefers borrowing to getting a job, but Lillian hopes for better times. Finally, deserted by all her friends and penniless, Lillian goes back to work in a department store"—Book review digest.

871. ————. *Loose ladies.* **New York: Harcourt, Brace, 1929. 299p.**
Short stories about New York City working-class women primarily who are experiencing love affairs—some are virtuous, some are 'bad', shallow and 'cheap.' One could well question the plausibility of a number of the author's characters.

872. Demarest, Virginia. *The fruit of desire*; a novel. New York: Harper, 1910. 331p.

> Released from prison after serving a term in place of his guilty brother, John Kenton finds a job in a small town as a bookkeeper for a railroad company. When his convict past is discovered and he is dismissed from his job, Kenton sets out for New York City accompanied by a girl who too has been running from trouble. The two are presumed to be married by those they meet; but the young woman is anti-marriage and the plot from this point concentrates on how she works her way through her objections.

873. DeMille, Nelson, 1943- . *The Gold Coast.* New York: Warner Books, 1990. 500p.

> "John and Susan Sutter are members in good standing of Long Island's blueblood Gold Coast. John practices tax law and Susan likes to paint, but mostly they ride their horses, have drinks at the club, go skeet shooting, sail on the yacht, and engage in oh-so-witty banter with each other and their snooty peers. Life changes dramatically one spring day when Mafia don Frank Bellarosa moves into the estate adjoining the Sutters' own impressive digs. Frank is reasonably charming, a hail-fellow-well-met sort of guy ostensibly looking for a little peace and a lot of status. While the locals recoil, John and Susan are intrigued. Then the IRS catches John with his taxable income pants down. Bellarosa has 'friends' who can help John, but the price he pays is all too high. With the don under investigation for a drug-related murder, John agrees to represent him, perjures himself along the way, and finds out that Susan is getting it on with his client. The conclusion of this talky tale—filled with generally unlikable characters—is steeped in blood and melodrama"—Booklist.

874. ————. *Plum Island.* New York: Warner Books, 1997. 511p.

> Plum Island is a federally restricted piece of land off the southern shore of Long Island that contains government research facilities. Likeable Tom and Judy Gordon, both scientists who had worked there, were unexplainably murdered—because of their research on Plum Island or because they were too close to a treasure-trove? New York detective John Corey, recovering at his uncle's home on the Island from gunshot wounds, pressed by the local authorities, agrees to help investigate the puzzling homicides.

875. Deming, Philander, 1829-1915. *Adirondack stories.* Boston: Houghton, Osgood, 1880. 192p.

> The Adirondack wilderness depicted by Deming in his tales was a harsh environment that offered little in the way of economic activity or security to the human settlers. They either endured in relative silence the adversities visited upon them or were sometimes driven to extremities of behavior. Nevertheless the beauty of the region shines through Deming's narratives. What was true of the vast area over 115 years ago remains much the same

today. Contents: Lost.—Lida Ann.—John's trial.—Joe Baldwin.—Willie.—Benjamin Jacques.—Ike's wife.—An Adirondack neighborhood.

876. ————. *The story of a pathfinder*. **Boston: Houghton, Mifflin, 1907. 259p.**

In part autobiographical (the writer's experiences as a court and legislative reporter in Albany) with four long short stories about young men in the aforementioned city and Upstate New York who, in two instances, carry promises made to their lady loves to extremes. 'In slavery days' deals with a presumed Black man of superior intellect who ultimately refuses to abide by the snubs and humiliations proffered by White acquaintances—the irony of his situation is made manifest in the story's final three paragraphs. Contents: The story of a pathfinder: The courts; Story writing.—A lover's conscience.—A stranger in the city.—Mr. Green's promise.—In slavery days.—The secret story.

877. ————. *Tompkins and other folks*; **stories of the Hudson and Adirondacks. Boston: Houghton, Mifflin, 1885. 223p.**

Characteristic sketches of New York State life and scenes: In the title story Tompkins recalls his younger days in Upstate New York, including an 'unromantic' love affair, before decamping for Chicago and a career in auctioneering. 'The court in Schoharie' describes a work-week in the court of a Catskill village. Contents: Tompkins.—Rube Jones.—Jacob's insurance.—Mr. Toby's wedding journey.—Hattie's romance.—The court in Schoharie.—An Adirondack home.

878. **Denison, Mary Andrews, 1826-1911.** *Captain Molly*; **a love-story. Boston: Lee and Shepard, 1897. 251p.**

A young woman turns away from her background of comfort and wealth and offers her services to the Salvation Army. She is assigned to several slum areas in New York City and acquires the title of 'Captain Molly', working tirelessly to better the conditions of the poor. Her personal life is brightened by a burgeoning romance.

Denison, Mrs. C.W., 1826-1911. See: Denison, Mary Andrews, 1826-1911.

879. **Denison, Thomas Stewart, 1848-1911.** *An iron crown*; **a tale of the Great Republic. Chicago: T.S. Denison, 1879. 560p.**

"The contrasted story of Tom Norwell, a rich wastrel, and Arthur Wilson, a young man fresh from the farm. Tom loses his fortune gambling in the stock market and ends up a lonely man when his fiancée dies of tuberculosis. Arthur makes a fortune in a rich gold strike, and then loses it in a panic engineered by a stock manipulator. He settles down to a quiet country life with the young schoolteacher he marries. There are two strikes, one by miners, the other by railroad workers, both violent and neither having much relevance to the already confused plot. The author is writing a condemnation of Wall Street manipulators and a warning to young men to avoid get-rich-quick schemes. The strikes are only another example of the economic chaos Wall Street is creating"—Blake, F.M. The strike in the American novel.

880. **Derby, Aleck, pseud.** *Ida Goldwin*; **the perils of fortune. New York: R.M. Witt, 1876. 323p.**

Ida Goldwin, rightful heir to her father's Irish estates, is spirited away in infancy to America by hirelings of her uncle, Edward Goldwin. Reared in the slums of New York City by a brutal Irish couple Ida falls into the hands of devious, greedy Madame Veazie who names her Cora Veazie. Meanwhile Edward Goldwin with his two sons, William and Arthur, migrates to Rochester, N.Y. William chooses a life of debauchery; Madame Veazie manipulates Arthur, a bank clerk in New York. He falls in love with Cora/Ida; however he is railroaded to Sing Sing after the failure of Madame Veazie's plan to poison Edward Goldwin. Cora/Ida flees from the Madame and finds refuge with the kind Madam Küster. Detective Hawk infiltrates Madame Veazie's vicious circle, secures the release of Arthur Goldwin and enables repentant Edward Goldwin to reclaim his niece. Goldwin also forgives his prodigal sons and Arthur marries Ida.

881. **Desmond, Alice Curtis, 1897- .** *Alexander Hamilton's wife*; **a romance of the Hudson. Illustrated with photos and with drawings by the author. New York: Dodd, Mead, 1952. 273p.**

"Fictionalized biography of Alexander Hamilton and his wife . . . Betsy Schuyler, daughter of the famous Revolutionary General Philip Schuyler. Includes a good deal of historical background about the life in New York State in colonial times and later. Includes information for finding the historic houses, etc. mentioned."—Book review digest.

882. **Desmond, Harry William, 1863-1913.** *The heart of woman*; **the love story of Catrina Rutherford contained in the writings of Alexander Adams, trans-Mitted to Harry Desmond. New York: J.F. Taylor, 1902. 311p.**

The American Revolution in its early days with New York City as a primary locale: The leading male character is a patriot who is in love with two women; when he selects Catrina Rutherford, another man (who is also attracted to Catrina and whose sympathies lie with the British cause) does his best to create friction between his rival and Catrina. The story brings in a number of historical figures and scenes including military activity in the contending armies and a British prison ship.

883. **Devinne, Paul.** *The days of prosperity*; **a vision of the century to come. New York: G.W. Dillingham, 1902. 271p.**

A futuristic novel in the wake of Edward Bellamy's *Looking Backward*. The protagonist, a journalist, meets a strange doctor in one of New York City's East Side cafés. The latter induces the journalist to fall into a deep sleep that lasts for a hundred years. He awakens in the year 2000 and begins charting a way of life and behavior, which will be most beneficial to mankind.

884. Devlin, Ellen, 1949- . *Hide and seek.* New York: Putnam, 1986. 286p.

Eleven-year-old Joan Flanagan is a newcomer to 'Meriden', an Upstate New York town on the Hudson. The first friend she makes there is Una McGraw who has a beautiful but retarded sister, Semmie. Una and Semmie live with their disquieting mother, 'Mrs. Mildred'; the latter has separated from her husband and son and is presently cohabiting with an odious man, a drug pusher and user, as Una and Joan discover when Una steals needles and white powder from him. He is most likely the person who is attempting to seduce poor Semmie. Nevertheless, Mrs. Mildred McGraw states her intention of marrying this despicable individual and moving to Boston. Joan persuades the two girls to run away. This act is followed by a series of disclosures and penalties that right the situation.

885. Devoore, Ann. *Oliver Iverson*, his adventures during four days and nights in the City of New York in April of the year 1890. Chicago: H.S. Stonc, 1899. 181p.

Poet and hero, Oliver Iverson of 'Peach Valley' in Upstate New York, decides to try his luck in the State's largest city. In the course of his trip to New York City he meets a clergyman, John Penfield, his daughter Charlotte, and an agreeable old gentleman, Joe Cross. Cross offers him lodging at his Second Avenue mansion. The old gentleman passes himself off as a philanthropic soul who reforms criminals and returns them to society. Oliver soon learns otherwise. Cross's mansion is actually a conduit for culprits sought by the law. The Rev. Penfield is in trouble with Cross's gang because he was in part responsible for the incarceration of one of them. Oliver takes matters into his hands; with the help of old Jacob, Cross's manservant, he fights off the gang and shields Mr. Penfield and Charlotte until the police arrive. Charlotte and Oliver (already married) and Mr. Penfield retire to Oliver's home in Peach Valley.

886. Dey, Frederic Van Rensselaer, 1861 or 5-1922. *The last woman*, by Rose Beeckman [pseud.] Front. by Howard Chandler Christy. Illustrated by by Bert Knight. New York: W.J. Watt, 1909. 317p.

The story of two men of great wealth—the older of the two has a beautiful, proud daughter who is carrying on a love affair of sorts with the younger man. The father needs the trifling sum of twenty million dollars to get him out of financial difficulties, and proposes to the younger man that they tell the daughter that the loan hinges upon immediate marriage to her lover. This, of course, brings about many complications, fits and starts as the scene shifts between New York City and Montana.

887. ————. *The three keys,* by Frederic Ormond [pseud.]. Front. by Harrison Fisher. New York: W.J. Watt, 1909. 301p.

After he has gone through his inheritance Morris Lathrop, a New York man-about-town, contemplates suicide. Then a friend, unaware Lathrop is penniless, asks for a loan to carry him through a fiscal crisis. Lathrop is able to fulfill the request only after Jack Millington, on his way to Chicago, leaves three keys with Lathrop that give him access to Millington's safe deposit boxes. He removes securities from one of the boxes and presents them to the man who asked for the loan. When Millington reappears in New York without warning, Lathrop is faced with a problem.

888. Di Pego, Gerald, 1941- . *Forest things.* **New York: Delacorte Press, 1979. 216p.**

A widow, Edith Rendon, owns Tilema Lodge in the Adirondacks but Til Sharkis, a handyman, is the real caretaker of the resort. Not only that, he is a ladies' man who has been intimate with the widow and is most attractive to whatever women happen to be nearby. The Chase and Demitter families are presently guests at the lodge. The author has a penchant for discussing nature, and introduces a stock 'old man of the mountain' character within the plot. However, when Lyn Chase, 16, precocious beyond her years, almost falls off a cliff, Sharkis is there to save her and these two flee together into the woods.

889. Dick, Herbert G. *Sounding brass*; **a novel. New York: Supplied by the American News Co., 1889. 182p.**

Helena Crosby, a Southern beauty, is selfish and manipulative. She walks away from her fiancé, wealthy New York socialite Jack Ormsby, and marries a bank clerk, Pierre Laneau. Laneau is actually Pierre Mignot, son of a count who is finally ready to forgive him his wayward ways. On the boat to France Pierre dies; Helena gives birth to a male child and leaves him with Theresa de Brolini, Pierre's sister. She marries Mr. Kellogg, an Englishman, and establishes herself in New York social circles. Completely forgetting the son she left in Paris, Helena gives Marie Vincent, adopted daughter of Colonel Barker the millionaire, the affection that she withholds from her second child, plain daughter Florence. Pierre de Brolini comes to New York and is fascinated by Helena Kellogg, unaware that she is his mother. Ormsby confronts Helena with the truth; distraught and disoriented, Helena has a final meeting with Pierre and dies of heart failure.

890. Dick, Trella Lamson, 1889-1974. *Flag in hiding.* **Illustrated by Don Bolognese. New York: Abelard-Schuman, 1959. 175p.**

Randy, 14, and his younger sister, Cynthia, are in constant danger of retaliation by the Tories in their Hudson River Valley surroundings because of their father's active participation in the patriot cause. (He is a spy for General Washington.) The two young people place themselves in more jeopardy when they take care of a wounded rebel soldier.

891. Dickinson, Ellen E. *The King's Daughters*; **a fascinating romance. Philadelphia: Hubbard Bros., 1888. 275p.**

The 'King's Daughters' was an organization founded in 1886 to advance 'Christian living and usefulness in practical good works.' Wealthy Madame Lawrence Fry and her granddaughter, Marion Fry, tired of the constant round of their high society activities, turn to benevolent pursuits among the poor of New York City. Marion is especially energetic in this direction, spurred on by the King's Daughters. She is in love with a sculptor, J. Harvey Lincoln; the latter is frowned upon by her haughty cousin, Clinton Osgood, and not readily accepted by her grandmother. But on a trip abroad Lincoln joins Madame Fry and Marion in Switzerland and he and Marion are wed in Freyborg (Fribourg). Returning to New York City the married couple reside with Madame Fry, connect with the King's Daughters and shortly Harvey is teaching art in night schools. Madame Fry passes away tranquilly.

Dickson, Carter, pseud. See: Carr, John Dickson, 1906-1977.

892. Didier, Charles Peale. *Would any man?* Illustrated by the author. [Baltimore] Williams & Wilkins, 1898. 169p.

The protagonist in this novel is a beautiful young woman, a native of Virginia, who hopes that New York City will polish her talents as an artist. She shares an apartment with another aspiring girl, a music student. Our heroine is somewhat sidetracked when she falls in love with a man of honor. She is honest enough, however, to tell him that there is a skeleton in her past that would be damaging to their relationship. The question is: once the secret is revealed to him, would he still want to marry her, or 'would any man?'

893. Dillon, Mary C. Johnson, d. 1923. *Miss Livingston's companion*; a love story of old New York. With illustrations by E.A. Furman. New York: Century Co., 1911. 434p.

"The hero is a titled young Englishman [Sir Lionel Marchant] who, instead of taking his father's advice to look up the absent mistress of the broad acres joining his home, falls in love with an actress twice his age. To cure him of his infatuation his father sends him to America. There [in New York City] he falls into a conspiracy of matchmakers, the guiding genius of which is his father across the sea. All unwittingly he nibbles at the bait and in time is duly caught [by Mademoiselle Desloge, the charming companion of Miss Livingston]. Woven into the love interest of the tale are the machinations of a French scoundrel who involves the hero in embezzlement. Alexander Hamilton has his case and clears him through as brilliant a coup as one can find anywhere in fiction"—Book review digest. Celebrities other than Hamilton who appear in the novel are Aaron Burr, Robert Fulton, Gouverneur Morris and Washington Irving.

894. [Dimondstein, Boris] *Beyond human power*: ten years; a novel by the author of *The call within*. Edited by Lew Earl Winburg. New York: Bee De Pub. Co., 1930. 208p.

In 1909 the radical and pacifist, Russian-Jew Jacob Rachlin, his wife Judith, and the peasant Mickita leave Czarist Russia for America. They settle in New York City in an apartment near Bronx Park, which serves as a starting point for other immigrants from Russia fleeing from the Czarist tyranny. Jacob becomes a leading contributor to socialist periodicals and establishes, with Mickita's financial aid, the polemical journal Liberty. The outbreak of World War I finds Jacob taking a position of neutrality toward the conflict. When the United States enters the war, Jacob, like Eugene Debs, suffers for his pacifist views. He is elated when the Czar's regime falls before revolutionists, but again is persecuted during the 'Red scare' of the 1920s. The novel ends with Jacob's death in New York in 1929, the result of beatings and imprisonment at hard labor—before he can make his contemplated return to Russia.

895. Disney, Doris Miles, 1907-1976. *The hospitality of the house*. Garden City, N.Y.: Published for the Crime Club by Doubleday, 1964. 183p.

"Mystery story about Mandy O'Brien, eighteen years old, who flies from Boston to Syracuse to spend a week with her pen-pal [Janet]. She becomes conscious of an atmosphere of evil, and her premonitions of sinister happenings are realized"—Book review digest. "From her first glimpse of Janet and family, Mandy is uneasy. A side trip to the farm home of a critically ill grandmother adds qualms"—New York herald tribune book week.

896. Dix, Beulah Marie, 1876-1970. *Mother's son*; a novel. New York: Holt, 1913. iv, 331p.

The family of playboy Hugo von Mehring exiles him to America. The heroine, Betty Willard, a successful playwright, is instrumental in pulling Hugo out of the depths. Although he is not lacking in moral courage, she rejuvenates him. The tale is played out against the background of New York and Boston and vicinity.

Dixon, Martin J. *A child of the slums*. See Item #3633.

897. Dixon, Thomas, 1864-1946. *The foolish virgin*; a romance of today. Illustrated by Walter Tittle, New York: Appleton, 1915. vii, 352p.

"Mary Adams, a young school teacher in New York . . . is the typical 'sheltered' maiden of fancy. She refuses to look facts in the face and dreams of a 'knight' who will some day appear to claim her. In the end, of course, she makes the illogical, ill-considered marriage that would be expected and finds after a too brief honeymoon that she is married to a criminal. She fears that the child to be born to her will inherit his father's weakness, but is reassured by a doctor who preaches the importance of prenatal influence. Regenerative influences are brought to bear on the husband and the story ends happily"—Book review digest.

898. ————. *The one woman*; a story of modern Utopia. Illustrated by B. West

New York: Doubleday, Page, 1903. 351p.

The idealistic New York clergyman, Frank Gordon, has socialistic leanings, but his strong personality brings many people to his church. A wealthy woman, Kate Ransom, supports Gordon's ministry with sizeable gifts of money even when the church's conservative officers object to the overflowing crowds and the direction of the church. Ruth, Frank's wife, feels neglected because of her husband's absorption in his labors; he in turn believes he is in love with Kate Ransom, so he casts off Ruth and 'marries' Kate in a socialistic ritual. Mark Overman, an old friend of the clergyman, falls in love with Kate; in a fit of jealousy Frank Gordon kills him. Twice sentenced to execution Frank is spared at the last moment by the governor of New York State.

899. ————. *The root of evil*; a novel. Illustrated by George Wright. **Garden City, N.Y.: Doubleday, Page, 1911. 407p.**

Because he refuses to cheat in order to acquire a substantial income, a New York lawyer is dropped by the woman he loves. She in turn marries a scheming, exploitative millionaire. Disregarding her obvious greed and frivolousness, the lawyer persists in his love for the woman. Only after the rich husband is faced with financial ruin and, gripped by mortal illness, pleads for life before his medical advisors, does the woman lose her hold on the affections of the lawyer.

900. ————. *The way of a man*; a story of the new woman. Illustrated by **Stockton Mulford. New York: Appleton, 1919. 294p.**

In early 20th century New York City "a famous woman journalist, Ellen West, whose feminism takes in sex freedom, although she has not yet emancipated herself from any of the feminine frailties and obsessions that beautiful women are apt to be encumbered with, who in her own words has not yet 'evolved a soul of her own', falls in love with a man at first sight. She breaks down every objection of his to a free union and has her way only to find her coveted freedom ashes and dust. The story ends with Ellen's 'love-man' marrying Ellen's young niece and miniature copy minus her theories, and Ellen herself finding happiness as the wife of her millionaire admirer of long standing"— Book review digest.

901. **Dobyns, Stephen, 1941- . *The church of dead girls*. New York: Metropolitan Books, c1997. 388p.**

Almost a case history of the fall from grace of a serene, friendly town, 'Aurelius', in Upstate New York. The cause is the particularly horrible murder of three girls whose bodies, with their left hands severed, are discovered in a church loft. Aurelius changes into a place where neighbor distrusts neighbor and finger pointing is common. The community is especially distraught by the return to Aurelius of highly unpopular Aaron McNeal; Aaron's mother had been murdered years earlier and her left hand had been cut off. Witch-hunts and vigilante activity inevitably follow.

902. ———. *Saratoga backtalk.* **New York: Norton, 1994. 221p.**

Since Charlie Bradshaw has been called for jury duty, his associate Vic Plotz becomes the narrator and private investigator in this mystery. The owner of Battlefield Farms, Bernard Logan, hires Vic to check out his wife and her lover who may be plotting to murder him. Logan is killed nevertheless, trampled under horses' hooves. Several more deaths occur at Battlefield Farms and Vic makes some hard, blunt inquiries that only serve to alienate the possible suspects. Charlie now enters the case and it is his milder, sensitive approach that eventually leads to the solution.

903. ———. *Saratoga bestiary.* **New York: Viking Press, 1988. 256p.**

Charlie Bradshaw, Saratoga private eye, delivers the ransom money demanded by the party that stole the painting of a famous racehorse. When the painting is not returned, Charlie wants to know why even though he is dropped from the case. Then a store-owning friend is killed and again unwanted, Charlie investigates. However, Charlie is hired when his friends are robbed while gambling on the Superbowl. His task is to make sense out of these disparate investigations and to find a connection, if any, between them.

904. ———. *Saratoga Fleshpot.* **New York: Norton, 1995. 220p.**

Victor Plotz, sidekick of the Saratoga private eye, Charlie Bradshaw, has a key role in this story about a Saratoga racehorse, Fleshpot, which has been sold for a half million dollars. Plotz wonders if a switch has occurred when he notices that Fleshpot no longer nips people, as was his wont before the sale. Vic's powers of observation win him no popularity contest with the culprits who set up the switch (for such it was). Three murders later, the kidnapping of the real Fleshpot, and a parade honoring Saratoga's retiring police—and clarity of a sort is reached.

905. ———. *Saratoga haunting.* **New York: Viking Press, 1933. 207p.**

Saratoga private detective Charlie Bradshaw has reached the age when he is inclined to look back semi-nostalgically on his early years as a policeman intent on his career, but also locked into a wretched marriage. Oddly enough two cases out of the past are galvanizing elements in Charlie's present. Firstly, the skeleton of Grace Mulholland turns up in the rubble of a torn-down pool hall; she had presumably fled South years ago with thousands of dollars stolen from the insurance company she worked for. Secondly, a disturbed young fellow Charlie had taken an interest in turns out bad anyway and had served 20 years for armed robbery; he places blame for his troubles on Charlie.

906. ———. *Saratoga headhunter.* **New York: Viking Press, 1985. 208p.**

McClatchy, a dishonest jockey who has now turned on former corrupt associates, has been given sanctuary by the Saratoga private eye, Charlie Bradshaw. Nevertheless, hired killers smoke out McClatchy and Charlie comes home to find the jockey's headless body in his dining room. Charlie has been moonlighting as a milkman and has some difficulty taking on this investigation; the Saratoga police are no help, suspicious, as they are that Charlie isn't entirely innocent in the affair. Other murders occur, Charlie's car is bombed, and he utilizes a milk truck to chase down supposed culprits. Horse racing adds flavor to the story and Charlie retains special respect for some 'classical' criminal personages.

907. ————. *Saratoga hexameter.* **New York: Viking Press, 1990. 246p.**
"Three separate cases—a string of murders at a nursing home, a series of burglaries at a swank hotel, and the perverse harassment of a literacy critic at an artist's refuge—conspire to befuddle Saratoga sleuth Charlie Bradshaw and to keep him away from his favorite track as the short racing season slips inexorably away. What's worse, all three cases involve poetry in one way or another, and Charlie, who would rather be scoping out the Daily Double, must pass himself off as a poet to catch one of the evildoers. . . . Bradshaw [has as his confederates] a skirt-chasing house dick and an alcoholic investigator with a delicate cgo" –Booklist.

908. ————. *Saratoga snapper.* **New York: Viking Press, 1986. 260p.**
Resident private eye of Saratoga, N.Y., Charlie Bradshaw has a buddy, Victor Plotz, who takes a snapshot of a group at the bar of the Saratoga hotel Charlie's mother owns. Victor is then unfortunate enough to fall victim to a hit-and-run driver and has to be hospitalized. Charlie, curious about various incidents at the hotel, starts snooping around. One of the hotel's maids dies suddenly; a person in Victor's group photograph commits suicide; and robberies occur at several of Saratoga's liquor stores. When a particularly frightening crime takes place, Charlie protects individuals who are inadvertently drawn in the web.

909. ————. *Saratoga strongbox*; **a Charlie Bradshaw mystery. New York: Viking Press, 1998. 198p.**
Saratoga, N.Y. private investigator Charlie Bradshaw is dragged into an unpleasant situation because his devious buddy, Vic Plotz, has worked out an easy moneymaking scheme. Vic is promised $2,000 if he will pick up a package in Montreal for Felix Weber. Vic is unable to fulfill the mission himself so he hires someone who can and will split the fee fifty-fifty. Before the matter is brought to a conclusion both Charlie and Vic are mixed up with gangsters and a stripper; Charlie surmises that the 'strongbox' of the novel's title will provide a satisfactory resolution to everybody's problems.

910. ————. *Saratoga swimmer.* **New York: Atheneum 1981. 207p.**
Charles Bradshaw is a 'private eye' in Saratoga with more than his share of bad luck recently. He compounds it by allowing an ex-jockey to use his cottage as a hideout; the ex-jockey is murdered (decapitated) and two more slayings occur. The connecting factor in these grisly happenings seem to be

the racehorse, Sweet Dreams; this supposed big winner is actually an imposter, a fact that Charlie's investigations uncover. Charlie himself is almost murdered (a couple of times) and just escapes being burned to death in a stable fire.

911. Doctorow, E.L., 1931- . *Loon Lake.* **New York: Random House, 1979. 258p.**

Set in the 1930s the narrative "covers several picturesque years in the life of [Joe], a young roughneck from Paterson, the son of wretchedly poor mill hands, who runs away from home, joins a gang of hobos, becomes a criminal roustabout, and stumbles accidentally onto Loon Lake, the vast Adirondack estate of the steel tycoon, F.W. Bennett. One of the old industrialist's toys is a gangster's moll who sneaks out of Loon Lake with Joe, and the two settle down for a while in a steel town owned by one of Bennett's many companies. She leaves him, and Joe goes back to Loon Lake [and] is taken in by the old man"—Commentary.

912. ————. *Ragtime.* **New York: Random House, 1975. 270p.**

Although a good portion of the novel is laid in New York City, featuring anecdotal material about historical personages at the turn of the century, it opens in New Rochelle with an unnamed family as the centerpiece of the story. As the novel progresses, it continues to move back and forth from New York City to New Rochelle, and it is those New Rochelle interludes that provide the fictional underpinning of this important novel.

913. Dodd, Anna Bowman Blake, 1855-1929. *The republic of the future*; or, *Socialism a reality.* **New York: Cassell, c1887. 86p.**

"The vision of New York City two hundred years hence, when men and women are equal in all things, children educated by government, all work done by machinery, all competition abolished, all wealth equally distributed, all romance dead, is described in letters to a friend in Sweden. The letters are full of instructive truths, given in innocent comments, without seeming to bear any hidden lesson"—Annual American catalogue.

914. ————. *Struthers, and the comedy of the masked musicians.* **New York: Lovell, Coryell, 1984. vi, 312p.**

The first story is that which concerns us here. It deals with the experiences of a young couple that, having achieved business prosperity, leave their modest Tenth Street flat and launch out upon the tide of New York 'society' life. Their social strivings are due to the snobbery and Anglo-mania of the husband, but the young wife's unaffected freshness and attractiveness are the factors which finally place them within the 'charmed circle' at home and abroad"—Annual American catalogue.

Doesticks, Philander, pseud. See: Thompson, Mortimer, 1831-1875.

915. Doherty, Edward Joseph, b. 1890. *The Broadway murders*; a night club

mystery. Garden City, N.Y.: Doubleday, Doran, 1929. 298p.

Also issued under the title: Murder on the roof. When her alcoholic father, lawyer Anthony Sommers (long separated from his wife and children), is convicted of the murder of racketeer 'Spots' Larkin, Molly Sommers leaves family and fiancé in Wisconsin and comes to New York. Searching for pertinent data that will prove her father's innocence, Molly becomes a singer at the raunchy Corsairs' Club ('perched at the top of the Allegheny Building, sixty stories above Times Square'), scene of most of the story's action. She immerses herself in the culture of the city's bootleggers, gangsters, chorus girls, playboys, thieves, et al., even encouraging the amorous advances of 'Big Joe' Carozzo, owner of the nightclub, and various lowlives. Her quest is rather unsuccessful; however, Geoffrey Platt, wealthy socialite, part-time deputy police commissioner and frequent visitor at the Corsairs' Club, ties the strands of homicide and diamond thefts into a neat, solvable bundle and Molly's father is freed.

Doherty, Edward Joseph, b. 1890. *Murder on the roof.* **See note under Item #915.**

916. Donaldson, Alfred Lee, 1866-1923. *A Millbrook romance, and other tales.* **New York: T. Whittaker, 1893 [c1892] 155p.**

"Millbrook [New York] in the heart of Dutchess County, is the scene of an aged hero's recital of a quaint love story, which he relates to his willing listener because it resembles, excepting in one episode, Longfellow's Evangeline. Included with . . . [it] is: A sound from the past; The story of a picture; A reverie; A pair of gloves; The opal ring; A simple story"—Annual American catalogue.

917. Donaldson, Marion C. *Marguerite's mistake*; a novel. **Chicago: E.A.Weeks, c1899. 462p.**

The scenes of the novel are a suburban college town and its neighboring city (H___) in central New York and the Adirondacks. Orphan Marguerite Brown's mistake is her marriage to domineering Horace LeRoy, co-owner with his brother James of the LeRoy Brothers Bank. Horace is led into unwise investments in mining stock at the urging of wealthy Herbert Graham; the latter, angry and jealous because Marguerite chose Horace rather than him, is on a mission to ruin Horace and the bank. While vacationing in the Adirondacks, Marguerite, her brother Roy (a bank employee) and James LeRoy meet a girl, Helen Keene, cousin to Alexander Keene, Marguerite's new physician. Graham, her self-appointed guardian and administrator of her father's estate had placed Helen in an Adirondack convent. Horace LeRoy, broken by the damage he has done to the failed LeRoy bank and his animosity toward his wife's brother Roy, dies. Herbert Graham's schemes, including his misadministration of the Keene estate, are exposed, and he is tried and sentenced to 6 years' hard labor. James LeRoy and Roy Brown are appointed supervisors of the bank, reopened through the efforts of Helen Keene and friends. Marguerite finds love with Dr. Keene, as does Roy with Helen.

918. Donati, Sara, 1956- . *Into the wilderness.* **New York: Bantam Books, 1998. xii, 691p.**

Elizabeth (Lizzie) Middleton, still unmarried at 29, comes back to 'Paradise' in Upstate New York after a sojourn in England with an aristocratic aunt. She plans to teach school, but her father, Alfred, wants her to marry Dr. Richard Todd in order to flesh out his property holdings. When Nathaniel Bonner, brought up by Mohawks, comes her way, Lizzie falls madly in love and joins Nathaniel in an adventurous life in the neighboring borderlands and forests. Nathaniel not only covets Lizzie; he also has his eyes on Alfred Middleton's estates, which, should they fall to him, he would share with his Mohawk friends.

919. Donleavy, J. P. (James Patrick), 1926- . *The lady who liked clean rest rooms;* **the chronicle of one of the strangest stories ever to be rumored about New York. With eight original illustrations by Elliott Banfield. New York: St. Martin's Press. 1997. 126p.**

A Scarsdale, N.Y. Southern-born matron, Jocelyn Guenevere Marchantiére Jones, is faced with the departure of her husband who has been captivated by a woman half his age. Confused, irate, casting about for succor, she still clings to her ideals of correct womanly behavior (an inheritance of her Southern upbringing). She is rescued from a deeper fall into eccentricity and financial troubles by a generous bequest from a deceased Jewish gentleman whom she earlier would have considered a league beneath her socially.

920. Donnelly, Ignatius, 1831-1901. *Caesar's Column, a story of the twentieth century*, **by Edmund Boisgilbert, M.D. [pseud.] Chicago: Donohue Bros., 1890. 367p.**

An overwrought but fascinating, semi-utopian novel in which the narrator, Gabriel Weltstein, reports on the state of civilization in 1988-89, primarily in letters to his brother Heinrich. New York City with its ten million inhabitants is at the core of the story. Technological and scientific advances have far outstripped man's social and ethical development; capitalists/oligarchs (Prince Cabano chief among them), in conjunction with the police, the army, politicians, the legal and religious establishments, et al., rule the dehumanized and half-starved masses of the metropolis and the outside world. Gabriel's newfound friend, Maximilian Petion, is a member of the Brotherhood of Destruction; the Brotherhood destroys the forces of the oligarchy, but in so doing causes the collapse of civilization. Gabriel and Max and their families and supporters establish a 'garden in the mountains', a perfect society sheltered from the madness of the exterior world. 'Caesar's Column' is a ghastly monument composed of cemented human bodies and erected in the center of New York City per order of drunken, crazed Caesar Lomellini, commander general of the Brotherhood of Destruction.

921. Dooley, Roger Burke, 1920 or 1993. *Days beyond recall.* **Milwaukee: Bruce Pub. Co., 1949. 446p.**

"This is the story of the Irish Catholics of Buffalo during the early part of the twentieth century [between 1901 and 1919]; and above all of Rose Shanahan. In contrast to his heroine's spiritual and emotional development, Dooley shows us the deterioration of the stouthearted, self-reliant group into which she was born. Since his protagonist is a young woman and he writes through her eyes, Dooley emphasizes the social rather than the political and economic changes in Buffalo during her youth"—Catholic world. Followed by the author's *The House of Shanahan*, (q.v.).

922. ————. *Gone tomorrow*; **a novel. Milwaukee: Bruce Pub. Co., c1961. 369p.**

This is the final novel of a trilogy (see Days beyond recall and The House of Shanahan). The proud Shanahans and Crowleys and their relatives—the O'Farrells, the Fitzmahons and the Kilcoynes—go through the early Depression years (1929-1932) in Buffalo. Rose Shanahan's husband Steve is dead and she returns to teaching in the public schools while raising her son Robert. In a prologue and epilogue Robert Crowley, in 1959, now an architect in New York City, revisits Buffalo and some of the old familiar places and people.

923. ————. *The House of Shanahan.* **New York: Doubleday, 1952. 249p.**

Buffalo, New York in the 1920s is the scene of a novel that looks at a Roman Catholic family and its numerous members. The women of the clan are especially interesting: Rose Shanahan marries a policeman (Steve Crowley) and seems to be a fairly steady personage, while her cousin Isabel unsettles the family by marrying a Protestant, Judge Harrison Lovett, who happens to be rich; Genevieve Shanahan marries a rum-runner, Dennis, although she is in love with Philip Lovett. Dennis has his heart fixed on Noreen, the adopted daughter of Rose's cousin . . . and so it goes. If there is any message in the novel, it is that from a Roman Catholic point of view divorce is a sin and the author seems to agree.

Doonan, Grace Wallace, b. 1873. See under per pseudonym: Keon, Grace.

Dorrance, James French, b. 1879, joint author. *His robe of honor.* **See Item #924.**

924. Dorrance, Ethel Arnold Smith, b. 1880. *His robe of honor,* **by Ethel Smith and J.F. Dorrance. New York: Moffat, Yard, 1916. 324p.**

Julian Randolph climbs to a semblance of power through a combination of political and legal corruption in New York City. Then he meets Lora Nelson while working for the interests of a traction company. She was to be an ameliorating influence in his career. When he ascends to the judge's bench (owing to his party boss's influence) Julian almost makes a blatantly wrong decision in a particular case; he suddenly realizes that he can act honorably and be a judge for all the people. Lora strongly supports his new stance.

925. Dorsey, David, 1952- . *The cost of living*. New York: Viking Press, 1997. viii, 273p.

Richard Cahill of Rochester, N. ., is caught up in a race to supply his family—wife, daughter and son—with all the amenities of upper middle class existence. He narrates his own story as an advertising firm functionary who traps himself into involvement with drug dealing when his day-to-day job fails to provide him with sufficient financial resources. His family sees less and less of him and Cahill's troubles increase.

926. Dos Passos, John, 1896-1970. *Manhattan transfer*. New York: Harper, 1925 404p.

A kaleidoscopic novel in which Dos Passos describes New York City's physical beauty and ugliness and the tenor of its inhabitants' lives. The author portrays a few definite characters, e.g., Jimmy Herf, a newspaper reporter, and Ellen Oglethorpe, an actress—both unhappy—but his chief 'character' is the teeming metropolis in all its variety.

927. Doty, William Lodewick, 1919-1979. *Button, Button*; a mystery story. Huntington, Ind.: Our Sunday Visitor, 1979. 206p.

"An elderly cigar-loving monsignor in a small New York town investigates two gruesome murders"—Menendez, A.J. The Catholic novel.

928. Doubleday, E. Stillman. *Just plain folks*; a story of "lost opportunities." Boston: Arena Pub. Co., 1894. viii, 316p.

"A story dealing with the social problems of capital and labor, crime, immortality, demand and supply, justice and charity. The author finds the solution in obedience to the old command—love thy neighbor as thyself"—Annual American catalogue. The author's main character, John Hardhand, finds that farming yields few monetary profits and tries to 'succeed' in New York City. His venture there is less than successful, but he does imbibe a few of life's hard knocks and learns therefrom. Back to the farm he goes and applies himself well enough to amass a small fortune, allowing him to marry. At one point in the novel John speaks at Cooper Union as an advocate of Henry George's single tax.

929. Dougall, Bernard. *The singing corpse*. New York: Dodd, Mead, 1943. 206p.

"Hades broke loose at Moon River Inn, Westchester, where the entertainers include Maris Miles, a lurid jive artist, Dewey Macomber's swing band, and Linda Sheridan, wife of the narrator. Somebody liquidates Maris, and Chief Gil Foot also has to discover who fixed Fibber Malloy that time in Sarah Adam's gambling place. Seems like Macomber loves Penelope Carter, daughter of Mrs. Lorraine Nesbitt Stewart Carter Chase Bruning of Westbury and Park Avenue, not in the Social Register after 1935"—New York herald tribune books.

930. **Dougherty, Richard, 1921-1988.** *A summer world.* **Garden City, N.Y.: Doubleday, 1960. 235p.**

"Alex Flynn, young prep school graduate, narrates this story of the eventful and emotion-charged summer which he spends in 'the Trough', an upper New York State community dominated by Charles Bonham, a philanthropist"— Book review digest.

931. ————. *We dance and sing.* **Garden City, N. Y.: Doubleday, 1971. 336p.**

'Jason Corners' in western New York State is the new home of Jack and Kate Malloy who have forsaken the Broadway stage. The novel covers the 1920s to the late 1960s and draws a picture of small town life with its scandals and quiet moments, and the progress of the Malloy family, with some focus on Michael, son of Jack and Kate. The latter two age quite comfortably; they and friends mellow and develop their own individualities.

932. **Douglas, Amanda Minnie, 1837-1916.** *A little girl in old New York.* **New York: Dodd, Mead, 1896. 367p.**

The novel is set in the 1840s and its young heroine is 'Hanny Underhill' who leaves her rural surroundings for the excitement of New York City. Hanny's experiences in the city are generally pleasant ones, often touched with glints of humor. The author describes the political and religious currents of the period and captures the manners and customs of the people and the physical appearance of the city itself.

933. ————. *Lost in a great city.* **Boston: Lee & Shepard, 1881. 468p.**

A child and her nurse in attempting to cross Broadway are unaware of a horse bearing down on them. The nurse is injured and removed to a hospital, but the child (our heroine) runs away in fright until she winds up in one of New York City's gloomiest slums. A mercenary woman who sells her to a circus acrobat picks her up. His aim is to prepare the child for circus performances. For the next ten years our heroine is introduced to a bundle of experiences, pleasant and unpleasant, till she has the unexpected good fortune of being reunited with her father who had never ceased searching for her.

934. **Douglas, Hudson, pseud.** *The lantern of luck.* **Illus. by Howard Chandler Christy. New York: W.J. Watt, 1909. 377p.**

Stock speculation in New York City is the theme of the novel. An artist and a gambler in stocks and bonds are the two protagonists who dominate the action in the story. The 'lantern of luck' is a star that has been seen from the deck of a boat by several of the novel's characters.

935. **Douglas, Julia.** *Deerhurst*; or, *The rift in the cloud.* **Boston: A.I. Bradley, 1893. 383p.**

An English child is separated from his prosperous parents by an evil servant and taken to America where he is eventually adopted by a couple whose residence, Deerhurst, sits grandly on the shores of the Hudson River. Years later the now-grown youth is fortuitously returned to his biological parents.

936. Douglas, Malcolm. *He would be an actor*; a story of the stage. **New York: Metropolitan Pub. Co., 1903. 241p.**

Patsy Brannigan, weary of laboring on his parents' farm in the Mohawk Valley, decides to try his luck on the New York stage, woefully untalented though he may be. His inspiration is Mamie Dooley, a childhood friend, who, under the name Caddie Corrisande, has been a chorus girl and also 'reigning queen of burlesque'. With a new name, Hector De Vronde, Patsy makes the rounds of the city's casting offices. Failing to receive any offers of employment, he joins a touring company and lands the role of a country bumpkin in a play, 'A Spendthrift Idiot'. His performance is so ludicrous as to be perceived by critics as a masterpiece of comic acting. Using that as a crutch Patsy essays a disastrous Hamlet in the Upstate towns of 'Hamsterdam' and 'Chenectady'. With his career in limbo Mamie Dooley/Caddie Corrisande, fresh from a hit on the New York boards and influenced by a newspaper headline touting Patsy's supposed 'heroism' in saving the lives of two of his former associates, falls into his arms. Among the names to be found in this whimsical story are: John Grew (Drew), Charles Shohman (Frohman), Lillian Fussell (Russell) and Flam Pubert (Sam Shubert).

937. Downes, Anne Miller, d. 1964. *The captive rider*. **Philadelphia: Lippincott, 1956. 286p.**

In a small college town in Upstate New York Roger Parton cuts a powerful figure. He is rich, by all measures of the American 'creed' a success, yet he comes to the realization that he has paid a harsh price—real happiness has eluded him and he has lost the one woman who could have provided that for him.

938. ————. *The eagle's song*. **Philadelphia: Lippincott, 1949. 320p.**

"Historical novel covering the period from colonial times to the end of the First World War. The scene is an Upstate New York town on the Mohawk River, and the struggles between two families provide the action. The families are the Ayres, founders of the town, who provided men and women of integrity and loyalty to the dream in every generation; and the Concords, exponents of dishonesty and greed"—Book review digest.

939. ————. *High hills calling*. **Philadelphia: Lippincott, 1951. 320p.**

"A mill town in Upper New York State during the years before World War II is the scene. Rex Brice, brought up to regard wealth as his birthright is suddenly faced with the prospect of the failure of his grandfather's mills. From playboy to mill owner is Rex's part for the next few years. His love for a beautiful, fragile American girl, divorced from a French count, adds to

Rex's difficulties. With the loss of Eunice there comes the gradual realization of his love for the loyal childhood playmate, Cordelia"—Book review digest.

940. ————. *No parade for Mrs. Greenia*. **Philadelphia: Lippincott, 1962. 350p.**
The hero of the story is a crippled orphan, Alec Trumbull, who wears an iron brace on one of his feet; he has an artist's hands and discerning eye, however. Through the years Alec's talent flourishes, fostered by his own dedication and courage and by the people around this Upstate New York artist who come into his life bringing with them tragedy, hope and joy.

941. ————. *Until the shearing*. **New York: Stokes, 1939. 448p.**
In the early years of the 20th century Felix Thorpe, son of the actress Gail Porter, is placed in the care of his Grandfather Thorpe and Aunt Em in 'Clearwater', a village in Upstate New York. The sensitive lad is prone to startling influences from the Kershaw family. He falls in love with Josephine Kershaw, but she marries wealthy Alexander Kent. While working in his Uncle Henry's bank, Felix dreams of being a writer and a man of the theater. Felix's guardians frown upon Mars Kershaw, a charming, almost diabolically clever girl, but she is one person who understands Felix's spiritual and secular quests better than anyone.

942. **Downs, Sarah Elizabeth Forbush, b. 1843.** *Katherine's sheaves*, **by Mrs. Georgie Sheldon (Mrs. George Sheldon Downs). New York: Federal Book Co., 1904. 370p.**
Katherine Minturn matriculates at Hilton Seminary, "a noted institution located in a beautiful old town of western New York." She has taken the teachings of Mary Baker Eddy to heart and it is through Katherine's active interest that the author presents her advocacy of Christian Science.

943. ————. *A true aristocrat*; **a novel. New York: A.L. Burt, 1889. 350p.**
Cecile Vavasour, penniless after her parent's deaths, marries Howard Montgomery in New York and thus arouses the strong antipathy of Helen Langley, Howard's sister. On a return trip from England Howard leaves ship and unaccountably disappears. Presumed dead, his finances revert to the care of Colonel Langley, Helen's husband, and Cecile is forced to support herself and her infant daughter, Daisy. She establishes a successful wearing apparel business in New York with the help of a lawyer friend. Helen kidnaps Daisy and flees to California with the child, but Cecile and another friend, Dr. Gregory Mortimer, get her back. The scene shifts to Saratoga where Helen, still vengeful toward Cecile, is apprised of her deceased husband's bad investments and her own lowly birth. Howard Montgomery appears in Saratoga after being released from prison in England where he had been wrongfully accused of the crime of theft. He and Cecile are reunited at Saratoga's Congress House. With a stipend from Howard, Helen Langley leaves the United States for permanent residence ion Paris.

944. Drachman, Theodore S., 1904- . *Reason for madness.* **New York: Abelard-Schuman, 1970. 192p.**

Dr. Paul Maddock of the town of 'Escalon' in the Finger Lakes region is a psychiatrist charged with the slaying of his uncle. His good friend, Carl Coblen, returns to Escalon to set up a defense for the doctor. Coblen finds no evidence that will definitely clear Maddock and he is reduced to using the 'not guilty by reason of insanity' plea. Paul Maddock goes along with his line of defense since he presumes that he can quickly display recovery from temporary insanity and then get down to the business of looking for the actual killer together with Carl.

945. Drago, Harry Sinclair, 1888-1979. *The hidden things,* **by J. Wesley Putnam [pseud.] New York: Macaulay Co., 1915. 245p.**

Emily Fraser had hoped to make her mark as an illustrator in New York City, but faced with no opportunities is forced to take an offer to be an artist's model. She feels a sense of humiliation that interferes with her marrying the man she loves, but time heals and broader views prevail.

946. ————. *Wild fruit,* **by Grant Sinclair [pseud.] New York: G. H. Watt, 1926. 288p.**

Escapees from the Bolshevik Revolution: Nina Mananoff, daughter of an international banker; Prince Alexis Spkin [sic], a talented aeronautical engineer; and Vera Lassr, a ballerina, find their way to New York City. Nina, with the help of two American friends, Peggy Ayres and Reginald Van Thorn, opens a nightclub with a distinctive Russian décor and atmosphere. It is a smashing success. Nina, who believes herself in love with Prince Alexis, helps him further his aeronautical research. Van Thorn falls in love with Nina and discovers Alexis' duplicity toward Nina (Alexis is romantically involved with Vera) and towards investors in his engine with its floating feed valve. Nina is finally cognizant of the Prince's dishonorable behavior and turns to Van Thorn for solace.

947. Drake, Jeanie. *The Metropolitans.* **New York: Century Co., 1896. 267p.**

"A brilliant and gifted young man, who has been meanly deprived of his inheritance, wins his way to success as a composer and gains his reward as a lover by dropping his idle associates and accepting the gospel of hard work. The scene is laid mainly in New York City, but the author has introduced a decided novelty in shifting the scene during an important part of the development of the plot to the Arctic regions. Here the hero's character is finally rounded out by the hardship and privation that necessarily accompany life in an Eskimo igloo. Both a novel and a good-natured satire of New York society"—Annual American catalogue.

948. Dreiser, Theodore, 1871-1945. *An American tragedy.* **New York: Liveright, 1926. 2v.**

Clyde Griffiths is working in his wealthy uncle's collar factory in Upstate New York (city of Cortland?); he had fled the Midwest after an auto accident that resulted in a girl's death. Roberta Alden, another factory worker, is seduced by the lonely Clyde who is ignored by his uncle's family. When he meets a local society belle he envisions a marriage to wealth and social position; however, Roberta, now pregnant, is in his way, and he plans to drown her in a nearby Adirondack lake. Actually the boat holding both Clyde and Roberta overturns and she accidentally drowns. Clyde is tried for murder; an ambitious district attorney and public outcry combine to condemn Clyde to death. It was Dreiser's contention that the weak Clyde fell victim to the peculiarly American ambition for material success, no matter how attained, and that dooms the Clyde Griffiths of the world.

949. —————. *The "genius."* New York: J. Lane, 1915. 736p.

An artist of midwestern origins, Eugene Witla, rides the roller coaster of success and eventual failure in the New York City art world. The author paints a picture of the 'opening of a golden age of luxury in New York' and the tremendous changes it undergoes as technology, modern architecture and a building boom take hold.

950. —————. *Sister Carrie.* New York: Doubleday, Page, 1900. 557p.

In this classic realistic novel Carrie Meeker comes from a rural area to seek worldly success in Chicago, where she meets and infatuates businessman and tavern manager George Hurstwood. He inveigles Carrie into going to New York with him, financing the move with stolen money. Carrie achieves stardom on Broadway, while Hurstwood sinks into poverty; deserted by the uncaring Carrie, Hurstwood commits suicide in a dingy Bowery hostelry.

Dresser, Davis, 1904-1977. See under Debrett, Hal, the joint pseudonym of Davis Dresser and Kathleen Rollins Dresser.

Dresser, Kathleen Rollins. See under Debrett, Hal, the joint pseudonym of Davis Dresser and Kathleen Rollins Dresser.

951. **Drummond, Dale.** *The evolution of Peter Moore.* New York: Britton Pub. Co., **1919.**

Bertha Hunter from Haynesville marries Peter Moore in New York City. He goes off to World War I as a volunteer in the British Army. Bertha takes a job as saleslady in a fashionable Manhattan clothing store and lives a rather gay life outside of work. A millionaire falls in love with her and proposes marriage. Bertha is inclined to accept the offer despite its bigamous connotations for Peter's letters bore her. Meanwhile Peter finds a 'soul-partner' in an English girl. The author provides a happy ending by arranging for two very convenient deaths.

952. —————. *A woman who dared*; a novel. New York: Britton, 1919. 312p.

This is the story of the peculiar life of a New York businessman's wife—Katherine Boroughs who to her husband Haskall is a beautiful figurine, a showpiece to be displayed at various social functions, but otherwise to be confined to her luxurious home. Haskall gives her no personal allowance or spending money and frowns on her attempts to broaden her social contacts. Katherine meets Eric Lucknow, explorer and socialite, a wealthy man; they fall in love. However, Katherine remains true to the conventions of the day, staying with Haskall through all his infidelities and business failures. A serious automobile accident and a succession of strokes enfeeble Haskall and he mellows a bit, even to the point of adopting the illegitimate child he fathered and whom Katherine had brought into their home. Katherine establishes a successful millinery business despite her husband's disapproval. Haskall eventually passes away and the 'woman who dared' to be true to her own self, her own sense of values, is free to marry Eric.

Drury, John P., 1918- . joint author. *A career for Carol.* **See Item #953.**

953. Drury, Maxine Cole, 1914- . *A career for Carol,* **by Maxine Cole Drury and John P. Drury. Illus. by Foster Caddell. New York: Longmans, 1958. 216p.**

"To earn money to go to a famous music school to which she has won a scholarship, seventeen-year-old singer Carol Latimer, in partnership with her younger brother [Dennis], tries her hand at lobstering in Long Island Sound. Although the story of Carol's ups and downs in the lobster business and in her friendship with two completely dissimilar boys is not exceptional, the plot is for the most part believable, the narrative is well-paced and suspenseful, and the characters are well-drawn"—Booklist.

954. Dryden, Bridget, pseud. *Passion is the wind.* **New York: John Day Co., 1928. 323p.**

The Manhattan department store, Nightingales, with its varied personnel, is a chief 'character' in this novel. It is the solace of Brooke Bonnell, head of the book division and mistress of unhappily married Harold Michelson, the store's buyer of pottery and Oriental goods. When their torrid love affair begins to wane as far as Brooke is concerned (she has become the desideratum of bachelor Marcel Amidon, rare book collector and general manager of Nightingales) Michelson commits suicide. To Brooke, who dismisses the idea of marriage, the store remains a refuge from the theatrical career her unstable family had hoped she would pursue.

955. Drysdale, William, 1852-1901. *The young reporter*; **a story of Printing House Square. Illus. by Charles Copeland. Boston: W.A. Wilde, 1895. 298p.**

"Richard Sumner was, in printer's parlance, a 'printer's devil' in the office of a weekly county newspaper, when he made his first hit by a skillful piece of reporting, which secured him a place on the reportorial staff of a well-known New York daily. His adventures thereafter are given, notably how he handled his Sing Sing assignment and the robbery of a well-know millionaire's grave, how he interviewed President Diaz [of Mexico], etc., with a final account of his literary venture"—Annual American catalogue.

956. Du Bois, Mary Constance, 1879-1959. *The lass of the silver sword.* **With illus. by Charles M. Relyea. New York: Century Co., 1909. ix, 418p.**

The heroine, leader of a band of girls at a boarding school (Hazelhurst), probably has a Joan of Arc complex, but she organizes her friends into a company of knights who give their word to help one another at all times and maintain good academic standing. They carry their adventurous spirits and capacity for wholesome activity to an Adirondack camp in the winter. Our heroine continues to be their inspirational pacesetter.

957. Du Bois, Theodora, 1890- . *The Devil and destiny.* **Garden City, N.Y.: Published for the Crime Club by Doubleday, 1948. 186p.**

"The Jeffrey McNeills, who go about their amateur detective work in a nice, unobtrusive fashion, ponder the problem of which one of the guests at a musicale given on an estate near New York drowned the dipsomaniac hostess by pushing her into the swimming pool. One of the principal suspects is a young lady who is convinced that she's under the thumb of Satan himself, and some psychiatric research that Dr. McNeill has been doing in a hospital proves useful in clearing things up"—New Yorker.

Dubois, Alan, pseud. See: Wood, Clement, 1888-1950.

958. Duff, Beldon. *The Central Park murder.* **Garden City, N. Y.: Published for the Crime Club by Doubleday, Doran, 1929, 285p.**

Theft of a pearl necklace and murder involve several unlikely characters: Virginia Trowbridge, a society girl; Captain O'Connor of the British Secret Service; the 'Scorpion', a super-crook; Elsie Scully; Adrian Pitt-Martin; and William Petty, who may or may not be an accountant, but who turns out to be the hero of this not very well-crafted mystery.

959. Dufour, Yvonne. *Monique.* **New York: Dutton, 1930. 249p.**

New York City, its skyscrapers and its promise of a civilization still finding its way, enthrall Monique de Bussac, a cultured French woman married to an American businessman. Her marriage has all the elements of success; the one character in the novel that strays beyond the ordinary conventions is Adrian, her husband's cousin, a talented musician who fancies himself irresistible to women.

960. Duganne, Augustus Joseph Hickey, 1823-1884. *The tenant house*; or *Embers from poverty's hearthstone.* **New York: R.M. deWitt [c1857] 490p.**

"A sentimental and melodramatic portrayal of the poverty-stricken, interwoven lives of the tenants of two sprawling [New York City] tenements, Foley's Barracks and Kolephat College.Noble newsboys, overworked seamstresses, gouging rent collectors abound"—Blake, F.M. The strike in the American novel.

961. Duganne,Phyllis, *Prologue.* **NewYork: Harcourt, Brace and Howe, 1920. 304p.**

"This is the story of Rita Moreland's life during her teens, when she is developing from little girlhood to womanhood.The only child of a rather unsatisfactory marriage, she has some difficulty in adjusting herself to life. The story tells of her family life, her schooling, and her home in New York, where she vibrates between Fifth Avenue and Greenwich Village, her friends, and more especially her relations with the masculine sex. She alternates between perfect happiness and periods of bored discontentment with everything and can't seem to 'find herself'. The [First] World War finds her at work in an office, but the end of the war brings back to her Donald, with whom, at the story's close, she stands at 'the beginnings of things'"—Book review digest.

Duncan, Sara Jeannette, 1862?-1922. See: Cotes, Sara Jeannette Duncan, 1862?-1922.

962. Duncan, Norman, 1871-1916. *The soul of the street*; **correlated stories of the New York Syrian quarter. New York: McClure, Phillips, 1900. 168p.**

Khalil Khayat, editor of the Arabic daily, Kawkab Elhorriah (Star of Liberty), observes life around Washington Street in Lower Manhattan, gives advice to little Billy Halloran, crippled son of the alcoholic Mrs. Halloran, tries to console Alois Awad when the latter learns that his beloved Haleem, daughter of Salim Khouri, has married Jimmy Brady, etc. Contents: The lamp of liberty.—In the absence of Mrs. Halloran.—The greatest player in all the world.—For the hand of Haleem.—The under-shepherd.—The sprit of revolution.

963. Duncombe, Frances Riker, 1907-1994. *Cassie's village.* **Illus. by W.T. Mars. New York: Lothrop, 1965. 221p.**

"Like the other residents of Katonah [New York] Cassie equates the village with stability. It is a shock to discover that the building of the Croton Dam will raise the water level and leave the whole territory submerged. The more daily concern of the 12-year-old Cassie involves looking after her widowed father and her school activities. Of particular importance to her is one of her best friends who has started to take an interest in boys, especially one 'fast' boy known to have encouraged some of the younger ones in stealing cigarettes. . . . The setting and characters are well conceived and the transplanting of the village is well handled"—Kirkus reviews.

964. ———. *Death of a spinster.* **New York: Scribner, 1958. 185p.**

Bayfield Center in Westchester County is the locus of the presumed suicide on one of the town's outstanding people; the body is come upon by a part-time bookkeeper of the Opportunity Shop. One learns that Bayfield Center is proud of its past (beginning with the American Revolution), yet it has several mysteries residing in that past and in the present. Investigation into the 'suicide' reveals some of them.

[Dunlap, William] 1766-1829. *Memoirs of a water-drinker.*
See note under Item #965.

965. **[Dunlap, William] 1766-1839.** *Thirty years ago*; or, *Memoirs of a water-drinker.* **By the author of Memoirs of George Frederick Cooke; Biography of Charles Brockden Brown . . .[etc.] New York: Bancroft & Holley, 1836. 2v.**

Also published under the title: *Memoirs of a water-drinker.* Zeb Spiffard, the hero, is a teetotaler with an actress-wife who, like her mother, is an alcoholic, although he doesn't know this right away. He himself has carved a niche on the New York stage as a comedian. When Zeb does come upon his wife's drinking, he leaves her and she commits suicide. There are two subplots, one of which makes a heroine of the chaste Emma Portland; she escapes an attack by a so-called general and falls into the arms of a humdrum (but on occasion 'heroic') clerk by the name of Henry Johnson. The work takes on the coloration of a typical 'temperance' novel.

966. **Dunn, Julia E.** *The bewildering widow*; a tale of Manhattan Beach. New York: W.B. Smith, 1881. 228p.**

The young widow, Mrs. Smiley, and her niece, Dora Smiley, are temporarily 'encamped' at Manhattan Beach (Coney Island) with financial betterment on their minds, and that translates into finding suitable husbands. Possibilities present themselves in the persons of Mr. Flurrey with his valet Émile, Jack Louder, rugged, wealthy miner, and his secretary, Phil Preston. Mrs. Smiley skillfully wins the attention of Flurrey and Louder and in the end selects the bachelor Flurrey; Louder is content with Flora, one of two daughters of Mr. Pillow (the other daughter, Violet, fancies herself in love with the English fortune-hunter, Levander Kidd, but withdraws in due time). Dora Smiley and Phil Preston prove to be a well-matched couple.

967. **Dunning, Charlotte, b. 1858.** *A step aside.* **Boston: Houghton,Mifflin, 1886. 333p.**

"A poor French drawing master, his talented comfort-loving daughter of nineteen, their boarding-house keeper (who keeps a house on a side street running off First Avenue in the heart of New York City), and two or three more of her boarders are the characters in this realistic drama, representing life among the respectable, educated poor. A poor clerk in a manufacturing company and his employer both fall in love with Miss Valrey, and she, after engaging herself to Langmuir, the clerk, takes 'a step aside' for a few months into the comforts of his employer's family, where she is teaching French to a very disagreeable little mischief-making girl. Langmuir gets into business trouble, and then Miss Valrey returns to him; they marry on nothing, and go on to live in the country. There is little action, but the story of irksome poverty is well told"—Annual American catalogue.

968. ————. *Upon a cast.* **New York: Harper, 1885. 330p.**

There are two 'heroes' in this novel. One of them flips a coin with heads coming up twice in a row; the upshot is that he registers at the Langham Hotel where he meets the heroine. She spends her leisure hours in a Hudson River village called 'Newbroek.' Although she is active in boating, riding, lawn tennis and other sports and enjoys picnics and hikes, she also has a keen, serious mind and a rather charming personality that is very attractive to the two male protagonists. It remains for her to select the one whom she will presumably marry and she does this fairly precipitously.

969. Dunning, Phillip Hart, 1891/2-1969. *Broadway*; a novel, by Philip Dunning **and George Abbott. New York: Doran, 1927. 288p.**

A novelization of the very popular Broadway play of 1926/27. Roy Lane and Billie Moore, dancers at the Paradise Night Club of Nick Verdis, are in the middle of a love affair which is interrupted when the smooth, wealthy gangster/bootlegger, Steve Crandall, takes a fancy to the rather naïve, virginal Billie. While Roy tries to wean Billie away from Crandall, the latter shoots his rival, 'Scar' Edwards, and elicits a promise from Billie not to tell what she saw after Edwards' murder. Detective Dan McCorn investigates the crime. There is a confrontation between Roy and Crandall; however, Crandall himself is killed by Edwards' girl friend, Pearl, who had been 'planted' in the chorus line at the nightclub. Detective McCorn knows by now who killed Edwards and Crandall, but he protects Pearl by declaring Crandall's death a suicide. Roy and Billie get back together again.

970. Durrant, Lynda. *Echohawk.* **New York: Clarion Books, 1996. 181p.**

When he was only four years of age, Mohican Indians killed Jonathan Starr's parents in a raid on their Hudson Valley cabin, and Glickihigan, a warrior, adopted Jonathan as his son. Now thirteen, Jonathan or Echohawk, his Indian name, is fully immersed in Indian culture and language. Glickihigan has familiarity with the settlers' language and he decides to send Echohawk and his Mohican brother for instruction by a teacher and his wife in Saratoga. Pictures from his early white past begin to crowd Echohawk's memory, but he rebels when he discovers that his white instructor intends to keep him from ever seeing Glickihigan again.

971. Dutton, Charles Judson, 1888-1964. *The crooked cross.* **New York: Dodd, Mead, 1926. 243p.**

"An eminent scientist returns to his home in New York State from China where he has discovered new and startling material for a book on the origin of man. Three friends, detectives of fame, are invited to dine with him. They find their host in the library, stabbed through the heart, a crooked cross traced upon his forehead. It develops on inquiry that the dead man's visitor was a

Chinaman on an unknown errand, that his secretary, an attractive young woman, left the house in the afternoon in a state of high excitement, and that the doors of a bookcase in the library had been smashed and several volumes stolen. With these facts to start upon the three detectives open their investigation and unravel the mystery"—Book review digest.

972. ————. *Out of the darkness.* **New York: Dodd, Mead, 1922. 282p.**

"The unraveling of what at first seems to be a simple robbery, to be later complicated by a series of exciting happenings, taxes even the keen wits of the criminologist John Bartley. The evidence of traffic in illicit whiskey at 'Circle Lake' near Saratoga, the scene of the story, and the spiritualistic practices of the sister-in-law of the murdered man, add considerable zest to the mystery, which is cleverly solved in the most unexpected manner"—Book review digest.

973. **Dutton, Louise Elizabeth.** *The goddess girl.* **New York: Moffat, Yard, 1915. 385p.**

After passing her early years as a conventionally reared girl in a small town, Rose Saxon goes to New York City and soon finds herself confronted with a problematic situation for which she is entirely unprepared. It is simply that the man she loves, Richard Carmichael, has wooed her in a manner far removed from the 'orthodox' one she has been expecting. The climax comes when Rose makes her decision to accept or reject Richard's proposal of marriage.

974. *Duty versus will*; or, *Decision makes the man.* **A tale for old and young. New York: Leavitt, Trow, 1849. 251p.**

Yale undergraduate Thomas Ensington, after his father's death, leaves school and seeks his fortune in New York City. An old friend, Harry Millison, helps Tom get a job with the firm he is working for, but Harry is already on the edge of corruption. Drinking and gambling are the sources of his downslide; while Tom works hard, Harry steals money from the company and has the accusing finger pointed at Tom. Tom, his mother, sister and brother are put through several trials before Harry confesses his guilt in a note found after his suicide. The author moralizes at every opportunity and seems quite certain that New York City is largely responsible for turning innocent, honest young men from the country into intemperate, thieving scoundrels. This work is sometimes attributed to William H. Rossiter.

975. **Early, Jack.** *Razzamatazz; a novel.* **New York: F. Watts, 1985. 331p.**

The townspeople of 'Seaville', Long Island, depend on summer tourism for a large part of their livelihood; a series of unsolved knife killings so disconcerts them that they fire Police Chief Hallock (his replacement is totally incompetent). All of these murders have taken place 25 years after a nightclub, 'Razzamatazz', had burned down. Reporter Colin Maguire comes to Seaville to investigate the crimes; he meets and falls for Anne Winters, a female minister, and joins forces with Hallock. The killer captures Anne;

Colin and Hallock have to work fast to save her and unmask the murderer. They have been working with such clues as old newspaper clippings and the killer's own egoistic monologues.

976. Eastburn, Joseph. *Kiss them good-bye*; **a novel. New York: Morrow, 1993. 300p.**

'Ravenstown' in Upstate New York is the home of a boys' preparatory school whose students are threatened by an unbalanced killer; he/she has already slain several of them in a hideous way. Nick Fowler, formerly with the Buffalo police, investigates; his approach is not very popular with his Ravenstown superiors and Maureen McCauley, an attractive reporter who has confidential information printed by her newspaper, impedes his probes. Nick moves ahead, however, and uncovers the killer.

977. Eastman, Edward Roe, 1885-1970. *The destroyers*; **a historical novel. Ithaca, N.Y.: American Agriculturist, 1947. 250p.**

"Lulled into a sense of false security because of the nearness of Fort Alden, the little settlement of Cherry Valley, south of the Mohawk, is suddenly attacked by marauding Indians and Tories one fall day in 1778. How young Nate and the old scout Joel, among the few who escape this massacre, join up with General Clinton's forces to be 'eyes and ears for his army' . . . is related with authentic detail in this historical novel of the Sullivan-Clinton expedition"—Bookmark.

978. ————. *No drums*; **a historical novel. Ithaca, N.Y.: American Agriculturist, 1951. 280p.**

The novel limns farm people of Tioga County in the Southern Tier of New York State and their struggles to survive the weather and illness while simultaneously supporting the Union cause in the Civil War. Three of the Wilson men—father and two sons—enlist in the Union Army. The author does describe their military adventures, but the civilian reaction to the alarums of war is his chief concern. Ann Clinton, the heroine, marries Mark Wilson just before his induction into the army. When his death is reported, Ann numbly becomes the wife of Henry Bain—he is widely detested in the country for his Copperhead activities and his profiteering from the war. Ann faces a dilemma when Mark shows up after surviving the horrors of Andersonville Prison.

979. ————. *The settlers*; **a historical novel. Watkins Glen, N.Y.: Century House, 1950. viii, 280p.**

The story of several families that migrated from the Hudson Valley and its patroon-based agricultural settlements to the Genesee Valley 30 years after the end of the American Revolution. Jim Miller, teacher/doctor, young farmer Asa Williams, his mother Constant and sister Hannah, two young women, Martha Ball and Polly Stevens—are most prominent among the many characters in the novel. The trials and tribulations of settlers in the Genesee

Valley (swamp fever, malaria, consumption, the War of 1812, etc.) are graphically portrayed. To those familiar with the Finger Lakes region of central New York the author's descriptions will ring true. Several errors have crept into the text, however: e.g., the poet Tennyson (1809-1892) is quoted by Jim Miller; a certain 'McDonald' is named as victor in the naval Battle of Lake Champlain (1814)—the correct name is McDonough (Thomas).

980. ————.*Tough sod*; a novel. New York: American Agriculturist, 1944. 240p.
The farmers of 'Briarton' and vicinity in the Upstate New York County of 'Lanark' outvote the 'standpatters', Ezra Chittenden and his allies, and set up a Farm Bureau office. Allen Clinton, the young farmer hero, is installed as president of the Bureau; his position brings him in conflict with his girlfriend, Helen, daughter of Chittenden. Also, when tuberculin testing of dairy cows is introduced, one of Chittenden's supporters, without Chittenden's knowledge, sells Allen one of his cows, obliterating the inspector's condemnatory stamp in the process. Allen is brought to trial for selling milk from a diseased cow. The culprit's confession clears Allen. Helen Chittenden and Allen go their separate ways; the latter begins to turn his attention toward Betty Tyler, a young woman whose parents have died and whom Allen has known since childhood days.

981. ————. *The trouble maker.* New York: Macmillan, 1925. 315p.
"The dairymen of New York State are dissatisfied with their treatment at the hands of the milk dealers; prices are low and the milk is occasionally refused at the station and turned back without reason to the dairyman who brought it for sale. Jim Taylor is interested in forming a co-operative organization, but his neighbor, John Ball, is opposed. Dorothy, Ball's daughter, is thus torn between love for Jim and loyalty to her father. Some of the dairymen agree to call a milk strike. Serious trouble arises during the agitation and Jim is unjustly accused. He is brought to trial, but his detractors are discovered and he is acquitted. The Dairymen's League wins its fight for fair prices. Jim is the community hero, and the book concludes with a wedding"—Book review digest.

982. Eastman, Max, 1883-1969. *Venture.* New York: A. & C. Boni, 1927. 398p.
"The story of Joe Hancock, a Harvard youth, with no fixed place in society, who comes to New York, there sets up as a 'portrait poet', then goes into business as a coffee distributor and finally is caught between two currents—the romantic and the ruthlessly practical—and stranded"—New York evening post.

983. Eaton, Walter Prichard, 1878-1957. *The runaway place*; a May idyl of Manhattan, by Walter Prichard Eaton and Elise Morris Underhill. New York: H. Holt, 1909. 257p.
A whimsical tale about an unemployed man and a girl on vacation who meet in Central Park by the statue of General Sherman (by Saint Gaudens). They

continue to meet day after day in the middle of Manhattan and begin to reveal to one another their dreams, hopes and philosophy. They are no longer strangers, there is even a hint of the intimacy of love as they visit and gaze at the paintings and statues of the city's museums. What will follow the end of her vacation and their return to the realities of their usual everyday lives?

984. Eberhard, Frederick George, 1889- . *Super-gangster.* **New York: Macaulay Co., 1932. 254p.**

In a castle on the Hudson rules a master of crime who fancies himself an underworld Napoleon (his consort is appropriately named Josephine and his aides are named after Napoleon's marshalls). The castle contains surgical instruments and machine guns, and its owner is more than capable of horrible, macabre executions of those who stand in his way.

985. Eberhart, Mignon Good, 1899-1996. *Another woman's house.* **New York: Random House, 1946. 276p.**

In a Westchester County setting Alice Thorne is acquitted of the charge that she had murdered Jack Mander. Her husband Richard is loved by Myra and Alice's release compounds the problems of Richard and Myra. The list of suspects for the murder now also includes Myra's brother Tim, Lady Carmichael alias Aunt Cornelia, and Barton the butler. Another murder occurs followed by other startling happenings and a strange quirk of fate. It is up to Myra to unravel the tangled skein.

986. ———. *Nine o'clock tide.* **New York: Random House, c1977. 166p.**

"When impulsive Meade thought she'd been jilted, she married Long Island millionaire Sam and moved in, along with her effete brother and tart Aunt Chrissy. But now true-love Andy has returned and presto—Sam takes a fatal tumble from the scenic terrace: a muscle-relaxant in his drink (that Meade mixed!) and a wee push. So poor, mixed-up Meade is the cops' chief suspect, though everybody—family, friends, blackmailing servants—has a secret: secret marriages, secret non-marriages, secret old crimes"—Kirkus reviews.

987. ———. *The unknown quantity.* **New York: Random House, 1953. 237p.**

"When Arthur Travers, a rather devious oil operator, asks his young wife to put up a man who will pose as him at their country place near New York for a week in his absence, she is both bewildered and reluctant. Travers is a plausible specimen, however, and when he tells her that the success of a secret government mission to which he has been assigned depends on this maneuver, she agrees. The events that follow are rather hard on her peace of mind. Word comes from San Francisco that a man thought to be Travers has been found stabbed in a park; the caretaker of the country estate and a mysterious prowler are murdered, and a beautiful adventuress turns up and accuses the heroine and her companion not only of being lovers, but also of having killed Travers for his money"—New Yorker.

988. ———. *Witness at large.* **New York: Random House, 1966. 174p.**

An estate on Long Island Sound is the site of two murders (and almost a third—the narrator's), which come about because the co-owners of a publishing house have opposing views on the sale of their company. Just about all the residents on the island are among the suspects in the case. 'Sister', the adopted daughter of the senior publisher, tells what is happening in a spirit of disbelief.

Edelstein, Mortimer S., joint author. *The bride laughed once.* **See Item #2968.**

989. Edgehill, Rosemary. *The bowl of night*; a Bast mystery. **New York: Forge, 1996. 220p.**

The pagan Hallow Fest is held each year at 'Paradise Lake' in Upstate New York. Karen Hightower ('Bast') and her lover, Julian Fletcher, have come from the occult bookstore in New York City where both are employed to attend workshops and sell books. But Bast happens upon the still body of the Rev. Jackson Harm, a fiery opponent of all cultists; his murder may be connected with a primitive ritual. Bast (and the local policeman, Lieutenant Wayne) studies the various suspects: witches, warlocks, and other practitioners of the esoteric arts; but it is also possible that the culprit could be a non-participant in the festival.

990. Edmonds, Walter Dumaux, 1903- . *Bert Breen's barn.* **Boston: Little, Brown, 1975. 270p.**

Tom Dolan, from the North Country of Upstate New York, is thirteen when, in order to be more supportive of his mother Polly Ann and his two sisters, he decides to look into the purchase of the Widow Breen's barn. He takes a job in the Ackerman and Hook feed mill in Boonville and puts aside part of his wages for the future. Eventually he negotiates with Mr. Armond who has recently bought the Breen property to sell him the barn. The deal consummated, Tom transfers the barn board by board (helped by an elderly friend) to his mother's place. Tom and Polly Ann also uncover a hoard of money concealed by Bert Breen shortly before his death, and Tom ends up with a sizeable savings account in the Boonville bank.

991. ———. *The big barn.* **Boston: Little Brown, 1930. 333p.**

"Deals with the Erie Canal country. Ralph Wilder's big barn, near Boonville (in the 1860s) dominates the countryside and the action of the story. Wilder's two sons, in love with the same girl, Rose, supply the love motif. Henry, the book-loving son, hates his savage and domineering father; Bascom, the younger, is old Wilder's pride. Rose's growing love for the farm makes her turn away from Henry, her husband, toward Bascom—and the Civil War brings the triangular situation to a climax"—Book review digest.

992. ———. *The Boyds of Black River.* **New York: Dodd, Mead, 1953. 248p.**

An episodic novel (in six chapters) told through the medium of youthful Teddy Armond, neighbor to the Boonville Boyds. The time is the early 1900s; the patriarch of Boyd House, Uncle Ledyard Boyd, and young Doone Boyd, are farmers, hunters and horse breeders into whose way of life enter retired Admiral Porter and his daughter Kathy who, although born and raised in the Black River country, had spent years in New York City and Long Island. The taciturn Doone and Kathy fall in love, marry and present the Admiral with a grandchild. A dog fight, a race between the Admiral's auto and the horse Blue Dandy, the hunting down of a wily deer (Old Ephraim), the threat of vampish Candida, faced down by Kathy—these and other incidents flesh out the narrative.

993. ————. *Chad Hanna*. Boston: Little, Brown, 1939. 548p.
Chad Hanna, stable boy at the Yellow Bud Tavern in Canastota, a village in central New York, runs off to join Huguenine's Great and Only International Circus. Unsophisticated as he may be, Chad soon exercises his native ingenuity to establish himself as an asset to the circus as it wends its way through the hamlets of central New York. He falls in love with and marries Caroline Trid, although the flamboyant circus rider, Albany Yates, complicates the relationship for a while. The time of the story is the 1830s; the novel is notable for its depiction of old-time circus people and their patrons from the small towns they served as one of the prime sources of entertainment of the period.

994. ————. *Drums along the Mohawk*. Boston: Little, Brown, 1936. 592p.
An outstanding novel portraying the struggles of ordinary people in the Mohawk Valley from 1776 to 1784. The protagonists are Gilbert (Gil) Martin, his wife Magdelana (Lana), and the indomitable Widow McKlennar. Their human foes are the Tories, the British regulars and their Indian allies who repeatedly raid the Valley. The settlers, with little or no assistance from the Continental Congress, have to defend themselves as best they can. Historical figures and fictional characters are mixed together with most satisfying results.

995. ————. *Erie water*. Boston: Little, Brown, 1933. 506p.
A fictional chronicle of the construction of the Erie Canal from its inception in 1817 to its completion in 1825 at Lockport. Hired by the canal contractor Caleb Hammil, Jerry Fowler is an ambitious young man who, however, stops long enough to wed Mary Goodhill, an indentured woman whose papers he purchases. The difficulties faced by the canal builders are a dominant theme of the novel. Historical characters move rather quickly through the story. Jerry, immersed in his work on the canal, loses the hitherto quiescent Mary who runs off with the itinerant cobbler, Henry Falk.

996. ————. *In the hands of the Senecas*. Boston: Little, Brown, 1947. 213p.

The narrative has to do with the fate of certain members of families in 'Dygartsbush', a settlement close by Fort Herkimer, which is attacked by Seneca Indians in 1778. The hamlet is destroyed; taken captive are two youngsters, Pete Kelly and Ellen Mitchell, several women and one man. Harsh as their captivity often is, most of them survive and are eventually reunited with those who escaped the initial attack. One particularly poignant incident is the reunion of young bride Delia and her husband John Borst after she has borne a child to an Indian warrior during her captivity.

997. ———. *Mostly canallers*: collected stories. Boston: Little, Brown, 1934. vii, 467p.

"Many of the characters [in these stories, chiefly about life on the Erie Canal in its early days] are inherently tragic, yet their tragedy has been allowed to become picturesque. And so one takes away the feeling that the author has stopped short sometimes of his inevitable truth"—New York herald tribune books. Contents: The trapper.—At Schoharie Crossing.—Death of Red Peril.—Citizens for Ohio.—Bewitched.—Blind Eve.—The voice of the archangel.—Water never hurt a man.—Dinty's deed.—Big-foot Sal.—The cruise of the Cachalot.—The three wise men.—Spring song.—Black wolf.—Who killed Rutherford?—Mr. Dennit's great adventure.—The old Jew's tale.—The end of the towpath.—Dust in September.—An honest deal.—The swamper.—It comes at twilight.—The devil's fancy.—Ninety.

998. ———. *Mr. Benedict's lion.* Illustrated by Doris Lee. New York: Dodd, Mead, 1938. 160p.

In 1812, shy Mr. Benedict, a teacher of English at Mrs. Satterlee's Female Seminary, is delegated to go to New York City to purchase a piano for the school. Losing the address of the musical instrument dealer he returns to the seminary with a lion in tow. The lion is actually a pregnant lioness. All is confusion until a pretty student steps forward to solve the crisis and Mr. Benedict finds romance.

999. ———. *The night raiders and other stories.* Boston: Little, Brown, 1980. 102p.

Two of the stories deal with large-scale farm operations near Boonville, N.Y. in 1908; the other two with the Erie Canal. Contents: Perfection of Orchard View.—Raging canal.—Charlie Phister's famous bee shot.—The night raiders.

1000. ———. *Rome haul.* Boston: Little, Brown, 1929. 347p.

Dan Harrow drifts away from the farm existence of his early years to life as a hoogee (a towpath driver youth) and eventually ownership of an Erie Canal boat, the Sarsey Sal. Romance is provided for Dan by Molly Larkins, a young woman taken aboard the Sarsey Sal as cook. In this period (the 1850s) the railroads are beginning to impinge on canal travel and it is Dan's decision to leave the Canal and embark on farming ventures; this move has unforeseen consequences anent Dan's relationship with Molly.

1001. ———. *The South American quirt.* **Boston: Little, Brown, 1985. 186p.**

Twelve-year-old Natty Dinston must contend with an angry, critical and demanding father when he comes for the summer to a farm in Upstate New York in 1915, his sickly mother having gone back to the city. But he does find time to walk the fields and woods in the company of his dog, observe farm life and even strike up a few friendships. The arrival by mail of a whip fashioned from a rhinoceros hide is a signal for further confrontation between father and son.

1002. ———. *Two logs crossing*; **John Haskell's story. Illus. by Tibor Gergely. New York: Dodd, Mead, 1943. 82p.**

In this story for teenagers, John Haskell, the son of a shiftless farmer and careworn mother, seeks, after his father's death, to provide support for his mother and his younger sisters and brothers. He takes up trapping in Upstate New York's forests with the experienced assistance of an Indian. An elderly judge develops an interest in John's activities and is a factor in the youth's strides toward success.

1003. ———. *The wedding journey.* **Drawings by Alan Tompkins. Boston: Little, Brown, 1947. 119p.**

An almost elegiac novella describing the course of an Erie Canal packet boat from Schenectady to Buffalo and its curious load of passengers and crew, especially an uncertain young married couple, Roger and Bella Willcox. It evokes the raucous character of canal travel across upper New York State in 1855 and provides technical details of that mode of transportation. Roger loses the couple's honeymoon money at cards with a pair of sharpers. Bella forgives him; no longer able to afford a hotel near Niagara Falls, they pass several idyllic days on a farm in Lewiston. On first seeing Lake Erie Bella exclaims: "It must be like the sea, Roger." The author remarks: 'She had never seen the sea. She was destined never to see it; but she did not know that.'

1004. ———. *Wilderness clearing.* **Illustrated by John S. de Martelly. New York: Dodd, Mead, 1949. xi, 156p.**

Young Maggie Gordon and Dick Mount are the major characters in this novel about the conflict between the patriot settlers and their adversaries, the Tories and their Indian allies (the 'Destructives'). The 'wilderness clearing' is an area on Black Creek west of Little Falls, New York, in which Robert Gordon, Maggie's father has established a farm.

Edward, James Joseph, 1928- . See under his pseudonym: James, Rebecca, 1928-

Edwards, Albert, pseud. See: Bullard, Arthur, 1879-1929.

1005. Edwards, C. *The rejected symbol.* **New York: J.S. Ogilvie, 1894. 288p.**

"The red flag of anarchy is the rejected symbol. Rev. Darby Jones, the supposed pastor of a church in 'Bumbletown', a thriving town on Long Island, tells, in a rather flippant way, his incidental history, especially dwelling upon a rather questionable passage with one of his parishioners and presenting his general views of socialism and anarchism"—Annual American catalogue.

1006. Edwards, Charles R. *A story of Niagara.* **To which is appended Reminiscences of a Custom House officer. Buffalo: Breed, Lent, 1870. 335p.**

His presumed uncle, Judge Jared Bailey, unknowingly maligns Benjamin Bailey of 'Fallington', N.Y., the hero of this rather formulaic novel, to Deacon William Summers of Niagara. The result is the termination of Benjamin's correspondence with the woman he loves, Laura Summers, the Deacon's daughter. With his appointment from Washington to secret service on the Niagara frontier to help intercept smuggling activities, Benjamin begins to learn more about Judge Bailey's nefarious intentions and activities. Needless to say the Judge's real origins and his involvement in clandestine aims are fully brought to light and Benjamin is able to bring to a successful conclusion his courtship of Laura with her father's approval. The author's description of Niagara Falls shortly after the close of the Civil War is of some interest.

1007. Edwards, Henry, novelist. *Annie*; **a New York life. New York: Manhattan Pub. Co. [186-?] 108p. (in double columns).**

After her stern father's death, Annie (the narrator) leaves Newport, R.I. for New York City and service with the fascinating Mrs. Beesey whom she had met earlier in Newport. And thus begins Annie's introduction to the world of high-level prostitution in the metropolis, for Mrs. Beesey and the two women Annie serves after leaving her first employer are courtesans. Their profession is no hindrance to Mrs. Beesey, Marian Willis and Pat Celeste in their pursuit of more permanent attachments, for all marry well and wealthily. Annie observes but never essays to join the world's oldest profession. Rather she returns to her home and marries the former woodsman, Woodruff, whom she had earlier spurned; Woodruff has acquired a comfortable living and the demeanor of a gentleman.

1008. ————. *The belle of Central Park*; **a story of New York life. New York: Advance Pub. Co. [1866?] 100p. (in double columns).**

Coming from the country to New York City to live with her aunt in Harlem, Fanny Graham is seduced and subjected to a mock marriage by Clarence Morgan. After he deserts her, Fanny falls into the snare of Charles Spencer and serves as his mistress. She eventually leaves him and plots revenge on her two faithless lovers. The story digresses here as Ida Clarence, Fanny's friend, comes under the influence of a Madame Careau and her husband, a doctor. Madame Careau tells fortunes and Fanny and Ida together had visited her earlier. Clarence Morgan and Charles Spencer receive their just due; Morgan is imprisoned for burglary on information provided by Fanny; Spencer is found dead one morning in his apartment. The reformed Fanny chooses a life of seclusion henceforth.

1009. ————. *Fashion and famime.* **Life in New York. New York: Advance Pub. Co. (186-?] 98p. (in double columns).**

Cecilia (Sissy) Gale, a farm laborer's daughter in Yonkers, is seduced and impregnated by the young aristocrat, Percy Amherst. Percy's parents persuade Sissy to enter a 'home' in New York City to have her child; they then take Sissy's baby boy from her. Sissy, adopting the name Fanny White, decides she will use her beauty and increasing knowledge of male ways to get what she wants with no permanent attachments. She lives successively with lovers in Brooklyn and Yorkville. Then she meets under rather odd circumstances Arthur Shamrock Waite and her interest is piqued. Returning to her parents' cottage in Yonkers, Fanny/Sissy again meets Waite who proposes marriage. After she turns him down and Waite learns more about Fanny's past, she takes up residence in Kinderhook. Alcide Everingham, pastor of a church there, falls in love with Fanny. With some reluctance she agrees to marry him. Everingham's accidental death releases Fanny; Shamrock Waite proposes again and Fanny accepts this time.

1010. ————. *The poor of New York.* **From the play of 'The Poor of New-York'. New York: Hilton, 1865. 96 (i.e., 46)p. (in double columns).**

With highly exaggerated flourishes the author describes the Fairbrother family—wife and mother, son Paul and daughter Antoinette—reduced to near beggary and starvation soon after the banker Gideon Bloodgood has appropriated the dying Captain Fairbrother's $100,000. Bloodgood pays hush money to his co-conspirator Badger and uses the stolen funds to build his own fortune. Whatever help the Fairbrothers receive comes from those almost as poor as they and from Mark Livingston, Paul's friend, on the edge of financial ruin himself until Bloodgood loans him money on the condition that he marry Bloodgood's daughter Alida. The once flush Badger, now scrabbling for mere existence, still retains the receipt Bloodgood made out to Captain Fairbrother when the latter's money was placed in Bloodgood's 'trust.' Ultimately the reformed Badger and Mark Livingston force Bloodgood to reimburse the Fairbrother family. Livingston, free of any obligation to wed Alida Bloodgood, turns to his true love, Antoinette Fairbrother.

1011. Edwards, Page, 1941-. *Peggy Salté.* **New York: Boyars, distributed in the U.S. by Scribner, 1983. 215p.**

Peggy Salté has lived all her life (66 years) in an Upstate New York village. Her widowed father, Charles Salté, reared her and while still a schoolgirl she married Charlie, a brutal, insensitive hunting/fishing guide. Peggy manages to rid herself of Charlie and turns to Alston Tucker, a childhood friend and an artist. He becomes Peggy's lover and in due time marries her.

1012. Egan, Maurice Francis, 1852-1924. *Belinda*; **a story of New York. Philadelphia: H.L. Kilner [1910]. 276p.**

At the age of fifteen Belinda Murray moves with her grandmother from Washington, D.C. to New York City. There they share the life of tenement-dwellers and are introduced to a provocative Catholic priest who quickens their interest in the practice of Catholic Christianity.

1013. ————. *The boys in the block.* **New York: Benziger Brothers, 1897. 85p.**

"The block in the story is a short row of houses in a New York street leading into the Bowery. The boys of this street are composed of two cliques, an Irish-American party and an Italian faction. The priest of the parish acting the part of mediator finds his task almost hopeless, until a scrimmage between two of the Irish-Americans and an Italian results in a broken violin, which leads to a peaceful understanding"—Annual American catalogue.

1014. ————. *The disappearance of John Longworthy.* **Notre Dame, Ind.: Office of the Ave Maria, 1890. viii, 306p.**

John Longworthy, a moderately wealthy bachelor author of two books on politics and social problems, disappears from a cab at Broadway and Canal Street. Miles Galligan, also a bachelor, a man of no particular occupation (more or less supported by his maiden sisters, Esther and Mary), decides to find out what really happened to Longworthy. Miles eyes suspiciously Arthur Fitzgerald, a lawyer interested in Mary Galligan, and Rudolph von Bastien, owner of a photography studio. Bastien throws out hints that he knows of Longworthy's fate; yet Bastien's prime concern is the cultural and economic improvement of New York City's poor, deprived classes, and Esther Galligan shares his views. As the reader might surmise, Rudolph von Bastien is John Longworthy in disguise. He converts to Catholicism and becomes engaged to Esther Galligan. With Longworthy's help Miles Galligan wins a seat in New York State's Assembly. A double wedding (Esther and Longworthy, Mary and Fitzgerald) concludes the novel.

1015. ————. *Jasper Thorn*; **a story of New York life. Philadelphia: H.L. Kilner, 1897. 303p.**

"The story of a New York boy who is for a time reduced to poverty and obtains a position as office-boy; his father had gone on a sea voyage and is reported as lost, but finally returns to tell of some remarkable adventures. Jasper has a millionaire aunt who in vain tempts him to leave his mother and become her heir, the condition being that he give up his [Catholic] religion"— Annual American catalogue.

1016. ————. *The vocation of Edward Conway.* **Reprinted from the Ave Maria. New York: Benziger Bros., 1896. 322 p.**

"The scene is on the banks of the Hudson near West Point. Edward Conway, coming from Virginia to visit his Northern relatives, explains to his cousin Bernice some of the doctrines of the Catholic Church. Bernice is so affected by his teachings that she rejects her own faith, the Protestant, becoming a Catholic; she is also heroine in the story which gives Edward Conway's reasons for entering the priesthood"—Annual American catalogue.

1017. Eggleston, Edward, 1837-1902. *The faith doctor*; **a story of New York. New York: Appleton, 1891. 427p.**

"New York City in the neighborhood of Second Avenue, and around Stuyvesant Square and Washington Square furnishes the localities for the story . . . [which] is realistic, presenting a vivid picture of many phases of city life and the many off characters to be found in the metropolis"—Annual American catalogue. The heroine, Phillida Callender, believes implicitly in the power of faith and thus achieves a number of striking 'cures' among New York City's poor, people she meets in the mission Sunday school. However, Phillida does not wish to be known as a faith healer and refuses to help a Christian Scientist, Miss Bowyer, who wants to gain access to rich and powerful families of the city.

1018. Eggleston, George Cary, 1839-1911. *Blind alleys*; **a novel of nowadays. Illustrated by E. Pollak. Boston: Lothrop, Lee & Shepard, 1906. 414p.**

"The characters who find themselves groping in the 'back alleys' of modern New York life as they strive honestly to be helpful to those less fortunate are a young newspaper man who has become separated from the wife he loves, a young doctor who received funds for his education from some mysterious source and knows not his own parentage, a fabulously wealthy spinster and the girl who passes as her ward, and others who are hedged about by circumstances more or less unusual. The story of their various complications and how they are finally straightened out is given in great detail"—Book review digest. An explanation of the title is given by the doctor who says: "My experience leads me to think that nearly all our efforts to better our fellow men, whether positively or negatively, lead us into blind alleys."

1019. Eldred, Warren L. *The Townsend twins, camp directors*. **Illustrated by C.M. Relyea. New York: Century Co., 1913. 376p.**

"Thaddeus and Thomas, the twins, are two wide-awake and resourceful high school boys who organize a summer camp. Under the direction of a young doctor [they and a] group of [eight other] boys spend a happy summer in the Adirondacks"—Book review digest.

1020. Eldridge, Frederick William, 1877-1937. *A social cockatrice*. **Boston: Lothrop Pub. Co., 1903. 412p.**

The story of two wealthy sisters from New Orleans: one a social-climbing, unprincipled woman who lets nothing stand in her way while she jockeys for entry into New York City's 'Four Hundred'; the other, beautiful, kind, as good as her sibling is evil. Unfortunately the latter gets in the way of the former and she is trampled along with a number of innocents and not so innocents.

1021. Elfman, Blossom, 1925- . *The strawberry fields of heaven.* **New York: Crown Publishers, 1983. viii, 372p.**

Peter Berger, saddled with a frigid wife, has been using prostitutes to satisfy his sexual needs. Tiring of that and intrigued by reports of 'free love', he brings Katherine, his wife, and their children to the Oneida Community (1848-1879) in central New York State. Katherine is at first very reluctant to participate in the Community until Sarah, a long-time member, indoctrinates her, and soon Katherine is having a passionate affair with the Community's gardener. Peter discovers that 'complex marriage' as practiced by the Community comes at a price and observes the effect of living in the Community has on his children.

1022. Eliot, Anne, pseud. *The dark beneath the pines.* **New York: Hawthorn Books, 1974. 219p.**

"A picture-prim, pre-World War I mystery-romance with appropriate fashion touches (blue serge or a white fichu) which follows another trail of the lonesome pine to a camp in Upper New York State where Andrea's great-uncle has not only disappeared, but so have his safe deposit valuables and some pictures, all complicating the simpler life of fishing and fireside singing. The story's as clean as that white birch settee and almost sturdy enough for the Adirondack rocker"—Kirkus reviews.

1023. Ellin, Stanley, 1916-1986. *Stronghold.* **New York: Random House, 1974. 322p.**

"Out of Raiford Prison (Florida) back to his old hometown in Upstate New York comes James Flood along with three other criminals. Together the 'Big Daddy' of this operation hopes to pull off a quick 4 million by holding up the local bank run by Quaker Marcus Hayworth whose two daughters (one of whom, Janet, Flood had known ten years earlier—now on pills and crystals) have joined another kind of communal culture. Flood seems equal to everything, except Janet. . . . The Quaker setting is the only difference between thee and all those other [works about violence]"—Kirkus reviews.

1024. Elliot, Henry Rutherford, 1849-1906. *The common chord*; a story of the **Ninth Ward. New York: L. Cassell [1887] viii, 294p.**

"The 'common chord' is the rich, solid, satisfactory chord of C major, in which the author has pitched the story of the lives of some inhabitants of the Ninth Ward of New York City, which he pronounces the American ward of that cosmopolitan town. He introduces almost half-a-dozen characters, but each one is a little masterpiece of word painting. A description of the Battle of Fredericksburg introduces the hero, who afterward drifts to New York and becomes the good influence in the lives of the characters with whom he is thrown"—Annual American catalogue.

Elliot, Norman, joint author. *A survival of the fittest.* **See Item #2263.**

1025. **Elliott, Charles Wyllys, 1817-1883.** *Wind and whirlwind*; **a novel by Mr. Thom White [pseud.] New York: G.P. Putnam, 1868. 307p.**

When first we meet the young heroine, Luly, she has just witnessed the death of her mother on the doorstep of wealthy Edward Percival's Broadway mansion. An Irishwoman, Mrs. Mulloy, takes the child with police permission and brings her up as one of her own. The childless Percivals, Edward and his wife, Matilda, come upon Luly during one of Matilda's charitable forays into the slums of the city and with no objection from Mrs. Mulloy adopt the girl. Mr. Percival, we learn, had a love affair with Sarah Eustis of New Jersey some years before. He had lost touch with Sarah but knew that she bore a baby daughter; his search for that child had been a long and fruitless one. It is obvious to the reader that Luly is that long-lost daughter, but it takes a series of misadventures before Percival and Luly are fully aware of their blood relationship. Matilda Percival, never very close to her husband, becomes increasingly jealous of his fixation on Luly and she and Edward finally separate; a year later she dies.

1026. **Elliott, Francis Perry, 1861-1924.** *The haunted pajamas.* **With illus. by Edmund Frederick. Indianapolis: Bobbs-Merrill, 1911. 355p.**

"A story of mystery, adventure and romance centering around a pair of bright, red, silk pajamas sent from China as a present to a New York clubman [Richard Lightnut who, as his name might imply, is not very smart]. Gauzy and delicate of texture, they yet cast a spell over the wearer, conjure up weird shapes, and bring about no end of midnight adventures. The ludicrous situations [in which Dick and his friend Billings find themselves], the attempts at explanation, the love tangle and the final straightening out are intimately associated with the mischief-making pajamas"—Book review digest.

1027. **Elliott, Sarah Barnwell, 1848-1928.** *The making of Jane*; **a novel. New York: Scribner, 1901. 432p.**

Reduced to poverty by the Civil War and the necessity of providing for a large family, Jane's Southern parents assent to her adoption by her father's female cousin in New York City. This woman is a stern, cold person determined to weld Jane into her notion of a proper lady. Jane escapes from her aunt's home and tries to make it on her own. In the course of the novel the author expands her own ideas on the place of women in a society based on money and social position.

1028. **Ellis, Edward Sylvester, 1840-1916.** *Brave Tom*; **or,** *The battle that won.* **New York: Merriam Co., 1894. 231p.**

"Tom Gordon is a country lad who, left an orphan, goes with a chum to New York City to seek his fortune. The boys are soon separated. Kidnappers carry off Jim and Tom has varied adventures as a newsboy in New York and on a railway route. They finally meet again, and after Jim's death Tom finds work with a rich merchant in a Hudson River town, where he finally wins his way into partnership, and marries his employer's daughter"—Annual American catalogue.

1029. ————. *Honest Ned.* **Philadelphia: H.T. Coates, 1894. 2360.**
"Opens with the discovery that a valuable black diamond has been abstracted from the safe of a firm of diamond brokers in Maiden Lane, New York City. Circumstantial evidence points directly to Edmund Melton, a young clerk in the employ of the firm, and the interest of the story centers in the unraveling of the mystery and the clearing of the lad's good name through the detective skill of a fellow clerk"—Annual American catalogue.

1030. ————. *Iron Heart, war chief of the Iroquois.* **Philadelphia: H.T.Coates, 1899. iv, 386p.**
The New York frontier in its early days with Indians and Whites in conflict over ownership of the land is the scene of this novel. The chief characters are: Iron Heart, warrior chieftain of the Six Nations, a White scout, and two young twin pioneer lads with their crippled brother.

1031. ————. *The rangers of the Mohawk*; a tale of Cherry Valley. **New York: Beadle and Adams, 1862. 96p.**
Historical events surrounding this tale are the siege of Fort Schuyler by St. Leger and the massacre at Cherry Valley perpetrated by Tories under Walter Butler and Mohawk Indians. Butler and Captain Eugene Heath of the patriot army are chief characters. Both men are suitors of Edith Gardner (the author starts out with the surname Gordon), daughter of a staunch Loyalist. Butler is painted as a reprehensible, merciless villain. Much of the narrative is concerned with a skirmish at the Gardner house between Heath, his scout Buck Bailey and their Oneida allies and Butler with his Mohawks and scout Honyost Schuyler. Before the story concludes Butler has been slain by the Oneida Catfoot, Honyost Schuyler has changed sides in the conflict (to his future profit) and Heath, wounded, is nursed by Edith and wins her love.

1032. ————. *Red Jacket, the last of the Senecas*, by Colonel H.R. Gordon [pseud.]. **New York: Dutton, 1900. iv, 347p.**
A fictionalized version of General John Sullivan's campaign in the Finger Lakes region of New York State in which he punished the Iroquois for their raids on American settlements in the Mohawk Valley and elsewhere. Sullivan himself and Red Jacket, the famous Seneca orator, are historical personages who take leading roles in the novel, although the two scouts, the veteran Jed Stiffens and the 16-year-old Jack Ripley, play the largest roles (one assumes, without any real proof that Stiffens and Ripley are fictional characters). In any

case, the author's story has enough verve and dash to quicken the pulse of any young (or old) reader. One detects, however, a tendency to dwell on the savagery of the Iroquois in war without placing enough blame on the White settlers who were so rapidly dispossessing the Iroquois of their lands.

1033. ————. *Righting the wrong*. **New York: Merriam Co., 1894. 217p.**
"Takes up the adventures of Edmund Melton [of New York City], forming a sequel to 'Honest Ned' in the same series. In the present story young Melton is driven by his guardian's harshness to run away from home, and is suspected of taking with him a package of diamonds belonging to his employers. A professional detective is employed to track him, but the boy is finally found and the puzzle solved by the young fellow clerk who figures in 'Honest Ned' [q.v.]"—Annual American catalogue.

1034. ————. *Seth Jones*; or, *The captives of the frontier*. **New York: I.P. Beadle [1860] 123p.**
Also published in 1907 (New York: Dillingham) under the title: *Seth Jones of New Hampshire*. Alfred Haverland and his family seek to escape the depredations of Indians on their western New York home, but their daughter Ina is captured by them. A mysterious woodsman who calls himself Seth Jones appears and offers his help. Everard Graham, Ina's lover, and an Indian fighter, Ned Haldidge, join him. The core of the tale revolves around the attempts of the men to wrest Ina from her captors, the Mohawks. After exciting adventures Ina is freed. Seth, whose real name is Eugene Morton (he had been thought killed during the American Revolution) is joined to the woman he has long loved, Mary Haverland, Alfred's sister. In the style of the day the author pictures the Indian, as 'devils' who cannot be trusted.

1035. **Ellis, John Breckenridge, 1870-1956.** *Something else*; a novel. **With illus. by Ernest L. Blumenschein. Chicago: McClurg, 1911. 438p.**
Reared by a New York Harbor tugboat captain and his wife, Irving Payne has no knowledge of his real parents. As he steps into the milling city Irving finds work as a clerk at 20 dollars per week and lodges in a third floor apartment room—then begins his search for an explanation of his origins. The novel evolves into a varied portrait of seething New York: activities by the 'Black Hand', rent riots on New York's East Side, the rantings of soap-box orators and anarchists, a glimpse of the very rich, etc. Irving does unlock some of the secrets of his past and also meets an upper class family and a girl who holds in her hands the promise of love.

Ellis, Sarah Stickney, 1812-1872, supposed author. *Two ways to wedlock.* **See note under Item #3422.**

1036. **Ellsworth, Louise C.** *Furono Amati*; a romance. **New York: United States Book Co., 1893. 164p.**

The hero is introduced as an Italian bootblack nine years old, dozing under a bench in Madison Square, New York City. Into his squalid tenement house comes a whole-souled German, possessor of an Amati violin, with which he charms the musical soul of the boy. In a fit of passion, because he cannot make the Amati sing for him, the boy destroys the valuable instrument. Later he becomes the fashion and marries a girl of good family. He discovers that she loves his music more than himself and he destroys her as he had done the violin, because she would not sing for him. But 'they were both loved.'

1037. ————. *A little worldling*; a novel, by Ellis Worth [pseud]. New York: American News Co., 1890. 320p.

'Nixie', the 'little worldling', the daughter of a failed actor, is at his side when he dies. Her father wills Nixie on his mother, a disapproving, austere lady of puritanical demeanor who lives with her half-brother and a sister in a large, well-appointed house somewhere in the State of New York. Nixie's bright outlook and cheery disposition does not seem to fit too well in the somber household presided over by her grandmother. Nevertheless, when Nixie's youngish great-aunt falls unwisely in love, Nixie stands by her; eventually Nixie is able to make her relatives happily accept the various pleasures the world has to offer.

Elman, Richard, 1934-1997. see under his pseudonym: Spyker, John Howland.

1038. **Elmore, Mrs. A.** *Billy's mother*. **New York: J.S. Ogilvie, 1885. 233p.**

A young physician becomes interested in an aged, friendless woman, known to certain denizens of New York as "Billy's mother', for it was a lad by that name that she had been searching the streets of the big city for a very long time. The doctor succeeds against all odds in tracking down the missing boy, a former sailor who had over the years become a prosperous farmer with a family to support.

Embury, Emma Catherine, 1806-1863. *The blind girl.* **See note under Item #1039.**

1039. **Embury, Emma Catherine, 1806-1863.** *Constance Latimer*; or, *The blind girl*. **With other tales. New York: Harper, 1838. 169p.**

Also issued under the title: *The blind girl . . .* (with additional short stories). The title story moves its scene from an opulent villa on the Hudson to a rented apartment in New York City and ends on Long Island. Constance, struck blind after a bout with scarlet fever, studies at a new institution for educating those who have lost their sight. Her father loses much of his fortune and goes abroad to recoup his losses. Constance becomes a music teacher, refuses marriage to the son of a benefactor and continues teaching and writing after her father returns and provides his family with a modest income. 'The Village tragedy' takes place in 'D'Autremont', a village in northern New York.

Presumably based on a true incident, it relates how the rigid and exacting James Churchill so exacerbates the unfortunate Walter Howland that he murders Churchill—Howland blames Churchill for the elder Howland's decline into idiocy and his own loss of farm and livelihood. Contents: Constance Latimer.—The son and heir.—The village tragedy.

1040. Emerson, Alice B. *Ruth Fielding of the Red Mill*; or, *Jasper Parloe's secret.* **New York: Cupples & Leon, 1913. 204p.**

> The first of a series of at least 18 'Ruth Fielding' novels, it and a 2nd title (Ruth Fielding at Briarwood Hall) have an Upstate New York setting. In this introductory story, Ruth, recently orphaned, comes to live with her miserly great-uncle, Jabez Potter, and his housekeeper, Aunt Elvirah Boggs. Ruth finds little love or attention from Jabez, but has a sympathetic supporter in Aunt Elvirah and such neighbors as Helen and Tom Cameron and Doctor Davison. Through trial, error and good works Ruth gradually mellows the proprietor of the Red Mill, Jabez. When she and the Camerons return Jabez's treasured strong box (taking it from Jasper Parloe's hiding place—for it was he who had walked off with it during a flood) Jabez is prepared to finance Ruth's further education at Briarwood Hall.

1041. Emerson, Jill, pseud. *A week as Andrea Benstock*; a novel. **New York: Arbor House, 1975. 252p.**

> Andrea Benstock, weary of her change-of-partners existence in New York City, heads back to Buffalo where she meets and marries a lawyer, a decent but rather naïve man. Despite the trappings of a comfortable, upper middle class life, tedium, unfaithfulness and failure to communicate beset the marriage. Andrea leaves but finds no comfort in frantic sex, the low-paying jobs she is forced to take, and her loneliness. Back she goes to Buffalo for another chance at resolving her problems.

1042. Emery, Anne, 1907- . *A spy in old West Point.* **Illustrated by Lorence F. Bjorklund. Chicago: Rand, McNally, 1965. 191p.**

> Jock Fraser, 14, lived on a farm in Croton-on-Hudson at the time of Benedict Arnold's formulation of plans to put West Point in British hands. He became involved with persons participating in that event and was present when Major André was captured. A rather routine, not very memorable piece of fiction.

1043. Emery, Russell Guy, 1908- . *Rebound.* **Philadelphia: Macrae Smith, 1955. 190p.**

> Larry Warren, whom the reader may have met in the author's 'Warren of West Point', is dropped from the Army basketball team because of a senseless incident that has involved him. Coming back to the Point after taking part of a year off and sacrificing his summer leave, Larry leads the basketball squad to a win over Navy and an invitation to a tournament.

1044. —————. *Warren of West Point.* **Philadelphia: Macrae, Smith, 1950. 202p.**

At 6 feet, 6 inches Larry Warren from Nebraska is a very tall plebe. There is some question in his mind as to whether he can adapt to the Academy's ways. However he takes up basketball and cross-country running. His talents in both sports assure Larry's gradual entry into the mainstream of plebe life.

1045. Empey, Arthur Guy, 1883-1963. *The madonna of the hills*; **a story of a New York cabaret girl. New York: Harper, 1921. 403p.**

"This story of a New York cabaret girl and of the New York underworld shows human nature at its lowest, and incidentally at its highest. It presents an appalling picture of the graft game with which human sharks outwit one another and prey upon the unwary, of the role played in it by the police, and of the dangers to which women are exposed in this murky flood. Mollie Eastman's mother was caught in it and went down and Mollie herself struggled long against the tide and kept herself pure—thanks to the kind mothering of Mrs. Henderson—even after she was engulfed. When she realized the fact that she had been trapped into a gambling den and that the man whom she thought she loved was a criminal, she fled into the mountains and allowed the past to fall away from her. The one-time cabaret girl marries a country parson after an enthusiastic Italian artist has painted her picture as the Madonna of the Hills"—Book review digest.

1046. Engel, Howard, 1931- . *Murder on location*; **a Benny Cooperman mystery. New York: St. Martin's Press, 1985. 222p.**

Private detective Benny Cooperman is in Niagara Falls searching for the missing wife of the real estate agent who hired him. She is an aspiring actress, and since a movie is being shot at the Falls, Benny figures she may be angling for a role in the production. Her husband has a gnawing fear that his wife has been murdered. However Benny alternately finds the missing person twice and loses her twice. While Benny's investigation continues, a murder does take place—the victim is a young actor/writer; then a movie actress of star caliber commits suicide and gangsters get into the act.

1047. England, George Allan, 1877-1936. *The air trust*. **Illus. by John Sloan. St. Louis: Phil Wagner, 1915. 333p.**

"A billionaire conceives the notion of controlling the distribution of the air itself. . . . He has the Socialist Party outlawed, sets up a great Air Trust power plant at Niagara Falls, and prepares to put his scheme into action." (Rideout, W.B. The radical novel in the United States, 1900-1954). The socialists go underground and one of their leaders, Gabriel Armstrong, leads an attack on the plant. It goes up in flames, the billionaire dies and his radical daughter joins her lover Gabriel.

1048. ———. *The alibi*. **With a front. by Modest Stein. Boston: Small, Maynard, 1916. 363p.**

Arthur Mansfield is the victim of Slayton, a cashier at the bank where he works, who sees in Arthur's appeal for financial help an opportunity to settle his own monetary difficulties. Slayton steals bank funds and places the blame for it and a resulting murder on Arthur. Mansfield spends two years in Sing Sing before an individual who knows of Slayton's crimes clears him; Slayton, beset by blackmail and a guilty conscience, finally confesses and kills himself.

1049. ————. *Darkness and dawn*. **Boston: Small, Maynard. 1914. 672p.**

"Allen Stern, engineer, and Beatrice Kendrick once his stenographer, wake up in his office in the Metropolitan Tower to find the city [New York] they have once known is a crumbling ruin in a forest of oak and pine; that wild animals and a strange race of savages, only half-human, have overrun Manhattan Island; that they are the only surviving members of their kind. The strange catastrophe that overwhelmed the Earth in the year 1920 had put them to sleep, and they have awakened only after many centuries. Then begins a series of perilous. . . adventures, and with the finding of a race of devoluted Americans whom they teach and inspire, the upbuilding of a new civilization in which an aristocracy of idleness is unknown where there is no slavery, where mankind is free"—Book review digest.

1050. **Enright, Richard Edward, b. 1871.** *Vultures of the dark*. **New York: Brentano's, 1929. 360p.**

A well-organized band of criminals, headed by a presumably respectable citizen, the brains of the organization, finds the victims of their robberies in the upper ranks of New York society. Detective Sergeant Roger Warren is assigned to help break up the gang; in the course of his investigation he and the daughter (Audrey) of the master criminal fall in love. Actually the reader will know who these criminals really are from the very beginning, but may well be intrigued by the interplay of the police and the thieves.

Epstein, Samuel, 1909- . See under his pseudonym: Campbell, Bruce, 1909-

1050a.**Esaki-Smith, Anna.** *Meeting Luciano*. **Chapel Hill, N.C.: Algonquin Books, 1999. 252p.**

After graduating from college Japanese-American Emily Shimoda is back in Westchester County, N.Y., living in her mother's house and waitressing at a Japanese restaurant. Emily's mother, Hanako, a recent divorcee and an opera lover, goes through several life-changing stages, one of which involves making over her home with the collusion of an intrusive Greek-American contractor. Although Hanako likes to tell Emily stories of her Japanese past, she insists that Emily become a full-fledged American. This is rather confusing to Emily and she has to look sharply at her own past experiences, find her own way and still be sensitive to her mother's needs.

1051. **Estabrook, Barry.** *Whirlpool.* **New York: St. Martin's Press, 1995. 280p.**

It is an extremely hot summer for Upstate New York and the Adirondacks would seem to offer some relief from the heat. Unfortunately that vacation retreat is rocked by three tragic events: the murder of a millionaire whose body is found by a trout fisherman; a chemical spill that decimates the trout population; and a shotgun blast that ends the life of a hiker. To New York State trooper Garwood Plunkett falls the task of making sense of these seemingly related incidents. The millionaire's widow, Percy Quinnell, a former girlfriend of Plunkett, must be deemed a prime suspect; she hasn't wept for her husband and is trying to force out her late husband's partner and take over the Quinnell business. Plunkett's life may be in danger because he is so near the solution of several contiguous crimes.

1052. *Estelle Grant*; or, *The lost wife*. **New York: Garrett, 1855. 350p.**
Emory brings his reluctant bride, Estelle Grant, and her family from St. Louis to his Hudson River residence; Estelle must leave behind the man she is in love with, James Ely (he turns up later in the novel, a widower with a small son). Emory is a vicious personage whose wealth derives from a swindle he perpetrated on a trusting associate from Texas; he is also a seducer and is presently endeavoring to ruin the virtuous Helen Wallace, the daughter of the man he swindled. Estelle flees her hellish marriage and ends up in New York City with a faithful servant and an infant son she thoroughly despises. Under a pseudonym Estelle now enters into a degrading criminal life that takes her to New Orleans and back to New York, leaving a trail of defrauded men in her wake. James Ely, her only true love, reenters her life; she passes off Ely's son to Emory, claiming that he is Emory's own. As the reader would suspect, the reprehensible characters in the novel come to bad ends, the true son of Estelle and Emory among them. Restored to Helen Wallace is the money stolen from her father by Emory; Helen and her husband, a reformed rake, Bob Barker, adopt Emory's (i.e. Ely's) son.

Evans, Florence Wilkinson. See: Wilkinson, Florence.

1053. **Evans, Ida M.** *The jeweled herd*. **New York: J.H. Sears, 1927. 301p.**
The young couple, Ira and Alma Packard, are scraping a bare existence from their New York City environment and living in a modest apartment facing an elevated railroad. Nevertheless Alma assures the folks back home in her letters that she and Ira are doing quite well. The imminent visit of a wealthy girl friend forces Alma to concoct an elaborate scheme wherein Ira is to act as a Greenwich Villager who has deliberately adopted poverty to emphasize the needs of half-famished mankind. Almost predictably Ira attains celebrity among some well-heeled eccentrics in their jewel-bedecked finery. One unexpected consequence of the scheme is the drifting apart of Alma and Ira.

Evans, Hugh Austin. See under his pseudonym: Austin, Hugh.

1054. **Everett, Ruth.** *That man from Wall Street*; **a story of the studios. New York: G.T. Long, 1908. 300p.**

A fictional attempt to portray bohemian, artistic life in New York City through the experiences of three women artists who share a flat and whose sexual mores are described by the author as far below the standards she herself clings to.

1055. Ewing, Hugh Boyle, 1826-1905. *A castle in the air*. New York: H. Holt, 1888. 273p.

"The Decker estate, consisting of a vast property in New York City, and millions in gold lying in the vaults of the Amsterdam banks, is the basis of this 'castle in the air.' The 'Decker estate' originated in the minds of two impecunious and unscrupulous lawyers. They found members of the Decker family in all parts of the country ready to believe their story, and give money to aid the plausible scheme of dividing up the land and the gold. These men's misdeeds, the people they rob and ruin, the brilliant hopes they raise, and the bitter disappointments which follow them are all parts of a well-told story"—Annual American catalogue.

1056. *Ex-judge*. New York: Bretnano's, 1930. 274p.

Idealistic young lawyer, David Gaunt, joins the Tammanela Social and Political Club, marries the daughter of a political boss, and acquires a judgeship. He learns too late that he owes his august position to the influence of the underworld and corrupt politicians. The scene of the novel is pointed to as "a large American city whose identity is rather meaninglessly obscured." New York is a most likely candidate (Tammany Hall, et al.).

1057. Exley, Frederick, 1929-1992. *A fan's notes;* a fictional memoir. New York: Harper & Row, 1968. 385p.

"The story of Mr. Exley, the son of a hero-worshipped high school athlete from Upstate New York, doomed by the accepted insanities of America to live out his life as a fan, not just of the New York Giants [and Frank Gifford], toward whom most of his real passion and affection get channeled, but of the process of daily survival"—The nation.

Fabend, Firth Haring, 1937- . See: Haring, Firth, 1937-

Fabian, Warner, pseud. See: Adams, Samuel Hopkins, 1871-1958.

1058. Facilis, pseud. *Two women who posed*. New York: J.S. Ogilvie, 1897. 136p.

"Most of the action occurs in the art studios of New York City. One of the women who posed was a society girl who frequented the studios because bohemian life attracted her; the other was a professional model, who earned a living by posing in costume. A well-known artist plays an important part in the lives of both women, although he is not the hero of the ... novel"—Annual American catalogue.

1058a.Fagan, Louis John, 1971- . *New boots.* **Johnstown, N.Y.: A-Peak Publishing, 1999. 178p.**

Cornelia ('Connie') McRamsee is 17 in 1911 when she and her wealthy parents depart from their spacious estate in Albany for a summer at an Adirondack resort. The only child and heiress, Connie becomes friendly with a stable boy, Samuel Flint, and the two eventually fall in love to the dismay of the elder McRamsees and the man they had 'selected' as their future son-in-law, Robert Stimes. Stimes may be socially acceptable but he is a cad with a tendency to drink too much. The outcome is a tragic one. Connie's great-grandson is the audience to which she reveals her story when she is 100 years old.

1059. Fagan, Norbert. *The crooked mile.* **New York: Fawcett Publications, 1953. 170p.**

The racetrack at Belmont, Elmont, Long Island, is the scene of the novel. The author's story is based on the reactions of the people who work at Belmont: the jockeys, trainers, the owners and the police. The hero is a rather ambivalent character who contends with the clever underworld element and its efforts to control the racing competition. The persons who are intimately connected with the details of horseracing are portrayed as consummate professionals.

1060. Fairbank, Janet Ayer, 1879-1951. *The Cortlandts of Washington Square.* **Indianapolis: Bobbs-Merrill, 1922. 399p.**

Ann Byrne becomes the ward of the old bachelor, Hendricks Cortlandt, when her mother, a widow, marries Hudson Cortlandt of Washington Square and both die at sea. Over the protest of the Cortlandt family Ann takes up nursing when the Civil War starts. The family gets wind of her quite unusual experiences near the front lines and are able to use them as a means of moving her towards what they deem a most fortunate marriage. But before the marriage comes off, Ann meets a most appealing young man and chooses to follow him, again to the family's consternation.

1061. Fales, William E.S. *Bits of broken china.* **New York: Street & Smith, 1902. 171p.**

Short stories about the people who dwell in New York City's Chinatown. Contents: Poor Doc High.—The Red Mogul.—The temptation of Li-Li.—A Mott Street incident.—The end of the hall.—The mousetrap.—The turning of the worm.

1062. Falkner, Leonard, 1900- . *Murder off Broadway.* **New York: Holt, 1930. 236p.**

"The murder of Beverly Bancroft, Broadway actress, baffled Inspector Luff. But his friend, John Ballinger, who knew enough about art to be able to tell a false painting or copy from an original, employed his art-detective methods to this murder case—in which, incidentally, a portrait was involved—and discovered the murderer"—Book review digest.

1063. Falkner, William C., 1826-1889. *Lady Olivia*; a novel. New York: G.W. Dillingham, 1895. 334p.

"A romantic love-story told by an old man approaching his hundredth birthday. The hero and heroine were born upon the banks of the Hudson River on the same day in 1757. The events immediately preceding the American Revolution give color to the chequered lives of the faithful lovers"—Annual American catalogue.

1064. *The Family of the Seisers*; a satirical tale of the City of New York. New York: Printed for the author by J.M. Elliott, 1844. 2 pts. in 1v. (in double columns).

The chief plot of the novel is the attempt by rich Louis Seiser, banker, and member of the firm of Grasp, Gripe, Grip and Seiser, to seize by fraud the rightful shares of the poor and improvident Seisers (including Mrs. Billington Seiser, widow, and her two children; Augustus Seiser, spendthrift; Edward Seiser, industrious but not prosperous) from an English estate. Captain John (Thunderbolt) Seiser, with the assistance of an English classmate, Billington Brent, presents Louis Seiser with proof of this criminal act and the latter expires on the spot. The anonymous author of this piece endows many of his characters with such picturesque names as: Tom Scrape, Sam Crisp, Madame Chinchilles, Twittey La Pump, Alderman Iky Snoll, Lob Tiershedder, Baron Clam, Motley Piper, the Messrs. Pork, Bungspunger and Pleabiter, et al.

1065. Fane, Frances Gordon, b. 1867. *The way of a man with a maid.* New York: G.W. Dillingham, 1901. 301p.

Grief and grim misfortune are the inevitable results when Dorothy Tremaine, a New York City artist, is attracted to a young English writer, John Barrington, and marries him—for Barrington had claimed that he was divorced from his first wife, when in actuality the so-called divorce was illegal and void.

1066. Farina, Richard, 1935-1966. *Been down so long it looks like up to me.* New York: Random House, 1966. 329p.

A novel that, among other things, purportedly portrays student life at Cornell ('Ithake'—or Mentor?) University in the 1950s. The protagonist, Gnossos Pappadopoulis, seems to spend most of his time with his friends getting high on alcohol, mescaline, and other substances, pursuing flat-chested Pamela, and occasionally taking off for such destinations as Cuba and the western United States.

1067. Farish, Terry, 1947- . *Shelter for a seabird.* New York: Greenwillow Books, 1990. 163p.

Andrea Tagg had been in a home for pregnant young women, had given birth to a baby that was put up for adoption, and had left the shelter to return to her home on an island off Long Island. There is a noticeable change in 16-year-old Andrea, although her parents and friends ignore it and treat her as if she had never undergone her recent crisis. Andrea retreats into her private self, coming out only when a young AWOL soldier, Swede Stuhr, introduces himself. He is the son of wealthy parents and at first Andrea shies away from him, but is ultimately drawn into a deep relationship with the lonely soldier.

1068. Farnham, Mateel Howe, 1910-1957. *The Tollivers.* **New York: Dodd, Mead, 1944. 240p.**

"Some thirty years of life in a small town called 'Otsego' [in Upstate New York] is described in this story. The Tollivers were a flamboyant family, consisting of a mother and three startlingly beautiful daughters. Mr. Tolliver only entered the picture twice, and then for brief intervals. But the three daughters delighted or shocked Otsego for many years; married well; caused scandals; and went their unorthodox ways. The narrator is Louise, the sensible daughter of the town judge, who aided, advised and comforted various members of the family for years"—Book review digest.

1069. Farnol, Jeffery, 1878-1952. *The definite object*; **a romance of New York. With front. by F. Vaux Wilson. Boston: Little, Brown, 1917. vii, 363p.**

"Geoffrey Ravenslee was suffering from the boredom of too much money. Life offered him a variety of diversions but no definite object. A young amateur burglar, attempting to break into his house, brings the needed change. Geoffrey decides that instead of turning young Spike over to the authorities, he will accompany him to his home in lower New York and see something of life from another angle. He finds all that he has been looking for—adventure, of course, and with it romance, for Spike, the would-be burglar, proves to be the adored younger brother of a very lovely sister"—Book review digest.

1070. Farrington, Fielden. *A little game.* **New York: Walker, 1968. 150p.**

Two boys, Bob Reagan and Stu Parker, leave the Hastings Military Academy on the Hudson to spend Christmas vacation with Bob's mother, Elaine, and her new husband, Paul Hamilton, at Shore Road in Great Neck, Long Island. Elaine and her son are very close, but Bob despises his stepfather. Paul is well aware of his stepson's hatred; when Laura, the housekeeper, shows him entries from Bob's diary that display his plans to kill Laura, Paul and Stu, Paul springs into action. He quizzes Stu and hires a private investigator to trace Bob's movements at the Academy. The denouement comes in the snow-covered grove back of the house—Paul and Stu and eventually Elaine face an armed, desperate Bob.

1071. Farris, John. *The captors.* **New York: Trident Press, 1969. 256p.**

Carol Watterson is kidnapped from Jake's for Steak on the Saw Mill River Parkway (Westchester branch). Whatever ransom may be demanded for her release is unlikely to be provided by her stepfather, a political pamphleteer. Carol's grandfather, General Morse, a dealer on the world's arms market, could easily come up with the cash. But then Carol, suffering from her ordeal, returns to her home—and no money has changed hands.

1072. Fast, Howard, 1914- . *The unvanquished.* **New York: Duell, Sloan and Pearce, 1942. viii, 316p.**

Of all the historical characters in the novel George Washington takes by far the commanding role as he matures into an effective leader of the mixture of earnest and ragtag patriots who suffered disaster after disaster in battling the British and their Hessian mercenaries on Long island (chiefly Brooklyn), Manhattan Island, and along the Hudson (Westchester). The novel winds to an end as the rebel army moves into New Jersey and Washington is about to advance on the Hessians in Trenton on Christmas Eve. The author draws a stark and convincing picture of New York City under brief occupation by an exhausted, demoralized, unwelcome patriot army and then by the victorious British that is followed by a resumption of ordinary business and social activities.

1073. Fauley, Wilbur Finley, 1872-1942. *Jenny be good.* **New York: Britton Publication Co., 1919. 326p.**

"The story opens in a New England seacoast village. Jenny, the descendant of Puritan forbears, lives with an old grandmother who never lets her forget her family's past greatness. On the other side of her heritage little is said, for Jenny's mother had married a Portuguese fisherman. But it is from the foreign strain that Jenny inherits the musical genius that is to make her famous. Before she reaches that height, however, she goes through many experiences, including a period as a factory worker in New York. Scenes in the upper levels of [New York] society alternate with pictures from the life of the poor [in that city]"—Book review digest.

1074. ———. *Queenie*; **the adventures of a young lady. Front. by G.W. Gage. New York: Macaulay, 1921. 306p.**

Queenie, the heroine of this mystery, has several encounters with life in New York City, the most striking of which is her residence in a mansion presently occupied by a servant who is impersonating his wealthy, reclusive employer; Queenie is the niece of the impersonator's wife.

1075. Fauset, Jessie Redmon, 1884?-1961. *Plum bun*; **a novel without a moral. New York: Stokes, 1929. 379p.**

"Angela Morgan is an educated colored girl fair enough to pass for white. Changing her name she goes to New York City to live in Greenwich Village and embarks on an unhappy love affair with a white man. Her younger sister, who is unmistakably colored, also goes to New York, but lives in Harlem, and the sisters rarely meet. Anthony Cross enters the lives of both girls, but does not know they are sisters. He too is 'passing'. A complicated situation arises, causing the three much pain before their problems of love and color are adjusted"—Book review digest. First published in 1928 in London (E. Mathews & Marrot).

1076. ————. *There is confusion.* New York: Boni and Liverright, 1924. 297p.

Joanna Marshall, gifted and Black, strives for full acceptance as an artist, but more often than not finds her color an insuperable impediment. And so it is with other middle class Black characters in this novel that is set in New York City (Harlem and upper Manhattan) chiefly and Philadelphia. Joanna infuses Peter Bye, who is inclined to indolence, with late blooming ambition. Together they achieve happiness and pride in their accomplishments that White prejudice cannot dampen. Faust, one of the first Black female graduates of Cornell University, effectively strikes at the artificial barriers White's have erected against Black entry into the mainstream.

1077. Fawcett, Edgar, 1847-1904. *The adopted daughter.* Chicago: F.T. Neely, 1892. 262p.

"The 'adopted daughter' is the child of a maid servant and an uneducated Irishman, who is adopted in infancy by a wealthy New York woman and reared as her daughter and heiress. Years later, when the real parents have become rich people—the father being a millionaire political boss—they insist on reclaiming their daughter. She is a beautiful, cultured, proud young girl, engaged to a rich New Yorker, when her parentage is revealed to her. The bravery with which she faces the situation determines her future happiness and assures the keeping of the secret of her birth. New York life is delineated with the author's accustomed insight"—Annual American catalogue.

1078. ————. *The adventures of a widow*; a novel. Boston: J.R. Osgood, 1884. 341p.

The widow comes from New York City's upper class; she is tired of its fripperies and aspires to be the hostess of a salon devoted to intellectual conversation and good literature. Ralph Kendelon, an Irishman and assistant editor of the journal Asteroid, provides support. The salon does attract members of New York's literary cabal and the hostess has mixed reactions to its views. The novel is a device for the author to criticize the literary establishment from several angles and to condemn the personal vilification that some of the city's newspapers print.

1079. Fawcett, Edgar, 1847-1904. *An ambitious woman*; a novel. Boston:Houghton, Mifflin, 1884. 444p.

The ambitious woman is Claire Hollister whose humble origins are no barrier to her marrying a Wall Street financier who also holds high position in the fashionable society of the day. Claire is more than willing to do just about everything to maintain her status and her goals, however questionable the ethics involved. The author provides a mix of other characters representing various levels of 'society': a Bowery bum, a beguiling stockbroker with malleable principles, an aristocratic lady who chooses her acquaintances based on their bloodlines, and an heiress to a brewer's millions.

1080. ————. *The confessions of Claud*; a romance. Boston: Ticknor, 1887. 395p.

"A study in heredity. 'Claud', or Otho Clauss, is the inheritor of a sad family history. He is the son of a German peasant who ran off with the daughter of a wealthy Breton bourgeois; failing to gain her father's forgiveness, he came to America and is gaining a precarious living, when the story opens, in an obscure part of New York, as a cultivator of fine vegetables. He is a morose, jealous man, and from striking his wife, at length murders her, and is hung for the crime. Claud, with the tragedy darkening his life, is adopted by a wealthy lady, who takes him abroad. The evil traits he has inherited bear fruit in his own painful life"—Annual American catalogue.

1081. —————. *A daughter of silence*; **a novel. New York: Belford Co., 1890. 255p.**
New York City and Hoboken, New Jersey are the locales of most of the novel's scenes. "The 'daughter of silence' is Brenda Monk, a beautiful but passive woman who becomes engaged to Guy Arbuthnot. During the period of their engagement Ralph Allaire, an erstwhile friend of Brenda's, murders Brenda's father. Brenda visits Allaire in his prison cell and hands him the knife he used to kill her father. Allaire stabs himself and dies. Brenda comes out of his cell, confesses to Arbuthnot that she had been Allaire's mistress for three years and then kills herself with the same knife"—Harrison, S.R. Edgar Fawcett.

1082. —————. *A demoralizing marriage.* **Philadelphia: J.B. Lippincott, 1889. 205p.**
"A young and lovely woman who is the possessor of three millions, but who is not within the enchanted circle of fashionable life, and a young and handsome man who is within the circle, but who is without money, are the pair who make what turns out to be a 'demoralizing marriage.' The husband is false to his vows, and recklessly extravagant; his wife discovers his deception, charges him with it, and orders him out of 'her' house. A Rhode Island divorce promises to be the result, but the false husband conveniently dies abroad. Another marriage experience concludes the story. The scene alternates between New York and Newport, and some capital descriptions are given of society people"—Annual American catalogue.

1083. —————. *Divided lives*; **a novel. Chicago: Belford, Clarke, 1888. 250p.**
New York City, 'Ponchatuk' (Long Island) and Ogdensburg (northern New York State) are the chief locales of the novel. The love affair of poet Hubert Throckmorton and Angela Laight is sundered by jealous Alva Averill when she tells Angela that Hubert has fathered an illegitimate child. Angela breaks with Hubert and marries wealthy Bleakly Voght. At the point of death Alva confesses to Hubert her sin and points to Voght as the true father of the child with a young woman named Jane Heath as the mother. Hubert and Voght have several confrontations culminating in Voght's death at Ponchatuk when Hubert's hunting rifle accidentally discharges. Brought to trial on a charge of murder Hubert wins a 'not guilty' verdict from the jury, but the general public feels he has gotten away with murder. Hubert tells Angela he does not want to

involve her in his dubious future, but auspicious investigation by Hubert's friend Callahan O'Hara and Angela reveals that Jane Heath's brother, Julius Heath, is the real murderer. Heath had been in Voght's service under the alias of Bradbourne, and had shot Voght, firing his pistol simultaneously with the firing of Hubert's rifle. And all ends well with the former and future lovers.

1084. —————. *The evil that men do*; a novel. New York: Belford Co. [c1889] 1339p.

"With the sickening, repulsive realism of Zola, Mr. Fawcett depicts the life of Cora Strang, a poor and friendless sewing-girl, whose home is in one of the meanest tenements of New York City. Her degraded associates and her squalid surroundings and the temptations, which assail her on all sides, are powerfully depicted. Her miserable career, ending in her ruin and subsequent death by violence in the streets, carries its own moral"—Annual American catalogue. The Rosenheims, owners of a clothing shop, are Cora's employers. She secured the job through her landlady, but is later ordered out of her living quarters because the landlady's brother, who has designs on Cora, downgrades Cora's behavior to his sister.

1085. —————. *Fabian Dimitry*; a novel. Chicago: Rand, McNally, 1890. 296p.

"Fabian Dimitry, a young successful playwright, falls in love with a young English girl, but learning that insanity is hereditary in her family, he does not ask her to marry him. His intimate friend, after first trying to combat Dimitry's scruples, marries the girl himself. After several months circumstances bring Dimitry to live with her former friend, a practicing physician in New York City. He then discovers that the hereditary curse has taken the form of kleptomania in his friend's wife. He once more sacrifices himself to shield his former love"—Annual American catalogue.

1086. —————. *A gentleman of leisure*; a novel. Boston: Houghton, Mifflin, 1881. 323p.

Brought up in the English gentlemanly tradition, the American, Clinton Wainwright, returns after 20 years for a three-month stay in New York City. It is an opportunity to study and contrast the two societies, English and American. Among the 'upper class' Americans he meets and assesses are: the rich Bodenheims, German-Americans who (though Mr. Bodenheim is thoroughly unlikable) do possess a distinct Old World charm; the Grosvenors, too aware of 'class differences'; Townsend Spring, daring, speculative, rich today, poor tomorrow, and then rich again; Ruth Cheever, the heroine, vivacious, forthright, not in least in awe of Wainwright's 'superior' English cultural upbringing. After due consideration Clinton decides that, with all its faults, American society is for several reasons, not the least of which is its social integration, preferable to its English equivalent. He will settle in America and marry Ruth Cheever.

1087. —————. *An heir to millions*. New York: F.J. Schulte, 1892. 307p.

Anthony Bainbridge's admiration for the socialist Stanley Southmayd displeases his father who threatens to disinherit Anthony. Mr. Bainbridge dies of a stroke before his threat is carried out and Anthony is now in possession of millions. He continues to associate with Southmayd and meets the latter's daughter, Winifred, formerly a schoolteacher in Utica, N.Y. The young millionaire further explores the social and fiscal questions of the day (with Southmayd often present), but also falls deeply in love with Winifred Southmayd. Winifred, Anthony discovers, is more conservative than her father; Anthony meanwhile has the welfare of his mother to consider and must answer his sister Evelyn's concerns about his direction. At the story's conclusion Southmayd, in ill health, aware of his failure as a reformer and realizing that he really cannot achieve conjugal happiness with his fiancée, Juliet Olyphant, commits suicide. Their own union mitigates Anthony and Winifred's sorrow.

1088. ————. *A hopeless case*. **Boston: Houghton, Mifflin, 1880. 275p.**
Agnes Wolverton, an orphan, who has been living in Brooklyn with her relatives, the Cliffes, changes residence when the Cliffes depart for the West. She now lives with her cousin, Mrs. Augusta Leroy, and the latter's bachelor brother, Rivington Van Corlear, in an old Knickerbocker mansion in Lafayette Place, New York. Agnes wants intellectual stimulation, the company of writers, artists, savants, but Mrs. Leroy is determined to place the attractive Agnes in fashionable society which Agnes finds is concerned only with outward show, manners and 'sophisticated' conversation. It is Agnes's final decision, which she explains to the astonished Augusta Leroy, to rejoin the West-dwelling Cliffes. Who is the 'hopeless case' – Agnes or New York Society?

1089. ————. *The house at High Bridge*; a novel. **Boston: Ticknor, 1887. 395p.**
"Fawcett [is] writing about a family which was in itself a strange contradiction in social values, for the husband, Herbert Coggeshall, a novelist, belonged remotely to such people as the Van Twillers, the Van Corlears and the Ten Eycks, but his wife was the daughter of a man 'who kept a popular eating house not far from Bowling Green.' They live in modest circumstances in High Bridge, a New York suburb, not through preference but necessity. Their lives while quite commonplace as compared with the rich Satterthwaites and Auchinclosses of [the author's] 'Olivia Delaplaine' are just as typical of their particular class in the social scale as are the former. One daughter, Isabel, after education in Europe, returns to New York completely 'at home in good society and well versed in all its arbitrary regulations.' The other daughter, Sadie . . . [takes] her characteristics from her mother who is more or less 'ordinary' and materialistic . . . The characters [in the novel] are [generally] typical suburban dwellers with the normal usual dissatisfaction on the part of some because they must live on the outskirts of the metropolitan centre which is for them the only source of pleasure and happiness"—Dunlap, G.A. The city in the American novel, 1789-1900.

1090. ————. *How a husband forgave*; a novel. New York: Belford Co., 1890. 228p.

A story of 'fashionable' New York City society. "Wallace Waldo, the husband of the title, falls in love with and marries Cecilia Brinckerhoff. After the marriage Cecilia becomes friendly with Wallace's friend, Paul Godfrey, a novelist, and the two spend a great deal of time with each other, as Wallace is always busy at the office. It turns out that Wallace is not really at the office; he is in the company of Charlotte Parselle, an old flame, and Kitty Claye, a woman of notoriety. Cecilia finds out and attacks Wallace, who feels not only contrite but also misunderstood—a woman should not be so possessive, he argues, and she should understand a man's needs. Needless to say, Cecilia does not. Wallace goes abroad with Kitty and Cecilia stays at home and has an affair with Godfrey. . . When Wallace returns he learns of Cecilia's affair; she admits her indiscretion, but in the end, husband and wife reconcile, have a son, and retire to home life sans social affairs"—Harrison, S.R. Edgar Fawcett.

1091. ————. *A man's will*; a novel. New York: Funk & Wagnalls, 1888. 308p.

"Presents a startling picture of the prevalence of intemperance among the business men of New York City, and in the homes of those who move in the best society. The story is merely a thread of connection between the various scenes in country houses, banks, brokers' offices, and rich homes, where the curse of drink is doing its disastrous work. Two physicians are introduced, one advocating temperance, the other total abstinence. The downward career of a handsome, talented, rich young banker is the theme, and his final cure through a sensible mother, a faithful wife, a devoted physician, and—a man's will"—Annual American catalogue.

1092. ————. *A mild barbarian*; a novel. New York: D. Appleton, 1894. 272p.

"The 'mild barbarian' is a young fellow of twenty-four who, after having lived all his life with an invalid mother in the complete seclusion of a small New England town, falls heir, soon after his mother's death, to a million-dollar fortune and a townhouse in New York. His unworldliness and frank naiveté are ill suited to the society life in which he is launched, and where he creates more or less social havoc. He loves a fashionable New York society girl, but there are mutual misunderstandings, and it is only after considerable unhappiness and long separation that the course of true love is finally smoothed"—Annual American catalogue.

1093. ————. *Miriam Balestier*; a novel. Chicago: Belford, Clarke, 1888. 192p.

New York City is the locale of the first half of the novel where Miriam Balestier wrestles with her dysfunctional family (brother, sister and mother) while trying to establish herself in light opera and the theater. Her rival for the leading role in an opera, the collaborative work of her brother and Miriam herself, is Paula Chalcott, presumably a good friend but murderously jealous of Miriam when producer Louis Matarand prefers Miriam for the role. The train to San Francisco, boarded by Miriam and Paula, derails shortly after leaving New York. Paula is killed and Miriam is injured. She is taken in by Sylvia and Mrs. Atherton and meets Sylvia Atherton's fiancé, Cecil Broadstaffe, a farmer in the village of 'Glassborough'. The latter falls in love with Miriam and she with him. However, Miriam, for Sylvia's sake, leaves Glassborough with Louis Matarand who claims to be in love with her; Miriam says to herself, "I will never marry that man."

1094. ————. *New York*; a novel. **London, New York: F. Tennyson Neely, 1898. 344p.**

"George Olson returned to New York after serving a term at Sing Sing for falsifying bank entries at the instigation of the cashier and the nephew of the vice-president. His efforts to gain an honest living led him to see the folly, the infinite selfishness, fashion, society, struggling pretension, overbearing plutocracy, stonyhearted aristocracy of the vast city. The author describes the missions, charitable schemes, hospitals, settlements, and other means of so-called help for fellow men. A young Unitarian clergyman and a rich, simple-hearted girl bring about . . . [George's] moral health, and incidentally point many lessons to would-be reformers"—Annual American catalogue.

1095. ————. *A New York family*; a novel. **With thirty-six illus. by Thomas Nast and others. New York: Cassell Pub. Co., 1891. v, 277p.**

"Fritz Eberhard, a German, began his career in America as a Hoboken grocer. Prosperity attended him, and he married Mary Smith, the daughter of a New York restaurant keeper. Fritz soon Anglicized his name, and was known to the public as Frederick Everard. He then moved to New York, took a partner, and set up the establishment of Everard & Flagler. The novel deals with the success and failures of the Everard family. The scenes are in well-known New York localities. The action is divided between the Everards and members of the Tweed Ring. Some of Tweed's exploits are introduced. The personality of Tweed, Sweeney and others of the Ring are described. Many of the characters are real personages"—Annual American catalogue.

1096. ————. *Olivia Delaplaine*; a novel. **Boston: Ticknor, 1888 [c1887]. 476p.**

A study of New York social life and character. "Olivia Delaplaine, born a Van Rensselaer, is left penniless at her father's death through his reckless extravagance. Spencer Delaplaine, her father's old partner and a man more than double her age, asks her to marry him. At first she indignantly refuses, thinking she can bravely endure her poverty and change of surroundings. A small experience of boarding house life leaves her very weak when a second temptation comes. It is represented to her that Mr. [Spencer] Delaplaine is dying and wishes to marry her [so] that she may inherit his fortune. She marries him and he does not die. Her married life and its tragical ending are well described. The character sketching is quite lifelike"—Annual American catalogue.

1097. ————. *Outrageous fortune*; a novel. New York: C.T. Dillingham, 1894. **431p.**

"Basis Moncrieffe, the protagonist of the novel, views himself as a martyr of destiny, moved in life by external forces that do not allow him the freedom to assert a willful choice. Encouraged by his friend, Whitewright, Moncrieffe sets up his medical practice in Riverview, New York, a small suburban community of wealth; there he soon realizes that his actions are determined by his desire to achieve success and recognition and by his instinctive rather than rational responses to situations. He falls in love with Eloise Thirlwall, but chance occurrences prevent him from proposing marriage to her; other chance occurrences thrust him into the company of the wealthy young socialite, Elma Blagdon; and in a bewildering moment of confusion, swept by the dictates of circumstances and passion, he agrees to marry her. The marriage is unsuccessful, but there is no way out for Moncrieffe until chance, once more, interferes and changes his destiny. Elma dies and Moncrieffe, for the first time in his life, experiences a sense of freedom. He quickly marries Eloise before the forces of fate can regroup and shape his life anew"— Harrison, S.R. Edgar Fawcett. Whitewright has a pessimistic outlook on life and is well aware of the latest scientific developments. It is his rational conclusion that man is relatively unimportant in life or death.

1098. ————. *Purple and fine linen*; a novel. New York: G.W. Carleton, 1873. **483p.**

A novel of New York society in which the virtuous Helen Jeffreys weds the licentious Fuller Dobell, who is enamored of the scandalous Edith Everdell. Dobell, wounded in a duel with Melville Delano, is taken to Edith's home to recover. Disguised as a nurse Helen appears there and points out to her husband the duplicity of scheming Edith. Dobell then gives up Edith and returns to his wife.

1099. ————. *A romance of old New York*. Philadelphia: J.B. Lippincott, 1897. **204p.**

The scene of this novel is New York City in the 1820s. [It] "follows the affairs of two sisters, Charlotte and Pamela Verplanck and their respective gentlemen callers, Mark Frankland and Gerald Suydam. Pamela, the spoiled and spiteful sister, insists she is in love with Charlotte's beau, Mark Frankland and the Verplanck family insists, therefore, that Frankland marry Pamela. The couples following the advice of Aaron Burr, who is all-knowing in affairs of the heart, straighten themselves out and depart for the happiness-ever-after land"—Harrison, S.R. Edgar Fawcett.

1100. ————. *Rutherford*. New York: Funk & Wagnalls, 1884. **301p.**

Like Clinton Wainwright in Fawcett's 'A hopeless case', Duane Rutherford returns to New York City after a long respite in Europe (12 years). Rutherford, however, has no conception of recent American developments and he, too, attempts to acquire an understanding of the American character. His 'mentors' are Constance Calverly and John Penrhyn; to Rutherford these two – Constance, beautiful, energetic, fetchingly feminine, and John, ruggedly handsome, individualistic and frank – are representations of the admirable spirit of America. Rutherford finds most disconcerting the Anglophile Stuyvesant, a poseur, and Philip Romaine, a poet who disdains America and gravitates to French culture. Mrs. Underclique, on the other hand, is a straightforward, freethinking American woman, knowledgeable of Europe, but decidedly favorable to the American scene. The duality is too much for Rutherford; he ends up as an itinerant, belonging to no particular world.

1101. ————. *Social silhouettes* (being the impressions of Mr. Mark Manhattan). Edited by Edgar Fawcett. Boston: Ticknor, 1885. 368p.
"An amusing series of character sketches of New York society people whose identity is hidden under fictitious names. . . .There are twenty-seven portraits in all, most of them showing up the meaner and weaker side of human nature"—Annual American catalogue. The periodical, the Bookman, in 1904, after Fawcett's death, commented that 'Social silhouettes' "will be found invaluable to any one who wishes to reconstruct a certain period of New York life."

Fawcett, Edgar, 1847-1904. *A story of three women*. See note under Item #1103.

1102. ————. *The vulgarians*. Illustrated by Archie Gunn. New York: Smart Set Pub. Co., 1903. 213p.
"Leander, Ernestine, and Lola Troop live a modest life in Stratton, California. They all move to New York City after their father's death leaves them with unexpected millions. In New York they meet Marian Warrender, who assumes the task of civilizing the three young people and of acquainting them with the bored sophisticates of New York. Marian cultivates their manners, rearranges their values, and alters their speech. The novel carries the project to the point where Lola is polished enough to marry into New York society, and Leander is disillusioned enough to return to Stratton to marry his uneducated sweetheart, Annie Shelton. . . . Lola, enamored of her new existence, takes on all the attributes of the older culture; Leander, on the other hand, is impressed by what he sees, but ultimately rejects it in favor of the untutored, pristine simplicity of the raw West"—Harrison, S.R. Edgar Fawcett.

1103. ————. *Women must weep*; a novel. Chicago: Laird & Lee, 1892. 331p.
"The author seems to have a theory that no matter how favorable the environments of marriage, women who take upon themselves its condition must weep sooner or later. This is verified in the individual experiences of the three daughters of a New York druggist, whose heart histories take up most of the story in which several phases of New York society are represented. The

reader is also given a passing glimpse of the present political outlook. Inherited drunkenness produces its inevitable results"—Annual American catalogue. A later edition was issued under the title: A story of three girls (Chicago: Laird & Lee, 1895).

1104. Fay, Theodore Sedgwick, 1807-1898. *Hoboken*; **a romance of New York. New York: Harper, 1843. 2v. in 1.**

The protagonist Harry Lennox, despite in his own view the absurdities, improbabilities and mythologies of the Bible and the Christian religion, finally deems himself a Christian. His life as a member of privileged New York society had been rocked by the apparent rejection of his profession of love by Fanny Elton and, while he was in Europe, the death of his beloved brother Frank in a duel that should never have occurred. Harry himself duels and kills an English lord, a former soldier who is indirectly responsible for Frank's death. The searching, wandering and once agnostic Harry returns to his family in New York and a happier future with his parents, his sister Mary and Fanny. The Hoboken of the title is the scene of two duels that involved Frank Lennox and British Captain Glendenning (a tragic figure). One of the more interesting characters in the novel is a Mr. Emmerson, a confidante of the Lennox family, who embodies, in a softer manner, many of the qualities of Dickens' *Uriah Heep.*

1105. ————. *Norman Leslie*; **a tale of the present times. New York: Harper, 1835. 2v.**

The novel's early scenes are laid in New York in the first third of the nineteenth century, portraying upper class social activities; then the story shifts abruptly to Italy and Rome. Norman Leslie, the hero, is accused by his enemy, the bogus Count Clairmont, of being instrumental in the disappearance and apparent murder of Rosalie Romain who had been in love with Leslie. Leslie's affections, however, were directed towards Flora Temple. The latter's testimony at Leslie's trial for murder is largely responsible for his acquittal. Leslie, still guilty in the eyes of the public, flees to Italy and a new life. It is there that the devious plotting of Clairmont and his confederates is unmasked. Rosalie Romain reappears as the insane wife of Clairmont. Clairmont is killed in a confrontation with Leslie. Cleared, Leslie returns to New York with Flora who is now his wife.

1106. ————. *Sidney Clifton*; **or,** *Vicissitudes in both hemispheres.* **A tale of the nineteenth century. New York: Harper, 1839. 2v.**

A New York businessman, Mr. DeLyle, gives Sidney Clifton employment after the death of Sidney's supposed father, Glenthorne, an accused criminal. Sidney's industry irks DeLyle's son Edward and he clandestinely has Sidney charged with robbery. Believing Julius Ellingbourne to be his accuser Sidney duels and badly wounds him. Thereupon Sidney leaves New York for England, leaving behind Julia Borrowdale, the woman he loves, and trailed by another charge of robbery, this time the theft of funds from his employer's safe. In London Sidney makes new friends and achieves literary fame and finally discovers that his true father is James Borrowdale, a Bostonian who had adopted Julia after his infant son (Sidney) was abducted and lost to him.

Feagles, Anita M[acRae] 1927- . See under her pseudonym: Macrae, Travis, 1927-

1107. **Feinstein, John, 1956- .** *Winter games*; **a mystery. Boston: Little, Brown, 1995. 277p.**

The Shelter Island community is excited about a Lithuanian immigrant, Rytis Buzelis, a star basketball player; visions of a state championship for his high school team dance before its eyes, as Bobby Kelleher, a tired Washington reporter, discovers when he tries to get some rest in his hometown. Recruiters from numerous colleges besiege Buzelis and one of them, Scott Harrison, an assistant coach and a friend of Kelleher, is murdered. Kelleher and Tamara Mearns, a local reporter, together contact Buzelis's domineering father, Rytis's sister, a superstar model, and a flashy sports broadcaster. They also have a run-in with some hoods who want no interference with their plans.

1108. **Feldman, Ellen, 1941- .** *God bless the child.* **New York: Simon & Schuster, 1998. 251p.**

A bookstore on the eastern end of Long Island is the new venture of Bailey Bender who has deserted the world of TV news production. Bailey has another object in mind: finding the baby she put up for adoption 20 years ago. Before that occurs Bailey is mixed up with the wealthy Prinze family—she knew Mr. Prinze from her TV days; his son, Charlie, is a suspect when the corpse of a pregnant woman is found in the Prinze house. Mack, a recuperating Vietnam veteran, provides Bailey with sympathy and affection.

Felton, Ronald Oliver, 1909- . See: Welch, Ronald.

1109. *The Female wanderer.* **An interesting tale founded on fact. Written by herself. [n.p.] Printed for the proprietor, 1824. 24p.**

The protagonist, Cordelia Krats, is a member of an affluent family in the Upstate New York town of 'Agadnacas' (Sacandaga?) who falls in love with Edwin ————. When she persists in her affection for a young man of uncertain prospects, Cordelia's parents disown her. She makes her way across New York State to Buffalo disguised as a man. Cordelia learns that Edwin is about to marry a Miss Eliza because he has been notified by letter of Cordelia's 'marriage.' After adventures as a sailor on the high seas Cordelia (still as a man) returns to central New York and begins teaching. Informed of her family's loss of fortune and Edwin's purchase of their farm, Cordelia finds him still unmarried, doffs her male garb, and the two lovers are reunited. 1815 to 1818 is the time period of this short piece. The work is sometimes attributed to <u>Cordelia</u> Stark.

1110. **Fenisong, Ruth, 1909- .** *Snare for sinners.* **Garden City, N.Y.: Published for the Crime Club [by] Doubleday, 1949. 189p.**

Rambler's Roost, a dilapidated Catskills farm, is the domain of the weird Van Broek family. When a squatter on their property is murdered and an orphan they had recruited from a children's asylum disappears, the Van Broeks become the target of an official investigation. Participating in the query are a Mr. Giles who poses as a magazine editor and the local police. To Giles belongs the major share of credit for the answers to the riddles.

1111. ————. *The wench is dead.* **Garden City, N.Y.: Published for the Crime Club by Doubleday, 1953. 219p.**

The wife of New York detective Gridley Nelson recognizes the artist that a beautiful divorcée has been attracted to as a man wanted for murder. The Long Island estate of a friend of the divorcée and the artist's nearby house are the scenes of a mystery that includes a new homicide. Mrs. Nelson and her husband look into the past and present of all the parties that might be involved.

1112. **Fenwick, Elizabeth, 1920- .** *The passenger.* **New York: Atheneum, 1967. 151p.**

Seventeen-year-old Tobey Lewis has been at his grandmother's in Upstate New York most of the summer. He has just finished repairing his ancient automobile and is preparing to hit the road to Cleveland. However, regulations forbid his driving out of the State unless an adult with a valid license accompanies him. The latter turns out to be a woman named Carol who works at the local supermarket; actually she isn't much older than Tobey, but she comes bearing a dark secret, which Tobey eventually unravels.

1113. ————. *The silent cousin.* **New York: Atheneum, 1966. 192p.**

A decaying Hudson River family is beset by numerous crises, not the least of which is a visitation by the Grim Reaper. The climax is a properly grisly one.

1114. **Ferber, Edna, 1887-1968.** *Dawn O'Hara, the girl who laughed.* **Front. in color by R. Ford Harper. New York: Stokes, 1911. 302p.**

Peter Orme's brilliance is cancelled out by his lack of self-control until he passes into insanity. His wife, Dawn O'Hara, an Irish-American journalist, puts aside the misery he has inflicted on her and continues to work in New York City to support herself and Peter until she suffers a breakdown and takes time off for several months. Upon recovery Dawn leaves New York for Milwaukee and another newspaper assignment. She receives encouragement from her sister, a magnanimous brother-in-law, the sports editor of the paper and a German-American physician who falls in love with her and urges Dawn to divorce Peter and marry him. At this point a recovered Peter leaves the asylum for the mentally ill and Dawn has decisions to make.

1115. ————. *Emma McChesney & Co.* **Illus. by J. Henry. New York: F.A. Stokes, 1915. 231p.**

Ferber is one of the first if not the first writer to portray the 'new' American businesswoman who stands on equal terms with many of her male counterparts. Emma McChesney of the Buck Featherloom Petticoat Company, located at the lower end of Broadway, is a driving force, successful at both marketing and designing fashionable undergarments. The New York garment trade is her milieu, but she does take time off to marry T.A. Buck, son of the company's founder. At the suggestion of her (second) husband Emma tries three months away from the office and factory, at the end of which it is obvious that she may expire from boredom; back into harness she happily goes.

1116. ————. *Personality plus*; some exploits of Emma McChesney and her son Jock. With fifteen illus. by James Montgomery Flagg. New York: F.A. Stokes, 1914. 161p.

Emma McChesney (more trenchantly described in Ferber's Emma McChesney & Co., q.v.) is a businesswoman of many talents who has a large share in the success of the New York City clothing firm, the Buck Featherloom Petticoat Company. In the present novel her son Jock, who has evidently inherited some of her acumen, takes a major role as he builds a career in advertising.

1117. ————. *Saratoga Trunk*. Garden City, N.Y.: Doubleday, Doran 1941. 352p.

"Life in New Orleans and Saratoga in the 1880s as seen through the lives of Clint Maroon, once a Texas cowboy, and his beloved Clio, the daughter of a New Orleans aristocrat and his mistress, a beautiful adventuress. Driven from New Orleans because she killed her lover, Clio's mother fled to France and there brought up her daughter. After her mother's death, Clio, devastatingly beautiful and outrageously clever, returned to New Orleans, determined to marry a wealthy man. There she met and loved Clint Maroon. In Saratoga, where Clint went to play the races, and where Clio joined him, they met the Morgans and Vanderbilts and other railroad barons, and Clint decided he would make his fortune in railroads rather than horses. Sixty years later, when Clint was eighty-nine and had given away most of his enormous wealth, he tried to tell his life story to the press, but nobody believed him—nobody but his still lovely Clio"—Book review digest.

1118. Ferber, Nat Joseph, 1889-1945. *New York*. New York: Covici, Friede, 1930. 345p.

Despite the title the book "confines itself [almost] exclusively to the activities of Russian and Polish Jews who emigrated to America in the Eighteen-eighties. Julius Midas, the central figure, is symbolical of the money-grubbing type who after making his millions (in this case from real estate) can think of nothing more sensible to do than to give away large sums to charity"—Saturday review of literature. However, the author does allude to many New York 'types'—real estate dealers, denizens of Broadway, prominent Manhattanites, and builders—giving his novel the 'flavor' of the metropolis.

1119. ————. *The sidewalks of New York.* **New York: Covici, 1927. 363p.**

Illegitimate Sam is brought up by the Posternocks when they arrive in New York City from their Russian homeland. Sam received little love or care from his foster parents and his youth is one of gang wars and scrabbling. As he grows to manhood Sam takes various jobs, begins studying on his own, and is railroaded into a marriage with a woman he dislikes. Accepted into the inner circles of the politician and high State officeholder, John Stone, Sam takes the fall when Stone, a vivid character, defrauds the public of several million dollars. Divorced from his wife, Sam finally finds happiness with Goldie, daughter of an unwed seamstress—Goldie, as a nubile young girl had drifted unwittingly into the clutches of a vice ring.

1120. ————. *Spawn;* **a novel of degeneration. New York: Farrar & Rinehart, 1930. 371p.**

"To 'Pike Hollow', an isolated farming community in the Catskills, came Heinrich Reimer, in 1844, to establish himself as an autocratic land owner with many tenant farmers in his fealty. Inbreeding, illegitimacy, and all the evils of indiscriminate mating prevail from one generation to another in this isolated settlement. The interest of the story centers about Madge Chilvers who, in spite of her grandmother's admonitions that she must be properly married, is not quite strong enough to live otherwise than her environment and the traditions of the valley dictate"—Book review digest.

1121. Ferguson, William Blair Morton, 1881 or 2-1967. *The riddle of the rose.* **New York: McBride, 1929. 330p.**

"From the first page, when the story opens on Fifth Avenue in the late afternoon, till it ends in Hillcrest, a little town on the Hudson, we are lost in a maze in which the clues are so inextricably entangled, the characters are so ensnared, that we feel we are walking alone in the dusk and seeing strange shapes among the trees, or wandering through some mediaeval castle with drawbridge and moat where evil deeds were done of old. For the 'Crimson Rambler' stalks through the pages in ancient armor which diffuses a ruddy glow"—Boston transcript. The mysterious deaths in Hillcrest are each marked with a red rose, presumably left behind by the murderer.

1122. Ferriss, Lucy, 1954- . *Against gravity.* **New York: Simon & Schuster, 1996. 303p.**

Memories of her youth in a sleepy town in the Hudson Valley flood in on young adult Gwyn Stickley ('Stick'). She recalls how the crash of the Challenger space shuttle seemed something of a focal point as she progressed to her apathetic high school days and distanced herself from her hard-working parents. Stick stands by her sexually active friend JoAnn as the latter tries to keep her fundamentalist parents in ignorance of her illegitimate baby. Other clandestine incidents in her small town come to mind. She can accept the tragic sense of life as symbolized by the Challenger disaster of which Stick says: "They slipped the surly bonds of earth to touch the face of God."

1123. **Feuer, Elizabeth.** *Lost summer.* **New York: Farrar, Straus & Giroux, 1995. 185p.**

The story turns around the relationships of a group of girls from the city that sometimes unwillingly, as is true in 12-year-old Lydia's case, spend the entire summer in a Catskill camp. Lydia tries to avoid getting involved when the bullying Carla picks on the other girls in her lodge (especially awkward Karen). Lydia grieves over her parents' recent divorce, and sympathetic Karen suggests that the detached Lydia invite her father to Parents' Weekend at the camp. Lydia responds and guardedly reaches out for self-acceptance and understanding of those around her.

1124. **Field, Louise Maunsell.** *Katherine Trevalyan.* **New York: McClure Co., 1908. 347p.**

Against a sharply-perceived background of frivolous New York society the story's heroine, Katherine Trevalyan, an orphan with a lot of money and high ideals, but unsophisticated, marries a fortune-hunter and cardsharp who takes hold of one-half of her wealth. Katherine, thoroughly disillusioned, divorces him, and then meets a worthy man. The latter has a friend who sees to it that Katherine's former husband suffers for his duplicities. She falls in love again, but this time with a man who is more than willing to accept her on equal terms.

1125. —————. *The little gods laugh*; a novel. **With front. by J. Newton Howitt. Boston: Little, Brown, 1917. 316p.**

Nita Wayne suffers disillusionment as she leaps from the world of New York City's high society to the necessity of earning her own way in the world of commerce. But along the way she gains a clearer grasp of life's realities and tolerance for its foibles. Donald Forsythe is in sympathy with her and eventually they fall in love. Donald's selfish wife Elsie clings to him until she sees gain for herself in asking for a divorce. That allows the two lovers to pursue further their relationship.

1126. —————. *Love and life.* **New York: Dutton, 1923. 286p.**

"From the old white house among the New England hills where she had lived a secluded life with her archaeologist father, Lynneth Frear is transplanted on her father's death into the fashionable home of her aunt in New York. Lynneth had resolved to earn her own living, but she yielded for a time to her aunt's determination to give her a conventional introduction to society. Her taste of the diversions of the younger set strengthens her in her resolve to become independent and she finds work in a bookshop. Love comes to her swiftly and is as swiftly snatched away when her aviator-husband is killed, but she continues to face the world bravely, holding on to every memory of her happiness and striving to make it a creative force in her life"—Book review digest.

1127. ————. *A woman of feeling*. **New York: Dodd, Mead, 1916. 293p.**
"Studies of three women . . . One of these, Vida Dareth, is a social parasite, living a life of ease and luxury for which she makes no adequate return either to her husband or to society. Margaret Lane is a big-hearted woman of the best twentieth-century type, keen-minded and alive, and awake to the demand for social service. Between these two stands Sylvia Farnham with her girlish enthusiasm and half-formed character. From the beginning Vida is her ideal, although for a brief moment she has a glimpse, through the eyes of Dr. Alan Macneven, of a more useful and nobler type of life. But Sylvia is one of the little people and she chooses a future that promises to be the counterpart of Vida's. This is fortunate, for it leaves Dr. Macneven free to turn back to his more worthwhile association with Margaret Lane"—Book review digest.
Vida has a fling with Maurice, an artist; her husband offers to divorce her sans alimony, an offer Vida refuses—she prefers the privileges of wealth to life with a poor artist. New York City is the scene of these little dramas.

1128. **Fielding, Howard, 1861-1929.** *Equal partners*. **Illus. by Seymour M. Stone. New York: G.W. Dillingham, 1901. 269p.**
Elsie Miller, a young New York actress, is the victim of an attempted murder as a knife thrust just misses her heart. Among the suspects are: Miss Brenda, a prominent socialite; Clarence, Elsie's boyfriend and owner of the knife; Dr. Blair; and Jack Robinson, bearer of $500 to Elsie. Earlier Elsie had escaped death by poisoning. After the would-be killer is apprehended, Elsie marries Clarence and Brenda marries a Mr. Kendall.

1129. **Fielding, Joy, 1945- .** *The deep end*. **Garden City, N.Y.: Doubleday, 1986. 303p.**
The peaceful Long Island calm that once surrounded Joanne Hunter is irrevocably broken by the exit from her life of a restless and disgruntled husband, the growing senility of Joanne's grandfather, the endless quarrels of her two adolescent daughters, threatening phone calls, and the presence on the Island of a killer designated 'the Suburban Strangler.' Joanne receives little comfort from her best friend, Eve Stanley, a psychoanalyst, who is convinced that the pains she endures are signs of a fatal illness (it's all psychosomatic according to Eve's husband). Lonely and sometimes stricken by fear, Joanne has to call upon all her remaining strength to deal with her problem.

1130. **Findley, Francine.** *From what dark roots . . .* **New York: Harper, 1940. 292p.**
The period covered by this novel is 1839 to 1860. It concerns Adam Burkett, a young Southerner who tires of bearing the brunt of family troubles in Natchez, Mississippi and decamps with his wife Sarai to a farm in northern New York State near the town of Malone. He makes a successful transition

and becomes an important figure in the community, certain that his family name will be carried on into the beckoning future.

1131. ———. *The root and the bough.* **New York: A.H. King, 1933. 320p.**

Adam Burkett and his Upstate New York farm exert a strong influence on his thirteen children; they left home but seem to be returning one by one. "Sarai gave her husband 13 sons and daughters and then lived on after his death in the midst of the strange army to which she had given birth. ... They were all Burketts—cold, domineering, unconsciously cruel—and she was not. Neither was Celia who came to that strange house to bury her husband who was Adam's sixth son. The bond between Adam's widow and his son's widow creates the beauty and significance of the early chapters. ... And Celia's discovery that her child, Merry, is another of the harsh, independent Burkett breed makes poignant the rest of the story"—New York herald tribune books.

1132. Fischer, Bruno, 1908-1992. *The bleeding scissors.* **New York: Ziff-Davis, 1948. 237p.**

Leo Atkins, in search of his wife Judith and her sister Paula Runyon, goes to the New York theatrical district to figure out why Judith gave him so little data about her lack of success in the theater. A woman who had some pertinent information is murdered before he can get to her. However his search does yield results as the mystery comes to a dramatic end.

1133. ———. *The dead men grin.* **Philadelphia: McKay, 1945. 248p.**

An Upstate New York village and its nearby swamp and woods are the venue of several murders. The town is one in which privacy is a premium. Private detective Helm moves into a situation fraught with terror and identifies the individual responsible for it all.

1134. ———. *House of flesh.* **New York: Fawcett Publications, 1950. 189p.**

A professional basketball star vacationing on a beach not far from New York City comes upon a house whose owner has been accused of having a homicidal past but who has never been charged with any crime.

1135. ———. *The paper circle.* **New York: Dodd, Mead, 1951. 242p.**

A quiet Upstate New York community is greatly disturbed when the bodies of two women are found in its midst. Private detective Ben Helm starts snooping around; he uncovers not only a wartime profiteering scandal, but also provides the solution to the two murders.

1136. ———. *The restless hands.* **New York: Dodd, Mead, 1949. 245p.**

"Ben Helm, one of the better-adjusted private ops, is retained by a leading citizen of a Hudson River town to try to keep his younger daughter from being strangled—a fate that befell her sister just a year before. Helm's list of suspects is on the pastoral side, but since it also includes a small-time racketeer with metropolitan connections, the detective meets with the requisite amount of gunplay before he's tidied things up"—New Yorker.

1137. ————. *The silent dust.* **New York: Dodd, Mead, 1950. 244p.**
A weekend invitation to a Long Island cottage involves Ben Helm and his actress wife in a murder. Their hostess is the victim; she was writing an autobiographical novel and evidently her manuscript revealed secrets that the murderer preferred to keep hidden. And then the murderer strikes again and easy-going Ben has to adopt a tougher-than-usual stance if he's going to solve the case.

1138. ————. *Mrs. Sherman's summer.* **Philadelphia: Lippincott, 1960. 254p.**
The Sherman family (German-American Jews) is gathered around the matriarchal Adelaide on Long Island in the summer of 1911. Adelaide Sherman is a commanding figure in her own right, but it is her oldest son, Joe, who wields the power. Joe, president of Sherman & Co., bankers, is ruthless and liable to change his mind and direction at any moment. It is his determination to be in complete control that sets off contentions that engulf the family on that fateful summer.

1139. **Fischer, Marjorie, 1903-1961.** *Pleasure first.* **New York: Macaulay, 1929. 287p.**
"Nicki, who was a count, and Mary, his loving American wife, were quite happy together [in New York City]. Then Nicki meets a fascinating young artist with red hair, and the two are clandestinely happy at Red's apartment. Mary turns for consolation to her dependable friend John, and goes to Paris with him. But Mary finds she loves Nicki in spite of his unfaithfulness and returns to New York to be with him. Then Red makes up her mind to marry John, and does. She is quite happy for a while. Then she sees Nicki again who promises to call on her occasionally and she is much happier"—Book review digest.

1140. **Fish, G. Williston.** *Short rations.* **Illustrated by C.J. Taylor. New York: Harper, 1899. 189p.**
"A series of sketches of American army life at West Point and in garrison in a fort on the Minnesota plains. The connecting link of the stories is a love affair between Lieutenant McVey and Ruth Lancaster that begins when McVey is a cadet at West Point. The first half-dozen sketches describe the social life of the national military academy, and then the scene shifts to Fort Snelling in Minnesota"—Annual American catalogue.

1141. **Fish, Rachel Ann.** *The newel post.* **New York: Coward-McCann, 1950. 376p.**
"A family chronicle in which Lucy Prescott, mistress of a large estate in upper New York State, is the central character. Madame Lucy has always been a domineering woman who ruled her farm and her three sons with the same grim determination. The marriage of Paul, the oldest son, to a girl who had

not been selected by his mother set off a train of events which brought heartache and tragedy in its wake"—Book review digest.

1142. **Fish, Robert L., 1912-1981.** *A handy death*, **by Robert L. Fish with Henry Rothblatt. New York: Simon and Schuster, 1975. 221p.**

"Attorney Hank Ross . . . defends former [New York] Mets pitcher Billy Dupaul on an eight-year-delayed-action murder charge. He was originally convicted of assault, but when his victim dies years later as a direct result of the bullet wound, another trial is necessitated. The story also involves an Attica [New York] prison riot that begins during a convict baseball game"—Breen, J.L. Novel verdicts.

1143. **Fisher, David E., 1932- .** *Variation on a theme.* **Garden City, N.Y.: Published for the Crime Club by Doubleday, 1981. 182p.**

"The chatty, urbane narrator here is Henry Grace, 42, a minor playwright who 20 years ago had a summer-stock ménage à trois with chum Turner and beautiful Sarah. But Sarah married Turner and that was that till a recent, rekindled Sarah/Henry affair. So when Sarah is discovered murdered, Henry is sure that Turner did it—even though the two men were together, at a movie, at the time of the crime." It turns out that Turner is using several orgy-mates as an alibi, but when Henry tries to find them (they are in a photo mailed to Henry) at least one of them is murdered and another, "a sexy, would-be actress is traced to a secluded Upstate New York cabin. ... The book's disappointing last section ... is an endlessly stretched-out siege at the cabin: psychotic Turner versus Henry with the sexy girl in the middle"—Kirkus reviews.

1144. **Fisher, Dorothy Canfield, 1879-1958.** *Rough-hewn.* **New York: Harcourt, Brace, 1922. 504p.**

Columbia University is the scene of the novel when Neale Crittenden studies there for his undergraduate degree, plays football and expands his knowledge of women. Neale meets Marise Allen, a European-educated girl, falls in love, and marries her. Tiring of life in New York City Marise and Neale find their way to country living in Vermont.

1145. **Fisher, Rudolph, 1897-1934.** *The walls of Jericho, 1928.* **New York: Knopf, 1928. 307p.**

"A cross-section of Harlem showing every strata of society and every shade of color from white and those who pass as white, yellow, yellow-brown, chocolate and black. The story shows up the stormy relationships of these groups with each other. Shine, the young hero, is a piano mover of prodigious size and strength. He thinks himself hardboiled. It takes Linda, pretty housemaid to the uplifting Miss Cramp (white), to teach him the truth. These two [Shine and Linda] fall in love, and though nearly swamped by Harlem squalls, make port"—Book review digest.

Fisher, Stephen Gould, 1912-1988. See: Fisher, Steve, 1912-1988.

1146. **Fisher, Steve, 1912-1988.** *Homicide Johnny.* **New York: Arcadia House, 1940. 256p.**

The owner and columnist of a newspaper published in Mamaroneck, Long Island is poisoned and a new doctor in town undergoes the tarnishing of his reputation. An attractive local librarian assists the detective who takes charge.

1147. —————. *The night before murder.* **New York: Hillman-Curl, 1939. 255p.**

Johnny West, a detective based in Westchester, has a slew of theatrical people to deal with when he researches a situation that is about to end in murder. Some of the characters who come together seeking to recharge or enhance their careers are: a once successful actress who fears that she is slipping badly; a young actress confident of a climb to the top; a playwright who has worked in experimental theater but has illusions of composing dramas that will place him among the greats; a promoter looking for vehicles that will bring him substantial financial rewards; a former journalist who had actually written a play of merit; and another actress who has plodded along and still awaits that ultimate achievement.

1148. **Fitch, James Monroe, 1878-1942.** *The ring buster; a story of the Erie Canal.* **New York: F.H. Revell, 1940. 224p.**

The title of this novel refers to Governor Samuel J. Tilden of New York and his success in breaking up a group of politicians (Republicans and Democrats) who were benefiting from poor administration of the State's canals. Grover Cleveland has an important role as a Buffalo lawyer although the story's chief protagonists are: Tim Brady, an Erie Canal towpath 'hoggee' bound to rise; Mary Wade, an 'upper class' young woman, whose brother Bill is a canal engineer; Ezra Baldwin and Silas Latham, corrupt contractors supposedly maintaining and repairing the canal; Jerry Sykes, town drunk; Red Moll, innkeeper and former wife of Jerry; and Budd Haynes, a reformed bully, who sides with Bill Wade and Tim Brady in collecting evidence against the corrupt ring.

1149. **Fitzgerald, Francis Scott Key, 1896-1940.** *The beautiful and damned.* **New York: Scribner, 1922. 449p.**

Covering a period from 1912 to the first years following the end of World War I the novel has as its protagonist Anthony Patch who partakes generously of upscale New York City entertainment and living. His marriage to Gloria Gilbert is not a very happy one; the two of them are forced to scale down their life style, but eventually they inherit a fortune, which, however, does not compensate for a ruined marriage and Anthony's own decline.

1150. —————. *Flappers and philosophers.* **New York: Scribner, 1920. 269p.**

"Here are to found originality and variety, with imaginativeness of the exceptional order that needs not to seek remote, untrodden paths, but plays upon scenes and people within the realm of ordinary life [chiefly in New York City and environs]"—Catholic World. Contents: The offshore pirate.—The ice palace.—Head and shoulders.—The cut-glass bowl.—Bernice bobs her hair.—Benediction.—Dalrymple goes wrong.—The four fists.

1151. ————. *The great Gatsby*. **New York: Scribner, 1925. 218p.**
"The power of the novel derives from its sharp portrayal of wealthy society in New York City and Long Island as seen through the eyes of the Midwestern narrator, Nick Caraway"—Benet's reader's encyclopedia of American literature. Wealthy Jay Gatsby tries to reclaim his lost love, Daisy Buchanan, but Daisy's husband Tom, Tom's mistress Myrtle, and Gatsby's own checkered past (and present) are obstacles to any happy solution; tragedy stalks these glamorous but irresponsible characters.

1152. ————. *This side of paradise*. **New York: Scribner, 1920. 305p.**
Snobbish Amory Lane, a Princeton student, is at first fascinated by New York City, but as he himself later falls into a state of boredom and semi-dissipation the city takes on a different hue. His personal life plunges further downward when Rosaline Connage who marries a young man with greater prospects than Amory's rejects him.

1153. **Fitzhugh, Percy Keese, 1876-1950.** *Along the Mohawk Trail*; **or** *Boy Scouts on Lake Champlain*. **Illustrated by Remington Schuyler. New York: Crowell, 1912. vi, 394p.**
"In the present story the Boy [Scouts] spend a summer on Lake Champlain. The action begins when Gordon Lord and Harry Arnold, through stopping to do a 'good turn' as Scout law demands, miss the train that is taking the party away. The two boys start out unaided to find their companions, and as the destination of the party was uncertain at the start, their way is beset with many difficulties"—Book review digest.

1154. ————. *Tom Slade at Temple Camp*. **Illustrated by Wa. S. Rogers. New York: Grosset & Dunlap, 1917. 209p.**
Tom Slade exposes the boys who attend a summer camp in the Adirondacks, established and funded by the generous Mr. Temple (he is the father of Mary Temple, Tom's friend) to knowledge of the forests, their plant and animal life, that he himself has already acquired.

1155. **Fitzsimmons, Cortland, 1893-1949.** *The Bainbridge murder*. **New York: McBride, 1930. 270p.**
"In which Arthur Martinson, an amateur private investigator, and Detective Kopff display enviable deductive powers in reasoning out the murder of Simon Bainbridge, a Long Island millionaire and philanderer found dead at the Roslyn Inn with a bullet hole in his shoulder and a glass of aromatic spirits of ammonia on the washstand"—Books (New York herald tribune).

1156. ———. *The Manville murders.* **New York: R.M. McBride, 1930. 252p.**
"The Manvilles were a land-poor family living on the South Shore of Long Island and local tradition conferred on them the title of 'The Mad Manvilles.' Any approaching marriage in this family presaged a disaster of some sort. Four brothers are killed, each on the eve of his wedding, and the police are unable to stop the wholesale slaughter. With the arrival of Arthur Martinson, private investigator, the mystery is cleared up, but not until the family is entirely wiped out"—Bookman.

1157. ———. *Mystery at Hidden Harbor.* **New York: Stokes, 1938. 300p.**
"Miss Ethel Thomas, the brisk middle-aged maiden who generally detects in Fitzsimmons's mysteries, chalks up another success. She arrives at 'Hidden Harbor' ... [a Long Island] summer resort just as trouble is about to break; for Mary Verity has unaccountably married Henry Baldwin, a stick with money, and Jerry Carter, her real sweetheart, is due back on his yacht. Jerry lands, hears the news, and Henry is found dead at the yacht club. Sure, they suspect Jerry, and Miss Ethel has a time of it chasing down clues. With the assistance of Abbie Abernathy, a special investigator, she has the villain all but handcuffed when the cops reach the scene. There are two other victims—one human, one canine. With the exception of the lovable Ethel, the inhabitants of Hidden Harbor are a strange lot"—New York herald tribune books.

1158. ———. *No witnesses!* **New York: F.A. Stokes, 1932. 311p.**
A Long Island district attorney, always looking for an opportunity to bolster his reelection chances, is rather happy to poke into the matter of a male and a female corpse found in the old Potter Place on Three Mile Road in 'Great Cove', Long Island. Tom Davin, a detective who walks in the D.A.'s shadow, doesn't necessarily approve of the latter's notions and approaches. e.g., despite the damning evidence, Davin moves fast to prevent the D.A. from indicting the woman targeted as chief suspect in the double murder. Questionable characters adequately populate the story and Davin has a problem keeping them all straight before he comes up with the right answers.

1159. Flack, Ambrose. *Family on the hill*; a novel. **New York: Crowell, 1945. 247p.**
"Stories about a lively family of Czechs, eighteen in number, living in a tumbledown house in upper New York State. Hunger, poverty, sorrow, and good fortune, all come their way, but the Otters take everything in their stride, and from their store of common sense they supply the mental health needed by some more unfortunate members of the community"—Book review digest.

1160. ———. *Room for Mr. Roosevelt.* **New York: Crowell, 1951. 244p.**
Family life in Syracuse, N.Y., in 1908-1909 is the focus of the novel. The pater familias is a cobbler who admires Theodore Roosevelt and for his birthday is given a portrait of the President. That picture occupies an honored place in the household and even exercises some influence on the family's affairs. The peculiarities of several of their neighbors are broached, but a high

point is attained when Mr. Roosevelt himself drops in on the family one afternoon.

1161. Flanner, Janet, 1892-198. *The cubical city.* **New York: Putnam, 1926. 426p.**

"In an elaborate style that tends to make difficult reading, the author gives the story of Delia Poole's life in New York, the 'cubical city.' Delia is a luscious blonde from Ohio, a designer of stage scenery under contract to Goldstein, the producer. To Delia the last love is always the only one. She feels this now, of Paul. Yet when he urges her to marry him before he leaves for the Philippines, Delia admits that marriage is not her aim. The lovers spend two days together and Paul goes away alone. The year of his absence brings on a period of Delia's relations with other men, yet his return does not make for the immediate happiness of the lovers"—Book review digest. A most striking aspect of this novel is its depiction of the vibrancy of New York City and its inhabitants.

1162. Fleming, Barry, 1899- . *Country wedding.* **Lakemont, Ga.: Copple House-Cotton Lane Press, 1982. 127p.**

The Mantry house in 'Eastharbor', Long Island, is being prepared for the wedding of daughter Beatrice to Walter Rutledge Pickens. Invited guests include Philip Eldridge, a former boyfriend of Beatrice's; Paul Ewing, 20, who has tried to convince Beatrice (she's older than he—24) to give him a chance, but is now turning to Eastharbor's femme fatale, the married Connie Wells; Connie herself who has evoked Philip Eldridge's interest so keenly that he has proposed that she run off to Montauk with him; Martin, the young minister who will perform the marriage ceremony. Mixing these and others produces several touchy, sticky situations—e.g., Beatrice is contemplating calling the whole thing off and pursuing piano studies in Europe; Paul Ewing waves a gun at Philip Eldridge and forces him to leave for New York City where he is supposed to board a ship for South America. A semblance of order returns to Eastharbor and by the end of the novelette the Long Island community seems likely to be the scene of a wedding after all.

1163. Fleming, Ian, 1908-1964. *The spy who loved me.* **New York: Viking Press, 1962. 211p.**

"Appears to be the first-person story of a young woman. According to her story, Vivienne Michel appears to have been involved, both perilously and romantically, with the same James Bond whose secret service exploits [Fleming] have [sic] written from time to time. ... This is the story of a night of terror in the Dreamy Pines Motor Court in the Adirondacks"—Publisher's note.

1164. Fleming, Thomas J., 1927- . *Remember the morning.* **New York: Forge, 1997. 379p.**

Taken prisoners in 1721 by Seneca Indians from the Lake Ontario region, Catalyntie Van Vorst, a Dutch girl, and black Clara are inducted into the tribe.

After 12 years they are exchanged and return to 'civilization.' Catalyntie now falls under the domination of an uncle, with Clara as her slave. In the ensuing 30 years the American colonies undergo Indian attacks, slave rebellions, and economic and class struggles. Catalyntie becomes a seeker after power and wealth while idealistic Clara nurses the sick and sustains the poor. Both women are two thirds of a triangle; the other third is Malcolm Stapleton, a colonist who possesses sterling qualities.

1165. ————. *The wages of fame.* **New York: Forge, 1998. 461p.**

A continuation of the author's Remember the morning (q.v.). The time frame here is 1827 to 1861 and the chief characters are George Stapleton, a politician and Hudson Valley land baron; his wife, Caroline Kemple Stapleton, a woman eventually ruined by her feverish quest for celebrity; and John Sladen, George's comrade and Caroline's lover who abets her misdeeds.

1166. *Florence De Lacey*; or, *The coquette*. **A novel by the author of** *Abel Parsons, a tale of the Great Fire.* **New York: E. Winchester, 1845. 106p. (in double columns).**

The scene: New York City and Saratoga on the eve of the presidential election (Martin Van Buren vs. William Henry Harrison). Wealthy and beautiful Florence shies away from marriage, but is pursued by man-of-the-world Edward Melville and other would-be suitors. She begins to take an interest in Arthur Wemyss, a law student, who labels her a coquette. Peter Hardscrabble, a rather indolent but good-natured fellow, is befriended by Edward Melville's brother, Richard. When Wemyss is convicted for cashing a forged check, it is Peter who recalls seeing that check first in the possession of Richard Melville. As the complex plot unfolds we are apprised of Edward Melville's desertion of a wife and his criminal behavior, abetted by his brother Richard. Florence realizes her deep affection for Arthur Wemyss who is cleared of all charges against him.

1167. **Florey, Kitty Burns, 1943- . *Family matters.* New York: Seaview Books, 1979. 294p.**

An associate professor at a university in Syracuse, N.Y., Betsy Ruscoe, is impregnated by a footloose commercial photographer, Judd Vandoss. Pro-choice Betsy disconcerts pro-choice people on the campus when she decides to bypass an abortion and have her child. To complicate matters she has a number of family problems—her mother Violet is terminally ill with cancer and Betsy is asked to search for her long-lost grandmother. Crawford Divine, Betsy's department chairman, offers to marry Betsy. She refuses. When her mother dies, her grandmother is located and Judd Vandoss is out of her life, Betsy's problems diminish. She is still awaiting the arrival of her baby.

1168. **Foley, Rae, 1900-1978. *The hundredth door.* New York: Dodd, Mead, 1950. 246p.**

"Meredith McGrath on the eve of her twenty-first birthday, unwisely accepts an invitation to visit her relatives in their Adirondack lodge. She had been orphaned in a particularly unpleasant way (her mother was executed for the murder of her father), and as she stands to inherit the family fortune, she can't reasonably expect a hearty welcome. Though she tries to assure herself that you can't inherit murder, her father's lawyer, who controls her money, is killed soon after her arrival in such a way that she is bound to be suspected. John Harland, a detective who goes in for analysis rather than action, finally narrows the field down to one suspect who has an overwhelming motive"— New Yorker.

1169. Folsom, Franklin, 1907-1995. *Beyond the frontier.* **New York: Funk & Wagnalls, 1959. 246p.**

> The author fictionalizes the youthful experiences of Horatio Jones who had enlisted as a ranger in the American Revolutionary army. When the Seneca Indians ambushed his company, Horatio fell into their hands and was put through the usual ordeals—the forced march, the gauntlet. He survived and gradually grew to so appreciate the Indian life style that he remained with the tribe despite opportunities to escape.

1170. Foote, Mary Hallock, 1847-1938. *The Royal Americans.* **Boston: Houghton, Mifflin, 1910. 386p.**

> "A story of pre-Revolutionary days. Catherine Yelverton, left motherless from the date of her birth, the night of the fall of Fort Ontario in 1756, grows into young womanhood in a peaceful Dutch village near the Hudson. She is taken to England where for a time she lives with her father's people, but of her own choice she returns to the land of her birth, and when the Revolutionary War breaks out proves herself a true American. Her life story is interwoven with that of a French girl who is rescued from captivity among the Indians by Catherine's father [an officer in the Royal Americans]. This girl, strange and unhappy, an Indian by nature even after years of 'civilization', makes a sacrifice in the end which means the happiness of Catherine and her lover"— Book review digest. Ethan Allen and the Schuyler family are historical personages who appear in the story.

1171. Footner, Hulbert, 1879-1944. *Antennae.* **New York: Doran, 1926. 350p.**

> "In this psychological study of youth and sex the author follows the development of two New York boys, contrasts and antagonists from their first meeting. Wilfred Pell is of West Eleventh Street, respectable, timid, yet secretly longing to be bad. Joe Kaplan is a typical child of the slums, dirty and vicious, and armed with a mean hardness that carries him everywhere and renders him proof against knocks. It is in the cards that he will succeed at Wilfred's expense, taking the other boy's job, and when the time comes, winning his girl. As the youths mature, their every contact rouses in Wilfred the old loathing and fascination, and in Joe contempt and jeers for the other's ineptitude. In their final encounter Joe is rich and powerful and Wilfred is still

a struggling writer, yet somehow it is not Wilfred who comes off second best"—Book review digest.

1172. ————. *The owl taxi.* **New York: Doran, 1921. 309p.**

"Gregory Parr [a once rich New Yorker], in the middle of a December night, suddenly found that he was in possession of a decrepit taxi for which he had just bartered the last two hundred dollars of his inheritance. Deciding to make the best of his bargain, he was about to admit his first fare, when to his horror he found the taxi already occupied by the body of a dead man. This gruesome event led to his meeting a charming young girl masquerading as a boy, and from then on he was ... [involved] in exciting adventures. They had to do with the political affairs of the little republic of Manaquay; the girl, with the best interests of the country at heart, was fighting treachery in her own household. Gregory is with her heart and soul in her fight, and after a series of stirring pursuits, the country is saved from the further perfidy of the villain"—Book review digest.

1173. ————. *A self-made thief.* **Garden City, N.Y.: Doubleday, Doran, 1929. 285p.**

"The story of a once upright New York lawyer, who plunges suddenly into a life of crime and vice which leads ultimately to his destruction. He rashly bets three other men that he can accomplish alone a single act of daring bank banditry and escape detection. After winning his wager the thrill of the escapade lures him into committing similar crimes, all the while he outwardly maintains his accustomed respectability ... he experiments with heroin and is soon its victim ..., murders two of his confederates and then in crazed bravado divulges the truth of the harrowing murders, the guilt for which no one hitherto had dreamed of laying to him"—Saturday review of literature.

1174. ————. *Thieves' wit; an everyday detective story.* **New York: Doran, 1918. 345p.**

Ben Enderby and his female assistant attempt to retrieve pearls stolen from the actress, Irma Hamilton. Their research leads them to a fashionable Fifth Avenue shop, which serves as a cover for a band of jewel thieves. A woman who gets her orders from an unknown master criminal directs the band. The stolid but solid Enderby pursues his objectives to a satisfactory conclusion (in his own words).

1175. ————. *The under dogs.* **Garden City, N.Y.: Doran, 1925. 325p.**

"An exciting yarn of the New York underworld in which Mme. Storey, an extraordinary woman and a famous detective, joins a criminal gang in order to save one of its members. As Jessie Seipp, Mme. Storey makes a daring robbery, breaks up the gang and exposes the master crook who is the invisible boss of its operations, and restores to her husband and respectability the young girl she has risked her life to save"—Book review digest.

1176. *For each other*; a novel. **New York: G.W. Carleton, 1878. 264p.**

Two Westchester society belles, Constance Clayton and Ethel Grosvenor, have marital experiences that lead to unhappiness and tragedy. The time is the late 1870s. Constance is in love with Armour Molyneux; he marries her although he harbors a secret longing for Mary Ashmead, a country girl he had saved from an onrushing train. Ethel 'marries' (it's a mock wedding) Rigdon Brooke, a fraud and a thief. While Ethel and Rigdon are honeymooning in Paris, Brooke, in a shootout with Ethel's angry father, Addison Grosvenor, and James Dudley, a former suitor of Ethel's kills Grosvenor and is himself supposedly shot to death by Dudley. Dudley marries the confused and grieving Ethel; back in New York Rigdon Brooke locates Ethel and persuades her to run off with him; and not long thereafter the ever abusive Brooke dies when he ingests poison Ethel had purchased. The crestfallen Dudley sickens and dies, leaving his estate to Ethel. Meanwhile Constance becomes increasingly despondent as she realizes Armour Molyneux is in love with Mary Ashmead and she commits suicide. Eventually Armour and Mary are wed; their first female child is named Constance.

1177. Forbes, James, 1871-1938. *The chorus lady*; novelized from the play by John W. Harding. Illus. from scenes of the play. New York: G.W. Dillingham, 1908. 329.

The heroine, engaged to her father's stableman, decides to pursue a career in the theater, believing she can help her parents with the money she earns. Her younger, weaker sister follows in her footsteps and has a difficult time resisting the blandishments of a man who is financing the career of her sister's fiancé. The New York City scene is well drawn and the heroine picks up the argot of the time and place and makes the requisite sacrifices for her family.

1178. Ford, James Lauren, 1854-1928. *Bohemia invaded, and other stories*. **With front. by A.W.B. Lincoln. New York: F.A. Stokes, c1895. 176p.**

A collection of stories dealing with a variety of situations (political and social) and places in New York City from the Bowery to Harlem, Coney Island, etc., etc. Contents: Bohemia invaded.—Wedded bliss.—High etiquette in Harlem.—The talent in the napkin.—A dinner in Poverty Flat.—The better element.—The squarer.—The joke that failed.—Dan Briordy's gitaway shadder.—The wardman's wooing.—The change of the luck.—Mr. Synick's anti-bad-break.—Freaks and kings.

1179. ——————. *The brazen calf*. **With illus. by W. Glackens. New York: Dodd, Mead, 1903. 323p.**

The more lurid activities of New York City society's so-called 'Four Hundred' are certain to be reported in the pages of the city's sensation-mongering newspapers. Mrs. Catnip's boardinghouse, a brownstone on a side street off Fifth Avenue, between Washington Square and Central Park, is a gathering place for the type of woman who leans on church railings to view fashionable weddings. One of the novel's characters, a beauteous Southern widow, writes for one of the 'yellow' newspapers but enrolls her daughter in an upscale school in order for her to meet the 'right people.' Worshippers of the 'brazen calf' (style, fashion, wealth, etc.) are likely to be women with little taste or culture.

1180. ———. *Dolly Dillenbeck*; **a portrayal of certain phases of metropolitan life and character. Illustrated by Francis Day. New York: G.H. Richmond, 1895. 392p.**

"The career of a pretty young country girl, who comes to New York City with the intention of going on the stage, and finds a financial backer in T. Adolphus Dillenbeck, a reputed millionaire. ... The girl, who is clever and heartless, rises to the top of the ladder of fame, while 'Dolly' Dillenbeck goes mad through his dissipations, loses his fortune, and ends his life in an insane asylum. The worried theatrical manager, various types of actors and actresses, and society men are depicted"—Annual American catalogue.

1181. ———. *The great mirage*; **a novel of the city underneath. New York: Harper, 1915. 350p.**

"The popular imagination, fed by fiction and the Sunday supplement, has built up an imaginary New York which has no existence in reality. But it is this imaginary city, this mirage, which lures the country youth, boy and girl alike, to come and taste of its glittering success. It is to such a New York that Kate Craven comes, her brief experience on a country newspaper [and the recommendation of Ned Penfield who had preceded Kate in coming to New York] having won her a position on a metropolitan 'woman's page'. The story follows her career through various stages of enlightenment [she wrote an article that ruffled her co-workers; Penfield, anxious for his own job, gave her no support] and leaves her at last, married, safe and happy in the 'real New York of the cross-streets where it is still possible to live within one's means in quiet dignity and comfort'"—Book review digest.

1182. ———. *Hot Corn Ike.* **New York: Dutton, 1923. viii, 300p.**

"The central character ... is a down-at-heels fellow who for many years sold hot corn from a pot boiling on the street corner in 'de Ate' [the Eighth Assembly District of New York City] during the green corn season; during the rest of the year he has given precious service to the leader of the district, Michael Grogan, saloon keeper and political boss. A 'silk-stocking' reformer, sent into the district by an uptown club bent on doing good, invokes an ordinance against street encumbrances and drives Hot Corn Ike off [his] corner. ... Hot Corn is an astute person, however, and involves himself in the politics that surround a presidential campaign"—Book review digest. Coney Island in its early years, with its sleazy dance pavilions and roiling taprooms, is well drawn.

1183. ———. *The wooing of Folly.* **New York: Appleton, 1906. 294p.**

"The story of a family from South Boston who come to New York to 'attack' society. The father has made an immense fortune in Nevada in silver and spends lavishly in pursuit of his one absorbing purpose. There is a daughter, Folly, who is the object of innumerable fortune hunters, and a son, Byron, fresh from Dartmouth College, whom it takes but a very short time to learn all the ways of the fast set of the metropolis. The story is told in letters, all the characters confiding their innermost secrets to correspondents"—Annual American catalogue.

1184. Ford, Norman Robert. *The black, the grey and the gold.* Garden City, N.Y.: Doubleday, c1961. 450p.

"Examination of the West Point honor system based on a fictional reconstruction of the cribbing scandal there a few years ago. ... Ford's protagonist, Major Landseer['s] quarrel is not with honor, but with the way the honor system has been perverted to serve the interests of football, expediency, and even personal rancor. The real story of the book is ... the twenty-year clash between Landseer, an unassimilated individual, and the 'system' personified by Col. Luther Philipbar. The clash is developed early in flashbacks to an earlier West Point and the pre-war Army, partly through the investigation of the accused cadets, and partly in a triangular relationship between Landseer, Philipbar and Charlotte Stockham, mistress of 'Stockhamfield', a Storm King Mountain estate intimately bound up with the Academy"—New York herald tribune books.

1185. Ford, Paul Leicester, 1865-1902. *A checked love affair*; and the Cortelyou feud. With photogravures by Harrison Fisher and with cove   decorations by George Wharton Edwards. New York: Dodd, Mead, 1903.112p.

In the first story a young bank clerk falls in love with Freda, the bank president's daughter. They have a quarrel and split. A Mrs. Baxter invites each of them separately to her Hudson River home. The couple, still estranged, decides to go back to their New York City homes as quickly as possible. Their luggage claim checks get switched and each discovers the other's love letters, still retained despite the lovers' quarrel. Reconciliation and marriage follow. In 'The Cortelyou feud' Mr. Pellew, invited by Mrs. Baxter to dinner, finds himself seated next to Kate Cortelyou. The two are members of long-feuding families, so everyone expects them to be most uncomfortable. But Kate and Pellew talk amiably together and realize that the so-called feud is ridiculous. The denouement is a growing affection enhanced by frequent attendance at afternoon teas and finally marriage.

1186. ————. *The Honorable Peter Stirling and what people thought of him.* New York: H. Holt, 1894. 417p.

"The Hon. Peter Stirling comes to New York City fresh from Harvard College. He puts out his sign as a lawyer in the most crowded part of Broadway, and for two years he has not a single client. He has some means, and while waiting he makes a study of New York City tenement house life, and finally uses his legal ability and great eloquence to bring home to the authorities the wrongs of the poor, the abuse of trusts, the general corruption of city life. The view of the evil that exists is optimistic in spite of the plain words spoken of bossism, railroad thievery, milk adulteration, liquor laws, and the thousand other disgraces of New York City. A stream of romance makes the truth palatable for the general reader"—Annual American catalogue. Ford disclaimed the notion that Peter Stirling was modeled on Grover Cleveland.

1187. ————. *The story of an untold love.* **Boston: Houghton, Mifflin, 1897. 348p.**
Donald Maitland, philologist/orientalist, leaves his studies and writings in Europe, Africa and Asia to come back to New York City where he hopes to earn enough money to begin paying off a debt of honor. Said debt is owed to Maizie Walton, a young woman brought up in the Maitland home under the elder Mr. Maitland's guardianship until she inherited a sizeable fortune from her aunts. Maizie's uncle, Mr. Walton, convinced Maizie that the Maitlands, father and son, had without her knowledge used up her earlier funds to support the extravagant Mrs. Maitland and their own trips to Europe. A sympathetic New York financier, Foster Blodgett, helps Donald find employment as editor of a journal supported by oil tycoon Whitely; the latter appropriates Donald's editorials, reviews and books as his own work. Donald, under the pseudonym Rudolph Hartzmann, accepts this odd situation because it allows him to get close to Maizie, the woman he has loved from their early years together. Maizie eventually realizes Whitely's deceptions, refuses his proposal of marriage, forgives the Maitlands and returns Donald's love. This novel is in the form of a journal kept by Donald from Feb. 20, 1890 to Jan. 10, 1895.

1188. ————. *Wanted—a chaperon.* **With illus. by Howard Chandler Christy; decorations by Margaret Armstrong. New York: Dodd, Mead, 1902. 109p.**
Confused by the numbers and directions that attach themselves to New York City's streets countrified Lydia Greenough, on her way to a pre-Christmas party, steps from her carriage during a heavy snowstorm into the wrong house. She spends a good part of the evening with the gentlemanly but temporarily disabled Allan Murchison, a bachelor and chemist, who is intrigued by her naiveté and forthrightness, a contrast to the social 'butterflies' he has hitherto not too happily associated with. Lydia's aunt, Mrs. Travers, with whom Lydia is staying, is horrified by the breach of convention her niece has committed. Murchison's apologies and his high position and income mollify Mrs. Travers; it requires little imagination to diagnose what the upshot of all this will be.

1189. ————. *Wanted—a matchmaker.* **With illus. by Howard Chandler Christy; decorations by Margaret Armstrong. New York: Dodd, Mead, 1900. 111p.**
A little New York newsboy, Swot McGarrigle, is the most interesting character in this short novel. Swot meets with an accident while peddling his

papers (he is struck by a carriage at 42nd Street) and is accompanied to the hospital by Constance Durant, a passenger in the carriage. There Dr. Armstrong and Constance 'collaborate' in restoring Swot to health. Simultaneously Swot is involved in bringing his two healers together into a most promising relationship.

1190. Ford, Sewell, 1868-1946. *Cherub Divine*; a novel. New York: Kennerley, 1909. 395p.

The novel's protagonist, 'Cherub' Divine, had started out as an errand boy on Wall Street and had climbed to the top of the financial ladder. He purchased a country estate on Long Island. Some time later he decided to examine more closely his acquisition. It turned out to be a rather confusing 'ordeal'; the servants of the former owner came with the house and then Cherub met the former owner himself and his daughter. She had been married to a European nobleman, but was now living once again with her father. Cherub masters the situation, however, and discovers love with a former countess in the process.

1191. ————. *Inez and Trilby May*. With illus. by Marshall Frantz. New York: Harper, 1921. 292p.

"The two girls of the story are Inez Petersen, a big Swede good to look at but dull and passive, and Trilby May Dodge, quick of wit and long of talk. They hail from Duluth, Minnesota, and have come to New York for adventure and to find an uncle of Inez, supposed to be rich and living under an assumed name, which she does not know. Their adventures are many and of a farcical nature, Inez looking the part and Trilby May furnishing the inspiration. The uncle is really found, he proves to be rich, and after due caution, he warms up to Inez"—Book review digest.

1192. ————. *Odd numbers*; being further chronicles of Shorty McCabe. Illus. by F. Vaux Wilson. New York: Clode, 1912. 309p.

Shorty McCabe is the proprietor of a physical culture studio who discourses on the odd people he has come upon or become interested in as they tramp the streets of New York City. Some are quite mad, some belong to the wealthy class, some come in from the country, some are living on alimony, etc.

1193. ————. *On with Torchy*. Illus. by Foster Lincoln. New York: Clode 1914. 317p.

Torchy is a true son of Manhattan and also a direct descendant of the medieval knight; his job as messenger and office boy in New York City may be humble, but Torchy is a very resourceful lad who is entrusted with several peculiar commissions and odd tasks that require quick thinking. He establishes a friendship with a 'Miss Vee', a young woman far above him socially; she has an aunt who watches over her 'like a hawk', but Torchy nimbly outwits the old lady on occasion.

1194. ————. *Shorty McCabe*. Illustrated by Francis Vaux Wilson. New York:

M. Kennerley, 1906. 316p.

In his own words Shorty McCabe, who teaches physical education in New York City, tells how he has gained the patronage of some of the wealthiest people in the city; then he informs us of his adventures in their company. When Shorty does go to Italy with one particular fellow, he becomes a critic of European customs, stating, "What I need is a life sentence to stay in little old New York."

1195. ————. *Shorty McCabe on the job.* **New York: E.J. Clode, 1915.**

The author's New York character, Shorty McCabe, has been appointed administrator of the estate of eccentric Pyramid Gordon. This group of stories tells how Shorty (in his own inimitable language and philosophy) deals with the conundrum that Pyramid has left $3,000,000 to a number of people with whom he had been on most unfriendly terms.

1196. ————. *Side-stepping with Shorty.* **Illus. by Francis Vaux Wilson. New York: Kennerley, 1908. 325p.**

Twenty sketches in which Shorty McCabe sees a good deal of life in New York City; he uses his brand of slang to tell us about it. His "unconventionality of expression ... make[s] his story as breezy as the sidewalks round about the Times Building on a windy day"—New York times book review.

1197. ————. *Torchy.* **Illus. by George Brehm and James Montgomery Flagg. New York: Clode, 1911. 311p.**

"Presents a red headed New York office boy and sets him to telling his autobiography. It is at any rate the essential vulgarity of the scene and its actors, such as may or may not please in its picturesque phrasing and uninvited repartee, but which is, nonetheless, the 'genius loci's.' Torchy is more clever than well-bred, and the last thing in the world he would think of keeping is 'his place.' On the contrary, by not keeping his place, or any consciousness of it, he rises in the world—after the fashion of storybook heroes. His apologists will observe that his heart is in the right place, as also that he has a head on his shoulders"—The independent. Torchy's weakness for pretty girls is illustrated by several amusing entanglements with them and his ever present wish to gain their good graces.

1198. **Forgione, Louis.** *Reamer Lou.* **New York: Dutton, 1925. 279p.**

"Reamer [a young Italian-American] comes from a mining town near Scranton [Pa.] to work in the Staten Island shipyards. He and his fellow workers know no higher law than physical strength, no keener joy than the fierce gratification of the senses. He glories in the perfection of his big frame and the sense of power it gives him over the men—and women—he meets. The story covers a comparatively short period, telling of the young man's friendships and loves, his loyalties and betrayals"—Book review digest.

1199. ————. *The river between.* **New York: Dutton, 1928. 254p.**

Demetrio and Oreste, father and son, share a home on the edge of the Palisades above the Hudson River. These two immigrants are relatively prosperous contractors; Demetrio is much the smarter of the two; Oreste is slow-witted with a huge physique. Rose, Oreste's wife, had already walked off because of constant quarrels with her father-in-law, but has returned. Now she and Demetrio reach an understanding; both unite against Oreste and leave home for the big city—Demetrio, half-blind, adopts a beggar-like existence, and Rose becomes a street prostitute. They finally come back to Oreste in dramatic fashion, with much yet to be resolved.

1200. Forman, Henry James, 1879-1966. *The captain of his soul.* **New York: McBride, Nast, 1914. 468p.**

"The story is in three parts. In part one, Gilbert Spottswood, newly arrived in New York, looks for work, writes a play, dines at Frisquita's on Eighth Street, and falls in love with Mary Fairweather. In part two, attaining a promising position in Wall Street, he forsakes his early ideals, hob-nobs with the capitalists [among them, Coleman, a powerful financier], dines at Sherry's and forgets Mary in an ignoble love affair with Mrs. Holroyd. In part three, after facing despair and contemplating suicide, he becomes master of himself. One of his plays is accepted, and, with Mary, he faces the realization of some of his dreams"—Book review digest.

1201. ————. *The fire of youth.* **Boston: Little, Brown, 1920. 364p.**

"This is the story of the country boy who comes to the city, goes wrong, but eventually finds the right path again. Anthony West is the son of a Nebraska editor, a man whose humble country paper, the Beacon, is known from one end of the land to the other. Anthony goes to Harvard and following the death, first of his father, and then mother, enters New York journalism. But quicker means of making money appeal to him and he goes into a broker's office, falls into the coils of an adventuress, is disillusioned and tastes the dregs of life. Then the girl from home comes to New York and hope picks up again. The [1st] World War breaks out, and when his service in the army is finished, he is ready to go back to Little Rapids [Nebraska] to the position Jim Howard has kept waiting for him on the Beacon"—Book review digest.

1202. Forman, James Douglas, 1932- . *The Cow Neck rebels.* **New York: Farrar, Straus & Giroux, 1969. 272p.**

A novel about the American Revolution with its center of attention on the Battle of Long Island. Some of the characters in the story are: a militant Scots grandfather; a weak-kneed father who runs from any danger; his wife who considers war stupid and unnecessary; their two sons, Malcolm and Bruce—Malcolm is a made-to-order gamecock, while introspective Bruce is the actual hero; Rachel, the pretty girl who comes between Malcolm and Bruce and is the daughter of the feuding grandfather's hated foe.

1203. **Forman, Justus Miles, 1875-1915.** *Buchanan's wife*; a novel. **Illustrated by Will Grefé. New York: Harper, 1906. 290p.**

"Beatrix Buchanan [25], for two years married to a man whom she does not love, finds her lot unbearable. [Her husband owns an estate on the seacoast in the vicinity of New York]. The 'droop to her mouth' reveals the state of her mind and incidentally betrays the fact that she had not made the way all sunshine for her husband. Grown cynical and harsh, with the 'desperately shy sweetness' entirely crushed, having nothing to nourish it, [Mr.] Buchanan disappears one night from the world. The day of Beatrix's happiness must dawn. She tricks the man she loves by purposely lying when called to identify a body resembling her husband. After her [new] marriage a little 'gray tramp' steps into her rose garden with mind as well as lungs gone. It is the pitiable shadow of her [first] husband and in her misery she ministers to him till death"—Book review digest.

1204. ————. *Journey's end*; a romance of today. **Illustrated by Karl J. Anderson. New York: Doubleday, Page, 1903. 240p.**

Bereft of funds after his father passes away, a young Englishman seeks a living in New York City. He starts out as a clerk in a photography shop and then utilizes his literary talents to make a name for himself in playwrighting circles. The death of a cousin, an English duke, poses a dilemma for the young dramatist. He can return to England, inherit a ducal estate, and marry his first love there, or stay in America and marry the actress who has been largely responsible for his success in the theater.

1205 ————. *The opening door*; a story of the woman's movement. **New York: Harper, 1913. 328p.**

"A novel offering a sane and temperate interpretation of the woman's movement. Hope Standish, a young girl just out of a fashionable finishing school, destined for a debutante season and a career in society, is drawn, almost against her will into the ranks of workers for equal suffrage [by her grandmother in New York, a miss King]. She makes a failure as a platform speaker, falls in love, marries, becomes a happy mother, and believes that she has abandoned the 'cause' forever. But she finds that she is still enlisted in its ranks, finds new ways of working for it, not antagonistic to other duties, and convinces a doubting husband of its justice and reasonableness"—Book review digest.

1206. **Forsslund, Louise, 1873-1910.** *The ship of dreams.* **New York: Harper, 1902. 306p.**

The sleepy hamlet of 'Meadowneck', Long Island is the locale of this rural idyll. Imogen, the 'Little Red Princess', is the heroine; she is the granddaughter of 'Mad Nancy', a woman who had 50 years before been driven to the poorhouse by Barnabas Fanning of Pepperidge Manor. Barnabas's nephew, Robert Fanning, falls in love with Imogen despite the bad blood between the Fannings and the kin of Mad Nancy; Imogen's seven brothers are reputed to be pirates and Imogen's family has laid a curse on the Fannings. But love conquers all; Robert's pure affection for Imogen and her love for him dispel the curse on Pepperidge Manor and its residents. The novel has other interesting characters: viz., Daddy Danes, a.k.a. 'Old Gol', and his wife Pernelia B., who dispenses six peppermint drops for a penny along with choice bits of gossip; and 'Simple Simon' who watches over Imogen, the Little Red Princess, when she seems detached from those who love her.

1207. —————. *The story of Sarah*, by M. Louise Forsslund (M. Louise Foster). New York: Brentano's, 1901. viii, 433p.

The heroine of the story (the scene of which is an inlet of the Great South Bay of Long Island) is Sarah, a young woman with sterling qualities who still adheres to many of the customs of the original Dutch and English settlers. Sarah's relationship to the people who man the sea rescue station on the coast and the activities of the lifesavers themselves are the crux of the novel.

1208. Fort,Charles 1874-1932. *The outcast manufacturers*. New York: B.W. Dodge, 1909. 328p.

An odd number about a dubious operation, the Universal Manufacturing Company, quartered in New York City with I. Birtwhistle as president, Asbury Parker, secretary, and a newcomer from New Jersey, Sim Rakes, as treasurer. The female characters are chiefly Irishwomen who take in boarders or work for the company. There are few clues as to what the Universal Manufacturing Company actually produces and when it goes under the 'directors' are reduced to looking for employment, however lowly.

1209. *The fortunate discovery*; or, *The history of Henry Villars*. By a young lady of the State of New-York. New York: Printed by R. Wilson for S. Campbell, 1798. 180p.

A 'remote village in the northern part of the State of New-York' is the home of Henry Villars and family, seeking refuge from the din of war [near the end of the American Revolution].Captain William Bellmore, a wounded British officer, accompanied by his friend Henry Hargrave, is taken in by the Villars family until he recovers. The scene shifts to New York City where secrets are opened up. Henry Hargrave turns out to be Mr. Villars' son (presumably drowned at sea as an infant) and the brother of Louisa Villars, Bellmore's ladylove. Hargrave, as grandson of Lord Beauclair (his mother is Lord Beauclair's disowned daughter, Maria Villars), is also heir to the deceased nobleman's estates. The story concludes in England with Hargrave as the new Lord Beauclair and the other chief characters gathered around him

1210. *The fortunes of a young widow*; a narrative ... A veritable revelation of New York life in the nineteenth century, by an old inhabitant. New York: Stearns, 1850. 111p. (in double columns).

Fanny, an orphan, had been raised by the grocer Nathan Clark; he had married her when she reached maturity. Nathan died and left Fanny $2,000 per annum provided she did not remarry. Banker Rufus Small, anxious to appropriate Nathan's money for his own uses, tried various ruses to get Fanny to break the will's terms. After he suffered crushing financial losses, Small committed suicide. His widow encouraged a former lover, the mechanic James, to woo Fanny. James reflects on his wasted life, ignores Mrs. Small and secures Fanny's consent to marry him. Fanny and James purchase a small farm with the residue from her first husband's estate—after the lawyers and accountants straighten out the tangled affairs of the late banker Small, the estate's executor.

1211. **Fosburgh, Hugh, 1916- . *The sound of white water.* New York: Scribner, 1955. 192p.**

The novel centers around a canoe trip down the 'Big River' in New York State taken by three men: bachelor Pete Gay, fiftyish, who serves as a guide, is a hunter and trapper; the younger Ben Pierson is on vacation from his job in the lumber industry and is well acquainted with Pete; Tony Farr, a college classmate of Ben, has little experience with the outdoor life. Their main object is to get in some good fishing, but their interrelationships are what may interest the reader more.

Fosdick, Charles Austin, 1842-1915. See under his pseudonym: Castlemon, Harry, 1842-1915.

1212. **Foster, David Skaats, 1852-1920. *Elinor Fenton*; an Adirondack story. Philadelphia: J.B. Lippincott, 1893. 300p.**

"While making a business visit to a small lumber settlement in the depths of the Adirondacks, Ethan Hardy loses his way in a rocky gorge and at the same time loses his heart to the mountain nymph who rescues him from his predicament. The plot of the story turns on a murder committed many years before the events described, and the final solution of the mystery is unexpected and satisfactory"—Annual American catalog. 'Fentondale' is the village around which the story is centered (probably it can be identified as Lyons Falls, New York). Foster rewrote this novel in 1915 (changing the names of the characters) under the title: Our Uncle William, also, Nate Sawyer.

1213. ————. *Flighty Arethusa*. With three illus. and cover design by Paul Wilhelmi. Philadelphia: Lippincott, 1910. 326p.

A rather wild adventure story—the two chief characters are Richard Armstrong, an aeronautical engineer and pilot, and Arethusa Moreland, a practical, sensible young lady. They meet when Richard lands his plane near a lake in Upstate New York, close by a bungalow occupied by Arethusa and her friends. When Arethusa tells Richard of a hidden treasure bequeathed her by her grandfather, the two of them set out to find it. They locate the hoard, but are hotly pursued by villains looking for the same treasure.

1214. **Foster, George G. d. 1850.** *Celio*; or, *New York above-ground and underground.* **New York: DeWitt & Davenport, c1850. 144p.**

Celio, escort of the beautiful, partially handicapped Mrs. Adelaide Carleton, is a man of many talents—writer, musician, critic, and a wit. Captain Earnest on the other hand consorts with the New York underworld as well as with the so-called 'good people.' But ultimately he is a benign figure who employs Celio as editor of a newspaper he is financing. When Mr. Carleton dies, his business associate, Job Pipson, apprises Adelaide of her husband's failed investments. Rather than submit to Pipson's overtures, she becomes a seamstress. Celio (who is in love with Adelaide), Nina, the Carleton's adopted daughter, and Adelaide are reunited in the Carleton mansion after Capt. Earnest forces Pipson to yield the mortgage on the house. Nina attains success as an opera singer, but Pipson plots his revenge on all the aforementioned principals. On the brink of reaching his goal Earnest and a couple of Earnest's shady friends thwart Pipson. Of course, all ends well and even Job Pipson, in old age reforms.

1215. **Foster, Henrie.** *Ellen Grafton*; or, *The den of crime.* **A romance of secret life in the Empire City. Boston: Star Spangled Banner Office, 1850. 91p. (in double columns).**

"The scout and the savages": p.[69]-91. New York City in 1835 is portrayed in part as a place where unsuspecting young women fall easy prey to pleasure-seeking men devoid of any scruples. Henry Lambert and his friends Wilson and Jones form a 'den of crime', where Lambert especially seduces ladies who accept his false promises of marriage. Ellen Grafton is one of them, but she has champions in her brother and a Mr. Russell, who ultimately wrest Ellen from Lambert's influence. Murder is often used as a device to silence would-be witnesses. Lambert and others of his kind get their comeuppance and the 'den of crime' vanishes in a ring of fire.

Foster, Mary Louise, 1873-1900. See: Forsslund, Louise, 1873-1910.

1216. **Foster, Maximilian, 1872-1956.** *Crooked.* **Philadelphia: Lippincott, 1928, c1927. 304p.**

"Bertha Maddox is tired of a four-room [New York City] flat, tired of home-made dresses, of being a 'clerk's wife.' Her husband, Charles, … is an easygoing, honest sort of fellow, who has been a clerk in a real estate firm for some five years. … Bertha … goads him on … in her craze for money, until he abandons his ideals and becomes 'crooked.' … Charlie, the long-suffering, the all-enduring … revolts. In his first and only moment of independence or reality, he is tossed into another woman's arms, there to remain, we presume, happily ever after"—Book review digest.

1217. —————. *Keeping up appearances*. **Illustrated by Lester Ralph. New York: Appleton, 1914. 284p.**

"When a young [married] man, receiving thirty-five dollars a week in a small Ohio city, is offered five thousand dollars a year to go to New York, visions of unlimited wealth and a dash into society inspire prompt acceptance. ... Adventures in house hunting are as amusing as they are probable. Jim thinks he will take a house at about a thousand dollars a year, and is surprised to find nothing less than a thousand dollars a month. He soon discovers that $5,000 a year in New York is much less than $1,800 in Ohio. Home life [of the young couple] is lost, he [and his wife] live at the rate of $8,000 instead of $5,000 and the end soon comes"—Boston transcript. The story concludes with the two, striving more or less successfully, to pull themselves out of their financial rut.

1218. —————. *Rich man, poor man*. **Illustrated by F.R. Gruger. New York: Appleton, 1916. 322p.**

Orphaned, penniless Babby Wynne was a girl of all-work in a New York City boardinghouse when she was suddenly whisked away to a Fifth Avenue mansion and placed under the guardianship of her rich, disagreeable grandfather, Peter Beeston. Bab had not lacked attention in her earlier environment—the landlady had a mother-daughter relationship with her; a bank clerk, whose family had been stripped of its funds through the machinations of Peter Beeston, looked fondly upon Bab; a shy, little old man had predicted a bright future for her. Now as a young lady of means, i.e. backed by Beeston's wealth, two men—one rich, the other poor, both exemplary suitors, seek Bab's hand in marriage.

1219. —————. *The trap*. **New York: D. Appleton, 1920. 282p.**

"Henry Lester was very wealthy, in fact uncomfortably so, for when he fell in love he couldn't be sure that Sally Raeburn, the object of his affections, wouldn't marry him for his money rather than love of him. So he didn't ask her to marry him, but instead laid a neat little trap for her. At his country estate on the Hudson he assembled a house party, and among those present were Mrs. Dewitt, a former sweetheart of his, and Mr. Hastings, a young man of reputed wealth, and of course Sally. How the trap, when it was sprung, caught not only Sally but Henry himself, is told"—Book review digest.

1220. —————. *The Whistling Man*. **New York: Appleton, 1913. 313p.**

A tale of mystery that begins in a small French inn and concludes in a private office in Wall Street. In between there are scenes of action in a comfortable country house on the Hudson. Leonard Craig, the hero, has spent most of his life in Europe; when his father dies of fright upon the sudden appearance of the 'Whistling Man' in the aforementioned inn, Leonard decides that the answer to his father's fears lies in New York City. The Whistling Man follows, tracking down his victims and blackmailing them, until Leonard unmasks him. Beautiful women and Wall Street financiers are very visible, and it is Leonard's good luck to find a love interest among the former.

1221. Foster, Robert Frederick, 1853-1945. *Cab no. 44.* **New York: F.A. Stokes, 1910. 323p.**

The story hinges on a $10,000 bet between two New York businessmen as to whether or not the city's police force is capable of nabbing a thief who has stolen a pocketbook 20 minutes before they are actually on the case. A young Englishman offers to assume the role of robber; however, it is disclosed that this volunteer may very well be a murderer as well as a thief. Before the tale concludes not only the police but also the two bettors and other characters (including an introduced 'heroine') have been completely baffled by what is happening.

1222. Fowler, Gene, 1890-1960. *Trumpet in the dust.* **New York: Liverright, 1930. 357p.**

Gordon Dole is brought up in a religious family in a small western town. He falls in love with an aspiring actress, Nada, who leaves for New York. Gordon marries Margaret; then he too leaves for New York and a sometimes-brilliant career as a reporter. The emptiness he feels, however, leads him to resume his affair with Nada, but in the end he returns to his wife.

1223. Fox, Barry. *Hide-Away Island.* **New York: Greenberg, 1934. 278p.**

The pregnant Beth Woodward divorced her distrustful husband and made a new home on an island near Long Island's South Shore. It was a simple but comfortable dwelling place, refurbished with the help of some Coast Guardsmen from what had been a summertime shanty. One of the Guardsmen, Jim, was on hand to deliver her baby. Beth named the infant Steve and was settling down with her child, when she found romance entering her life once again.

Fox, David, pseud. See: Ostrander, Isabel Egenton, 1883-1924.

1224. Fox, Gardner, F., 1911- . *Arrow in the hill,* **by Jefferson Cooper [pseud.] New York: Dodd, Mead, 1955. 244p.**

This story of the French and Indian conflict veers between New York State and Virginia and points in between. The commanding figure is Stephen Brant who has been raised by Mohawk Indians (he was an orphan at five years of age). Stephen forms a friendship with George Washington, orates before his Iroquois friends to persuade them to make war on the French and gets into romantic entanglements with several women, Indian and White.

1225. Fox, Paula, 1923- . *One-eyed cat.* **Scarsdale, N.Y.: Bradbury Press, 1984. 216p.**

In the 1930s in a Hudson River town Ned Wallis is warned by his father, the Rev. Mr. Wallis, not to use the air rifle he was given on his 11th birthday.

Ned finds the confiscated gun, takes it out at night and fires it. The thought that he may have hit someone takes hold in his mind. Ned comes across a one-eyed cat while visiting old Mr. Scully, a cat lover. He is now certain that the cat was his victim and his conscience bothers him. Much as Ned might wish to confess his misdemeanor he puts it off until the story's end. Characters who touch Ned in one way or another are his invalid mother, a stern but kind father, the Wallis's touchy housekeeper, the aforementioned felinophile, Mr. Scully, and a number of the townspeople.

1226. ————. *Poor George.* **New York: Harcourt, Brace and World, 1967. 220p.**
George Macklin and his chiding wife live in Westchester County. He commutes to Manhattan to teach in a private school. George has always managed to hide behind an air of innocence and to avoid anything 'corrupt'. But when Ernest, a young unconscionable student, arouses George's interest, he finds himself in emotional turmoil that has no surcease. Thus his life at home in Westchester with a fretting wife crumbles beyond repair.

1227. **Frank, Waldo, 1889-1967.** *City block.* **Darien, Conn.: Frank, 1922. 320p.**
These short chapters or stories (with linkage as certain characters appear in more than one scene) were suggested by a block of flats in which Frank lived in the winter of 1915—ca. the 500s of Manhattan's East Seventy-seventh Street. Frank called 'City block' a 'lyric novel.' "The structure is simple: a series of episodes in the lives of people who live in the same block, showing something of the currents and counter-currents in their lives, suggesting the continuum of which all their lives are a part"—Bittner, V. The novels of Waldo Frank.

1228. ————. *The dark mother*; a novel. **New York: Boni & Liveright, 1920. 376p.**
Vibrant New York City plays a very prominent role in this novel about David Markand and his introduction to the competitive world of business under the auspices of his uncle, Anthony Deane. David attracts and has affairs with various women while he continues his friendships with Tom Rennard and Tom's sister Cornelia. The latter commits suicide when David seems to lose interest in her—he is wrapped up in a liaison with Helen Daindris. David succeeds as a businessman and Tom condones corruption as he practices law. David, however, still retains a sense of alarm as he notices wrongdoing being accepted as endemic to the social order.

1229. ————. *Rahab.* **New York: Boni & Liveright, 1922. 250p.**
"The underlying fact of the story is a tragedy in a romantic girl's [Fannie Luve's] life that leaves her stranded in New York, cast off by her husband— once a drunkard and later a convert to Christ, however dead to the spirit—and robbed of her child. From this her history is, eternally, a gradual descent in the social scale, from industrial worker to kept woman and, at last, companion to courtesans. Her internal development however is a 'falling up to God.' The

somewhat incoherent narrative portrays a series of states of mind, of exalted moods, in which Fannie's mind and soul are in turmoil but in which she never loses her sense of spiritual purity, or striving after God and truth"—Book review digest.

1230. ————. *The unwelcome man*; a novel. **Boston: Little, Brown, 1917. 371p.**
Quincy Burt was a late arrival in the Burt family and from all indications he was an unwanted one. More or less ignored by his siblings and father, but loved almost furtively by his mother, Quincy moved from Long Island to the Upper West Side of Manhattan with them. His college years were unremarkable, although chiefly through the urging of a college chum, they may have incited him to look closely at a more vibrant New York than he had hitherto known. Quincy's experiences with women are unfulfilling; he backs away from an attempted seduction by a professor's wife and loses the girl he is courting. He sinks into the bloodless world of business, further alienated from his family and himself.

1231. Frankel, A.H. *In gold we trust.* **Philadelphia: Wm. Piles, 1898. 332p.**
The novel is an unsympathetic portrayal of pursuers of wealth whose greed often is at the expense of their immigrant neighbors and even their own relatives: Wolf Zamzumewsky who acts the part of a prosperous clothing merchant, the better to trap into marriage wealthy Jewish ladies; Micha Kalbi who pushes his daughter into marriage with Wolf; Zimri Lachmandritzky, banker and proprietor of a pawnshop, who absconds to Europe with the funds of his clients; Balsam Amalik, bunko artist dealing in real estate investments; and Schmandritzki who steers fortune-hunters towards rich young women. The decent characters in this disjointed, rather crude novel include: Nathaniel Disraeli, a vegetarian, and his wife Myrtle; Daniel Ephrathy, Nathaniel's friend and eventual liberator of Nathaniel's children, Ammiel and Tirzah, from destitution; Antonia, a servant of the Disraelis of Slavic descent, who stays by the children after the elder Disraelis' deaths.

1232. Franken, Rose, 1895-1988. *Strange victory,* by **Franken Meloney [pseud.] New York: Farrar & Rinehart, 1939. 281p.**
Paige Griswold is not in love with her presumed fiancé, George Hastings; to escape marriage to him she has taken a job as governess and companion to the nervous young ward of Michael Herron at his estate on Long Island. Paige was down to her last dollar and she worked for Michael under an assumed name; that seemed to create some obstacles in their relationship, but the problems disappeared finally and the course of true love took over.

1233. Fraser, Georgia. *Crow-Step.* **New York: Witter & Kintner, 1910. 401p.**
"When at the close of the [American] Revolution Aerson Delenaut's Dutch mansion [Crow-Step, the old 'Stone House' of "Gowanus', Long Island] is restored to domesticity after an enforced period of service as military redoubt, its master carries a heavy hatred in his heart for the 'renegades' who had

brought misery upon them all. It is not surprising then that a certain British officer was repulsed in his overtures to win Delenaut's younger daughter. The tale follows intimately the affairs of the household, the sacrifices and spiritual communing of the older daughter, the fickleness of the younger daughter; and tells how a father's interception of letters affected in turn the lives of his daughters and his own state of mind"—Book review digest.

1234. ————. *Wishes come true.* **New York: H. Vinal, 1926. 258p.**

Lila Destin, a clerk in a fashionable Fifth Avenue clothing shop, stumbles upon an expensive string of pearls—and this lucky find eventually leads to Lila's transport to a carefree, comfortable life among the upper-class society of Long Island.

1235. **Frazer, Elizabeth.** *The secret partner.* **New York: Holt, 1922. 206p.**

A story of conflict between a Wall Street tyrant and the man his daughter loves. "Far away from the heat and dirt of New York, Celia, the daughter of Klaggett King, enjoys the scenery of Hunter's Ranch and the company of Pinkney Sloane. Sloane is trying to raise a loan for the Sloane Salvage Company through the help of the same King, a powerful Wall Street financier, and unknowingly is at the same time falling in love with King's daughter. King, haunted by a dream, which disturbs even his waking hours, seems to be wrestling with a powerful adversary whom he believes he must conquer to win success, and of course success means the ruin of some of his most formidable business opponents, so Sloane is the victim. Finally King dies after one of his nightly struggles with his dream partner, which is in reality his own powerful will, and Sloane's company gives him [Sloane] the chance of making a huge success in which, of course, Celia shares"—Book review digest.

1236. **Frederic, Harold, 1856-1898.** *The Copperhead.* **New York: Scribner, 1893. 197p.**

In a 'little farmland township of northern New York' Abner Beech, a farmer previously much admired by his neighbors as a man of substance, is subject to scorn and exclusion when he states his strong opposition to the waging of war against the South by Mr. Lincoln's Union Army. The abolitionist 'Jee' Hagedorn is especially uncompromising in his diatribes against anyone who opposes emancipation and the war necessary to achieve that goal. It is only after the Beech family loses its house by accidental fire and son Jeff Beech, who had joined the Union Army against his father's wishes, comes home to his sweetheart, Esther Hagedorn, that a reconciliation of sorts is effected between Abner Beech and the community that had tagged him with the sobriquet of the 'Copperhead.'

1237. ————. *The damnation of Theron Ware.* **Chicago: Stone & Kimball, 1896. 512p.**

The Methodist clergyman, Theron Ware, had hoped to secure the pulpit at 'Tecumseh', New York, but was instead assigned to 'Octavius' (Utica?), a disappointment to both him and his wife Alice. Theron is frequently in dispute with the hard-shelled Methodists of Octavius; to add to his woes he and Alice fall into debt. Exposed to the scholarly Catholicism of Father Forbes, the science of Dr. Ledsmar and the pleasure seeking of the beauteous Celia Madden, Theron's commitment to his ministry falters despite support from the evangelist Sister Soulsby and her husband. In the end Theron leaves the church and sets out for Seattle. The novel epitomizes the continuing decline of orthodox, mainline religion in America at the close of the 19th century.

1238. ———. *Harold Frederic's stories of New York State.* **Edited by Thomas F. O'Donnell, with an introduction by Edmund Wilson. Syracuse, N. Y.: Syracuse University Press, 1966. xvi, 340p.**

Five of the seven stories in this collection have appeared in other works by Frederic in this bibliography. The two new items are: The deserter and A day in the Wilderness. In the first, Moses Whipple, worried about the elderly father he had left behind in their Adirondack shack, deserts his Civil War army post and makes his way home. Young, semi-orphaned Job Parshall, at work on miserly Elisha Teachout's farm, leaves his job to help out Moses and Asa Whipple. A sympathetic deputy marshal, Norman Hazzard, searching for the deserter, is not prepared to turn Moses over to the military authorities even when he finally locates him. When the war ends the two Whipples, dispossessed of their stubby farm by Teachout, are living freely in the Adirondacks and Job has been taken under the protective wing of Hazzard. 'A day in the Wilderness' takes a drummer boy, Lafe Hornbeck, from 'Juno Mills' (near 'Octavius' in Upstate New York) through the horrible Union-Confederate clash in the scrub forests of Virginia where he comes upon a wounded Union officer whom he drags from the burning woods to safety. That individual turns out to be a cousin from Ohio with whom Lafe makes his home after the war.

1239. ———. *In the valley.* **Illustrated by Howard Pyle. New York: Scribner, 1890. 427p.**

The background of the novel is the Mohawk Valley in the stirring period just before and during the American Revolution. Daisy Mauverensen, an adopted daughter, is dearly loved by her 'brother', Douw. When Daisy marries Philip Cross, a Tory, Douw, deeply disappointed, joins the American forces under General Nicholas Herkimer and is a participant in the Battle of Oriskany. Philip Cross is wounded in the battle, but Douw shields his enemy from outright death. Eventually Cross does die and Douw is free to marry the widowed Daisy.

1240. ———. *The Lawton girl.* **New York: Scribner, 1890. xi, 472p.**

'Thessaly', a town in Upstate New York, is the site of a major industry, the Minster Ironworks, which Kate Minster, daughter of its founder, Stephen

Minster, now watches over. Jessica Lawton was brought up in a wretched home; seduced by Horace Boyce, she had left Thessaly and adopted a corrupt life style. Jessica decides to return to her hometown, forget her past, and earn an honest living. In alliance with Kate Minster, Jessica becomes involved with upgrading the lives of the workingwomen of Thessaly. But Boyce, who had arrived in town simultaneously with Jessica, is scheming with Wendover, a predatory New Yorker, and Schuyler Tenney, a local businessman, to take over the Ironworks. They are blocked by Reuben Tracy, the lawyer, a former schoolmaster. Tracy wins the battle, but in due course Jessica dies. The good work begun by Kate and Jessica and Tracy's victory are Frederic's paean to an enlightened capitalism.

1241. ————. *Marsena and other stories of the wartime.* **New York: Scribner, 1894. 210p.**

The four stories in this collection dwell on the reactions of the citizens of 'Octavius' and other towns in Upstate New York to the deadly Civil War. Marsena Pulford, deeply in love with Julia Parmalee, the wife of Lt. Dwight Ransom, leaves his photography studio in Octavius to join the Union Army. The conceited, self-centered Julia, interested only in projecting her own image, completely ignores the dying Marsena when he is pointed out to her in an Army field hospital; she also pays little heed to her wounded husband as she curries the favor of her latest conquest, the slightly hurt Colonel Starbuck. Other stories deal with the trepidation of home-front citizens as they read the casualty lists, the return of a soldier to the woman he once rejected for her now deceased sister, and the resentment of a taciturn widow at the townspeople's neglect of her undistinguished husband who had fallen in battle along with a well-liked young officer who is given a celebratory funeral. Contents: Marsena.—The war widow.—The eve of the Fourth.—My aunt Susan.

1242. ————. *Seth's brother's wife*; **a study of life in the greater New York. New York: Scribner, 1887. 405p.**

Seth Fairchild, a green country boy, with the help of his brother, Albert, gets a job on a newspaper in an Upstate New York city. Albert, a wealthy New York lawyer, tries to buy his way into nomination for Congressional office, but is murdered by one of his own political team. Seth teeters on the edge of a serious affair with his brother's wife, but breaks it off in time. Albert's widow succeeds in gaining the attention of her husband's opponent for the nomination and marries him. Seth climbs steadily in the profession of journalism and finally assumes editorial responsibilities. The novel provides an excellent picture of life and personalities in rural New York State.

Freedgood, Morton, 1912- . See under his pseudonym: Godey, John, 1912- .

1243. **French, Lillie Hamilton, 1854-1939.** *Mrs. Van Twiller's salon.* **Records by**

George Leake; expurgations by Lillie Hamilton French. New York: J. Pott, 1905. 359p.

Mrs. Van Twiller establishes a salon that she hopes will be a meeting place for the most visible people intellectually, socially, and artistically in New York City. Among those attracted to her residence are: an artist, several popular men-about-town, a university professor, an army officer (a major), and a recorder of the social life of the city, et al. Their conversations and activities are the chief substance of the novel.

1244. **French, Michael, 1944- .** *Us against them.* **Toronto, New York: Bantam Books, 1987. 151p.**

Sheriff Covington of the small town of 'Olancha' in the Adirondacks keeps a sharp eye on the doings of seven youths led by proud, arrogant Reed. The latter persuades the other lads to join him in a mountain cabin, but then forces them to follow him deeper into the woods. Reed has a fatal argument with the father of the twins, Amber and Jade, who has come in search of the two. Reed flees, leaving his followers to explain as best they can (presumably with words favoring Reed) the death of Reed's adversary. However they come to the realization that they are morally obligated to tell Sheriff Covington the facts, with no embellishments.

1245. **[French, Sireno]** *Down the banks*; **a romance of the Genesee, by Iron Point [pseud.] Dansville, N.Y.: A.O. Brunnell, 1877. 112p.**

The author is much too rhetorical for the slim tale he has to tell. His spending all of Chapter I describing it evidences that he has a fondness for the Genesee River region. The plot itself—the time period is ca. 1787—concerns the efforts of 'Doctor' Raatsbein (in essence a White 'medicine man') to 'civilize' the mix of Indians and settlers, and, since he is enamored of an Indian maiden, Blue-Legs, to get rid of his scold of a wife via kidnapping or some other method. Mrs. Raatsbein upsets her husband's plans and exacts her revenge. The young Indian, Foxfoot, the eventual bridegroom of Blue-Legs, rescues Raatsbein, his wife and their baby son from an almost fatal fall. The Indians in the story generally do not come off too well; the author dwells on their fondness for hard liquor and their 'uncouth' customs.

1246. **Friedman, Sanford, 1928- .** *Rip Van Winkle.* **New York: Atheneum, 1980. 279p.**

In the summer of 1931 Andrew Spector came in contact with primitive reindeer-worshipping people living clandestinely in an unexplored corner of the Catskills. Through the years Andrew harbored this unusual secret until in 1969, a victim of arteriosclerosis, Andrew dropped some vague hints about his early discovery. His family assumed that his remarks had some connection to his current physical state and their own family concerns.

1247. **Friel, Arthur Olney, 1885-1959.** *Hard Wood.* **Jacket and front. by R.J. Cavaliere. Philadelphia: Penn Pub. Co., 1925. 333p.**

The novel's setting is the upper Hudson River Valley in that period when New York State's canals were thriving. 'Hard' Wood, the hero of the story, had, as a youth, whipped 'Copperhead' Cooper in the village schoolyard and had thereby made an enemy for life. 'Copperhead's' family kept distance between themselves and the other settlers in the burgeoning backwoods society; they distilled hard liquor and on one occasion, when they were hopelessly drunk, set fire to Hard's home. Homeless and deprived of his deceased mother's prized possessions, Hard swore he would exact retribution from the Coopers. Somewhere on the road to revenge Hard fell in love with Jane Cooper, the restoration of whose eyesight he was partly responsible for, and his rage cooled.

1248. *The frontiersmen*; a narrative of 1783. **New York: Stringer & Townsend, 1854. 166p.**

The locale of this post-American Revolution tale is a primitive region in the former Tryon County (Mohawk Valley) N.Y. The leading characters are: Ralph Weston and Ichabod Jenkins, two veterans and frontiersmen in search of new ways of making a living, the settler Matthew Barton and his daughter Ruth, Guthrie, a one-time Tory, and the Tuscarora brave, Eagle's Wing, or Canendesha. The above-named are besieged in Barton's cottage by a raiding party of Senecas who are out to avenge the killing of Seneca warriors by Eagle's Wing. Hand-to-hand combat, capture and escape, the slaughter by the Senecas of two unfortunate Yankee lawmen when Weston and the others refuse to hand Eagle's Wing to his vengeance-seeking foes—these are among several bloody incidents that occur before the besieged (less the traitorous Guthrie who is almost literally 'thrown to the wolves' by Ichabod Jenkins) are rescued by Oneidas and Tuscaroras.

1249. **Froscher, Jon.** *The Woodstock murders*; or, *Happiness is a naked policeman.* **Woodstock & New York: Overlook Press, 1998. 247p.**

A young gay friend, Buddy Keepman, accompanies Sam and Wendy Schaeffer, theatrical performers in their late 60s to Woodstock, N.Y. Supposedly liberal Woodstock, they are sad to discover, has its quota of prejudice and homicide. A local matriarch who has been instrumental in their move becomes a murder victim. Her husband and two sons (a nasty duo) are also killed. Tom Wilder of the New York State Police is left to ponder who wiped out that family—was it the Schaeffer's housekeeper, raped several times by the sons; the black gardener, the object of the son's racial calumnies; or the two lesbians who were censured in public by them?

1250. **Frost, Lesley, 1899-1983.** *Murder at large.* **New York: Coward-McCann, 1932. 238p.**

"Judge Bertand Whitaker, incurably ill, decides to have himself murdered. He invites eight acquaintances and a detective to his Long Island mansion, reads them portions of a diary (to be published) involving them all in horrible crimes and scandals, and the butchery begins. We counted six or seven corpses before long, including the nasty judge … but the handsome sleuth … who loves Joel, will probably escape"—New York herald tribune books.

1251. Fuessle, Newton Augustus, 1883-1924. *Jessup*. New York: Boni and Liveright, 1923. 280p.

"Jessup had been brought up by her grandmother in ignorance of her origin. When her grandfather one day blurted out the secret, her one thought was to get away where she could live among strangers. Five years later she was in New York, resolutely determined to make a place for herself in the world. Beauty, talent and a strong will brought her success, first on the stage and then as a costume designer. To give herself a background she invented some satisfactory ancestors and displayed their portraits. She married a young architect of aristocratic family whose love for her was not strong enough to overcome his suspicions of her nameless birth, and when the chance recognition of one of her fake ancestors by a friend led to the discovery of her deceit, her husband divorced her. The story leaves her starting out to face the world again, if without ancestors or husband, yet with confidence in herself and her abilities"—Book review digest.

1252. Fuller, Anna, 1853-1916. *One of the Pilgrims*; a bank story. New York: G.P. Putnam, 1898. vi, 331p.

The setting of the novel is New York City, in particular the Pilgrim Savings Bank. Frank Truxton is a junior clerk, well liked by all the employees. Frank had dropped out of college when his father died in order to care for his mother. She too passed on and Frank decides to stay with the bank. He has inherited some real estate and rental properties in the city. He meets Ruth Ware, a young woman with upper social strata connections; she has been assisting several working families with various problems and deposits some of their earnings in the 'Pilgrim.' Frank suffers a cruel blow when a $10,000 gold certificate he had placed in his cash drawer is, without his knowledge, carried by a gust of wind to the floor, where it is picked up by Tim, janitor Barney Flynn's helper, and taken to his home. Frank is accused of theft; he loses his job and casts about for other employment. Tim relents and places the certificate in Frank's old linen bank coat. Barney Flynn brings the coat to Frank and the gold certificate is found. Frank's good repute is reinstated and he and Ruth Ware plan a future together.

1253. Fuller, Caroline Macomber, b. 1873. *The bramble bush*. New York: Appleton, 1911. 307p.

The novel takes as its motif bohemian life in and around New York City. The hero of the story, Brant Harbeck, is a cartoonist and book illustrator who is enthralled by music. His mother had hoped he would study for the ministry, but that was an illusory wish. In the company of Miss Noel Gordon (a more talented artist than he) Brant spends the summer on Dipper Island; they find a congenial group of writers and artists and have some quite amusing 'adventures.' Brant espies Patty Lang, a frustratingly beautiful girl, and falls

323

hard for her. He continues to struggle for a living until a measure of prosperity comes along—a substantial fee for popular songs he has been composing on the side. This allows Brant to help out his mother and to pursue his romance with Patty.

1254. **Fuller, Edward, 1860-1938.** *John Malcolm*; **a novel. Providence, R.I.: Snow & Farnham, 1902. 432p.**

A wealthy, retired businessman, John Malcolm, lives alone in a big house in Clinton Place, New York City. He had a son and a daughter who had long since left the family hearth. Neither had met with good fortune. The son was suspected of criminal activity; the daughter had run off with a frivolous Englishman. Now they have returned to New York; machinations centered on the elderly man's wealth begin.

Fuller, Samuel Richard, b. 1879. See under his pseudonym:
Brainerd, Norman, b. 1879.

1255. **Fulton, Chandos, 1839-1904.** *A brown stone front*; **a story of New York and Saratoga. New York: H.L. Hinton, 1873. 147p.**

The first half of the novel takes place in Saratoga where Mrs. Brown has an eye to matching her daughter Adele with a suitable mate. Adele falls in love with the Southerner, Colonel Thomas, but he soon moves out of the picture and William Dick, a dilettantish, wealthy young fellow who at first resists the notion of marriage, steps in. Dick proposes to Adele, they are married and take up residence in New York City. It isn't long before cracks appear in their marriage. William Dick is a clubman who favors light entertainments while Adele is a conventional but accomplished young woman who pursues the arts. An increasing amount of Adele's time is spent with Señor Viva, a Spaniard with musical talents and his own fortune. The Dicks are caught in a web of scandalous rumors. Señor Viva assures William that he has made no overtures to Adele and then sails for South America. Adele is so dismayed by the so-called 'affair' that she becomes quite ill. Upon her recovery Adele and William come to an agreeable understanding and their marriage will probably be more firmly grounded in the future.

1256. **[Furman, Garrit] 1782-1848.** *Redfield*; **a Long Island tale of the seventeenth century. New York: O. Wilder & Jas. M. Campbell, 1825. 214p.**

Tamane, daughter of Wyandance, sachem of the Mattowacs (who were settled a short distance from Montauk Point) comes upon Redfield, a shipwrecked sailor, lying on the shore half-dead. The Indians restore Redfield to relative health and take him to the nearby home of Mr. Norwood and his daughter Clara. With money given him by a doughty Captain Cutwater, Redfield purchases a boat and begins trading for furs, circumnavigating Long island and touching at points on the Connecticut shore and New Amsterdam. When the Narragansett Indians declare war on the Long Island tribes, Tamane is taken prisoner. Redfield purchases Tamane's freedom and at the novel's close he is married to Clara Norwood, while Tamane weds the young Indian chief Pombam. The book is noteworthy for the data it presents about the Indians of Long Island.

1257. **Futrelle, Jacques, 1875-1912.** *The diamond master.* **Illustrated by Herman Pfeifer. Indianapolis: Bobbs-Merrill, 1909. 212p.**

Young E. Van Cortlandt Wynne convinces New York's diamond experts that he could flood the market with his cache of perfect diamonds, if he so chose. The much-exacerbated merchants hire detectives to follow his movements. Using carrier pigeons and assistance given him by the girl he loves, Wynne deceives the detectives and the diamond merchants. The diamonds are actually in the hands of the girl's grandfather, and it is only after the old man's murder by a vagrant that one learns they were manufactured by a secret process in his house. Wynne is paid by the diamond cabal to destroy the process, and the market's stability is retained.

1258. ————. *The simple case of Susan.* **New York: Appleton, 1908. 233p.**

Susan and her husband are a New York City couple who seem to be getting along quite well. Then she, known by her friends to be rather scatterbrained, gets involved in certain situations that cause her to lie to her husband in order to avoid any jealous reaction on his part. The upshot is that a gentleman friend's affair of the heart is endangered and Susan is terrified at the thought of her husband finding out that she played a role in all of this.

1259. **Futrelle, May Peel, b. 1876.** *Secretary of frivolous affairs.* **Indianapolis: Bobbs-Merrill, 1911. 311p.**

"A carefully reared young girl suddenly faces the necessity of self-support and finds that her beauty, modesty and breeding are assets that she can use advantageously in managing, quite above the commonplace, the 'frivolous affairs' of an experienced New York hostess who seems less of a task-master and employer than a friend and benefactress. A bogus count and a shrewd accomplice steer the story into channels of melodrama"—Book review digest.

G., M.A. *Jeanne; the story of a Fresh Air child.* **See Item #1807.**

Gaberman, Judie Angell, 1937- . See: Arrick, Fran, 1937-

1260. **Gabriel, Gilbert Wolf, 1890-1952.** *Brownstone front.* **New York: Century Co., 1924, 365p.**

"Mr. Gabriel has shrewdly chosen the house with the brownstone front as the symbol of a New York that was, not so long ago. It is of a day when La Gioconda was a daring opera, when Dolly Gray was a song of the day, and when the Boy Orator of the Platte, was storming the citadel of politics, when the Spanish-American War was about to break, when Brooklyn was actually another city in fact as well as in jest—it is of yesterday. The story is of no consequence, nor does it pretend to be. It is the tale of how Robert Ladd recuperated the family fortunes by inventing the Ladd bicycle lamp (everyone went bicycling, you know) and then the Ladd Street arc lamp, and of how he lost his heritage when the old brownstone house passed away with his mother"—Literary review of the New York evening post.

1261. **Gale, Elizabeth, d. 1951.** *The winged boat.* **Illus. by Harve Stein. New York: Putnam, 1942. 190p.**

A story for young people that reconstructs the village life of Indians along the shores of the Hudson. The explorer Henry Hudson is a leading figure as he takes his ship, the Half Moon, up the river and becomes friendly with two Indian lads whom he suggests taking along on his return voyage to Holland.

1262. **Gale, Sarah Helen.** *The Grail brothers*; or, *Was it an accident?* **New York: F. Tennyson Neely, 1899. 285p.**

"The story opens in 'Graftonville', a picturesque village about two hundred miles from New York City. The principal characters are two brothers, Rex and Nathaniel Grail, their sister Natalie and her betrothed, William Matthews, a New York lawyer. While yachting Nathaniel Grail is drowned. Following this sad accident is Natalie's marriage. Events that follow thirteen years later are given, evidently to prove certain theories about spiritual influence and personal impressions"—Annual American catalogue.

1263. **Gallagher, Grace Margaret.** *Vassar stories.* **Rev. ed. Boston: E.H. Bacon, 1907. 269p.**

First ed. published in 1899. Vassar College in Poughkeepsie, N.Y. was founded in 1861. Originally it was called Vassar Female College. It went coed in 1968. Contents: In the matter of roommates.—The molding of public opinion.—Her position.—A sense of obligation.—Neither a lender nor a borrower be.—The clan.—At the first game.—On baccalaureate Sunday.

1264. **Gallico, Paul, 1897-1976.** *Miracle in the wilderness*; a Christmas story of colonial America. **New York: Delacorte Press, 1975. 53p.**

It was Christmas Eve in 1755 at the home of Jasper and Dorcas Adams on the northwestern New York frontier. Before preparations for their celebration of Christ's birthday are complete, Algonquin Indian hostiles appear and take them and their first-born son, Asher, captive. The Adams's are marched towards Canada and possible death. Their hope for survival rests on Jasper's ability to explain to their captors some strange forest sightings that puzzle and frighten the Indians.

1265. **Galt, John, 1779-1839.** *Lawrie Todd*; or, *The settlers in the woods.* **London: H. Colburn and R. Bentley, 1830. 3v.**

The Scots writer Galt based the hero of his novel and incidents therein on the life of Grant Thorburn (1773-1863), a famous seeds man (who actually used the pseudonym, Lawrie Todd, on some of his writings). Like Thorburn, Galt's hero, Lawrie Todd, emigrates to America from Scotland; he takes employment in New York City as a nail maker, but soon opens a store, and then joins the Yankee, Zerobabel L. Hoskins, in a commercial venture in Upstate New York—the Genesee Valley, e.g. Most curious are the names of the settlements established or about to be established in the region: Babelmandel, Judiville, Olympus, etc. Lawrie Todd marries three times and has several children (one of whom, Charles, takes his place as partner to Mr. Hoskins). The novel concludes with Lawrie Todd taking leave of his friends and associates (and the often vexatious John Waft) in 'Judiville' and returning to Great Britain with his wife to spend remaining days in England and Scotland.

1266. *Garangula, the Ongua-Honwa chief*; a tale of Indian life among the Mohawks and Onondagas, two hundred years ago. By a citizen of Milwaukee. Milwaukee: Strickland, 1857. 160p.

"Diedrich Lansing, the hero, and Katrine Van Dervear, the heroine ... were the descendants of the first Dutch settlers on the Mohawk River, and in the midst of the magnanimous Indians with whom they had entered into friendly relations" (Preface). The two lovers must overcome the disapproval of Katrine's father; he wants Katrine to marry her cousin, Yakup Stuyvesant of New Amsterdam. Diedrich is a close friend of Garangula, son of Black Kettle, the Mohawk chieftain, and fights with him against the French and the Canadian Indians. Baron Lansing, Diedrich's uncle, leaves his estate and title to his nephew; Diedrich's landed rights are confirmed by the Crown even after New Amsterdam falls to the English and that smoothes the way for Diedrich and Katrine to marry.

1267. Gard, Anson Albert, b. 1848. *My friend Bill*; many stories told in the telling of one. New York: Emerson Press, 1900. viii, 336p.

Bill and Ruben are two young men who leave their hometown, Highmont, for the possibilities and excitements of New York City. Actually Ruben, the narrator, appears more often than Bill, but both pursue affairs of the heart— Bill with Anita Alleyn Leighton, daughter of a British officer, and Ruben (who succeeds to a fortune when oil is found on his Aunt's Rachael's farm) with Helen DeHertburn, the grown-up young woman he had saved from a runaway horse in her childhood. The story wanders far afield when it relates the adventure of Edward DeHertburn (brother of Helen and a particular friend of Ruben's) in Italy.

1268. Gardenshire, Samuel Major, 1855-1923. *The silence of Mrs. Harrold*. New York: Harper, 1905. 462p.

"A prominent New York lawyer meets a beautiful woman on an ocean steamer returning to New York. He woos and wins her—but under a condition that he will never in any way seek to penetrate the mystery of her past. Their married life in New York City is for seven years an ideal one, when John Harrold's long sleeping desire to know something of his wife's early life is rudely awakened. A story follows, of ingenious construction, which gradually unravels an unusual plot. The characters are men and women of today—millionaires, actors, businessmen, lawyers, etc. The Theatrical Trust plays no small part in the story"—Annual American catalogue.

1269.   **Gardiner, Cecilia A. *Light ahead*. New York: Phillips & Hunt, 1884. 443p.**

The protagonists in this story, intended for girls in their teens, are young people of both genders who are New York City residents; they endure all 'the changes of this fitful life'—rich today, poor tomorrow—but keep their eyes, hearts, and minds alert for the 'light ahead.'

1270.   **Gardner, John, 1933-1982. *Nickel Mountain*; a pastoral novel. With etchings by Thomas O'Donohue. New York: Knopf, 1973. 312p.**

The hero of the novel, "Henry Soames, is the fat owner of a truck route diner deep in the forests of the Catskills. A nice girl named Callie, who helps in Henry's diner, gets pregnant by a rich man's son, who then skips town. Soames marries her out of kindness. They go through the agony of childbirth. As the boy grows up, their domestic peace is variously threatened in small ways, among them a long summer's drought and the arrival of a religious fanatic who gives the child nightmares by talking about the devil. The child's real father skulks back and they forgive him"—Time.

1271.   **————. *The Resurrection*; a novel. New York: New American Library, 1966. 241p.**

"James Chandler returns from San Francisco to his childhood home in a small Upper New York State town. With him come his wife and three young daughters. Awaiting him is his aging mother. … The forty-one-year-old philosophy professor has leukemia. He has come back home to die. … [The] fact of death … as he calls forth the full resources of his intellect in an attempt to reconcile himself to it … [touches] all those with whom he comes in contact: his wife, his daughters, his mother; the three old spinster sisters who have survived from his youth; an adolescent girl … [and] a man named John Horne"—Publisher's note.

1272.   **————. *The Sunlight dialogues*. Drawings by John Napier. New York: Knopf, 1972. 656p.**

Fred Clumly, chief of police in Batavia, New York, and a veteran hippie/quasi-magician, the Sunlight Man, air their differences in long dialogues. The Sunlight Man is actually the prodigal son of Mr. and Mrs. Hodges, heads of a family that has gone steadily downward after early prominence in Batavia. Of subsidiary interest are the endeavors of a professional criminal, Boyle/Benson, to bring order into his private life. Chief Clumly pleads for clarity in an increasingly aimless society, echoing the author's own belief in the need for a moral order.

Garet, Garet, 1878-1954. See: Garrett, Garet, 1878-1954.

1273. **Garis, Howard Roger, 1873-1962.** *Larry Dexter and the bank mystery*; or, *A young reporter on Wall Street*. **New York: Grosset & Dunlap, 1912. 208p.**

> Larry Dexter is a reporter for the New York Leader who takes on the task of tracing the million dollars stolen from the Consolidated National Bank. Also on his mind is scooping rival New York newspapers. Originally the bank's money—to be transferred to another bank for payments—was placed in a steel-lined valise, but at some point a switch was made and bricks were substituted for the missing funds. The most likely suspect is Harrison Witherby, a 'runner' for Consolidated National and a master of disguise (he has theatrical ambitions). Larry pursues clues around Manhattan, New Jersey, Chicago and back to New York before a written confession surprises him, bank officials and police.

1274. ————. *The white crystals*; being an account of the adventures of two boys. **With illus. by Bertha Corson Day. Boston: Little, Brown, 1904. 243p.**

> A boy brought up in New York City, Roger Anderson, has a sickly constitution that country living might improve, so he is sent to his uncle's farm near Syracuse, N.Y. There he and a cousin embark upon a series of adventures that involve, among others, the discovery of salt on the farm property and the upsetting of the devious plans of two surveyors to take over some valuable property.

1275. **Garis, Lillian C. McNamara, 1873-1954.** *Cleo's conquest.* **Illustrated by J.M. Foster. New York: Grosset & Dunlap, 1927. 252p.**

> A story for juvenile girls, one of a series of 'Cleo' books by Garis. Cleo Kimball, her sister Nonnie, and Nellie (or Ellen) Glennon are New York City girls who elect to spend part of the summer in the Adirondacks at 'Camp Climax' or 'Lake Lookout.' They do live in tents when the weather permits, but have barracks available for stormy skies. They have their own cooks—all told it isn't a very rugged existence, although they do hike, boat and make pottery, which they bake in a kiln in the village of 'Bencherly.' Lorna Thornton is one camper who doesn't 'fit in', who seems to invite trouble; it falls to Cleo to become Lorna's friend and pull her through her difficulties.

1276. **Garland, Hamlin, 1860-1940.** *The light of the star*; a novel. **New York: Harper, 1904. 277p.**

> George Douglass, an architect by profession, of stables and barns, a Midwesterner, and incidentally a drama critic, comes to New York where he writes a play, meets an actress, Miss Merival, who acts chiefly in lurid plays and melodramas. She falls in love with Douglass and resolves to produce his play with its high-minded American theme. It is not a success; people walk out before it is over. Douglass goes back to his native West. Miss Merival keeps working with the play until it finds its audience—wholesome and earnest Americans. Douglass writes another play and comes back East to its opening performance. It is successful under Miss Merival's guidance. Evidently the author's purpose is to elevate the tastes of audiences for native-

grown, wholesome American plays. Not one of Garland's better efforts; it lacks humor and style.

1277. **Garrett, Garet, 1878-1954.** *The driver.* **New York: Dutton, 1922. 294p.**

"This story of high finance dates back to the Coxey Army episode and tells of the evolution of one, Henry M. Galt, obscure speculator on the [New York] Stock Exchange, into the monarch of Wall Street and economic dictator of the country. It shows him driving ahead with aggressive bluntness, his eyes riveted with fanatic intentness on his one goal.Overriding every obstacle, gaining his end [profitably reorganizing a great railroad from its wreckage], making enemies and turning them into friends, and at last changing from a repellent, awe-inspiring figure into a sympathetic one"—Book review digest.

Garrison, Frederick, pseud. See: Sinclair, Upton, 1878-1968.

1278. **Gartland, Hannah.** *The house of cards.* **New York: Dodd, Mead, 1922. viii, 327p.**

"Back in headquarters Inspector Kane of 'the [New York] Force' filled his pipe and settled himself down comfortably into his desk chair. 'Dead easy!' he soliloquized, 'Dead easy!' But this was soon after that morning when Patrolman Dooley had found Gregory Barwood, wealthy clubman, and one of the most skilful card players in New York, sitting in one of the carved chairs of his luxurious reception room with a bullet hole in his forehead. But the solution of the 'Barwood mystery' is not as 'dead easy' as Inspector Kane at first thinks. On the contrary it grows more and more complicated as the evidence in the case accumulates. Many are the clues followed by Inspector Kane and his subordinates, by various special detectives, by Attorney General Wallace, and by Jimmy Macoy, the cub reporter whose wide-open eyes discovered what the police missed, and whose perseverance and young American ignorance of the verb 'to fail' led him at last to the heart of the mystery"—Boston transcript.

1279. **Gaskin, Catherine, 1929- .** *Corporation wife.* **New York: Doubleday, 1961. 356p.**

"In telling the story of the effect that giant Amtec Industries has on little 'Burnham Falls', N.Y. Miss Gaskin has combined two themes: the small town novel and the business novel—a story of four women. One of the ladies, Jeannie Talbot, with a quick sharp mind, 'sensuous graceful body, mature to the point of lushness', supplies the necessary melodrama. The three other women are victims of Amtec's grimly paternalistic control of its executives' wives"—New York herald tribune book review.

1280. **Gatenby, Rosemary, 1918- .** *Deadly relations.* **New York: Morrow, 1970. 254p.**

Stephen Wylie is on a quest for a girl named Sheila who had the cottage next to his when he was on vacation fishing the nearby lakes and streams. He tracks her to the town of 'Harrodston', New York that is seething with political complexities and is under the administration of an idealistic mayor; in addition there is the threat of instantaneous demise.

1281. **Gates, David, 1947- . *Preston Falls*; a novel. New York: Knopf, 1998. 337p.**

Despite a shaky marriage Westchester residents Jean and Doug Willis take off on Labor Day weekend to their farmhouse in 'Preston Falls' in Upstate New York. Mr. Willis decides he needs an extended leave from his public relations job and his family; he hangs around with the natives, plays his guitar and reads Dickens, but also exhibits some odd behavior patterns. He follows his wife and two children to their campsite, has a confrontation with a park ranger and disappears; Jean searches for her almost paranoid husband and he eventually shows up in the couple's Westchester home, telling Jean that he has no rational explanation for his strange conduct.

1282. **Gates, Henry Leyford, 1880-1937. *House party*. New York: Grosset & Dunlap, 1932. 301p.**

Philaine North's house party, a rather wild affair held at her father's lavish Long Island estate is visited by tragedy.

1283. **Gauntier, Gene, b. 1885. *Cabbages and harlequins*; a novel. New York: Coward-McCann, 1929. 326p.**

The New York theater has an important role in this tale of Minnie from Missouri who steps on the performing stage of the 1890s in the big city and whose children also act in Broadway theaters. "The first marriage of Minnie Brown, an inexperienced country girl, ended in failure. Leaving her baby with her parents, she ran away to marry Lancelot LeRoy, a repertoire company star, who wanted her money. When Min presented him with twins, a boy and girl whom she named Jack and Jill, LeRoy left her. The rest of the story is concerned with Min's struggle to bring up her children, and their growing success on the stage. Both reach Broadway fame, but Jill pays for an indiscretion with death, and Jack marries a haughty English titled actress. Min, once more alone, goes to live with the son of her first marriage on his ranch in Wyoming where she becomes a happy grandmother to his children"—Book review digest.

Gawaso, Wanneh, pseud. See: Parker, Arthur Caswell, 1881-1955.

1284. **Gayler, Charles, 1820-1892. *Fritz, the emigrant*; a story of New York life. Founded upon Mr. Gayler's popular drama of 'Fritz' as played by Joseph K. Emmett all over the world. New York: Frank Leslie's Pub. House, 1876. 89p. (in double columns).**

New immigrants Fritz and Katrina, arriving in New York, are hassled by two undesirables, James Crafton and Phil Bobbet, gamblers/counterfeiters. Katrina is kidnapped and Fritz, with the help of some worthy Irish people, frees her. Crafton and Bobbet are incarcerated at Auburn State Prison. Fritz and Katrina buy a farm in Upstate New York near the village of 'Sprayville' and begin to raise a family. The escape of Crafton and Bobbet from Auburn arouses the Upstate community; they are cornered by Fritz and the local police and killed. The main story is preceded by a prologue that explains the origins of Moppy, a young orphan whom Katrina and Fritz had emancipated from her horrible existence as a slave in Phil Bobbet's unsavory dance/music hall.

1285. **George, Alice.** *Dolly's doings.* **Illustrated by Hattie Longstreet. Philadelphia: Penn Pub. Co., 1914. 215p.**

Dolly was quite convinced that she was the best judge of how to get things done to her own satisfaction. When she went to New York City to reside in an apartment house, she struck up a friendship with the doctor's daughter who lived one floor down. They enjoyed one another's company and studied together, but Dolly also began to realize that she, by no means, had the best answers to her own problems and certainly not to those of others.

1286. **George, Henry, 1862-1916.** *The romance of John Bainbridge.* **New York: Macmillan, 1906. vii, 468p.**

"A novel of reform in politics. John Bainbridge is a lawyer of some means who does chiefly unpaid work for the poor. Hearing of so much wrong, 'graft' and wickedness in high places, he accepts the position of New York City alderman to make a beginning at stopping corruption. He meets a young artist in glasswork working under her mother's name who is also given to high ideals. She proves to be the daughter of the great magnate whom John Bainbridge rates the biggest scoundrel of all, but she has only known him as a kind, indulgent father. John does up-hill work, and the plot shows methods of city 'graft.' The author favors his illustrious father's ideas of municipal ownership"—Annual American catalogue.

1287. **George, Jean Craighead, 1919- .** *My side of the mountain.* **Illus. by the author. New York: Dutton, 1959. 178p.**

Sam Gribley is a boy from New York who decides to leave his city home and endeavor to survive by his own wits in the Catskills. In a diary he records his experiences as he becomes increasingly dependent on his natural surroundings. He proves his self-sufficiency, but in the end he perceives that contact with fellow humans is most important to him. He returns to civilization, but carries back a heightened appreciation of the forests and their wildlife.

Germaine, Lottie. See under her pseudonym: Merrilies, Meg.

1288. **Gerson, Noel Bertram, 1914-1988.** *Savage gentleman.* **Garden City, N.Y.: Doubleday, 1950. ix, 306p.**

Jeffrey Wyatt, an Englishman indentured to a prosperous frontier family living near Schenectady, New York, falls in love with Leah Hill, a daughter of the estate owner. He is captured by Seneca Indians, outwits them, escapes and finally wins the love of Leah. These fictional events take place in the early years of the 18th century (ca. 1702-1713).

1289. ————. *The twisted saber*; a biographical novel of Benedict Arnold, by Phil Vail [pseud.] New York: Dodd, Mead, c1963. 310p.

Arnold's life is intertwined with New York State's historical past. The author has a good deal of sympathy for his complex 'hero' and gives much attention in his novel to Arnold's naval feat at Valcour Island on Lake Champlain, his raising of the siege of Fort Stanwix (Rome, N.Y.), his brilliant service at the Battle of Saratoga, and, sadly, his attempted betrayal of West Point into British hands.

1290. Gerstenberg, Alice, 1885-1972. *The conscience of Sarah Platt.* Chicago: McClurg, 1915. 325p.

"The author intends her story to be a plea for a larger life and greater freedom for women. Brought up by the strict conventions of a generation ago, Sarah Platt, [teacher in a New York City school], lets the one lover of her life go from her, believing that maidenly modesty forbade her to show her feeling for him. After twenty-five years of tragic loneliness on her part, he comes back [to New York] and offers her a belated chance of happiness. But the habits of years prove too strong. Sarah is unable to break the conventional barriers that hold her and the story ends in tragedy"—Book review digest.

1291. Gessner, Robert, 1907-1968. *Treason.* New York: Scribner, 1944. 383p.

The novel is divided into four parts. In Part one ('Despair') the American rebels are evacuating in great confusion the City of New York following their rout by the British and we are introduced to the protagonist, Matthew Clarkson, an officer in Washington's army. Part two ('Devotion') describes military operations around the Upper Hudson Valley, particularly the Saratoga campaign in which Benedict Arnold plays a vital role. Part three ('Loyalty') moves the scene to Philadelphia and vicinity as Arnold tries to defend himself from charges of misconduct, marries Peggy Shippen, and receives sympathy and support from Matthew who is deep into his own love affair with Sally Cornell, daughter of a neutral but Tory-oriented merchant. Part four ('Treason') finds Arnold in command of West Point. Matthew Clarkson is still unaware of Arnold's intentions. Arnold's treasonous plot unravels when André is captured and Matthew, benumbed, has to confront the unpleasant truths about his former hero. Haym Salomon, the Jewish financier so valuable to the American cause, is a rather prominent character in the novel.

1292. Gibbs, Alonzo, 1915- . *A man's calling.* New York: Lothrop, 1966. 192p.

"The setting is … eighteenth century Long Island, the central figure is a girl, and she's an idealized character. Delanie is the darkly colored eighteen-year-old ward of the Dutch couple, Tunis and Annamelia Van Cott. She knows only rumors about her origin, and she would like to feel more a part of the Van Cott family. Tunis is a surveyor, and when he starts training Delanie as his assistant, she is gradually accepted as a daughter by the Van Cotts. When Tunis is bedridden, Delanie in turn teaches her neighbor and old friend, Seth Clydesdale, how to survey too and their romance is measured out along with the job they are completing for Tunis. Delanie is unblemished and her story rolls along without much development. Her triumph at being recognized by the Van Cotts as one of them is ineffective because you never really see her left out, and her discovery about her background seems anticlimactic; although it's meant to prove that 'we are all brothers and sisters in God's sight.' There are some violent incidents (Tunis' original assistant breaks his back saving Seth; Tunis is caught and dragged by a deer; a peddler is lost in a snowstorm, develops gangrene and dies)"—Kirkus reviews.

1293. **Gibbs, George Fort, 1870-1942.** *The bolted door.* **New York: Appleton, 1911. xi, 346p.**

New York City is the primary locus of this story in which "according to an eccentric man's will, his niece, Natalie Judson, and his wife's nephew, Brooke Gerriott must marry within a year in order to inherit his large fortune. She is a spoiled child with more pride and spirit than common sense, and he is a rugged young engineer who, after Yale, had chosen a hard Western field for practical work and whose head lately had been full of inventions. ... How these two incompatible people work out their problems to a happy solution is told with plenty of emphasis on the frailties of human nature"—Book review digest.

1294. ————. *Fires of ambition.* **New York: Appleton, 1923. 442p.**

"This story is concerned with the career of Mary Ryan, bright, witty, adaptable, but above all ambitious and reliant on her good looks to obtain the material prosperity which she most desires. It is almost through the pages of a biography that we follow her career and mark how her essential hardness becomes more dominant. In the end, though she gains a full measure of prosperity, she loses the love of Joe Bass, which, all unconsciously, she had longed for most. The scene is almost entirely in New York"—The Times (London) literary supplement.

1295. ————. *The forbidden way.* **New York: Appleton, 1911. 387p.**

The opening scene is in a Western mining camp where Jeff Wray (while wondering who his father is) marries a charming young woman, Camilla, and strikes it rich. Wray and Camilla move to New York City and join fashionable society there and on a large Long Island estate. Camilla meets a former acquaintance, Cortlandt Bent, and comes to believe he is her real love. Misunderstandings grow between Jeff and Camilla. After long, mutual recriminations the couple resolve their differences and even find a core of happiness. The mystery of Jeff's father is solved when business transactions bring the father and son face to face.

334

1296. ————. *The house of Mohun.* **New York: Appleton, 1922. 355p.**

"This story is apparently a defense of the rising generation and especially of flapperdom. Cherry Mohun has all the marks of her time and type, but when faced by adversity, her qualities of honesty, independence and confidence, somewhat arrogantly used in the days of her pride, prove her salvation. It is the tale of a nouveau riche family [in New York City]—the father a successful promoter, the mother an equally successful social climber, the children left to go their own unrestrained ways. When the crash [of 1921] comes, it is the lovely young Cherry who takes the brunt, who proves the mainstay of her sick father, who bolsters up her weak mother and finds a way for herself out of the ruin"—Book review digest.

1297. ————. *Mad marriage.* **New York: Appleton, 1925. 367p.**

The story moves from the countryside around the Delaware River to New York City where the artist and idealist, Peter Randle, makes the acquaintance of the successful artist, Wingate, enters into bohemian life, and falls in love with a girl, 'Tommy' Keith. Peter, already married to the pretty but ordinary Josie, decides that however unhappy his marriage has turned out to be and despite his yearning for Tommy, he cannot divorce Josie.

1298. ————. *Youth triumphant.* **New York: Appleton, 1921. v, 418p.**

The story of a girl from the slums of New York fighting for happiness. "Patsy Slavin was a gutter-snipe and, dressed as a boy, sold papers in the street. One day she ran away, hid in an automobile and while asleep, was driven to a Westchester home of wealth. The two maiden ladies of the estate were persuaded by their nephew Sydney to keep and adopt the child. It turned out that her parentage was shrouded in mystery, and after she had grown to womanhood this uncertainty so troubled her pride that she finally ran away again. In the meanwhile the investigations set on foot by her adopted relatives cleared up the mystery. When Patsy was found and assured of being the issue of a legal union, she no longer hesitated to accept Sydney's love"—Book review digest.

1299. Gilbert, Edwin, 1907-1976. *Native stone.* **Garden City, N.Y.: Doubleday, 1976. 469p.**

The novel is built around the problems that three young Yale architects face at the outset of their careers. Rafferty Bloom, of mixed Irish and Jewish blood, is an idealist, while his friend Vince Cole is a moneygrubber. Albany Austin, Boston Brahmin, is so concerned with his faltering marriage that his architectural career assumes second place in his life. The setting is, at the outset, Connecticut, and then New York City becomes the chief locale.

1300. Gilbert, Nelson Rust. *The affair at Pine Court*; a tale of the Adirondacks. **With illus. in color by Frank H. Desch. Philadelphia: Lippincott, 1907. 391p.**

The scene of the action is a lodge in the Adirondacks where a wealthy host, a New York businessman, entertains a variety of guests. He has aroused the enmity of the natives by punishing trespassers and poachers on his extensive properties. One of the guests stirs the greed of the host's neighbors, including a number of outlaws, by indicating he possesses a method of acquiring vast riches. Those anxious to grasp the secret besiege the lodge. Before order and safety are restored the outlaws have threatened the host, the guests (two of whom are shot) reveal their true character, and three romantic affairs are in progress.

1301. **[Gilder, Jeannette Leonard] 1849-1916.** *Taken by siege*; **a novel. Philadelphia: Lippincott, 1887. 294p.**

Rush Hurlstone graduates from the staff of the paper 'Free Lance' in his hometown of 'Farmsted', New York to the big city and an opening on 'The Dawn'. As he settles into life in New York he becomes acquainted with several important people, foremost among them Helen Knowlton, the prima donna, with whom he immediately falls in love. His wayward brother, John, leaves his fiancée, Amy Bayliss, in Farmsted and also comes to New York. John is not only engaged unknowingly in a fraudulent mining stock scheme but unfortunately, falls in love with Leoni Cella, a ballet dancer, and impulsively marries her. As the date of his scheduled wedding to Amy draws near, John commits suicide. In the meantime Rush's journalistic career prospers, interrupted by his having to carry the news of his brother's death to grieving relatives in Farmsted. Oddly enough Leoni Cella and Amy Bayliss share their sorrow and become close friends. Rush works for two years in Europe and then returns to New York. Helen Knowlton comes back from her London engagement and she and Rush have a significant meeting.

1302. **Giles, Fayette Stratton.** *Shadows before*; **or,** *A century onward.* **New York: Humboldt Pub. Co., 1894. 286p.**

"Another of the visions of what the world will be one hundred years later. New York [City] in 1993 is the scene. A Japanese professor on a visit to New York asks questions which bring out comparisons between the old and new dispensations. There are long discussions on the effects of accepting Herbert Spencer, Darwin and Huxley as authorities, also on railroads, government, education, marriage relations, dress, longevity, burial customs, etc., etc. A thread of romance gives form to many excellent theories of national and individual life in coming years"—Annual American catalogue.

1303. **Giles, Marie Florence.** *The end of the journey.* **New York: G.W. Dillingham, 1897. 216p.**

"An American story with the scene laid on the Hudson, not far from New York City. The heroine, Vera Courteney, is a noble and beautiful woman whose wonderful strength of character and stern devotion to duty are the results of a great temptation and sorrow which is vaguely hinted at in the course of the story"—Annual American catalogue.

1304. ————. *Though your sins be as scarlet.* **London, New York: F. Tennyson Neely, 1898. 294p.**

"The position the Catholic Church takes upon divorce is brought out in a story of New York life of today. The careers of two sisters are the chief themes. One marries a rich old man for his money and position, the other lives with a divorced man, or at least one who claims to be divorced, without the ceremony of marriage. A contrast is drawn between the conventional and unconventional virtues of the two heroines"—Annual American catalogue.

1305. Gill, Josephine Eckert. *Dead of summer.* **Garden City, N.Y.: Doubleday, 1959. 192p.**

Laurie Bankhart, a newly coined college graduate, looked forward to a relaxing, even carefree summer. It was not to be. Her Upstate New York vacation was interrupted by sudden deaths (three in all, including a judge—one of them may have been a suicide). If Laurie is puzzled by these happenings so are the local and State police.

1306. Gill, William. *The woman who didn't.* **New York: G.W. Dillingham, 1895. 192p.**

"Reginald Golday had been a colonel in the Southern army. While penniless and stranded in New York City he met Geraldine Barkis, a lovely Virginia girl, to whom he had once been engaged. She was earning her living as a seamstress. Reginald found a $20 gold piece and in a few years became a millionaire. Geraldine had promised her mother never to marry a rich man and for years refused to listen to Reginald's wooing. After disaster had ruined him, she married him at once, and they found happiness in a little cigar store on South Fifth Avenue"—Annual American catalogue.

1307. Gillespie, Robert B., 1917- . *Deathstorm.* **Carroll & Graf, 1990. 200p.**

When Fred Engelhardt and his wife are killed in an explosion, Ralph Simmons, retired newspaper executive, and his wife, give the Engelhardt daughter, Eileen, a place in their Long Island home. She is certain her parents were murdered. Rudi Mannheim, like Ralph, a former soldier in the German army, agrees with her. Rudi's suspicions fasten on a former Nazi who lives in the neighborhood and who 50 years earlier had investigated Ralph in Germany because of his pacifist views. Other murders occur and Ralph and Eileen are clearly in danger before Fred's murderer surfaces along with incredible revelations about Fred himself.

1308. Gilliat, John R.V. *The loyalty of Langstreth*; a novel. **Chicago: Morrill, Higgins, 1893 [c1892]. 273p.**

"The 'smart set' of New York City, it is claimed, furnished the types from which the author studied his characters. It is the familiar story of a woman who prefers wealth to honest love, and permits her heart after marriage to return to her former lover"—Annual American catalogue.

1309. ———. *Mrs. Leslie and Mrs. Lennox*; a novel. New York: Cassell Pub. Co., 1892. 327p.

> Jack Gordon was habitually in the company of two New York society women, Mrs. Leslie and Mrs. Lennox. In love with Mrs. Leslie he was well aware of the impossibility of acknowledging that, so he pretended Mrs. Lennox was the object of his affections. This represented a measure of 'self-sacrifice' on his part and involved several points of honor.

1310. Gilligan, Edmund, 1899-1973. *Strangers in the Vly*. New York: Scribner, 1941. 261p.

> "A legendary tale of the Rip Van Winkle country in the Catskills. It concerns three dwarfs, exiles from Europe, who have fled to America and seek to hide themselves in the mountains. They are brought to the village called The Vly by a Yankee sailor whom they have befriended but who knows them as 'little bundles of wickedness'. What influence the simple folk and wild scenery of The Vly had on the little men and what the little men did in return is told in this fantasy"—Book review digest.

1311. Gillman, Nathaniel Isaiah. *Circumstantial affection*; a realistic romance of the New York ghetto. Illustrated by H.E. Nelson. New York: F. Tennyson Neely, c1900. 119p.

> The Lerner and Pasternak families have little love for one another despite the efforts of Moses Pasternak, unschooled storeowner, to enter into marriage with Lillian Lerner. Lillian has the good sense to break off the engagement to her cousin Moses and marries a formerly rejected suitor, Samuel Aronson. Lillian's brother, Edwin, casting about for an occupation, finally settles for the study of medicine. Fellow student Joseph Greenstein, hard up for money to pay his medical fees, woos and weds homely Nancy Flynn. Their divorce soon follows; Nancy begins to judge all Jews as carbon copies of her former husband. Edwin, now a full-fledged physician, falls in love with beautiful, wealthy Lucy Brown, marries her and struggles to pass the State medical exams and disappears into obscurity. Moses Pasternak, facing bankruptcy, dies in a quarrel with George Hirshman, a poor carpenter from Harlem, who had at one time been an accomplice in one of Pasternak's tangled schemes.

1312. [Gilman, Caroline, Howard] 1794-1888. *Love's progress*, by the author of *The Recollections of a New-England housekeeper, The Southern matron*, etc. New York: Harper, 1840. 171p.

> The heroine is Ruth Raymond; we follow her through her youth and early adult years—as a schoolgirl in a village on the banks of the Hudson, her friendship with the entomologist, Dr. Gesner, and the stirrings of love for Alfred Clarendon. The death of Mrs. Raymond is followed by the further shock of Mr. Raymond's progressive madness and his mystifying hatred of Clarendon. Ruth dutifully clings to her father who has flashes of sanity. But the final scene of the novel takes place at Trenton Falls, N.Y. —Mr. Raymond

flings himself and Ruth into the churning waters. He drowns, but Clarendon is able to pull Ruth to safety.

1313. Gilman, Dorothy, 1923- . *A nun in the closet*, **by Dorothy Gilman Butters. Garden City, N.Y.: Doubleday, 1975. 191p.**

"Bouncy Sister John and herb buff Sister Hyacinthe of a tiny impoverished order take over an inherited turreted manse in Upstate New York and find not only the future Sister Ursula, but visiting Mafia and hirelings, friendly flower children, migrant workers, caches of loot and dope in and about the premises. Sister John's pansy cheer is a bit hard to take"—Kirkus reviews.

1314. Gilman, Mildred Evans, 1898- . *Headlines***. New York: Liveright, 1928. 309.**

Immigrant life on Staten Island; the stories behind the tabloid headlines. Contents (partial): Grim reaper takes toll.—Wife beater gets stiff term.—Says he is not tot's father.—Rum raid nets six.—Mysterious apparition terrorizes neighborhood.—Jazz-mad youth slays family.

1315. Gilman, Wenona, 1860-1900. *A wondering beauty***; or,** *The temptations of a great city***. New York: Munro's Pub. House, 1891. 186p.**

The notorious Madame Celestine de Mornay intercepts Gladys Bertram, a virginal country girl from Upstate New York, as she detrains at Grand Central Station. The Madame, impressed by the fresh beauty of Gladys, takes the innocent girl to her house of assignation and offers Gladys up for sale to the highest bidder. Three men – Nicholas Merton, an avaricious banker, and the roués Dwight Olin and Hugh Barnes–vie for her favor. Gladys finally realizes her precarious position and tries as best she can to ward them off. Her little sister Tess, held by Madam de Mornay, is a pawn in the desperate game. Salvation comes in the form of Laurence Rushton, a New York socialite and gentleman of taste, who has fallen in love with Gladys. Merton and Barnes recede into the background, and Olin, ardently loved by the jealous Madame de Mornay, is fatally wounded by her. She then commits suicide. Tess is restored to Gladys and she and Laurence Rushton eventually marry.

1316. Girvan, Helen Masterman, b. 1891. *Patty and the spoonbill***. Decorations by Vaike Low. New York: Funk & Wagnalls, 1953. 218p.**

Patty Small's uncle is missing a rare Audubon bird print, and she, while spending the summer with him on Long Island, is quite helpful in the retrieval of that valuable item. She also finds the time to develop a friendly relationship with a girl whom she had hitherto abhorred.

1317. Glagsow, Alice. *Bright tiger***. New York: L. MacVeagh, Dial Press, 1930. 309p.**

"New York in the years during and directly following the Civil War furnishes the background for this social romance. Stanton Plumer, ward of Darius Atterbury, is fourteen at the time of the Draft Riots. The story traces his subsequent adventures as a young man-about-town who has risen to success in the profession of political architect, and his various affairs with certain belles of the period. He becomes the lover of beautiful Alida Wyatt, his half-brother's fiancée, who dies from an illegal operation. Following the reversal of his fortunes, Stanton marries the chaste and pretty Hermine Geiger, daughter of a German banker"—Book review digest. Boss Tweed, Jay Gould, Jim Fisk and Josie Mansfield are historical characters in the novel.

1318.   [Glasgow, Ellen] 1874-1945. *The descendant*; a novel. New York: Harper, 1897. 276p.

Tired of being reminded of his illegitimate birth Michael Akershem leaves the Virginia farmer's family that brought him up. In New York City he obtains a job on a socialist newspaper, The Iconoclast; a non-believer in marriage, a free soul, he meets and lives with Rachel Garvin, a painter, for a while. When he is accused of betraying the socialist reform movement Michael kills a young assistant who had looked up to him. After serving a prison term Michael, his health shattered, returns to Rachel, now a successful artist. But it is obvious that Michael is on the path of early demise.

1319.   ————. *Life and Gabriella*; the story of a woman's courage. Front. by C. Allan Gilbert. Garden City, N.Y.: Doubleday, Page, 1916. 529p.

Brought up in the traditions of Southern womanhood Gabriella Carr easily succumbs to the physical charms of George Fowler and marries him. She quickly discovers that Fowler is unreliable and a heavy drinker and severs ties with him. Gabriella is thrown on her own resources; she, with her two children, settles in New York City and over the years becomes a success as a milliner, and eventually assumes ownership of Dinard's, a fashionable shop for women. Her New York sojourn furthers her dissociation from the decadent gentility of her native Richmond. George Fowler dies from delirium tremens in Gabriella's apartment and she, at the age of 38, finds a more suitable spouse in the rugged but softly appealing Ben O'Hara.

1320.   ————. *Phases of an inferior planet*. New York: Harper, 1898. 324p.

In the New York City of the 1880s Anthony Algarcife, a scholar skeptical about traditional Christian beliefs, falls in love with Mariana Musin who lives in the same apartment house, the 'Gotham', as he. Neither Algarcife's immersion in Darwinism, the creation of his own concept of religion or the affair with Mariana provides him with any lasting comfort. Eight years later he has become an Episcopal priest, but he still does not accept the dogmas of the Church, finding his chief solace in helping the poor. His passionate feelings for Mariana are revived, however, and she is ready to receive him when she suddenly contracts pneumonia and dies. Anthony thinks seriously of committing suicide—and then realizes that the members of his church and those bending under the yoke of poverty require his services.

1321.   ————. *The wheel of life*. New York: Doubleday, Page, 1906. 474p.

The novel's heroine, Laura Wilde, a poet with Virginian ancestry, is an acute observer of the foibles of New York society. The sophisticated representatives of that society—Perry Bridewell, Gerty Bridewell and Arnold Kemper especially—come across as hypocritical, flippant, conceited, selfish and ultimately cynical. For a short period Laura is engaged to Arnold Kemper, but she withdraws when she realizes that despite possessing a few good qualities Kemper is essentially an egoist and pleasure-seeker with few principles, a manipulator of human emotions. The 'hero', if such he can be called, is Roger Adams, New York editor of the International Review; Adams is an idealist and a Spencerian, whose former passion for his errant wife, Connie, has evolved into a 'love, so sexless, so dispassionate that its joys were like the joys of religion.' The relationship of Laura and Roger Adams is largely one of teacher and student.

1322. **Glass, Montague Marsden, 1877-1934.** *Abe and Mawruss*; **being further adventures of Potash and Perlmutter. Illustrated by J.J. Gould and Martin Justice. Garden City, N.Y.: Doubleday, Page, 1911. 379p.**

Abe Potash and Morris ('Mawruss') Perlmutter, cloak and suit outfitters of New York City, exercise their business acumen and extend sympathy and assistance to their employees (occasionally outmaneuvering themselves); their English often suffers grammatical 'dislocations' and is frequently interspersed with German and Yiddish words and idioms.

1323. ————. *The competitive nephew.* **Garden City, N.Y.: Doubleday, Page, 1915. vii, 350;.**

Ten humorous short stories concerned with the clothing trade and various phases of Jewish life in New York City. This is the world of Abe Potash and Morris Perlmutter, familiar to readers of Glass's writings. Contents: The competitive nephew.—Opportunity.—The sorrows of Seiden.—Serpents' teeth.—Making over Milton.—Birsky & Zapp.—The moving picture writer.—Coercing Mr. Trinkmann.—'Rudolph, where have you been?'— Caveat emptor.

1324. ————. *Elkan Lubliner,* **American. Garden City, N.Y.: Doubleday, Page, 1912. 323p.**

A collection of stories dealing with two clothing manufacturers, Marcus Polatkin and Philip Scheikowitz, and especially with their one-time office boy, Elkan Lubliner of Wooster Street, New York City, who rose to assistant cutter in their factory, became a salesman, and finally achieved partnership in the business. Contents: Noblesse oblige.—Appenweier's account.—A match for Elkan Lubliner.—Highgrade lines.—One of Esau's fables.—A tale of two Jacobean chairs.—Sweet and sour.

1325. ————. *Lucky numbers.* **Garden City, N.Y.: Doubleday, Page, 1927. 290p.**

Of the seven short stories in the collection five take place in New York City and vicinity and poke fun at the Jewish citizenry of the area. Familiar characters used by the author in other works – Potash and Permutter, 'Abe' and 'Mawruss' (Morris), their wives, relatives and friends and enemies – are present here. Two of the stories use Hollywood as the setting. Contents: Lucky numbers.—Such a mother!—Well, why not?—Yes, Mr. Rosenthal?—Be warned by Mr. Walpole.—That's the way it goes.—Under new management.

1326. ————. *Potash & Perlmutter*; **their copartnership ventures and adventures.** **Philadelphia: Altemus, 1910. 419p.**

"Photographic sketches of ... [Jewish-American] types found on the East Side of New York. [Abe] Potash and [Morris] Perlmutter, Henry D. Feldman, Sammet Brothers, and a host of others live as really as Pickwick, Becky Sharp or Falstaff. We talk of them as if they were living people. They come to us dripping with faults; they shock us by their manners and their meanness, by their money-lust and sharp practices, but they grow on us until we accept them as relatives—that is, we see their faults merged with a universal humaneness, a humaneness that we share ourselves. In fact Mr. Glass has interpreted ... a certain type of the Jew, and done it successfully"—Bookman.

1327. ————. *Y'understand.* **Garden City, N.Y.: Doubleday, Page, 1925. 317p.**

Short stories about Jewish-Americans in New York City graced by the author's generous sense of humor, often using the Yiddish-American dialect. Contents: Blood is redder than water.—Cousins of Convenience.—They will do it.—It's never too late.—You can't fool the camera.—Never begin with liens.—The sixth McNally.—Keeping expenses down.

1328. ————. *You can't learn 'em nothin'.* **Garden City, N.Y.: Doubleday, Doran, 1930. 320p.**

Stories of Jewish-Americans in business or in love in New York City and, to a lesser extent, in Hollywood. Contents: You can't learn 'em nothin'.—The man who disliked acrobats.—Maybe druggists don't have troubles too.—"It wasn't what they thought it was."—They cared nothing for money.—"Mr. and Mrs. Max Dainin request the pleasure" (if you can call it that).—You've got to keep right after them.—He always wrote her everything.

1329. **Glemser, Bernard, 1908-1990.** *The blow at the heart.* **New York: Appleton, 1953. 279p.**

John Gilhooley is a warm-hearted and accomplished Irish-American commercial artist in New York City who relocates to a Long Island community so that his daughter might benefit from a pleasant suburban environment. It isn't long before he is bemoaning his decision; he certainly has no great fondness for many of the people he must now associate with.

1330. **Glenn, Isa.** *Southern charm.* **New York: Knopf, 1928. 301p.**

Mrs. Habersham's daughter, Alice May, was the picture of genteel Southern womanhood. Her other daughter, Laura, had been raped and had thus been 'spoiled.' She was sent away with a modest income to make her own way in the world. Twenty years later in New York City Laura and her mother meet accidentally. Laura was well-groomed, self-assured and supporting herself. After visiting Alice May and her husband Roger in their Park Avenue apartment, Mrs. Habersham realized that doll-like Alice May was rather boring. There is an effort to bring a meeting of minds between Laura and her mother. Mrs. Habersham also has to deal with the hovering presence of Aunt Sallie and Cousin Nathalie.

1331. **Glentworth, Marguerite Linton.** *The tenth commandment*; a romance. **Boston: Lee & Shepard, 1902. viii, 350p.**

> With a background of New York City and London the novel tells the story of Edythe Barratoni, a beautiful, successful actress who marries a rich, aristocratic New Yorker, Geoffrey Merrall. She bears Geoffrey four children in the nine years she is by his side, but she eventually tires of her children and husband and leaves. Among the characters who appear in the story are: the eccentric Barratoni family; Lonapetti, an Italian prince who plays the violin; Gleshko, a pianist; and the Rev. Rodgers Courtney. However, this gallery aside, Geoffrey is the only truly memorable or sympathetic person portrayed by the author.

1332. **Glidden, Minna Wesselhoft.** *The Long Island murders.* **New York: Phoenix Press, 1937. 252p.**

> A Long Island community is witness to a number of strange murders. Among those who investigate the homicides are: the 'Automaton', persistent hunter of wrongdoers, his partner, Carey Brent (actually a U.S. Secret Service agent), and the deceptively simple 'Butterfly' (Madam or Mademoiselle?).

1333. **Glover, Douglas, 1948- .** *The life and times of Captain N.*; a novel. **New York: Knopf, distributed by Random House, 1993. 185p.**

> Tories, Indians and rebels fight for control of the Mohawk Valley. 'Captain N' (Hendrick Nellis), a leading Tory, has lost the respect of his son Oskar who sympathizes with the rebels. Oskar is compelled to serve with the King's forces; yet he secretly pens letters to General Washington and takes seriously the role of writer. The novel contains excerpts from 'Oskar's Book on Indians' as well as the statements and fantasies of two white women; one of the latter, a captured German immigrant girl, is a full participant in the Indian way of life.

1334. **Gluck, Sinclair, b. 1887.** *Blind fury.* **New York: Dodd, Mead, 1930. 302p.**

> "A brilliant and respected financier is ruined on the [New York] Stock Exchange, his residence set fire to and he himself is brutally murdered. Captain McCoy of the police and Christopher Morgan, a newspaper man, solve the mystery"—Book review digest. "A ruined man takes revenge on the men who broke his life and scattered his family. There is much excitement, considerable hocus-pocus of raw-head and bloody bones, mystic tit-tat-toe cards that presage sudden death, and a terrific finale"—Saturday review of literature.

1335. ─────. *The man who never blundered.* New York: Dodd, Mead, 1929 [c1928] 304p.

A master criminal known as 'the Governor' gives the lawmen of New York City conniptions. He informs the police of impending robberies and gets away with them despite the 'best laid schemes' of his adversaries. Lieutenant McCoy of the New York Police Department, Pierre LeToque of the Paris Surété, and Morgan, a journalist, combine to thwart the Governor. But it isn't the officials that are most responsible for putting an end to the Governor's career—that credit goes to the newspapermen.

1136. ─────. *The white streak.* New York: Clode, 1924. 319p.

Harry Burnham has 'just returned to his [New York] home after a long stay abroad following the [first World] War [and] takes to the trail of the man who, on the very night of the boy's coming back, shoots … [his] old father in the study of the family mansion. A safe has been opened and the incriminating report taken of a local investigation. This fact and the murdered man's last words—those of the book's title—are the only clues which Harry has to work … [with]"—New York world. The New York City underworld plays a significant role in the mystery.

1337. Godey, John, 1912- . *The gun and Mr. Smith.* Garden City, N.Y.: Published for the Crime Club by Doubleday, 1947. 279p.

"Miss Rosalie Lamson, a concert pianist, finds herself in for an extremely peculiar weekend on a Long Island estate. One of the guests in the house, who has fits and is the pretender to a European throne, gets shot at, and the others—prominent industrialists, foreign agents, and what not—become quite tough with Miss Lamson when she tries to intervene in the subsequent conniving"—New Yorker.

1338. Godfrey, Hollis, 1874-1936. *Dave Morrell's battery.* **Illustrated by Franklin T. Wood. Boston: Little, Brown, 1912. 289p.**

David Morrell is hard-pressed to keep his newly developed storage battery (which has features that surpass any similar product on the market) out of the hands of some predators from New York City. He is endeavoring to secure loans that will enable him to start up a manufacturing plant for the production of his invention. Fortunately David has a sharp mind; loyal friends abet him and the combination keeps the city 'slickers' at bay.

1339. Godwin, Gail, 1937- . *The finishing school.* New York: Viking Press, 1983. 322p.

The story is told by Justin Stokes some 30 years after she, as a 14-year-old, came from a South of gentle manners with her widowed mother to Upstate New York to live with Justin's aunt, a practical lady with middle class values. Justin is much taken with the sophisticated woman next door, Ursula De Vane, 44, who shares a large house with her brother, a pianist. Justin can often be found in a cabin in the neighboring forest (her 'finishing school') while she learns more about Ursula's early years.

1340. Gold, Michael, 1894-1967. *Jews without money*. Woodcuts by Howard Simon. New York: Liveright, 1930. 309p.

An 'autobiographical' novel in which the narrator discusses life in a Chrystie Street tenement and on New York's East Side. The narrator's mother champions the downtrodden; his sister Esther is killed when a wagon rolls over her, a death similar to that of his boyhood friend Joey Cohen. Esther's mother refuses compensation from the wagon-owning company despite her husband's reservations. Echoes of Jewish radicalism, revolutionary Marxism and prophecy sound throughout the novel. A classic of proletarian literature, it has influenced other writers (e.g., E.L. Doctorow's *Book of Daniel*).

1341. Goldfluss, Howard E. *The power*. New York: D.I. Fine, 1988. 324p.

Hungry for power and celebrity beautiful socialite Loren Sturdivant, running-mate with would-be governor Joe Klyk, is not too perturbed when she is wounded slightly by an insane accountant who interrupts a meeting of the candidates with labor groups. Loren is not the only one using whatever is available in the climb to the top. e.g., an influential moneyed player kicks around a minority leader in the New York Assembly in order to assure his son's election to the body; a lawmaker escapes penalties, which should have been assessed against his industrial firm for pollution. Loren herself is fully aware of a bold, unwarranted movement to impeach the standing governor, which, if allowed to succeed, would redound in her favor.

Goldfrap, John Henry, 1879-1917. See under his pseudonym: Payson Howard.

1342. Goldsborough, Robert, 1937- . *The bloodied ivy*; Nero Wolfe mystery. New York: Bantam Books, 1988. xii, 189p.

Goldsborough recreates Rex Stout's detective Nero Wolfe in this story (related by Archie Goodwin, Wolfe's right-hand man) that deals with the possible murder of right-wing Professor Hale Markham at an Upstate New York university. Professor Cortland, Markham's liberal friend, calls on Wolfe who first of all questions student Gretchen Frazier and Professor Elena Moreau, both of whom were in love with Markham. Next he queries the dead man's faculty colleagues (Cortland too). When one of the suspects commits suicide, Wolfe picks up a most pertinent piece of evidence that will inevitably lead him to the culprit.

1343. Goldthwaite, Eaton K., 1907- . *Don't mention my name*. New York: Duell, Sloan & Pearce, 1942. 307p.

Also published in 1944 under the title: The case of the nameless corpse. "In which Elbert Jones, accountant, and Sam Clarke, drug man, experience jitters and worse while vacationing in the Adirondacks. First corpse discovered by them may be Judge Appleby, who might somehow be connected with the strange disappearance of Ben Fettridge, a financier wanted by the government because of the Franconia Bonding Company folding. As Sam cries early in the game, 'If this ain't the doggonedest thing!" Sergeant Joe Brinkley of the State cops does what he can, often in the midst of pandemonium. his unpretentious offering has secrets, action and a touch of homespun in the characters"—New York herald tribune books.

Goldthwaite, Eaton K., 1907- . *The case of the nameless corpse.* **See note under Item #1343.**

1344. ————. *First you have to find him.* **Garden City, N.Y.: Published for the Crime Club by Doubleday, 1981. 175p.**

"When narrator Frank Merson—a mild-mannered local newspaperman—gets socked by a total stranger while riding the Long Island Railroad he's pretty sure the punch was meant for his notorious, womanizing twin brother Fred. But what about the subsequent break-and-entering job on Frank's apartment? Or the fact that art-gallery owner Fred seems to have run off with Dominique, his partner's wife? Some of the mystery is cleared up when Frank's assailant turns up dead ... and turns out to be an angry Philadelphia art-collector whose paintings have been stolen, and then sold by Fred to another collector! Eventually... after Frank has searched for Fred, wound up in bed with Dominique, been abducted by thugs, and done some sleuthing at an Upstate museum—some family secrets and missing papers are shown to be at the center of the goings-on"—Kirkus reviews.

1345. **Gollomb, Joseph, 1881-1950.** *Tuning in at Lincoln High.* **New York: Macmillan, 1925. 255p.**

Tim, a student at Lincoln High in New York City, is the butt of his taller and more muscular peers' jokes and gibes. He wins their respect, however, when he goes out for football and through perseverance and a measure of talent becomes a quarterback on the team.

1346. **Golub, Marcia.** *Wishbone*; a novel. **Dallas, Tex.: Baskerville, 1994. 335p.**

Mabel Fleish's novel, 'Bone', features a Satanic character based on her teenage crush, Beauregard Barbon, a boy who delighted in torturing small animals and studying witchcraft, and who eventually killed himself. Living in a New York State college town, married to Professor Percival Furnival, Mabel is kidnapped by a former lover who is certain that she used his life, not Beauregard's, as the linchpin of her novel. He takes Mabel to a shack in the mountains, ties her up and tortures her. Percival and a colleague, Rufus Wutzl, organize a search for the missing woman. Meanwhile reporter Herm Kwestral believes Beauregard is not at all dead and that he has good leads as to his whereabouts.

1347. Goodman, Allegra. *Kaaterskill Falls; a novel.* **New York: Dial Press, 1998. 324p.**

From Washington Heights to Kaaterskill, a community in Upstate New York founded by early Dutch settlers, comes each summer an Orthodox Jewish sect led by Rav Kirschner. From 1976 to 1978 relationships in Kaaterskill are portrayed: longtime residents descended from Yankee and Dutch stock are apprehensive as their real estate holdings are eroded, and even liberal, secular, socially upscale Jewish summer dwellers who preceded their Orthodox brethren are perturbed. The Orthodox group has its share of family conflicts. For example, Rav Kirschner is close to death and is worried about his two sons—Isaiah, who may lack the necessary qualities to succeed him, and Jeremy who prefers intellectual sophistication to his father's religion.

1348. Goodrich, Arthur Frederick, 1878-1941. *The yardstick man.* **New York: Appleton, 1910. 325p.**

A New York businessman, Mr. Jones, is so committed to commercial success that he neglects his wife and her emotional needs. Enter a former schoolmate of Jones, a carefree fellow from the West who forms an attachment to Jones's private secretary, but who more importantly shows Jones that his devotion to business has turned him into a person who has used yardstick standards to gauge his life and has overlooked the truly worthwhile aspects of living. When suddenly confronted by financial failure Jones has to reassess his attitudes toward his wife and his career.

1349. Goodwin, Maud Wilder, 1856-1935. *Flint, his faults, his friendships, and his fortunes.* **Boston: Little, Brown, 1897. viii, 362p.**

"Jonathan Flint is introduced at the age of thirty-three to the other characters, men and women summering at a New England seashore resort. All the summer boarders again meet in New York, and the author … portrays the great city at the present day, with all its interests and customs. Incidentally the work of the Salvation Army is described. The hero is a writer of books that make people think, and also the editor of a great magazine"—Annual American catalogue.

1350. ————. *Four roads to Paradise.* **Illustrated by Arthur L. Keller. New York: Century Co., 1904. ix, 347p.**

Anne Blythe can keep the millions she inherited from her late husband only if she does not remarry. Swirling around her are such characters as: Bishop Alston, an elderly uncle; Stuart Walford, assistant rector in a New York City church attended by the upper echelons of society; Tom Yates, a lawyer, rough around the edges but nevertheless a kindly man; Newton, a one-time physician who follows the latest developments in the sciences; Blair Fleming, another lawyer, but admirable all the same. A Fifth Avenue club is a meeting place for the four last-named gentlemen. All hold a ripening love for Anne and all envision a 'Paradise' that enfolds Anne and one of them.

Gordon, Colonel H.R., pseud. See: Ellis, Edward Sylvester, 1840-1916.

1351. **Gordon, Grace.** *Patsy Carroll at Wilderness Lodge.* **Illustrated by R. Emmet Owen. New York: Cupples & Leon, 1917. vi, 340p.**

Wilderness Lodge at Lake Placid in the Adirondacks is the destination of Patsy Carroll, her aunt, and three friends. While there the group is drawn into a search for a missing will, which they finally locate; their efforts are instrumental in the restoration of an inheritance to a young companion.

1352. **Gordon, Homer King, b. 1896.** *Sally of Show Alley.* **New York: Crowell, 1928. 366p.**

Sally Larkin, Irish and pretty, seeks a career in Broadway's musical theaters. Discovered by Lee Lindy, a dissolute producer, Sally takes a job in the chorus line, but sticks to her high personal ideals. Princetonian Rod Savage, infatuated by Sally's beauty and essential goodness, introduces her to his family. His father recognizes Sally as a chorus girl; there is a breakup and Sally returns to the stage. Just as disillusioned Sally is about to pay the price for success, playwright Jean Samson, in love with Sally all along, marries her.

1353. **Gordon, Howard [William].** *The African in me.* **New York: Braziller, 1993. 156p.**

In his collection of nine stories the author portrays the Afro-American experience in Upstate New York from the 1950s to the 1990s. Racism and violence are constants; e.g., during school recesses the children on their own divide along racial lines; a black boy is taught by his parents to 'keep his cool' and stand his ground when racist jibes are directed at him; the younger of two brothers is dying of cancer, alienated from the older one who suffers from the cancer of hatred.

1354. **Gordon, Hugh, pseud.** *The blind road.* **New York: Moffat, Yard, 1912. 285p.**

A man from New York City takes to wife a beautiful young woman from a small town, brings her to his home and looks forward to a happy married life. Unfortunately his wife is evidently transformed by marriage and the temptations of the metropolis. While he concentrates on making money to support his establishment, she indulges her whims, her freedom from previous restraints, unjustifiably suspects her husband of indiscretions and allows another man to enter into her thoughts. Within two years the marriage bond is broken; they separate and enter the divorce courts. The fault lies more with the wife than with her spouse who had taken seriously the role of devoted husband.

1355. **Gordon, Julien, d. 1920.** *Eat not thy heart.* **Chicago: H.S. Stone, 1897. 319p.**

"The magnificent country house on Long Island belonging to the Marstons, wealthy New Yorkers, is the scene. The story opens when Joe Bush is hired to be the farmer or superintendent. His wife is a handsome woman of a coarse type who forces her society upon Mrs. Marston, imitates her ways and costumes, and becomes insanely jealous of her, the result being almost a tragedy and the dismissal of the Bush family. There are other character contrasts, some flirting, love-making, and witty conversations"—Annual American catalogue.

1356. ————. *Marionettes.* **New York: Cassell Pub. Co., 1892. 320p.**
"The Marquise Le Moyne was a New York girl who had married a Frenchman. As her father and mother had separated when she was a child, she only learns to know her father after her mother's death, when she returns to New York to aid in the settling of some money matters. She is then past thirty, rich, beautiful, and a widow with a little boy of eight years. The scene of the story is in an old country house, the home of the Marquise's father and brother. Here the Marquise has a sad love experience, which, though not unusual, is freshly and cleverly told"—Annual American catalogue.

1357. ————. *Poppaea.* **Philadelphia: J.B. Lippincott, 1894. 320p.**
"The New York girl oddly named after the Roman empress marries for money a man more than twice her age for whom she simply feels gratitude for the luxury with which he surrounds her. After several seasons among the 'smart' set of New York and Paris, where her beauty and grace make her a conspicuous figure, she meets her fate in the person of a brilliant journalist whose father (an American) had married a Parisian. The many vicissitudes of Poppaea's sad love story, with its sudden and tragic ending are related with much power"—Annual American catalogue.

1358. ————. *A Puritan pagan*; a novel. **New York: Appleton, 1891. 367p.**
"A dual nature, half pagan, half Puritan, is admirably illustrated in the person of young Norwood, a clever patent lawyer of New York City. A sin against his wife, which he falls into through his pagan thirst for pleasure, is repented in sackcloth and ashes, his morbid Puritan conscience leading him to confess to his wife the wrong he has done her. She is young and lovely, with little knowledge of the world, and bitter and unforgiving. The confession disgusts her and she leaves her husband, flying to the protection of a rich and fashionable aunt, who gives her her first glimpses of society. How this pair works out the problem of their separate lives is the story. The analysis of character is remarkably well done and the scenes from fashionable diplomatic life in Washington, Newport and Paris vividly done"—Annual American catalogue.

1359. ————. *Vampires.* **Mademoiselle Réséda. Philadelphia: J.B. Lippincott, 1891. 299p.**
"The first story opens with a wonderful description of second-class boardinghouse life in New York City. The red-haired boarder Paton, softhearted and sympathetic, is completely taken possession of by an intriguing mother and a sickly daughter, who prove the 'vampires' of his short life. Mademoiselle Réséda is a penniless, ravishingly beautiful governess who

makes some of her sister women's lives uncomfortable for a time"—Annual American catalogue.

1360. Gorman, Herbert Sherman, 1893-1954. *Gold by Gold.* **New York: Boni and Liveright, 1925. 380p.**

Emboldened by the acceptance for publication of his poetry, Karl Nevins of the New England town of 'Springvale' leaves wife and career for the pleasure domes of New York City. Settled in the Latin Quarter of Manhattan he samples the fleshpots of the city and goes downhill physically and financially rather quickly. At rock bottom he is finally aware of his debauchedness and leaves New York for Springvale and a renewal of his former life there.

Gossip, George Hatfield Dingley, 1841-1907. See under his pseudonym: Trepoff, Ivan.

1361. Gould, Edward Sherman, 1808-1885. *John Doe and Richard Roe*; or, *Episodes of life in New York.* **New York: Carleton, 1862. 312p.**

Richard Roe, banker, churchman and supporter of charities, comes under the purview of citizen/bachelor John Doe when Roe is present (presumably chloroformed) as a felon, Wilson, a former employee of Roe's escapes from the Tombs. Doe brings suit against Roe for recovery of money he claims was fraudulently appropriated by Roe from the estate of Joseph Peters (Doe is the brother of Elizabeth Peters, Joseph's widow). The hypocritical Roe, we soon learn, has been swindling a number of persons who had entrusted him to invest their funds. Doe finds Wilson who gives him incriminating documents which indicate Roe has been 'cooking' his books, altering and transposing his accounts. Doe and his bright young lawyer face Roe in the courts—Roe realizes he cannot win and settles out of court to the tune of $120,000. This is not his only loss: his daughter Margaret and his second (rather young wife) walk away from his house.

1362. Gould, Elizabeth Lincoln, d. 1914. *Grandma.* **Illustrated by Mary Pemberton Ginther. Philadelphia: Penn Pub. Co., 1911. 263p.**

"A New England grandmother goes to New York City to look after a socially ambitious daughter-in-law on the point of a nervous breakdown. She proves less successful as a nurse for neurasthenic ills than as a wholesome tonic to morally sluggish natures. ... [She] elevates the business ideals of her son, penetrates a little the crust of silliness and selfishness incasing his wife ... and improves the morals and digestion of her deceitful, sweet-devouring little granddaughter"—Book review digest.

Gould, Stephen, pseud. See: Fisher, Steve, 1912-1988.

Goulding, Edmund, 1891-1959. *The Broadway melody.* **See Item #2012.**

1363. Grady, Frank P. *Sergeant Death.* **New York: Barrows-Mussey, 1936. 256p.**

"Millionaire John Barter [is] found dead (throat cut) down by the boathouse at his Long Island estate. At first Inspector Peter Bernadone, from Headquarters, blames Clark, the valet, because he's an ex-convict, but it soon looks as though several women, a bunch of spiritualists, or the Millvale strikers might figure in the case. [A] letter received by [the] 'Evening Bulletin' runs: 'there are others to follow. The punishment of the next world is highly uncertain. The only punishment I can bring to them in this world is to put them out of it'—[signed] Jack Ketch. Who is Jack? The next murder occurs in a wax works on Coney Island, and the next on an archery range. And why did Barter leave his secretary $100,000? There's a girl too. … Inspector Bernadone is assisted by Inspector Ketcham, a wisecracking county detective—New York herald tribune books.

1364. Graeve, Oscar, b. 1885. *The brown moth.* **New York: Dodd, Mead, 1921. 329p.**

"Lola Kargo, the 'brown moth' of the story, is one of the thousands of unnoticed New York working girls whose motive force in life is to 'get on' in the world. She is engaged to be married to Dan Briggs, a spineless fellow in her own humble station. Dan, fired by desire to please Lola, commits a petty theft and is forced to flee the city. Lola helps him to escape, rebels against the sordidness of her life, and pays back the money to her employers in order to buy her freedom. She falls under the spell of William Ogden, her wealthy employer, whose service she leaves after they discover a mutual passion. Ogden provides Lola with enough money to establish her in a small shop, and she continues her quest for happiness amid minor adventures. She finally finds it in marrying the prodigal, sick Dan, after nursing him back to health, remaining unto the end the same obscure and humble brown moth. New York local color is a strong feature of the book"—Book review digest.

1365. ————. *The keys of the city.* **New York: Century Co., 1916. 274p.**

"The story of a little boy who spends his childhood in Bay Ridge, a suburb of Brooklyn overlooking distant Manhattan. To David Wells, a fisherman's son, it's the city of dreams, which he is some day to conquer. The conquest begins low down, in an insurance office in Wall Street, but after three years of drudging at work that gives no scope to his imagination, David sees that this is not the way upward for him. He ultimately finds his opportunity, climbs to the top, wins money and ease, marries and enters an assured place in the social world. Then he meets Nora Davenport, the playmate of his childhood, and finds that all his achievements are as nothing. The reader is left in doubt as to the future of David and Nora"—Book review digest.

1366. ————. *Youth goes seeking.* **New York: Dodd, Mead, 1919. 297p.**

"A boy in a highly respectable house in Brooklyn is forced into his uncle's business instead of being allowed to go to college according to his bent. After some years of it, during which he attempted various kinds of welfare work among the employees, he follows the advice of a radical friend, breaks away

351

and goes to live in New York among the very moderns, the social insurgents. The life among them is sketched with much fidelity. Henry Baker dives into it and becomes as one with the brilliant, argumentative, experimenting and dreaming crowd. Finally the serious illness of his uncle takes him back to Brooklyn and the leather business. He takes Sadie, the girl he has rescued, with him as his wife and devotes himself to larger reforms in his uncle's business, and finds contentment"—Book review digest.

Graham, John, pseud. See: Phillips, David Graham, 1867-1911.

1367.   **Grainger, Arthur M.** *Golden Feather*; or, *The buccaneer of King's Bridge. A warlike romance of the rivers and bay of New York; being a tale of love and glory of the War of 1812-'15.* **New York: F.A. Brady [1860?]. 90p. (in double columns).**

"Golden Feather is the name given by a friendly Delaware chief to Rosale (Rose) Lee, daughter of Adam Lee, proprietor of an inn on Spuyten Duyvel Creek. Rose takes a neutral position in the war, even helping a wounded English officer/spy, Arthur Percy, return to British lines. Her brother, Robert, is a problem; he makes lecherous advances towards her and takes up buccaneering after killing the pirate captain who had slain Adam Lee. Robert seizes Rose and sets sail from New York, pursued by Rose's lover, Ralph Turner. Robert tells Rose that Adam Lee who had killed her father on the high seas adopted her. The climax comes in Jamaica where Rose's mother and brother, Countess Neville and Arthur Percy (Neville) greet her. Robert Lee is placed under arrest; Ralph Turner and Rose, now happily married, depart for New York.

1368.   **Grant, Dorothy Fremont, 1900- .** *Night of decision*; a novel of colonial New York. **New York: Longmans, Green, 1946. 279p.**

An historical novel of colonial New York under the governorship (1682-1688) of Colonel Thomas Dongan, a Catholic notable for keeping the Iroquois Indians on friendly terms with the colony. Jacob Leisler is given the role of villain, leading a revolt in 1689 (the novel covers the years 1683-1690) against Stuart appointees. The chief fictional characters include Becky Kartright, her strict Protestant father of Hempstead, Long island, and Tom, and Irish Catholic shipwrecked on Becky's doorstep. Tom is slated to serve as Dongan's military aide. He and Becky marry counter to the wishes of her father.

Grant, Douglas, pseud. See: Ostrander, Isabel Egenton, 1883-1924.

Grant, Ethel Watts Mumford, 1878-1940. See: Mumford, Ethel Watts, 1878-1940.

1369.   **Grant, Robert, 1852-1940.** *An average man.* **Boston: J.R. Osgood, 1884. 300p.**

Arthur Remington and Woodbury Stoughton, two Harvard graduates, are thrust into the maelstrom of upper class New York social life as they establish a law practice in that city. They draw apart when Stoughton enters the political arena and marries wealthy Isabel Idlewind, while the less worldly Remington struggles career-wise, but finally wins the love of feminist Dorothy Crosby. Unhappy in his marriage Stoughton leaves Isabel, who files for divorce. Remington and Dorothy have a successful union and they try to patch the rift between Stoughton and Isabel.

1370. ————. *The confessions of a frivolous girl*; a story of fashionable life. **With vignette illus. by L.S. Ipsen. Boston: Houghton, Mifflin, 1880. 220p.**

Alice Palmer does all the things expected of a wealthy young girl 'coming out' into the New York social world. She is not, however, the title of the novel notwithstanding, a 'frivolous' girl, but a rather careful measurer of her future options. For the present she does enjoy the surface pleasures of New York and Newport. When she finally marries, she selects a quietly attentive and devoted man whom she comes to love deeply, if not passionately. Alice's diary is the nucleus of the story.

1371. ————. *Face to face*. **New York: Scribner, 1886. 396p.**

After long sojourns in New York City and Newport, Evelyn Pimlico, an English girl, is left $15,000,000 by an old family friend, Wilbur Pierce Brock. Mills in the Hudson River Valley are a part of the inheritance and Evelyn tries to manage them with a view to improving living conditions and wages of the workers. As an associate she has Andrew DeVito, presumably a socialist, who yet has a penchant for various aspects of luxurious living. DeVito leaves her employ and returns a few years later when the workers are striking. The strike gets out of hand as a Valley factory and the home of Ernest Clay, a wealthy young American and an inventor (who for a long time has been in love with Evelyn) are put to the torch. DeVito also loves Evelyn, but he risks his own life when he saves Ernest from the flames engulfing 'Seven Oaks', Clay's home. As DeVito expires from injuries received in the fire, saddened Evelyn turns slowly to Ernest and declares: "Dearest, we have our lives before us."

1372. ————. *Mrs. Harold Stagg*; a novel. **With illus. by Harry C. Edwards. New York: R. Bonner's Sons, 1890. 240p.**

Emma Stagg and her husband Harold, a New York banker, adopt the three orphaned children of Harold's brother Silas and take them from Illinois to the eastern metropolis. It is Mrs. Stagg's intention to make a comfortable New York marriage for one of the children, Eleanor. The latter has her coming-out party and is courted by a young millionaire. But she opts for an academic career and eventually returns to Illinois as a college professor, much to Mrs. Stagg's consternation. Eventually Eleanor accepts the marriage proposal of a young scientist. Mrs. Stagg remains a formidable New York lady who is certain that Eleanor made the wrong choice.

1373. ————. *Unleavened bread*. New York: Scribner, 1900. 431p.

"The ambition of a young American girl born on a farm to become 'somebody' is the motive of a strong story presenting various phases of American town and city life, especially as seen in politics and women's clubs. The story is divided into three parts—the emancipation, the struggle, the success—depicting with realism and satire the different steps by which Selma White achieves social success. Divorced from one husband, she quickly marries a second whose death in a short time is brought about by the struggle of living in New York City. This opens the door for a third husband, a member of the Legislature, who becomes governor of his state [New York], and finally a U.S. senator"—Annual American catalogue.

1374. Granville-Barker, Harley Granville, 1877-1946. *Souls on Fifth*. **With front. by Norman Wilkinson. Boston: Little, Brown, 1916. 61p.**

"Fifth' is Fifth Avenue, and in this fantasy … [the author] sets forth the plight of the souls of departed Americans who haunt it. Instead of going to Paris, as good Americans are said to do when they die, these Americans had come back to Fifth Avenue. Like the man spoken of in Acts, who 'died and went to his own place', these people have come back to theirs"—Book review digest.

Granville-Barker, Helen Manchester Gates, d. 1950. See: Huntington, Helen, d. 1950.

1375. Gratacap, Louis Pope, 1851-1917. *Benjamin the Jew*. **New York: T. Benton, 1913. 492p.**

The novel tells the story of Benjamin Nessi, a Russian Jew, from childhood to untimely death. After a pogrom in Russia Benjamin's father, Joseph, a goldsmith, decides to leave for America where he settles on New York City's East Side and achieves prosperity in business. Benjamin is remarkably handsome; to some he is destined to become the 'Redeemer of the Jewish people.'

1376. ————. *The mayor of New York*; **a romance of days to come. New York: Dillingham, 1910. 471p.**

The novel presupposes that the City of New York has achieved statehood and that its mayor is also its governor. Personal wealth assumes primary importance; its possessors are the new aristocracy. The agnostic mayor/governor falls in love with Helen Lorimer, a Catholic whose prominent family opposes any close connection between the two. After a stormy trial and accompanying disturbances the mayor/governor falls victim to gunfire. The heroine (Helen) grieves for her loss, but she eventually marries a Catholic gentleman who proves to be a happy choice for a husband.

1376a. Graver, Elizabeth, 1964- . *The honey thief*; **a novel. New York: Hyperion, 1999. 263p.**

The widow Miriam Baruch (DiLeone) moves with her kleptomaniac daughter Eva from Manhattan to the Finger Lakes region of New York State. She finds employment as a paralegal in one of the towns of the area but makes her home in a farmhouse some distance away. Miriam's deceased husband, Francis DiLeone, was Catholic; Miriam is Jewish. Apprehensive about Eva's mental state and her bad habit of shoplifting Miriam continually worries while Eva is angry about being wrenched from her urban habitat to a rural place that offers her little to do and no close friends. Eva's (and perhaps Miriam's) salvation appears in the guise of a former lawyer from Philadelphia, Mr. Burl, who has taken over his grandparents' farm and is now an apiarist. He befriends Eva and teaches the disturbed girl the complexities of beekeeping and gathering honey; this new interest and companion help Eva subdue hidden fears that have driven her to steal.

1377. Graves, Robert, 1895-1985. *Sergeant Lamb's America*. New York: Random House, 1940. xiii, 380p.

Roger Lamb, a sergeant in the British army, recounts, among other memoirs, his experiences during the British campaigns in northern New York, in 1776 and 1777 (the story ends just after Burgoyne's surrender at Saratoga). All in all a well-balanced statement of what an honest and perceptive soldier thought of the business at hand.

Gray, Walter T., supposed author. *Bijah Beanpole in New York*. See note under Item #3483.

Grayson, Eldred, Esq., pseud. See: Hare, Robert, 1781-1859.

1378. *The great wrongs of the shop girls*. The life and persecutions of Miss Beatrice Claflin, daughter of the late Claflin, founder of the well known New York firm of Claflin & Co. From a narrative furnished by the Ladies' Philanthropical Society. How Miss Claflin became the white slave in the dry goods palace of a merchant prince! Her incarceration in a private insane asylum! Two years in a mad house! How patients are treated therein! [Philadelphia: Barclay & Co., c1886] 20-64 p.

Thomas Hilton, Sr. cheats the Widow Claflin out of her inheritance, forcing Beatrice, the widow's daughter, to take a clerk's job in the Hilton department store. Thomas Hilton, Jr. lusts after Beatrice and the girl's woes continue until George Bentley, an accountant in the Hilton firm (following a prison term on charges trumped up by Hilton, Sr.) uncovers Hilton's chicanery. The police shoot Hilton, Jr. during a robbery.

Greaves, Richard, pseud. See: McCutcheon, George Barr, 1866-1928.

1379. Greeley, Robert F. *Old Cro' Nest*; or, *The outlaws of the Hudson*. A romance of American forest life in the olden time. New York: Ward, 1846. 110p. (in double columns).

The Crows' Nest (a crag) and Kaaterskill Clove are familiar natural features in the Catskills. The author designates the village where most of the action of his story takes place as Kaaterskill in the mid 17th century. The outlaws who occupy forest areas near the village are led by 'Basil Redgrave' (a.k.a Gilbert Pembroke, brother of Geoffry Wylde (a.k.a. Geoffry Pembroke), an aristocratic recluse who lives with his niece Winifred in a large house in the forest. The hero is Archibald Earle, a hunter in love with Winifred. Leonard Wylde, disagreeable 'son' of Geoffry, is forced into collaboration with the outlaws, but it is he who finally leads soldiers to the outlaws' lair. By the tale's end both Gilbert and Geoffry are dead and 'Crazy Kate', the village seeress/witch, is disclosed to be the wife of Geoffry, surreptitiously separated from him shortly after their English marriage. Archibald Earle, switched at birth with Leonard, is Kate and Geoffry's true son.

1380. ————. *Violet: the child of the city.* **A story of New York life. New York: Bunce, 1854. 336p.**

The story of two families: Mr. Pryce Benedick, his wife, their children, of New York City and Westchester—wealthy, spoiled, snobbish; and widower Walter Lyle, his daughter Violet, and a son presumably lost at sea. Violet and Lyle a former acquaintance of Benedick, follow the latter to New York in search of a good living, but failure slips them into poverty. A benign figure, Mr. Humphreys, with his protégé Herbert, try to soften the blows that fall on the Lyles; Herbert eventually falls in love with Violet. The fortunes of the Benedicks begin to decline and Mr. Benedick looks on helplessly as his family comes apart. When Mr. Humphreys finds himself in debt and at odds with the powers that be and is imprisoned, Herbert and the dubious, former felon Timothy Flint affect his release. Mr. Humphreys, it turns out, is actually Pryce Benedick's brother, Humphrey. Humphrey Benedick settles his brother's shattered estate, finding resources enough to set things right with Mr. Lyle, the broken Pryce, Violet and Herbert, and several other characters.

1381. **Green, Anna Katharine, 1846-1935.** *Behind closed doors.* **New York: G.P. Putnam, 1888. v, 523p.**

"The scene is New York and the heroine the beautiful daughter of the wealthy family of Gretorex. She is about to marry a famous New York doctor, and a misunderstanding occurs on the very eve of the marriage, which calls in the aid of a detective. The wedding, however, takes place, but has a startling interruption in a wild scream from no one knows where, which throws the bride into a painful state of terror and faintness. The death of a young girl by prussic acid the same night is traced to the Gretorex mansion, and the reader is at once in the depths of an apparently inexplicable mystery"—Annual American catalogue.

1382. ————. *The circular study,* **by Anna Katharine Green Rohlfs. New York: McClure, Phillips, 1900. 289p.**

Police detective Ebenezer Gryce solicits Amelia Butterworth's help in cracking the case of the mechanic, Felix Adams, who is murdered in his New York City brownstone dwelling. As they peel off the layers of mystery surrounding the homicide, Ebenezer and Amelia uncover unpleasant facts about Adams. They receive assistance from Caleb Sweetwater, a young member of the Metropolitan Police Force.

1383. ————. *Cynthia Wakeham's money*. **New York: G.P. Putnam, 1892. iv, 336p.**

"A telegram received by a New York lawyer, asking him to come without delay to 'Flatbush', Long Island to make the will of Cynthia Wakeham, starts a characteristic story by the author of 'The Leavenworth case.' The lawyer's search for the woman's heirs is rich in mysteries and horrors. The heroine is an exquisitely beautiful woman with a strange scar on her face, who almost falls a victim to the unreasoning hatred of her father and uncle"—Annual American catalogue.

1384. ————. *Dark Hollow*. **With illus. by Thomas Fogarty. New York: Dodd, Mead, 1914. 381p.**

Detective Caleb Sweetwater 'displaces' Ebenezer Gryce as chief investigator of the murder of socialite Edith Challoner in a New York hotel. In order to more clearly observe one of the suspects, Sweetwater 'becomes' a carpenter and lives in a working-class boarding house.

1385. ————. *A difficult problem, the staircase at the Heart's Delight, and other stories*. **New York: F.M. Lupton Pub. Co., 1900. 344p.**

Of these six mystery stories, four have a distinctively New York City aura (the first-second, fifth-sixth). Contents: A difficult problem.—The gray madam.—The bronze hand.—Midnight in Beauchamp Row.—The staircase at the Heart's Delight.—The hermit of — Street.

1386. ————. *The doctor, his wife and the clock*. **New York: G.P. Putnam, 1895. 131p.**

"A mysterious murder committed July 17, 1851, in the night, arouses the inhabitants of Lafayette Place and at the same time the keen scent of a New York detective who, while following up a slight clue, hears an astounding confession from Dr. Zabriske, who claims that he is the murderer; at the doctor's hearing, his wife making the defense that it would be impossible for him to hit a direct mark on account of his blindness, and he contending that his sense of sound would enable him to hit a target, a clock is fastened to a tree and the doctor directed to aim. The results of the test are surprising and tragic"—Annual American catalogue.

1387. ————. *The golden slipper and other problems for Violet Strange*. **Front. by A.I. Keller. New York: G.P. Putnam, 1915. iii, 425p.**

This collection of short fiction features Violet Strange an upper-class young lady from a Fifth Avenue home, who works undercover as a private detective to raise money for her own clandestine purposes. Her clients are members of her own class. Violet pursues her cases with professional demeanor; they generally involve theft, the hushing up of scandal in order to preserve reputations, uncovering facts that will help the wrongfully accused, and even the solution of murders. Contents: The golden slipper.—The second bullet.—The intangible clew.—The grotto spectre.—The dreaming lady.—The house of clocks.—The doctor, his wife and the cook.—Missing page 13.—Violet's own.

1388. ————. *Hand and ring.* **New York: G.P. Putnam, 1883. 608p.**
'Sibley' is a small town situated [in] Upstate New York. Details of life in the community become important when the widow Clemmens is murdered, seemingly under the very eyes of its citizens. Green examines land entitlements, hidden relationships, routines of business and social life, railroad schedules and travel opportunities. Although far from the clamor and crime of Manhattan, this distant town has its secrets"—Maida, P.D. Mother of detective fiction.

1389. ————. *Initials only.* **Front. in color by Arthur I. Keller. New York: Dodd, Mead, 1911. 356p.**
Two brothers—Oswald and Orlando Brotherson—one (Oswald) good, the other (Orlando) evil, fall in love with the same woman, Edith Challoner, a beautiful New York debutante. Edith's death, at first unexplained, ultimately reveals a fiendish plot by Orlando Brotherson. Since Edith would not marry him, Orlando was determined that she would be no one's bride, especially his brother's. The method by which Orlando disposed of Edith is most ingenious.

1390. ————. *The Leavenworth case*; **a lawyer's story. New York: G.P. Putnam, 1878. iv, 475.**
"New York City was a likely choice for the setting of ... Green's first detective story. Readers who followed New York's high society, its debutantes and lavish dress balls, were eager to catch a glimpse of life behind the doors of Fifth Avenue"—Maida, P.D. Mother of detective fiction. New York millionaire Horatio Leavenworth is found murdered in the library of his Fifth Avenue home; later, Hannah Chester, the Leavenworth's ladies' maid, is a homicide victim in Saratoga Springs. Two prime suspects are Mary and Eleanore Leavenworth, Horatio's beautiful nieces and likely heirs to his fortune. Ebenezer Gryce of the New York Police and Everett Raymond, a young lawyer, are the sleuths who combine to solve the murders. Gryce makes his appearance in several others of Greene's works. 'The Leavenworth case' is one of the first pieces of detective fiction to be written by a woman.

1391. ————. *Lost Man's Lane*; **a second episode in the life of Amelia Butterworth. New York: G.P. Putnam, 1898. ix, 403p.**

Amelia Butterworth, a highly ethical, upper-class woman and an amateur sleuth, steps center stage in this mystery set in an Upstate New York town (some 90 miles from New York City). She has to deal with a psychopathic murderer as she agrees to stay at the Knollys' house in Lost Man's Lane, the scene of several unexpected disappearances. Amelia solves the secrets of the house, but is at risk from the trapped murderer. Police detective Ebenezer Gryce puts in a timely appearance to shield his friend and occasional helper from harm.

1392. ―――――. *Marked "personal."* **New York: G.P. Putnam, 1893. vi, 415p.**
"Twenty-five years back of the story lies the cause of the package marked 'personal.' Twelve years back lies a connecting link during the time of the New York Draft Riots of 1863. On his wedding-day, Samuel White, with everything to live for, is found dead in his room two hours after the ceremony. His son and young second wife employ friends and foes to get at the mystery of his death"—Annual American catalogue.

1393. ―――――. *A matter of millions*; a novel. **With illus. by Victor Perard. New York: R. Bonner's Sons, 1890. 482p.**
"A few hours before his death Michael Delancey bequeaths a fortune to Hamilton DeGrow of Cleveland, with a proviso that the latter will search in New York for a girl of specified name and characteristics, and in compliance with his last wishes bestow upon her the three millions of dollars in question. On DeGrow's action in regard to this trust is dependent a story of sensational interests and tragic consequences. The action takes place in New York and Great Barrington, Massachusetts"—Annual American catalogue. Possible claimants to the fortune are Virginia Rogers, Jenny Rogers, and Jeanette Rogers, each from totally different backgrounds.

1394. ―――――. *The millionaire baby.* **Illustrated by Arthur I. Keller. Indianapolis: Bobbs-Merrill, 1905. 358p.**
"The spiriting away of a baby, the heiress to three fortunes, furnishes a plot for a unique detective story. The detective himself, in the race with others for the fifty thousand dollar reward, narrates the steps that lead to the mystery-solving stroke—this latter involving surprise even for the wily disciple of Sherlock Holmes"—Book review digest. The suburbs of New York City and several nearby towns on the Hudson River are the locales of the story. Green's characters are often given fictional names that conceal their true identities.

1395. ―――――. *The mystery of the hasty arrow.* **With front. by H.R. Ballinger. New York: Dodd, Mead, 1917. vii, 432p.**
In his last case "a rheumatic Inspector [Ebenezer] Gryce is called to a New York City museum to investigate the murder of a young French girl shot with a bow and arrow belonging to the museum collection. The case is difficult because witnesses are not truthful and hidden alliances must be unveiled if the

puzzle is to be solved"—Maida, P.D. Mother of detective fiction.... The author displays her sympathy for women as society's victims by developing one character, Ementrude Taylor, abandoned by her husband and with child, but still a strong survivor.

1396. ————. *One of my sons.* **New York: Putnam, 1901. v, 366p.**

Archibald Gillespie, a railroad tycoon, is murdered in his home on Fifth Avenue. Son and heir Leighton Gillespie, who gives in to his father on every point, has a wife, Milles Fleurs, who is addicted to drugs and ends up in a lower Manhattan slum; Green contrasts the lives of the upper class with the ghetto existence of Lower Manhattan. Ebenezer Gryce, the detective on the case, hears the coroner state that old Mr. Gillespie's death was caused by the ingestion of prussic acid. He also learns that Gillespie fully expected one of his sons would be held responsible for his death.

1397. ————. *A strange disappearance.* **New York: G.P. Putnam, 1880. [c1879] 280p.**

New York Police Detective Ebenezer Gryce solves the kidnapping of a young married woman (Luttra) with a past. He not only frees her from the criminals holding her, but also succeeds in preventing them from exposing Luttra's past indiscretions, thus saving her marriage.

1398. ————. *The sword of Damocles*; **story of New York life. New York: G.P. Putnam, 1881. vi, 540p.**

The 'sword of Damocles' is the haunting dread of a bank president that a criminal act he committed in his early life will be revealed for all the world to see. In addition he has the onus of being suspected of stealing bonds from his own bank.

1399. ————. *That affair next door.* **New York: G.P. Putnam, 1897. iv, 399p.**

The body of Louis Van Burnham is found in Gramercy Park and proof is available to establish the death as a murder. The police detective, Ebenezer Gryce, and the amateur sleuth, Amelia Butterworth, have a go at identifying the murderer, but fail quite markedly. The two try again, cooperating more closely this time, and come up with the right answers.

1400. ————. *To the minute [and] Scarlet and black*; **two tales of life's perplex-ities. New York: G.P. Putnam, 1916. iii, 226p.**

"The mystery in the first of these two stories centers about an old house. Neither Albert Mann nor his cousin Judith can understand the interest Seth Fullerton takes in the house that has been willed to Judith by her grandfather. She soon comes to see that his wish to marry her is only the outcome of his desire to gain possession of the house. Failing in that, he offers to buy it for three times its actual value. The two people wisely decide to wait for an explanation before accepting his offer. A house is also the scene of the second story, Scarlet and black. A New York doctor who is starting on a trip to

Europe turns back to his home to secure valuable papers he has left in an unlocked drawer and finds that two beautiful Russian women have taken possession in his brief absence. He decides to let the steamer sail without him while he remains to solve the mystery of their presence"—Book review digest.

1401. ————. *The woman in the alcove.* **With illus. by Arthur I. Keller. Indianapolis: Bobbs-Merrill, 1906. 371p.**

The novel takes place in Manhattan and in a New Mexico mining town. It is "a mystery story which runs a rapid and exciting course to the inevitable solution [and] opens upon a brilliant private ball. A gorgeously appareled woman with a diamond on her breast too vivid for most women is murdered in an alcove, and the gem hidden in the woman's glove is discovered later in the possession of innocent Rita Van Arsdale. Her lover is accused of the deed, and the interest of the story becomes identified with this determined young woman's efforts to free him of the charge of guilt"—Book review digest. Detective Caleb Sweetwater, the chief investigator, poses as a valet for one of those suspected of the crime.

Green, Asa, 1789-1838. See: Greene, Asa, 1789-1838.

1402. **Green, Edith Pinero, 1929- .** *Rotten apples.* **New York: Dutton, 1977. 245p.**

"Dearborn (Dearie) Pinch [is] a suave, crabby septuagenarian whose salad-day chums (and enemies) are being killed off one by one. Eschewing the services of the police or those of playboyish son Benjamin, Dearborn visits the potential victims and possible suspects; all but Dearborn belonged to the secret 1930s Rotten Apple Corps, a club for undetected do-badders. And Benjamin follows his father, asking similar questions to the same people. … Eventually the Pinches and the surviving Rotten Apples get together at a defunct Longevity Clinic on Long Island for more talk and a few scary-house antics"—Kirkus reviews.

1403. **Green, George Dawes.** *The juror.* **New York: Warner Books, 1995. viii, 420p.**

Annie Laird, a sculptor and a single mother, has been selected to be a member of the jury that is sitting in judgment in the Westchester trial of crime boss Louis Buffano. She receives a promise from 'The Teacher', Buffano's associate that her life and the life of her son Oliver will end unless she votes 'Not guilty.' Annie is at first overwhelmed by fright and then resolves to set a trap for The Teacher. The latter meanwhile seems to have developed a romantic attachment to the woman he has threatened.

1404. **Green, Helen, b. 1882.** *At the actors' boarding house and other stories.* **New York: Nevada Pub. Co., 1906. 380p.**

The volume contains 56 short and short short stories, the majority of which take place in and around the Irving Place (New York City) boarding house of landlady Mrs. De Shine and her husband. Eccentricity is the norm of many of the show business people that are portrayed by the author. Some of her stories have an American West locale. Partial contents: The honeymoon of Sam and Caroline.—Emma the slavey makes good in vaudeville.—The rise and fall of Dooley's dog act.—The way of a music hall song bird.—The troubles of two working girls.—The creating of a top line act.—The finish of Duffy the Dip.—How the soubrettes broke a lease.—The manager's new wife.—Mary had to have her Broadway.—The comedian's wives.—The rival landlords and the bridal party.—Pinafore and 'The Duke' skin a corporation.—New York Arabian nights.—The adventures of Clarence, the messenger boy.—The love of One-Arm Annie.—The way it goes on Broadway.—Romance of an acrobat and a darning needle.—Clancy the copper, and the kid.

1405. ————. *The Maison De Shine*; more stories of the actor's boarding house. New York: B.W. Dodge, 1908. 298p.

The actors' boarding house, the Maison De Shine, is on Irving Place, New York City; its residents are chiefly vaudevillians whose lives away from the stage are the primary theme of the novel. The New York Times critic of the day said: "This doesn't look a bit like New York. It's funny and … it may be true, but it seems only as near to anything real as the average vaudeville performance appears like life. …There is any amount of detail as well as dialect concerning her people … but you cannot get over the feeling that they are … unreal."

1406. ————. *Mr. Jackson*. New York: B.W. Dodge, 1909. 299p.

John and Mary Smith, innocents from 'Shackopee', Iowa, on their very first visit to the big town (New York City), are fortunate (or unfortunate) enough to fall into the purview of the charming Mr. Jackson, a fellow reminiscent of 'Raffles' (the debonair theif created by E.W. Hornung).

1407. **Green, Judith H.** *Winners*; a novel. New York: Knopf; distributed by Random House, 1980. 305p.

Although Amanda Weldon and her husband are only going through the motions of marriage, she stays with him because she wants to share the power that would accrue to him should be become a successful candidate for governor of New York State. Amanda shares with the reader her observations as her husband's campaign gets under way, but she also fills free time with play writing, watching over her two daughters and having affairs with partners of both genders.

1408. **Green, Mason Arnold, b. 1850.** *Bitterwood*; a novel. New York: G. W. Carleton, 1878. 288p.

The Widow Carter, daughter Kate and son Harris are prominent residents of 'Bitterwood', a town in Upstate New York. Paul Jeffrey, son of the owner of Jeffrey & Co., plow manufacturers, is Harris's closest friend. The company's chief clerk, Seth Wellington, is the brain behind the firm; his lack of business ethics is mixed with a certain sense of decorum and the goals of gaining wealth and marrying Kate Carter. When Harris Carter tries to bail out one of Jeffrey & Co.'s chief debtors, Wellington has already set in motion his takeover of the Jeffrey property. The Civil War breaks out; Paul Jeffrey raises a company of volunteers, but trumped-up charges of misuse of the company's funds send him to Auburn State Prison. Seth marries Kate; he neglects her, concentrating on his business activities. The failure of his marriage and the burden of his checkered past bring Seth to an early grave. The Jeffreys and Carters, putting aside any animosities, try unsuccessfully to reconstruct their former affluence in the town. Kate, living in the decaying Carter mansion with her turned-to-farming brother ponders her marriage to Seth and Seth's true character—was he totally amoral or could he have submitted to his wife's good influences?

1409. **[Greene, Asa] 1789-1838. *The perils of Pearl Street, including a taste of the dangers of Wall Street.* By a late merchant. New York: Betts & Anstice, and P. Hill, 1834. 232p.**

William Hazard clerks at a store in 'Spreadaway' in Upstate New York until he reaches the age of 21. Then off he goes to New York City. He works at several retail establishments before striking out on his own as a wholesaler. When he fails William takes a clerk's job and saves enough from his wages to establish Hazard, Griffin & Co. Unwise speculation in cotton and hops futures drive him into bankruptcy; a winning lottery ticket enables William to achieve a modest measure of fiscal stability. In the long run, however, William is the prey of dishonest businessmen and ill-advised flyers in Wall Street. Rather than return to Spreadaway William stays in New York as a lecturer on bookkeeping. A few final words form William Hazard: "[I am of the opinion] that the man who is no honester than the law compels him to be is little better than a downright knave."

1410. **Greene, Homer, 1853-1940. *The Riverpark rebellion and A tale of the towpath.* [Illustrated by H.W. Peirce]. New York: T.Y. Crowell, 1892. 274p.**

"Riverpark Academy, the scene of the [first] story, stands for the Riverview Military Academy of Poughkeepsie, N.Y., where the author long ago spent two years under the preceptorship of the late Colonel Otis Bisbee, who appears under the name of 'Colonel Silsbee.' The 'rebellion' is a vivid scene from a boy's life at school, which may or may not be all true, although it has a background of fact. In 'A tale of the tow-path' the Pennsylvania canal region is vividly described"—Annual American catalogue.

1411. **Greene, Marjorie Sherman. *Cowboy of the Ramapos.* New York: Abelard-Schuman, 1956. 189p.**

A 17-year-old boy living in Orange County, New York during the American Revolution takes on the task of frustrating the efforts of a band of Tories (the 'Cowboys') to divert the shipments of food badly needed by Washington's soldiers.

1412. **Greene, Ward, 1892-1956.** *Ride the nightmare.* **New York: J. Cape & H. Smith, 1930. 327p.**

"Jake Perry believed in living selfishly and in getting what he wanted. He started his career as a newspaper artist; he ended as a well-paid cartoonist. Throughout he is a poseur; for the sake of his pose as an individualist he drinks, mistreats his faithful wife, and numerous other women as well, practices sadism, and, as a final gesture, attempts suicide"—Book review digest. The scenes range from a Southern city to the studios of Greenwich Village and the penthouses of Park Avenue.

1413. ————. *What they don't know*; **a novel. New York: Random House, 1944. 218p.**

"Story of a middle-class American family, living in suburban Long Island during the present war [World War II]. Mrs. Crockett ran all the town activities that she could and took in war refugees on the side; Mr. Crockett was hampered in his business by the W[ar] P[roduction] B[oard]; Nancy [Crockett] was young and beautiful and finally married her George, and young Henry Crockett went overseas. The Crocketts were a fairly typical family: compulsive, disorderly, kind, rude, jolly, and ambitious"—Book review digest.

1414. **Greene, Waverly.** *George Forest*; **a story of the present day. New York: G.W. Dillingham, 1897. 204p.**

"Illustrates the present-day theory that intemperance is more a disease than a vice; the author's hero is a man who drinks to excess. He marries a woman much older than himself, and in a fit of passion and intemperance one day strangles her. Intermingled with this story is the story of an Englishwoman of noble birth who marries a man socially beneath her, comes to America and opens a boarding house in New York"—Annual American catalogue.

Greenhorn, pseud. See: Thompson, George, fl. 1848-1858.

1415. **Gregor, Elmer Russell, 1878-1954.** *Jim Mason, backwoodsman.* **New York: Appleton, 1923. vi, 282p.**

Jim Mason grew from boyhood to manhood in the frontier town of Schenectady, N.Y. during the exciting days of the French and Indian Wars. As a backwoodsman he played a role in making sure that the Mohawk Indians would be on the British/American colonials' side during the conflicts. This novel was followed by: Jim Mason, scout; Captain Jim Mason; Mason and his rangers (q.v.)—all dealing with the hero and his Iroquois friends fighting with Sr. William Johnson against the French and their Indian allies. The Battle of Lake George figures prominently in 'Jim Mason, scout.'

1416. ————. *Mason and his rangers.* **New York: Appleton, 1926. 244p.**

"Jim Mason is assigned to a duty that, if accomplished, will save the fort at Oswego from falling into the hands of the French. His adventures take him among the Mohawks, and the author's account of his stay in the Mohawk camp shows a fine spirit of research and a talent for extracting the colorful"—Saturday review of literature.

1417. Gregory, Alyse, b. 1884. *She shall have music.* **New York: Harcourt, Brace, 1926. 263p.**

"Sylvia [Brown] is the daughter of wealthy middle class parents. To her mother, busy trying to do the correct thing, Sylvia's oddness is a source of chagrin, while her father has never pretended to understand her. Thus the child early learns that the best policy is not candor, but concealment of her precious ideas. She finds a real friend in Marcel, the gardener's boy next door, but as they grow older their friendship terminates on something like scandal. Marcel goes abroad, Sylvia to New York where she attempts to find out about herself and life, and what she is to do with both. Having learned, perhaps, she returns home and meeting Marcel who, to her parents' relief, is not the gardener's son after all, their love permanently revives"—Book review digest.

1418. Greig, Maysie, 1902-1971. *The luxury husband.* **Boston: Small, Maynard, 1927. vi, 324p.**

New York City in the age of jazz, flappers, and speakeasies is the scene of this story of two young lovers who quarrel, make up and marry, even though Ray has to depend on Barbara's money as their chief means of support. After a while Ray's pride makes the situation distasteful so far as he is concerned and he resumes his serious jazz composing. Barbara realizes that her husband is trying to make his own contribution to their marriage and she comes to value him even more.

1419. ————. *Satin straps.* **New York: L. MacVeagh, Dial Press, 1929. 301p.**

New York upscale clothing store clerk and sometime model, Jacqueline Grey, went out 'on the town' one evening in a gown 'borrowed' from Madame Heloise's shop. The escapade brought her to the attention of three men: Ted, the artist, who scorned the soft life of the so-called gentlemanly class; old Marquis de Rembon who had a roving eye that appreciated beautiful young women; Bruce, stylish socialist, yet stuffily self-important. With flair, beauty and 'a little bit o' luck' Jacqueline becomes part of that world of wealth, celebrity and high society and, as an extra dividend, found love awaiting her.

1420. Grendon, Felix, b. 1882. *The love chase.* **Boston: Small, Maynard, 1922. 494p.**

"A novel of bohemian life in New York, but this time for a change the subject is not Greenwich Village, but the smaller and less advertised colony of artists and radical intellectuals which is scattered over the East Side in the Thirties, Forties and Fifties. The story is centered in a young woman who flees from the rigors of a puritanical house in Brooklyn to the free and easy atmosphere of the radical colony, takes a flier in free love, and being converted to matrimony by this experience, finally settles down with the right man. Some large-scale opportunities in diamond smuggling and an international spy complication are thrown in—for what reason it is difficult to see"—Literary review of the New York evening post.

1421. ———. *Nixola of Wall Street.* **New York: Century Co., 1919. 384p.**

A thin novel about the world of commerce in New York City and the part that Nixola Hill and her employer play in it. She is private secretary to the president of the Pacific Mercantile Company, Carleton Boyd. Boyd is of a rather aristocratic mien who has an inflated belief in the encompassing importance of business in the social scheme of things, a view Nixola does not share. However she is so valuable an assistant to Boyd that he looks more closely at her; they merge as husband and wife.

1422. **[Grey, Jeannie H.]** *Tactics*; or, *Cupid in shoulder straps.* **A West Point love story, by Hearton Drille, U.S.A. [pseud.] New York: Carleton, 1863. 250p.**

The social rather than the military aspects of life at West Point and vicinity are the focus of the novel despite the military terminology used for chapter headings. Isagone Smith from California visits her aunt and uncle, Violetta and Lt. Adelbert Bobaline, at the Point; she is promptly renamed Ione and becomes the center of attraction for several officers. Ione's engagement to the mercurial Lt. Saberin is short-lived, especially after Saberin's friend Lt. Mera, discovers Saberin is also engaged to a Southern belle, Pauline DeSaye. The Civil War brings about changes in the lives of the novel's characters. Saberin is wounded and turns to an early love, Mary Greenleaf. Ione accepts Lt. Mera's proposal of marriage and Pauline DeSaye finds happiness with her 'enemy', wounded officer Lt. Alton.

1423. **Grey, Leslie.** *Corners of the heart.* **Huntington Station, N.Y.: Rising Tide Press, 1993. 201p.**

Prejudice against gay people is a central theme in the novel. Katya Michaels, an English professor, lives with an adopted son, Sam, just outside 'Deer Falls' in Upstate New York. She is attracted to Chris Benet, a painter who does odd jobs to support herself. Both Katya and Chris have memories of unhappy pasts that impede their relationship. Katya is threatened over the phone by a caller who says: "If I can't have you, I'll take that little blond boy" [Sam]. The local police evince little concern despite recent attacks on lesbians in and out of town (two were murdered). Chris rescues Sam from a deliberately plotted 'accident.' Their search for their homophobic enemy continues.

1424. **Griffis, William Elliot, 1843-1928.** *The pathfinders of the Revolution*; a story **of the great march into the wilderness and lake region of New York in 1779. Illustrated by W. F. Stecher. Boston: W.A. Wilde, 1900. 316p.**

A semi-fictional account of General John Sullivan's expedition, the purpose of which was to break the power of the Iroquois Indians, allies of the British Crown. Griffis states in his preface that he has utilized 'the local traditions of New York's [Finger] Lakes region, many old letters, and local and ancestral traditions' in presenting a very detailed story, with a mix of historical and fictional characters, of Sullivan's campaign.

1425. Griffith, Helen Sherman, b. 1873. *Letty at the Conservatory.* **Illustrated by Paula B. Himmelsbach. Philadelphia: Penn Pub. Co., 1915. 319p.**

Letty comes from a well-to-do family; she enters the Conservatory in New York City for the serious study of music. Many of the other young women in the school tend to look upon Letty as just another dilettante with a desultory interest in the musical arts. However, her dedication is quite obvious by the end of the story and she wins the respect of her peers.

1426. Griffith, Susan M., b. 1851. *The ladder of promise.* **Richmond, Va.: Presbyterian Committee of Publication, 1899. 327p.**

The young hero, Tom Knox, is an orphan and newsboy, living by his wits on the street, when he is taken in hand by a Christian gentleman, Merril Merton, who introduces Tom to the possibility of turning his life around. Tom absorbs Merton's 'message', begins attending church and the nearby mission house. Henceforth he commits himself wholeheartedly to Christ and acquires an education through the auspices of the Merton family. Tom carries the 'good news' to his former street comrades; he rises in the world working in Mr. Merton's store, discovers hidden musical talents, and begins to unravel the mystery of his parentage. The novel concludes years later with Tom as a college professor and gospel singer who meets his mother's father and the father who had divorced his mother and left her and very young Tom penniless.

1427. Grinnell, David. *Edge of time.* **New York: Avalon Books, 1958. 221p.**

Scientists experiment with the transference of life from other planets and Upstate New York becomes a destination for some of these alien life forms. The result is altered, dangerous and ultimately uncontrollable situations that attract a reporter and a photographer.

1428. Griswold, Hattie Tyng, 1840-1909. *Fencing with shadows.* **Chicago: Morrill, Higgins, 1893. 404p.**

A seamstress, Lizelle Gay, tenant of a garret in a tenement located in New York City's Fourth Ward, is on the verge of starvation when a warm-hearted neighbor provides her with food. Good fortune is Lizelle's when Victoria Armstrong, a young woman from New York's upper social class, takes Lizelle from her cramped, dark quarters and employs her as a servant. Victoria, incited by her involvement with Lizelle, begins to look into and to better the living conditions of the poor of the city.

1429. [Griswold, V.M.] *Hugo Blanc, the artist*; a tale of practical and ideal life. **By an artist. New York: Hilton, 1867. 411p.**

Hugo Blanc of 'Denwood', a village outside of New York City, desires to be an artist—or so he tells his friend, Louis Grattan, a painter. Grattan perceives

Hugo's talent, but the latter is commanded by his father to enter the world of commerce. Hugo rebels and runs off to New York. He is preceded by Grattan who, together with his friend, Byrnie, another painter, tries to sell his works with little success despite connection with the Art Union of New York. Hugo has an accident, recovers and meets Byrnie and Grattan. Grattan's despondency is countered by the optimism of Hugo and Byrnie and Hugo makes a break-through with the sale of two of his paintings. A defining moment in Grattan's life occurs when he learns that he is heir to a great estate in England. This news is carried by the father he never knew, a certain Mr. Grey (real name: Hewson) who had been separated from his son, Louis Grattan Hewson, when the latter was an infant. Father and son depart for England; Hugo, reconciled with his father, has a definite place in the art world of New York.

1430. **Gross, Milt, 1895-1953.** *Dunt ask!!* **Illustrated by the author. New York: Doran, 1927. 235p.**

A leading character in this humorous slice of Bronx apartment life is Looy Feitelbaum who keeps a 'dairy', which Mrs. Feitelbaum reads. Looy is always on the verge of getting a job or threatening to leave, but he never does either, although Mr. Feitelbaum is most willing to give him the boot. Another noteworthy personage is Mrs. Noftolis, the social climber, whom Looy essays to bring down to earth. The characters speak in a version of 'Yiddish-American.'

1431. —————. *Nize baby.* **Illustrated by the author. New York: Doran, 1926. 207p. Half-title: Gross exaggerations.**

Sketches of mostly Jewish tenants of Bronx and East Side apartment houses told in their own fractured English and recorded as overheard. Mrs. Feitelbaum and Mrs. Yifnif are the interlocutors.

1432. **Grossinger, Tania, 1927- .** *Weekend,* **by Tania Grossinger and Andrew Neiderman. New York: St. Martin's Press, 1980. 280p.**

The Congress Hotel in the Catskills is one of the borscht circuit resorts in 1958, whose survival is questionable because of competition for airlines, etc., offering tourists access to a mountain of choices. It is Fourth of July weekend; the hotel management is anxious to provide its usual high standard of service to the young women in search of mates, husbands looking for sexual adventures, children, divorcées, et al. They and the hotel staff, the doctors and the hotel owner, a widow with a 13-year-old daughter—all have stories to tell. Over all this looms the danger of an outbreak of cholera.

1433. **Grumbach, Doris, 1918- .** *The book of knowledge*; a novel. **New York: Norton, 1995. 248p.**

Caleb and Kate Flowers, Roslyn Hellman and Lionel Schwartz spend the summer of 1929 as happy companions in the beachside town of 'Far Rockaway', N.Y. Caleb and Kate are the children of a widow who tends to keep to herself. Roslyn and Lionel have fathers who are Manhattan stockbrokers. The subsequent Great Depression and the 15 years following mark a cessation of the pleasant existence of the young people. Caleb Flowers and Lionel Schwartz meet again at Cornell University and begin a homosexual relationship that Caleb terminates when it threatens his career plans. Roslyn's lesbian inclinations, exposed during a summer camp stay, are quickly quashed by social conventions. Kate turns to religion to still her sexual longings for her brother.

1434. **Guernsey, Clara Florida, 1836-1893.** *The silver rifle*; a story of the Saranac Lakes. **Philadelphia: American Sunday School Union, 1871. 256p.**

John and Allan FitzAdam accompany their father, uncle and cousin on a vacation to the still wild Adirondacks. John takes along the valuable silver rifle bequeathed him by the late Edmund DeForest. On a side trip to an isolated lake in the mountains the two lads are led by Sam Kremlin, a young guide. Overcome by covetousness and the urgings of a cowardly, snobbish acquaintance of the two boys, Sam walks off with the rifle and fishing equipment, leaving John and Allan to find their own way out of the wilderness. They barely survive; lost, they come upon a wounded Sam about to be attacked by a panther. John kills the beast with two quick shots from the silver rifle that he had picked up from the ground close by Sam. Sam claims he had repented of his theft and was on his way back to the boys. A search party comes upon the scene and all head back to 'civilization.' Sam suffers permanent paralysis from the waist down—the author points her moral; the love of money has been at the root of Sam's tragic fate.

1435. *'Guilty or not guilty?'* **The true story of Manhattan Well. New York: Carleton, 1870. 396p.**

A novel based on a murder that occurred in 1799 in New York City wherein the body of a young woman, Gulielma Sands, was found at the bottom of an abandoned well near Spring and Greene Streets. 'Elma Sands' progress from her parents' farm in Cornwall [on the Hudson] to a home with 'Cousin Catharine' Ring in New York City, her education at the fashionable Miss Willson's School and friendships with socially prominent young people are recounted. News of her parents' death devastates 'Elma, but she recovers and is engaged to businessman Levi Weeks. On the fatal night 'Elma leaves the Ring home, presumably accompanied by Levi, and never returns. Her body is recovered; Levi Weeks seems a logical suspect. Arrested and brought to trial, Weeks is acquitted for lack of evidence beyond the purely circumstantial. The general public, dissatisfied with the verdict, causes Levi to flee New York to Kentucky where he marries but dies shortly thereafter.

1436. **Gunter, Archibald Clavering, 1847-1907.** *The adventures of Dr. Burton.* **New York: Home Pub. Co., 1905. 223p.**

A tale concerning the mysterious death of a governess employed by a wealthy family in New York City. Dr. Burton, who has joined Dr. Stohl in a very

369

lucrative medical practice, is seen by some as rather lackadaisical, but he actually has a keen scientific mind that he uses to improve the lot of those he deals with; he applies his intelligence in researching the governess's death. The author slips in two characters who happen to be Mormons and uses them to explain some odd goings-on.

1437. ————. *The changing pulse of Madame Touraine.* New York: Home Pub. Co., 1905. 228p.

Among the diverse characters in this short novel set in new York City are: a family doctor who doubles as a criminologist; a dressmaker for the rich with a hidden past; a debutante in debt to the dressmaker, loved by a young man with few financial resources; and his rival for the girl's love, a venal financier. A forged check and an alibi provided by 'the changing pulse of Madame Touraine' are elements that propel the plot.

1438. ————. *Her senator*; a novel. New York: Home Pub. Co., 1896. 261p.

Overhand Guernsey uses funds entrusted to him by Arthur Ellison to enrich himself. Ellison's death releases him from the fear of disclosure. Ellison's two daughters, Evelyn and Mathilde, are placed by Guernsey in an orphanage outside New York City. Evelyn runs away from the orphan asylum and in a few years becomes a theatrical performer with bohemian leanings with an improvident husband, Claude Auchester Montressor. Guernsey's son, James Bertram Guernsey, takes Mathilde out of the orphanage to his Western ranch. In time James is elected to the U.S. Senate; Evelyn, after divorcing Montressor, ends up in Washington, D.C. looking for a bribable senator to further her Gelatine Trust interests. She tries and fails to corrupt the son of the man who stole her inheritance; in a turnaround she falls in love with James Guernsey and he with her.

1439. ————. *The man behind the door*; a novel. New York: Home Pub. Co., 1904. 281p.

During a performance at the Metropolitan Opera Jack De Lacy gets into a fracas with a man he believes is Charles Livingston for making disparaging remarks about Jack's fiancée, Maria Pierson. Later Jack goes to Livingston's apartment for satisfaction and is locked in the library by Livingston's valet, Jobson Smithson Johnson. Livingston, Maria, Alice Montague Marvin (a striking widow Jack has temporarily been smitten with) and banker Harvey Kelsey are already in the apartment. Jack hears Kelsey expressing his love to Maria and strains to break out of the library. Then tragedy strikes when the valet Johnson is murdered—it has become obvious that it was Johnson, not Livingston, who had been the person Jack confronted at the opera. Of course Jack is a suspect; however he clears himself by tracking down the killers, two jealous Sicilians infuriated by Johnson's getting too close to performer Zerlina, whom both loved. Kelsey recognizes Jack as the man who saved him from drowning in Long Island Sound and cedes Maria to him.

1440. ————. *Phil Conway*; a novel. **New York: Home Pub. Co. [1903]. 297p.**

Philip Caskill Conway maintains comfortable bachelor quarters in one of New York City's finest apartment houses. His surprise and his concern is piqued when he is informed by a young man, apparently of German origins, that some individual (or group?) is making plans to terminate his (Conway's) life. Conway's informant is an accomplished investigator who sets about (with Conway's approval and assistance) uncovering the plot and fingering the villains[s].

1441. Gurney, A[lbert] R[amsdell] 1930- . *The Snow Ball.* **New York: Arbor House, 1984. 240p.**

Fiftyish Cooper Jones looks back nostalgically to his youth when he and his friends were high schoolers in Buffalo before the outbreak of World War II. They were younger members of Buffalo's exclusive and conservative families when one of the social events of the year was the Snow Ball. The Ball has been inactive for many years and Cooper sets about reviving it. Cooper married his high school sweetheart but he has reserved a special place for the heiress Kitty Price and insolvent, engaging Jack Daley. These two were a romantic pair but went their separate ways—Kitty has a third husband and Jack is lieutenant governor of a state in the Midwest. As might be expected Cooper's restoration of the Ball generates more disillusion than happy recollections.

1442. Gurwit, Samuel Gordon, b. 1890. *Alias the promised land.* **New York: J.H. Hopkins, 1938. 380p.**

Three New York City characters with dubious reputations—a gold-digging, beautiful young woman (Sue), an expert at rigging card games (Colonel Cantillion, father of Sue), and his somewhat violent associate who probably would not hesitate at murder ('Fash')—invade a college town not far from New York City with the intention of despoiling the unsuspecting 'rubes'. As the reader might guess this is one of those tales where the would-be marauders end up thoroughly reformed, adapting themselves to the estimable life style of their intended victims.

1443. Guthrie, Ramon, 1896-1973. *Parachute.* **New York: Harcourt, Brace, 1928. 299p.**

"Lieutenant Rickey, wounded in the air service in France [during World War I] is sent to a reconstruction hospital in a small New York town. Known as 'Tony the Wop' he is a disconcerting addition to the social life of the town until Natalie Gortion and her husband take him up. His affair with Natalie, her friendship with the sardonic Sayles and their united venture in commercial aviation are incidents in the story which centers around the character of the 'big Wop from Peoria'"—Book review digest.

1444. Gutwillig, Robert. *After a long silence.* **Boston: Little, Brown, 1958. 350p.**

'Arden University', a center of action in the first half of this novel, is obviously Cornell University; an Ivy League school, Arden is situated on a hill in central New York overlooking a large lake (Cayuga). Two students, Tom Freeman and his buddy, Chris Hunt, are more interested in partying than in scholarship. In the New York City half of the book Tom takes employment as a low-level mass media person. Chris dies in a car crash and Tom decides to go to graduate school.

H.F.P. See: Parker, Helen Eliza Fitch, 1827-1874.

1445. **Habberton, John, 1842-1921. *The Chautauquans*; a novel. With illus. by Warren B. Davis. New York: R. Bonner, 1891. 351p.**

The country village of 'Brinston' becomes excited about starting a Chautauqua series within its confines. The town debates it, studies it, works on it at great length and several of the villagers (including Mr. Broad, owner of the Brinston Foundry, Mr. Dawn and Mrs. Purkis) go to the campground at Lake Chautauqua when Recognition Day and other events are in full swing. Most of Brinston's citizens agree that the benefits derived by young and old in the community have been substantial after it joins the Chautauqua circuit.

1446. ————. *Couldn't say no.* **New York: Belford Co., 1890 [c1889]. 229p.**

Frederic Valtrey returns to New York from a European tour and immediately plunges into the pleasures the city offers a young man with money and social position. Unfortunately Fred knows no restraints; his partiality for women and gambling soon drains away his patrimony and he deserts his wife Ethel. He becomes a tramp-like wanderer on the face of the land. At one point when he is out West Fred's death is announced in print. When he comes back East he is witness to the wedding of Ethel Valtrey and Philip Royal, her business partner. Shortly thereafter Fred slips away and dies.

1447. ————. *Country luck.* **Philadelphia: J.B. Lippincott, 1887. 260p.**

" 'Nine men of every ten who amount to anything in New York come from the country', says the father of the heroine, a city merchant who has become rich by 'iron looking up.' After boarding with his family in a country farmhouse, this hearty old gentleman gives the oldest son an invitation to visit them in the city. Against his better judgment this talented young man runs down to 'York' for a couple of weeks and gets drawn into a combination of circumstances which he in time controls with 'country luck'"—Annual American catalogue.

1448. ————. *Out at Twinnett's*; or, *Gnawing a file.* **A story of Wall Street ways and suburban mysteries. New York: J.A. Taylor, 1891. 197p.**

Paul Frayston walked away from Wall Street, mining stocks, etc., and vanished; some theorized that his sins had caught up with him and he had committed suicide. A keen onlooker, Mr. Maile, had an eye out for properties that Frayston had left 'in a condition of uncertainty as to ownership', and he decided to acquire them by whatever means necessary. Into the picture comes an old sailor by the name of Twinnett who is living on a small island off Long Island. Twinnett is a talented cook and has a daughter, May, who hires out as a governess. The Burnhams, good friends of Frayston, have always believed him to be an honest man whatever Maile's opinion. Of course, Twinnett turns out to be Paul Frayston; he blocks Maile's efforts to get the real estate he coveted.

1449. Hackenburg, Frederick L. *This best possible world*; a novel. New York: R.O. Ballou, 1934. 310p.

Although much of the novel portrays Tammany politics, Assemblymen from New York City and their activities in the State capital (Albany) are also the author's concern. Among the figures in the State legislature are: James (Jim) McLarner, ambitious, silver-tongued State senator, who uses his talents well enough to achieve governorship of the State; Margaret Doyle, former mistress of businessman Frank X. Dempsey, who uses the money he left her to live comfortably and gain enough support from society women to take a seat in the State Assembly; Morris Bender, a young idealistic lawyer who reluctantly consents to take a seat in the Assembly offered by the Tammany political machine; Sig Roth (known as Bacsi), intellectual, cynical observer of human foibles, who comes to Albany as 'Assistant Doorkeeper of the Assembly' and is eventually elected to that august body as a member from the Downtown Tammany District of New York City.

1450. Haddam, Jane, 1951- . *A great day for the deadly*. New York: Bantam Books, 1992. 284p.

Gregor Demarkian, a retired FBI agent, is beckoned to 'Maryville', N.Y. by worried John Cardinal O'Bannion where postulant Ann Reilly's body has been found covered with water moccasins, snakes that are not indigenous to temperate climates. As an expert on toxic substances Demarkian determines that hemlock was the poison that killed Ann. The various suspects are lined up and happenings like a malfunction in the local bank's computer system and an intimidating letter to the Mother Superior and the nuns of the Sisters of Divine Grace and Ann Reilly's tender feelings for evasive individuals are investigated.

1451. Haight, Ada Clementine Acker, b. 1879. *Croton waters*. New York: Pageant Press, 1951. 121p.

A girl from an old Westchester family takes the plunge into a deep love affair. The scene of the story is the Croton-on-Hudson and Croton Reservoir region.

1452. Haldeman, Charles, 1911- . *The snowman*. New York: Simon and Schuster, 1965. 186p.

'Joseph's Landing' in Upstate New York is the setting of a tale that has its share of symbolism. When the town doctor, Donatien Villiers, hardly a sterling character, is killed in a hunting accident, Dr. Mendel Cadmus, a young Jew, takes his place. Mendel is on friendly terms with Geneva, a mute girl who had been traumatized by a childhood rape, and with Charley Villiers, a wounded veteran, Donatien's son. Anti-Semitism is quite visible in Joseph's Landing and Dr. Cadmus is not around very long. After his death Geneva recovers her voice and she and Charley place a medallion on their snowman (an effigy of Cadmus?). Charley is convinced that his father's evil spirit still stalks the inhabitants of Joseph's Landing.

1453. **Hale, Edward Everett, 1822-1909.** *Four and five*; **a story of a Lend-a-Hand Club. Boston: Roberts Bros., 1891. 194p.**

"The four were all boys who had a camp together one summer in the Kaatskills. When they broke up in the autumn, it was determined that each should bring another boy with him on returning the next summer. The club, increased to eight, obtained a ninth member, which gave it its name, 'Four and five', quite oddly. The boys on a tramp become separated, and one, after wandering all day in the woods, comes upon the hut of an old Negro woman. She illustrates the mottoes of the club so thoroughly and lends a hand so cheerfully that the boys make her a member"—Annual American catalogue.

1454. **Hale, Louise Closser, 1872-1933.** *Home talent.* **New York: Holt, 1926. 293p.**

"Charlie Flagg is a great favorite in amateur theatricals at the High Platte Masonic Temple. She would like to go to New York, and Ben Dorsey thinks she should. Circumstances and friends combine to make it possible. She meets a matinee idol and his gently managing wife, and is offered a part in the play. The stage folk are kind to her and help her to success, but much as she loves the theater she comes to love Ben more"—Book review digest.

1455. **Hale, Nancy, 1908-1988.** *Black summer*; **a novel. Boston: Little, Brown, 1963. 312p.**

Seven-year-old Robert Kean spends the summer with an aunt and uncle in a New York suburb at the request of his parents back in Virginia. It is an unhappy experience for the sensitive Southern boy who finds these Northern Yankees superficial people who make no effort to understand him however often they talk about love, obligations, support, etc.—they do not put them into practice.

1456. **Hall, Brian, 1959- .** *The Saskiad.* **London: Decker & Warburg, 1996. 423p.**

Saskia is only 13, but she is able to keep the decrepit Upstate New York commune she lives in together. Looking for a supportive friend she picks a newcomer to her school, Jane Singh. Saskia and Jane are meshing well together when Saskia suddenly receives word from her absent father who has rarely acknowledged her existence—he wants her to go with him on a journey the whereabouts and goals he does not identify.

1457. **Hall, Charles Everett.** *Some honeymoon!* **Illustrated by Robert Gaston Herbert. New York: G. Sully, 1918. 280p.**

A Wall Street Pooh-Bah and bachelor (35 years of age), John Ryder, is more than enthralled by the beautiful Miss Mont, a passenger on the liner returning the two from Europe. They leap into marriage and then the enigmas unfold. Strangely enough Mrs. Ryder is unaware of her true name and trouble appears in the person of a Mr. White. Then Mrs. Ryder abruptly vanishes. A combing of New York and pointed inquiries disclose that there are actually two Miss Monts, sisters who have not seen or been in touch with one another since they were children.

1458. **Hall, F. Cameron.** *A country tragedy.* **New York: F. Tennyson Neely, 1898. 284p.**

The tragedy occurs in Upstate New York. A man who has led a hermit-like existence (no one knows anything about his past) is murdered. Another man, a doting father with a cherished daughter, is charged with the homicide. It is at his trial that the pertinent facts are carefully and thoroughly unveiled.

1459. **Hall, Gertrude, 1863-1961.** *The unknown quantity.* **New York: H. Holt, 1910. 300p.**

The heroine, a widow with the gentle demeanor of an Amelia Sedley (Thackeray's antithesis to Beck Sharp of 'Vanity Fair'), accompanied by her very young son, comes to New York to look into some business matters in which her late husband had an interest. She meets an array of New Yorkers of diverse occupations and economic status, and becomes especially close to her lawyer, Tracy Balsh, who falls in love with her yet has to fight against his liking for strong drink. In the process of earning her own living the widow serves as companion to her lover's eccentric mother. There is a secret in the widow's past that could cast a dark cloud over her future.

1460. **Hall, Gertrude Calvert.** *The Nowadays girls in the Adirondacks; or, The deserted bungalow on Saranac Lake.* **Illustrated by E.C. Caswell. New York: Dodd, Mead, 1915. 302p.**

A story for young adults about four girls on leave from college who make their way to a bungalow on Saranac Lake that is presumably occupied by the brother of one of the girls. However they encounter no one when they enter the dwelling. After an unsuccessful preliminary search the girls hire an experienced guide and comb the nearby forests and a mountain before they receive an answer to the mystery.

1461. **Hall, Holworthy, 1887-1936.** *The man nobody knew.* **Illus. by Clarence F. Underwood. New York: Dodd, Mead, 1919. 315p.**

With war and facial surgery behind him Henry Hilliard returned to his hometown of Syracuse, N.Y. where he had previously failed under the name of Dick Morgan. When a successful new life seemed to be opening before him, Hilliard was almost stopped by the dishonesty of his business partners. He recovered, however, and in the process found happiness with the woman he loved.

1462. **Hall, Richard Walter, 1926-1992.** *Family fictions*; a novel. New York: Viking Press, 1991. 273p.

The novel is framed in the 1930s to the 1960s. For reasons of status and a personal need to shut out an 'inferior' past, Margaret Schanberg, with her family safely settled in New Rochelle, N.Y., changes the family name to Shay. Her husband Judd is a successful businessman; she is now an active Episcopalian. Their two children, Mag and Harris, are good students. But as the years go by the Shays feel the strain of Margaret's continuing denial of the Schanberg past. Harris, a homosexual, builds up an antipathy toward his mother. Mag, married, with children, has her own family life to live. In the '60s after Judd is dead Harris and his mother do reconcile in part.

1463. **Hall, Ruth, b. 1858.** *The black gown.* Boston: Houghton, Mifflin, 1900. 318p.

Ca. 1750 in Albany, N.Y. Cornelis Sleight (a.k.a. Neal) falls in love with the pretty but insipid Eve Verbeck. Eve is attracted to the position in society that the British officer, Cecil Loveland, offers her and the two are married. Disconcerted Neal goes on a trading expedition into Indian country. Upon returning to Albany Neal learns Eve is the widow of a presumably deceased Loveland and he starts keeping company with Annetje Kierstiede. Cecil, captured by the French during the French and Indian conflict, is released and comes back to Eve. Neal realizes his true love is Annetje. The author limns a knowledgeable picture of the manners and customs of Albany's inhabitants in colonial years.

1464. ————. *A downrenter's son.* Boston: Houghton, Mifflin, 1902. 304p.

The Antirent Wars of 1839-1846 in Upstate New York are the background of this novel. The hero is the son of a farmer who is protesting the perpetual lease on the land he tills. Other very visible characters, historical and fictional, participate in the political maneuvering that ends with the substitution of fee-simple tenure for perpetual leases.

1465. ————. *The Pine Grove house.* Boston: Houghton, Mifflin, 1903. viii, 290p.

'Northwood', the scene of the novel and the location of a boarding house, The Pine Grove House, is somewhat north of New York City. The 'upper' gentry of the village tend to look down on the 'lower' classes in the town and the boarders at the shabby gentile House. Helen Loring, the 'heroine', and her mother are lodged at the House; Helen's brother, Anthony, is a less than honest speculator who makes love to Amy Grant, a wealthy spinster in the town. Amy's brother, Christopher, finds Helen an attractive, well-bred young lady. Helen's friend, Maud Talbot, is enamored of Harold Smith, another House boarder, who in turn is fascinated by Sara Joralemon, a beautiful young lady with a questionable past. This medley is resolved in the novel's final chapters when Anthony Loring dies after a carriage accident, but not before retracting a marriage proposal to Amy Grant, unmasking the Joralemons, father and daughter, and clearing the way for Harold Smith's marriage to

Maud Talbot. Christopher Grant finally takes the step of proposing to Helen Loring.

1466. **Hallworth, Joseph Bryant, b. 1872.** *Arline Valére*; **a story of life, reproduced in facsimile from the original manuscript of Joseph Hallworth, with sketches by the author. Boston: L.C. Page, 1901. 161p.**

A sentimental portrayal of the life of the poor in New York City's tenements, Arline Valére being one of those affected by the poverty all around her. An outstanding feature of the story is the many drawings by the author in the margins; evidently he has used real-life models for his pictorial representations.

1467. **Halsey, Forrest, b. 1878.** *The stain.* **With illus. by Thomas Fogarty. Chicago: F.G. Browne, 1913. 343p.**

"The heroine, Louise Gray, a young woman acting as secretary to a rising [New York] lawyer, [Robert Norris], is a kleptomaniac. In moments of intense nervous excitement or physical exhaustion she is obsessed with the desire to steal. An alienist believes the defect to be an hereditary one, but because her parentage is unknown nothing can be proved. At her trial [in the New York courts] for stealing a bracelet, it is revealed that she is the illegitimate daughter of the judge who is trying the case; [the latter] is a grafter and a thief on a big scale"—Book review digest.

1468. **Halsey, Margaret, 1910- .** *The demi-paradise*; **a Westchester diary. New York: Simon and Schuster, 1960. 216p.**

This novel purports to be the diary of Helen Fitzgibbons, a Westchester matron, who seems to be having an ideal suburban life, although she is fully aware of some of its disadvantages. The 'diary' covers only an 8-month period, but during that time Helen has a dispute with the American Legion when her friend Cynthia's great-aunt Persis is to be a speaker in its hall, but is found to be on the Legion's blacklist; the invitation to speak is rescinded, yet it is later reinstated.

1469. **Hamilton, Alice King.** *Mildred's cadet*; **or,** *Hearts and bell-buttons.* **An idyl of West Point. Philadelphia: T.B. Peterson, 1881. 302p.**

The summer romance of Mildred Ray and Cadet Stanleigh Cameron seems certain to remain just that—for Mildred has been affianced at her parents' urging to the elderly but wealthy Horatio Pemberton, while Stanleigh is about to be married to Miss 'Lil' Castle. However, when Stanleigh has a life-threatening accident at the Riding Hall of West Point, Mildred rushes to his side. Mrs. Cameron and Mildred help Stanleigh recover and the two lovers, Mildred and Stanleigh, marry.

1470. **Hamilton, Cosmo, 1872-1942.** *Who cares?*; **a story of adolescence. With illus. by Richard Culter. Boston: Little, Brown, 1919. 342p.**

After her mother remarried, Joan Ludlow, 18, was placed 'temporarily' in the home of her very strict grandparents. Joan rebels, runs off to New York City and marries Martin Gray, 24, an orphan but well heeled. Joan's credo is: 'I shall make life spin in whatever way I want it to go. My motto's going to be a good time as long as I can get it, and who cares for the price?' She refuses to live with her husband and pursues all the delights that fashionable New York circles have to offer. Gilbert Palgrave, a friend of Martin and very much in love with Joan, justly accuses her of playing the coquette who uses sex to draw men to her and then 'slams the door' on them. In due time, worn thin by her fast life, Joan returns to Martin as a dutiful wife. Martin says: 'You were so young and you had to work it off; I knew all that and waited.'

1471. **Hamilton, David Osborne. *Pale warriors*; a novel. New York: Scribner, 1929. 332p.**
A tale, with a New York City and European background, about a fascinating woman (Beatrice) without a heart who holds in thrall an army of admirers. She has few scruples when it is a matter of getting what she wants. The men who grovel at her feet do not seem to realize that they arc likely to be walked upon as Beatrice rushes to her next appointment or conquest.

Hamilton, W.J. pseud. See: Clark, Charles Dunning, 1843-1892.

1472. **Hamlin, Myra Louisa Sawyer, 1856-1927. *Nan in the city*; or, *Nan's winter with the girls*. A sequel to *Nan at Camp Chicopee*. Illustrated by L.J. Bridgman. Boston: Roberts Bros., 1897. 251p.**
Nan Ratcliffe spends a winter in Brooklyn with Mrs. Reginald Prince. Study at the famous Pratt Institute is supplemented by hours on the tennis courts and workouts at the school gym. Nan also keeps up with her violin exercises, and a wisp of romance courses through the story.

1473. ————. *A politician's daughter*. **New York: D. Appleton, 1886. 321p.**
The story opens in New England and then shifts to New York City. Miss Harcourt is well versed in the politics of the day, but is also a woman of culture, wit and tact. For a husband she claims a Boston Brahmin whom she loves, turning aside the proposal of a political ally of her father.

Hamm, Margherita Arlina, 1871-1907, joint author. *Ghetto silhouettes*. See Item #3515.

1474. **Hammock, Claude Stuart, b. 1876. *Why murder the judge?* New York: Macmillan, 1930. 223p.**
"Judge Stilwell was poisoned with prussic acid. Eight people [who had dined with him in his New York West Side apartment shortly before the homicide] had the opportunity and the means to commit the murder. The problem before Probus Throne, detective, aided by his astute Japanese butler, Nikko, was to discover the reason for the murder. The tale reaches a climax, leading to the

solution in the old mansion of Peter Van Dorn at Spuyten Duyvel"—Book review digest.

1475. **Hammond, Henrietta Hardy, 1854-1883.** *A fair philosopher*, **by Henri Daugé [pseud.] New York: G.W. Harlan, 1882. 296p.**

Drosée Alwyn, her sister Josephine ('Josephus Appleblossom'), and her father, John Alwyn, move from New York City to 'Fairvalley', a resort town in the Catskills, 'sponsored' by wealthy friends, the Fieldings. John Alwyn is a failed man of letters, but Drosée is the author of several fairly successful, serious works. Louis Seaford, after three tries, convinces young and beautiful beautiful 'Jo' Alwyn to marry him. Drosée's growing attachment to a student of the law, Wilmer Rudolph Wilmer, is interrupted when he rescues her from a fire in a local church. The sorely injured Drosée does, however, finally accept Wilmer as her future husband while recovering from her almost fatal wounds.

1476. **Hammond, William Alexander, 1828-1900.** *Doctor Grattan*; **a novel. New York: Appleton, 1885 [c1884] 417p.**

Doctor Grattan, a widower and the only physician in a small village in central New York State and a writer of novels, has a daughter, who with her sunny disposition lends a bright edge to what is essentially a rather gloomy story. A Mr. Lamar comes to town and has a home built for himself and his daughter. Lamar suffers from memories of a past that include his accusing himself of being an ex-slaver—he had translated a biography of a dealer in slaves and hallucinated that he had taken a heroic part in incidents of the slave trade. After Lamar dies in bed under rather suspicious circumstances, Dr. Grattan marries Lamar's daughter who had been left a barely adequate income by her father; it had been widely assumed that she would be an heiress with a considerable fortune. The doctor is pleased that this is not so, for he is no fortune seeker.

1477. **————.** *Mr. Oldmixon*; **a novel. New York: Appleton, 1885. 456p.**

Hammond's interest in the hereditary factor in mental disease has given rise to a story based in central New York State in which that condition plays a leading role. The chief figure in the novel is Mr. Oldmixon, a quite out-of-the ordinary elderly man who has 'second sight.' His well-educated nephew has unfortunately inherited the family's tilt toward mental illness. The heroine is Barbara Henschel, daughter of a taxidermist and one herself, who is inextricably drawn into the web of the Oldmixon family.

1478. **————.** *Robert Severne, his friends and enemies.* **A novel. Philadelphia: J.B. Lippincott, 1867. 369p.**

Bibliophile Robert Severne, an Englishman now a confirmed New Yorker, and a frequent customer of rare book dealer and chemist John Holmes, falls in love with Holmes's granddaughter, Margaret Leslie. Simultaneously he is trying to reform Sarah Tompkins, thief and habitué of the city's mean streets.

Correspondence left by Sarah's mother discloses that Sarah is Margaret's half-sister; their father, Richard, had abandoned his wife Leslie, Margaret's mother, for his mistress, Sarah's mother. Severne faces a crisis brought on by his unscrupulous lawyer, Bagley Freeling, who uses Severne's feelings of responsibility for the death of his wife, Francisca Severne. Robert Severne returns to England to face trial on a charge of murder. He is cleared when his fiancé, Margaret, chances upon a book in Holmes's collection that contains notes in the suicidal Francisca's hand; these marginal scribblings confirm her attempt to make Robert, the husband she hates, appear to be her murderer.

1479. ————. *A strong-minded woman*; or, *Two years after*. **New York: Appleton, 1885. 503p.**

Lalage Moultrie, restored to her father years after she had been kidnapped and reared by an outlaw and killer out West, is now in New York City. Engaged to the Polish nobleman Tyscovus, it is incumbent on her to educate herself to meet her lover's standards. 'Lal' is introduced to a strong women's rights group; assertive enough to act for itself, give lectures, and even found a medical college for women. But in the end Lal does not abide by its opinions; in fact, one of the women's leaders, Kate Meadows, marries Tom Burton, a Congressman—and Lal marries Tyscovus—and both defer to their spouses.

1480. **Hancock, Harris Irving, 1868-1922.** *Dick Prescott's first* [-fourth] **year at West Point … Philadelphia: Altemus Co., 1910-11. 4v. [Vol. 1] has imprint: Akron, Ohio, Saalfield Pub. Co.**

The appointments of Dick Prescott and his friend Greg Holmes to West Point are described in the author's book for boys: The high school captain of the team (1st vol. of The high school boys series), Prescott is the straight arrow type, zealous for an army career and rigidly conforming to the 'system.' Holmes is less enthusiastic, almost sending in a letter of resignation to the commandant. Both have their share of fisticuffs with yearlings or classmates on points of honor. The stock villain is Bert Dodge, a rival of Dick's since high school days; an excellent student, Dodge has a sneaky, jealous streak that ultimately leads to his (involuntarily) leaving West Point. Throughout the set the story is on hold as the author informs the reader of the customs, traditions and regulations of the United States Military Academy and aspects of the daily life of the cadets (hazing of first year men, presumably illegal, is discussed).

1480a. **Hand, Elizabeth, 1957- .** *Black light*. **New York: Harper Collins, 1999. 288p.**

An Upstate New York artists' colony and a town named 'Kamensic' are the scene of this atmospheric tale. The young heroine, 17-year-old Charlotte 'Lit' Morgan, and just about every resident of the community, is invited to a party hosted by Alex Kern, movie director and native of Kamensic; it is held in debauched Kern's stately hilltop house, 'Bolerium'. Kamensic has a past that includes an alarming number of suicides by young people and an air of menace hangs over Kern's glittering fete.

1481. Hankins, Marie Louise. *Women of New York.* **Written and illustrated by Marie Louise Hankins. New York: Marie Louise Hankins & Co., 1861. 349p.**

"The New York female is a most wonderful study for moral philosophers and readers of human nature. … And New York women go to the extreme of good or bad in whichever position they may stand. Find a more perfect specimen of her sex than a virtuous New York lady, descended perhaps from the old Knickerbocker stock.… Look then, upon the other side. Can there be a more intensely vulgar, ignorant, prejudiced, wicked and remorseless creature than a 'low' New York female?" (p. 13-15). The author then proceeds to spin 32 fictionalized tales of typical New York women, e.g.: Ruth Martin, the spiritual medium.—Maggie Brewer, the milliner's girl.—Angelina Plump, the lap-dog's mother.—Mrs. Biffles, the philanthropist.—Olive Roland, the dashing widow.—Signorina Adelina, the opera singer.—Mrs. Biddy McKay, the female vagrant.—Priscilla Wiggins, the man-hater.—Aunty Green, the old peddler woman.—Helen Bray, the ballet girl.—Lillie Bell, the female writer.—Mrs. Grampus, the boarding-house keeper.—Susan Bradley, the clergyman's wife.—Stella Risdon, the old man's darling.—Clara Collier, the disowned daughter.—Madame DeWall, the woman in black.—Madame Rand, the fortune teller.—Sophia Renville, the perfect lady.—Medora Jacobs, the confidence woman.—Miss Johannas, the bogus lady.—Julia Morris, the adventuress.

Hanley, Mr. R.J., b. 1867. See: Fane, Frances Gordon, b. 1867.

Hanna, Frances Nichols. See: Nichols, Fran.

1482. Hansen, Ron, 1947- . *Mariette in ecstasy.* **New York: E. Burlingame Books, 1991. 179p.**

The setting of this novel of spiritual fervor is the quiet, natural world of rural Upstate New York at the beginning of the 20th century. Mariette Baptiste is 17, the daughter of a local physician, when she becomes a postulant in the Convent of Our Lady of Afflictions. She impresses the nuns with her religious passion but disrupts their cloistered, regulated life of prayer and work when she goes into trances and is covered with stigmata that quickly disappear. Disbelief, envy and veneration are some of the feelings the nuns display and to which the Mother Superior and Mariette must respond.

1483. Hanyen, Jim, 1918- . *All the way home.* **Manassas, Va.: E.M. Press, 1994. 202p.**

The writer Michael Van Veldt is in his 40s when he comes back in 1975 to the town, 'Greenlea', N.Y., where part of his youth transpired. He meets and falls in love with the beautiful Inez, daughter of an imprisoned political activist. After Michael pretends concern for Inez's father, his romance with her fizzles out. A sexy real estate manipulator and another old flame next catch his fancy even while he is trying to patch things up with his ex-wife, Maria, also a Greenlea native.

Hapgood, Mrs. Hutchins, b. 1872. See: Boyce, Neith, b. 1872.

1484. **Harbaugh, Thomas Chalmers, 1849-1924.** *The hidden lodge*; or, *The little hunter of the Adirondacks*. **New York: Beadle & Adams, c1878. 15p. (in triple columns).**

Reissued in 1886 under the title: *Piney Paul, the mountain boy.* The search for a young girl kidnapped and taken to the Adirondacks to be raised by an old Indian involves the villain, Cecil Crane, his cohorts—two White woodsmen and several Indians—and Piney Paul (Paul Burleigh), the hero, who is completely at home in the Upstate New York wilderness. The heroine, known to certain Indians as Little Arrow, is actually the heir to an estate taken over by Crane and his wife. It remains for Piney Paul to rescue Cicely from the clutches of Crane (who intends to kill her) and other miscreants, which he does after narrowly escaping death himself. He kills Crane and brings Cicely back to her former home; Paul and Cicely are eventually married.

Harbaugh, Thomas Chalmers, 1849-4924. *Piney Paul, the mountain boy.* **See note under item #1484.**

1485. **Harben, William Nathaniel, 1858-1919.** *The divine event.* **New York: Harper: 1920. 357p.**

"A story of psychical phenomena. Hillery Gramling, unhappy over the death of his brother, in consultation with a medium is sent to New York's East Side to live among the poor. There he comes in contact with Lucia Lingle, a beautiful young girl who seems to be under the shadow of some awful, mysterious tragedy. He falls in love with her and is anxious to help her. He is aided by Professor Trimble, psychologist, alienist, mental scientist, who becomes deeply interested in Lucia's case. Through the mediumship of Madame DuFresne they discover the exact nature of her trouble—that her half-brother is trying to prove her insane so that he may take over her inheritance. Together they fight the thing out, encouraged always by the supernatural aid they receive through Madam DuFresne, from those on the other side of death. In the end through their combined efforts, Lucia is freed from the awful curse that has hung over her, and has the promise of happiness"—Book review digest.

Harding, John William, b. 1864. *The chorus lady.* **See Item #1177.**

1486. **Harding, John William, b. 1864.** *The City of Splendid Night.* **Front. by Carol Aus; other illus. by C. Grunwald. New York: G.W. Dillingham, 1909. 330p.**

New York is the 'City of Splendid Night.' A chief character in the story is a schoolteacher from a rural community who comes to New York looking for a different line of work. After a bout with near-starvation, from which he is delivered by an artist's model, he accepts a position as a secretary to a writer who is trying to regain the love of a former wife. The artist for whom the model poses plays an important role in the novel. A *New York Times* reviewer said of the novel: "The best things in it are the many pages of description of the varied aspects of New York City by night and by day, under various conditions of weather. These show sensibility to beauty and good descriptive power."

1487. Harding, William Harry, 1945- . *Rainbow*. New York: Holt, Rinehart & Winston, 1979. 375p.

"Rainbow Roberts is the greatest con man of the 1920s, but he's hung up on killing the father who deserted him as a kid and seemingly was responsible for the death of Rainbow's beloved Aunt Ruth. She was a card sharp like his dad and has trained the boy to go into every gambling situation with a rightful edge. … So Rainbow goes about scamming his way until 'the Biggest [Scam] of All' is planned for Saratoga Springs where Rainbow is bowled over by green-eyed Iris Winslow, who is also a con artist. … What's more, Iris' father sets Rainbow up in a superscam by pretending he can fix the races at Saratoga if Rainbow will settle a very hefty sum on him. Iris doesn't know the full extent of her alcoholic dad's deal with Rainbow and hopes that her new lover is Mr. Right. Vivid backgrounds of the wealthy, topnotch gambling scene, and a gift for crackling, right-on dialogue full of outright laughs [offer] engaging … entertainment"—Kirkus reviews.

1488. Hardy, Francis H., pseud. *To the healing of the sea*; a novel. Philadelphia: Drexel Biddle, 1900. 302p.

'Black Friday' (Sept. 24, 1869) is witness to the ruin of a New York City stockbroking firm whose chief executive suffers less than most because of a friend who comes to his aid. The former takes an ocean trip, hoping to partake of 'the healing of the sea.' On shipboard he meets a girl with whom he falls in love—his concerns with the financial markets no longer seem that important. The author aptly describes the frenzy of Wall Street speculation.

1489. Hare, Robert, 1781-1858. *Standish the Puritan*; a tale of the American Revolution, by Eldred Grayson, Esq. [pseud.] New York: Harper, 1850. 320p.

Three college friends – William Standish, George De l'Eur and Julius Caesar Snifling – go in different directions when the American Revolution breaks out. Standish achieves the rank of colonel (later brigadier general) in the Continental Army; de l'Eur remains loyal to the Crown, as does Snifling. Throughout the novel Standish, despite his strong patriotic stance, takes many risks to assure the well-being of the Tory De l'Eurs (he falls in love with Edith De l'Eur). British-occupied New York and environs are the scenes of much of the story. With his guerrilla tactics Standish gains notoriety as a harasser of the British troops there and in the Connecticut countryside. Excessive sentiment and suffering characterize the women prominent in the tale, but in the end they find happiness as do Standish and De l'Eur. However, Snifling, loyal only to his own cupidity, loses his fortune. Hare has created one unique personage in Zimri Freeborn, an impoverished Yankee, who trudges between British and American lines with his 'perpetual motion' machine strapped to his back.

1490. **Haring, Firth, 1937- .** *Greek revival.* **New York: Dutton, 1985. 350p.**

Returning to the small Upstate new York town where he had first met and loved Tina Penney, Jack Troy hopes to revive their love affair. However, both are married to others and have children to look after. When the 20-year-old drowning murder of Clarice Heard is again a news item, both Tina and Jack are aware of the guilt of Micky Kolyrion, their childhood bully, who now deals in drugs. Hugh Gardiner, Tina's lawyer husband, assumes responsibility for retrying the case. Jack and Tina must come forward to point the finger of guilt at Micky. Jack has another problem—that of identifying his real father.

1491. **Harland, Henry, 1861-1905.** *As it was written*; **a Jewish musician's story, by Sidney Luska [pseud.]. New York: Cassell, 1885. 253p.**

This occultish tale takes place entirely in New York City and recounts the strange experiences of the 'hero', Ernest Newman, a violinist, who falls in love with Veronika Pathzuol, a beautiful Jewish young woman who supports her aged uncle. When Veronika is murdered, Neuman becomes the chief suspect, but he is acquitted when brought to trial. Several years later the chance discovery of the papers of Neuman's father (who died when Neuman was two) reveal a curse that can be lifted only by Ernest's carrying out vengeance on Nicholas Pathzuol or his descendants for Nicholas's seduction of the elder Neuman's wife.

1492. ————. *Grandison Mather*; **or,** *An account of the fortunes of Mr. and Mrs. Thomas Gardiner*, **by Sidney Luska [pseud.]. New York: Cassell, 1889. 387p.**

The novel is "concerned with ... a novelist and his attempt to achieve fame. The novel has obvious autobiographical elements: Tom Gardiner uses the pseudonym of 'Grandison Mather'; he is helped by an older writer, a prominent member of the [New York] literary establishment, modeled after Stedman; Tom's wife, Rose, is a singer who completes her husband's second novel (an odd prophecy, for though Aline never did this during her husband's lifetime, she did complete his final novel, left unfinished at his death). When Tom and Rose, because of monetary troubles, move from their elegant apartment, they settle in 53 Beekman Place; and their landlord is a Mr. Grickel, a German Jew, who leads a congregation of liberal Jews called the Society for Humane Culture, clearly Harland's description of Felix Adler and the Ethical Culture Society. At the end of the novel, Tom is elected to the Authors Club, as indeed Harland was. The novel concludes on a sentimental note about the joys of marriage"—Beckson, K. Henry Harland ... p. 39.

1493. ————. *Mrs. Peixada*, **by Sidney Luska [pseud.]. New York; Cassell,**

1886. 317p.

"A young lawyer, Arthur Ripley, the only Gentile in the story is the hero. His first case is the tracking of Mrs. Peixada, a young woman of twenty-three, accused of shooting her husband and his coachman. She was acquitted on the grounds of insanity and then disappeared. The story is almost all acted in Beekman Place in New York City. A new will has been uncovered that entitles the brother of Mrs. Peixada to the estate. The central irony occurs when Ripley marries a woman named Mrs. Lehmyl, who lives in Beekman Place, and who is, in fact, Mrs. Peixada. … Again indicted, she unexpectedly pleads guilty but explains in a letter that she killed in self-defense after learning that her husband and his coachman were thieves planning a murder. On the sole basis of the letter, the charges against her are dropped, and she is freed. Ripley, ailing from the shock, is restored to health by Mrs. Peixada, and they leave New York to live in Europe"—Beckson, K. Henry Harland… p.25.

1494. —————. *My Uncle Florimond*, **by Sidney Luska [pseud.]. Boston: D. Lothrop, 1888. 198p.**

Gregory, the young hero of the story, is an orphan living with his kindly French grandmother and a cruel uncle, her brother, in Norwich. He has never seen his 'Uncle Florimond', but idealizes him anyway. When his grandmother dies Gregory comes to New York in search of Uncle Florimond; a number of Jews in the city serve as his protectors and helpmates—the author takes the opportunity to dwell on aspects of Jewish home life. In a sense this short novel is about Gregory's realization that the 'heroic' uncle (as opposed to the cruel one in Norwich) does not really measure up to the high standards Gregory had presumed he possessed.

1495. —————. *The yoke of the Thorah*, **by Sidney Luska [pseud.]. New York: Cassell, 1887. 320p.**

"Elias Bacharach, a Jewish artist, falls in love with a young Christian maiden [Christine Redwood] who charms him for a time into forgetting the teachings of Judaism. The result is a betrothal, of which Elias speaks fearfully to his uncle, the Rabbi Gedaza, who contents himself by giving the doctrines of the Thorah on intermarriage, and prophesying that this event will not transpire. The rabbi's prophecy is fulfilled; Elias is seized on his wedding day by a strange malady, which dulls his sensibilities and leaves him a prey to feelings, which cause him to forget honor and lose sight of his love for Christine. … With the recovery of his senses comes a knowledge of his loss and the dramatic ending of a novel which gives a very true picture of Jewish life [in New York City]"—Annual American catalogue.

1496. Harper, David, pseud. *The hanged men*; **a novel of suspense. New York: Dodd, Mead, 1976. 218p.**

"A former FBI agent is into 'town-taming', or 'cleaning up the messes otherwise responsible citizens have let their towns become.' Unlicensed and unauthorized, Stone works on a percentage with the certain odds that the little guys get caught while the big crooks stay free. His current assignment is to find the killers of three syndicate-linked hoods hanged along a rural road in upper New York. The Adirondack setting is as invigorating as the characterization of Stone as a tough-as-nails good guy"—Booklist.

1497. **Harper, Harry.** *File no. 115*; or, *A man of steel*. **New York: J.S. Ogilvie, 1886. 149p.**

"A detective story. On a January afternoon Harry Hastings, clerk in a jewelry establishment, received a note saying, 'You are hereby notified that on next Thursday afternoon you shall disappear from among men; you shall vanish utterly, and be known no more'. He puts himself in the hands of a brilliant detective, who shadows him on the day mentioned as far as Broadway and Grand Street, New York City, where a block in the street makes the detective lose sight of him, and when the wagons move on, his client is gone. His efforts to recover the track and the explanations of the methods and motives of the villains concerned, make up the story"—Annual American catalogue.

1498. **Harper, Karen, 1945- .** *Eden's gate*. **New York: Charter Books, 1989. 300p.**

Claire Chandon, a French actress who keeps a journal, has attached herself as a laundress to the British/colonial army during the French and Indian War in the Mohawk Valley. She attracts the ardent attentions of the American frontiersman, Ethan Trent. The two enter into a marriage of convenience. Claire is, of course, torn between two loyalties: her French compatriots and the British/Americans, their enemies. The author paints a colorful picture of New York State in the mid-18th century with its mixture of upper class Englishman, mercurial Americans, French noblemen, Dutch entrepreneurs, Germans, Scots-Irish, farmers and artisans.

1498a. **Harr, John Ensor, 1926- .** *Dark Eagle*; **a novel of Benedict Arnold and the American Revolution. New York: Viking Press, 1999. 512p.**

The author intends to capture the first six years of the Revolution with Benedict Arnold as the central character, portraying his successes as a combat commander, especially in his New York State ventures—Saratoga, etc.—and his attempt to put West Point in the hands of the British with Major John André's complicity. Arnold's later career as a British officer and his marriage to Peggy Shippen (supposedly she loved André but consented to be Arnold's wife) are recapitulated.

1499. **Harrigan, Edward, 1845-1911.** *The Mulligans*. **Illus. by L.F.A. Lorenz. New York: G.W. Dillingham, 1901. 451p.**

The Mulligans are one of those clans, be it Irish or German, that flourished in the Sixth Ward of the Lower East Side of New York City. Dan Mulligan, good natured and good-humored, cruises the barrooms, barbershops, corner groceries, policy shops, etc., of the area. The Mulligans and the Skidmore Guards participate in the patriotic celebrations that come along and Mrs.

Cordelia Mulligan exhibits the finery she brought back with her from Paris. The author has a good ear for the dialect of the time and place.

1500. Harris, Corra May White, 1869-1935. *A daughter of Adam.* **New York: Doran, 1923. 333p.**

Nancy MacPherson made the transition from rural life in 'Redfields' to the challenge of New York City. After ten years in the big town she had scored a signal success as a novelist and had become engaged to a man closely tied to the New York scene. The serious illness of her father drew Nancy back to the family farm; his death left Nancy little choice but to take charge of her inheritance and to ward off the artifices of Black Manson. She gained a new appreciation of the land and country existence, cut her ties to the city, disengaged herself from her fiancé in New York and married a local farmer.

1501. Harris, Cyril, 1891- . *The trouble at Hungerfords.* **Boston: Little, Brown, 1953. 274p.**

Near Peekskill, New York in the 1850s the Hungerford family own an ironworks and a sawmill in which are employed immigrant Irishmen who are forced to live in company housing. The new schoolteacher, John Balfe, organizes the workers and challenges the Hungerfords. Several buildings, including George Hungerford's home, are torched. George Hungerford calls for the State militia; the soldiers rout Balfe's armed laborers. When the confrontation and shootings are over, several people are dead, including young Max Hungerford, the workers are jobless and the Hungerfords' enterprise is in abeyance. Balfe, the agitator and visionary, will most likely be brought to trial; Juliet Hungerford will bear his child and Burt Hungerford will resume his laboratory experiments.

1502. ————. *Trumpets at dawn.* **New York: Scribner, 1928. 429p.**

An engrossing historical novel that covers the American Revolution from June 1775 to May 1783. It begins and ends in New York City and Long Island with occasional twists toward military campaigns in the Hudson Highlands, New Jersey and Yorktown. Sam Wyatt and his sister Kitty, supporters of the rebel cause, have a falling out with their Loyalist parents. Sam serves five years in Washington's army as an artillery officer; special missions take him back to familiar haunts in New York and vicinity. Kitty marries, without parental consent, Charles Townsend, Sam's friend and fellow officer. Sam also marries; his wife, Hannah Honeyman, is the daughter of a humble pumpmaker. The novel concludes with Sam's meeting his parents just as they, impoverished by the Revolution, are preparing to migrate to Nova Scotia.

Harris, Kathleen, pseud. See: Humphries, Adelaide.

1503. Harris, Lee. *The christening day murder.* **New York: Fawcett Gold Medal, 1993. 213p.**

'Studsburg' is another of those Upstate New York towns whose inhabitants had to be relocated when an expanded reservoir covered most of the village. A long dry spell uncovered the old Catholic church and inquisitive former nun Christine Bennett, while visiting a childhood friend, finds there the corpse of a young woman. Stirring up little interest from the local police, Chris questions older residents in the area as to the identity of the dead woman. But they too are reluctant to give out much information. Chris's boyfriend, New York Police Department Sergeant Jack Brooks gives Chris some practical help, but it is primarily Chris's own persistence and skill at sorting out what data she has been able to collect that leads to the right answers.

1504. **Harris, Leonard, 1929- .** *The Hamptons.* **New York: Simon and Schuster, 1981. 333p.**

East Hampton, Long Island, is the destination of New York's fashionable set as Labor Day weekend in 1977 arrives. The summer colony there is on tenterhooks, for it opines that Bea Fletcher, the novelist, is about to lay bare its peccadilloes. Several outsiders put in their appearance: a WASPish publisher eager to secure rights to Bea's book; a female paperback editor who throws roadblocks at competitors; and a TV performer who hopes to star in the inevitable filming of the novel. But there are also those in New York State who would like to block publication: the governor and his financial aide; and the millionaire Freddie Kohl, the cannibalistic Wall Street whiz. It is Freddie, not Bea, who is dispatched to the great beyond. A young detective who tries not to be over-awed by all the celebrities is charged with sifting the facts and fingering the murderer.

1505. **Harris, Mark, 1922- .** *Speed*; **a novel. New York: Fine, 1990. 285p.**

The novel's narrator, a stand-in for the author himself, recalls his youth in Mount Vernon, New York, near the middle of the 20th century. His younger brother, Speed, is handsome a fine athlete, intelligent and good-hearted, but all this seems discounted by a persistent, uncontrollable stutter. Thus, while the narrator enjoys the usual round of youthful activities, he feels a sense of guilt and even responsibility for his brother's handicap, especially since the family favors him over Speed—his superior in many ways. A double burden of guilt and sorrow follows the narrator into his own successful adulthood.

1506. **Harris, Miriam Coles, 1834-1925.** *Richard Vandermarck*; **a novel, by Mrs. Sidney S. Harris. New York: Scribner, 1871. 330p.**

'American Women Writers' calls this 'one of the earliest literary portraits of the Wall Street businessman hero', but actually there is little about the business world in its pages. New York City and comfortable countryside homes are the locales of the story that is chiefly concerned with the heroine and narrator, Pauline d'Estrée, and her somewhat peculiar relations with Richard Vandermarck, her uncle/guardian's junior partner in business. Richard's first proposal of marriage, almost stated as a duty, fails to bring the expected (?) response from Pauline. Six years pass; Pauline becomes her surpassingly wealthy uncle's sole heir. She hears rumors of Richard's impending marriage to Charlotte Benson—and then Richard and Pauline close the gap separating them and their union becomes a very distinct probability.

1507. ————. *The tents of wickedness.* **New York: Appleton, 1907. 474p.**

The heroine has been educated in a French convent at the request of her late mother. When she returns to New York she has little knowledge of the 'sophisticated' world and is scandalized by the 'smart set' types she meets as she steps out into society. Her father is too preoccupied with his business and entertainments to be of much use as a counselor. But she finally locates a friend among her father's associates, although she and her new found friend are occasionally separated by mutual misunderstandings. Her Catholic religion is a source of strength for the young woman.

Harris, Mrs. Sidney S. See: Harris, Miriam Coles, 1834-1925.

1508. Harrison, Bruce. *A-100; a mystery story.* **New York: Dutton, 1930. 249p.**

"Near the bodies of three murdered people in the quiet [Brooklyn] neighborhood of Cedar Street Inspector Dan Golan finds scrawled in chalk: A-100. The strange fear of a pet monkey in the shop of Professor Schmidt, one of the victims, finally gives the detective a clue in the case"—Book review digest.

1509. Harrison, Constance Cary, 1843-1930. *The Anglomaniacs.* **New York: Cassell Pub. Co., 1890. 296p.**

The Anglophiliac tendencies of certain New York society types is satirized through several characters in this novel: Mrs. Floyd Curtis, one of the 'nouveau riche' and her striking daughter, Lily Clay, who married an Englishman, was left high and dry by him, and was now making use of her own resourcefulness; a countess with bad manners and a good-for-nothing son; an impoverished, scholarly professor. Mrs. Curtis tries to persuade Lily to connect with the countess's son, but Lily, in love with professor, resists.

1510. ————. *A bachelor maid,* **by Mrs. Burton Harrison. With illus. by Irving R. Wiles. New York: Century Co., 1894. 224p.**

A comedic novel about late 19th century New York society. Rebelling against her father's championing on every occasion his choice for a son-in-law, Gordon, a rising young lawyer, Marion Irving confides in Sara Stauffer, an opportunistic women's rights advocate. Sara attempts to grab Gordon for herself, and when that fails, she induces Mr. Justice Irving, Marion's father, to marry her. Dismayed, Marion leaves home and shares living quarters with Miss Mignon Cox who has just broken off with her lover, Clifford. These two young women eventually realize that they may have acted too hastily; actually Marion has always been fond of Gordon and Mignon has never lost her affection for Clifford.

1511. ————. , *The circle of a century,* **by Mrs. Burton Harrison. New York: Century Co., 1899. 225p.**

A two-part novel. Part one takes place in 1789 in New York City, which is recovering from the Revolutionary War's ravages. Captain Laurence Hope is loved by Eve Watson, the heroine, whose aristocratic but impoverished family she serves, and by Lucilla Warriner, a rich widow. When Laurence is sorely wounded in a duel with Arnold Warriner, Lucilla's cousin, the two women hasten to his bedside to nurse him to recovery. It is then that Eve tells Lucilla that she has married humble, faithful Luke Adamson despite her continuing love for Laurence Hope. Lucilla, her path to Laurence now clear, is no longer jealous of Eve. Part two is laid in New York of 'today' (the late 1890s). The hero, Rex Adamson, is a direct descendant of Eve Watson Adamson. The Adamsons are fabulously wealthy; the Hopes and the Warriners are still struggling economically. Rex has a lukewarm relationship with Euphrosyne Warriner; his deep love is reserved for Lucy Hope and she is engaged to scapegrace Jack Warriner, Rex's friend. During the War of 1898 Jack and Euphrosyne die in Cuba (Jack saves Rex's life) and the way is open for Rex to woo Lucy. The male line of the Warriners is extinct.

1512. ————. *Good Americans,* **by Mrs. Burton Harrison. New York: Century Co., 1898. 220p.**

A novel about a young lawyer, Peter Davenant, who questions what he considers an exaggerated posture of worship before all things European that seems so common among the wealthy, leisure class of New York society at the turn of the century. Davenant marries Sybil Gwynne who has been brought up among the 'Four Hundred' and the two have the usual 'ups and downs' before they adjust to his concept of an Americanism that does not defer slavishly to alien models.

1513. ————. *The story of Helen Troy.* **By the author of** *Golden Rod, an idyll of Mount Desert.* **New York: Harper, 1881. 202p.**

A novel about 'dressing-room society' in New York City with occasional excursions to a resort town called 'Hillsdale' (Lenox, Mass.?). The beauteous and wealthy Helen Troy is the heroine. The hero, Arthur Russell, who is in love with Helen, has no money, but sets about establishing himself in the business of mining. Eventually he returns to New York and wins Helen's hand in marriage.

1514. ————. *Sweet bells out of tune.* **With illus. by C.D. Gibson. New York: Century Co., 1893. 231p.**

"Eleanor Halliday, the beautiful daughter of an old Knickerbocker family, marries for love Gerald Vernon, the only child of a wealthy widow, who hopes through the Halliday connection to gain an entrance into New York society. This wedding in a crowded fashionable New York church opens the story, which follows the career of the young couple on their bridal tour to

Florida where Eleanor's disillusion begins and she discovers that her husband is a very selfish, ordinary young man. Outside of this story is Eleanor's younger sister's love-tale and clever satirical sketches of English and American society characters"—Annual American catalogue.

1515. ————. *The unwelcome Mrs. Hatch*. **New York: D. Appleton, 1903. 191p.**
A story of New York life first related in a play performed by Minnie Madden Fiske, among others. This 'weeper' concerns a faithless husband and a wife who decides that two can play the game. In the lurid divorce that ensues Mrs. Hatch loses custody of her daughter. Twelve years later on the eve of her daughter's marriage her former husband refuses to allow Mrs. Hatch to see her daughter. A deathly illness overtakes Mrs. Hatch; her daughter, returning from her wedding trip, finally is made aware of her mother's presence and Mrs. Hatch dies in her daughter's arms.

1516. **Harrison, Henry Sydnor, 1880-1930.** *Captivating Mary Carstairs*, **by Henry Second [pseud.]. Boston: Small, Maynard, 1911. 346p.**
Separated from his wife for 12 years [New Yorker] Elbert Carstairs longs to see their child, Mary, but Mary adamantly refuses to see her father despite her mother's pleas. Mr. Carstair's young friend, Lawrence Varney, is commissioned by him to abduct Mary and bring her to New York. Varney and a friend take Carstair's yacht up the Hudson to the town where Mary lives. The two would-be kidnappers assume that Mary is a 12-year-old. She turns out to be a clever girl of eighteen. Numerous complications arise, town politics edges into the picture and Varney unfortunately bears a close resemblance to Ferris Stanhope, a novelist, who is despised by the townsfolk because of his dastardly manipulation of one of the town's innocent young girls.

1517. **Harrison, Lewis.** *Not to the swift*; **a tale of two continents [by] Lewis H. Watson (Lewis Harrison). New York: Welch, Fracker, 1891. 399p.**
Despite the subtitle New York City (with a few scenes in Washington, D.C.) is the primary locale of the novel. Two Southerners, James Cateret and his daughter Madeleine have established residence on Washington Square. Madeleine is the brainier businessperson of the two, speculating successfully on stocks with the advice of Commodore 'Vanderfelt' and James T. Dawes. Her Southern sympathies are aroused with the outbreak of the Civil War. She fails to recruit her lover, the artist Hugo Bernhard, for the Confederacy; Hugo severs any further relations with her and raises troops for the Union. Madeleine's next move is entanglement with an anti-Union Jesuit cabal and then a link-up with the conspiracies of John Wilkes Booth and Madam Surratt. She is imprisoned and upon her release embarks for Europe. Hugo marries Grace Richmond, one of Madeleine's erstwhile friends.

1518. ————. *A strange infatuation*. **New York, Chicago: Rand, McNally, 1890. 313p.**

A newly minted doctor, Frank Willian, a native New Yorker, meets the heroine at Carlsbad, Germany. She is the daughter of a Russian nobleman who is using his vast wealth to improve the lot of laboring men and women. These characters are brought together again in New York City where the arch villain of the story, Robert Weir, suddenly appears. Weir has a strange influence fueled by occultism over the heroine and that is what Dr. Willian must challenge.

1519. Hart, Frances Noyes, 1890-1943. *The Bellamy trial.* **Garden City, N.Y.: Doubleday, Page, 1927. 324p.**

"Because of the prominence of the principals in Long Island society, the Bellamy trial is the sensation of the hour. Stephen Bellamy and Susan Ives (Mrs. Patrick Ives) are accused of the murder of Stephen's wife. It is the State's contention that Patrick Ives and Madeleine Bellamy were caught in a clandestine affair and that the guilty woman was killed by the accused from motives of jealousy and revenge. Incriminating circumstances are brought out at the trial, but the defendants are their own witnesses and public sympathy is for them. The trial is over [but] there is still a surprise for the reader in the final chapter"—Book review digest.

1520. Hart, James S. *Scoop,* **by James S. Hart and Garrett D. Byrnes. Boston: Little, Brown, 1930. 310p.**

"Snakes Shiel, star reporter [on a New York newspaper] is sentenced to ten days in jail for driving his car while drunk. In prison he runs across evidence of a political scandal concerning the practices of a certain judge in dealing with pardons for convicts—a story that Shiel follows up for his paper. The campaign for reform and justice is considerably complicated when Shiel falls in love with the sister of a murderer whose freedom has just been bought"—Book review digest. "It [the novel] will appeal to young men from the provinces who want to see how life ticks in a city room"—Atlantic bookshelf.

1521. Harte, Julia Catharine Beckwith, 1796-1867. *Tonnewonte*; **or,** *The adopted son of America.* **A tale containing scenes from real life. Watertown, N.Y.: J.Q. Adams, 1824-25. 2v.**

"The action opens in New York [City] during the yellow fever scourge of the autumn of 1796, moves to France, and then back to pioneer western New York, contrasting American democratic social institutions with the injustice of European aristocratic regimes"—American historical novels (Scribner book store).

1522. Hartshorn, Nancy, pseud. *Nancy Hartshorn at Chautauqua.* **New York: J.S. Ogilvie, c1882. 212p.**

Nancy (wife of Deacon Hartshorn) relates, in dialect, her experiences at Chautauqua. She accompanies her persuasive friend Mandy Hopkins and Mr. and Mrs. Baker to the famous camp/meeting ground despite the Deacon's opposition. In Nancy Hartshorn's parlance 'Chetauquy's Ampletheater' is impressive, and after speculation about the 'C.L.S.C.' and the 'C.L.C.S.' she discovers those initials stand for the 'Chetauquy Lit'rary' and 'Sientifick Sosiety' and the 'Chetauquy Lib'ral Criticizm Sosiety'. Nancy attends Chautauqua's famous Sunday school and lectures by 'Ram Shunder Bozy'; the tent she shares with Mandy and the Bakers is flooded. She is much taken with the singing of a black choral group—but is ready after a week to return to her 'neglected' husband.

Harvester, Hiram, pseud. See: Colvin, Addison Beacher, b. 1858.

1523. **Harvey, James Neal.** *The headsman*; a novel. **New York: D.I. Fine, 1991. 372p.**
The beheading of a teenager in her bedroom in 'Braddock', N.Y., and a continuing sequence of murders there reawakened the legend of the town's 18th century executioner who presumably comes back at various intervals to carry out his gruesome tasks. Nervous town fathers, a team of pushy State investigators, and his reporter girlfriend who smells a big story hamper chief of Police Jud MacElroy in his probes. Jud enlists the aid of a troubled psychic who seemingly has the power to see through the murderer's eyes a village that does not want fearsome secrets exposed.

1524. **Harvey, Marion, 1900- .** *The house of seclusion*. **Boston: Small, Maynard, 1925. vi, 329p.**
The murder that has to be solved is that of a decidedly odd character who just happened to be very wealthy – Mr. Fielding. He was killed in his own house in New York City, a house filled with artifacts from all corners of the globe.

1525. **Hasbrouck, Louisa Seymour, b. 1883.** *At the sign of the Wild Horse*. **Illus. by Ruth King. New York: Century Co., 1930. 215p.**
Veronica Ashe's summer with her cousins in a Catskill artists' colony is filled with adventure. One caustic critic called the work 'a silly story of silly people, written for equally silly people to read.'

1526. **————.** *Those careless Kincaids*. **Illus. by Manning DeV. Lee. New York: Century Co., 1928. 248p.**
The sisters Rosemary and Delight Kincaid are summer guests (in the St. Lawrence region of Upstate New York) of a conventional hostess who is surprised by their tendency to get into scrapes. There is humor in the conversations and situations the sisters fall into; e.g., a four-year-old boy amuses them with his passion for tools, such that he takes screwdrivers as bedtime companions rather than teddy bears or the like.

Hastings, Roslyn, joint author. *Plain unvarnished murder*. **See Item #1980.**

1527. **Hatch, Eric, 1901-1973.** *A couple of quick ones*. **New York: R.M. McBride, 1928. 201p.**

Martin Jones, a young-man-about-New York City and Long Island, keeps a journal in which he records that he has inadvertently gotten himself married to a woman he never seriously intended to take as a life partner. The horrible realization comes to him while he is awakening from a sound sleep at the Pickwick Arms, in Greenwich, Conn.

1528. ————. *Five days.* Boston: Little, Brown, 1933. 285p.

His 'friend', Milton Sands, took Beadleston Preece's money and lost it all on the Stock Exchange. Preece was forced into bankruptcy, auctioning off all the articles in his Long Island mansion. On the verge of hanging himself 'Beadle' is interrupted by the burglar Swazey. These two snatch Sands' yacht and pilot it out of Hempstead Harbor, engaging in a bit of 'piracy' on Long Island Sound and vicinity. Among other activities Beadle rescues a beautiful Southern girl, daughter of a recently deceased scow captain, and gives a comeuppance of sorts to Carlotta Townsend who had in the past taken delight in putting Beadle down.

1529. ————. *Romance prescribed.* New York: Farrar & Rinehart, 1930. 280p.

"Jarnal Harvey was a young author who thought very highly of himself. In fact his sense of humor had almost died because of his own imagined importance. His publisher, Colonel Fisher, determined to change all that. As a consequence Jarnal spent a summer on the Colonel's houseboat [on Long Island Sound] and rediscovered himself, his sense of humor, and various other things and people"—Book review digest.

**Hatton, Fanny Locke, 1870?-1939, joint author. *Years of discretion.*
See Item #1530.**

1530. **Hatton, Frederic, 1879-1946. *Years of discretion*, by Frederic Hatton and Fanny Locke Hatton. Novelized from the play by the authors. With illus. by Alonzo Kimball. New York: Dodd, Mead, 1913. 349p.**

A woman of 48 who has observed the conventions characteristic of behavior in upper-class social circles in Boston decides to throw off these 'shackles.' She goes to New York and quickly draws the attention of four eligible bachelors. After she marries a 'young fellow of fifty' the wedded pair confess to one another that middle age has its compensations and that their pretense of youthfulness had been a burden.

Haubold, Herman Arthur, 1867-1931. See under his pseudonym: Trepoff, Ivan.

1531. **Haven, Alice Bradley, 1827-1863. *The Coopers*; or, *Getting under way.* New York: D. Appleton, 1858. 336p.**

Although his business activities are based in New York City Murray Cooper agrees with his wife Martha that they should find a permanent home in the Hudson River countryside. Martha receives good advice of household economy from Mrs. Henderson, the mother of Murray's business partner, Steven. Martha is also inclined to worry about her husband's overspending but by the novel's conclusion the success of the Cooper-Henderson partnership is assured, and Steven Henderson has surprised everyone with the announcement of his engagement to Lizzie Grant Cooper.

Haven, Emily Bradley Neal, 1827-1863. See: Haven, Alice Bradley, 1827-63.

1532. **Havill, Edward, 1907- . *The low road*; a novel. New York: Harper, 1944. 227p.**
"Quiet story of a young married [pioneering] couple [Clay Treman and wife Karen] living in a cabin on the shores of Keuka Lake in northern New York State. Their lives and those of their few neighbors are simple in the extreme. The book is concerned mainly with the few months just before the birth of their first son"—Book review digest.

1533. **————. *The Pinnacle*; a novel. New York: W. Sloane, 1951. 248p.**
"The setting is the the Pinnacle grape-growing region of Upstate New York; the plot is concerned with the love of two men for the same woman. Holley Mathew, returned to his father's rundown farm after the [Second World] War, lived alone, getting his food from the forests and lakes. Jim Vining, after a university education, decided to make a living on the land. Both men loved Silky Cornel. The situation was climaxed by the tragic death of Holley"— Book review digest.

1534. **————. *Tell it to the laughing stars*; a novel. New York: Harper, 1942. 325p.**
Urban life had been a 'downer' for both Steve Lanely and his wife Ellen, so they removed to a rustic dwelling on a ten-acre farm near Keuka Lake in central New York State. Steve had not made much of an impact as a commercial artist and he figured that he might regenerate his marriage and the direction of his life in the simple surroundings that he had chosen for Ellen and himself.

1535. **Hawthorne, Hildegarde, 1871?-1952. *A country interlude*; a novelette. Boston: Houghton, Mifflin, 1904. 161p.**
The heroine (Imogen) of this slight tale tells her friend Anne (who is wife to a member of Congress) in a series of letters about the pleasures of country life at Briar Rose, an old family home on the Hudson. Imogen and her mother had spent an eventful winter in New York City and find needed rest at Briar Rose. Into this pastoral scene comes a young artist who pleasantly and romantically interrupts Imogen's solitude and causes her to turn from young Bert, another of her admirers.

1536. **Hawthorne, Julian, 1846-1934. *An American Monte Cristo*. London: Butterworth, 1888. 2v.**

Keppel Darke, a New York painter, is accused of the murder of his sweetheart's [Olympia's] guardian, but escapes to Europe and coincidentally obtains a fortune from French crown jewels, whereupon he returns to New York City under the name of Count de Lisle and proceeds to unmask the real murderer and wins the hand of Olympia.

1537. ————. *An American penman*; from the diary of Inspector Byrnes. New York: Cassell, 1887. 280p.

After losing money at Monte Carlo and presumably having his Russian estates stripped away, Count Ivan Fedovsky goes to New York to begin a new life. He fails, although he loses his heart to Sallie Vanderblick, but then he entangles himself in a robbery that attracts the attention of Inspector Byrnes. The latter gives Fedovsky a secret mission to Europe to help uncover international forgers known as 'penmen.' In the course of his European venture Fedovsky learns that an old girl friend, Vera, was an accomplice of the forgers; she commits suicide and Fedovsky gets his estates back.

1538. ————. *Another's crime*; from the diary of Inspector Byrnes. New York: Cassell, 1888. 242p.

"A young man unjustly accused of a theft of twenty-five hundred dollars by a woman who had professed to love him, is the chief figure. His career is ruined by the suspicion, and he escapes from New York before the affair comes to trial. He is reported to have been lost on a vessel he sailed away in, and his sister resolves to clear his memory of the stain that rests upon it. The usual detective work follows, with Inspector Byrnes as the prime mover of events"—Annual American catalogue.

1539. ————. *Beatrix Randolph*; a story. Illustrated by Alfred Fredericks. Boston: J.R. Osgood, 1884. vii, 280p.

Beatrix Randolph, the daughter of a once-rich Virginian who had made his home just outside New York City, tries to soften the losses her father had incurred by unwise speculation; her brother is of little help, for his wasteful habits had further depleted the family's fortune. Beatrix has a singing voice of operatic quality; she starts out by impersonating a Russian prima donna who fails to show up for the performance the impresario General Moses Inigo had planned for the grand opening of his opera house in New York City. Beatrix impresses both music critics and the opera-going public. When she reveals her true identity she is embraced for the talented American original she is.

1540. ————. *A dream and a forgetting*. Chicago: Belford, Clarke, 1888. 209p.

Primarily set in the New York social world. Fairfax Boardwine, a poet and the hero, loves Mary Gault, a girl from the country. One of Mary's dreams, related to her lover, is the source of Boardwine's successful poem. He leaves Mary and goes to New York and involvement with Mrs. Cartaux, his publisher's wife. An adaptation of Boardwine's poem into a play fails and

Mrs. Cartaux dumps her erstwhile lover, Boardwine. He admits his error and returns to Mary who is waiting for him in her rural home.

1541. ————. *The great bank robbery*; from the diary of Inspector Byrnes. **New York: Cassell [1887]. iv. 235p.**

"The basis of the story is the robbery of the Manhattan Savings Institution on the corner of Broadway and Bleecker Streets, New York, which took place early in the morning of October 27, 1878. Mr. Hawthorne has thrown his imagination around the narrative, investing it with a great deal of artistic finish. A woman moving in good society is brought into the story, as a partner of the thieves, aiding them in many ways with information, etc."—Annual American catalogue.

1542. ————. *John Parmelee's curse.* **New York: Cassell, 1886. 270p.**

"John Parmelee's curse is the opium habit, contracted in the hope of finding consolation for his breaking heart, after witnessing his wife's downfall, and the utter wreck of her womanhood, from the same vice. The picture of Parmelee's home is a sad and realistic one and the figure of his little daughter, Sophie, most pathetic. The story turns on an attempt that is made to rob the bank of which Parmelee is cashier. He has been warned that the robbery is planned, and makes an honest endeavor to save the funds in his charge. His ungovernable love for opium gets him into a very suspicious tangle of circumstances that bring him to New York City and into a den of thieves and a Chinese opium joint"—Annual American catalogue.

1543. ————. *Love—or a name.* A story. **Boston: Ticknor, 1884. 304p.**

The hero, Warren Bell, hesitates as he considers his next course of action: should he marry the girl from New England that he had spent his childhood years with but has not been in contact with for a long time; or should he enter the stew of New York City politics which is rife with corruption? The author effectively sketches that sleazy political world.

1544. ————. *Section 558*: or, *The fatal letter.* **From the diary of Inspector Byrnes. New York: Cassell, 1888. 246p.**

Disguised under the fictional name, 'Maxwell Golding', Jay Gould, the crafty New York financial manipulator, is really the protagonist of Hawthorne's novel. Golding/Gould is the receiver of several anonymous letters that state he will forfeit his life unless he makes restitution to one who had lost everything when he/she had invested in one of the stockbroker's risky stock offerings. Inspector Byrnes is contacted to see whether he can identify the letter-writer, which, of course, he can, utilizing all his investigative skills.

1545. ————. *Six Cent Sam's.* **Illustrated by J. Henderson Garnsey. St. Paul, Minn.: Price-McGill Co., 1893. 332p.**

Six Cent Sam's is a "secluded and mysterious New York eating-house, where the inner man may be satisfied for six cents; the proprietor is a mysterious person, who disguises his true name, and is said to be 'a mixture of St. Paul and the Devil'. All classes meet at his restaurant—rich and poor, the ignorant and the cultured. Among the queer rules of the place is the following: 'If one guest offers to treat another and the offer is accepted, the guest is bound to entertain his host with a true story of his adventures'. Hypnotism, spiritualism and other 'isms' play conspicuous parts"—Annual American catalogue.

1546. ————. *A tragic mystery*; from the diary of Inspector Byrnes. New York: Cassell [1887]. iv, 269p.

"The first of a series of detective stories, for which Inspector Byrnes of New York will furnish the facts and Julian Hawthorne the literary workmanship. The crime upon which the detective work hinges is a murder, committed in West 26th Street, New York City. The victim is a French wine merchant. Suspicion flies backward and forward from inhabitants of New York's choicest localities to frequenters of its lowest slums. A woman is cleverly pressed into the detective service. A young engraver, sent from England on secret detective service to get at the key to a cipher used between members of secret Irish societies, is the final means of getting at the facts, which are concealed almost to the close in a most ingenious manner"—Annual American catalogue.

1547. Hawthorne, Violet. *Sweet deadly passion*. New York: Ballantine Books, 1976. 219p.

The family that resides in a Long Island mansion has a beautiful daughter, Lori, who is distraught when her husband disappears; she suspects that he has been intending all along to run away with her bitterly candid sister. The heroine in the story, Karen, listens to all comers and soon finds herself enmeshed in a situation that evolves into outright murder.

1548. Hay, Elzey, pseud. *A mere adventurer*; a novel. Philadelphia: Lippincott, 1879. 174p.

A son's venture into criminal activity and a father's unwise stock market speculations impoverish the heroine's family; she grinds out a living by teaching and other employment. She decides to exercise her literary talents in New York City; success comes to her in a newspaper office, and she falls into a number of uncommon adventures. And of course romance enters her life as she continues to meet many unusual people in a city that specializes in out-of-the-ordinary human beings.

1549. Hayes, Daniel. *Flyers*. New York: Simon and Schuster, 1996. 203p.

Gabe Riley is only fifteen, yet he has a passion for filmmaking. His mother disappeared while he was very young and his father is an alcoholic. Gabe does have a number of friends, although they might be considered rather weird. The story takes place in Upstate New York and centers around odd happenings on property belonging to one of Gabe's neighbors. The author reflects on various issues and relationships common to all readers, e.g., falling in love (he says) is "a little like getting a bad cold—sometimes the symptoms persist longer than others, but it's only a matter of time before you feel yourself again."

Hayes, Henry, pseud. See: Kirk, Ellen Warner Olney, 1842-1928.

Hays, Elinor Rice. See: Rice, Elinor.

1550. **Hazel, Harry, pseud.** *Jack Waid, the cobbler of Gotham.* **Philadelphia: A. Winch, 1856. 97p. (in double columns).**

By day Jack Waid is an honest cobbler with a shop in New York City's 'Five Points.' At night he is the gentlemanly 'Colonel Belleville', master thief. With the assistance of Cockney sailor Rob Rodney and desperate banker Thorncliffe the Colonel heists cash and jewels from Thorncliffe's bank. Virginia Thorncliffe, the banker's niece, suspects her uncle's complicity and speaks to Albert Mandeville, a clerk at the bank. Mandeville begins to investigate and turns up damning evidence against Waid and his accomplices, but the thieves are able to pin the robbery on Mandeville and he is arrested. Rob Rodney makes the mistake of spreading cash from the robbery around the city; the money is traced and eventually the real culprits are caught. Virginia Thorncliffe's testimony at Mandeville's trial clinches the case against Waid, Rodney and Thorncliffe. Virginia persuades her uncle to restore the treasure to the bank and he departs quietly for Europe. Mandeville and Virginia marry.

Hazeltine, Horace, pseud. See: Wayne, Charles Stokes, b. 1858.

1551. **Hazelton, Frank.** *The mysteries of Troy*: **founded upon incidents which have taken place in the city. Troy [N.Y.]: Troy Pub. Co., and sold at Smith's Periodical Rooms, 1847. 39p.**

Laura Lerow is a native of a village a few miles east of Troy, N.Y. who finds employment in that city as a milliner. She leaves behind a young farmer, her fiancé, George Graham. Clarence Merton, the son of rich parents (they reside in western New York State), is a clerk in the Troy firm of Wholesale, Retail & Co. Merton, a playboy who associates with a 'fast' crowd, beguiles the innocent Laura, invites her to Saratoga, seduces her and leaves Laura pregnant. When Laura shows Merton their infant son, he persuades her to move to a boardinghouse in Albany where he often visits her. In good time Clarence Merton gives up his carefree activities and marries Laura. George Graham, Laura's former sweetheart now in the employ of Clarence's father, marries Eliza Merton, Clarence's sister.

1552. **Hazzard, John Edward, 1881-1935.** *The four-flusher.* **New York: G.W. Dillingham, 1908. 190p.**

An epistolary novel—the young 'hero', a New Yorker, is trying to impress his peers, to make them believe he is really something he is not. Thus the analogy to a poker game where the 'four-flusher' is a bluffer. A woman cousin is the one who receives correspondence from him relating his triumphs and tragedies.

Hazzard, John Edward, 1881-1935. *Turn to the right.* **See Item #2457.**

1553. **Heald, Aya.** *Shadows under Whiteface*; **a novel. New York: Vantage Press, 1956. 264p.**

"Set in the Adirondack Mountains in and about Lake Placid [the novel] brings into dramatic focus the intense, innermost feelings of some of the native people of that region. … [It] reconstructs the tense story of an arrogant, heartily disliked millionaire [Eric Baxter] and his relations with the mountain and village people; [it] is the fictional account of the modern killing of a man everybody hates"—Publisher's announcement. Other characters in the story are: Colonel Cameron Fairchild, retired army officer; woodsman Jim Fawcett and his daughter Yolanda; Marie-Jo, a French-Canadian woman in love with Jim; Smoky Jo, Marie-Jo's father.

1554. **Healy, R. Austin.** *Sweetfeed.* **Manchester Center, Vt.: Marshall Jones Co., 1996. 231p.**

The demise of two women who have had ties to horse-racing at Saratoga—Claire Valova, former ballerina and social luminary, dies in New York City, while veterinarian Anne Bifford dies during a Caribbean vacation—arouses the investigative instincts of Mike Flint, formerly with the CIA and the New York City police. There is something rotten going on at Saratoga that has reverberations in the world of horseracing all the way to the Caribbean. Trainer Howard 'Sweetfeed' Thompson, 80, has sullied a fine career by feeding the animals a debilitating, even poisonous mush. Flint is only one of several private eyes snooping around; and the CIA, FBI, and the Navy have begun making inquiries.

Hearton Drille, U.S. ., pseud. See: Grey, Jeannie H.

1555. **Heberden, Mary Violet, 1906- .** *The lobster pick murder.* **New York: Published for the Crime Club by Doubleday, Doran, 1941. 273p.**

"Desmond Shannon, private detective, is six foot three, with red hair and green eyes. He speaks Arabic fluently, can lick twice his weight in a fistfight and shoots to kill in a pinch. …He wants to know who stuck a sharp instrument through the medulla oblongata of Dr. Henry Morne, a mean plastic surgeon residing at 'Kenilworth' on the Hudson. Some think it was Eleanor Morne. 'She's guilty as hell', says police chief Pierson, but Pierson is a fool. … Shannon shows him up at every turn with the help of hints from a coin, a thread of blue silk, a table of logarithms, and a white scarf. Other suspects include relatives and neighbors, some of them fascinating in more ways than one. Romance, too, but Desmond Shannon is the main show"—New York herald tribune books.

1556. ————. *They can't all be guilty*. Garden City, N.Y.: Published for the Crime Club by Doubleday, 1947. 224p.

In an Upstate New York town an innocent man has been convicted of murder. Desmond Shannon is urged to look into what appears to be an open-and-shut case. He accepts the challenge and finds himself confronted by additional killings and a communist plot. Shannon's satisfaction comes when he is able to rescue the young man from capital punishment and prove his innocence.

1557. Hecht, Daniel, 1950- . *Skull session*. New York: Viking Press, 1998. 418p.

Suffering from Tourette's syndrome, Paul Skoglund copes as best he can, supported by his father and regular doses of haloperidol. This drug, however, has a deleterious effect on his capabilities and leaves him struggling to find steady, remunerative employment. Then his Aunt Vivien asks him to work on her old house in 'Lewisboro', New York, on the Hudson, and he accepts the offer. The home has been vandalized, perhaps by some local adolescents, who have disappeared without a trace. Morgan Ford of the State Police enters the case, while Paul (still groping for self-understanding) and his girlfriend, Lia, discover several ominous facts about the house.

1558. Hedden, Worth Tuttle, 1896-1985. *Wives of High Pasture*. Garden City, N.Y.: Doubleday, Doran, 1944. 285p.

This fictional account of John Humphrey Noyes' Oneida Community in central New York State substitutes the term 'communistic Christianity' for what Noyes' group was practicing. A young English traveler gives his impressions of what is happening in 1857 as the movement gains and loses members. One young woman is especially averse to the concept of 'complex marriage' that encourages sexual freedom and she ultimately leaves.

1559. Heiman, Judith, 1935- . *The young marrieds*. New York: Simon & Schuster, 1961. 255p.

Story of the "marriage of Peggy and Ken Mosely—a marriage that began in a glow of romance and that seems, to outsiders, to be everything a marriage should be. There is an adorable child, a comfortable home (in suburban 'Hawthorne Farms' [New York]—a community of $50,000 houses), increasing success for Ken in his job. But to Peggy, once the romantic glow has worn off, life seems increasingly empty—PTA meetings, supermarkets, bridge clubs, a husband who is more and more preoccupied with business, dreary gossip with the girls. …She involves herself with a young novelist who introduces her to the excitement of his bohemian world and, walking out of her Westchester Doll's House, she begins to build a life of her own. At first her freedom is intoxicating, but once again the glow fades away"—Publisher's note.

1560. *Helen Leeson*; a peep at New York society. Philadelphia: Parry & McMillan, 1855. 367p.

Helen Leeson, a belle of upper class New York society, fully expects to marry either a member of European nobility (preferably) or at least a man from her own wealthy circle. To her utter surprise she is 'abducted' after a ball by Walter Grey and is forced to marry him when Walter's father threatens to expose the rank dishonesty of Robert Leeson, Helen's father. At first very distant from her husband, Helen gradually mellows as she hears of Walter's good works and kindnesses. Walter departs for Europe and Helen becomes aware of a deepening love for him. A rumor that Walter has died is belied when Helen and Walter meet in Switzerland. Robert Leeson sustains financial setbacks and dies in semi-repentance for his past wrongdoing. Walter and Helen Grey, at home in New York, extend gracious welcomes to beloved relatives and friends.

1561. Heller, Murray. *Placid's view.* **Fleischmanns, N.Y.: Purple Mountain Press, 1997. 179p.**

The Lake Placid region in the Adirondacks is the backdrop of this mystery that concerns a murder that is charged to a student in a local college. Mike Diamond, a faculty member, is aroused from his passive, academic 'slumbering' to activity that will disprove the charge. Assisting him in his search for the murderer are his girlfriend, Judy, and Jake, an Indian artist.

1562. Hemyng, Bracebridge, 1841-1901. *Jack Harkaway in New York*; or, *The adventures of the Travelers' Club.* **New York: Beadle & Adams, 1885. 31p. (in double columns).**

Jack Harkaway and Lord Maltravers are rivals for the love of the American, Lena Van Horsen. While in London they duel and Maltravers is wounded. The scene switches to New York where Maltravers kills his manservant, Bambino, when the latter threatens to expose Maltravers' marriage to Adele Bellefontaine. Maltravers then prepares to lead Lena to the altar, but Adele appears. In an ensuing struggle Maltravers accidentally kills Adele; he escapes the clutches of the law, nevertheless. Lena and Jack take the marriage vows.

1563. Henderson, William James, 1855-1937. *The soul of a tenor*; a romance. **Front. in color by George Gibbs. New York: Holt, 1912. 366p.**

"The need of a local habitation and a name led to the choice of the Metropolitan Opera House as the theater of scenes in the drama"—Prefatory note. The tenor, Leander Barrett (stage name: Leandro Baroni), married to the exquisite Helen Montgomery, sings with technical virtuosity, but lacks the passion and 'soul' of a true artist. It is through a love affair with Nagy Bosanska, a soprano of Hungarian gypsy origins, that Barrett (or Baroni) is gradually made aware of his shortcomings. He concludes his passionate relationship with Bosanska, but is cognizant of the debt he owes her for leading him 'to the gateway of art', and returns to his true love, Helen, whom he had neglected for so long. This is the only novel by Henderson, a music critic, and he suffuses it with the aura of the world of performing artists in grand opera.

1564. Hendryx, James Beardsley, 1880-1963. *Without gloves*. New York: Putnam, 1924. iv, 389p.

> The hero, Shirley Leonard, a former truck driver, takes the name of Mike Duffy when he turns pugilist. His New York City ring career is one of framed fights and double crosses; and when he does lose a championship fight, his manager wants to have him killed. His love affair with Dago Lottie, a shoplifting gun moll, comes to naught. Leonard/Duffy finally takes off for the North Woods and a new life in a lumber camp.

1565. Henry, Arthur, 1867-1934. *The house in the woods*. New York: A.S. Barnes, 1904. ix, 323p.

> Three people: a journalist (the 'I' of the narrative), Nancy, a businesswoman, and her companion Elizabeth—weary of the demands of New York City existence—gradually lengthen their stays in the Catskills until the narrator and Nancy decide they will take permanent residence there. And so the narrator and natives of the area build 'the house in the woods'. The former city people establish close ties with their country neighbors and their natural surroundings, and prepare to meet the demands of a rural existence.

1566. —————. *Lodgings in town*. New York: A.S. Barnes, 1905. 327p.

> The narrator of this story, a sometime poet, comes to New York City to make a living and 'do' the New York scene. Despite the attractions of the city, which are vividly described, the narrator and a helpmate decide to leave town and try the relative isolation of a Catskill farm. He continues to write and maintains ties with the people he knew in his New York boarding house. When country life begins to pall, the twosome come back to the city and then go on a tour by automobile to experience new sights and sounds.

1567. —————. *The unwritten law*; a novel. New York: A.S. Barnes, 1905. 401p.

> A German engraver and his wife living in Manhattan and Brooklyn are able through hard work to save $10,000; and after many years of marriage the couple are blessed with two daughters. Unfortunately their savings are wiped out by the failure of the bank in which they had deposited their small fortune. The family struggles for mere existence. The daughters' lives too are visited with many of the societal problems of the day. To alleviate their condition these characters turn, not to the formal law and decrees of the social order, but trust in the 'unwritten law' that derives its authority from tradition and custom.

1568. Henry, Harriet, 1897?-1974. *Jackdaw strut*. New York: Morrow, 1930. 310p.

> "The jackdaw in the story is Stephany Dale who wanted peacock feathers. She lives in New York and is determined to purchase money and position, the things that count with her. Nicky loves Stephany—but he is only a poor boy

struggling with his first novel. Then Stephany, meeting the wealthy and correct Charles, enters the society of her heart's desire. Charles, however, learns of her lowly birth; and Stephany, once more a jackdaw without feathers, goes back to work and poverty. Nicky, of course, comes along again, romance blooms, and all is well"—Book review digest.

1569. *Henry Russell*; or, *The year of Our Lord two thousand*. A novel. New York: W.H. Graham, 1846. 115p. (in double columns).

The novel deals with a communty/association in the year 2000 A.D. ("Somewhere within the limits of the State of New York ... stood the palace of the community A——") whose inhabitants live according to the utopian ideals of Charles Fourier, the French social reformer. Young members of the community: the hero Henry Russell, William Templeton, Mary St. John, Kate Templeton, and Julia Watrous, with their love affairs and adventurous hikes in the mountains (the Catskills?) and alongside wild streams, are the chief characters. The climax is a meeting in the community of worldwide kindred spirits who are moving toward the complete abolition of war and all forms of slavery and in which Henry Russell takes a leading role.

1570. Hepburn, Elizabeth Newport. *Alison Vail*. New York: Holt, 1926. 300p.

"A Southern girl [daughter of a Southern mother and a New England father] comes to New York to follow an artistic career. Her first love affair long since over, she is happy in the comradeship of Hector Trench, a fellow artist. Because Hector is poor, lame, and in his own eyes ineligible, he leaves without speaking of love to Alison when the chance comes to study abroad. Meanwhile Alison meets again the hero of her first affair, now married unhappily, and between them there springs up afresh the glamour of their early passion. The situation is difficult for all of them, husband and wife, Alison and Hector, but time resolves it into love and happiness"—Book review digest.

1571. Hepworth, George Hughes, 1833-1902. *Brown studies*; or, *Camp fires and morals*. New York: E.P. Dutton, 1895. 332p.

Clarence Fleming, almost 40, is successful, but dead tired, and unlucky in love, too. He closes up his office and takes off to the 200 acres in the Adirondacks he had purchased several years ago. Accompanied by his faithful dog, Leo, he speculates on the fate of the woman he had loved and lost, Margaret; she had married and had settled in Florida. Clarence hallucinates that Margaret's husband has died and a letter confirms the fact. Clarence heads back to New York and hunts for Margaret. His intuition tells him that she is in the Berkshires. Evidently he found her, for he writes: 'Last month Margaret and I were married.'

1572. *Her Highness*; an Adirondack romance. Boston: R.G. Badger, 1910. 309p.

In the vein of Anthony Hope's Prisoner of Zenda and George Barr McCutcheon's Graustark this novel transports Ottilie, Princess of the House of Von Hapsberg, and her secretary/companion, Hilda Von Scheller, to the Adirondacks where they are hiding from a so-called representative of the German Kaiser who presumably has given his consent to a marriage between the Princess Ottilie and a German noble she detests. The heroes are two very much look-alikes, Josiah Haskins (a writer presently staying in the cabin of the guide Bill Pickett) and Captain Henry Elsesser of the U.S. Army, attached to diplomatic missions. Josiah, Elsesser and Bill Pickett are fully engaged fighting off the would-be abductors of Ottilie, and the forests and waters of the Adirondacks are the 'battleground'. By the story's end we learn that the rather mercurial Elsesser is the spouse of Princess Ottilie and Hilda has collared the very willing Josiah for her mate. Perhaps the most realistic character in this 'romance' is the Adirondack guide, Bill Pickett, who holds to his opinion that the situation and the people in it are quite ridiculous.

1573. Herbst, Josephine, 1897-1969. *Money for love*. New York: Coward-McCann, 1929. 296pp.

The need for money governs young New Yorkers and especially Harriet Everist, or so it appears. She has loved Bruce Jones, but he ended their affair and now she is in love with Joseph Roberts and needs money so he can build a career in medicine, perhaps. Harriet is able to wheedle only $1,000 from Bruce who humiliates her. She combines the thousand with funds from an aunt and she and Joseph head for Europe.

1574. [Hern, Henry, pseud.]. *A stepmother's victim*. A true narrative of the sufferings, trials and perils of the lovely daughter of Daniel Stuart, Esq., the New York millionaire, at the hands of his second wife, who, after his death, cruelly persecuted her and finally drove her out of the house, after breading off her intended marriage. A most heart-rending incident of high life. Philadelphia: Old Franklin Pub. House, 1886. 62p.

There are actually two highly sensational narratives here. In the first Ellen Stuart, persecuted by her stepmother and the latter's two daughters, rejected by her lover, and lured to the 'Institute of Free Love' in Oneida County, N.Y., a virtual bawdyhouse, finally finds her way back to Brooklyn, destitute and quite ill. She dies before she can claim a rightful share of her father's estate. In the second story Belle Allen, daughter of pious Methodists, joins a theatrical troupe, marries a rigid, unsympathetic man who deserts her and sinks into prostitution as her stage career founders. She dies of consumption in Terry McCauley's Cremorne Mission in New York City.

1575. Hershfield, Harry, 1885-1974. *Super-city*. New York: The Elf, 1930. 364p.

The novel "gives a picture of the devout, hard-working small business man of [New York's] East Side which belongs in any portrait gallery of New York types. …Mr. Hershfield's clubmen are not convincing, but Manny Traub, the Rivington fur jobber, is as authentic as Abe the Agent. Mr. Hershfield … has used him as a peg on which to hang reflection on Jewry and Jewish life. … He has much truth to say about New York—the 'super-city' where everyone mutinies and no one deserts"—Saturday review of literature.

1576. **Herzog, Dorothy. .** *Some like it hot.* **New York: Macaulay, 1930. 248p.**
Patricia Marsen, a vibrant, 'modern' New York girl, is besieged by a bevy of young men eager to take possession of her. She goes through a couple of wild, restless experiences, but is basically 'decent' and latches onto Peter Moore, a fellow who needs some thawing out; Patricia is up to the task.

1577. **Hess, Fjeril, b. 1893.** *Shanty Brook Lodge.* **Illustrated by Ruth King. New York: Macmillan, 1937. x, 292p.**
Cornelia ("Kit") Carson joins a troop of Girl Scouts summer camping in the Adirondacks despite the qualms of her snobbish mother who believes Kit's companions are hardly her equals socially. Shanty Brook Lodge on the banks of Fallen Leaf Lake is their destination. Resourcefulness and adaptation to a natural environment are benefits derived from their experiences. Part of the troop veers off and bicycles around the youth hostel loop in New England.

1578. **Hess, Isabella Rosa, b. 1872.** *Saint Cecilia of the court.* **New York, Chicago: Revell, 1905. 212p.**
The name in the title belongs to a quick-tempered little girl who resides in a heavily populated enclave in downtown Manhattan. One of her favorite acquaintances is Jim Belway, a shoe repairman, whose friendliness touches everyone he comes in contact with. When Cecilia's brother injures his back and is sent to the hospital, Cecilia, in one of her visits, gets to know a doctor and a wealthy patient (the latter struggling to conquer his affinity for hard liquor). These two adults are instrumental in opening up new possibilities for 'Saint Cecilia.'

1579. **Hess, Leonard.** *Tomorrow's voyage.* **New York: I. Washburn, 1929. 308p.**
The novel dwells on a poor New York City family and especially on Samuel Jones who has dreams based on the ships that pull into the docks he visits. "Through the misty, sea-dreaming eyes of Samuel Jones we are presented with Hell's Kitchen as it flowered in all its pristine and fetid grossness during the dog days of Anthony Comstock. What Samuel wanted was to ride the high seas beside fragrant Amanda Stark on the good ship Venture. That demanded brawn and all Samuel had was dreams. [And what he found was] tragedy—in the guise of Carrie Sodger, the neighborhood Cleopatra"—Saturday review of literature.

1580. **Heyward, Dorothy Hartzell, 1890-1961.** *The Pulitzer Prize murders.* **New York: Farrar & Rinehart, 1932. 361p.**
A 'haunted' house on Long Island is occupied by a company of littérateurs who must face the unexpected jolt of murder in its midst. A stolen manuscript and a clock that 'stopped short … never to run again' add to the mystery. An

'over-the-hill' yet tenacious detective appears and draws on his long experience in resolving the matter.

1581. ————. *Three-a-day*. **New York: Century Co., 1930. 301p.**
"The loves and adventures of a vaudeville trio [based] primarily in New York City]: Jan, the harpist, loved by her two companions: Ricardo, a young composer who played the violin; and Tad, a rich man's son who preferred his flute and gift for entertaining to inheriting millions"—Book review digest.

1582. **Hicks, Clifton.** *The little lion*. **New York: Island Workshop Press, 1946. 256p.**
The scene is Upstate New York and Iowa, ca. 1850 to the 1870s. William and Sarah Taylor raised a goodly lot of children, the most interesting of whom was Sam, he of quite small stature, who did not let this 'handicap' impede him from entering one of the State's universities and displaying his gift for rhetoric and cultivating exquisite manners that were favorably commented upon.

Hicks, Jennie E. See under her pseudonym: Sparkle, Sophie.

1583. **[Higgins, Thomas W.]** *The Crooked Elm*; or, *Life by the wayside*. **Boston: Published for the author by Whittemore, Niles and Hall, 1857. 452p.**
The novel is played out against a background of New York City, the Hudson Valley, Saratoga Springs, Virginia, Niagara Falls, northern New York State, Europe and Quebec. New York lawyer William Hastings becomes involved in the affairs of Walter Belmonte. Fearing he will lose his inheritance from a wealthy uncle, Mr. Rivington, Belmonte has one of his confederates, Robin Moulton (a.k.a. Michael Merle or Mr. Mowbray), kidnap Flora Rivington, a child adopted by Rivington. Hastings, in love with Belmonte's wife, Cornelia, begins to wonder whether Flora is his long-lost daughter from an early marriage. Belmonte lays plans to murder Walter and Mr. Rivington at the Crooked Elm, a Hudson Valley landmark. The plot fails and Belmonte flees to New Orleans, to be heard from no more. Cornelia dies in Europe. On a trip to Niagara Falls and Quebec Hastings runs into Flora (she had been reared by Moulton who had disassociated himself from Belmonte) and acquires conclusive proof that she is indeed his daughter. Father and daughter go back to New York and Hastings marries Kate Coleman, a young woman who has been in love with him for a number of years.

1584. **Hildick, Edmund Wallace, 1925- .** *Bracknell's law*. **New York: Harper and Row, 1975. 216p.**
The Englishman Ron Bracknell and his wife Pat were residents of a typical suburb, Palmers Point, fairly near New York City. Ron was on one of his business trips when Pat found an old notebook in which her husband had outlined his rationale for murdering various individuals. Fascinated by Ron's 'diary', she begins keeping one of her own. Together the two go on a killing spree, culminating in the setting on fire of a freakish motorcycle band.

1585. Hill, Carol Denny, 1904- . *Wild.* **New York: John Day Co., 1927. 246p.**

The New York City experience of Helen Hutchinson, a small town girl who matriculates at Barnard College in Upper Manhattan—related from a diary she keeps. The academic work palls on Helen after a while, so she begins to sample the lighter offerings of the city—the night clubs/speakeasies, theaters, restaurants, studios, etc.—and surrenders herself to a young man named Carl, who seems to be the most stable of the males who cluster around her.

1586. Hill, Fowler, 1901?-1973. *Plundered host.* **New York: Dutton, 1929. 270p.**

Peter was brought up in the country, watched closely by a prissy aunt and a cold father. Their solicitude for his sexual mores and other aspects of his growth left him with little understanding of the more complex spheres of life. He progressed through college, still a perplexed young man and it was only when he moved to New York City that he began to acquire knowledge and experience that would fit him for an enigmatic world.

1587. Hill, Grace Livingston, 1865-1947. *A Chautauqua idyl.* **Boston: D. Lothrop [1887]. 102p.**

A short novel in which the author attempts to capture the spirit of the Chautauqua Movement; towards that end she makes use of the birds, flowers, fishes and squirrels as characters in her novella.

1588. ―――――. *Dawn of the morning*, **by Grace Livingston Hill Lutz. With illus. in color by Anna Whelan Betts. Philadelphia: Lippincott, 1911. 320p.**

The time and place of the novel are 1826 in New York City. Dawn Van Rensselaer, the heroine, is educated in a Quaker school. She is a meek girl who has an abiding dislike for her stepmother and stands in awe of her father. Her schooling completed Dawn is pushed towards a marriage with a man she detests. However, it comes out that he is already married, and his younger brother stands in his place before the altar with Dawn. Her eye averted Dawn does not realize who her partner is until the ceremony is over. Bullied by a resentful mother-in-law Dawn runs away. Her husband finds Dawn after months of fruitless searching and assures her a happy future.

1589. ―――――. *Ladybird.* **Philadelphia: Lippincott, 1930. 294p.**

An intelligent but artless girl from the West, in search of her mother's relatives, comes to New York City and is almost immediately thrust into sophisticated society. She copes as best she can with her new life. Fortunately she meets various individuals who are willing to help her get through complex situations, and she has rewarding connections with the people she originally came to see.

1590. ―――――. *Phoebe Dean.* **With illus. by E.L. Henry. Philadelphia: Lippincott, 1909. 330p.**

"When the fates endowed Phoebe Deane with a love of beauty and a delicate refinement that craved books and a pleasant environment, they offset their kindness by leaving her orphaned in a New York State farmhouse, a drudge dependent on the bounty of her half-brother and his sharp-tongued wife. The dismal life the young girl led here is pictured in an appealing and pathetic fashion, and when a wicked old widower, who is their neighbor, begins to persecute her with his attentions and she is made the object of false scandal to further his suit, it seems that she must marry him and lose all hope of happiness. But the man who is worthy of her rescues her at the right moment and all is well. The time of the story is 1830 and there is a vague historical background"—Book review digest.

1591. Hill, Marion, 1870-1918. *The toll of the road.* **Front. by Stockton Mulford. New York: Appleton, 1918. 321p.**

"A young village girl [Gert Hall], just twenty, is braiding her hair under the maple tree in her front yard, when she is addressed by a marvelous stranger, who proves to be a theatrical manager [from New York City] and who sees in her the ideal actress for a role in a new play he is producing. The girl refuses, but when the young man [Terry Powers] she is engaged to be married to forbids her to accept the proposition, she straightway accepts it. After a year on the road in which her views of life are considerably widened, she is forced to choose between the sweet certainties of home and motherhood and the stage and the open road. She chooses the latter, swayed by the magnetism of a man of brilliant achievement but questionable reputation"—Book review digest.

1592. Hillhouse, Mansfield Lovell, 1858-1908. *Storm King*; **a story of want and wealth. New York: G.W. Dillingham, 1895. 293p.**

"A story of today, with its scene in New York City. The hero, a struggling lawyer, is reduced to beggary, when a remarkable series of events enables him to make use of his invention of an airship; he is helped in the realization of this long-nursed project by the 'Storm King', also an inventor in this line. The latter possesses the secret of a wonderful destructive power; this, with the airship they build, is the basis of an immense future"—Annual American catalogue.

1593. Hilliard-d'Auberteuil, Michel René, 1751-1789. *Miss MacRae*; **Roman historique. A Philadelphie, [Bruxelles?]: 1784. xii, 131p.**

A novel based on the capture, murder and scalping of Jane McRae by Indians allied with the British forces; the daughter of an American patriot, she was on her way to join her fiancé, a British officer in Burgoyne's army. In 1958 a facsimile reproduction, together with a translation by Eric LaGuardia ('Miss McCrea; a novel of the American Revolution') was issued by Scholars' Facsimiles and Reprints, Gainesville, Fla.

1594. Hilton, Marian A. *The garden of girls*; **a story. New York: Tandy-Thomas**

Co., 1909. 360p.

New York City is the destination of two Southern girls who have to make a living since the small sum left them by their deceased father has dissipated. In the city they encounter the Morse girls with whom they pool their earnings and share an apartment. Sometime later they engage in poultry farming on Long Island. A newfound and influential friend is a nonconforming fellow who raises frogs for the restaurant market. One of the girls is suddenly heir to a sizeable fortune, but dies shortly thereafter leaving behind a comforting and beneficial will.

1595. **Hindus, Maurice Gerschon, 1891-1969.** *Magda.* **Garden City, N.Y.: Doubleday, 1951. 314p.**

"Mike Koziol, an immigrant from Poland, leaves the confines of Brooklyn to get his own section of land in Upstate New York. He finds and falls in love with Magda, already married. He leaves the state, establishes his farm, but returns to New York to find Magda"—Inglehart, B.F. and Mangione, A.R. The image of pluralism in American literature.

1596. **Hine, Al, 1915- .** *Brother Owl.* **Garden City, N.Y.: Doubleday, 1980. vii, 301p.**

A biographical novel about the Mohawk Joseph Brant in all his varied roles—as warrior, diplomat, translator of the Bible into Mohawk, the father who slew his own son.

1597. **Hines, Dorothy Palmer.** *No wind of healing.* **Garden City, N.Y.: Doubleday, 1946. 250p.**

"The scene of this story is a sanatorium located in a village in the Adirondacks. The chief character is a young married woman, Christina Ward, who has spent several years here and is contemplating the time when, cured at last, she must return to her husband and a different kind of life"—Book review digest. "At times the dialogue is distressingly poor. Her descriptions of scenery, however, are beautiful. The countryside and the village come to life"—Saturday review of literature.

1598. **Hinkemeyer, Michael T., 1940- .** *Lilac Night*; a novel of revenge. **New York: Crown Publishers, 1981. 306p.**

Long Island residents Jack and Carol Kenton (he's a possible candidate for the New York State governorship) are harassed by vengeance seekers: Vic Brand III, a former lover of Carol, who makes several attempts on her life; black Cleophus Watts, who lost his son to an accident involving Carol's family limousine; college and business enemies of Jack; General Twister's widow—he committed suicide after Jack revealed his corrupt practices; Ed Peters, Jack's insurance agent, who finds a nude photo of Jack and Ed's wife Pauline together—she was later run over by a truck. Ed plots to kill Carol on Lilac Night, July 4.

1599. ————. *The Order of the arrow.* **New York: T. Doherty Associates, 1990.**

313p.

"Starts out like a standard novel about a psychopathic mass murderer, here determined to kill an impending nymphomaniac for an imagined slight. This is in the Chicago area. Then said impender gets married on a moment's acquaintance, has all her itches continuously scratched, and we find ourselves on fantasy island (witchcraft island?) somewhere off Long Island. But the psychopath has not given up his passions, and our sated nympho has still the odd brain cell to wonder if she has gone from the frying pan into the fires of hell"—Armchair detective.

1600. Hinman, Walter N. *Under the maples*; a story of village life. Chicago, New York: Belford, Clarke, 1888. 299p.

'Mapleville' in north central New York State is the hometown of several village 'characters' and two young men, Ira Davies and Arthur Huntington, both of whom must make their own way in life—Arthur when his father, the Colonel, fails in business, and Ira, who buries his grandmother Aunty Davies, and is entrusted with the care of Babe, daughter of a touring actress, Dora Fielding. Arthur studies law and enters the political arena; Ira matriculates slowly through medical school and returns to Mapleville to open a practice. Wrongly accused of arson, Ira escapes to New York and uncovers secrets relating to Babe's now deceased mother. At the novel's end Ira marries Babe Fielding while Arthur weds Laura Warren of Mapleville.

1601. Hirsch, Lee, 1881- . *Murder steals the show*. New York: F. Fell, 1946. 299p.

The murder of Mrs. Radcliffe Lewes at the local ('Woodlyn Park', New York) playhouse as she was about to star in the play, 'His Lordship's Love Affair', brings Detective Sergeant Jack Keff to the scene. Keff is no great shakes as an investigator, but he knows enough to ask Dr. Richard Bart of the State mental asylum and a talented criminologist, for assistance. It is Bart who issues the final report in the case and points to the murderer. Keff is the story's narrator; his half-literate account has a piquant flavor.

1602. Hirschfeld, Burt, 1923- . *Fire Island*. New York: Avon Books, 1970. 509p.

An unhappy group of people—two married couples and two unmarried men—take a house for the summer on Fire Island, the popular resort lying off the southern shore of Long Island. One of the married men is more interested in money and his own wants than in caring for wife and children with tragic consequences; the other three men include an abject failure, a murderer (for financial gain) and a 'ladies' man' who outwardly exudes bravado but is inwardly insecure. One summer follows another and the desperate search for pleasure goes on and on.

1603. ————. *Return to Fire Island*. New York: Avon Books, 1984. 304p.

The novel features the same characters that appeared in the author's earlier 'Fire Island.' They are cynical and acrimonious as ever, ashamed of their dissipations and unfaithfulnesses but loathe to give them up. One of them,

Nick, a former professional football player, in love with the daughter of an early Fire Island settler is well aware of his limited talents and abandons his dream of sports broadcasting. There are other characters outside the circle of the worldly, indulgent sophisticates—e.g., a mother and daughter who reach an accommodation and a husband and wife who are attempting to patch up a crumbling marriage.

1604. Hitchcock, Jane Stanton. *Trick of the eye.* **New York: Dutton, 1992. 275p.**
Faith Cromwell, 39, unmarried, a painter of fine detail, is commissioned by Frances Griffin, a very rich art collector, to redo the ballroom of The Haven, Griffin's mansion on the North Shore of Long Island. The widow tells Faith that the ballroom was specially built for her daughter Cassandra's social debut. Cassandra had been murdered (stabbed) 15 years ago, not long after her marriage. Obsessed by the unsolved crime even as she starts to paint, Faith and her friend Harry Pitt decide to take a crack at unraveling it.

1605. Hobhouse, Adam. *The hangover murders.* **New York: Knopf, 1935. 238p.**
The alcohol-soaked, hangover atmosphere of a wild party the morning after at a Long Island locale is privy to a murder of one of the guests—followed by two more homicides and a suicide. Danny Harrison weaves his way through a passel of sodden characters to arrive at a solution to the crimes.

1606. Hobson, Laura Z., 1900-1986. *First papers.* **New York: Random House, 1964. 502p.**
Two families, one Jewish, the other WASPish Unitarian, mingle on Long Island shortly before and during the First World War. Stefan Ivarin, a teacher and editor of the Jewish News, his wife Alexandra, and their children Eli and Fran, and Evander Paige, a lawyer, are the chief characters. With their liberal and radical ideas the Jewish group, and to a lesser extent, Paige, suffer harassment from the community's mainstream.

1607. Hodges, Arthur, 1868-1949. *The bounder*; a vulgar tale. **Boston: Houghton Mifflin, 1919. 450p.**
"Pictures certain phases of New York life largely bohemian. Most of the characters live in the Kilkenny, a mediocre apartment house which seems to be located in or near the Broadway theater district. Fred Filbert, the 'bounder', son of a country lawyer, has spent four years at a coeducational college in the Middle West 'cramming a variety of undigested facts which were promptly forgotten, playing on the college baseball team, getting drunk at times, and pursuing those students of the other sex who were reputed to be of easy virtue.' He comes to New York, gets into journalism, and writes two mediocre novels. Selfish, ignorant and thick-skinned, he nevertheless manages to appeal to 'the beautiful and mysterious' Dora St. David who lives at the Kilkenny"—Book review digest.

1608. ————. *The essential thing.* **Front. by Harrison Fisher. New York: Dodd,**

Mead, 1912. 379p.

Money is the fuel that drives New York society. Geoffrey Hunter's fiancée tells him that 'the one essential thing in life to people who have money is money.' When Geoffrey's funds disappear, she turns him away. He finds a means of recouping his losses, and it is then that he appreciates the other woman who stood by him, and he marries her.

1609. ———. *Pincus Hook*. **With illus. by Frederic R. Gruger. Boston: Small, Maynard, 1916. 438p.**

The Sixth Avenue art dealer, Pincus Hook, hoped to bring gifted artists to the attention of the public, especially to that part of it that had the money and the time to think seriously of sponsoring these gifted creators of art. He knew Claudine Molitor, a rich young Fifth Avenue resident, and he knew Chris, a struggling artist—and he was largely responsible for introducing them to one another and watching the growth of an intimate relationship.

1610. **Hoffman, Alice, 1952- .** *Angel Landing*. **New York: Putnam, 1980. 220p.**

Minnie Lansky, 74, a vegetarian, runs a boarding house in 'Fisher Cove', Long Island; the Cove is no longer a fashionable address for vacationers or residents. When a nuclear power plant on the Island is blown up, Minnie finds herself involved with three perplexed young people: Natalie, her niece, is a dissatisfied social worker; Carter Sugarland, Natalie's boyfriend, is completely caught up in 'Soft Skies', his anti-nuclear movement; Michael Finn, a welder responsible for the destruction of the plant, has withdrawn from human intercourse. Natalie takes the frustrated Michael in hand, acting as his therapist and weighing the possibility of falling in love with him.

1611. ———. *The drowning season*. **New York: Dutton, 1979. 212p.**

In this novel "the grandmother, called Esther the White, has chosen to live cut off from the dangers and joys of normal human experience; she rules over a clannish family in a secluded compound on Long Island. Every July and August her son Phillip tries to kill himself by walking into the water, and these months have become known as 'the drowning season.' This summer his daughter, Esther the Black, has just turned eighteen and is exploring her first chance to flee from her hated and hating grandmother and from the strange world of the compound"—Publisher's note.

1611a. ———. *Local girls*. **New York: Putnam, 1999. 197p.**

The fifteen stories in Hoffman's book look at the discordant lives of several young Long Islanders; Gretel Samuelson whose Jewish parents have gone through a divorce brings them into focus. Gretel's brother Jason has taken a dead-end job at the local food market and shoots up heroin even though a Harvard education had been a possibility for him. Her own brushes with delinquency are countered by Gretel's attention to the needs of her beloved, cancer-stricken mother and the support of her cousin Margot Molinaro and best friend Jill Harrington. These young suburban women are able to overcome the crises in their lives and find solace in their natural surroundings.

1612. ————. *Seventh heaven.* **New York: Putnam, 1990. 256p.**
A housing development on Long Island in 1959-1960, where the residents seem to be happy and secure, is the setting for the novel. About the time the plucky, recently divorced Nora Silk, with her sons Billy and baby James, moves in, things start to change. Many of the housewives resent the presence of the sexy, self-assured Nora, and the façade of solid family life erodes. In the long run Nora, upbeat despite the cul-de-sac she may be in, becomes a healing presence.

1613. **[Hoffman, Charles Fenno] 1806-1884.** *Greyslaer*; **a romance of the Mohawk. By the author of** *A winter in the West* **... New York: Harper, 1840. 2v.**
"The scene is the Mohawk Valley at the time of the Revolution. ...The hero, Max Greyslaer is a patriot agitator who falls in love with Alida De Roos, but they cannot marry until the shame of a secret (but, as it turns out, invalid) marriage has been cleared from her name"—Benet's reader's encyclopedia of American literature. Sir William Johnson appears in the novel.

1614. **Hoffman, Mary Jane.** *Felix Kent*; **or,** *The new neighbors.* **New York: P. O'Shea, 1871. 430p.**
"'Tasso' was a pleasant little village in the central part of New York, surrounded on all sides by high ranges of hills" (p.[7]). The next town is 'Livy'; obviously we are in that part of New York State that features places with classical/Italianate names. Felix Kent, stripped of his money by Homer Spafford, his daughter Florence's husband, occupies the farm left to his second (deceased) wife by her father. Living with him are his children, Clara, Leo, a medical student, and Florence and her two children, Theodore and Frank. Michael Bryan, a neighboring farmer whom Kent had saved from addiction to alcohol, is a constant friend and advisor. A railroad accident injures Leo Kent and George, Michael's son; a Mr. Milton is critically injured. Milton's real identity?—Homer Spafford. On his deathbed Homer asks forgiveness and leaves his estate to Florence and sons. Most of the novel's characters depend on their Catholic faith to sustain them.

1615. **Hoffman, Paul.** *Seven yesterdays.* **New York: Harper, 1933. 226p.**
Semi-autobiographical novel about boyhood and adolescence in the Upstate New York city of 'Naples' in 'Mohican Country' during the years 1910-1930. The family of the main character is a German Protestant one. "With its picture of German-American characters and traditions and its simple sincerity, Hoffman's novel has, in the words of an admiring New York Times reviewer, 'a quality of wistful charm and sensitivity rare in contemporary writings'"— O'Donnell, T.F. Oneida County: literary highlights <u>in</u> Upstate literature. Syracuse, 1985.

1616. Holden, Jonathan, 1941- . *Brilliant kids.* **Salt Lake City: University of Utah Press, 1992. 178p.**

Running away from bad debts, narrator Tom Jenkins, a bridge hustler, ends up in the western New York village of 'Powawathia' in 1959. He gets a bridge game going (for stakes, of course), teaming up with Charlotte Griller; she must have money for treatment of her brother Danny who has polio. Other people on stage are: Dr. Norbert Bell, a dispenser of practical, pastoral advice à la Norman Vincent Peale; his daughter Linda, in need of an abortion; Will Baxter, professor of philosophy and religion. The bridge game is occasionally interrupted by Tom's elucidation of bridge hands and the doctor's philosophical musings.

1617. Holding, Elisabeth Sanxay, 1889-1955. *Angelica.* **New York: Doran, 1921. 289p.**

"Beauty and a passion to make something of herself were Angelica's assets; her drawbacks were dire poverty and a street gamin education [she had been brought up in New York City tenements]. She finds her way into a rich household where one of the two sons, Eddie, is a successful businessman and a correct prig: the other, Vincent, a poet, dissolute, irresponsible and emotionally unbalanced. Eddie sets about to improve Angelica's mind and manners with a view to marrying her, but Vincent takes her by storm. They have a wild week together and Angelica returns to her janitress mother to become a mother herself. The rest of the story shows us Angelica, on the one hand fiercely determined to live down her past and coldly calculating to marry Eddie and become mistress of the big house; on the other, still hopelessly exposed to Vincent's power over her. Even after his death on a transport his face haunts her and impels her to the abject confession on her wedding day which puts an end to her dreams of success"—Book review digest.

1618. ————. *The death wish.* **New York: Dodd, Mead, 1934. 279p.**

The police of a Long Island suburb at first call the death of a long-suffering husband's wife an accident, but change their minds. Another husband has the selfsame wish to dispose of his wife nefariously. Before the case is closed there are several more unexpected entanglements.

1619. ————. *The girl who had to die.* **New York: Dodd, Mead, 1940. 200p.**

The scene of most of this novel is Long Island. Jocelyn Frey is a twisted and neurotic girl who tells John Killian that she fully expects to be murdered. Killian is torn between love and hate for Jocelyn; he really doesn't know whether she is incredibly evil or that he has behaved badly towards her. When her body turns up on the sands of Long Island, it is a matter of conjecture whether she is actually a murder victim. Certainly Killian had been under her influence, as had several other men.

1620. ————. *Kill joy.* **New York: Duell, Sloan & Pearce, 1942. 281p.**

Also published as: *Murder is a kill-joy* (New York: Dell, 1946.)

"Maggie MacGowan has taken a commercial course in high school and wants to be a private secretary instead of a maid in Mrs. Mayfield's house in New York. When Miss Dolly, Mrs. Mayfield's niece, says that she is writing a book and asks Maggie to help her with the typing, Maggie goes with her to a pretty unpleasant house on a tidal creek near Long Island Sound. Horror and humor are delicately mixed in this fine mystery"—New Yorker.

1621. ————. *The old battle-ax.* **New York: Simon and Schuster, 1943. 247p.**
Mrs. Harriott's sister, from whom she had been separated for 25 years, returns from France. Mrs. Harriott, a widow with a Long Island address, is rather dismayed by the changes she observes in her sister's appearance and behavior. She does not have long to reflect on them, however, for her sibling is murdered that very night. The motive for the murder is left for the reader to determine; it does not have anything to do with sabotage as Lizzie Bascom, a local seamstress, supposes.

1622. ————. *Rosaleen among the artists.* **New York: Doran, 1921. 290p.**
"Rosaleen is a poor orphan who aspires to be an artist but whose qualities of heart far outweigh both her talent and her intellect. Nick Landry, socially from another world, divines her true character and falls in love with her at first sight. They drift apart and Rosaleen is thrown among [New York] artists where she resists the attentions of a distinguished painter, but marries him out of pity when he is poor and threatened with blindness. With intense loyalty and benevolence she endures her abject poverty, his ingratitude and abuse, until he casts her from him in a fit of passion. Rosaleen's genius for self-effacement, sacrifice and resignation then devotes itself to a married sister and her family, and she is a worn-out, discouraged and dejected woman of thirty when at last she is free to marry Nick. This eventuality the always-devoted friend now faces halfheartedly, while fierce determination is born in Rosaleen to assert herself. She has found a new power"—Book review digest.

1623. ————. *The shoals of honour.* **New York: Dutton, 1926. 330p.**
Basil Hazeltine was a well-bred New Yorker who lived by his wits and his personality. He had no money and quite often had to ask for a loan from his cousin Lewis. There was a Mrs. Huested who was quite taken with him, plied him with gifts and hoped to draw him into marriage. Things were looking up for Basil, but there was omnipresent his love for the girl, Jocelyn, and in the final analysis he just could not give in to Mrs. Huested's entreaties. He saw the opportunity to turn his life around, with Jocelyn's love as his support and encourager.

1624. ————. *The silk purse.* **New York: Dutton, 1928. vi, 362p.**
Archie Grier, back in New York after six years in South America and Jamaica, is not sure that the girl he loved, Kathie, is still available. His conjectures are still up in the air when he is trapped into marriage with Anthea, Kathie's cousin, a shallow, flapper-like girl without a serious thought

in her head. And so this nice, polite young man is left with a wife he does not love and the fleeting hope that Kathie is still waiting.

1625. ———. *The unfinished crime.* **New York: Dodd, Mead, 1935. 249p.**
Surprisingly, when a murder is carried out in a suburban town near New York City, the individuals who should be showing the most solicitude are the very ones who fail to tell the police about it or even put in a call for an investigator. It does come out in the end, however, and those who do look further uncover blackmail, a curious scrap of paper and a smidgen of love.

1626. ———. *The unlit lamp*; **a study of inter-actions. New York: Dutton, 1922. vi, 334p.**
"In the first part of the story one follows the transition of Claudine from the happy and intellectually stimulating Mason family home on Staten Island to be the bride of Gilbert Vincelle in his Brooklyn home, where his mother rules in a hopelessly arid mental and social world. Gilbert is stupidly selfish; that Claudine manages to continue as his wife is testimony to the comparative indestructibility of marriage, even though the cement holding them together eventually is the natural one—children. Andree, the first born, a girl of unusual temperament, grows up in the uninspiring atmosphere of the Vincelle family and herself marries surprisingly over the violent objections of her parents; and the second half of the novel is devoted to getting this couple through the difficulties of individual adjustment to each other"—Literary review of the New York evening post.

1627. Holland, Isabelle, 1920- . *Counterpoint.* **New York: Rawson, Wade Publishers, 1980. 295p.**
Kate Malory takes a leave from her job as senior editor at a New York publishing firm to help in the supervision of her sister's unruly children in a Westchester village. Kate's sister is a wasted, almost useless person whose husband, presently absent on a business trip, was formerly Kate's lover.

1628. ———. *Flight of the archangel.* **Garden City, N.Y.: Doubleday, 1985. 321p.**
The story features "the past and present unsavory goings-on in a hideous Upstate New York mansion: three murders; a missing sibling and a muddled marriage; rumors and scattered facts about drug dealing; and a puzzle involving three cats. Young journalist Kit Maitland, separated from abusive, alcoholic husband Simon—a cousin of Kit's beloved half-brother Joris, missing and long assumed dead—is assigned to some snooping in the Van Reider mansion of 'Rivercrest', which the Episcopal Church is about to sell to an unknown guru. A corpse, a bludgeoned boy, and a ginger cat will eventually link with other murders, and at the close some kin are violently (and fantastically) reunited"—Kirkus reviews.

1629. ———. *Tower Abbey*; **a novel of suspense. New York: Rawson Associates Publishers, 1978. 345p.**

"Diana Egremont is seeing things—specifically, the ghost of a nonexistent twin—so she convinces old acquaintance Candida Brown to stay with her in Tower Abbey, Westchester County. Candida … doesn't believe in ghosts and assumes Diana's flakiness comes from her drinking problem—until she too feels the uncanny chill in a certain bedroom, is pushed down a disused staircase by unseen hands, and is almost done to death twice by hallucination"—Kirkus reviews. Other people show up—e.g., Diana's young son James; Simon, an Episcopal priest, an old flame of Candida's; and old friend Eric who warns her against Simon. Buried treasure and newly discovered murders and exorcisms add to the stew.

1630. Holland, Josiah Gilbert, 1819-1881. *Nicholas Minturn*; a study in a story. **New York: Scribner, Armstrong, 1877. 418p.**

Dissatisfied with the quiet life at his estate at 'Ottercliff' in the Hudson Highlands, Nicholas Minturn goes on an aborted ocean voyage where he meets the love of his life, the crippled Miss Larkin and her guardian, Mr. Benson, a banker. After a heroic performance in saving passengers from a sinking vessel, Nicholas settles in New York City; he broaches a radical plan for ridding the city of 'pauperism', but is rebuffed by the philanthropists, the clergy and those whose jobs depend on their overseeing the poor. Meanwhile Benson is in desperate financial straits, his debts are overwhelming, he has wrongfully taken possession of bonds that are Nicholas's property, and his bank is on the verge of collapse. Nicholas whisks Miss Larkin away from Benson's guardianship. She shows signs of recovery from her lameness. Our hero pursues his own plan for relieving the hardships of the poor with some success and becomes engaged to Miss Larkin. Benson takes his own life, but makes it look like murder; in so doing he ensnares 'Captain Hank', the ruffian who had turned the bonds he had stolen from Nicholas over to Benson. Hank is executed for murder. The novel ends on a happy note for Nicholas and Miss Larkin and their friends.

1631. Holland, Norman Norwood, 1927- . *A death in a Delphi seminar*; a postmoden mystery. **Albany: State University of New York Press, 1995. 334p.**

Police detective Lieutenant Justin Rhodes investigates the death of Trish Hassler, a graduate student at a Buffalo, New York university who had been attending a seminar led by Professor Norman Holland. Trish, an argumentative, offensive person, was much disliked and one or more of her fellow students may be responsible for her untimely end. Rhodes asks Holland to analyze his students' compositions for clues and to trail, alone, a covert intruder. There are more student deaths before the case is closed satisfactorily. The author uses various documents as a device for laying out the story.

1632. Holland, Rupert Sargent, 1878-1952. *The Boy Scouts of Snow-Shoe Lodge.* **With illus. by Will Thomson. Philadelphia: Lippincott, 1915. 293p.**

This novel is intrinsically aimed at teen-age boys; it describes the activities of a midwinter camping expedition of a troop of Boy Scouts. They utilize lean-tos and cabins on the edge of an Adirondack lake and skate, sled, make good use of snowhoes and generally learn much about the wildlife in the vast forest regions, lessons the reader too can handily absorb.

1633. Holley, Marietta, 1836-1926. *Miss Richard's boy and other stories.* **Hartford, Conn.: American Pub. Co., 1883. 410p.**

In these New York State stories the protagonists are most often young women on their own, working as schoolteachers, dressmakers, music teachers, maids, etc. These women receive little encouragement from the men around them, so they depend on their own intellectual resources and will. Contents: Miss Richard's boy.—The outcast.—The deserted wives.—Mrs. Wingate's charity.—The Dorcas Society.—Belinda, Caroline, and Henrietta.—Little Christie's will.—John's wife.—The plain Miss Page.—Kate's wedding gift.—Kitty Ross.—A woman's heart.—Katy Avenal.

1634. ————. *My opinions and Betsey Bobbet's.* **Designed as a beacon light to guide women to life, liberty and the pursuit of happiness, but which may be read by members of the sterner sect without injury to themselves or the book. By Josiah Allen's wife [pseud.]. Hartford: American Pub. Co., 1873. 432p.**

"In a series of episodes taken from country life, local characters are introduced and developed, most notably members of Samantha's family and Betsey Bobbet. The novel chronicles the events that eddy around Samantha [Allen]: quiltings, church meetings, visiting and the Fourth of July in 'Jonesville'. The book also describes Samantha's trip into New York City, where her country manners are set against the genteel sophistication of city folk. She meets Elizabeth Cady Stanton, Victoria Woodhull, Henry Ward Beecher, Susan B. Anthony, U.S. Grant, Schuyler Colfax and Horace Greeley"—Winter, K.H. Marietta Holley.

1635. ————. *My wayward pardner*; or, *My trials with Josiah, America, the Widow Bump, and etcetery*, **by Josiah Allen's wife (Marietta Holley). Illus. by True W. Williams. Hartford, Conn.: American Pub. Co., 1880. xvi, 490p.**

Samantha Allen worries about her husband's attentions toward the Widow Bump, his get-rich schemes that entail renting out a presently unused cottage and taking in summer boarders, and his determination to attend any 'pleasure exertion' that hoves into view. She has long discussions with Caleb (or Kellup) Cobb, the tightfisted undertaker who assumes that all the unattached (and attached) women in the Upstate New York village of 'Jonesville' are pining away with love for him. The Mormon, Elder Judas Wart, suggests to Samantha that she become his second wife, thus inciting her to a long diatribe anent polygamy and Mormonism. Samantha defends women at every opportunity, but she still defers to the mercurial Josiah on occasion and is delighted to be his helpmate.

1636. ————. *Samantha among the brethren.* By Josiah Allen's wife (Marietta Holley). New York: Funk & Wagnalls, 1890. xiv, 437p.

> Samantha argues the right of women to fully participate at church conferences despite Josiah Allen's objections. A subplot portrays a spinster and a missionary who fall in love, but almost lose one another because of their churchly commitments. Samantha also attacks literal interpretation of the Scriptures.

1637. ————. *Samantha at Coney Island and a thousand other islands,* by Josiah Allen's wife (Marietta Holley). New York: Christian Herald, 1911. xiv, 349p.

> Samantha pursues Josiah to Coney Island, which she judges unfavorably when put up against the sights of the St. Lawrence River's Thousand Islands. Coney Island has gone through a fire and Samantha mentions this, but her real interest still centers on the Thousand Islands.

1638. ————. *Samantha at Saratoga*; or, *Flirtin' with fashion*, by Josiah Allen's wife (Marietta Holley). Illustrated by Frederick Opper. Philadelphia: Hubbard Bros., 1887. 561p.

> This novel is one "most concerned with the so-called fashionable world [and] abounds with women whose gentility is the target of Holley's humor"—Morris, L.A. Women humorists in nineteenth century America. As vacationers at the resort both Samantha and Josiah dress in their own unique styles that are at variance with those of other vacationers who take the path of fashionable excess. Also published with the subtitle: Racing after fashion.

1639. ————. *Samantha vs. Josiah*; being the story of the borrowed automobile and what became of it. Illus. by Bart Haley. New York: Funk & Wagnalls, 1906. 395p.

> "The cautious Josiah begins by hitching his old mare to the borrowed auto, thus combining to his satisfaction 'fashion and safety', but later he becomes more reckless and he and his wife meet with many characteristic adventures. A large part of the book is taken up with lively argument in which Josiah, by powerful and amazing reasoning, wholly masculine, attempts to refute certain instances of spiritual manifestation brought forward by his wife, who has developed a sudden and alarming belief in ghosts"—Book review digest.

1640. ————. *Sweet Cicely*; or, *Josiah Allen as politician*, by Josiah Allen's wife (Marietta Holley). New York: Funk & Wagnalls, 1885. ix, 381p.

> Josiah's niece, Cicely, marries Paul Slide—He is an alcoholic and dies a drunkard. Samantha and Josiah then care for her and her son. Josiah decides to run for the U.S. Senate, which impels Samantha to go to Washington where she interviews several prominent politicians (including President Chester A. Arthur). Josiah thinks better of his plan and Samantha is back in 'Jonesville.' Cicely's health declines and she dies, leaving Paul, Jr. behind. Paul follows soon after, a victim of scarlet fever—his mother had feared that like his father Paul would turn to strong drink. The novel proved popular with supporters of

temperance and with readers who cherished Holley's rustic humor, domesticity and sentimentalism.

1641. ─────. *The Widder Doodle's courtship and other sketches*, **by Josiah Allen's wife. New York: J.S. Ogilvie, 1890. 175p.**

> Short stories featuring the 'Jonesville' folks who appeared frequently in Holley's other books. Contents: The Widder Doodle's courtship.—A pleasure exertion.—How we took in summer boarders.—The sufferens of Nathan Spooner.—The Widder Doodle as a comforter.—Betsey Bobbet: her poem.—Deacon Slimpsey's mournful forebodings.—Borrowing 'Peterson'.—Melankton Spicer'ses wife.—How the Bamberses borrowed Josiah.—What came of borrowin' Josiah.—A nite of trubbles.—The surprize party.—Tirzah Ann's summer trip.—The Jonesville quire.

1642. Holmes, A.M. *The end of Alice.* **New York: Scribner, 1995. 271p.**

> The narrator is a pedophile who has spent 23 years in Sing Sing and has recently been the recipient of letters from an unnamed 18-year-old girl. The latter is in Scarsdale for the summer with her unfeeling parents; at low ebb yet defiant, on the verge of adulthood, she seduces a 12-year-old boy who lives nearby. Her erotic obsessions are filtered through the prisoner's febrile mind and reverberate through his own carnality. Her letters also bring back memories of his sexually abusive mother and his killing of 12-year-old Alice Summerfield who, as he tells it, lured him into sexual intimacy.

1643. Holmes, Mary Jane Hawes, 1825-1907. *Cousin Maude, and Rosamond.* **New York: Carleton, 1864. 374p.**

> 'Cousin Maude' takes up 234p.; 'Rosamond' and other pieces, with which we are not concerned, the remaining pages. 'Cousin Maude' has for its locale 'Laurel Hill', the home of penurious Dr. Kennedy, and is a little south of the Finger Lakes town of Canandaigua. The doctor, a widower with a daughter, Nellie, remarries; his second wife is Matilda Remington who already has a child, Maude. The union is an unhappy one; Matilda bears Dr. Kennedy one child, Louis, a crippled but intelligent boy. Maude is 16 when her mother dies. Two young men from the Rochester area appear in Laurel Hill, James and 'J.C.' De Vere. J.C. is engaged to Nellie, yet falls in love with Maude. It is James De Vere, however, who sustains the several characters at Laurel Hill when they are faced with crises. J.C. marries Nellie with the expectation that she will inherit Dr. Kennedy's estate. Maude goes blind after smallpox; James marries Maude and takes her to France where she regains her sight. James uses his money to help the doctor, bankrupted by the extravagance of a third wife; his assistance extends to the crippled Louis, J.C. and Nellie.

1644. ─────. *Edna Browning*; or, *The Leighton homestead. A novel.* **New York: G.W. Carleton, 1872. 423p.**

> Bachelor Roy Leighton first encounters Edna Browning in a railroad coach while on the way to see his younger half-brother, Charlie Churchill, at the

academy in Canandaigua. Roy and Charlie's mother are surprised and not too pleased when Charlie passes over steady Maude Somerton to marry Edna. Charlie is killed in a railroad accident; Edna survives. She refuses Roy's offer to stay at the Leighton homestead on the Hudson, and helps Jack Heyford take care of the child Annie in Chicago. Returning briefly to her Aunt Jerusha's home in 'Allen's Hill', Ontario County, N.Y., Edna is next in 'Rocky Point', New England, with her great uncle, Phil Overton, teaching school under the name Louise Overton. Meanwhile Roy is on the verge of marrying Georgie Burton, the niece of a friend of Mrs. Churchill. Georgie consistently demeans Edna and Maude champions Edna. Edna/Louise Overton leaves Rocky Point and comes to the Leighton manor as companion to Mrs. Churchill. Georgie's lurid past catches up with her; she dies after being forgiven by her brother, Jack Heyford, who had taken responsibility for her illegitimate child, Annie. Roy, now aware that Louise and Edna are one and the same, marries her. Maude Somerton and Jack Heyford discover their need for one another.

1645. **[Holt, Henry] 1840-1926.** *Calmire.* **New York: Macmillan, 1892. 742p.**
"Fleuvemont, a rich country seat just outside of New York City, is the home of Muriel Calmire and his uncle. Muriel suffers greatly from undigested and unassimilated information on religious and social conditions. His opinions and conceptions of life are chiefly spoken to his young cousin, Nina Wahring, a healthy, lovable, commonsense girl, full of desire to understand the impulsive, poetic, unbalanced young reformer. Under her influence he finally passes from chaos into Kosmos, the two divisions of a very serious novel"— Annual American catalogue.

Hooke, Charles Witherle, 1861-1929. See under his pseudonym: Fielding, Howard, 1861-1929.

1645a. **Homes, A.M.** *Music for torching.* **New York: Morrow, 1999. 368p.**
A married Westchester couple, Elaine and Paul, experience a downslide in their union and an unrelieved sense of boredom with neighborly social evenings, barbecues, etc. With their house suffering fire damage they move in with Pat and George, supposedly a model couple, dropping their sons off with people they hardly know. Paul starts to use drugs and slips into sex with a crony's girlfriend. Elaine has little resistance when Pat introduces her to lesbianism. All of the above lead to chilling aftermaths for Elaine, Paul and their children.

1646. **Hope, Edward, 1896-1958.** *Manhattan cocktail.* **With illus. by Irving Politzer. New York: L. MacVeagh, Dial Press, 1929. xiii, 302p.**
Humorous tales and sketches of life in Manhattan—clerks, their wives and sweethearts, Frankie and Johnny look-alikes, the whole range of characters who throng the streets and housing of the city, all are grist for the author, a columnist for the New York herald tribune.

1647. Hope, Laura Lee. *The Blythe girls: Helen, Margy and Rose*; or, *Facing the great world*. **Illustrated by Thelma Gooch. New York: Grosset & Dunlap, 1925. iv, 214p.**

"The Blythe girls, three in number, were left alone in New York City. Helen, who went in for art and music, kept the little flat uptown, while Margy, just out of a business school, obtained a position as a private secretary, and Rose, plain-spoken and businesslike took what she called a 'job' in a department store—Publisher's announcement. Three other titles in the series with varying subtitles further explore the three girls' experiences in the metropolis. The title above is the first of nine novels in the series, published from 1925 to 1932.

1648. Hopkins, Herbert Müller, 1870-1910. *Priest and pagan*. **Boston: Houghton, Mifflin, 1908. vii, 372p.**

The opposing forces in this novel are: a half-Jewish Episcopal priest at St. Basil's Cathedral in the Bronx who has his faults but is sincere when it is a matter of his religious faith; a wealthy young New Yorker, the 'pagan', possessing scholarly proclivities but lacking a moral sense. A young woman from a family in straitened circumstances intrigues both. She is a willful creature who chooses to wed the 'pagan'; the latter has been living under an assumed name since being declared dead for over a year. The story's ending is a surprising one even if it does defy comprehension. The Bronx is portrayed in loving detail while many of its landmarks are still in place.

1649. Hopkins, Joseph Gerard Edward, 1909- . *Retreat and recall*. **New York: Scribner, 1966. 223p.**

In this sequel to the author's 'Patriot's progress', young Doctor Joseph Frayne is temperamentally a dove but becomes something of a hawk as the American Revolution breaks out in full fury. The British capture him at the fall of Fort Washington near New York City; after he escapes Frayne poses as a Loyalist and spies under the nose of Lord Howe, digging up useful data for the rebel army.

1650. Hopkins, Stanley, Jr., pseud. *Murder by inches*. **New York: Harcourt, Brace, 1943. 288p.**

A defense plant on Long Island is the target of Nazi espionage. At the same time the editor of a Long Island paper is poisoned. The sophisticated Mr. Murrell tries his hand at detection; by his side is a young woman who is the story's narrator.

1651. ————. *The parchment key*. **New York: Harcourt, Brace, 1944. 218p.**

"Frightful villainies afoot in Long Island, including the poisoning of a Great Dane and worse, are spotted by Peter Murrell and wife Angey, as well-raised persons mill around in superior jig-saw fashion. This guessing game provides a generous number of honest clues, all the problems you could ask and a climax adorned with certain profundities which may be a part of the youth movement"—New York herald tribune books. "Unexplainable 'accidents' in [a] Long Island home bring Peter Murrell to [the] scene. He unravels [the] strange case of [a] maladjusted personality"—Saturday review of literature.

Hopley-Woolrich, Cornell George, 1903-1968. See: Woolrich, Cornell, 1903-1968.

1652. **Hoppus, Mary A.M.** *A great treason*; **a story of the War of Independence. New York: Macmillan, 1883. 595p.**

An historical novel that starts with the Boston Tea Party and ends with the evacuation of New York City by the British. The story has three heroes and three heroines who take different sides in the conflict. As the title implies a large part of the work is given over to details of Benedict Arnold's plot to hand over the fort at West Point to the enemy. The author draws an excellent picture of the manners and customs of people in the Revolutionary era.

1653. **Horan, James David, 1914-1981.** *King's rebel.* **New York: Crown Publishers, 1953. 376p.**

"Captain Robert Carhampton, a British officer, is the central figure. After two years among the Indians in New York State he goes to New York [City] to resign his command. Returning to wed the rebel girl he loves, he arrives in time for the massacre at Cherry Valley and only just manages to save his beloved Ann"—Book review digest. [Horan] "writes of military campaigns, Indian rituals and border settlements as if he had seen them. In describing the scalpings, the hand-to-hand fights, the burning of defenseless homes, he pulls no punches"—New York herald tribune book review.

1654. **Horgan, Paul, 1903-1995.** *The fault of angels.* **New York: Harper, 1933. viii, 349p.**

"The city of 'Dorchester' [i.e. Rochester] New York is dominated by Henry Ganson whose millions have endowed Dorchester with an opera, a symphony orchestra, and a large school of music. Vladimir Arenkoff comes to Dorchester to conduct the opera, and with him is Nina, his wife. Nina is young, spontaneous; she approaches Dorchester with a directness and simplicity that disarms everybody from Mr. Ganson to Leona Schrantz, the loose-living landlady. She immediately recognizes the artificiality of the community that Mr. Ganson has created, and the inarticulate reality of the individuals who compose it. Her ambition is to make it possible for these Americans to live as she lives, spontaneously and directly; her attempts, and her gradual discovery that this is the last thing these Americans want, are the embodiments of Mr. Horgan's theme"—Saturday review of literature.

Hornblow, Arthur, 1865-1942, joint author. *The easiest way.* **See Item #3507.**

Hornblow, Arthur, 1865-1942, joint author. *The gamblers.* **See Item #1976.**

1655. **Hornblow, Arthur, 1865-1942.** *Kindling*; a story of today from the play of Charles Kenyon. Illus. by William F. Taylor. New York: Dillingham, 1912. 375p.

Pregnant Maggie Schultz views with trepidation the imminent birth of her baby in a cheerless New York tenement. Her husband deplores bringing into such an impoverished environment newborns and Maggie fears he might kill the infant. When Maggie steals money that she hopes will provide a means of escaping from the New York slums, her husband discovers the reason for the theft and thinks anew his rigid attitude.

Hornblow, Arthur, 1865-1942, joint author. *The money makers.* **See Item #1978.**

1656. ————. *The profligate*; a novel. Illustrated by Charles Grunwald. New York: G.W. Dillingham, 1908. 383p.

"The 'profligate' is the foster son of a New York merchant. He is first held responsible, then finally cleared, of the charge of murdering his foster father. Idler, gambler, criminal are the epithets that he determines to live down when he finds that he loves a good woman. In order to prove beyond question his innocence of the crime [with which he was originally charged] he resolves to find the real criminal. When the latter is traced to his hiding place, he is discovered to be the profligate's own father. Sacrifice and readjustment follow"—Book review digest.

Hornblow, Arthur, 1865-1942, joint author. *The third degree.* **See Item #1979.**

1657. **Horowitz, Gene, 1930- .** *The ladies of Levittown*; a novel. New York: R. Marek, 1980. 321p.

Harold Selden, a returning veteran of World War II and his wife Evelyn, are among the first residents of Levittown, Nassau County, Long Island, one of two like-named communities offering affordable housing for people like the Seldens. Evelyn is the more important character of the twain; she and her female friends are anxious to sustain and further their own ambitions for inward growth, realizing, however, that they must also continually deal with sexual hang-ups, children and sicknesses that interrupt everything.

1658. **Horwitz, Julius, 1920-1986.** *Landfall.* New York: Holt, Rinehart and Winston. 1977. 205p.

In Larchmont, an affluent community in Westchester County, Elaine seduces her son, 15-year-old Michael, so that he may tap once again into the highly sensory feelings he had as a child. Her husband Philip does not agree with her 'experiment.' The three characters take turns revealing their 'take' on the peculiar situation created by an overindulgent mother.

1659. **Hosmer, William Howe Cuyler, 1814-1877.** *Yonnondio*; or, *Warriors of the Genesee.* A tale of the seventeenth century. New York: Wiley & Putnam,

1844. 239p.

The narrative (in flowery epic poetry format) is based on the French/Huron invasion of Seneca Indian country (in the Finger Lakes region of New York State) in 1687 led by the Marquis De Nonville. The Baron Le Troye, one of De Nonville's officers, is also a father in search of his daughter Blanche who had eloped with the cavalier De Grai to the New World. De Grai, portrayed to the Baron as a scheming seducer, has found refuge for himself and his wife Blanche with the Senecas. De Grai rescues Blanche, who is captured by the Hurons. The Baron is taken prisoner by the Senecas and condemned to death at the stake, but De Grai successfully pleads for the Baron's life. Father and daughter are reunited and De Grai is acquitted of any wrongdoing by the confession of a dying Jesuit who reveals himself as the individual (at the time a soldier) who had planted suspicion in the mind of the Baron Le Troye. 'Yonnondio' was a title with which the Iroquois designated the various governor-generals of New France.

1660. Hotchkiss, Chauncey Crafts, 1852-1920. *A colonial free-lance.* New York: Appleton, 1897. viii, 312p.

"The time of the tale is 1778, and the scene old New York, mostly of that period during the occupancy of the British, changing to Long Island Sound and to Martha's Vineyard. The central character and the one that tells the story is Captain Donald Thorndyke, master of the Yankee schooner Phantom, and a noted smuggler sailing under the British flag, but at heart a patriot. The fortunes of war bring him to New York and in contact with General Sir Henry Clinton … [who in this novel is unfavorably portrayed]. The narrative is a succession of dramatic and highly sensational episodes, ending with the surrender at Yorktown"—Annual American catalogue.

1661. ————. *Maude Baxter.* Illus. by Will Grefé. New York: Watt, 1911. 319p.

Much of the action of this novel of the American Revolutionary period takes place on Long Island. The American hero, who happens to be visiting in London, is pressed into service on a British warship. He escapes and finds his way back to Long Island, only to discover that a cousin has taken possession of his home and that his fiancée is pledged to wed an Englishman. His tasks are to remove his brash cousin from his (the hero's) house and to win back the girl he loves.

1662. ————. *The red paper.* Illus. by Will Grefé. New York: Watt, 1912. 299p

Late one evening in their New York home John Wentworth's father tells his son that his life is near the end, and that his fortune is in the hands of a blackmailer. However, he still retains a coveted, mysterious piece of red paper that John is to give to his father's ward, Grace Merridale, who will reach adulthood in just two months. Later that night old Mr. Wentworth dies and John is plunged into a whirlpool of adventure that begins in New York and concludes in Texas. That 'red paper', two consummate villains and a beautiful girl are an integral part of the story.

1663. **Hough, Frank Olney.** *If not victory.* **New York: Carrick & Evans, 1939. 335p.**

"Story of Westchester County in the American Revolution, stressing the years 1776 to 1778. The hero is Abe Kronkhyte, a nineteen-year-old Quaker youth. Driven to despair at the conditions of war in his home region Abe deserts his Quaker family and throws himself wholeheartedly into the struggle. At the end of two years he is a valued member of the Continental Army"—Book review digest. Westchester was designated as a neutral ground at the outbreak of the war, but it turned out to be the site of several bloody engagements. Molly, an enticing barmaid, is the only female in the novel who is even slightly interesting.

1664. ————. *The neutral ground.* **Philadelphia: Lippincott, 1941. 526p.**

"Historical novel about the effects of the American Revolution upon Westchester County, New York. The Westchester Guides, that dashing but loosely organized company [of patriots] has as a member the young rakehell Robert Trowbridge. Sam Hilton, owner of a large Westchester estate, and a gentler sort than Robert, belongs to the opposite party. The picture is of the war in both camps, as the men ranged over the Westchester countryside, trying to bring the neutrals into one party or the other"—Book review digest.

1665. ————. *Renown.* **New York: Carrick & Evans, 1938, 497p.**

Benedict Arnold is treated sympathetically in this fictional representation of his life. The novel follows Arnold from his pre-Revolutionary Connecticut days to his career in the Continental Army, focusing largely, of course, on the events surrounding Arnold's almost successful betrayal of West Point, the capture and execution of Major André, Arnold as an officer in the British Army, and his last years in England.

1666. **Houston, Margaret Bell, d. 1966.** *Gypsy weather.* **New York: Appleton-Century, 1935. 274p.**

Dirk Joris first saw circus rider, Hope Devins, when he left the great stone house on the Hudson to take in a tent show in New Jersey. Upon returning to the Joris estate he was just in time to watch his liquored-up brother, Rupert, marry Hope. By now Dirk was in love with Hope; Rupert was not—the woman he really loved had just discarded him. There was a deep mystery surrounding Hope that Dirk was able to unravel only after Rupert's death.

1667. **Howard, George Fitzalan Bronson-, 1883-1922.** *Birds of prey*; being pages from the book of Broadway. **Illus. by Wallace Morgan. New York: Watt, 1918. vi, 392p.**

A novelette and a dozen short stories frame a rather bitter depiction of the people who inhabit New York's theatrical world. Most of the stories are about chorus girls, vaudeville and musical comedy. Several of the male characters are quick to give their chorus girl friends advice as to the best way to fleece the rich playboys who pursue them. The author takes potshots at so-called "bestsellerdom" and the lack of taste in literature and the arts of Americans in general.

1668. Howe, Frank Howard. *A college widow*; **a novel. New York: Belford, Clarke, 1890 [c1889]. 198p.**

While a guest of Jessie Druce, retired salt manufacturer of Syracuse, N.Y. ('Salt City'), the widow Mrs. Jerome Curzon, her funds exhausted, lays plans to marry her son Tom to Jessica, Druce's daughter. Unfortunately Tom Curzon, a student at the University of Rochester has been trapped into marriage to a 'college widow.' This is the main plot of a farcical short novel. A secondary plot revolves around Mrs. Curzon's attempt to induce her daughter Marion to accept the marriage proposal of Congressman Alfred Pleasants, a millionaire and a man twice Marion's age. The dilemmas are worked out to the satisfaction of all the chief characters. Tom learns that his 'wife' is already married to another man who disappeared years ago and then reappeared. Jessica Druce marries Fred Rathbone, a clergyman's son and stockbroker; there was no spark between her and Tom Curzon. Marion is saved from marriage to Pleasants and turns to her true love, Major Vernay, Fred Rathbone's business partner. The story moves from Syracuse to the resort town of Long Branch, New Jersey, then back to Syracuse (and Rochester).

1669. Howe, William Wirt, 1833-1909. *The Pasha papers*: **epistles of Mohammed Pasha [pseud.], real admiral of the Turkish Navy, written from New York to his friend Abel Ben Hassen. Translated into Anglo-American from the original manuscripts ... New York: Scribner, 1859. 312p.**

A satire on American society in which, through 19 letters, the Pasha [i.e. Howe] observes the social, financial, religious and legal aspects of New York City life (but also brief remarks on Boston, Washington D.C. and Mount Vernon). The 'translator' purports to be Chief Justice, Secretary of State and ex-Worshipful Grand Punster of Glenwood, an [imaginary] state 'situated on the eastern bank of the Hudson River'—New York City is 18 miles below it.

1670. Howell, Jeanne M. *A common mistake*. **St. Paul, Minn.: Price-McGill Co., 1892. 290p.**

New York society is the venue of a novel in which Sylvia Gilchrist, a wealthy, beautiful and mercurial girl, makes a 'common mistake' in expecting the unwavering loyalty of her suitors. Another 'mistake' she commits is falling in love with and becoming engaged to a Polish count, Alexis Inorinski, whose constancy cannot be taken for granted. In fact, the Count is deep into an affair with Mrs. Eva Severance. Her oldest friend, Mr. Ballantyne, apprises Sylvia of the liaison. She sinks into depression and within a short time the remorseful Count, Ballantyne and Sylvia's indulgent uncle, Dan Gilchrist, discover her lifeless body.

1671. Howells, William Dean, 1837-1920. *The coast of Bohemia*; **a novel. New York:**

Harper, 1893. 340p.

Her devotion to art impels Cornelia Saunders to leave Pymantoning, Ohio and come to New York City to study at the 'Synthesis.' There she meets Charmian Maybough, a wealthy young fellow student, who 'presides' over a small circle of artists and writers. Charmian, who is really just a dabbler in art and bohemianism, befriends Cornelia. Cornelia renews acquaintance with Walter Ludlow, an impressionist she had met earlier in Ohio and who had encouraged her artistic talent. Eventually Walter and Cornelia fall in love and return to Pymantoning where they are married. Cornelia's plans for years of study are thus short-circuited, although she does continue to paint.

1672. ————. *The day of their wedding*; a novel. New York: Harper, 1896. 158p.

"A Shaker couple, Lorenzo Weaver and Althea Brown, having decided to leave the order and marry, travel to Saratoga, where they spend the day in several stages of indecision before resolving the conflict between their personal and religious feelings. But the concentration on the emotions and the experience of this unworldly couple as they encounter the obtaining realities of the 'world-out-side'—of which, Saratoga, with its elegancies and idle diversions and mixed humanity of vacationers and exploiters serves as a particularly effective symbol—produces a small triumph of sensibility. ... It is an effective realistic modulation that has Althea and Lorenzo overcome their final doubts about marriage after their day of hesitations, only to have Althea then decide, after the ceremony, that she must return to the [Shaker] Family for the simple reason that, whether it taught her right or wrong, 'It's too strong for me now, and it would be too strong as long as I lived.' ... Lorenzo receives this announcement [without]... recrimination or reproach, and [makes] his own decision to resume the Family life rather than live in the 'world-outside' without her"—Bennett, G.N. The realism of William Dean Howells, 1889-1920 (p. 123-124).

1673. ————. *A hazard of new fortunes*; a novel. New York: Harper, 1890. 171p.

"The plot involves the relationship of a rich [but morally obtuse] man, [Jacob] Dryfoos, to the magazine he has casually bought and also the difficulties he and his family encounter after suddenly becoming wealthy, in scaling the social barriers of New York. Basil March ... is made the editor of the magazine [Every Other Week]; he resigns rather than discharge a free-spoken radical [Mr. Lindau] from his staff [Lindau resigns anyway. Basil has this to say about the magazine: 'I don't believe there's another publication in New York that could bring together, in honor of itself, a fraternity and equality crank like poor old Lindau, and a belated sociological crank like old Woodburn, and a truculent speculator like old Dryfoos, and a humanitarian dreamer like young Dryfoos, and a sentimentalist like me, and a nondescript like Beaton, and a pure advertising essence like Fulkerson']. Dreyfoos's son, Conrad, turns radical and both he and the outspoken staff member die from injuries received in a labor riot"—Benet's Reader's encyclopedia of American literature.

1674. ——————. *Letters home.* **New York: Harper, 1903. 299p.**

The heroine of this epistolary novel is America Ralson, daughter of the head of the Cheese and Churn Trust. The Ralsons have come to New York City from Wottoma, Iowa, primarily to give America a push towards entry into the Four Hundred. America herself is more interested in the opportunities to meet young men and in sampling the pleasures a big city offers. Wallace Ardith, a would-be writer, also comes from Wottoma to New York and initiates a romance with America. Unfortunately Ardith becomes entangled with another young lady, Essie Baysley, and it is Mr. Ralson who 'buys' Ardith away from the Baysleys for America's sake. The time frame is 1901-1902; the 'letters home' (five by America) pass between relatives and friends and include eye- and ear-catching descriptions of the New York of the turn of the century.

1675. ——————. *An open-eyed conspiracy*; **an idyl of Saratoga. New York: Harper, 1897. 181p.**

Once again the Basil Marches are at the center of a Howells' novel. On this occasion they are vacationing in Saratoga when Basil's sympathies are aroused by a naïve beautiful girl, Julia Gage from 'DeWitt Point', who seems to be lonely and bored. The Marches go about bringing Julia together with their friend, Gerald Kendricks, a contributor to Mr. March's magazine, Every Other Week. The two young people discover a mutual attraction and Mrs. March has good reason to 'fear' that bringing them together may lead to a more serious attachment.

1676. ——————. *Their wedding journey*; **a novel. New York: Harper, 1871. 601p.**

"This novel, describing Basil and Isabel March's honeymoon trip by boat and train to New York City, Rochester, Niagara Falls, and Canada, is largely autobiographical and treats with loving fidelity the people and scenes of everyday American life"—Benet's reader's encyclopedia of American literature. Basil March is a character who appears in several other Howells' novels (e.g., *The shadow of a dream* and *A hazard of new fortunes*) and who turns from insurance to the literary world.

1677. ——————. *The world of chance*; **a novel. New York: Harper, 1893. 375p.**

The protagonist, Percy Bysshe Shelley Ray, a native of 'Midland', takes the manuscript of his novel to New York City in the hope of having it published, a matter of chance in itself. He falls in with the Hughes family with its radical social and economic doctrines and pays some attention to Peace, an attractive, unmarried daughter. Ray is an 'innocent abroad' in the great city with its teeming streets, huge publishing offices, the variety of its citizens—and the acquaintances he makes tend to be social and political 'radicals': e.g., Ansel Denton, former Shaker, husband of Jenny Hughes, who destroys a printing process he has invented rather than cause the loss of many workers' jobs; David Hughes, head of the family; Henry Chapley, a Tolstoyan and senior partner in the firm that publishes Ray's work; et al. Ray returns to Midland with a dab of sophistication and a few lost illusions, and with no commitment to Peace Hughes.

1678. Howie, Edith. *Murder for Christmas.* **New York: Farrar and Rinehart, 1941. 314p.**

"Among those present at Carter Davis's Christmas house party at his snowbound country mansion [near Niagara Falls] were Daphne, his 4th wife; Lydia, his third wife; Judith, his daughter, pretty tired of having one stepmother after another; Tanya Ludokova, a lady wildcat with green eyes; Nicholas Andranoff, a dancer with green eyes, but his are 'agate-shaped'; Charles Kinross, a repulsive actor-manager; Alden Hoyt, with a nasty habit of playing Saint-Saëns' Danse Macabre; and a scattering of others filled with most unreasonable hate. … They all hated one another. … Also on hand were Peter Holgate, private detective, and his wife Marcia, a narrator of the foreboding school who tells the story with plenty of suspense and commendable ease. … Peter sleuths with neatness and dispatch, getting the right person at the right moment with a confession to prove it. Santa Claus comes into the story too"—New York herald tribune books.

1679. Hoyt, Francis Deming, 1843-1922. *The coming storm.* **New York: P.J. Kennedy, 1913. v, 283p.**

Harvard graduate George Stuart practices law in New York City; he is also an ardent supporter of socialist causes and theories. Alfred Drayton, Stuart's best friend and a fervent Catholic, has no use for George's socialism, so the two frequently end up in heated arguments about modern society and capitalism vs. socialism. A thread of romance is present in the love that George has for Gertrude Drayton, Alfred's sister.

1680. Hoyt, Nancy, 1902- . *Bright intervals.* **New York: Knopf, 1929. 246p.**

"Lydia, daughter of mad Stephanyis and West Highland Graemes, meets and marries your perfect and typical New York businessman. They play, and then quarrel. Too little money, too great a need for gaiety, American style, on his part, and happiness, foreign style, on hers, nearly turn the divorce trick. But not quite. There is an interval of happenings and suspense, then the conclusion, which, if not, alas, true to life, is true to light fiction"—Outlook and Independent.

1681. Hubbard, Lindley Murray. *An express of '76*; **a chronicle of the town of York in the War of Independence. Illustrated by I.B. Beales. Boston: Little, Brown, 1906 [c1905]. xii, 340p.**

A novel of the American Revolution focusing on the early days of the conflict and the disastrous (from the American point of view) campaign in and around New York City. Interesting females figure in the story, including the mysterious Lady Claremont, a Quaker maid and other young women. Historical personages like Washington, Franklin, Burr, Hamilton and [Israel]

Putnam wander in and out of the plot. The author says that he made use of data he found in the journal of his ancestor, 'General Jonathan Hubbard.'

1682. Hubbell, Harriet Weed, 1909- . *Cannons over Niagara.* **Philadelphia: Westminster Press, 1954. 192p.**

Hostile Indians take Eben Bascom prisoner. When he escapes from them and returns home, he discovers that his father has enlisted in the American army that is engaged in the War of 1812. Eben too takes up soldiering, serving in campaigns around the Niagara frontier; he eventually rejoins his father after the British have destroyed Buffalo in December 1814.

1683. Hudson, Henry, 2nd, pseud. *Spendthrift town*; **a novel. Boston: Houghton, Mifflin, 1920. 402p.**

"New York City is the 'spendthrift town' of the title. Claire Nicholson is the central character, a young girl brought up in a conservative and aristocratic family who has never moved from their Ninth Street house, and whose creed is 'Work hard, take care of your property, increase it if you possibly can, and let all idealists and spouters and impractical people alone.' At twenty [Claire's age] a series of misfortunes come upon the family, bringing death, dishonor and poverty into Claire's experience of life, and when wealthy Dudley Orville asks her to marry him, she consents. It doesn't take many years for her to discover that Dudley values material things too highly and his marriage vows not at all. But she has by now realized, too, that she loves Felix Malette, a young Englishman whom she had previously scoffed at for regarding material things too lightly. She realizes that she has wronged both Dudley and herself by marrying him and they separate, but she refuses to get a divorce as Dudley wishes. She is finally driven to doing so to obtain the allowance that she needs, but feels herself degraded, and feels that it would be impossible ever to make use of a freedom secured as she had secured hers. Nevertheless the closing page sees her sailing for Europe where Felix is"—Book review digest.

1684. Hudson, William Cadwalader, 1843-1915. *The diamond button.* **Whose was it? A tale from the diary of a lawyer and the notebook of a reporter, by Barclay North [pseud.]. New York: Cassell, 1889. iv, 247p.**

A diamond button is picked up at the scene of the murder of Henry Holroyd Templeton—Union Square, New York City. A young lawyer, Henry Holbrook, and a reporter, Tom Bryan, join forces to track down the owner of the button. In the course of their investigation Holbrook falls in love with the murdered man's daughter, Annie Templeton. It becomes obvious as time goes on that Mr. Templeton was unfortunate enough to be mistaken for the person the murderer was really anxious to eliminate.

1685. ————. *The Dugdale millions*; **a novel. New York: Cassell Pub. Co., c1891. 319p.**

The main events in this novel of detection and exposure occur in New York City and just above Dobbs Ferry on the Hudson. The lawyer, Mr. Hetlow, designates his confidential clerk, Dick Mason, to find out whether a closer heir than his daughter Bessie, to the millions left by Samuel Dugdale of England exists. Harold Pierson comes forward, claiming to be the grandson of Samuel Dugdale—his father, Edmund Dugdale, and wife died in poverty in New York. Several friends are instrumental in helping Dick, an orphan, uncover startling information about the real Dugdale heir who just happens to be the chief investigator himself. Dick and Bessie acknowledge their love for one another and their marriage is followed by residence in England while they sort out their acquired wealth.

1686. —————. *J.P. Dunbar*; **a story of Wall Street. New York: B.W. Dodge, 1906. iv, 441p.**

"A story of modern high finance giving many details of how stocks are manipulated and one interest worked against the other to gain control of the market. An imaginary trust, called the Universal Supply Company, has been worked at great profit with wholly watered stock. J.P. Dunbar, a successful operator, is almost ruined by a supposed friend. A woman speculator plays a controlling part in the plot. The uncle of J.P. Dunbar is an original character [who has harsh opinions about] ... present business methods"—Annual American catalogue.

1687. —————. *Jack Gordon, knight errant, Gotham*, **1883, by W.C. Hudson (Barclay North [pseud.]). New York: Cassell Pub. Co., 1890. iv, 247p.**

"The events all spring from the dastardly actions of Cyril Renfrew, a popular actor attached to a New York theatre. Using his fascinations upon the silly girls who hover around him to obtain from them compromising letters, he afterwards uses these letters for the purpose of blackmail. One day he is discovered dead in his room, apparently murdered. His desk is found full of love letters from his victims. A detective is sent from headquarters to work the case up; three people he finds have visited the actor on the day of the murder, two women and a man. Around these three characters the interest clusters. The detective work is clever and 'Jack Gordon' freshly drawn"—Annual American catalogue.

1688. —————. *The man with a thumb*, **by W.C. Hudson (Barclay North). New York: Cassell Pub. Co., 1891. iv, 266p.**

When Mrs. Ella Farish (a.k.a. Madame Delamour) and her daughter Anne are savagely murdered on the same night in two different houses in New York City, Simon Cathcart, wealthy and famous 'amateur' detective, investigates. He hires as his assistant John Dorison (a.k.a. James Dudley) whose past includes a false accusation of robbing his deceased father, Reuben, of money and honor. Cathcart and Dorison comb the streets and byways of New York City searching for clues and reasons for the murders. Suspects include the elder Herbert Clavering Eustace and his son and Harry Langdon, a Chicagoan, who has close ties with Dr. Arthur Fassett, another man under a cloud. Evidently the Farishes were holding documents that were wanted by at least two of the above-mentioned. After the person who committed the murders has been apprehended, John Dorison finds himself possessor of a fortune left him by his father (it had been committed for safe keeping to Mr. Eustace) and successful suitor for the hand of young Evelyn Eustace.

1689. ————. *On the rack*; a novel. New York: Cassell Pub. Co., 1892. iv, 283p.
Clarence Fellows is presumably a murder victim after he has been seen in a violent altercation with Frank Pemberton in the neighborhood of Twentieth Street in New York City. Pemberton is taken into custody when circumstantial evidence points in his direction. Frank has a rather rough go of it before a pawned watch turns out to be a key factor in the case. The watch had been tracked to the shop of a Mr. Mandelbaum on Rivington Street. A reporter from a large New York daily has a significant role in the story.

1690. ————. *Should she have left him?* New York: Cassell Pub. Co., c1894. vi, 273p.
"Dorothy Courtenay and Henry Trescotte, both prominent members of New York society, marry for love. After a few months of exceedingly happy married life they are confronted by a lawyer who questions the legality of their marriage on account of a former episode in the life of the groom. The lawyer advises a separation. Dorothy's action in this crisis is the cause of the query involved in the title"—Annual American catalogue.

1691. ————. *Vivier, of Vivier*, Longman & Company, Bankers; a novel, by Barclay North (W.C. Hudson). New York: Cassell, 1890. iv, 280p.
Another of Hudson's twisty, complex mysteries, taking place in New York City, Albany and Blooming Grove, Orange County, N.Y. The chief roles in the novel are taken by: James Vivier, banker; his son, Ned, a Columbia graduate and currently a bon vivant; Stanley Lysaght, an artist and Ned's bosom friend; Harry Molleson, gambler, always searching for the 'main chance' and avowed enemy of James Vivier; Ines Alloway, girl of mystery loved by Stanley Lysaght; and Ella Newton, artist's model, Ned's lady love, and her 'mother', Mrs. Newton. The two girls are objects of investigation by Molleson and others who are trying to determine their relationship (if any) to Stanley Lysaght's deceased uncle who presumably had a daughter, heir to a fortune that seems to have vanished without a trace. Illegitimacy and unauthorized use of funds are two more items that are raised before the story ends. However, Ned and Stanley and Ella and Ines are finally assured of happy futures.

1692. Hueston, Ethel Powelson, b. 1887. *Brotherly Love Unlimited*. Indianapolis: Bobbs-Merrill, 1951. 283p.
An Upstate New York organization called Brotherly Love Unlimited, which, as the name implies, is committed to the performance of good deeds, is the target of a group of communists. A little old lady, aware of their intentions, takes a stand against the interlopers and upsets their plans.

1693. **[Huet, M. M.]** *Eva May, the foundling*; or, *The secret dungeon*. **A romance of New York. By the author of Seven brothers of Wyoming, Alexander Tardy, & c. New York: Garrett, 1853. 105p. (in double columns)**

Eva May, consigned to the county poorhouse in the village of 'Greenburgh' north of New York City, is the illegitimate daughter of Eliza Moreton who died while Eva was in her infancy. Eva comes under the protection of the schoolteacher Ephraim Lanky; as she matures Eva is lured to New York City by the broker John Bearem who attempts to seduce her. Rescued by Frank Noble, a fireman, Eva's troubles do not end. Men in the hire of the corrupt Greenburgh lawyer, Holdfast Sharp, kidnap her; he hopes to get his hands on the estate willed Eva by her mother's father, John Moreton. Again Eva is saved by the intervention of Frank Noble and her jailer, a deaf and dumb dwarf. She meets her remorseful father, Eustace Delany, a wealthy Englishman permanently settled in New York. The machinations of the villains continue, but their plans go awry and violent death is meted out to them. Eva, Frank Noble, Ephraim Lanky, Eustace Delany, et al. find true happiness.

1694. ——————. *Silver and pewter*; **a tale of high life and low life in New York. New York: H. Long, 1852. 106p. (in double columns).**

A tale of two 'losers'—Frederick Carter, the 'silver' of the title, well-born, a partaker of the fleshpots of New York, and Job Poore, the 'pewter', low-born, and a career criminal. Arrested following a riot, the two meet in prison. Fred, enamored of Mary Meek, the rich fiancée of lawyer Edward Masterton, hires Job to abduct her. Mary is rescued after Nancy, Job's sister and Fred's mistress, tells Masterton what the two blackguards are up to. Job and Fred then formulate a check-forging scheme against the account of Fred's father. Again they are thwarted when Bess McCord, Job's discarded mistress, informs the bank. Job murders Bess and commits suicide as the police close in. Fred jumps bail and accompanies his indulgent parents to Europe. On his return to New York Fred clashes with Nancy and while running off falls and dies when his head strikes a curbstone.

1695. **Hughes, Rupert, 1872-1956.** *Beauty*. **With illus. by W.T. Benda. New York: Harper, 1921. 410p.**

"As an Adirondack house party in late autumn was hurriedly breaking camp to escape an approaching blizzard, Clelia Blakeney, a young girl of great beauty, beloved of all and especially of the men, was found missing. Search was fruitless and the guests departed, leaving Gad Larrick, of Texas and New York, with several others of the party, to make further search. Larrick later discovered Clelia embedded in the frozen waters of the lake, a bloody gash on her forehead and her hands folded as if in prayer. They mystery of her death still undiscovered, but her beauty immortalized in sculpture, Larrick, heart-broken and otherwise broke, went back to Texas. He straightway acquired a second fortune in cinnabar and was soon followed there by Nancy Fleet, a faithful admirer of the New York days, who brought him not herself only, but a simple though hardly to be dreamed of solution to Clelia's death"—Book review digest.

1696. ———. *Colonel Crockett's co-operative Christmas.* **Philadelphia: G.W. Jacobs, 1906. 66p.**

Colonel Crockett of Waco, Texas had had the not very pleasant experience of eating a Christmas dinner alone in a poorly patronized New York City restaurant and he vowed never to do that again. So he latched onto a plan to finance a repast on that special holiday that would be attended by himself and any strangers in town, men and women, who wanted to dine in company. The colonel pulled it off in the auditorium of Madison Square Garden. It was a smashing success and he described it all in letters to his wife back home.

1697. ———. *Empty pockets*; **a novel. Illustrated by James Montgomery Flagg. New York: Harper, 1915. 606p.**

The novel's complex plot encompasses: a rather irresponsible woman-chasing millionaire, 'Merry Perry' Merithew; Muriel Schuyler, Perry's latest female acquaintance whose wealthy father frowns on some of her missions of mercy; 'Red Ida' and her spouse, the gunman Shang Ganley, who formulate plans to kidnap Muriel and hold her for ransom. Perry, along with a Dr. Worthing, comes to Muriel's aid, but amorous Perry is murdered, his body found on the roof of a New York tenement. A clever young newspaper reporter takes a hand in untangling the mystery surrounding Perry's murder.

1698. ———. *The golden ladder.* **New York: Harper, 1924. 354p.**

"Drawing upon legend, tradition, history and his own romantic fancy, Rupert Hughes has made a story of the life of that beautiful and daring adventuress Betty Bowen who became Mme. Jumel, and who, in the days of her prime, hobnobbed with royalty itself. Mr. Hughes describes his real-life heroine as one bred in the gutter, and in appreciation of her rise to a certain glittering fame he gives to the book the title of 'The golden ladder.' Many names are in Mr. Hughes's pages of men and women of two worlds who were eminent in one way and another in the days that knew Hamilton and Burr. At the end of the story is a chapter giving the history of the old Jumel mansion, that relic still prized and preserved in Upper Manhattan"—The world (N.Y.).

1699. ———. *Ladies' man.* **New York: Harper, 1930. 465p.**

"The astonishing career of Jamie Darricott was cut short by a death as spectacular as it was baffling. Dressed in gorgeous carnival costume and pushed by unseen hands, he went hurtling down from a top story window of a New York hotel, while a Broadway crowd gaped below, and in the ball room the carnival grand march waited for the man who was to have led it. More than one person had said: 'Somebody ought to kill Jamie Darricott', and this lurid story of his life shows good reasons why"—Book review digest.

1700. ――――. *Long ever ago.* **New York: Harper, 1918. 301p.**

Short stories featuring the Irish in New York City. The Morahan family 'stars' in several of them. Contents: The Murphy that made America.—Michaeleen! Michaelawn!—Sent for out.—Except he were a bird.—Long ever ago.—At the back of Godspeed.—Canavan, the man who had his way.—The after-hour.—The bitterness of sweets.—Immortal youth.

1701. ――――. *Love song.* **New York: Harper, 1934. 532p.**

Hughes' knowledge of music stands him in good stead as he infuses this novel of the career of Meriel, a Polish girl from a Midwestern town on her way to the Metropolitan Opera, with vocal methodology, the techniques of Meriel's teachers, and the discouragements and triumphs of singers, musicians and composers.

1702. ――――. *Miss 318*; **a story in season and out of season. New York: Revell, 1911. 128p.**

The New York department store saleslady known in this novella as 'Miss 318' is a brusque, efficient person who clandestinely nurtures her romantic interest in a lackluster floorwalker. Inevitably she suffers disappointment when her 'Lochinvar' favors another young lady who works in the store. One critic believes Hughes presents a rather accurate picture of the tough life of sales clerks in their huge workplaces.

1703. ――――. *Miss 318 and Mr. 37.* **New York: Revell, 1912. 128p.**

The "theme is the inhuman risk taken by big 'selling' concerns like the Mammoth [a New York department store] within the letter of inadequate fire-laws. From the opening pages the red specter of fire is seen hovering about Miss 318 and her thousand fellow employees"—The nation.

1704. ――――. *The real New York.* **Drawings by Hy. Mayer. New York: Smart Set, 1904. 384p.**

In this semi-fictional work, out-of-towners—e.g., an artistic young woman from the Pacific Coast, a clergyman from the Midwest, a sporting man from Chicago, a Londoner, et al.—are assigned to guides, resident New Yorkers, who give them whirlwind tours of familiar landmarks and neighborhoods of the city.

1705. ――――. *The thirteenth commandment*; **a novel. With illus. by James Montgomery Flagg. New York: Harper, 1916. 559p.**

The author proposes that the so-called thirteenth commandment is simply: 'Thou shalt not spend more than thou earnest.' It is an admonition that two New Yorkers—Daphne, the heroine, and her fiancé, Clay Winters—ignored momentarily. The example of her own brother's monetary troubles when his wife outspent their income brought Daphne up short. She reconsidered her engagement to Clay and set out to earn a living as an actress; that failed, as did several other ventures. Success came when Daphne opened up a lingerie shop; it prospered and Daphne (on the last page of the novel) renewed her engagement to Clay telling him she would defray one half the cost of their wedding ring.

1706. ————. *We can't have everything*; a novel. Illustrated by James Montgomery Flagg. New York: Harper, 1917. 636p.

Kedzie Thropp, native of a small Missouri town, visits New York City with her parents. She walks away from her parents and begins a career all her own. From candy-store clerk she graduates to movie acting and marriage to an adman, Tommie Gilfoyle. Tommie is dumped for Jim Dyckman, one of the wealthiest men in New York. Jim's real love was Charity Coe, but she had married Peter Cheever. Charity leaves the unfaithful Peter and Kedzie leaves Jim for the Marquis of Strathdene. The winners in all this are Jim and Charity who finally find happiness together. Kedzie has made her bed and now …

1707. ————. *What will people say?* A novel. New York: Harper, 1914. 510p.

An Army lieutenant, Harvey Forbes, recently returned from duty in the Philippines, is thrust into the high life of New York City's 'smart set.' At first appalled by the total lack of discipline in this young crowd, he becomes a participant and falls for Persis Cabot, one of the set's most flamboyant exemplars. Harvey's obvious inability to support Persis munificently motivates her to marry the sickly, slow-witted millionaire, 'Little Willie' Emslee. Persis and Harvey clandestinely meet, driven by their mutual passion. Emslee discovers his wife's infidelity and stabs Persis. Even as she lies dying, Persis wonders 'what will people say about the scandal she and Harvey have created'?

1708. ————. *What's the world coming to?* Illustrabed by Frank Snapp. New York: Harper, 1920. 388p.

"Bob Taxter, coming home from the [first World] War [to New York], learns that he has inherited ten thousand dollars. His first thought is that now he will be free to marry April, the girl he has loved and quarreled with since childhood. But he finds that April too has inherited money, a much larger sum than his own. He straightway sets about making more and turns his attention to oil. And quite opportunely Joe Yarmy and his sister Kate appear on the scene. The old homestead in Texas is all ready to gush oil. Bob bites, but April is skeptical. They quarrel and she returns his ring. Bewildered, Bob finds himself engaged to marry Kate. But there has been another skeptic, old Uncle Zeb, family retainer of the Taxters, now a 'professor of vacuum cleaning.' It is he who thwarts the wedding plans, redeems the ten thousand dollars and the Taxter diamonds. This is the story, but the book abounds in an astounding array of other matters, doggerel verses current at the time, statistics, price lists, quotations from the Brewers' board of trade, and the author's opinions on prohibition and social conditions generally"—Book review digest.

438

1709. ―――. *Within these walls*. New York: Harper, 1923. 363p.

"New York [City] and its progress through half a century is Mr. Hughes's theme. … His story begins with the flight of a bride and bridegroom from the cholera-stricken town in 1832. It continues through the tempestuous episodes that come into the lives of David Robards, his wife and their children, through the wild nights of a city threatened with destruction by fire, through the years that begin and enlarge a water supply to quench the thirst of rapidly growing millions. Personal and political intrigue pervades a story in which the joys and the penalties, the burdens and the woes of sex have a significant part"— Boston transcript.

1710. ―――. *Zal*; an international romance. New York: Century Co., 1905. 356p.

"A Polish pianist comes to New York to make his debut. At first he is not successful and is, in fact, severely criticized in reviews. With the aid of his parents he is able to maintain himself, and his talent is recognized a year later"—Inglehart, B.F. & Mangione, A.R. The image of pluralism in American literature.

1711. [Hull, Charles]. *Redeemed*; a novel, by C.R.B., New York: G.W. Dillingham, 1894. 272p.

Samuel, city editor of the New York 'Moon', hires Frances Peel, late of Syracuse, N.Y. and Cornell University, as a reporter. Peel also accepts a 'commission' from wealthy Morris Jacobs to discomfit Jacobs's unfaithful Gentile wife, Clara. Rose, Peel's wife, fills in when her drunken husband fails to complete a newspaper assignment and catches the sympathetic and improper attention of Jordan. The Jewish actress and former courtesan, Stella Videll, enters the picture. Although she is a friend of Clara Jacobs, Stella feels sorry for Morris and nurses him to recovery after he has a bad fall. Francis Peel and Clara Jacobs are killed in the same accident and Stella, comforting Rose, urges her to become an actress. Rose takes her advice and triumphs on the London and New York stages. Before he dies Morris Jacobs draws up a new will that will assure financial security for Stella, Rose and his faithful retainers. Stella uses her portion to alleviate the pain of the city's unfortunates.

Hull, Edward, supposed author. *Adsonville.* **See note under Item #37.**

1712. Hume, John Ferguson, b. 1830. *Five hundred majority*; or, *The days of Tammany*, by Willys Niles [pseud.]. New York: Putnam, 1872. 200p.

"The target is Tammany Hall, as directed from behind the scenes by Burton Seacrist. Although Seacrist is beset by problems such as the presence of a hostile press, uncertain support from the city's criminal element, a rival faction, the Mohicans, and even a newly created reform party, he wields immense power and rules successfully for some time. Although various opposition groups combine to defeat him at the end of the novel, most readers would anticipate Seacrist's speedy return to power"—Milne, G. *The American political novel.*

1713. Hummel, George Frederick, 1882-1952. *Heritage.* **New York: F.A. Stokes, 1935. 674p.**

"'Norwold', Long Island, a hidebound little village, which was really an outpost of New England, is the scene of this long chronicle. With the coming of the railroad in 1846 things began to change. The railroad brought a new type of inhabitant, of which the Wellers, sturdy German immigrants, were the shining lights. George and Henry Weller, twin sons of the original Wellers, and Beth Beebe, about whom they quarreled, are the central figures"—Book review digest.

1714. ————. *Tradition.* **New York: Coward-McCann, 1936. 430p.**

A sequel to the author's 'Heritage' (q.v.). 'Norwold', Long Island, is again the locus of a family chronicle—the Wellers, the Beebes and the Howells are interrelated and one follows their fortunes from 1914 to ca. 1935. Peggy Howell, grandniece of the wealthy Henry Weller, leaves college when she marries the handsome Irishman and World War I ace, Joe McCarthy. The latter takes up bootlegging and his occupation is ultimately the reason for Peggy leaving him and pursuing a career of her own in New York City. The twin Weller brothers, Henry and George, for decades bitter enemies, reconcile in their old age and die almost simultaneously. The village of Norwold maintains a central position in the narrative; it survives successive waves of prosperity and the doldrums of depression.

1715. Humphreys, Ida Frances, b. 1852. *Janse Douw's descendants.* **Philadelphia: Dorrance, 1923. 173p.**

The story's scene is Setauket, which the author locates on Long Island's east coast, although the real Setauket will be found on the map on the north central coast of the island. Mrs. Florence Dow, a widow living in the old family mansion, has a falling out with her son Frank, whose speculations may have impinged on Dow property. Her cousin, young Eliza Jakway, is a companion and helper of the widow, and hopefully more than just a friend of Nathaniel Dow, Mrs. Dow's nephew. The Dows' new gardener, in disguise, is Jarvis Marshall, a former lover of the widow; he had run away from Setauket years ago after having chief responsibility for the accidental shooting of Mrs. Dow's husband, leaving her the onus of explaining all the circumstances surrounding the tragedy. His disguise penetrated, Jarvis leaves Setauket a second time, but he confesses all in the local paper and leaves his share in a prosperous stone quarry to Mrs. Dow, 'her heirs and assigns, forever.' By this time Frank has patched things up with his mother and Eliza and Nat are to be married. Mrs. Dow passes away quietly to the consternation of her servants, friends and family.

1716. Humphries, Adelaide. *Make way for romance,* **by Kathleen Harris [pseud.].**

New York: Arcadia House, 1940. 270p.

When her fiancé, Jim Carson, suddenly breaks his engagement to Joan Marshall, she is both embarrassed and angry because she had given up her sales job at Storrington's in New York and was not about to ask for reinstatement at the store. Joan decides to spend the money she had saved for her marriage on a vacation at a winter resort in 'Seabrook', an Adirondack village. There she meets ski instructor Max Richmond who was also jilted by his fiancée. In addition Max had assumed the blame when his DWI fiancée had run down a pedestrian; Max had served three months for manslaughter. At first cool to one another, Joan and Max end up planning their marriage. The appearance of Joan's old boyfriend, Jim Carson, at the Adirondack resort puts a crimp in their plans. Misunderstandings multiply. Max returns to the practice of medicine and Joan becomes governess to the child of a couple on their way to South America. The reader knows, of course, that reconciliation will eventually come about as it always does in popular novels.

1717. Huneker, James Gibbons, 1860-1921. *Painted veils*. New York: Boni and Liveright, 1920. 294p.

"Huneker used as background the art world of New York City … introducing many people under their real names. In addition he digressed readily into discussion of the art movements of the day. The morals of the fictional characters are for the most part free-and-easy"—Benet's reader's encyclopedia of American literature. The leading characters are Easter Brandès, a would-be opera singer, who fascinates several men, among them: Ulrick Invern, an aesthete; Paul Godard, a wealthy young man-about-town; and Alfred Stone, a journalist/music critic. Ulrick gives himself over to fleshly pleasures with Dora, a prostitute he shares with Godard. He also fancies himself in love with Mona Milton whom he impregnates. Easter, under the sponsorship of Lilli Lehmann, is a smashing success in Europe. When she returns to New York for her debut at the Metropolitan Opera, she creates havoc in the lives of her acquaintances. Syphilitic and partially paralyzed Ulrick goes back to his first love, the city of Paris, where death overtakes him. Mona, after a serious illness and miscarriage, marries Paul Godard. Easter seduces Milt, Mona's virginal brother; he will eventually become a priest and missionary. Alfred Stone observes as the corrupt Easter stars in German opera and has New York at her feet.

1718. Hungerford, Edward, 1875-1948. *The copy shop*. New York: Putnam, 1925. 342p.

The young journalist hero of this novel is Wendell P. Groome of 'Uxdale', New York. He has a stubborn streak and a propensity for getting his name bruited about. Thus he is able to pick up employment on the Tremont Republic and from there go on to the New York Planet. Wendell is almost forced into the ranks of the unemployed by an irate city editor, but preserves his job and later reaches the heights as editor-in-chief of 'The Republic.'

1719.   **Hunt, Peter, pseud. *Murders at Scandal House*. New York: D. Appleton-Century. 1933. v, 296p.**

> "This is a lurid tale of an especial gruesome series of murders [one of the victims is a too-knowing chauffeur of a wealthy family, the Burrells whose body is found in an Adirondack swamp] … It hardly seems possible that the man whom we cannot help suspecting can be guilty, but all trails lead to him. … 'Old Lydia' [Whyte-Burrell], the head of the Burrell family, is a tippling, profane old woman, but she is a good sport and is kind to those who are unfortunate. She has a kind heart in spite of her eccentricities and she is the best drawn character in the story"—Boston transcript.

1720.   **Hunter, Evan, 1926- . *Don't crowd me*; a novel of suspense. New York: Popular Library, 1953. 190p.**

> A young employee of an advertising agency goes camping on Lake George in Upstate New York where he becomes acquainted with a glamorous nymphomaniac. Before his two weeks' vacation is over he also takes responsibility for bringing a murder to light.

1721.   **Hunter, Frederick. *The Spaniard*; or, *The cruiser of Long Island*. A story of sunshine and sorrow. Boston: F. Gleason, 1849. 100p. (in double columns).**

> The subtitle is misleading. Very little of the action takes place on Long Island or in its waters—rather more in New York City and Westchester County. Actually England is the scene of much of the story whose hero, Clarence Defoe, flees from New York after being charged falsely with robbery, is pulled from the sea by 'Old Willie', then sails to England where he is mixed up in a variety of undertakings and is patronized by 'The Spaniard.' In quick bursts the reader learns that the Spaniard and Old Willie are one and the same, identical with a William Dufour, husband of a noble lady who with her child was separated from him. That child is Clarence Defoe (Dufour), brought to New York by his mother, but evidently not apprised of his parentage. The Spaniard/Old Willie/William Dufour assumes his rightful title—Lord Wortley—and father, son and mother are at last reunited.

1722.   **Hunting, Henry Gardner, 1872-1958. *Sandy's pal*; or, *How fire forged a friendship*, by Gardner Hunting. New York: Harper, 1915. 346p.**

> Larry Start, a lad from the slums of New York, forges a friendship with Bob Sands ('Sandy') when he saves the latter's dog Spin[oza] from a kennel fire in 'Hazelhurst', Long Island. Both boys are hired by Sterling & Co., a New York advertising agency, as office and errand boys. Suspicion falls on them when a fifty-dollar bill vanishes from their boss's desk. Further adventures, including Larry's temporary disappearance, culminate in the discovery of the missing bill which had been in the office all the while, stuck to a piece of cardboard. The boys' next move?—catching up on their formal education.

1723.   **Huntington, Cornelia, b. 1803. *Sea-Spray, a Long Island village*, by Martha Wickham [pseud.]. New York: Derby & Jackson, 1857. 460p.**

The novel opens with a shipwreck off the Long Island coast near the village of 'Sea-Spray'. Among those rescued are Ada and Walter Evelyn and their son Ernest; their daughter Edith drowns. The Evelyns settle in the village; Captain De Koven, another shipwreck survivor, travels westward through New York State. Various village characters are introduced, but the chief focus is on the Evelyns. Walter Evelyn is perturbed by his wife's mercurial moods and her aversion to would-be friendly and helpful people. The death of young Ernest leaves the couple childless. The arrival of the Reverend Ernest Atherton and his daughter Ellen is the occasion for startling revelations about Ada before she married Walter. Captain De Koven reappears in Sea-Spray and provides what solace he can to the tragedy-haunted Evelyns and Athertons.

1724. Huntington, Elizabeth, 1893-1928. *The son of Dr. Tradusac.* **New York: Duffield, 1929. 365p.**

Abner, the son of Dr. Tradusac, was brought up in one of New York's finest brownstone dwellings with all the advantages accruing therefrom. However, he was ill-prepared for some of the problems he had to face as he grew older. Especially bitter to him were his experiences with the two women he married: Stella, a sensual maid-servant who found him an easy mark; then Charlotte from whom he received only blighted hopes and finally grief.

1725. Huntington, Helen, d. 1950. *An apprentice to truth.* **New York: Putnam, 1910. 405p.**

Marah Langdon leaves her father's home in Vermont (he is an impoverished doctor and has another daughter besides Marah) to answer the call of a cousin in New York City for a companion. Marah's cousin turns out to be a conceited, malevolent woman with an unsavory skeleton in her past that she confesses to Marah. Marah endures three years of her cousin's abusive behavior and then blurts out to her sister the dark secret. This has unsettling effects for the principals in the story.

1726. ————. *Eastern red.* **New York: Putnam, 1918. 289p.**

"A novel of New York society picturing the aimless and harried round of women's lives in the leisure classes. Elsie Harcourt is unhappy with her husband, but has long come to accept this unhappiness as normal as well as inevitable. In Europe the year before she had met Ralph Aston, an expatriated American who had not seen his own country for ten years. He returns to spend a winter in New York and the love that has been awakened between these two speedily develops. But Elsie, through weakness or discretion, stops short of definite action, and Aston goes back to France. Along with this story runs that of a little vaudeville singer, [Rose Durand], also unhappily married, who chooses a tragic way out. The novel offers many criticisms of America, but its America is too plainly New York society"—Book review digest.

1727. ————. *Marsh lights.* **New York: Scribner, 1913. 395p.**

For the sake of his wife but against his own wishes John Wallace gives up a promising career in military service to go into business (for which he has little flair) and mingles with New York society. Wallace's greedy wife attracts another man who has an affair with her and pulls off some profitable deals on Wall Street in her favor. It is John Wallace's 'turn' to wander from his spouse; he falls in love with a woman who has no interest in the gala doings of smart society. Just when he is about to go away with her, the woman dies suddenly.

1728. ————. *The moon lady*. **New York: Scribner, 1911. 301p.**
New York City at the beginning of the second decade of the 20th century is the scene of the novel. Humphrey Wilde has an overriding problem—to ensure that his mother, a novelist and an intelligent, scintillating lady, does not become hopelessly addicted to alcohol. The girl he hopes to marry, Linda Arnold, is affronted by his dedication and mistakenly interprets Humphrey's relationship to his mother. It takes the combination of Humphrey's unstinting exertions and his mother's culminating sacrifice to resolve the situation.

1729. ————. *The sovereign good*. **New York: Putnam, 1908. iv, 386p.**
Fidelia King is 12 years older than her ardent admirer, Neil Duncan, but that seems to be no obstacle to their growing love for one another. True, she is rich and belongs to one of the prestigious families in New York City, while he, poor and without notable ancestry, is still a gentleman, a lover of literature and the fine arts and an incipient dramatist. At the end of a busy New York social season Fidelia and Neil are ready to take serious steps leading to a lasting union.

1730. **[Huntington, Jedediah Vincent] 1815-1862. *Blondes and brunettes*; or, *The Gothamite arcady*. New York: D. Appleton, 1858. 316p.**
Also published in 1860 under the title: *A tale of real life*; or, *Blondes and brunettes*. The 'heroines' of the novel are the daughters of a successful New York merchant, Patrick Blake, Irish and Catholic and husband of a woman from the city's upper class who has converted to Catholicism. Xanthine (blonde) and Melanie (brunette) are courted by the two 'heroes'—Donald McAboy, an artist of Scottish descent, and his cousin, Thomas McAboy Tremaine, an aristocrat with spendthrift ways. Both are Protestants ('Negatives'); the girls are Catholics ('Positives'). Blake distrusts Tremaine but takes a liking to Donald McAboy. With or without his approval the two young men marry Xanthine and Melanie in Catholic ceremonies. When Tremaine reverts to his old irresponsible habits, neglecting his wife Xanthine, she, childless, turns for solace to writing. The marriage of Melanie and Donald is a happy one. They have a son and Donald's paintings sell briskly in New York although they lack the quality of real genius.

1731. ————. *The forest*. **New York: Redfield, 1852. 384p.**

This novel is considered by some to be the earliest 'Adirondack' romance. The time of the story is the 1830s. Alban Atherton, while hunting in the Adirondacks, receives word that the patroon De Groot is ill and under the care of a priest and his Indian converts. Alban, his second cousin Jane, Mary De Groot, the patroon's devout Catholic daughter, and guides start out for the Indian village deep in the Adirondacks. Mary and Alban are in love; upon their arrival the recovering De Groot assures Alban he approves of the latter's engagement to his daughter. Mary makes a pilgrimage to the grave of Catherine Tegahkowita (or Kateri Tekakwitha), the saint of the Iroquois. The wife of an untrustworthy trapper, Duncan, accompanies her. Duncan robs De Groot, kidnaps Mary and forces his wife to join them. Mary and Mrs. Duncan escape; in pursuit Duncan kills his wife and is in turn shot to death by Alban.

1732. ————. *Rosemary*; or, *Life and death*. **New York: D. and J. Sadlier, 1860. 522p.**

"A melodramatic tale of love, crime, intrigue, and marriage, set in New York. Most of the principal characters are Irish, and all of them Catholic. Cahal O'Malley, a wealthy New York lawyer, is head of the family. His son, Rory, graduate of a Jesuit college is a medical student in a New York hospital. … The plot is a tangle of kidnappings, rescues, near escapes, and confusion of motives. The significance of the book is that it places Irish Catholics in the key roles in a full scale romantic novel"—Bolger, S.G. The Irish character in American fiction, 1830-1860.

Huntington, Jedediah Vincent. 1815-1862. *A tale of real life.* **See note under Item #1730.**

1733. **Hurd, Grace Marguerite.** *The Bennett twins***. New York: Macmillan, 1900. xi, 313p.**

The orphaned Bennett twins, Donald and Agnes, are reared by their Uncle Ned Lowe, a banker, and Aunt Lilla. Instead of following his uncle into banking, Donald aspires to be an artist and Agnes wants to study singing. Their dubious uncle watches them depart his house for the uncertainties of New York City. Their trial begins. Donald enters the Hayes School of Art while Agnes, with the help of the janitor's wife, tries to make a comfortable home for them in a cramped apartment. At times they are nearly broke and very hungry, but they endure. Donald wins several art competitions and Agnes begins singing before small groups of people. At the novel's conclusion, as they prepare to leave the city temporarily, Agnes says: 'Goodbye New York, you monster!…It's the whole world that likes you well enough while you keep time to the wonderful tune it roars, but grinds you under foot the minute you lose heart and fall out of step.' Don replies: 'That's all right; we'd have ground it under our heels if we could. I don't bear it any grudge. … We've got to have it out with New York yet.'

1734. **Hurlbut, Ella Childs.** *Mrs. Clift-Crosby's niece***. New York: Tait, 1893. 178p.**

A young woman, Bessie Lowery, dies in childbirth in a New York City hospital. The attending physician, Dr. Edwin Strong, befriends Bessie's infant and finds out that the father, Jack Howland, has also died. Dr. Strong convinces Howland's sister, Mrs. Isabel Clift-Crosby of Fifth Avenue, to adopt the baby girl—to whom the name Rella is given—despite the qualms of her husband, Dexter. Sixteen years go by. Rella and her cousin, Edith Clift-Crosby, 19, make their debuts in society. Rella is not the most endearing girl—she has a mind defined as 'cold, hard and brilliant.' She upstages Edith on at least one occasion but then falls deeply in love with the Count de Cassar despite the presence of more reliable suitors. When Dr. Strong receives a cable from Europe describing the Count's illegitimacy, his disputed title and separation from his wife, the Count falls into despair and commits suicide. Rella's character undergoes a complete change for the better, but she wastes away and lapses into death within a year.

Hurlburt, William James, b. 1883. *The writing on the wall.* **See Item #2249.**

1735. **Hurst, Fannie, 1889-1968.** *Appassionata.* **New York: Knopf, 1926. 300p.**
Looking at the lack of joy in the marriages of her mother and sister, Laura Regan, one of nine children, ponders whether her imminent union with Dudley will be any better. Her longing for a vocation leads her to look closely at the Catholic Church. When she may be permanently lamed because of an auto accident, Laura exempts Dudley from any promises towards her and prays for guidance. After she begins her novitiate in the church, another young man professes his love for her. In the struggle between flesh and spirit the Church wins out.

1736. ————. *Every soul hath its song.* **New York: Harper, 1916. 376p.**
Shop girls, traveling salesmen, immigrants and others who make up the diverse population of New York City are the cast of these short stories. Contents: Sea gullibles.—Rolling stock.—Hochenheimer of Cincinnati.—In memoriam.—The Nth commandment.—T.B.—Summer resources.—Sob sister.—The name and the game.

1737. ————. *Gaslight sonatas.* **New York: Harper, 1918. 270p.**
Tales of middle and working class New Yorkers during the First World War. Contents: Bitter-sweet.—Sieve of fulfillment.—Ice-water, pl——!—Hers not to reason why.—Golden fleece.—Nightingale.—Get ready the wreaths.

1738. ————. *Humoresque, a laugh on life with a tear behind it.* **New York: Harper, 1918. 333p.**
Eight stories of Jewish life in New York City—the ups and downs of ordinary people with a dash of sentimentality. "Swift and graphic are the strokes with which the author sketches in her characters, the atmosphere, and the conversation through which the story is developed. She knows her people and handles them with a very human and understanding touch"—New York

evening post. Contents: Humoresque.—Oats for the woman.—A petal on the current.—White goods.—'Heads'.—A boob spelled backward.—Even as you and I.—The wrong pew.

1739. ————. *Just around the corner*; a romance en casserole. New York: Harper, 1914. 360p.

Short stories of New York City working girls written with sympathy and humor. Contents: Power and horse-power.—Other people's shoes.—The other cheek.—Marked down.—Breakers ahead.—The good provider.—Superman.—The paradise trail.—The squall.

1740. ————. *Lummox.* New York: Harper, 1923. 329p.

"Bertha, huge of body and white of skin, half Swede, half Slav, was born somewhere on the waterfront of New York. Silent and brooding, she was the receptacle of inherited memories of her mixed ancestry. Although inarticulate she gave the impression of strength that was more than physical, and many there were who drew from it. Her life was spent in hard labor, sometimes as domestic servant, sometimes as day worker. Once a young poet, son of an employer, sensed the drama of the unconscious in the uncouth body and the result was a single book of inspired verse for an otherwise mediocre talent and for Bertha a son in the flesh. More silent than ever and more lonely—her baby signed away to rich foster-parents—Bertha stumbled through life and stumbled at last, when middle age made her less sought after as a worker, upon a family of neglected, motherless children"—Book review digest.

1741. ————. *Mannequin.* New York: Knopf, 1926. 297p.

"The main theme is the hoary one of a kidnapped child brought up in unscathed innocence amid squalor and sin, pursuing an industrious and virtuous life surrounded by roseate temptations, and reunited finally, on the last page, to wealthy and loving parents. Incidental thrills are obtained through a murder trial where the innocent heroine [Orchid Sargossa], firmly enmeshed in the toils of circumstantial evidence, is on trial for her life before a judge, who, quite unknown to either, is her own father!"—Saturday review of literature. New York City is the scene of this melodramatic novel.

1742. ————. *The vertical city.* New York: Harper, 1922. 280p.

Short stories about New York City. The title story is one of six sketches of the hazards of life in the skyscraper city. There is a daughter's heroic sacrifice and devotion to a drug-addicted mother in 'She walks in beauty.' In 'Back pay' a girl who has thrown over a high-minded lover for money and led a life of luxury as the mistress of a war-profiteer, experiences a change of heart and turns her back on her former life when she finds her true love in a base hospital blinded and dying. The remaining tales are: The smudge.—Guilty.—Roulette.

1743. Hurst, Hawthorne. *Via Manhattan.* New York: A.H. King, 1930. 276p.

447

Sonia Devlin, blues singer of New Orleans Creole origin, decamps to New York City after being deserted by a wealthy young man whom she had hoped to marry. Graduating from nightclub engagements to the musical theater, Sonia, assisted by a tabloid columnist, meets eligible bachelors and marries one of the richest among them. She has a plan to divorce him and secure hefty alimony payments (she wants revenge on men in general) although it becomes apparent that he is deeply in love with her. In any event Sonia's husband dies and she goes back to the lover who had been the original cause of her disillusionment with the male species. In the author's view an exorbitant price must be paid for success on Broadway, and a newspaper columnist can wield more influence than most theatrical entrepreneurs.

1744. Hyde, Florence Élise. *The unfinished symphony*; a novel. Boston: Bruce Humphries, c1934. 359p.

Although the author names the city in which the story takes place Laconia, it is obvious that Ithaca, N.Y. is the true locale of the narrative, for familiar landmarks are identified very clearly—Cayuga Lake, the Clinton House, Rothschild's department store, Buffalo Hill, the 'conservatory' (later Ithaca College), the several churches in the downtown area, etc. The novel itself is extremely formulaic and sentimental. Theron Merridale, a hard-nosed businessman, rejects his two children, Jerrold and Helen, when they refuse to follow his plans for their futures. An enraged father also casts Alida Converse, the beautiful, innocent girl Jerrold is in love with, out of her home when she confesses to sexual intimacy with an ambitious politician, Norman Pride, who disengages himself from Alida to marry a young woman from a prominent family. Forgiveness and reunions are the themes of a final, rather maudlin Christmas scene in the Ithaca home of Helen (Merridale) Stepney and her husband Stephen (as he plays Schubert's Unfinished symphony on the piano). Timeframe: shortly before and shortly after the First World War.

1745. Hyde, Mary Caroline, d. 1904. *Yan and Nochie of Tappan Sea*. Boston: Roberts Bros., 1895. 115p.

The Hudson River Valley and New York City are the stages on which this tale is played out. The period is that of the American-British conflict in the late eighteenth century with Whigs and Tories at one anothers' throats. The chief incident, the release of one of the story's prime characters from a British prison ship, happens on Christmas Eve with a metal likeness of St. Nicholas playing a role.

1746. Hyde, Miles Goodyear, 1842-1928. *The confessions and letters of Terence Quinn McManus*. Boston: Badger, c1911. 189p.

The young Irish-American, Terence Quinn McManus, has definite goals: to secure an education and to climb the ladder of success on the world's terms. He tells his own story with a touch of his Irish brogue. Settled in New York City he describes in many humorous letters the sights of the metropolis, his happenstances, and the commencement of an affair of the heart.

Ide, Frances Otis Ogden, 1853-1927. See under her pseudonym: Ogden, Ruth, 1853-1927.

1747. *Illma*; or, *Which was wife?* **By Miss M.L.A. New York: Cornwell & Johnson, 1881. 353p.**

Robert Montague, a lawyer, generally taken to be the fiancé of Maud Erskin of Cooperstown, is spellbound by the beauty of Illma Ericson, the daughter of a farm couple living near Cooperstown. Montague arranges a mock wedding and takes his 'bride', Illma, on a honeymoon to a Montague property in 'Hillsboro.' Illma realizes she has been duped when the engagement of Robert Montague and Maud Erskin is announced. She gives birth to a baby girl and wanders aimlessly around the countryside. Her child taken from her, a physician from Albany, David Wilson, and his sister, nurse Illma back to health. As the years roll by Illma achieves success as an opera singer in Europe. Her daughter, she learns, was adopted by General Ilsby and his wife and given the name Ethel Ilsby. Illma gives up her career and returns to her parents' farm. Maude Montague dies; Robert asks Illma's forgiveness and reconciliation. She rejects him and marries Dr. Wilson. Mr. Ericson kills his daughter's seducer; Ethel is reunited with Illma. Montague's estate is settled, with his two daughters by Maud and his daughter by Illma receiving equal shares. Ethel marries an artist, Arthur Avery.

1748. **Inglehart, Donna Walsh.** *Breaking the ring*; **a novel. Boston: Little, Brown, 1991. 148p.**

Two sisters, Emma and Jesse, and their gloomy friend Maggie, natives of northern New York State, come upon a bag of cocaine while exploring a 'haunted' island in the St Lawrence River. They quickly get rid of the bag and leave the island. When the returned narcotics smugglers are unable to find the cocaine in the very spot they had left it, they feel certain that it has been stolen. The girls spend the succeeding days trying to elude the suspicious criminals, although Jesse is able to find time for romance and Maggie comes to terms with her parents' divorce.

1749. **Ingraham, Joseph Holt, 1809-1860.** *The beautiful city vender*, **and its sequel,** *Herman de Ruyter.* **Tales of city life founded on facts. New York: Williams Bros., Morning Star Office, 1849. 96p. (in double columns).**

Ignoring his mother's pleas Herman de Ruyter, like his father, takes the criminal path. He and a ruffian named Shears burglarize the home of Mr. Carrol, the guardian of Maria Cecilia, an orphan. Herman kills Shears when the latter tries to kidnap Maria and puts the girl into his mother's hands. The years pass; Maria is a clerk in a Broadway cigar store and Herman, now a seaman, hopes to marry her. Mr. Carrol comes into possession of various items relating to Maria and identifies her to Lord Delorme, an English visitor, as the nobleman's daughter who had disappeared in London while still an infant. The enraged Herman returns to his former criminal activities and is slain by an acquaintance. After Mrs. De Ruyter's death Lord Delorme takes his daughter home to England. This work was also published ca. 1850 under the title: *The beautiful cigar girl*; or, *The mysteries of Broadway*.

1750. ————. *Burton*; or, *The sieges*. **A romance, by the author of** *The Southwest* **and** *Lafitte*. **New York: Harper, 1838. 2v.**

In vol. 1 we meet the chief protagonist, Edward Burton, an officer in the American army, disguised as a monk and seeking information about the strength of British-held Quebec. He meets and professes love for Eugénie de Lisle, a young heiress held in thrall by her greedy uncle. After the American attack on Quebec, led by General Richard Montgomery and Benedict Arnold, fails, Burton (back in uniform) and Eugénie escape to New York. Vol. 2 is largely devoted to the contest of American and British troops for control of New York City. Burton reveals his libidinous nature—he has three women in love with him almost simultaneously. Eugénie is apprised of Burton's caprices and turns to a more reliable lover. Historical characters—Washington, his wife Martha, General Israel Putnam, Lord Howe, et al.—assume fairly important roles in the story; e.g., Eugénie takes an active part in disrupting a British plot to kidnap Washington. Edward Burton's future is left for the reader's speculation. Published in England in 1839 (London: A.K. Newman) in 3 vols. under the title: *Quebec and New York*; or, *The three beauties*.

1751. ————. *Captain Kyd*; or, *The wizard of the sea*. **A romance by the author of** *The Southwest, Lafitte, Burton, & c*. **New York: Harper, 1839. 2v.**

The first part of this fanciful tale takes place in South Ireland; most of the second part is laid in New York City and its adjacent waters. Ingraham's conceit is that the individual who later became the notorious pirate Captain Kyd (Kidd) was born in Ireland, the bastard son of an Irish outlaw and a fisherman's daughter, but raised as Robert of Lester (the Lesters were members of the nobility) because he was switched at birth with the true infant child of the Countess of Lester. When the false Robert discovers his bastardly origins he eventually turns to piracy, but not before being engaged by the colonial governor of New York, Lord Bellomont, for service against pirates and the French. In New York Lester/Kyd professes his love for Kate Ballamont (i.e. Bellomont) daughter of the governor. When Lester/Kyd is arrested for piracy and transported to England to be hanged, Kate dies of a broken heart. The true heir of the Lesters is finally recognized—he had spent his youth as a fisherman's son with the name Mark Meredith (later Robert Fitzroy).

1752. ————. *The Dancing Feather*; or, *The amateur freebooters*. **A romance of New York. Boston: G. Roberts, 1842. 32p. (in double columns).**

Henry Hayward, a Harvard student no longer able to meet his college expenses, sails to New York City to seek employment. A pirate boat, the Dancing Feather, attacks his ship. Hayward saves the two daughters of

Colonel Powell, Kate and Annette, from drowning. The grateful father asks Henry to be his guest for an extended visit, but Henry is determined to find a job. Unsuccessful and slipping into poverty Henry learns the identity of several of the pirates and takes an oath not to tell the authorities. The pirates' leader imprisons Henry when he refuses to join the gang. Hetty, ward of one of the pirates, facilitates Henry's escape. Colonel Powell once again offers his services to Henry and he accepts. The denouement is the beginning of a promising literary career for Henry and his marriage to Kate Powell. The Dancing Feather perishes in Mexican waters.

1753. ————. *Frank Rivers*; or, *The dangers of the town*. **A story of temptation, trial and crime. Boston: E.P. Williams, 1843. 32p. (in double columns).**

Ellen ————, strikes the fancy of two young men intrigued by her beauty. The first, Hart Granger, a New England college student, seduces her and takes her to New York City as his mistress. The second, Frank Rivers, well-born employee of a New York firm, recalls Ellen as the girl who had nursed him after he fell ill in New England. Abandoned by Granger, Ellen decides to profit from her charms. She seduces Frank yet refuses his offer of marriage and plies her 'trade' in a fashionable brothel. Bearing Hart Granger's child Ellen hears of his impending marriage to a socially prominent woman and threatens to reveal his sordid past. Granger murders her using a weapon that belongs to Frank Rivers. Granger flees to Europe; Frank is charged with murder but gains acquittal. With public sentiment running strongly against him, Frank exiles himself to Europe.

1754. ————. *Leisler*; or, *The rebel and king's man*. **A tale of the rebellion of 1689. Boston: H.L. Williams, 1846. 90p. (in double columns).**

An historical novel based on the tumult in New York City in 1689 when the minions of James II were being forced to vacate their administrative posts as William and Mary ascended the throne of England. The controversial Jacob Leisler took authority when Governor Dongan and Lieutenant-Governor Nicholson fled the city. Mayor Courtlandt, Colonel Bayard and Robert Logan opposed him; the latter (later the Earl of Rochfort) was in love with Leisler's daughter Bertha, but still labored, successfully as it turned out, to unseat Leisler whom he considered a usurper. Bertha Leisler was the wife of Logan (the Earl) and in England when her unfortunate father was charged with treason and condemned to death.

1755. ————. *The miseries of New York*; or, *The burglar and the counsellor*. **Boston: 'Yankee' Office, 1844. 48p. (in double columns).**

A trio of benign criminals unites to bring the devious, murderous attorney, Tait Gardner, to justice, their particular brand of justice. The burglar Sampson ('Sams') Cameron, his sister Catharine (Kate), and the smuggler Harry Alstyne also try to save the young marrieds, Henry Gardner (Tait's son) and Jeanne Wetmore, who have fallen into extreme poverty. It is too late for Jeanne who dies of illness and lack of nourishment, but Henry joins the trio in their private trial of his father. The verdict is 'guilty'; Tait Gardner is hanged and Harry Alstyne's vessel, the Flying Foam, on which the trial was held, sails away from New York's waters and out of 'history.'

1756. ———. *Rivingstone*; or, *The young ranger hussar*. **A romance of the Revolution. New York: De Witt & Davenport, 1855. 66p.**

Most of the action takes place in New York City and environs during the British occupation. Schuyler Rivingstone is a young patriot in love with Grace Lee, a recent convert to the American cause; her father, a major in Washington's army, is captured and imprisoned in Amboy (New Jersey). Schuyler joins the British Colonel Simcoe's Queen's Rangers Hussars as he plots to rescue Major Lee from his confinement. Isabel Rivingstone, Schuyler's sister, loves another young patriot, Logan McLeod; she is a Loyalist with her conversion to the rebel cause occurring at the tale's end. Schuyler, with the assistance of Simon Bean, a Jerseyman, and twelve men from McLeod's command, pulls off the release of Major Lee. Simcoe succeeds in destroying Washington's flotilla, but he is captured by American troops. All ends happily for the two pairs of lovers.

1757. ———. *The treason of Arnold*; a tale of West Point during the American Revolution. By the author of *Lafitte* … [etc.] Jonesville (Templeton), Mass.: J.M. Barnes, 1847. 46p.

Ingraham's fictionalized version of Arnold's treason has Major John André in the forefront. Another character, 'Jack Smithson', is, according to the story, the 'Yankee' courier who carried Arnold's letters (outlining his plans for turning West Point over to the British) to Sir Henry Clinton in New York City. He later served as a reluctant guide to André when the latter was within the American lines (one wonders whether 'Jack Smithson' is Ingraham's version of Joshua Hett Smith, a supposed 'rebel' who was implicated in the André-Arnold affair but was later acquitted of any treasonous activities).

1758. **Ingram, Eleanor Marie, 1886-1921.** *A man's hearth*. **With illus. in color by Edmund Frederick. Philadelphia: Lippincott, 1915. 313p.**

Caught in an unpleasant situation a young New York millionaire, bachelor Tony Adriance, takes an unusual step to wriggle out of it. In short, his best friend's wife is planning to divorce her husband and marry Tony. While roaming in Central Park Tony hits upon the notion of establishing a household of his own devising. In record time he finds and marries a suitable bride. The 'sacrifice' is not so burdensome after all, and despite lingering questions it leads to several necessary reconciliations.

1759. ———. *The twice American*. **Illus. in color by Edmund Frederick. Philadelphia: J.B. Lippincott, 1917. 336p.**

When he was a boy of the streets in New York City David Noel had received kindness from a beautiful young girl. As a young man he earned a fortune and returned to New York to search for that girl whom he fancied as his 'princess.' Apprised that she had been married David meets another young woman to whom he is strangely attracted. It is this second girl that turns out to be the 'princess' he had been seeking all along. This novel had been copyrighted in 1916 by the Frank A. Munsey Company under the title: *The house of the little shoes.*

1760. **Ingram, J.K.** *Amelia Somers, the orphan*; or, *Buried alive!* **Boston: Wright's Steam Power Press, 1846. 36p.**

> The dying and wealthy John Somers of New York City, a widower, leaves his daughter Amelia under the guardianship of his brother Richard. The latter covets Amelia's money and arranges to have her poisoned. The presumably deceased Amelia is entombed; she rises from her coffin, leaves the tomb (through the door left ajar by grave-robbers) and is taken in by the kindly Mrs. Haraldson, a widow and tenement-dweller. Amelia passes herself off as a boy with the name Charles Forbes and begins selling books and magazines on the streets of New York. Amelia/Charles goes to Upstate New York to ply her trade and is rescued from a bully by Horace Winslow, a farmer's son. She writes letters to Richard Somers, stating that she is alive and aware of his crime. Somers murders his wife and an accomplice, the only people other than Amelia aware of his scheme. Driven by fear and conscience Somers finally commits suicide. Amelia's fortune is restored to her and she marries Horace Winslow.

Iron Point, pseud. See: French, Sireno.

1761. **Irving, Alexander, pseud.** *Deadline.* **New York: Dodd, Mead, 1947. 229p.**

> The body of a much-disliked copywriter (a young woman) turns up in one of the trunks housed in a Westchester County department store. Police Lieutenant Sinclair, with the assistance of a useful friend, questions a small army of suspects and comes out with some answers.

1762. **Irving, Clifford, 1930- .** *On a darkling plain*; a novel. **New York: Putnam, 1956. 320p.**

> The novel "recites the interwoven empires of Mike Donnenfeld, Joe McFarlane, and Pete Reed. The three protagonists of the piece are undergraduates at Cornell during the first half of the book. They then transport themselves to New York City for post-graduate adventures. Though not without their introspective moments, Mike, Joe, and Pete search primarily for social and sexual gratification through the story, hence the collegiate portions of the narrative emphasize the extra-curricular side of student life in Ithaca"— Kramer, J. E. *The American college novel.*

1763. **[Irving, John Treat] 1812-1906.** *Harry Harson*; or, *The benevolent bachelor*. **By the author of** *The attorney*. **New York: S. Hueston, 1853. 364p.**

> 'Michael Rust' (Henry Colton), the villain of the story, prowls New York, seeking ways to enhance his fortunes. He has drawn his brother's two children

away from their home and placed them in the hands of Mrs. Blossom, a female counterpart of Dickens' Fagin. Rust hopes the children will stay out of sight and that he will be in line to inherit his brother George's wealth. But Harry Harson and his allies who become guardians of the children disrupt Rust/Colson's plans; Rust learns that his own daughter whom he long ago deserted has turned to prostitution. When he locates her, he kills one of her clients who had promised to marry her. Rust is found guilty of murder and takes his own life. An erstwhile assistant of Rust, the lawyer Kornicker, tries to help the ailing daughter of Rust, but it is too late. Harson restores the two children to their father, George Colton, helps Kornicker set up a legitimate law practice, and is the go-between for two young lovers, Ned Somers and Kate Rhoneland, persuading the hitherto reluctant Mr. Rhoneland to accept Ned as his son-in-law.

1764. ————. *The Quod correspondence*; or *The attorney*. by John Quod[pseud.]. New York: J. Allen, 1842. 2v.

John Quod (Irving's pen name) unfolds the story of a murder that occurred in New York City on the premises he now occupies. Reuben Bolton, a crooked attorney, and George Wilkins, his confederate, forge the will of the late John Crawford so that the bulk of Crawford's estate will fall into the hands of Bolton. Wilkins, with Bolton's aid, also hopes to shed his devoted wife, Lucy, and wed a wealthy widow. Lucy leaves her husband, but suspects his participation in the forgery. Wilkins drifts into sickness and near-madness; Lucy dies and Bolton, fearful that Wilkins may reveal their plot, tries to kill him. Wilkins recovers from Bolton's attack. Bolton's plan is upset when Crawford's true will, dated a month beyond Bolton and Wilkins's forgery, turns up. A short while later Bolton is murdered by Wilkins and Wilkins himself dies.

1765. ————. *The Van Gelder papers, and other sketches.* Edited by J.T.I. New York: Putnam, 1887. 316p.

Purportedly a history of Long Island as told through sketches of worthy denizens of the Island; but also are included sketches of Upstate New York characters. Contents: Teunia Van Gelder.—Nick Wanger's adventure.—Derrick Van Dam.—Ralph Craft.—Zadoc Town.—Rulif Van Pelt.—Obed Groot.—Harry Blake.—John Monroe.—A visit of St. Nicholas.—Little Sharpshins.

1766. Irving Washington, 1783-1859. *A history of New York from the beginning* of *the world to the end of the Dutch dynasty ...* by Diedrich Knickerbocker [pseud.]. New York: Inskeep & Bradford, 1809. 2v.

Under the guise of a fictional character named Diedrich Knickerbocker, Irving gives a satirical account of Dutch and British rule of the colonial city—a mixture of fact and legend, or 'fictional' history that also describes humorously many of New York City's early landmarks.

1767. ———. *The sketch book of Geoffrey Crayon, gent.* **New York: Printed by C.S. Van Winkle, 1819-20. 7 pts in 1 v.**

> The Sketch book is primarily a collection of essays and a few short stories. Including it in a bibliography of New York State fiction rests partly on the influence that *Rip Van Winkle* and *The Legend of Sleepy Hollow* had on the development of the American short story. Both of these tales from the Sketch book have an Upstate New York locale: Rip is wandering through the Catskills when he meets the strange character who offers him the liquor that is responsible for Rip's 20-year sleep; Sleepy Hollow, schoolmaster Ichabod Crane's place of work, where he meets the headless horseman, is present-day Tarrytown on the east bank of the Hudson River.

1768. Irwin, Florence, b. 1869. *The mask*; **a novel. With front. by Paul Stahr. Boston: Little, Brown, 1917. 325p.**

> "The mask referred to in the title is the one which the author assumes that we all wear to hide our thoughts and feelings. Elsa, Alison and Terry are the daughters of a father who is a clergyman and a mother who is a 'dodger of real issues.' The girls lead a sheltered life in the town of 'Coningsboro', and grow up innocent and inexperienced. Alison inherits money from an aunt, marries a temperamental young author, Phil Howland, and goes with him to New York. Her husband proves to be selfish, lazy, a gambler, and neglectful of his wife. The way in which Alison bears everything, even the loss through Phil's carelessness of her baby, how she remakes her husband, body and soul, form the main theme of this story of married life. The handling of one episode … between Alison and a friend of Phil's recalls the descriptive power of Mr. Theodore Dreiser"—Book review digest.

1769. ———. *The road to Mecca.* **New York: Putnam, 1916. 422p.**

> Ellie (later Nora) Prentiss was a small-town girl who aspired even in little 'Allenbury' to social position. When her husband became wealthy through the fortuitous discovery of coal on his farm, the Prentisses moved to New York City. Ellie/Nora began her climb to recognition in New York and Newport society; despite her rise she ultimately found little joy in all of this. The dispassionate, humorless, yet slightly satirical telling of Nora's story by the author mirrors that fact.

1770. Irwin, Grace Luce. *The diary of a show-girl.* **Illustrated by Wallace Morgan. New York: Moffatt, Yard, 1909. x, 177p.**

> The heroine of this 'rags to riches' tale is a pretty young woman from the West whose first job in New York is clerking in a department store that pays her 'starvation' wages. Because of her good looks, pleasing voice and talented feet she decides to apply for a spot in a chorus line of one of New York City's theaters. She is accepted and in a relatively short period rises to leading roles. Attracting many male admirers she judiciously accepts the marriage proposal of an honorable, prosperous young man. Theatrical terminology is much used in the telling of the story.

1771. Irwin, Inez Haynes, 1872-1970. *Lady of kingdoms.* **New York: Doran, 1917. 494p.**

"A village on Cape Cod is the scene of the early part of the story and the two young women who have grown up in its repressive atmosphere are joint heroines. ... Southward Drake is a beautiful, flashing girl who early exhausts the opportunities Shayneford offers. Her friend, Hester Crowell, is colorless and uninteresting, her latent qualities remaining undeveloped. A party of New Yorkers who spend a summer in a camp in the neighborhood bring contact with the outer world. The two girls visit New York and are introduced to its many side[ed]ness. Southward ultimately marries, and Hester, breaking through the barriers of reserve that have held her, deliberately chooses the difficult way of unmarried motherhood as the solution for her problem"— Book review digest.

1772. ———. *P.D.F.R.; a new novel.* **New York: Harper, 1928. viii, 360p.**

"Margaret [Rhodes] returns to New York after twenty-five years in Africa to find her niece [Una Bellamy] the center of a gay, unprincipled group of young people who are trying to hide under much surface frivolity a depth of bitterness and jealousy. The niece is fascinated by a man of force and charm who is, the aunt feels sure, a bounder. Margaret finds proof of her suspicions just in time"—Book review digest.

Irwin, Laetitia McDonald, b. 1890. See: McDonald, Laetitia, b. 1890.

1773. Irwin, Wallace, 1875-1959. *North Shore.* **Boston: Houghton, Mifflin, 1932. 321p.**

"Shelby Barrett of the Kentucky Barretts turns professional horse-woman. On a Western ranch where Nicko, a temperamental widow, employs her Shelby meets Johnny Wyatt and elopes with him. She finds herself plunged into the sporting and social set of ['Wyattsville'] Long Island with practically no money and plenty of debts, but her grit pulls her through"—Book review digest.

1774. ———. *Venus in the East.* **Illustrated by May Wilson Preston. New York: Doran, 1918. 314p.**

"This is the story of Buddy McNair, of Axe Creeke, Colorado, who, having cleaned up a lot of money through his 'supercyanide process of gold reduction', starts for New York to spend it. How Buddy hires a hotel valet to turn him out properly dressed; how he discovers the uncrossable line between Manhattan and the Bronx; how he scrapes acquaintance with the society beauty, Mrs. Pat Dyvenot, by the gift of a pearl necklace; and how havoc is wrought in his heart by the 'sweet blue eyes' of that 'real woman', Martha Harrison, is amusingly told"—Book review digest.

1775. Irwin, William Henry, 1873-1948. *The red button.* **Illustrated by Max J.**

Spero. Indianapolis: Bobbs-Merrill, 1912. 370p.

"The murder of Captain John Hanska in the third floor room of a second-rate boarding-house [in New York City] is the incident that opens this story. The discovery of the murderer is the matter with which the plot is concerned. Suspicion falls on young Lawrence Wade who called on Captain Hanska on the evening of the murder, and the third degree system of Police Inspector McGee and the finer methods of Mme. Rosalie Le Grange, ex-medium, are both used in determining his guilt or innocence. The discovery of an attachment between Wade and Constance Hanska, widow of the dead man, fixes suspicion more firmly [on Wade], but in the end the cleverness of Rosalie reveals the truth. The grimness of the tale is relieved by the presence of a group of interesting minor characters, chief among them Betsy—Barbara Lane, a girl with all the attractiveness her name suggests"—Book review digest.

1776. **Isaacs, Susan, 1943- .** *After all these years.* **New York: HarperCollins, 1993. viii, 343p.**

Placing her story in fashionable 'Shore Haven', Long Island, the author satirizes the pretensions and habits of the community's 'socially and fiscally elite' residents. The chief character, Rosie Meyer, in her forties, a 'suburban schoolteacher with a bit of a Brooklyn accent', has come to the end of the party that has celebrated her 25th wedding anniversary. She walks into her kitchen and on the floor spies the still body of her husband, his death caused by the thrust of a butcher's knife. She is quick to realize that she will be the police's main suspect; Rosie figures that her best bet is to hide out and hope that she can piece together the facts behind her husband's demise.

1777. ————. *Compromising positions.* **New York: Times Books; dist. by Harper & Row, 1978. 248p.**

"The locale of [the] … novel is Shoreham Acres, Long Island. The narrator is Judith Singer, mother of two toddlers, and wife of Bob, who is vice-president, at eighty thousand dollars a year, of the family public relations firm. Judith turns detective when the local periodontist is found dead of a puncture at the base of his skull and the wives of the most successful men in the neighborhood confess to her that M. Bruce Fleckstein, D.D.S., probed and photographed more than just their gums (thence the title). With the help of … Police Lieutenant Nelson Sharpe—whose assistance is not only technical but amatory—the case is solved"—New Yorker. "Somewhat of a sociological study. The lives of the people of Shoreham are bared"—Best Sellers.

1778. ————. *Magic hour.* **New York: HarperCollins, 1990. 412p.**

Long Island's Hamptons have a mixed population; there are the long-term residents who hold workaday jobs and then there are, e.g., recent purchasers or builders of upscale homes, Manhattan snobs and 'artistic' types, and the summer resort dwellers. The social climbing Sy Spencer, a movie producer, is shot to death near his Southampton swimming pool and detective Steve Brady is faced with a panoply of suspects: the about-to-be-fired star of Spencer's latest film who is also his mistress; an ex-wife; a screenwriter bankrupt of ideas; and a mobster who was once a friend of the murdered man. Brady has gone through the mill: Vietnam, drugs, alcohol, and is allowing his attraction to Spencer's ex-wife to get in the way of solving the homicide.

1779. **Isaacson, Louis.** *Deepening purple*; **a novel. New York: H. Vinal, 1928. 389p.**

Post World War I in New York City, with a sidelong glance at Baltimore, is the scene of the novel. The chief characters are: Reginald Lansdowne, an architect, graduate of Columbia University and war veteran; Christine Netumiere, a beautiful girl in her late teens; Christine's family—father Jacques, an expert auto mechanic, mother Ellen, and brother Raoul; Alfred Robinson, a New York University alumnus and a civil engineer; George Fosdick, prosperous shoe store owner; and a number of Christine's girl friends, most prominently Winifred Saunders and Adair Simpson. The major portion of the story deals with Reginald's long, unrequited love for Christine, who cares only for material things and is determined to get them. The narrative is frequently interspersed with the philosophical artistic musings of Reginald, Alfred and Raoul. The reader may tire of Reginald's endless infatuation for erratic Christine. It is only after she has been seduced and impregnated by married George Fosdick and has gone through an almost fatal abortion that Christine discovers humility and solitude. Reginald has meanwhile embarked on an ambitious history of architecture.

1780. **Isham, Frederic Stewart, 1866-1922.** *Black Friday.* **With illus. by Harrison Fisher. Indianapolis: Bobbs-Merrill, 1904. 409p.**

A novel of New York society and its financial markets. Elinor Rossiter, whose once prosperous family is now on the brink of insolvency, marries Richard Strong, a rugged, honest financier. He concentrates on his business affairs; romantic Elinor, feeling neglected, turns for solace to Charlie Dalton, a young man 'on the make' hoping for a connection to Strong. On Black Friday, Sept. 24, 1869, Jim Fiske and Jay Gould attempt to corner the domestic gold supply; Strong, among others, persuades President Grant to dump government gold on the market, collapsing the corner. Dalton loses heavily—both money and Elinor's respect when she discovers he has kept his marriage to a French entertainer a secret from her. A Parisian interlude follows during which both Dalton and Elinor's fathers die and Strong searches in vain for her. Strong returns to New York. A short while later Elinor comes back to Richard, realizing that she is and always has been very much in love with him.

1781. ————. *A man and his money.* **Illustrated by Max J. Spero. Indianapolis: Bobbs-Merrill, 1912. 368p.**

A young New Yorker by the unlikely name of Horatio Heatherbloom has run through his funds and now faces the need for gainful employment. One of the jobs he takes is that of a 'dog's valet'; his employer is a quirky woman who just happens to be the aunt of Elizabeth Dalrymple with whom Horatio is in love. Unfortunately Elizabeth has little esteem for poor Horatio. When Elizabeth unaccountably vanishes, Horatio, suspected of being involved in her disappearance, tracks down the missing girl and with a display of derring-do pulls her to safety.

1782. ————. *The social buccaneer*. **With illus. by W.B. King. Indianapolis: Bobbs-Merrill, 1910. 347p.**

A modern Robin Hood works by day as a small-salaried clerk in New York, and steals thousands of dollars from men of unlimited resources; he hands the money over to the city's charitable organizations. On the verge of being caught he manages to escape and spends two years in China making amends for his criminal career and winning back the friendship and love of a girl he feared he had lost.

1783. **Israels, Josef, 1906- .** *Rebecca the wise*. **Garden City, N.Y.: Doubleday, Doran, 1930. 313p.**

"A young Jewish girl comes from Oklahoma to New York and gets a job in a newspaper office. She believes that she has put her race and background behind her, falls in love with an Irish newspaperman, and marries him. Rebecca soon realizes her mistake, however, and a return visit to her parents brings her to a better understanding of herself and her destiny"—Book review digest.

Ivory Black, pseud. See: Janvier, Thomas Allibone, 1849-1913.

J. Mc. *The witch-woman's revenge* ... **See Item #3722.**

J.S. of Dale, pseud. See: Stimson, Frederic Jesup, 1855-1943.

Jaber, Diana Abu-, 1959- . See: Abu-Jaber, Diana, 1959-

1784. **Jackson, Bruce, 1936- .** *The programmer*; a novel. **Garden City, N.Y.: Doubleday, 1979. 281p.**

"40-year-old Eddie Argo, deputy computer programmer for the city of Buffalo, [is] a gentle fellow saddled with a TV-rerun-obsessed wife, a distant son, a lazy boss, an inadequate salary, skyrocketing bills—and torture-by-computer. ... He escapes by using his office computer to write himself a city check for $25,000, then by planting his identification on a dead drunk's drowned, disfigured body." He gets revenge on computers by figuring out how to hook in and steal from major commercial enterprises ...e.g., American Express. "He also rediscovers sex in the person of freewheeling mountain neighbor Carla. But an FBI agent, Francis X., decides to put Eddie out of business"—Kirkus reviews.

1785. **Jackson, Charles, 1903-1968.** *The outer edges*. **New York: Rinehart, 1948.**

240p.

"A novel about the brutal murder of two little girls by a moronic seventeen-year-old boy, and the consequences of the murder upon other members of the Westchester community where it occurred, and on two other people outside the community. Those who are affected by the murder include a successful public relations man and his family, a bored Westchester wife, an intellectual New York City student, and a nurse in a Catskill sanitarium"—Book review digest.

1786. ————. *A second-hand life*. **New York: Macmillan, 1967. 337p.**
In the early decades of the 20th century in a small Upstate New York town (the author has a sure, illuminating grasp on the vicissitudes of small-town American life) Winifred Grainger and Harry Harrison are two unlikely subjects for a close, friendly relationship. Winifred has been obsessed by the need for sex ever since she was seduced at an early age (11) by a neighbor. Harry, on the other hand, to whom Winnie confides her sexual encounters, has no other intimate friends outside of Winnie and obviously little or no sex life. The two lives stand in stark contrast; they meet once again years later when both attend the funeral of one of Winnie's former lovers.

1787. ————. *The sunnier side*; **twelve Arcadian tales. New York: Farrar, Straus, 1950. 311p.**
These short stories for the most part are cast in the form of reminiscences of the boyhood and adolescence of Don Birnam spent in 'Arcadia' (very likely Newark, Wayne County, N.Y.) in the early years of the 20th century. They are semi-autobiographical, the young narrator rather closely identified with the author himself. Jackson's stories fall in the tradition of Sherwood Anderson's 'Winesburg, Ohio.' Contents: The sunnier side.—The band concert.—Palm Sunday.—The sisters.—In the chair.—Tenting tonight.—The benighted savage.—How war came to Arcadia, N.Y.—'By the sea.'—A night visitor.—Sophistication.—Rachel's summer.

1788. **Jackson, Charles Ross, 1867-1915.** *Quintus Oakes*; **a detective story. New York: G.W. Dillingham, 1904. 318p.**
Rodney Stone of New York City is the narrator. He and his friend, Dr. Moore, make the acquaintance of Quintus Oakes, master detective, who is also a resident of the city (Long Acre Square off Broadway). Oakes relates to them his experiences in the Upstate New York town of 'Mona', where the mysterious Mark Mansion is located. The wife of the house's owner, Mrs. Odell Mark, had been driven insane by an unprovoked attack by an unknown person (or ghost?). Odell Mark, himself assaulted, had vacated the mansion (he had tried unsuccessfully to unload it on his brother Winthrop). The three New Yorkers, determined to solve the weird events surrounding Mark Mansion, come to Mona. Oakes and the local police chief cooperate in the investigation. The murder of Winthrop Mark and several other individuals quickens the need to find the criminal[s] responsible. The community of

Mona is, of course, paralyzed by events and it eventually falls to Oakes to meet the culprit[s] in a life and death struggle.

1789. **[Jackson, Frederick].** *The victim of chancery*; **or,** *A debtor's experience.* **By the author of** *A week in Wall Street.* **New York: 1841. 208p.**

In 1837 a well-respected New York City merchant, Mr. Adams, seeks help in his financial difficulties (originating in the disastrous fire of 1835). He is shortly taken into the chancery court (the author depicts New York State's Chancery Court, as especially demeaning), facing Mr. Heartless, the lawyer Gouge and the wealthy Mr. ——, all of whom claim not only his property for debt but also that of his wife. Mr. Adams languishes in debtor's prison while Mrs. Adams on her own and with the aid of Amelia, sympathetic daughter of Mr. ——, and her fiancé, Henry Allen, find a way to enable Mr. Adams to discharge his obligations. His tormentors drop away and the case, for lack of plaintiffs, is ended by default.

1790. **Jackson, Frederick, 1886-1953.** *The third act.* **New York: D. FitzGerald, 1913. 349p.**

Confident of his ability to write plays Johnny Cauldewell leaves his country town and the girl he loves for a try at New York City. Flattered by a beautiful actress who finds him attractive and assures him that his dramatic piece is a work of art, Johnny loses his grip on reality. Of course he is in for a very rude awakening and it is the girl back home who pulls him through the disappointments.

1791. **Jackson, Gabrielle Emilie Snow, b. 1861.** *The Joy of Piney Hill.* **New York: Appleton, 1907. ix, 239p.**

A poor and friendless girl, Joy lives with an aunt who would be happy to get rid of her. A nameless, kind woman is behind an opportunity that allows Joy to enter Piney Hill, a school for girls located on the outskirts of New York City. There Joy finds the love and friendliness that had been missing in her life; and it is brought to light that Joy is actually the niece of her patroness.

1792. **Jackson, Margaret Doyle, b. 1868.** *The horse-leech's daughter.* **Boston: Houghton, 1904. vi, 349p.**

A portrayal of certain American social types perhaps most sharply observed in New York City. The male characters are chiefly those who play the financial games of Wall Street, have residences on Riverside Drive and comparable addresses, and support wives and daughters eager to show off the latest fashions. One woman especially, the daughter of pliant Thompson Werner, insists that she must have the wherewithal to buy many items if she is to maintain her position in society. Her husband caters to her wishes. Enter a brutish villain who manipulates her to his own satisfaction and her ultimate chagrin.

Jacobs, Charles Pelton. See: Pelton, Charles J.

1793. Jacobs, Harvey, 1930- . *American Goliath*; **inspired by the true, incredible events surrounding the mysterious marvel known to an astonished world as the Cardiff Giant. New York: St. Martin's Press, 1997. 346p.**

> The subtitle says it all. The novel recounts the origin and unearthing of the famous fake prehistoric Cardiff Giant on an Upstate New York farm and its exploitation. Among the historical characters present in the narrative are: P.T. Barnum (he created a 'twin' when he could not get hold of the 'original' Giant), General Tom Thumb, Boss Tweed, J.P. Morgan, Edwin Booth, Cornelius Vanderbilt, John D. Rockefeller, et al.

1794. ————. *Summer on a mountain of spices.* **New York: Harper, 1975. 340p.**

> The Willow Springs Hotel in Monticello, Sullivan County is the destination of vacationing New York City Jews. The Catskills have always been a favorite spot for them, although in recent years there has been a definite downslide in the numbers that head for the area. The novel covers ten ordinary days in the summer of 1945 with numerous characters wandering in and out of the hotel, not really making much impact plot-wise or any otherwise.

Jacobsen, Norman, b. 1884, joint author. *Esmeralda.* **See Item #2772.**

1795. Jacobson, Harold S. *For the freedom of the Mohawk.* **Illustrated by Richard H. Rogers. New York: Dutton, 1931. 320p.**

> "The exploits of two boys, John and Roger Allen, in the Mohawk Valley during the Revolutionary War. Sent by General Herkimer to spy upon General St. Leger's army, Indians capture the boys. They escape and find refuge in Fort Stanwix. The climax of the story is the Battle of Oriskany"—Book review digest.

1796. James, George Payne Rainsford, 1799-1860. *Ticonderoga*; **or,** *The Black Eagle* **. A tale of times not long past. London: T.C. Newby, 1854. 3v.**

> A new edition (London: G. Routledge, 1859—viii, 248p.) had title: *The Black Eagle, or, Ticonderoga*. In some respects the English author James's novel bears a fairly close resemblance to Cooper's *The Last of the Mohicans*, which he likely used as a model. Leading characters are the woodsman Woodchuck (Capt. Jack Brooks); Lord George H——, British soldier and guest of the Prevost family; Edith and Walter Prevost and their father; Black Eagle, Oneida chief and his daughter Otaitsa ('the Blossom'). In self-defense Woodchuck kills a vengeful Oneida brave; tribal law demands that Woodchuck or another white man must forfeit his life.

James, George Payne Rainsford, 1799-1860. *The Black Eagle.* **See note under Item #1796.**

1797. James, Henry, 1843-1916. *Julia Bride.* **Illustrated by W.T. Smedley. New York: Harper, 1909. 83p.**

The novella's heroine is a strikingly beautiful New York girl whose mother had been married thrice; Julia ambles through six engagements before she falls in love with a staid young man who is very likely to be censorious of Julia's and her mother's flippant attitude towards the marital state. Julia asks some of her former fiancés to put her in a good light with the young man, but the latter turns their words to his own social uses, and poor Julia suffers deep mortification.

1798. ————. *Washington Square*; a novel. **Illustrated by George Du Maurier. New York: Harper, 1881. 266p.**

Catherine Sloper, plain, shy and rather dull, is pursued by Morris Townsend, a fortune hunter who has his eye on her inheritance. He leaves her when he learns that her father, Dr. Austin Sloper, will disinherit her should she marry him. Townsend returns to Catherine after Dr. Sloper's death, but she has mettle enough to reject him and resume her spinster's life at Manhattan's Washington Square.

1799. **James, Rebecca, 1928- .** *Storm's End.* **Garden City, N.Y.: Doubleday, 1974. 282p.**

Storm's End, a huge, foreboding house in Upstate New York, was the home of Constance Britton's youth, and it is the place to which she, an amnesiac, returns when she is released from the hospital. She hardly recognizes Storm's End, her husband Hale or her secretary Irene. Even the household employees view her as an oddly suspicious interloper. Papers endowing her with three million dollars have to be signed, however. Virtually the only friend she can turn to for help is Dr. Gallard, an outsider with knowledge of her secretive past.

1800. **James, Susan, 1944- .** *Foul deeds.* **New York: St. Martin's Press, 1989. 245p.**

'Charles University' in Upstate New York is the scene of killings that have a Shakespearean resonance. A star student who was to play Cordelia in a production of King Lear is discovered hanging in the university theater's costume chamber. Shortly thereafter an English professor is stabbed through a curtain, reminiscent of Polonius's death in Hamlet. When two more slayings occur, Polly Winslade of the police and Tom Hammock, professor of journalism, investigating the homicides, have only a few shreds of evidence that the culprit might be someone on the university's English faculty. Academic strivings and rivalries as portrayed by the author do not make the investigation an easy one.

1801. **Janis, Elsie, 1889-1956.** *Counter Currents*, **by Elsie Janis and Marguerite Aspinwall. New York: Putnam, 1926. 354p.**

Jinny Gregory, a young rancher, decides to try the 'New York scene'; she finds a compatible group of young people with whom to socialize, has a romantic adventure, but most unexpectedly gets mixed up with a circle of international jewel thieves and smugglers.

1802. ————. *A star for a night*; a story of stage life. **With pictures from the play taken especially for the book. New York: W. Rickey, 1911. 205p.**

> The much-used plot of a girl, Martha, from the 'sticks' (in this case, Indiana) who has ambitions of playing on the New York stage is much in evidence here. An 'angel' in the form of a roué who has designs on the innocent maiden provides the backing for the would-be actress's venture onto the boards. Martha displays little talent, the play flops, and she is about to flee the big town when an opportunity to play a starring role in marriage to a model young man presents itself.

1803. **Janvier, Thomas Allibone, 1849-1913.** *Color studies.* **New York: Scribner, 1885. 227p.**

> The four stories look at artistic life in New York, touching on Greenwich Village, Fourth and Tenth Streets, and the Jefferson Market area. Contents: Rose Madder.—Jaune D'Antimoine.—Orpiment & Gamboge.—Robertson's medium.

1804. **Jarrold, Ernest, 1850-1912.** *Mickey Finn idyls.* **With an introd. by C.A. Dana. New York: Doubleday & McClure, 1899. 281p.**

> The scene is 'Cooney Island', Ulster County, New York, and the protagonist, ten-year-old Irishman, Mickey Finn, gets into scrapes and misadventures at home and abroad, watched over by his colorful, no-nonsense mother and a quarryman father.

1805. ————. *Tales of the Bowery.* **With an introductory poem by Gerald Brenan. New York: J.S. Ogilvie, 1903. 190p.**

> Twenty sketches of denizens of the Bowery—mostly Irish roisterers, saloon keepers, down-on-their-luck men and women, with a scattering of Blacks and Italians and a few 'swells' out slumming.

1806. **Jarvis, Stinson, 1854-1926.** *She lived in New York*; a novel. **New York: Judge Pub. Co., 1895. 304p.**

> Estelle Crosby belongs to that set of late 19th century New York 'society' whose negative qualities the author describes as follows: "The absence of traditions and of all kinds of reverence and religion, the minimum of education, the absence of elevating tendencies and good lineage, and the ignorance of the coercive etiquettes of other countries." On the other hand "its positive qualities are new wealth, greed for pleasure, and a sense of humor." Estelle's marriage to Charley Crosby is a disaster although they do have a beautiful child, Winifrede (Winna). Estelle drifts into affairs with Richard Alleyne and the artist Vernon. Charles sues for divorce and gains custody of Winna. Estelle refuses Charley's offer of remarriage and he commits suicide. Contributions from Alleyne, Vernon and notorious Mandy Van Duren are insufficient to maintain Estelle's accustomed lifestyle. Betrayed by her best friend and even as a member of New York's demimonde, her beauty faded,

Estelle faces destitution. Richard Alleyne visits her one last time. Estelle elicits his promise to take care of Winna and leaps to her death.

Jarvis, Thomas Stinson, 1854-1926. See: Jarvis, Stinson, 1854-1926.

1807. *Jeanne; the story of a Fresh Air child*, by M.A.G. Illustrated by Edward T. Jewett. Albany, N.Y.: Press of Brandow Print. Co., 1893. 50p.

"Written for the benefit of the Fresh Air Work at Albany, N.Y." Girls of the village of 'Hilton', companions of elderly Miss Priscilla Martin, bring a poor girl from the tenements of New York City to the countryside. Jeanne is a crippled child who lives with her caring mother and two brothers on Water Street. She marvels at the beauties of her temporary natural surroundings in Hilton but must eventually return to her crowded city quarters. Before she dies Jeanne writes a letter to her benefactors, urging them to continue bringing other underprivileged children to the country in perpetuity. "After all, the growing good of the world is partly dependent on unhistoric acts" (p.50).

1808. **Jeffers, Albert, 1900-1976.** *Screen for murder.* New York: Mystery House, 1941. 256p.

A philanthropist is murdered on his Hudson River estate; the weapon used bears the fingerprints of the chief male suspect, but there are others who could have committed the crime: a nephew who is the murdered man's heir—he insists he has been reclaimed from evil by the love of a fine woman; the members of a secret Italian society, The Brotherhood, might have dispatched the philanthropist. Detective McNamara plays his cards well; he acts as if the case has him bewildered, but that is only a ploy—he winds up with conclusive identification of the murderer.

1809. **Jeffers, Harry Paul, 1934- .** *What mommy said*; a novel. New York: St. Martin's Press, 1997. 247p.

Precocious Sebastian Duncan hears his dead mother's voice telling him that she was a murder victim, not a suicide. Sebastian's grandmother has the case reopened. Shortly thereafter Matilda Allen, a wealthy widow, is strangled. Arlene Flynn from the district attorney's office investigates both deaths occurring in the same Upstate New York locale. Widower James Duncan, a suspected philanderer, and now rolling in money, is a chief suspect in his wife's 'murder'. But the actual killer is someone rather detached from the main threads of the novel.

1810. **Jen, Gish, 1956?- .** *Mona in the promised land.* New York: Knopf, 1996. 303p.

The Chinese-American Chang family are new residents in 'Scarshill' (Scarsdale?), New York in 1968, most of whose inhabitants are Jewish and upper middle class. Mona Chang takes a good look around and decides that 'if you want to know how to be a minority there's nobody better at it than the Jews', and so she adopts their attitudes and folkways. Mona's parents are understandably chagrined, and then she extends her social concerns further—

she and her latest boyfriend determine that Alfred, the good-looking black number two chef at the pancake house owned by the Changs, should be housed at the sumptuous home of Barbara Guglestein, Mona's best friend.

Jen, Lillian, 1956?- . See: Jen, Gish, 1956?- .

1811. **Jenkins, Marshall.** *A freshman Scout at college*; **a story of life at Columbia at the time of the abolition of football. Illustrated by August Spaenkuch. New York: Appleton, 1914. 316p.**

The 'freshman' is a lad from the West, a Boy Scout, who has entered Columbia University in 1906, a time when the school was about to (temporarily) drop football as an intercollegiate sport (the cessation lasted from 1906 to 1914). The novel gives data concerning Columbia's 'last' football game, a regatta at Poughkeepsie, N.Y. in which the hero takes a winning role, and a flag-pulling contest between the freshmen and sophomore classes. Our hero utilizes valuable lessons from his Scout training in several of his collegiate activities (including a first aid demonstration).

1812. **Jenkins, Stephen, 1857-1913.** *A princess and another.* **New York: B.W. Huebsch, 1907. xviii, 405p.**

"The hero appears to us when a child brought to New York by a Frenchwoman whose services are sold in payment for her passage. The child is not her own, but the secret of his birth remains concealed for many years. The young woman is presently wooed and won by a Quaker farmer of the neighborhood [Westchester County] and the boy there finds a happy home among respectable people. His education is provided for and at the outbreak of the [American Revolution] War he is … in [his] early twenties. He has an adventurous career, not becoming an ardent partisan of either cause, but serving for a time, more by accident than from conviction, in the Tory ranks. He gets into trouble with the colonial forces, being found within their lines and taken for a spy, although his errand is of private concern only. Things look dark for him at first, but the devotion of the heroine [the young woman with whom the hero is in love] produces the evidence that clears him at the critical moment, and at the same time he discovers his long-lost father is one of the French officers taking part in the trial"—The dial.

1813. **Jennison, Peter S., 1922- . *The mimosa smokers.* New York: Crowell, 1959 [c1958]. 213p.**

Through their early years in Europe and adulthood in Rhinebeck, New York Turo and Roz Cave, Hugh Seton and Carol Chase were bound together by mutual neuroses, twinges of conscience and troubled thoughts interspersed by moments of joy. When they try to revitalize the pleasant memories, they are met with unexpected tragedy.

1814. **Jepson, Edgar, 1863-1938. *Tangled wedlock.* New York: McClure Co., 1908. 343p.**

The heroine of the novel must fend for herself with little help from her mother, one of those pursuers of 'high culture'. The heroine weds a once-married sculptor; they separate and she marries the sculptor's cousin. The latter dies and the sculptor, who had been living with his first wife, returns once more and for all to his second spouse. Bohemian life in New York is a distinctive feature of the story with its ventures into vegetarianism, spiritualism, hypnotism, the latest developments in exploration of the mind, etc.

1815. **Jessup, Henry Wynans, 1864-1934.** *Abimelech Pott, the Don Quixote of the bar*; a novel. **New York: W. Neale, 1928. 187p.**

Southerner Abimelech Pott wound up his father's estate, invested wisely in virgin timberlands and then relocated to New York City where he dabbled in law. The case of an Irish woman, Mary Moloney, awakened his interest, however. She had lent her father her fortune, $10,000, and was told by her brother that their parent had died and she was no longer in a position to collect the loaned money from the decedent's estate. Pott and another, sharper lawyer were able to win back most of Mary Moloney's money. Abimelech now vowed to seek a seat in the New York State Legislature in order to introduce legislation to overthrow Section B29 of the State's Civil Law Code, which prevented an interested survivor from testifying to a transaction with a decedent.

1816. ————. *Hearsay*; the story of a lie. **New York: W. Neale, 1928. 147p.**

Young New York lawyer Jonathan Bream finds a way to stop a suit for slander against a beloved maiden aunt who had unwittingly repeated a piece of malicious hearsay involving the saintly Mrs. Brown. The crooked physician, Dennis Mulcahey, is not as fortunate when he tries to mulct the rather dissolute Mr. Brown of a thousand dollars, accusing him of fathering a child by a maid in the Brown household. Another novice New York lawyer, Alexander Snow, turns the tables on Mulcahey, threatening a suit for slander on behalf of the supposedly pregnant maid who had never been touched by her employer. The doctor pays up and Mr. Brown is reconciled with his wife.

Joanna, pseud. See: McCornick, Joanna.

1817. **Jocelyn, Lydia A., b. 1836.** *Lords of the soil*; a romance of Indian life among early English settlers, by Lydia A. Johnson and Nathan J. Cuffae. **Boston: C. M. Clark Pub. Co., 1905. 467p.**

Conflict between greedy English colonists and the Indian tribes of Long Island in the early part of the 17th century is at the center of this novel. The settlers are determined to seize the lands the Indians ('the lords of the soil') have always possessed. Woven into the story is the love affair of the beautiful Indian girl, Heather Flower, and an English officer of noble antecedents. However, he is already engaged to a white woman. Heather Flower and her tribe vow revenge for her lover's dishonesty. The author expresses her interest in the Indian way of life by providing details of their rites, dress, etc.

1818. **John Norton's conflict.** *A story of life in New York City.* **Buffalo: Express Print. Co [1866 or 7?]. 23p. (in double columns).**

The dilemma facing lawyer John Norton is whether to defend young Roby Burns and his companion Donohue against a charge of murder or to ignore them and allow the real culprits to walk away free—one of those guilty of the homicide happens to be Mark Ruthven, scion of an eminent Madison Avenue family and the cousin of the woman Norton loves, Gertrude Morrison. His conscience impels Norton to answer the pleas of Meg Burns, Roby's mother, a friendless, hard-bitten widow displaced from her former London home to the lower depths of New York City. By defending Roby and Donohue, winning their freedom and indirectly causing the imprisonment of Mark Ruthven, Norton incurs the displeasure of the Ruthvens. He fears he has lost Gertrude forever, but she faces down her relatives and comes to him. Roby dies not long after his release and Meg follows the path of Christian penitence and service.

1819. *John Van Buren, politician*; **a novel of to-day. New York: Harper, 1905. 258p.**

John Van Buren, a "young Upstate lawyer [from Schenectady] … comes to New York [City], joins Tammany Hall, wins the favor of 'Boss Coulter' and is sent to the State Legislature where he is speedily made acquainted with the darker aspects of legislative life. The story of his adventures in politics and of his love-making … is told in a volume that is a curious combination of novel and guide to the sights of New York"—Outlook.

Johnes, Mrs. E.R. See: Johnes, Winifred.

1820. **Johnes, Winifred.** *Miss Gwynne, bachelor*; **a novel. New York: C.W. Dillingham, 1894. 285p.**

Two young women just out of college 'invade' New York in tandem to pursue art studies. With adequate money to support their basic needs, they relish their freedom from responsibilities. But then one of them embarks on the seemingly inevitable romance and its outcome is in sad, jarring contrast to her former life.

1821. **Johns, Orrick, 1887-1946.** *Blindfold.* **New York: Lieber & Lewis, 1923. 259p.**

"During the first few chapters the interest wavers between Ellen Sydney and Potter Osprey who are destined to become the parents of the principal character. Then the light dims on Ellen and goes out completely on Potter whose opportune return is saved for the tragic denouement. Meanwhile the illegitimate Moira emerges from childhood a rather charming girl settled in New York and combining the brains of an artistic amateur with the habits of a flapper. Her experiences are interesting but not unusual. But the author depends for his climaxes on two such aged melodramatic devices as the heroine's discovery—also by the convenient means of a letter—that the girl he loves is his own daughter. Of course their reactions are orthodox; the girl goes out into the world and the father shoots himself"—Detroit news.

1822. [Johnson, Alexander Bryan] 1786-1867. *The philosophical emperor*: **a political experiment; or,** *The progress of a false position…* **. New York: Harper, 1841. 112p.**

"A … tale set in Johnson's never-never land, Boresko … presided over by a philosophical emperor (Andrew Jackson), so-called for his fondness for 'experimenting in the science of government'"—Todd, Charles L. Alexander Bryan Johnson. Nicholas Biddle is His Majesty's confectioner with whom he eventually has a falling out because the confectioner refused the order of His Majesty's plum-keeper (the Secretary of the Treasury) to fire one of his shopkeepers. This political allegory attempts to explain why Martin Van Buren met defeat in 1840 at the hands of William Henry Harrison; it was the consequence of the earlier dispute between Nicholas Biddle and Emperor Andrew Jackson.

Johnson, Anna, b. 1860. See under her pseudonym: Daring, Hope.

Johnson, Enid. See: Jones, Jennifer, the joint pseudonym of Enid Johnson and Margaret Lane.

1823. Johnson, Evelyn Kimball. *An errand girl*; **a romance of New York life. New York: G.W. Dillingham, 1889. 341p.**

Orphaned by the premature death of their parents, the Hurlbert children—Guy, Grace and Olivia—are separated. Guy makes his home with a great aunt, Mrs. Withington, dressmaker; Grace is taken in by her wealthy grandfather, Major Dunn, changes her name to Helen Dunn and becomes the stereotypical 'spoiled brat'; Olivia is placed in the care of foster parents, the kind Malonys, who call her Pansy Blossom. When the Malonys die, Olivia is given employment by Mrs. Withington as an errand girl. Guy undergoes a series of troubles; unemployment, malaria (contracted out West) and a false accusation of murder and theft, but he finally achieves success in the banking-house of Dunn & Fairweather. Towards the novel's end the three siblings are cognizant of their close bonds. Grace/Helen Dunn is consumed by jealousy when her fiancé, Jasper Montrose, Major Dunn's stepson, falls in love with Olivia. Both Grace and the Major die, Guy becomes a partner in his firm, and Olivia, now 'properly educated', weds Jasper Montrose.

1824. Johnson, Hugh Samuel, 1882-1942. *Williams of West Point.* **New York: Appleton, 1908. viii, 292p.**

The protagonist in the story, Bob Williams, has risen to the top of his class at West Point when he is challenged by Brinsley Bartlett who is himself an outstanding and popular cadet. Their confrontation can only be settled, according to the Academy's code, by combat between the two. Williams refuses to fight; deemed a coward by his classmates, how he reclaims their respect is the crux of the story.

1825. Johnson, Owen McMahon, 1878-1952. *Blue blood*; a dramatic interlude. **Boston: Little, Brown, 1924. 247p.**

"The old house of Majendis was in grave danger of bankruptcy, so the young daughter Rita was deliberately sacrificed in return for the millions of an old philanderer. After six years of suffering, his death left her free. While Rita was in Montana her cool pride had yielded to the personality of Dan Haggerty. Back in New York she found her father had played in Wall Street against Dan with disastrous results. For the second time she saved the family name—this time by a bargain with Dan to come to him whenever he called, if he would save her father. Time passed and she was not summoned. In despair at the suspense and humiliation she arranged a meeting between Dan and another suitor to decide her choice for her. An unexpected pistol shot revealed to herself the real object of her love"—Book review digest.

1826. ————. *Making money.* **With 8 illus. by James Montgomery Flagg. New York: Stokes, 1915. 327p.**

The money marts of New York City beckon four college friends to test their ability to achieve financial success. The story focuses on Thomas Beauchamp Crocker ('Bojo'), the hero, who makes a quarter of a million dollars on Wall Street but in the process ruins several men, one of whom commits suicide. Bojo turns away from speculation; when his father is in trouble Bojo comes to his aid. He marries Patsie Drake, the girl he has fallen in love with; her father was a victim of over-speculation on Wall Street. Bojo now concentrates on the family business, the Crocker Mills.

1827. ————. *Max Fargus.* **New York: Baker & Taylor, 1906. 315p.**

The novel's title character, Max Fargus, is the prosperous owner of a chain of New York oyster houses who is smitten by an out-of-work actress posing as a guileless girl from a rural district. Nevertheless, he hires a crooked lawyer to look into her background; the shyster tells the girl that his report to Fargus will be a favorable one provided she shares her good fortune with him. She seems to agree with him, but after Fargus marries the girl, Fargus puts in motion a plan that punishes the dishonest lawyer while leaving Mrs. Fargus (who really is not as bad as some other sleazy New Yorkers in the story) with Max Fargus's money.

1828. ————. *The salamander.* **With illus. by Everett Shinn. Indianapolis: Bobbs-Merrill, 1914. 529p.**

Again we confront the familiar plot of the young woman who has high hopes of experiencing 'life' in its myriad shades in the crucible of New York City. Doré Baxter is clever, certain that she can handle any untoward situation, and obviously exercising a fascinating influence over a swarm of admirers (and she even pulls one young man away from his addiction to strong drink). But by the time of the novel's conclusion Doré has taken the path to a conventional marriage and she herself becomes a paragon of conservatism.

1829. ————. *The sixty-first second.* **Illustrated by A.B. Wenzell. New York: Stokes, 1913. 383p.**

The disappearance of a valuable ruby ring at a bohemian-like New York party hosted by the ring's owner impels her to ask the pilferer to place the article on the table after the lights have been turned out. At the 61st second a metallic sound is heard, but when the lights go on again, there is no ring in view. Detective McKenna is called in to solve the puzzle; while he is at work, the guests, including Wall Street brokers and a young fellow just out of college, go about their business. The latter is especially involved with a young actress and an adventuress with an intellectual turn of mind.

1830. ————. *Virtuous wives.* **With illus. by C.H. Taffs. Boston: Little, Brown, 1918. xii, 352p.**

Amy Forrester is so wrapped up with her New York social engagements and her quest for more exciting stimuli that she sadly neglects her businessman husband. Their growing estrangement finally awakens Amy, and after recriminations, suffering and near scandal she finds her way to a truer understanding of her wifely obligations and esteem for her husband.

1831. ————. *The woman gives*; **a story of regeneration. With illus. by Howard Chandler Christy. Boston: Little Brown, 1916. 458p.**

The regeneration of Daingerfield, a painter of great promise, by Inga Sonderson, another artist, is the main plot of the novel. Daingerfield inevitably falls in love with his savior and asks Inga to marry him. Inga is not particularly fond of the marriage bond but consents to marry him only if he will let her go when she feels the need to strike out on her own again. This occurs when Inga comes upon another man who is in danger of sinking into dissipated oblivion. All of the foregoing takes place in New York and the studios of the Bohemian artists' colony with its aspiring musicians, painters, writers, models, et al.

1832. **Johnson, P. Demarest.** *Claudius, the cowboy of Ramapo Valley*; **a story of Revolutionary times in southern New York. Middletown, N.Y.: Slauson & Boyd, Press Steam Print, 1894. 206p.**

"The story opens in the autumn of 1774, in that part of New York which is now known as Rockland County. Claudius Smith, the Tory leader of a reckless band of mountaineers, is a real person, who is still spoken of in that part of the country as 'the scourge of the Highlands'. His bloody deeds were finally expiated on the gallows. The story has a central romance, and gives an excellent account of the historical Revolutionary events which occurred in the locality"—Annual American catalogue.

1833. **Johnson, Paul.** *Killing the blues.* **New York: St. Martin's Press, 1987. 294p.**

Moldering away in the Catskills and facing difficulties in his marriage, erstwhile 1960s radical Casey comes upon an unidentifiable corpse—removed are its head, hands and feet. The local police are stumped, but Casey believes the remains are those of the wife of Roger Kugel; she had vanished some months ago. Kugel is a cop and something of a hero to his Catskill neighbors, although Casey sees him as a brutal, half-mad individual. Aided by his friend Gary, a seedy rock musician from the 60s, and by a local policeman who doesn't see eye to eye with the powers that be, Casey is determined to carry on his investigation to a conclusion.

1834. Johnson, Rossiter, 1840-1931. *Phaeton Rogers*; **a novel of boy life. New York: Scribner, 1881. vi, 344p.**

Phaeton Rogers is a teen-age boy with a knack for inventing useful items and for solving whatever practical problems come up in the course of the days. He is a native of the Rochester, New York area.

1835. Johnson, Samuel Paige, b. 1852. *Zebadiah Sartwell, the miller of Whallonsburgh.* **Illustrated by William L. Hudson. Foreword by Stephen G. Clow. New York: Broadway Pub. Co., 1903. xii, 318p.**

Zebadiah is a wit and a homespun philosopher who has sold his farm and moved with his wife and daughter, Abieola, to town—'Whallonsburgh', Essex County, New York on the edge of or in the Adirondacks—where he is now the village's miller and postmaster. When not 'minding the store', Zeb is busy spinning his limitless supply of yarns, performing acts of kindness towards those with physical disabilities, and setting one young man in particular, Frank Stewart, his mill assistant, back on the honest path from which he had temporarily strayed. The coming of a railroad, a husking bee, a post-office robbery, the double wedding of Abieola Sartwell/Jack Spaulding and Frank Stewart/Jane Spaulding are some of the events that enliven the narrative.

1836. Johnson, Sandy. *Walk a winter beach.* **New York: Delacorte Press/Eleanor Friede, 1982. 361p.**

"After 20 years with the New York Police Department Lieutenant Jake Ryan is made the new head of a special homicide team dubbed Ryan's raiders. And Jake is soon very personally involved in a homicide; his wife Nora is shot to death in a revenge setup aimed at Jake. The culprit? Tommy Angel, whom Jake had sent up to Attica for molesting a minor. ...So following a lead, Jake heads out to Montauk Point in the winter—where, tracking down Tommy, he'll meet Scotty Stanton, who's starting up a service ferrying passengers about Long Island in her monoplane. Among Scotty's clients: her Montauk neighbor Max Landau, a top Mafioso. And the wretched Tommy Angel is hiding out in the boathouse on Landau's palatial estate. Jake and Scotty fall in love; Jake tries to corner Tommy and get a man-to-man confession from him. But then, when Tommy attempts to rape Scotty, Jake kills him—and the novel's last section drags on into the departmental investigation of this legally iffy killing"—Kirkus reviews.

1837. Johnson, Virginia Wales, 1849-1916. *Tulip Place*; a story of New York. New York: Harper, 1886. 195p.

"Tulip Place is an aristocratic street of New York City in which live the two families of St. Nicholas and the Belts. Their fortunes and misfortunes make up a pleasant story. Camilla Belt at 21 inherits a fortune of ten millions from her grandfather who was an inventor of a sewing machine. Her travels, her dress and luxurious way of living, her ambition to marry a title, and the pursuit of her numerous admirers are full of interest and graphically related"—Annual American catalogue.

Johnson, W. Bolinbroke, pseud. See: Bishop, Morris, 1893-1973.

1838. Johnston, Brian, 1944- . *The Dutch treat murders*; a Winston Wyc mystery. New York: Windsor Pub. Corp., 1991. 256p.

Architectural historian Winston Wyc is hired as a consultant to the Oblates of Tranquil Deliverance who have a problem in deciding what to do with their quarters, Smelton Castle in the Hudson River Valley. Should it be preserved as an historical structure or, as businessman Justin Barefoot suggests, should it be put up for sale along with the property around it? Then Barefoot's body is discovered floating in the Hudson River. Local reporter Mary Bartlett gets in touch with Wyc and they form a team. A second corpse, that of a stranger, appears in the Hudson. Wyc and Bartlett espy suspicious-looking nuns and an elderly man who looks like Bozo the Clown on drugs. They wonder why Smelton Castle and its grounds have become so valuable that one would kill to gain possession of them.

1839. ————. *The gift horse murders*; a Winston Wyc mystery. New York: Windsor Pub. Corp., 1992. 288p.

Following the murder of Minerva Trotteville in the Hudson Valley town of 'Wistfield'—she was clubbed down and trampled by a runaway horse—architectural historian Winston Wyc appears as consultant to a restoration project on the house that had been occupied by the murdered lady. Shortly after Wyc's arrival another murder happens, that of the president of the society which has facilitated the restoration undertaking. Wyc, in the course of his work and snooping, has an affair with Cassandra Trotteville, Minerva's sister, and it remains for the feisty 70-something Dr. Janice Wetmore (who had originally hired Wyc) to point to the killer who tries to dispatch her.

1840. ————. *With mallets aforethought*; a Winston Wyc mystery. New York: Penzler Books, 1995. 256p.

The creation of a Sturbridge (Mass.)-like historic village at 'Longmeadow' in Upstate New York has been initiated by the stockpiling of dismantled buildings by millionaire Clement Corbally. Other people get into the act—TV luminary Niles Northingham has visions of a television show based on the project; Corbally's sons, Clement Jr., a gay avant-garde artist, opts for an amusement park; his other son, Sackett, a sham Episcopal priest, is against the whole project, and hires Winston Wyc to come up with suggestions. Murder rears its ugly head and Wyc ends up using his amateur investigative powers instead of his architectural knowledge.

1841. **Johnston, James Wesley, 1847?-1936.** *Dwellers in Gotham*; **a romance of New York, by Annan Dale [pseud.]. New York: Eaton & Mains, 1898. vi, 392p.**

Through a variety of characters the author touches upon aspects of New York's social, economic and religious life. Two young friends—Edward Vaughen and John Disney, Vaughen especially—debate the possible ameliorating effects of a socialist order on the disparities they see all around them. John is inclined to take the world as he sees it, although he worries his parents and his sister, Madge, when he discusses some of Vaughen's ideas. Mark Brompton, Edward's uncle, is a typically sharp New York businessman who looks after his sister's (Mrs. Vaughen's) interests when her husband dies. Disney Senior is a prominent physician who gets himself entangled in some unethical business practices. The young clergyman Hugh Dunbar remains true to his vocation of serving the poor. By the novel's conclusion several changed lives are on view. Edward Vaughen now has his own business, aided by Brompton. John Disney is a successful but fair-minded businessman. Madge Disney comforts and helps the unfortunate. Mark Brompton becomes a benign employer, generous to his workers.

1842. —————. *The mystery of Miriam.* **Boston: H.B. Turner, 1904. 459p.**

A talented young New York clerk is taken into his employer's confidence and performs most creditably, but when he falls in love with the boss's daughter he is fired. However, the two lovers marry—a short while later she falls ill and dies. The hero changes his name and strikes up an acquaintance with a girl who is reminiscent of his late wife. The girl was born on the same day as his first love, and she has a knack for very capably handling his business and family affairs.

1843. **Johnston, Velda.** *Along a dark path.* **New York: Dodd, Mead, 1967. 228p.**

Susan Sayre goes back to her grandfather's Victorian mansion in Upstate New York to search for memories, both of her radiant mother who died in that house and of her own first six years of life there under the care of her mother.

1844. —————. *The fateful summer.* **New York: Dodd, Mead, 1981. 225p.**

The now aged Emma Hoffsteader, the narrator, recalls a summer years ago she spent with her friend, Amanda Dorrance, at the Dorrance family summer home on Long Island. Amanda, an adopted daughter, is dearly beloved by her father, John Dorrance. She is treated very casually by John's wife, Clara, who treasures her twins, Larry and Lucy. When Amanda falls in love with Michael Terence Doyle, son of the owner of several hotel bars, John Dorrance is furious and drives Michael away with the threat of bankrupting the young man's father. He also separates the twins, sending Larry to military school and Lucy to Boston. Amanda, pregnant by Michael, meets her biological mother, Rose Shannon, an alcoholic in genteel poverty—the reader will figure out who who Amanda's biological father is. Tyrannical John Dorrance is murdered and Michael Doyle is a prime suspect because one of his cuff links was discovered near Dorrance's body. Unhappy Amanda has a miscarriage. Emma Hoffsteader applies her powers of detection and unveils the murderer, although not before she almost becomes another murder victim.

1845. ————. *The late Mrs. Fonsell*; a novel of suspense. New York: Dodd, Mead, 1972. 215p.

"What happened to the late Mrs. Fonsell wonders Irene, who married a son and was bearing his child when he's lost at sea—leaving her to accept, in his lieu, Jason Fonsell, born on the wrong side of the family's blanket. All … of this takes place out of Sag Harbor [Long Island] before the turn of the century and there's an old house with a portrait and perhaps a presence—a deadly assailant"—Kirkus reviews.

1846. ————. *The light in the swamp.* New York: Dodd, Mead, 1970. 186p.

The novel is a gothic/mystery piece that features an old dilapidated house on a Long Island estate owned by Catherine Morrell's Aunt Marion and Uncle Loren, relatives she has not seen for years. The widow Catherine, accompanied by her five-year-old daughter, comes to the estate (her mother's childhood home) for needed rest. However, there is a moody, chilling atmosphere about the place, which is guarded by Dobermans. A shot is fired into Catherine's car and a snoopy history professor strides through the family cemetery. And though Aunt Marion and Uncle Loren try to be good hosts, Catherine feels they are very uncomfortable with her presence.

1847. ————. *The people from the sea.* New York: Dodd, Mead, 1979. 234p.

"A young woman renting an isolated Long Island house, where she hopes to recover from emotional trauma, finds she shares her new quarters with a ghostly trio who place her in danger by impelling her to track down their murderer. A nice blending of the occult, romance and suspense"—Booklist.

1848. ————. *The underground stream.* New York: St. Martin's Press, 1991. 169p.

While recovering from a nervous breakdown at 'Hampton Harbor', Long Island, an old whaling port that was transformed into a resort and which played a role in her family's history, Gail Loring is transported back in time to 1840. The tragic marriage of Martha Fitzwilliam to violent Samuel, Gail's ancestor, passes before her eyes. Samuel Fitzwilliam is the Monster of Monroe Street to the citizens of Hampton Harbor and his discovery of the love affair between Martha and sea captain Jared Cantrell has calamitous consequences. As the story shifts back to the present Gail turns away the importunities of Martin Crowley, a real estate salesman, and faces the future with hope.

1849. **Johnston, William Andrew, b. 1871.** *The apartment next door.* **With illus. by Arthur William Brown. Boston: Little, Brown, 1919. 301p.**

German espionage in New York City during World War I is the concern of the United States Secret Service. Surprisingly enough the American agents are abetted by Joan Strong, a young woman prominent in New York social circles and who lives on Riverside Drive. In the course of her contacts with two of the Secret Service men there is developed a smidgeon of romance.

1850. —————. *The house of whispers.* **With illus. by Arthur William Brown. Boston: Little, Brown, 1918. 292p.**

"Secret passageways, mysterious tapings, strange whispering voices, all of these belong to ancient haunted houses and yet here they are in a modern apartment house facing Central Park. Spalding Nelson, a young man on a small salary, is asked by his great-uncle, Rufus Gaston, to occupy the Gaston apartment during the absence of its owners. He has been but a short time in the place before he becomes aware of the queer happenings that had driven his terrified uncle and aunt away. He finds too that Barbara Bradford, the beautiful girl next door, is involved in a strangely complicated situation. He is just stumbling onto a clue when a murder is committed in the house, and he finds himself under arrest as the suspected murderer. The story follows it course to the satisfactory explanation, tracing all the mysteries back to one source"—Book review digest.

1851. **Jones, Charles Reed, b. 1896.** *The King murder*; **a Leighton Swift detective story. New York: Dutton, 1929. 265p.**

There are few if any clues to the murder of Miriam King, a beautiful woman with a wide circle of friends, especially among the male contingent. She is found in her New York City apartment apparently the victim of poison. The homicide might never have been solved had not the so-called 'Death King' confessed to it.

1852. —————. *The Van Norton murders.* **New York: Macaulay, 1931. 301p.**

It is up to the gentlemanly criminologist Leighton Swift to fathom the reasons behind the murders of several members of the Van Norton family, all of which occur in its Long Island mansion, and subsequently bring the murderer or murderers to justice.

1853. **Jones, Eugene.** *Who killed Gregory?* **New York: Stokes, 1928. x, 292p.**

"Was it a ghost or a big ape or a human hand? No one seemed to know, and detectives had a way of getting knocked unconscious, so the proposition looked all the more hopeless. Somehow in the huge Long Island house [the 'Grange'], with its barred windows and air of mystery Wilton Gregory had been struck down, in a room to which there was absolutely no access, except through the door—which was locked on the inside. Who killed Gregory?"—Book review digest.

1854. **Jones, James Athearn, 1791-1854.** *The refugee*; a romance, by Captain Matthew Murgatroyd of the Ninth Continentals in the Revolutionary War [pseud.]. New York: Wilder and Campbell, 1825. 2v.

> Sometimes claimed to be the first fictional account of New York City during the early years of the American Revolution. The hero is Gilbert Greaves, son of a loyal British subject; both father and son leave their home in the upper Hudson Valley, are given commissions in the English forces and serve in the New York City-Long Island campaign of 1776. But Gilbert has second thoughts despite warm friendships with several English officers and deserts to the Americans after a confrontation with a despicable British general officer. Captured in battle, Gilbert is imprisoned; he escapes briefly but, recaptured, he must stand trial for desertion and treason. His father is infuriated by Gilbert's actions and almost disowns him. Condemned to death Gilbert is pardoned at the last moment by Sir Henry Clinton. As the story winds down both of the Greaves go to England to claim old family estates. Gilbert marries Ellen Keith, daughter of a wealthy New York Tory. George Washington and several of his generals and aides, John Paul Jones, the aforementioned Sir Henry Clinton are just a few of the historical personages who play occasionally significant roles in the novel.

1855. **Jones, Jennifer, pseud.** *Dirge for a dog.* New York: Published for the Crime Club by Doubleday, Doran, 1939. 277p.

> "Here we have what appears to be a case of allergy to cat fur in a Miss Hannah Bostwick, rich old lady of 'Cool Brook' [N.Y.], completely surrounded by sinister servants and other enemies who would be capable of shooing cats in her direction. ...Daisy Jane Mott, a genial, if somewhat awkward narrator, tells also of a grim torso-killing and unearths some hideous secrets [and foils attempts on the life of New York heiress Bostwick]. The dog involved is named Balthazar. Another dog found the body making two dogs in all"—New York herald tribune books.

1856. ———. *Murder al fresco.* New York: Published for the Crime Club by Doubleday, Doran, 1939. 277p.

> "Daisy Jane Mott, fearless real estate broker and deducer of Reuterskill ... tells what really happened in the affair of Yggdrasil Farm [in Upstate New York] when Lotus Carmichael (Mrs. J. Ogden Carmichael) dropped dead in the third act of 'Gypsies for a Night', produced by an amateur cast in the courtyard of the estate. Lotus was supposed to stab herself with a rubber stiletto, and you know how these things turn out in mysteries—but you don't know who did it, or how or why. Just watch Daisy Jane as she concentrates on the suicide note, the typewriter, the adhesive tape and the other clues. Several of the performers look guilty, and so does Jasper, the butler"—New York herald tribune books.

1857. ――――. *Murder-on-Hudson.* **New York: Crowell, 1937. 303p.**

A real estate agent, unmarried Daisy Jane Mott, proves to be a detective smarter than the local police when she unlocks the mystery behind the killing of a banker whose corpse she stumbled across in an uninhabited mansion. The town on the Hudson in which the homicide occurs has its quota of odd characters and an outcropping of sinister scoundrelism.

1858. **Jones, Jesse Henry, 1836-1904.** *Joshua Davidson, Christian, the story of the life of one who in the nineteenth century was 'like unto Christ', as told by his body servant*; **a parable. Edited by Halah H. Loud. New York: Grafton Press, 1907. xviii, 308p.**

It is in upper New York State that Rebekah, daughter of a Lutheran father and a German-Jewish mother, marries Joshua. He is a believer in and teacher of Christian social doctrines: Christians are 'latter-day Jews' since Christianity is basically a continuation of Judaism in another form. At the story's end Joshua's teachings and advocacy of the laboring classes and strikers so antagonize the prominent business interests that they share a good deal of the responsibility when Joshua is lynched.

1859. **Jones, John Hilton.** *The Dominie's son.* **A novel. New York: [Manufactured by G.P. Putnam] 1874. 264p.**

Joshua Arbuckle, son of the recently deceased pastor of a church in 'Keesleyville' in the Chenango Valley, is given a clerkship in the New York City business firm of William Denniston, an old family friend. Joshua boards with the Dennistons; his memories of Rosetta Keesley, younger daughter of Keesleyville's physician, are still fresh. His father had taught Joshua well, for the young man spends many hours outside his job helping New Yorkers who have fallen on hard times. Rosetta comes to New York to further her education; within a few years she becomes the wife of Joshua in a ceremony performed in Keesleyville. Various bequests provide Joshua with a large capital base; while honeymooning in England and Scotland Joshua and his wife meet Sir Neville Arbuckle who is actually a rather close relative. With his growing fortune Joshua devotes a large portion of his money to assist farmers in Keesleyville and vicinity with their mortgages as well as endowing charitable institutions in Great Britain. Back in New York Joshua invests wisely in real estate and his fortune grows, granting him ever more funds for worthy purposes. The author intersperses commentaries on musical culture, philosophy of life, etc.

Jones, Justin. See under his pseudonym: Hazel, Harry.

1860. **Jones, Louis Clark, 1908-1990.** *Spooks of the valley*; **ghost stories for boys and girls. Illustrated by Erwin H. Austin. Boston: Houghton, Mifflin, 1948. iv, 111p.**

The folklore of the Upper Hudson River region provides the impetus for these stories of ghosts of the past including Captain Kidd, Aaron Burr, Henry Hudson, and others. Two young boys are introduced to help draw the stories together in a narrative wherein the ghosts ask the modern pair for help in resolving their particular problems.

1861.   Jones, Matthew F. *The Cooter farm*; a novel. **New York: Hyperion, 1991. 458p.**

In this convoluted gothic tale narrated by 10-year-old Ollie Cooter, a marginal dairy farm in Upstate New York is run by his redneck uncles 'Hooter' and 'Scooter', while Ollie's father is on the road selling high-grade bull semen. The two uncles' sister, Mary Jean, is 13, and she is Ollie's constant companion. The Cooter farm goes downhill—Scooter is a hypochondriac and ignores Hooter's incessant taunts, which annoy Scooter's wife. Hooter is 'a piece of work'—an adulterer, dangerously murderous, and incestuous. 'The Power', an evil force (perhaps a ghost) that resides in a deserted house, is discovered by Mary Jean; she and Ollie release it, hoping it will kill Hooter. Tragedy and humor mingle in the novel; however, the two young people, as they strive for maturity, are heirs to anxiety and alarm.

1862.   Jones, Ruth Fosdick. *Escape to freedom.* **Illus. by Dorothy Bayley Morse. New York: Random House, 1958. 236p.**

Timothy Blaine, 12, discovers that his house in Buffalo, New York is a 'terminal station' and his father is a 'conductor' defying the Fugitive Slave Law to help slaves across the Niagara River into Canada. "And it takes Tim himself through many a dangerous mission and narrow escapes from Southern owners in pursuit of their 'property'"—Chicago sunday tribune.

1863.   Jones, Stephen, 1935- . *Turpin.* **New York: Macmillan, 1968. 307p.**

The veterinarian Turpin is an ardent lobster fisherman who, when not indulging in his favorite pastime, deals professionally with some very peculiar clients in his Long Island practice.

1864.   Jordan, Elizabeth Garver, 1867-1947. *The girl in the mirror.* **Illustrated by Paul Meylan. New York: Century Co., 1919. 297p.**

A mystery and love story taking place in New York City, its underworld and more legitimate 'upper world'. "The young son of a rich family, having sown some wild oats, settles down to work and writes a successful play in collaboration with a chum. His sister, on starting out on her honeymoon, commends Laurie to the care of his friends, Bangs, his fellow collaborator, and Epstein, their manager. When about to begin work on another play, Laurie sees in his mirror the reflection of a beautiful girl with a pistol at her head. He dashes out of the room and into the studio building were he knows the girl to be. This is the beginning of a deep mystery involving a series of thrilling incidents, which will nigh end fatally. As the climax is reached the mystery clears and reveals itself as a hoax played on Laurie by the friends in collaboration with the beautiful girl, an actress, to keep him out of mischief"—Book review digest.

1865. ————. *The life of the party.* **New York: Appleton-Century, 1936. 298p.**
Halcyon Camp, the Long Island estate of millionaire Casper Kneeland, is the scene of several worrisome happenings; Kneeland is being blackmailed; a Pekinese is slain (by Dr. Craig, a vivisectionist?); Mrs. Spencer Forbes has a strange hold over Aunt Hosanna, etc. Young Rex Hale, an unemployed engineer, does some sleuthing and eventually unmasks a most unexpected wrongdoer; he also saves the girl he loves.

1866. ————. *May Iverson's career.* **New York: Harper, 1914. 177p.**
The writer May Iverson, educated in a convent, gets a job on a New York newspaper and begins to realize that she has much to learn about human vagaries. She utilizes her powers of observation, acquires valuable experience while working on the newspaper and eventually gains signal success with her first published book and a play. Then she walks away from her burgeoning career as a writer to take a chance at love and marriage.

1867. ————. *Miss Blake's husband*; a novel. **New York: Century Co., 1926. 379p.**
In her quest for the perfect husband wealthy Marjorie Blake boards a train going East; after a railroad accident kills her traveling companion, two strangers, a man and a woman, insert themselves into her company. They advise her to try New York; there she meets the man that she has been seeking. Yet Marjorie and her lover are not free until the two aforementioned strangers' interest in her future is thoroughly explained.

1868. ————. *Miss Nobody from Nowhere.* **New York: Century Co., 1928. 186p.**
Suffering from amnesia and in need of a job a young woman wanders aimlessly on New York's Fifth Avenue. A young man happens by who recalls the girl as a registrant at his hotel, listed under the name of Miss Eve Personne of Nulleport—'Miss Nobody from Nowhere'? Falling in love with Eve he appoints himself her guardian; however, she slips away from him and finds work in a nightclub. A few nights later she encounters various friends who set about jogging her memory of things past and Eve recovers.

1869. ————. *The night club mystery*; **the experiences of a highly unconventional young man unexpectedly brought into contact with sinister forces. New York: Century Co., 1930. 314p.**
"Barry Cabot of Wheaton, Mass. developed a case of hero-worship at the age of nine for a magnificent stranger named J.C. Bleecker, who went fishing with him. Years later, when Barry was a striving young bank employee in New York, he ran across his childhood friend again when J.C. Bleecker, known as Brian Strong, gambler, was framed by the police following a nightclub murder. Barry didn't frequent nightclubs, but he had gone to this one to

protect young Janet, his childhood playmate, from the very racy crowd of which she had become a member. Barry not only protects his sweetheart, but beats up a few underworld thugs as well and saves his good friend"—Book review digest.

1870. ————. *Red Riding Hood*; a novel. **New York: Century Co., 1925. 356p.**
The Schuylers are very prominent in the New York social world and Mrs. Morgan Schuyler feels the need for a secretary to handle her many appointments. An advertisement brings forth a young woman of obvious culture but with no references or even a recallable name. Mrs. Schuyler dubs her 'Hope Emerson'. Answering the telephone on one occasion, Hope is startled by a wolf-like howl. Then she and the Schuylers get involved with a rather peculiar bunch and a wild sequence of events follows. By the story's end Hope finds her true identity and that of 'the wolf'.

1871. ————. *Tales of the city room*. **New York: Scribner, 1898. ix, 232p.**
A connected series of stories about women journalists on major newspapers in New York City. Ruth Herrick of 'The Searchlight' and Helen Bancroft of the 'Evening Globe' figure prominently in several of the 'tales' which deal with investigative reporting on the city's life and politics. Contents: Ruth Herrick's assignment.—The love affair of Chesterfield, Jr.—At the close of the second day.—The wife of the candidate.—Mrs. Ogilvie's local color.—From the hand of Dolorita.—The passing of Hope Abbot.—A point of ethics.—A romance of the city room.—Miss Van Dyke's best story.

1872. ————. *The wings of youth*; a novel. **New York: Harper, 1918. 319p.**
"The wealthy aristocrat masquerading as a penniless and friendless stranger is quite common of late in fiction. Here a new note is added to the situation—a note old in itself, but new in this combination. Lawrence Devon and his sister Barbara are the last of a long established family of high social standing— Lawrence, however, is a young wastrel and passes from failure to failure. Not only his own habits handicap him, but also the fact that he and his past are widely known. To give him a 'sporting chance', his young sister, in whose hands rest all the Devon wealth, makes a compact with him to go to New York under assumed names, with only fifty dollars each, and for one year to earn their way by their own efforts and independent of each other. Lawrence is to promise to give up drink, cards, and other bad habits, and if he keeps every condition of the compact, is to receive at the close of the year ten thousand dollars. Most of the book is occupied with the story of their struggles in the big city, their adventures, the friends they meet, the kinds of success they achieve. In the end Lawrence is entirely reclaimed from his early dissipations and Barbara marries a son of one of New York's best families"— Book review digest.

1873. **Jordan, Kate, 1861 or 2-1926.** *The creeping tides*; a romance of an old neighborhood. **With front. by Lucius Wolcott Hitchcock. Boston: Little, Brown,**

1913. 354p.

In a Greenwich Village setting John Cross, a retired English soldier in poor health and saddled with a dubious past, meets Fanny Barrett who is also trying to forget past horrors and is wary of the future. Several well-defined minor characters surround the two. John and Fanny come together, for both are anxious to keep their pasts hidden and to reach for peace and security.

1874. ————. *The other house*; a study of human nature. New York: Lovell, Coryell, 1892. 183p.

"A young woman, tired of everything, goes to live in seclusion with her chaperone in a suburb of New York City. Her neighbor is a successful physician who first meets her on entering her house by mistake with his own latchkey. The doctor is married and his wife soon grows jealous of the inhabitants of 'the other house'. Meeting a missionary friend of the doctor's, the heroine grows interested in work among the poor. After attending an evening service at the Sunset Mission she confesses her history to the doctor. The consequences are far-reaching"—Annual American catalogue.

1875. ————. *Time the comedian*. New York: Appleton, 1905. 333p.

Bored with life in a small manufacturing town in New York State, tired of her husband, and saddled with a ten-year-old daughter, a selfish woman is allowed to visit New York City for several months. There she and her husband's best friend make plans to elope, but when he hears of her husband's suicide, he refuses to consider marrying the widow. He does, however, grant her substantial funds for her expenses. Years later he falls in love with the widow's daughter, but the latter's knowledge of the correspondence between her mother and her former New York lover, ends any hope of marriage.

1876. Jordan, Robert. *Thanksgiving*. New York: Dutton, 1970. 315p.

The story surrounds "a group of young people: Chris and Elinor, a happy radical couple, Eric and Linda, who can't make up their minds whether they are a couple or not, and Peter—dour, efficient and apparently the odd man out—whose expertise in demolition makes him an essential member of the clan. They are brought together by a common contempt for American society in general and a loathing of the American Vietnam policy in particular, and plan to blow up [the Amagansett] Country Club in an exclusive part of Long Island [during Thanksgiving] in order to bring its well-heeled residents to an understanding of the monstrous acts wrought in the name of the Silent Majority"—Times of London literary supplement.

Josiah Allen's wife, pseud. See: Holley, Marietta, 1936-1926.

1877. Judah, Samuel Benjamin Helbert, 1799-1876. *The buccaneers*; a romance of our own country, in its ancient day; illustrated with divers marvellous histories and antique and facetious episodes; gathered from the most authentic chronicles & affirmed records extant, from the settlement of the Nieuw

482

Nedlerlandts, until the times of the famous Richard Kidd: carefully collected from the laborious researches, and minute investigations, of that excellent antiquary and sublime philosopher yclept Terentius Phlogobombos. In five books. Boston: Munroe & Francis; New York: C. S. Francis, 1827. 2v.

The author's only attempt at fiction results in a murky, hardly readable historical 'romance' populated by comic characters (e.g., Sportus Vanderspeigl, his wife Yokupminshe, their servant Yonne, Tribulation Wholesome, et al.) and by historical figures—Captain William (here called Richard) Kidd, the pirate; Jacob Leisler, lieutenant-governor of New York; and the latter's arch-enemy, Colonel Henry Sloughter. Books 1-2 recount some of the early history of New York City under Dutch and British rule and Captain Kidd's dealings with the ferry master Vanderspeigl and the pirate's supposed booty-seeking forays in the areas around the city. Books 3-5 deal with Leisler and the troubles he faced from his enemies as he endeavored to rule New York as a popular leader, but eventually was executed on trumped-up charges of treason.

Judson, E[dward] Z[ane] C[arroll], 1823-1886. See: Buntline, Ned, 1823-1886.

1878. **Judson, Jeanne, b. 1890.** *Beckoning roads.* **Illus. by Grant T. Reynad. New York: Dodd, Mead, 1919. 259p.**

"Marguerite Shay, of Irish-Spanish descent, lost her parents before she was five years old, and went to live on the Canadian wheat ranch of her father's friend and her guardian, John Gratiot. She grew up with only men for companions, taught by Cecil Barrington, a young Englishman who lived on the ranch until Marguerite was fourteen years old. At seventeen Gratiot took her to St. Louis and put her in school, whereupon she married Humphrey Wells, not because she cared deeply for him, but because she hated school. She soon left Humphrey to live in New York where she earned her living by working for Baron Brinker, proprietor of a high class gambling house, who wanted someone whose name he could 'use at a bank and with bankers', so that his own name need not appear in stock transactions. Marguerite fell out with Baron, tired of her fast friends, went to work as a cloak model, and finally, having discovered that she loved her husband, went 'back to the white high road'"—Book review digest.

1879. ————. *The stars incline.* **New York: Dodd, Mead, 1820. 286p.**

"Upon the death of her mother Ruth Mayfield is sent to New York City to live with an aunt whom she has never seen who is a celebrated, emotional actress, and who has the unique distinction of having divorced three husbands. Ruth in her early teens dabbled below the surface of mysterious, occult things; to her amazement she discovers an actively evil hypnotic influence among her aunt's servants. George, the powerfully built, red-eyed Hindu, not only very nearly kills Gloria Mayfield's first husband by his mystic power of thought and faith, but also comes close to wrecking Gloria's future. Ruth, however, quietly intervenes, and after much anxiety, has the happiness of seeing Percy Pendragon, Gloria's first husband, miraculously restored to health, Gloria restored to Percy, and George's sinister power utterly broken. Ruth's own love affairs together with her frustrated ambition to be a great artist, offset the mystic atmosphere that hangs over Gloria and her household"—Book review digest.

1880. **Judson, William, pseud.** *Cold River*; a novel. **New York: Mason & Lipscomb [1975], c1974. 213p.**

"A bitter hard winter looms ahead in October 1921 when Lizzie, 14, and Tim, 13, are taken by their woodsman father on a canoe trip into the Adirondack wilderness. Within a few days an accident kills their father and for two months the children, equipped with little but memories and ingenuity, are alone in the woods"—Christian science monitor.

1881. **Justice, Maibelle.** *Love affairs of a worldly man.* **Chicago, New York: F. Tennyson Neely, 1894. 311p.**

"'There was something lofty, yet not haughty' in Alvin Geoffrey's manner, 'which indicated the finished man of the world', but likewise, 'there was that simplicity and neutralness in his demeanor which are the results of the very highest breeding', and, as a leader of New York society explained, 'were he not so fabulously rich and his family of such distinction, he would be completely ostracized by good society'. He had married an actress in his early youth, but, according to the same authority, 'It became a very cold day outside to him when he tried to introduce his wife into our society'—and so the actress left him after six months. Being a bold ... man, it falls to his lot, of course, to be loved by the heroine"—The critic. But even after Geoffrey's former actress/wife dies, the new woman in his life will not enter into any permanent connection with him.

Kagey, Rudolf Hornaday, 1904-1946. See under his pseudonym: Steel, Kurt.

1882. **Kahler, Hugh MacNair, 1883-1969.** *Hills were higher then.* **New York: Farrar & Rinehart, 1931. 284p.**

In a collection of eight interconnected stories the author's chief player is Andrew McNaughton, a kindly elderly man who had wandered the hilly farms of Upstate New York from his childhood. McNaughton's outstanding characteristics are his instinctive sense of fairness and his ability to make the right choices, a beacon for others to follow.

1883. **Kahler, Woodland, b. 1895.** *Smart setback.* **New York: Knopf, 1930. 236p.**

"Rylda Wade [a member of New York City's 'smart set'] is bored with life. Her mother is a society leader, her husband a banker. She meets Kent Crawford at a party, and in the course of trying to get him to give her life a plot, becomes his mistress. But Kent's ideas aren't of much use to her, so she finally gives him up and goes into the fashion business in an endeavor to give meaning to life"—Outlook.

Kaler, James Otis, 1848-1912. See: Otis, James, 1848-1912.

1884. **Kamins, Jeanette.** *Everything but a husband.* **New York: St. Martin's Press, c1962. 344p.**

The novel revolves around the husband-seeking (primarily) of five young women from New York City during a long weekend in a Catskill resort. They may be seeking 'prey' but their male counterparts prey upon them too. Flashbacks and fast-paced dialogue are major ingredients of the story.

1885. **Kandel, Aben, 1899- .** *Black sun.* **New York: Harper, 1929. 250p.**

"A story of love and disillusionment beginning in Greenwich Village and ending …in [Brightplains, a New York suburb]. Michael loved Louise casually, but Louise demanded marriage. Then there was a baby and Michael gave up his dream of a newspaper job to take a place on a trade journal. The next step was the loss of that job with its consequent misery. He traveled through all the phases of discouragement until we leave him finally turning back with relief to his home and Louise and the baby"—Book review digest.

1886. **Kane, Edward Charles.** *A gentleman born.* **New York: G.W. Dillingham, 1900. 340p.**

Brought up in the slums of New York the young hero of this tale is actually the true heir of a huge estate who had been stolen away from his original home by hirelings of an unsavory man high in the social circles of the 'smart set'; the latter looked on the young child as an impediment to his plans to marry the boy's mother. Of course the story concludes with the restoration of the young man's rights and the 'comeuppance' of the villain.

Kane, William Reno, b. 1885. See under his pseudonym: Wright, Mason, b. 1895.

Karlstein, Heinrich Oscar von, pseud. See: Valentine, Ferdinand Charles, 1851-1910.

1887. **Karp, David, 1922- .** *Leave me alone.* **New York: Knopf, 1857. 303p.**

"Arthur Henry Douglas is an editor in a good publishing house, lives within his salary in Manhattan and is persuaded to move to [the North Shore of] Long Island. There his community life becomes involved with the issue of a new library which is cut through by racial and religious lines; his professional life is colored by the need for the replacement of Sprague, the chief editor, the demands of the owner of the business and the possibility of financial compromise, when a chance in a broker's office comes up. The effect of both areas of conflict reflect on his marriage, point up the clash between the humanities and pragmatic living, and draw in the net of timidity"—Kirkus reviews.

1888.   Kaufelt, David Allan, 1939-   . *The Fat Boy murders*; a Wyn Lewis mystery. New York: Pocket Books, 1993. 230p.

The Long Island town of 'Waggs Neck Harbor' is struggling economically; the mayor, Phineas Browne, envisions a development plan that will attract the much-needed expenditures of a swarm of tourists. Jackson Hall, distinguished artist, and a former schoolmate of the mayor, has meanwhile returned to Waggs Neck Harbor, his hometown. Hall in his youth had often been the target of cruel tricks performed by the 'Fat Boys', a club of well-heeled lads that included in its membership Phineas Browne and Percy Curry, now a local character. When both Browne and Curry die suddenly a current of alarm and of rancor sweeps through the town. Wyn Lewis, lawyer and realtor—her father had been one of the Fat Boys—takes on the task of making sense of the tangled skeins.

1889.   ————. *The winter women murders*; a Wyn Lewis mystery. New York: Pocket Books, 1994. 214p.

Chic residential (and fictional) 'Waggs Neck Harbor', Long Island, is stirred by the death of the Annual Literary Arts Symposium's founder and the arrival of Rhodesia Comfort Noble, the founder's daughter from California (with her lover); Ms. Noble assumes control of the symposium and contemplates changing its character and its planning board. Wyn Lewis, a local realtor/lawyer, is perturbed when her lover, Tommy Handwerk, is mesmerized by novelist Annie Vasquez, one of the scheduled speakers at the symposium. Things really heat up when two of the speakers are throttled and Wyn, with the assent of the chief of police, looks into the murders.

1890.   Kauffman, Bill, 1959- . *Every man a king*. New York: Soho Press, 1989. 227p.

John Huey leaves his hometown in western New York State and finds employment on a popular but inebriated New York State senator's staff. From there he goes to a right-wing research organization and then embarks on a career as a political columnist. With success apparently assured, John Huey blows it all when he appears on Face the Nation and gives voice to an opinion that has racial bias connotations. The ensuing furor terminates his political itinerary and back he goes to hometown Batavia, N.Y. Huey settles down and eventually finds solace and love with Wanda, a factory worker.

1891.   Kauffman, Reginald Wright, 1877-1959. *The house of bondage*. New York: Moffat, Yard, 1910. 466p.

The main plot of the novel depicts the betrayal and downfall of a girl of sixteen from a Pennsylvania factory town willingly taken away from unsympathetic parents by a smooth-talking traveling salesman. Broken promises of marriage and her determination not to return to a hated home lead the girl to a captive existence in a New York brothel run by Rose Legère. When she

486

breaks away from Legère's and crawls back home, she is refused entry. Back to the mean streets of New York she goes, homeless and slowly dying. The author has harsh words for the graft and political chicanery in the metropolis that have a cruel impact on young working women. The 'system' ensures that females who have 'fallen' have little or no chance of ever recovering.

1892. ————. *Mad Anthony's drummer.* **Illustrated by Thomas Fogarty. New York: Macmillan, 1929. 211p.**

The capture of Stony Point on the Hudson, July 1779, by 'Mad' Anthony Wayne is the basis of this historical fiction. Sam, a drummer boy with the American Revolutionary Army, presumably has a hand in the victorious assault on the British-held fort.

1893. ————. *Miss Frances Baird, detective*; **a passage from her memoirs, as narrated to and now set down by Reginald Wright Kauffman. With a front. in color by William Kirkpatrick. Boston: L.C. Page, 1906. vi, 269p.**

The lady detective, Frances Baird, was not among the favored of her supervisor for she had failed to perform adequately in a couple of cases to which she had been assigned. However she did show up at an estate on the Hudson where two robberies and a murder had taken place. The detectives who preceded her and were supposed to be guarding some very expensive diamonds were of no help. Baird used her intuition and her natural smarts to disentangle the crimes and bring her back to the good graces of the chief of detectives.

1894. ————. *Running sands.* **New York: Dodd, Mead, 1913. vii, 353p.**

At age fifty a successful Western miner comes to New York to enjoy the fruits of his labor and perhaps to end his bachelor status. He feels as vigorous as a man half his age and falls deeply in love with a girl of eighteen. She is not sure how far she wants to go with him, but they do marry. And then she finds herself drawn to an Austrian near her own age. Her husband, aware of his wife's predicament, is willing to withdraw from the marriage, even contemplating suicide to free his wife (divorce is out of the questions, since the Austrian's religion forbids him to marry a divorced woman). The husband backs away from the notion of killing himself and returns for better or worse to his wife.

1895. ————. *The spider's web.* **Illustrated by Jean Paleologue. New York: Moffat, Yard, 1913. xix 409p.**

Idealistic Luke Huber comes to New York City as an assistant in the district attorney's office quite certain that he is in a position to combat corruption and greed. But he 'comes to see the sin of compulsion exerting itself against humanity in all the powers that conduct modern society'. He resigns and is himself nominated for district attorney by the Municipal Reform League—but even there he is confronted by graft. Going into business for himself Luke is once again made only too aware of the insidious reach of the moneyed interests. A personage known as 'The Man', 'The King', or 'The Modern Napoleon', sits in his Wall Street office and pulls the strings from which his puppets dangle.

Kavanaugh, Ian, pseud. See: Webb, Jean Francis, 1910- .

1896. **Kay, Terry, 1918- .** *Shadow song.* **New York: Pocket Books, 1994. 258p.**
It is 1955 and Madison Lee ('Bobo') Murphy has come from rural Georgia to work at a Catskill resort. Bobo's introduction to Jewish folkways is eased by elderly Avrum Feldman who is held in high esteem by Bobo even though many of the guests think his lifetime devotion to the late opera legend, Madame Galli-Curci, borders on the demented. Bobo and Amy Lourie, a 'Jewish princess' from New York City, have an innocent summer-long romance and then go their separate ways. After 38 years Bobo returns to the Catskills to attend Avrum's funeral. Amy is also present and the two fall in love with one another again.

1897. **Keeler, Harry Stephen, 1890-1967.** *Sing Sing nights.* **New York: Dutton, 1928. ix, 397p.**
In Sing Sing Prison, Ossining, N.Y., three men have been sentenced to death for the murder of a highly unpopular New York man-about-town. They 'kill' time before the appointed hour for their execution by swapping stories. Each of the three prisoners is a writer of fiction; they are apprised that he who tells the best story will receive a pardon.

1898. **Keenan, Henry Francis, 1850-1928.** *The aliens*; **a novel. New York: Appleton, 1886. 453p.**
"A city of western New York some fifty years ago [ca. 1836] is the chief scene of the story. The aliens are a family of Irish emigrants who come there with a little money, but who are finally separated and condemned to much sorrow and misery through the father's brutality. The mother dies in a poorhouse, and the children have various fortunes—their adventures and opposite lives taking up a greater part of the book. The family of the 'Governor of Warchester' furnished a contrasting picture, from a different grade of life—the son 'Darcy' being one of the heroes, and having his fortunes inextricably mixed with those of the 'aliens'. The story is brought down to the time of the Mexican War"—Annual American catalogue.

1899. ————. *The money makers*; **a social parable. New York: D. Appleton, 1885. vi, 337p.**
The novel's chief protagonist is Alfred (Fred) Carew, a New York journalist with high ethical standards who has tasted the carefree life of the free-spending, spoiled sons of the titans of finance and commerce, but tends to side with the laboring classes. When he assumes editorship of a newspaper in the Upstate New York city of 'Valedo' his is a liberal voice that mediates between the 'plutocracy' and the factory workers. His main opponents are

wealthy, unscrupulous Aaron Grimstone and his political allies. The novel concludes with a wild riot by workers incensed by layoffs and the manipulations of corporate owners and Grimstone's suicide with Carew back at his editorial desks of two newspapers in Valedo. The author notes that greed is back in the saddle and that moneymaking remains 'not only the law, but the gospel of life'.

1900. Kehoe, William John. *A sweep of dusk.* **New York: Dutton, 1945. 442p.**

Curt Fahrner of Upstate 'Graceville', New York graduates from high school on the eve of World War II and enters nearby 'Ames University'. Away from his mother's possessiveness Curt is gradually developing a life of his own when the sudden death of his father brings on the mental collapse of Mrs. Avis Fahrner with a subsequent call for Curt to leave Ames and come back home to Graceville. Upon the shoulders of Curt's Aunt Malvina falls the burden of soothing Avis, her sister, while Curt and his two sisters, un-disciplined Ginnie and dissatisfied Dody, are bystanders. Curt drifts away from Stevie, the girl to whom he had given his fraternity pin, and loses any meaningful contact with his college friends. As the novel concludes one is inclined to predict a drab future for Curt—tied to a helpless mother, a dull job and the increasing importunities of a hometown girl of long acquaintance.

Keilstrup, Margaret, 1945- . See under her pseudonym: Lorens, M.K.

1901. Kelland, Clarence Budington, 1881-1964. *Dance magic.* **New York: Harper, 1927 [c1926]. 270p.**

"To Ripley Chandler, as to all inhabitants of Ripley-Bridge, dancing was of the devil. Therefore Chandler's harsh course at the discovery of his daughter's [Johalla's] talent followed as naturally as that she should run away from [the drab New England farm] and find her place on the New York stage that her dancing justified. The story of her romantic career discloses a liberal number of the thrills, the perils and the disillusionments of [New York] stage life"— Book review digest.

1902. ————. *Double treasure.* **New York: Harper, 1946. 248p.**

Four men and a girl search that piece of shore on Long Island which some old documents claim is the site of treasure buried there in 1699 by pirates. Several questionable characters who obviously have the same objective as they harass the searchers. The cast includes an Oriental knife-thrower, an Armenian, the twins Gallan and Quelch, and a corpse with a gold coin imbedded above each of its eyes.

1903. ————. *Hard money.* **New York: Harper, 1930. 474p.**

"In the early days of the nineteenth century young Jan Van Horn, son of a Dutch peddler, sailed his sloop down the Hudson River to New York. His object was to learn all he could about money, and his quest was successful beyond even his dreams. With the knowledge gained on that trip Jan entered upon his career as a banker, and from then until his death in 1845 he was a figure to [be] reckoned with in the banking world"—Book review digest.

1904. ————. *The lady and the giant.* **New York: Dodd, Mead, 1959. 246p.**
Syracuse, N.Y. is the place and the time is 1869, just after Black Friday. The Cardiff Giant has been uncovered on Stubby Newell's farm and the mysterious Madam Cissie Janeway and her saturnine butler Oscar have moved into a house just across from the Foxes. Orrin Applegate, a lawyer just out of the newly-founded college, Cornell in Ithaca, and his companion from childhood, the beautiful young Lossie Fox, are more than a little curious about the free-spending Madam Janeway, the probable hoax—the Cardiff Giant— and the recently arrived medicine show with its odd cast of characters. With the help of the friendly Erie 'canawlers', Zacharias and 'Maw' Wheelright, and hardheaded detective work, Orrin and Lossie arrive at the solution of two murders and the circumstances surrounding Madam Cissie Janeway's lavish expenditures in Syracuse. A most entertaining novel.

Kelly, Adelaide Skeel, 1852-1928. See: Skeel, Adelaide, 1852-1928.

1905. **Kelly, Ethel May, b. 1878.** *Beauty and Mary Blair*; **a novel. Boston: Houghton, Mifflin, 1921. 282p.**
"A story of adolescence told with vivacity and humor, from the viewpoint of eighteen, sophisticated years, by Mary Blair herself. She lives in a New York apartment with a father and a mother who have never had any sense of responsibility toward their children, a married and emancipated sister, and a twelve-year-old brother who observes and comments upon the infelicities of his parents. In the midst of this disintegrating household Mary Blair pursues her search for beauty with youthful honesty and ardor and even with a touch of idealism"—Book review digest.

1906. ————. *Home, James.* **With illus. by Ralph Burton. New York: Knopf, 1927. 118p.**
A girl from Park Avenue society with 'flapperish' tendencies marries her chauffeur, Jimmie Jakes, who is an admirable person with a broad sense of humor; each takes turns telling his/her story in 'New Yorkese' language.

1907. ————. *Over here*; **the story of a war bride. Front. by Charles Dana Gibson. Indianapolis: Bobbs-Merrill, 1918. 259p.**
To Beth, an 18-year-old New York City society belle, America's entrance into the First World War is not of any great significance. Then she falls in love with Tommy, a patriotic young soldier. They marry in haste; Tommy is trained in Plattsburgh, N.Y. and is then shipped to France. By now the war has taken on new meaning to Beth, especially since she is pregnant, a fact she keeps from her husband. Tommy dies in combat before the baby is born. In a burst of patriotism Beth decides that her baby son, Obadiah, will follow in his father's footsteps and choose a military career.

1908. ————. *Wings*. **New York: Knopf, 1924. 214p.**

"This book is written backwards. In the first section, Epilogue, is given the story of the love of Priscilla Anne Prendergast, nineteen-year-old flapper, for Paul Hutchinson, thirty-five, a poet and editor of a highbrow [New York] magazine. In Book Two, called The End, is told the story of Hutchinson's infatuation years earlier for a charming married woman. In Book Three, The Beginning, Hutchinson's first considerable love affair comes to light. By the device of having the women meet one another the author links up the story and makes it complete"—Book review digest.

1909. Kelley, William, 1929- . *The Tyree legend*. **New York: Simon and Schuster, 1979. 512p.**

Returning to 'Kaatskill' County in Upstate New York to attend the funeral of his alienated wife Deidre, Oscar Tyree, a brilliant painter, gets to know Gaybee Kalkbergh and asks her to marry him. Gaybee is murdered and suffers the same mutilation as a young girl who had been killed and hung outside Tyree's home many years before. The similar circumstances lead to Oscar's arrest and trial for murder. At the same time Deidre's family the prominent Breesvorts, get involved in the court proceedings; Duff Breesvort, the son, a lawyer, stops his drinking and playboy activities in order to take up a defender's role at the trial.

1910. Kellogg, Walter Guest, b. 1877. *Parish's fancy*. **New York: John Day Co., 1929. x, 293p.**

A fictionalized version of a triangle in which Contessina Ameriga (or Maria Amerigo) Vespucci, mistress of 'Prince' John Van Buren (son of President Martin Van Buren) is gambled away in a poker game in Evans Mills, N.Y., to George Parish of Ogdensburg. The Contessina is a direct descendant of the explorer, Amerigo Vespucci; however, the unfortunate woman, in love with Parish, spends her remaining days in Parish's mansion at Ogdensburg, dying of a broken heart when Parish marries another woman.

1911. Kelly, Florence Finch, 1858-1939. *On the inside*. **New York: Sanford, 1890. 238p.**

Harry Reberfell's friend, Ambrose Brokken, uses his wife Clara's money to create business opportunities, but also keeps a mistress, Helen Lestrange. Reberfell himself is something of an anarchist, disapproving of current American economic practices. He is much interested in a newcomer to New York City, Isbelle Fairmount, a typist with intellectual curiosity but very protective of her reputation and her innocence. When Isbelle goes to Brokken's office for dictation he attacks her. She escapes and tells Helen (who has befriended her) of the attempted rape. Brokken is also in trouble of another kind when his partner's wife, Mrs. Dellaury, accuses him of murdering her husband whose body was found in the doorway of Reberfell's apartment. Brokken is brought to trial and is acquitted, partly because of his mistress's perjured testimony. Then charges of forged instruments fall on Brokken, now a ruined man; he is adjudged guilty and is sentenced to 14 years in prison. Helen Lestrange is found guilty of perjury and receives a 10-year sentence. She leaves her two children by Brokken in Isbelle's hands. Reberfell and Isbelle find they have much in common.

Kelly, George C., d. 1895. See under his pseudonym: Payne, Harold.

1912. Kelly, Jack, 1949- . *Apalachin*. New York: Dutton, c1987. 278p.
In 1957 members of the American 'Mafia' got together in Apalachin, N.Y., to discuss territorial imperatives and allied problems. This novel hones in on the activities of several mobsters in another Upstate New York locale (it could well be Buffalo) a year after the above gathering. The 'big shot', Manny ('the Mover') Petrone, has a domestic crisis fueled by an alcoholic wife. Link, a car thief and auto racer, continues clandestine meetings with a married woman; George is syphilitic and an incipient pedophile. The novel is a graphic canvas in its depiction of the 1950s and life as led by a lower middle-class group that was not averse to occasional violence.

1913. Kelly, Myra, 1887-1910. *Little aliens*. New York: Scribner, 1910. 291p.
Aspects of life among the recent immigrants on New York City's teeming East Side, stories that run the gamut from humor to tragedy. Contents: Every goose a swan.—Games in gardens.—A brand from the burning.—Friends.—The magic cape.—'Bailey's babies'.—The origin of species.—The etiquette of Yetta.—A bent twig.

1914. ————. *Little citizens*; the humours of school life. Illustrated by W.D. Stevens. New York: McClure, Phillips, 1904. 352p.
Stories about children of New York's East Side of varying ethnic groupings: e.g., Jewish, Italian, Irish. They go to a large public school full of mischief and display the prejudices of their adult mentors. Contents: A little matter of real estate.—The uses of adversity.—A Christmas present for a lady.—Love among the blackboards.—Morris and the Honorable Tim.—When a man's widowed.—H.R.H. The Prince of Hester Street.—The land of heart's desire.—A passport to Paradise.—The touch of nature.

1915. ————. *Wards of liberty*. Illus. by Frederic Dorr Steele. New York: McClure Co., 1907. xv, 310p.
Short stories dealing in a humorous way with new immigrants to New York City and based on the author's own observations while she was a teacher in schools located in the city's slums and ghettoes. Contents: In loco parentis.—A soul above buttons.—The slaughter of the innocents.—A perjured Santa Clause.—Little Bo-Peep.—The wiles of the wooer.—The gifts of the philosopher.—Star of Bethlehem.

1916. Kelsey, Vera. *The bride dined alone*. Garden City, N.Y.: Published for the

Crime Club by Doubleday, Doran, 1943. 184p.

"An excellent psychological dissection of Dana Madison, a young Long Island matron who likes to marry money so that she can keep her foot on the neck, or necks, of her long-suffering family. The mortality rate among Dana's husbands and employees mounts rapidly, and so does the suspense"—New Yorker.

1917. **Kemp, Harry [Hibbard], 1883-1960.** *More miles*; **an autobiographical novel. New York: Boni & Liveright, 1926. 437p.**

In part an autobiographical novel about a boy adrift in the big city who finally settles in Greenwich Village (prior to World War I), sharpens his poetic sensibilities and explores the art of love. Several of the author's characters are based on real personages who were habitués or residents of the Village.

1918. **Kendall, Jack.** *Playing for keeps.* **New York: Avon Books, 1989. 216p.**

When the bodies of three teenagers turn up in the vicinity of a Long Island village there is evidence that the killings are connected with arcane ceremonies conducted by malevolent individuals. The local youth social worker, Arnold 'Zip' Zipke, cooperates with the police in the search for the perpetrator[s] of a horrible crime.

1919. **Kendrick, Baynard Hardwick, 1894-1977.** *Clear and present danger*; **a Duncan Maclain mystery. New York: Published for the Crime Club by Doubleday, 1958. 190p.**

In one of his latest cases Captain Duncan Maclain, a blind private detective, investigates the murder of Henry Wilkins who had uncovered uranium deposits in the Hudson Valley. The strike attracted a variety of individuals: prospectors, crooks, would-be-investors, et al. The F.B.I. also appeared on the scene; unperturbed, Maclain continued with his search for the murderer and evidence.

1920. **Kennedy, William, 1928- .** *Billy Phelan's greatest game.* **New York: Viking Press, 1978. 282p.**

As this novel begins it is "1938, and the Democratic machine of the McCall brothers has Albany and all its gambling in a firm grip. When Charlie Boy McCall, sole heir of the family, is kidnapped, the brothers call on journalist Martin Daugherty to quash the city's biggest story since Legs Diamond was shot to death in an Albany rooming house seven years earlier. Billy Phelan, [a young gambler], whose livelihood is controlled by the McCalls, is recruited as a reluctant informer, and Daugherty watches as the loner, for whom he feels a paternal admiration, clashes with the machine"—Atlantic.

1921. ————. *The flaming corsage.* **New York: Viking Press, 1996. 209p.**

The marriage of Edward Daugherty, son of rigid Irish Catholics from North Albany, to Katrina Taylor, daughter from an old, proud, Albany Protestant family, is frowned upon by all but the lovers. When he achieves success as a playwright, Edward tries to smooth over family differences with gifts and a banquet. Fire engulfs the dining room; there is one death and Katrina is injured. Edward has an affair with an actress and Katrina cozies up to Francis Phelan (later the alcoholic protagonist of Kennedy's 'Ironweed'). That is only the beginning of a series of tragic incidents.

1922. ————. *The ink truck*. **New York: Dial Press, 1969. 278p.**
"All that needs saying is that this is not a book about an anonymous city but about Albany, N.Y., and a few of its dynamics during two centuries"— Author's note (1984 reprint). The conflict that drives the novel is a protracted newspaper strike that is dragging to a hopeless end despite the continuing leadership of the hero, Bailey, a former columnist. Bailey stoops to arson, the target being a building used by the strikebreakers, a mixture of gypsies and plug-uglies. The fire accomplishes nothing and invites extreme counter-actions by the newspaper owners. Bailey in his search for the meaning of it all encounters dirty union politics and his own fantasies.

1923. ————. *Ironweed*; **a novel. New York: Viking Press, 1983. 227p.**
Francis Phelan, a former professional baseball player, ran out on his family 23 years ago following the tragic death of an infant son for which he held himself responsible. It is 1938 and Francis is still on the bum, drinking with his lady friend Helen, turning an occasional dollar by digging graves, and getting involved in various violent incidents in Albany's shantytown. He is welcomed by his wife Annie, son Billy, and daughter Peg at a dinner in their home, but then goes on another drinking spree. Helen dies of a stomach tumor and Francis seeks refuge under the 'holy Phelan eaves' in the family's attic after another killing in shantytown.

1924. ————. *Legs*; **a novel. New York: Coward, McCann & Geoghegan, 1975. 317p.**
In this fictional account Albany attorney Marcus Gorman tells the story of his relationship to the notorious gangster/killer Jack 'Legs' Diamond, concentrating on the last two years of Legs' life, much of which is spent in Upstate New York (the Catskills and Albany, the city where the 'invincible' Legs is finally killed by two gunmen). There are a few scenes in Diamond's Hotsy-Totsy Club in New York City and a feckless trip to Europe. According to Gorman, Legs Diamond envisioned expanding his bootlegging and speakeasy operations to the Catskills and neighboring regions.

1925. ————. *Quinn's book*. **New York: Viking Press, 1988. 289p.**
The author uses Daniel Quinn, a young lad who eventually becomes a skillful reporter, as narrator of a story that is set in Albany and other Upstate New York locations. Daniel records his obsession with the actress Maude Fallon, the labor unrest that characterized the period, Civil War events, the whole gamut of disasters, natural and human, from 1849 to 1864. He encounters

along the way a procession of charming, rascally, picaresque role-players who make the pages come alive.

1926. ————. *Very old bones.* **New York: Viking Press, 1992. 292p.**

The Phelan family of Albany, N.Y. is once again the focus of a Kennedy novel. Orson Purcell, illegitimate son of the artist Peter Phelan, is the story's narrator. A Phelan family gathering in 1958 is the occasion for Purcell's filling the reader in on his own life and projecting data concerning the whole range of Phelan family members, whether they are living or deceased. A shocking crime that occurred years ago but which has attained a special place in Albany's annals has also affected the peace of mind of the Phelans (if ever such peace existed).

1927. Kent, Elizabeth, pseud. *The house opposite*; **a mystery. New York: Putnam, 1902. iv, 276p.**

On a very warm day in New York City a young doctor, seeking relief from the summer's heat, goes to the roof of his home. Glancing over at a stylish apartment building on Madison Avenue, 'the house opposite' his, the doctor witnesses some violent happenings. Later a man's body turns up in that apartment building and the search is on for the perpetrator of what is obviously a homicide.

1928. Kent, James, novelist. *The Johnson manor*; **a tale of olden times in New York. New York: Putnam, 1877. 304p.**

Col. James Johnson, Sr. (no relation to the Sir William Johnson family) lives at the 'Manse' in the Mohawk Valley 20 years after the American Revolution with his son James (Jim) Jr. and his half-sister Katharine. During the war Katharine had survived a long Indian captivity in which a suitor, the Tory William Latimer, had been involved. Now half-insane she babbles frequently about her 'missing' child. When Latimer's brother, George, a distant cousin of James Johnson, Sr., passes away, he leaves his daughter Margaret under Johnson's guardianship. William Latimer, wanted by New York State authorities for various crimes and misdemeanors, reappears searching for Katharine and hoping to share the money she inherited. Documents turn up that prove William and Katharine are husband and wife. The Mohawk chieftain, Joseph Brant, provides evidence that Margaret is their child—Brant had protected both Katharine and Margaret from further harm during their captivity. Katharine dies and William Latimer is captured, put on trial and condemned to death. He escapes but on the point of recapture drowns himself to avoid the stigma of a formal execution. Margaret bravely survives all the revelations and confrontations with her father; she and James Johnson, Jr. are betrothed.

Kent, Willis, pseud. See: Collison, Wilson, 1893-1941.

1929. Kenyon, Michael, 1931- . *Kill the butler!* **New York: St. Martin's Press,**

1992. 221p.

Henry Peckover of Scotland Yard happens to be on Long Island when Lou Langley, a prosperous man in his eighties, is killed outside his home by a pickup truck. There is some contention that this was no accident and the local police have drawn up a list of suspects among whom are: Millicent, 79, Lou's widow; the two married daughters and their mates; the caretaker, a British historian to whom Langley has left his mansion, and who supports Lou Langley's belief that President Roosevelt was well aware of the Japanese intention to attack Pearl Harbor. Henry Peckover agrees to being planted in the Langley house as a butler (named Jervis). He and his right-hand man, Constable Twitty, also fortuitously on the scene, unveil the pertinent data.

1930. Keon, Grace, pseud. *Not a judgment* ———. **New York: Benziger Bros., 1906. 318p.**

The novel contrasts two women who come from widely different backgrounds. Mollie, a child of New York City's East Side slums, is determined to become a blessing, 'not a judgment' to all she comes in touch with. A brother who has committed murder and a mother defeated by poverty handicap her. Mollie moves upward by dint of her tenacity and noble character, achieving happiness with a doctor who loves her. Juxtaposed to Mollie is a spoiled society belle who eschews the empty values around her and offers her services to the needy as a member of a Catholic religious order.

1931. Kerr, M.E., 1927- . *Gentlehands.* **New York: Harper & Row, 1978. 183p.**

Sixteen-year-old Buddy Boyle of 'Seaville', Long Island (and Montauk) is attracted to upper class Skye Pennington who resides with her parents on an estate with the name Beauregard. Buddy's father and mother are dubious about his new girl friend; Skye Pennington is far above their station in life. However Buddy continues to see Skye, but he also deepens his relationship with Grandfather Trenker, Mrs. Boyle's estranged father, a cultured, kindly man who likes Buddy. Eventually Buddy moves in with Mr. Trenker at Montauk. The climax of the story arrives when Grandfather Trenker is unmasked as a refugee Nazi who had committed atrocities during the Third Reich. His nemesis is Nick De Lucca, a reporter and Pennington guest searching for the person responsible for his Italian-Jewish cousin's death at Auschwitz.

1932. ———. *Him she loves?* **New York: Harper & Row, 1984. 315p.**

Henry Schiller, 17, is a new boy in a Long Island town who has the misfortune of falling hard for beautiful Valerie Kissenwiser. Valerie's father, Al Kiss, is a well-known comedian who takes a violent dislike to Henry's hanging around his precious daughter. Al uses poor Harry, tagged as 'Heinrich', as a foil in his nightclub and TV gigs; the windup question Al asks is: 'Him she loves?' Henry concludes that he must in some way assure Al that he is no inept, timorous soul and Valerie couldn't choose a better partner than gentile he.

1933. ————. *What I really think of you.* New York: Harper & Row, 1982. 208p.

Opal Ringer, 16, of 'Seaview', Long Island, is jeered by her peers because her father preaches undeviating fundamentalism to a vociferously accepting congregation. The Rev. Guy Pegler is in sharp contrast to Rev. Ringer; he delivers 'feel-good' television sermons and his family 'fits in'. Opal and Jesse Pegler, Rev. Pegler's disaffected son, meet unexpectedly and share views. When Ringer performs a 'miraculous' cure Pegler invites the 'healed' girl to be a guest on his TV show. The upshot is embarrassment and turmoil for everyone involved, especially for withdrawn, introspective Opal, and she reacts in a startling way.

Kerr, Orpheus C., pseud. See: Newell, Robert Henry, 1836-1901.

1934. [Keyes, Hervey]. *The forest king*; or, *The wild hunter of the Adaca.* **A tale of the seventeenth century [sic]. New York: Wheat & Cornett, Printers, 1878. 63p.**

Deals with the exploits of Esock Mayall, the 'forest king', an expert woodsman who is adept at dealing with the Indians of the Mohawk Valley, friendly and hostile, and with the dangerous mammals (panthers, bears, wolves) of the forest. Married several years before the outbreak of the American Revolution to Nelly Gordon, a prosperous farmer's daughter, he has taken his bride to the Valley of the Adaca (present-day Otego area). The Mayalls survive the Revolution, but Nelly's parents are killed by Tory and Indian raiders. In the years following the conflict, Esock, Jr. grows to manhood and marries the adopted daughter of an old Indian chief; she is a White girl who was taken from her Canadian home after her mother was slain by the Indians. She has taken the name of Blanche, but later learns that her true forename is Dora. Blanche/Dora and Esock, Jr., accompanied by the elder Mayalls and their children and the old chieftain leave the Adaca for the Mohawk Valley.

1935. Keyser, Harriett A. *Thorns in your side.* **New York: G.P. Putnam, 1884. 238p.**

Opens with the Battle of Aughrim, Ireland, in 1691 where the English forces of William III overwhelmed those of James II; many Irish supporters of James fell in the battle. Almost 200 years later descendants of those who fought on both sides are in New York City—namely, the Rev. Dan Guardian of St Agnes, an Anglican church, and Terence O'Farrell, a laborer and terrorist filled with hatred of all things English. Strains of anti-Catholicism and disdain for the 'Romanists' Irish are manifested throughout the novel. The Rev. Guardian (with his daughter Sybilla) is a kindly man who cannot divest himself of antipathy towards Roman Catholicism and its Irish adherents. With knowledge of explosives gained from the Russian Skobeloff, O'Farrell dynamites St. Agnes, despite warnings to the Guardians by Jasper Arnold who has converted from Catholicism to Anglicanism. On a visit to the hamlet of

Aughrim the Reverend is murdered by O'Farrell (who had followed the Guardians), fulfilling a premonition Sybilla had envisioned.

Kildare, Leita, joint author. *Such a woman.* **See Item #1937.**

1936. **Kildare, Owen Frawley, 1864-1911.** *The good of the wicked*; **and** *The party sketches.* **New York: Baker & Taylor, 1904. 148p.**

Fictional pieces about New York characters (especially those floating around the Bowery—obviously members of the 'lower classes'). The author, a journalist who had previously been a newsboy, bouncer, prizefighter, and a latecomer to literacy (at the age of 30), does not apply to himself the statement: 'They who know the least about New Yorkers are born New Yorkers' (p. 108). 'The Party' of 'The Party sketches' is a young woman who points out aspects of the natural world to the narrator and whom he cares enough about to make her 'his girl' as they taste the sights of the city, the Hudson, Coney Island, etc. Contents: The good of the wicked.—The responsibility for slang.—The party sketches [including fifteen separate sketches].—Little stories from the streets [Canal Street and the Bowery; Cooper Square; Twenty-fifth Street; Catherine Street].

1937. —————. *Such a woman*, **by Owen and Leita Kildare. Illus. by Joseph C. Chase. New York: G.W. Dillingham, 1911. ix, 316p.**

Nora is a woman from the slums of New York; conscientious and faithful despite the layer of inertia and corruption her environment has encrusted her with. Recognition of her good qualities by several people who offer her friendship, kindness and assistance results in Nora's redemption and improvements in her neighborhood.

1938. —————. *The wisdom of the simple*; **a tale of Lower New York. New York, Chicago: Revell, 1905. 353p.**

The East Side of New York, the Bowery district in particular, is the 'home' of a boy of the streets who seeks to pull himself out of the slums and into a better life. A one-time friend becomes his bitter rival in both ward politics and in his effort to win the love of Lucy, the only girl he has ever been close to.

1939. **Killian, Kevin.** *Shy*; **a novel. Freedom, Calif.: Crossing Press, 1989. 276p.**

Teenage culture is a significant part of this novel that explores the darker side of life in Smithtown, Long Island. Killian's characters are the dropouts from 'normal' society—malcontents, losers, unattached souls, etc. The author even inserts himself as a writer who is working on a book about his slain homosexual lover. Two of the teenagers one meets are: Harry Van, so cognizant of his fading youth, and Paula, who takes David Bowie's music as a chief source for her awareness of the world.

1940. **Kilpatrick, Katherine.** *Trouble's daughter*; **the story of Susanna Hutchinson, Indian captive. New York: Delacorte Press, 1998. 247p.**

The novel is based on the Indian captivity of Anne Hutchinson's daughter, Susanna, who is nine when the story begins. The Hutchinsons have fled from the Puritans in search of religious freedom but are massacred on Long Island in 1643 by the Lenapes. Survivor Susanna, initially resistant to the ways of her Lenape captors, through the years develops psychic powers and an appreciation of the Lenapes' struggles for survival.

1941. Kimball, Gwen, pseud. *The Cardiff Giant.* **New York: Duell, Sloan & Pearce, c1966. ix, 150p.**

Nate Hull is forcibly drawn into his Uncle George's scheme involving the famous 'Cardiff Giant'; a 10½-foot 'artifact' dug up at Cardiff in Upstate New York in 1899 and billed as an ancient American aborigine. Nate finally breaks away from his uncle and pursues truth and study with the encouragement of Cornell University's president. If intended as historical fiction the novel does not stand up well; the true perpetrators of the hoax are generally taken to be David Hannum and E.N. Westcott, the novelist Edward Noyes Westcott's father.

1942. Kimball, Paul. *Mrs. Merivale.* **New York: Clode, 1926. 320p.**

Left with a large sum of money by her late husband, Mrs. Merivale finds the fashionable suburb of 'Northway' too small for her ambitions. Off she goes to New York City where she splurges on a new wardrobe, rents an apartment, and sets herself up as a vocal teacher, attaining an excellent reputation in that occupation by sheer bluff and her ability to convince herself and others of her talent. Her friends in Northway lionize Mrs. Merivale when she returns there for a rest from her 'arduous' teaching career. Persuaded to retire from her musical vocation Mrs. Merivale enters an advantageous second marriage. An announcement of her retirement is carried in 'The Musical Mercury'.

1943. Kimball, Richard Burleigh, 1816-1892. *Henry Powers (banker). How he achieved a fortune, and married*; a novel. **New York: G.W. Carleton, 1868. 335p.**

A chronicle of the progress of Henry Powers as he seeks his fortune in the maelstrom, 'the great Babel' (New York City). Fresh from New Hampshire he starts at the bottom in Gardner, Lynde & Co. in 1857. By 1860 he is head of a department. The Civil War begins, the firm spins into financial chaos, and Henry enlists. Surviving serious war wounds he returns to the financial wars. He joins tricky Horace Deams in several dubious schemes, learning all the while the stratagems of prosperous commercial entrepreneurs. Leaving Deams, Henry and a new partner, Holman, secure loans, buy dry goods at extremely low prices and resell them at a handsome profit. In 1864 Henry and Holman buy up gold on margin, watch its steep rise and dispose of it before the market collapses. By now they have a well-established banking house, Powers & Holman. Henry also attains success in matters of the heart as he woos the estimable Mary Wirth—her father is a leader in New York's financial and social circles.

1944. ————. *To-day*; a romance. New York: Carleton, 1870. 480p.

Tom Castleton, Alfred Du Barry and the orphaned, wealthy Clara Digby were fellow students at a fashionable school in Westchester County. Charley Graves and Harry Ellsworth are 'Wall-Streeters' and William Holt is at the bottom of the employment ladder but on his way up. All the above merge as they pursue their careers in the metropolis and are active socially. Idealistic, priggish Tom Castleton, a lawyer involved with the problems of the poor, loses Clara Digby to restless Alfred Du Barry. Financial reverses impoverish the newly married Charley Graves and Virginia Randall, a former debutante. They have a benefactor in William Holt, prosperous at last; after Charley is killed in a train accident, William marries Virginia. Du Barry walks away from Clara to pursue an earlier love and Castleton takes his place. Harry Ellsworth marries a plain, socially awkward but wealthy young woman and passes from view.

1945. ————. *Undercurrents of Wall Street*; a romance of business. New York: Putnam, 1862. 428p.

The narrator, Charles E. Parkinson, had lost his silk goods importing firm in the economic crisis of 1837, had borrowed from his wife's estate and from friends and started up a fairly successful wholesale grocery business in 1843—it too went under. As the story opens the year is 1858 and Parkinson, now 61, is trying valiantly to make a living as a 'Man-Friday to several [commercial] note-brokers'. He is a widower, has three children and a deceased friend's daughter, Matilda Hitchcock, to provide for, and has been on the threshold of destitution for a number of years. The author, through Parkinson, provides the reader with a detailed picture of Wall Street operations—legal, barely legal and criminal. The Parkinson ménage's economic woes come to an abrupt end when elderly Charles receives a letter from an old college friend in Canandaigua, N.Y., apprising him of a bequest of $5,000; and Matilda is designated the true heir of a wealthy relative whose estate had mistakenly been ceded to another young woman.

1946. ————. *Was he successful?* A novel. New York: Carleton, 1864. 407p.

Hiram Meeker is the ultimate trimmer, a complete hypocrite who wears the trappings of piety but is interested only in himself and moneymaking. He fancies himself a ladies' man in his Connecticut hometown, 'Burnsville', then leaves that village for a career in New York after acquiring some business basics. He works briefly for a couple of firms and decides to strike out on his own. With an eye to marrying wealthily Hiram worms his way out of one engagement when his fiancée's father faces bankruptcy. However, Hiram leads Arabella Thorn, a prune-faced spinster older than he and the possessor of over $250,000, to the altar. His real estate investments in a growing New York make Hiram a millionaire. Happiness eludes him; his children are generally great disappointments and in the end he is reduced to sitting by a window in his fashionable home, a victim of semi-paralysis, watching the passing parade and reminiscing. Reader, what think you? Was he successful?"

1947. **King, Basil, 1859-1928.** *The city of comrades.* **New York: Harper, 1919. 405p.**

A victim of addiction to alcohol, Frank Melbury, an architect in New York, had slipped further into degradation. Turning to crime he tried burglary, and that brought him in touch with Regina Barry, a noted architect's daughter. Stirred by love, Frank, with the help of faithful friends, gets back on the right track and begins molding a rewarding career and a place in responsible society. Despite various personal interruptions Regina and Frank find one another again during World War I in which Frank serves as a soldier and Regina as a Red Cross nurse.

1948. —————. *The empty sack.* **New York: Harper, 1921. 445p.**

Two families—The Collinghams of the affluent New York suburb of 'Marillo Park'—and the lower middle class Folletts of 'Pemberton Height' on the New Jersey side of the Hudson—find their lives irretrievably intertwined. Josiah Follett loses his job at Bradley Collingham's Manhattan bank, plunging his family into a precarious economic situation. Bradley's son Bob marries Jennie Follett, even though she believes she is really in love with the artist for whom she models. Josiah dies of despair and malnutrition. His son Teddy steals from the Collingham bank to pay the bills oppressing the Follett family, flees and is tracked down. On the verge of suicide Teddy inexplicably kills one detective and wounds another. Bob Collingham befriends the doomed Teddy and with the consent of his parents safeguards the Folletts. Following Mrs. Follett's death Jennie understands that Bob is the man she loves. Implicit in King's novel is a condemnation of an economic system that underpays its workers and casts them adrift for efficiency's sake.

1949. —————. *The high heart.* **New York: Harper, 1917. 419p.**

Left penniless when her father dies, Alexandra Adare takes a position as governess in the New York and Newport homes of the Rossiters. Mrs. Rossiter's brother, Hugh Brokenshire, falls in love with Alexandra, raising a storm in the family. The patriarchal and autocratic J. Howard Brokenshire is especially offended, but Alex brings him to heel with her knowledge of a scandal involving J. Howard's daughter, Mrs. Rossiter.

1950. —————. *The inner shrine*; a novel of today. **New York: Harper, 1909. 355p.**

In a story that starts out in Paris but ends in New York City a young woman of French-Irish parentage is slandered by a conniving Frenchman; her husband challenges him to a duel and is killed. The wife is filled with self-reproach, but in due time she must find a way to reconstruct her life and demonstrate her own sense of worth.

1951. —————. *The lifted veil.* **Illustrated by James Montgomery Flagg. New York: Harper, 1917. 340p.**

A complex story that involves Arthur Bainbridge, rector of a prestigious New York City church, with a veiled lady who tells him of sins in her past. Bainbridge offers her spiritual guidance and the hope of God's forgiveness and a better future. The lady has a suitor in Sir Malcolm Grant, a Canadian banker; she asks Bainbridge in a letter to disclose to Grant what she has told the rector about herself. Bainbridge refuses to do so and eventually the lady dismisses the banker. Some time later Bainbridge falls in love with Clorinda Gildersleeve, a vibrant young widow. Inevitably Clorinda is the veiled lady who assumed Bainbridge was aware of her identity all along. The two lovers have a problem to resolve before they can take further steps.

1952. ————. *Satan as lightning*; a novel. **New York: Harper, 1929. 280p.**
Owen Hesketh took the fall, albeit unwillingly—4 years in a New York State prison—for an illegality committed by his business partner. Released he returns to New York City determined to defend his sullied honor and to make the real criminal pay in some measure for his failure to come forward and assume the penalty Owen was forced to pay. Owen does restructure his life and even regains the devotion of the girl he has long loved; but he also puts aside thoughts of vengeance. "Probably the excellent picture of New York will go a long way towards making the book worthwhile for many readers"— Saturday review of literature.

1953. ————. *The way home*; a novel. **Illustrated by W.H.D. Koerner. New York: Harper, 1913. 546p.**
"It begins in the [eighteen-] seventies when Charley Grace is a boy of five in the rectory of St. David's Church in Lower Manhattan. It extends over a long period of time, leaving Charley a man nearing forty and facing the possibility of death, according to a specialist's calculation, within two years. Charley is an idealistic boy with the conviction that he is designed for the ministry, but certain incidents in his mother's experience, in his father's and in his own, convince him of the insincerity of the Church and the hollowness of Christianity. He forsakes his early ideals, determined to live by one law, that of self. He does so, and wins the success he desires, but wins it at the expense of satisfaction and self-respect. He faces the need of something outside of self that is greater than he, and finds the way to its realization"—Book review digest.

1954. ————. *The wild olive*; a novel, by the author of *The iInner shrine*. **Illustrated by Lucius Hitchcock. New York: Harper, 1910. 346p.**
A young New Yorker, John Norrie Ford, goes to work in the Adirondacks for his great-uncle, the much despised Chris Ford, a lumber baron. When Chris is murdered, Norrie is the most likely suspect. He escapes into the Adirondack wilderness and eventually winds up in South America where he prospers and takes on airs of arrogance and cocksureness. Through all his troubles Miriam Strange, 'the wild olive', has stood by him, strongly believing in his innocence. Ford comes back to New York City, still on the run, but now

engaged to the flighty, unreliable Evie Colfax. Miriam too is engaged, to Charles Conquest, but both she and Norrie Ford realize that they are in love with one another. With the magnanimous Conquest's help Miriam persuades Norrie to turn himself in to the police. It is likely that Norrie will be cleared, that Miriam will set him on a right course, and that the two will find happiness together.

1955. **King, Charles, 1844-1933.** *Cadet days*; **a story of West Point. New York: Harper, 1894. 293p.**

"A graphic picture of West Point life. Beginning with George Graham's application for nomination by the Congressman of his district, Captain King carries his hero through the full four years' course at the Military academy. All the details of cadet life—the miseries of 'plebehood', the rise to the dignity of 'yearlings' and third-class men, the grind of drill and study—are exemplified in Graham's career, as he makes his way from the humble standing of a 'plebe' to the glories of graduation as first captain of his class"—Annual American catalogue.

1956. —————. *From school to battle-field*; **a story of the war days. Illustrated by Violet Oakley and C.H. Stephens. Philadelphia: J.B. Lippincott, 1899 [c1898]. 322p.**

"The story opens in 1860 in New York City. The chief actors are schoolboys of a then famous school, whose famous head, nicknamed 'Pop', was worshipped by his boys. Scenes are given from school life of ante-bellum days, illustrating the final causes, which made two young men enlist for the war then just dawning. The old fire-depot comes in for a sketch, and New York City life of that day is pictured with much cleverness"—Annual American catalogue.

1957. **King, Edward, 1848-1896.** *Joseph Zalmonah*; **a novel. Boston: Lee & Shepard, 1893. iii, 365p.**

"Joseph Zalmonah leaves Russia to find liberty in America. He exchanges the slavery of inherited power for the slavery of capital and works away his life trying to show his countrymen in New York City their rights and duties. He brings over his wife and child, but finds them almost in the way in his life work among the tailors ground down by the 'sweating' system in the Jewish quarters of New York. The end is tragic"—Annual American catalogue. This is one of the first novels to take note of the sweatshops, of Russian Jews being exploited by the German-Jewish owners of clothing firms—the latter pay contractors who in turn hire and 'sweat' the workers.

1958. **King, Harold, 1945- .** *The Hahnemann sequel*; **a novel. New York: Windsor Pub. Co., 1984. 399p.**

For some reason, unfathomable to him, David Townsend is kidnapped and carried to a medical research institute in Upstate New York called Weeksbriar. Before he can be thoroughly used in any experiment David escapes with the assistance of Dr. Sara Mills (first a hostage and then David's lover). David discovers that he was the intended donor of his heart to his deathly ill twin brother Stuart. The latter is the only scientist cognizant of the uses of an enzyme that blocks the aging process and increases mental acuity. To save his own life David must go back to Weeksbriar and make certain that Stuart dies.

1959. **King, Pauline.** *Alida Craig.* **With illus. by T.K. Hanna, Jr. New York: G.H. Richmond, 1896. 289p.**

"Alida Craig is a young girl painter who has established herself in a studio building in New York City and has begun to be successful after a hard experience in learning her art. Among her friends and patrons is a man who, after confessing his love for her, tells her of his previous engagement to a celebrated actress. The story gives the outcome of this young man's troubles and ends with a surprising revelation. Some very delightful women, married and unmarried, in every class of society, are skillfully brought into the tale"— Annual American catalogue.

1960. **King, Rufus, 1893-1966.** *The fatal kiss mystery.* **Garden City, N.Y.: Published for the Crime Club by Doubleday, Doran, 1928. vii, 264p.**

"In a far ravine in the Adirondacks three young scientists were trying a terrifying experiment. Everything happened to mar the success of the work, but the kiss was the starting point. Drusilla [Duveen] absolutely disappeared when her fiancé [a young physicist] kissed her. The experimenters were alarmed, and there followed the most harrowing days of all their lives"—Book review digest.

1961. **————.** *Profile of a murder*; **a new Valcour mystery. New York: Harcourt, Brace, 1935.**

The wealthy Beatrice Mundy meets with death by strangulation at her vacation estate in the Adirondacks. Lieutenant Valcour of New York City comes to the scene of the murder and faces dangerous predicaments before he tracks down the killer.

1962. **King, Sherwood, 1904- .** *If I die before I wake.* **New York: Simon & Schuster, 1938. 309p.**

"Considerably tangled yarn of amoral Long Island socialites, with three violent deaths and a weird denouement"—Saturday review of literature. A chauffeur, Larry Planter, invites trouble when he agrees to kill or fake killing someone for $5,000. The man who hired him for that purpose is found dead, and two other murders follow. Before the situation is clarified and the guilty party pinned down, Larry is almost a candidate for capital punishment.

1963. **Kinney, Thomas.** *Devil take the foremost.* **Garden City, N.Y.: Published for the Crime Club by Doubleday, 1947. 150p.**

"Miss Jennie Mayfield, a New York model, marries into one of those conventionally psychotic families, becomes pregnant, and almost at once finds it prudent to feed her vitamin pills to the cat, since several of her in-laws seem resolved to prevent her from producing an heir. Jennie discovers that life around the old mansion in the Hudson River Valley is pretty perilous until the various family aberrations result in a general administration of cyanide, thus smoothing things out"—New Yorker.

1964. [Kinzie, Juliette Augusta McGill], 1806-1870. *Walter Ogilby*; **a novel, by the authoress of** *Waubun*. **Philadelphia: Lippincott, 1869. 2 v. in 1 (610p.).**

This novel has some value as a description of social life in Dutchess County, N.Y., in the 1830s. Walter Ogilby, a wealthy bachelor, develops a romantic attachment to Alice (Ally) Morton of 'Ashfield', Conn., visiting niece of the Ellsworths of Milbank. Ally's cousin, Gertrude ('Gitty') Ellsworth, wanting Walter for herself, tries to keep the two apart. She misinforms Walter that her brother, John Peter, a West Point cadet, and Ally are engaged. To Ally's dismay Walter severs his contacts with her. It is only several months later while in New Haven that Walter hears that John Peter Ellsworth is about to marry Ally's best friend. Walter and Ally reconcile, are married in Ashfield and return to Walter's estate, Ferndale, in Dutchess County. Gertrude must accept defeat; her future is bleak as she spends her days in distant retirement from old friends and acquaintances.

1965. Kip, Leonard, 1826-1906. *In three heads*. **The Argus Christmas story. Albany: Argus Co., 1874. 70p.**

In 1758 Gisbort Van Twiller invites the prominent people of the colony of New York to a Christmas party to be held in his Albany, New York mansion; not invited are the Hillebrandts who have fallen on hard times. Meanwhile Van Twiller's daughter Geretie, in love with Heybert Hillebrandt, turns down the proposal of the wealthy Rollof Van Schoven, displeasing her father. The three dwellers in the mansion—Gisbort, Geretie and Gisbort's sister Lysbeth—share a similar dream in which a Dutch official (later identified as Cornelis Hillebrandt) from Peter Stuyvesant's era seems to be reaching for an important item. On the night of the party a mahogany desk Gisbort had purchased at an auction of Hillebrandt properties is accidentally smashed and the long lost Hillebrandt patent falls out of a secret panel. Heybert, now a British army officer, with a good part of the Hillebrandt property restored to the family, is accepted by Gisbort as Geretie's suitor.

Kirk, Eleanor, pseud. See: Ames, Eleanor Marie Easterbrook, 1831-1908.

1966. Kirk, Ellen Warner Olney, 1842-1928. *The apology of Ayliffe*. **Boston: Houghton, Mifflin, 1904. 323p.**

Ayliffe Grant resides in Washington Square, New York City with four aging aunts. Her life there is a relatively placid one, although she is prodded by her conscience and is much given to prayer. She removes to a rural estate on Long Island Sound where she meets a yacht-owning young millionaire. The two fall in love, are swept out to sea during a storm and are shipwrecked, but they survive and ultimately marry.

1967. ————. *Ciphers.* **Boston: Houghton, Mifflin, 1891. 311p.**

"A rich and very handsome widow [Mrs. Lee Childe who reappears in New York society via a brilliant reception] is beset by two lovers, one who wants her money more than he does herself, and another who loves her for her own sake but will not tell her because he is poor and obscure and does not dare. The first tells the second, in a friendly way, that it is absurd for him to aspire to the hand of such a woman, and he believes him and on the strength of it engages himself to a girl for whom he feels sorry and to whom he thinks he can be of assistance. Time passes, and he does not see the widow until one day she asks him to dine with her, and in the course of the conversation betrays the fact that she is and always has been in love with him. He is in despair because of his engagement to the other woman. He tells her of it, and they part, but the atmosphere is cleared later by the girl's discovering she cares for someone else more than she does for her fiancé, by breaking with him, and leaving him free to be happy"—The critic. Writers, journalists, artists and people with various other talents who choose New York as the center of their activities are noteworthy elements in the novel—nevertheless some of them might be deemed 'ciphers', others significant figures.

1968. ————. *A daughter of Eve,* **by the author of** *The story of Margaret Kent.* **Boston: Ticknor, 1889. 447p.**

"David Litchfield is old, deaf, and a millionaire. Olive Barrymore gives up the man she loves and marries him, because her mother wants his money to save the family honor. Olive is not without a conscience and is deeply humiliated at her family's money demands upon the old man who is a good husband to her. She resigns her right of dower in his estate and begs him to use his money to carry out his own desires. He dies suddenly and it is found [that] the bulk of his money is given to a humanitarian scheme, though Olive is abundantly provided for. The man she had loved returns to her and tries to sustain her resolution to carry out her husband's wishes. But carried away by the importunities of her impecunious family she at last agrees to break the will. James Merion, her former lover, tries to prevent this and makes it the test of her love for him. The scene is laid in New York"—Annual American catalogue.

1969. ————. *His heart's desire.* **A novel. Philadelphia: J.B. Lippincott, 1878. 417p.**

The setting is a 'Knickerbocker' mansion overlooking the Hudson River. Of the many characters in the novel the chief ones are: Clement Chilton; his nephew Philip Gray; Walden St. John; his sister Nora who has a mysterious past; Nora's niece Florence St. John; Colonel Etheridge, a middle-aged man of the world in love with Florence; young Clarence St. John; John Wilton, village blacksmith and philosopher; his daughter Annie; and the villain, Mr.

Sistare, who hopes to marry Nora St. John. Sistare uncovers one of Nora's secrets but 'his heart's desire' is forestalled by the revelation that she has actually long been married to misogynistic Clement Chilton. Sistare is murdered by Annie Wilton who then drowns herself. Philip Gray marries Florence, despite Chilton's misgivings. Nora discovers her long-lost male child although he dies almost simultaneously, and reconciles with Clement Chilton. "Such is life on the Hudson. … Let no one who has not read presume upon his knowledge of the Hudson"—The nation.

1970. —————. *Marcia*; a novel. **Boston: Houghton, Mifflin, 1907. 391p.**
At the age of twenty-one Marcia Dundas is the heir of a large piece of real property, but she has no money to spend on its upkeep. Resolving to keep the estate she takes a job in New York cataloging a wealthy woman's art objects; she also starts writing fiction. Two men are attracted to Marcia—one is a hugely talented 'bohemian' who drops her when a bewitching actress catches his attention. Marcia of course ends up with the man who really cares for her, while almost simultaneously having unanticipated riches dropped into her lap.

1971. —————. *Queen Money*, by the author of *The Story of Margaret Kent*. **Boston: Ticknor, 1888. 513p.**
"The scenes and characters are taken from the literary, [artistic] and fashionable circles of New York. The struggle that goes on everywhere in the great metropolis for money, at the expense of all that is good and noble, is the subject illustrated. The leading characters are a prominent reviewer and his wife who entertain all the 'lions' in turn expressing some caustic opinions of their brethren and their work. A young man, Otto March, who has an unprofitable experience in Wall Street, and who seems for a time to be going to lose his lady-love also, is the chief hero"—Annual American catalogue.

1972. —————. *The story of Lawrence Garthe*. **Boston: Houghton, Mifflin, 1894. 435p.**
"Ought a girl to marry a divorced man whose wife is still living? is the question Mrs. Kirk sets before her heroine. Lawrence Garthe has been divorced for five years when he meets and loves Constance Garner, who knows him only as a widower with a little son. Then, when their happiness seems assured, Garthe's wife appears—the rich and fascinating widow of a fourth husband—tempts him to return to her, and, failing, makes the whole story known to Constance in revenge. he fifth marriage of the divorced wife determines Constance's action and Garthe's future. As usual, Mrs. Kirk has chosen New York for her scene, and 'society' people for her actors; there is a second love story in lighter vein, and the book abounds in the bright conversation characteristic of the author of 'Queen Money' and 'Ciphers'"— Annual American catalogue.

1973. —————. *The story of Margaret Kent*; a novel, by Henry Hayes [pseud.]. **Boston: Ticknor, 1886. 444p.**

"The story is that of a woman, beautiful and accomplished, left by an easy-going husband, absent in South America, to earn her own living and that of their child, by literary work in New York. She [Margaret] is a 'social success', without money to back it up, backbitten by inhuman women, loyally admired by men; the contrasts of her life are drawn with great dramatic power; social and literary life in New York is acutely studied"—Annual American catalogue.

1974. **Kirke, Genevieve.** *An unwedded wife.* **Chicago: Morrill, Higgins, 1892. 320p.**
Jessie Kingdon is a typist in a New York office with whom her married employer falls in love. She resists involvement with him, but gradually accepts his overtures. The affair moves from New York City to San Francisco and back to New York, providing details of Jessie's life before and after her entanglement.

1975. **Klavan, Andrew.** *Corruption.* **New York: Morrow, 1994. 332p.**
Corruption in an Upstate New York city—which is under the thumb of political boss Cyrus Dolittle, the local sheriff—is fought by bureau chief Sally Dawes of the Daily Champion. Dolittle's choice for county executive is likely to win election and Sally intends to stop him. Sid Merriwether, a Harvard graduate and cub reporter, and rumpled Ernie Rumplemeyer are assigned to look into the demise of a realtor with Dolittle tie-ins. A drug bust ends with the killing of the boyfriend of Dolittle's daughter. Merriwether draws information from the dead boy's mobster employer and the aggrieved girl gives some interesting data to Rumplemeyer. Sally and the Daily Champion are cautioned by Dolittle and company to back off, which, of course, they will not do.

1976. **Klein, Charles, 1867-1915.** *The gamblers*; **a story of to-day, by Charles Klein and Arthur Hornblow. Illus. by C.E. Chambers. New York: Dillingham, 1911. 351p.**
The 'gamblers' are denizens of Wall Street who use every means at their disposal to manipulate the stock market in their favor. One of them is a young banker who is facing a prison term; he had temporarily lost the regard of the woman he loved, but she comes back to him in his time of need.

1977. ————. *Maggie Pepper.* **New York: H.K. Fly, 1911. 317p.**
'Maggie Pepper' was a play before this novelized version appeared. The heroine, Maggie, buyer for a large New York department store, offers suggestions for increasing sales. Young Holbrooke, who has the chief stake in the store, is pleased with Maggie's ideas and spends more and more of his time with her. That leads to a bust-up between Holbrooke and his fiancée, a girl with high social connections. Maggie's sister-in-law and the latter's shady second husband are no help to Maggie and she must use her own ingenuity to right matters.

1978. ———. *The money makers*; a story of today, by Charles Klein and Arthur Hornblow. **Illus. by Paul Stahr. New York: Dillingham, 1914. 340p.**

> A novelized version of a play by Klein. The story's principal is James Rodman who makes millions through crooked stock manipulations while his wife and children have little place in his life. Overcome by a sudden revulsion of what he has been doing Rodman begins to give back the money he has stolen from the stockholders. His children refuse to stand by him, but his ever-faithful wife is willing to make any sacrifice to help him.

1979. ———. *The third degree*; a narrative of metropolitan life, by Charles Klein and Arthur Hornblow. **Illus. by Clarence Rowe. New York: G.W. Dillingham, 1909. 356p.**

> "The son of an old New York family marries a girl of character, but one whose parentage is unworthy of the recognition of the husband's family. They disown the son; he sinks into dissipation and debt; and is finally accused of murder. He becomes a victim of the police officialdom, but is saved from the 'chair' by his clear-headed, stout-hearted wife who believes absolutely in his innocence, and whose wit and good sense enable her to win against the tremendous odds imposed by the law"—Book review digest.

1980. Klein, Kate. *Plain unvarnished murder*, **by Kate Klein and Roslyn Hastings. New York: Arcadia House, 1959. 222p.**

> Martha Matthews, the proprietor of an antiques store in Upstate New York, was always on the lookout for suitable articles to place on sale. However, when she drove to a nearby farm to make several purchases she was confronted by a cadaver and the likelihood of murder.

1981. Klein, Norma, 1938- . *Lovers.* **New York: Viking Press, 1984. 282p.**

> A comedy of infidelity involving a Westchester couple, Marilyn Greene, her husband Mo, and her lover Benjy Fetterman. Mo has had several extra-marital affairs, but he has always been solicitous of his wife and has hustled a good living. Marilyn loves both her husband and Benjy—the latter and his wife are neighbors of the Greenes—and keeps her marriage intact while having weekly trysts with gentle Benjy for two decades.

1982. Klein, Norman, 1897-1948. *The destroying angel.* **New York: Farrar & Rinehart, 1933. 307p.**

> "G. Howard Leland of River Farm near Rhinebeck [Dutchess County, N.Y.] believes himself to be on the spot and Kennedy [Jones, the detective] is called in. Then Charlie Farmer, who has been meeting Leland's young wife in the old house in the woods, is found murdered. Watch Will Douglas, who may have rubbed Charlie out over a horse trade; Madeline Douglas, who's horsy enough to do anything; Aunt Regina, who ought to be in a sanitarium; Julian Eggett, a stableboy with a touch of shell-shock; and so forth. And what about the poisoned mushrooms that Mr. Leland raises just for the fun of it? Our author delineates the Rhinebeck set with what we suppose is utter faithfulness

and tells his tale in strict chronological sequences, gradually setting up to a melodramatic climax that should knock you for a corpse. Four killings in all"—New York herald tribune books.

1983. Klempner, John, 1898-1972. *Letter to five wives.* **New York: Scribner, 1946. 204p.**

Which of the five suburban Long Island housewives is about to lose her husband to the divorcée, Addie Jones, who sends a note to each of them announcing a plan to run off with one of their spouses? The women are left to speculate on what in their husband-wife relationship could induce the man of the house to steal away from his hearth in the company of the attractive Addie.

1984. Kluger, Richard, 1934- . *When the bough breaks,* **a novel. New York: Doubleday, 1964. 328p.**

A novel about a "conflict of values that splits a suburban community near New York City. Forest Glen Road, an outlying residential section of 'Somerset Township', overlooks an unspoiled wooded tract. And when plans to rezone the woods and sell them for industrial and residential development are made, the Forest Glen group vows to save the small forest that buffers their homes and way of life from suburban blight. ...They discover that the law allows them to secede from the town and take the woods with them—if their plan to create an independent village of Forest Glen is approved by referendum. As the day of the vote approaches, the process of law is abandoned, and forces in the town bring increasingly vicious pressure to bear on the Forest Glen group"—Publisher's announcement.

1985. Knevels, Gertrude, 1881-1962. *The diamond rose mystery.* **New York: D. Appleton, 1928. 305p.**

"Lee Henderson kept a small shop in Greenwich Village and her uncle, a kindly, middle-aged minister, lived with her. When her uncle was killed, Lee undertook a dangerous mission for him and found herself in quantities of trouble. She met with all the members of that gang of women known as the 'Wildcats' and nearly lost her life, but she found the diamond rose and restored it to the owner. And that was the beginning of her happiness"—Book review digest.

Knight, Adam pseud. See: Lariar, Laurence, 1908-.

Knipe, Alden Arthur, 1870-1950, joint author. *The flower of fortune.* **See Item #1986.**

Knipe, Alden Arthur, 1870-1950, joint author. *The lost little lady.* **See Item #1987.**

Knipe, Alden Arthur, 1870-1950, joint author. *A maid of old Manhattan.*

See Item #1988.

Knipe, Alden Arthur, 1870-1950, joint author. *The shadow captain.* **See Item #1989.**

1986. **Knipe, Emilie Benson, 1870-1958.** *The flower of fortune,* **by Emilie Benson Knipe and Alden Arthur Knipe. Illustrated by Emilie Benson Knipe. New York: Century Co., 1922. 354p.**

"A story for older boys and girls with New York City just after it had been taken from the Dutch for a background. Judith Van Taarl, at the age of sixteen, is left an orphan, and at her father's dying request, takes charge of his large import business. In disposing of some stocks she finds a friend in Salvador Dacosta, a Portuguese Jew, who tells how to get word to him if she ever needs him. Every one in New York thinks Judith is immensely wealthy, but she knows that only strict economy and the sale of a precious tulip of a strange variety will enable her to meet her obligations. Word of the tulip's value gets noised about and it is stolen. After many mishaps and with the aid of her friend Dacosta, the tulip is found safe, and Judith's happiness assured"—Book review digest.

1987. ————. *The lost little lady,* **by Emilie Benson Knipe and Alden Arthur Knipe. Illustrated by Emilie Benson Knipe. New York: Century Co., 1917. 410p.**

The Civil War Draft Riots of 1863 in New York City are in the background of this novel for young adults. Nora O'Neill, 13, the heroine, snatches an obviously Southern girl from a band of ruffians and takes the frightened maiden to her home. Nora and her father are quite well off, but she has had a lonely existence, which the rescued girl, Bébé, now fills. Although Bébé is adamant in her refusal to disclose anything in her past, the two girls grow very close to one another. Nora worries that relatives will take her friend away and that she will never see Bébé again.

1988. ————. *A maid of old Manhattan,* **by Emilie Benson Knipe and Alden Arthur Knipe. Illustrated by Emilie Benson Knipe. New York: Macmillan, 1917. 292p.**

"A story of New Amsterdam under the rule of Peter Stuyvesant. Annetje, the maid of old Manhattan, had spent her early childhood with the Indians. She knows that they had loved and treasured her highly, for even after they had sent her to live with white people, their protective watch over her continued. Of her parentage she knows nothing, but she has sometimes been made to feel that she is not Dutch like her companions. Twice it is given Annetje to warn the governor of impending danger. The first time, when an Indian attack threatens, she intercedes with her red friends and the town is saved. The second time her warning is not heeded. The English ships come and New Amsterdam becomes New York. But the ships bring to Annetje the secret of her birth, and Peter Stuyvesant, no longer the governor, sanctions his son Balthzar's choice of a wife"—Book review digest.

1989. ————. *The shadow captain*; an account of the activities of one Christopher Ronsby in the town of New Yorke during several months of the year of Our Lord 1703, by Emilie Benson Knipe and Alden Arthur Knipe. New York: Dodd, Mead, 1925. 347p.

"A narrative compiled from notes gathered and set down by Launcelot Dove, one-time chief lieutenant of the famous Captain William Kidd. The action of the story takes place in New York in 1703, two years after the execution of … Kidd. The captain's hidden treasure and his attractive widow, like a lodestar, draw numerous suitors to the feet of Mistress Kidd, but two villains, James Stuart and Lord Carstairs, do the most vigorous courting. A revelation in the moonlight—the shadowy form of the captain himself—eventually brings defeat to the treasure-seekers and the reward of loyalty to the widow"—Book review digest.

1990. Knowles, Robert Edward, 1868-1946. *The dawn at Shanty Bay*. New York, Chicago: Revell, 1907. 386p.

"A story whose scenes are laid in a Scottish settlement in western New York. The hero is a crusty Scotsman. He inherits his creed and his theory of life from his Covenanter father who 'got till his rest without hardly hearin' tell o' Christmas or any o' thae new-fangled schemes for worshipping Almighty God'. But before the end of the story Ronald Robertson changed his mind about Christmas and several other things"—The dial.

1991. Knox, Ann. *Featured on Broadway*. New York: Century Co., 1930. 333p.

Idena Dare, a gardener's daughter with a finishing school education, marries upper crust Dick Stamford, divorces him and buys a boardinghouse on West 26th Street in New York City. She sells the house and becomes the mistress of Melville Del Rio, lion tamer and leading actor and owner of a second-rate play with which he and Idena tour the country. 'Discovered' by a theater manager and a playwright/director Idena stars in a smash hit on Broadway. The financier Lewis Wingate motivates Idena to break off her long-term affair with Del Rio. Wingate commits suicide when ruined financially by Mark Leaning, another of Idena's admirers. During World War I Idena is in London, appreciative of 'the intimacy and bonhomie of the London theater, after New York, where showmanship was a business and the stage a factory'. Idena's theatrical career dims; she fails to revive it in New York and goes back to England, a forgotten star, but still an acceptable social figure.

1992. Koch, Claude F., 1918- . *Light in silence*. New York: Dodd, Mead, 1958. 312p.

"A study of a highly specialized community: the Catholic College of the Ancient Order of St. Bardolph, which stands above Niagara Falls. …The death of the saintly, muddle-headed prior, Cletus Paul, and his succession by a worldlier, very much less sympathetic character, leads to a number of crises in the lives of the teaching staff. One of them, which has vital consequences, is the attempt by the psychology instructor to confront the aged and amiable Father Didymus with a rationale for his vision of the saint. ...The indisputable hero is Brother Joseph, the craggy artist, who has never had a true vocation. In his case the crisis is intensified by his feelings for Ann, the sister of one of the younger brothers, a widow with three children, who keeps a bookshop in the town. For a time he leaves the Order and goes out into the world but he returns in the last chapter"—New statesman.

1993. **Koch, Stephen, 1941- .** *Night watch.* **New York: Harper & Row, 1969. 212p.**

Parentless Harriet and her brother David are left on their Long Island estate under the care of an aunt, an alcoholic, wraith-like, odious creature, hardly a befitting guardian for the two adolescents. Harriet is spied upon by David who sees her having sex with a strange man in the estate's garden. That only serves to draw the two young people together to explore further their sexuality and incestuous proclivities.

1994. **Koenig, Laird.** *The little girl who lives down the lane.* **New York: Coward, McCann & Geoghegan, 1973, c1974. 254p.**

Rynn, a 13-year-old English girl, is living alone in a house in eastern Long Island, left there by her father, a poet. Her only friend is a crippled boy, Mano, who has to leave her when he is taken ill and is sent to the hospital. Then Frank, an adult with perverted sexual tastes, begins to move in on her. Rynn may expect some help from a neighborhood police officer, but she is essentially dependent on her own imaginative resources for survival.

1995. **Komroff, Manuel, 1890-1974.** *Echo of evil.* **New York: Farrar, Straus, 1948. 233p.**

After serving some twenty years in prison for murdering her faithless husband Anna Rudd is reluctantly taken into the Hudson Valley home of her sister, Hester Hallows. Laura, 20, oldest child of Roy and Hester Hallows, is kind to her Aunt Anna and the latter suddenly blurts out her past to the girl. The disturbed Laura in turn tells George Dray, her wealthy young fiancé; the story moves through the small town. Its impact destroys the peace of the Hallows family and it has far ranging and demoralizing effects on them, Anna, and certain of the townspeople.

1996. **Korolenko, Vladimer Galaktionovich, 1853-1921.** *In a strange land.* **Translated from the Russian by Gregory Zilboorg. New York: Richards, 1925. ix, 214p.**

Two Russian immigrants, Matvai and Dimma Lozinsky, are overwhelmed by the complexities of life in New York City—the English language, the technological marvels, the lack of civility in a society that boasts of its classlessness and 'liberty'. Dimma tries to come to terms with her new surroundings; Matvai makes no concessions as he wanders aimlessly around the city, on one occasion witnessing a labor rally led by Samuel Gompers. At the novel's end sympathetic persons place Matvai on a train headed for the Midwest, a region more suitable to him. The novel resulted from Korolenko's visit to the United States in the 1890s and it contains, as the translator states, "a few amusing incongruities and a rather peculiar conception of American traits. These incongruities, however, seem …a useful illustration of how difficult it is even for a great master to render accurately the life of a foreign people." The original Russian title is: Bez iazyka (literally Without the language—Matvai and Dimma have no prior knowledge of English).

1996a. Kowalski, William. *Eddie's bastard*; a novel. **New York: Harper Collins, 1999. 384p.**

In the small Upstate New York town of 'Mannsville' Billy Mann is raised by his grandfather. Billy's father, Eddie, died in Vietnam and Billy is the 'bastard' offspring he left behind. Grandfather Mann embellishes the Mann family history and Billy is fascinated, using it as a crutch for his own solitary childhood and adolescence. He does, however, befriend Annie Simpson, despite her slovenly, white trash family background. Ultimately Billy can point to several solid accomplishments of his own and provide some substantiality to the Mann family legends.

1997. Kraft, Eric, 1944- . *At home with the Glynns*; **the personal history, adventures, experiences & observations of Peter Leroy (continued). New York: Crown Publishers, 1995. 179p.**

Peter Leroy, now proprietor of a hotel in 'Babbington', Long Island, again recalls his youth in the mid 1950s. At that time he got to know the Flynn family—the father Andy, an abstract painter; Rosetta, Andy's wife and an obsessive contestant in commercial giveaways; and the 13-year-old twins, Margot and Martha. Peter watches art films with the Glynn sisters and then progresses, quite innocently, to nighttime visits in their bed, undressed, which only serve to stimulate his sexual fantasies.

1998. ————. *Leaving Small's Hotel.* **New York: Pecador USA, 1998. 346p.**

Peter and Albertine Leroy's hotel on Small's Island, not far from the town of 'Babbington', Long Island, is in poor financial health, yet Peter entertains guests following dinner with readings from his memoirs. It is Albertine who must shoulder the burden of maintaining a semblance of order and fiscal viability. Then comes Peter's decision to put the hotel up for sale, and he must ask himself whether his nonchalance has been at the expense of Albertine's worries and pain.

1999. ————. *Little follies*; **the personal history, adventures, experiences & observations of Peter Leroy (so far). New York: Crown Publishers, 1992.437p.**

As a youngster Peter Leroy resided in 'Babbington', Long Island, so-called clam capital of the world. Peter's father was proprietor of a gas station and his grandfather sold Studebakers. New Peter lives in a rather passé hotel on an island which can be seen from Babbington. While he reminisces about Babbington's Clam Fest, the parading boats on the Bolotomy River, and his eccentric neighbors and acquaintances, Albertine, his wife, looks after the hotel.

2000. ————. *What a piece of work I am*; a continuation. **New York: Crown Publishers, 1994. 275p.**

Kraft's Peter Leroy (see the author's 'Little follies') is a post-World War II adolescent in 'Babbington', Long Island in this novel. He is in love with the exotic Ariane ('Tootsie') Lodkochnikov, a waitress at a clam bar in Babbington. Ariane takes Peter into her confidence as she is about to leave town, sharing with him her experiences in Babbington—e.g., her local notoriety as a performer in avant-garde theater. However, Ariane turns out to be a figment of Peter's imagination.

Krausé, Lyda Farrington, b. 1864. See: Yechton, Barbara, b. 1864.

2001. Kringle, Kate, pseud. *The beautiful girl*; or, *Burning of the robber's den*. **A tale of the Revolution. New York: New York City Pub. House, 1846. 50p.**

Frederick Wycoff of Albany transacts fur-trading business in Utica and heads for home. Warned by a friendly Indian, Dutta, of a particular inn, Frederick still takes shelter there when a storm threatens. He soon realizes that he is in a den of thieves, but he is intrigued with the landlord's niece who bears the name Gazema Mortine. When it becomes clear that the robbers may dispose of both him and Gazema, Frederick breaks away from the inn while Gazema feels obligated to stay by her guardian, the landlord. Frederick is attacked on the road by one of the band. Dutta comes to his aid and Frederick shoots the criminal. A few weeks later Dutta tells Frederick that Mohawk Indians have burned down the inn, slaughtered the thieves and carried off Gazema. Dutta and Frederick make their way to the Indian camp and rescue her. The expected romantic ending follows.

2002. Kummer, Frederick Arnold, 1873-1943. *The brute*. **Illus. by Frank Snapp. New York: Watt, 1913. 314p.**

Donald Rogers, a small businessman in New York, is meeting with little success and he, his wife Edith and their child are 'living on a shoestring' day by day. An old friend of Edith's, Billy West, comes into New York with a fortune and Edith, bored with her life in the Rogers' Harlem flat, fancies she loves West and agrees to leave her family for him. But while West is in Denver taking care of some personal and financial concerns he suddenly dies, leaving everything he had to Edith. She reluctantly takes the money with no explanation to Donald. Of course he finds out the circumstances surrounding the inheritance and deals with it in his own way.

2003. Kunstler, James Howard, 1948- . *Blood solstice*. **Garden City, N.Y.: Doubleday, 1986. 266p.**

"Grover Graff, 29, investigative reporter for the Times-Herald of Albany, N.Y., (coyly referred to as 'The Capital' throughout), is the chatty narrator-hero of this cheerfully derivative thriller—which centers ...on a fiendish religious cult. Grover...keeps digging into the doings of... the Children of Abraham, especially when a suburban couple begs him to search for their daughter who disappeared after joining the cult's California branch"—Kirkus reviews. He heads for San Francisco and then back East to Vermont, harassed by the cult. He quits his newspaper job and fights the cult under his own auspices—finally he exposes the criminal activities of the cult.

2004. ————. *The Halloween ball.* **Toronto, New York: Bantam Books, 1987. 340p.**

A one-time watering place in Upstate New York, 'Excelsior Springs', is now the refuge of those uninterested in jockeying for positions on the so-called ladder of success. They are happy enough to 'drop out' and take menial jobs while eyeing the upscale coeds of 'Greer College' and also dealing as best they can with the mentally ill people released into the community from New York State's psychiatric institutions. Artist Sandy Stern is on the verge of being evicted by his landlord and agrees to assist Joel Harlow, a drug dealer, with setting up a Halloween celebration. The ball takes place and with it a potpourri of sputtering affairs, sexual and otherwise; and the town once again relaxes while Sandy's landlord pushes plans to upgrade it and its population.

2005. ————. *Thunder Island.* **New York: Bantam Books, 1988. 266p.**

'Thunder Island' is more or less a stand-in for the well-known Fire Island that lies off the central southern shore of Long Island. Andy Newmark, a New York City teenager, is employed for the summer as a maintenance worker at an island resort. He is worried about the draft (the Vietnamese Conflict is on), but freely explores alcohol, sex and drugs when not working. He is Jewish and the club that employs him is basically Catholic in membership. Andy is able to handle the prejudice he encounters, his parents' divorce, social misfits, etc., and comes out fairly confident of his ability to enter into the outer edges of the adult world.

2006. **Kussy, Nathan, b. 1872.** *The abyss.* **New York: Macmillan, 1916. 508p.**

Sammy Gordon, a young Jewish boy of New York City's 1880s, endures the poverty of the slums (Mulberry Bend) because his mother gives him love and guidance. When she dies Sammy runs away rather than be placed in an institution. He begins associating with thieves and tramps and is arrested for vagrancy. The police know him now and even when he tries to go straight he is destined to fail. Returning to the haunts of his childhood and hounded by the police, Sammy is about to descend deeper into the abyss of criminal activity.

2007. **Kutak, Rosemary, 1908- .** *I am the cat.* **New York: Farrar, Straus, 1948. 249p.**

While a guest at a Long Island mansion, a young Army psychiatrist is only too well aware of three fatalities occurring around him. These so-called 'accidents' are actually the handiwork of a solitary killer who is finally brought to justice by a persistent, hard-working assistant district attorney. The psychiatrist offers his psychological analyses as a way of getting at the core of the matter.

L., B.H. *Chevrons*; a story of West Point. **See Item #2112.**

2008. **Labree, Lawrence.** *Rebels and Tories*; or, *The blood of the Mohawks!* **A tale of the American Revolution. New York: De Witt, 1851. 202p.**

John Upton, harassed by Nahum Leffers to pay overdue rent, even as Upton's beloved wife is dying and just before her interment, vows vengeance. Upton abandons his infant son, leaves New York City and disappears into the forests of northern and central New York. Years later during the American Revolution Upton's son, Roger, is an agent for the British, Nahum Leffers is a clandestine Tory raider, and John Upton, known by awed Indians as 'Wild Medicine', is an ally of Americans fleeing from the British and Indians. The Battle of Oriskany, the several raids of Indians and Tories in the Mohawk Valley, and, in greater detail, the massacre at Cherry Valley, are woven into the novel. Despite the introduction of other interesting characters and situations the author is chiefly concerned with the fates of John and Roger Upton and Nahum Leffers, none of whom survive their hatreds and vengeful actions.

Lady of New York, A. *Changing scenes.* **See Item #612.**

Lady of New York, A. *Married above her.* **See Item #2246.**

2009. **Lafore, Lawrence Davis, 1917-1985.** *Learner's permit*; a novel. **Garden City, N. Y.: Doubleday, 1962. 308p.**

'Acropolis' in New York State is the seat of 'Parthenon College', founded by a Protestant sect. Nicholas Torrente, a high school graduate, assumes the mantle of a real Ph.D. who is in Europe and begins teaching at Parthenon. After being voted the best instructor on the faculty Torrente's true academic background is uncovered; the school's president talks with Torrente and learns that he, a former military policeman (with a clear understanding of the 'psychology of sex') has possibilities as an administrator. The conclusion of this comic novel finds Nicholas the dean of students.

2010. **Laiken, Deidre S., 1948- .** *Death among strangers.* **New York: Macmillan, 1987. 258p.**

'Bakersville' in Upstate New York is the scene of the murder of a little-known teenage girl; police officer George Murphy, recently divorced, calls on his girlfriend, Elizabeth Kern, a social worker, for assistance in the search for clues. A professional photographer appears in Bakersville and Elizabeth finds herself attracted to him while George continues to work on the homicide. As her relationships with the two men deepen, Elizabeth herself may be in danger of becoming the victim of the yet unknown murderer.

2011. ————. *Killing time in Buffalo*; a novel. Boston: Little, Brown, 1990. 275p.
Two university students spend the summer of 1967 in Buffalo in a grungy apartment building facing Days Park, a hangout for hippies and druggies. Renee and Fran, together with many of their generation, believe that money is obscene, but it's ok to shoplift. Renee has a husband, Barry, but he hasn't been seen for a while. The two girls are into drugs and Renee has the notion that she is a target for murder. Her older brother, Leon, has been her protector in the past, but even he is unable to watch over her on every occasion, e.g., when intruders have evidently been in the girls' apartment.

2012. **Lait, Jack, 1882-1954.** *The Broadway melody.* **Novelized by Jack Lait from the scenario by Edmund Goulding. New York: Grosset & Dunlap, 1929. 242p.**
This execrably written novelization of the motion picture purports to give novices the inside story of how a big Broadway musical or revue is put together. The show is being produced by Joseph Zanfield (a thin disguise for Florenz Ziegfeld); the main characters in the story are two sisters, Hank and Queenie Mahoney from the vaudeville circuit, and a songwriter and 'hoofer', Eddie Kerns. Kerns is engaged to Hank but feels himself being drawn more and more to the younger Queenie. As Queenie assumes a more prominent role in the production, Hank faces the inevitable breakup of the Mahoney Sisters' act and realizes that Eddie and Queenie are falling in love. After the stereotypical misunderstandings and 'heartbreak', Hank backs off and prepares to return to vaudeville with a new partner. Queenie passes up an opportunity to marry the rich playboy, Francis Warriner, choosing, of course, to follow her true love, Eddie Kerns.

2012a. **Lamalle, Cecile.** *Appetite for murder.* **New York: Warner Books, 1999. 290p.**
Despite carrying a frequently drunk partner Charly Poisson has had great success with their Upstate New York restaurant, La Fermette. Unfortunately Charly's quest for edible wild mushrooms in the countryside results in his turning up a woman's body. It's a police matter, but Charly can't resist snooping and he begins to conjecture that a regular customer at the restaurant, affluent Walter Maxwell, is deeply involved in the probable murder. Such suspicions spell trouble for the restaurateur when he is the caterer for a festive gathering at Maxwell's home.

2013. **Lancaster, Bruce, 1896-1963.** *Guns of Burgoyne.* **New York: Stokes, 1939. 424p.**
A revised and condensed version of the above was issued in 1952 (Boston, Little, Brown) under the title: Guns in the forest. Lancaster's novel follows Burgoyne's invasion of New York and the British debacle at Saratoga; the

518

narrative is told from the point of view of a young Hessian officer, Kurt Ahrens, serving in the English army. Ahrens falls in love with a girl who is in sympathy with the American patriots.

2014. ————. *The secret road.* **Boston: Little, Brown, 1952. 259p.**

A novel about the origins of the American Secret Service during the American Revolution. Robert Townsend, one of Washington's chief informants, serves the patriot cause on Long Island and vicinity in 1780; Major John André, the British officer, plays a very important role in the story.

2015. **Landon, Herman, 1882-1960.** *Murder mansion.* **New York: Liveright, 1928. 302p.**

"Introducing Donald Chadmore, a scion just out of prison (for a boyhood prank), who returns to darkest New York, gets mixed up in the diabolical schemes of some killers, is accused of murdering his millionaire uncle in the Museum of Mystery, and discovers that love is all, or almost all"—New York herald tribune books.

2016. ————. *The voice in the closet.* **New York: Liveright, 1930. 348p.**

Lieutenant Delmar of the New York Police detective division is given the task of solving the murder of Duncan Forbes, millionaire husband of a much younger woman who was entertaining guests in their Park Avenue apartment when the crime was committed. Several of the suspects seem anxious to eliminate Delmar also, but he survives and doggedly pursues the case to a proper conclusion.

2017. **Lane, John Russell, b. 1867.** *The house between the trees*; **a novel. Boston: C.M. Clark Pub. Co., 1909. 365p.**

In this novel, many of whose scenes are laid in the Catskill region of New York State, a young man loses his mind when his car accidentally hits a little girl. His parents adopt the injured girl; she graduates from college and medical school and practices surgery with a brilliant touch. By means of an extremely sensitive operation she is able to bring her adopted brother back to a normal life. The latter portion of the book features a mysterious being who sits in 'the house between the trees'. His neighbors are unable to identify this presence, but at last he makes himself known to all the curious.

Lane, Margaret. See: Jones, Jennifer, the joint pseudonym of Margaret Lane and Enid Johnson.

2018. **Langdale, Hazel Louise Raybold, b. 1889.** *Jon of the Albany Belle.* **Illus. by Sandra James. New York: Dutton, 1943. 211p.**

A story for teenage boys laid in an Erie Canal era, the 1850s; the hero, Jonathan Hedges, leaves the family canal boat, the Albany Belle, and stumbles into several unexpected adventures before he returns to the Belle. Not only is he twice a kidnapping victim, but he also participates in the Underground Railroad and finds the gold that was buried on his grandfather's farm.

2019. ————. *Mark of Seneca Basin.* **Illus. by Sandra James. New York: Dutton, 1942. 215p.**

Mark Kingsbury, 14, is an orphan brought up in a hamlet on the Seneca River and present at the celebratory opening of the Erie Canal and the huge parade of boats from Buffalo to New York City. He has the good fortune to find his grandfather and clear up many of the secrets that shrouded his family from him.

2020. **Lange, Dietrich, 1863-1940.** *The Iroquois scout.* **Illustrated by Harold James Cue. Boston: Lothrop, Lee & Shepard, 1923. 308p.**

The Iroquois scout is Ganadoga, a young Oneida, who scouts for the American forces in the Revolutionary conflict as fought in eastern New York State. Two white boys from the Hudson Valley are counted as his friends and associates.

2021. **Lanham, Edwin Moultrie, 1904-1979.** *Death of a Corinthian.* **New York: Harcourt, Brace, 1953. 252p.**

Drifting in Long Island Sound is a boat whose owner, a Connecticut yachtsman, is not on board. There is some indication that treachery involving his wife or certain men he has associated with may be the key to the mystery. One of those under suspicion is aware and determined enough to do some sleuthing of his own in order to find some answers. A good description of boating on the Sound is an added dividend for the reader.

2022. **Lanza, Clara Hammond, 1859-1939.** *The dweller on the borderland.* **Philadelphia: J.J. McVey, 1909. 477p.**

A young teacher with wife and child seeks a new start in life in New York City. He is hired by a beautiful lady to act as tutor to her nephew. The teacher keeps his marital status a secret from his employer and he also tells his wife little or nothing about the lady's attractiveness or her artistic talent. The Catholic faith enters the picture for the lady is a strong adherent, while the teacher teeters 'on the borderland' between Catholicism and other beliefs until his wife dies, whereupon he is converted.

2023. ————. *Horace Everett*; a novel. **New York: G.W. Dillingham, 1897. 275p.**

After a long stay in Europe Horace Everett—whose mother had overseen his education there—decides to go back to his native shores to look up his father's people, wealthy New Yorkers. Mrs. Everett is a capricious person who marries a Frenchman of questionable character just before Horace's departure; mother and son quarrel and Horace leaves. Settled in New York, Horace is on the way to a satisfying career when his mother shows up, bereft of funds, which were stolen by her disappearing husband. Horace takes her in but is forced by this circumstance to sever his engagement to a charming young woman.

2024. ————. *A modern marriage*; a novel. New York: J.W. Lowell Co., 1890. 344p.

A New York City couple to all appearances is enjoying a happy, carefree marriage. However, the wife succumbs to the blandishments of a successful but cynical poet who toys with her affections. In the end she has to face the consequences of her lapse in judgment.

2025. Lardner, Ring, 1885-1933. *The big town*; how I and the Mrs. go to New York to see life and get Katie a husband. Illus. by May Wilson Preston. Indianapolis: Bobbs-Merrill, 1921. 244p.

The narrator, a cigar salesman named Finch, persuades rich widow Ella and her daughter Katie to test life in New York and incidentally find Katie a husband. Katie is almost a nonentity but does become involved with several candidates whom she drops abruptly when their true character emerges. Fascinated by Broadway and its theaters, she does marry a second-rate comedian, while Finch and Ella, now married too, return to South Bend, Indiana and the relative calm of small city life.

2026. ————. *Lose with a smile*. New York: Scribner, 1933. viii, 174p.

Danny Warner is a not very talented baseball player with the Brooklyn Dodgers with a hometown (Centralia, IL.) sweetheart, Jessie Graham. Threatened with release to the Jersey City farm team Danny balks and starts to look for work in New York City as a crooner, although singing is hardly his forte. When Jessie decides to come to Jersey City to visit relatives, she asks Danny to meet her at Pennsylvania Station—and there the book ends. Casey Stengel makes an appearance as roommate and friend of Danny.

2026a. Lardo, Vincent. *The Hampton affair*. New York: Putnam, 1999. 320p.

East Hampton, Long Island farm boy Galen Miller drowns his lover, a 40ish woman, in a deserted lake. He is trying to escape poverty and a drunken father and has dreams of film stardom. The murder is witnessed by Michael Anthony Reo who decides to keep it quiet because of his own troubled marriage to a woman from one of East Hampton's richest families and his fear of unwelcome publicity in some tabloid. The detective in the case is Eddy Evans. The author eventually explains why Galen Miller chose to murder his lover.

2027. Lariar, Lawrence, 1908-1981. *Death paints the picture*. New York: Phoenix Press, 1943. 256p.

"Some fiend unknown slew Hugo Shipley, popular illustrator and playboy, in his Woodstock manor, and it's up to Homer Bull, a comic stripper, to nab same. He does so with the assistance of Ham McAndrews, a knowing cartoonist, who acts as right-minded narrator, Sheriff Swink and a stooge yclept Shunk Smith. Among those present are Nicky English, nasty columnist,

Grace Lawrence, a model once married to Homer, and Mike Gavano, racketeer"—New York herald tribune books.

2028. ————. *Knife at my back*, **by Adam Knight [pseud.]. New York: Crown Publishers, 1952. 246p.**

Steve Conacher, skip-tracer (whose job is to track down missing persons or persons who have left without paying their bills) at a Catskill resort, is so intent on pursuing Haskell Lasker's wife that he is inadvertently involved when she becomes a murder victim.

2029. ————. *Win, place, and die!* **By Adam Knight [pseud.]. New York: Appleton-Century-Crofts, 1953. 248p.**

A harness-racing driver's death at a track in the New York area impels his nephew to nose around Long Island racing circles in order to uncover the person or persons responsible for what looks like the murder of his uncle.

2030. **Larkin, Robert T.** *Wild deuces.* **New York: Macaulay, 1928. 377p.**

New York City's 'Hell's Kitchen' is the locale of this tale about criminals who prey on unsuspecting citizens. Heroin addiction, mugging, and plans to gain wealth through crooked financial dealing are elements of the novel. One of the women caught in the maelstrom is Mary Smith who tells her lover that she would prefer a husband who has no criminal record.

2031. **Larner, Jeremy, 1937- .** *Drive, he said.* **New York: Dell Pub. Co., 1964. 190p.**

A "seriocomic novel about a college basketball player who seeks to find a meaning to his life beyond studies and athletics. The protagonist is Hector Bloom, a student at 'a small university upstate along the Hudson from New York City.' Hector and his non-athletic friend Gabriel Reuben seduce professors' wives, take drugs, experiment with radicalism, and in a variety of other ways seek to get beyond the narrow strictures of traditional college life. Gabriel dies when, on a drug trip, he sets fire to a college building. But at the end of the book Hector is alive, well, and still engaged in his search"—Kramer, John E., Jr. The American college novel.

2032. **Larsen, Nella, 1893-1963 or 4.** *Passing.* **New York: Knopf, 1929. 215p.**

"The story of two fair-skinned Negroes, both white enough to be Caucasians. Clare Kendry is living a dangerous life, 'passing' in white society and married to a man who is ignorant of her Negro blood. A chance meeting with Irene Redfield, a childhood friend who has remained loyal to her race, inspires Clare with a longing to associate with her own people. The tragic climax occurs at a Harlem party where Clare is discovered by her white husband"—Book review digest.

2032a. **Larsgaard, Chris.** *The heir hunter*; **a novel of suspense. New York: Delacorte Press, 1999. 356p.**

Alex Moreno, Albany, N.Y. lawyer and her former partner, Nick Merchant, once again collaborate as they try to determine who and where the heir[s] of the 22- million-dollar estate of Gerald Jacobs of Hudson, N.Y. are. The duo's investigation is unwelcome to at least one individual who is aware of Nick and Alex's illegal search of the late Mr. Jacobs' house; a policeman looking into the 'burglary' is shot and Nick is accused of the crime. He takes off for Europe and digs up some interesting data concerning the hidden past of the deceased millionaire.

2033. Lathen, Emma, pseud. *Banking on death.* **New York: Macmillan, 1961. 166p.**
"John Thatcher, effective vice-president [of the enormous Sloan Guaranty Trust], aging, sedate and amused, is accidentally embroiled in a fuss about a minor but curious trust, and between visits to the Harvard Club and the Buffalo Police Department, soon finds himself wound up in a matter of murder [the murder occurs in Buffalo]"—New York herald tribune books.

2034. ————. *Going for the gold.* **New York: Simon and Schuster, 1981. 251p.**
Lathen's banker/detective, John Thatcher, is once again a presence when French skier Yves Bisson is shot during the 1980 winter Olympics at Lake Placid. When Sloan Guaranty Trust's branch manager, Roger Hathaway, reports that he has paid $500,000 for Euro-checks that turn out to be phony, Thatcher suspects a swindle involving the murdered athlete. The ski contestants are checked over and Thatcher notes that Bisson's rivals, Gunther Euler and Tilly Lowengard, may well be accomplices in duplicity. A wild confrontation on the mountain slopes results in providing evidence pertinent to the solution of the case.

2035. ————. *A stitch in time.* **New York: Macmillan, 1968. 185p.**
Long Island is the scene of a novel in which a suicide, Pemberton Freebody, leaves his $100,000 life policy to Hanover University. The Atlantic Mutual Insurance Company claims the policy is void because Freebody took his own life. The University's answer is to ask the courts to adjudicate; the insurance company counters by calling Dr. Wendell Morton from the Southport Memorial Hospital to testify.

2036. ————. *Sweet and low.* **New York: Simon and Schuster, 1974. 223p.**
Two murders at the Dreyer Chocolate Company, which is located in Upstate New York at the chocolate center of the world (so the author suggests), call for an investigation by John Putnam Thatcher of the Sloan Guaranty Trust.

2037. Lathrop, George Parsons, 1851-1898. *Would you kill him?* **A novel. New York: Harper, 1889. iv, 384p.**
"On the historic shores of Otsego Lake, a young lieutenant in the regular army engaged himself to the daughter of a large grain speculator. At his instigation the officer leaves the army and puts his private fortune into grain, taking New York City as his basis of operation. A total failure in speculation breaks up

friendship between the parties and Ida Vail cancels her engagement. The young man becomes a successful businessman and active politician, gets in with a set devoted to a new religion, women's rights, fine china, etc., and loses his heart to a Vassar graduate. Her friend, Lill Britton, 'a sort of semi-detached, unmarried mother-in-law of the malignant type', becomes the terror of his life, and by her machinations he almost commits a crime"—Annual American catalogue.

2038.   **Latimer, Margery, d. 1932. *This is my body*. New York: H. Smith, 1930.351p.**
The "heroine is an hysterical, egocentric girl whose talk is all of the 'realities of life', but who has not learned the reality of her own insignificance. She would rather be a great writer than a moral woman (aims which appear to her incompatible), but she has a moral woman's body and soul. She pursued her ambition through a co-educational college with its opportunities for superficial sex experience, and on into Greenwich Village with its equal opportunities for the same. The novel abounds in scenes of recrimination and misunderstanding at home and of hypocrisy in classrooms and deans' offices, in description of poetry society and meetings and in …orgies and talk about love, life and art"—Outlook and independent.

2039.   **Lauferty, Lillian 1887-1958. *The crimson thread*. New York: Simon & Schuster, 1942. 370p.**
"Hilda Glenn was a writer of daytime radio scripts. …She wrote 'Love's wages' … a show just entering the last thirteen weeks of its third year as the story begins. Then Hilda returned to her old home, Glennacres, at 'Havenhurst-on-the-[Long Island] Sound', and Hades started to pop when she found a dying dog on the beach. Murders [of a young philanderer, a little girl and a servant at the Long Island estate] are to come as Hilda picks up the threads, including Commodore Knowlton, who may or may not have been involved in the death of the heroine's parents some years ago—dashed over a precipice. Here are generous helpings of mystery gambits of many kinds, some of them highly exciting, and the yarn grows more so toward the end"— New York Herald tribune Books.

2040.   **————. *The street of chains*. New York: Harper, 1929. 374p.**
"Descendants of the Gruenturm Jewish family have established themselves in New York, and the Delavans are a minor branch of it. The mingling and conflicting elements of Jewish and Gentile blood in the children of the present generation are the theme of the story. Carlie [Delavan] remains true to the Gruenturm tradition; while Tress, hating everything pertaining to the Jewish race, marries a Walton of Boston to escape"—Book review digest. "The background of Jewish life is beautifully and sympathetically given"— Saturday review of literature.

2041.   **Laughlin, Clara Elizabeth, 1873-1941. *Children of tomorrow*. Illustrated by Lucius W. Hitchcock. New York: Scribner, 1911. 445p.**

New York City in the first decade of the 20th century is the scene of this novel which is sociological and atmospheric in its intense exploration of the lives of a diverse group of characters—actress, journalist, social reformer, shop-girl, politician, matron, bohemian, the unhappily married, et al. Street scenes in Lower Manhattan, its editorial offices, restaurants, theaters and other places of amusement, night court, a glance at the East Side of New York and its slums—all are described zestfully and accurately. "The book has a value independent of its incidents—in its sincere and often vivid presentation of New York life as it is lived by the workers and dreamers in contrast to the spenders"—The nation.

2042. *Law and laziness*; or, *Students at law of leisure*. **New York: Printed for the author at the Golden Rule Office, 1846. 48p.**

In four sketches the author delineates the 'activities' of his heroes Bob and Henry and 'the friend', students at law who already embody the 'combination of the lawyer by license, and the idle man by nature'. In Sketch I, Henry is in New York City with an ambitious schedule of study curtailed by the lure of good times with Bob and friend. By Sketches II-III, Henry and Bob are in Utica boning up for the law examinations, regretting the wasted years in New York. To their surprise the examiners pass them both. In Sketch IV, Henry is now a full-fledged attorney-at-law with a student in his law office in New York City and searching for clients.

2043. **Law, Janice, 1941- .** *Time lapse.* **New York: Walter, 1992. 199p.**

When Henry Brook, champion swimmer and movie idol, is drowned while he is on the set, an estate in Upstate New York, the insurance company hopes the death is judged to be a suicide so it will not have to pay on a policy worth several million dollars. The company hires private investigator Anna Peters (the story's narrator); she is an admirer of Brook, but finds some unpleasant truths about him. Brook's mistress, an underage girl, and his ex-wife had sufficient reasons for wishing him dead. Other suspects turn up as the estate's manager (perhaps an eyewitness to Brook's demise) is viciously attacked, as is Anna. She ultimately figures out just how Brook was killed.

2044. **Lawson, Thomas William, 1857-1925.** *Friday, the thirteenth*; a novel. **Front. in color by Sigismond de Ivanowski. New York: Doubleday, Page, 1907. 226p.**

The frenzy and sometimes-sad consequences of gambling in New York's stock market are on display in this novel whose 'hero' is brilliant but flawed. One of his projects is to put an ex-governor of Virginia back on his financial feet, for he is in love with the Virginian's daughter. So, as a member of the Stock Exchange, he endeavors to corner the sugar market, fails, and brings disaster to many, including his ladylove.

2045. **Lea, Fanny Heaslip, 1884-1955.** *With this ring.* **New York: Dodd, Mead, 1925. v, 237p.**

"The small town of 'Columbia' accepts the inevitability of her [Lila Kemp's] spinsterhood. But Lila tries out a pet theory of her own. Planning a month's vacation in New York, she buys some smart clothes and a platinum wedding ring, and under the name of Mrs. James Duval, she seeks adventure in the big city. She finds it in the trig-looking person of Anthony Thorne who falls head over heels in love with her. The complications that follow are both fearful and funny for Lila—but she returns to Columbia with every prospect of becoming Mrs. Anthony Thorne"—Book review digest.

2046. Leary, Paris, 1931- . *The innocent curate.* Garden City, N.Y.: Doubleday, 1963. 208p.

In the village of 'Schinderhook' in Upstate New York a simple-minded Episcopal curate, Sonny Bell, is certain that he has witnessed a minor miracle (stigmata and the like). His rector considers miracles to be in poor taste, interfering with his drive towards a bishopric. Ultimately also involved in the hullabaloo are an Oberlin girl student who believes in free love and a fund-raising salesman of religious objects who would like to use the curate for his own profit.

Lechleidner, Mary L., 1947- . See under her pseudonym: Parr, Delia, 1947- .

2047. Lecky, Walter, pseud. *Mr. Billy Buttons*; a novel. New York: Benziger Bros., 1896. 274p.

The setting of Lecky's novel is a village in the Adirondacks. Many of its inhabitants are of French-Canadian origin, respecters of their old priest, a Frenchman. The local doctor and an eccentric guide by the name of Billy Buttons are the story's narrators; they tell of the people of the village, the tenor of their lives and their aspirations.

2048. ————. *Père Monnier's ward*; a novel. New York: Benziger Bros., 1898. 304p.

Little Genevieve Bain loses her mother in one of New York's poor neighborhoods; her father cannot be found. Sal McClintock, an Irishwoman, and jobless journalist Charles O'Connor look after her briefly until an entertainer, Emil Parenti, persuades her to travel the country roads of Upstate New York with him. Parenti dies without warning in an Adirondack village and Genevieve is placed in the hands of kindly Catholic priest, Père Monnier, and his faithful servants, Napoleon Brousseau and Anna ————. At 16 Genevieve falls prey to the scoundrel, Captain James Dade Fortune. Fortune takes her to New York where, after a mock marriage, he abandons her. Once again Sal McClintock and Charles O'Connor (and his wife) are there to comfort her. The good priest hastens to New York and brings Genevieve back to his mountain village. She survives for only a few weeks to the great sorrow of Père Monnier and his servants.

2049. Lederer, Paul Joseph, 1944- . *Manitou's daughters.* New York: New

American Library, 1982. 283p.

Peter Van der Veghe, a Dutch naturalist, pushes up the Hudson from New Netherlands hopeful of establishing a settlement on lands that contain the present-day city of Albany. Deserted by the band of men who accompanied him, Peter is befriended by the Oneidas and their 'headwoman', Crenna. She and Peter fall in love and she parts from her people, following Peter as they put up a trading post at the Albany site. The British arrive on the scene with the intention of forming alliances with the Oneidas and other tribes against the French and their Algonquin allies. Crenna's attempts to halt any further negotiations between the Oneidas and the British have tragic consequences.

2050. **Lee, Day Kellogg, 1816-1869.** *Summerfield*; or, *Life on a farm.* **Auburn, N.Y.: Derby, 1852. xv, 246p.**

Matthew Fabens leaves his parents' home in eastern New York State and establishes roots in the 'Waldron Settlement' on the banks of Cayuga Lake. He marries Julia Wilmer, an orphan raised by the Mason family. A son, Clinton, is born to the Fabenses, but while he is still just a 'tad' Clinton disappears; a widespread search is unsuccessful and Matthew and Julia reconcile themselves to their loss. A daughter, Fanny, helps assuage their grief. Matthew's farm prospers and he becomes justice of the peace for the village. A newcomer, William Fairbanks (and his clerk Almon Frisbie), opens a store; he impresses Matthew, although Julia Fabens is rather suspicious. Fairbanks is a frequent borrower from Matthew, the bank, and other people in the community. Matthew even contemplates forming a business partnership with Fairbanks. Comes the rude awakening. Fairbanks and Frisbie abscond, leaving behind a string of debts. Matthew survives his loss of $1,000 dollars by selling a strip of his farmland. With the help of George Ludlow, a poor but ambitious young man in love with Fanny Fabens, Matthew is able to make his farm profitable again. At the wedding of George and Fanny the minister introduces a stranger as the long-lost Clinton Fabens. The author intends to explain Clinton's absence ('abduction') in a later novel.

Lee, J. Wilke. See under his pseudonym: St. Remy, Dirck.

2051. **Lee, Margaret, 1841-1914.** *A Brooklyn bachelor*; a novel. **New York: F.F. Lovell, 1890. 207p.**

"The story of a man [Samson Dorrien] whose self-satisfaction and conceit were impenetrable. Nothing could induce him to marry, because he was such a superior person from every point of view that no woman was worthy to bear his name and share his home. He had so much to offer, and the women he had known had nothing; how could he be expected to unbend to them? He does, though, and when he least expects it. …Brooklyn street, Philharmonic choruses and Theodore Thomas's orchestra are tin-typed in…[these] pages"— The critic.

2052. ————. *Divorce.* **New York: F.F. Lovell, c1882. 411p.**

The author peoples her novel with middling-wealthy persons, Fifth Avenue residents who are church-goers and rather ordinary conversationalists. The heroine, Constance, marries for love, but her spouse, though he professes strong attachment to 'superior' Constance, betrays her, lays waste her fortune, "descending at the last to vulgar brutality and the long deceit involved in getting a 'Connecticut' divorce from her. …What he does is simply to live out his own nature, as she does hers" Catholic world.

2053. —————. *Dr. Wilmer's love*; or, *A question of conscience.* A novel. New York: Appleton, 1868. 416p.

Just before he leaves New York for Buffalo Dr. John Wilmer is at the bedside of the dying Arthur Ferris along with Mathilda, Ferris's second wife, Ferris's daughter Arabella (Belle) and Joseph Masters, executor of the Ferris estate. Six years pass and Wilmer meets Mathilda Ferris and Belle in Niagara Falls and is puzzled by the girl's poor physical and mental state. Returning to New York Wilmer finds Belle in an insane asylum. He begins to suspect that Mathilda is driving Belle into madness in order to appropriate Belle's share of the Ferris estate. Wilmer and Joseph Masters take Belle to Wilmer's mother and sister outside Albany. The doctor is distressed when Belle marries a neighbor, Claude Lecount. Lecount abuses Belle and is killed in an accident. After service in the Union Army during the Civil War Dr. Wilmer is informed by Pauline Lecount, Claude's sister, that she had arranged the marriage of Belle and Claude despite her awareness of the deepening love of Belle and Wilmer for one another.

2054. —————. *Lorimer and wife*; a novel. New York: G.W. Harlan, 1881. 259p.

New York businessman and socialite Barry Lorimer marries Claire Lascoigne, to his sister Amanda's surprise and dismay, for Claire has no money and no 'appropriate' social connections. The marriage totters and the couple agree to separate. Claire in trying to become self-supporting learns much about the hardscrabble existence of New York's working class women. Meanwhile selfish Amanda (Lorimer) Bartlett's long-suffering husband receives information that Claire is actually his granddaughter, she being the child of Mathilde Prevôte who was the daughter (unknown to Mr. Bartlett) of his first wife, Ada Clarkson. Mr. Bartlett, always fond of Claire, welcomes her into his household, simultaneously arranging for the reconciliation of Barry and Claire—Barry must admit he has been too stubborn. With Mr. Bartlett's support Claire also sets about ameliorating the living conditions of working women.

2055. Lefcourt, Peter, 1941- . *Abbreviating Ernie*; a novel. New York: Villard, 1996. 301p.

Ernie Haas, a urologist in Schenectady, is a cross-dresser who enjoys having sex with his wife in odd places. However, Ernie has a life-ending heart attack when he is in the middle of sex with Audrey while she is handcuffed to their kitchen stove and she cannot free herself. She reaches for an electric knife and cuts off his penis. She is now able to move about; then a burglar and the police suddenly invade her house, and her subsequent trial draws the usual reporters, lawyers, moviemakers, publishers, et al.

2056. Lefèvre, Edwin, 1871-1943. *The golden flood.* **Illustrated by W.R. Leigh. New York: McClure, Phillips, 1905. 198p.**

"The financial lives of the richest man in the world and the president of the greatest New York bank hang by a thread. Every week a young man deposits an Assay Office cheque representing gold bullion. The first was for $100,000, the latest for $10,000,000. He refuses to tell where he got the gold or how much more there is to come. The fear is it will become as cheap as silver; then what will happen to the gold-bearing bonds of the bank? And—where does the gold come from?"—Annual American catalogue.

2057. ————. *H.R.* **New York: Harper, 1915. 336p.**

'H.R.' may be a bank clerk but he is no milquetoast. He accosts the bank president, courts the president's daughter—and is fired. New York becomes his 'city for conquest'. He whips up a bold financial plan that succeeds beyond even his expectations. Politics as well as other avenues of action beckon and again he wins, becoming the topic of admiring conversation throughout the city.

2058. ————. *The making of a stockbroker.* **New York: Doran, 1925. 341p.**

"John Kent Wing goes into a Wall Street brokerage office to learn the business. ...He is offered an initial salary of $3 a week. ... [At the story's end] he is junior partner in a firm offering a certain man a salary of $1,000,000 a year. The story of the phenomenal rise of the great brokerage house makes interesting reading. It describes to the uninitiated public the legitimate methods by which the huge enterprises of big business are financed and set afloat"—Book review digest.

2059. ————. *Reminiscences of a stock operator.* **New York: Doran, 1923. 299p.**

"A tale, autobiographical in manner, of a successful Wall Street speculator and stock-plunger. At the age of fourteen and just out of grammar school, he became a quotation-board boy in a stock-brokerage office. He was quick at figures, had a good memory, and was a good observer. He became interested in the behavior of stocks as a game. At fifteen he was known as the 'boy plunger' of the bucket shops. Needless to say he became the biggest and most successful speculator of Wall Street"—Book review digest.

2060. ————. *Sampson Rock, of Wall Street*; **a novel. New York: Harper, 1907. 393p.**

Sampson Rock's stock market speculations and shady maneuvers to gain control of the Virginia Central Railroad are disapproved of by his son. The latter 'gets in the swim' in an attempt to outfox his father. And he also continues to court a beautiful young woman who will inherit a fortune.

2061. ————. *Wall St. stories*. **New York: McClure, Phillips, 1901. 224p.**

Himself a former stockbroker Lefèvre's short stories paint pungent pictures of the manipulators, tipsters and cagey financiers who use their comprehensive knowledge of the bulls and the bears of the stock market to gain control of railroads, etc. O'Henry-like surprise endings are not infrequently utilized by the author. Contents: The woman and her bonds.—The break in turpentine.—The tipster.—A philanthropic whisper.—The man who won.—The lost opportunity.—Pike's Peak or bust.—A theological tipster.

2062. **Leffingwell, Albert, 1895-1966.** *Rope for an ape*, **by Dana Chambers [pseud.]. New York: Dial Press, 1947. 256p.**

"Nile Boyd, a newspaperman, finds the household of his prosperous friends, the Lomaxes, up near Tuxedo in a state of alarm when he pays them a visit. A murderer—or possibly an ape—seems to be heaving things out of trees at the help and the house guests, and Boyd himself is nearly exterminated a couple of times when he tries to find out why"—New Yorker.

2063. **Lehman, Eric Gabriel, 1954- .** *Quaspeck*; **a novel. San Francisco: Mercury House, 1993. 339p.**

The Gajewskis are a highly dysfunctional Upstate New York family in the early 1970s. Carl, a one-time hippie, is at the head of a coalition fighting a developer who has plans for turning the 'Quaspeck Lake' area into an elegant resort. That doesn't sit well with Carl's father, Walter, a construction worker in need of a job. Carl's home happens to be in the way should the developer start building. Cee Gajewski, Carl's sister, tries to commit suicide, leaves college and is impregnated by an ex-druggie and homosexual. Jason, Carl's younger brother, rapes his girlfriend and dashes off to the gay underground of Greenwich Village.

2064. **[Leigh, Oliver Herbrand Gordon].** *Dollarocracy*; **an American novel. Illustrated by Frank Ver Beck. New York: J.A. Taylor, 1891 [c1892]. 211p.**

"In developing the 'floating' of a big railway scheme into commercial existence, and the political wire-pulling of a 'rising' ex-senator, the author satirizes 'peanut' politics, modern journalism, and the vulgarities of the 'Dollarocracy'. The collapse of his financial schemes and crushing political defeat force the ex-senator to realize that there are better things in life than a position in the 'Dollarocracy'. The action is chiefly in New York City"—Annual American catalogue.

2065. ————. *The family physician, by one of his victims*. **New York: W.D. Rowland, 1892. 164p.**

"Dr. Gryffon, a New York doctor, is seemingly a means of making evident the influences of the physician in the household. The novel is based on sensational incidents and a discreditable professional career, in which the doctor appears in the role of a social magnet, who is rather sinned against than sinning"—Annual American catalogue.

2066. Leiser, Joseph, B. 1873. *Canaway and the Lustigs*. Cincinnati: Young Israels, 1909. 134p.

A story of Jewish life in a small town in western New York State; the leading characters are two Jewish boys who cope with daily life in an environment quite different from that which their father experienced in the 'old country' in his own childhood (he tells them all about it). But withal the boys are well aware of the Jewish holidays and observe them accordingly.

2067. Lemann, Nancy, 1956- . *Sportsman's paradise*; a novel. New York: Knopf; distributed by Random House, 1992. 225p.

"Set in the sleepy Long Island resort of Orient Point which has been discovered by Southerners who had moved North. ...[Storey Collier] carries a torch for ...Hobby Fox. She thinks of him as a burnt-out case—'courtly and windblown and stoic'—but in his 36 years he has been a major league ballplayer, a New Orleans prosecutor and the foreign editor of an important New York City newspaper. ...[Events] gradually reveal the couple's past affair and tell why a heartless decision made five years earlier blights any chance for happiness now"—Time.

2068. Lennox, Charlotte Ramsay, 1720-1804. *Euphemia*. London: Printed for T. Cadell and J. Evans, 1790. 4v.

Approximately half of the novel is set in America (New York City and Upstate New York primarily). Euphemia and her feckless husband, Lieutenant Neville, leave England for the colonies, hoping for a more secure financial future. Their son, Edward, is lost in the forests near Schenectady and receives upbringing at the hands of the Mohawk Indians. Reunited with his mother, Edward acquires the polish of a gentleman; he accompanies his mother to New York City where he finds favor, although he has a rather dim view of the city's fashionable society. The Neville family returns to England and Euphemia finds solace and comfort when she is left a fortune by her husband's uncle.

2069. ————. *The life of Harriot Stuart*. Written by herself. London: J. Payne, and J. Bouquet, 1751. 2v.

Lennox's novel is notable for perhaps being the first to include quite a few descriptions of American places (e.g., the Hudson River, Albany, the Mohawk Valley). The daughter of a man of noble lineage, Harriot sails with him and his wife to America where she attracts the attention of several suitors; her favorite is Dumont, a wealthy New York merchant's son despite his being of the Catholic faith. She has several adventures around Albany, Schenectady, etc., including capture by the Mohawk Indians. After her father's death Harriot is invited by an aunt to reside with her in England. Before and after reaching England Harriot undergoes another series of adventures, at sea and on land, before she falls into the arms of her true love, Dumont, who has converted to Protestantism.

2070. **Lentricchia, Frank, 1940- .** *Johnny Critelli*; **and,** *The Knifeman*: **two novels. New York: Scribner, 1996. 268p.**

The first 'novel' is ostensibly about an almost mythical character, Johnny Critelli, who circulates in Utica, New York's Italian-American community. But the author seems more interested in portraying the childhood and life in general in the 1950s of Italian families groping for their place in a strange setting. 'The Knifeman' is also laid in Utica with a protagonist, Richard Assisi, a gynecologist, who evolves into a cold-blooded serial killer.

2071. **Leonard, George, 1946- .** *The ice cathedral.* **New York: Simon & Schuster, 1984. 221p.**

Making a living as a clammer on the South Shore of Long Island, Mark Kessler kills a man who had attacked him. He develops a taste for bloodshed and becomes a serial killer, retreating sporadically into a silent, solitary, fantasy world under the ice of the Great South Bay. Hunted for reward money Kessler forces his pursuers into a suicidal posture, but in the end, despite his arrogant intelligence, Kessler is cornered.

2072. *Leonie*; **or,** *The sweet street singer of New York.* **By the author of** *For mother's sake*, *Marco*, **etc., etc., etc. New York: N.L. Munro, 1884. 151p.**

The villainous Gerard Varley, and his equally vile servant, Antonio Bucarelli, cast young Leonie (child of Varley and his deserted wife Isabel, a.k.a. Mlle. Marie Delsarte) adrift in New York City's wretched Five Points where she is forced to earn a living as a street singer. Wealthy Geoffrey Trevelyan falls in love with Leonie and marries her. Their troubles begin in earnest as Geoffrey's cousins, Cleora and Gaston Meers, with Bucarelli's aid, attempt to separate the two lovers, by death if necessary. Geoffrey suffers imprisonment by the conspirators and a shipwreck, and Leonie, in despair, almost commits suicide. Geoffrey and Leonie surmount innumerable other dangers, but are reunited finally along with Leonie's mother. Bucarelli, already having murdered Varley, turns on Cleora, the woman he loves, and kills her. His life ends on the scaffold; Gaston Meers dies in Sing Sing.

2073. **Lerman, Rhoda, 1936- .** *Call me Ishtar.* **Garden City, N.Y.: Doubleday, 1973. xii, 247p.**

A comedy about an off-center family; the 'heroine' is a suburban housewife in Upstate New York (around Syracuse) who is the reincarnation of Ishtar (Sumerian-Assyrian deity of love, Queen of Heaven, Whore of Babylon, etc.). Her husband works with polyester in his Canadian plant and manages a rock band; her son is more than a little weird (pulling out his teeth for no discernible reason). Mythology and deranged modern suburban life are brought together in a wild series of images.

2074. Leslie, Eliza, 1787-1858. *Althea Vernon*; or, *The embroidered handkerchief.* **To which is added,** *Henrietta Harrison*; or, *The blue cotton umbrella.* **Philadelphia: Lea & Blanchard, 1838. 276p.**

Rockaway Beach, Long Island, is the primary locale of the first tale, with a few scenes in New York City. Althea Vernon by chance picks up the costly cambric handkerchief of the heiress Miss Fitzgerald and carries it with her to social affairs. Wyndham Selfridge, in love with Althea, is perturbed by Althea's attachment to an article she, it is generally agreed, cannot afford. Is she frivolous, a worthy candidate for a wife? When the handkerchief is dropped again and badly damaged, Selfridge buys a replacement. Althea then confesses the true status of the embroidered handkerchief, satisfying her lover that she is a serious young lady. 'Henrietta Harrison', accompanying her uncle to 'Markhamville' in Upstate New York, is appalled by his purchase of a cheap, dowdy cotton umbrella, and does her best to hide it from friends on the boat going up the Hudson. The tale becomes a travelogue as places of interest Upstate are visited, including especially the Shaker settlement at Niskayuna. The umbrella, rescued by its would-be destroyer (Henrietta), becomes the means by which her future husband recognizes Henrietta when he is passing through Markhamville.

2075. Leslie, Madeline. *Rawlin's Mills.* **Boston: I. Bradley, 1882. 346p.**

Maxmilian Westerford starts out in life as a young Knickerbocker, but by his late teens his parents have sold their home in New York City as the metropolis expands into their hitherto rural-like area. Max has a vision of becoming very rich in manufacturing, however using his wealth to create a Utopian community of workers and employers where poverty has ceased to exist. Rawlin's Mills in 'the village of P——, lying along the banks of the ——' (p. 94) has many of the worst features of the 'industrial revolution', and it becomes the Christian mission of Max, who obtains a clerkship in the factory's office, to turn the situation completely around. He accomplishes this with his own perseverance, the assistance of a like-minded businessman, Mr. Rand, Marion Terry, daughter of one of the mill owners, his mother Gerty, and various other characters who gradually accept the Christian message of neighborly compassion—'Love is the fulfilling of the law of God and his Son]'.

2076. Lessing, Bruno, 1870-1910. *Children of men.* **New York: McClure, Phillips, 1903. 311p.**

"The stories [23 in all] have to do with the Jews of the East Side [of New York]. …In the reek of the sweatshop, and amid the tawdriness of the Essex Street ballroom, or in the silence of the synagogue, and behind the noise and fumes of the squalid café, the same drama of life is going on forever, precisely as we see it played before us everywhere. The Jewish girl with red-gold hair, loving a Christian to her death, the pushing, greedy, vulgar half-American young men who are ashamed of their own people, the learned rabbi, the drunken miser, the thief redeemed by a woman's deep devotion—here are all the elements of tragedy and comedy and farce. Love, hate, avarice, self-sacrifice, ambition—it is the whole gamut of the passions and virtues, making these children of the ghetto close akin to all of us who read"—The bookman.

2077. **Lester, Eugenia Campbell, 1929- .** *Frontiers aflame*: **Jane Cannon Campbell, Revolutionary War heroine when America had only heroes, by Eugenia Campbell Lester and Allegra Branson. Interlaken, N.Y.: Heart of the Lakes Pub., 1987. 304p.**

A novelization of the experiences of Jane Cannon Campbell and her family during the American Revolution in central and western New York State (and the Mohawk Valley), concentrating primarily on their Iroquois Indian captivity. Following the Cherry Valley massacre (Nov. 11, 1778) the captives were marched to Kanadesaga (present-day Geneva, N.Y.) and then taken to Fort Niagara. As negotiations for their exchange or release went on, the prisoners moved via Lake Ontario and the St. Lawrence River to Montreal and then began the journey homeward down Lake Champlain to Crown Point and from there southward to Albany where Colonel Samuel Campbell met up with his wife on Nov. 11, 1780, exactly two years after the Cherry Valley incident and the beginning of the long Indian captivity of Jane and her children.

Levine, William b. 1881. See under his pseudonym: Levinrew, Will.

2078. **Levinrew, Will, pseud.** *Murder on the Palisades*. **New York: McBride, 1930. viii, 345p.**

"A cryptic message is sent to a New York newspaper announcing the imminent death of Conrad Manx, the son of a well-known physician dwelling in a lonely spot on the Palisades. The death, the communication states, would be by meningitis. Three weeks later the death occurs. This strange message and its verification rousing the curiosity of the editor, he calls in the eminent Professor Brierly and a brilliant young reporter for conference. The stage now being set for mystery and murder, the tale proceeds, furnishing fresh crimes and new suspects in nearly every chapter"—Boston Transcript.

2079. **Lewis, Alfred Henry, 1857-1934.** *The Apaches of New York*. **New York: G.W. Dillingham, 1912. 272p.**

"All the Apache tales … deal with crime and social decadence, stick-ups and safe-cracking, Tong Wars and house-breaking, gang rub-outs and opium smoking, confidence games and prostitution. Lewis's purpose was 'to show you how the other half lives in New York'"—Ravitz, Abe C. Alfred Henry Lewis. Contents: Eat-Em-Up Jack.—The baby's fingers.—How Pioggi went to Elmira.—Ike the Blood.—Indian Louie.—How Jackson slew the Doc.—Leoni the Trouble Maker.—The wages of the snitch.—Little Bow Kum.—The cooking of Crazy Butch.—Big Mike Abrams.—The going of Biff Ellison.

2080. ————. *The Boss and how he came to rule New York*. **New York: A.S. Barnes, 1903. xiii, 409p.**

The nameless narrator of this novel (the 'Boss' of the title) comes as a young Irishman, the son of an immigrant blacksmith, under the tutelage of the cunning Tammany politician, Big John Kennedy. He learns well the methodology of acquiring political power and worldly wealth in teeming New York City; on the death of Big John he steps into the role of Tammany's leader. His only two 'friends' are the cynical and brilliant financier, James Morton, and the idealistic reformer, the Rev. Bronson. His own family life is filled with tragedy; beloved wife 'Apple Cheek' has a short life, leaving behind a frail daughter, Blossom. The Boss's sister Anne, Blossom's tutor, and Blossom herself succumb to illness and the Boss retires from politics. Lewis's novel gives the reader crude but cogent insight into the ways of machine politics in New York at the turn of the century.

2081. ————. *Confessions of a detective.* **Illustrated by E.M. Ashe. New York: A.S. Barnes, 1906. 280p.**

A retired New York City policeman of Irish stock looks back on his experiences as he rose from a novice cop on the beat to a shrewd, discerning detective. He deals effectively with bullies like 'Red Bob' and Tammany politicians like district leader McBulto. Honest himself, the detective frankly takes note of the graft that seems endemic in all departments of the city's government. The second half of the book contains stories of another highly skilled detective in the New York Police Department, Inspector Val. Contents: Confessions of a detective.—The Washington Square mystery.—The man who flew.—The murder at the Santa Marie.—The stolen red diamond.

2082. ————. *Sandburrs.* **Illustrated by Horace Taylor and G.B. Luks. New York: F.A. Stokes, 1900. 318p.**

Fifty stories and sketches of East Side slum life in New York City; most of them are in the language used by denizens of the Bowery.

2083. **Lewis, Edgar Donald.** *Minisink*; **kingdom forbidding loyalty. New York: Exposition Press, 1949. 220p.**

The Minisink region of New York State that runs from Hudson River to the headwaters of the Delaware and Susquehanna Rivers was a hotbed of Loyalist activity during the American Revolution. This historical romance portrays the difficulties patriotic settlers had in dealing effectively with Tories and Indians.

2084. **Lewis, Sinclair, 1885-1951.** *The job*; **an American novel. New York: Harper, 1917. 326p.**

"A story of modern business and of a woman's place in business life. Una Golden, who comes from Panama, Pa. to New York, is an ordinary girl with blond hair and eyeglasses. The story covers ten years of her life, from 1905 to 1915, from the age of twenty-five to thirty-five. In that time she studies at a 'commercial college', holds various jobs, and lives the life of a working girl, in a boarding house, 'home', and light housekeeping flat. Midway in this period she finds the job getting on her nerves, and takes the way of escape offered, marriage. But marriages made from that motive start with a handicap, and Una's is a failure. She returns to the job with new resolution, determined to conquer. She does, becomes a successful business woman, and then begins to consider the possibility of a second marriage in which conflicting claims of home and a career are both to be satisfied"—Book review digest.

2085. ————. *The trail of the Hawk*; a comedy of the seriousness of life. New York: Harper, 1915. 408p.

The hero of Lewis' novel is Carl ('Hawk') Ericson, a Minnesotan and college dropout who tries several paths of activity—porter in a saloon after drifting through several New York breadlines, a short but brilliant stab at airplane piloting, e.g.,—before he enters the motor car business in New York City. Carl meets a girl, Ruth Winslow, from an aristocratic New York family, and marries her. When Carl first experienced the city he recoiled from the poverty he saw and the 'strange' mix of its milling population. Now confined to office work, the pressures of city life and the claustrophobia of a New York apartment Carl, the caged 'Hawk', together with Ruth, flees to Buenos Aires and the management of the Van Zile Motor Corporation there.

2086. Lewisohn, Ludwig, 1885-1955. *The broken snare.* New York: B.W. Dodge, 1908. 289p.

Frances Garnett, though well educated and attractive, has been living with her parents, a doctor and his wife, for several years in what has been an increasingly vapid, unstimulating existence. Into their Morningside Heights apartment Dr. Garnett brings Julian Ware, a sophisticated man who considers marriage a despotic institution. Frances and Julian fall in love; he explains to Frances his beliefs concerning love and marriage and she, rather than break off their liaison, quits her New York home and follows Julian southward as 'Mrs. Ware'. They reconsider their situation after several embarrassing incidents.

2087. ————. *Don Juan.* New York: Boni and Liveright, 1923. 305p.

The novel closely examines the problems of marriage, divorce and personal freedom. It is laid in Manhattan and travels between Greenwich Village and Fifty-ninth Street. The characters are a man and his wife and the two other women with whom he is in love. He is especially weary of the constraints society has foisted upon him as he contemplates the three women with whom he has become involved.

2088. ————. *The island within.* New York: Harper, 1928. 350p.

Arthur Levy, son of an affluent German Jew who had migrated to America and settled in New York in the 1870s is a graduate of Columbia University medical school and is now practicing psychiatry. He marries Elizabeth Knight, a gentile and an agnostic even though her father is a Presbyterian minister. Arthur finds it impossible to fully acclimate himself to American culture. He leaves his wife and children, immerses himself in his heritage and traditions, and joins a Jewish mission to the Balkans.

2089. Lewton, Val, 1904-1951. *Yearly lease.* **New York: Vanguard Press, 1932. 298p.**

A Westchester village ('Sawpits' originally, but then a change of name to 'Chester Manor') is the site of an apartment house that goes by the name, the Bishop's Arms Apartments, a 'refuge' from the hustle and bustle of New York City. Hans Fife, writer of pulp fiction, and his pregnant wife, Helen, have taken rooms there; they are short of funds and Hans has little success squeezing pay from his publisher. Berenice Church lives below the Fifes; she is an old girl friend of Hans with an adulterous husband and a yen for reconnecting with Hans. Laura Bishop Sauvage Singleton, daughter of 'Lucky' Larry Bishop (he who had erected the ungainly mansion that eventually became Bishop's Arms Apartments), is a new resident who has drifted into lesbianism. She is especially interested in the young (19) and handsome Jean Pomeroy, a girl anxious to get away from her officious and flirtatious mother. By the story's end Hans has reawakened to his marital responsibilities (after a fling with Berenice) and sells several of his writings to the relief of his worried wife, now a mother; Berenice has dumped her faithless husband Bill; and Laura and Jean are lovers.

2090. Libbey, Laura Jean, 1862-1924. *Leonie Locke; or, The romance of a beautiful New York working-girl.* **New York: G. Munro, 1889. 287p.**

The pitfalls awaiting the poor working girl in wicked New York City are the theme of this formulaic, extravagantly sentimental tale. Penniless Leonie Locke finds work at Messrs. Lincoln & Carlisle, furriers, but the sexual harassment of Charlie Hart, the foreman, is more than she can endure. She leaves, but not before she attracts Gordon Carlisle, one of the owners. Leonie's father dies and she continues to have employment problems, and is pursued by the never-say-die Hart. Because of Carlisle's growing love for her, Leonie aggravates his mother and Doris Lancaster, an upper class young woman hopeful of marrying Gordon Carlisle. Of course, despite the vicissitudes Leonie endures; she triumphs in the end.

2091. ————. *Little Leafy, the cloakmaker's beautiful daughter; a romantic story of a lonely working girl in the City of New York.* **New York: J.S. Ogilvie [c1891]. 237p.**

Orphan Leafy Clifton, 17, sews cloaks with her aunt; her beauty stirs the passions of Frank Harris, a roué and part owner of Messrs. Fenton & Harris. Frederick Forrester, son of a wealthy man, asks Leafy to marry him after he pulls her from a fire and the clutches of Harris. The elder Forresters reject the girl; cast out on the mean streets Leafy leaps into the East River. This time Harris is her rescuer and he expects her to marry him. Leafy flees Harris and survives a railroad accident. Taking the name of one of those who died Leafy ends up in the home of Colonel Alden in 'Cloverdale' (New York?); he believes her to be a long-lost niece. The Alden villa is not especially safe for Leafy, for she is the target of another niece of the Colonel eager to eliminate any competition for the Colonel's fortune and affections. By the tale's conclusion Forrester and Harris are in Cloverdale and Leafy's relationship to the Colonel is substantiated. Of course now Forrester and Leafy are accepted by one and all (Harris excepted) as a married couple.

2092. *The Liberal American*; a novel, in a series of letters, by a lady. London: Printed for W. Lane, Leadenhall-Street, 1785. 2v.

The English heroine, Miss Sophie Aubrey, sails with friends to New York City, where she meets and marries Mr. Elliot, 'the liberal American.'

2093. Liddon, Eloise S., 1897- . *The riddle of the Russian princess*. Garden City, N.Y.: Published for the Crime Club by Doubleday, Doran, 1934. 297p.

"About what happened when Norman Fairchild, an author, was stabbed with the Renaissance dagger at his home, Villa Daphne, on Long Island Sound. The trouble is over a golden brooch …once the property of Catherine the Great, and the murderer may be Princess Catherine Bobrinsky (descendent of the empress), or old Dorcas Weatherby (thinks she's a reincarnation of same), or Roger Thornton (in love with [the] corpse's wife) or somebody else altogether—why not Joe Zakowsky, the gardener? So-so detecting by a couple of young lady guests and others"—New York herald tribune books.

2093a. Lieberman, Robert, 1941- . *Baby*; a novel. New York: Crown Publishers, 1981. 344p.

Doris Rumsey, 59, a rather humpbacked librarian at Boynton Junior High in Ithaca, N.Y., gives virgin birth to a golden-haired child in a hedgerow just outside the village of Lansing. The awe-struck Doris immediately gives it the name Baby. Back in her Ithaca home Doris is even more surprised when Baby breaks into what is undeniably a song. *The Ithaca Journal* and Syracuse newspapers feature the story and Irwin Shockley, professor and composer, becomes a major figure in the exploitation of Baby's peculiar talent. Exposed to the media, the excitement of New York City, a kidnapping and the 'cult' formed around her, Baby eventually loses her musical voice. Doris Rumsey dies and Ruth Shockley, divorced from Irwin and remarried, adopts Baby. Familiar places in Ithaca and environs are in large part the setting of the novel.

2094. Liebovitz, David, b. 1892. *Chronicle of an infamous woman*. New York: Macaulay, 1933. 336p.

"The saga of Martina [Harley] who first appeared in a small Adirondack village as the devoted nurse to an ailing husband, Dr. Harley. When he died, it was rumored that Martina had poisoned him. That rumor, coupled with her great attraction for men, proved her undoing. She wandered about, now supporting herself by teaching music, now taking lovers, and supplying the countryside with gossip. She tried to rehabilitate herself in the eyes of the

538

villagers, but rumor grew and spread. Her story ends with a tragedy—Book review digest.

2095. **Liederman, Judith, 1927- .** *The pleasure dome*; **a novel. New York: Arbor House, 1981. 383p.**

The Eastman and Goldmark families are owners of resort hotels on Long Island and in Florida. When capable Jesse Goldmark dies, his alcoholic son Matthew fights with brother-in-law Harlan Chase for control of the Goldmark properties. Family quarrels become a way of life. Laina Eastman, rape victim of Chase when she was a teenager, cannot and evidently does not want to escape his fascinating hold on her, in part because she is married to homosexual David Goldmark, a composer. The novel offers an interesting glimpse of Jewish traditions and phraseology.

2096. **Lief, Max, 1899- .** *Hangover.* **New York: Liveright, 1929. 318p.**

A wild weekend party in a New York City penthouse is the opening scene of this rather gross novel, with the guests drawing a bath for an inebriated young woman. That is only the first of a series of distasteful incidents that fill out the story; the author is straightforward and does not offer any satirical commentary as he parades his theatrical characters and gossipy journalists. Lief, it has been noted, has adopted fictitious names for individuals who are actual players in the Broadway and glamorous New York scene.

2097. **Lieferant, Henry, b. 1892.** *Grass on the mountain,* **by Henry and Sylvia Lieferant. New York: Dutton, 1938. 443p.**

"The scene is an Upstate New York town. The Lyenbeck factory was the chief reason for the town, and for nearly a hundred years the Lyenbeck family had presided with almost feudal splendor over town, factory and workers. The second theme of the novel is the story of the supernatural experiences of Thorry and the sudden cure of her blindness"—Book review digest.

Lieferant, Sylvia, b. 1896, joint author. *Grass on the mountain.* **See Item #2097.**

2098. **Lighthall, William Douw, 1857-1954.** *The Master of Life*; **a romance of the Five Nations. Chicago: A.C. McClurg, 1909. vi, 262p.**

The author casts a romantic (though fictional) aura over the early years (before the appearance of the white man) of the Iroquois and their confederacy. Hiawatha, taking his inspiration from the 'Master of Life' (an Indian god who lived beneath the 'Great River'), is designated as the founder of the League of the Five Nations. The Iroquois are portrayed as people of nation-building talents with a close kinship to nature and possessing poetic sensibilities.

2099. **Lillie, Lucy Cecil White, b. 1855.** *Elinor Belden*; **or, *The step brothers.* Philadelphia: H.T. Coates, 1896. 328p.**

"Elinor Belden's father is killed in a railroad accident, and she and her mother, after his debts are paid, have very little to live upon. They come to New York to live with a stepbrother of Elinor's, but his wife treats them so heartlessly that they take refuge in a house downtown with some relatives of a former maid. Here they are quite comfortable, and Elinor carries out a long-cherished scheme of becoming a writer, in which Miss Montressor, a middle-aged authoress of note, assists her. Elinor also has a love-story"—Annual American catalogue.

2100. ————. *For honor's sake*; *a sequel to the Squire's daughter.* **Philadelphia: Porter & Coates, 1891. 450p.**

"The thread of Dorothy Kent's history is taken up after the death of Squire and Mrs. Kent, when she is the ward of General Bering. The story deals with the trials and triumphs that attend the heiress Dorothy and some incidents that precede her marriage to Alfred Thorndyke. The scenes are mostly in New York and Connecticut"—Annual American catalogue.

2101. ————. *A girl's ordeal.* **Philadelphia: H.T. Carter, 1897. v, 413p.**

"Between Mr. [Mark] Read, who gains and loses and regains his fortune, his second wife and stepdaughter with their affiliations, his own daughter [Constance] and her friends, Fenton and his scapegrace brother, the rather vulgar heiress Miss Armitage, and all the rest, affairs are pretty well mixed up. As a matter of fact it is not true to life and it is too complicated"—Literary world (Boston). Constance has the feeling that she is not welcomed by her stepmother in the Reads' New York City home, so off she goes to become a paid companion to a wealthy young woman of her own age.

2102. ————. *Ruth Endicott's way*; or, *Halgrave's mission.* **Philadelphia: H.T. Coates, 1896. 286p.**

Ruth Endicott's 'way' is to 'be there' whenever someone she meets is overwhelmed by seemingly insurmountable problems. She herself had suffered through her father's death and the realization that the inheritance he was to leave her had disappeared. She came to New York to earn her living and secured a place as secretary to a prosperous man who faced the possibility of total blindness. When not on the job Ruth lived rather snugly in the home of an elderly relative.

2103. ————. *The squire's daughter*; a story for girls. **Philadelphia: Porter & Coates, 1891. 350p.**

The above novel and its sequel, 'For Honor's Sake' (q.v.) are intended by the author to stimulate young women to make 'correct' moral choices in their lives, as does her protagonist. "Dorothy [Dolly], daughter of Squire Kent of 'Johnsburg', is the heroine. Although the story opens in Connecticut, most of the action is in New York. Dolly pays a visit to Pauline Molesworth, and during this time she meets General Bering. The incidents which follow this meeting and her acquaintance with Alf[red] Thorndyke form the substance of the story"—Annual American catalogue.

2104. Lilly, Jean. *Death in B-minor*. New York: Dutton, 1934. 319p.

On the Fourth of July weekend the featured entertainment of a house party at a Long Island home other than the fireworks is the piano playing of Benjamin Whipple. As Whipple plays the last measure of a Liszt sonata the host is shot and falls dead before the startled guests. The local district attorney handles the case and solves it.

2105. ————. *Death thumbs a ride*. New York: Dutton, 1939. [c1940]. 252p.

Prominent political personalities vacationing in the Adirondacks are the victims of jewel heists and murder. An officer of the law who is also on holiday in the same place takes on the responsibility of clearing the air.

2106. Lincoln, Jeanie Thomas Gould, 1846-1921. *The Luck of Rathcoole*; being the romantic adventures of Mistress Faith Wolcott (sometimes known as Miss Moppet) during her sojourn in New York at an early period of the Revolution. Boston: Houghton, Mifflin, 1912. 262p.

In 1789, while George Washington is being inaugurated, Scots-Irish Nugent Carmichael is in New York looking for a lost necklace, the Luck of Rathcoole, which is vital to his family's prosperity and to his own survival. Miss Faith Wolcott attracts his attention and innocent she is somehow drawn into Carmichael's search. The inevitable romance develops and the novel draws quickly to a conclusion satisfactory to readers of this type of fiction.

2107. ————. *An unwilling maid*; being the history of certain episodes during the American Revolution in the early life of Mistress Betty Yorke, born Wolcott. Boston: Houghton, Mifflin, 1897. 263p.

Connecticut is the early scene of the novel. It is there in her home that Betty Wolcott meets the gallant British Captain Geoffrey Yorke who saves her sister Moppet from drowning. Betty's brother Oliver, an American officer, captures Yorke but Betty helps Yorke escape. Months later Betty visits her sister Clarissa (married to Gulian Verplanck, a Tory) in British-occupied New York City. There Betty finds out that Oliver and Kitty Cruger, a guest in the Verplanck mansion, are in love. Captain Yorke reappears, to Betty's dismay, for though she is falling in love with him, she feels that her patriot views forbid her marrying him. Kitty and Betty, with covert assistance from Yorke, help Oliver—he has been spying on the British—escape from the city. When the war ends and the peace treaty is signed, Oliver and Kitty wed. Geoffrey Yorke, presumed to be in England turns up again and tells the ecstatic Betty that he has cut ties to his native land and has cast his lot with the new nation.

2108. Lindsey, William, 1858-1922. *The backsliders*. Boston: Houghton, Mifflin, 1922. 362p.

"When the Reverend John Gray entered upon his first charge as a pastor of the Methodist Church of 'Wesley', an out-of-the-way country town in the Adirondacks, he was twenty-five years old, steeped in classic and Biblical lore, but absolutely ignorant of life. He had never been young. The story tells how, in the first few months of his ministry, he grew up to the tall stature of a man and a Christian in the true spirit of Christ. The village, though small, contains a full assortment of human types from all of whom in turn he learns something new about Christianity. Above all it is a girl, not one of his flock and a so-called infidel who takes upon herself the role of teacher"—Book review digest.

2109. Linney, Joseph Robert. *The touch of human hands*; **a novel. Philadelphia: Dorrance, 1947. 478p.**

The author draws on his own experiences to portray the operation of an iron mine and an ore-dressing mill in the Adirondacks. The manager and chief engineer, Jim Lane, is under constant pressure from the mining company president and the restless, hard-living miners. 'Tiger Mountain', the primitive village where most of the action takes place, is faithfully served by Swedish Doctor Alex Larson and the socially concerned community nurse, Betty Dale, with whom Jim falls in love. Jim has a passionate affair with the chief executive's foster daughter, Sally O'Neill, and weathers labor troubles that include a strike of several weeks duration. In a rousing conclusion Jim and several of his workers are trapped by a mine cave-in; rescue efforts are headed by Steve Jordon, Jim's chief assistant, heretofore an antagonistic union leader. Jim returns to his first love, Betty. Sally, recovering from an auto accident and a miscarriage, finds consolation in Steve.

Lipez, Richard, 1938- . See under his pseudonym: Stevenson, Richard, 1938-.

2110. Lippard, George, 1822-1854. *The Empire City*; **or,** *New York by night and day*. **New York: Stringer & Townsend, 1850. 100p. (in double columns).**

"Sets up the tale of the 1823 will of the wealthy Gulian Van Huyden, who commits suicide when he discovers his wife and his brother are lovers. The estate is to be divided among seven descendants of 'Our Ancestor', who landed on this shore in 1620, 'penniless, a beggar and a vagabond' …on Christmas Day 1844 …The seven [are]—including a corrupt statesman, Gabriel Godlike, a satirical amalgam of Webster, Clay and Calhoun; a lecherous minister, Herman Barnhurst; the financier Israel Yorke; the merchant prince, Evelyn Somers; the Southern slaveholder Harry Royalton; and the dandy Beverly Barron—a typical pantheon of Lippard villains. The seventh is Arthur Dermoyne, a minor character who is said to be a reformer, a deist …When he appears he is tracking the seducer of the innocent Alice Burney. Lippard brings The Empire City to an abrupt close, never really completing any of the multiple plots, and not even reaching the climactic Christmas Day of 1844. Arthur Dermoyne is married off to a daughter of Van

Huyden in the last paragraph, and shares in the estate"—Denning, Michael. Mechanic accents ... London, New York, 1987.

2111. ————. *The Midnight Queen*; or, *Leaves from New-York life.* **New York: Garrett, 1853. 110p (in double columns).**

Includes three unconnected stories. In the first story ('The Midnight Queen') Frances Van Huyden, reared by Rev. Walworth in the Hudson Valley, is forced by her dissolute and mostly absent mother into a shameful way of life in New York. She is dying when Rev. Walworth's son, Father Luke, her only true love, comes to offer her solace. The second tale ('The Life of a man of the world') concerns Frank Van Warner whose beloved Eva is murdered by his loathsome first wife. His second wife, Eugenia (with their child Mary) stands by him as he drifts into madness but does recover. The protagonist of the third story ('Margaret Dunbar') believes her husband is dead and marries a scoundrel, Stanley Burke. However Harry Dunbar has survived and comes to New York searching for Margaret. He finds her—too late. Burke murders Harry, steals Harry's gold and then accidentally drowns. Forlorn Margaret suffering from consumption, roams the streets of New York with an air of death about her.

2112. ————. *New York*: *its upper ten and lower million.* **Cincinnati: H.M. Rulison, 1853. 284p.**

A melodramatic novel about heirs to a fortune who commit frightful acts in their contention for riches. The author states that these 'horrors [are not] born of romance, but of that under-current of real-life, which rolls on evermore, beneath the glare and uproar of the Empire City.' The novel is undergirded with descriptions of familiar New York City landmarks (Broadway, the Astor House, East River, etc.), a scathing portrayal of the heartless well-to-do, and sympathy for the less fortunate of the milling metropolis.

2113. **[Lippincott, Bertha Horstmann] 1880-1963.** *Chevrons*; **a story of West Point, by B.H.L. Illustrated by the author. Philadelphia: Lippincott, 1901. 264p.**

Harold Wayne, captain of a company of West Point cadets, had been grievously hurt by a young woman with whom he had been deeply in love and as a consequence had distanced himself from any more contact with the society of women. He is brought back to reality and romance by a young, patriotic, high-reaching girl; she spends her summer near West Point just before the outbreak of the Spanish-American War. Wayne serves heroically in that conflict and also wins the girl's heart.

2114. **Lippmann, Julie Mathilde, 1864-1952.** *'Burkeses Army'.* **Illus. by Harriet Mead Olcott. New York: Holt, 1915. 341p.**

"The story of a spoiled child of fortune who comes to live in a slum and thereby learns something of life and is transformed in character. When her grandfather, the great Alexander Guthrie, had insisted on her going to Europe with her Aunt Jean and himself, Amy had dared to defy him. She chose instead to join her father; and her father, James Burke, who had queer ideas, had gone to live in lower New York to study the conditions of the poor. From her new acquaintances, Nora Cavanaugh, Borisovna Orloff and John Graham, Amy gets a new point of view. A fire in a shirtwaist factory of which Alexander Guthrie is the owner is one of the realistic incidents of the story, but in some of its developments it bears a resemblance to the fairy tale. [e.g.] Nora becomes a great singer, John is found to be the heir to a title, etc."—Book review digest.

2115. ————. *Martha-by-the-day*. New York: Holt, 1912. 201p.

"Claire Lang is one of the many young girls [of good character but with little money] who start out in highest hope to match youth and strength and talent against the grim indifference of New York. But fate is kinder to Claire than to many, for while she fails as the many fail, she finds Martha-by-the-day [a kindly Irish charwoman] who rescues her when she is down to her last carfare, with room rent to pay. It is through Martha that she finds herself installed as governess to one of the little sons of the rich, a child who has been spoiled by an indulgent society mother and only partially held in check by a stern young uncle"—Book review digest. Claire and that uncle over time form a promising relationship.

2116. Liscomb, Harry F. *The Prince of Washington Square*; an up-to-the-minute story. New York: Stokes, 1925. ix, 180p.

Jack, the newsboy hero, is described as follows: "The Prince of Washington Square was a handsome, manly and superbly muscled youth of fifteen with a buoyant disposition toward his compatriots. His ebony hair had been combed and parted flawlessly in the centre." Jack's adventures take him from Washington Square to Harlem, and they are told in the idiom of the place and time. The author is said to be a mature 19-year-old lad.

2117. Listfield, Emily, 1957- . *Acts of love*. New York: Viking Press, 1994. 373p.

Tragedy strikes a family in rural Upstate New York when Ted Waring shoots his wife Ann during a vicious quarrel. The couple's two daughters, Julie, 13, and Ali, 11, witnessed the killing. Ted insists that the shooting was an accident but is refuted by Julie who says she saw her father take aim. The story then veers backward and explores the early years of the marriage, with Ann claiming most of our sympathy while Ted is a morose man with a longing to be free, although he does stand by his family. Ann's younger sister drifts pointedly into the picture, but the question of Ted's innocence or guilt is overwhelmed by the ugliness of the situation.

2118. Litchfield, Grace Denio, 1849-1994. *A hard-won victory*. New York: G.P. Putnam, 1888. 384p.

Our heroine, Jean Ormsby, enters the New York City ménage of the Van Voorsts—ruled over by a physically disabled matriarch—as companion to the old lady. Jean, an orphan, who has money in her own right, bequeathed by her deceased grandfather, is certain that she has been placed on earth to do good. The sophisticated, worldly Mrs. Van Voorst is a capable enough manager of her family despite her paralysis. However, Jean does insinuate herself into the affairs of the younger Van Voorsts, even though she has a benign touch. In the long run Jean profits character-wise from her involvement with the family.

2119. ———. *Only an incident.* **New York: G.P. Putnam, 1883. iii, 226p.**

It had been accepted by the good folk of 'Joppa' (presumably a cover name for Cazenovia, New York) that the Rev. Denham Halloway and pretty, beloved Phebe Lane would be a well-matched couple. Then Phebe's friend Gerald (i.e. Geraldine) Vernor comes from New York City to Joppa for a summer and the young minister is smitten with her charm and beauty. Denham confides to his sister, 'Soeur Angélique', that he has fallen in love with Gerald although there is an ember of love remaining for Phebe. While nursing a young woman with 'the fever' Phebe contracts the disease herself and dies. In New York City Gerald, now Mrs. Ogden De Forest, learns that the Rev. Denham Halloway has left his Joppa parish. Gerald says to Ogden: "I don't suppose I have thought twice of Denham Halloway since [we left Joppa]. Ah, so it was! That brief summer meeting, which had had so potent an influence on the lives of those other two, had in her life been 'only an incident'" (p. 226).

2120. **Livingston, Armstrong, b. 1885.** *The doublecross.* **New York: R.D. Henkle, 1929, [c1928]. 316p.**

"A diamond necklace is the cause of all the trouble. A group of smugglers have tried to get it into this country, but the agent to whom they have entrusted the mission has been robbed. In the closing pages good turns out to be bad and bad good in the persons of many characters [many of whom are members of New York society], and the necklace is recovered while a huge counterfeiting plot is exposed"—Springfield Republican.

2121. ———. *Night of crime.* **New York: Sovereign House, 1938. 315p.**

A serial killer stalks the fancy-dress ball held at a Long Island estate. Jimmy Traynor flushes out the killer while the unaware guests continue to enjoy their revels.

2122. *Lizzie Lee's daughter*; or, *A rich father's remorse!* **Being a true narrative of how, after disowning and turning out his daughter, Lizzie Lee, because she eloped with and married his coachman, he also gave away her child to a strange woman. How, after the mother's death in the almshouse, he became stricken with remorse for his cruelty, and commenced to search for the child he had given away; her final rescue after a most exciting series of adventures and incidents; and how the coachman tried to abduct and kill her, & c., & c. Truly a most romantic incident of real life in Fifth Avenue, New York City. [New York: 186-?] 62p.**

This work is listed in Wright's American fiction but is not available in its microfilm series.

2123. **Lloyd, Beatrix Demarest.** *The pastime of eternity.* **New York: Scribner, 1904. 364p.**

A novel in which music and the city (New York) play significant roles. The protagonist is a man whose wealth and leisure afford him little satisfaction for his marriage is an unhappy one and he feels isolated from the 'real' world. He begins to take consolation in his love for music and devotes himself to studying and playing the violoncello. Two new sympathetic and loving women come into his life and through them and their musical interests he finds regeneration.

2124. **Lloyd, Nelson McAllister, 1873-1933.** *Mrs. Radigan, her biography, with that of Miss Pearl Veal, and the memoirs of J. Madison Mudison.* **New York: Scribner, 1905. viii, 344p.**

"The story is told through a young real-estate man, himself a climber of the climbers, who depicts his business as offering the open sesame to society, because 'all the cotillion leaders are in real estate or architecture, as dancing is a branch of their business'. When Mrs. Radigan [who has come from Kansas City, rich and expecting to purchase entry into New York society] inquires of him: 'Do tell me, how do people get to know you in New York?' he replies, 'They don't', and then proceeds to enlighten her on the quickest way of getting to know them, which is, of course, to cultivate real estate men by making their ostensible business calls at their offices. Notwithstanding these assurances to Mrs. Radigan, he is not at all averse to making assurance doubly sure by grasping one of the points of the Radigan star in its swift ascent and being carried up himself"—Bookman.

2125. **Lockridge, Frances, d. 1963.** *Murder out of turn.* **New York: Stokes, 1941. 294p.**

Detective Lieutenant Weigand of the New York City police is on a holiday at 'Lone Lake', sixty miles northeast of Manhattan, visiting the Norths (Pam and Jerry), when he is called in on a double murder, one of the victims being Jean Corbin, a lady in the advertising business. The Norths and Weigand collaborate to bring the case to a satisfactory conclusion.

2126. ———. *The ticking clock,* **by Frances and Richard Lockridge. Philadelphia: J.B. Lippincott, c1961/62. 184p.**

A 31-room mansion in an isolated area of Westchester County is the inheritance of Constance Dale from her great-aunt, Adelaide Farmer. Connie has taken a break from her job in Hollywood to come east and look at the formidable structure and perhaps find a way of unloading it on a prospective buyer. While she is spending a day and night in the house she becomes aware that there are other people in it. Overhearing their conversation Connie stumbles onto a kidnapping plot. Four men and one woman have snatched the child of a wealthy Westchester couple and are using the mansion as a hiding place as they press their ransom demands. In an effort to upset the criminals' plans Connie falls into several dangerous and very unpleasant situations before the New York State Police, the kidnapped child's father and Connie's rather distant relation, artist/illustrator Jonathan Farmer, arrive on the scene.

For other works by Frances Lockridge written in collaboration with husband see: Lockridge, Richard, 1898-1982.

2127. Lockridge, Richard, 1898-1982. *Accent on murder*; a Captain Heimrich mystery, by Richard and Frances Lockridge. Philadelphia: J.B. Lippincott, 1958. 223p.

At his Westchester County home, retired academician Walter Brinkley entertains several friends. The following day Carolyn Wilkens, a naval officer's wife, is discovered on a neighboring beach, her body riddled with shotgun pellets. Captain Merton Heimrich of the New York State Police is baffled until Brinkley, a scholar of regional dialects, provides him with the distinctive clue—the peculiarity in the chief suspect's speech patterns. This is one of a series of mysteries (about a dozen) by Lockridge (and, on occasion, his wife Frances in collaboration) that were set in Westchester County and featured Captain Heimrich (see infra).

2128. ————. *Burnt offering*; a Captain Heimrich mystery, by Richard and Frances Lockridge. Philadelphia:Lippincott, 1955. 189p.

"The burnt offering is the town's most influential if not its oldest or most beloved citizen. The investigation requires understanding not only of the people [in Upstate New York's Putnam County], observed so alertly by the Lockridges, but of the town's ['Van Brunt's'] history, while the tug of an ancient name vies with the simple weight of money"—New York herald tribune books. Captain Heimrich is the chief investigator, confronted with an incinerated body and various violent events.

2129. ————. *Death and the gentle bull* (a Captain Heimrich mystery), by Richard and Frances Lockridge. Philadelphia: J.B. Lippincott, 1954. 224p.

"Captain Heimrich …is summoned to a stud farm [in the Hudson Valley] where it seems there is some doubt as to whether a two-hundred-and-fifty thousand dollar prize bull actually did trample the proprietor [Mrs. Margaret Landcraft], an indomitable old lady, to death. The landscape is cluttered with heirs, none of whom have much interest in livestock and all of whom need money, so the narrowing-down process takes quite a while [even with the help of one of Heimrich's best New York State troopers]"—New Yorker.

2130. ————. *The distant clue*; a Captain Heimrich mystery, by Richard and Frances Lockridge. Philadelphia: J.B. Lippincott, 1963. 187p.

Excellent detective work by Captain Merton L. Heimrich of the New York State Police solves the questionable deaths of two elderly residents of Putnam

County. Homer Lenox was hard at work on his 'The Families of Putnam County, New York' when he suddenly died either from a self-inflicted wound or perhaps was shot by his mild friend, Professor Loudon Wingate, the 'Van Brunt' librarian, who himself later ended up dead. Which was it? Delightful details of life in Putnam County are an added bonus for the reader.

2131. ————. *First come, first kill*; a Captain Heimrich mystery, by Richard and Frances Lockridge. Philadelphia: J.B. Lippincott, 1962. 190p.
"Captain Heimrich, New York State Police, has a personal interest in finding who shot the old man who died in his driveway. ...The corpse is that of a vanished Upstate [New York] judge and his murder is linked to his wife's second marriage and to his inheriting daughter, but the situations disclosed have little relation to the killer when revealed"—Kirkus services. The author provides a warm portrait of Putnam County, N.Y. life.

2132. ————. *Foggy, foggy death*; a Captain Heimrich mystery, by Richard and Frances Lockridge. Philadelphia: J.B. Lippincott, 1950. 223p.
"There may have been a reason for the little boy to wander away in the fog, and for his unhappy young mother to be found drowned in a foot of water at the bottom of the garden, but why should anyone want to kill the handyman, who had done nothing worse than make off with a Cadillac and a sizable jewel case? These are only a few of the problems that confront ...Heimrich in a bleak mansion [in a village] north of New York, dominated by the inflexible matriarch"—New Yorker.

2133. ————. *I want to go home*; a Captain Heimrich mystery, by Richard and Frances Lockridge. Philadelphia: J.B. Lippincott, 1948.
"Jane Phillips, a former Wave, has an eventful journey from California to her home in Westchester ...since somebody seems to be intent on keeping her from reaching the bedside of her Great-Aunt Susan, a well-heeled old lady with an allergy to shrimps. Things aren't much quieter after Miss Phillips arrival, either; her aunt has been bumped off, she finds, and both the police and one of her own admirers are having quite a time pinning the job on the right party"—New Yorker.

2134. ————. *Let dead enough alone*; a Captain Heimrich mystery, by Richard and Frances Lockridge. Philadelphia: J.B. Lippincott, c1955. 191p.
"People who go to New Year's Eve house parties in the country [the Hudson Valley] probably deserve exactly what they get, but John Halley's guests have an even worse time than most, and he himself winds up frozen in the lake. Captain Heimrich of the New York State Police has quite a job figuring out what happened when all the lights went out, and is not quite in time to prevent a second murder, but, as usual, the killer makes that one fatal small mistake"—New Yorker.

2135. ————. *Murder can't wait*; a Captain Heimrich mystery. Philadelphia: J.

B. Lippincott, 1964. 189p.

"Lieutenant Shapiro, New York Police Department, goes to ['North Wellwood' in] Westchester County to find out about Stuart Fleming, and his information about bribes offered, and perhaps paid, to football players at Dyckman University. When he found Captain Heimrich at the headquarters of [New York State] Troop K, he learned of Fleming's murder"—Book review digest. Heimrich and Shapiro try to figure out whether Fleming was killed because of a point-shaving fix in syndicate gambling or because of wrought-up emotional tensions.

2136. ————. *Murder roundabout*; a Captain Heimrich mystery. Philadelphia: J.B. Lippincott, 1966. 186p.

The Westchester community of 'Van Brunt' is not too downcast or surprised when former movie queen Annette (LeBaron) Weaver is murdered in her home. She had made no secret of her disdain for the town's social leaders who chose to ignore the thrice-married Annette. Unfortunate Leslie Brennan, young, still somewhat immature wife and part-time real estate agent, is drawn into the situation; she is trying to sell the Weaver home and inadvertently discovers Annette's body. However, it is the Weaver's cleaning woman, not Leslie, who first tells the police of the murder. As Captain Heimrich and his New York State Police crew look into the case, Leslie suddenly finds herself being stalked in the nearby woods by someone who may well be the murderer.

2137. ————. *Practice to deceive*; a Captain Heimrich mystery, by Richard and Frances Lockridge. Philadelphia: J.B. Lippincott, 1957. 188p.

"The Lockridges …have turned their attention to a tidy little murder [of Olive Senley, stabbed] in a motel in Upstate New York, which is, of course, Captain Heimrich's territory. The victim has had three husbands, all, naturally, suspected; a hurricane supplies a good deal of upset as well as what appears to be an unbreakable alibi; and the Captain's romance with female decorator [and widow Susan Faye] is reasonably unobtrusive"—New Yorker.

2138. ————. *A risky way to kill*; an Inspector Heimrich mystery. Philadelphia: J.B. Lippincott, 1970. 192p.

An ad printed in a Westchester County weekly, the Van Brunt Citizen, stirs up memories of the 'accidental' death of 20-year-old Virginia Gant (thrown from her horse) who at the time was living in neighboring Putnam County with her stepfather, Paul Wainright, and her mother, Florence. Lyle Mercer, reporter, and her boss, Robert Wallis, editor and publisher of the Van Brunt Citizen, pique Inspector Merton Heimrich's curiosity about circumstances surrounding the year-old death of Miss Grant. The so-called fatal ingestion of too many sleeping pills by Mrs. Florence Wainright [could it have been suicide or was it murder?] is a key incident as the case winds down to its conclusion.

2139. ————. *Show red for danger*; a Captain Heimrich mystery, by Richard and Florence Lockridge. Philadelphia: J.B. Lippincott, 1960. 191p.

Hollywood (Allied Pictures) invades Putnam County, New York, the home turf of Captain Merton L. Heimrich of the New York State Police, who is presently wooing the widow, Susan Faye, owner of a fabric shop in 'Van Brunt'. Susan, accompanied by the Captain, drives to the artist Brian Collins's residence to look at one of his designs; they run into what appears to be a murder, followed by a suicide. The much married movie glamour queen, Peggy Belford, lies dead in the Collins house, apparently shot by the artist who then turned the gun on himself. But, of course, appearances are deceiving; Susan notices the big splash of red on Collins's design and posits that he was signaling red for danger. Heimrich gets to work interviewing a cast of motion picture actors, directors, et al. Near the story's end Heimrich uses Susan as bait to draw out the murderer, a ploy she highly resents despite the protective measures (which went awry) he had prepared.

2140. ————. *Spin your web, lady!* a Captain Heimrich mystery, by Richard and Frances Lockridge. Philadelphia: J.B. Lippincott, 1949. 218p.
"Murder on the outer edge of [New York City's] suburbia [read Putnam and Westchester Counties] where one of an exasperated bunch of Martini addicts has wound a wire around the neck of a young woman who had been going in for blackmail and Scotch whiskey on an extensive scale. Another member of this muddled circle of friends succumbs to the garotte before Captain Heimrich, a State Police detective, finally makes sense out of the clues, which are, understandably, tenuous"—New Yorker.

2141. ————. *Stand up and die*; a Captain Heimrich mystery, by Richard and Frances Lockridge. Philadelphia: J.B. Lippincott, 1953. 219p.
"Captain Heimrich…is confronted with a rather nasty problem involving a young lady, who gets chopped up on a country lane [in Westchester], and her grandmother, who is eliminated in a much less messy and far more scientific fashion in her bed. There are a good many suspects, including a young Marine, who provides the customary heart interest; quite a lot of subsidiary violence; and a solution that, not altogether naturally, backs into the files of the London Lancet"—New Yorker.

2142. ————. *With one stone*; a Captain Heimrich mystery, by Richard and Frances Lockridge. Philadelphia: J.B. Lippincott, 1961. 192p.
"Captain Heimrich, honeymooning with Susan, has a hasty return to Hawthorne barracks [in the Hudson Valley] when the young second wife of wealthy newspaper owner Bedlow is found dead. He picks up the already established threads, is faced with the murder of Bedlow, and in fitting the criminal to the crime, eliminates a definite suspect and turns up another. An able exploit for Westchester's thorough-going Captain"—Kirkus service.

2143. ————. *With option to die*; a Captain Heimrich mystery. Philadelphia: J.B. Lippincott, 1967. 192p.

"'North Wellwood, Town of Wellwood', County of Westchester and State of New York—a village lying in a valley with green hills tumbling around it" (p. 9)—is very conservative and presently upset by the possibility of a country club being formed in its midst, a club which will be open to all regardless of race. A number of people in the village are disdainful of those residents who are 'liberal' or even 'socialistic' in their politics. One of the latter is Faith Powers, a retired professor and former school board member, who is found in her totaled car with a bullet in her brain. Newcomers to North Wellwood, 'outsiders' Ann and Eric Martin, are harassed; the local weekly's office is bombed; Afro-American lawyer Thomas Peters, another newcomer, is shot at and right-wing fanatics are prowling the area searching for communists. Obviously the situation requires the investigative skills of Captain Merton Heimrich and Lieutenant Charlie Forniss of the New York State Police.

2144. **Logan, Algernon Sidney, 1849-1925.** *Not on the chart*; a novel of today. **With illus. by Gordon H. Grant. New York: G.W. Dillingham, c1898. 277p.**

Josiah Forbes, a conscientious New Englander educated at Harvard, with army service and a teaching position in a Western college, is, at the age of 35, an insurance clerk in New York City. "He had learned to like the noise and seeming confusion of New York" and frequently met for discussions on literature, the arts and cultural currents with his friend Reginald Moulton. Josiah has an affair with Nellie Vance, a working-class girl, which he reluctantly breaks off when he marries Bertha Parker, a well-educated young woman with high moral standards. Josiah opens a law office in New York that attracts few wealthy clients. Nellie, unhappily married, appears in Josiah's office and their romance flares up again briefly. Nellie's later suicide further depresses Josiah and he takes his own life while his wife and their son are in church. Reginald Moulton has also failed to achieve anything in the New York business world and has lost the woman he loved; he leaves the city and returns to his native small country town to practice law.

2144a. **Logue, John, 1933- .** *On a par with murder.* **New York: Dell Pub., 1999. 288p.**

Golfer Buddy Morrow is the center of attention at the 1955 U. S. Open being played on Long Island's Shinnecock Hills golf course. He takes the 'homage' in stride, concentrating on his game and incidentally signing for $2,000,000 with an athletic manufacturing company. His sudden death occasions the revelation of his real identity and the suicide of his wife. Reporters John Morris and Julia Sullivan believe Morrow has been murdered by someone other than his wife and begin to line up possible suspects—and there are many.

2145. **Lombardi, Cynthia, d. 1942.** *At sight of gold.* **New York: Appleton, 1922. viii, 341p.**

The heroine is Clara, from Rhode Island, who eventually becomes an operatic prima donna. The villainess, Geraldine, with her father, steals gold from the hero, Antonello, who has found buried treasure. Of course, Geraldine is foiled and everything ends happily for the hero and heroine. This all takes place in New York City, moving from a small Italian boardinghouse to the salons of upper crust society.

2146. **Long, Haniel, 1888-1956.** *Spring returns.* **Pref. by Anne Morrow Lindbergh. New York: Pantheon Books, 1958. 245p.**

'Pauolinus', a village in the Finger Lakes region of Upstate New York, is the setting of this novel whose 'hero' is Roger Wake, an orphan related to the prominent Drummond family. Although only 19, Roger has healing powers derived from spiritual sources that enable him to pierce the emotional and psychological problems that beset the deranged, suicidal (or even homicidal) tendencies of Isabel Drummond Forbes, wife of the steel magnate Robert Forbes. Roger also presides over a household of diverse young people while Judge Drummond and his wife are abroad. The Finger Lakes country is at one point portrayed as the nurturing ground for strong, independent women, Indian and White.

2147. **Long, Manning, 1906- .** *Bury the hatchet.* **New York: Duell, Sloan and Pearce, 1944. 249p.**

"A good-natured laugh-and-thrill story about multiple slaughter on Iroquois Island up the Hudson inhabited by Liz Parrott, her G-2 husband [Gordon], her cat and a group of problem neighbors. First crime raises the question of homicidal Navajo, Mohawk or Cayuga, though there seem to be no red men around. A locked room and a haunted piano add to the complications"—New York herald tribune books.

2148. ————. *Vicious circle.* **New York: Duell, Sloan and Pearce, 1942. 277p.**

Invited to spend Christmas at 'Upper Cutting', N.Y., by her husband Gordon's relatives (Aunts Hester and Mina) Liz Parrott (and Gordon) have no choice but to use their detecting powers when they are confronted by two sudden deaths. Cousin Clifford figures in their investigation; he has just written a book on Russia, but all copies of it at Upper Cutting have vanished. What connection does the disappearance of these books have to do with the two deaths, i.e., murders, and further attempts at homicide? Liz and Gordon must clear up the situation before they can return to Brooklyn.

2149. **Longstreet, Abby Buchanan.** *A débutante in New York society*; **her illusions and what became of them, by Rachel Buchanan [pseud.]. New York: Appleton, 1888. 363p.**

"This story is told in the form of [40] letters written by 'Flossy', the young débutante, to her aunt in the country. She details her 'coming out', her love affairs and her sister's love affairs, her mother's struggles to secure for them wealthy husbands and her father's disapproval of these worldly schemes, and show that in spite of her training she is a true, warm-hearted girl. The author displays a keen appreciation of the weaknesses of society"—Annual American catalogue. In her final letter, Flossy, now 19, is about to be married to Roger Lenox who has a country home in England but is searching for a house in New York.

Longstreet, Rachel Abigail Buchanan. See: Longstreet, Abby Buchanan.

2150. **Longstreet, Stephen, 1907- . *Decade, 1929-1939*. New York: Random House, 1940. xii, 398p.**

In the last ten years of his life the patriarch of a wealthy family ensconced in the Hudson River Valley—John Christian Rowlandson—oversees the dissolution of his finances and the death of especially loving members of his circle. Throughout the tragic sequence of events his attitude is one of stoical acceptance; his spirit is not daunted.

2151. **————. *Eagles where I walk*. New York: Doubleday, 1961. 477p.**

A novel of New York State just before and during the American Revolution with emphasis on the great landowners of Dutch descent in the Hudson Valley—the Philipses, Schuylers and Van Cortlandts—some of whom rallied to the American cause, others kept their allegiance to the British Crown. Dominant figures in this panoramic story are Captain (later Major) David Cortlandt, a surgeon in the American Army, and Roxanne Philipse, his wife. Cortlandt cares for the wounded during the Long Island and New York City campaigns; his duties carry him to northern New York State where the Americans face the Burgoyne invasion. The treason of General Benedict Arnold at West Point is one of the climactic chapters in the novel. At the story's end David and Roxanne Cortlandt head southward to escape David's possible arrest for challenging Colonel Jameson to a duel. In an epilogue David Cortlandt is in his eighties (in 1824) and the Marquis de Lafayette, on a triumphal tour in America, is renewing acquaintance with old comrades-in-arms, including David Cortlandt.

2152. **Longstreth, Thomas Morris, 1886-1975. *Ade of the Marcy Mounted*. Illustrated by William C. Blood. New York: Century Co., 1926. xii, 254p.**

Ade Durham, a surly farm manager's late teenage son, living in the Lake Placid region of the Adirondacks, has one ambition: to someday join the ranks of the Royal Canadian Northwest Mounted Police. In pursuit of that dream he forms his own version of that organization, calling it the Marcy Mounted Police (members: Ade himself; Roddy, nephew of his employer, Miss Matilda, and Brush Parsons, a blacksmith's son). This unofficial body unintentionally finds itself involved with a murderous gang that smuggles Chinese across the Canadian/New York State border. Ade feels sympathy and affection for Nicholas Poldinsky of noble Polish lineage and a former 'Mountie', who had been pulled against his will into the gang's activities. Ade and his colleagues barely escape with their lives from the smugglers; he then pleads for Poldinsky with the commandant of the Canadian Mounted Police with surprising results.

2153. ————. *At Mountain Prep*. Illus. by Robb Beebe. New York: Appleton-Century, 1939. 265p.

> Three student athletes from 'Elmville', New York grab the opportunity to spend a year at a highly respected preparatory school in the heart of the Adirondacks. Irv Torrence (the narrator), Frank Harmon and Les Wells, the 'Three Mosquiteers', have rewarding experiences despite conflicts with Seeley 'Comet' Garvin and 'Snaky' Smith, Mountain Prep's premier athletes. The two most interesting fellow students they meet are Theodore 'Tweeter' Henderson, dedicated amateur ornithologist, and the eccentric, inventive Clarence Eakins, better known as 'Goofer' or the 'Duke'. Irv and Frank spend another year at the 'Prep', Irv combining a postgraduate course in journalism with publicity work for the school and Frank as an athletic coach.

2154. ————. *Mac of Placid*. New York: Century Co, 1920. xi, 339p.

> "Anson MacIntyre is born in the 'wolf winter' of 1869 and he tells his own story up through the Eighties. His beginnings are not promising, but two things unite to make a man of him, his deep love for his native woods and his love for Hallie Brewster—these two forces and one other, his friendship with Robert Louis Stevenson. For no less [a] person than Stevenson appears as a character. ...The two skate together on Saranac Lake and become intimate companions, Mac's romantic devotion to Hallie and his rivalry with Ed Touch appeal to the fiction writer's [Stevenson's] imagination and he takes a hand in the wooing. Other real people, the Bakers and Dr. Trudeau, are mentioned in the story"—Book review digest.

Looker, O.N. pseud. See: Urner, Nathan D.

2155. **Loomis, Charles Battell, 1861-1911.** *Minerva's manoeuvers*; the cheerful facts of a 'return to nature'. Illustrated by Frederick R. Gruger. New York: A.S. Barnes, 1905. xi, 415p.

> "A New York couple seeks a country life that the wife may recuperate. They secure a furnished cottage for the summer, and take with them a colored cook, born and raised in New York [City]. She is the Minerva of the story. She hates the darkness and silence of the country, fears every sound, longs for companionship and is utterly ignorant of everything in nature, animate and inanimate. She is always on the point of returning to New York, and it is her master and mistress's attempts at amusing and conciliating her that make fun of the book"—Annual American catalogue.

2156. ————. *A partnership in magic*. Illustrated by Herman Heyer. Boston: Lothrop Pub. Co., 1903. 270p.

> Leaving a rural home and a harsh stepfather, a boy who has a strange 'talent' for finding edible fruit on the bare branches of trees accompanies a friend to New York City where they open a fruit business. Their venture is a resounding success, but the stepfather comes to the city determined to find the 'runaway' and there follows a series of rousing and humorous incidents.

2157. Lorens, M.K., pseud. *Sorrowheart.* **New York: Doubleday, 1993. 387p.**

'DeWitt Clinton College' in 'Ainsley', N.Y., receives a new chancellor in James Macauley, while simultaneously a serial killer has transfixed town and gown. English professor Winston Marlowe Sherman who doubles as a writer of mysteries learns from his girlfriend, Sarah Cromwell, of a female body she came across in the orchard of Sorrowheart, Elsa Worthing's residence. This is number four of the killer's victims. Winston has been fencing with Chancellor Macauley who hopes to water down the college's courses and to encourage condemnation of Sorrowheart and its eventual takeover by the college—so Winston isn't too excited about pursuing the serial killer further until he realizes that the murderer's schedule points toward another homicide very shortly.

2158. Lorimer, George Horace, 1868-1937. *The false gods.* **New York: Appleton, 1906. 91p.**

"A reporter from the Boston Banner comes to New York to write up a 'good story' for his paper, of which a Mrs. Athelstone, who claims to be a reincarnation of Madame Blavatsky, the Theosophist, is to be the heroine. He uses great ingenuity in reaching Mrs. Athelstone, who refuses to see reporters. He meets her surrounded by mummies and Egyptian statues of great antiquity, an air of mystery over everything. How his great 'find' works out is left to the reader to discover"—Annual American catalogue. Part of this droll mystery deals with the death of a noted Egyptologist whom the reporter suspects has been murdered by the scholar's wife.

2159. Loring, Emilie Baker, 1864?-1951. *There is always love.* **Boston: Little, Brown, 1940. 292p.**

Linda Bourne deemed it best for all concerned (including her sister and mother) that she leave New England and seek a job in New York City. In pursuit of Linda were three would-be lovers: Greg Morton, Skid Grant (from her hometown), and Pedro Lorillo, a Brazilian. Dissatisfied with her job in a big business concern Linda welcomed the opportunity to serve as companion/secretary to a wealthy old lady she had met while touring the woman's large castle on the Hudson. Two of Linda's suitors were competing for commissions they would receive should they sell the castle. The owner possessed a valuable collection of jewels that were in danger of being stolen.

Lothrop, Harriet Mulford Stone, 1844-1924. See under her pseudonym: Sidney, Margaret, 1844-1924.

Lough, Brigette Roux, See: Roux-Lough, Brigette.

Low, Lois Dorothea, 1916- . See: Paxton, Lois 1916-.

2160. Lowe, Corinne Martin, b. 1882. *Confessions of a social secretary.* **New York:**

Harper, c1916. 255p.

"Gives what appears to be an honest account of the inner workings of the households of a society leader [of New York], including town house, country house, and Newport cottage. There are details concerning the management of servants, the arrangement of house parties, the planning of dinners, etc. Society, if this be a true picture, must be a deadly dull affair. There is a slight thread of fiction in the story of the rich young girl [Veronica Grey] who chose to marry a 'real man' [rather than the viscount selected for her]"—Book review digest. Several of the characters seem to be based on real people in the Four Hundred and other social groupings in New York City.

2161. ————. *Saul.* **New York: McCann, 1919. 347p.**

Saul Furinski's father worked himself into exhaustion at a garment maker's machine and Saul made himself a promise that he would reach higher than that ever as he left the tenements of East Side New York and mixed with contractors, designers and buyers in the garment industry. Successively he was a clothes designer, a contractor, and a promoter of new ideas—but as he rose he lost touch with the simple human decencies until one day he realized the mean-spirited man he had become and began to regain his sense of beauty and humanity.

2162. **Lowell, Robert Traill Spence, 1816-1891.** *A story or two from an old Dutch town.* **Boston: Roberts Bros., 1878. 322p.**

The three stories (actually novellas) take place in 'Westenvliet' (i.e. Schenectady), the first two during the early years (the 1820s) of the 19th century, the last in the colonial period (about the 1730s?). 'Abram Van Zandt, the man in the picture' concerns a prosperous baker (the title character) who is obsessed with a painting 'forced' upon him by a deceased debtor. The 'man in the picture' is an almost exact likeness of Van Zandt, although the painting is discovered to be by the Flemish (?) master, Adriaen van der Velde (1636-1672). 'Mr. Schermerhorn's marriage and widowhood' is about a talented man who is so unnerved by the loss of his beloved wife that he fails for most of his remaining years to acknowledge the son that issued from the marriage. 'Master Vorhagen's wife' is not really his spouse, but a young woman pushed by her father to view the pompous schoolmaster Vorhagen as her only chance for a husband. She ('Jannetje' Sickels) is 'saved' from such a union when the combination of schoolboys' pranks and a drunken but aggressive constable result in Vorhagen's flight from Westenvliet.

2163. **Lubin, David, 1849-1919.** *Let there be light*; **the story of a workingmen's club, its search for the causes of poverty and social inequality, its discussions and its plan for the amelioration of existing evils. New York: G.P. Putnam, 1900. vi, 526p.**

"[Lubin's] book [is in] the form of a story [set in New York City] in which he tries to show the viewpoint of the wealthy capitalist [Henry Morton] who has risen from the ranks, and of his well-to-do nephew and niece [Joseph and his wife Dorothy] who represent the leisured, cultural class, in contrast with that of the intelligent working man, whether conservative trade-unionist, socialist agitator, or humble acceptor of the status quo. These represented by American, Italian, German, Irishman and Negro, he groups around the central figure, Ezra [Selner], a Jew gifted with the fine speculative brain characteristic of his race, who by argument, debate, criticism and thought has attained a degree of spiritual freedom which enables him to view events not as isolated phenomena but as links in a chain of cause and effect. The prevailing social and economic order comes up for discussion before the Twentieth Century Club in a series of debates"—Agresti, O.R. David Lubin; study in practical idealism. Boston, Little, Brown, 1922. Joseph Morton and his wife, Dorothy Hamilton Morton, become friends and supporters of Ezra Selner and by the story's conclusion are floating the idea of a Church Universal, which would ultimately be the means of transferring the balance of worldly (and economic) power to the mass of people.

2164. **Luby, James Patrick Kenyon, 1856-1925.** *The Black Cross Clove*; a story and a study. **New York: B.W. Huebsch, 1910. 368p.**

The relationship of Stephen Eltringham (a young New York painter and the ostensible hero of an often strange story) to two young women is one of the driving forces behind the novel. The first of the two women is another New Yorker, a girl with strong ties to her home, but who also possesses inner strength. The other is an illiterate but shrewd girl of Indian blood, a native of the Catskills (where several of the scenes are laid) who hopes to become an actress in New York. However she is so caught up in a transcendent love for a mythic, spirit-like figure, Minnesook, that she is unable to tear herself away from his neighborhood—The Black Cross Clove, where he is immured. There follows a tragic coupling of the village girl with her diaphanous lover; an epilogue tells us the fate of the other characters in the story.

2165. **Ludlow, James Meeker, 1841-1932.** *The baritone's parish*; or, *All things to all men.* **New York, Chicago: F.H. Revell, 1896. 40p.**

Philip Vox, a baritone who sings in the Rev. Dr. Wesley Knox's church, accompanies the clergyman to the Bowery where he performs for an appreciative audience. To his surprise Vox hears a beautiful tenor voice emanating from a besotted young man. Vox takes the tenor, Charles Downs, for his 'parish'; eventually Downs conquers his drinking problem and wins back his patient wife who had endured through all his bouts with alcohol.

2166. ————. *That angelic woman*; a story. **New York: Harper, 1892. 149p.**

George Goldie, a wealthy young man with no serious vocation immersed in the more frivolous aspects of New York City's social life, meets Amy Walford, a nurse in one of the city's hospitals. Under the spell of her idealism and concern for others Goldie is inspired to awaken and use his good qualities that have long been dormant. His new direction and one action in particular lead to an unanticipated denouement in the affairs of himself and Amy.

2167. **Ludlum, Jean Kate.** *At Brown's*; an Adirondack story. **New York: Hunt & Eaton, 1890. 341p.**

The Adirondack mountains in all their beauty, the variety of people she meets and the discovery of her own ability to influence the direction of her life—all play a part in helping a young woman overcome the physical and emotional fatigue she had suffered while caring for her long-ill mother up to and including the latter's death.

2168. —————. *John Winthrop's defeat*; a novel. **With illus. by Victor Perard. New York: R. Bonner's Sons, 1891. 28p.**

New York City and Fire Island form the chief background for this novel of a courageous woman, Alecia Graham, who bears with fortitude the dissipation of her husband's and her own fortune by his unwise speculations. The lawyer, John Winthrop, is stern and unbending in his insistence that Harold and Alecia Graham pay off their creditors in full. Harold Graham dies shortly thereafter in San Francisco and Alecia turns back to New York. John Winthrop and Alecia seem destined to cross paths in the ensuing months—Alecia even becomes friends with John's mother. The man whom Alecia would be expected to view as an enemy saves her from drowning off Fire Island, but the consequence is that Winthrop is brought to the point of death. The inevitable occurs—a joint recognition of love. John has meanwhile learned that circumstances surrounding Harold Graham's debts dictated a far more lenient stance toward the Grahams in their crisis.

2169. —————. *Under oath*; an Adirondack story. **With illus. by Warren B. Davis. New York: R. Bonner's Sons, 1890. 337p.**

Allan Mansfield is on his way to Lake Placid when he is stopped and imprisoned by two highwaymen. A vaguely familiar woman helps him escape on condition he keeps quiet about his detention for at least a year. Arriving at the Placid resort Allan is greeted by Edith Hallston, the lady he loves, Marie Castlemon, Edith's companion, and Arthur Montgomery, a wealthy Canadian. Several strange events occur at the resort—e.g., Montgomery disappears and Allan is shot from ambush. After convalescing Allan sees Montgomery again, this time in Montreal. A masquerade ball in New York City is the climactic episode in the novel, for it is then that the several interrelationships of the principal characters are explained and Allan Mansfield and Arthur Montgomery are able to unmask the criminal behind the dangers they have been exposed to.

2170. **Luehrmann, Adele.** *The curious case of Marie Dupont.* **Illustrated by Frank Snapp. New York: Century Co., 1916. 324p.**

This mystery is set primarily in New York City. It concerns an amnesiac, Marie Dupont, whom several people say was once a dancer in Paris. Nevertheless Guy Amarinth wants to marry Marie even though he is not much in love with her. Hugh Thorley begins his investigations into Marie's case, which seems to be complicated by the murder of Alix Flora, a dancer, on the day a famous Rumanian heirloom disappeared. Marie herself recalls only her own childhood and the immediate past and has little interest in the stolen necklace or the people clustered around it. Of course all is resolved when a tensely dramatic situation helps Marie regain her memory.

2171. Lull, De Los. *Father Solon*; or, *The helper helped*. **New York: W.B. Ketcham, 1888. 367p.**

"Father Solon is introduced at a Thanksgiving dinner at the old family homestead in Yonkers, New York, surrounded by his wife, children, and grandchildren, after thirty-seven years of married life. The son, Willis, an irresolute boy of twenty, and Carrie, a lovely girl of seventeen, are still at home. The old father loses everything through devotion to a friend, the old house is abandoned, and Carrie goes to work in the village factory. Willis is enticed to Salt Lake City by a Mormon priest, and much space is given to his adventures there until he is found and released by his devoted sister and father"—Annual American catalogue.

2172. Lupton, Leonard. *River man.* **New York: L. MacVeagh, Dial Press, 1930. 309p.**

"The glimpse of life [in a shanty boat] on the [Hudson] River and the road, and the record of the mental processes of the hero from the time he encountered a stray copy of [Jim] Tully's 'Beggars of life' and felt the first awakening of an ambition which eventually led to his evolution from a tramp to a newspaperman, make very interesting reading"—Boston transcript.

2173. Lurie, Alison, 1926- . *Only children.* **New York: Random House, 1979. 259p.**

This novel spans the long Fourth of July weekend [of 1935]. Bill and Honey Hubbard and their eight-year-old daughter Mary Ann, and Dan and Celia Zimmern and their daughter Lolly (and Dan's sullen adolescent son from a previous marriage) abandon New York City and its suburb, Larchmont, for the Catskill farm owned by Anna King, headmistress of the progressive school the two girls attend. This innocent outing doesn't turn out to be a relaxing weekend. ... Instead the grownups start romping in an unseemly way and end up fighting, while the two little girls look on, bewildered"—New Republic.

2174. ————. *The war between the Tates.* **New York: Random House, 1974. 372p.**

The setting of the novel is the community of 'Corinth', New York during late 1969 and early 1970. The action involves the conflicts between Brian and Erica Tate and their two adolescent children. "Erica is bored and restless, Brian's career as a political scientist is at a standstill, and their well-behaved children have become revolting—in both senses of the word—teenagers. ... Erica discovers that her husband is sleeping with a blond student named Wendy. Brian tries to make peace by announcing that he is breaking off the affair and his wife promises to forgive him. ...Brian not only takes up with Wendy again, but [also] makes her pregnant; and the war between the Tates is joined"—Publisher's note. It is very probable that Cornell University and Ithaca are models for Corinth and the college where Brian teaches.

Luska, Sidney, pseud. See: Harland, Henry, 1861-1905.

2175. **Lute, Uncle, pseud.** *Paul Hart*; or, *The love of his life.* **Philadelphia: T.B. Peterson, 1881. 420p.**

Rising from New York newsboy to the world of business Paul Hart receives help from the merchant Raymond Lawrence and Chauncey Greentree, grain speculator. Lisette, Lawrence's daughter and Paul have a mutual attraction. Lawrence tells Paul he cannot allow any further intimacy with Lisette. Greentree marries Paul's mother and Paul, after several business reverses, leaves New York for Mobile, Alabama. His death at sea on a ship bound for South America is reported in the newspapers. This upsets Lisette; she is almost cajoled into marriage with a lawyer, Julius C. Spauldwin, backing off when she recognizes him as the man (under another name) who tried to abduct her several years earlier. His mother and Greentree no longer among the living, Paul turns up in New York as a simple workingman with an alias. Lisette is not deceived; she recognizes her lover and this time Mr. Lawrence assents to their marriage.

2176. **Luther, Mark Lee, b. 1872.** *The crucible.* **With illus. by Rose Cecil O'Neill. New York: Macmillan, 1907. vii, 341p.**

Her hot temper and immaturity combined with a miscarriage of justice put Jean Fanshaw in a New York State reformatory for women. A brief escape is ended when an artist in the neighborhood persuades Jean to complete her jail term. When Jean is released she heads for New York City and tries making an honest living in a variety of jobs: garment maker, clerk in a department store, artist's model, and cashier. Jean is finally rescued from the uncertainties of life for a young woman in the big city by the artist who had earlier been her supporter.

2177. ————. *The henchman.* **New York: Macmillan, 1902. 376p.**

"The scene is a New York town [in the 'Demijohn' district in the northwestern part of the State] ... [where] the ambition of a local leader [Shelby, is] to become governor of the State. ... He is a politician of a coarse type who pulls wires, makes demagogic speeches and enters into corrupt bargains ... [climbing] the ladder ... until his ambition is achieved. ... [However] there are certain latent possibilities of the finer sort in his nature, and these gradually come to the surface, while the responsibilities of power exert upon him a sobering and even uplifting influence." When the presidency of the United States seems within his reach, he refuses it rather than submit to the immoral authority of the leader ('Old Silky') of the party machine. "As a picture of ... New York politics the book is closely studied from the actual political life of the times"—Dial.

2178. ——————. *The mastery.* New York: Macmillan, 1904. 402p.

"Primarily a strictly localized story of New York politics, although it embodies a love story which crops out now and then when the exigencies of the political situation permit the hero to spare a breathing spell for sentiment. In the end he proves especially triumphant in love and politics"—Dial. The hero 'boss', much to his surprise, is nominated for governor of New York State when his party fails to come up with a better choice. The woman he is in love with is just about as knowledgeable as he is about the game of politics. Election night in New York City is graphically portrayed.

2179. ——————. *Presenting Jane McRae.* **With illus. by James Montgomery Flagg. Boston: Little, Brown, 1920. 333p.**

"When Jane McRae is first presented she is acting as a waitress in her step-father's hotel in a small 'Upstate' New York town. Here she comes in contact with Stuart Pendleton, a young civil engineer, and with Arthur Gault, a movie singer. With Stuart she falls in love, but refuses to marry him when she learns of his previous entanglement with another woman. Leaving unbearable conditions at home she goes to New York to support herself. At the end of her resources, she again meets Arthur Gault, who is now a moving picture director. He gets her a small part in his picture and finally persuades her to marry him. She becomes more and more successful as an actress, but is not happy. She realizes that her marriage to Arthur was a mistake, but does not see the way out. But when the [First World] War comes and frees her from him, the manner of his death leaves her still with an unanswerable question. 'It did not occur to her that she was free'"—Book review digest.

Lutz, Grace Livingston Hill, 1865-1947. See: Hill, Grace Livingston, 1865-1947.

2180. Lyman, Olin Linus, b. 1873. *The trail of the Grand Seigneur.* **With col. Illus. from paintings by J. Steeple Davis and Clara Angell. New York: New Amsterdam Book Co., 1903. 432p.**

An historical novel of the War of 1812 as fought on the New York State-Canadian border, Sacketts Harbor, Watertown and Frontenac being major sites in the story. The two heroes are Gilbert Warburton and John Godfrey; both accept captaincies in the American militia and participate in several battles. They jointly rescue a French émigré, Vincent de Montfort, and his daughter, Renée, when the latter two are taken captive by 'Red Rolfe' (a.k.a. William Barclay) and his Indians. Warburton and Godfrey capture a British spy, Lt. Percy Stranahan, and Warburton poses as Stranahan in order to secure knowledge of British military and naval positions and fortifications. He and Godfrey fall into enemy hands and are about to be hanged as spies when a wily American, Sergeant Cyrenus, effects their escape. The three run into Rolfe and his Indian allies. In a fateful struggle Rolfe kills Godfrey (his half-brother) and is in turn slain by Godfrey's dog Gypso. Warburton returns to Sacketts Harbor and the woman he loves, Renée de Montfort.

2181.	**Lynch, Daniel, 1946- .** *Brennan's Point.* **Latham, N.Y.: British American Pub., 1988. 530p.**

A family saga covering three generations of wine makers in the Finger Lakes region of New York State. The patriarch, Liam Brennan, is an Irish immigrant who acquires knowledge of wine production from Christian Weidener and marries the latter's daughter, Helga. Helga and her father are killed in a steamboat explosion. The tragedy turns Liam into a self-pitying drunkard until the governess of Liam's and Helga's daughter, Helen, takes him in hand, marries him and gives birth to a son, Kevin. Although the Brennan winery is successful, ill fortune stalks Liam's children—Helen's marriage and motherhood result in her abuse of alcohol; Kevin is severely wounded in World War II, but still takes of care of his children after his wife leaves him. The Brennans of the third generation have to deal with a move by strong outside interests to take over their winery.

2182.	**Lynch, Lawrence L., pseud.** *A blind lead*; **daring and thrilling adventures, clever detective work, by Lawrence L. Lynch (E.M. Van Deventer). Chicago: Laird & Lee, 1912. 324p.**

Two women leaving a fashionable woman's club in New York City are snatched and whisked away in an automobile. The kidnapped victims are: Miss Iris LaCroix, the only daughter of a Wall Street financier, millionaire and grain speculator, Jerry LaCroix, and Miss Helmuth, newcomer to the city about whose past (and present) there is much conjecture. Excitement builds as efforts to free the abducted proceed; amidst all the agitation there is time out for a romantic interlude.

2183.	—————. *The lost witness*; or, *The mystery of Leah Paget.* **Chicago: Laird & Lee, 1890. 557p.**

"The disappearance of Leah Paget ushers in the story [that has New York City as its chief locale]; the solving of the mystery first takes...[one's] entire attention, then it becomes blended with a crime that involves a double murder; here everything else gives way to the finesse of a noted English detective, who succeeds in clearing up the sensational mysteries, and bringing about an unexpected ending to an intricate detective story"—Annual American catalogue.

2184.	**Lynde, Francis, 1856-1930.** *Mr. Arnold*: **a romance of the Revolution. Front. by John Wolcott Adams. Indianapolis: Bobbs-Merrill, 1923. 336p.**

Historical novel of the American Revolution against the background of Manhattan with historical figures: Benedict Arnold, Alexander Hamilton, et al., figuring prominently. A major theme is Arnold's treason and patriot attempts to capture him in his new capacity as a British officer.

Lynds, Dennis, 1924- . See under his pseudonyms: Collins, Michael and Sadler, Mark.

Lyons, Ivan, 1934- , joint author. *Sold!* **See Item #2185.**

2185. **Lyons, Nan, 1939- .** *Sold!* **[by] Nan and Ivan Lyons. New York: Coward, McCann & Geoghegan, 1982. 270p.**

'Perry Falls' is a small New York town where Dorothy ('Duffy') Patterson has an auctioneering business housed in the Patterson family barn. In the course of her searches for saleable items Duffy uncovers 66 bejeweled Fabergé eggs, which are among the few belongings of Natalie Corbett, a maiden lady. There is a rush, when news of the jewels gets out, by collectors, Duffy and her boyfriend Ben Perry, et al., eager to acquire them. Charles Wyndham, owner of a famous Manhattan gallery, uses his sex-laden charm on Duffy as he too wants the prestige of being the auctioneer for the Fabergé eggs. The author tells how solitary, unassuming Natalie came to own the art objects in the first place.

M.A.G. *Jeanne*; **the story of a Fresh Air child. See Item #1807.**

M.L.A. *Miss Illma*; **or,** *Which was wife?* **See Item #1747.**

2186. **Mabie, Louise Kennedy, d. 1957.** *The wings of pride.* **New York: Harper, 1913. 323p.**

"Olive Muir, the spoiled beauty who is the heroine of this story, has been brought up to believe herself the daughter of a wealthy New York woman. She learns, through a sudden turn of circumstances, the truth—that she is but an adopted child, that her parents are poor, that her father is a drunkard, that the despised little Western girl who had been a visitor in the New York home is her sister. From this blow to her pride the girl rises with admirable courage, and when she is called to the Ohio town in which her mother lives to assume the position of daughter in the humble home, she finds in the new life possibilities of happiness unknown in the old. The young Western lawyer, Kent Ordway, has much to do with this transformation, and the full rounding out of the romance is accomplished by the marriage of Alice, the sister, to the New York man to whom Olive had been half-heartedly engaged"—Book review digest.

2187. **MacCarthy, Emma W.** *Assemblyman John*; **or,** *His wife's ambition.* **Chicago: Belford, Clarke, 1889. 134p.**

"John Fairfax, a large paper manufacturer, had no ambition to be Assemblyman from a Hudson River district, but Mrs. Fairfax was determined, and by coaxing and spoiling induced him to accept the nomination. Then she finds a politician's wife has not an easy time. Woman suffragists, temperance lecturers, and all kinds of women with ideas and missions besiege her, and help the author amuse her readers"—Annual American catalogue.

2188. **MacConnell, Sarah Warder, 1869-1953.** *Many mansions.* **Boston: Houghton,**

Mifflin, 1918. 345p.

Brought up in a boarding house in New York City by two kind but undiscerning aunts, Perdita Hardwick dreams of having her own well-furnished home. She fulfills a tiny part of that dream by earning her living as an interior decorator beautifying other people's houses. She and Terence Kildare meet one summer and fall in love. A lover's quarrel separates them—Terry goes off to Canada while Perdita stays in New York, receiving unsatisfactory attention from other men. It is in the order of things that Terry and Perdita will eventually be reconciled.

2189. **Macdonald, Everett.** *Slimtonian Socker.* **Philadelphia: Jacobs, 1922. 368p.**

Two veterans of the First World War, Slimtonian (Slim) Socker and his buddy, Peter (Pop) Huggins, both natives of 'Kuddleville', Indiana, are determined to 'make it' in New York City. At the moment their fortunes are at very low ebb; that they are surviving at all is due to Thomas Hallock, foreman of an all-night garage on East 24th St., who allows them to quarter there. Opportunity beckons when wealthy widow Cora Waterson believes Slim to be her nephew, Samuel Stormman, who had presumably died soldiering in France. A mediocre racehorse, Heelwin, which was sold to Slim and Pop for a nominal sum by its grateful owner, Patrick McCormick (Slim saved his daughter's life), suddenly becomes a big winner at the racetrack and Slim and Pop are in the money. Eventually Slim can no longer continue the subterfuge he has visited on Aunt Cora. His confession to her is waived aside and our fortunate heroes find romance with two vivacious young women.

2190. **MacDonald, John D., 1916-1986.** *On the run.* **New York: Fawcett, Gold Medal, 1963. 144p.**

Old Thomas Brower is slowly dying in his home at 'Bolton', a hamlet north of Syracuse, N.Y. He entrusts his round-the-clock nurse Paula Lettinger with a mission to bring Sidney Shanley, one of his two grandsons, to Bolton. That's a problem since Sid is being hunted by hit men hired by mobster Jerry Wain whose face Sid had disfigured. Paula does find and bring reluctant Sid to the little village in Upstate New York. The other grandson, George Shanley, a shifty gambler, also comes to Bolton. Tom Brower explains to his grandsons the provisions of his new will. Danger looms when hit man Mr. Jones (a.k.a. Eldon Bartold), working out of Troy, N.Y., appears in Bolton, disguised as a photographer for the New York State Historical Commission. His maneuvers to eliminate Sid form the climax of the story, a tragic one for several of the main characters.

2191. **Macdonald, Zillah Katherine, b. 1885.** *Two on a tow.* **Illus. by Harvey Kidder, Boston: Houghton, Mifflin, 1942. 230p.**

Twin brothers, Jarvis and Jerry, are hands on their grandfather's barge as it carries freight on the Erie Canal in its heyday. Of more than fleeting interest are the author's detailed descriptions of the way the Canal's locks worked, how barges were strung together and then pulled by a single tugboat, and the competition between the several canal boat masters for major shares of the freight business and speeding delivery to the various destinations.

2192. ————. *Windywhistle.* **New York: D. Appleton, 1929. 226p.**

A young native of Windywhistle, Nova Scotia, Thistle Throckmorton, is determined to go out into the wide world. With the rudiments of stenography and typing she sets out for New York City with her grandmother. After several absorbing months working for $18 a week, wherein she acquires new friends, she stumbles upon the owner of the other half of a golden cross, the first part of which she had discovered at her home place in Nova Scotia.

2193. **Mace, Merlda.** *Motto for murder.* **New York: J. Messner, 1943. 213p.**

Her three grandchildren, other members of Mrs. Hammond's household, and Tip O'Neil, a guest unrelated to the Hammond family attend a party given by Grandmother Hammond at her home in the Adirondacks. When corpses begin to appear here and there, Tip is delegated to investigate since the party is snowed in and there is no way to get hold of the police—the house has no telephone.

2194. **MacGowan, Alice, 1858-1947.** *The last word.* **Boston: L.C. Page, 1903 [c1902]. viii, 439p.**

The heroine of this light piece of fiction is a girl from Texas who sets as her goal success in journalism in New York City. She is bright, imaginative, and rather flippant, but takes her first job on a newspaper in the city quite seriously. The squalor of New York's East Side moves her to pity and she hopes some day to help palliate conditions there; however she is enthused by the beauty, fashion and elegance she sees on Broadway and vicinity—where everyone seems happy and prosperous. Obviously a successful career is ahead for her, if not short-circuited by the love affair that begins to occupy a niche in her life.

2195. **MacGrath, Harold, 1871-1932.** *The girl in his house.* **Illustrated by Howard Giles. New York: Harper, 1918. 148p.**

At the conclusion of an unhappy love affair James Armitage leaves New York and wanders in the wide world for six years. When he returns to his native city he discovers that Boardman, his agent, has sold his house and disappeared with half of his fortune. Now living in the former Armitage home is a beautiful young woman names Doris around whom swirls an atmosphere of mystery. James seeks and gradually finds answers to basic questions: why Boardman walked away with so much of his money and just who Doris really is.

2196. ————. *Half a rogue.* **With illus. by Harrison Fisher. Indianapolis: Bobbs-Merrill, 1906. 448p.**

New York playwright Richard Warrington decides to abandon the metropolis and settle permanently in his Upstate New York hometown of 'Herculaneum'.

Kate Challoner, a brilliant actress, surprises Warrington when she announces her forthcoming marriage to John Bennington, owner of a prosperous steel mill in Herculaneum and Warrington's best friend. Kate has long had deep feelings for Warrington but he never reciprocates. Kate finds happiness in her marriage. Richard runs for mayor of Herculaneum and bumps into the ambitions of Daniel McQuade, political boss. McQuade fears Warrington's possible election might negate his construction contracts with the city and tries to derail Warrington by hinting at a past clandestine affair between Warrington and Kate; he also instigates a strike at the Bennington mills. John Bennington closes his factories rather than accede to what he deems extreme union demands. Warrington is able to convince John of his innocence of any liaison with Kate, but he loses the election. In the end Warrington is comforted by the love of John's sister, Patty, who drops her suspicions of Richard's New York City 'dissipations'.

2197. ————. *Pidgin Island*. **Illustrated by Arthur W. Brown. Indianapolis: Bobbs-Merrill, 1914. 340p.**

The U.S. Secret Service seemed like a good place of employment for John Carpenter; however, Carpenter now cannot shake the feeling that what he is doing is underhanded, sneaky. Fishing offers him relief from the pressures of his job. This time Uncle Billy, the guide who had always been available at the Thousand Island resort that John had frequented for years, was accompanying a young woman angler. Diana was John's equal at the sport, and she was also adept at staking out the smugglers operating near Pidgin Island, for she too was in the Secret Service. John and Diana cooperate in nabbing the criminals and, predictably, fall in love.

2198. **MacIsaac, Frederick John, 1886-1940.** *The vanishing professor*. **New York: H. Waterson, 1927. 266p.**

An underpaid physics professor, Frank Leonard, from eastern 'Omega College', failing to receive a raise in salary, quits his position and departs for New York City. He possesses a black box that contains rays that allow its knowing holder to become invisible. Frank uses its powers to rob the city's banks, until John Craven, a former student of his, appropriates the box for like use. Frank repents, makes a second black box and goes after Craven. A sidelight of the novel is Frank's wooing of a Vassar graduate whose father has a distinct scorn for academics and their paltry salaries.

2199. **Mack, Willard, 1873-1934.** *Anybody's property*. **New York: Macaulay Co., 1917. 298p.**

A young man who had made a fortune in a Mexican silver mine wonders what New York City has to offer. Dick Tracy is taken in hand by a friend and shown the sights and sounds of Broadway. He meets several sophisticated, worldly women, one of whom, Dot Wheeler, has retained a certain glimmer of innocence despite being buffeted by the cruel, uncaring city. The hero takes her by the hand, Dot responds with love, and the two leave Broadway and the city streets far behind.

2200. MacKellar, William, 1914- . *Kickoff.* **New York: Whittlesey House, c1955. 184p.**

Football in a Long Island high school is the novel's center. A star soccer player from Scotland matriculates at the school; it is up to him to apply in some way the skills he displayed in British soccer to the game of American football.

2201. Mackenzie, Rachel, 1909-1980. *The wine of astonishment.* **New York: Viking Press, 1974. 154p.**

In the early years of the 20th century the Upstate New York village of 'Pliny Falls' witnesses a tragedy of "two gentle women fallen on evil days. They follow the death of their Mama ('one of the landmarks gone') where in Upstate New York Mama had not only apotheosized the first family (Henderson Preserving Company) but the First Presbyterian Church, leaving Martha and Esther, both skirting their thirties, to make bereft nightly visits to the cemetery. But eventually for Martha there will be David Rathbone the minister, until Esther, always headstrong, falls in love with choir tenor, Oliver, who disregards his wife and his youngsters, alienates the town and causes Martha to lose David who—in failing to correct the situation with his Christian Home sermons—feels he has 'betrayed his calling'. Comes the Depression and Oliver is immured in the old, once proud pillared, Greek Revival Henderson home with Esther and Martha—their lives flaking away with the paint in penury and ostracism"—Kirkus reviews. Reprinted by Books & Company, Turtle Point, N.Y., in 1997.

2202. MacKinnon, Mary Linehan. *One small candle.* **New York: Crown Publishers, 1956. 250p.**

"A slice of mid-eighteenth-century American farm life [in Upstate New York]. Ellen, an immigrant girl, marries the widowed Denis and devotedly rears his children. But all that Denis offers Ellen is hard work and ten years of marital chastity as he silently grieves for his first wife. In a moment of deep resentment Ellen has an affair with another man and carries his child. This kicks up a crisis and forces Denis to accept Ellen on more mature terms"— Saturday review.

2203. Maclean, Charles, 1946- . *The silence.* **New York: Viking Press, 1996. 308p.**

The placid existence of wealthy Tom and Karen Welford and their little boy Ned on a Long Island estate is shattered when Ned's parents begin to argue and their marriage is suddenly on the cusp of dissolution. Karen turns for help to Victor Serafin. Bad choice—Serafin is a scumbag who hatches a plan to kidnap frightened Ned and murder Tom and Karen's clandestine lover, Joe Haynes. The latter happens to be Ned's biological father.

2204. Maclean, Charles Agnew. *The mainspring.* **With illus. by Edmund Frederick. Boston: Little, Brown, 1912. 313p.**

A fight to gain control of an important network of railroads by opposing New York financial circles almost by accident drags Ashmore, a reporter on the prowl for a good story, into the fray. He enters the Long Island home of the dying J. Craven, one of the leading contestants. Ashmore is prevailed upon (chiefly by the presence of a charming but serious young lady) to impersonate Craven's son and thereby have access to unlimited funds to pour into the struggle. He is kidnapped, escapes, participates in the overthrow of the party led by Mr. Farnum, and is well on his way to winning the aforementioned young woman.

Macnie, John, 1853-1909. See under his pseudonym: Thiusen, Ismar.

MacPherson, Mrs. M.E. See under her pseudonym: Hartshorn, Nancy.

2205. Macrae, Travis, 1927- . *Death in view.* **New York: Holt, Rinehart and Winston, 1960. 246p.**

"A suburban [north of New York] group, with the patterned exchange of partners centering around Alice Eckert, is suspended in distrust when she is murdered and the resulting investigation and disclosures upend the lives of the five families involved. Near-sighted Kate, known to be not wearing her glasses, has seen the killer; when her secret of contact lenses is learned, there is more trouble"—Kirkus services.

2206. ————. *Trial by slander.* **New York: Rinehart, 1960. 246p.**

"Janet, after the death of her husband, John, becomes involved with Jason Whiting, a professor, who hopes to be free of his incompatible marriage with Antonia, a vulgar and vicious woman. People talk, and talk more when Antonia is found murdered—with John's gun clearly fingerprinted by Jason. Only Janet believes in Jason's innocence despite the trial, which finds him guilty, and she is able to prove her point. ...The everyday familiarity of the suburban scene (Westchester), domestic detail and the romance keeps this plausible"—Kirkus service.

2207. Macvane, Edith, b. 1878 or 80. *The thoroughbred.* **Illustrated by Charles Grunwald. New York: G.W. Dillingham, 1909. 303p.**

Jim Palliser, cashier in a New York City trust company, is accused by the president of the bank of making off with a half million dollars of the bank's deposits. Palliser's wife staunchly defends him, preventing his attempted suicide and then taking steps to clear her husband of the charge. The real culprit, the trust company's president, is discovered largely through her efforts.

2208. Madison, Lucy Foster, 1865-1932. *Captain Kitty, Colonial.* **Illustrated by Marguerite Davis. Philadelphia: Penn Pub. Co., 1923. 309p.**

Kitty Gerritt is a young Dutch girl experiencing life in Manhattan some nine or ten years (about 1765) before the outbreak of the Revolutionary War. Her brother Dirck is impressed into the British Navy to the consternation of his aunt and uncle, his guardians (both Kitty and Dirck are orphans), but he takes to life at sea and chooses to return to his ship despite the possibility of punishment for desertion (when he left without permission to visit his family). It is the period of the Stamp Act and the widespread anger of the colonials because of it and the disdain the King's soldiers and sailors show for them are illustrated. When the Act is repealed the city celebrates and declares its allegiance to King George even though there are forebodings of further trouble. The book is noteworthy, however, for reasons stated in the introduction: "The whole tale makes a wonderfully clear picture of the life of the early Dutch inhabitants of Manhattan. The author...is faithful to historical detail [accurately describes New York's physical and cultural landmarks of the time], and has given truthful local color."

2209. **Magoun, Jeanne Bartholomew.** *The mission of Victoria Wilhelmina*. **New York: Huebsch, 1912. 146p.**

It is the mission of Victoria Wilhelmina, daughter of a New York office woman and her employer, to comfort her mother and assuage any bitterness that might linger from her sad experience. Victoria's mother had been a naïve country girl who came to New York to make her living; the man who employed her confused her moral sense, led her down 'the primrose path' to illegitimacy and then walked away from her. Guilt had eaten away at her soul ever since.

2210. **Magruder, Julia, 1854-1907.** *Labor of love*; **a story for boys. Boston: Lothrop Pub. Co., 1898. 144p.**

"How love won a boy of some innately good impulses who had gone astray back to the right path is told in this story. Frank Morris picks up a five-dollar note in the streets of New York, and indulges his gaming propensities by buying a valise at an auction of unclaimed baggage. In the valise he finds clothes, money, and a letter from a rich uncle to his poor nephew that he has never seen, inviting him to his home. Frank impersonates the nephew; but remorse overtakes him, and he confesses and redeems himself"—Annual American catalogue.

2211. ————. *Struan*. **Boston: R.G. Badger, 1899. 330p.**

"Lucien Struan was a musician of great renown. Jenny Lacy, a little country girl with a good voice, fell in love with his picture at the age of fourteen. When she was nineteen she went to New York to take singing lessons from Struan, then forty-two years old. After many striking conversations Struan and Jenny are married. Their married life brings out their very opposite characters"—Annual American catalogue. They face their differences and take measures to resolve them.

2212. ————. *The Violet.* **With illus. by Charles Dana Gibson. New York: Longmans, Green, 1896. 210p.**

"A story of fashionable New York. 'The Violet', named so by admiring friends, is a Mrs. Bertrand, an Englishwoman come over to chaperone Louise Wendell in her first season in society. She is highly recommended, but has evidently a story, as she shrinks from all unnecessary contacts with society. Louise's cousin and guardian—Pembroke Jerome—a rich widower, falls in love with Mrs. Bertrand, and by degrees her unhappy past is unraveled"— Annual American catalogue.

2213. **Maguire, Gregory, 1954- .** *Missing sisters.* **New York: McElderry Books, 1994. 152p.**

In 1968 an orphanage in Upstate New York managed by nuns is the home of Alice, a 12-year-old who has hearing and speech difficulties. Alice's friend and mentor, Sister Vincent de Paul, badly hurt in a fire, is placed in a nursing home. Alice has not been informed of this and she fears that the sister may have died. She promises God that she will not accept an offer of adoption until she really knows Sister Vincent's ultimate fate. By a stroke of luck Alice discovers that she may have been separated from a twin sister very early in life and she uses all her innate cleverness and courage to find her.

2214. **Maher, Richard Aumerle.** *Gold must be tried by fire.* **New York: Macmillan, 1917. 303p.**

"A story of industrial conditions in northern New York. The scene is a mill town, dependent wholly on the paper manufacturing industry for its existence. Daidie Grattan, who three years before had thrown a wrench into her machine and walked out of a cotton factory, comes to 'Barton' to work in the mill. In the years following her act of rebellion the girl had gone through a bitter experience, but she had found healing at the hands of a Catholic sisterhood and with new courage had come out into the world with the hope of helping other girls. Not until she is employed in his mill does she discover that Hugh Barton is the man who had once saved her life in a crisis. The situation between the two is worked out against a background of industrial unrest, labor warring with capital, the independent manufacturer fighting for his life against the trust"—Book review digest.

2215. ————. *The heart of a man.* **New York: Benziger Bros., 1915. 414p.**

"Pictures conditions in a 'one-mill town' [in Upstate New York] in which everything—mill, bank, store, houses—is under the control of one man, the mill owner. The characters are John Sargent, who represents capital, Jim Loyd, who stands for labor, and Father Driscoll, representing the Catholic Church. And it is the latter power that in a crisis controls the situation, curbing the hand that would do violence on the one part, and awakening a rudimentary sense of justice on the other. The scene is a manufacturing town in the lower Adirondacks and with little disguise recent events in industrial towns similarly situated are reproduced. The Catholic point of view is most evident in the author's attitude toward socialism"—Book review digest.

2216. ————. *The shepherd of the North.* **New York: Macmillan, 1916. 342p.**

"The central character of the story is a big-hearted Catholic bishop who is indeed a shepherd to the people of the Adirondack hills where the scenes are laid. It is while he is on a visit to a French-Canadian village on the remote borders of his parish that Ruth Lansing comes under his protection. Her father, although he is a Protestant, is willing to leave his daughter to the care of the good bishop. Ruth is placed in a convent and, surrounded by the all-pervasive Catholic influence, becomes a ready convert. Her… lover, Jeffrey Whiting, is less easily persuaded and it is only after his soul has been tried that he finds comfort in the Catholic faith. Much of the action of the story is concerned with a fight between the hill people, led by Jeffrey, and a powerful railroad corporation that attempts to get possession of their land"—Book review digest.

2217. ————. *The works of Satan.* **New York: Macmillan, 1921. 370p.**

A country town in Upstate New York, 'where everybody knows everybody', and where the residents have perhaps more than their share of peculiarities, is the home of a rural editor, an innocuous fellow, who has been mockingly dubbed 'Satan' by some of the townspeople. 'Satan' wanted to liven things up and so he began spreading harmless (?) little rumors that produced great commotion. George G. was faced with a run on his bank and suddenly found himself in the village jail. His bookkeeper, Betty Saunders, in love with George, actually busted him out of jail and an informal marriage followed. Satan, sorry for all the havoc he had wrought, helped George find the supposedly stolen money that had gotten George in trouble in the first place.

2218. Maitland, James A. *The old patroon*; or, *The great Van Brock property.* **Philadelphia: T.B. Peterson, 1879. xxi, 392p.**

The Van Brock property is an estate in abeyance whose claimants include members of old Knickerbocker families. The scenes of the novel, laid far in the past, shift back and forth between New York State and New England. It yields provocative data about a number of the old New York 'clans'.

2219. Malamud, Bernard, 1914-1986. *Dubin's lives.* **New York: Farrar, Straus & Giroux, 1979. 362p.**

The distinguished biographer, William B. Dubin, and his wife Kitty, have lived for about 25 years in an old house in Upstate New York near the town of 'Center Campobello' and not far from the Vermont border. Dubin is currently working on a book about D.H. Lawrence; his occasional walks, day or night, on the country roads often end with Dubin getting lost or having a mishap (can't overcome those urban, academic, New York Jewish origins?). His sexual life goes into overdrive when he meets Fanny Bick, a sometime college student whom his wife has temporarily employed as a housekeeper. The

Fanny/Dubin affair continues throughout the novel and in various locations; Fanny is 22 and Dubin is 56. By the time Kitty has become fully aware of her husband's infidelity Fanny has purchased a farm not far from the Dubin home and Dubin learns that Kitty has been seeing the psychiatrist Evan Ondyk for much more than professional reasons. At the novel's conclusion one wonders how much longer Dubin and Fanny will connect as sexual partners and friends and whether Kitty will stay with Dubin. Dubin's life has some resemblance to Dubin's lives (his biographies).

2220. **Malkiel, Theresa Serber, 1873 or 4-1949.** *The diary of a shirtwaist striker*; a **story of the shirtwaist makers' strike in New York. New York: Co-operative Press, 1910. 96p.**

In her diary Mary, the heroine, notes her change from an almost mindless, carefree young woman to a union supporter who undergoes all the hazards and exhaustion associated with her job in a New York shirtwaist factory. When the women workers go on strike (in 1910) Mary is among them; she does jail time, but the strike succeeds and Mary convinces her stubborn, equivocal fiancé Jim, that she has the 'right stuff'.

2221. **Malkus, Alida Sims, b. 1895.** *Pirates' port*; a tale of old New York. Illustrated **by Lyle Justis. New York: Harper, 1929. x, 251p.**

Fourteen-year-old Anneken Jans is aware that smuggling is occurring on her father's estate. The year is 1700 and New Amsterdam is the scene of a major portion of the story. Anneken's awareness results in her being involved in a strange and stirring sequence of events from which she emerges relatively unscathed.

2222. **Mallory, Kate.** *Sarton Kell.* **New York: Morrow, 1977. 324p.**

The heroine, Olivia, is a Southerner enrolled at the Art Students' League in New York City. The time is the 1890s. She meets and marries Chris Sarton, half-Indian son of deceased Milo Sarton and his second wife, Annie-Lo, a Mohawk. Olivia and Chris leave the city for a new home at 'Sarton Kell' near Lake Champlain. Other people enter Olivia's sphere: Chris's half-brother Tod, Tod's amicable wife Alix, and the matriarchal widow, Annie-Lo. Olivia learns that Milo had been quite detached from his wife just before he died and this alienation had left a lot of unanswered questions in its wake.

2223. **Malm, Dorothea, 1915- .** *The woman question.* **New York: Appleton-Century-Crofts, [c1957]. 277p.**

Mary Whitby, a schoolteacher, is present at the Women's Rights Convention in Seneca Falls, New York, and is inspired by the devotion of Elizabeth Cady Stanton, Lucy Stone, Lucretia Mott, Susan B. Anthony and others to equal rights for women. Her fiancé, William Bonchurch, had at one time thought himself in love with Mary's younger sister, but was now devoted to Mary. However he was not to have Mary for his wife until he acknowledged that she would be an equal partner in their venture.

2224. Malone, Paul Bernard, b. 1872. *A plebe at West Point.* **Illustrated by F.A. Carter. Philadelphia: Penn Pub. Co., 1905. 430p.**

> Because of his courage in battle during the Philippine campaign at the turn of the century Douglas Atwell is admitted to the United States Military Academy (West Point). The novel tells of his experiences there during his initial year, including an account of the traditional hazing of underclassmen that just a few years before had been a topic of much controversy.

2225. ————. *A West Point cadet.* **Illustrated by F.A. Carter. Philadelphia: Penn Pub. Co., 1908. 419p.**

> Douglas Atwell is in his last years at the U.S. Military Academy. Once again he is a vital cog in West Point's football fortunes and is at the forefront of a step towards abolishing hazing at the Point. He is compelled to answer the accusation of a rival that he has acted dishonorably; Douglas fights the charge for two years before he is finally cleared.

2226. ————. *A West Point yearling.* **Illustrated by F.A. Carter. Philadelphia: Penn. Pub. Co., 1907. 383p.**

> In this sequel to the author's A Plebe at West Point, Douglas Atwell is now in his second year at the U.S. Military Academy. As in the earlier volume hazing is a focus; it is represented as a grave threat to the Academy's discipline. Atwell is president of his class and under his leadership hazing is confronted and effectively controlled despite interference by the class bully and other resentful classmates. Douglas also has a prominent role in the annual Army-Navy football game.

2227. Maloney, Ralph Liston, 1827-1973. *The great Bonacker whiskey war*; **an entertainment. Boston: Little, Brown, 1967. 212p.**

> One of the few assets unlucky Bailey Miller has is the fastest fishing boat in 'Bonack Bay', Long Island. A lot of amateur bootlegging is going on—it is the 1920s when hardened criminals headed by Cullum Pearse (a former member of the Irish Republican Army) move in. Pearse and his gang commandeer Bailey's boat and Bailey is forced to accompany them on their bootlegging operations. It is up to Bailey to figure out how the rumrunners may be frustrated.

Malzberg, Barry N., 1939- , joint author. *The running of the beasts.* **See Item #2766.**

2228. Mancur, John Henry, fl. 1834-1847. *Christine*; **a tale of the Revolution. New York: W.H. Colyer, 1843. 60p.**

> The western end of Long Island and the village of Flatbush (later a part of Brooklyn) with its mixture of patriots and Tories await with trepidation the advance of invading British forces under Howe and Clinton. The heroine, Christine, is the daughter of British sympathizer Gabriel Mellen who is

determined to marry her off to Nicholas Corlear, a Tory. Young patriot Adrian Van Horne, in love with Christine, participates in the Long Island campaign and is taken prisoner by the British; when he is released, he joins Washington's forces at New Brunswick. He returns to Flatbush with Corlear's capture as his goal; despite his misgivings Gabriel finally assents to the union of Christine and Adrian. With the war's end Corlear moves to Canada while Gabriel Mellen stays on his property, but has little faith in the viability of the new government.

2229. ————. *The deserter*; a legend of Mount Washington. **New York: W.H. Colyer, 1843. [61]-132p.**

At head of title: No. 2. Tales of the Revolution. One gets the impression that the author is more interested in describing the military situation in New York City and environs with General Washington facing Lord Howe than he is in spinning his tale. Arthur Merrill, an American officer, keeps to quarters in the home of Madame Dancourt and her daughter Eugenie when he is wounded. A sympathetic British soldier, James Hayward, helps Arthur elude detection by the occupation army and Arthur returns to the American lines. Hayward deserts the British army and eventually gets back to England. After action at Mount Washington (Washington Heights, New York City) Arthur Merrill finds Mrs. Dancourt and Eugenie safely within the American lines and takes the young woman's hand in marriage.

2230. ————. *Wilfred Lovel*; a revolutionary romance. **Philadelphia: A.J. Rockafellar, 1843. 62p. (in double columns).**

"The scene of this novel is laid in New York, soon after the cession of that city by the Dutch to the English [1689-ca. 1691]"—To the Public (p. 3). Wilfred Lovel, a young London skylarker, is shipped off to New York by his uncle in the hope that he will settle down and acquire a useful commercial activity. Wilfred carries an introduction to Jacob Leisler, the controversial historical personage who had been selected by a Committee of Safety as lieutenant governor of the Colony of New York to defend it against the minions of James II of England, French invasion, etc. Wilfred falls in love with Styntie, Leisler's daughter, follows the brief career of Leisler, and witnesses the questionable execution of Leisler and Leisler's son-in-law for treason as ordered by the new governor, the weak, incompetent Henry Sloughter.

2231. **Mangione, Jerre Gerlando, 1909- . *Mount Allegro*. Illustrated by Peggy Bacon. Boston: Houghton, Mifflin, 1943. 292p.**

The author is an American of Sicilian descent. He fictionalizes his childhood and memories of life in Rochester, New York's 'Mount Allegro', a 'colony' of Italian and Sicilian immigrants and newly naturalized citizens. Relatives and friends, with all their laughter, quick tempers and sudden changes of mood are portrayed as the young protagonist passes into his early adult years. He makes a pilgrimage to Sicily, the former home of his parents.

2232. Manley. R.M. *Some children of Adam.* **New York: Worthington Co., 1892. 310p.**

"A novel that presents a social study of American life as seen in New York. The characters which figure in the uncommon and sometimes sensational incidents will be recognized as typical ones of the metropolis"—Annual American catalogue. The two 'heroes' are Franklin Raymond and Arthur Wareham, both men of wealth and social standing. Arthur is in love with his cousin, Katherine Croxton, but feels that she is interested in Franklin. The latter however has become intimately acquainted with a young Frenchwoman, Désirée, daughter of Achille Renaud, who has turned to crime to support himself. Franklin's first meeting with Désirée was as a concerned individual responsible for an accidental injury to the girl. He soon falls in love with her, but a commitment to a plan of his aunt, Mrs. Westmeath, precludes his marrying Désirée for the nonce. After the swindler Achille Renaud falls to his death while contemplating the murder of his innocent daughter for money given her by Franklin, the latter goes forward with his determination to marry Désirée. Arthur discovers that Katherine is his to win after all.

2233. Manvill, Mrs. P.D. *Lucinda*; or, *The mountain mourner*: **being recent facts, in a series of letters from Mrs. Manvill, of the State of New York, to her sister in Pennsylvania. Johnstown [N.Y.]: W. & A. Child, 1807. 150p.**

Tale of a woman betrayed by her lover. The heroine, while residing in Marcellus, N.Y. is seduced by Mr. Brown who promises to marry her. Discovering that she is pregnant Lucinda wanders distractedly to relatives in Scipio, Troy, Charlton, towns in central and eastern New York, and her final stopping place, Greenfield, near Kayaderosaras Mountain, Saratoga County. A sympathetic father and stepmother give her shelter and sympathy, but Lucinda, after the birth of a female child, wastes away from shame and grief to an early death. Her child is adopted; Mr. Brown in remorse states that he will help defray the expense of his daughter's rearing. The novel received several reprintings in the last half of the nineteenth century.

2234. Mapes, Victor, 1870-1943. *The gilded way*; a novel. **New York and Washington, D.C.: Neale, 1910. 326p.**

The early scenes of this novel transpire in New York City where Margaret Benton has become the bride of a multimillionaire's son. The marriage is a disaster; her spoiled husband and his college chums are given to dissipation and neglect of common decencies, 'the gilded way'. Divorce seems to be the only path available for Margaret. In poor health she enters a sanitarium in the Adirondacks, renews old acquaintances and ties and paves the way, one hopes, to a new tomorrow.

2235. Marasco, Robert. *Burnt offerings.* **New York: Delacorte Press, 1973. 260p.**

The Rolfe family of Queens—Ben and Marian, son David and Aunt Elizabeth—rent a huge old house on Long Island for the summer. They pay very little for use of the neglected structure, but with it comes the condition that they feed a permanent resident, 85-year-old 'Mother', three times a day; she never leaves her room and a tray of food must be placed outside her door. The house gradually exerts a chilling effect on the Rolfes. Ben begins picking on David and suffers hallucinations; Marian ignores her husband, immersing herself in housework, as her hair turns gray; Aunt Elizabeth loses her energy and dies. Is there a logical, if ominous explanation for what is happening?

Marbourg, Dolores, 1870- . See Bacon, Dolores, 1870- .

2236. **March, Joseph Moncure, 1899-1977.** *The set-up.* **New York: Covici, Friede, 1928. 184p.**

A verse-narrative of the life and death of a black prizefighter, Pansy Jones of Harlem; it is a bloody affair in which Jones double-crosses his managers and wins a fight he was supposed to throw.

2237. **————.** *The wild party.* **With illus. by Reginald Marsh. Chicago: P. Covici, 1928. viii, 113p.**

March's second verse-narrative in which he describes a 'no-holds-barred' party of New York City bohemians. "The guests are all theatrical people. They drink, then they sing, then they make love, and finally go to sleep, while a sordid and passionate little triangle drama works itself out to the inevitable revolver shot and arrival of the police"—New statesman.

2238. **Marcin, Max, 1879-1948.** *Are you my wife?* **Illustrated by Z.P. Nikolaki. New York: Moffat, Yard, 1910. 311p.**

The young 'hero', a lawyer in New York City lacking clients but with a long list of debts, agrees to marry a mysterious woman in exchange for a half million dollars. There is a stipulation—he must not let anyone know of the marriage. Of course he is curious about the whole thing and spends $100,000 in an effort to solve the puzzle. At the end of four years he will be divorced from his bride and receive the promised sum, so it really is not in his interest to dig too deeply.

2239. **Marfield, Dwight, 1868-1955.** *The mandarin's sapphire.* **New York: Dutton, 1938. 307p.**

Calvin Winters, old sea captain, dies in his sinister mansion on the Hudson. It looks like murder; among the suspects are: Blossom Lily, Eurasian girl and her mentally retarded brother, Tuan; Silver Lily, her mother; Chang Koo, the gardener; two great Danes, a weasel-bat and a cockatoo. Idahoan Crete Monroe, a one-time prospector, digs for the answer, finds it and hands it to Inspector Skane and Trooper Malloy.

2240. **Marion, Frances, 1887-1973.** *Molly, bless her.* **New York: Harper, 1937. 320p.**
Down on her luck, or perhaps a 'washed up' comedienne, the performer Molly Drexler has to find another way to make a living. So Molly takes a crack at

housekeeping for a grumpy Mr. Graham and his lonely son in their Long Island home. Once established in the new position Molly brings in a medley of down-and-out actors and actresses to replace the servants already in the Graham ménage. Their presence provides benefits for the Grahams and also eventuates in a theatrical comeback for Molly and her friends.

2241. Markey, Gene, 1895-1980. *Stepping high.* **Illustrated by Jay. Garden City, N.Y.: Doubleday, Doran, 1929. 310p**

Benny is a dancer on the vaudeville circuit whose wife Flo suddenly finds herself a headliner in musical comedies and a darling of certain elements of New York society. Benny is pushed into the background, but is noticed favorably by an attractive young lady. Remaining true to his wife Benny refuses to get involved with the pleasant miss; when Flo's brief moment in the spotlight is over, Benny is waiting for her. "Mr. Markey writes with the lift, the humor, and at times the pathos of Tin Pan Alley at its best. ... The prevailing character sketches [are those] which Broadway quite often finds plausible"—Boston transcript.

2242. Markham, Richard. *On the edge of winter* ….**New York: Dodd, Mead, 1881. 236p.**

Five boys and five girls celebrate Thanksgiving in an old farmhouse in the Hudson Highlands. In addition to narrating the activities of the ten young people the book contains stories and poems about the American past.

Marks, Mary A.M. Hoppus. See: Hoppus, Mary A.M.

2443. Marks, Percy, 1891-1956. *Between two autumns*; **a novel. New York: Reynal & Hitchcock, 1941. 349p.**

"When Tinker Larme stopped for shelter on a stormy night at the Steele home in Westchester, he promised to be the solution of the Steeles' problems. Under his influence Mrs. Steele, suffering from shock after an accident, gradually grew better; in emergencies, Tink was a good gardener, carpenter and cook; and he could drive Mr. Steele to the station or play tennis with him. But during the year Tink remained with the Steeles he was the unconscious, unintentional cause of several catastrophes—as the [psychological] flaw in his personality is gradually revealed"—Book review digest.

2244. ――――. *Lord of himself.* **New York: Century Co., 1927. 336p.**

Carl Peters and Cynthia Day, characters in the author's The Plastic age, are leading personages in this novel. Carl is now a New Yorker with a good income, a wealth of friends and a propensity for good times—they make it difficult for him to live up to his mother's hopes for him. The fact that he begins to find Cynthia most attractive only adds to his problems; he must wrestle with his fears and move in several directions before he gains full control of himself. Music plays a role in the story; e.g., Ivan Leshakoff, a prodigy from New York's East Side, is portrayed with a sure, convincing touch.

2245. **Marlowe, Amy Bell.** *The girl from Sunset Ranch*; or, *Alone in a great city.* **New York: Grosset & Dunlap, 1914. vi, 324p.**

Helen Morrell ('Snuggy') leaves the ranch she, an orphan, owns and heads East to broaden her education and meet an uncle she has never seen. Willets Strangeway and his three daughters receive Helen coldly, certain that this country niece/cousin will be an embarrassment to them and their social circle. Helen finds a good friend in Sadie Goronsky, a poor Jewish milliner, and later is welcomed by several other New Yorkers, among them Dud Stone, a young lawyer, and his sister Jessie. Our heroine has another overriding reason for coming to New York—to clear her late father, Prince Morrell, of a charge of embezzlement. Able detective work by Helen and Dud uncovers the true thief, Fenwick Grimes, her father's former business partner; Willets Strangeway was secondarily involved in Grimes' activities. Helen returns to her ranch after accepting the apologies of her cousins and uncle, and presenting Sadie with her own millinery shop. Love-struck Dud Stone follows her.

Marquis, Don, 1878-1937, joint author. *Pandora lifts the lid.* **See Item #2417.**

Marple, Allen Clark, 1901?-1968. See under his pseudonym: Youmans, N.O.

2246. *Married above her*; a society romance. By a lady of New York.   Philadelphia: T.B. Peterson, 1884. 566p.

Grace Howard, a poor orphan raised by her grandparents in the village of 'Riverside' on the Hudson, has an unfortunate marriage with Raymond Irving, age 45, of New York; the latter keeps looking back at a lost love, a woman named Anita whom he presumes is dead. The story takes place during the American Civil War; its scene shifts back and forth from Riverside to New York City and a seaside resort. Many characters and subplots appear in this long, drawn-out novel. In the end Grace is divorced from Raymond when the 'deceased' Anita turns up in the flesh and Raymond confesses his long-ago marriage to her. 'Anita' is a woman well known to Grace, for she (under the name of Mrs. Mary Myers, and homeless) had been taken in by Grace's grandmother. Frank Everett, a wealthy friend of the Irving family, and for a long time in love with Grace, is conveniently present to woo Grace who is now free of any ties to her former husband.

2247. **Marshall, Edward, 1870-1933.** *Bat*; an idyl of New York. Illus. by Ike Morgan and Haygarth Leonard. **New York: Dillingham, 1912. 288p.**

Perdue, a young man from the country starting out on his career as an architect, meets 'Bat' (Beatrice) when he rents a room in a New York boarding-house managed by Bat's grandmother. Bat is just a slip of a girl and when Perdue is appointed her guardian after the grandmother's death, he hardly knows just how to deal with Bat. With the passage of time Perdue's love for Bat and her love for him solves the problem.

2248. ————. *Broadway Jones*; from the play of George M. Cohan. Illus. from scenes in the play. New York: Dillingham, 1913. 322p.

Glittering Broadway draws a young man from a country village when he inherits a fortune. His deep pockets attract the artful denizens of the city and our hero soon has empty pockets and a pile of debts. An elderly much-divorced lady offers him security if he will be her constant 'companion'. He worms his way out of this proposition and in the end finds the girl who is right for him.

2249. ————. *The writing on the wall*; a novel founded on Olga Nethersole's play by William J. Hurlbut. Illus. by Clarence Rowe. New York: G.W. Dillingham, 1909. 350p.

The novel "portrays relentlessly the terrible state of things existing in a tenement house district of New York [City]. A tenement house landlord and a young man devoting his life to tenement house reform are rivals for the hand of a New York society girl. The former wins her, and then follows a revelation of her husband's irresponsibility and greed coupled with infidelity to her. The tangled threads are finally untwisted through a tragic fire in one of the tenements in which the little son is killed"—Book review digest.

2250. Marshall, Marguerite Mooers, 1887-1964. *The drift*. New York: Appleton, 1911. 255p.

A fictional autobiography in which, through her letters, a young woman with literary aspirations tells how she fell in love with an unhappily married man in her hometown and then left for New York while her lover began divorce proceedings. She becomes a journalist and submerges herself in the New York way of life, but she eventually suffers debilitating despondency and yields to the suicidal impulse when her lover writes that his wife is pregnant and he has to stay with his family.

2251. Martel, Henry. *The social revolution*; a novel. New York: G.W. Dillingham, 1891. 302p.

Mark Richardson meets the heroine, Anna Fielding, in a New York City beer garden where she works as a waitress. He is attracted by her beauty and modesty; although he tells her he is no saint, their ongoing relationship remains at a platonic level throughout the novel. Mark encourages Anna to take more suitable employment; she becomes servant/companion to Mrs. Luther Marsh, an unhappily married woman, while Mark, evidently with independent means, embarks on a crusade against the hypocrisy of the city's churches which neglect social problems but fawn upon their wealthy parishioners. Mr. Marsh attempts to seduce Anna; she leaves the Marshes, studies stenography (supported by money Mark has forced from the libidinous Marsh) and enters the employment of Ezra Haynes who, along with Marsh, is a member of the aptly named 'Church of the Holy Hypocrites'. Haynes tricks Anna into entering his summer home where he and Marsh lie in wait. Mark rushes to her rescue, but he, Anna, Haynes, Marsh and others are killed in an explosion set off by Mark's adherents who use his tirades against the abuses of capitalism to justify violent means towards the end of 'the social revolution'.

2252. **Martin, Edward Sandford, 1856-1939.** *The courtship of a careful man, and a few other courtships.* **New York: Harper, 1905. 184p.**

A half-dozen short stories of New York life "having a peculiar quality of their own. Quite modern in effect, they have a background of good breeding distinctly American. The conversations among different members of the families represented are clever and exhibit a complete and happy knowledge of the world" (Outlook). Contents: The courtship of a careful man.—A party at Madeira's.—The making of a match.—A disguised providence.—Josephine.—Found, a situation.

2253. **Martin, George Madden, 1866-1946.** *The angel of the tenement.* **New York: Bonnell, Silver, 1897. 134p.**

'Angel' is a child who has no recollection of her earlier life. Found in a grimy New York tenement she is taken in by a kindly but poverty-stricken woman who lives in the building. From there on Angel experiences the harshness and the few moments of joy that are endemic to those who dwell in the slums of the inner city.

2254. **Martin, Nell Columbia Boyer, b. 1890.** *Lord Byron of Broadway*; a novel. **New York: R.D. Henkle, 1928. 336p.**

The author has infused her novel of the rise to fame of a writer of popular songs with a flavoring of Broadway characters (vaudevillians, chorus girls, actors, et al.) and dialogue.

2255. **Martin, Virginia Bird.** *Bed and board.* **New York: Farrar & Rinehart, 1938. 279p.**

Miriam, the distaff side of a young married couple in a New York suburb, suffers increasing boredom and turns for variety to coquetry; as the marriage sours and Miriam's 'affairs' become more serious, the two marrieds are suddenly brought back together by mutual shock at the death of a beloved friend.

2256. **Martyn, Wyndham, b. 1875.** *All the world to nothing.* **With illus. by H.H. Leonard. Boston: Little, Brown, 1912. 403p.**

New Yorker Richard Chester has excellent social connections, but they are of little use to him when his speculations go sour and he is left with no money. He refuses to ask his older brother for help and considers approaching a loan shark he had once heavily overpaid in settling a loan. By an odd twist of fate Chester ends up in Norah Lester's apartment; Norah stands to inherit

$250,000 from her grandfather's estate on the condition that she get married before midnight. Chester's assent to be the bridegroom propels him into a most disconcerting set of adventures.

2257. —————. *The death fear.* **New York: McBride, 1929. 326p.**

"John Addison, prominent New York financier, is beset by a nameless fear that he will explain to no one. After an attack on his life, the police are thrown off the scent; but Anthony Trent, millionaire sportsman and amateur criminologist, is not fooled. He starts an investigation in the midst of which Addison disappears. Undismayed, Trent digs deeper and finally locates both the missing man and the would-be murderer"—Bookman.

2258. **Marvin, Eleanor.** *Mary Allen.* **Illustrated by Alice Beard. Garden City, N.Y.: Doubleday, Page, 1916. vii, 238p.**

A novel for older teenagers. What there is of a plot is simple and straight-forward. Mary Allen has a talent for design; Jim Grant, a friend, takes several of her sketches to New York and she herself enrolls in one of the city's art schools. She enters a prize competition and wins a scholarship that provides her with a year's study in Paris.

2259. *Mary Beach*; or, *The Fulton Street cap maker.* **New York: W.F. Burgess, 1849. 97p. (in double columns).**

A tale of the pitfalls unsophisticated country girls from Vermont face when they come to the metropolis to earn a living (in this case by sewing caps). Two friends, Mary Beach and Jane Haines, are enticed into accepting smart living quarters by two libertines, Frank Prentice and Thomas Green, who pretend to be suitors for marriage. Luxury-loving Jane is easy prey for the blandishments of Green who impregnates her. Mary is made of stronger stuff and puts off Prentice until she is finally tracked down and rescued from her quarters (in a house of ill repute) by her brother William, Jane's former lover, George Morrison, and John Winchendon, a kind, elderly Quaker who had been helpful to Mary when she first came to New York City. Jane commits suicide; Mary chooses to become the wife of John Winchendon.

2260. **Mason, Caroline Atwater, 1853-1939.** *A minister of the world.* **New York: A.D.F. Randolph, 1895. 154p.**

Reverend Stephen Castle is rather happy with his New England pastorate of Thornton. Then he makes the acquaintance of Miss Loring, a New Yorker, and is flooded with a host of new ideas. His call to a fashionable church in New York City results in a change of his ministerial methods, in sharp contrast to those he utilized in Thornton.

2261. **Mason, Edith Huntington.** *The politician.* **Illustrated in full color by the Kinneys. Chicago: McClurg, 1910. 409p.**

The protagonist of the novel is an ambitious New Yorker who has an insatiable desire for political power. To reach his goal adequate financial resources and a 'suitable' marriage are necessary. But in regard to the latter condition he can't quite see putting the girl he loves in a position that might result in her suffering neglect as he exclusively pursues his own dreams. He has to find his own solutions to the problem.

2262. **Mason, Francis Van Wyck, 1897-1978.** *Seeds of murder.* **Garden City, N.Y.: Published for the Crime Club by Doubleday, Doran, 1930. 302p.**
"A right smart story of what happened to a wealthy Wall Street broker who defrauded his friends and subjected his wife to endless cruel indignities. Captain North of the U.S. Army Intelligence and his doctor friend are present at broker Delancey's weekend party in his Long Island home. A double tragedy that throws the whole house into an uproar takes place shortly after their arrival, makes a complete fool out of the local police lieutenant, and is all the more mysterious because of tomato seeds found beside the bodies of the 'suicides'"—Bookman.

2263. **Mason, Louis Bond, 1869-1936.** *A survival of the fittest*; a novel by L. Bond Mason and Norman Elliot. **Chicago: Nile Pub. Co., 1892. 195p.**
"Catherine Shirley is left an orphan and penniless at eighteen. She is protected and enabled to become a painter by Mrs. Vanderslyce, a warm-hearted, irresponsible woman, addicted to drink and narcotics. Carried away by gratitude, Catherine shields this friend's good name after her death by accident. The consequences of this act are far-reaching. New York City and a Florida watering-place are the settings for a story of the frivolity and heartlessness of fashionable life"—Annual American catalogue.

2264. **Mason, Roy, b. 1879.** *When I am rich*; a novel. **Illus. by Roy Martell Mason. New York: G.W. Dillingham, 1909. 343p.**
Upon his graduation from college Chester Taylor has no money and few prospects. A gambling man from New York's East Side advises him to take as his motto, 'keep feelin' cheerful inside all the time'. Chester figures that clothes might make the man, that an imposing, snappy exterior will bring him the attention of people of substance. He orders expensive wearing apparel and then takes an apartment in a high rent district. He bluffs his way into several Wall Street deals, picks up a lot of cash, and gathers in the girl he loves.

2265. **Masters, Hilary, 1928- .** *Clemmons*; a novel. **Boston: D.R. Godine, 1985. 294p.**
Gravitating from Broadway press agent to Upstate New York real estate agent Clemmons finds himself in a father-of-the-bride situation when one of his daughters decides to get married in a meadow that had once been the scene of a famous illicit prizefight in the 19th century. He asks the wife from whom he has been separated to help him plan the minutiae that accompany a wedding. Clemmons reminisces and begins visiting old haunts and lovers in Boston Corners, N.Y., mid-Manhattan, Provincetown and suburban Virginia while contemporary events like the Kennedy assassination come and go.

2266. ———. *Hammertown tales.* **Winston-Salem: S. Wright, 1986. 128p.**

The author, son of Edgar Lee Masters of 'Spoon River' fame, set the scene of this collection of short stores in an Upstate New York village that has been in decline ever since a major freeway bypassed it in the 1950s. Some of the tales feature 'natives'—persons born and raised (and who will likely stay) in the town; others deal with people who have professional careers in the city to which they commute from Hammertown. These professionals have in some instances taken over and remodeled old houses in the village; they 'live' in Hammertown but do not necessarily feel that are establishing firm roots there.

2267. Masterton, Graham, 1946- . *The house that Jack built.* **New York: Carroll & Graf, 1996. 385p.**

Craig Bellman is fascinated by a deteriorating mansion, 'Valhalla', that sits on a hill in the Hudson Valley, north of Cold Spring. Because she wants her husband's failing confidence restored, wife Effie goes along with Craig's plan to rebuild Valhalla which had once been the home of egoistic Jack Belias, a wealthy textile manufacturer, who had strangely disappeared in 1937. But the mansion has cast a weird spell on Craig; his sexual appetite becomes ravenous and he may be tied to the deaths of several associates. Effie's research indicates that the evil occultist Belias could quite possibly be using Craig as the medium of his return to Valhalla. A thunderstorm in the Hudson Highlands triggers the climax of this eerie spin-off that does offer illuminating data on the history of the Hudson Valley.

2268. Matheson, Richard, 1925- . *Earthbound.* **New York: TOR, 1994. 223p.**

David and Ellen Cooper, married 21 years, are on the verge of final separation. In a move to save their marriage the Coopers leave Los Angeles for a beach cottage on Long Island. A strange woman, Marianna, insinuates herself into their lives and seduces David. Marianna is ultimately revealed as a succubus, and David succeeds in casting her off and rescuing his wife in a 'cliff –hanger' of an ending.

2269. Mathews, Cornelius, 1817-1889. *Big Abel, and the Little Manhattan.* **New York: Wiley and Putnam, 1845. 93p.**

Lankey Foyle ('Little Manhattan') and Abel Henry Hudson ('Big Abel') wander through the City of New York, which they claim as rightfully belonging to them. In their week-long journey they meet a number of denizens of the city and note some of the metropolis's physical changes. Lankey imagines a return to the past of his Indian forbears (when Manhattan Island was a green land) while Big Abel, cognizant of his distinguished ancestor (Henry Hudson) is very much aware of the sounds of 'a great city setting forth toward the mighty future he is called to fill'.

2270. ———. *The career of Puffer Hopkins.* **Illustrated by H.K. Browne, Esq. (Phiz). New York: D. Appleton, 1842. 319p.**

Puffer Hopkins, presumably an orphan, is an ambitious young politician in New York City who receives good advice from a mysterious Mr. Hobbleshank. An effective speechmaker, Puffer rises, participating in local electioneering and broadening his acquaintances. In due time Puffer is acknowledged as Hobbleshank's son; Hobbleshank explains his absence from Puffer's childhood and youth and his contention with the evil broker, Fyler Close.

2271. **Mathews, Frances Aymar, ca. 1855-1923.** *Billy Duane*; **a novel. New York: Dodd, Mead, 1905. viii, 361p.**

As his political career soars Claiborne Courtlandt Duane (better known as Billy Duane), a Republican, wealthy and cultured, uses his Madison Avenue address as headquarters while his wife is in Europe with their ill son. On her return Mrs. Duane is apprised that Billy is mayor-elect of New York. She finds Billy's cronies and his concentration on politics distasteful and indulges her fondness for the roulette wheel. The estrangement of the couple deepens. Mrs. Duane stops gambling when the police raid the establishment she patronizes. In the end, however, the love Billy and his wife have for one another leads to reconciliation.

2272. ————. *A Christmas honeymoon.* **Illustrated in color by Herbert Bohnert. New York: Moffat, Yard, 1912. 152p.**

The story covers a span of thirty years, beginning in Washington, D.C. and concluding in New York City. Betty Revere and Peter Van Zandt marry and take up residence in his Washington Square home. A few weeks later Betty learns to her dismay that Peter is a violinist (it must have been a whirlwind, uninformative romance). Betty unfortunately has had a long-standing dislike of men who devote themselves to music to the exclusion of other facets of their being. Misapprehension thenceforth colors the relations of the twain; amity is restored by the intervention of a child.

2273. ————. *The flame dancer.* **Illus. by C.F. Neagle. New York: G.W. Dillingham, 1908. 371p.**

The author's novel is a candid 'put-down' of the upper strata of New York society. Two of the ignoble characters are a man who marries for money and a woman who casts her net for a millionaire (with no success). Oriental mysticism, hypnotism, a love affair and a mysterious theft are elements in the story.

2274. ————. *The New Yorkers and other people.* **New York: G.A.S. Wieners, 1900. 436p.**

Of the ten stories in this collection only the first four concern themselves with New York City types; the author evinces a penchant for coincidental happenings and the relationships between worldly Europeans and their 'forthright' American acquaintances. In the novella, 'In Clinton Place', an American couple recently arrived from Europe successfully 'con' an Italian-

American banker into investing in their worthless 'invention', but lose their protégé to an honest young American who sees through their schemes. Partial contents: The New Yorkers.—In Clinton Place.—The foreigner.—Two of a kind and the joker.

2275. ————. *The undefiled*; a novel of to-day. **New York: Harper, 1906. 277p.**
Very attractive Judith Harriman is pursued by a number of prospective suitors, among them the Duke de Montresor, a Parisian who comes to New York in the hope of taking her with him back to France. He fails. Judith marries the vain Conningsby, a writer of popular literature, and discovers that she can't stand him. Taking back her maiden name Judith hires out as private secretary to Bob Travers, a New Yorker who has worked his way up to affluence. He recognizes Judith as a girl he had saved from danger in France; ever since he could not put her out of his thoughts. An auto accident takes the life of Conningsby and Judith is free to be wooed and won by her employer.

2276. **Mathews, Harry, 1930- .** *Cigarettes*; a novel. **New York: Weidenfeld & Nicholson, 1987. 292p.**
This novel about the art world "is divided into fifteen chapters, each headed by the names of the two principal characters involved: Allan and Elizabeth, Oliver and Elizabeth, Oliver and Pauline, Owen and Phoebe; I. Owen and Phoebe: II, etc. The setting alternates between Saratoga Springs and New York City, and the dates (also given in the chapter headings) jump from 1963 to l936 and 1938 and then back to 1962-1963"—New York review of books.

2277. **Mathews, Robert Valentine.** *The lost legion.* **New York: E.C. Hill, 1910. ix, 164p.**
The two Gair sisters are a sharp contrast: one (Margaret) is admirably self-sacrificing; the other, sophisticated and selfish, has married a New York physician who suddenly goes blind. She abandons her husband, while Margaret leaves her Montana school and hurries to her brother-in-law's side in New York. Margaret's voice matches that of her sister and the sightless physician assumes that his wife is still standing by him. Margaret does nothing to disabuse him.

2278. **Matschat, Cecile Hulse, 1895?-1976.** *Preacher on horseback.* **New York: Farrar & Rinehart, 1940. viii, 429p.**
"A story of mid-nineteenth century days in western New York and Michigan. The chief characters are Janos Sandor, an immigrant from Hungary, who studies medicine then becomes a minister, and his wife Rica, daughter of a wealthy Long Island family, who becomes in time a true pioneer woman. In part the novel is based on reminiscences of the author's mother-in-law"—Book review digest.

2279. **Matteson, Stefanie.** *Murder among the angels.* **New York: Berkley Prime Crime, 1996. 250p.**

Charlotte Graham, a 70-something actress, and her friend, police chief Jerry D'Angelo of 'Zion Hill' (Hudson Valley site of a religious sect with Swedenborgian beliefs) are intrigued when both of two recently unearthed skulls turn out, after reconstruction, to resemble the features of Lily, the granddaughter of the sect's founder. Victor Louria, a cosmetic surgeon who now occupies the founder's house, had been married to Lily who supposedly drowned while in Mexico. Lily's angelic face can also be found in paintings that are displayed for public viewing in the community. Did Louria commit murder?—he admits he had operated on the two women. He has a rock-ribbed alibi and Charlotte and Jerry have to look elsewhere for explanation of the mystery.

2280. **Matthews, Brander, 1852-1929. *The action and the word*; a novel of New York. Illustrated by W.T. Smedley. New York: Harper, 1900. 261p.**
Carla, a fascinating Creole, becomes a member of upscale Manhattan society through marriage, but suffers growing disenchantment with her life and her gentle, amiable husband, Evert. he 'liberated' woman she might have graduated into is, however, subdued by the necessity of caring for her sick child and a final, almost enthusiastic acceptance of the 'father/husband knows best' syndrome.

2281. **————. *A confident tomorrow*; a novel of New York. Illustrated by William L. Jacobs. New York: Harper, 1900. 300p.**
"The hero is a young western man who had worked his way through college and served his literary apprenticeship on a Kansas newspaper. Looking for a wider horizon he comes to New York, under engagement to edit a subscription book for a leading publisher. He also has the manuscript of a novel in his grip from which he expects to gain fortune and fame. His letter of introduction to a famous novelist admits him to the best literary society of New York City. His literary experience is realistic and practical; there is a love story and many charmingly described scenes of New York life"—Annual American catalogue.

2282. **————. *His father's son*; a novel of New York. New York: Harper, 1895. 248p.**
"Winslow Pierce is the son of Ezra Pierce, an old Wall Street speculator who, although sharp in speculating practices, is professedly religious, and has a horror of gambling, drinking and sensuality. His son marries, lives in his father's house, has a nominal position in the business, and draws $10,000 a year. He goes from bad to worse, drinks, supports traveling opera companies, speculates with … [company] funds, finally forges, is protected by his father, bustled off to Europe, and is last heard as the 'hero' of a divorce scandal"—Annual American catalogue.

2283. **————. *The last meeting*; a story. New York: Scribner, 1885. 268p.**

The author places his story in the circles of 'high society' in New York City. The artist Frederick Olyphant has fallen in love with the society belle, Winifred Marshall; Winifred's guardian (Colonel) Lawrence Laughton, is also in love with her, but he contains his emotions. At a party hosted by Laughton, Frederick, after a tiff with Winifred, disappears mysteriously into the night. For several months intensive searches fail to reveal his whereabouts. Then several months later word comes from Olyphant that he has survived a shanghaiing engineered by his mortal enemy, Constantin Vollonides, a leading figure in the dangerous Brotherhood of the Sea. The latter drowns at sea when his boat collides with the ship on which Olyphant is serving his impressment. The artist reappears in New York and he and Winifred resume their love affair.

2284. ——————. *A tale of twenty-five hours,* by **Brander Matthews and George H. Jessup. New York: D. Appleton, 1892. vi, 189p.**

Paul Stuyvesant wrongly believes that his fiancées brother Charley, an artist in New York City, has stolen a painting by Titian. His investigation takes him to the pawnshop of Michael Zalinski, a Polish Jew, who may or may not be a 'fence'. As it turns out neither Charley nor Zalinski are guilty of wrongdoing. Charley had only clandestinely made a copy of the painting and had purchased old frames from Zalinski.

2285. ——————. *Tom Paulding*; **the story of a search for buried treasure in the streets of New York. New York: Century Co., 1892. 254p.**

"An interesting bit of Revolutionary history is woven in with the story of Tom Paulding's search for buried treasure. Tom Paulding lived above Central Park in a house on the Hudson built by his great-grandfather. It is in looking over this ancestor's papers that he obtains a clue to the lost money. With a couple of his school friends he has an exciting hunt for the treasure, only to discover on finding it that the 'golden guineas' are worthless counterfeits"—Annual American catalogue.

2286. ——————. *Vignettes of Manhattan.* **New York: Harper, 1894. viii, 180p.**

Each of the twelve pieces in this collection has "a little story in which fictitious characters figure [although] they are set in real scenes from contemporaneous New York life." E.g., the short story 'Before the break of day' has the Bowery as its locale and a heroine named Maggie who is hardly a copy of Crane's tragic character (of whom Matthews was well aware); Matthew's Maggie is ambitious, determined to participate in the American dream of eventual riches. Contents: In the little church down the street.—The twenty-ninth of February.—At a private view.—Spring in a side street.—A Decoration-Day revery.—In search of local color.—Before the break of day.—A mid-summer midnight.—A vista in Central Park...—The speech of the evening.—A Thanksgiving Day dinner.—In the midst of life.

2287. ——————. *Vistas of New York.* **New York: Harper, 1912. 242p.**

"A dozen little stories and sketches, snapshots or flashlights of one or another of the shifting aspects of this huge and sprawling metropolis of ours." Contents: A young man from the country.—On the steps of the city hall.—'Sisters under their skins'.—Under an April sky.—An idyl of Central Park.—In a hansom.—The frog that played the trombone.—On an errand of mercy.—In a bob-tail car.—In the small house.—Her letter to his second wife.—The shortest day of the year.

2288. **Matthews, Patricia, 1927- .** *Gambler in love.* **New York: Bantam Books, 1984. 308p.**

The bustling Erie Canal provides Catherine ('Cat') Carnahan and her father with an adequate living; they carry freight on their boat to various destinations in Upstate New York. When the gambler Morgan Kane is mugged by robbers, Cat comes to his rescue—Morgan has given up the gambler's life. He joins the Carnahans, taking on his share of the work, and he and Cat become lovers. The crooked Simon Maphis seeks revenge after Cat turns down his marriage proposal; Morgan and Cat have a lovers' quarrel, providing Simon with an opportunity to advance his nefarious plans.

2289. **Maxwell, Maria.** *Ernest Gray*; or, *The sins of society.* **A story of New York life. With six illus. by M'Lenan. New York: T.W. Strong, 1855. 335p.**

Ernest Gray, unable to find work, is driven to theft to provide food for his wife, Jane, and their child, Steve. Caught and sentenced he endures callous treatment from the prison guards at Sing Sing. After Mrs. Gray's death, the Clements, father and son (Robert) who have taken responsibility for earlier troubles Gray had with the law, bring Steve into their household. Ernest, released from prison, is killed while fighting robbers who have broken into the Clements' home. The adult Steve (or Stephen) Gray has a brilliant career in the practice of law. Robert Clements devotes himself to the reformation of released convicts. To the author an uncaring society (with some exceptions) is the real culprit for the inability of Ernest Gray and poor people and petty felons like him to cope with their circumstances.

2290. **Maxxe, Robert.** *Arcade.* **Garden City, N.Y.: Doubleday, 1984. 332p.**

Carrie Foster, a widow with two children—Nick, 12, and Emily, 7—runs a gourmet food shop in a quiet Long Island resort town. A video arcade opens down the street and Nick spends a lot of time there. When one of the untalented video game players is drowned and the tragedy is termed a suicide, Carrie and her boyfriend Lon Evans, start investigating. Carrie is convinced that some inhuman force is programming the children. She and Lon kidnap one of the machines; Lon finds super-sophisticated signs of 'bio-chips' and a means of feeding intelligence into the machine. But he is not certain that there is anything inherently sinister in this.

2291. **Mayer, Nathan, 1838-1912.** *Differences*; a novel. **Cincinnati: Bloch, 1867. 462p.**

The first portion of the story takes place in Tennessee. Louis Welland, a German-Jewish political refugee, falls in love with Antonia Goldman. Hazelton (or Hassel), an enemy of Welland of long standing, spreads a rumor that Welland is an abolitionist. Welland flees to New York City (escaping a lynch mob) and stays at the Fifth Avenue home of the Reichenaus. The Goldman's son, Charles, is also in New York, pursuing a love affair with Emma Reichenau, a Christian. There are misunderstandings between the quartet of lovers, Welland and Antonia, Charles and Emma, and it is only after the end of the Civil War (in which Welland joins the Union Army and Charles the Confederates) that the romantic tangle is corrected. "A significant strain in the novel is the disdainful description of the club life and the attitudes of and toward Jewish nouveaux riches in New York. These vulgar rich are intended to stand in sharp contrast to the aristocratic Goldmans and Welland, as well as to the liberal non-Jewish Reichenaus"—Harap, L. *The image of the Jew in American literature.*

2292. **Maynard, Cora.** *The letter and the spirit.* **New York: F.A. Stokes, 1898. 330p.**
"The misery that lurks under silks and jewels, and the heavy hearts that attend exhibitions, galleries and festivities in fashionable [but hollow] New York society are uncovered in this story of modern married life of wholly unsympathetic natures"—Annual American catalogue. One of the chief characters in the novel, Walter Durant, discovers too late that he had unthinkingly and impulsively married a cold, zealously religious creature. He realizes the woman he should have wed has been taken by his associate, Ned Worthington.

2293. ————. *Some modern heretics*; **a novel. Boston: Roberts Bros., 1896. 382p.**
"Winfred Grey, novelist and dramatist and somewhat of an anarchist, in other people's opinion, is made acquainted by accident in Central Park with Vida Radcliffe, the beautiful daughter of a New York millionaire. Grey has mortally offended Mr. Radcliffe by expressing his opinion about the rich who acquire wealth at the expense of the health and morals of the poor, and Radcliffe has sworn to be revenged upon him. This revenge, Grey and Vida's love, a strike, a panic in a theater, some broad views of capital and labor, and some broader ones relative to individual responsibility, are among the contents of this story"—Annual American catalogue.

2294. **Maynard, Lawrence M.** *The pig is fat.* **New York: Farrar & Rinehart, 1930. 278p.**
"The evil effects of Prohibition is … [the] theme in this novel of post-Volstead days. The story opens with New York City's last mad celebration the night before the dry law went into effect. Following this, it traces the course of converting former saloons into speakeasies, the growing graft and corruption of the bootleg racket, and its effect upon August Wagner, old-time saloon keeper, and his young son Benny. Benny becomes a tool in the hands of the

corrupt alderman's son Chick, and ends a dope fiend in spite of all of Louise Warren's efforts to save him"—Book review digest.

Mc., J. *The witch-woman's revenge* ... **See item #3722.**

2294a. McCafferty, Jane, 1960- . *One heart*; **a novel. New York: Harper Collins, 1999. 304p.**

The 40-ish sisters, Gladys and Ivy, are employed as cooks at an Upstate New York school and summer camp. They have lived uneasily together after Gladys' husband James left her following the accidental drowning of their 3-year-old daughter and the death of James' son in Vietnam. Gladys' recovery from these strains is brought about by her 'adoption' of Raelene, a lonely girl from Philadelphia. In another twist, Gladys' former husband becomes Ivy's lover.

2295. McCahery, James R. *Grave undertaking*. **New York: Knightsbridge Pub. Co., 1990. 316p.**

"[The] seventy-one-year-old widow [ex-radio actress Lavina London] likes to think well of people, but she is nevertheless highly skilled at sniffing out their guiltiest secrets. The sleepy town of 'Boulder', nestled in the Catskills, seems to have plenty of secrets. Lavina is on the scene when funeral director Leo Frame is found murdered in his most expensive display casket, and she continues to be where the action is as the investigation of Sheriff Tod Arthur progresses. Other business associates of Frame ... join Leo's nearest and dearest as the major suspects. Lavina, sometimes in the guise of a gullible customer, cross-examines them all. She learns more than she ever wanted to know about burial crypts before she catches the murderer"—Wilson library bulletin.

2296. McCall, Dan, 1940- . *Triphammer*. **New York: Atlantic Monthly Press, 1990. 237p.**

The author's protagonist is an Irish-American policeman in Ithaca, New York named Triphammer who narrates his own experiences as he goes about dealing officially with the unstable, disturbed human beings that cross his path. Triphammer is a good, warmhearted man and tries to interact with his son while cultivating a romantic relationship with a young woman, a Jewish academician. He thinks much about the nature of his job as a public guardian and his (unfortunate?) use of liquor as a crutch.

2297. McCardell, Roy Larcom, b. 1870. *Jimmy Jones*; **the autobiography of an office boy. Boston: Dana Estes, 1907. vii, 310p.**

Priding himself on his toughness and versatility Jimmy Jones, a New Yorker in the 'know', describes in his own peculiar Bowery language the story of his young life. Jimmy's chief drawback is his inclination to associate with various undesirable characters. An uncle tries with little success to make a businessman of Jimmy, but the latter pines for the sea and actually begins studying for possible appointment to the U.S. Naval Academy. His old companions get in the way, however, and Jimmy simply runs away from any further study.

2298. ————. *Conversations of a chorus girl.* **Illustrated by Gene Carr. New York: Street & Smith, 1903. 184p.**

Lulu Lorimer, peroxide blonde chorus girl, pours out her reminiscences, sad and blissful, in New York or on the road, to the drama editor of one of the metropolis's papers. At the front of the book is a month-by-month calendar in which Lulu records her theatrical year. Along the way she describes the New York types with whom she comes in close contact; Dopey McKnight, Louis Zinsheimer, Mama Amy de Branscombe, et al.

2299. ————. *The wage slaves of New York.* **Illustrated by H.T. Smith. New York: G.W. Dillingham, 1899. 196p.**

"A ridiculous novel with no redeeming feature except for the social historian. The strikers ask for a share of the profits in a New York silk mill and help the real but defrauded owner of the mill, Arthur Harrison, to regain his inheritance. He reorganizes the factory as a 'socialistic experiment' and all is sweetness and light"—Blake, F.M. *The strike in the American novel.*

2300. **McCloy, Helen, 1904-1993.** *The deadly truth.* **New York: Morrow, 1941. 278p.**

"Claudia Bethune, practical joker, who will do anything for a laugh, puts scopolamine in the cocktails before a dinner party which is being given at her estate on Long Island. The truth serum works too well, her guests tell all, and Mrs. Bethune gets choked with her own emerald necklace. [There are] five charming suspects in this swift, witty story"—New Yorker.

2301. ————. *Mr. Splitfoot.* **New York: Dodd, Mead, 1968. 211p.**

Dr. Basil Willing, a forensic psychiatrist, is accompanied by his wife as he leaves the city for a skiing vacation in the Hudson River Valley. A blizzard and the breakdown of his car force the two to take shelter in the house of a novelist. A playful poltergeist enters the home; then a vengeful spirit is responsible for a murder that occurs in a room the host claims is haunted.

2302. ————. *Panic.* **New York: Morrow, 1944. 217p.**

Following her uncle's death from what seems to be a heart attack, Alison Tracy treks to the lonely Adirondack cabin where it happened. She finds a message in cipher on her uncle's bed that may hold the key to unanswered questions. Breaking the code is no easy task, but Alison does it—and with it the killing ends.

2303. **McCornick, Joanna.** *By Hudson's banks*; a novel. **By Joanna [pseud.]. San Francisco: Bancroft Co., 1889. 392p.**

'Summerville', where a major proportion of the novel takes place, is "a quiet little home in a sparsely populated region in the suburbs of our metropolis"

[New York City]. Angelica Franklin, her father David and her cousin Sarah Current reside there. Karl Kingswell, a close friend, opens a law office in New York in partnership with Edmund Grandfield. Both are frequent visitors at Summerville. Karl falls in love with Lucy Floyd, a flighty girl with high social aspirations. Married in the village of 'Ferryfoot' they lease an apartment in New York. Grandfield asks for Angelica's hand; his status as a divorced man sways her toward rejection. With Grandfield in Europe Karl mismanages the law practice. The Franklins of Summerville are faced with heavy debts, but the receipt and application by Sarah Current of funds long denied her pull them through. Grandfield returns to New York, reorganizes the law practice, and is given Angelica's consent to marriage now that the woman he divorced has died. Karl's financial situation improves, yet Lucy, much of her beauty gone, wallows in disappointment over her relatively low position on the social scale.

McCoy, Madeleine. See under her pseudonym: Mace, Merlda.

2304. **McCray, Florinc Thayer.** *Environment*; **a story of modern society. New York: Funk & Wagnalls, 1887. 404p.**

Early scenes of the novel take place in 'Stoneham', Connecticut—introduced are the Mertons, Raymond and his wife Mary, their daughter Adaline, her suitor Robert Trevor, and Dr. Frank Eustace. The major locale however is New York City, its 'fashionable' society and its publishing scene. The merchant Harry Meredith's second wife, Florence (Sterling) seems rather fragile but is on excellent terms with her stepdaughter Beatrice. When Harry goes to China on business, Florence, bereft of the soothing presence of her husband, plunges impetuously into the social whirl of the city. Her earlier addiction to alcohol returns as her health problems mount (e.g., a bout with pneumonia, a fractured knee). Beatrice tries to hold a crumbling household together, abetted by a new attending physician, Dr. Frank Eustace. Florence's recovery is assured by Harry's return. Dr. Eustace and Beatrice find one another. As for Adaline Merton—recently employed by the publisher Thomas Macey after consultation with him concerning her deceased father's book on the dyeing of textiles—she no longer favors Robert Trevor, but finds true love in the arms of her employer.

2305. **McCulloch, James Edward, b. 1873.** *The mystery of love*; **a narrative of settlement life. New York, Chicago: Revell, [c1910]. 272p.**

A novel about two dedicated women who established themselves in New York's 'Hell's Acre' and gave freely of their love and energy to better the lives of their slum-dwelling neighbors. Their experiences in a city mission encapsulated joy and despair, laughter and tragedy.

2306. **McCulloch, Robert W., 1867 or 8-1946.** *Me and thee.* **New York, Boston: Lothrop, 1937. 257p.**

On the verge of a marriage that she felt offered little chance of happiness Kate Harmon sought refuge in the Shaker colony at Mount Lebanon, New York. But even in that peaceful community the troubled past seemed to be catching up with her. However she quietly fought back and ultimately came upon a brighter future.

2307. McCullough, David Willis, 1937- . *Think on death*; **a Hudson Valley mystery. New York: Viking Press, 1990. 257p.**

In this story the town of 'Smyrna' is in the Catskills (there is a village in Chenango County, N.Y. with that name). 'Smyrna', a utopian community in the 19th century, is now the center of a successful manufactory. Ziza Todd, a Presbyterian minister, is living in the town while she works on her graduate thesis. When Aunt Nan Quick dies—she of the family that had been so instrumental in Smyrna's history—many people come from afar to her funeral. Just before the ceremony Ziza finds a skeleton in Aunt Nan's closet, the remains of a long vanished Quick heir who left a widow, Naomi, a New York copy editor. Among those who join forces to seek answers to the strange happenings in Smyrna are Naomi, Ziza, police detective Nick Story, Hagadorn Mills, official historian of Smyrna, and Melody Horn, a young business school graduate, an 'outsider' who has been appointed head of the manufacturing firm.

2308. McCutcheon, George Barr, 1866-1928. *The alternative.* **With illus. by Harrison Fisher and decorations by Theodore B. Hapgood. New York: Dodd, Mead, 1909.**

Van Pycke Sr. and Van Pycke Jr. do not necessarily agree on everything, although both are New York men-about-town. The father has gone through the Van Pycke fortune and the only hope for recouping adequate funds for his lifestyle is marrying his son off to a wealthy widow. The son dislikes the idea and chooses his own alternative, entry into a business career. The first of his family to really knuckle down to hard work Junior also meets a charming woman who will make a splendid helpmate. Van Pycke Sr. continues on his careless path resentful of his son's deviation from the 'gentlemanly' (though feckless) Van Pycke ways.

2309. ————. *Blades.* **New York: Dodd, Mead, 1928. 344p.**

Jasper Elias Bernadotte (or Barnaby the Barnacle) Blades is a much-in-demand New York dandy and former athlete who flits from job to job. Then an uncle he has never met leaves Barnaby a piece of holdings in a rather austere colony on the Canadian border. To acquire the inheritance Barnaby must go to the sectarian settlement and undergo a three months' trial period. Perhaps surprisingly Barnaby accepts the conditions, ends his relationship with an alluring married woman, leaves New York and starts on the road to a new way of life where religion and romance are in the mix.

2310. ————. *Brewster's millions,* **by Richard Greaves [pseud.]. Chicago: H.S.**

Stone, 1903. 325p.

The young New Yorker, Montgomery Brewster, is faced with a dilemma. In order to inherit seven million dollars from a little known uncle, he must spend the million dollars he received from his late grandfather within one year, leaving himself completely broke—the uncle and the grandfather despised one another. As he starts throwing money about, his girlfriend questions his suitability as her fiancé and his friends, unaware of the conditions Monty is trying to fulfill, endeavor to temper his wild spending sprees. To be sure Monty succeeds in getting rid of that million in the nick of time and his explanations are accepted by his bewildered acquaintances.

2311. ————. *The city of masks*. **With illus. by May Wilson Preston. New York: Dodd, Mead, 1918. 314p.**

"Thanks to the impecunious or otherwise embarrassed aristocrat of Europe, desiring to live for a time in retirement, New York is a paradise, is the suggestion of this novel. Here various and sundry lords and dukes and countesses, of as many different lands, live quietly, if not shabbily, assembling once a week at the home of one of their number, a marchioness, to shuffle off their disguises and treat one another with the respect due their stations. The heroine of the tale is Lady Jane Thorne (Miss Easdale, the governess) and the hero is Lord Eric Temple (Thomas Trotter, the chauffeur). In the end, which comes in July 1914, these two, their temporary difficulties dissolved, are allowed to return to their English home. An amusing situation is created by the presence in the group of Mr. Cricklewick, an Englishman with the soul of a butler, who has amassed great wealth in America and who in the presence of these blue blooded aristocrats, is impelled to act the part of a butler"—Book review digest.

2312. ————. *Cowardice Court*. **With illus. by Harrison Fisher and decorations by Theodore B. Hapgood. New York: Dodd, Mead, 1906. 140p.**

Shaw, a young American, owns a home and land in the Adirondacks adjoining that of Lord and Lady Hazelhurst. A feud springs up between Shaw and the Hazelhursts when the former refuses to sell 500 acres of Adirondack woodland to the acquisitive latter. Lady Penelope Baslehurst begins dickering with Shaw to Lady Hazelhurst's dismay; the seeds of love are sown between Penelope and Shaw. A thunderstorm, a haunted house, some unscheduled shootings and intrusions, etc., occur before things are settled—Penelope emerges as the winner.

2313. ————. *The hollow of her hand*. **With illus. by A.I. Keller. New York: Dodd, Mead, 1912. 422p.**

"It is a story of modern New York built about a strikingly unusual situation. Mrs. Challis Wrandall has been to the roadhouse outside the city to identify her husband's dead body; she is driving her car home late on a stormy night when she picks up in the road the woman who did the murder—the girl who had accompanied her husband to the lonely inn and whom the whole country is seeking. She takes the girl home, protects her, befriends her and keeps her secret. Between Sara Wrandall and her husband's family there is an ancient enmity born of their scorn for her inferior birth. Events work themselves out until she is forced to reveal to them the truth about their son's death and his previous [infamous] way of life"—Book review digest.

2314. ————. *Shot with crimson*. **With illus. by F.R. Gruger. New York: Dodd, Mead, 1918. 161p.**

McCutcheon's 'patriotic contribution' to America's participation in the First World War takes the form of a thriller dealing with pro-German activities in New York City. Mrs. Carstairs, the wife of a distinguished New Yorker, and much appreciated in her own right, extends her sympathies to the German war effort. After an explosion at a munitions factory and the leakage of vital official data, a U.S. Army captain's investigations point to the involvement of Mrs. Carstairs with German spies and sympathizers.

2315. ————. *What's-His-Name*. **With illus. by Harrison Fisher. New York: Dodd, Mead, 1911. 243p.**

"What's-His-Name" is the negative, invertebrate, self-effacing husband of a successful New York comedienne—alluded to as Miss Nellie Duluth's husband, or more often, as Mr. What's-His-Name. Unable to meet a single situation in life in a manly, courageous manner, with a personality entirely effaced by that of his dazzling wife, he retires to a suburb and plays successfully, be it said, the role of nursemaid to his five-year-old daughter. The story records his failures and his wife's successes; finally, her failure and the dawn of his little day that he had earned through years of patient self-obliteration"—Book review digest.

McDermott, William A., 1863-1913. See under his pseudonym: Lecky, Walter.

2316. **McDonald, Laetitia, b. 1890.** *Silver platter*. **New York: Farrar & Rinehart, 1934. 370p.**

"Victoria Rupp, daughter of a sturdy, sensible manufacturer from Louisville, Married Philip Pyne, a charming but ineffectual member of an old Long Island family. For two years she was happy in playing the role of young society matron. Then her father died, and with his death went much of her sense of security. The realization of her love for her father's lawyer, Carter Logan, and the aftermath of the 1929 crash, reawakened Victoria's old independence, and she decided upon a courageous course"—Book review digest.

2317. **McEvoy, Joseph Patrick, 1895-1958.** *Simon and Schuster present Showgirl*. **New York: Simon-Schuster, 1928. 215p.**

"This scrapbook of letters, telegrams, dialogues and newspaper clippings gives us the musical comedy story of [such New York characters as] Dixie

Dugan, the golden-hearted, gingery-tongued, fast-stepping female hooker; Danny Kerrigan, greeting card salesman; Alvarez Romano, 'sun-kissed tango dancer from the coffee belt'; Jimmy Doyle, ghost writer on the Evening Tabloid"—New Republic.

2318. **McGee, Dorothy Horton.** *Sally Townsend, patriot.* **New York: Dodd, Mead, 1952. 282p.**

Fictionalized account of the daring actions during the American Revolution of Sarah Townsend, a Long Island girl, who (with the help of her brother) collected useful information for the American rebels from British officers posted at Oyster Bay.

2319. **McGhee, Alison, 1960- .** *Rainlight.* **Watsonville, Calif.: Papier-Mâché Press, 1998. 177p.**

The Williams family lives in a village that squats in the shadow of the Adirondacks. It is traumatized when loving father Starr is killed while pulling a slow-witted boy from the track of an oncoming truck. Particularly affected is Starr's daughter, Mallie, a 9-year-old, who tires in a variety of ways to make her deceased father a 'living' presence for herself and her younger brother.

2320. **McGivern, William Peter, 1922-1982.** *Savage streets.* **New York: Dodd, Mead, 1961. 277p.**

'Riverdale', a Long Island suburb is divided: Faircrest is upper middle-class, 'respectable'; Hayrack houses blue-collar wage earners and some tough, gang-oriented youths. The latter have begun harassing and extorting money from Faircrest boys. Faircrest parents respond by notifying the police and then confronting the 'delinquents' when the law does little. The encounters get uglier, until a rape and an unintentional killing bring things to a critical juncture. Certain elements in Faircrest try to dodge any responsibility for what has happened, but others prepare to go to the police with a true account of the tragedies.

2321. **McGonigle, Thomas, 1944- .** *Going to Patchogue.* **Elmwood Park, Ill.: Dalkey Archive Press, 1992. 212p.**

This quasi-fictional stream-of-consciousness work takes a rancorous Irish-American writer (Tom McGonigle himself), age 40, back to the scenes of his youth in the village of Patchogue, Long Island. There while walking around the town he reflects on the common concerns of life, his travels, he drinks and converses with old acquaintances, etc. and gives the reader a potpourri of Patchogue history. When he returns via the Long Island Railroad to his New York apartment he briefly contemplates suicide, but then decides 'to wait another year'.

McGrady, Mike, 1933- , joint author. *Establishment of innocence.* **See Item #115.**

2322. McGurk, Slater, pseud. *The big dig.* **New York: Macmillan, 1968. 179p.**

The setting of this detective novel is the eastern end of Long Island. It is there that the master criminal, Doc Krilly, is concocting plans for a major bank heist. Police Sergeant Tip O'Connor, a well-read and pleasant fellow, is well aware of the pretty young schoolteacher, Anna Rubin; she has insatiable curiosity about the people who live nearby.

McHugh, Augustin, 1877-1928, joint author. *Office 666.* **See Item #755.**

2323. McIntosh, Maria Jane, 1803-1878. *The cousins*; **a tale of early life. By the author of** *Conquest* **and** *self-conquest*; *Praise and principle*; **etc. New York: Harper, 1845. 205p.**

A sentimental story whose purpose is to inculcate virtue in its young readers. Its two 'heroines' are Mary Mowbray and Lucy Lovett—the former a girl from Georgia sent by her widower father to the Lovett home in New York City for formal education; the latter, Mary's cousin, is a rather vain and selfish girl whose early contacts with Mary are not of a friendly nature. Both attend Miss Butler's School in the city with Mary frequently outshining Lucy in general studies. A visit to the countryside of Upstate New York has an unfortunate consequence—Lucy falls into a bog, is taken ill and is forced to rely on crutches when the family returns to New York City. Meeting with an older, crippled but patient, kindly woman, Eliza Bennett, Lucy gradually sheds her bitterness and absorbs the lessons of forgiveness and endurance. At the story's end Lucy accompanies Mary to the Mowbray home in Georgia where the warmer climate may speed Lucy's recovery.

2324. ————. *Two lives*; **or,** *To seem and to be.* **New York: D. Appleton, 1846. 318p.**

When Grace Elliott's widower father dies, she and her cousin Isabel Duncan, an orphan, are packed off to New York City and a rich uncle, where they are to receive their education and enter society. The two young women are opposites; Grace, self-centered yet needing attention; Isabel, steady and independent but willing to aid Grace, even by rejecting the Reverend Falconer's offer of marriage because she thinks Grace is in love with him. Grace is soon engaged to a man who breaks their engagement, whereupon she marries a rather worthless French marquis; he abandons Grace in Paris. Isabel meanwhile supports her Uncle Elliott, now penniless. She welcomes the forlorn Grace into her New York City quarters. Eventually Isabel finds happiness with the faithful Rev. Falconer.

2325. McIntyre, John Thomas, 1871-1951. *Ashton-Kirk, investigator.* **Illus. by Ralph L. Boyer, Philadelphia: Penn Pub. Co., 1910. 336p.**

The author's protagonist is another of a multiplying fictional character type—the wealthy New Yorker who has an affinity for unriddling mysteries. Ashton-Kirk cannot, of course, ignore the plea of a beautiful girl to free her lover from the clutches of a Mr. Hume. When Hume is murdered the girl's fiancé is a prime suspect, and Ashton-Kirk has to separate the many threads that intertwine the homicide.

2326. ————. *In the dead of night.* **With illus. by Frances Rogers. Philadelphia: Lippincott, 1908. 282p.**

From the moment the hero comes at night into New York City he is immersed in a mystery in which a beautiful young woman he comes to admire figures. He is skillful enough to fend off leading questions about his involvement and uses his own 'stock in trade' to untangle the trickier elements of the puzzle that at one point finds him taking on the identity of another man.

2327. ————. *The museum murder.* **Garden City, N.Y.: Published for the Crime Club by Doubleday Doran, 1929. 307p.**

When the curator (Mr. Custis) of the John Gregory Museum, Murray Hill, New York, is found stabbed to death, investigator Duddington Chalmers tries to protect Mona Rogers, Custis' secretary, and Billy Gregory, an artist, both of whom seem to be hiding some very pertinent data. The two young people are best served by Duddington's solution of the homicide.

2328. ————. *"Slag."* **New York: Scribner, 1927. 249p.**

"A cross-section of the New York City slums—breeding place of malcontent and crime. In a poolroom rendezvous Groloch is planning a burglary with Needle and Rush. They need five dollars for dynamite. Innocent of their purpose Cochak the Slav supplies it. He is a consumptive, wasted with disease and on fire with muddled socialistic ideas. Minnie Karsh is Groloch's girl. Too dumb to be of use to him she moons about on the night of the burglary, until she hears a police whistle and the pop of guns, and knows that the attempt has been a failure. She finds the three burglars in a loft, hiding from the police. Groloch is wounded. Cochak joins them, and still in the dark as to the real issue, goes berserk at the arrival of the police and dies"—Book review digest.

2329. **McKay, Claude, 1890-1948.** *Home to Harlem.* **New York: Harper, 1928. 340p.**

McKay's hero, Jake Brown, following World War I and a sojourn in Europe, comes back to Harlem; a Harlem that is not a paradise but nevertheless has thus far insulated itself from false white values. And so Jake's paean: "Oh to be in Harlem again after two years away. The deep-dyed color, the thickness, the closeness of it. The noises of it. The sugared laughter. The honey-talk on the streets. And all night long, ragtime and 'blues' playing somewhere, dancing somewhere! Oh the contagious fever of Harlem" (p. 15). Jake moves happily through Harlem, connects with a generous prostitute his first night there; she leaves and Jake searches for her. In the central portion of the novel Jake takes a job as a railroad porter; the rather plotless story concludes with Jake once again back in Harlem which is now hardly Edenic, but a crowded, even somewhat dangerous place outflanked by pushy white society.

2330. McKean, Thomas, 1869-1942. *The master influence*; a novel. **With illus. in color by Will Grefé. Philadelphia: Lippincott, 1908. 308p.**

Most of the scenes in the novel are laid in New York City with a brief interlude at the end in Sicily. The heroine is bored by the 'smart set' to which she belongs and looks for more satisfying fulfillment. A job in a hospital gives her some satisfaction; however, she strongly suspects that her temperament precludes a romantic attachment. That is disproved when a masterful young politician enters her life and becomes her 'master influence'.

2331. ————. *The mercy of fate.* **New York: Wessels & Bissell Co., 1910. 366p.**

"Fate is indeed merciful to this man who makes of himself a millionaire by dogged persistence, rises socially [in New York society] and evolves a character which men admire, but who, having sinned in his youth to the undoing of his first love, comes back from the Klondike and takes a frivolous young actress for his mistress. Then after he has outgrown her and thrown her off, he marries a girl who loves him so much she forgives him all. An English edition of this novel has been issued under the title 'The punishment' in the last chapter of which the hero falls dead on learning that the girl he is to marry is his own daughter. Up to that critical point the stories seem to be identical"—Book review digest.

2332. McKenna, Edward L. *Hardware.* **New York: McBride, 1929. 287p.**

"James [Cronin] begat Michael and Michael begat Neil and Frank; and this is the story of their lives and their connection with politics and the liquor trade. The chapters narrating the rise of Michael [Cronin] from South Brooklyn saloon-keeper to district political boss are the best in the book and constitute an excellent picture of the hard-boiled machine politician who is also an honest man"—Outlook.

2333. McKnight, Carolyn. *The house in the shadows.* **New York: St. Martin's Press, 1979. 197p.**

The Cinderella motif is conspicuous in this story of the orphan Amanda Wallace who is given shelter by her Uncle Ezra at Nethercliffe in the Catskills. Amanda is forced into a servant's role and is treated shabbily by Ezra's daughters, her cousins. Sympathetic neighbors—the secretive Micah Van Deusen and the elderly artist Blaisdale Spain—provide Amanda with friendship; she eventually escapes the Nethercliffe household and takes off her rags for resplendent dress. Two young women are murdered, several damning enigmas from Ezra's past are uncovered, Amanda faces down his daughters, and she has a frightening confrontation with the murderer. The novel is laid in the 1830s and the atmosphere of the Hudson Valley and adjoining regions is well conceived.

2334. McLaurin, Kate L. *The least resistance.* **New York: Doran, 1916. 374p.**

"Evelyn Lane of this story was a woman who was out of place on the stage. A cottage with a garden would have been the right setting for her and a husband

and a baby or two her fitting preoccupations. But an early and romantic marriage with a handsome actor attached her irrevocably to theatrical life, for after her separation from him she continued to act because it was the one thing she knew how to do. In a half dozen or so years she runs the whole gamut of theatrical experiences—stock work, vaudeville, long periods of unemployment, one-night stands and finally Broadway success, won in the way which is said to be open to young beautiful girls of elastic virtue. The path of least resistance seemed to be the inevitable one, even at the end when she lays down her weary body and slips away out of the world, she seems to be following it"—Book review digest.

2335. McMahon, John Robert, b. 1875. *Toilers and idlers*; a novel. New York: Wilshire Book Co., 1907. 195p.

Using an alias a young foundry owner takes a job in his New York plant in order to study the conditions under which his workers complete their tasks. When he draws up plans to improve the situation, he finds it impossible to implement them because of obstacles thrown in their way. Beyond his business concerns he is fortunate in his relations with two young women from whom he learns much about human and ethical behavior.

2336. McMahon, Thomas Patrick. *The Hubschmann effect*. New York: Simon & Schuster, 1973. 167p.

"What do a chronic runaway boy, the three children brutalized by six others, the mother who drowns her youngster, and another father who turns on his own, all have in common? The oral contraceptive drug, which was tested on a small scale in a suburban community [some miles from New York]? Or perhaps the ex-Dachau Dr. Hubschmann who takes his own life? A grand jury investigation, which proceeds by testimony here, refusal to talk, tapes, statements, speculations, will mobilize your attention and (mis)direct it, occasionally, while leaving a few afterthoughts"—Kirkus review.

2337. McMorrow, Thomas, b. 1886. *The sinister history of Ambrose Hinkle*. New York: Sears, 1929. 311p.

New Yorker Ambrose Hinkle ('Little Amby') started out as a street-wise kid, was apprenticed to a lawyer, went through a frustrated love affair, made a specialty of keeping sleazy characters out of the law's clutches and innocent parties in, but eventually lost much of his prosperity; he then turned to thoughts of self-reform. The novel contains humorous touches.

2338. McNally, Clare. *Addison House*. New York: Avon Books, 1988. 298p.

Social worker Doreen Addison has taken an old, worn Victorian mansion in Upstate New York and has turned it into a shelter for 'throw-away' children, youngsters who have been abandoned by family and society. Whatever Doreen's good intentions, the story lapses into the stereotypical haunted house routine with the evil spirits and other ghostly elements that infest the mansion creating mischief and injuries for the children and the workmen repairing the house.

2339. McNaughton, John Hugh. 1829-1891. *Onnalinda*; **a romance. New York: G. P. Putnam, 1884. 250p.**

The background of this narrative poem is the battle in 1687 near Irondequoit Bay fought between the Seneca Indians and the punitive forces of the Marquis of Denonville, Governor of New France. Onnalinda is a Seneca maiden whose love story is the centerpiece of the narrative.

2340. McPherson, James Lowell, 1921. *Goodbye Rosie.* **New York, Knopf, 1965. 372p.**

Harvey Swithin Dark (or d'Art) is a fundraiser for 'Thebes University', an Upstate New York institution located on a former Army base. He is the medium through which a large endowment is made in honor of his maternal grandfather by a former opponent. Harvey is enthralled by Margaret, the illegitimate daughter of the grandfather, but she marries Janko, Harvey's friend from Europe, a 'professional' student. Naomi, an assistant professor at the university, makes no secret of her passionate interest in Harvey. It is quite understandable that Harvey finally has an emotional breakdown.

McPherson, Mrs. M.E. See under her pseudonym: Hartshorn, Nancy.

McQuade, Ann Aikman, 1928- . See: Aikman, Ann, 1928- .

2341. McRoyd, Allan. *Death in costume.* **New York: Greystone Press, 1940. 282p.**

"Inspector Franklin Grady and [his] long suffering assistant track [the] killer of ex-vaudevillians from [the] Broadway stage to [a] Long Island palace"— Saturday review of literature. "Why was Ms. Lucia Drew, wife of a Long Island millionaire, strangled in the dressing room at the Troy Theater, where she was about to substitute for Iris Ryder in an old vaudeville act? Was the killer after Lucia or Iris? … Inspector Franklin Grady, New York Homicide Squad, … proceeds to question husbands, former husbands and sundry about past and present. … McRoyd offers plenty of contrast in social strata, exhibits ranging from Christian Van Nuys of the North Shore set, to Flip Ryder, a former tumbler now raising dogs in 'Riverhead' [Long Island]. … Grady's routine is all right with the jasmine perfume, the anonymous letter and the scrap of paper reading "ENT APP"—New York herald tribune books.

2342. McVickar, Henry Goelet. *The purple light of love.* **New York: Appleton, 1894. 176p.**

"The purple light of love comes into the life of John Edgar when he has reached fame and fortune as a successful railroad lawyer. The woman is a calculating widow and the man dies of a broken heart. Fashionable New York and Newport circles, clubs and decks of yachts are made the background of an earnest, honest man's life tragedy"—Annual American catalogue.

2343. **Mead, Shepherd, 1914- . *"Dudley, there is no tomorrow!" "Then how about this afternoon?"* A novel. New York: Simon Schuster, 1963. 288p.**

"Dudley Bray is a light-headed and light-hearted hero who has a habit of tripping gaily into catastrophe. He has arrived in 'Queensport', on the North Shore of Long Island, in order to protect his ex-wife Gloria, whose second husband, Tom, has just driven his Cadillac into the Sound and been drowned. … In his six crowded days on Long Island Dudley becomes a self-appointed private eye, discovering the true circumstances of Tom's death and saving the railroad station for his ex-wife's use. Most of all, he and Gloria discover that they may not be divorced until death do them part"—Atlantic monthly.

2344. **Meadowcroft, Enid La Monte, 1898-1966. *Along the Erie towpath.* Illus. by Ninon MacKnight. New York: T.Y. Crowell, 1940. 227p.**

A novel for juveniles. "David Burns, one of six orphaned youngsters, runs away from his Aunt Polly to take a canal job on the Flying Cloud at thirty-five cents a trip; later he works for the book boat aptly named 'Encyclopedia'; and finally is reunited with his brothers and sisters in Buffalo, where the family watches DeWitt Clinton and the Seneca Chief begin the celebration marking the opening of the Erie Canal in 1825"—Wyld, L.D. The Erie Canal and the novel (In: *Upstate literature.* Syracuse University Press, 1985).

2345. **————.*We were there at the opening of the Erie Canal.* Historical consultant: Sylvester Vigilante. Illus. by Gerald McCann. New York: Grossett & Dunlap, 1958. 182p.**

The Erie Canal is in the latter stages of construction when Chris Martin, his sister and two brothers take up quarters in their aunt's home in 'Cannon', New York. Chris is the most adventurous of the four young people; after helping capture an elusive thief, he turns his talents toward completion of the Canal.

2346. **Meaker, Marijane, 1927- . *The girl on the best seller list*; an original Gold Medal novel, by Vin Packer [pseud.]. Greenwich, Conn.: Fawcett Publications, 1960. 174p.**

Another of the 'Peyton Place' or 'Kings Row' species—this time the town with its very personal secrets exposed is 'Cayuta', New York, in the Finger Lakes region, with a population of 12,360—oddly enough there is a real Cayuta, N.Y. (population about 1,000) which is about 12 miles SE of Watkins Glen. Gloria Wealdon has written a best-selling novel (title: Population 12,360) which has shocked the town; her characters are fictional counterparts of the following: Milo, her husband and physical education teacher at the high school (and Cornell graduate); Freddy Fulton, local merchant and Milo's best friend; Fern, Freddy's wife and Gloria's only friend in Cayuta; their daughter Virginia; the psychologist, Dr. Jay Mannerheim; Stanley Secora, hired man of all trades and war hero, et al. It is quite obvious that the hated, vengeful Gloria will get her comeuppance—accidentally or intentionally.

2347. ————. *Hometown.* **Garden City, N.Y.: Doubleday, 1967. 532p.**

A family saga covering the period from World War I to the end of World War II in 'Cayuta', Upstate New York, about 90 miles east of Rochester. Cayuta has endured growing pains and has become rather important as an industrial and transportation center. The Ware family is in the grocery business and the novel dwells on their intergenerational conflicts and extramarital activities. Other people come into the story—Jews, Italians, et al.—and subsidiary plots are developed. American boosterism, among other aspects of small-city American life, is etched with humor and understanding.

2348. **Mearson, Lyon, 1888-1966.** *Footsteps in the dark.* **Front. by George W. Gage. New York: Macaulay, 1927. 319p.**

A mystery story centered in a house in New York that is permeated by an oriental atmosphere. Near the telephone slumps the body of a deaf and dumb man whose niece shared with him the secret of a guilt-ridden past. The arcane 'Seven' had complete control of the deceased, were responsible for his death and were hopeful that his passing would redound to their advantage. The girl's lover completes the cast of characters in a tale laced with supernatural terror and enigmas.

2349. **Meek, Sterner St. Paul. b. 1894.** *Rip, a game protector.* **New York: Knopf, 1952. 266p.**

A story about poaching on public preserves in Upstate New York and enforcement of the wildlife conservation laws. The ranger entrusted with tasks in these areas is helped greatly by Rip, a well-trained dog.

2350. **Meeker, Nellis J.** *Beverly Osgood*; or, *When the great city is awake.* **A novel. By Jane Valentine [pseud.]. New York: G.W. Dillingham, 1900. 335p.**

The story is narrated by Beverly Osgood. On one of his frequent visits to New York he meets Nina Palermo. Her father was of noble Italian ancestry, her mother was an Irishwoman. With death near, Nina's mother places her in the care of Mrs. Lunis, Beverly's landlady. Nina is fired from her job in a department store when she resists the overtures of store manager Roscoe Delano. Nevertheless Roscoe settles Nina in excellent living quarters and she begins to call herself 'Countess Palermo'. A completely unanticipated flow of money from her father's estate releases Nina from any further dependence on Delano's 'generosity'. As Nina expands her social contacts, Bertram Arlington, a friend of Beverly, falls in love with her, to his family's consternation. She is the chief suspect when Roscoe Delano, a guest in her house, is shot to death. One of Delano's abandoned 'conquests' proves to be the murderer. Acquitted, Nina marries Bertram.

2351. **Mehling, Harold.** *Assumption of guilt.* **New York: Carroll & Graf, 1992. 287p.**

The townspeople of an Upstate New York town, 'Hudson Ferry', assume that Laurie Coles is guilty of abusing her young charges at the nursery school in which she teaches. Harry Hull, her defender, is inexperienced in criminal law, but he stays the course and mounts a rather effective case for his client. The author sheds light on all the people most closely involved (and that includes the jury), but it is up to the readers to reason whether Laurie Coles is innocent or guilty.

2352. **Mele, Frank.** *Polpetto*; **a novel. New York: Crown Publishers, 1973. 248p.**
A flat, juiceless chronicle of an Italian immigrant laborer in Rochester, New York in the early 1900s; he partakes of the American dream and has the ambition of seeing his first-born (a son) study medicine.

2353. **Mellett, John Calvin, b. 1888.** *Ink;* **a novel. Indianapolis: Bobbs-Merrill. 1930. 286p.**
"Red-headed Arthur Morton, a born newspaperman, lands in 'Columbia' [a small New York city] in search of a job on a bootlegger's truck. Instead of a job he acquires a newspaper and boldly sets to work, minus cash but with courage and convictions, to deliver the city from municipal corruption. His short but meteoric career is typical of the experiences of an editor in any stagnant town controlled by a few men"—Bookman.

Meloney, Franken, pseud. See: Franken, Rose, 1895-1988.

2354. **Meloney, William Brown, 1905-1971.** *Many are the travelers.* **New York: Appleton-Century-Crofts, 1954. 344p.**
John Milnor, illegitimate son of Matt Tracy, Sr. and Elizabeth Milnor, is named heir to the Tracy estate in 'Haviland', New York (Poughkeepsie is the nearest city of any size) after his half-brother, Matt, Jr. and Matt's wife Alyce had committed suicide. Along with the estate John takes responsibility for the surviving Tracys, many of them females; they had been designated by one individual as 'a mixed-up kettle of fish'. Milnor himself is the narrator of the story. At the novel's conclusion John Milnor is married to Françoise, Alyce's daughter, Matt Tracy, Jr.'s stepdaughter.

2355. ————. *Mooney.* **New York: Appleton-Century-Crofts, 1950. 306p.**
"Tim Mooney was the town undertaker and sold furniture besides in the little New York State town of 'Haviland'. Tim was drunk a good deal of the time, but he was kindly even when drunk. Through Mooney's musings, alcoholic or otherwise, we learn to know the people of Haviland"—Book review digest.

2356. ————. *Rush to the sun.* **New York: Farrar & Rinehart, 1937. 275p.**
A novel with 'Haviland' and the surrounding area in Upstate New York as the setting. The farmer Alf Adams shares his farmhouse with his widowed sister, Jessie, and her 17-year-old daughter, Mary, although Jessie has land of her own that she is leasing. Chris Barret, the hired man, whom Alf despises and distrusts, seduces Mary, impregnating her. With an eye on Jessie's property Chris inveigles Jessie into marriage. When Mary goes into labor, loses her

child and is near death, Jessie senses Chris's responsibility for her daughter's crisis. After Chris forces himself on Jessie in the hayloft, he falls, half-pushed by Jessie, and breaks his neck. Completely drained, Jessie slips away into death herself, while Mary slowly recovers. Alf's ongoing romance with Sylvia Potter, Mary's schoolteacher in Haviland, culminates in their marriage. Together they shelter and comfort Mary.

2357. **Melville, Herman, 1819-1891.** *Pierre*; or, *The ambiguities*. **New York: Harper, 1852. viii, 495p.**

A large portion of the novel takes place near 'Saddle Meadows' (the Berkshire Hills of western Massachusetts in all likelihood), but the most pointed action and the climax occurs in New York City where Pierre Glendinning, residing with his supposed half-sister Isabel in a peculiar tenement known as the Church of the Apostles, disowned by his mother and snubbed by his wealthy boyhood friend, Glen Stanly, loses control of his precarious situation. He becomes sexually involved with Isabel; his former fiancée Lucy Tartan, moves in with the couple, and Stanly and Fred Tartan denounce the once virtuous Pierre. Driven to emotional extremities Pierre kills Stanly and commits suicide with Isabel, after Lucy has expired at his feet.

2358. **Mercer, Charles Edward, 1912-1988.** *There comes a time.* **New York: G.P. Putnam, 1955. 312p.**

"The minister of a fashionable New York church resigned his charge when he was sixty-three and went out to the Finger Lakes region where he was born, in an attempt to regain a living faith. In his efforts to untangle the snarled lives of some of the inhabitants, and in the opening of the long boarded-up church, Adam Brock was able to renew his faith"—Book review digest.

2359. **Meredith, Miss Ellis, b. 1865.** *Under the harrow.* **Boston: Little, Brown, 1907. 267p.**

Occupants of the 'fourth-floor back' of a rooming house on New York's West Twenty-third Street are three young women who are striving to make a decent living in the metropolis. More often than not their efforts yield disappointment and crushing defeat. What small achievements they can point to are overwhelmed by the rejections of their literary and artistic submissions. Despite the above the three celebrate life and are participants in several affairs of the heart.

2360. **Meredith, Katharine Mary Cheever.** *Green Gates*; an analysis of foolishness. **New York: Appleton, 1896. vi, 257p.**

'Green Gates', a Long Island country home, is the scene of the major portion of the story. The plot deals with the sad, unrewarding love of a young woman for a married man. Fashionable life in both New York City and the Long Island countryside is described in between the plenitude of dialogue between the main characters.

2361. ———. *The wing of love.* New York: McClure, Phillips, 1905. 162p.

The story takes place in a rooming house in the 'bohemian' section of New York City. Three bachelors, one of whom is a journalist, occupy three of the house's attic rooms; a widow and her little daughter rent a fourth room. The girl charms the young men; especially charmed is the journalist, and it is he who, although poor and proud, is enabled by a chain of fortunate coincidences to win the love of a woman who is the most beloved aunt of the little girl.

2362. Meredith, William. *Not of her father's race.* New York: Cassell Pub. Co., 1890. iv, 291p.

"Jennie Andersen was the child of a white father and a mulatto mother, and born out of wedlock. In Virginia, her home, though as white as her father, she was adjudged a Negro, and grew up with the Negroes, and was educated with them. Her father comes into possession of a large sum of money and sends Jennie north to finish her education. She grows up so beautiful and attractive that he acknowledges her as his daughter and introduces her to New York society. Her career here, the admiration she excites, and the effect her true story has upon those who know her, point a striking moral"—Annual American catalogue.

2363. Merrick, Leonard, 1864-1939. *Lynch's daughter.* New York: McClure Co., 1908. 316p.

An English portrait painter in New York on a commission falls in love with Betty Lynch, daughter of a millionaire, but will not marry her until she meets his stipulation of refusing any money offered her by that 'devastating trust magnate, the debaucher of politics, the infamous multi-millionaire'. Betty finally agrees to Keith's terms; they marry and live in England. Poverty and a sick child in need of medical care bring about a break in the marriage and Betty returns to her father in New York. Still in love with Keith she gives up any claim to her father's wealth and goes back to her husband who is on the verge of recognition for his talents.

2364. Merrilies, Meg, pseud. *The woman with good intentions.* New York: G.W. Dillingham, 1896. 213p.

A girl from Canada becomes the wife of a New York stockbroker and the two enjoy a life of privilege and luxury until the bottom falls out of the stock market and he is ruined. She decides that she must help him pay off his debts, but that requires sacrificing her honor at the urging of the chief creditor.

2365. Merwin, Samuel, 1874-1936. *Lady can do.* Boston: Houghton, Mifflin, 1929. 232p.

"The Cuppys of Long Island are very rich, but not very admirable people, as Elsie Penn, their newly engaged secretary, soon discovers. Mr. Cuppy had presented Mrs. Cuppy with a beautiful Chinese headdress; that night Mr. Cuppy is murdered in a rather gruesome fashion. A number of Chinese servants seem to be involved; Mr. John Dane, a nice young artist, finds himself even more severely entangled. But Elsie, who has fallen in love with Mr. Dane, helps solve the mystery [whose answers are to be found in New York's Chinatown]"—Book review digest.

2366. ————. *The trufflers*; a story. Illus. by Frank Snapp. **Indianapolis: Bobbs-Merrill, 1916. 456p.**

Peter Ericson Mann patterns the leading character in his play, 'The trufflers', after Sue Wilde, a minister's daughter, who has chosen the free, pleasure-seeking life of a Greenwich Village habitué. Henry Bates, or 'The Worm', as he is called, had suggested the play's theme to Peter. When Sue rebuffs Peter's romantic inclinations, Henry steps into the breach. The play proves successful, although Peter is probably unaware that within it there emerges a satirical sketch of himself.

2367. **Michalesi, Alice.** *Written in the stars*; a novel. **Boston: Bruce Humphries, c1954. 285p.**

"Although fiction, this novel of the American Revolution is based on a carefully studied historical background" (p.3). The author has worked with and translated various German sources in order to portray the activities of Hessian forces in the British invading army. One of the novel's major characters is an impressed Hessian soldier, Friedrich Heubauer who, after the war's end, chooses to stay in the new nation, marrying a young American of German ancestry. The two chief fictional personages are the lovers, Cora de Galisson du Lac, an orphan and Jim Handley, a marginal farmer. The novel opens in Upstate New York. Cora and Jim serve the American cause, Jim as a soldier and mover of needed supplies to the American army, and Cora, in America and in France, encouraging French participation in the American cause. Historical events covered in the story are: the American victory at Trenton, St. Clair's evacuation of Fort Ticonderoga, Burgoyne's invasion and his surrender at Saratoga, Valley Forge, Yorktown and Washington's inauguration as President in New York City. Cora and Jim (now Colonel) Handley maintain homes near Ticonderoga and in New York.

2368. **Midwood, Barton, 1938- .** *Bennett's angel*; a novel. **Latham, N.Y.: British American Pub., 1989. 255p.**

Waking up one morning in 1959 David Bennett, 21, a graduate student in an Upstate New York college, is unable to remember any details of the previous night, although he knows he had been in a bar. As he tries to jog his memory he wonders whether he and his friend Dmitri Leskow (who does yoga exercises and attends prayer sessions with Hasidic Jews) had a homosexual episode. The story is padded with a lot of philosophizing about sex, redemption, the act of forgetting and the interior life of young students.

2369. ————. *Bodkin*. **New York: Random House, 1968. 211p.**

"Takes place in a home for wayward and disturbed boys, the majority of them Negro. The home ... is located in a remote wintry region of Upstate New

York; most of the story takes place at night. … [The] adult staff members and boy inmates [are] equally unstable. … Semi-literate Negro watchmen spice their sentences with such words as 'mayhap' and 'alas'. … Several clumsy attempts are made to murder the director of Ulser. …Doberman, a mysterious tramp appears and then disappears; a child is found dead. … The staff nurse, Miss Rose, goes mad and gives narcotics to her charges to put them temporarily out of their misery"—Book world.

2370. **Mighels, Ella Stirling Clark, 1853-1934.** *The full glory of Diantha.* **Chicago: Forbes, 1909. 432p.**

"A story in which the heroine [Diantha March], a bookkeeper … [in the office of the Lockwood Lumber Company in New York City] refuses to marry the junior partner of the firm employing her only because her wooer is not the elemental man of her dreams. She accepts a position in [the firm's branch in] a Western mining camp, finds her primitive man, loves him, and still later learns that the rudimentary strength of the 'hero' is so crude that he lacks the refining interest in his species upon which all social intercourse is based. A continual clash of wills finally terminates relations between them and Diantha … [returns to New York] and the man, strong of spirit, who had suffered and triumphed for her sake"—Book review digest.

2371. **Mighels, Philip Verrill, 1869-1911.** *Thurley Ruxton.* **Illus. by James Montgomery Flagg. New York: D. FitzGerald, 1911. 378p.**

A novel with Graustarkian elements although most of it takes place in turn-of-the-century New York City. Thurley, formerly a tutor to college students, is living with a wealthy woman in New York when Princess Thirvinia of Hertzegotha slips quietly into the city. Thurley bears so close a resemblance to the royal person that she is assumed to be the princess, and her hostess does nothing to discourage the misidentification. Then the princess's fiancé shows up and Thurley is kidnapped. A manly young American hero rescues Thurley and explanations prove satisfactory to all parties involved.

2372. ————. *The ultimate passion*; a novel. **New York: Harper, 1905. 365p.**

An idealistic New York politician maneuvers to get his name in nomination for the presidency, enlisting the assistance of a corrupt political ring and hoping to learn enough about its modus operandi so that he can effectively deal with the ring in time. From the three women who are in love with him he selects the one who stirs 'the ultimate passion' within him. Meanwhile he encounters extreme difficulty in trying to free himself from his unsavory supporters and his political campaign withers and fades away.

2373. **Miles, Robert Harrison Parker, 1866-1940.** *Three men and a woman*; a story of life in New York. **New York: G.W. Dillingham, 1901. 290p.**

A young couple from Vienna—she a country girl and he a medical student—migrates to America and locates in New York City. While her husband establishes a successful medical practice, his wife pursues an active social life and separates from her spouse. She adopts several shady schemes, drifts into crime and ends up in prison. A lover she had taken after leaving her husband is convicted and sentenced to death by electrocution.

2374. Millay, Kathleen, 1897?-1943. *Against the wall.* **New York: Macaulay, 1929. 442p.**

It is more than likely that 'Matthew College', the center of activity in this novel, is actually Vassar (Matthew Vassar was the founder of Vassar College in Poughkeepsie, N.Y.). The leading lady is Rebecca Brewster, 'refugee' from a barely functioning Maine family, who finds Matthew College's milieu not at all to her liking. She spends two years there trying to deal with the snobbery, prejudices and interminable partying. In the end she jumps ship and heads for New York City and independence.

2375. ————. *Wayfarer*; **a novel. New York: Morrow, 1926. 344p.**

"This is the love story of a Maine farmer and a Greenwich Village maid. John Bartlett comes to New York to rest and see life. He faints on a bench in Washington Square Park and is cared for by Martha Little and her group. John stays on in the Village, sampling its gay life till his funds give out. Then having fallen in love with Martha he marries her and takes her back to Maine with him. Entranced, she begins to play at housekeeping on the farm. The play imperceptibly turns into real work, and as the years pass life grows hard and flat. When a young man with money and charm enters her erstwhile Eden, Martha runs off with him, leaving good, dependable John to wait with hope for her return"—Book review digest.

2376. Miller, Agnes. *The Colfax book-plate*; **a mystery story New York: Century Co., 1926. v, 375p.**

The lower Fourth Avenue section of New York was once the home of a number of second-hand bookstores. Darrow's was one of those repositories of rare volumes and Peter Darrow was one of its buyers. He purchased for himself and his girl friend a volume containing bookplates by Colfax despite interest in the book by other parties. When one of Darrow's best customers is murdered in the store, the bookplate evidently has been a leading cause. Miss Fuller, one of the Darrow staff, narrates the story.

2377. Miller, Alice Duer, 1874-1942. *The beauty and the Bolshevist.* **New York: Harper, 1920. 111p.**

The love story of Ben Moreton, a radical socialist editor of a New York paper, the 'Liberty', and Crystal Cord, daughter of a wealthy conservative. Ben goes to Newport to talk his brother out of marriage to Eugenia Cord, Crystal's sister, but falls in love with Crystal. Crystal has the task of reconciling her father to the notion of her alliance with a man with whom he has little in common.

2378. ————. *Ladies must live.* **Illustrated by Paul Meylan. New York: Century**

Co., 1917. 249p.

Christine Fenimer and Nancy Almer, 'society ladies' of New York and Long Island, were alike in that both desired wealth and used their beauty to captivate any number of men. Nancy to be sure was married to a wealthy man; Christine was a bachelor girl. Max Riatt, a rich Midwesterner, attracts both Nancy and Christine at a Long Island house party. Christine wins; she and Max are married, although he is not yet in love with her. While Max is away on business Christine makes the social scene accompanied by Lee Limburne, her man of the moment. When Max finally does fall in love with his wife, his business is collapsing. Surprisingly Christine becomes aware of her love for Max and remains by his side.

2379. ————. *Less than kin.* **New York: Holt, 1909. 230p.**

"Vickers, a young man who had fled to South America under the cloud of a crime, sees the opportunity to return when a fellow countryman dies whom he resembles and who during his twelve years had been importuned by an aged father to come home [to his New York family]. Vickers slips into Lee's shoes and is received as the long lost prodigal, but finds, not at all to his liking, that in assuming Lee's identify, a most unsavory reputation [in New York circles] goes with it. [The story tells] how he took the dilemma by the horns and even won an obdurate maiden"—Book review digest.

2380. ————. *The reluctant dutchess.* **New York: Dodd, Mead, 1925. 175p.**

Jacqueline, a New York debutante, was engaged to the Duke of Dormiger through arrangements, unknown to her, made by her stepmother and the Duke. Although she really likes the rather quiet Duke, Jacqueline is infuriated when she discovers the origin of her engagement and breaks it off. She proposes to Paul, a former boy friend. However, the Duke has plans of winning Jacqueline back.

Miller, Hanson Orlo, 1911- . See: Miller, Orlo, 1911-.

2381. **Miller, Helen Topping, 1884-1960.** *Christmas at Sagamore Hill with Theodore Roosevelt.* **New York: Longmans, Green, c1960. 56p.**

In this novella the author puts a fictional gloss on a Roosevelt family gathering at newly elected Governor (New York State) Roosevelt's Oyster Bay, Long Island house during the Christmas season of 1898.

2382. **Miller, Isabel, 1924- .** *Patience and Sarah.* **New York: McGraw-Hill, 1969. 218p.**

Two young lesbians are forced by family pressure in 19th century Connecticut to split up, but they get back together again and leave Connecticut for a farm and a log cabin in Greene County, N.Y. Patience, the older of the two, has the skills that will ensure their survival; Sarah is uneducated and rather innocent, yet determined to live as she sees fit.

2383. Miller, Joaquin, 1841-1913. *The destruction of Gotham.* **New York: Funk & Wagnalls, 1886. 214p.**

> As much a polemic as fiction in which Miller, in his familiar bombastic style, rails against the heartlessness of New York and the stark contrasts in the lives of the poor and the bloated rich. A young woman, Dot or Dottie Lane, arrives exhausted and half-starved and penniless in the city and fails to find her cousin Hattie at the address she had been given. She becomes the prey of New York's predators and soon loses her innocence, is impregnated by the millionaire Matherson and then abandoned. Walton, a reporter, hopelessly in love with Hattie, now Matherson's mistress and intended bride-to-be, tries to take care of Dottie and Dollie, Dottie's daughter by Matherson, in their struggle for existence. After Dottie's death from exhaustion and malnutrition, Walton takes Dollie to Matherson who rejects his child. The novel ends with the cataclysmic destruction by fire of the city as roving bands of vengeful poor sack the citadels of the rich; Walton flees the conflagration with the near-to-death Dollie.

2384. Miller, Maurice E., 1890- . *Seneca drums.* **New York: Vantage Press, 1969. 203p.**

> As the American Revolution ends John Dunlap's title to lands in the Delaware River basin is voided because it was given under a 'King's Grant', no longer recognized as valid in the newly independent nation. Three of his sons, Andrew foremost, decide to migrate to the Finger Lakes region of central New York State—Andrew had served under General Sullivan in the punitive campaign against the Iroquois. The trek from New Jersey through Pennsylvania to the 'promised land' is described in detail. Once settled in the Military Tract on the shores of Seneca Lake and environs the several Dunlap families endure frightful storms, near-starvation, the attacks of wild beasts, the forays of a vengeful human enemy, and sudden drastic changes in the weather. Eventually the whole Dunlap clan, with the exception of a son gone to Virginia, is gathered together around the Finger Lakes of New York.

2385. Miller, Orlo, 1911- . *Raiders of the Mohawk*; **the story of Butler's Rangers. Illustrated by John MacLellan. New York: Macmillan, 1954. 182p.**

> Daniel Springer, an historical character, is a central figure in this novel for the young. Daniel is a Tory who joins Captain Walter Butler's Rangers as they carry out raids against the American rebels in the Mohawk Valley.

Miller, Phyllis, 1920- , joint author. *House of shadows.* **See Item #2506.**

2386. Miller, Victor B[rooke], 1940- . *Hide the children.* **New York: Ballantine Books, 1978. 300p.**

> Four kidnappers abduct a busload of 25 children ranging in age from five to seventeen from a prestigious school outside the city of New York. The children are tormented and brutalized with the result that the captives imitate the captors and even commit murders. The children's parents are uncertain as

to whether they should really pay for offsprings' release; but back under their parents' care the children exhibit an unearthly fear of grownups. The officials investigating the situation evince little sensitivity; to them their jobs are more important than the case at hand.

2387. Millis, Walter, 1899-1968. *Sand castle.* **Boston: Houghton, Mifflin, 1929. 304p.**

Annie, a "solitary little girl grows up into a poised and self-contained young woman with an individualistic outlook on life. The story, which is largely a character study, tells how love put her philosophy to the test. Her lover is a whole-souled, sensitive young man unhappily married. The story is set in Greenwich Village and Cape Cod"—Book review digest.

2388. Mills, Weymer Jay, 1880-1938. *Caroline of Courtlandt Street.* **Illus. by Anna Whelan Betts; decorations by W.E. Mears. New York: Harper, 1905. vii, 290p.**

The heroine of this novel of New York City some years after the American Revolution is 'Lady' Caroline; she is patronized by her father's aristocratic relatives because her mother was an actress. Caroline too has high hopes of an acting career and much of the story takes place among people of the theater. As it turns out Caroline does not go on the stage; she wins at the game of love and gains a place in the higher social scene. The novel provides the reader with a realistic picture of New York's most important buildings and theaters of the period.

2389. ⸻. *The ghosts of their ancestors.* **Pictures by John Rae. New York: Fox, Duffield, 1906. 142p.**

Jonathan Knickerbocker has an inordinate love of money and family status. He has three daughters, the youngest of whom is mischievous and buoyant, and in love with the organist at St. Paul's in the New York of the 1830s. On Easter Eve Knickerbocker's sisters and 'the ghosts of his ancestors' appear and show what a boisterous, hard-drinking, uncouth bunch they really were. Poor Jonathan is forced to surrender his notions of the family's superiority and gloomily acquiesces to the marriage of his daughter to a man without the 'proper' forbears.

2390. ⸻. *The girl I left behind me.* **Pictures and decorations by John Rae. New York: Dodd, Mead, 1910. 90p.**

It was in New York City of the 1840s that an impoverished Irishman, Sir Cyril Stephenson, was pierced by love's arrow when his eyes met those of a pretty American girl, and he asked her to a ball in the Astor House. The brief romance expires sadly for he is honor-bound to return to Ireland and the young woman he is engaged to marry. This short piece touches on landmarks fashionable at the time of the story—e.g., Niblo's Garden.

2391. ⸻. *The Van Rensselaers of old Manhattan*; **a romance. Illustrated and**

decorated by John Rae. New York: F.A. Stokes, 1907. 215p.

"A novel set in the days of New York when trocades, powder and patches were worn. The heroine rejoices in the name of India and is a hoyden, as her starched old Tory relative inappropriately but politely informs her. Still, she is so attractive that her path is literally besieged by the gallants of the day. … The other characters include the hero, a young Tory of fallen fortunes, a desperate and most repulsive villain, and an actress; while George Washington appears upon the scene, though very cursorily"—Outlook.

2392. Minster, Annie Maria, pseud. *Glenelvan*; or, *The morning draweth nigh.* **New York: A.B. Burdick, 1861. 384p.**

"Among those upward-reaching hills that form the eastern bank of the noble Hudson, on a southern slope, lies Glenelvan" (p. [7]). Annie Maria (Minnie) Minster is one of three daughters and she is the narrator of events in the lives of the Minster family and in the lives of her friend Albertine Gunnison, Albertine's brother Fred, and her Anglo-Indian cousin Haidee Hastings. However far Minnie may wander from Glenelvan and her father, she always returns to the beloved homestead. Tragedy strikes the Minsters when Minnie's sisters—Mildred (and her spouse) and Rose—and Mrs. Minster, and Minnie's brother Edgar (to whom Haidee was betrothed) are lost at sea. Albertine Gunnison wastes away when she discovers that her husband's (Mr. Bovie's) first wife had not died, as he had believed, and he must return to her. Minnie herself marries George Washington Guilder, the adopted son of her aunt, Madam Guilder, and goes South with him. Haidee finally gets over the loss of Edgar and marries Minnie's cousin, Henry Clay Guilder. The last lines of the novel are: "For me, my home is now with husband and child, without father, at Glenelvan"—(p. 384).

2393. Minton, Maurice Meyer. *The road of the rough*; a simple story of life in New York City. Illus. by G.A. Traver and George Varian. New York: Illustrated American Pub. Co., 1893. 150p.

Angrily struck by 'Gentleman Tom' McCarty, a street lad from New York's Sixth Ward, whom he had called a thief, Frederick Raingold, ruthless Wall Street financier, exacts his vengeance; Tom is sentenced to Sing Sing Prison for two years and eight months. But Raingold's life is unraveling; his wife's sole concern is the cultivation of New York's socially elite, and his son Frederic, Jr. is a purposeless, thoughtless person saddled with gambling debts; Raingold's mistress, the actress Mildred Vane, tires of being a 'kept woman' and resumes her stage career. Only Mary, Raingold's daughter, a charming girl who faces reality with firmness of purpose and actively serves the needs of the city's poor and forgotten, is a solace to the increasingly wretched millionaire. As his health fails Raingold provides for the future needs of his family in his will and faces another unpleasant truth about his past—the hatred of another woman he had used badly and the revelation of the paternity of Gentleman Tom.

2394. Mitchell, John Ames, 1845-1918. *Gloria victis*. **New York: Scribner, 1897. 269p.**

Stephen Wordsworth is the adoring son of a professional thief and murderer; he has a quick temper and a penchant for criminal mischief, but he also possesses the glimmerings of honesty and faithfulness. Semi-adopted by the saintly clergyman Dr. Thorne after his parents disappear, Stephen commits a homicidal act and runs away to the circus and life as a trapeze artist. He falls in love with a performing partner, Filippa Zabarelli. A glance at a ring given by Stephen to Filippa brings back to Mrs. Zabarelli the memory of Stephen's father and his theft of her small reserve of money. Angered by her accusations Stephen strikes out and kills Mrs. Zabarelli's daughter. Filippa is brought back to life by a mysterious healer (we recall that Dr. Thorne always insisted that Jesus Christ is forever walking on this earth) and Stephen is forgiven. New York City and environs are the scene of the story along with a New England interlude.

2395. ————. *The silent war*. **Illus. by William Balfour Ker. New York: Life Pub. Co., 1906. 222p.**

The scene of the novel is New York City where the potentates of financial empires are 'threatened' by the socialist People's League that seeks to gain justice by all possible means for all those who have been ruined by the trusts. Complications arise in one millionaire's family when a son falls in love with the daughter of a People's League member.

2396. Mix, Jennie Irene. *At fame's gateway*; **the romance of a pianiste. New York: Holt, 1920. 307p.**

Adventures in love and in music of an American girl from an oil town who comes to New York in search of musical fame. "Josephine Prescott was a musical prodigy in the little town of 'Parksburg' and the admiration of her townspeople made it possible for her to continue her studies on the piano with a famous teacher in New York. There her personal charms secured her many friends among musical and literary people whose bohemian life she shared. A great violin virtuoso chose her for his inspiration and she loved the man in him while the artist left her indifferent. Her teacher, the great Brandt, dubious about her artistic testing, tried her out: one year, two years. In the third year he tells her that, with all her talent, she will never be a great artist, for she lacks understanding. Despondent and with all her hopes shattered, she again hears the great violinist and suddenly awakens to the realization that she understands and thrills to his music, and that she no longer loves the man but the artist. And outside of the hall on the sidewalk romance stands waiting for her"—Book review digest.

2397. Moffat, Edward Stewart, b. 1876. *Go forth and find*. **Illustrated by Lester Ralph. New York: Moffat, Yard, 1916. 370p.**

Disconcerted by the staid, predictable path of a young woman's life in Rittenhouse Square, Edith Wallace strikes out on her own, taking an office job in the business world of New York. Simultaneously a wealthy man's son makes a decision similar to Edith's and ends up in the same office with Edith. Joined together by mutual attraction the two are oddly enough (or unwittingly) about to fulfill the expectations of their two upper crust families.

2398. Moffatt, William David, 1866-1946. *Not without honor*; **the story of an odd boy. Philadelphia: Arnold, 1896. 261p.**

Daydreaming, impractical Pennington ('Pen') Rae with his literary ambitions is ridiculed by many in the small town of 'Wilton Junction'. So he betakes himself (with his mother's wistful encouragement) to New York City to make his mark in the world of letters. Pen is a failure in his first two stabs at regular employment: as a factotum in the New York Herald office and as a clerk in a bookstore. But he continues to write with the encouragement of a Herald editor, Austin Terry, his friend Carl Moran, a book salesman, and others. His breakthrough comes with the successful publication of his fiction in a newly created magazine. That leads to a permanent position as literary editor for the periodical. By the story's end Pen and his family and friends are present at the first performance on Broadway of his short play. Pen is also instrumental in restoring his long-absent father—separated by mutual agreement from Mrs. Rae—to the family hearth.

2399. Moffett, Cleveland, 1863-1926. *The battle.* **Illus. from scenes in the play. New York: G.W. Dillingham, 1909. 303p.**

A prose narrative version of the author's drama, which was produced under the same title. The 'battle' is the venture of a very wealthy man into the slums of New York City to find the son who had walked away from him and all he stood for.

2400. ————. *A king in rags.* **New York: Appleton, 1907. 333, [1]p.**

New York City's poor are the concern of the hero of this novel, a young street preacher and diver with the assumed name of Phillip Ames. 'Margaret', the heroine, is curious to know more about Ames and his friend, deep-water diver and idealist, Mr. Gentle. She works with the tenement dwellers of New York's East Side. John J. Haggleton, the 'richest man in New York', is a slumlord who is targeted by those who are trying to improve social conditions in the metropolis. By the end of the story Haggleton learns of the existence of his long missing son (guess who he might be) and has committed (just before his death) a large amount of money to provide better housing for those in need. The close association of Phillip Ames/Haggleton and Margaret leads inevitably to a mutual declaration of love.

2401. Mohin, Ann, 1946- . *The farm she was*; **a novel. Bridgehampton, N.Y.: Bridge Works Pub., 1998. 245p.**

Through her journal spinster Irene ('Reeni') Leahy recounts her 20th century life on a sheep farm in 'Donohue Flats', a town in central New York. Social caseworker Esther Pomeroy looks after Reeni who is now pretty much confined to her bed. Pleas from Esther and Reeni's minister fail to persuade her to enter a nursing home. The story reverts to Reeni's younger years when, at 18, she took on the management of the farm after her father died. Her only love affair, with a veterinarian, occurred when Reeni was 37; it ended in duplicity and Reeni never really recovered from the hurt.

2402. **Mok, Paul P., 1934- .** *The year of the quicksand.* **New York: Trident Press, 1967. 371p.**

A small Upstate New York town witnesses the suffering of its school superintendent's wife, Katie Harris, from terminal cancer. She has always been her family's mainstay and it is son Jeff, a veteran, who kills her to end the pain she is in. Mr. Harris leaves his superintendent's position, stays around long enough to see Jeff freed on a temporary insanity plea, and then commits suicide. Young Billy Harris, Jeff's brother, stumbles into a love affair with both daughter and wife of the town's premier manufacturer, but tries to grow out of the complex situation and takes faltering steps to responsible adulthood.

2403. **Monfredo, Miriam Grace.** *Blackwater spirits.* **New York: St. Martin's Press, 1995. vii, 328p.**

The third in the author's series of novels that portray mid-19th century Seneca Falls, N.Y. through the eyes of Glynis Tryon, an energetic librarian, who is a participant in many of the historical events that rocked that small city. Cultures clash when half-Indian Iroquois deputy Jacques Sundown is put on trial for murder and Neva Cardoza, a young Jewish female doctor from New York City, comes to Seneca Falls to practice medicine. The popular spiritualist movement and the efforts of temperance advocates to stem the flow of hard liquor arouse passions.

2403a. ———. *Must the maiden die?* **New York: Prime Crime, 1999. 384p.**

Librarian and feminist Glynis Tryon is available when the local constable asks her help in solving the mysterious death of businessman Roland Brant. The story takes place in Seneca Falls, N.Y. during the spring of 1861 when the Civil War has just broken out. Among those who may have been connected with Brant's demise is the Brant's pretty but mute kitchen maid who disappeared the day of Brant's death.

2404. ———. *North Star conspiracy.* **New York: St. Martin's Press, 1993. xvi, 332p.**

With its mix of historical and fictional characters the novel deals with the Underground Railway in central New York State, with special emphasis on Seneca Falls (in the 1850s). Glynis Tyron, librarian at Seneca Falls, assumes a pivotal role. When Niles Peartree falls in love with a mulatto slave, Kiri, in Richmond, Virginia, the two escape north; this sets off a manhunt by slave catchers. Glynis helps Kiri elude her pursuers; however, Niles is arrested and an ensuing trial establishes Kiri's white paternity. Still to be resolved are three murders that occur in Seneca Falls; here, Glynis uses her detection skills and points out the individual responsible for the triple slayings. The women's rights movement is alluded to in various sections of the novel.

2405. ————. *Seneca Falls inheritance*. **New York: St. Martin's Press, 1992. 259p.**

The birth of the women's rights movement in Seneca Falls, N.Y., (1848) is prominently featured in this novel (Elizabeth Cady Stanton is among the historical figures present). Glynis Tryon, a spinster librarian, is the heroine. Shocked by the sudden deaths of wealthy Friedrich Steichen and his wife, Glynis is even more taken aback when a woman who claims to be Steichen's daughter shows up in Seneca Falls. Before she can substantiate her allegation, the woman is murdered. Suspect is Karl Steichen, Friedrich's son, who denies the murdered woman is any relation. The latter's husband comes to town to push his claim to part of Steichen's estate. Glynis snoops, and when the sheriff is ill, investigates a second related murder.

2406. ————.*Through a gold eagle*; a Glynis Tryon mystery. **New York: Berkley Prime Crime, 1996. 400p.**

Glynis Tryon, librarian, returns by train to her post at Seneca Falls, New York, after a year's stay with her brother's family in Illinois. n the train a man had been murdered, but not before he had briefly addressed Glynis, mentioning Seneca Falls and giving her a pouch containing money and a ring. It is May 1859 and Seneca Falls is buzzing with the national concerns of the time—women's suffrage, banking reform, abolition of slavery, etc. Closer to home, however, are the circulation of counterfeit money, break-ins and thefts of weapons, and the sudden deaths of seven people in town. Glynis finds a connection of these happenings to the financing of John Browne's attack on Harper's Ferry and partisan efforts to solve the slavery question by war if necessary. She knows too by the exciting conclusion who is behind the crimes and the commotion.

Monroe, Forest, pseud. See: Wiechmann, Ferdinand Gerhard, 1958-1919.

2407. **Montague, Charles Howard, 1858-1889.** *Two strokes of the bell*; a strange **story. Boston: W.L. Harris, 1886. 185p.**

Ansel Lewis of 'Winterside', Long Island, heir to the property of Benjamin Crooke, his uncle (Mrs. Crooke has been listed as dead), wanders in an amnesiac cloud to 'Bromberg', a village in Upstate New York. There he is cared for by Dr. Boodleby until he suddenly runs half-cured to New York. A friend, Sylvester Wayne, gives Ansel some facts about his (Ansel's) earlier life. His relationship to a French adventuress, Sidonie Lamonte, is disclosed. More importantly Ansel is gradually aware that in his recent past he had married a Miss Amy Bueford contrary to his uncle's wishes. After more twists and turns (Benjamin Crooke has passed away) and after the vengeful Sidonie wounds Ansel with a bullet from her pistol, Ansel and Amy are reunited.

Ansel no longer has an inheritance, for Mrs. Crooke 'materializes' from London to claim her husband's estate.

Montalvo, Marie de. 1950. See: De Montalvo, Marie, d. 1950.

Montross, Lois Seyster, 1897-1961, joint author. *The talk of the town.* See Item #2409.

2408. **Montross, Lois Seyster, 1897-1961. *With land in sight.* New York: Appleton-Century, 1939. 305p.**

He was only eighteen when he left home to try the 'laid-back' life of Tahiti and it was ten years later that Kent Salidin learned his grandfather had left him a million dollars and sizeable property in 'Vineyard', New York. Kent had his own ideas on how to live, based largely on his contact with Asian philosophies and South Sea ways. Yet it took only a few months of Vineyard for Kent to begin toeing the line—to accept the manners and customs of his friends and neighbors in Vineyard.

2409. **———. *The talk of the town*, by Lynn Montross and Lois Seyste Montross. New York: Harper, 1927. 296p.**

"Cynara lives on Gramercy Park and frequents Greenwich Village. She is sleek, fair-haired, attractive, and by virtue of her love for Ames Carruth, a Village artist not quite divorced, and of her sudden marriage to Mark Hexter, she is a rather wistful heroine. Her cousin Nettie comes from the backwoods with a little bag of parlor tricks—she renders selections compounded of bathos and abandon—is hustled onto the musical comedy stage, and is presently the talk of the town. Though there is a good deal of Nettie in the book, the story belongs really to Cynara"—Book review digest.

Moore, Bertha Pearl, 1893?-1925. See: Pearl, Bertha, 1893?-1925.

2410. **Moore, H.H. *Ida Norton*; or, *Life at Chautauqua.* Introd. by T.L Flood. Jamestown, N.Y.: M. Bailey, Chautauqua Press, Fair Point, 1878. 293p.**

Raised as an orphan in a children's home Ida Norton is taken by George Sands and his daughter Florence to the village of 'Fair Point' (Chautauqua, N.Y.). Ida spends many hours attending activities at the newly founded Chautauqua Assemblies, but when George Sands dies in the explosion of the steamer Chautauqua, his widow, Florence and Ida must support themselves. Matriculating at the Fredonia Normal School Ida renews acquaintance with Fred Granger, a childhood friend. Fred tells Ida he loves her; however both have studies to pursue. Ida meets her real mother, Ida Herron, who has married a second time and lives in Philadelphia. Her concentration on languages takes Ida to Pennsylvania and Paris; in Paris she develops an interest in Jesuit relations with the Iroquois and the war between the Senecas and the neutral Indians. Fred comes to Paris and accompanies Ida on a danger-fraught homeward voyage. They marry in Philadelphia.

2411. Moore, Lorrie, 1957- . *Who will run the frog hospital?* **A novel. New York: Knopf, 1994. 147p.**

Berie Carr, the narrator, while on vacation in Paris trying to weather a seemingly doomed marriage, harks back to her youth in 'Horsehearts', a tourist town in the Adirondacks close by the Canadian border. It was in the summer of 1972 that Berie, 15, was cashier at the amusement park, 'Storyland'; her best friend was sexually active Sils who played the role of Cinderella in one of the Park's productions. Sils and Berie had various escapades in Storyland until Berie, after stealing from her cash register to help Sils pay for an abortion, was sent to a Baptist camp by her parents.

Moore, Marie Lorena, 1957- . See: Moore, Lorrie, 1957- .

2412. Moore, Susan Teackle Smith. *Ryle's open gate.* **Boston: Houghton, Mifflin, 1891. 256p.**

A summer spent in an inconspicuous Long Island fishing village gives the narrator (accompanied by her 11-year-old son, Robin) an opportunity to observe closely the often-quaint characteristics of its inhabitants and their response to the environment.

2413. Morette, Edgar. *The Sturgis wager*; **a detective story. New York: F.A. Stokes, 1899. 260p.**

"A detective story of New York City, with a villain compared with whom Dr. Hyde is an innocent baby. The latest appliances of science are at his command. Roentgen rays, vats of chemicals in which human bodies are dissolved without leaving a trace, registers through which gas is turned on to asphyxiate reporters and detectives, etc., etc. A bank defalcation and a murder occurring in New York City on the last day of 1896 start a train of reasoning in a reporter that leads to very remarkable detective work which traces crime to a rich, respectable, learned scientist"—Annual American catalogue.

2414. Morford, Henry, 1823-1881. *Shoulder-straps*; **a novel of New York and the Army in 1862. Philadelphia: T.B. Peterson, 1863. 482p.**

With the Civil War in the background several upper class New York families cope with their personal problems. Josephine Harris ('Joe' or 'Josey') is the chief character of the many that appear in the novel. She is especially close to Bell Crawford; Bell has two brothers, John, a private in active service with the Union Army, and Richard, long an invalid in the Crawford home. A cousin, 'Colonel' Egbert Crawford is eager to replace Richard in the affections of still another cousin, Mary Crawford of 'West Falls' in Upstate New York—Mary is heiress to her father's fortune. Josephine unravels Egbert's plot to poison Richard and forces Egbert to flee. Egbert Crawford's redemption comes when he dies heroically, leading a Union cavalry charge against the Confederate foe. Another plot has Emily Owen defying her father, Judge Owen, by refusing to marry his choice, the bogus Colonel John Boardley Buncker, clinging to her lover, the printer Frank Wallace. 'Joe' Harris finds a lover of her own, the journalist/quasi-detective Tom Leslie.

Morgan, Carrie A. See under her pseudonym: Dick, Herbert G.

2415. **Morland, Catherine. *The legacy of Winterwyck*. New York: Pinnacle Books, 1976. 182p.**

The Covingtons, occupants of a Hudson Valley manor, are a conceited lot, wary of any 'outsiders' who do not fit into their closed world, so they are rather upset when one of the sons comes home with a bride from Boston who does not possess the 'right' social background. The bride's sister comes to the Valley to visit and is appalled to come upon a comatose sister and a just deceased brother-in-law. The Covingtons are not much perturbed by the tragedies; they are too busy entertaining other houseguests.

Morley, Blythe, 1923- . See under his pseudonym: Hopkins, Stanley, Jr.

2416. **Morley, Christopher, 1890-1957. *The haunted bookshop*. Garden City, N.Y.: Doubleday, Page, 1919. vii, 289p.**

"Roger Mifflin [of Morley's Parnassus on wheels] is now a secondhand book dealer in Brooklyn and indulges in delightfully eccentric talks about books. He finds a spellbound listener in Aubrey Gilbert who promptly falls in love with Titania Chapman, beautiful daughter of one of Roger's friends, who is learning the book trade. In sharp contrast to their idyll is the German bomb plot of which the bookshop becomes the tragic scene, but in which only the perpetrator and the dog Bock are killed"—Book review digest.

2417. **————. *Pandora lifts the lid*, by Christopher Morley and Don Marquis. New York: Doran, 1924. 290p.**

The 'heroine' of this entertainment, Pandora Kennedy, her closest friend Marjorie Conway, and five other students at the exclusive Miss Van Velsor school, for a cabal whose purpose is to convert the capitalist Alexander J. Crockett (with the unwitting assistance of Gloucester Gray, young teacher of English at the school) to socialism and world peace. All the above board the yacht 'Pandora' and set sail for their retreat, Thatcher's Island in Long Island Sound. They are unaware that the island, in the absence of its owner, is being used in a bootlegging operation headed by Jericho McGowan, Long Island hotel-keeper and marina operator. After some wild adventures and escapades—falling into the hands of McGowan and his semi-piratical crew— Pandora and the girls, the surprisingly resilient Crockett, and the rather befuddled Gray return safely to school and home (McGowan has been of inestimable help, for he fended off his now unruly, mutinous cronies). The story is told in alternate sections by Marjorie Conway and by Melville Kennedy, Pandora's uncle, who, in concert with Tom Carmichael, a rash young aviator, has been searching for the missing persons.

2418. ————. *Tales from a rolltop desk.* Front. by Walter Jack Duncan. Garden City, N.Y.: Doubleday, Page, 1921. viii, 262p.

"These little stories have all grown, in one mood or another, out of the various life of [New York City's] Grub Street, suggested by adventures with publishers, booksellers, magazine editors, newspaper men, theatrical producers, commuters, and poets major and minor"—Dedication. "All the tales breathe the breath of New York, the clatter and hurry, the thrill and adventure of city streets and busy people"—Springfield Republican. Contents: The prize package.—Advice to the lovelorn.—The curious case of Kenelm Digby.—Gloria and the garden of Sweden.—The commutation chophouse.—The pert little hat.—Urn burial.—The battle of Manila envelopes.—The climacteric.—Punch and Judy.—Referred to the author.

2419. Moroso, John Antonio, 1874-1957. *The people against Nancy Preston.* New York: Holt, 1921. 257p.

"His attempts to study the application of criminal law at first hand twice landed a young lawyer, Michael Horgan, in Sing Sing Prison for a term of years. When he went in a third time, under sentence of ten years at hard labor, it was because on his second release he undertook to protect and care for Nancy Preston, widow of a one-time burglar, and her little son. His re-arrest and conviction, on a framed-up charge, was a case in point of the miscarriage of justice through greed and stupid zeal. The same stupid zeal also marked Nancy for its prey. She falls under suspicion of murder and it is only the desperate efforts of Michael, who escapes from prison and calls upon his influential friends for aid, that Nancy is saved from the last extremity"—Book review digest.

2420. ————. *The quarry.* With illus. by Thomas Fogarty. Boston: Little, Brown, 1913. 324p.

"How through the machine-like workings of the New York police system a guiltless lad, ignorant in his innocence, may be accused, tried, convicted, and sent to Sing Sing for life on a charge of second-degree murder, is the theme of this story. Five years of the sentence are served; then through the connivance of his cellmate, Jim Montgomery makes his escape. In spite of all efforts to track him he finds peace and freedom in a small Southern manufacturing town. Under an assumed name he wins to a position of dignity and honor. But Kearney, the detective [from New York] who first arrested him, is still on the track of his quarry. He hunts him down, intent on getting the fingerprints, which will assure his identity. When the net is about to close around the victim, a sudden and unforeseen act on his part defeats the hunter's purpose"—Book review digest.

2421. ————. *The stumbling herd.* Front. by Harvey Dunn. New York: Macaulay Co., 1923. 306p.

The orphan Rosie Rosetti is just four years of age when she is adopted by the childless Kaminskys who live on New York's East Side. A short while later

Rosie persuades her foster parents to take in another orphan, Danny Lewis. The relations between Rosie and Danny become the novel's chief focus. Rosie's fondness as 'sister' to Danny evolves into her impassioned love for him, but it is only after the Kaminskys have passed away that Danny returns Rosie's affection in kind.

2422. **Morris, Charles, 1833-1922.** *Handsome Harry, the bookblack detective.* **New York: Beadle & Adams, 1886. 31p. (in double columns).**

In which Harry Hunter, Boss of the Bootblacks in his section of New York City, joins forces with Edward Livingston to thwart the villainy of Hall Stanway and helps save Mr. George Gordon's commercial ventures. Alice, Gordon's daughter, is betrothed to Edward. Despite some schooling offered by his grateful friends, Harry prefers to stay in the business he knows best, boot blacking.

2423. **Morris, Clara, 1848-1925.** *A pasteboard crown*; a story of the New York stage. **With a front. from a drawing by Howard Chandler Christy. New York: Scribner, 1902. vi, 370p.**

The novel follows the career of a young woman on the New York stage who has the misfortune of falling in love with an actor-manager of high repute who is actually a married man with few scruples or principles. Her tragic denouement is redeemed in part by the author's introduction of the actress's sister with her happy marriage and motherhood.

2424. **Morris, Gouveneur, 1876-1953.** *The penalty.* **Illustrated by Howard Chandler Christy. New York: Scribner, 1913. ix, 347p.**

"In a New York setting [the author] pictures Beauty and the Beast. Beauty is an especially attractive young woman sculptor; the Beast is an almost unbelievably horrible legless beggar. In spite of the hints and warnings of her men friends Barbara Ferris persists in having Blizzard, the beggar, in her studio as a model. Blizzard, who is represented as vice incarnate, falls madly in love with the beautiful young sculptor and is ready to move heaven and earth, or all the forces of New York's underworld to possess her. The fact that her father, a famous surgeon, is responsible for the loss of his legs, seems to put her further in the man's power. The story comes, however, to a conventional ending. Barbara marries the respectable young man lover and the atrocious villain is robbed of his attributes by the removal of a blood clot on his brain"—Book review digest.

2425. ————. *The seven Darlings.* **Illustrated by Howard Chandler Christy. New York: Scribner, 1915. viii, 325p.**

The Darlings, six girls and one boy, had only one asset, their recently deceased father's well-appointed summer camp in the Adirondacks (other than their own personal good-looks). They decided to turn the camp into a resort, the 'Four Seasons', and advertised in the newspapers, featuring a photo of the revised camp with the seven owners alongside it. The response was immediate; young men, from Downstate New York especially, made reservations. Over the next weeks the Darlings' venture promised to be a great success and the six female entrepreneurs were affianced to six eligible bachelors.

2426. ————. *When my ship comes in.* **Illustrated by Frank Snapp. New York: Scribner, 1915. 361p.**

A Broadway producer, McKay Hedden, returns Paul Henley's rejected play to the owner with a note of thanks, but not before stealing Henley's plot, altering it a bit, and then putting it on the stage with an ingénue, Silver Sands, in the lead role. The play, entitled 'When my ship comes in', is a hit. Hedden romances Silver; her thoughts, however, are with Paul (whom she had saved from drowning at Cape Cod several months earlier). The story concludes with Silver and Paul drawing close to one another, and the real playwright (Paul) gaining a measure of restitution from Hedden.

2427. **Morris, Hilda, 1888-1947.** *The main stream.* **New York: G.P. Putnam, 1939. 327p.**

"Novel of American life which follows the fortunes of the Denwoods, a New York State farm family from the last years of the nineteenth century to the present. It charts the course of the lives of each of the three who left the farm, with stress on the life of Flora, the youngest, who, after years of teaching in New York City, returned gladly to the farm"—Book review digest.

2428. ————. *The Tuckers tune in.* **New York: G.P. Putnam, 1943. 312p.**

"In the guise of a novel based on the life of an American family living in a small New York town [in the 1920s to the 1940s] the author traces the effect of radio on American mores. … The Tuckers begin their radio listening on an old crystal set; throughout the years their financial status and that of their neighbors was measured by the style of the radio they owned"—Book review digest.

2429. ————. *The vantage point.* **New York: Putnam, 1940. 311p.**

At 46, and a widow, Amy Trent no longer has her job as a teacher in a girls' school. To earn a living she turns her Westchester home into a boarding house. The boarders she takes in include some malcontent elderly and young relatives. Among her other concerns are her son's romantic complications. Amy's good understanding nature allows her to bridge the new and old ways and incidentally to rekindle the flame between her and a former lover.

Morrison, James Woods. See: Morrison, Woods.

2430. **Morrison, Woods.** *Road End.* **New York: Putnam, 1927. 351p.**

"A young man out of money and a job and too proud to ask for help from home hires out as a chauffeur to an eccentric old lady and her pretty niece who live in 'Cove Haven', Long Island, in a house called Road End. In the first day at his new job a jewel theft is discovered. That is only part of the excitement; a maid is murdered and there are ghosts in the house. The new chauffeur is not above suspicion, but when his luck is at low ebb, an unlooked-for confession saves him"—Book review digest.

Morrison, Roberta, pseud. See: Webb, Jean Francis, 1910-1991.

2431. **Morse, Lucy Gibbons, b. 1839.** *Rachel Stanwood*; **a story of the middle of the nineteenth century. Boston: Houghton, Mifflin, 1893. 441p.**

Anti-slavery agitation is rife in the New York City of the 1850s and the Quakers, Mr. & Mrs. Stanwood, use their home as a way station for the Underground Railroad. Their children variously support their parents' activity: Dick considers 'nigger' a swear word; Betty tells her schoolmates that she belongs to the 'Abolitionist Church'; the older Rachel is supportive of 'just causes'—she is a beautiful, high-spirited girl who captivates Horace Desborough, a lawyer with proslavery leanings. However, when 'the chips are down', Horace refuses to return a fugitive slave to his Southern master. The novel renders an account of an 'Antislavery Fair' held in the city and such historical personages as William Lloyd Garrison, Frederick Douglass, Ole Bull, and Lydia Maria Child appear in the story.

Morse, Murray, 1921- . See: Morse, Ray, 1921- .

2432. **Morse, Ray, 1921- .** *Cadets at Kings Point.* **New York: Aladdin Books, 1949. 249p.**

Three young men with quite different backgrounds attend the Merchant Marine Academy at Kings Point, New York, a training school for officers of the commercial fleet. Their daily experiences find them (Jim, Lee and Salty) trying out for the football team, dealing with a bully in their midst, and tussling with their academic assignments.

2433. **Moss, Robert, 1946- .** *Fire along the sky.* **New York: St. Martin's Press, 1992. 349p.**

The novel's protagonist is Skane Hardacre, remote kin to Sir William Johnson and one of the latter's agents. Hardacre keeps a journal that gives an account of his activities in furthering the goal of Sir William—to bring the Indians and the colonial setters of New York and neighboring territory into a cooperative and peaceful existence. Hardacre and his companion, Sir Robert Davers ('Fire Along the Sky' to the Indians) are witnesses to the failure of Johnson's plan as white and Indian cultures clash and the land-grabbing ventures of the settlers multiply.

2434. ————. *The Firekeeper*; **a narrative of the eastern frontier. New York: Forge, 1995. 512p.**

'The Firekeeper' is the name given by the Iroquois Indians to Sir William Johnson whom they trust implicitly to deal fairly with them. This novel is a sequel to Moss's 'Fire Along the Sky'. When the French and Indian War (which began in 1756) broke out, it was Sir William who kept the Six Nations on the British side of the conflict and was active as a soldier in campaigns around Lake George.

2435. ————. *The interpreter*; a story of two worlds. New York: Forge, 1997. **346p**

In the early 1700s a Palatine German youth newly arrived in the colony of New York, Conrad Weiser, has a falling out with his father who sends him to live with the Mohawk Indians. This historical novel depicts how Conrad (1696-1760) mastered the language and customs of the Indians and returned to 'civilization' to serve as an Indian agent in Pennsylvania. Conrad's later life is sketched, but of chief interest is the author's portrayal of the Mohawks and their persistent efforts to keep their way of life. At one point in the story several Mohawk chiefs leave for England to press their case with the authorities in charge of colonial affairs.

2436. **Mowatt, Anna Cora, 1819-1870.** *Evelyn*; or, *A heart unmasked*. **A tale of domestic life. Philadelphia: G.B. Ziebar, 1845. 2v.**

An epistolary novel with a New York City setting wherein Katherine Bolton writes to a friend anent the marriage of Evelyn, the beautiful daughter of the improvident Willards, to the fastidious Walter Merritt. The fashionable New York world Evelyn and Walter cultivate 'is composed of the dashing and wealthy, especially those who are nominally rich'. The appearance of Colonel Hubert Damoreau in that circle signals Evelyn's downfall. She falls in love with the Colonel and deserts her husband and Lilla, her infant child. Evelyn runs away from the Colonel also and enters a life of despair and deprivation in the Bowery and other sections of the city. Walter Merritt sues for divorce and then commits suicide. The death of little Lilla preceded that of Merritt and Evelyn dies of grief at the dissolving of her family. Colonel Damoreau, disfigured by acid thrown in his face by a young woman who deemed him responsible for her father's death, disappears. Evelyn's sister, Ellen, she of the curved spine, plays a role as the narrator's friend, benefactor of the poor, teacher and translator of French works.

2437. ————. *The fortune hunter*; or, *The adventures of a man about town*. **A novel of New York society, by Mrs. Helen Berkley [pseud.]. New York: J. Winchester, New World Press, 1844. 108p.**

Impecunious Augustus Brainard is advised to settle his debts by marrying an heiress. Estelle (a.k.a. Esther) Clinton, daughter of a retired hardware merchant, is a most likely candidate, even though Augustus inconveniently falls in love with the poor but stunningly beautiful Arria Walton. The outcome is that Brainard is dismissed by both women and falls into the trap of marrying Priscilla Adair, a fortune hunter herself. When knowledge of his wife's economic circumstance is made known to Brainard, he flees abroad. The novel has several other plots, notably the love stories of Rachel, the plain sister of Estelle, and Arria Walton who is in love with Edgar Chadwick, a medical student. Only her uncle and a long-lost father know Arria's mysterious origin.

Mowbray, J.P., pseud. See: Wheeler, Andrew Carpenter, 1835-1903.

2438. *Mr. Winkfield*; a novel. New York: American News Co., 1866. 160p. (in double columns).

Moses Winkfield believes he is a student of human nature, yet shortly after he arrives in New York City he is unable to prevent himself from being victimized on several occasions. He is keen enough, however, to recognize a fraud in the Reverend Hunkyfell who exercises a great deal of influence on the Tomlins family. Among Winkfield's friends and acquaintants are: Thomas Titman of Dibbletown, exposer of confidence men; Mr. Bunter, the ardent suitor of Miss Tomlins; the wealthy Wagfulls (Miss Wagfull is Winkfield's fiancée); the artist Mr. Pinksitt; the bogus Count and Countess Hetherington; the short-tempered Miss De Pompenkops (object of the affections of Winkfield's uncle, Effingham Toplady); the diplomat George Henry Bottlewasher; and Judge Pootoops—a veritable gallery of (American) Dickensian characters. The novel concludes with Rev. Hunkyfell in full flight from New York and the marriages of Bunter and Miss Tomlins, Moses Winkfield and Miss Wagfull.

2439. **Mullen, Clarence, 1907- . *Thereby hangs a corpse*; a Tony Lantz and Eddie Wright mystery. New York: Mystery House, 1946. 256p.**

The sleuthing duo of Tony Lantz and Eddie Wright are in an Upstate New York town that has been the scene of a number of murders; one of the corpses has Tony's calling card in his pocket! Tony and Eddie are soon dealing with a mix of gangsters, prizefighters and bold women.

2440. **Muller, Charles G., 1897- . *The Commodore*, by Charles Geoffrey Muller. With drawings by Elsa Hartman. New York: Harper, 1929. 272p.**

The hero of this tale for teenagers and young adults is Douglas Johnson (familiarly known as 'Fatso'). He and two friends pick up Bob Blanchard at the latter's cottage and all of them go along with Fatso's suggestion that they spend the summer at Shinnecock on Long Island. Although he knows little about sailing, Fatso is determined to learn so that he may enter the boat races for the famous Baldwin trophy. His friends somewhat reluctantly go along with Fatso. Needless to say Fatso is at the tiller when the vessel Halcyon garners first place in the last deciding race; he acquires a new name in honor of the victory—'Commodore'.

2441. ————. *Hero of Champlain*. New York: John Day Co., c1961. 192p.

During the War of 1812 a young midshipman in the command of Captain Thomas Macdonough participates in the Battle of Lake Champlain (1814). Despite the subject the author fails to make his narrative very memorable.

2442. Muller, Julius Washington, b. 1867. *Rulers of the surf*; a story of the mysteries and perils of the sea. **New York: Appleton, 1910. vi, 324p.**

"A story whose earlier pages deal vividly with the experience of the life-savers and fishermen on the fighting side of Long Island. ...The savagery of the open sea and the uncalculated bravery of those who daily cope with it are sketched with a good deal of vigor and color. There are chapters on deep-sea fishing, which suggest the vividness of A.H. Bullen's first books; and nothing better has been written in celebration of our national life-saving service. For the rest sea adventures are intermingled with romance with a plot of considerable ingenuity involving abduction by a pirate, pursuit of treasure under the sea, an escape in an open boat from the hands of the abductor"— The nation.

2443. Mumford, Ethel Watts, 1878-1940. *Dupes.* **New York: Putnam, 1901. v, 288p.**

The 'dupes' are those fashionable people in the upper strata of New York society who are eager to absorb the teachings of a quasi-theosophical mystic, Mme. Bouzales. She claims prophetic powers and the force of her personality dominates the story.

2444. ————. *Whitewash.* **Illustrated by A.G. Learned. Boston: Dana Estes, 1903. 319p.**

A mystery story involving a dashing young man who claims to be a Polish patriot and insinuates himself into the good graces of several eminent New York families—and a young woman who believes she recognizes him as a thief and murderer who committed his crimes in a French inn where she and members of her party had spent the night.

2445. Munroe, Kirk, 1850-1930. *Under orders*; the story of a young reporter. **New York: G.P. Putnam, 1890. vii, 348p.**

"Just as Myles Manning is within a year of finishing at X——— College, his father has financial difficulties which cause Myles to leave college and seek a means for earning a living. By the advice of a friend he becomes a reporter on a New York paper. He begins at the very beginning, and has some humiliating first experiences. But as he becomes accustomed to his position, many exciting and amusing episodes fall to his lot. Practical knowledge of a reporter's work may be learned from the story"—Annual American catalogue.

2446. Munsey, Frank Andrew, 1854-1925. *Afloat in a great city*; a story of strange incidents. **New York: Cassell [1887]. 388p.**

"The story opens at night on the lights and gayety of Broadway, New York, but the scene swiftly changes to a squalid den at Cherry St. and the East River, where a revolting scene takes place between a street arab and two personages of shady repute; after this, Ben the arab again repairs to Broadway, and becomes involved in difficulties which lead to his being smuggled on board a vessel bound for Australia; his adventures from thenceforth include two wrecks, an unexpected discovery, and an accession to wealth"—Annual American catalogue.

2447. ————. *The boy broker*; or, *Among the kings of Wall Street*. New York: F.A. Munsey & Co., 1888. 243p.

Emulation of his hero by young readers of this story is the author's purpose in writing about Herbert Randolph, a young, rural Vermonter who rises to financial success in Wall Street. Two newsboys, Bob Hunter and Tom Flannery, are also models of achievement; they attain significant results despite being novices at the arts of detection—Bob has a knack of preparing viable plans and carrying them out.

2448. Murdoch, Anna. *Coming to terms*. New York: Harper Collins, 1991. 230p.

Disabled Uncle Percy is joined in Poughkeepsie, N.Y. by his niece, Joelene Mathissen, and her teenage son, George, who have driven from California to take care of him. In Percy's backyard stands a huge, finely built ark that represents his life project. George finds a huge large amount of cash in the upholstery of Joelene's car, placed there by his mother's former lover, Ernie. He buys gifts with part of the money; meanwhile Ernie has come to Poughkeepsie to recover his loot. Before the story concludes George and his eccentric great-uncle have come to understand one another and Percy's ark plays a key role in a parade through town following a blizzard.

2449. Murdoch, David, 1801-1861. *The Dutch dominie of the Catskills; or, The times of the 'Bloody Brandt'*. New York: Derby & Jackson, 1861. 471p.

Also published in 1865 under the title: *The Royalist's daughter and the rebels*; or, *The Dutch dominie of the Catskills*. There are two 'heroines'—Elsie, daughter of the patriot Martin Schuyler, and Margaret, daughter of Sir Henry Clinton. Two Indians in the pay of the villainous British Colonel Clifford abduct Margaret. Elsie takes to the woods after her home is set on fire by Brant's Mohawks and snatches Margaret from her captors. The two women hide in the forests of the Catskills until rescued by a cooperating group of patriots and Loyalists. The Dutch dominie of the title, the Rev. Schuneman, is a commanding figure, a fiery patriot respected by friend and foe. The novel digresses quite often and the Dutch characters sometimes lapse into their hard-to-understand native dialect.

Murdoch, David, 1801-1861. *The Royalist's daughter and the rebels*. See note under Item #2449.

Murgatroyd, Captain Matthew, pseud. See: Jones James Athearn, 1791-1854.

2450. Murphy, David. *Old Moneypenny's*. Cleveland: Cleveland Plain Dealer Print, 1900. 147p.

A murky novel that does give a rather vivid picture of election parades and other election activities in New York City in 1876. However the plot of the story is difficult to fathom. Nicodemus Maffling, a displaced Southern aristocrat, acquired his medical education in New York and is now campaigning for the position of city coroner. His wife and his foster daughter Betty have taken a boarder, William Dumbar, a broker who is more likely a bucket-shop operator. Several odd characters put in their appearance, among them Neddie Shawn, an employment-seeking lad who runs errands for Dumbar and various Wall Streeters. What seems to be an assured victory for Maffling turns into defeat; he places the blame on William Dumbar, although why and how the latter influenced the outcome of the election is not really made clear. The story concludes with Dr. Maffling, burned in effigy by a mob, shooting Dumbar. 'Old Moneypenny' is the name given to the Maffling residence.

2451. **Murray, John F., 1923-1977.** *The devil walks on water*; a novel. **Boston: Little, Brown, 1969. 273p.**

Southampton, Long Island has a busy social life in the 1930s despite the overhanging gloom of the Depression. Briney Mitchel comes from a wealthy Irish Catholic family and has endearing Celtic traits, although he is something of a loudmouth. He is a bit enamored of a WASPish debutante, Midge Crocker, but does not give up his liaisons with a married woman and a maid employed in the Mitchel household, and he still frequents a local bordello. Southampton is hit by a hurricane and a tidal wave; Briney comes to the rescue of Midge who is clinging to a floating piece of roof; both are naked by the time they reach dry land.

2452. **Murray, William, 1926- .** *The self-starting wheel.* **New York: Dutton, 1960. 221p.**

"The scene is a Long Island summer resort. … The hero of the novel is Max Daniels … part mystic, part lunatic, part practical joker, part philosopher. … He arrives fresh from living on an Indian reservation where he has had a vision of a new religion. He bursts into the sun, martini, sex society to set himself up as a new Messiah. Before he has finished he has … created chaos and destroyed the emotional, moral and physical stability of the resort world"—New York herald tribune book review.

2453. **Murray, William Henry Harrison, 1840-1904.** *The Adirondack tales.* **Springfield, Mass.: Press of Springfield Print and Binding Co., 1897-98. 5v.**

John Norton, the 'Old Trapper', the author's fictional creation—wise, humorous, big-hearted, brave, an old-fashioned New England man, who lived his life in the woods of northern New York State—is featured in many of the tales of Adirondack life. Not all the material published in the five volumes relates to the Adirondacks. The author, a former clergyman and an orator of some note, traveled widely in America and abroad, so some of the items reflect that. Contents: v. 1. The story of the man who didn't know much.—v.

2. The Story of the man who missed it.—v. 3. Mamelons and Ungava, with supplementary notes.—v. 4. Stories of description and humor.—v. 5. Sermons, lectures and addresses.

2454. ————. *The story that the keg told me,* and *The story of the man who didn't know much.* **Boston: Cupples and Hurd [1889]. xvi, 454p.**

One of a series of "Adirondack tales ... to be completed in six volumes. Three volumes are already written, representing ... graphic sketches of the Adirondack region. ... These special stories have John Norton, the trapper, for their hero; in fact, he runs all through the scenes, speaking words of wisdom on many subjects connected with the woods and with nature"—Annual American catalogue.

2455. **Musgrave, Florence, 1902- .** *Stars over the tent.* **Illus. by Robert Candy. Boston: Houghton, Mifflin, 1953. 214p.**

"When Susan was twelve she left the orphanage where she had lived since her mother's death when she was three. Susan's father played the violin in a traveling Chautauqua circuit and Susan was to play the cello. The story tells of Susan's efforts to learn to like the new life, and her joy in belonging to someone"—Book review digest.

2456. **Musick, John Roy, 1849-1901.** *Calamity Row*; or, *The sunken records.* **Chicago: Rand, McNally, 1887. 265p.**

"Calamity Row is supposed to be situated along the river on the East Side of New York City. A beautiful young girl who waits on customers in a fifth-rate thread and needle store is the heroine, and her parentage is established after a complicated story by means of the 'sunken records'. Four young physicians play prominent parts. A chapter is devoted to a description of a dissecting room in a medical college at midnight, which gives gruesome details that lead to the identification of the heroine's mother. A fair description is also given of second-class New York boarding houses"—Annual American catalogue.

2457. **Musson, Bennet, 1866-1946.** *Turn to the right.* **From the play by Winchell Smith and John E. Hazzard. New York: Duffield, 1917. 291p.**

Deacon Tillinger does not deem Joe Boscom a fit suitor for his daughter Elsie. Frustrated, Joe heads for New York City, leaving behind his mother and her peach farm. The city is not kind to Joe and he is sentenced to a year in Sing Sing for his suspected participation in a robbery. While in prison he makes two friends: Muggs, a pickpocket and Gilly, a safecracker. Released, Joe returns to the farm, which his mother fears she will lose if she can't raise money owed Deacon Tillinger. Joe's two jail mates learn of the crisis facing Joe and his mother. They devise a complex but successful plan (utilizing their particular skills) to rescue their friend from debt. The story ends happily for everyone but the Deacon. Joe and his mother are owners of a flourishing peach orchard and Joe marries his sweetheart Elsie; Muggs and Gilly 'turn to the right' and settle down to an honest rural existence.

2458. Myers, Cortland, 1864-1941. *Would Christ belong to a labor union? or, Henry Fielding's dream.* **New York: Street & Smith, 1900. 216p. Reprinted in 1902 under the title:** *Henry Fielding's dream*; **or,** *The labor union.*

Henry Fielding had left a Vermont farm, his widowed mother and a brother to make a living in 'the great city' (New York); his sister Elsie came with him, sharing an apartment in the metropolis. Henry, working steadily in a factory, had come to believe that the church has 'lost the spirit of the Bible and has no real relation to the greatest needs of today'. Nevertheless, he, Elsie and a friend, Richard Hamilton, attend a service in which Rev. David Dowling answers the question in the novel's title in the affirmative. Elsie meets wealthy Grace Chalmers in mission school. Brother and sister return to Vermont to attend their mother's funeral. When they return to the city the Rev. Dowling accompanies Henry to a meeting of Labor Union 10; his powerful preaching wins the hearts of 29 members of the union. Henry is himself converted; he meets and is charmed by Grace Chalmers. Then Elsie breaks the unfortunate news that she is suffering from acute, incurable arthritis. Advancement at the factory enables Henry to acquire ownership of the workplace. Taking a home for himself and Elsie in the suburbs, Henry marries Grace and applies Dowling's Christian principles to his factory, asking for the workers' cooperation in the industry's management and sharing profits with them.

2458a. Myers, Mildred Davis, 1926-2001. *Miss Emily*: **Emily Howland, teacher of freed slaves, suffragist and friend of Susan B. Anthony and Harriet Tubman. With excerpts from her diaries and letters. Charlotte Harbor, FL: Tabby House, c1998. xiv, 238p.**

The author has fashioned a novel (replete with imagined conversations), which is, of course, based on Emily Howland's diaries, correspondence and other papers. The story begins in 1856 (when Emily is 29) and concludes in 1927 (she is now 100). Between those years Emily has been active in the abolition movement, the pursuit of women's rights and suffrage and especially with the education of former slaves with the Civil War years assuming a prominent role. Her deep friendships with Frances Seward (wife of William Seward, Lincoln's Secretary of State), Harriet Tubman, Susan B. Anthony and other noteworthy personages are delineated. Although Ms. Howland spent much time establishing schools for recently freed slaves in Washington, D.C. and Virginia she always returned to her family in Sherwood, N.Y.; her later years were devoted to the founding of the Sherwood Select (later the Emily Howland) School and continuing efforts to gain women the right to vote.

2459. Myers, Peter Hamilton, 1812-1878. *Ellen Welles*; **or,** *The siege of Fort Stanwix.* **A tale of the Revolution. Rome, [N.Y.]: W.O. M'Clure, 1848. 48p.**

A novella in which the author describes events in the lives of Charles Dudley, patriot; Ellen Welles, daughter of Loyalist Captain Welles; and Enoch Waldon, Tory, shortly before, during, and after St. Leger's siege of Fort

Stanwix. Ellen elects to stay near Charles Dudley during Indian raids but is tricked into entering the British camp by Waldon. Ellen's father is killed during the siege; when it is lifted, Dudley pursues the retreating British forces and with the help of Oneida Indian allies and his friend Rogers succeeds in freeing Ellen from Waldon's camp. Narrowly escaping by canoe from Waldon and his Mohawks, the party meets the patriot force of Marinus Willett that routs the Mohawks and kills Waldon.

2460. ————. *The first of the Knickerbockers*; a tale of 1673. New York: G.P. Putnam, 1848. 221p.

The resentment and antagonism felt by the Dutch towards their English conquerors in the colony of New York are at the core of this novel. The heroine Effie's father, Evert Knickerbocker, loses his extensive properties because of his failure to produce deeds to his estates. Effie's lover, Rudolph Groesbeck, arrested and condemned to death by the British authorities because of complicity in a move to restore Dutch rule, escapes from prison with the help of Jed Knickerbocker, Effie's brother. The arrival of a Dutch squadron in New York harbor results in the displacement of the English standard for a brief while, but long enough for several happy resolutions. Former Governor Peter Stuyvesant is a participant in the action of the story; the author carried artistic license rather far in this instance, since Stuyvesant actually died in 1672 or before the events described in the narrative (Myers states 1682 as the date of Stuyvesant's death!).

2461. ————. *The king of the Hurons*, by the author of *The first of the Knickerbockers* and *The young patroon*. New York: G.P. Putnam, 1850. 319p.

In 1703 a crippled French warship is forced to enter New York Harbor and is commandeered by the English authorities. The Baron Montaigne (King of the Hurons) escapes his English enemies, but leaves behind his daughter by a first marriage, Blanche Montaigne. The latter, using her cousin's surname, Roselle, is allowed to stay in New York; when her real identity becomes know, Blanche, with the help of a sympathetic young Englishman, Heinrich Hunt, and the Huron allies of the Baron, flees northward up the Hudson River and Lakes George and Champlain. Pursued by the Iroquois the party reaches fortified Castle Montaigne area near the tip of Lake Champlain. Heinrich, on his way back to New York (after being reprieved from death at the hands of the Baron's firing squad) falls in with a British-Indian expedition against the Castle. In the ensuing battle Heinrich takes a neutral stance; however, the Baron is killed and the Castle torched. Blanche and Heinrich proceed to Montreal and eventually to England, then back to New York. The novel was reprinted in England in 1857 under the title: Blanche Montaigne: the prisoner of the border.

2462. ————. *The miser's heir*; or, *The young millionaire*. Philadelphia: T.B. Peterson, 1854. 222p.

A village outside New York City is the stage for a major portion of the novel. Ralph Werter is hopeful that his guardianship of sickly Sidney, a young son of the late, rich Hugh Werter, will not be an extended one for Sidney's demise would leave Ralph in full possession of his brother's estate. Sidney has a friend in Addison Jay, a retired sea captain's son, and Ralph makes things as difficult as possible for this 'interloper'. As several years pass and Sidney and Addison meet to discuss further Sidney's inheritance, Ralph (who has been using his nephew's money to build a fine home for his family in New York City) loses his patience and poisons Sidney. Also put out of the way is the doctor who provided Ralph with the lethal substance. Ralph's plans go awry nevertheless, because Addison discovers that Hugh Werter had a son by an earlier wife, a woman he had deserted. That son, Addison's friend, Edward Hazelton, is thus the true heir of the bigamous Hugh.

2463. ————. *The young patroon*; or, *Christmas in 1690*. A tale of New York. By the author of *The First of the Knickerbockers*. New York: G.P. Putnam, 1849. 142p.

A miniature portrait of Anglo-Dutch upper-class society shortly after the British takeover of 1664. The young patroon, Harry Livingston, nephew and heir of General Van Ness of 'Kenterhook' on the Hudson, becomes engaged to the imperious Gertrude Van Corlear of New York City. Gertrude's brother Seth, in order to save his friend Harry from a disastrous marriage and fix Harry's attention on the other Van Corlear daughter, sweet, unassuming Jessie, hatches an ingenious plot with the aid of a young relative of the late General. This young man, Derick Van Ness, assumes the identity of the General's son, Bleecker, who was presumably lost at sea, and lays claim to the Kenterhook estate. When Seth finally reveals the deception, Harry has already discovered Gertrude's selfish motives (she rejects him when she believes him 'disinherited' by Bleecker Van Ness) and turns to lovelorn Jessie.

2464. *Mysteries from the Finger Lakes*; short stories from *Six Lakes* arts magazine (formerly *In-between*). Seneca Falls, N.Y.: Six Lakes Arts, Inc., 1989. 149p.

The authors of the seven stories in this collection are natives of Upstate New York and four of the stories have an Upstate New York locale or 'flavor'. Contents: The carnival killer, by David E. Downey.—Mystery by the lake, by John Fouracre.—Perfection, by James MacNeal.—The scam, by Richard Ciciarelli.—The short story writer, by John Fouracre.—Wheels for the dead, by Barbara Mater.—Will of the wind, by Jack LaValley.

2465. Nabokov, Vladimer, 1899-1977. Garden City, N.Y.: Doubleday, 1957. 191p.

Timothy Pnin, like Nabokov himself, is in his middle years, an exile from his native Russia, and now teaching in an Upstate New York college (Nabokov taught at Cornell University from 1948 to January 1959). Pnin has difficulty adjusting to American culture and to a world that seems increasingly filled with horrible human actions. His eccentricities are perhaps his saving grace.

2466. Nagy, Gloria. *A house in the Hamptons* (one summer near the end of the lie); a novel. **New York: Delacorte, 1990. 374p.**

The yuppies of the late 1980s are alive but not too well in their enclaves in the fashionable Long Island Hamptons. The girl that publisher Harry Hart and psychiatrist Donnie Jamieson cherished in high school has become a resident of Easthampton 25 years later. Her presence has a disquieting effect on the two men with their families in second houses in the Hamptons. The author acidly portrays the denizens of this consumer-oriented and status-seeking culture.

2467. Nassar, Eugene Paul, 1935- . *Selections from a prose poem: East Utica.* **Designed, and with original woodcuts by Robert Cimbalo. [Utica, N.Y.]: Munson-Williams-Proctor Institute [c1971]. 44p.**

Prose-poem about a Lebanese-American community in Upstate New York. "Covering the years 1944-64 Nassar's work takes the reader along an 'infamous, colorful, insulted' Bleecker Street, into the mills on Broad Street and 'the Ah'we', Lebanese-Syrian coffee house on Elizabeth Street. It crosses ethnic lines to let the reader hear the Banda Rosa, Italian musicians 'tooting, wriggling and drumming ... for the Madonna and her son and Santa Rosalia, patron saint of Sicily'. ... East Utica is, in essence, the story of a sensitive young person who, though born in the New World, is aware of strong ties to the Old; who realizes (sadly at times) that he may be of the last generation of Americans to feel the strong pull of ancient traditions and loyalties, and who knows that the term 'the American dream'—now in disrepute—derives much from the vision and values of his immigrant parents and neighbors who, while they looked to the future, refused to forget a proud past"—O'Donnell, Thomas F. Oneida County: literary highlights (in: Upstate literature. Syracuse University Press, 1985).

2468. Naylor, Henry Rodley, b. 1840. *The mystery of Monastery Farm.* **New York: Eaton & Mains, 1908. 135p.**

The Bank of England is robbed and the detectives assigned to the case are at a loss to explain the disappearance of the funds and the perpetrators. The story shifts to 'Monastery Farm' in western New York. Suspicion falls on a young English employee there; it is well founded, for the suspect confesses and promises to restore at least some of the stolen money. One of his co-conspirators is also picked up by the investigators.

Neal, Alice, 1827-1863. See: Haven, Alice Bradley, 1827-1863.

2469. Neal, John, 1799-1876. *Brother Jonathan*; or, *The New Englanders.* **Edinburgh: W. Blackwood, 1825. 3v.**

"Young New Englander Walter Harwood ... travels to New York through a countryside gearing up for war. He ... seeks to join General Washington's forces. In New York he encounters the grimier aspects of life, is led to a house of prostitution, and meets the seductive Mrs. P. He finds other girls susceptible to his fresh country charms, and undergoes a baptism of war at Brooklyn Heights, followed by an encounter with Nathan Hale. Walter escapes as Hale is hanged. From there on the gothic elements introduced by [the Byronic Jonathan] Peters engulf the story. … He returns to the better world of the New England coast. Walter's initiation into the city [New York], and passion has awakened the sleeping genius in him. His change is marked by his boyish New England dialect becoming the speech of 'genius'—Sears, Donald A. John Neal. Boston, 1978.

2470.   ———. *True womanhood*; a tale. Boston: Ticknor and Fields, 1859. 487p.
"The opening chapter paints a good picture of contemporary New York society. Reflecting contemporary events, Neal traces the rapid rise of crime following the financial panic of 1857-1858. … Again good social history is set forth in chapters dealing with the 'business-man's prayer meeting' at the Episcopal Church on Broadway"—Sears, Donald A. John Neal. The heroine of the novel, Julia Parry, is very religious, but she is also strong-willed and free-spirited. She is instrumental in reforming her capricious cousin, Arthur Maynard, but when he proposes to her she refuses on the grounds of their consanguinity. Another wooer, the lawyer Winthrop Fay, who had defended Julia's Uncle George (accused of fraud), is turned away. Julia says: "I do not believe marriage is a condition absolutely indispensable for the happiness of woman, or for the development of true womanhood." Neal was an early male advocate of women's rights.

2471.   Neggers, Carla, 1955- . *Tempting fate.* New York: Berkley Books, 1993. 341p.
Saddled with two irresponsible parents Dani Pembroke was actually reared in Saratoga by her grandmother. As an adult she achieves some success as an entrepreneur, balancing her own independence against the enticements of the wealth possessed by elderly members of the Pembroke family. She wants to know why her mother disappeared from her life and is surprised when Zeke Cutler, a private detective, comes to Saratoga searching for the same answers. Dani and Zeke decide to work together; the weight of the past menaces the stability of Dani's business enterprises, and it is the hitherto not fully trusted Zeke Cutler who props up Dani's capacity for weathering her difficulties.

2472.   Neiderman, Andrew, 1940- . *Sisters.* New York: Stein & Day, 1971. 155p.
A novel of suspense involving two spinsterish sisters who run a candy store in a Catskill resort town and a drifter who agrees to work for them during the summer vacation season. Murder comes into the picture when the sisters compete for the romantic attentions of the handsome young man.

Neiderman, Andrew, 1940- ., joint author. *Weekend.* See Item #1432.

2473.   Nella, Milton. *His one desire*; being an account of the growth of the greatest wish of his heart, and how he secured the attainment thereof. New York: J.S. Ogilvie, 1892. 258p.

After being away from his Syracuse home for several years, a young typesetter returns. He meets a girl from Rochester and sets his heart on winning her hand in marriage. His suit is successful. Syracuse and Rochester in Upstate New York are the cities the young couple are most familiar with, although Nashville, Tenn. also becomes a part of their itinerary.

2474.   **Neuberger, Ruth Felicia Adams, b. 1870.** *His uncle's wife.* **New York: A. Harriman Co., 1912. 175p.**

An irresponsible young man does have the decency to gather up a girl he has run down on his way to catch a boat for Europe and deposit her at his uncle's Dr. Leighton's home in New York City. The girl suffers from amnesia and believes the doctor's house is her own home. Dr. Leighton goes along with the deception in the hope of tracing down her true identity. When memory finally returns to her, she is able to fathom the reason for the wedding ring on one of her fingers.

2475.   **New, Clarence Herbert, 1862-1933.** *Franc Elliott; a story of society and Bohemia.* **New York: G.W. Dillingham, 1895. 271p.**

"Franc was a girl and a painter and a 'bohemian' of New York who seemed to spend the most of her time being made love to. The tale may be very true to life; bohemians can best judge that. It is certainly 'realistic' in the modern sense of the word, and it is unquestionably stupidly dull, as much of real life is"—Daily picayune, New Orleans.

New Yorker, A. *Annals of the Empire City.* **See Item #106.**

2476.   **Newell, Audrey.** *Who killed Cavelotti?* **New York: Century Co., 1930. 306p.**

Detective Doyle is faced with a puzzle: how was it possible for the womanizing ex-opera star, Guido Cavelotti, to be stabbed to death in his locked New York hotel apartment? To be sure there was a young woman in the apartment with Cavelotti, his latest sexual conquest; but it is the consensus that she did not commit the murder. Cavelotti was hated by a number of people, any one of whom would gladly have promoted his removal from society in New York or elsewhere.

2477.   **Newell, Hope Hockenberry, 1896-1965.** *A cap for Mary Ellis.* **New York: Harper, 1953. 200p.**

Mary Ellis Stebbins and Julie Saunders are two outstanding black girls who are selected as fine representatives of their race to attend an Upstate New York nursing school. They undergo three years of training with the chief focus on the earlier part of the training period. There is also a hint of romance entering the life of Mary Ellis.

2478.   **Newell, Robert Henry, 1836-1901.** *Avery Glibun; or, Between two fires; a romance, by Orpheus C. Kerr [pseud.].* **New York: G.W. Carleton, 1867. 2v. in 1 (301p. in double columns).**

"The novel contains many plots; it is in fact several novels—a gothic romance involving a magnetic villain called the King of Diamonds, strange women of many identities, and babies switched in their cradles; a political satire revolving around the attempts to buy the New York State senatorial election; a social comedy of manners among the new rich; and the chronicle of the title character's rise to manhood. ... Avery Glibun's adventures take him [e.g.] from a wealthy home dominated by a cruelly sinister father ... to a Dickensian boarding school, to a gypsy camp, to a secret hideout in the New York underground, to the offices of a literary journal, to the accounting department of a large dry goods store. The book also offers extended and detailed pictures of conditions among the criminal classes of New York, the literary bohemians, and its retail clerks"—Dictionary of literary biography, v. 11, pt.2.

2479. ————. *The walking doll*; or, *The Asters and disasters of society*. **New York: F.B. Felt, 1872. 391p.**

Arrogant, self-centered and rude, Jack Aster (but the hero all the same) leaves his father's house because his stepmother so desires it—she hopes that Jack will be disinherited in favor of her own offspring. Jack ends up in New York driving a horse car to support himself, making the acquaintance of toymaker Geoffrey Dapple, the toymaker's daughter, and Lucy Lardner, a merchant's daughter. Jack's seemingly outlandish behavior is explained in part by the revelation of his being both John Phillip Aster and John Francis Aster, identical twins unknown to one another. The author airs some of his social concerns: he notes that the New York rich very often ignore the poor; he is disturbed by the plight of children of the hard-drinking poor; incompetent physicians, discourteous sales clerks, and corrupt Tammany politicians are berated.

2480. **Newhouse, Edward, 1911- .** *This is your day.* **New York: Furman, 1937.**

Striking farmers in Upstate New York are the target of an idealistic young communist who tries to organize them into a coherent, potent organization. The novel also touches upon his experience of love and marriage.

2481. **Newlove, Donald, 1928- .** *Leo & Theodore.* **New York: Saturday Review Press [1973, c1972]. 341p.**

The author's unusual fictional heroes are Siamese twins born in Upstate New York on October 29, 1929, the day the New York stock market collapsed. Stella, their mother, marries a succession of well-off but essentially loutish, cruel men in an effort to support the twins. Leo and Teddy receive little formal education (they complete only eight grades), but that doesn't get in the way of their enjoyment of life as they drink heavily, have sex, wear whatever comes to hand, drive crazily, rob, and play jazz. Leo marries Thelma and Teddy takes a lover, Salome; they nurse a rich old man, drive a run-down ambulance, and when they are approaching their thirties, meet Cynara Roseweink, a 15-year-old brainy beauty who, in love with both of the twins, proposes that they compose an opera.

2482. **Nicholls, Charles Wilbur de Lyon, 1854-1923.** *The décadents*; a story of Blackwell's Island and Newport, by C. de Lyon Nichols (Shelton Chauncey). New York: J.S. Ogilvie, c1899. 172p.

Elsie Lane, a nurse in the Blackwell Island Hospital, takes an interest in the reformation of alcoholic Dennis M'Inerney, a former habitué of the Bowery and East Side dives, but presently an unpaid helper/resident of the Hospital. Unknown to her Dennis is plotting with a felon, Mike Harrigan, now a plumber/internee in the Island's prison, to determine how much money Elsie has inherited from her deceased father. A Dr. Sniffins who is unable to persuade her to marry him pursues Elsie. When she takes a leave of absence to serve as a private nurse to Mrs. Griswold in Newport, she suggests Dennis as a caretaker for an ill neighbor of Mrs. Griswold. Both Dennis and Mike appear in Newport only to be arrested for breaking and entering. So much for Elsie's goodheartedness. The author frequently sprinkles descriptions of New York City's islands and institutions throughout the text.

2483. ————. *The Greek madonna*, by Shelton Chauncey [pseud.]. New York: G.W. Dillingham, 1894. 315p.

"The scene is laid in New York City. The hero, whose name is 'Shelton Chauncey', is first a student of Trinity Theological Seminary, and afterwards a chaplain in one of the hospitals on the city's islands. The story is a rambling narrative of his affection for two women, his courtship taking place mostly on the elevated roads. His special religious ideas, which seem to run to High Churchism, he symbolizes under the figure of the Greek Madonna. Names of fashionable New Yorkers are freely mentioned and incidents of local history drawn in regardless of chronology"—Annual American catalogue.

2484. **Nichols, Anne, 1891-1966.** *Abie's Irish Rose*. New York: Harcourt, 1927. 324p.

A novel based on the long-running play. Abie Levy, Jewish, and Rose Mary Murphy, Irish, fall in love and are married by a Methodist minister without the knowledge of their families. Abie introduces his 'girlfriend' to his widowed father, Solomon as Rosie Murpheskie and preparations are made for Abie and Rose Mary to be wed by Rabbi Samuels. The truth comes out when Patrick Murphy, Rose Mary's father, walks into Solomon Levy's New York apartment with the priest, Father Whalen. By this time the couple has been married by the rabbi and then undergone another ceremony conducted by Father Whalen. A year later at Christmas time Patrick Murphy and Solomon Levy finally accept the situation and one another as they delight in their twin grandson and granddaughter in Abie's and Rose Mary's New York apartment.

Nichols, Charles Wilbur de Lyon, 1854-1923. See: Nicholls, Charles Wilbur de Lyon, 1854-1923.

2485. **Nichols, Fan.** *Be silent, love*. New York: Simon & Schuster, 1960. 219p.

"People who have crippled themselves—Kay Hubbard with her subjection to married David Drake; David by his determination not to jeopardize his business career; and Bill Webb, math teacher and football coach, whose past mistakes in sport still scar—bound together in a hit and run killing [of a Hudson Valley high school football star]—are an uncommendable, but understandable, trio. [The] boy's death severs Kay's and David's relationship and David, running, kills again, turns on Kay and writes his own finis"—Kirkus Services. Also published under the title: *The girl in the death seat* (New York: Ace, 1961).

Nichols, Fan. *The girl in the death seat.* **See note under Item #2485.**

2486. **Nichols, John Treadwell, 1940- .** *The sterile cuckoo.* **New York: D. McKay, 1964. 210p.**

> When the heroine, Pookie Adams, "first stumbles on the hero, Jerry Payne, waiting at a cross-country bus stop, he sees only a skinny, scrubby-haired girl, balancing a toothpick on her tongue. Then she bursts into speech and Jerry … remains bewitched until her last syllable. Her pursuit of Jerry is launched with … determination. When fate places the couple at neighboring Eastern colleges, Jerry succumbs to his first frantic affair. … As their romance plunges into its second year, they make a final attempt to slow to a more normal pace, but on a New York weekend, somewhat the worse for an overindulgence in Tiki Puka Pukas, their affair staggers to a close"—Publisher's note. The novel contains many scenes that evoke places in Oneida County, New York.

2487. **Nichols, Thomas Low, 1815-1901.** *Ellen Ramsay*; or, *The adventures of a greenhorn, in town and country.* **New York: For sale by booksellers and periodical agents generally, 1843. 61p. (in double columns). (Stories of American life. Nichols's monthly series, no. 1.)**

> The familiar tale of the country boy who wants a taste of metropolitan life and falls into the various snares that await him in the big city. Edward, the greenhorn, leaves behind his parents' New Hampshire farm and his ladylove, Ellen Ramsay, and with $300 'tackles' New York City. Confidence men and women, gamblers, et al., soon relieve Edward of much of his stake; he tries to sell some of his literary pieces with little success and almost succumbs to the charms of a lady from his hometown who has run away from her elderly husband. This lady, however, helps Edward reclaim from J. Rollins Smith (a.k.a. Jenkins), her seducer, a large part of his original funds and together they start back to New Hampshire. Edward's father dies; he takes over the farm and, after misunderstandings stemming from his New York City sojourn are cleared up, eventually marries Ellen Ramsay.

2488. **————.** *The lady in black*; a study of New York life, morals, and manners. **New York: Sold by the principal booksellers in the United States, 1844. 44p. (in double columns).**

The artist Frederick Austin has long been the lover of Mrs. Aurelia Nelson, a neglected wife, when he finds himself irresistibly drawn to the fresh young beauty of Sarah Thornton, sister of his friend Jack Thornton. Jack Thornton in turn is enamored of 'the lady in black', Isabella Walton, a sophisticated woman who is artist Austin's chief model. Mrs. Nelson learns of her lover's deep affection for Sarah and in despair takes her own life. Shaken by Mrs. Nelson's suicide and believing that Sarah does not return his love, Austin wastes away until Isabella becomes the medium through whom Sarah and Frederick are brought together. Although Jack is very much in love with Isabella, she prefers to remain only his good friend. The author, Nichols, digresses at several points in the story with his observations on morals and social behavior.

2489. ————. *Raffle for a wife.* **New York: Burgess, Stringer, 1845. 72p.**
Jonathan Hallett, merchant of New York City, and his wife, childless, adopt a poor, starving orphan girl whom they name Mary. She blossoms into a beautiful young woman with whom five men-about-New York town fall in love. These five decide to raffle off their opportunities for courting Mary—whoever throws the highest number with the dice will be the first to ask Mary for her hand in marriage, and so on. On a vacation trip to Niagara Falls Mary is rescued from near death when she slips over a cliff, by Edward Temple, a farmer/artist. In Saratoga Mary is courted by one of the five rafflers, Mr. Judevine; Temple appears and declares his love to Mary, although he has been led to believe she is engaged to Judevine. But that misunderstanding is dispelled and Temple, not one of the five, is the winner.

2490. **Nichols, Walter Hammond, 1866-1935. *A Morgan rifleman*; a story of the American Revolution. Illustrated by W.P. Couse. New York: Century Co. 1928. viii, 308p.**
"While Washington, Hamilton and other historical characters are introduced … its outstanding personage is Benedict Arnold, who is seen by the Morgan rifleman, John Homer [during campaigns in New York State, etc.] in moments of bravery as well as of less creditable feelings. The reader obtains a better understanding of Arnold's strange personality than most of Arnold's countrymen now possess"—Saturday review of literature.

2491. **Nicholson, Meredith, 1866-1947. *The siege of the seven suitors.* Illustrated by C. Coles Phillips and Reginald Birch. Boston: Houghton, Mifflin, 1910. 400p.**
Action takes place in Octavia Hollister's country house just outside New York City. She has two unmarried nieces who are heirs to her fortune. The elder niece attracts seven suitors, all of whom are temporarily lodged at a nearby inn. Her sister, Hezekiah, takes great pleasure in sowing confusion and general mischief among the competing claimants. The most likely candidate is an architect who has been assigned to make repairs and improvements in the heating system of Aunt Octavia's house. Selection of the winning suitor is to be based on the results of a test that all must take.

Niles, Willys, pseud. See: Hume, John Ferguson, b. 1830.

Nitsch, Helen Alice Matthews, d. 1889. See under her pseudonym: Owen, Catherine.

2492. **Noble, Annette Lucile, 1844-1932.** *Miss Janet's old house.* **New York: National Temperance Society and Publication House, 1884. 425p.**

> The spinster Miss Janet, 50, presented a stern, even hard-shelled exterior to the world but underneath was a person with a deep concern for the downtrodden. Her 'old house' provides shelter for poor families that are striving to get back on their feet. The novel is directed towards portraying the bleak lives of tenement dwellers in New York City and the curse that strong drink places on many of them.

2493. **————. *"Out of the way."* New York: American Tract Society, 1880. 240p.**

> Perhaps the most noteworthy character in this novel is Hannah Nichols, a Quaker, who quite 'stealthily' performs good works throughout New York City. The story opens, however, with two upper class ladies, Mrs. Grey and Mrs. Stuart (abetted by their inspiration, seamstress Kaziah Hallenbeck) visiting a charity ward on an island outside the city where they meet a girl of German extraction, Elsie. Another girl, Mary, is introduced as she toils for tenement-dweller Catherine Rian. The fortunes of Elsie and Mary are followed; neither one is 'quite' an orphan—Mary's father has disappeared while Elsie's German mother appears briefly at the story's end. The girls' work experiences are rather unrewarding; at last Elsie finds a home with Hannah Nichols whom she adores and Mary is taken into the service of wealthy Mrs. Stuart. Quaker Hannah, everyone's 'Friend', never ceases in the performance of her good deeds.

2494. **Nolan, Jeannette Covert, 1896 or 7-1974.** *Treason at the Point.* **Illustrated by Henry C. Pitz. New York: J. Messner, 1944. 224p.**

> A fictional look at General Benedict Arnold's treasonable plot concerning the American fort at West Point as seen by three young patriots: Jed Drake, a courier for the American forces; his sister Emmeline, who was a servant in the Arnold home; and their younger brother, Kirby.

2495. **Norris, Charles Gilman, 1881-1945.** *The amateur.* **New York: Doran, 1916. 379p.**

> "The story of one of those hopeful young persons who come to New York intent on conquest. Carey Williams has had some success in commercial art work in his home city and has won a prize in a poster contest. This is enough to send him to New York. The fact that there are 25,000 artists in New York City alone, a bit of information offered by the distinguished illustrator to whom he applies for advice, dampens his enthusiasm somewhat, but although he is a man of somewhat weak fibre, he perseveres and the story follows him

through discouragement, popular success, and failure (including a period when he hung around with a rakish group and ended up innocently implicated in a misdemeanor), and leaves him in the end [trying to overcome his amateurism and] looking forward to what may be a second and more firmly-founded success"—Book review digest.

2496. ――――. *Pig iron*. **New York: Dutton, 1925. 466p.**
"Samuel Osgood Smith is a self-made millionaire. Born the son of an unsuccessful schoolmaster/farmer, he goes at 19 or 20 to New York where an uncle finds work for him. The religious atmosphere of his uncle's home offsets the influence of his new friends, but does not keep him from falling in love with a pale little prostitute and living with her. His love for Evelyn is real, and it is a bitter blow when she leaves him. It marks the end of his dream life and the beginning of his business success. Marriage to Paula, his employer's daughter, makes possible a social career. He seems to have acquired everything a man could want. But in the process sentiment and affection and all comradeship with his wife and children have been lost"—Book review digest.

2497. ――――. *Seed*; **a novel of birth control. Garden City, N.Y.: Doubleday, Doran, 1930. 436p.**
Bart Carter and his wife Peggy leave the Carter ranch for New York City where Bart seeks fame as a writer. The Carter women always had a tradition of bearing a lot of children and Peggy, a Carter by marriage, is no exception. She is also a strong Catholic decidedly against any form of birth control. As their marriage cools Bart has an affair with another woman, one who can further his literary career. Bart's milieu is increasingly one that encompasses New York and Long Island suburbia. Peggy leaves him, taking the children back to California. Ten years go by when Bart, now a literary success, longs for Peggy and his children, so he asks her to take him back.

2498. **Norris, Kathleen Thompson, 1880-1966.** *The heart of Rachael.* **Front. by Charles E. Chambers. Garden City, N.Y.: Doubleday, Doran, 1916. 408p.**
Rachael is calculating enough to aim for social prominence in New York by marriage to Clarence Breckenridge. His addiction to alcohol and his general indolence, however, signal Rachael to sever her bond to Breckenridge. After the divorce she marries Dr. Gregory; with her newfound happiness Rachael sheds her former coldness to become a caring, loving woman. Her world crumbles again when the doctor is obsessed by a scatterbrained little actress. Rachael starts to rethink the topics of marriage and divorce; she and her children leave Dr. Gregory. A reunion with her abashed husband occurs only after one of their children is in critical condition after an accident.

2499. ――――. *The love of Julie Borel.* **Garden City, N.Y.: Doubleday, Doran, 1931. 348p.**

Two girls, Julie Borel and Pen Barnes, from a town in the Hudson River Valley are in love with the same man, the Vicomte Tony de la Ferronays, teacher in a woman's college. Tony is as poor as Julie and she is at the beck and call of the Barnes family. Pen is the stereotypical spoiled little rich girl. The Vicomte must choose between them. He does; when he vacillates because of an unusual circumstance, Julie takes hold and she does the choosing this time around.

2500. ———. *Mother*; a story. **New York: Macmillan, 1911. 172p.**

Increasingly restive and weary of the stresses of school teaching in a small New York State town Margaret Paget leaves her mother and brothers and sisters to become live-in companion to a wealthy lady in New York City. She is brought in touch with upper-class society and believes that its ideas about motherhood and the raising of children coincide with her own. When love comes into her life, Margaret begins to rethink her attitudes. She goes back home cognizant now of the sacrifices and satisfactions that her mother had derived from her concentration on family life.

2501. **Norris, Mary Harriott, 1848-1919.** *Afterward.* **St. Paul, Minn.: Price-McGill Co., 1892. 470p.**

Temptation compels a respectable New York broker, Henry Winchester, to write out a falsified check and to steal other people's bonds. It is his unaware wife, Madeleine, who has to bear the brunt of his misdemeanors. She is shut out of polite society and strives to regain her good repute. That happens only after she has distanced herself from Henry Winchester and is about to be married to honorable Mark Dascom.

2502. ———. *The gray house of the quarries.* **With an etching by Edmund H. Garrett. Boston: Lamson, Wolffe, 1898. 498p.**

"The 'gray house of the quarries' was an old homestead on the Hudson, surrounded by the farms of descendants of the early Dutch settlers, where greed and avarice are pictured, in striking contrast to the liberality of the inhabitants of the gray house. Susanne Kildare, a child of the quaint old house, is the heroine. Susanne's ancestry is traced, and episodes of her childhood, girlhood and wifehood are introduced in a story which deals with questions of heresy, and which pictures also the social conditions of New York at the … [turn of the century]"—Annual American catalogue.

2503. ———. *John Applegate, surgeon*; a novel. **St. Paul, Minn.: Price-McGill Co., 1893. 334p.**

"The scene is New York. John Applegate, a medical specialist and confrére of Dr. Huntington, loves Margaret Huntington, generally supposed to be the doctor's daughter; in an incidental conversation, however, between Drs. Applegate and Huntington, it is revealed that the latter adopted Margaret for the purpose of testing whether education or heredity is strongest in the evolution of human character. The interest is in the final solution of this social problem, and in the unlooked for developments of the young woman's wooing"—Annual American catalogue.

2504. **Norris, Zoe Anderson.** *The color of his soul.* **New York: Funk & Wagnalls, 1902. 220p.**

This piece of fiction is actually a series of sketches that dwell on life in the bohemian section and the newspaper offices of New York City. A central character is a confused young man who epitomizes the ideas of a radical professor who expounds at some length on socialistic and matrimonial themes.

North, Barclay, pseud. See: Hudson, William Cadwalader, 1843-1915.

2505. **North, Nelson Luther, 1830-1904.** *Ask and receive,* **including stories and folklore of the Adirondack and Lake Champlain regions. Chicago: Scroll Pub. Co., 1901. 83p.**

Augustus De Mott, member of a family that resides on an island in Lake Champlain, relates several stories, true and fictional, to Mr. Jones, a visitor. Lt. Thomas McDonough, later the victor in the Battle of Lake Champlain in the War of 1812, is the main character in one story. The fortunes and misfortunes of a Frank Perry in New York City are the subject of another tale. The Adirondacks, Plattsburgh and Dannemora (now Clinton State) Prison are the scenes of several of De Mott's narratives (including the 17th century love story of the Italian Fransioli Lentilla and Wa-Wi-Watha (Beautiful Little Water), an Iroquois maiden.

2506. **Norton, Andre, 1912- .** *House of shadows* **[by] Andre Norton and Phyllis Miller, New York: Atheneum, 1984. 201p.**

An historic house in Upstate New York presided over by Great-Aunt Hendrika is the temporary home of Susan, Mike and younger brother Tucker. None of the three is comfortable there; Tucker especially sees youthful ghosts from the past that have some relationship to paper dolls he and Susan have discovered. Are they asking Tucker to help them? Mike, Susan and Hendrika encounter via Tucker manifestations of a tragedy that took place over 200 years ago. They work together courageously and sympathetically to rid the house of its indwelling evil spirits.

2507. **Norton, Charles Ledyard, 1837-1909.** *The Queen's Rangers;* **a story of Revolutionary times. Illus. by William F. Stecher. Boston: W.A. Wilde, 1899. 351p.**

During the British occupation of New York City by General Sir William Howe and British command of the sea approaches by Admiral Richard Howe, three young American patriots find themselves stranded in the city. Together they undergo a series of adventures on land and sea before they are able to formally join the American forces.

2508. Oakley, E. *Eliza Atwood*; or, *The resemblance*. **An authentic tale. New York: S. Raynor, 1848. 163p.**

Eliza Atwood's mother tells her the sad story of Eliza's aunt, Eliza Wardrop, a young woman in the Hudson Highlands in love with Richard Edwards. He is in New York City carving a career in the world of commerce. Richard's health declines and Miss Wardrop experiences a similar drop in physical well-being. In Saratoga Springs for physical and spiritual improvement Eliza Wardrop has presentiments of her lover's death. Richard dies and Eliza Wardrop follows shortly thereafter. Eliza Atwood's life begins to follow a similar pattern. Her fiancé in New York, Theodore Scudder, goes on an ocean voyage to help his deteriorating health. However he does improve markedly and marries Eliza. The chain is broken. Oddly enough the author intersperses on pages 13-55 of her novel a story of the Indians who lived near the cascade of Melsingah (or Melzingah) and its tributary Matoavoan (or Matteawan) that, we are told, are about 60 miles from New York City, 'at the foot of the northernmost ridge of the [Hudson] Highlands'.

2509. Oakley, Hester Caldwell. *As having nothing*. **New York: G.P. Putnam, 1898. 330p.**

"Two New York girls are the heroines. One has a studio on 55th Street; the other is the daughter of rich parents. [The more interesting of the two], Elizabeth Wallace, had studied art abroad, and when her father's death left her the only support of her mother and herself she tried to get work at book illustration, finally succeeding beyond her expectation. There are two men in the story, one a rising novelist, the other the son of the senior member of the Boston publishing house of Linton, West & Co. They both find inspiration in the heroines"—Annual American catalogue.

2510. Oates, Joyce Carol, 1938- . *American appetites*. **New York: Dutton, 1990. 340p.**

Oates examines the attitudes of upper middle class residents of an affluent Hudson River suburb of New York City through her story about Ian McCullough, researcher at an institute for human behavior studies, and his graceful wife, Glynnis, who makes all the right social moves. Ian, half-drunk, has a quarrel with Glynnis, which terminates in her death caused by her body crashing through a plate glass wall. Ian is picked up on a charge of murder and goes to trial. Did Ian push his wife to her death, or did she fall accidentally and fatally?

2511. ————. *Because it is bitter and because it is my heart*. **New York: Dutton, 1990. 405p.**

"In a small city in Upstate New York in the decade before the upsurge of the Civil Rights movement, when racial prejudice seemed inflexible and habitual, we are introduced to two families struggling to advance themselves—the Courtneys, who are white, and the Fairchilds, who are black. The invisible color line separates them; each family is secure (or so it seems) in its own world, but there is a strange, virtually subterranean link. When Iris Courtney is a young girl, she is the only witness to a murderous street fight between Jinx Fairchild and a white man who has threatened her. A bond of passion and guilt is formed between the two … and the consequences are fateful. Parallel to this story of extraordinary passion are the lives and struggles of the two families and of the country in which they live; each moves from a time of high promise to an age of embittered violence"—Publisher's announcement.

2512. ———. *Bellefleur.* **New York: E.P. Dutton, 1980. 558p.**
"In this gothic novel Oates weaves a shimmering tapestry made up of odd and contradictory threads: a hermaphroditic birth, a vulture that devours an infant, a dwarf with 'powers', a vampire, a cannibal, religious mystics and clairvoyants. Such are the trappings of … the Bellefleurs, an old and powerful American family whose estate is located in the Adirondacks and whose history is an interpretation of American history from pioneer days to the present"—Benet's reader's encyclopedia of American literature.

2512a. ———. *Broke heart blues*; a novel. **New York: Dutton, 1999. 369p.**
It was assumed that lower-class teenager John Reddy Heart, a recent arrival in 1967 in a community not far from Buffalo, N.Y., had killed his mother's no-good lover and then run off. The police eventually picked up the lad, but in the meantime he had become a legend in the minds of his peers. These young people meet 30 years later as middle-aged adults at their high school reunion. One of them, Evangeline Fesnacht, opens up scrapbooks that contain data about John Reddy Heart and his trial.

2513. ———. *First love*; a Gothic tale. Designed and illustrated by Barry Moser. **Hopewell, N.J.: Ecco Press, 1996. 85p.**
Josie, 11, and her selfish, abusive mother, Delia, who has just left her husband, have settled for the summer in the home of Josie's great-aunt, Esther Burkhardt, in mid-20th century Upstate New York. Esther is a morose, almost unapproachable person. Her son, Jared, Sr., a Presbyterian minister, had died 20 hears ago following his church's destruction by fire. Jared, Jr., 25, a seminary student, is the third adult in the household. He is a monster, sexually molesting Josie and scaring her into silence with dire warnings. Possessed by guilt and emotionally distraught Josie upsets everyone with her weird, troublesome actions and her self-scourging.

2514. ———. *Foxfire*; confessions of a girl gang. **New York: Dutton, 1993. 328p.**
In 'Hammond' in Upstate New York (Lockport is its real counterpart) during the 1950s a group of girls headed by steadfast, daring 'Legs' Sadovsky band together to express their own brand of rebellion against the hypocrisies of class society and especially against the abusive power of men. The story of this sisterhood ('Foxfire') is told by Maddy Wirtz years later from a notebook she compiled during her membership in the 'outlaw' gang (or 'juvenile delinquents' in contemporary terminology).

2515. ———————. *I lock my door upon myself.* **New York: Ecco Press, c1990. 98p.**

The protagonist of Oates's novel, with its setting a farm in Upstate New York at the turn of the century (19th & 20th), is Edith Freilicht, called Calla by her mother (who later died in childbirth) and by Tyrell Thompson, Calla's black lover. Calla had been forced into a loveless marriage and she had little zest for the life she led on the family farm until Thompson came along. He was a dowser (one who uses a divining rod to locate ground water) and had dropped by to offer his services. The love affair of Calla and Tyrell is laden with sexuality and eventually desolation.

2516. ———————. *Man crazy*; **a novel. New York: Dutton, 1997. 282p.**

Chautauqua County, more specifically the banks of the Chautauqua River [i.e. Creek?] is the home of Ingrid Boone and her youngish alcoholic mother, Chloe; they are hiding from a Vietnam veteran, Ingrid's father Luke. Luke is a violent, brutal man; Chloe sleeps around with a variety of worthless men. With such role models it is not surprising that adolescent Ingrid finds solace in drugs and self-abuse. Gang-raped by outlaw motorcyclers who force her to live a prisoner in a filthy hovel, Ingrid is finally hospitalized and undergoes extensive therapy. There is now the possibility of a brighter future for Ingrid, especially when an elderly psychiatrist falls in love with her.

2517. ———————. *The mysteries of Winterthurn.* **New York: Dutton, 1984. 482p.**

The three mystery-oriented novelettes in this collection have an Adirondack setting (at the turn of the 19th-20th centuries). They are wrapped in Gothicism with underpinnings of diabolism, rape, infanticide, suicide, madness, murder and romanticism. Xavier Kilgarvan applies his keen powers of detection and peels back layers of grisly secrets while his love for the bewitching Perdita sustains him. Contents: The virgin in the rose-bower; or, The tragedy of Glen Mawr Manor.—Devil's Half-Acre; or, The mystery of the 'Cruel Suitor'.— The bloodstained bridal gown; or, Xavier Kilgarvan's last case.

2518. ———————. *Unholy loves*, **a novel. New York: Vanguard Press, 1979. 335p.**

British poet Albert St. Denis's imminent arrival at 'Woodslee University' in Upstate New York arouses great expectations from the English faculty. But it's all a downer. Alcoholic enfeebled St. Denis is killed when his apartment catches fire. Meanwhile Brigit Stott, a novelist, and other faculty and administrators have problems of their own. Brigit is able to make use of her colleagues' lives and their reactions to the St. Denis affair.

2519. ———————. *We were the Mulvaneys.* **New York: Dutton, 1996. viii, 454p.**

High Point Farm outside the Upstate New York town of 'Mt. Ephraim' is the home of a prominent family, the Mulvaneys. Michael Mulvaney is the owner of a roofing company; his wife Corinne is the good housewife and mother with a sideline in antiques. The four Mulvaney children (3 boys and a girl) are: Judd (the story's narrator); Mike, Jr. ('Mule'), the athlete; Patrick

('Pinch'), the intellectual; and beautiful Marianne, cheerleader, and, in 1976 at the age of 17, raped by a schoolmate. This episode has tragic, far-reaching consequences for the Mulvaneys. From this point on the family splinters. Michael Sr. can't stand having his tainted daughter around and sends Marianne to a relative. The roofing firm collapses and eventually the farm is lost. The boys sadly, angrily and destructively work out their frustrations. Ten years pass and the author ends her novel with the Mulvaneys grasping hope for the future.

2520. ————. *What I lived for*. **New York: Dutton, 1994. x, 608p.**
To the general public Jerome Andrew Corcoran, a millionaire through dabbling in real estate, is a councilman in 'Union City', N.Y., and an old friend of the mayor. In private 'Corky' pursues women avidly and drinks to excess. Union City is faced with precipitous decline unless new industry comes in and urban renewal takes hold. On a May morning Corky volunteers to direct traffic as the police deal with an emergency situation—the suicide of a young black woman with city hall connections and a close acquaintance of his stepdaughter. Corky begins looking more closely at his city and his relationship with his ex-wife, stepdaughter, friends, political partners, et al. With all his peccadilloes Corky still retains a sense of what is right.

2521. ————. *You must remember this*. **New York: Dutton, 1987. 436p.**
A novel with incestuous overtones as Enid Marie Stevick, a 15-year-old living with her family in an Upstate New York industrial town during the 1950s, falls in love with her Uncle Felix, 30, a one-time pugilist. Enid had already attempted suicide. The feverish affair of niece and uncle ignores the suffocating drabness of a very conventional community.

2522. **Ober, Norman [Alfred]. *Bungalow Nine*. New York: Walker, c1962. 263p.**
Jason and Ann Cutler are a young couple vacationing in a summer bungalow colony known as 'Hector's' in Upstate New York. A show business pair, the Cutlers find the activities at Hector's rather strenuous. Typically, a party night in the casino is followed the next morning by a softball doubleheader, then card games for the women and intense poker for the men, and so on. The Cutlers look rather patronizingly upon the frantic fraternizing and status-seeking of other Jewish-American guests.

2523. **Obolensky, Ivan, 1925- . *Rogues' march*. New York: Random House, 1956. 433p.**
A panoramic novel about a Hudson River town called 'Red Bank' (it is close by Poughkeepsie) in the years 1884 to 1945. At the outset Nathaniel Dill brings his New England bride, Amy Judith Todd, home to the Dill mansion in Red Bank, to the disappointment of a local belle, Stella Robeson. The story then chronicles political and economic events in the town: David Tenvroos and Stella Robeson and her relatives rise to affluence; James Endicott Harper, the undertaker, and his wife Janet's turbulent domesticity; the love affairs of

the male Dills; the crime and punishment of Doc Vetch; etc. Steven, the lawyer son of James Harper, is the leading character as the novel moves toward the middle of the 20th century; he is called upon to be a defense attorney for the Nazis facing the Allied trials at Nuremberg.

2524. O'Brien, Meg. *The Daphne decisions.* **A Jessica James mystery. New York: Bantam Books, 1990. 219p.**

Presently employed as an investigative reporter for the Weston Free Press ('Weston' is a residential community for the affluent a few miles from Rochester, N.Y.) Jessica (or Jesse) James believes she may be on the trail of a real estate scam that Empire Tech and Development of Albany has some part in. Actually there are a number of people closer to home—in Rochester and Weston—who are suspiciously involved, among them Ian Webber, Jesse's mentor and editor of the Weston Free Press, Judge Malcross, certain members of the Rochester Mafia and Jesse's lover Pav. She pokes around in the two towns, barely escaping with her life, and enlists the help of Marcus Andrelli, the mobster, and three friendly Rochester street kids often in trouble with the law. Grady North, Rochester police detective, is deeply troubled by the dangerous situations in which Jesse places herself. The 'Daphne' in the title is Daphne Malcross, daughter-in-law of the Judge, and a murder victim. By the novel's end there is a smidgeon of hope that some of those involved in the corrupt real estate scheme and murder will be punished. Jesse writes the story, sells it to the Rochester Herald and is offered a job by that paper.

2525. ————. *Eagles die too.* **New York: Doubleday, 1992. 245p.**

The personal life of the Rochester, N.Y. reporter, Jessica (or Jesse) James continues to be quite rocky and haphazard. Researching an article, Jesse takes a course on executive bodyguarding, fails it, but is offered flying lessons by the instructor, Mac Devlin. Jesse's mother, Kate, arrives from California with a dubious new husband, Charlie. Kate, Charlie, Mac, and Sam Garner, a flying acquaintance of Mac's get together at a place owned by mobster Marcus Andrelli, a former lover of Jesse, but refuse to let Jesse know what they are up to. The usually capable Jesse has to turn to Tark, one of Andrelli's gang, to fill herself in.

2526. ————. *Hare today, gone tomorrow*; **a Jessica James mystery (book 3). New York: Bantam Books, 1991. 232p.**

Rochester, N.Y. reporter Jessica (Jesse) James is saddled with her mother and the latter's current boyfriend, Charlie Browne, who have come from California with a painting that was obviously stolen from an art gallery. Jesse hopes to shield her mother from Charlie's criminal tendencies and plies her investigative skills in both her own Upstate New York neighborhood and the West Coast. In the course of her inquiries Jesse solves several crimes, including the 1950 murder of Charlie's mother, fights her own alcoholism and begins to fathom her mother's emotional problems.

2527. ————. *Salmon in the soup*. **New York: Bantam Books, 1990. 245p.**
Jessica ('Jesse') James is a hardboiled reporter for the Rochester, N.Y. Herald recovering from alcohol abuse and currently absorbing the doctrines of a psychiatrist/guru. She has also had an affair with the mobster Marcus Andrelli. When Andrelli is charged with murdering a former city attorney, Barbara Sloan, while he and Barbara were hatching a child pornography scenario on his yacht, Jesse suspects Andrelli has been framed. Her own investigation brings her in touch with cops, unsavory characters, and a former high school Adonis she had a crush on.

2528. O'Connor, Varley. *Like China*. **New York: Morrow, 1990. 272p.**
Ex-model Katha Pinnell is twenty-five; formerly a Westchester resident, she has moved to Long Island and is married to Tommy, a 'control freak' who has lowered her sense of self-worth. Despite her growing dislike of violent Tommy, oddly enough Katha pities him and begins searching for something to give meaning to her own life. She believes she has found it when she comes upon a young boy, Peter Kramer; he and his two brothers, Sam and Big Dan, have been forsaken by their parents. They are just about surviving in East Hampton, Long Island often with goods stolen by Big Dan, oldest of the trio. Katha's gradual bonding with the troubled youngsters promises to be a healthy, heartening development for all parties.

2529. O'Cork, Shannon. *End of the line*. **New York: St. Martin's Press, 1981. 232p.**
"T.T. Baldwin ... [is] sent with boozy colleague Floyd, to cover a shark-hunting tourney out of 'Scrimshaw Township' on Long Island. Their ulterior motive ... [is] to investigate the disappearance of a priceless necklace belonging to the zany mother of local Squire Gordon Kittridge and the disappearance of Orthodox Jewish diamond dealer Avram Stein, who was dealing with Kittridge for the necklace. But more serious crime surfaces—when, on T.T.'s first shark expedition, accountant Jeremy Junker falls overboard and winds up dead via sea-wasp venom. And from thereon the overcrowded narrative heaps up melodrama on all sides: the reappearance of Stein, now revealed (sans earlocks) as a government agent; Stein's flaming affair with sexy marina owner Elsie (whose husband beats her); a corrupt local cop who's in a smuggling scam with Kittridge; the movements of two copies of that necklace; plus the death of local gossip columnist Georgia Keene, Kittridge's supposed fiancée. Finally, then, there's a wild midnight shark-hunt finale to unmask the culprit"—Kirkus reviews.

2530. ————. *Sports freak*. **New York: St. Martin's Press. 1980. 171p.**
"Sleuth T.T. Baldwin, spunky girl photographer for the New York Graphic, covering the opening game of the High Mountain Climbers, a new NFL team in Upstate New York ... is right on the scene when Lou Lamont, rookie superstar, hits the ground during the game and doesn't get up—it's murder. T. T. investigates ... and uncovers a veritable Peyton Place—full of illicit couplings, starting out with team owner Marcella Snowfield—sixtyish widow

with a more than motherly interest in football players. But the none-too-substantial motive in fact reaches back to the past; and it's tracked down by routine police work while the body count rises and T.T., in the idiot-heroine manner, nearly gets herself killed"—Kirkus reviews.

2531. **O'Daniel, Janet, 1921- .** *The cliff-hangers*; a novel. **Philadelphia: Lippincott, 1961. 267p.**

About "the making of cliff-hanger [movie] serials in Ithaca, New York fifty [now about ninety] years ago. Matt Hillyer, producer and scenarist as well as director of the movie company, daringly hires a new leading lady, a famous popular dancer. [Matt and his chosen actress do not see eye-to-eye and engage in a battle of wills.] ... Moreover, the exotic movie people set the formerly placid little university town on its ear"—Publisher's note.

2532. —————. *O Genesee.* **Philadelphia: Lippincott, c1957. 350p.**

In 1799 Cyrus Fairchild, a tenant farmer in the Albany region pulls up stakes and travels westward to homestead in the Genesee River Valley. His guide is Marcus Hook, a restless frontiersman and trader. Cyrus achieves property and stature in the community while the non-conforming Marcus is discomposed by a love affair with Abby Candless, a parson's daughter, which ends tragically. Marcus then forms a friendship with Helen Fairchild, Cyrus's daughter, though she has a commitment to Josiah, a lawyer. When the War of 1812 arrives, the Genesee community suffers Indian depredations; Marcus proves his mettle by turning away a contemplated attack by British forces.

2533. **O'Donnell, Jessie Fremont, 1860-1897.** *A soul from Pudge's Corners.* **New York: G.W. Dillingham, 1892. 313p.**

"A question of conscience is involved in the first story. A minister, who believes it is a sin to marry a divorced woman, has a painful experience in a miserable, out-of-the-way village in New York State"—Annual American catalogue. Contents: A soul from Pudge's Corners.—Two points of view.—Miss Athalina's mind cure.—Miss Pamela's journal.—An afternoon's imprisonment.

2534. **Oemler, Marie Conway, 1879-1952.** *Two shall be born.* **New York: Century Co., 1922. 411p.**

An improbable tale featuring a New York traffic policeman, Brian Kelly (whose father just happens to be extremely wealthy), and Marya Jadwiga Zuleski, daughter of a Polish nobleman, who has been given secret papers relating to Poland's freedom movement and sent to New York by her father. Russian, German and Japanese agents are on her trail and Brian comes to her aid, hiding her and then marrying the beleaguered young woman. Brian, his father, and Baron Rittenhouse (the latter putting a new spin on his German secret service loyalties) are instrumental in rescuing Marya from Russian hands.

2535. Offit, Sidney, 1928- . *He had it made*; a novel. New York: Crown Publishers, 1959. 317p.

A 'go-getter' New Yorker takes a summer job in one of the resort hotels of the Catskill 'borscht circuit'. It isn't long before he has won the good will and support of his fellow employees and many of the guests—with a single exception: one of the hotel's tougher retainers who fancies himself irresistible to the fairer sex.

2536. Ogburn, Dorothy, 1890- . *The will and the deed.* New York: Dodd, Mead, 1935. 264p.

Old Horatio Walters, eccentric millionaire, left his estate to his daughter Ollie. She falls to her death—was she pushed or was it an accident? There's a number of relatives and others who act suspiciously: sophisticated Carthew Walters; Lester Neville, Ollie's husband; Sybil Blake, a singer; and the inevitable butler, Brandon. There's a family skeleton to boot. Detective Morrison, rooting around the gloomy mansion on the Hudson where it all takes place, has to overcome his initial puzzlement before he comes up with the answer.

2537. Ogden, Harriet Verona Cadwalader. *Then came Molly.* Front. by Elizabeth Pilsbry. Philadelphia: Penn Pub. Co., 1922. 318p.

"The story of a girl who ventures from the seclusion of a Southern plantation into the tumult of life in New York and the delicious excitement of study in an art school. Being gifted with a genus for painting, she rapidly outstrips all her competitors and is rewarded by becoming the target of their jealousy. But she perseveres until in the end she is in sight of the success that her talent merits; and, incidentally, after various difficulties and misunderstandings, she succeeds in an entirely different field—and is well on the road to having her engagement announced"—Literary review of the New York evening post.

2538. **Ogden, Ruth, 1853-1927.** *Loyal hearts and true.* Illustrated by H.A. Ogden. New York: F.A. Stokes, 1899. viii, 322p.

The protagonists of this story for young people have the Brooklyn Navy Yard and the old docked ship, the U.S. Fremont, as their 'playground'. Incidentally they learn quite a bit about the U.S. Navy and what life aboard a Navy ship entails for the ordinary sailor. The youngsters are also witness to preparations for prosecution of the Spanish-American War of 1893.

2539. ————. *A loyal little Red-coat*; a story of child-life in New York a hundred years ago. With over 60 original illus. by H. A. Ogden. New York: F.A. Stokes, 1890. 217p.

This is a story for juveniles, but it has interest for older readers because it scrutinizes the question of ownership of houses taken from Tories during the American Revolution and occupied by patriots. The tale's little heroine is Hazel Boniface whose father was a colonial who accepted a captaincy in the King's Army. Hazel has friends on both sides of the recent conflict, but she herself remains loyal to the British Crown. The lawyer, Colonel Alexander Hamilton, late of Washington's staff, has a prominent role in the story.

2540. O. Henry, 1862-1920.

In all, O. Henry (William Sydney Porter) wrote 140 stories that recorded the people, sights and sounds of New York City and environs. "The New York one meets in O. Henry's stories is both real and unreal. Its essence is there, firmly and indelibly embedded in scores of passages ... the changeless, turbulent, indestructible spirit of the place. ... The endless allure of New York with its thousands of beckoning contrarieties, inducements and denials he was to celebrate in story after story"—Current-Garcia, E.O. Henry. Below are listed the seven collections which contain most of those stories.

The four million. New York: McClure, Phillips, 1906. 261p. (25 stories.)

The trimmed lamp. New York: McClure, Phillips, 1907. [c1906]. 260p. (25 stories.)

The voice of the city. New York: McClure, 1908. 228p. (25 stories.)

Options. New York: Harper, 1909. 257p. (8 'New York' stories.)

Strictly business. New York: Doubleday, Page, 1910. vi, 299p. (22 stories.)

Whirligigs. New York: Doubleday, Page, 1910. [c1910]. vi, 314p. (12 'New York' stories.)

Sixes and sevens. New York: Doubleday, Page, 1911. 283p. (15 'New York' stories.)

2541. O'Higgins, Harvey Jerrold, 1876-1929. *The adventures of Detective Barney.* Illus. by Henry Raleigh. New York: Century Co., c1912-15. 305p.

Based on a play by O'Higgins and Harriet Ford the story concerns a young man brought up on New York's East Side who fancies himself a detective. He seizes the opportunity to do some investigating for a well-known private detective agency and falls into seven instructive undertakings. Barney's acquaintance with life on the streets of New York proves invaluable.

2542. ————. *Don-a-Dreams*; a story of love and youth. New York: Century Co., 1906. 412p.

The hero of the story is a young Canadian, dubbed 'Don-a-Dreams' because he has imagination and a capacity for timeless daydreaming, but seemingly lacks practical sense and has failed in college. His failures continue in New York City where he loses job after job, but then comes a renaissance when he takes up playwriting and creates several successful theatrical pieces. That allows Don-a-Dreams to rekindle his love for a childhood sweetheart,

Margaret, bring her to New York and marry her. Their happiness is a surety, yet Margaret must confess that she, like many others in his circle, has moments when she finds her husband incomprehensible.

2543. ———. *Old Clinkers*; a story of the New York Fire Department. With illus. by Martin Justice. Boston: Small, Maynard, 1909. 277p.

Captain Keighley, chief of a New York City firefighting boat, the 'Hudson', is known as 'Old Clinkers' to many of his colleagues. Keighley is non-political and tries his best to insulate his crew from political rumbles that swirl around 'The Jigger Jumpers', a recently formed benevolent association.

2544. ———. *The smoke-eaters*; the story of a fire crew. New York: Century Co., 1905. 296p.

Stories of the team of Hook and Ladder Company No. 0 of New York City taken from actual accounts. The firemen have a saying: that they 'eat smoke and spit black buttons'. Chief among these firefighters are: Captain Meaghan who is about to collect his pension after 35 years of noteworthy service; Lieutenant Gallagher who wins a staunch reputation and marries the Captain's adopted daughter; and Sergeant Pim whose humor at grim moments relieves a lot of tension.

Ohl, Mrs. Josiah Kingsley, b. 1866. See: Andrews, Annulet, b. 1866.

2545. O'Kane, Leslie. *Death and faxes*. New York: St. Martin's Press, 1996. 216p.

Back in her hometown in Upstate New York with her two children while her husband is completing an engineering project in the Philippines, greeting card designer Molly Masters initiates a faxable greeting service. She is about to answer a letter from a high school teacher she had lampooned in the school paper in her teen years when that person suddenly dies. Molly then receives several faxed notes that not only accuse her of hastening the teacher's death but which also imply reprisals against her and the children. Members of Molly's graduating class who recall her satirical piece are still around: Tommy Newton, the policeman looking into the teacher's demise; Stephanie Saunders, PTA president; and Jack Vance, elementary school principal, who had been a football star in high school. The murder of another classmate's husband motivates Molly to concentrate on the present activities of all her former classmates.

2546. *Old Haun, the pawnbroker*; or, *The orphan's legacy*. A tale of New York, founded on facts. New York: Livermore & Rudd, 1857. 463p.

Little Anna Hervey, after her parents' deaths, is adopted by Dr. Benjamin Foster, a kindly bachelor. Anna is unaware that she is the closest relative of William Leonard, a retired resident of New Orleans with real estate holdings there. But another relative, James Cornell, hoping to take over Leonard's properties for himself, hires the vicious, unscrupulous pawnbroker, Carlos Haun, of Chatham Street, New York City, to track down Anna. Cornell and

Haun quarrel over division of the spoils when the former does acquire Leonard's estate. The two brawl; Haun kills Cornell, is arrested and dies as he attempts to escape from his jail cell. Meanwhile investigative work by Dr. Foster's lawyer and friend, Daniel Pierce, abetted by Anna's childhood companion, Mich Lynch, helps identify Anna's right to the Leonard fortune. Years later Anna, now a belle of New York society, breaks her engagement to the dissolute son of the Rev. Dr. Randall and finds her true love to be Mich Lynch; the latter, with the support of lawyer Pierce, has become a successful attorney.

2547. **Oldboy, Oliver, pseud.** *George Bailey*; **tale of New York mercantile life. New York: Harper, 1880. 288p.**

George Bailey, an honest young clerk, is on the verge of marrying his employer's only daughter when a presumed friend, a fellow employee (and a religious hypocrite) commits a forgery, which he cleverly pins on George. Convicted by circumstantial evidence George is consigned to a New York State prison for two years. On his release George sets about to clear his name and resume honorable employment.

2548. **Older, Cora Miranda Baggerly, 1875-1968.** *Esther Damon*, **by Mrs. Fremont Older. New York: Scribner, 1911. 355p.**

A story of the regeneration of two former 'outcasts'. The heroine is the daughter of rigidly conventional religious parents who are determined to push her into missionary work. Esther rebels and pursues a lifestyle that marks her as a 'scarlet' woman. She meets Robert Orme who is also regarded by the inhabitants of the Upstate New York town as a drunken 'loser' and a bad influence. Nevertheless Orme surprises everyone by establishing a Utopian community, performing good works and turning Esther's life around.

Older, Mrs. Fremont, 1875-1968. See: Older, Cora Miranda Baggerly, 1875-1968.

2549. **Oliphant, Laurence, 1829-1888.** *The tender recollections of Irene McGillicuddy*. **New York: Harper, 1878. 94p.**

Irene (the "I" of the novella) is transplanted from a Fifth Avenue mansion to the 'modest luxury' of a villa in Richmond (the New York City borough) and compares herself favorably to her peers in English (London) society. Irene is beautiful, accomplished and well able to take care of herself. Visitors from England—the Earl of Chowder and Viscount Huckleberry—excite the mothers of Irene and her best friend, Flora Temple, with the prospect of a noble title in their families. The Earl of Chowder's parents, however, do not deem Irene a suitable match for their son despite her wealth. Flora does capture Huckleberry and the Viscount hustles her off to London. Irene falls in love with penniless Obadiah Tompkins, an English scientist-writer. Over the objections of the title-seeking Mrs. McGillicuddy Irene and Obadiah marry.

2550. Oliver, Roland, pseud. *Back stage*; a story of the theater. New York: Macmillan, 1924. ix, 285p.

"Another story of the 'inside' of the New York world of the theatre, another case of the meteoric rise of a brilliant young dramatist, of his troubles with Semitic managers, actresses, and other queer folk. This one deals chiefly with the developments of the semi-amateur Greenwich Village playhouses and is fairly closely drawn from the living models, and therein it holds some novelty, though for the most part the action is familiar enough in its lines. But the value of the story lies in its people, chiefly the amiable and very British young Peter Millard. Peter gets a newspaper job, drifts into the Village theatrical world and writes a playlet which is a 'wow', and thus attracts the Olympian notice of a Broadway magnate"—Literary review of the New York evening post.

2551. Olmstead, Florence. *Father Bernard's parish.* New York: Scribner, 1916. 302p.

"A novel of New York [City] life that has many of the qualities of a story of a country town. The New York that the author suggests is a New York of innumerable small communities, each with interests and activities of its own. Father Bernard's parish lies along Columbus Avenue up near 100th Street and his parishioners, the butcher, the baker, the cobbler and many other persons of local importance, are characters in the story. In particular it has to do with two love stories. Lena, the waitress in Zukerman's lunch-room is the heroine of one, and little Annie Halligan, who, until George Wagner came to clerk in the drug store, had thought herself called to the Church, of the other"—Book review digest.

2552. O'Nan, Stewart, 1961- . *The names of the dead.* New York: Doubleday, 1996. 399p.

To add to the miseries of his incessant Vietnam War memories and his current humdrum job of delivering snack cakes to stores in Ithaca, New York, Larry Markham is abandoned by his wife, Vicki, and their son, slow-learning Scott. While Larry tries to put his family back together, his father's health goes downhill and Larry feels himself drawn to a neighbor, Donna, who has been helping out in Vicki's absence. Topping all this is Larry's suspicion of being targeted by another Vietnam veteran, a mental hospital fugitive seeking to punish Larry for some unknown grievance.

2553. ————. *A world away.* New York: H. Holt, 1998. 338p.

The rather dysfunctional Langer family moves to Long Island's Hamptons during World War II to help care for James's father, recent victim of a stroke. James had been involved with one of his high school students and his offended wife, Anne, acquired her own lover. The Langers have two sons— adolescent Jay and Rennie, a 'conscie' turned medic and now lost somewhere in the Pacific. Rennie's wife recently gave birth and is added to the Langer household. There is a lot of forgiveness to be achieved, anxieties to be soothed and growing-up to be done.

2554. Oppenheim, James, 1882-1932. *The beloved.* **New York: Huebsch, 1915. 268p.**
An impassioned affair between Ralph Hardy, a poet with a New England background, and Trixie Dugan, a third-rate movie actress of dubious reputation in New York, leads eventually to her rebirth. Greenwich Village is the scene of much of this story. So great is the power of their love for one another that when Ralph dies Trixie dedicates herself to her career as an actress and through grief and remembrance of Ralph's simple purity and goodness rises to stardom; her presence on film is inspirational to many who watch her.

2555. ————. *Doctor Rast.* **New York: Sturgis & Walton, 1909. 321p.**
Although he could have had a quietly rewarding life as a country doctor, Dr. Rast searches his conscience and accepts instead the practice of medicine among the poor Jews of New York City's East Side. He faces and tries to mitigate their tragedies, physical and emotional: the child who dies from overwork, the young lovers who are staring at death or separation, the critically wounded from an excursion boat catastrophe, the would-be suicide, etc.

2556. ————. *Idle wives.* **New York: Century Co., 1914. 426p.**
Taking a leaf from Ibsen's *The Doll's House*, the novel's heroine, Anne Wall, realizes that she is a virtual nonentity in her Riverside Drive apartment home; her husband is fixated on his business strivings, her servants keep the physical aspects of the home in order and her children, watched over by an efficient governess, hardly recognize her. When Anne supports her brother Richard who plans to marry Alberta Davies, his stenographer and the mother of a child deemed illegitimate by society, her husband, mother and sister are condemnatory. Anne walks out of her home and takes a job as probation officer at Manhattan's Night Court for young women afoul of the law (prostitution, etc.). Her new living quarters are with Alberta in a tenement located in one of New York's poor districts. The situation is resolved when Anne's husband draws back and agrees to give Anne freedom of choice and wide latitude in the future.

2557. ————. *The Nine-Tenths*; **a novel. New York: Harper, 1911. 319p.**
Joe Blaine, rather careless proprietor of a print shop on New York's East Side, is wiped out by a fire, which takes the lives of a number of his employees. Conscience-stricken he joins the workers' movement and starts a labor paper called 'The Nine-Tenths' and participates in a strike of the garment workers. His on-and-off love affair with a woman named Myra is part of the story, but the author's chief interest is in picturing the city's industrial life and Joe's quandaries.

2558. ———. *Pay envelopes*; tales of the mill, the mine and the city street. **Illustrated by Harry Townsend. New York: B.W. Huebsch, 1911. 259p.**

The first, third, eighth, ninth and tenth stories of the collection are New York City based. They are pervaded with the sights, sounds and smells of the big city, whether, e.g., recounting the desperate search of a discharged worker and father for employment during a depression (The great fear) or the resignation of a Bohemian immigrant, a peasant woman, to her hard life as the chief support of a lazy, drunken baker in a slum tenement (The broken woman). Contents: The great fear.—Meg.—Saturday night.—The cog.—Slag.—A woman.—Joan of the mills.—The empty life.—The young man.—The broken woman.—Stiny Bolinsky.

2559. ———. *Wild oats*. **With a foreword by Edward Bok. New York: Huebsch, 1910. 261p.**

The author reintroduces his fictional Dr. Rast, physician to the Jews who live on New York's East Side. The doctor observes and endeavors to alleviate the physical and emotional pain caused by young people who in sowing their 'wild oats' do not realize or perhaps do not care that it often wounds their elders and the innocent.

2560. **Optic, Oliver, 1822-1897.** *Brake up*; or, *The young peacemakers*. **Boston: Lee and Shepard, 1872. 303p.**

This is the fifth in a series of novels known as the Lake Shore series: the others are, Through by daylight; Lightning express; On time; Switch off; and Bear and forbear. All have the Finger Lakes region of New York State as their locale, perhaps more specifically, Cayuga Lake and environs—in 'Brake up' the author uses anagrams for familiar places in the area, e.g., Hitaca (for Ithaca); Ucayga (for Cayuga); Ruoara (for Aurora). The story itself deals with the rivalry between Colonel Wimpleton's steamship line and Major Toppleton's railroad line. The narrator, Captain Wolf Penniman, is instrumental in bringing the two antagonists together and consolidating the two transportation companies. Colonel Wimpleton has a weakness for brandy, but after several embarrassing drunken episodes, he 'brakes up' (puts an end to) his tippling.

2561. *Oran, the outcast*; or, *A season in New York*. **New York: Peabody, 1883. 2v.**

Refused Margaret Hosmer's hand in marriage because of his ignoble birth, Charles Warner settles in New York City and acquires a good friend in wealthy young Mr. Chillingsworth. Margaret and her father, Major Hosmer, leave the village of 'Bloomsbury' and also take up residence in New York. Haselrig Vane Olmsted, a libertine, sees Margaret as a desirable conquest and plans to keep his rival, Charles, far from her. When General Hezekiah Olmsted, the villain's father, is murdered, Charles is accused—his stolen wallet was planted on the General's body. Testimony from the strange Oran clears Charles. Oran Lorton Olmsted, the half-brother of Haselrig Vane Olmsted, was sired by the General and his slave mistress. A further revelation establishes Haselrig Vane Olmsted as the father of Charles Warner and Chillingsworth by different mothers. Major Hosmer relents after the death of Charles Warner's uncle/guardian, Ralph Warner, and agrees to the marriage of Margaret and Charles. This novel is sometimes attributed to Charles James Cannon.

2562. **Orenstein, Frank, 1919- . *A killing in real estate*. New York: St. Martin's Press, 1989. 218p.**

'Appleboro', N.Y., an attractive and historic town, is under siege by a bulldozing developer, Carl Van Houten, and is in danger of losing its charm. Van Houten had been pressing farmer Jason Belding for the use of his land and Belding had balked. The farmer's body, its skull crushed, turns up and police inquiries uncover interesting financial data—many in the community had a stake, win or lose, should the Belding land be developed. Detective Hugh Harrison calls on Harriet Lorimer, the town's know-it-all, for assistance. But she turns out to be the sole trustee of the Belding property. Another homicide occurs while the town's inhabitants buzz around and do their own snooping.

Ormond, Frederic, pseud. See: Dey, Frederic Van Rensselaer, 1861-1922.

2563. **[Ornitz, Samuel Badisch] 1890-1957. *Haunch, Paunch and Jowl*; an anonymous autobiography. New York: Boni and Liveright, 1923. 300p.**

The fictional life of a Lower East Side Jew, Meyer Hirsch, who carefully plans his advancement and utilizes all available tools—gang membership, theft, extortion, bribery, strikebreaking, alliances with Irish politicians, etc.— to rise to a judgeship on the Superior Criminal Court of New York. He regards with contempt the efforts of several compatriots to better the living conditions of Jewish and other recent immigrants. Meyer's political ambitions are short-circuited by his marriage to his long-time servant/mistress, Gretel. The novel presents a brutally frank, searing portrait of the New York City slums of the late 19th and early 20th century and the struggles of immigrants to achieve success on American terms. 'Haunch, Paunch and Jowl' is the nickname applied to Hirsch as his girth increases with his worldly prosperity.

2564. **————. *A Yankee passional*. New York: Boni and Liveright, 1927. 514p.**

To New York City of the 1890s comes a Yankee mystic, Dan Matthews (the name recalls Harold Bell Wright's popular piece—*The calling of Dan Matthews,* published in 1909). Earlier Dan had worked in a mortuary in a New England village and had been encouraged in his spiritual yearnings by Mame, wife of a quack. Dan's mission in the Bowery attains national stature, yet in the end his piety and goodness is called into question and the naysayers are responsible for driving Dan to an early grave.

2565. **Orton, Helen Fuller, 1872-1955. *The gold-laced coat*; a story of old Niagara. New York: F.A. Stokes, 1934. x, 226p.**

Philippe, a young French lad, sailed from France in 1758 to join his father, a soldier at Fort Niagara, bringing with him his parent's gold-laced coat. His father was killed in battle with the British; Philippe retrieved the coat and kept it as a family heirloom until he exchanged it with the Seneca Indian captors of an English girl, thus obtaining her release. One reviewer (in the Books section of the New York herald tribune) called the story "a thoroughly reliable picture of the settlement of western New York and one that brings out a good trait of Indians often overlooked—remembering a favor received from a white man."

2566. **Orton, Jason Rockwood, 1806-1867.** *Camp fires of the Red Men*; or, *A hundred years ago.* **Illustrated by Walcutt. New York:J.C. Derby, 1855. 401p.**

Captain Charles Warwick, the adoptee of a British colonel, had spent his early years among the Iroquois, not knowing either his father or mother. He is one of the survivors of the wreck of a Spanish vessel off the New Jersey coast. Don Manuel Torrillo, his daughter the Lady Viola, Ferdinand de Cassino, and assorted soldiers, servants, et al., also survive. The Spaniards head up the Hudson River and into the wilderness; their destination is Montreal from whence they will sail for Europe. Woodsman Michael Johnson guides the party and Charles Warwick, already in love with Viola, follows closely behind. Hostile Iroquois impede the party's progress. Ferdinand de Cassino lays plans to trap Lady Viola into marriage. Charles, Michael Johnson (he reveals himself as Charles's father) and friendly Mohawks checkmate De Cassino. Charles kills the villain and he and Viola return to New York City to be married. The author discourses at some length here and there on the customs, organization, etc. of the Iroquois.

2567. **Osborn, Mary Elizabeth, 1989- .** *Another pasture.* **Boston: Bruce Humphries, 1938. 115p.**

In this well-written novella Anna Fraser, well into spinsterhood and teaching at a woman's college in Upstate New York, revisits her childhood hometown in the Catskills. Anna has no living relatives and she finds herself slipping comfortably into the simple country ways and perhaps surprises herself by accepting the marriage proposal of Hiram Bashford, a good-natured, awkward, uneducated farmer. Marriage and the plain cycles of life in the Catskills begin to pall on Anna; she laments the lack of intellectual companionship and feels imprisoned by the mountains that she had longed for when she was still in the 'groves of academe'. "But Anna knew that life was over now, and she could not go back, much as she wished to. The Catskills would be cold and barren soon, and winter would close in. ... It was always some different kind of life from her own that she wanted; and there would be no release for her, ever. She understood that now. Resolutely, she turned away from the window" (p. 115).

2568. ———. *Days beyond recall.* **New York: Coward-McCann, 1942. 108p.**

"A brief novel, which tells the story of dwellers in a small valley in the Catskills. The once fertile farm lands of the valley are worn out and its inhabitants struggle for bare existence. Mr. Hewitt sends young Gwennie into town ('Haynes Hollow') to work for Dan Martin, but Gwennie's innocence and her love for the boy, Russell, save her from the fate Dan Martin planned for her"—Book review digest.

2569. ————. *Listen for a thrush*. **Philadelphia: Westminster Press, 1955. 188p.**
The pattern of a young girl's life and her inability to relate to the people in a Catskill community are briefly interrupted when a visitor from Asia becomes her short-term friend. His departure means the resumption of her isolation from the town.

2570. **Osborne, O.O.** *The quest*. **New York: Fawcett Publications, 1952. 280p.**
A Hudson River Valley businessman's endless quest for women in all their variety becomes a serious drag on his professional and personal life.

2571. **Osborne, William Hamilton, 1873-1942.** *The catspaw*. **With illus. by F. Graham Cootes. New York: Dodd, Mead, 1911. 333p.**
When successive burglaries take place in a small town not far from New York City, Kittredge St. John is suspected as the culprit, but he worms his way out with airtight alibis. Roxane Bellders joins with St. John in planning further daring and patently illegal activities. When they seem to be in harm's way from pursuing lawmen St. John and Bellders use their talents for trickery and escape.

2572. ————. *The red mouse*; **a mystery romance. New York: Dodd, Mead, 1909. 321p.**
A novel that looks at the interaction of machine politics, graft, law, and personal interests in New York City at the turn of the century. A gambling house the district attorney is determined to shut down figures prominently, for it is where a murder takes place that implicates Lawrence Challoner, the 'hero'. Up to that point Challoner had been sponging off his wife's money; his arrest and trial called forth Mrs. Challoner's unstinting support of her husband and made him realize what a waste his life had been.

2573. ————. *The running fight*. **With illus. by Harrison Fisher and George Brehm. New York: Dodd, Mead, 1910. 378p.**
The Panic of 1907 is at the center of the novel. The protagonist is a multimillionaire with a mansion (84 rooms) on Riverside Drive, New York; he has to contend with one of his subordinates who has set himself up in opposition to the financier. New York State's governor, although in office largely because of the millionaire's backing, refuses to commit the perjury that could help the protagonist. Even the millionaire's daughter has to do 'the right thing' when she learns the truth behind the financial turbulence.

2574. **Osmun, Leighton Graves.** *The clutch of circumstance*. **New York: Sully & Kleinteich, 1914. 320p.**

"The story of a young woman's struggle to earn a livelihood in New York. Ruth Lawson leaves behind her in the country village that has been her home, an invalid husband and her mother. She goes to the city to look for work, hoping to earn enough for herself and her home folk. Her experience is the usual one—failure, despair, and a breakdown in health. A chance friend, an actress, saves her, and when she is well again finds her an opening on the stage. Ruth wins a remarkable success, but at the moment of triumph finds that a price is demanded of her. For the sake of those at home she stands ready to pay it—but in the end is released from the demand. Her husband, however, cannot believe her story, and against the narrowness of his point of view stands out the generosity of [Benjamin] Rudolf, the theatrical manager"—Book review digest.

2575. **Ostrander, Isabel Egenton, 1883-1924.** *Above suspicion*, **by Robert Chipperfield [pseud.]. New York: R.M. McBride, 1922. 302p.**

"Geoffrey Peters, a mason and carpenter in the little Long Island town where Joseph Benkard is murdered, runs the criminal to earth and manages to solve a baffling mystery. Benkard, a wealthy resident, is found dead on his veranda, with his head crushed in. There does not appear to be one tangible clue in the whole affair. Peter finds one, however, and he follows it up with complete success"—Book review digest.

2576. **————.** *Annihilation.* **New York: Macmillan McBride, 1924. 310p.**

"Mystery overhung an exclusive residence block in New York [City] known as New Queen's Mall. First, Hughes, Henry Orbit's valet, hurrying along the waterfront in the rain, suddenly dropped dead. The autopsy found that he was the victim of a powerful poison. Then little Horace Goddard mysteriously disappeared, and later, the pretty French bonne, Lucette, died as she sat in her chair listening to Mr. Orbit playing the organ. But McCarthy, ex-special deputy of the police department, happened to be on the spot when Hughes fell, and his sure instinct put him on the right scent of the arch villain to whom the taking of a human life was an exhilarating experience"—Book review digest.

2577. *The fifth ace*, **by Douglas Grant [pseud.]. Front. by George W. Gage. New York: Watt, 1918. 314p.**

The novel crosscuts between Mexico and New York City. The heroine, Willa Murdaugh, was reared by a foster father, Gentleman Geof, in a mining camp in Mexico. He was an honest gambler who instilled that virtue in Willa. When it came out that Willa was the granddaughter of a wealthy New Yorker, Giles Murdaugh, she was dispatched to New York City. With her frank Western ways Willa was a puzzle and embarrassment to certain of her newly discovered relatives. She was smart enough to trap by herself a blackguard named Wiley who had a hand in the death of Gentleman Geof. Kearn Thode, who first met Willa in Mexico, renews acquaintance with her in New York society and eventually gains her assent to his proposal of marriage.

2578. ———. *The heritage of Cain*. **Illustrated by George W. Gage. New York: Watt, 1916. 310p.**

Victoria had always been horrified by her husband's (Dysart Van Rensselaer's) conviction that evil tendencies were passed from generation to generation. Then Mrs. Van Rensselaer is murdered while she and Dysart are hosting a party at their Adirondack hunting lodge. A suspicious incident that several of the guests took note of was the disappearance of a newly hired maid (an out-of-work actress) shortly after the homicide. Solving the crime is dependent on a searching look at people closely tied to Victoria's past.

2579. ———. *How many cards?* **New York: McBride, 1920. 314p.**

"A murder in New York society forms the raison d'être for this detective story. Eugene Creveling is found dead in his library early one April morning. McCarthy, the ex-roundsman detective of previous stories, constitutes himself the chief investigator. He interviews the family social and business friends and servants of the murdered man, and finds as he says, 'every last one of them bluffing and hedging and lying' except the O'Rourkes, former friends of his in the old country, whose integrity he could swear by. He can't understand what the others are all working for, but gradually their motives are uncovered, and although they have a bearing on the character and habits of the dead man, the identity of the murderer still remains a mystery. Then in a flash the solution is revealed to McCarthy by a passing glimpse of a woman's handwriting, the last woman in the world he would want to suspect. But through an act of what he calls Providence she is not brought to justice, and after all perhaps Creveling got no more than he deserved for playing with a woman's honor"—Book review digest.

2580. ———. *The man in the jury box*, **by Robert Chipperfield [pseud.]. New York: R.M. McBride, 1921. 324p.**

"The little town of 'Sunnymead' [New York] is stirred one day by the murder of Gilbert Latimer, a newly arrived and wealthy citizen. Sergeant Barry Odell, of the Homicide Bureau of the New York Police Department, happens to be in the vicinity and undertakes to work the case. There is incriminating evidence, which at first seems to lead to a farmer living nearby, then to Mrs. Latimer herself, and there are other suspects in the household as well. Barry carries his investigations farther afield, and when the case comes to trial, the criminal is discovered in a dramatic finale, to be the one who has not been previously mentioned in connection with the case at all"—Book review digest.

2581. ———.*The man who convicted himself*, **by David Fox [pseud.]. New York: Alexandrian Society, 1930. 308p.**

"The 'Shadowers, Inc.' is a unique detective society composed of six ex-criminals who have decided to use their exceptional talents in an honest way, rather than decidedly otherwise as heretofore. There is a handwriting expert, a jewel and art connoisseur, a toxicologist, 'the greatest safecracker of the age', and a smooth villain who has dealt in various forms of fraud, from oil stock to psychical phenomena. At the head of this band is Rex Powell whose brain conceived the scheme. Their aim is restitution, not prosecution, and they work privately and discreetly. Their first case is one of robbery in an exclusive Riverside Drive home, but as it progresses it provides scope for the activities of each one of the Shadowers. That they are successful in apprehending the robber almost goes without saying, but their greatest success lies in the fact that they actually force the man to convict himself"—Book review digest.

2582. ————. *The tattooed arm.* **New York: R.M. McBride, 1922. 278p.**
"There is much gossip in the little Long Island town of 'Brookles' where the Drake family had resided for many years. Why three elderly gentlemen should suddenly act as if bereft of their senses is the mystery Sergeant Miles and 'Scotty', his able assistant, have to solve. Miss Patricia Drake, whose father is one of the brothers afflicted, in desperation and unbeknown to other members of the family, calls in the help of detectives. After many exciting weeks a wily scheme is unearthed, in which counterfeiters, rogues from Australia, and a tattooed arm play important parts, and even the shrewdest reader will be puzzled at the outcome of the story"—Book review digest.

2583. ————. *The twenty-six clues.* **New York: Watt, 1919. v, 277p.**
"A retired police detective and a New York City fireman … are the chief actors in … The twenty-six clues. The case grows out of the finding of a young woman's body in the 'museum' of a dabbler in criminal investigation whose hobby is the collection of relics connected with famous crimes and criminals. She is the wife of this man's next[-door] neighbor. A 'scientific' investigator directs suspicion against the secretary of the man in whose house the body is found"—Springfield Republican.

2584. ————. *Unseen hands,* **by Robert Orr Chipperfield [pseud.]. New York: McBride, 1920. 307p**
The family mansion of the Lorns on Madison Avenue is the scene of at least two murders. Mrs. Lorn expires from blood poisoning when she is pricked by an infected needle. Julian, the Lorns' oldest son, is discovered in a bathroom with his throat cut. Someone, most likely an 'insider', with detailed knowledge of the Lorns, their customs and behavior, seemingly wants to expunge the remaining members of the family too.

2585. **Otis, James, 1848-1912.** *An amateur fireman.* **New York: E.P. Dutton, 1898. v, 324p.**
"A little New York City bootblack spent most of his leisure time hanging around the engine house of his district and longing to be a fireman. His friends and neighbors discouraged him, but little by little he did odd jobs for the firemen, and finally showed great courage and capacity in a few dangerous fires. From being an amateur he becomes an expert, of whom the 94th Company is proud. [The story] describes accurately the duties of the Fire Department [of New York]"—Annual American catalogue.

2586. —————. *The boy spies of old New York*; the story of how two young spies prevented the capture of General Washington. New York" A.L. Burt, 1899 [c1898]. vi, 265p.

In 1776 two patriots, Dennys Howland and Lloyd Dacre, overhear a plot to have General Washington either captured or killed. They go to General Israel Putnam with their information and offer to infiltrate the conspiratorial group (which includes William Tryon, Royal Governor of New York). Their offer accepted, the two lads have many close calls as they dig for further information. Caught talking to one of Putnam's soldiers, Dennys and Lloyd are found guilty of spying and assume that they will be executed. Their rescue from a British prison ship is carried out by the soldier Paul Stubbs and Caleb Billings, a boatman who had regretted his small part in the British conspiracy. The plot comes to naught and the two boys join the Continental Army.

2587. —————. *The boys of Fort Schuyler.* Illustrated by George Foster Barnes. Boston: Estes and Lauriat, 1897. 265p.

An historical novel about several young American lads who were helping defend Fort Schuyler (better known as Fort Stanwix) in the Mohawk Valley when it was besieged by British and Indian forces under Brigadier General Barry St. Leger and Captain Joseph Brant in 1777. Leaders of the American contingent were Colonel Peter Gansevoort and Lieutenant Colonel Marinus Willett.

2588. —————. *The boys' revolt*; a story of the street Arabs of New York. Illustrated by W.P. Hooper. Boston: Estes & Lauriat, 1894. 193p.

After the boy bootblacks of New York strike against the conditions under which they must work and form a union (which prejudicially excludes 'Eyetalians'), the union's president (the 'Boss Shiner') is found to be corrupt, milking the union treasury for his own benefit. The bootblacks finally end the strike; it has been for them an educational experience with lessons good and bad and with some amusing aspects.

2589. —————. *Corporal 'Lige's recruit*; a story of Crown Point and Ticonderoga. With six pages of illus. by J. Watson Davis. New York: A.L. Burt, 1898. 247p.

The 14-year-old Isaac Rice joins the patriot army under Ethan Allen, Benedict Arnold and Seth Warner, which is preparing to march on Fort Ticonderoga and Crown Point. His mentor is Corporal Elijah Watkins (Corporal 'Lige'), a veteran of the French and Indian Wars. In Vermont Nathan Beman, a lad of Isaac's age, well acquainted with the interior of Ticonderoga, offers to spy for the Americans for a price. Beman's father is a patriot, his mother a Loyalist; Nathan sits on the fence, waiting to judge which side in the conflict has the best chance of success. After several escapades Isaac and Nathan are able to relay pertinent information about British and Tory movements—and Nathan finally foregoes his mercenary ways and joins the American cause.

2590. ————. *Dorothy's spy*; a story of the first "Fourth of July" celebration, New York 1776. New York: T.Y. Crowell, 1904. 161p.

Two girls, Dorothy Dean and Sarah Lamb, daughters of ardent patriots, prepare to attend the reading of the Declaration of Independence. The Americans still hold New York, but General Howe is poised on Long Island and about to strike Washington's army. Dorothy and Sarah see patriots pursuing a man whom they are denouncing as a British spy. If captured he will be hung, so the two girls impulsively offer the spy refuge in the Dean home. This causes no end of trouble for the girls' parents when they are informed of the stranger's presence. Once again Dorothy helps the spy (Lt. Fitzroy Oakman of H.M. 44th Foot) escape—through a window—thus relieving the elders Dean and Lamb from the prospect of turning the lieutenant over to the authorities and certain death on the gallows. After the British occupy New York, Lt. Oakman repays his debt to the Deans and Lambs by saving their homes from destruction by a Tory mob.

2591. ————. *How the twins captured a Hessian*; a story of Long Island in 1776. New York: T.Y. Crowell, 1902. 102p.

Twins Rutgert and Nicholas, young sons of Captain Lambert Suydam of the rebel army, like most boys of their age, are fascinated by the panoply of soldiering. After they are eyewitnesses to the actual gore and confusion of combat as British troops rout the American defenders on Long Island, they quickly lose their enthusiasm for certain things military. They and their mother, under the guidance of the old veteran, Jacob Klemper, attempt to escape the area of fighting and cross the water to New York. That they are able to do so is owing to a safe conduct pass given them by a wounded, exhausted Hessian officer whom the twins had 'captured'—i.e., they had locked the officer in a cellar they had used as a hiding place. The Hessian had been unaware of the boys' presence in the cellar and did not realize they had slipped out, locking the door behind them. Fearful that their 'prisoner' would starve if he could not find a way out, the boys left their escape path to go back and release him. The officer, Count Shonnebraum, repaid their humane act with one of his own—the safe conduct pass.

2592. ————. *Jenny Wren's boarding-house*; a story of newsboy life in New York. Illustrated by W.A. Rogers. Boston: Estes and Lauriat, c1893. 173p.

Five New York newsboys—Pinney White, Tom Downing, Ikey Jarvis, Sam Tousey and Jack Phinney—pool their resources to help Jenny Parson (a.k.a. 'Jenny Wren') rent a building to be turned into a boardinghouse under her management. The project is in place when a baby is left on the doorstep and Pinney is arrested when he innocently takes money from a stranger to deliver a package that turns out to be stolen goods. The lawyer, F.H. Barstow, wins Pinney's release, but the boarding-house burns down. The baby (dubbed 'November' by the newsboys) is reclaimed by its mother, Mrs. Hooper. She, in gratitude for the good care given her missing infant, turns over a vacant structure she owns rent-free to Jenny and the homeless boys to be used as Jenny's new boardinghouse.

2593. ———. *Jerry's family*; a story of a street waif of New York. Illustrated by George Foster Barnes. Boston: Estes and Lauriat, 1895. 195p.

> An unlikely pair is Jerry Bascomb, a New York street boy, and the homeless woman and her baby he takes under his wing. Jerry uses his small earnings to provide living quarters for the three of them off East Broadway. Their survival after an accident that temporarily disables Jerry is assured by the intervention of his friends and a restorative removal to the country.

2594. ———. *Jinny and his partners*. Boston: A.I. Bradley, 1894. 250p.

> The ingenuity of New York street boys is the motif of this novel. "Scotty Jarvis and Jinny Harmon, two boys who were partners in a licensed vendor's trade and a pushhouse or shanty near Chambers Street Ferry; this venture necessitating them to take in two new partners, Ollie Barber and Ben White. After moving into their new home Jinny finds a lost child; this incident causes confusion in the house and results in the advent of Tillie Towser who helps in the discovery of the child's identity"—Annual American catalogue.

2595. ———. *Joel Harford*. Illustrated by C. Copeland. New York: T.Y. Crowell, 1898. 200p.

> Joel Harford is another boy with a rural background who believes that New York City may offer him an opportunity to 'get on' in the world. Two bootblacks who cover territory around New York's City Hall take Joel in hand, introducing him to the insecurities the underclass faces each day. Robbed, beaten, the target of many hard knocks, Joel endures and ultimately develops a prosperous little business of his own.

2596. ———. *Josiah in New York*; or, *A coupon from the Fresh Air Fund*. Boston: A.I. Bradley, 1893. 259p.

> "The amusing adventures of a country boy from 'Berry's Corners' in his first visit to New York City; he [Josiah] misses his friends at Jersey City, and from this point has a succession of mishaps, finally discovering Tom and Bob, the two friends he has come to visit. These boys are street gamins whom Josiah's father had entertained for the Fresh Air Fund, and they do not fail in introducing Josiah to the dime museums, the 'peanut' gallery of the circus and other attractions of the metropolis"—Annual American catalogue.

2597. ———. *Larry Hudson's ambition*. Illustrated by E. Keen. Boston: L.C. Page, 1901. 261p.

> In the Horatio Alger, Jr. mode, Larry Hudson is a bootblack on the streets of New York whose goal in life is to own a home and a farm. Deacon Eli Doak, proprietor of Herdsdale Farm, in the city with his family to celebrate the 4th of July, is robbed by a 'con' man, and Larry is at the ready to help the Deacon retrieve his mulcted funds. As a reward the bootblack receives an invitation to

the Herdsdale Farm. Within a short period Larry is taken in by the Doak family and proves to be a model of integrity and perseverance.

2598. ————. *Left behind*; or, *Ten days a news-boy*. **New York: Harper, 1885. 205p.**

The story of a boy, Paul Weston, a Chicagoan, who missed the boat in New York Harbor that was taking his parents (and presumably him) to Europe. 'Left behind' he places himself in the hands of several sympathetic New York street boys; they give him a batch of newspapers and he essays the occupation of newsboy with little success and less enthusiasm. His new-found friends purchase Paul a ticket for a return to Chicago. Almost simultaneously they come across a bulletin asking for news of the missing Paul. They start for the Fifth Avenue Hotel mentioned in the bulletin and surprise the clerk with their numbers and motley appearance. But Mr. Weston comes down, thanks the boys, and recompenses them for their kind concern for Paul.

2599. ————. *The Minute boys of Long Island*; a story of New York in 1776 as **told by Ephraim Lyttle [by] James Otis. Illustrated by L J. Bridgman. Boston: Dana Estes, 1908. 342p.**

Three teen-age boys are present at several of the early events of the American Revolution—e.g., the Declaration of Independence's first reading, the pulling down of King George III's statue, the British invasion of Long Island, and the occupation of New York City after American resistance is routed.

2600. ————. *The Minute boys of New York City*. **Written by Adam Skidmore [by] James Otis. Illustrated by L.J. Bridgman. Boston: Dana Estes, 1909. 327p.**

Several boys favoring the American cause are caught up in the agitation that continued to grip New York City in 1775 as various committees supporting the Second Provincial Congress and the Independence movement were formed.

2601. ————. *The Minute boys of the Mohawk Valley*. **Illustrated by A. Burnham Shute. Boston: Dana Estes, 1905. 365p.**

This story is based on letters written in 1777 by Joel Campbell of Cherry Valley, N.Y. It tells of several lads who were recruited in Vermont and came to Upstate New York to participate in the American struggle to maintain control of the Mohawk Valley versus invading British, Tory and Indian forces.

2602. ————. *Our uncle, the Major*; a story of New York in 1765. **New York: T.Y. Crowell, 1901. 102p.**

Prior to the repeal of the Stamp Act in April/May 1766 the citizens of New York City had been rioting in protest against that special tax. Caught in the commotion were two youngsters, Janet and Percy Courtyce, niece and nephew of Major James, the King's officer commanding Fort George, who had threatened to severely punish the rioters. Janet and Percy, deserted by their servants, flee a rabble that recognizes them as children of the privileged Royalist class. They find a protector in humble Mistress Brower who guides them through the dangerous, crowd-filled streets of New York to Major James' home, Ranelagh, near the intersection of Anthony Street and West Broadway. The former touch of arrogance that Janet and Percy had displayed towards those 'beneath' them socially had cooled considerably because of the kindness shown them by Mistress Brower.

2603.   ————. *Peter of New Amsterdam*; **a story of old New York. New York: American Book Co., 1910. 158p.**

A story for young readers that explores the home life of a young Dutch boy in New York when it was under Dutch domination. Peter deals with some unfriendly Indians, trading with them and buying land they offer to sell; the tale closes with the coming of the English and their takeover of the colony.

2604.   ————. *The princess and Joe Potter.* **Illustrated by V. Oakley. Boston: Estes & Lauriat, 1898. 249p.**

A good turn is not always seen as such by those most closely involved. A newsboy, Joe Potter, comes upon a small girl near Grand Central Station who has obviously lost touch with the person watching over her. He gathers in the little stranger and cares for her as best he can, but when he sees a newspaper piece asking his whereabouts, Joe thinks the police are targeting him. He flees with his 'princess', receives help from several of his friends and has several escapades before the reunion of child and parents takes place.

2605.   ————. *Teddy and Carrots, two merchants of Newspaper Row.* **Illustrated by W.A. Rogers. Boston: Estes & Lauriat, 1896. 225p.**

Walking all the way from Saranac Lake to New York City, Teddy sets up as a newsboy. Competing news vendors begin picking on him and on one occasion he is arrested for violating a city ordinance. To his aid comes 'Carrots', a sympathetic bootblack. He joins forces with Teddy. The two face all their trials together and by the end of the story Teddy and Carrots are making a solid place for themselves as entrepreneurs on a small scale.

2606.   ————. *A traitor's escape*; **a story of the attempt to seize Benedict Arnold after he had fled to New York. New York: A.L. Burt, 1898. 234p.**

If the author is stating fact in his introductory note this story is based on an actual account by Oliver Whitefield, the narrator. Sergeant Champe, a non-commissioned officer in Major Henry Lee's American contingent, pretended to be a deserter to the British in order to get at Benedict Arnold and eventually return him to the American lines to be tried for treason. Oliver Whitefield and David Rhinelander, two 17-year-old boys joined the Sergeant in his effort. Of course the mission failed because Arnold was not in the expected place at the right time. Oliver and David had to flee New York City pursued by the Tory brothers, Jethro and Ben Stork. They were captured by the Storks but were released by a patriot, Mr. Maxwell, and in turn took the Storks prisoner and turned them over to Major Lee. Champe was enrolled in the British-sponsored American Legion yet found a way to escape and rejoin his American compatriots.

2607. **Ottolengui, Rodrigues, 1861?-1937.** *The crime of the century.* **New York: G.P. Putnam, 1896. viii, 349p.**

The author pursues several chilling threads in his novel, viz.: the central incident—the arrest of a young man accused of the murder of his father, a rich New Yorker; the kidnapping and later abandonment of an infant; the victimizing of a trusting, innocent young woman by a wealthy philanderer. However, the 'crime of the century' in the author's view is the inhumanity of society's treatment of those who step outside the law's boundaries.

2608. **————.** *A modern wizard.* **New York: G.P. Putnam, 1894. v, 434p.**

Laid in New York City the novel tells of "a young woman, supposed to have been unmarried, and believed to have died from diphtheria [who] is proved to have been poisoned by morphine. She is shown to have been the wife of Dr. Emmanuel Medjora, who had attended her in her last moments, and he is arrested on suspicion. A trial for murder follows, the evidence, which is sensational and dramatic, being given at length. Medjora is the 'modern wizard' and though not proven guilty of the crime at the time, is soon implicated in others. His powers come from his knowledge of hypnotism and science; he inoculates his victims with the germs of disease, or forces them to obey his will, even to their own destruction"—Annual American catalogue.

Oudenarde, Nicholas Aegidius, pseud. See: Paulding, James Kirke, 1778-1860.

2609. **Ousler, Fulton, 1893-1952.** *About the murder of Geraldine Foster*; a Thatcher Colt detective mystery, by Anthony Abbott [pseud.]. **New York: Covici-Friede, 1930. xii, 280p.**

The police commissioner of New York City, Thatcher Colt, is at the top of his form as he arrives at the solution to the murder of Mrs. Foster. The story's narrator is Colt's secretary who has an unfortunate propensity for attracting attention from the wrong people.

2610. **————.** *Stepchild of the moon.* **New York: Harper, 1926. 527p.**

"Walter Fairchild was ... a poet, perhaps, at heart, a writer of advertising copy by profession. In his second courtship and marriage Walter sought eagerly all that he missed in the first. With Florence, his second wife, he dedicated himself to the making of beautiful memories. There were, however, irremovable factors at work against this happiness. Foremost was Florence's jealousy of the dead wife and hatred of the other woman's son. Then there was Ducarel, a grotesque, exotic figure whose malign influence shadowed their lives. Against these odds the couple fought to keep their ideal of beauty intact, but they were only stepchildren of the moon"—Book review digest. "[The work has] considerable significance as a comment upon contemporary New York"—Saturday review of literature.

Ousler, Grace Perkins, 1900- . See: Perkins, Grace, 1900- .

2611. **Overbaugh, De Witt Clinton. *The Hermit of the Catskills*; a tale of the American Revolution. New York: G.W. Dillingham, 1900. 233p.**

The story is based on events in the Revolutionary War that occurred around Hardenburgh Hall in Rosendale, Ulster County, N.Y. In a skirmish with Tories and Indians Captain Donald McGregor, a courier for General Washington, and the girl he loves, Bretta Rutsen, are captured. Old Cyrus, McGregor's Negro servant, and the 'Hermit of the Hudson' come to the rescue as McGregor is about to be burned at the stake. After Kingston, N.Y. is set on fire by Sir Henry Clinton's troops, an unsuccessful attack on Hardenburgh Hall is mounted by forces led by the Tory John Leffens and his son Paul, McGregor's bitter enemy. The Leffens are taken prisoner and Paul is hanged; his father is put in jail and released at the war's end. At a hearing in which Leffens tries to assert his claim to land owned by the Rutsen family, the Hermit of the Catskills steps forward and announces that he is Vicomte Phillip de Rutsen, Bretta's uncle. He disproves Leffens' claim. McGregor and Bretta marry.

2612. **Overton, Grant Martin, 1887-1930. *Island of the innocent*. New York: Doran, 1923. 332p.**

Brought up conventionally in a Fifth Avenue home Dace Sherril takes a job in the kitchen of a New York hospital. She has an on-again, off-again relationship with a man she really doesn't want to marry, but her fears and doubts conspire to envelope her in a shroud of despair. Then she meets a young writer, Avery Floyd, and they build a solid foundation for mutual understanding and future happiness.

2613. **————. *World without end*. Garden City, N.Y.: Doubleday, Page, 1921. 317p.**

"Years after it all happened, this story of a mistaken marriage was pieced together by the children and sufferers from the union. When Leda Stanborough came over from England [to Long Island] to marry Martin L'Hommedieu, according to an arrangement made by letter, she found that the man she loved with all her heart was not in love with her but with her sister Lucy, and that it was Lucy whom he was expecting. It gave the first twist to his mind that later developed into violent insanity and caused his death. It was also, in a subtle way, the cause of the psychic bond between Leda and her beautiful daughter Helen, which guided the latter even after the mother's death. Religion, mythology, worldly mystery and occultism are some of the threads woven into this story of many strands"—Book review digest.

671

2614. **Owen, Catherine, pseud.** *Gentle breadwinners*; **the story of one of them.** **Boston: Houghton, Mifflin, 1888. 186p.**

"The story of a young girl who is left friendless and penniless through her father's death. She does not possess any brilliant accomplishments or gifts, but is proud and independent and determined not to be a burthen to her friends or relatives. After failing at dressmaking, she turns her knowledge of fine cooking to account. The book relates her experience in selling her mincemeat, preserves, fancy cakes, candy, etc., to the Woman's Exchange in New York City, and her success not only in gaining a living but in building up a permanent business. All the recipes she uses are given"—Annual American catalogue.

2615. **Owen, George Washington, d. 1916.** *The Leech Club*; **or;** *The mysteries of the Catskills.* **Boston: Lee & Shepard, 1874. 298p.**

The Civil War is over but lawyer Horace Lackfathe, formerly an idealist, now has a dim view of humankind. He wanders into the Catskills; there he encounters a ghostly assemblage of pleasure-seekers from which he flees. He next comes in touch with the Leech Club whose members are busy dividing up the spoils accruing from their political offices. The Club has its opponents with whom it deals harshly. Horace joins the core of the Club's adversaries who have been forced to flee into the forests pursued by the Leech Clubbers. Horace's friend, Mr. Graphic, and the 'Hermit of the Catskills' offer their assistance and the crooked politicians taste defeat. Horace Lackfathe speaks for the prosecution at the ensuing trial and several members of the Leech Club are convicted. The author offers no explanation for the manifestations of ghosts and other gossamer-like apparitions—evidently they are just 'mysteries of the Catskills'.

P., H.F. See: Parker, Helen Elizabeth Fitch, 1827-1874.

2616. **Packard, Frank Lucius, 1877-1942.** *The adventures of Jimmie Dale.* **New York: Doran, 1917. vi, 468p.**

"He was a member of one of New York's most exclusive clubs. He was known as an idle young man, but he had a complete and scientific knowledge of his father's business, the manufacture of safes. There was nothing Jimmie Dale did not know about combinations and locks. So, unknown to his society and club friends, he led a double, no, a triple life, acting now the part of the Gray Seal, a clever and mysterious cracksman who always leaves his mark, a gray seal, behind him, and again the part of Larry the Bat, a denizen of the underworld. The chief mystery of the tale centers in the personality of the unknown woman whose commands Jimmie obeys, and who, whatever the means adopted, always had a worthy end in view"—Book review digest.

2617. ————. *Doors of the night.* **New York: Doran, 1922. 297p.**

Billy Kane is wrongly accused of the murder of his employer, his father's old friend, David Ellsworth; he slips out of the police net and hides in the underworld of New York's East Side. There he takes on a new identity, is accepted by certain lawless elements and becomes known as 'The Rat'. Following a series of adventures that include a rescue from death by a 'Woman in Black', Billy unmasks the real killer.

2618. ————. *The further adventures of Jimmie Dale.* **New York: Doran, 1919. 340p.**

Jimmie Dale, in disguise as 'Smarlinghue', an underworld character and drug addict, mixes with New York City's criminals and enters their secret places, all with the purpose of exposing them to the authorities. His undercover work is abetted by a mysterious woman whose orders he follows.

2619. ————. *Jimmie Dale and the blue envelope murder.* **Garden City, N.Y.: Doubleday, Doran, 1930. 289p.**

Jimmie Dale, who masquerades as the Gray Seal (alias Larry the Bat), tours the nightclubs of Broadway as he seeks to avenge the murder of his old comrade Ray Thorne.

2620. ————. *Jimmie Dale and the phantom clue.* **New York: Doran, 1922. 301p.**

Packard's Jimmie Dale, New York society figure and crime fighter, returns to his forays against the city's underworld when Marie, the woman he loves, is threatened by a gang she and Jimmie have tangled with before. In their last confrontation the gang's chief had been crushed, but now a new leader has taken over. After Jimmie and Marie elude the gang's nets on several occasions, they finally get the better of their pursuers.

2621. ————. *The red ledger.* **New York: Doran, 1926. 318p.**

Henri Raoul Charlebois of 2½ Dominic Street, Manhattan, keeps a record of the rights and wrongs done him in a big red ledger. He is settling accounts one by one, kindnesses and injustices. Ewen Stanway, a jobless, financially strained young man, is the son of an individual who gave Charlebois a 'lift' years ago and the latter hires Ewen to assist in settling the various affairs. Perhaps most important is the shielding of a beautiful girl, the 'Orchid' (or the 'Princess' Myril of Karnavia) from assassination by the Yersel-Thega, a band of thugs from New York's underworld and elsewhere. The sinister Prince Stolbek, anxious to get his hands on the Orchid's inherited wealth, is a member of that gang. Charlebois and Stanway have a final climactic fight with the villains. They triumph and the Orchid/Myril falls into the waiting arms of her lover, Ewen Stanway.

2622. ————. *The White Moll.* **New York: Doran, 1920. 306p.**

"The 'White Moll' is the name Rhoda Gray has earned for herself in New York's East Side district by always playing on the square with its denizens. So Gypsy Nan, when dying in a slightly penitent frame of mind, entrusts her with the secret of a crime about to be committed. Rhoda tries to stop it, but is arrested, charged with committing it. She escapes, but her career of charity as the White Moll is thus wrecked and she is forced for safety to disguise herself as Gypsy Nan, in which role she finds herself in the midst of a criminal gang. She resolves to circumvent their schemes, and so plays the double part of Gypsy Nan, who is hand in glove with them, and the White Moll, their bitterest enemy and a fugitive from justice. Her part is hard, but her luck is good, and with the 'Adventurer' as her ally she finally, after many exciting experiences, breaks up the gang and brings it to punishment. Then she makes the gratifying discovery that the Adventurer is not the thief she had thought him and that they had been working for the same ends"—Book review digest.

Packer, Vin, pseud. See: Meaker, Marijane, 1927-.

2623. **Pahlow, Gertrude, 1881-1937. *The cross of heart's desire*. New York: Duffield, 1916. 296p.**
"Marcia Dale had been reared in the belief that woman's chief duty is to charm. Above all she must never appear to be intellectual; men abhor intellectual women. In this belief Marcia flutters down the stairs to greet Spencer Blake, the young millionaire, and, remembering her mother's admonition to keep her three-quarter view turned towards him, she proceeds to charm. But Spencer Blake is a serious-minded and earnest young man intensely interested in factory reform. He is at first puzzled and then bored and shortly takes his departure. Humiliated by the experience Marcia leaves her home to go to New York. Here a wealthy cousin has offered her a position as secretary to his pseudo-philanthropic society. As Marcia grows, she finds her position here intolerable and later is given work with an organization that comes into actual contact with the poor, and when she again meets Spencer Blake, she has a new and broadened viewpoint"—Book review digest.

2624. **Paine, Albert Bigelow, 1861-1937. *The bread line*; a story of a paper. New York: Century Co., 1900. 228p.**
Three young unconventional New Yorkers (who have little money) and an unprincipled associate start a family newspaper they hope will be subscribed to by thousands of readers. Despite their enthusiasm and the drudgery of drumming up interest in their venture they seem doomed to fail. One of the men, an artist, has drawn his conception of the bread line that formed one wintry night at Fleischmann's Bakery in New York City and one wonders how long it will be before the would-be journalists take their places in that line.

2625. **———. *From van dweller to commuter*; the story of a strenuous quest for a home and a little hearth and garden. New York: Harper, 1907. iv, 416p.**
A man and his wife and their two daughters who have tried to live comfortably in the crowded flats of New York City turn to suburban living and roles as commuters. With gentle humor the author describes their new way-of-life, which is destined to be a common feature of the 20th century.

2626. ————.*The lucky piece*; **a tale of the North Woods. New York: Outing Pub. Co., 1906. 250p.**

The Adirondacks are the stage for this tale that starts out telling how a girl of the region came into possession of a Spanish 'lucky piece'. Several years later a wealthy New York couple and their daughter come to the mountains to stay at their summer camp. Close by them is the daughter's supposed boyfriend, a spoiled, ambitionless young man. Two love stories develop: that of the Adirondacks girl who takes the rich young man in hand and teaches him to live purposefully; the New York City girl meets and falls in love with a self-educated Adirondack guide and engineer. The Spanish lucky piece once again comes into play as it helps clear up certain puzzling incidents and misinterpretations.

2627. ————. *The van dwellers*; **a strenuous quest for a home. New York: J.F. Taylor, 1901. iv, 191p.**

"'Van dwellers', the term applied by landlord and agent to those who move systematically and inhabit the moving-man's great trundling house no less than four to six times a year" (p. 78). A family from the West is confronted by some dismaying facts about finding suitable living arrangements in New York City. To begin with, the apartments they survey and even occupy for short periods are exceedingly small—and inadequate heating, unsympathetic janitors, piecemeal deliveries of household items from the department store, the poor fare at the boarding house they try—they encounter all of them. When last heard from the family has settled for a house in the suburbs with a backyard and a vegetable garden. Words of advice are offered to would-be future New York City apartment dwellers.

2628. Palier, Emile. *Social sinners*. New York: Abbey Press, 1900. iv, 229p.

Barbara Eckert, a German-American girl brought up in the country, is perhaps representative in the author's telling of hundreds of young women who believe they have the talent and perseverance to achieve great things in New York. Barbara takes the plunge but, as is too often the case, ends up working for meager wages and sliding farther and farther down in the social scale.

2629. Pall, Ellen, 1952- . *Among the Ginzburgs*; a novel. Zoland, 1996. 245p.

As their father, Meyer, lies upstairs near the point of death in the Ginzburgs' Catskills farmhouse, his five children are gathered downstairs discussing past and present. Meyer had deserted them and their mother 28 years ago, and although they had taken him in this one last time, they have mixed reactions to his presence, let alone their own sibling differences and feuds.

2630. Palmer, Bruce, 1932- . *The karma charmer*. New York: Harmony Books, 1994. 245p.

Woodstock, New York, near the place of the famous rock festival (1969), is the scene of this novel. The junk dealer (or 'recycler'), Dick Howser, experiences changes in his lifestyle when a local college student, Leslie Zak,

21, boards with him. The two are soon engaged in a passionate love affair, which Leslie intends to break off when she graduates, and heads for a career on Wall Street. Then Howard, Dick's 10-year-old son, whom he hasn't seen for 7 years, turns up in Woodstock. Father and son do not want to lose Leslie, and they devise all sorts of exotic, outrageous stratagems to keep Leslie in Woodstock.

2631.   **Palmer, Stuart, 1905-1968.** *Miss Withers regrets.* **Garden City, N.Y.: Published for the Crime Club by Doubleday, 1947. 223p.**

A body floating in a Long Island swimming pool brings spinster Hildegarde Withers out of retirement. Murder charges are brought against the former boyfriend of the victim's wife. To Hildegarde falls the task of proving his innocence.

2632.   **Pangborn, George Wood, b. 1872.** *Roman Biznet.* **Boston: Houghton, Mifflin, 1902. 280p.**

Roman Biznet, the hero, inherits a passion for music from his grandfather—he plays the cello and composes—but like his father he is of a quarrelsome, deceitful nature. Many of the story's scenes take place in an Upstate New York settlement. Roman, always popular with the ladies, has contacts with three orphaned girls who have been adopted by a narrow-minded aristocrat: Elizabeth, poetic but messy; Kitty, who has no interest in self-improvement; Maude, who has a patrician manner but has the bad habit of eavesdropping. A Dr. Winthrop is one of the few likeable characters in the novel. The story ends with a fight between Roman and his father. "They bit, tore, scratched, fighting grotesquely as anthropoids may have fought before men were."

Pansy, pseud. See: Alden, Isabella Macdonald, 1841-1930.

2632a.   **Pappano, Marilyn.** *Father to be.* **New York: Bantam Books, 1999. 384p.**

'Bethlehem', N.Y. is the scene of psychiatrist J.D. Grayson's attempt to be the foster father of four young children who have been cast off by their parents. Looking over his shoulder is Kelsey Malone, a dedicated social worker. Grayson must finally confess to himself that he has failed to make much impression on the children who refuse to communicate with him. He realizes that Kelsey Malone holds more attraction for him, at least for the moment, than the recalcitrant kids.

2633.   ————. *Some enchanted season.* **New York: Bantam Books, 1998. 374p.**

The Xmas-New York season lights up the fantasized town of 'Bethlehem', New York, and its citizens. One of them, Maggie McKinney, had been disfigured in a very serious auto accident and she still has a touch of amnesia. However she knows that she and her husband Ross are on the verge of divorce, largely because of Ross's extramarital affair. Ross is suffused by guilt. As the holiday season takes hold in Bethlehem, Ross looks anew at his flaws and sets about amending them, while Maggie absorbs the lessons of forgiveness.

2634. **Parker, Arthur Caswell, 1881-1955.** *Gustango gold*, **by Arthur C. Parker (Gawaso Wanneh). Illustrated by Frank Dobias and Robert Goldfield. Garden City, N.Y.: Doubleday, Doran, 1930. viii, 258p.**

The son of a Secret Service agent forms friendships with several Indian youths on a reservation in northern New York State; with their help David Burton is able to explain how a hoard of gold was stolen from an express train and how to set about recovering it.

2635. ————. *Red Streak of the Iroquois*, **by Arthur C. Parker (Gawaso Wanneh). Illus. by I. Heilbron. Chicago: Children's Press, 1950. 191p.**

The Indian youth Red Streak is guided by Hiawatha, the legendary Iroquois chief, to look towards the leadership of his people—the time is the late 16th century.

2636. **Parker, Helen Eliza Fitch, 1827-1874.** *Constance Aylmer*; **a story of the seventeenth century, by H.F.P. New York: Scribner, 1869 [c1868]. 347p.**

Reissued in 1889 with sub-title: A tale of the times of Peter Stuyvesant.
English Puritan and orphan Constance Aylmer comes to America and the home of her aunt, the Quaker Lady Deborah Moody, and her son Sir Henry Moody, close by New Amsterdam. Constance forms friendships with several of the Dutch colonists: the Zwallers, Baltazaar and Nicholas Stuyvesant, Elsie Roosevelt, et al. She also falls in love with Edward Mordaunt, a visitor from Virginia, and they are engaged. In a pique of jealousy Edward suddenly marries Elsie Roosevelt; despondent Constance returns to England and the society of Lord Grey, his wife and daughter. She meets a staunch Cromwellian, Lord Huntington, and reassesses her affairs of the heart. Mordaunt appears in England and Constance tells him that she now loves another (Lord Huntington). Elsie, presumed lost at sea, is rescued and taken by the Indian Lyano to New Amsterdam, which is suffering from Indian incursions. Mordaunt goes back to America and his wife Elsie. Lady Deborah and Sir Henry Moody give up their lands in New York and move to Virginia.

2637. **Parker, Jane Marsh, 1836-1913.** *Barley Wood*; **or,** *Building on the rock*. **New York: D. Dana, Jr., 1860. 320p.**

The chief locale of the novel is Barley Wood, a Presbyterian female seminary at 'Litchfield' in the Genesee Valley. The heroine, Agnes Ryland, daughter of a Presbyterian minister, questions the value of a religious revival in the 1850s, which has gripped central New York State. She herself is searching for a church that she can faithfully adhere to as most representative of Christian teachings. To her father's discomfiture Agnes chooses Episcopalianism after study and long conversations with the Rev. Bellamy, an Episcopal priest. The revival peters out and Agnes accepts the headship of a parish school near Litchfield; after her father's death she marries Roscoe Field, a new convert from long-time skepticism and even agnosticism. Peopling the novel are other interesting characters: Ellen Burton Butler, another skeptic, who saves Mollie Raymond, a 'born again Christian', from eloping with a leading figure in the revival, the spurious Prof. Cartzen; and Carrie Seabury, a sickly student at the seminary, herself an Episcopalian, who is in part responsible for Agnes's interest in Episcopacy.

2638. ————. *The Midnight cry*; a novel. New York: Dodd, Mead, 1886. iv, 298p.
The Genesee Valley in the 1830s and 1840s—more specifically the district known as 'Barley's Flats'—is the setting of a story in which Millerism and the Millerites (with their belief in the imminent end of the world—most likely in 1843 or 1844) play a prominent role. Priscilla Ottoway, a strong, independent woman, lives at Barley's Flats in semi-seclusion with her Negro servants, Phil, a boy she took in as an infant from his dying mother, and Nan or Annie, her niece from New York City. Annie marries Christopher Burke, a former boy preacher; Burke leaves Annie and goes to England to investigate a possible inheritance. Annie comes back to Barley's Flats with her daughter Marjory. As Marjory matures she begins to follow Millerite pronouncements, taking a special interest in Letitia Barkenstone, a handsome woman and a powerful preacher for Millerite views. Eventually Christopher Burke returns to the Genesee Valley to spread the doctrines of Millerism. The deaths of Priscilla Ottoway and Annie Burke leave Marjory dependent on Phil. Letitia Barkenstone goes on a mission to the Middle East and dies in Palestine.

2639. Parker, Maude, ca. 1890-1959. *The intriguer*. New York: Rinehart, 1952. 248p.
"Elizabeth Little … reports some mighty queer occurrences somewhere on Long Island. They center about a celebrated actress and a family of soberly skatty [sic] if wealthy neurotics. Elizabeth is everybody's confidante, and when she isn't, she picks up information by sitting in adjacent booths. Nearly all of it gives her a sort of noble pain as well as a certainty of impending disaster. The disaster comes after pages of unconcealed gasps, flashes of righteous indignations, chuckles of social certitude and reports on gowns and cummerbunds. Elizabeth's understanding is enormous and her compassion wells up all the time"—New York herald tribune books.

2640. Parr, Delia, 1947- . *The minister's wife*. New York: St. Martin's Paperbacks, 1998. 307p.
Illegitimacy has left its mark on Emilee Clarke, yet she is determined to overcome her 'shameful' origin by marrying a man of the cloth. The time is the early part of the 19th century and the place is a town in Upstate New York. Emilee's husband is actually a former clergyman who has a wastrel son, Jared; the latter has returned home to seek forgiveness. Abused by her husband Emilee falls in love with Jared. Emilee and Jared restrain their passion and then Emilee's husband attempts to murder her. Emilee survives but is still a married woman and that places Jared in an awkward position. If

he and Emilee consummate their love, discovery would destroy Emilee's hard-won respect.

2641. Parrott, Katherine Ursula, 1902- . *Strangers may kiss.* **New York: J. Cape & H. Smith, 1930. vii, 373p.**

The people we meet in the novel are those New Yorkers, restless, semi-bohemian, sometimes disoriented—men and women journalists who drink too much, smoke too much, and do a lot of promiscuous bed-hopping. The heroine, Lisbeth, is perhaps not too much different from the above, but she cannot forget the man, Alan, she began to love when she was only seventeen. It could be said that she was essentially a one-man woman. Lisbeth and Alan have brief meetings, long separations and a tragic denouement at the story's conclusion.

2642. Parsons, Alice Beal, 1886-1962. *I know what I'd do.* **New York: Dutton, 1946. 252p.**

Back home to little 'Pawlet', his native town in Upstate New York, after combat service in World War II, Al Miller hears gossip that his wife Sally had an affair with Jim Phelan, the town's sporting goods store owner, while he was away at war. Al confronts Phelan, they scuffle and Al kills Phelan. Margaret Manton, a well-know writer who lives in Pawlet, takes more than a passing interest in the events leading up to Al's arrest for murder and in the trial following. Things tilt in Al's favor; he wins acquittal and he and Sally resume their commitment to one another.

2643. ————. *John Merrill's pleasant life*; **a novel. New York: Dutton, 1930. 268p.**

Thomas Castle has been the great benefactor of Pawlet, an attractive factory town on the Hudson, bringing prosperity to it with his industrial enterprise. As his successor-to-be he selected the clever John Merrill, a hard worker. Merrill's wife, Mary, an inconsequential woman, dislikes Castle because of his mistress and illegitimate children. Merrill buries himself in his home and his books, even embarking on an extra-marital affair. His work suffers; his refusal or inability to recognize talent convinces Castle that he should be fired. Before that can happen, Castle dies and Merrill takes over. He is now accepted as the town's leading citizen, but it is quite obvious that he does not at all measure up to his patron, the deceased Thomas Castle.

2644. ————. *A lady who lost.* **New York City: Gotham House, 1932. 284p.**

The professor, scientist and writer, James Hillyer, is spending a summer in 'Pawlet', New York, on the Hudson. He becomes involved in various ways with three women: platonically with Mrs. Rowe who feels like a stranger in Pawlet even after 10 years residence there; the flashy Mrs. Nash from New York City who is not accepted by virtuous Pawlet society; and Mary DuVall, labor organizer, attractive and energetic, but no lady. Mrs. Rowe condemns the strike of the town's factory workers as a matter of law and order, but then displays her independence when she supports a young woman suspected of a murder and hounded by the local newspaper.

Parsons, Julia Warth. See: Warth, Julian

2645. **Partington, Norman. *The Sunshine Patriot*; a novel of Benedict Arnold. New York: St. Martin's Press, 1975. 221p.**

Benedict Arnold is the key but shadowy figure in this not very successful fictional account of the siege of Quebec, the Valcour Island (on the New York side of Lake Champlain) naval battle, the defeat of Burgoyne at Saratoga, etc. Arnold is traced from 1774 to his attempted betrayal of West Point in 1780.

2646. **Partridge, Bellamy, 1878-1960. *Big freeze.* New York: T.Y. Crowell, 1949. 236p.**

In the late 1830s and early 1840s the Croton Dam and Aqueduct project was of vital importance in providing New York City with a multi-use water supply. A young engineer, David, worked on the project that was beset by political and construction problems, but David found solace in the love of Japsie. Horace Greeley, James Fenimore Cooper and Nathaniel Parker Willis appear sporadically in the novel.

2647. **————. *Excuse my dust.* Illustrated by Stephen J. Voorhies. New York: Whittlesey House, McGraw-Hill, 1943. xiii, 359p.**

In the first decade of the 20th century the town of Phelps in central New York (33 miles southeast of Rochester) experienced the pangs that accompanied the introduction of the motorized vehicle. The author's semi-fictional, semi-autobiographical work has as its main character Tom Hunter, a farm boy who has a singular talent for fixing anything mechanical. The narrator (Partridge) introduces other members of his cast, a number of whom are quite certain that the new-fangled auto can never take the place of a reliable horse. Tom opens a bicycle shop, but increasingly turns his attention to the new mode of transportation. By the 2nd and 3rd decades of the century paved roads are well on their way to solving the problem of the clouds of dust stirred up by the motor vehicles. Interspersed in the story are sketches of the progress of the early auto and improvements that gradually made it a most viable means of moving people and goods.

2648. **————. *A pretty pickle.* New York: Brewer and Warren, 1930. 364p.**

George Harrington is the son of a pickle manufacturer but has little interest in the business. He picks up his Cousin Mary at the train station and brings her to his Long Island home; when she turns out to be no relative of his, George falls into a myriad of complications that evoke much laughter from everyone but himself. He also has to deal with a burglary and a Japanese butler who is forever listening behind closed doors although he never acts upon what he hears.

2649. ————. *Thunder shower.* **New York: Arcadia House, 1936. 280p.**

"'Simpson Falls [in Upstate New York] is proud of its ancient elms and its modern concrete, and its citizens—like the setting—are complacently old-fashioned as well as consciously modern. The plot hinges upon a political feud engendered by a love affair—a village free-for-all open to both the younger and older generations. Like a thunder shower, it clears the air and leaves almost everybody… smiling and refreshed"—New York herald tribune books.

2650. Pascal, Ernest, b. 1896. *The age of love.* **New York: Harcourt, Brace, 1930. 291p.**

"Jean Hurd, who had a job with a New York literary agency, grew bored with authors and editors, and fell in love with Dudley Crome, young business man. After two months of married life she discovered that his interests and friends were not hers. A baby did little to bring the young couple together. Jean hired nurses for it and went back to work. She still had an ideal of love—and when she met Justin Marsh, that ideal seemed fulfilled. She went to live with Justin, and Dudley refused to let her have custody of the baby. The story, which ends on a note of compromise in Justin's death, is an indictment of the marriage based wholly on physical attraction"—Book review digest.

2651. ————. *Cynthia Codentry.* **New York: Brentano's, 1926. 318p.**

"A biographical study of a modern young woman whose father, a famous actor, desired to have her go on the stage. From her girlhood Cynthia has never been interested in domesticity of the suburban type. After making a brave effort to become an actress Cynthia gives up the stage and for a time endeavors to stifle her restlessness by being formally engaged to a worthy, hard-working young man who is a poor but ambitious sculptor. But in order to put it from her mind she plays with Sybil who has money and whose home is a three-ring-circus. Florida and Long Island with their gay life [are] engagingly pictured by the author. Cynthia's point of view does not include her fiancé's studio. He fades from the picture. In time she becomes Mrs. Tweed. … A divorce from Tweed enables Cynthia to start forth in search of fresh excitement. Again she seeks Willie, but in the end she turns to a man of a totally different type"—Boston transcript.

2652. Patrick, Q., pseud. *Death and the maiden.* **New York: Simon and Schuster, 1939. 308p.**

'Wentworth College', a school near New York City, yields up the murdered body of one of its coeds, Grace Hough. Grace was a dubious character with several enemies and her roommate, Lee Lovering, the novel's narrator, throws false leads in the path of Lieutenant Timothy Trent of New York City's Homicide Squad, chief investigator. It is Trent's task to unravel the many twists and turns in the case, which he is eminently qualified to do. Q. Patrick is the joint pseudonym of Richard Wilson Webb and Hugh Callingham Wheeler.

2653. Patrick, William B., 1949- . *Roxa*: voices of the Culver family. Brockport, N.Y.: BOA Editions, 1989. 181p.

The hardships faced by a New York State farm family in the 1840s is the theme of this novel—sickness, natural calamities, human frailties and infighting, etc. The mother of the brood, Hannah Culver, implores loudly for all to confess their sins and get ready for Judgment Day. Teenager Amelia is sensitive to the voices and actions of the natural world. The youngest member of the family, Roxa, takes note of a snowstorm in June that decimates the Culvers' flock of sheep with poetic phrases: 'Who let the dark and snow begin? I, said the wind.'

2654. Patterson, Emma Lillie, 1904-1984. *Midnight patriot.* Decorations by Millard McGee. New York: Longmans, Green, 1949. 304p.

The American Revolution and the effect it had on the lives of people who lived in Peekskill, New York and vicinity is the theme of the novel. The hero and heroine are 'average' young people with no particularly outstanding qualities, but with a deep sense of loyalty to the cause they support. The author portrays clearly the conflicting allegiances of Tories and Colonials and the local setting of the story.

2655. Patterson, Frances Taylor. *White wampum*; the story of Kateri Tekakwitha. New York: Longmans, Green, 1934. 304p.

Kateri Tekakwitha, the subject of this fictionalized biography, was an Indian girl of a Mohawk tribe who was converted to the Catholic faith and took the vow of chastity in 1679; she died in 1680. The story is based on the known facts concerning her life and on the author's knowledge of the manners and customs of the Indians of those times. It is also the story of the struggle between two religions, Indian and Christian.

2656. Patterson, Innis. *The Eppworth case.* New York: Farrar & Rinehart, 1930. 316p.

The millionaire Courtney Eppworth, a collector of pornographic literature, is found dead in his Westchester summerhouse. A second victim of Death's visit is Mrs. Block, his housekeeper. Sebald Craft, scholar-detective, a friend of the New York police commissioner, has several suspicious persons to query concerning these sudden departures, among them: Dr. Carl von Herner, a Viennese vivisectionist; Stuart Farnese, former star athlete; Corinne Adams; Marianne Nash, Eppworth's beautiful niece, the possessor of a rather unsavory past.

2657. Patterson, Joseph Medill, 1879-1946. *A little brother of the rich*; a novel. Chicago: Reilly and Britton, 1908. 361p.

The protagonist is the son of a rural Indiana parson; he graduates from a distinguished Eastern college and, shedding his 'countrified' origins, climbs to affluence as a New York stockbroker. So intent is he on the pursuit of money and social position that he gives up the one woman he really loves. She in turn achieves fame as an actress and has influence on his later life. The author is quite candid in his revelation of the less palatable aspects of so-called fashionable social life in New York City and Newport circles.

2658. **Paul, Louis, 1901-1970.** *Summer storm.* **New York: Crown Publishers, 1949. 253p.**

A Hudson River summer home is the scene of a weekend party hosted by a well-known neurologist. His guests include a number of people who have little in common. After the men in the group go back to New York, the women are left to face their differences and to experience a sudden dangerous storm that threatens not only their personal safety but also the house itself.

2659. **Paulding, James Kirke, 1778-1860.** *The book of St. Nicholas.* **Translated from the original Dutch of Dominie Nicholas Aegidius Oudenarde [pseud.]. New York: Harper, 1836. 237p.**

The stories here listed treat the Dutch in New York State and are in large part based on the folklore of this colonial people. Two of the tales are especially worth taking note of: The little Dutch sentinel of the Manhadoes and Cobus Yerks. The first is a ghost story wherein Jan Sol, a garrulous little braggart claims to have seen a gigantic specter while on watch; the news upsets the citizens of New Amsterdam. It turns out that the sighting is really a handsome youth from New Jersey intent on seeing his secret wife Blandina. The second tale, Cobus Yerks, has some resemblance to Irving's Legend of Sleepy Hollow. Cobus, a superstitious Dutch farmer living near the Saw Mill River (east side of the Hudson) disappears from a village inn after drinking too much whisky. When found in deep sleep in the bushes Cobus is awakened and spins a story about a demon pursuing him and his wagon. Cobus's huge dog takes the reins from his master and lashes the horses. Cobus is then overcome by the smell of brimstone and falls asleep. Partial contents: The little Dutch sentinel of the Manhadoes.—Cobus Yerks.—A strange bird in Nieuw-Amsterdam.—Claas Schlaschenschlinger.—The origin of the bakers' dozen.—The ride of Saint Nicholas on New Year's Eve.

2660. ————. *The Dutchman's fireside*; a tale. **By the author of** *Letters from the South, The backwoodsman,* **& c., & c. New York: Harper, 1831. 2v.**

The scene of this once very popular novel is chiefly the Hudson River region and New York City; its hero is a shy but valiant Dutch lad, Sybrant Nestbrook. It is the time of the French and Indian War and Sybrant participates as a volunteer in the British forces, meeting with such historical figures as Sir William Johnson and others. The girl Sybrant loves, Catalina Vancour, his cousin, makes her mark in the social whirl of New York City and flirts with two flamboyant British suitors, much to rustic Sybrant's dismay. Sybrant's military career is a splendid one that earns the commendation and support of Sir William Johnson, and Sybrant eventually wins the heart of Catalina—he had at one point in the story saved her from an Indian attack.

2661. ———. *The Old Continental; or, The price of liberty.* **By the author of *The Dutchman's fireside*, & c., & c. New York: Paine and Burgess, 1846.**

> Paulding's hero is based on his own cousin John and his patriotic activities during the American Revolution. The tale also examines the effects the conflict had on the people of the 'Neutral Ground' (an area between New York City and the Hudson Highlands—much of present-day Westchester County). The capture of the British spy, Major André, is a leading and climactic point in the novel. There is a vivid description of a British prison ship.

2662. Paxton, Lois, 1916- . *The quiet sound of fear*. New York: Hawthorn Books, 1971. 137p.

> Kay Brandon is profoundly disturbed by the sound of footsteps outside her Hudson River home, which is located in a somewhat isolated spot. She is working on the papers her deceased father left and does not want to go to the police with her qualms, presuming they might advise her to get away from her lonely house. Kay is 24 years old and has decided that she can handle most situations that might intrude upon her privacy.

2663. Payne, Elizabeth Stancy McGovern, d. 1944. *Easy Street*. Philadelphia: Penn Pub. Co., 1930. 306p.

> The Goodwillies—George, his wife Maida and daughters Tinka, Linnet and Budge—share a lavish apartment on the 'wrong side of Central Park'. They are living on 'easy street', i.e. on the installment plan. The Thornes—Christopher Petree Thorne, sister Nancy and their mother, Mrs. Silas Thorne—have a house on Washington Square, aristocratic forbears and little money. When Christopher and levelheaded Linnet Goodwillie fall in love, life-styles are bound to clash. An accident and a fire disable George Goodwillie and wipe out his car dealership, forcing his family to accept spare quarters east of Lexington Avenue and over a shop.

2664. Payne, Harold, pseud. *The Gilded Fly*; a political satire. St. Paul, Minn.: Price-McGill, 1892. 331p.

> A clique of politicians and police administrators calling itself 'The Gilded Fly' seek to line its pockets by collecting monetary 'contributions' from the 'lowlifes' of New York, including owners of disreputable night spots, saloon keepers, professional thieves, et al. A satirical if unrelieved portrait of a morally, politically and socially corrupt New York City.

2665. Payne, Jessie. *Black sheep*. Philadelphia: Macrae Smith, 1930. 318p.

> The 'yuppies' of 1930s New York City, many of them in advertising or publicity, draw Payne's focus. Marne Lewis, left an orphan when she was only 16 years old, is grinding out a living when she meets Larry Underhill, a publicity agent. Larry is bright but fallible, and a married man; nevertheless the two fall in love. When Larry fails on all counts to fulfill her expectations,

Marne has the good sense to forget him and get on with her other concerns. She eventually attains happiness in marriage with a more responsible man.

2666. Payne, Will, 1865-1954. *The losing game*; a novel. **Illus. by F. Fr. Gruger. New York: G.W. Dillingham, 1910. 352p.**

By means of a bucket shop operation that tampers with quotations from the New York Stock Exchange, two telegraph office workers are well on the road to personal prosperity even though it results in the ruin of thousands of gullible investors. The two—a man and a woman—are talented though corrupt, but it is the woman who puts an end to the venture, driven in part by jealousy.

2667. Payson, Howard, pseud. *The Boy Scouts of the Eagle Patrol.* **New York: Hurst, 1911. 302p.**

Rivalry in 'Hampton', Long Island between a Boy Scout patrol organized by Rob Blake and friends and boys of the town who were denied membership is a disrupting force in the community. The Scouts undergo many trials and mishaps before the situation is stabilized and misunderstandings allayed.

2668. Payson, William Farquhar, 1876-1939. *The copy-maker*; [a novel of journalistic life in New York]. **Illus. by H.B. Eddy. New York: New Amsterdam Book Co., 1897. 192p.**

The first person narrator, Samuel E. Forbes, locked out of the house by his father, joins the staff of New York City's The Daily Bread. His assignments are varied: e.g., he is selected to write the story of a poor family, but receives only 5 or 6 lines in the newspaper for all his work; he attains reportorial heights when he investigates with huge success the murder of Madeline Marteau, a famous actress. But his life as a journalist is relatively short-lived; an uncle leaves him a comfortable inheritance whereupon Sam and his wife go on a world tour. He takes note of the saying of his newspaper acquaintances: "The shoes of one newspaper invariably fit another."

2669. ————. *The triumph of life*; a novel. **New York: Harper, 1903. v, 424p.**

Young author Enoch Lloyd accepts financial success at the cost of his moral scruples. The two women in his life are opposites in character: Celeste Moreau, sophisticated daughter of a New York hotel proprietor; and Marion Lee, daughter of Lloyd's publisher—one degrades, the other elevates—and the choice is Enoch's. Will he embrace the virtuous, honorable woman and simultaneously turn away from his own errors of judgment?

2670. Pearl, Bertha, 1893?-1925. *Love child.* **New York: T. Seltzer, 1923. 253p.**

"A tale of a family of Jewish immigrants of the East Side [of New York City] that depicts their futile ambitions, their vague longings for beauty and their dreary day-by-day activities. Mira, practical, bustling through life, has never even glimpsed the inner life of her husband, Yekel, a drunkard and a dreamer. Annie, the child who so strangely resembles a girl he once loved, is touched by his position and gropingly attempts to meet him on common ground. In spite of her efforts they drift further away from sympathetic understanding. When Yekel finds Annie drunk at her sister's party, he loses his last hold on life and ends it. Annie, presumably, is to follow in his path of slow dissolution"—Book review digest.

2671. ————. *Sarah and her daughter.* New York: Seltzer, 1920. 521p.

"The scene of the story opens on Henry Street in the ghetto and portrays the American Jew in every nuance of his racial peculiarities. The abject poverty and suffering, the breaking under suffering, the resiliency, the ethical slips in the fierce struggle for existence, the hysteria and nervous breakdowns, the seriousness and absence of a sense of humor and the fundamental goodness of heart that always has the last word to say, are all there and every type finds its place down to the tragic figure of the orthodox survivor of a dead religion. In Sarah and her daughter Minnie, the immigrant Jew and the first generation, with the resulting sad conflicts between parent and child, are represented"— Book review digest.

2672. Pearl, Jack, 1923- . *Callie Knight.* New York: Saturday Review Press, 1974. 344p.

The scheming, ambitious protagonist of this novel is a woman, Callie (short for Caliban), Knight who plies her tricks along the upper Hudson River Valley. She will bed down just about any man (including Ham, son of her first husband) who will be a stepping stone in her ascension to wealth and influence. She achieves her goal, playing the grand lady during the Depression, and then having the inevitable fall to the miserable station she occupied before her march to 'glory'.

Pearl, Jacques Dain, 1923- . See: Pearl, Jack, 1923.

2673. Pearson, Henry Clemens, 1858-1936. *Her opportunity.* Boston: J.H. Earle, 1889. 462p.

"The author's views upon certain social questions are illustrated in a story whose scenes alternate between the most fashionable quarter and the dirtiest slums; in localities familiar to every New Yorker the votary of fashion mingles freely with the ill-paid workman, and even the beggar or the most vicious rough. The heroine is young, beautiful, wealthy, and of high social position, when she becomes an instrument of reform and gives herself up to a scheme to better the conditions of the paper-box makers. Upon her furtherance of this scheme and her manner of dealing with a political question the interest depends, although the book has side issues, dealing with intemperance and its attending evils, and the bearing that mission work has upon this evil"— Annual American catalogue.

2674. Peck, Dale, 1967- . *The law of enclosures.* New York: Farrar, Straus & Giroux, 1995. 306p.

The novel yields two records of the marriage of a couple, Henry and Beatrice, in the latter 1900s. The first discusses their early married life on Long Island; the second describes their retirement years in the Finger Lakes region of Upstate New York. Also included is an autobiographical account of a narrator's (Dale Peck's) disturbed childhood in which he suffered an abusive father, the death of his mother when he was three years of age, and life with three strange stepmothers.

2675. **Peck, Robert Newton, 1928- .** *Fawn*; **a novel. Boston: Little, Brown, 1975. xiii, 143p.**

Fawn Charbonfears, a boy of mixed French and Mohawk blood, is present at the British-French battle for control of Fort Ticonderoga in 1758. His father is with the French defenders while Fawn sides with the British; he asks young Benedict Arnold to help him draw up a plan to keep his father from harm. The British failure to invest the Fort more or less assures the safety of the elder Charbonfears, however, and the lad is much relieved.

2676. **Peck, Theodora Agnes, b. 1882.** *White Dawn, a legend of Ticonderoga.* **New York, Chicago: F.H. Revell, 1914. 306p.**

A Scots girl, Grace Stuart (whose father allies himself with the French), after the fall of Ticonderoga in 1758, and accompanied by her Indian foster brother, moves to warn Lord Howe of French maneuvers.

2677. **Peake, Margaret Bloodgood, 1838-1908.** *Born of flame*; **a Rosicrucian story. Philadelphia: J.B. Lippincott, 1892. 299p.**

"The story opens in the Rosedale Insane Asylum. Clothilde Gilroy is dying. Before her death however, she bequeaths her physician, Dr. Aubrey Grotius, a package of letters that reveal her fatal secret and the strange antecedents of her mother. These, with the diary of Dr. Grotius, and the experiences of Grotius, Dana, and Elfrieda Cathmore, with the action of an Indian mystic, Sulmal, are a means of ventilating theories of mysticism, transcendentalism, spiritualism, etc. Although one of the scenes is in Benares, India, many of them, it is claimed, are real places in New York State"—Annual American catalogue.

Pell, John Leggett Everitt, b. 1876, joint author. *Hell's Acres.* **See Item #2688.**

2678. **Pellegrino, Charles R., 1953- .** *Dust.* **New York: Avon Books, 1998. x, 387p.**

Drastic changes in the earth's ecosystem result in a plague of mites that attack humans. A cluster of these mites kills the wife of Richard Sinclair, a paleobiologist. He and his daughter flee their Long Island home and find refuge close by in a research laboratory. Sinclair begins to explore the causes of this and other infestations and disasters. An opportunistic former TV talk-show host presents himself to scared Long Islanders as a 'religious' person on whom they can depend for succor.

2679. Pelton, Charles J. *The old one looks on*. New York: Clode, 1927. viii, 309p.

A story of artistic and bohemian life in New York told largely through the frequent conversations of the characters; featured are the inhabitants of a row of houses in a downtown section known as London Terrace.

2680. Pendleton, Edmund, 1845-1910. *A Virginia inheritance*; a novel. New York: D. Appleton, 1888. 303p.

"The scene is laid partly in New York City and partly in Virginia, and the leading characters are a city lawyer [Felix Perry] of good social standing, the members of an old Virginia family [the Chesters of Chatterton], a hot-headed youth from the same state, and sundry people moving in fashionable circles. By the terms of a will the Virginians are threatened with the loss of their old home, which passes to a city cousin who engages the lawyer to conduct negotiations. The oldest daughter of the house is a charming girl, strong-minded, but ingenuous and captivating, and the lawyer finds himself face to face with a very complicated problem. The ways of sleepy, delightful old Virginia and of New York in some of her social and commercial aspects, are faithfully delineated [and contrasted]"—North American review.

2681. Penfeather, Amabel, pseud. *Elinor Wyllys*; or, *The young folk of Longbridge*. A tale. Edited by J. Fenimore Cooper. Philadelphia: Carey and Hart, 1846. 2v.

"An insipid study of manners among Upstate New York gentry, the book features a heroine who is said to be exemplary, but we see her only at balls, dinners, and parties, and get little opportunity to judge. Elinor is an orphan living with a wealthy and indulgent grandfather and aunt; her only trouble in life is that her cousin Jane is very beautiful while she is very plain"—Baym, N. Woman's fiction. Sometimes attributed to James Fenimore Cooper or Susan Fenimore Cooper.

2682. Penrose, Margaret. *Dorothy Dale in the city*. New York: Cupples & Leon, 1913. 246p.

One of a series of novels for young people in all of which Dorothy Dale is the leading character. This story tells of her experiences in New York during a Christmas break from boarding school. Dorothy's itinerary is the usual one for relative newcomers to the metropolis; exploring the huge department stores, theater-going, dealing with a dishonest apartment house agent, a sleigh ride in the Park—and an unusual mission to New York's East Side to help some needy people.

2683. Pentecost, Hugh, 1903-1989. *Death delivers a postcard*, by Judson P. Philips. New York: I. Washburn, 1939. 304p.

"Why did John Lawrence, Long Island millionaire, look worried and rush out to change his will when he received an unsigned postcard adorned with a view of the old Dutch Reformed Church of 'Hillsdale', Conn.? Is there anything sinister in the engagement of his daughter, Janet, to Basil Garth, the actor?

And who was the stranger (if such he be) shot dead on the lawn of the Lawrence estate? These problems are up to Carol Trevor, head of a detective agency given to her by Maxwell Blythe, her ex-husband, as a divorce present, [to solve]"—New York herald tribune books.

2684. ————. *Kill and kill again*. **New York: Dodd, Mead, 1987. 163p.**
'Bridgetown' in Upstate New York is the home of the Manchester Arms Corporation and of Martha Best, secretary to the company's president. Her body is discovered in the trunk of her car, a yellow Mercedes; the police conclude that some insane stranger has killed her and do little to carry the matter further. Martha's brother Wally, a rock star, isn't satisfied with the local police verdict; his sister had hinted to Wally that scandal had touched one of the firm's executives and Wally suspects Martha was murdered by someone in the company's hierarchy. Julian Quist is hired by Wally to manage public relations for his mayoral campaign, allowing Wally to concentrate more on studying pertinent documents that may point to the murderer.

2685. ————. *Murder clear, track fast*. **New York: Dodd, Mead, c1961. 212p.**
The unsolved murder of a sportsman killed the year before in Saratoga draws the attention of the junior partner in a New York law firm. He comes to the Upstate New York resort town during the racing season and tries to put the pieces together. The mystery novel is noteworthy for its authentic descriptions of Saratoga and its horseracing stables.

2686. **Perkins, Frederic Beecher, 1828-1899. *Scrope*; or, *The lost library*. A novel of New York and Hartford. Boston: Roberts Bros., 1874. 278p. (in double columns).**
Adrian Scrope Chester, a librarian from Hartford, in the course of tracking down a valuable book collection, the 'Scrope Library', learns much about the past and present Scrope family. He comes across several actual or purported Scrope descendants in New York City, among them: old Mr. Van Braam and his daughter Civille; Tarbox (Scrope) Button, publisher and seller of subscription books; Button's daughter Ann (Adrian's fiancée); and 'Cousin' Scrope (Brabazon Aymar de Vere Scrope of Scrope) from England. At the novel's windup Adrian has fallen in love with Civille Van Braam, broken off his engagement to Ann Button, been appointed executor of his will by the crestfallen and ill Tarbox Button (his wife, daughter and son have failed him), and has located the 'Scrope chest' which contains a number of extremely rare books; those books are returned to their rightful owner, Mr. Van Braam. "Certain parts of New York … are described with the utmost exactness, and deep familiarity with life in this city is shown"—Nation.

2687. **Perkins, Grace, 1900- . *Boy crazy*. New York: Covici, Friede, 1931. 235p.**

Her millionaire family is dismayed when their pride and joy, Hope Ross, so very popular with the young men in her circle, falls deeply in love without their knowledge. The Rosses are Westchester County residents.

Perry, Clair Willard, 1887-1961. See: Perry, Clay, 1887-1961.

2688. **Perry, Clay, 1887-1961.** *Hell's Acres*; **a historical novel of the wild East in the 1850s, by Clay Perry and John L.E. Pell. New York: L. Furman, 1938. 400p.**
"In 1851 the State of Massachusetts ceded some 1,200 acres of land around the present town of Boston Corners [sic] to the State of New York. For two years this land was not officially claimed by New York, and during the interim this section became the home of a gang of horse thieves working with racetrack gamblers from the Bowery. The story tells how the ring was broken up and the law finally enforced"—Book review digest. Characters involved in the above are: Jean Randall, a lovely heroine; Derk Williams, trampish blacksmith, who turns out to be a hero and the heroine's 'prince'; Black Bart, who runs the Black Grocery Tavern and acts as fence for the thieves; and Irene, Queen of 'Jimmytown'.

2689. **Perry, Lawrence, 1875-1954.** *The romantic liar.* **New York: Scribner, 1919. 255p.**
Wall Streeter "Robert Trent, for business reasons, decides to impersonate Robert Pinkham. In this role he comes in contact with Eleanor Lowell whom, as Pinkham, he is supposed to marry and thereby under the terms of her father's will, they will inherit certain valuable mining stock. Eleanor's uncle, to whom her fortune will go if the terms of the will are not carried out, is aware of Trent's real identity. But for sentimental reasons, Robert, once into the deception, wants to withdraw gradually and gracefully in his own way, so he and the uncle make mutual concessions, which work well until Robert suspects Uncle Caleb of having his own interests too strongly at heart. Then Uncle Caleb unmasks him. Eleanor spurns him, and the fat is in the fire until strong-minded Auntie comes to the rescue and clears up all business and sentimental misunderstandings"—Book review digest.

2690. **Perry, Richard, 1944- .** *Montgomery's children*; **a novel. San Diego: Harcourt Brace Jovanovich, 1983. 282p.**
The town of 'Montgomery' in the Catskills is the home of a number of Afro-Americans whose lives the author follows from 1948 through 1980. Meredith Malone had slain her sightless, retarded child, but had waited many years before turning herself in to the police. The boy's father is now a drug dealer who has the police chief on his payroll. The novel records further incidents of turbulence and human depravity—incest, child abuse, infidelity, suicide, infestations of earthworms—while a glimmer of love offers some hope for the future.

2691. ————. *No other tale to tell*; **a novel. New York: Morrow, 1994. 315p.**

Perry's rather gloomy novel features aspects of Afro-American life in Kingston, N.Y. in 1966 as seen through the experiences of 40ish Carla March, a single mother. Carla's affair with the recently divorced Miles Jackson ends with a quarrel—and the story flashes back to Carla's bond with adopted white brother Max, later a preacher who has captured a large following.

2692. Perry, Thomas, 1947- . *Vanishing act.* **New York: Random House, 1994. 289p.**

Jane Whitefield's Upstate New York house serves as a refuge for people fleeing from spousal abuse, from assassination at the hands of hit men, from false arrest, etc. Jane is a 'half-breed', a member of the Seneca Wolf clan; she finds that connection most useful when she helps John Felker (an accountant being charged, falsely, he says, with embezzlement) retreat further Upstate and finally to an Indian reservation in Canada where he can start life anew.

2693. Perutz, Kathrin, 1939- . *A house on the Sound.* **New York: Coward-McCann, 1964. 212p.**

The novel is an "account of a dinner (and bathing) party on Long Island Sound. … Host and hostess are a middle-aged publisher and his just grown-up daughter. … The themes—half-relationships—emerge: jealousy, a love too old to be revived, a sadoerotic ambiguity between two young men, an incestuous ambiguity between father and daughter, a sexual act gratuit"—New statesman.

2694. Peters, John A. *Two odd girls***; or,** *Douglas Rock's secret.* **New York: G.W. Dillingham, 1898. 529p.**

The 'two odd girls', residents of the Sharon Springs, N.Y. area, achieve fame: the first by writing one of the most popular novels of the year; the other by painting a work shown at the Columbian Exposition of 1893. Other characters in Peters' novel are an impoverished girl engaged to a Methodist minister and the wealthiest man in town who is determined to win her for himself.

2695. Petersen, Herman, b. 1893. *The covered bridge.* **New York: Crowell, 1950. 376p.**

The chief character in this novel is Zoann O'Day, a very capable woman who runs a farm in the Chenango Valley of central New York State during twenty years following the conclusion of the Civil War. Her ambitions for her son are partly responsible for stirring up a feud that involves a covered bridge that joins two sections of the O'Day farm. She is forced to settle differences after her son falls in love with the daughter of one of Zoann's long-standing opponents.

2696. ————. *The road.* **New York: T.Y. Crowell, 1952. 277p.**

The novel's locale is Upstate New York, very likely Madison County, where the Loomis Gang rustled horses and cattle and terrorized communities of farmers and small businessmen in the 1850s and 1860s. In the story at hand the Loomis Gang's name becomes the Huggins Gang; it is this band that the heroine, Hannah Barty, spends years combating to a bloody windup when the remaining vicious Huggins's are virtually wiped out (but not before they have intimidated and even murdered several worthy citizens). Hannah marries Simeon Hume upon his return from the West where he had hoped to improve his fortunes and incidentally escape the law. Together they raise money by trapping in the great swamp that serves as a hiding place for the Hugginses, hiring out and digging up $2,500 in gold coins buried by Hannah's Uncle Amos who died in the Civil War. With these funds Hannah and Simeon purchase a farm 'on the road' (the most prosperous farms are located there), a property that the Huggins family coveted. This action-filled tale draws an excellent picture of the hard lives and struggles of the inhabitants of Upstate New York in the mid-19th century.

2697. **Peterson, Charles Jacobs, 1819-1887.** *Grace Dudley*; or, *Arnold at Saratoga.* **An historical novel. Philadelphia: T.B. Peterson, 1849. 111p. (in double columns).**

Colonel Dudley looks with disfavor on Capt. Henry Malcolm's affection for his daughter Grace; the Colonel observes that Malcolm is hardly his daughter's equal in class and future prospects. Grace obeys her father's wishes and puts aside her true feelings for the young American officer. However all this changes when proof is forthcoming that Malcolm is the heir to the Glenville estates in Scotland, superseding Grace's own claim to said estates. Malcolm/Glenville and Grace are finally joined in marriage. Aside from this plot a large part of the novel is concerned with Benedict Arnold's heroic actions in the Saratoga campaign and his resentment at being passed over for promotion. He intimates to Malcolm the possibility of his defection to the British; Malcolm is of course shocked and does his best to keep Arnold faithful to the American cause for he knows Arnold to be a soldier of distinctive talents.

2698. **Peterson, Keith, 1954- .** *The trapdoor.* **Toronto, New York: Bantam Books, 1988. 184p.**

John Wells of the New York Star investigates a rash of suicides at Grant Valley High School [in Upstate New York]. He had lost his own daughter to suicide. Wells begins to doubt the deaths were self-inflicted. He is maligned by the sadistic editor of the Grant County newspaper and faces the hostility of the community and threats from the murderer, but he persists and finally solves the mystery.

2699. **Peterson, Ray.** *Cowkind.* **New York: St. Martin's Press/Wyatt, 1996. viii, 195p.**

Animal and human characters share the pages of this tale of a dairy farm in Upstate New York in the 1960s and early 1970s. The three most prominent members of the dairy herd are: the assertive Smitty, daydreaming Aretha, and Peanut who courts disaster when he runs away from the farm to hook up with the circus. The cows are not supremely happy when the latest technology is applied to their milk-producing capabilities; they would like to turn the clock back, if the humans would only listen. The latter include: industrious farmer Bob; Edna, his sober wife; and the teens, Gerry and Renee who have no intention of carrying on the family business. Tragedy stalks the human family and Bob has to deal with it.

2700. Phelps, Almira Hart Lincoln, 1793-1884. *Ida Norman*; or, *Trials and their uses*, **by Mrs. Lincoln Phelps. New York: Sheldon, Lamport & Blakeman, 1855. 2 v.**

The original 1848 edition (Baltimore, Cushing & Brother) of this novel was issued in one volume; this is the expanded 2-volume edition. Ida Norman is an exemplar for the person who undergoes harrowing situations but yet comes out of them a better, stronger individual. In volume two Ida finds a husband and Julia Selby, a former coquette, becomes a model teacher and prefers to remain unmarried. New York City and its upper level social life form the backdrop of the chief portion of the novel.

Phelps, Mrs. Lincoln, 1793-1884. See: Phelps, Almira Hart Lincoln, 1793-1884.

2701. Phelps, Robert, 1922- . *Heroes and orators*. **New York: McDowell, Obolensky, 1958. 304p.**

The narrator, Roger, is a novelist living near an artists' enclave in the Catskills; his wife, Darcy, is pregnant with their first child, but Roger neglects her as he runs around the countryside with his irresponsible, girl-chasing cousin, Glib Trask. The two grab odd jobs in the Catskill region and both have a fixation on nubile Elizabeth who is currently living with Margot, a commercial artist. His lust for Elizabeth unrequited, Roger is by the novel's end ready to return to Darcy, now in New Rochelle. Glib continues getting drunk, brawling and bedding down Elizabeth and other women who are enthralled by this free-wheeler.

Philips, Judson Pentecost, 1908-1989. See: Pentecost, Hugh, 1908-1989.

2702. Phillips, Alexandra. *Forever possess*. **New York: Dutton, 1946. 352p.**

The place and period of this historical novel are the Hudson Valley and New York City in the last two decades of the 17th century. A New York merchant's daughter, Annetje Hoosen, marries patrician Henri Devalon and joins him on his large country estate. Jacob Leisler's popular protest against the British and Dutch aristocrats and oligarchy in New York has repercussions throughout the colony. Annetje and Henri air their differences and a separation takes place, but after Henry is accused and held by Leisler and his allies Annetje comes to his rescue. Henri and Annetje are now bonded together, never again to divide.

693

2703. ———. *Where the apple reddens.* **New York: Putnam, 1941. 312p.**

'Madras' is an Upstate New York city where the seven Kreuter sisters (six are widows) have an influence owing to their ownership of a large brewery. Irena Kreuter, ever mindful of her social advancement in Madras, decides to pull the local celebrity, Shamus McNeil, an Irish man of letters, into her orbit. McNeil lives in seclusion, ignoring the people of Madras, but readily available to his publisher and litterateurs from New York City. Irena pursues Shamus, but neither Irena nor Shamus benefit from her stratagems. Gretchen, Irena's niece (she is the narrator) and Shamus's nephew, Brian, distance themselves from their designing elders and go their own way with the help of Colin O'Toole, a genuine poet and patriot.

2704. Phillips, David Graham, 1867-1911. *The cost.* **Illustrated by Harrison Fisher. Indianapolis, Bobbs-Merrill, 1904. 402p.**

The two protagonists of the novel are in sharp contrast: John Dumont, the financier, bestrides Wall Street and corrupts politicians to do his bidding; Hampden Scarborough is an almost saintly public figure free of any taint as he pursues his political ambitions. A New York divorce case finds Dumont named as a correspondent, and his wife, Pauline Gordon Dumont, who had already left him, turns to Scarborough for comfort. Dumont never really recovers from the scandal, although he temporarily assumes control of his company, which has been raided by his enemies, and death is not far away.

2705. ———. *The deluge.* **With illus. by George Gibbs. Indianapolis: Bobbs-Merrill, 1905. 482p.**

Matt Blacklock plays the Wall Street game most successfully, depending solely on his own intuition and resources. He does, however, evince a certain sense of responsibility toward the less fortunate members of society. A battle ensues between Blacklock and a group of financiers determined to ruin him. The plutocrats retain control of the financial and industrial markets, but Blacklock does survive, bolstered by the affection of his wife, the cultured Anita Ellersby.

2706. ———. *The fortune hunter.* **With illus. by E.M. Ashe. Indianapolis: Bobbs-Merrill, 1906. 213p.**

Carl Feuerstein, penniless actor and fortune hunter, agrees to marry Hilda Brauner, daughter of a delicatessen store owner. Her true love is Otto Heilig, a novice in the delicatessen business. But Feuerstein had already eloped with Lena Ganser, daughter of a thriving brewer in Uptown Manhattan. When his duplicity is revealed to the industrious and home-loving German-Americans of New York's East Side, the depressed Feuerstein commits suicide in Meinert's Beer Garden on South Street.

2707. ———. *The grain of dust*; a novel. **Illustrated by A.B. Wenzell. New York: Appleton, 1911. 427p.**

Frederick Norman is the driving force behind the New York corporation law firm of Lockyer, Sanders, Benchley, Lockyer & Norman, although he is the youngest (and least scrupulous) member. He breaks his engagement to Josephine Burroughs and courts Dorothea Hallowell, one of his employees. The two marry, though Dorothea believes she does not really love Frederick and Frederick suspects he was seduced by Dorothea's personal attractiveness. The passage of time and close association finally brings them to a happy and loving adjustment.

2708. ————. *The great god success*; a novel, by John Graham [pseud.]. New York: F.A. Stokes, 1901. iv, 299p.

Howard the 'hero' is a New York journalist determined to 'succeed' by whatever means is available to him. He is not much affected by the sudden death of his mistress Alice and even when he achieves a top position in metropolitan journalism he just as quickly sells himself to the Coal Trust. His reward is an ambassadorship to France.

2709. ————. *Light-fingered gentry*. New York: D. Appleton, 1907. vii, 451p.

A divorced couple, Neva Carlin and Horace Armstrong, leave Indiana for New York City, Neva to study painting with Boris Raphael and Horace to become an officer in the Mutual Association Against Old Age and Death (O.A.D.). Neva, besieged by Raphael's declarations of love, still retains affection for Horace, even as she learns that the O.A.D. is an unscrupulous firm. Horace responds to Neva's pressure and forces the rebuilding of the Association to a level of honesty and fair response to its customers. The couple reconciles to the passionate dismay of Raphael.

2710. ————. *The price she paid*; a novel. New York: D. Appleton, 1912. 378, [1]p.

The beautiful but penniless socialite, Mildred Gower of Hanging Rock (near New York City), accepts marriage to venomous General Siddall because his enormous financial resources seem to promise a life of comfort. When the General refuses to give her a personal allowance Mildred leaves him and goes to New York in search of a singing career. Her 'sponsor' is Stanley Baird, a married man, who is in love with Mildred and imposes no conditions when he provides her with funds to live on while she studies. General Siddall continues to hound Mildred but is finally bested by Donald Keith, a friend of Baird, who dredges up Siddall's bigamous past. And it is Keith, the man Mildred loves, who is the catalyst impelling her to cast aside her hitherto desultory efforts to achieve success as a singer and really buckle down to sustained effort. Mildred has a choice to make: marriage vs. a career in grand opera.

2711. ————. *Susan Lenox: her fall and rise*. New York: D. Appleton, 1917. 2v.

The heroine of Phillip's masterpiece, born illegitimately in an Indiana town, is forced into marriage with a slobbering, almost animal-like farmer. She escapes to showboat life as an actress and singer; when the boat is destroyed,

695

Susan drifts into factory work and eventually prostitution. New York City (especially the Tenderloin and the Lower East Side) is the scene of Susan's full entry into prostitution and drug addiction. A lover from her past, Rod Spenser, gives her reasons for putting her sordid activities behind. Susan meets a theater director and playwright, Robert Brent, who prepares her for the stage. Brent leaves for Europe, Spenser deserts Susan, and she renews a relationship with another old lover, Freddie Palmer. The latter, jealous of Brent, has him murdered. Susan finally realizes her ambition of becoming a great actress, for Brent has left her his estate and she is no longer dependent on any man. 'She has learned to live. But she has paid the price'.

2712. ————. *White magic*; a novel. **Illustrated by A.B. Wenzell. New York: Appleton, 1910. 392p.**

Spoiled Beatrice Richmond is madly in love with artist Roger Wade despite her father's disapproval; the latter keeps Beatrice confined to his estate in northern New Jersey until she breaks away to New York City, pursues Wade, and decides that in spite of her background as a sheltered society woman she can succeed on her own in the city as a fashionable dressmaker or in some other occupation.

2713. ————. *A woman ventures*; a novel. **With front. by William James Hurlbut. New York: F.A. Stokes, 1902. vii, 331p.**

Emily Bromfield enters the 'man's world' of newspaper reporting in New York City; she marries another reporter to satisfy the conventions of the day, although she adopts the role of mistress rather than that of wife. The practice of her profession brings her into contact with labor-capital conflicts and with the wretched life of slum and tenement dwellers. However, Phillips in the end places more emphasis on Emily's romantic affairs than on her reportorial career.

2714. **Phillips, Ephraim. *Lost in the Adirondacks!* Triumphs of a Southern beauty. A tale of love at Piseco! A faithful lover's tragic end! Truth stranger than fiction. Adventures in 'Forest and stream' [by] ex-Sheriff Ephraim Phillips. Indited by a friend. New York: Chas. Burrows, Printer, 1890. 60p.**

A little more than half the booklet tells of the arduous, dangerous trek the narrator and Allen Enos made through a wild stretch of the Adirondacks to mark a trail from Piseco Lake to a lake named after Mr. Stevens of New Jersey who often summered in northern New York State. The rest of the work recounts the tale of the Southern Howland family that fled from the Civil War to the Upstate New York town of Ilion. The daughter, Lucretia, presumably widowed by the war, welcomes the attentions of Orlando Porter of Herkimer and a marriage is about to follow. However, Alonzo Pinkney, Lucretia's husband, turns up (he survived Bull Run, etc.). Alonzo, Lucretia and Lucretia's mother go back to the South. Lucretia's father dies in Ilion. The dejected Orlando Porter is killed when his wagon rolls over on an Adirondack road.

2715. **Phillips, Henry Albert, 1880-1951.** *Other people's lives.* **New York: Boni and Liveright, 1924. 389p.**

"Duncan Wyatt finds that the 'leading of other people's lives' may be an idealistic theory but an unhappy practicality involving many complications. Young and full of the spirit of reforming, Duncan marries little Cynthia Burrell. Helpless child that she is, she receives the full brunt of her husband's ideas. Not satisfied with converting her, he attacks with his favorite slogan the entire 'Westminster Estates' [in Westchester County], a community where the residents buy their homes on the installment plan. Drawn into this suburbia, matters become complicated and others follow Duncan in sowing discontent. Yet they all believe they are idealists. Finally comes the crash of ideals, house and job for Duncan. From the débris Duncan gathers the necessary courage to enable Cynthia and him to live as they desire—and let others do likewise"— Book review digest.

2716. **Phillips, Ruth.** *Love is never late.* **New York: Macaulay, 1933. 316p.**

A novel about an attractive 40-year-old woman with a home on Long Island and a propensity for harking back too often to memories of a love affair in the past which threatens the stability of her present marriage.

2717. **Piatt, Donn, 1819-1891.** *The Reverend Melancthon Poundex*; **a novel. Illustrated by Edgar M. Ward. Chicago: Belford Pub. Co., 1893. 366p.**

"The Reverend Melancthon Poundex, an eminent divine, is reminded of an episode in his early life by reading the death notice of its heroine. This leads him to look up some old letters which, being interrupted while reading them, he hastily secretes in an old mattress. These letters are the indirect means of bringing about the interesting situations in a novel in which an erring minister, a woman suffragist, a disciple of free love, a talented artist, and an ingenuous heroine, have important parts. The scene is 'Pokohasset' and New York City; scenes and characters seem to recall those of the celebrated Beecher trial"— Annual American catalogue.

2718. **Picton, Thomas, 1823-1891.** *The bootmaker of the Fifth Avenue*; **a story of the petroliomania in New York City, by Paul Preston [pseud.]. New York: Hilton, 1866. 93p. (in double columns).**

Walter Devine is aware that at the age of 18, Genevieve, illegitimate daughter of Hubert Vane and Henrietta Desmond, will inherit a fortune. He kills Mary Vernon, Genevieve's caretaker, but is boldly interrupted by Christopher Last before he can seize Genevieve and the documents carried by Mrs. Vernon. Last takes the child and the papers to his cobbler's shop on Fifth Avenue. Fifteen years later Genevieve falls in love with Dr. Stephen Morand. She has always assumed that Christopher was her father. She doesn't know that there is so small a difference in their ages that Christopher could not have that relationship to her. The villain Devine reappears under an assumed name but fails to deceive Christopher and Genevieve meets her mother who is now married as Mrs. Littleton. Dr. Morand has turned into a fop; Genevieve forgets him and realizes that she and Christopher are meant to be a married couple. The subtitle refers to the rabid speculation in petroleum fields that gripped New York in the mid-1800s.

2719. **Pier, Arthur Stanwood, 1874-1966.** *The Plattsburgers.* **With illus. by Norman Rockwell. Boston: Houghton, Mifflin, 1917. 184p.**

The experiences of several fictional college undergraduates taking basic military training at Plattsburgh, N.Y. during World War I. "The training of the boys was less intensive than that to which the recruits at the later camps were subjected. Instead of being drilled in only the infantry branch of the service they were given an opportunity to get at least a smattering of knowledge about other branches. This story is generally true to the conditions that existed at the first camp; in minor details the routine that it describes does not correspond with the routine followed at subsequent camps"—Preface.

2720. **Pierce, Noel, 1907- .** *The second Mrs. Draper*; **a novel. New York: R.M. McBride, 1937. 248p.**

Kitty had gone through divorce and the memory of a tragic suicide was still with her, so when she married Rupert Draper she devoutly hoped that her life from now on would be one of tranquility. Rupert takes Kitty to his handsome Long Island home, which is subtly redolent of the first Mrs. Draper (deceased). And Kitty immediately awakens the resentment of Jim Draper, Rupert's son, who suspects that she is a mere adventuress, a fortune hunter who should never have been allowed to take the place of his mother whom he worshipped. Curbing Jim's hatred and reconciling him to her presence in the Draper household are tasks Kitty is ready to assume.

2721. **Pierson, Ernest De Lancey.** *A slave of circumstances*; **a story of New York. Chicago, New York: Belford, Clarke, 1888. 195p.**

"A story of New York City life introducing characters from all classes of society. The hero is found very poor and shabby and almost ready to commit suicide on a doorstep on Fifth Avenue by a member of the Impecunious Club. The Club looks up good-looking, talented men, puts them on their feet, introduces them to good families, and helps them win the affections of girls with money, upon condition that a percentage of the lady's capital shall after marriage be paid regularly toward the expenses of the club"—Annual American catalogue.

2722. ————. *A vagabond's honor*; **a romance. New York: Belford Co., 1890. [c1889]. 217p.**

"A fire in a [New York City] hotel during the night and the ensuing excitement and confusion cause a strange misunderstanding in the identity of two men who are rescued [but are] insensible and badly burnt. The one, George Heywood, a vagabond and a gambler, becomes rehabilitated in name and character—as he is supposed to be Jack Henley, who has been absent in

Australia for five years, and has returned to New York to visit a cousin and aunt, his only relatives. As Jack Henley, the vagabond is nursed by the beautiful Sylvia Dane, who fails to discover, in his disfigured face, that he is not Jack Henley. Of course they love each other, and the vagabond George Heywood is given a chance to make a display of his so-called 'honor' just as the real Jack Henley turns up as George Heywood"—Annual American catalogue.

Pignatelli, Constance Wilcox. See: Wilcox, Constance Grenelle.

2723. **Piesman, Marissa.** *Personal affects*; **a Nina Fishman mystery. New York: Pocket Books, 1991. 216p.**

New York City attorney Nina Fishman's best friend, Susan Gold, had been searching for a husband, largely through the personal ads section of the newspapers, but ended up in the Catskills with a man who murdered her by strangulation. Nina and detective James Williams also use the personal ads columns, hoping to attract the killer. Nina does meet two fellows at a hiking club outing, but they do not fit any psychotic pattern pointing to a killer. Nina receives a bunch of answers to her ads and has a number of idiosyncratic dates before she stumbles on the possible murderer.

2724. **Pinkney, Andrea Davis.** *Raven in a dove house.* **San Diego: Harcourt Brace, 1998. 208p.**

'Modine', New York, has long been a place where African-Americans could be comfortable. Nell Grady, 12, a summer visitor at her Aunt Ursa's home in Modine, attracts the attention of Slade, the best friend of her cousin Foley. Smitten by the older, 'sophisticated' Slade, Nell agrees to conceal a gun ('raven') for him in her now unused dollhouse. She is much troubled by her action and the consequences are all too real.

2725. **Pinsky, David, 1872-1959.** *Arnold Levenberg.* **Translated by Isaac Goldberg. New York: Simon & Schuster, 1928. 401p.**

Arnold Levenberg, a fairly affluent New York Jew, has pacifistic leanings. The First World War sorely tries his peace-centered ideals. In addition he has allowed himself to be manipulated by several attractive young women, Katherine Shufro being the most troublesome among them.

2726. **Plagemann, Bentz, 1913-1991.** *The boxwood maze.* **New York: Saturday Review Press, 1972. 212p.**

Spending the summer with her elderly, wealthy aunt in a castle on the Hudson, Lee Appleton walks innocently into several mysteries, one of which is the strange disappearance of a treasured family heirloom; another is the unexplained hostility of the estate's handsome gardener. Then a friend of Lee's childhood turns up and asks her to marry him.

2727. **Plain, Belva, 1919- .** *The carousel.* **New York: Delacorte Press, 1995. 342p.**

Grey's Food, an international corporation, is run from its upstate New York headquarters by Dan Grey, his uncle Oliver Grey, and the latter's two sons, Ian and Clive. Dan and his wife Sally are greatly disturbed when they learn that Tina, their 5-year-old daughter, has been sexually abused. Meanwhile the firm is rocked when Dan's sister, Amanda, wants to cash in her one-quarter share in the company so that she can finance an organization which will help despairing young women—and when Ian hopes to turn a profit by selling off Grey's Woodlands, a family treasure. Another crisis for the family and the company looms when Sally is certain of the identity of Tina's abuser.

2728. **Poate, Ernest M.** *Behind locked doors*; a detective story. **New York: Chelsea House, 1923. 320p.**

Another in the roll of murders that take place behind locked doors with the victim alone in his room and no other access to him other than through those doors. Major Conford has been killed with his own knife and the police question his niece Mildred and a surgeon at New York's Bellevue Hospital.

2729. **Poling, Daniel Alfred, 1884-1968.** *The heretic.* **Garden City, N.Y.: Doubleday, Doran, 1928. 233p.**

Cleaning up New York's waterfront is on the agenda of a young minister in a West Side parish despite demurs from the elders of his congregation and their disapproval of his assistant whom they deem a heretic. The minister also faces the strong arm methods of the waterfront thugs, rescues a young woman from harm at the hands of 'The Killer', faces down his son's murderer, and with the application of love and forgiveness brings order out of chaos.

2730. **Pollack, Eileen, 1956- .** *Paradise, New York*; a novel. **Philadelphia: Temple University Press, 1998. 251p.**

Lucy Appelbaum is only 19 when she assumes management of her parents' Eden Hotel in the Catskills. She develops a crush on the hotel's fix-it man, a scholarly African-American named Thomas Jefferson. The latter is pushed out of the Eden Hotel by Lucy's prejudiced grandmother; Jefferson purchases a bungalow colony and seeks to attract the world's greatest thinkers and mystics. Noteworthy is the odd mix of characters of various ethnic backgrounds that populate this Catskill resort area.

2731. **Pollard, Eliza Frances, d. 1911.** *A New England maid*; a tale of the American Revolution. **Illustrated by Frank E. Wiles. Boston: Caldwell, 1911. 288p.**

"A stirring story of the War for American Independence in which such historical characters as Washington, Major André and Benedict Arnold are introduced. The chief interest of the story rests with Hannah Arnold, sister of Benedict, and the failure of her efforts to save André"—Publisher's weekly. "The Puritan element in the midst of the war is illustrated with skill"— Saturday review of literature.

2732. **Poole, Ernest, 1880-1950.** *The car of Croesus.* **New York: Macmillan, 1930.**

230p.

"An exiled Russian prince and a clever young buyer of gowns buy a sumptuous car on the installment plan, embellish it with every luxury and rent it at $100 an hour to New Yorkers who want to be multimillionaires by the hour. The prince as chauffeur and the buyer as ladies' maid ride on the front seat, and by a clever system of mirrors and a Dictaphone learn about those who ride with them"—Book review digest.

2733. —————. *The harbor*. **New York: Macmillan, 1915. 387p.**

"The story ... is that of a boy [Billy] to whose eyes the world unfolds in the form of New York Harbor as it is seen from that part of Brooklyn known as Columbia Heights. Ever since he could remember he had looked down from the back windows of his home upon a harbor that to him was strange and terrible"—Maurice, A.B. The New York of the novelists. Ultimately the boy grows up into an educated man and a writer and falls in love with and marries Eleanor Dillon whose father laid plans for the harbor. Nevertheless Billy tends to be on the side of the laborers employed by his conservative father-in-law. And the vital force and beauty of the harbor will ever be reflected in Billy's life and literary works.

2734. —————. *His family*. **New York: Macmillan, 1917. 320p.**

"A deep sense of the continuity of life ... pervades this ... novel. Roger Gale, close on to sixty years old, living in the New York house that has been his home since his early marriage, tries to understand the new and bewildering currents of modern life as they are reflected in his three daughters. These three represent distinct types. Edith is the domestic and maternal woman, fiercely absorbed in her children. Deborah is the active woman, spending herself on social movements. Laura is the modern woman of society, living life gladly, throwing away old conventions and breaking into new paths, without fear and without regret. In each of them Roger sees his own life repeated. Each of the three has something of himself. It is the second daughter, Deborah, who is nearest to her father's heart. With her passion for mothering the world at war with instinct for personal motherhood, she is the most interesting study in ... [the] book"—Book review digest.

2735. —————. *His second wife*. **New York: Macmillan, 1918. 302p.**

"From a little town in Ohio Ethel Knight comes to live with her married sister in New York City. A few weeks of flurried shopping prepare her for her introduction to the gay life of the city, and then all her plans are cut short by her sister's illness and sudden death. In assuming charge of her sister's home and her small niece, Ethel is thrown into intimate association with her brother-in-law, Joe Lanier. Joe has always been fond of the young girl, so very different from Amy, his wife, and he comes in time to love her and to consider a second marriage. Married to Joe, Ethel finds that she has a very real rival in her sister's unseen presence. For Amy had made of Joe what she had willed. For her sake and to give the luxuries she demanded Joe had forsaken the ideals of his profession, architecture, to gamble in real estate and make big money. Ethel, who cares nothing for these things or for Amy's friends or the kind of life she had led, hopes to turn him back and revive the man he had once been. The story follows her not unsuccessful struggle"—Book review digest.

2736. ———. *Millions*. **New York: Macmillan, 1922. 279p.**
From her position as cashier in an Upstate New York bank Madge Cable is called to New York where her brother, Gordon, supposedly a millionaire, is close to death. The possibility of inheriting his wealth draws a large number of relatives to his side. An actress who may have been Gordon's mistress and whose name he pronounces in his moments of delirium, puts in her claim to be present at the solemn proceedings. Madge is resented by everyone, but she stays the course. Gordon's unforeseen recovery shatters his relatives' dreams; his so-called wealth is a mere supposition. Madge is not at all dismayed by her experience; she feels she has witnessed a significant slice of life.

2737. ———. *Silent storms*. **New York: Macmillan, 1927. 382p.**
"Barry McClurg, a widower of forty-eight and member of a Wall Street firm which is doing some of the big financing of the post-war world, marries for his second wife a brilliant young French girl of noble family, Madeleine de Granier, who has come to America on a lecture tour. They are sincerely if not wholly in love with each other, but the disparity in their years (Barry is almost twice Madeleine's age) and the clash of their temperaments, ideals and loyalties produce the 'silent storms' which make Barry's second marriage a failure, as his first had been. In the end, having sent Madeleine back to France with a liberal settlement, Barry turns with relief to his old comforter and consoler, Charlotte Wheelwright, his mother-in-law and the woman he should have married in the first place"—Book review digest.

2738. ———. *The voice of the street*; **a story of temptation. New York: A.S. Barnes, 1906. x, 285p.**
Jim is a street Arab in New York City with a magnificent voice who manages to separate himself from the degrading pressures of the 'street'; eventually he achieves fame as a singer. Simultaneously we are introduced to a girl who sacrifices her own future when she steals to support her father and 'Lucky Jim'.

2739. **Pope, Elizabeth Marie, 1917- .** *The Sherwood ring*. **Illustrated by Evaline Ness. Boston: Houghton Mifflin, 1958. 266p.**
"A mystery story … Peggy Grahame, newcomer to her [ancestral] American family estate near the Hudson, becomes attached to a young British scholar who arrives to study its history. In backward-in-time episodes … Peggy meets ghosts from the past and sees her ancestor, Barbara Grahame, falling in love with a clever British officer"—Horn book. These ghosts, however, are quite

useful in helping Peggy arrive at explanations of the puzzles that are imbedded in the old home.

2740. Popkin, Zelda, 1898-1983. *So much blood*; **a mystery novel. Philadelphia: Lippincott, 1944. 220p.**

World War II is in progress and Lieutenant j.g. Sam Tate, a Navy doctor, is recuperating from wounds suffered during the North African invasion. He is resting at a Long Island estate when a visiting psychologist is murdered and an attempt is made on the life of the shipbuilding owner. The FBI investigates, but it is Tate who uncovers most of the data that points to the perpetrator.

2741. Porter, Connie Rose, 1959- . *All-Bright Court.* **Boston: Houghton Mifflin, 1991. 224p.**

"All-Bright Court is a steeltown housing project. ... This community [which is made up primarily of black families that have migrated from the South] is the subject of the novel. It is located ... just outside Buffalo, N.Y. (a place to which the inhabitants of All-Bright Court rarely venture) in the heart of the Snow Belt and also the Rust Belt around the dying Great Lakes. All-Bright Court is dominated by the Capital Steel Company, which sometimes employs and more often lays off most of the workers. ...The novel centers on the Taylor family, Samuel, Mary Kate and their five children, and their friends and neighbors [in the 1960s and early 1970s]"—Women's review of books. The decline of the steel industry in and around Buffalo parallels the decay of All-Bright Court and the families that live in it and their dreams of a better life.

2742. Porter, Eleanor Hodgman, 1968-1920. *Cross currents*; **the story of Margaret. Illustrated by William F. Stecher. Boston: W.A. Wilde, 1907. 207p.**

The author provides a glimpse of the depressing conditions of child labor at the turn of the century in this story of a rich family's child, 5-year-old Margaret, who seems irretrievably lost in New York City, is picked up by a boy of the slums and brought to his cramped quarters. She grows up in a world of ugly, unclean streets and sweatshops. Four years later Margaret's distraught mother, almost bereft of hope, finds her daughter and trusts that Margaret's ordeal will eventually recede from the girl's memory.

2743. ————. *The turn of the tide*; **the story of how Margaret solved her problem. Illustrated by Frank T. Merrill. Boston: W.A. Wilde, 1908. 306p.**

Margaret, the lost and restored girl of the author's 'Cross currents', is 21 years of age when she completes her education. Her wealthy mother has long since passed away and Margaret's thoughts return to the friends she had made during her four years in New York City's slums. She decides to devote her time, energy and resources towards helping those who have no one else to alleviate their poverty and despair. Along the way love with the 'proper stranger' enters her life.

Porter, Harold Everett, 1887-1936. See under his pseudonym: Hall, Holworthy, 1887-1936.

Porter, Linn Boyd, 1851-1916. See under his pseudonym: Ross, Albert, 1851-1916.

Porter, William Sidney, 1862-1910. See under his pseudonym: O. Henry, 1862-1910.

Porter, Laura Spencer, joint author. Theodora. See Item #2733.

2744. **Post, Emily Price, 1873-1960. *Parade;* a novel of New York society. New York: Funk & Wagnalls, 1925. 382p.**
"Beneath her languid softness of manner Geraldine is cold and calculating. She jilts her first suitor to marry a man who can give her comparative wealth, an entrance into [New York] society, and the ease, which she has craved. Incapable of interest in anything besides her looks and her social position she gradually loses the only genuine friends she has ever known. Her husband kills himself. The shock rouses her to momentary honesty with herself, but the mental habits of years cannot be lightly shaken off. Old age overtakes her with nothing in life save the lying youthfulness of face and figure that assure her place in the fashionable parade"—Book review digest.

2745. ————. *Purple & fine linen.* **New York: Appleton, 1905. 346p.**
Camilla has completed her schooling and is ready to take her place in New York and Newport society. She is charming yet somewhat immature when she marries Anthony Stuart who is in his late thirties. Anthony's father is one of the richest men in New York, so Anthony can indulge his interest in the latest technologies. Although he showers Camilla with presents, Anthony otherwise pays small attention to her. Camilla turns for comfort to another man; however Camilla and Anthony reconcile just in time to avoid a complete marital rift.

2746. **Post, Mary A. *Poverty Hollow*; a true story. Brooklyn, N.Y.: T.B. Ventres, 1887. 59p.**
Poverty Hollow "was the name given on the maps of New York to a collection of miserable houses on the old Boston [i.e. Albany] turnpike-road near the end of Manhattan Island, and only a few miles from the city" (p.[5]). Mrs. B_____ gazes at this wretched place and decides that its inhabitants, however lowly or even criminal, must be Christianized. She gathers support for a Sunday school from various wealthy New Yorkers (Mrs. Alex. Hamilton, Madame Jumel, e.g.) but meets disapproval from pastor 'Dominie J———'. The success of the school wins him over, however. When Mrs. B___ moves from the area to the city she is sorely missed. Years later Poverty Hollow is swept away to be replaced by fine residences. Mrs. B—— moves to

a small village on the St. Lawrence and finally goes back to New York City's environs, taking care of her husband in their small cottage.

2747. Post, Melville Davisson, 1871-1930. *Randolph Mason, corrector of destinies.* **New York: Putnam, 1923. v, 319p.**

>Randolph Mason is a reformed New York lawyer who has devoted himself to righting the wrongs visited upon the defenseless; he and his clients use some subtle and often barely legal methods to outsmart the bad guys. Contents: My friend at bridge.—Madame Versay.—The Burgoyne-Hayes dinner.—The copper bonds.—The district attorney.—The interrupted exile.—The last check.—The life tenant.—The Pennsylvania pirate.—The virgin of the mountain.—An adventure of St. Valentine's night.—The danseuse.—The intriguer.

2748. ————. *The strange schemes of Randolph Mason.* **New York: G.P. Putnam, 1896. v, 280p.**

>"A collection of stories based upon the present criminal law of New York, showing its loopholes and weak points, and pointing out how an unscrupulous man might commit almost any crime and escape punishment with the advice of an unscrupulous lawyer. Randolph Mason is this kind of lawyer, and he successfully aids his clients to commit murder, robbery, and other criminal deeds, and also to escape punishment"—Annual American catalogue. Contents: The corpus delicti.—Two plungers of Manhattan.—Woodford's partner.—The error of William van Broom.—The men of the jimmy.—The sheriff of Gullmore.—The animus furandi.

2749. Post, Van Zo. *Diana Ardway.* **With illus. in color by Gayle Hoskins. Philadelphia: Lippincott, 1913. 327p.**

>Wealthy Diana Ardway, while on a summer vacation in the Catskills, is saved from a nasty spill from her unruly horse by Paul Worden, a playwright. The two would surely seem to be incompatible: Diana is impetuous, enthusiastic and accustomed to doing whatever pleases her; Paul is 'rough around the edges', a no-nonsense person who has little patience with anyone he considers 'spoiled'. Nevertheless, there is an indefinable connection between the two that bodes well (or ill?) for their futures.

2750. Potter, Frances Boardman Squire, 1867-1914. *The Ballingtons*; a novel, by **Frances Squire. Boston: Little, Brown, 1905. 445p.**

>With New York State as the backdrop this is "the story of two marriages [that of Ferdinand and Agnes Ballington and Tim and Miriam, the latter a Ballington]. In one the husband [Ferdinand] was rich but allowed his wife [Agnes] no money for herself and forced her to stoop to deception to aid her mother and sister in their dire distress. In the other the woman [Miriam] was rich, but when she could not make her husband [Tim] leave his position as bank-clerk and live on her income, [she] became reckless and almost lost her reputation for one of the Ballingtons. How far a husband or wife must respect

each other's individuality and grant each other freedom in the marriage relation is the author's study"—Annual American catalogue.

2751.   **Potter, Margaret Horton, 1881-1911.** *The golden ladder*; a novel. **New York: Harper, 1908. vi, 433p.**

John Kildare and Kitty Clephans first meet at their cheap lodgings in Chicago; John's intention to marry Kitty is frustrated by her sudden removal to New York and her fascination with the glitter of that city. John too goes to New York where he gradually ascends the financial ladder. Kitty, after running through a succession of lovers, turns to John again; he will not have her and Kitty returns to her rudderless life while John, although dissatisfied, takes refuge in his millions.

2752.   **Potter, Mary Knight, d. 1915.** *Councils of Croesus*. **Illustrated by W.H. Dunton. Boston: L.C. Page, 1903. 232p.**

Although Jack Wilton, a young architect, had been given "entrance to the inner temple of New York's social life," he was still looked upon by the widow Helen Lorraine as "a nobody, no family, no money." She is particularly perturbed by Jack's interest in her daughter Laura whom she hoped would marry someone like Sir Paul Martinmas or another man with impeccable social connections. As Jack becomes a frequent visitor to the Lorraine ménage Helen slowly develops affection turning to love for the young architect. She is crestfallen when she overhears a conversation between Jack and Laura in which they declare their mutual love. Laura, ever fearful that her mother would never consent to her marrying Jack, is pleasantly surprised when the aggrieved Helen bows to the inevitable. Concurrent is the romantic pairing of Harriet Aspinwall, the painter, Helen Lorraine's closest friend, and Tom Dinsmore who finally convinces Harriet that he has given up his hitherto dilettantish activities for a career in New York City politics.

2753.   **Pottle, Emery Bemsley, b. 1875.** *Handicapped*. **New York: J. Lane, 1908. 267p.**

A novel about a young man, Donovan O'Hara, who has little education but a knowledge of horses from which he makes his living; his character is a mixture of personal beauty and refinement inherited from his mother and a brutal streak that comes from his father. Love enters his life when he meets a well-bred young woman. The story contains a vivid description of the New York Horse Show.

Potts, Jean, 1910- . *Dark destination*. **See note under Item #2754.**

2754.   **Potts, Jean, 1910- .** *Death of a stray cat*. **New York: Scribner, 1955. 191p.**

Also published as *Dark destination* (Detective book club, 1955). "Marcella, the stray cat is strangled in a vacation cottage on Long Island at the outset of a Labor Day weekend. Her murder sets an affectionate husband [a New York bookseller] and [his] wife at odds, creates a good deal of local dismay and scares the wits out of a rather witless romantic named Lillian"—New York herald tribune books.

2755. Powel, Harford Willing Hare, 1887-1956. *The giant's house,* **by Harford Willing Hare Powel, Jr. and Russell Gordon Carter. New York: Appleton, 1928. 228p.**

Jack Farrington, just graduated from high school in a rural area, like so many young men in the 1920s, comes to the big town ('the giant's house', New York City—Jack is the giant killer) to find fortune, if not fame. However, he discovers, after many disappointments, that the metropolis is hard-hearted, grudgingly if at all offering only the barest necessities to most of those who storm its barricades. He finally throws in his towel, returns home, and happily, successfully organizes a place where boys can learn a craft and make their living therefrom.

2756. ————. *The glory of Peggy Harrison,* **by Harford Powel, Jr. and Russell Gordon Carter. Philadelphia: Penn Pub. Co., 1927. 313p.**

Her earnings in 'Millville', Conn. go towards the support of her mother, younger brother and disabled father, but they are so small that Peggy Harrison decides to try New York City. Unable to find work there, Peggy asks a chance acquaintance, wealthy hard-bitten millionairess for a letter of recommendation to Alan Crosby, owner of the Mammoth Department store. It works; however, no sooner does Crosby hire her than she is fired by a jealous supervisor who resents, among other things, Peggy's suggestions for increasing the store's sales. Dejectedly returning to Millville, Peggy is recalled by Evan Crosby, Alan's son who has tested the value of Peggy's ideas. She is named executive secretary of the store's employee association. As she and Evan work together on aspects of Mammoth's operations they fall in love and marry. The 'glory' of Peggy Harrison is Evan's wedding present to her—the purchase of Pemberton's Castle (or 'Folly') that towered above Millville and which Peggy had often wistfully wished she could someday own.

2757. ————. *Married money.* **New York: Norton, 1929. 298p.**

Wee Legg welcomes the opportunity to shuck off her Bostonian-inherited restraints when she marries Jerry McCoy, athlete and seller of bonds, inherits a million dollars, and begins to taste the offerings of New York City. Her money and champagne flow freely: nightclubs, fine restaurants, yachts, oversize parties, etc.—she tries them all until they reach the point of satiety. When she gives birth to a son, Wee takes the moment to turn her back on New York and return to the comparative quiet and normality of Boston and Beacon Street.

2758. Powell, Dawn, 1897-1965. *Whither.* **Boston: Small, Maynard, 1925. 305p.**

The constricting, petty and dull tenor of small town existence drives Zoe Bourne to the charged atmosphere of New York City. If variety is what she is seeking, Zoe has it: she boards at a house filled with actors and other arts-oriented people; the quest for remunerative employment results in an office job; she has a taste of the city's pleasurable diversions; there are also hard times and failures; but finally romance enters Zoe's life.

2759. Powell, Ella May, b. 1863. *Clio, a child of fate.* **Atlanta, Ga.: J.P. Harrison, 1889. 122p.**

The sudden deaths of her parents who have taken her to New York City to better utilize her talents leave Clio Guery an orphan. Even after she is taken in by an Irish couple, the Limericks, ill fortune stalks her. Mr. Limerick dies, Mrs. Limerick falls ill, and Clio and Nell, the Limericks' blind, adopted daughter fight poverty and near starvation despite the assistance of poor Antonio, an Italian sculptor. Then a stroke of luck brings Clio into the home of wealthy Mr. Van Corlear who recognizes a locket Clio is wearing as once belonging to his lost son, Alfred Van Corlear (a.k.a. Guery), Clio's father. Clio steps into the higher circles of New York society and is about to marry Douglas Mantel (although she really loves Antonio) when a jealous woman poisons her. Nell, her sight restored, marries Antonio—he sculpts Clio as she appeared in her wedding gown.

2760. Powell, Frances. *The By-Ways of Braithe.* **New York: Scribner, 1904. 361p.**

Braithe Manor, an exact replica of the ancestral Braithe home in England, sits on the Hudson, presently inhabited by descendants of its builder, wicked Vivian de Vere Braithe. The By-Ways are secret passages built into the manor. The 'present-day' Braithe heroine is very beautiful, virtuous and religious—a contrast to her many devious relatives—but also flirtatious. The hero is a great-grandson of a Braithe servant. The scion of the family is the devil's own. Lilian, the heroine's stepsister, is no better. Worst of all the distaff side of the Braithes is Jancy, a 10-year-old with physical deformities and a sharp, satanic intelligence.

2761. ————. *The house on the Hudson*; a novel. **New York: Scribner, 1903. 416p.**

The heroine is a descendant of any number of young women in the gothic and romantic English novels of the late 18th and 19th centuries. An American country house in the Hudson River Valley rather than a castle or imposing mansion in Europe is the setting wherein the heroine escapes from danger after danger, villain after villain, is rescued finally by a handsome, undaunted hero; the scoundrels, of course, receive appropriate penalties.

2761a. ————. *The prisoner of Ornith Farm.* **New York: Scribner, 1906. 315p.**

"A young girl drifts out to sea in an open boat off the New England coast on the night of her betrothal to a man she loves and is rescued by a strange man who carries her to his home, 'Ornith Farm', in Westchester Co., N.Y. This man, Rollis Lannion, although he has seen Hope Carmichael but twice in her girlhood, is deeply infatuated with her, and conceives an ingenious story to make her his own. He represents she is insane, that the name she claims is not her own, and keeps her a prisoner at the Farm for many weeks. Lannion is a man of mystery; his home is isolated and filled with strange people, the heroine going through a series of thrilling events"—Annual American catalogue.

Powell, R. Stillman, pseud. See: Barbour, Ralph Henry, 1870-1944.

Preston, Paul, pseud. See: Picton, Thomas, 1823-1891.

2762. **Price, Christine, 1928- . *Song of the wheels*. New York: Longmans, Green, 1956. 214p.**
"Jared, a boy in Upper New York State, finds that he is unable to stand by during the Farmers' Rebellion early in the eighteenth century. He joins the Levelers to fight against the rich and tyrannous landlords. His commander and perennial hero is Will Prendergast who leads a campaign which does much to establish the rights of tenant farmers"—Saturday review.

2763. **Price, Margaret Barnes. *Daddy's widow*; a Long Island story. New York: Broadway Pub. Co., 1916. 366p.**
'Aunt Molly' is the 'fixer', the person in a Long Island community who offers sound advice to young women with questions about marriage. In one case a widow whose husband was a scoundrel believes she has no right to a second marriage despite her love for the man presently courting her. Aunt Molly sets her mind at ease on that score. Molly herself dangles her wooer, Uncle Billy, on a string before she ties the knot with him.

2764. **Prime, William Cowper, 1825-1905. *The Owl Creek letters, and other correspondence*. by W. New York: Baker & Scribner, 1848. 203p.**
In 23 letters (to 'my dear L———') written from New York City, Saratoga, Ballston Spa, N.Y. and Stonington, Conn., the author, in a fictional and semi-autobiographical vein, describes hunting trips in the Adirondacks with a friend, Joe Wilis, the death of a child of 14 and her funeral service—she was the daughter, with the name of Mary, of a once well-established man who isolated himself and Mary in a lonely spot in Upstate New York. 'W———' then spends time on Long Island Sound and Block Island before returning to Upstate New York—to Saratoga, Ballston Spa, Mohawk country, and the Adirondacks. Interspersed are stories and legends he has come across in his wanderings.

2765. **Procter, Arthur Wyman, 1889-1961. *Murder in Manhattan*. New York: Morrow, 1930. vii, 276p.**
During a banquet honoring Dawson Deever, Chief of the New York City Police Department, who is about to retire, a murder interrupts the festivities. The victim is Garet Garmany who takes a keen interest in the subject of administrative reform within the Police Department. Two more murders occur that seem to be related to the first. Burroughs, a young detective assigned to

the case, depending more on his instincts and footwork than on the latest science-based methods of detection, moves from the world of high society to the East Side underworld and comes up with the murderer.

2766. **Pronzini, Bill, 1943- .** *The running of the beasts*, **by Bill Pronzini and Barry N. Malzberg. New York: Putnam, 1976. 319p.**

A serial killer on the loose in an Adirondack village has already murdered three women. Is the killer to be found among the following: a disaffected State Police officer, a weak-willed reporter dominated by his mother, a drunken former thespian, and an elderly, sadistic constable? The murders do not cease and the town's terror reaches an apogee before the killer is unmasked.

2767. **Prose, Francine, 1947- .** *Primitive people.* **New York: Farrar, Straus & Giroux, 1992. 227p.**

Working for a family in Upstate New York (the town is 'Hudson's Landing', an outwardly serene place) in exchange for room and board, Simone, an illegal Haitian immigrant, picks up data about American ways from her employer, Rosemary, and Rosemary's friends (the 'primitive people') that is hardly flattering to them. Rosemary is separated from her husband Geoffrey, a womanizer, but continues to live with her disengaged children, 10-year-old George and 6-year-old Maisie, in his ancestral home. Rosemary's best friend, Shelby, an interior decorator, is a short-tempered, sarcastic woman with a boyfriend, Kenny, who is the self-centered owner of a children's hairdressing establishment and whose sexual tastes are a matter of conjecture.

2768. **Prosper, John.** *Gold-Killer*; **a mystery of the new underworld. New York: Doran, 1922. 283p.**

"The blue-black marks on the neck of John Rice, killed in his box at the opera, show evidence that the much-feared Gold-Killer is again at work. A succession of murders, all among people of wealth and all apparently committed by a person of brute force, disturb Wall Street greatly. This last cold-blooded deed and the sorrow of Anne Rice for her father make the young intern, Dr. Tom Ware, resolve to find the murderer. He leaves no stone unturned, visits haunts of New York's underworld, gathers together clues through exciting experiences in which Anne sometimes shares. Their efforts are crowned with success and the identity of the murderer comes as a shock"—Book review digest.

2769. **[Proudfit, David Law], 1842-1897.** *The man from the West*; **a novel. Descriptive of adventures from the chaparral to Wall Street. By a Wall Street man. New York: Pollard & Moss, 1889. 245p.**

An imposter posing as Texan Henry Armitage milks cash from Armitage's brokers, Flam & Whipple of Exchange St., in Manhattan. Armitage hires the private detective, Rodman Bolster, to track down the swindler (Royal Sturges, 'the General'). Sturges's confederate is Tim ('the Cat') Cody. Armitage speculates on the Stock Exchange, giving a helping hand to a luckless investor, Herbert Henderson, and falling in love with Henderson's sister May. Sturges dies during a burglary he and Cody have planned. The latter, filled with hatred of Armitage, kidnaps May Henderson for ransom money; Detective Bolster foils him. The Texan's Wall St. risks, threatening at one point to bankrupt him, finally turn around in his favor. He becomes president of the Lycoming & Columbia Railroad, with Bolster as treasurer, and marries May Henderson.

2770. **Pryer, Charles, 1851-1916.** *Reminiscences of an old Westchester homestead.* **New York: G.P. Putnam, 1897. 174p.**

"As a reminiscence of the days and dreams of boyhood, rather than for their historic value, do I print these tales of mist and legend" (p.1). About half of the tales dwell on ghosts and a cloven-footed personage that the human characters claim to see wandering the byways of Westchester County. The other half is primarily stories springing from incidents in the American Revolution. Contents: Marvellous tales of Nicholas the Hunter.—Wonderful and mysterious tales of James the Fearless.—A queer old house.—A noted musician.—The Battle of Davenport's Neck.—The wood famine.—The treasure hunters.—Tales of the Old Homestead.

2771. **Pulver, Mary Brecht.** *The spring lady.* **With front. by Neysa McMein. Indianapolis: Bobbs-Merrill, 1914. 298p.**

"Rita, a New York society woman, grows suddenly tired of her empty, meaningless existence and runs away from a luxurious home and a generous husband to hide herself in a village in the Catskills. She lives close to nature … and is ready, after a variety of new and stimulating experiences, to rejoin her husband and start life again on a better and more sane footing. The author has been unusually successful in delineating her village characters and arousing a deep interest on the part of the reader in a number of lightly sketched village tragedies and comedies"—Book review digest.

Putnam, Arthur Lee, pseud. See: Alger, Horatio, 1832-1899.

2772. **Putnam, Nina Wilcox, 1888-1962.** *Esmeralda*; or, *Every little bit helps*, **by Nina Wilcox Putnam and Norman Jacobsen. With illus. by May Wilson Preston. Philadelphia: Lippincott, 1918. 172p.**

"Mrs. DeWynt, of an exclusive Long Island colony, is overwhelmed with bridge luncheons, Red Cross teas and other exhausting forms of 'war work' when her niece, Esmeralda Sprunt of California, appears on the scene. Mrs. DeWynt has looked to her niece for assistance and support, but Esmeralda's ideas of war work are widely different from her aunt's, and the exclusive household, with its horde of men servants, receives one shock after another as their 'typically Western' heroine gets into action. The story is told by the DeWynt social secretary, Mr. Penny"—Book review digest.

Putnam, Wesley, pseud. See: Drago, Harry Sinclair, 1888-1979.

2773. Pyle, Katharine, d. 1938. *Theodora,* **by Katharine Pyle and Laura Spencer Porter. Illustrated from drawings by William A. McCullough. Boston: Little, Brown, 1907. vi, 271p.**

When Theodora Winthrop is left at the Episcopal Sister's school in New York City while her father is abroad, she judges her fellow students. Theodora immediately dislikes Susie, an orphan with misfortune in her past. The Sisters take note of this and draw Theodora aside to point out to her the misconceptions and prejudices that have colored her attitude towards Susie. In time an almost inseparable bond of friendship and devotion is formed between Theodora and Susie.

2774. Queen, Ellery. *The copper frame.* **New York: Pocket Books, 1965. 160p.**

Gamblers operating in Chautauqua County, N.Y. have to deal with an honest police chief, one who cannot be bribed. They have two recourses: either the chief must be framed, or, failing that, they will have to permanently eliminate him.

2775. ————. *The finishing stroke.* **New York: Simon and Schuster, 1958. 244p.**

The story opens on a snowy/icy night in 1905 as John Sebastian and his pregnant wife try to reach their home in Rye. An accident eventually results in the death of these two, but not before Claire has been delivered of twin boys. The story skips to the eve of Dec. 24, 1929 through Jan. 6, 1930 at the mansion of Arthur B. Craig (in 'Alderwood', Westchester County) and concludes in the summer of 1957 when Ellery Queen can finally account for the two murders and other odd goings-on at the Alderwood mansion in 1929/30. Clues in the mysteries are bound up with boxes that are delivered to one or another of the 12 (actually 13) chief occupants and guests during the Twelve Days of Christmas (recalling the folksong of that title).

2776. ————. *The French powder mystery***; a problem in deduction. New York: Stokes, 1930. xvi, 316p.**

"During a Fifth Avenue department store window demonstration the murdered body of Mrs. French, wife of the owner of the store, falls from a suddenly opened wall-bed. Inspector Queen and his son Ellery take charge of the case. Ellery regards as the chief clue the finding of fingerprint powder on a pair of onyx bookends—and from this works to a solution"—Book review digest.

2777. ————. *The House of Brass.* **New York: New American Library, 1968. 210p.**

"Brass has twelve dictionary definitions, one of which is money which is what [blind] Hendrik Brass, a crank and a fraud, offers six people whose parents presumably once helped him. But his potential will is a death warrant and Richard Queen (he has a new wife) advances all kinds of speculations, which are quickly controverted"—Kirkus reviews. There is, by several accounts, six million dollars in the Brass mansion that sits imposingly on the Hudson. The six 'heirs' and Hugo, Hendrik Brass's misshapen servant, make a sterling list of suspects when Brass is murdered.

2778.   ————. *The Roman hat mystery*; **a problem in deduction. New York: Stokes, 1929. xv, 325p.**

The Queens, father and son, set out to learn "who poisoned Monte Field as he sat in his orchestra seat at the Roman Theater [in New York] … and what happened to his top hat. The suspects present at the performance include the dead man's former partner who had threatened him, a gangster who had been one of his clients, and Miss Frances Ives-Pope, whose handbag was found in his pocket"—Saturday review of literature.

2779.   **Quick, Dorothy, 1900- .** *Cry in the night.* **New York: Arcadia House, 1957. 222p.**

Responding to the epistolary cry for help from an old school companion, young Lana goes to an isolated house on Long Island and is soon puzzled by mysterious happenings and the ultimate event, murder.

2780.   **Quigg, Lemuel Ely, 1863-1919.** *Tin-types taken in the streets of New York*; **a series of stories and sketches portraying many singular phases of metropolitan life. With fifty-three illus. by Harry Beard. New York: Cassell Pub. Co., 1890. 297p.**

In his thirteen stories and sketches the author purports to draw portraits of several dissimilar New York types: the 'occupational' thief, the pawnbroker, the lawyer (he is hunting for the individuals who are unaware they are heirs to extensive property in England), the Tammany politician, et al. Contents: Mr. Ricketty. —Mr. Jayres. —Bludoffski. —Maggie. —The Hon. Doyle O'Meagher. — The same (concluded). — Mr. Gallivant. — Tulitz . —Mr. McCafferty. — Mr. Wrangler. — Mr. Cinch. — Grandmother Cruncher.

2781.   **Quiller-Couch, Sr. Arthur Thomas, 1863-1944.** *Fort Amity.* **New York: Scribner, 1904. vi, 337p.**

This historical novel opens with the attack by British and Colonial troops on French-held Fort Ticonderoga in 1758. Other scenes of the story are the regions around Lakes George and Champlain and the Canadian wilds in the Gulf of St. Lawrence. Romance has a role even while French and Indian and British/Colonial forces fight for control of Upstate New York and Lower Canada. An epilogue portrays American descendants one hundred years later gathered on an estate in the Hudson River Valley.

2782.   **Quintano, Dorothy.** *Weekend at the villa.* **Garden City, N.Y.: Published for the Crime Club by Doubleday, 1974. 183p.**

"A mystery about brother and sister, Francesca and Nikki, who spend time together with their socialite heiress mother at Tuxedo Park, N.Y., where they lose [her] to a watery grave—their father died in an accident too—after she has remarried, and Nikki feels guilty for months and years"—Kirkus reviews.

Quod, John, pseud. See: Irving, John Treat, 1812-1906.

2783. **Rabe, David, 1940- .** *Recital of the dog.* **New York: Grove Press, 1993. 308p.**

An unnamed artist with psychological problems living in Upstate New York shoots and kills a dog belonging to a neighbor, the Old Man, claiming that it had been snapping at his cows. The Old Man, unaware of the artist's act, tacks up posters of Barney, the missing animal. The artist/narrator then turns abusive toward his wife, snubs his son, and spies on the Old Man and eventually is metamorphosed into a dog himself.

2784. **Ragsdale, Lulah.** *Miss Dulcie from Dixie.* **Front. by C.H. Taffs. New York: Appleton, 1917. 285p.**

On the condition that she stays six months with her uncle in New York City, impoverished Southerner Dulcie Culpepper will inherit $1,500. In Dulcie's thoughts is the prospect of bringing her father and his brother together; they have been separated by the enmities engendered by the Civil War. Dulcie has to deal with an unsympathetic, scheming aunt, but Orvin Castleton, her uncle's stepson, shows her great kindness. Misunderstanding arises when Dulcie is led to suspect that Orvin is interested primarily in whatever money she is to receive now and in the future. By the story's end all misconceptions are erased and reconciliation take place.

2785. **Raine, William MacLeod, 1871-1954.** *The big town round-up.* **Boston: Houghton Mifflin, 1920. vi, 303p.**

The hero, rugged, generous Clay Lindsay, a no-nonsense Westerner (an Arizonan), takes on the big town, New York. The bad man with whom he has the inevitable showdown is the gangster Jerry Durand. The heroine is the beautiful Beatrice Whitford for whose love Lindsay has a rival in Clarendon Bromfield, the sophisticated but essentially effete Easterner.

2786. **Raison, Milton Michael.** *No weeds for the widow.* **Hollywood, Calif.: Murray & Gee, 1946. 241p.**

The novel has a Long Island setting; the two chief characters are a New York drama critic and a beautiful young woman who has been implicated in a murder and is also believed to be mentally unbalanced.

2787. **Ralph, Frank.** *The king's messenger*; or, *The fall of Ticonderoga.* **Philadelphia: McKay, 1904. 220p.**

The young hero of this story, Robert Masters, and his friend, Eben Hopper, are two Vermonters who spend a good deal of their time scouting the region around Fort Ticonderoga on the New York side of Lake Champlain. Robert is asked by Ethan Allen to slip into the British-held Fort and gather information on the strength of the garrison. Robert is held by the King's troops for a short while, but eludes his captors and is with the forces led by Allen against Fort

Ticonderoga. To Robert falls the task of opening the gates of the Fort through which the American troops enter.

2788. Ralph, Julian, 1853-2903. *An angel in a web.* **With illus. by W.T. Smedley. New York: Harper, 1899 [c1898]. 238 [1]p.**

Scene: A large estate (the Clock House) "near 'Powellton' a few miles to the northeast of Fishkill-on-Hudson; 'Lingard's Mill', not far from Fishkill"; and New York City.As Colonel Lamont lies near death, the spirits (the 'Etherians') of his deceased relatives gather round his bedside and discuss the probable heir to his fortune. Since the Colonel has disinherited his worthless nephew, Jack Lamont, the probable heir is the daughter of the Colonel's sister Helen; the latter had been disowned by the Colonel for marrying unwisely— Helen's daughter, Laura Balm, struggles after her mother's death. Laura suffers many indignities not the least of which is the persistent attention of her cousin Jack Lamont who sees her as a way to grasp the Colonel's fortune. Through all her trials Laura is supported by the spirit of Editha Lamont, the Colonel's late wife. In New York City Laura finally comes into her own, aided by Editha, the young lawyer Archibald Paton, the firm of Brown & Crossley, and the kindly beggar Christmas. Free from all troubles, Laura is left a note: 'In pain and sorrow, call on Editha'.

2789. ————. *The millionairess.* **Illustrated by C.F. Underwood. Boston: Lothrop Pub. Co., 1902. 422p.**

A novel of New York society featuring the talented and beautiful Miss Lamont, the heroine, a millionairess who is anxious to make good use of her wealth. Many of the scenes take place in her country home on the Hudson, and the fashionable Beaux Arts Club plays a fairly important part in the story. The author dwells on the differences between the so-called 'smart set' and the coterie of men and women who have achieved distinction in the arts or in public affairs.

2790. ————. *People we pass*; **stories of life among the masses of New York City. New York: Harper, 1896. vi, 209p.**

"The author never lived in any other tenement than the enormous hive called Manhattan Island; but there he has spent nearly all his life, and there, as everywhere else, the lives of the people of all sorts have been more studied by him than his books. During more than twenty years as a reporter on the [New York] Sun his duties took him into the tenements and among the tenement folk very frequently. ... These tales are, in the main, reflections of scenes that have actually been witnessed"—Preface. Contents: The lineman's wedding. —The mother song.—A day of the Pinochle Club.—Cordelia's night of romance.—Dutch Kitty's white slippers.—Petey Burke and his pupil.—Low Dutch and High.

2791. Rand, Edward Augustus, 1837-1903. *Behind Manhattan gables*; **a story of New Amsterdam, 1663-1664. New York: T. Whittaker, 1896. ix, 382p.**

"Katryne Schuyler, who had always supposed herself the daughter of Lysbet and Hans Schuyler, discovered an old chest containing papers whose purport Katryne determined to find out. Before she could do so, however, the box was stolen. The old chest and the quaint brass knocker on the Schuyler house are important factors in a story of colonial New York, which reveals Peter Von Twiller's secret and describes the wooing of Katryne and Gertruyd Smidt"— Annual American catalogue.

2792. **Randall, Florence Engle, 1917- . *Hedgerow*. New York: Harcourt, Brace & World, 1967. 307p.**

Meredith Costain is still trying to make a career as a ballet dancer in New York City when a summer job in Upstate New York as a babysitter for an 8-year-old girl beckons. She takes an uninvited interest in the family's activities (and those of its hired help) and is soon enmeshed in several very sticky situations.

2793. **Randolph, Marion, 1912-1975. *Grim grow the lilacs*. New York: Holt, 1941. 247p.**

"When George Reed, art patron and gentleman farmer residing at Black Rock Farm, in the Hudson Valley, up and married a second wife named Lilac, the stage was set for murder. Lilac had to have lavender lilacs planted all over the place. Worse … she kept bees. … People who loathed the sight of her were Frank Ritchie, a furious sculptor, inclined to drink; Dick Alder, a painter, writer & landscape gardener; Burton Cole, a malign critic of all the arts; and Tony, one of those stubborn stepdaughters. And there was some belladonna around too [the cause of Lilac's death]. Detecting honors go to Mrs. Andy Stevens, a nice neighbor who outsmarts the cops and gets the answer"—New York herald tribune books.

2794. **Ransome, Stephen, 1902-1977. *A shroud for Shylock*. New York: Doubleday, 1939. 268p.**

Jill Archer, actually head of the detective agency called Secrets, Incorporated, uses scientific methods to advantage in solving the murder of Edmund Gilroy who was killed with an old Spanish rapier. The action takes place in the Hudson River Valley and Jill proves superior to the local police in the case, which also involves a second murder. Bruce Lockridge, Gilroy's former son-in-law, had confessed to the murder and then presumably drowned while trying to escape the authorities. Why did Bruce confess? Was he protecting someone? Paula, Bruce's second wife, took a walk in the woods—why did she faint there? Where was Frank Alfara, Spanish proprietor of a New York nightclub at the time of the murder? Jill provides the answers.

2795. **Rapp, Marvin A. *Canal water and whiskey*; tall tales from the Erie Canal country. Illustrated by Norman Truesdale. New York: Twayne Publishers, 1965. 189p.**

A "'bottoming out' of New York State life along the Erie Canal—a collection of [43] folklore stories, tall tales, anecdotes, newspaper squibs and folk songs—the flotsam and jetsam of the canal era. ... The flavor of most of these stories is Irish" (p. 11-12).

2796. **Rauch, Constance, 1937- .** *A deep disturbance.* **New York: St. Martin's Press, 1990. 202p.**

Holed up in a rented barn in the Adirondacks, editor Madeleine Rafferty is hard at work on a novel her boss has given her time off to complete. She is accompanied by her daughters whom she wishes to keep away from her cocaine-sniffing husband and his pornographic activities. The barn's owner, Harry Littlefield, is still snooping around his property, searching for his vanished ex-wife. Madeleine stumbles onto a decaying body, which is identified as the missing woman. The question to be answered: was she murdered? Most of the novel's characters do not believe she was. Madeleine has another worry; she believes her children are in mortal danger.

2797. ————. *The landlady.* **New York: Putnam, 1975. 245p.**

Despite the admonitions of a friend, Jessica and her husband Sam rent a downstairs apartment in the Westchester house of elderly Mrs. Falconer who seems a little dotty but harmless. The married couple dismisses rumors that previous tenants had left suddenly and were sorely affected by their experiences in the house. Strange things begin to happen. Jessica's child, Patience, is petrified by a plastic doll left in her crib; it is impossible to escape the looming presence of Mrs. Falconer and Sam is never around when needed; Jessica fumbles with keys that do not fit the designated doors. Jessica tries as best she can to deal with the bizarre situations that confront her family. Finally ...

2798. **Raushenbush, Hilmar Stephen, b. 1896.** *Men atwhiles are sober.* **New York: A. & C. Boni, 1928. 337p.**

The characters in the novel are New Yorkers who are members of or who frequent the literary and theatrical cliques of the city. One of them, Lathrop Baker, is mentally tortured by his love for two women and his inability to make either of them content. Both of the women, Ruth, his wife, and Julia Anderson, have stronger natures than he. Lathrop is picked up drunk and taken to court after he had intended to deliver a speech to striking workers. Then he leaves his law firm after a stupid quarrel with a junior partner and spends months looking for employment, living the while in Chelsea in a furnished room. Wife Ruth quits his side and heads for Boston and her mother's home. Julia Anderson's affair with Lathrop falls flat; once again he must be stigmatized as one who never measures up in his own life or in the lives of others.

2799. **Rawlings, Marjorie Kinnan, 1896-1953.** *The sojourner.* **New York: Scribner, 1953. 327p.**

The large Linden farm in Upstate New York is the scene of the novel that covers the period from the end of the Civil War to World War II. When the patriarch Hiram Linden dies his widow, Amelia, and two sons, Asahel and Benjamin, take over the operation, but Benjamin heads West to the dismay of his mother who loves him and hates Asahel. Asahel marries Nellis Wilson; she bears him five children, all rather dull and avaricious with the exception of little Doll who dies in a blizzard—the responsibility is Amelia's who has become increasingly detached and disagreeable. Asahel continues to run the farm well, but his few friends, Amelia, and youngest son Willis pass away and Asahel grieves for and misses his brother Benjamin. Asahel and Benjamin do come together in California, but heart attacks fell them both. Asahel leaves the farm to a Polish family.

2800. **Rawson, Clayton, 1906-1971.** *The headless body*; **a Merlini mystery. New York: Putnam, 1940. 293p.**

The unusual background of a circus touring Upstate New York provides the surroundings for the startling death of the circus's proprietor and the beheading of the title character. The 'Great Merlini', a magician and illusionist with the show, demonstrates his skill as a detective.

2801. ————. *No coffin for the corpse.* **Boston: Little, Brown, 1942. 280p.**

"A corpse that won't stay buried, a ghost, and two murders on Long Island have the Great Merlini, New York magician, hanging on the ropes when he tries to unravel the problem. With the aid of Rose Harte, a reporter, and some sleight of hand by Merlini, the mystery is solved"—New Yorker.

2802. **Ray, Anna Chapin, 1865-1945.** *Day: her year in New York.* **Illustrated from drawings by Harriet Roosevelt Richards. Boston: Little, Brown, 1907. 317p.**

The story opens in 'Heatherleigh', summer home of the Argyle family, and then moves quickly to New York City where Day Argyle is to spend the winter prior to her first year of college. Day meets Sidney Stayres and Sidney's younger sister, Phyllis, Day's brother, and Jack Blanchard. Interest shifts to Phyllis; she is an undisciplined although sensitive girl who is especially in need of kind attention from the people around her.

2803. ————. *The dominant strain.* **Illustrated by Harry C. Edwards. Boston: Little, Brown, 1903. 350p.**

"A society novel purporting to treat realistically of fashionable and musical New York and the manner of their intermingling. Beyond this, the book is concerned with a problem and a moral, the latter being that it is unwise to marry a man with the hope of 'reforming' him"—The critic. The hero is Cotton Mather Thayer who is influenced by both Puritan and Slavic strains—his father was descended from New England Puritans and his mother was a Russian musician.

2804. ————. *Each life unfulfilled.* **Boston: Little, Brown, 1899. 257p.**

Elinor Tiemann and Tom Heaton first meet at a summer camp. When she arrives in New York for voice lessons under Maestro Manuel Arturo, Elinor learns that Tom Heaton is now blind and lives with his sister Bertha Emerson and her husband. Elinor becomes part of the Emerson social circle and spends many hours with Tom. He is deeply in love with Elinor but she looks upon him only as a dear friend. Tom studies Braille and publishes a fairly successful novel with Elinor serving as the model for his heroine—Elinor fails to get the connection. Jack Wyckoff, Tom's best friend, marries Elinor; while the couple are in Europe Elinor gains recognition for her concert stage appearances. Back in New York Elinor is acclaimed for her role in Handel's Arminio. Nevertheless her career falters; it has no continuity. Maestro Arturo contends that Elinor has not suffered and consequently her singing evinces a lack of emotional intensity. Neither Elinor Tiemann nor Tom Heaton have won the fulfillment they so desired.

2805. ————. *Sidney: her summer on the St. Lawrence.* **Illustrated from drawings by Alice Barber Stephens. Boston: Little, Brown, 1905. 332p.**

The summer that Sidney Stayres and her little brother Bungay spend with their cousins and friends in the St. Lawrence River region is filled with picnics, boating, hiking and the inevitable mishaps. Sidney's oldest cousin is a young man of 26 years with weakened lungs and the threat of further physical deterioration. She takes on the task of lifting his spirits and encouraging him to fight the good battle against his illness.

2806. ————. *Ursula's freshman.* **Illustrated by Harriet Roosevelt Richards. Boston: Little, Brown, 1903. 303p.**

When Ursula Thain from the Iowa prairies becomes a full-time resident of New York City, she brings with her the common sense that she nurtured in her previous country existence. Her cousin Jack, a Yale freshman, is a conceited chap obsessed with his own importance, and it is Ursula's mission to reshape his character—which she does.

2807. **Ray, Frederick Augustus, b. 1871.** *Maid of the Mohawk.* **Boston: C.M. Clark Pub. Co., 1906. 340p.**

"Romance of the picturesque Mohawk Valley in the days of the American Revolution when the Dutch held sway in the land. The maid [of the title] is loved by two gallant lads who both suffer heartaches on her account. Customs and manners of the period are worked into the … plot"—Annual American catalogue.

2808. **Raymond, Evelyn Hunt, 1843-1910.** *Among the Lindens.* **Illustrated by Victor A. Searles. Boston: Little, Brown, 1898. 289p.**

Young Beatrice (Bonny) Beckwith's timely assistance to elderly Philipse Chidly Brook, who has met with a couple of mishaps while visiting New York City, calls for a response from the old gentleman. The Beckwiths—Bonny, Isabelle, Robert, Roland and their mother, the widow Rachel Beckwith—are living in straitened circumstances in a New York flat when Mr. Brook brings them to his Hudson Valley town of 'New Windsor'. Under his kindly surveillance and with his help the Beckwiths are able to enter rewarding paths in their new environment.

2809. ————. *A sunny little lass.* **Philadelphia: G.W. Jacobs, 1906. 234p.**

Glory Beck and her blind grandfather, a former sailor, inhabit a cramped little house in Elbow Lane, a slum on the East Side of New York. Their dog, Bos'n, accompanied the old seaman wherever he might be. When Bos'n appeared one night without her grandfather, Glory was afraid that the authorities had taken him away to the Sailors' Snug Harbor, a rest home for indigent or disabled seamen. She put aside the articles she peddled on the street and began looking for him. Good fortune smiled on the girl and her elderly 'charge' when some good-hearted people gave them a shelter and the wherewithal to continue living together.

2810. **Rayner, Emma, d. 1926. *The dilemma of Engeltie*; the romance of a Dutch colonial maid. With a front. in full color by G. Gibbs. Boston: L.C. Page, 1911. 402p.**

Engeltie Van Waesberge has to contend with a father who places her in an awkward position vis-à-vis her fiancé, Hendrick De Grott. The latter quarrels with Mr. Van Waesberge and bolts from the village in New Netherlands that has long been his and Engeltie's home. Laurens Van Waesberge tells his daughter that she must choose as a husband one of the six eligible young men in town, and, failing that, marry elderly Peter Jacobsen. Engeltie is released from her predicament by the fortuitous return of Hendrick De Grott who makes peace with the rambunctious but somewhat chastened Van Waesberge.

2811. ————. *Free to serve*; a tale of colonial New York. **Boston: Copeland & Day, 1897. 434p.**

In the early years of the 18th century an English girl of good background, Aveline Nevard, books passage with her debt-ridden brother, Fulke, for America. Unknown to Aveline her brother has paid for his berth by giving the ship's captain the right to sell his sister into servitude. The friend who was supposed to give Fulke money to rectify the situation fails to show up and Aveline is bound to a Dutch household in New York. She draws the loving attentions of the two brothers in the family. Rivalry for Aveline's hand dredges up bitter enmities between the two men before Aveline makes her choice. The novel has a variety of characters enlivening its pages: Dutch, English, Puritan, French and Negro.

2812. **Read, Opie Percival, 1852-1939. *An American in New York*; a novel of today. Illustrated by Emlen McConnell and Howard Heath. Chicago: Thompson & Thomas, 1905.**

The author does not think very highly of such New Yorkers as are portrayed in this novel, much of which takes place in the Waldorf-Astoria. In contrast are the courtly visiting Southerner, a millionaire, dubbed the Colonel, and the beautiful widow he meets and converses with in the hotel's tearoom. The Colonel is accompanied by his adopted son and the widow by his niece. The Colonel is a most generous soul who is not averse to spreading his wealth around, but he is also capable of dealing handily with one of those superficial, intrusive and unprincipled New Yorkers.

2813. **Reagan, Thomas B., 1916- .** *Blood money.* **New York: Putnam, 1970. 183p.**
"In a psychologically valid development of Earl Boulton's personality Reagan dramatizes middle class desires which he fulfills through bank robbery. On what is to be his final job [robbing of a bank in Upstate New York] with the support of his wife and a hired gunsel [Boulton] is betrayed and betrays himself to come to a tragic end"—Booklist.

2814. **Reed, Isaac George.** *From heaven to New York*; **or,** *The Good Hearts and the Brown Stone Fronts.* **A fact founded on fancy. New York: Optimus Print. Co., 1876. [c1875]. 114p.**
Reed's short novel paints a satirical and condemnatory picture of the corruption, vulgarities, and meanspiritedness of New York City's 'upper classes'. The Brownstone-front family is the lurid exemplar, forcing daughter Mary out of their home when she refuses to marry Thomas Sewell whose money could pull them out of financial difficulties. Mary weds Melville Goodheart, a seminarian, and the two betake themselves to the Goodheart homestead at Irvington-on-Hudson. The three Goodheart brothers, Melville, Francis and Robert, enter various fields of endeavor—business, law, medicine, politics, the Church—but fail in all because of their refusal to compromise the Christian ethics set before them by a 'Mysterious Stranger' (actually Christ himself). Despite ruin, death and mental breakdown the brothers and Mary have gained the promise of eternal life while the less principled remain to be judged.

2815. **Reed, Kit, 1932- .** *Captain Grownup; a novel.* **New York: Dutton, 1976. 249p.**
Will Michael's ex-wife has just taken him for everything; he has lost his job and he has an unfinished novel lying around. So he migrates to 'Elder', New York, a tiny village, to teach English. There he meets Susan Hinners, a talented writer, who is poor and decidedly unbeautiful. Will becomes Susan's mentor and hopes to impress and regain his ex-wife, but he suddenly jumps up and leaves Elder, as empty-handed as ever.

2816. **Reeder, Red, 1902-1998.** *West Point first classman.* **New York: Duell, Sloan & Pearce, 1958. 209p.**
The last of the quartet of Reeder's stories about Clint Lane from his entry into West Point as a plebe to this, his final year and graduation. Clint continues his participation in varsity sports, extends his social contacts, and broadens his acquaintance with the responsibilities of leadership.

2817. ———. *West Point plebe*. **With a front. by Charles J. Andres. New York: Duell, Sloan & Pearce, 1955. 246p.**

Clint Lane's first year at West Point is a rugged one, made all the harder by one particularly persistent upper classman. Clint and his two roommates do, however, acquire discipline and the traditions of the military academy while also participating in the sports program.

2818. ———. *West Point second classman*. **New York: Duell, Sloan & Pearce, 1957. 238p.**

His third year as a cadet at West Point finds Clint Lane a key player on the football and baseball teams, taking an unplanned flight with a high-ranking officer, and settling a dispute with an unduly alarmed F.B.I.

2819. ———. *West Point yearling*. **New York: Duell, Sloan & Pearce, 1956. 253p.**

Sequel to the author's 'West Point plebe' (q.v.). Clinton Lane's second year at West Point is taken up with academic study, sports and social life, as well as field training at Camp Bruckner. He imbibes new lessons in leadership and army discipline despite having to walk off a number of demerits, the rivalry of classmates and difficulties with mathematics. Baseball and football are the two sports he plays with gusto.

Reeder, Russell Potter, 1902-1998. See: Reeder, Red, 1902-1998.

2820. **Reeve, Arthur Benjamin, 1880-1936.** *The film mystery*. **New York: Harper, 1921. 379p.**

During the filming of 'The Black Terror' in Tarrytown, N.Y. (in the library of Emery Phelps' home) the star, Stella Larson, suddenly collapses and dies. Crag Kennedy investigates. Medical examination reveals that Stella was poisoned with rattlesnake venom. She had several love affairs currently and had just divorced Millard, the screenwriter of 'The Black Terror'. Actually there are six people who are suspects in the murder of Stella Larson. Among them: Millard, and Emery Phelps, the banker and financial backer of Manton Pictures which held a contract for Stella's services.

2821. ———. *The gold of the gods*; **the mystery of the Incas solved by Craig Kennedy—scientific detective. New York: Hearst's International Library Co., 1915. vi, 291p.**

Craig Kennedy, scientific detective and hero of other works by the author, is here called on to solve a mystery of modern New York and ancient Peru. "The story opens with the theft from a village museum of an ancient Peruvian dagger. Immediately on the heel of this follows the mysterious murder in a New York hotel of a Peruvian capitalist [Don Luis de Mendoza]. The curator of the museum calls in Kennedy to recover the antique weapon, but the murder follows so swiftly that the scientist at once discovers the relation between the two events, and is thus drawn into a wider field of investigation"—Springfield Republican. Kennedy draws revelatory facts from several Wall Street financiers and from rancorous descendants of a dignified Incan family.

2822. ——————. *Guy Garrick*; **an adventure with a scientific gunman. New York: Harper, 1914. 326p.**

Auto thieves are 'on a roll' in New York City and the police have had little success in putting a halt to the crime wave. One car insurance company hires Guy Garrick to investigate the string of thefts; he accepts the help of Wellington, a playboy, whose car was the scene of a murder, and a young woman who turned up a clue and demanded that it be thoroughly checked out. The surprise in the case is, as Garrick fits the pieces together, that a supposedly trustworthy official is not what he seemed.

2823. ——————. *The stars scream murder*; **a Craig Kennedy novel. New York: Appleton-Century, 1936. 307p.**

"Craig Kennedy, the scientific detective, thinks maybe he could solve a murder by means of horoscopes (astrology). So he tries it out when old Maria Daskam turns up dead at Hampton Hall, Southampton [Long Island] with results that aren't conclusive—the X-rays helped a lot. Craig has to deal with some odd relatives of the deceased and a painting by El Greco. And he does so with much of his old-time skill. As for the stars, when a friend asked him, "Craig have you gone off your nut?," Craig just smiled. "He had found the fiend, hadn't he?"—New York herald tribune books.

Reilly, Bernard James, 1865-1930. See under his pseudonym: Yorke, Anthony, 1865-1930.

2824. **Reilly, Helen Kieran, 1890 or 1-1962.** *The farmhouse.* **New York: Random House, 1947. 246p.**

Seeking relaxation on a Dutchess County farm that has been inactive for a while, a writer is inadvertently pulled into a situation that includes the murder of a private detective from Manhattan, which in turn bodes ill for her friends and neighbors. Detective McKee moves into an idyllic country setting that brings forth clandestine crimes before the case is closed.

2825. **Resnicow, Herbert.** *The hot place.* **New York: St. Martin's Press, 1990. 231p.**

Warren, son of Ed Baer, an enterprising financier, finds the body of Barney Brodsky, the hated chairman of a Long Island country club in the club's steam room. The spa's manager, Bill Carey, is a likely suspect. The Baers have endorsed a gym Carey hoped to build, but Brodsky had opposed Catholic Carey's wish to marry his granddaughter. There are five club members who were not far away when Brodsky met his death. Ed Baer and his son Warren have permission from police sergeant Ben Palmieri to look for the murderer. Ed is a very likable Jewish father who would like Warren to marry and present him with several grandchildren.

2826. Reynolds, Bonnie Jones. *The truth about unicorns.* **New York: Stein & Day, 1972. 369p.**

A novel that presents an illuminating image of rural, small town living—the model is Oriskany Falls in Upstate New York during the late 1920s and early 1930s. Fantasy is an element in this story of the Westcott and Bascomb families who are inadvertently bewitched, but are shielded from gross evil by young Harly Wescott's teacher, Toynbee Upjohn, and a unicorn that wanders in a nearby forest.

2827. Reynolds, John Murray, 1901- . *Men of Morgan.* **Illus. by Manning De V. Lee. New York: Appleton, 1933. vi, 279p.**

This historical novel of the famous Morgan's rifles focuses on their major role in the defeat of General Burgoyne's forces at Saratoga.

2828. Reznikoff, Charles, 1894-1976. *By the waters of Manhattan.* **With an intro. by Louis Untermeyer. New York: C. Boni, 1930. 255p.**

The novel has essentially two parts: in the first part we follow in the steps of Sarah Yetta Volsky, who left her Jewish family in Russia at age twenty and came to America, finding employment as a clothesmaker in New York City's garment center and married; in the second her eldest son, Ezekiel, has his ups and downs while operating a bookstore in Greenwich Village.

2829. Rhoades, Nina, b. 1863. *The girl from Arizona.* **Illustrated by Elizabeth Withington. Boston: Lothrop, Lee & Shepard, 1913. 358p.**

Marjorie Graham is approaching her middle teens with a miniscule knowledge of the world outside her Arizona ranch home. She seizes the opportunity to join a cousin of her own age in New York City for the winter. Their living quarters are in one of the better hotels and both are enrolled in the winter term of a private school. With her natural ebullience and her open-ended honesty Marjorie cuts through many of the affectations that her urban peers have adopted and in time serves as a role model for a number of them.

2830. ⸺. *How Barbara kept her promise.* **Illustrated by Bertha G. Davidson. Boston: Lee & Shepard, 1905. 245p.**

Two English girls whose father, a British Army officer, was killed in the South African Boer War, are placed under the guardianship of their American uncle in New York City. The older of the two girls, Barbara, had promised her father that whatever happened she would always 'be there' for her sister. Barbara fulfills her pledge even though it demands self-sacrifice and dealing maturely with anxieties that would have frustrated a much older person.

2831. ⸺. *Ruth Campbell's experiment*; **a story. Illustrated by W.F. Stecher. Boston: W.A. Wilde, 1904. 288p.**

Returning to her uncle John Campbell's New York home after eight years in a Midwestern boarding-school, Ruth Campbell receives a lukewarm welcome and is asked to leave the house and support herself. Unable to find any other remunerative employment, Ruth uses an alias and enters her unaware brother's household as a 'lady helper', taking care of Arthur and Nellie Campbell's five children, cooking meals, mending, etc. She meets Percy Allen, a friend of the family, and between these two there seems to be a ripening awareness of mutual love. John Campbell dies intestate, leaving Ruth and Arthur equal inheritors of the miser's estate with a value of two million dollars. Ruth reveals her deception to Arthur and Nellie and fears that Percy will be unforgiving and unwilling to court a woman of wealth. After several painful episodes and misunderstandings it is Ruth who comes forward to profess her love to the still rather stiff Percy.

2832. **Rice, Craig, 1908-1957.** *The man who slept all day*, **by Michael Venning [pseud.]. A Gargoyle mystery. New York: Coward-McCann, 1942. 259p.**

A weekend party at Ravenswood, the lavish estate of the Faulkner clan, not too distant from New York City, is interrupted by the grisly murder of the host's obnoxious brother. Melville Flair is on the spot and he cools the guests down while he simultaneously examines the circumstances surrounding the crime.

2833. **Rice, Edward Irving, 1868-1927.** *Old Jim Case of South Hollow*. **New York: Doubleday, Page, 1909. xii, 253p.**

Old Jim Case is the village seer and reigning humorist of 'South Hollow', which is located in Onondaga County, New York. He holds court in the village's general store where he spins his yarns for an audience of boon companions. Jim claims his adherence to temperance and has a sermon on the subject always available. His greatest utility so far as the village is concerned is his in-depth knowledge of all that has gone on there and thus his capability of playing an enthusiastic role in making certain things happen.

2834. **Rice, Elinor.** *The best butter*; **a novel. New York: Morrow, 1938. 338p.**

The author satirizes the pretensions of a group of ultra-intelligent men and women living in a suburban town near New York City who hope that their efforts to produce an atmosphere of enlightenment and freedom from society's implicit restrictions will redound to their children's intellectual development.

2835. **Richmond, Grace Louise Smith, 1866-1954.** *High fences*. **Garden City, N.Y.: Doubleday, Doran, 1930. xii, 343p.**

Rose Collins and David MacRoss meet at a New York dinner party and continue to get together on other occasions. When their mutual attraction turns to love they must confront a dilemma. Both are writers. Rose sees no possibility of leaving her beloved New York, where her sophisticated writings flourish, and joining David in the countryside he loves far more than the city. How they settle their differing points of view is revealed at the story's conclusion.

2836. ————. *Lights up*. **Garden City, N.Y.: Doubleday, Page, 1927. 300p.**

Joan is a Long Island young woman who does not hesitate to stabilize the lives of those around her. Thus she takes an affectionate interest in the activities of a headstrong playwright, turns around a superficial society girl until she meets the requirements of proper wifedom, and furthers the progress of a young carpenter who eventually takes Joan herself into his 'protective custody'.

Ridgely, Albert Newton. See: Ridgely, Newton.

2837. **Ridgely, Newton. *By law of might*; of the campaign in Sunset, a romance of the real Wall Street. New York: H.A. Simmons, 1908. 398p.**
An inside, caustic look at the ethics, or lack of them in Wall Street transactions. It is the code of the 'Street' that its secrets are not for public airing and betrayal of them is the ultimate 'sin'. The plot swings around a perplexing murder in a stylish hotel in which two faithless wives may be implicated. The guilty party or parties are never picked up, for their apprehension could be devastating to other players on Wall Street and their wives.

Riefe, Alan, 1925- . See: Riefe, Barbara, 1925-

2838. **Riefe, Barbara, 1925- . *For love of Two Eagles*. New York: Forge, 1995. 378p.**
In this sequel to The Woman Who Fell from the Sky, Margaret Addison marries Two Eagles, the Oneida chief, after she learns that her French husband Lacroix (whom she married by proxy) is corrupt. Margaret has embraced Indian ways, but she does not know that her father has asked Seth Wilson to whisk her back to England. Within the Oneida tribe Margaret has a problem of her own; she was accidentally responsible for the death of her Indian husband's first wife and has incurred the hatred of Blue Creek, the dead woman's brother. Margaret, believing Two Eagles had died while protecting her from Blue Creek, is about to leave with Wilson on the first stage of her return to England when she and the live Two Eagles are reunited.

2839. **————. *Mohawk woman*. New York: Forge, 1995. 378p.**
Two young Mohawk Indians, Sky Toucher and Singing Brook, marry at their own convenience, thus breaking the tribe's long-standing tradition of arranged marriages. Sky Toucher is called away from his wife's side to act as a scout for the English/colonial forces as they confront the French and Indian enemy. When he is captured and imprisoned in Quebec, Singing Brook, ignoring widespread counsel from other Mohawks, starts out in mid-winter to attempt to procure the release of her husband.

2840. **————. *The woman who fell from the sky*. New York: Forge, 1994. 332p.**
On her way up the Hudson River to Quebec to join her French army officer husband, Margaret Addison, an English aristocrat, is the sole survivor of an Indian attack. A hunting party of Oneidas succeeds in wresting Margaret from

her captors; they give her the name of the Iroquois spirit, Ataentsic, 'The Woman Who Fell from the Sky'. The strange world of early 18th century Indian culture is at first difficult for Margaret to comprehend or even marginally accept. Of course, she has no choice as the days, weeks and months pass swiftly; by the end of the story she must make an unavoidable decision.

2841. Riesenberg, Felix, 1879-1939. *East Side, West Side.* **New York: Harcourt, Brace, 1927. 415p.**

"A collision on the East River sends John Breen's late home to the bottom and hurls John into the water. The East Side receives him and takes him to itself. Pug Malone, trainer, is making a fighter of John when the boy learns to read. Ambition wakes. The one time river rat forges ahead, leaves East Side for West Side, enters Columbia, and presently, through a man whose relationship neither of them at first suspects, is introduced to the homes and haunts of the fashionable. He becomes a civil engineer, woos and almost wins the niece of his wealthy sponsor. After years of struggle with and for the city [of New York] he refuses a tempting offer of moneyed leisure from the once loved Josephine and gives himself utterly to his great love, the city"—Book review digest.

2842. Riis, Jacob August, 1849-1914. *Children of the tenements.* **With illus. by C.M. Relyea and others. New York: Macmillan, 1903. ix, 387p.**

Essentially an expansion of the author's earlier 'Out of Mulberry Street' (q.v.). The earlier volume contained thirty stories and sketches about the economically depressed dwellers in Manhattan. The present work includes ten additional pieces for a total of forty.

2843. ————. *Nisby's Christmas.* **New York: Scribner, 1893. 52p.**

Three sad stories of life among New York City's poor—Nisby's Christmas; What the Christmas sun saw in the tenements; Skippy of Scrabble Alley—drawn from the author's own experiences on the city's East Side.

2844. ————. *Out of Mulberry Street*; **stories of tenement life in New York City. New York: Century Co., 1898. viii, 269p.**

Thirty short stories and sketches of the invariably grim lives of the denizens of the often shoddy tenements in the poorer sections of Manhattan based on the author's observations as a journalist. Italians, Jews and Irishmen are most frequently the 'ethnics' that populate Riis's pages.

2845. Rikhoff, Jean, 1928- . *Buttes Landing.* **New York: Dial Press, 1973. viii, 440p.**

The time frame of the novel is Jeffersonian America to the post-Civil War era. The Buttes family are owners of a lakeside farm, Buttes Landing, in the Adirondacks. Odden Buttes clears the virgin forest, cultivates the land, and marries a woman who relates well to animals. Despite the calamities that nature occasionally foists on them the Buttes cling to their farm, strong in their love of the land. Guthrie, a second generation Buttes, takes a half-Indian girl to wife and develops his skills as a woodsman, while Clyde, an exception to the Buttes rule of affinity for the soil, goes into politics. Through the generations Buttes Landing remains a symbol of one family's devotion to a place that nurtured them.

2846. ———. *One of the Raymonds.* **New York: Dial Press, 1974. 370p.**
"Fifteen-year-old Mason Raymond Buttes ... has the unenviable position of being a certified booklearner in a small Upper New York State town where qualities such as imagination and sensitivity are considered not only useless but downright liabilities—particularly when you own more money than anybody else around, and your politically ambitious father married your mother for her money, and then copped out via suicide, and your mother's marbles aren't entirely there either. Doing his damndest to live up to the expectations of much-admired Uncle Cobus—the strong silent expert Civil War hero figure who is everything his father wasn't—Mason goes through various rites of passage—miraculous survival during a snowstormed week in the woods, beating his cousin John in a hunting contest, taking a truly horror-filled trip through the ... Reconstruction South—only to find out after all, that the world where men delight in killing animals and each other is more macho than manly and there are other things to life than proving oneself"—Kirkus reviews.

2847. **Rinehart, Mary Roberts, 1876-1958.** *The swimming pool.* **New York: Rinehart, 1952. 312p.**
"The Maynard girls, wealthy as anything before the Crash, have been having a harder time since. Judith, of course, skims along best with her millionaire husband. Anne, though, is querulous and clad skimpily in her snobbery, while Lois, who tells the tale (indefatigably) lives with her brother in the crumbling old Westchester house writing detective stories to make ends meet and just getting by with a cook and a general maid. It is Judith's mysterious plight that starts the retrospective business and she is the focus of the tale. While everybody around the place seems to know a little about why she is avoiding taxicabs and locking her doors at night, it takes three hundred and twelve pages to assemble the information. The pages include a great deal of sedulously colloquial talk, a nightly routine of scurrying about in the shrubbery, bashings and shootings, and most of all, a rather strenuously contrived fog"—New York herald tribune books.

Rios, Tere, 1917- . See: Rios, Teresa, 1917-

2848. **Rios, Teresa, 1917- .** *An angel grows up.* **New York: Duell, Sloan & Pearce, 1957. 154p.**
Bianca Maria, a very intelligent Puerto Rican girl, loses her mother and is sent to a convent school on Long Island. Her inability or refusal to follow the

school's rules is especially noted by a perceptive Sister who takes on her case and persuades the young student to change direction.

Ritchie, Anna Cora Ogden Mowatt, 1818-1870. See: Mowatt, Anna Cora, 1818-1870.

2849. **Ritter, Margaret.** *Simon says*; a novel. Boston: Little, Brown, 1966. 248p.
"When Diana Braden, daughter of a divorced and famous pair of actors, left school to become an actress by way of apprenticeship in a New York summer theater, she met Simon. …Simon and Diana immediately become 'buddy chum pals', having in common frustrations and inadequacies which they could blame on their respective parents. Diana held Simon's friendship even when he failed her as a lover and so moved on to other loves as she sought meaning and satisfaction in her life. … The very proper Stanley Partridge III, marriage, and a subsequent child were not the answer and only added to Diana's questioning and sense of failure. It took a soul-searching visit to a psychiatrist and a wise Simon to set Diana on the path of understanding self and her relationship to the other people in her life"—Best sellers.

2850. *The River pirates*; a tale of New York. Taken from the records of the New York Police courts. New York: H. Long, 1853. 92p.
Young William Wainwright, son of the late ship's captain of the same name, falls into bad company—specifically the Mansons, a family of smugglers: John the patriarch, his sons Zachariah, Thomas and Edward, and beautiful but vicious daughter Harriet. When a Customs official is murdered during one of the thieves' raids, William is charged with the homicide, but escapes the gallows or a life in prison when evidence clearly points to the Mansons as the culprits. William turns his life around, goes to sea and marries, but is never quite able to shake off the Mansons who have evidently escaped the law. Zachariah, Edward and Harriet Manson plot to exact vengeance on William; however William's wife, his ship's steward and William himself, thwarts them. The only Manson eventually remaining alive is Thomas who enlists the help of the hypocritical Rev. Meekface Oily and flees to Europe.

2851. **Rives, Hallie Erminie, 1876-1956.** *A fool in spots*. St. Louis: Woodward & Thiernan Print Co., 1895. 234p.
The melodramatic situations in this novel are almost stultifying. Cherokee Bell, the Southern heroine, marries Robert Milburn, an alcoholic artist, whose supposed friend Willard Frost, is secretly endeavoring to ruin Milburn, competitor, and place Cherokee in compromising situations. Cherokee is at an impasse in trying to deal with her husband's alcoholism and falls in love with Marrion Latham, a wealthy, concerned companion of Robert. When Marrion exposes Frost for the rotter he is, the latter shoots him; Marrion recovers from his wounds. Robert gives every indication that he is on his way to getting rid of his bad habits and he and Cherokee go back to one another. New York

society and the city's art world contain most of the story's scenes, although a few are placed in the blue grass region of Kentucky.

2852. **Robbins, Clarence Aaron, 1888-1949.** *Red of Surley*; **a novel. New York: Harper, 1919. 333p.**

"This is the story of two lads, natives of a Long Island fishing village, and of their thwarted ambitions. Jerry, son of a wealthy sporting gentleman whose sins are visited upon his offspring, is a cripple. Early condemned to bookishness, he would be an author and marry his beautiful cousin. After bitter disappointments he devotes his life and money to a hospital for crippled children. Charley, called Red, son of a fisherman, is spared the consequences of his more robust father's sins, and, though sturdy, is a dreamer. Understood by no one but his friend Jerry, he feels himself to be a poet, and writes 'enough to fill a book'. He is handicapped by an unappreciative environment and his lack of education, and after Jerry has left him, becomes resigned to follow his father's calling and marry a one-time playmate"—Book review digest.

2853. **Roberts, Kenneth, 1885-1957.** *Rabble in arms, a chronicle of Arundel and the Burgoyne invasion.* **Garden City, N.Y.: Doubleday, Doran, 1933. 870p.**

The hero of this sequel to Roberts' novel 'Arundel' is Benedict Arnold. He is perceived by the author as the brilliant leader of men really responsible for Burgoyne's defeat at Saratoga. A major portion of the story is the recounting of the experiences of men from Arundel, Maine who participate in the Saratoga campaign. One of them, Peter Merrill, a seaman, is the narrator.

2854. **Roberts, Walter Adolphe, 1886-1962.** *The haunting hand.* **Front. by George W. Gage. New York: Macaulay, 1926. 309p.**

When silent movies were being made in New York Margot Anstruther, a medical student turned actress, threw a party for the cast of 'A Toreador's Love'. Later that night in her bedroom Margot sees a disembodied hand reaching out from under her bed. She recalls a newspaper report about the theft of radium from the Fellowe Institute. Two people who had occupied rooms in Margot's boarding house disappear and the director of the movie, Frederick Stoner, has an air of mystery about him that piques Margot. She believes that she must find answers to these odd occurrences.

2855. **Robertson, Constance Noyes, 1896 or 7-1985.** *Fire ball in the night.* **New York: Holt, 1944. viii, 342p.**

The role played by certain citizens of Syracuse, New York in the Underground Railroad just before the outbreak of the Civil War is the focal point of the novel. Mahala North, the heroine, had purposefully come to that city with her father, opening an inn near the Erie Canal that was to serve as a way station for the Railroad. She is the center of attraction for two men: Dallas Ord, an abolitionist of Southern origin, and John Palfrey, a leader of pro-slavery sympathizers.

2856. ————. *Five fatal letters,* by Dana Scott [pseud.]. **New York: Farrar & Rinehart, 1937. 308p.**

It seemed rather odd that the recently widowed Isobel Loveland should invite all those people to her house on an Adirondack lake in mid-February. The guests are: Gordon Loveland, her brother-in-law, and his wife Ann; Fran and Lindy Lindstrom; Hal and Regina O'Brien; the bachelor 'Slats' Howell; Jim Steele, a lawyer; Michael Ruby, spiritualist and medium; and Charlotte Costello, spinster and narrator of this tale. Dr. Oscar Sibellius and his wife are already with Isobel; he is a psychoanalyst and hypnotist, treating Isobel for emotional stress. When Regina O'Brien is murdered, Jim Steele begins his investigations of the circumstances, assisted by Charlotte. In quick succession two more murders occur; the victims are Dr. Sibellius and Gordon Loveland. At Steele's request Charlotte agrees to be a decoy, a probable fourth 'victim'; the scheme works and the murderer is unmasked.

2857. ————. *Go and catch a falling star.* **New York: Random House, 1957. 368p.**

The New York novelist, Norman Shields, under the duress of a writer's block, buys an octagonal Victorian mansion in the Upstate New York town of 'Hebron'; the house has a fascinating history and Norman does research on its past. Nell Sackett some 40 years before was mistress of the mansion; she was a beautiful woman who aroused a lot of controversy in Hebron. Suicide and insanity followed in her wake and the house had been empty for thirty years before Norman Shields acquired it. An orphan, Paula, appears as an enigmatic figure and Norman wonders what her relationship to Nell could have been. In unlocking the past Shields rustles up more excitement than he had expected.

2858. ————. *Seek-No-Further.* **New York: Farrar & Rinehart, 1938. ix, 351p.**

The author places her fictional spiritualist society, Seek-No-Further, with its Temple Commune, in 'Jericho Center', Upstate New York, in the late 1860s and early 1870s. Father Swan is the guiding force behind the Commune, which survives by selling its products and putting on concerts and festivals. His son Isaiah, college-educated, is skeptical about his father's theology, although he does cherish the place to which he has returned. Isaiah's sweetheart, Dinah Waite, does not question the Commune's control and is in danger of being captivated by the charlatan James Prince who inserts himself and his followers into the Commune. Isaiah strongly feels he must rescue Dinah and the Commune from Prince however harsh the measures required to do so.

2859. ————. *Six weeks in March.* **New York: Random House, 1953. 312p.**

"Story … [of] a large family living in upper New York State a few years after the Civil War. Elijah Lamb, the head of the family … [is] dying of a stroke when the novel begins. His wife, Meg, a tall and still beautiful woman is touched with insanity. … They have twelve living children and the memories of a beloved … son killed in the Civil War. Ruth Lamb, his young widow, had left her own home for Elijah's farm to nurse the old man"—Saturday review of literature. As Elijah's death approaches, the family gathers around him, thirty people in all; they are primarily motivated by interest in his accumulated wealth (with the exception of Ruth). They fight, conspire, storm about the farm looking for Elijah's fortune. Gypsies too come into the picture; they are a point of attraction for both Meg and Ruth. Two climaxes close the novel.

2860. ———. *The unterrified.* **New York: Holt, 1946. 503p.**

"The story of the struggle to force an early peace through a Union default because of a shortage of troops. Mrs. Robertson has focused this problem in the fictional King family of Troy [New York] whose innocuous patriarch, Senator [Ranyard] King, has brought a Southern wife, many years his junior, home to his estate on Perigo Hill. He is a Peace Democrat, solidly against the war and for a compromise with Jefferson Davis to restore the Union without further bloodshed. His new wife, an active Southern sympathizer, influences her two susceptible stepsons to such an extent they both espouse wholeheartedly her nineteenth-century version of the 'peace in our time' philosophy, throwing themselves into the fight against the draft, only to learn too late that her motives and the cause they have joined both stem from a desire for a Confederate victory"—New York herald tribune book review.

2861. **Robins, Elizabeth, 1862-1952.** *The Florentine frame.* **New York: Moffat, Yard, 1909. 334p.**

A rather implausible story about Chester Keith, loved by two women—a mother and her daughter. Prominently in the novel's background is Columbia University (here called 'Hudson College'). Keith marries the daughter in order to be near the mother, his real preference. Most conveniently the older woman dies and the wife, who has for sometime been aware of her husband's predilection, has to find a way to achieve happiness with him.

2862. **Robinson, Anthony, 1931- .** *The member guest*; **a novel. New York: D.I. Fine, 1991. 266p.**

Upstate New York lawyer Augie Wittenbecher takes advantage of a member-guest weekend at the 'Easthelmsford' Long Island Country Club (the ECC) to visit an old buddy, Gordon McSweeney. Gordon, Augie finds, is a troubled man—his marriage is collapsing, he has a dreary job that doesn't pay the bills, and alcohol has become his comforter. Catherine, Gordon's wife, targets Augie for seduction, but he steers clear of her; besides, he is attracted to Azy Flannery of a snobbish East Hampton family. Augie does, however, have a weekend date with Betty, a local girl. Catherine resents Augie's attentions to Azy. The ECC is upset by all this, and is further dismayed when Augie and Gordon compete too successfully against a number of the club's best athletes.

2863. ———. *The whole truth*; **a novel. New York: D.I. Fine, 1990. 316p.**

His wife Phyllis refuses to divorce Leonard Bradley, Upstate New York industrialist; he has visions of her vanishing without a trace. She actually does disappear, and a few days later her raped, sodomized body is found in nearby woods. Of course, Bradley is a chief suspect; he tells the police the whole truth of his relations with Phyllis. His hitherto neglected children stand by him. In another part of the Upstate New York town a tawdry drama with its principal actors—a truck driver and his battered wife and a policeman—has a bearing on the circumstances surrounding Mrs. Bradley's murder.

Robinson, Dorothy Atkinson, b. 1892. See: Blake, Dorothy, pseud.

2864. **Robinson, Gertrude, 1876-1958.** *Spindleshanks*. **Pictures by Peter Burchard. New York: Oxford University Press, 1954. 187p.**

Cal Doane, a lad who was living in the Hudson Valley in 1777, decides to undertake an extremely perilous spying mission directed at the British forces that, if successful, could provide useful information for the American rebels.

2865. **Robinson, Henry Morton, 1898-1961.** *The great snow*; **a novel. New York: Simon and Schuster, 1947. 277p.**

"For three weeks an unparalleled snow storm paralyzed New York City and the surrounding country; in the city people starved, on the farms they froze to death. In Ruston Cobb's luxurious house near the Hudson his sister-in-law and a visiting painter were marooned with Cobb, his neurotic wife and effeminate son. Cobb, a successful patent attorney, saw a civilization dependent on the mechanisms it had invented, now betrayed, when electricity failed, fuel oil ran out, snow plows were snowed under, while he himself self-confident, certain he was the pillar that upheld the family, discovered in himself new weaknesses, and after his own unfaithfulness was able to condone his wife's. The characters suffer from complexes of various kinds, and the book is filled with Freudian symbolism which makes it more than an adventure story, but limits it to mature readers"—Booklist.

2866. —————. *The perfect round*. **New York: Harcourt, Brace, 1945. 280p.**

In this story which is basically one of a contest between righteousness and malfeasance Wake O'Reilly returns from World War II, a battle-fatigued veteran, looking for a simple, quiet life in Hudson Valley and Catskill country. When he attempts to rehabilitate a broken-down carousel he finds himself in conflict with several nasty natives and crooked politicians, at one point being forced to fight off a vicious wolf dog. With the support of a local girl, Olivia, and his reawakened Catholic faith, Wake overcomes the destructive forces in his chosen community.

2867. **Robinson, Mabel Louise, 1874-1962.** *The deepening year*. **Philadelphia: Westminster Press, 1950. 247p.**

The Denby family's year in a Long Island summer resort (in the winter it is boarded up)—its five members undergo abrupt social and financial changes; most disheartening is the realization that their father may be losing his sight. They muster all their courage to meet their many problems.

733

2868. Robinson, Margaret Blake. *Souls in pawn*; a story of New York life. New York: Chicago, F.H. Revell, 1900. 308p.

Rev. Irving is in charge of a mission 'in the neighborhood of Twenty-third Street, New York, where the better class of sinners are supposed to congregate'. Richard Masterson, a saloon-keeper and lapsed Roman Catholic, is smitten by Katherine Irving, the Reverend's daughter, although he is married and has a beloved but sickly son. Katherine's affections are directed towards John Pierce, a rugged, fun-loving young Christian. Katherine's chief 'occupation' is bringing sinners into the mission's fold and she is instrumental in saving Alice Masland from further corruption by the hypocritical 'Christian Merchant' Grey; she and the aristocratic Ellen de Rutyer point the way to a better life for Katie Finnegan of the Chinatown slums. Distraught by Katherine's rejection of him, Richard Masterson is sentenced to Sing Sing Prison after a scuffle and accusation of thievery. It is there that Masterson is converted to the Irvings' brand of Christianity and upon release returns to his family. Christian Merchant Grey, angry at being exposed by Katherine, throws acid in her face. John Pierce marries the disfigured young woman in the presence of Mrs. de Rutyer, Alice Masland, Katie Finnegan and other friends.

2869. Robinson, Solon, 1803-1880. *Hot corn*: life scenes in New York illustrated, including the story of Little Katy, Madalena, the rag-picker's daughter, Wild Maggie, & c. With original designs engraved by N. Orr. New York: DeWitt and Davenport, 1854 [c1853]. 408p.

Fictional vignettes of the sufferings and abuse of female vendors ('hot [sweet] corn' on the cob is one of the sales items), dressmakers, and beggars in the streets of a seemingly uncaring mid-19th century New York City. The first-person narrator describes scenes of wretched poverty, drunkenness and prostitution as he walks around Broadway, Union Square, the Battery, the Five Points, Cow Bay, etc. The 'novel' is an indictment of a metropolitan society that to a large extent ignores or exploits its least fortunate members, especially homeless or slum-dwelling girls and young women.

2870. Roche, Arthur Somers, 1883-1935. *The age of youth*. New York: Sears, 1930. 299p.

Sophisticated denizens of New York City people this novel; it develops a situation that may be peculiar to that metropolis when a former chorus girl, Donna Raynor, determined to marry a very eligible bachelor, asks a New Yorker, Randolph Granby, for $25,000 to finance her quest. The 'patron' is not expected to get that money back; the only satisfaction he will receive for his outlay of money will be a grandstand seat at the game the girl is playing to win.

2871. ————. *Among those present*. New York: Sears, 1930. 298p.

Lacy Crandall, a young man from a socially prominent family, is so deeply in debt that he connects with professional thieves who talk him into a Raffles-like existence, circulating in the higher echelons of New York society and even stealing from the girl he hopes to marry.

2872. ————. *Come to my house.* **New York: Century Co., 1927. 264p.**
"'Johnny' Century is a young and popular member of a social set on Long Island. Hitherto indifferent to amorous advances, she accepts a poet's challenge to visit his house at night, and that on the night of her tentative engagement to Murtaugh Pell. The rash act has far-reaching consequences which seriously affect the girl and the two men who love her"—Book review digest.

2873. ————. *Find the woman.* **With four illus. by Dean Cornwell. New York: Cosmopolitan Book Corp., 1921. 311p.**
Clancy Deane of Zenith, Maine comes to New York City hoping to break into the movies and to experience romance and adventure. Two days after her arrival she is wanted by the police on the charge of murder. It all started when Clancy was helping Fay Marston of the Ziegfeld Follies with her dress; Fay asked Clancy to take the place of girl who was ill and dance at the Chateau de la Reine. There Clancy met a movie magnate by the name of Zenda and went to his apartment on Park Avenue with several other people where they played poker for high stakes. She fled when accusations of cheating and a fight broke out. The next day Clancy had an unpleasant interview with Morris Beiner, a theatrical agent; it ended with Clancy leaving Beiner through a window. The following morning she read Beiner had been murdered and that she is a prime suspect. It is all a 'frame-up'. She survives the frame-up because of a kind judge and his wife and a wealthy young man who has fallen in love with her.

2874. ————. *Plunder.* **With illus. by Will Foster. Indianapolis: Bobbs-Merrill, 1917. 322p.**
"The three richest men in the United States meet together in one room [in a New York City office building]. One controls coal, one transportation, one the food supply. An agreement is drawn up and their signatures are added. A gust of wind flips the paper out of the window! By chance it falls first into the hands of Handsome Harry Mack, the cleverest con man of two continents. Handsome Harry sees his way to making a million, but the opportunity passes by and the paper comes into the possession of Dixon Grant, a small-salaried clerk, who also sees visions of a million exacted by blackmail. But Grant's sweetheart, Kirby Rowland, has other plans and she persuades Grant to put the paper to other uses. With what results the story tells"—Book review digest.

2875. ————. *Uneasy Street.* **Illustrated by James Montgomery Flagg. New York: Cosmopolitan Book Corp., 1920. 339p.**
Before World War I Rodney Baird had worn the white collar of an office worker, but after he received a captain's commission in the army and was

discharged, he was introduced to New York high society by a millionaire friend. There he meets Eileen Elsing, dances away the night with her, loses his army pay and an expensive bauble Eileen had given him for safekeeping, and ends up badly in debt. Oddly enough he stumbles on a cache of money under his hotel bed and uses it for a time before he owns up to his misdeed. His confession puts him back in the good graces of the acquaintances he had made in social circles; he is especially forgiven by Eileen.

2876. ————. *The woman hunters.* **New York: Century Co., 1929. 337p.**
New York's underworld and its society, high, upper middle, and would-be, of Park Avenue and surroundings merge in this story. Vonny Candace, the heiress of 30 million, draws the attention of 'the woman hunters', chief among them Allen Gorham, a former professional gambler, and Kenneth Runyon, an underworld figure. Despite his past Gorham is from a socially prominent family and he really loves Vonny, money or no. Aided by his friend, private detective Mack Morgan, Gorham deals forcefully with Runyon, a jealous woman and a dishonorable financier and wins Vonny.

2877. **Rockey, Howard, 1886-1934.** *Masked longing.* **New York: Macaulay Co., 1930. 319p.**
Two sisters, Aileen and Vivienne Gray, aspire to the rewards success on Broadway and in the fashion world can bring. Levelheaded Aileen takes responsibility for Vivienne, a restless, fun-seeking model. One of Vivienne's escapades leaves Aileen horribly scarred just when stardom in a musical comedy beckoned. Publicist Jimmy Crane, in love with Aileen, and theatrical impresario Max Klein revamp Aileen, wearing a mask to cover her scars, into a radio and recording star. Vivienne gets into more trouble—this time a murder is involved—but is finally set straight and married by the artist Dwight Channing. A plastic surgeon repairs Aileen's features and the future looks brighter for her (and Jimmy Crane).

2878. ————. *This woman.* **Front. by P.J. Monahan. New York: Macaulay Co., 1924. 317p.**
"A story of New York society life which stresses the attitude displayed in regard to marriage and prohibition. Carol Drayton, with her dismissal papers from a reformatory school in her handbag, has the misfortune to have her bag taken. This leaves her absolutely penniless, and to keep from starving she sings on the street. She comes under the protection of the wealthy Rhinebeck-Sturdevants and Baptiste Stratini, a great music master. Charmed with her voice they sponsor her until she shall become an operatic star. Carol never reveals her identity even when the bag is returned with its evidence missing, so all the world wonders about her. The man she loves believes in her and waits throughout her time of study. Finally the greatest night of her life gives her the opportunity, not only to clear herself, but to expose the man who brought about her prison experience"—Book review digest.

2879. Rockwood, Caroline Washburn. *An Adirondack romance.* **New York: New Amsterdam Book Co., 1897. 181p.**

Faith Holland is the beneficiary in the will of Leigh Wadsworth, a quondam close friend of her mother Miriam. Because of Miriam's poor health Faith takes her to the Adirondacks where they form friendships with the Dean family, which is also touring this northern New York recreational area. The story evolves into a guidebook for the Adirondacks as the Hollands and the Deans undertake explorations of Saranac and Raquette Lakes, Lake Placid, etc. There are two romances that develop within this framework—that of Faith Holland and Jack Dean; and Daisy Dean and Ned Murray, the latter a companion of Jack. The mystery of Jack's father, the deceased first husband of Mrs. Dean, is explained to the satisfaction of all concerned.

2880. ————. *A masque of honor.* **A Saratoga romance. New York: Funk and Wagnalls, 1889. 167p.**

A trifle about 'upper-crust' society at play in the convivial whirl of Saratoga Springs. Several romances bloom, the most substantial one involving Jeanne Langley and Stephen Westland. Margaret Selden, Jeanne's companion, mistakes Stephen for his reprehensible twin brother Mark and consequently attempts to draw Jeanne away from Stephen. The appearance of Mark and his estranged wife Beatrice Campbell in Saratoga dispels Margaret's doubts about Stephen. The cynical young lecturer Richard Mannering Howard is fascinated by Beatrice; their love affair progresses when Mark conveniently becomes ill and dies. Margaret finds solace with Arthur Graham who had long fancied himself in love with Jeanne Langley.

2881. Roe, Azel Stevens, 1798-1886. *How could he help it? or, The heart triumphant.* **New York: Derby & Jackson, 1860. 443p.**

Herbert Jones, proprietor of a small store in New York City, supports his mother and sister Ellen. One of his customers, Gertrude Manners, from the slum of Hunker's Alley, draws his interest. When her mother dies the Joneses take care of Gertrude. Gertrude's grandfather, Robert Kirkland, regretting his past rupture with his daughter, Gertrude's mother, is near death on his Hudson Valley estate when he bequeaths his granddaughter a substantial income. Gertrude leaves the Joneses to live with her aunts Gerty and Lizzie and acquire an education. Years of separation take their toll on Herbert—he has long been in love with Gertrude. He is now a prosperous businessman when he hears that Gertrude is contemplating marriage to her cousin, young Robert Kirkland. By the end of the story misunderstandings and missteps of the 'hero' and 'heroine' have been resolved and Gertrude and Herbert are married.

2882. ————. *Like and unlike.* **A novel. New York: Carleton, 1862. 501p.**

Recommended by his pastor, James Beaufort of 'Pleasant Vale', Dutchess County, N.Y., is hired by the merchant, James Sterling, of New York City. James's excellent relations with the elder Sterlings and their daughter Matilda are countered by the hostility of Mr. Sterling's sister, Felicia Roff, and her son, Julius. The yellow fever epidemic of 1822 carries off Mr. and Mrs. Sterling, leaving Felicia Roff's husband in charge of the Sterling business. James is fired; Matilda, feeling a growing love for James, is expected by her aunt to marry Julius. James prospers at the firm of Russel & Co., but his concern for Matilda rises when he hears the Roffs are treating her as mentally unbalanced. He springs to her defense; Mr. Roff has a nervous breakdown and dies, his family left penniless. Matilda has joined James's mother in Pleasant Vale and generously provides Mrs. Roff with an income. James and Matilda are married in Pleasant Vale by his old pastor.

2883. ————. *Looking around.* **A novel. New York: Carleton, 1865. 312p.**
Reverend Robert Ransom, pastor of the Presbyterian Church of 'Woodburn' on the Hudson, provides a home for William Randolph Herbert who has run away from his disagreeable stepmother. William's father assents to Rev. Ransom's guardianship of his son. As he edges toward maturity William is offered a clerkship in Mr. Robert Stanley's wholesale drygoods firm in New York City. He lives with the Stanley family and draws ever closer to young Eva Stanley. When Mr. Stanley is near death he names his partner, Rufus Blanchard, as executor of his estate. William, distrustful of Blanchard, refuses a higher position in the Stanley business. After Mr. Stanley dies, Blanchard fires William. A few years later William, Eva and Blanchard and several friends are together on a Hudson River packet. Blanchard, a widower, hopes to marry Eva, his ward, and assume greater control of her inheritance. William tells Eva that Blanchard is not to be trusted and suggests she select another guardian. Rev. Ransom and a Mr. Tremain from New York decide the union of the hesitant lovers, Eva and William, is long overdue. With their marriage Blanchard recedes into an uncertain financial future.

2884. ————. *To love and be loved.* **A story. New York: D. Appleton, 1851. 190p.**
After the death of paterfamilias James T., the Edwards family—the widow and her three children—move to a small town 30 miles from New York. James, 18, the oldest of the children, has to find work to support the almost penniless family. He is hired as a clerk in the ship chandlers' firm of G. & A. Hunt in the big city and boards with Mr. and Mrs. Gerardus Hunt, Sarah, their niece, and Rudolph, their nephew. Rudolph resents Sarah's fondness for James. Blame is placed on James for the disappearance of $6,000 from Mr. Hunt's safe. Mr. Hunt's brother, Augustus, posts bail for James and the latter has his day in court. James's supporters gather data that incriminate Rudolph and Rudolph confesses. James takes Rudolph's place as the firm's junior partner. James is shot despite his offer of forgiveness to Rudolph; he recovers, marries Sarah and places his family in comfortable circumstances.

2885. **Roe, Edward Payson, 1838-1888.** *A day of fate.* **New York: Dodd, Mead, 1880. 450p.**

On the edge of a nervous breakdown Richard Morton, a New York newspaper editor, goes for a rest to a small town in Upstate New York where he attends a Quaker service and meets the Yocomb family. The Yocombs' pretty daughter Adah, Morton discovers, has only quite ordinary interests; he turns his attention towards Emily Warren, a local music teacher. Richard and Emily fall in love, but she must break off her engagement to Gilbert Hearn, a New York City banker. In an 'all's well that ends well' conclusion, Hearn discovers that Adah Yocomb, her materialistic impulses quelled, is ready to accept his proposal of marriage, primarily because she really does love him.

2886. ————. *A face illumined.* **New York: Dodd, Mead, 1878. 658p.**
Roe emphasizes the elevating influence of religion and 'proper friends' on the character of his heroine, Ida Mayhew, who hitherto has been a flirtatious and shallow young woman. The story takes place in large part in a hotel on the Hudson. On the point of suicide Ida comes under the influence of the elderly James Eltinge, a saintly Christian; the turnabout in her life impresses Harold Van Berg, a successful artist, who had been observing Ida at some distance. During his recovery from a serious accident Van Berg and Ida fall in love and share their mutual trust in God.

2887. ————. *From jest to earnest.* **New York: Dodd, Mead, 1875. 548p.**
'Highland on the Hudson' is the scene of Roe's story that treats of Lottie Marsden's tendency to pick in jest on a somber theological student the 'Lincolnesque' Frank Hemstead. Lottie, a society belle from New York City, gradually begins to understand the essential goodness and sweet nature of Frank and the cruel features of her own behavior.

2888. ————. *A knight of the nineteenth century.* **New York: Dodd, Mead, 1877. 582p.**
"The suburban city [of 'Hillaton'] … was not very distant from New York, and drew much of its prosperity from its relations with the metropolis. It prided itself much in being a university town, but more because many old families of extremely blue blood and large wealth gave tone and color to its society" (p.33). The spoiled and dissolute Egbert Haldane of Hillaton and New York drank too much; he was in love with Laura Romeyn. He decided to stay in Hillaton despite his poor reputation there; helped by the recluse Jeremiah Growther, Egbert started on the road to reform. He studied medicine, served as a doctor in the Civil War and acquired all the attributes of a caring individual and a Christian gentleman. He married Laura and the couple settled in Hillaton where he continued his good works.

2889. ————. *Nature's serial story.* **Illustrated by W. Hamilton Gibson and F. Dielman. New York: Dodd, Mead, c1884. xviii, 430p.**
In this story of the daily life of a farm family in the Hudson Highlands the author takes the opportunity to discourse at length on the main facets of nature during the seasons of the year.

2890. ————. *Near to nature's heart.* **New York: Dodd, Mead, c1876. 556p.**
"The novel begins on 17 June 1776, in the granite mountains around the Hudson Highlands. The hero is Theron Saville who, while on a lone canoe trip up the Hudson, comes upon a beautiful young woman, Vera Brown … an untouched child of nature. How these two finally come together and marry takes up a large portion of a complicated plot structure. Of principal interest is the appearance of General George Washington in the Revolutionary battles"— Carey, G.O. Edward Payson Roe.

2891. ————. *Opening a chestnut burr.* **New York: Dodd, Mead, 1874. 561p.**
Embittered and lacking any faith in God, New York businessman Walter Gregory retires briefly to his former country home on the Hudson, now owned by the Walton family. Gregory, along with his partners, had been swindled by a former friend, Charles Hunting. His developing interest in Annie Walton furthers Gregory's recovery from depression, and he returns to New York City and commercial affairs. During an ocean voyage to Paris, with Annie, her fiancé Hunting, and Walter Gregory on board, their liner collides with another ship. In the ensuing chaos the three, largely through the efforts of Gregory, survive. Hunting, unmasked as a coward and business cheat, loses Annie who marries Gregory; their future residence will be Gregory's old home at 'Highlands on the Hudson'.

2892. ————. *An original belle.* **New York: Dodd, Mead, 1885. x, 533p.**
Of especial interest in this novel about a Northern beauty, Marian Vosburgh, whose chief mission in life seems to be the 'conversion' of her several suitors into men of superior qualities, are full-scale descriptions of the Draft Riots of 1863 and the Battle of Gettysburg.

2893. ————. *What can she do?* **New York: Dodd, Mead, 1873. xii, 509p.**
The three daughters of a once wealthy New York businessman—Edith, Zell and Laura Allen—are ill equipped to earn a living when left almost destitute by the sudden death of their father. Giving up their Fifth Avenue home, Mrs. Allen and the three girls move to a place in the country where Edith takes charge, starts a garden for self-sufficiency, and meets the helpful Arden Lacey, a local farmer who has his own set of responsibilities. Zell runs off with a worthless man-about-town, Guillian Van Dam, and Laura, a hopeless romantic, leans on Edith. Through a series of fortuitous circumstances, the help of Arden, and an awakening of religious faith, Edith is able to achieve a sense of order in her family. She reverses her somewhat snobbish attitude towards Arden Lacey and eventually marries him.

2894. ————. *Without a home.* **New York: Dodd, Mead, 1881. 560p.**
Mr. Jocelyn, a wealthy merchant of New York City, relieves his neuralgia with opium, a drug he gradually becomes addicted to. His habit costs his family dearly; as the family's finances decline, Mildred and Belle, his

daughters find work in a retail store. They are not long in discovering that they are at the mercy of employers who compel them to stay on their feet for too long hours, and who can fire them ruthlessly. Roe foreshadows our present-day concern with drug addiction and unsatisfactory working conditions. Mildred becomes a professional nurse and ends up marrying Roger Atwood, a timid young man, who had wandered in and out of her life for a number of years.

Roe, William James, b. 1843. See under his pseudonym: Cervus, G.I.

2895. **Rogers, Lillian.** *The royal Cravatts*; **a novel. New York: Ives Washburn, 1927. 344p.**

"The study of a family of Russian Jews who emigrated to New York in the last years of the old century: Olga Kravitz and her sons and daughters, Gregory, Sasha and Volodya, and Marsha and Tanya, but it is Gregory who is described with the most insight. Gregory dominates the whole family, except the young and rebellious Tanya, and it is Gregory who decrees that they shall change their name from the common Kravitz to the regal-looking Cravatt. Miss Rogers describes his life, first as an assistant in a pharmacy on the edge of the New York ghetto, and then as the proprietor of a business which he purchases with his mother-in-law's slender savings"—Times of London literary supplement.

2896. **Rogers, Robert Cameron, 1862-1912.** *Old Dorset*; **chronicles of a New York country-side. New York: G.P. Putnam, 1897. v, 209p.**

Short fictional pieces about a village, 'Old Dorset', in southern New York State in the 1840s and of the characters that lived and died there. Contents: A Dorset prodigal.—The Denison vendue.—Madame Callander.—The expiration of Ezra Spicer.—The case of Pinckney Tolliver.—The last of the old church.

2897. **Rollins, Alice Wellington, 1847-1897.** *Uncle Tom's tenement*; **a novel. Boston: W.E. Smythe Co., 1888. 468p.**

"The writer institutes a parallel between the poverty which holds the masses in New York City in bondage and the slavery which formerly existed in the South. The one is as cruel a master as the other, separating families, crushing out natural feelings and being the root of all kinds of immorality. 'Uncle Tom's tenement' is one of the worst examples of a New York tenement in the 'Mulberry Bend'. Here the poorer people manage to exist who figure in the story. There are characters from Madison Avenue who occupy themselves in visiting the 'slums' and devising means for bettering the condition of the people. The work is a severe arraignment of the agents and owners of tenement property"—Annual American catalogue.

2898. **Roman, Eric, 1926- .** *After the trial*; **a novel. New York: Citadel Press, 1968. 250p.**

When she is selected to serve on the jury that is sitting in the trial of John Healy, accused of murdering (strangling) his wife, Susan Davies, married to the vice-president of the only bank in 'Ansburgh' on the Hudson, carries with her an open mind. Most of the townspeople have already concluded that Healy is guilty and Susan has to channel her doubts to the people she is serving with and persuade them to be much more circumspect in their deliberations.

2899. **Ronns, Edward, 1916-1975.** *They all ran away.* **Hasbrouck Heights, N.J.: Graphic Pub. Co., 1955. 189p.**

A former detective, who is now a lawyer with offices in New York City, goes to an Adirondack village to search for a dominant man in the community who has vanished without leaving any clue as to his whereabouts.

2900. **Rood, Henry Edward, 1867-1954.** *Hardwicke*; a novel. **New York: Harper, 1902. 311p.**

"Religious controversy in a small New York town is the substance of 'Hardwicke'. ...The principal character is a young clergyman whose faith in the fundamentals of Christian belief are unshaken, but who has read and thought too much to have any sympathy with the narrow and intolerant orthodoxy of the past. In accepting his village charge he finds himself a member of a community bound hard and fast in the trammels of a mechanical and repellent faith. His opinions quickly arouse suspicion and he finds himself, after a few weeks, the victim of an old-fashioned heretic hunt, with the whole village at his heels. The plot of his enemies to dismiss him in disgrace is shrewdly circumvented, and he withdraws voluntarily with most of the honors of the game, including the daughter of his most virulent antagonist [a Presbyterian elder]"—The dial.

2901. **Roof, Katharine Metcalf.** *The stranger at the hearth.* **Boston: Small, Maynard, 1916. 457p.**

"Nina Ferris, now the Contessa Varesca, returns to New York with her Italian husband to find her own city a different place from the one she had left a dozen years before. Everywhere the immigrants and the children of the immigrants are, in her eyes, de-Americanizing America. The book is a study of these new conditions, written around a slender plot furnished by Nina's evaluation of her husband's Latin qualities when forced into sharp contrast with those of Percy Loring, a hypocritically priggish writer of 'best sellers', and of Daniel Griscom, a forceful, clear-thinking American of the older type. A study of New York society forms a background to this character analysis"—Book review digest.

2902. **Roome, Katherine Ann Davis, 1953- .** *The letter of the law.* **New York: Random House, 1979. 208p.**

"Set at a fictive version of the Cornell Law School, this novel is written in journal format. The diarist, Ixias Smith, is a second-year Law student. An ambitious and highly competitive young woman, Ixias does anything to get good grades. At one point she even seduces and blackmails one of her professors. Occasionally humorous, but predominantly bitter in tone, this book probes the frenetic life of law students in considerable detail"—Kramer, J.E., Jr. The American college novel.

2903. Roosevelt, Elliott, 1910-1990. *The Hyde Park murder.* **New York: St. Martin's Press, 1985. 231p.**

Mrs. Eleanor Roosevelt, the First Lady, is resting at the family home in Hyde Park, Dutchess County, N.Y. in 1935 when she is asked by Adriana van der Meer, a neighbor, to help Adriana's fiancé, Bob Hannah. It seems that Bob's father, Alfred, has stolen funds from his stock brokerage and has plunged to his death—suicide or contrived to look like suicide? Mrs. Roosevelt suspects that Alfred Hannah was murdered. She cooperates with Bob and Adriana to point out plotters who are appropriating funds to send to Nazi Germany. Important names appear in the course of the novel: e.g., Joseph Kennedy, Mayor Fiorello LaGuardia, Louis Henry Howe and Harry Truman.

2904. Roosevelt, Robert Barnwell, 1829-1906. *Love and luck*; **the story of a summer's loitering on the Great South Bay. New York: Harper, 1886. iv, 350p.**

"Having exhausted almost all places of summer and winter resort, the fortunate people of whom this rollicking story treats resolve to build a yacht and spend the next summer sailing about from place to place. The plan is formed at Saratoga, which they find very hot; the boat is built at Garden City and launched on … [Long Island] Sound. The characters are well described, particularly the young man who spent all his time changing his suits and 'gurgling' his replies. … A fondness for frequent meals and plentiful supplies of champagne characterizes several members of the party"—Annual American catalogue.

2905. Rose, Marcia, pseud. *Second chance.* **New York: Ballantine Books, 1981. 440p.**

Four graduates of Upstate New York's 'Hampton College' come to their class's tenth reunion in 1980 and share their experiences since 1970. The class glamour girl, Kitty Cameron, has endured a marriage without love to prosperous Whitney Harris, recalling from time to time the memory of her true love, Dan Copeland. Her best friend, formerly plump, free-spirited Lee Rivers, has gained success as a singer but romance has passed her by as it has Benno Akkardijian, Dan Copeland's college roommate. The reunion is destined to effect major changes in all their lives.

2906. Rosenfeld, Paul, 1890-1946. *The boy in the sun.* **New York: Macaulay Co., 1928. 265p.**

David Bauer, a sensitive and artistic young Jew, has a difficult childhood in his uptown New York home with its bitter parental quarrels and its demanding father. He imagines himself as 'the boy in the sun' who will one day shed all the darkness and mortification he suffers in his youth. David finally does cast aside any feelings of inferiority and steps into manhood with an acceptance of his Jewishness and a sense of his own spiritual self-worth.

2907. **Ross, Albert, 1851-1916.** *A black Adonis*. **New York: G.W. Dillingham, 1895. 318p.**

"Shirley Roseleaf, aspirant for literary fame, writes a novel which is rejected by the reader of a leading New York publishing house because it lacks realism; about this time Millicent Fern has the manuscript of her novel returned to her on account of bad diction. Seeing a literary future for the disappointed authors, Archibald Weil introduces them [to one another], and advises them to write in collaboration. A story is the outcome in which [the black protagonist has a nefarious role]"—Annual American catalogue.

2908. ————. *His foster sister.* **New York: G.W. Dillingham, 1896. 303p.**

"Amos Walton, [62], a millionaire New York bachelor, is found dead in his house [No._, West 37th St.] with twenty-nine wounds on his body. His diamonds, watch, and chain are stolen, but a large sum of money in his pocket remained untouched. The question is who committed the murder, Mr. Walton's nephews [the cousins Edward and Charles Walton] being suspected—especially his heir, Charles, who had married the foster sister [Theresa Ball] of a gambler [and con man, Dan Bennett]"—Annual American catalogue. The story becomes very complex when 20 years later (the crime still unsolved) Theresa (Ball) Walton, a widow—Charles Walton presumably fell overboard, or was pushed, during an ocean cruise—has left daughter Lilian in the care of Dan Bennett. If Charles Walton is really dead, Lilian is his heir. Edward Walton disputes her claim and before the novel concludes he and Dan Bennett have been killed and Charles Walton reappears. The mystery of Theresa Ball and Lilian Walton's births is disclosed and the murderer of Amos Walton finally revealed.

2909. ————. *Love at seventy.* **New York: G.W. Dillingham, 1894. 311p.**

Willard Linnette, widower and owner of the Montvale Optical Works in a New York State town, is seventy years of age, but he declares his love for Eva, the daughter of his housekeeper, Mrs. Warren. Eva rejects his suit and eventually marries 'Guy Dalton', a rather mysterious character whose real name is Clarence Lincoln. Maude Arline is another enigmatic personage in the story and it is her fate to marry Willard Linnette's nephew, Roland, a dissolute young man who may be a candidate for regeneration by the novel's conclusion when Maude's surprising connection to the elderly Linnette is revealed.

2910. **Ross, Nancy Wilson, 1910-1986.** *The left hand is the dreamer.* **New York: W. Sloane, 1947. 390p.**

Fourteen years of a tepid marriage (for security) with a cousin, Christopher, have left thirtyish Frederika Perry frayed and discontented. Living in the Perry family mansion in Upstate New York with her two children whom she appreciates but pays little attention to, Frederika does have a sympathetic mother-in-law, Aunt Palm, an engaging, sometimes puzzling painter, to lean upon. Christopher goes off to serve in World War II and Frederika resumes her painting and historical studies. She has a teacher to whom she is attracted, a Viennese refugee of brilliant intellect; they have a drawn-out affair that is more intellectual than physical. Gradually Frederika establishes her own priorities and her own outlook on all that is going on around her, edging away from Aunt Palm, e.g., whose eccentricities are more and more pronounced.

2911. —————. *The return of Lady Brace.* **New York: Random House, 1957. 242p.**

"An American-born widow, Lady [Caroline] Brace, returns [rather reluctantly] to the Long Island home of her youth to face the problems of her own life which had not been settled. At once she becomes involved in the lives of her [beloved] brother Stephen, her two married daughters [Rosemary and Lydia] and her grandchildren. Her brother's attendant friend, an oriental monk [Venerable Sir] helps them all with his quiet wisdom"—Book review digest. Caroline retains memories of her first husband, an American, from whose violence death released her, and her British son who had died slowly from war wounds.

Rossiter, William H., supposed author. *Duty versus will.* See note under Item #974.

2912. **Rossner, Judith, 1935- . *Nine months in the life of an old maid.* New York: Dial Press, 1969. 183p.**

The sisters, Beth and Mimi Crane, and a housekeeper live at Yiytzo, an estate in Westchester County purchased for them by their parents, Josh and Lily, while the latter two work in Hollywood. Mimi, the stronger of the sisters, thrives; married to a poet she is expecting her first child. Beth has at least two mental relapses; her half-brother Vincent who is a fairly frequent visitor, which is more than can be said for the parents, pulls her through. One unsettling incident is the sale of a large piece of the Yiytzo estate to realtors. Beth has little to look forward to as she continues to live on the shrinking estate.

2913. —————. *To the precipice.* **New York: Morrow, 1966. 384p.**

"Ruth Kossoff, the bright Jewish girl from New York's Lower East Side ... accepts a summer position with a wealthy family at their Catskill home, and ultimately marries her employer, Walter Stamm, when her childhood sweetheart, David Landau, refuses to marry her. ... Now, some fifteen years after she had met the Stamm family, Ruth recalls the fevered days of her intoxicating affair with David; her first summer at the Stamm's home; the suicidal skiing accident which killed her beloved brother Martin; her attachment to Boris, Walter's son; the friction (and later affection) between herself and Helen, Walter's first wife; and the long agony of her loveless marriage which culminates in her bearing a child of David's"—Best sellers.

Roth, Arthur Joseph, 1925-1993. See under his pseudonym: McGurk, Slater.

Rothblatt, Henry B., 1916-1985, joint author. *A handy death.* **See Item #1140.**

2914. **Rothermell, Fred, 1901- .** *Fifth Avenue*; **twenty-eight x-rays of a street. Illustrated by the author. New York: Harcourt, Brace, 1930. 299p.**
Twenty-eight short stories about the underside of Fifth Avenue, the people who make it hum—the 20-dollar-a-week clerk in a high-priced store and its owner with all his worries about staying afloat, the street cleaner, cops on the beat, messenger boys, bus drivers, floorwalkers, charwomen, doormen and subway track-walkers. The crass commercialism of Fifth Avenue is emphasized.

2915. **Roueché, Berton, 1911-1994.** *Fago.* **New York: Harper & Row, 1977. 143p.**
Retired businessman Chick Hill, 62, and his wife Sue, in her fifties, retire to East Hampton, Long Island and vicinity. They have a problem. There isn't enough money coming in to enhance their lifestyle, so Chick devises a plan to defraud the insurance company by murdering a stranger and then faking his own suicide.

2916. **————.** *Feral.* **New York: Harper, 1974. 137p.**
"A young couple who have left the city life for year-round idyllic residence in semirural Long Island find themselves menaced by hostile, nocturnal hordes of abandoned, starving cats. A nagging moral issue blunts the vigilante-style solution"—Booklist.

2917. **Rouse, Adelaide Louise, d. 1912.** *Annice Wynkoop, artist.* **Illustrated by E.B. Barry. Boston: A.I. Bradley, 1898. 294p.**
"In the opinion of Annice Wynkoop's native village, the Wynkoops were an unlucky family. The story tells of Annice's aspiration to become an artist and how she accomplished this, giving her decidedly interesting experiences while a student at Cooper Union [in New York City], and dwelling upon the incident of Nan's prize picture, which proves to her admiring friends that 'ill luck' was a fallacy so far as she was concerned"—Annual American catalogue. The heroine is not only artistically successful but also fortunate in love.

2918. **————.** *The letters of Theodora.* **New York: Macmillan, 1905. 307p.**
Theodora Varney leaves a post as a college instructor to test her ability as a writer in literary but insensitive New York City. She describes her experiences in letters to her brother and to certain female friends. Rejection slips and boarding-houses are familiar features of her day-to-day existence. Theodora's

letters offer commentary on the important writers and currents of the period. Strapped for money she almost marries a Congressman; in the end she returns to an earlier love, a poet and teacher at Columbia University.

2919. **Rouse, Lydia L.** *Kezia and the doctor*; or, *The infidel's school*, **by Lydia E. [i.e. L.] Rouse. Philadelphia: American Sunday School Union, 1888. 150p.**

"The scene is laid under the shadow of the Catskills. Dr. Armstrong is an unbeliever, acute, fascinating, plausible, and bitter. Kezia Fleetwood is the doctor's sister-in-law. He paid her some attention before marrying her sister, Laura. Kezia is a well-to-do maiden who has no fear of the doctor, and does not feel it her duty to allow him to propagate infidelity without her earnest protest. She tells him plain truths in plain words. The story is a narrative of events during many years in the life of a rural [New York] community close to a busy town"—Annual American catalogue.

2920. **Rouse, William Merriam, 1884-1937.** *Bildad Road*. **New York: Orlin Tremaine Co., 1940. xi, 204p.**

"Bildad Road winds down from the granite-buttressed heights of Coon Mountain to the shores of Lake Champlain, and in all the Adirondacks there is no more joyously unregenerate highway. There the girls step faster to the music of a fiddle … [and] a man needs little more than a good dog and plenty of chewing tobacco in order to be happy. The mountain air nourishes a spirit that looks upon the world with a vision pleasantly fantastic" (Preface). The 17 stories in the book introduce us to a gallery of Adirondackers from Buffalo Smith, Simp Tuttle, Calico Sal and Grampy Adam Hardy to Matilda Strong, Oliver Crow (the 'Black Terror' of Bildad Road) and his twins, wiggly Molly and twisty Dolly, Jerry Trip and his father-in-law, blacksmith Zeb Plunkett, the trader Bill Scruggs, et al.

Routsong, Alma, 1924- . See Miller, Isabel, 1924-

2921. **Roux-Lough, Brigette.** *The Fresh Air kid*. **New York: Viking Press, 1990. 210p.**

Fourteen-year-old Leigh enters an entirely different world when she is taken as a Fresh Air kid to the Long Island home of the wealthy Bensons. The kindness of Mr. and Mrs. Benson is seconded by their two younger children who befriend Leigh without reservation. Cindy Benson, also 14, tends to dismiss Leigh; Cindy is boy-oriented while Leigh prefers basketball and 'shooting the breeze' with her male peers. When she returns to her Bronx home Leigh is aware that bridges can be built between people who come from entirely different backgrounds.

2922. **Rowans, Virginia, pseud.** *House party*. **New York: Crowell, 1954. 276p.**

This light satirical novel deals "with a weekend house party in the palatial but somewhat rundown Long Island residence of Mrs. Lily Ames, a charming lady of about fifty, whose relatives descend upon her to rest themselves and to straighten out their lives and their love affairs"—New Yorker.

2923. **Rowe, Anne (von Meibom).** *Men are strange lovers.* **New York: King, 1935. 288p.**

Janet Farnham had hoped to realize a small profit when she turned her Long Island estate into a small-scale resort for selected guests; she hadn't counted on the damaging hearsay and the jolting events that would have an impact on the people around her and on herself.

2924. **Rowe, Fynette, 1910- .** *The burning spring.* **New York: Current Books, A.A. Wyn, 1947. 245p.**

Jud Palmer is a good man who tries to hold his family together and wrest a living from the knobby farm in the Finger Lakes region of central New York at the time of World War I. His two sons, Ned and Harlow, and three women, Pink Bushnell, Sate Ritt and Lottie Bruno, sort out their relationships. Harlow marries the seductive and pregnant Pink; amorous Sate Ritt pursues Ned until he, without too much thought, marries Lottie Bruno, housekeeper par excellence, but whom he had heretofore looked upon as only a good friend. Jud gets along as best he can with his two daughters-in-law.

2925. ————. *The Chapin sisters.* **New York: Current Books, A. A. Wyn, 1945. 238p.**

Charlotte and Penelope Chapin occupy a big house in an Upstate New York town ('Bloomfield') in the mid and latter decades of the 19th century. They have an unexciting, humdrum existence—neither had any luck acquiring a husband; Penelope had a cold and virtuous demeanor, while Charlotte's beaux shied away from her as she became more aggressive. The two maiden ladies were employed at the Bloomfield Library and Museum and faithfully attended Sunday worship services—there was little beyond that, or was there? One finds out at the conclusion.

2926. **Rowson, Susanna Haswell, 1762-1824.** *Charlotte*; a tale of truth. **London: printed for W. Lane, 1791. 2v.**

Also published many times under the title: Charlotte Temple … The scene of this very popular novel (ca. 200 editions) is New York and Great Britain. Seduced by Colonel Montraville of the King's Army, Charlotte is abandoned, with child, in New York during the American Revolution. Her sad fate is to die in poverty, leaving behind her daughter Lucy.

2927. **Roy, Lillian Elizabeth, 1868-1932.** *Girl Scouts in the Adirondacks.* **New York: Grosset & Dunlap, 1921. 224p.**

The Dandelion Troop of Girl Scouts of New Jersey under the leadership of Mrs. Vernon travels by motorcar to its camp in the Adirondacks, which has been placed in readiness by Mr. Gilroy. Despite a series of mishaps the Girl Scouts, along with the reader imbibe much forest lore, take a canoe trip through the Fulton Chain of Lakes, save lives when a fire sweeps through an Adirondack lodge, and join a nearby troop of Boy Scouts in exploration of their surroundings.

2928. ————. *Polly in New York.* **Illustrated by H.S. Barbour. New York: Grosset & Dunlap, 1922. 292p.**

Polly Brewster and her friend Eleanor (Nolla) Maynard are enrolled in a private school in New York City; they also hope to study interior design and decorating as a future occupational choice. New York in the early 1920s as described in this novel for teenage girls (one of 'The Polly Brewster series') is not dissimilar in many way from the New York of the 1990s—Polly, a Westerner, is astonished by the huge numbers of people who 'catapulted back and forth like rockets'. And apartment hunting is as discouraging as always; the choices are few, the rents exorbitant. But these young women have no money problems; prices are of little concern to them. Except for one incident of almost being mugged, the two acclimate themselves handily to the metropolis and accomplish much of what they had expected to do.

2928a. Rozan, S.J. *Stone quarry.* **New York: St. Martin's Press, 1999. 288p.**

Schoharie, N.Y. is scenic and snug for the vacationing private investigator from New York City, Bill Smith. However, the small town soon proves to be a restless, even violent place, and Smith must leave his cabin to confront some demanding characters and situations—thefts of paintings, the two troubled Antonelli boys, a search for prominent citizen Mark Sanderson's runaway daughter, the possibility of a homicide or two—so he solicits the help of a partner, Lydia Chin.

2929. Ruben, Edward. *The path to fame.* **New York: O. Lauckner, 1887. 342p.**

The author traces his hero from early youth when he first expressed his dedication to painting to his move to New York City after his parents' deaths. He gradually climbs the ladder to artistic success and enhances his personal life by marrying a beautiful young woman he had met while winning fame as an artist. It is quite obvious that Mr. Ruben's real purpose in penning this novel is to use it as a vehicle for expressing his views on various subjects, including art, civilization, the social order and morality.

2930. Rud, Anthony M., 1893-1942. *The stuffed men.* **New York: Macaulay, 1935. 240p.**

Hempstead, Long Island and Westchester County are penetrated by a league of Chinese criminals who spread a particularly vicious mode of killing. Jigger Masters faces up to the monstrous gang and brings its activities to a fitting end.

2931. Ruff, Matt. *Fool on the hill*; a novel. **Boston: Atlantic Monthly Press, c1988. 396p.**

The author uses his old school tie, Cornell University, as the scene for a fantasy with overtones of frenzied activity by human and animal characters. Stephen Titus George, the chief 'actor', is a writer searching for romantic love and a good plot he can use. One of Satan's companions, a sorceress by the name of Calliope, provides Stephen with all he desires, and evidently he does not pay the price for dealing with this minion of the Devil. The Cornell campus here pictured is bereft of gray or even youthful professors, but students and other humans, dogs, cats and nymphs are numerous.

2932. **Ruggero, Ed. *The Academy*; a novel of West Point. New York: Pocket Books, 1997. viii, 448p.**

West Point is the locus of a series of scandals, which are often sex-driven. When Major Tom Gates is about to be reprimanded for his clash with Cadet Wayne Holder, the Major's wife, Kathleen, uses all her feminine wiles to get him off the hook, even calling on a publicity-hungry, budget-slashing senator for assistance. Among the scheming officers and civilians (mostly female) one finds a born-again Christian cadet who takes his own life when the girl he loves is persuaded to have an abortion.

2933. **Runkle, Bertha. *The Island*. New York: Century Co., 1921. 237p.**

"Each one of the small group of people in this story [of contemporary New York life] has a critical problem to meet and each tackles it sensibly and without melodrama. Mary Lea, having to choose between the absorbing interest of her life on the stage and the agreeable attentions of young Bill Carrington, elects to concentrate on her profession. Carrington's father, whom gossip has brought a distorted tale of Mary's relations with his son, goes to her in frankness for the truth and finds her unexpectedly rational and decent. Young Carrington, when he is convinced that Mary will not give up her work for him, makes a graceful retreat and marries, contentedly, one of his own social set. His father who in the meantime has come to love Mary deeply, decides that he is not, therefore, justified in obtaining a divorce from a faithful, if unsatisfying wife, while Mary, whose life Bill's father now fills completely, after some struggle with herself, comes to a like mind, and they go their separate ways with dignity"—Book review digest.

2934. —————. ***The truth about Tolna*. New York: Century Co., 1906. 359p.**

"Tolna, the golden-throated tenor, who is not what he seems … gives to this novel of modern New York society a real individuality. The whole action occupies but seven days. There are many people more or less rich and more or less socially ambitious involved in the plot, but they are merely vivacious adjuncts to the story of Tolna and his love for Honor, the cold beauty who was his boyhood's playmate, and of Denys Alden, the man who, having lost his own voice, rejoices in the triumphs of his protégé, living in his success until he even renounces to him Marjorie, the girl he loves, only to find that her heart is his, but not his to renounce"—Book review digest.

2935. **Ruppius, Otto, 1819-1864.** *The pedlar, a romance of American life.* [Translated by Emily R. Steinestel]. Cincinnati: Block, 1877. 83p.

> Translation of Der Pedlar; Roman aus dem amerikanischen Leben. August von Helmstedt, a lawyer and a refugee from the failed Revolution of 1848 in Germany, sails for New York where he is helped by the Jew, Isaac Hirsch, who finds him a job and teaches him English. The novel shifts then to the South where Helmstedt serves as Hirsch's secret business agent as well as working regularly for another employer whose daughter he eventually marries after being cleared of a charge of murder. Isaac Hirsch dies in New York while the Helmstedts are on their way to visit him.

2936. **Russell, Florence Kimball.** *From chevrons to shoulder-straps*; a story of West Point. Illustrated by John Goss. Boston: Page Co., 1914. vi, 324p.

> The hero of this story of the career of a cadet in his third and fourth years at the U.S. Military Academy is Jack Stirling, the chief character in the author's earlier novel In West Point gray as plebe and yearling (q.v.). Appended is information about appointments to West Point and the indoctrination and supervision of new entrants.

2937. **————.** *In West Point gray as plebe and yearling.* Illustrated by James K. Bonnar. Boston: L.C. Page, 1908. 401p.

> The novel covers the first two years of a group of appointees at the United States Military Academy (West Point). The three leading characters are Jack Stirling, an 'army brat' devoted to the military profession, and his two best friends, John Raymond from Missouri (dubbed 'Mizzoo'), and Thomas (Tom) W. Winthrop, son of the U.S. Secretary of State. The author (daughter and wife of army officers) describes at some length the customs, traditions and regulations of West Point and their effect on the plebes and yearlings. The code of honor that meant so much to the 'Point' leads to Tom Winthrop's withdrawal from the Academy when he confesses (with Jack's reluctant urging) to cheating on an exam and covering it up. John Raymond gradually comes to accept the strictures of cadet life while Jack accepts them without question.

2938. **Russell, John, 1885-1956.** *The society wolf,* by Luke Thrice [pseud.]. Illustrated by W.H. Loomis and Modest Stein. New York: Cupples & Leon, 1910. 304p.

> The story of a young man from Virginia who is determined to 'make his mark' in New York City. He gains entry into the highest social circles of the city through financial manipulation and the power and wealth that accompanies it. The woman he loves marries him. He has achieved his goals, but staying at the top requires that he continue to manipulate, to engage in activities that prey on the society he has joined.

2938a. **Russell, Paul Elliott.** *The coming storm.* New York: St. Martin's Press, 1999. 371p.

Tracy Parker accepts a teaching assignment at a preparatory school in Upstate New York. Homoerotic tensions heighten as headmaster Louis Tremper is physically drawn to Tracy and the latter becomes involved with a disturbed student, Noah Lathrop III. Tremper's wife Claire clearly understands her husband's homosexual tendencies and she and Tracy confide in one another, but she fears that she has become nothing more than on onlooker with no help of offer anyone.

2939. ————. *The salt point*. **New York: Dutton, 1990. 210p.**
The restless, world-weary characters in this novel inhabit Poughkeepsie, New York but find little point in their lives there. Their existence is compared to the always-changing nature of the 'salt point'—i.e. the place in a river where it turns into an estuary, changing from fresh to salt water. Leigh, a young hustler, wanders into town and is soon desired by gay hairdresser Anatole, his friend Lydia, and bisexual Christopher who has Anatole and Lydia in his stable of lovers. Leigh seems to be the only one who is able to move on and out; the others have to stay and confront their own demons.

2940. **Russo, Richard, 1949- .** *Mohawk.* **New York: Vintage Books, 1986. 418p.**
'Mohawk' is a fictional small town in Upstate New York inhabited by characters like subnormal Wild Bill Gaffney and his friends whose central meeting place is Harry's Mohawk Grill (one must assume that the author was not pinpointing the village of Mohawk in Herkimer County). The working class of the town supports itself with jobs in the unstable leather factories; its members are unable to escape from Mohawk, so they spend much of their time drinking and gambling and going through the motions of unhappy marriages. Some of the 'respectable' men of the town have a penchant for stealing from the local industries. The author expresses sympathy and understanding for these semi-rural folk trapped in situations that offer little hope of succor.

2941. ————. *Nobody's fool.* **New York: Random House, 1993. 549p.**
Sully is 60, carrying around the memory of a father who had been a bully; still Sully is 'nobody's fool' with the exception of his own self. Work is hard to come by in Upstate New York and even when he does find employment arthritis hampers Sully. And he has a further list of troubles: he faces eviction from his apartment, if the son of his sympathetic landlady (she is 80) has his way; his girlfriend's daughter is in the hospital with a broken jaw for which he is somehow blamed; Sully's former wife is on the verge of a nervous breakdown; his son from whom he has long been separated turns up at Thanksgiving without his wife; Sully is almost broke. His bad luck must be about to run out.

2942. ————. *The risk pool.* **New York: Random House, 1988. 479p.**
Russo's Upstate New York town of 'Mohawk' is again the scene of a novel about a freewheeling father, Sam Hall, and his son, Ned, the narrator,

introspective and impressionable. Soon after he returned from World War II Sam abandoned his wife Jenny and the newborn Ned. As the years pass Ned tries to reconnect with his irresponsible father who lives in a messed-up apartment above Mohawk's only department store, and his nervous, moody, dreaming mother. Sam Hall is contemptuous of all rules and restraints and is at the bottom of the insurance risk pool. The conclusion finds Sam slowly dying of cancer and Ned on his own, coming back now and then to visit his ill father, but with a commitment to his pregnant girlfriend, Leigh, later his wife.

2943. Ryan, Alan, 1943- . *Dead white.* **New York: TOR, 1983. 351p.**

This horror story unfolds in 'Deacons Kill' in Upstate New York. A record snowfall envelops the town and simultaneously a circus arrives with the storm. Most of the villagers take refuge in the Centennial Hotel and are only gradually aware of strange and even deadly incidents happening in the town. The acting sheriff, Richie Mead, investigates; however, elderly Doc Warren is the individual who has intuitive suspicions of the circus personnel and studies 70-year-old clippings that indicate the townspeople may be candidates for extermination.

2944. Ryerson, Florence, 1894- . *The Borgia blade,* **by Florence Ryerson and Colin Clements. New York: D. Appleton-Century, 1937. 274p.**

Under the alias Q. Silver, a slick professional thief appears with a fraudulent letter of introduction at the Long Island home of rich Vincent Welch. Silver of course intends to rob Welch, a collector of valuable artifacts, but he no sooner arrives than Welch is murdered. Realizing that police investigators will likely uncover his criminal past and pin the homicide on him, Silver takes on the guise of a detective and provides the local lawmen with plausible answers to the puzzle. Joe Lynch, Silver's assistant, tells the story; Joe is very uneasy because he is afraid that he and his boss may end up in the death chamber.

2945. Sabastian, Inez, b. 1895. *Don't call it love.* **New York: Macaulay, 1930. 288p.**

The locale of the novel is New York City, with side trips to Paris and the Bahamas. The chief protagonists, Denise and Camilla Paige, are both interested in Nick Lawrence, a poor young inventor. That doesn't suit Mrs. Paige who hopes to marry off her penniless daughters to wealthy suitors. Camilla agrees with the view that money is of prime importance. Denise takes a room in a flat, writes fashion notes for a metropolitan newspaper and continues seeing Nick. Camilla returns to New York after living abroad and vamps Nick, but he has the good sense to tighten his ties to Denise.

2946. ————. *Men call it love.* **New York: Macaulay, 1926. 320p.**

In this novel of love and marriage in New York "there hadn't been many men in Beulah's life; she responded readily therefore to Michael's charm and as readily married him. But she did not know how to hold him, and after a year he left her. For a while Beulah struggled along by herself until Jim Hubbard asked her to share an apartment with him. Her education concerning life and men had begun. When some time later Michael came back from abroad, she recaptivated him. Beulah had learned meanwhile how to hold him and their marriage began again"—Book review digest.

Sabastien, Inez, b. 1895. See: Sabastian, Inez, b. 1895.

2947. **Sachs, Emanie Louise Nahm.** *The octangle.* **New York: J. Cape & H. Smith. 1930. 127p.**

A psychological novel in which eight unconventional New Yorkers are forced to look hard and long at the murder of a friend, Linda Carter. Each of the eight is 'dissected' so thoroughly by the author that the alert reader is given enough clues and motives to solve the crime by himself/herself.

2948. ————. *Red damask*; **a story of nature and nurture. New York: Harper, 1927. 426p.**

"Abby Hahl is the daughter of wealthy German Jews in New York City. She early acquires a definite set of standards and ideals, and spends her life trying to live up to them. She gives her first love to the wrong man, and later, not greatly caring, marries a man who turns out to be temperamentally and physically unsuited to her. They have two children and are apparently settled when Abby finds herself really in love with Michael Heron. According to her standards there is but one thing to do and she does it"—Book review digest.

2949. **Sadler, Mark, pseud.** *The falling man.* **New York: Random House, 1970. 212p.**

"A battering case for private investigator Paul Shaw who accidentally kills a prowler in his office hired by someone else anxious to muffle the industrial report of an Upstate (New York) firm. There's Maureen, Paul's wife; Miranda, the dead youngster's flower girl; and there's Cassandra, another lure. ...But it all moves—like a high-powered coupe with a hard top"—Kirkus reviews.

2950. **Sadlier, Anna Theresa, 1854?-1932.** *Mary Tracy's fortune.* **New York: Benziger Bros., 1902. 169p.**

Mary Tracy is an orphan "adopted by [the McGowans] who inhabited a shanty among the rocks that skirted Central Park, New York." Her 'fortune' consisted of a few coins given her by various individuals; she hid the coins in the rocks near the shanty. When she was badly injured by a neighbor's butting goat, a young doctor took care of Mary and interested wealthy Mrs. Morrison, a resident of Fifth Avenue, in the girl. Mrs. Morrison treats all the inhabitants of the shantytown to a Christmas party and promises that henceforth Mary will receive all the support she needs to make her way in the world.

2951. ————. *The true story of Master Gerard.* **New York: Benziger Bros., 1900 [c1899]. 321p.**

An historical novel about New York City in the latter years of the 17th century. Solid Dutch merchants and artisans were of major import to the city; there were also a number of thrill-seeking gentlemen—Master Gerard among them—who had an appreciation for the fair-haired daughters of the Dutch. It was also a time of troubles when many citizens of New York feared Catholic conspiracies and possible French invasion and took control of the city with the enigmatic, anti-Catholic Jacob Leisler as their commander and governor.

Sadlier, Mrs. James, 1820-1903. See: Sadlier, Mary Anne Madden, 1820-1903.

2952. **Sadlier, Mary Anne Maddon, 1820-1903.** *Aunt Honor's keepsake.* **A chapter from life. New York: D. & J. Sadlier, 1866. 322p.**

"The brutal reform schools of New York discriminate against Catholics by forbidding prayer, religious services or family visitations. The hero in this story remains loyal to his religion and helps to convert many others"—Menendez, A.J. *The Catholic novel.*

2953. **Safford, Henry Barnard, b. 1883.** *Tory Tavern.* **New York: William Penn Pub. Corp., 1942. x, 389p.**

Roger, the son of a Loyalist, is a Long Islander who casts his lot with the patriots. He is informed that he can best serve the American cause by spying on British troop movements. In due course he is privileged to meet General Washington, Ethan Allen, John Jay and William Livingston.

2954. **Sager, Juliet Gilman, b. 1873.** *Anne, actress*; **the romance of a star. New York: F.A. Stokes, 1913. 346p.**

Anne Houghton has won a secure place for herself on the New York stage but has not reached the apex in her profession. The opportunity to star in a production presents itself. At that moment Anne's daughter, Elsie, 18, who has joined her mother in New York after formative years in California, is given a part in the play. With incredible malice the selfish Elsie underhandedly tarnishes the success her mother should have had. Anne finds solace and a lasting, loving relationship with a country doctor who has long been her constant admirer.

2955. **Salisbury, Henry Barnard.** *Miss Worden's hero*; **a novel. New York: G.W. Dillingham, 1891. 149p.**

The novel is a semi-Utopian tract that in its final episodes portrays New York City as a socialist paradise where all of society's ailments have been banished. 'Miss Worden's hero' is Cecil Lord, a life-long crusader for the rights of workingmen. Lord, Miss Worden, Mr. Mason, a carpenter, and the anarchist Conrad (i.e. Karl Conrad Müller) have more or less joined forces for mankind's betterment. Revolution breaks out in the city and the non-violent Lord is seized by soldiers fighting the anarchists and sent to Alaska as a convict-laborer. Years later Lord has organized industrial cooperatives and returns to

New York—Manhattan is now the center of factories, stores, warehouses and exchanges; their operators, workmen and managers alike, live comfortably in residential enclaves on Staten Island and Long Island. A 'religion' of universal brotherhood pervades the metropolitan area. Miss Worden and Cecil Lord meet again and will be together from that moment on.

2956. **Saltus, Edgar, 1855-1921.** *Eden*; **an episode. Chicago, New York: Belford, Clarke, 1888. 187p.**

"Eden [Menemon Usselex] is a well-informed, refined New York girl who marries a rich merchant many years her senior. After some months of unclouded happiness she begins to suspect her husband of devotion to another woman. Her best friends tell her all they can to worry her, and Eden finally leaves her husband and returns to her father. After many harrowing scenes the mystery is cleared up and Eden learns her husband's true relationship to the beautiful widow and also to his confidential clerk"—Annual American catalogue.

2957. ———. *Madam Sapphira*; **a Fifth Avenue story. Chicago: F.T. Neely, 1893. 251p.**

Hilda Nevius, the 'Madam Sapphira' of the title, is bored with her husband, Carol, and interested primarily in enjoying the fleshpots of New York and her adulterous affairs. In order to obtain a divorce from Carol and marry her lover of the moment Hilda diabolically maneuvers her unaware, faithful husband into two compromising situations. The breakup of the author's (first) marriage provided the impetus for this novel.

2958. ———. *Mr. Incoul's misadventure*; **a novel. New York: Benjamin and Bell, 1887. 216p.**

Harmon Incoul, a New York millionaire, accepts (not entirely) Maida Barhyte's condition that her marriage to him shall be an unconsummated one. Maida's lover, Lenox Leigh, incurs Incoul's suspicion and the latter draws up plans of revenge on both Leigh and Maida. Leigh is driven to suicide and Maida drinks poison provided by her husband. The two deaths do not affect Incoul in any way; he is simply going about his business affairs when last we see him. As the scene shifts form New York to Europe and back one may get a sense of the attitudes of upper class Americans in the 1880s.

2959. ———. *The pace that kills*; **a chronicle. Chicago: Belford, Clarke, 1889. 202p.**

New York City and Paris furnish the settings for this story. Roland Mistrial, a fortune hunter, elopes with Justine Dunellen, a New York heiress, even though her father has rejected Mistrial as a suitable son-in-law. Mistrial treats his wife shabbily, wrongfully accusing her of an affair with Guy Thorold, brother of one of Mistrial's former lovers. Justine leaves him, and Mistrial, his plans and future seemingly awry, commits suicide.

2960. ————. *The Paliser case.* **New York: Boni & Liveright, 1919. 315p.**

"The scene of this story of society life is laid in New York City, and most of the action takes place prior to the entrance of the United States into the [first] World War. The title is somewhat misleading. The book is not a detective story, the murder of Monty not occurring until about two-thirds of the tale has been told. The leading characters are Monty Paliser, son of an old millionaire who had 'agreeably shocked New York with the splendid uproar of his orgies'; Keith Lennox, slandered by the scheming Mrs. Austen; Margaret Austen, in love with Lennox, but too easily managed by her mother; Angelo Cara, the old violinist, really Marquis de Casa-Evora; and his daughter, Cassy of the 'cameo face', who loves Lennox, but goes through what she believes to be a binding marriage with Monty Paliser"—Book review digest.

2961. ————. *The perfume of Eros*; **a Fifth Avenue incident. New York: A. Wessels Co., 1905. 222p.**

"The novel is memorable chiefly for its use of two new women, the incipient flapper and the lower-class girl whose eventual professional success begins with her fall from virtue"—Sprague, Claire. Edgar Saltus. Marie Durand, the lower-class girl, graduates from mistress of Royal Loftus, whom she ultimately dismisses, to success as an opera singer. The flapper, Fanny Price, marries, divorces and waits for the man she really loves, Royal Loftus. When he is murdered, Fanny wastes away.

2962. ————. *A transaction in hearts*; **an episode. New York: Belford, Clarke, 1889. 188p.**

The protagonist, Christopher Gonfallon, is an Episcopal priest who has recently left a dull Bronx parish for a 'chic' Manhattan church. Although he is married, Gonfallon looks beyond his wife, Ruth, to her younger sister, Claire Bucholz, who is living in their house. His clumsy advances toward his cool sister-in-law are met with exasperating indifference, for Claire has her own plans; she marries a wealthy, arrogant young man for whom she has little love, but who did step forward to rescue her father from an ugly situation. Ironically Gonfallon officiates at Claire's wedding.

2963. ————. *Vanity Square*; **a story of Fifth Avenue life. Philadelphia: Lippincott, 1906. 304p.**

The Uxhills of Fifth Avenue have plenty of money and a seemingly trouble-free existence, which is just what troubles Mr. Uxhill. He suffers from ennui and pays little attention to his attractive wife and their only child, a girl. Mrs. Uxhill, on the other hand, is content with the way things are. The girl comes down with diphtheria and on the advice of their physician the Uxhills hire a trained nurse. The latter is the daughter of a famous bacteriologist whom she had served as a laboratory assistant. The nurse uses her knowledge of toxic substances to poison Mrs. Uxhill with the objective of taking her place by Mr. Uxhill's side; there is no doubt that he finds the nurse most fetching. However, Uxhill and the doctor wake up in time to upset the plot and the

Uxhills celebrate their happy reunion. Unfortunately the satanic nurse is allowed to go free and some time later is found to be preying on another unsuspecting couple.

2964. ———. *When dreams come true*; **a story of emotional life. New York: F.F. Collier, 1894. 187p.**

The hero is Tancred Ennever, a young aristocratic New Yorker and litterateur, who falls in love with Sylvia March. She proves to be a mercurial type who walks away from her engagement to Tancred. Eventually he turns to Madame Bravoura, Sylvia's friend, an experienced older woman. His relationship with her is an on and off one; after spending a summer in New York City working on his book, *The heroines of love*, he meets Madame Bravoura by chance in Como, Italy, and their futures are entwined.

2965. **Salvato, Sharon Anne, 1938- .** *Briarcliff Manor*; **a novel. New York: Stein & Day, 1974. 192p.**

"Briarcliff Manor is a large estate [on the Hudson] with its own mausoleum where Annabel Arbriar's mother lies interred after having been locked up the last years of her life. Annabel is also a briar in her father's flesh—particularly when she comes home to realize that he is about to wed a young woman who has quickly survived two earlier husbands and is a 'murderess.' On the other hand, to whom should she turn—estate manager Darien Varka, or her about-to-be-stepmother's cousin, either one of whom seem to be set on a course of demolition"—Kirkus reviews.

2966. **Samuels, Charles, 1902-1982.** *The frantic young man.* **With black and white illus. by Margaret Freeman. New York: Coward-McCann, 1929. 289p.**

Arthur Gordon, 18, alone in New York City, has literary aspirations, but his first order of business is to lose his virtue (by seduction?). This he does with the cooperation of an overweight lady quite a bit older than he, leading him to surmise that he has been the one seduced. So much for any romantic notions he may have had.

2967. **Sanders, Lawrence, 1920- .** *The sixth commandment*; **a novel. New York: Putnam, 1979. 350p.**

The Crittenden Research Laboratory, located in a declining Hudson River town not far from Albany, is the destination of Samuel Todd who investigates applicants for research grants. The Laboratory's owner, Mr. Crittenden, is one of the applicants; he is researching the 'pathology of mammalian cells' and is on the point of producing a formula that could extend human longevity. Todd snoops around the town and the Laboratory and finds out that an unreasonable number of deaths have occurred in the sanitarium that is a subsidiary of the Laboratory. Are these deaths related to Crittenden's experiments?

2968. **Sanders, Marion K., 1905-1977.** *The bride laughed once,* **by Marion K. Sanders and Mortimer S. Edelstein. New York: Farrar & Rinehart, 1943.**

281p.

The Broadway press agent had big plans to turn the Adirondack village of 'North Valley' into a winter playground for bored denizens of the city Downstate. But the big news coming out of the community is the murder of a wealthy young wastrel, with a ski pole as the chief instrument of mayhem. Dr. Seth Noble follows clues that will lead him to the culprit.

2969. Sanderson, James Gardner. *Cornell stories.* **New York: Scribner, 1898. 251p.**

Tales of undergraduate life at Cornell University, Ithaca, N.Y., in the latter years of the 19th century. Several later editions have appeared. Contents: The wooing of Melville R. Corydon.—Little Tyler.—Company D's revenge.—One who didn't.—One who did.—The elder Miss Archlen.

2970. Sands, Beatrice. *Weepers in playtime.* **New York: Lane, 1908. x, 265p.**

The novel is an exposé of the abuses heaped on the inmates of childcare institutions of New York City—the orphanages and children's homes at the beginning of the 20th century.

2971. Sanford, John B., 1904- . *Adirondack stories.* **Santa Barbara, CA.: Capra Press, 1976. 107p.**

Three of the stories: I let him die, Jasper Darby's passion and The king of the minnies, were reworked and became part of the novel Seventy times seven (q.v.). 'The fire at the Catholic church' tells of the trial for arson of Mr. Doyring who was incensed at his wife's passion for crosses; that plus the resentment of Rev. Titus of the Catholic priest's proselytizing efforts led to Doyring's arson and his confession thereof. However, the judge dismisses the case, stating that Doyring was blatantly lying. 'Once in a sedan and twice standing up'—a New York City lawyer tries to defend a local parson of Long Lake on an adultery charge; the parson solemnly but forthrightly admits to impregnating Marjorie Brown, servant girl looking after his house and his invalid wife. 'Adirondack narrative' is a woodland idyll with a New York City salesclerk, Alfred Gibson, and a farm girl, Hattie Bennett, the protagonists. Gibson returns to his workaday job; Hattie prefers to stay where she is, although Alfred importunes her to come to the city. Other stories: I let him die.—Jasper Darby's passion.—The king of the minnies.

2972. ————. *The old man's place.* **New York: A. & C. Boni, 1935. 263p.**

The only son of an Upstate New York farmer, a good lad who gave no one any trouble, goes off to World War II and comes back a changed man. With him are two companions, an evil pair setting a bad example for the farmer's son. When a girl comes to the farm things rise to a boil, and murder is an unintended consequence.

2973. ————. *The people from heaven.* **New York: Harcourt, Brace, 1943. 232p.**

The author tells his story with a mixture of verse and narrative prose. A small town in Upstate New York is the scene of a struggle between the forces of social tolerance and bigotry. The climax comes when a long-persecuted black woman breaks the fetters that have restrained her.

2974.   ————. *Seventy times seven*; a novel. **New York: Knopf, 1939. 195p.**
Aaron Platt is an Upstate New York farmer whose land, located in the vicinity of Warrensburg (Adirondack region), yields a bare living. Platt keeps pretty much to himself; he is unpopular with the citizens of Warrensburg. In contrast is Tom Paulhan, a shiftless wanderer, who takes to wife Grace Tennent, leaving her soon after the wedding. Platt, once friendly with Paulhan, is incensed by Paulhan's neglect of Grace (whom he himself loves) and his casual irresponsibility. When Paulhan stumbles into Platt's barn on a cold winter's night, half-starved, Platt ignores his needs and Paulhan subsequently dies of exposure and starvation. The townspeople accuse Aaron of the murder of the popular Paulhan, but the district attorney clears him of that charge—the law states: 'an omission is not the basis of penal action unless it constitutes a defect in the discharge of a responsibility specially imposed.' The author utilizes such devices as flashbacks and interspersed poetry.

2975.   **Sangster, Margaret Elizabeth, 1838-1912.** *Eastover Parish*; **a tale of yester-day. New York, Chicago: Revell, 1912. 224p.**
'Eastover' is the name the author applies to the village that is the scene of the story—Eastover may be equated with that part of Brooklyn known as Williamsburg. The time is 1852 and the ministers of the two churches in Eastover have been their parishioners' mentors for three generations, urging them to commit their lives to service to mankind and God. The author's point seems to be that such places as Eastover are the sources of the best people the country has to offer.

2976.   ————. *Island of faith*. **New York, Chicago: F. Revell, 1921. 175p.**
"Records the experiences of a young settlement worker on the East Side [of New York] and her successes in rather miraculously uplifting a 'submerged' family, beginning with a small boy whom she finds torturing a kitten, and including a wayward girl, a discouraged mother, and an afflicted child. It even extends to a successful young criminal, Jim, who, in spite of his hard heart, is led to see the error of his ways. There is a pleasantly interwoven love story between the heroine and a young doctor"—Literary review of the New York evening post.

2977.   **[Sargent, Epes] 1813-1880.** *Fleetwood*; **or,** *The stain of birth*. **A novel of American life, by the author of** *Philip in search of a wife, etc., etc*. **New York: Burgess, Stringer, 1845. 238p.**
Sentimentality reaches an apogee in this novel by a writer of the Knickerbocker School. Adelaide Winfield, an orphan, is reared by Mrs. Winfield in New York City and 'Soundside', Conn. Frederick Fleetwood is charmed by Adelaide and stands by her even though his lawyer states that Adelaide is the illegitimate daughter of 'an infamous mother'. As Adelaide

becomes the center of intricate plots, Fleetwood takes ill for several weeks. Nursed by Emily Gordon and despairing of Adelaide, he asks Emily to marry him. Just before their wedding Fleetwood is given proof that Adelaide is the legitimate daughter of the late Edward Challoner and his wife, the sister of Emily's father, Mr. Gordon. Adelaide stands to inherit Mr. Gordon's estate. Fleetwood rushes to the now mortally ill Adelaide. Before she dies Adelaide forgives her uncle, Gordon, Emily Gordon and Mrs. Winfield, all of whom kept the facts of her origin hidden. She entrusts a young friend, Florinda, to Fleetwood; it is implied, as Florinda matures, that she and Fleetwood will marry.

2977a. Saulnier, Beth. *Reliable sources.* **New York: Warner Books, 1999. 336p.**

'Gabriel', N.Y., is the seat of Benson University; the latter is in bad repute as a place where suicides occur too often in the nearby gorges. The most recent one is that of Adam Ellroy, boyfriend of Alex Bernier, a reporter for the Gabriel Monitor. Alex is certain that police reporter Adam's demise is no suicide and that Adam's investigative reports have driven someone to commit murder. Alex, with help from her allies on the Monitor, solves the crime. Saulnier, a columnist for the Ithaca, N.Y. Journal and staff member at Cornell University, very likely had Ithaca and Cornell in view while writing this novel.

2978. Sauzade, John S., b. 1828. *Garret Van Horn*; **or,** *The beggar on horseback.* **New York: Carleton, 1863. 376p.**

The narrator, Garret Van Horn, and his brother, Myndert, are educated at a Westchester school and then go their separate ways—Garret as a junior clerk in his Uncle Garret Van Horn's firm in New York City and Myndert to study mathematics and the profession of shipwrighting. Garret, bored by his job, carouses with companions who include the wily Dr. Edmund Ross. His despairing uncle secures him a berth on a ship bound for Europe. Garret jumps ship and has varied adventures in France and Algeria. Returning to New York he rejoins his uncle's household and works for the Gotham Trust and Banking Company. Garret has a falling out with his old companion in dissipation, Dr. Ross. The latter marries Mrs. Van Horn after her husband dies and then runs off with Lesbia Home, a woman Garret had planned to marry. His hopes of inheriting his uncle's fortune unrealized, Garret sinks lower and lower until his brother Myndert finds him a job. The two work together in the shipyards; Myndert looks forward to reviving his mutual Benefit Industrial Association.

2979. Savage, Richard Henry, 1846-1903. *Checked through, missing trunk no.17580.* **A story of New York life. Chicago, New York: Rand McNally, 1896. 2v.**

The 'heroine', Madeleine Ware, an orphan has the misfortune of marrying the rising young star (Seaton Bennett) of the law firm headed by her late father's best friend, Hiram Bashford. The politically ambitious Bennett meets the wealthy widow, Julie Martyn, influential in Tammany circles, and decides he must rid himself of an impediment, Madeleine. He has a rendezvous with

Madeleine in a secluded mansion near Mamaroneck, Long Island, and poisons her. Bennett hires 'Red Mike' Doolan to dispose of the body. Doolan maps out a plan of blackmailing Bennett, the cornerstone of which is a large trunk containing items that could be most damaging to Bennett. Doolan stores the trunk in a Manhattan warehouse. In the year and a half that follows Bennett takes a seat in Congress, marries Mrs. Martyn and basks in personal wealth and influence. But the unclaimed telltale trunk is 'unearthed', placed on the auction block and sold to a book dealer. Finally opened the trunk contains the evidence that seals Bennett's doom.

2980. ————. *A daughter of Judas*; a fin-de-siécle tale of New York City life. New York, Chicago: F. Tennyson Neely, 1894. 304p.

A New York City basking in the free-spending ways of its moneyed class is the scene that greets a Southern woman of indeterminate background just married to a native New Yorker who has vast sources of income. The marriage is a failure; the wife, ostensible heroine of the novel, takes measures to hold her own against her husband's daughters and falls in love with a bon vivant reputed to be a sexual adventurer. The result is that she has to find ways of extracting herself from several very ticklish situations.

2981. ————. *Delilah of Harlem*; a story of the New York City of today. New York: American News Co., 1893. 329p.

Harry Morton, manager of Morton, Burnham & Company's bank, is completely 'gulled' by gambler and confidence man Thomas Overton, and the latter's sometimes unwilling accomplice, the beautiful Marie Ashton (a.k.a. Kate, Delilah of Harlem, Eleanor Laurence). Morton's unbridled passion for Marie's favors and Overton's control over the debt-ridden confidential bank clerk, Abel Cram, are keys to Overton's theft of bonds and currency from the bank's vaults. Seth Wise, senior partner of Morton, Burnham & Co., unravels Overton's complex plotting, and Morton, cognizant at last of his gullibility, pursues Overton to Central America. Morton kills Overton during a Honduran revolution and Morton himself dies of yellow fever. Seth Wise persuades Marie Ashton, now a pillar of respectability in Europe, to assist in the recovery of the stolen bonds. The author characterizes New York City as "a burning fever. Night throws out the battalions of male and female bandits; day lets loose the hawk-eyed, anxious schemers who fight to the death under the banner of 'business.'…Misery throws the needy man and woman at the mercy of the strong".

2982. ————. *In the swim*; a story of currents and undercurrents in gayest New York. Chicago and New York: Rand, McNally, 1898. 361p.

"A novel that deals with several phases of social life in New York. The characters are Harold Vreeland, an adventurer from the West; Elaine Willoughby, who figures in the story as the 'Queen of Wall Street'; Alida Van Sittart, an heiress; Fred Hathorn, a broker; James Potter, a millionaire; and last, but not least, the lady's maid, Justine, and Hugh Convers, devoted to the interests of Elaine Willoughby. The story shows the part played by Hathorn, Vreeland and Convers in the history of Elaine, and reveals a secret of her past"—Annual American catalogue.

2283.   ——————. *The last traitor of Long Island*; a story of the sea. New York: Home Pub. Co., 1903. 341p.

Hiram Worth, third mate on a whaling vessel that has been at sea for three years, has acquired a fortune. His expectations of settling down with the girl he left behind are shattered when he learns that she has dropped him for another man. With the Civil War in progress the raging, vengeful Worth suddenly severs his Union loyalties and joins the Confederate Navy. He leads several warships to familiar fishing grounds and meets his rival; the novel's conclusion is hair-raising and brutal.

2984.   ——————. *The midnight passenger*; a novel. New York: Home Pub. Co., 1900. 278p.

"This work is so aggressively American in style as almost to require an interpreter. …The actors … from the New York gamin who 'joins the dashing villainy of the Bowery tough to the crafty longheaded scheming of the low-grade Israelite to the well-groomed clubmen' who constitute, we infer, the high-grade portions of society—are all racy of the soil. Mr. Savage has complicated the plot with the details of a large commercial business in which a multiplicity of characters are involved; and apart from the officials of the Western Trading Company, we have villains of a more cosmopolitan dye, such as the poisonous Fritz Braun, and the 'velvet-faced Magyar witch' whose enchantments are employed to lure the hero to his death and ruin"—Athenaeum. Of course she and Braun fail signally in their evil plans and receive overdue punishment.

2985.   [Savidge, Eugene Coleman] 1863-1924. *Wallingford*; a story of American life. Philadelphia: J.B. Lippincott, 1887. 308p.

Wallingford, a suburb of Philadelphia, is the hometown of two young men who follow different careers—the first becomes an architect; the second, Burt Sheldon, enters Bellevue Medical College in New York City. Working his way through the college to graduation, Burt is seized by the authorities for the murder of a young woman (Fanny). Several friends come to his aid, but Burt is brought to trial. Another individual from Wallingford, Ruby Fuller, an evangelist, provides the data that will determine Burt's guilt or innocence.

2986.   Sawyer, Ruth, 1880-1970. *The silver sixpence.* Illustrated by James H. Crank. New York: Harper, 1921. 331p.

"A story of the theater and of the actual business of putting on plays. Eudora Post inherits from her father, a professor of philosophy, a fortune of four millions, the existence of which had been kept a secret from her. The will provides that she shall not receive the full sum till she has profitably invested an initial payment of twenty thousand dollars. She elects to put this to use in backing a play by a young and entirely unknown author. Coming to New York to produce the play, she encounters every possible obstacle, but through the help of her youth and fighting spirit and an ability to attract warm and powerful friends, wins a Broadway success for her play and incidentally finds her own romance"—Book review digest.

2987. **Sayle, Helen. *Lady fashion artist*. New York: Arcadia House, 1957. 222p.**
Julie Winthrop, an unemployed commercial artist for the world of fashion, responding to a notice in the newspaper, takes a job as companion to an old gentleman whose home is a mansion on an island in the Hudson River. She gets a lot more than she bargained for, as the cliché goes.

2988. **Sayler, Harry Lincoln, 1863-1913. *The airship boys in finance*; or, *The flight of the flying cow*. Illustrated by S.H. Riesenberg. Chicago: Reilly & Britton Co., 1911. 295p.**
By virtue of their answer to the question—How was Old Brindle able to jump over Niagara Falls?—the airship boys are granted an audience with the great J.P. Morgan who provides them with financial assistance in the formation of the Universal Aerial Transportation Company.

2989. **Sayre, Theodore Burt, b. 1874. *Two summer girls and I*. New York: G.A.S. Wieners, 1898. 255p.**
"The narrative of the amusing aquatic and sentimental adventures of an idle, pleasure-loving young society man spending the summer months in a fashionable Long Island watering place. The story of his love affairs with two totally different types of society girl is told in an entertaining manner by the hero"—Annual American catalogue.

2990. **[Scaife, Roger Livingston] 1875-1951. *The confessions of a debutante*. With illus. by R.M. Crosby. Boston: Houghton, Mifflin, 1913. 140p.**
A short novel that presents a romanticized view of social life among the upper classes of new York City and Newport, Rhode Island. The story is told through 15 letters written by 'Peggy', the debutante, to her mother (Mimsy). Peggy is living at 1012 Fifth Avenue and enjoying the social life of a girl from the top rung of New York society. One of Peggy's side trips is to the Adirondacks, another to 'Castle Neck', N.Y. (somewhere on the Hudson). Among the personalities Peggy mentions are the actors John Drew and David Warfield.

2991. **Scarlett, Rebecca, pseud. *The monkey's tail*. New York: Scribner, 1934. vi, 406p.**
Sandra Ladd, at eighteen, is an incipient feminist afloat in a world dominated by the male of the species. However, she is presently on the horns of a dilemma—pregnant by one man but really in love with another. Her grandmother, the strong-willed feminist that Sandra may become, is sympathetic when Sandra relates her troubles. Supported by her grandmother Sandra

leaves her Hudson Valley home for New York City. The baby arrives; Sandra adopts a child, proves to be a helpful factor in a playwright's success, and finally is united with the man she wanted.

2992. **Schaefer, Edward P.** *The hidden voice*; or, *The ghost of the old Genesee.* **An interesting story of Rochester, N.Y. A novel. Rochester: Press of H.H. Smith, 1887. 134p.**

The Cameron family treks from Vermont to the banks of the Genesee River where Mr. Cameron prepares to build a sawmill. 'Nigger Joe', their guide and friend, together with his companion, the Indian Eagle Eye, upset the evil plans of two thieves and cutthroats, the neighboring innkeeper, Jim Dawsonie and Jack Johnsones. After the Camerons survive more harrowing encounters with human enemies and predatory animals, the 'ghost of the Genesee' is identified as Charley Rockburn, son of a wealthy Englishman. Wounded and suffering from amnesia he had wandered in the forest until a blow to the head restored his senses. Charley's father and his cousin, Arthur Burnham, appear at the Cameron camp after an encounter with Dawsonie and Johnsones. Eagle Eye slays the two villains at the price of his own life. Belle and Lily Cameron are engaged to the two young Englishmen and the Camerons decide to accompany their new friends to England.

2993. **Schereschewsky, Mrs. Samuel Isaac Joseph.** *Miss Ruby's novel.* **New York: T. Whittaker, 1889. 69p.**

"Upon the death of her sister Miriam, Miss Ruby feels a call to work for the poor in New York City. She hires two rooms in a tenement-house near Washington Market and becomes the good genius of the hard-worked wives and mothers and the sickly children of the neighborhood. While resting from overwork she plans a novel which shall carry her ideas of charity beyond the limits of her personal sphere"—Annual American catalogue.

2994. **Schieren, Harris Victor, b. 1881.** *The quitter.* **Boston: Small, Maynard, 1924. 285p.**

"The story deals with the transference of the love of a [suburban New York] wife from her husband to her child and the effect this has upon him. The quitter is the hero who accepts the change in his wife and her neglect of him with no effort of resistance. He makes no contact with his child and falls back on self-pity and love of another woman for comfort. How his problems work out and how his son grows up must be left to the reader"—Literary review of the New York evening post.

2995. **Schmitt, Gladys, 1909-1972.** *A small fire.* **New York: Dial Press, 1957. 343p.**

Frieda Hartmann, 36, voice teacher at a liberal arts college close by New York City, looks fondly upon Arthur Sanes, a concert pianist, and a new member of the faculty. At a recital in New York City Arthur collapses mentally and escapes to his parents' uptown Manhattan apartment. Frieda, the much stronger of the two musicians, marries Arthur and will obviously be the primary factor in his eventual recovery, if that occurs.

Schoeffel, Florence Blackburn White, 1860-1900. See under her pseudonym: Gilman, Wenona, 1860-1900.

Schubert, John D. See under his pseudonym: Morland, Catherine.

Schücking, Kathinka Sutro-, b. 1835. See: Sutro-Schücking, Kathinka, b. 1835.

2996. **Schultz, Alan Brener.** *Private secretary*; **the story of Mary Linden. New York: Simon & Schuster, 1929. 392p.**

"Mr. Schultz has turned an observant eye, directed by a brisk intelligence, upon the typical personnel of a New York office—almost any competent New York office—and drawn from it plenty of material to fill the pages of 'Private secretary' full to overflowing with the rattle, rivalry, innuendo and productive work of the metropolitan business day. As contemporary as the daily paper, the story of Mary Linden must approximate at innumerable points the experience of thousands of attractive looking young 'business girls'"— Literary review of the New York evening post.

2997. **Schuyler, Doris E.** *The Adirondack princess*; **an historical novel. Brookfield, N.Y.: Worden Press, 1982. 139p.**

The story begins in 1785 in the upper Mohawk Valley south of Rome, N.Y. Left alone when a fire kills her mother (her father and brothers were away) Emmie Van der Veer is taken in by Indians and treated with great respect; to them she is a 'princess' with her pale white skin and long golden hair. Emmie marries a young warrior, the son of the chief, whom she names Luke. Emmie and Luke leave the tribe to start a small farm; Luke gradually adapts to this new way of life, the white man's way. Through the years, though childless, the two prosper and form friendships with people in the settlements some distance from their cabin. Mr. Becker, owner of a trading post, and his wife are especially welcoming; he purchases Luke's furs and notices Emmie's talent for keeping accounts. When Mr. Becker dies and his wife leaves the post, it is deeded over to Emmie and Luke. At the story's conclusion in 1826, the Erie Canal is well under way and an inn has been added to the trading post.

2998. **Schwartz, Julia Augusta, b. 1873.** *Elinor's college career.* **Illustrated by Ellen Wetherald Ahrens. Boston: Little, Brown, 1906. 335p.**

"Pictures the life of four college girls, presumably of Vassar, through freshman, sophomore, junior and senior years. They are strongly contrasted. First is the college granddaughter, who enters the college solely because her mother, a former graduate, wishes her to; second, a girl who is in college for 'fun'; third, a handsome, dignified girl, who is in college because it is the proper thing; and last, a poor, plain, ill-dressed, tactless [girl] disagreeable to the others, but a genius. The college spirit overcomes selfishness and dislikes, and they eventually become loving comrades"—Annual American catalogue.

2999. ————. *Vassar studies*. **New York: Putnam, 1899. 290p.**

"Twelve college stories written with a double purpose. The essential motive is to embody in literary form for the alumnae [of Vassar College] … memories and impressions of college days. The secondary purpose is to endeavor to present to the public a truthful picture of life in a college community"—Annual American catalogue. Partial contents: In search of experience.—The history of an ambition.—The genius.—Heroic treatment.—The career of a radical.—A superior young woman.—That athletic girl.

3000. Scollard, Clinton, 1860-1932. *A knight of the highway*. **Clinton, N.Y.: G.W. Browning, 1908. 228p.**

The novel, set in the first decade of the 20th century, "recalls vividly that the growing of hops was once a major industry in Oneida County, New York. This pleasant story tells the modern reader more about the customs and traditions of hop-growing and hop-picking than any other source now readily available"—O'Donnell, Thomas F. Oneida County: literary highlights in Upstate literature (In: *Upstate literature* … Syracuse University Press, 1985).

3001. ————. *The son of a Tory*; **a narrative of the experiences of Wilton Aubrey, in the Mohawk Valley and elsewhere during the summer of 1777, now for the first time edited by Clinton Scollard. Boston: R.G. Badger, 1901. 307p.**

Despite his patriot leanings Wilton Aubrey follows his Tory father and joins the British regulars, Tory rangers and Indians under Barry St. Leger, Sir John Johnson and Joseph Brant as they march from their collection point at Oswego to besiege Fort Stanwix. When his father sickens and dies, Wilton heeds his true feelings and deserts to the Americans in the fort. Thereafter he takes part in several hazardous ventures that benefit the patriot cause and result in the lifting of the siege. At this excellent historical novel's conclusion (just prior to Burgoyne's invasion and the Battle of Saratoga) Wilson is reunited in Albany with his lover, Margaret Wells, who had left her home in the Mohawk Valley after news had reached her of Wilton's 'death.'

3002. Scoppettone, Sandra, 1936- . *Gonna take a homicidal journey*. **Boston: Little, Brown, 1998. 229p.**

'Seaview', Long Island, is the vacation destination of private detective Lauren Laurano and her girlfriend Kip. They arrive in Seaview just as the 'suicide' of local solid citizen Bill Moffat occurs; Moffat had been the leading opponent of fast-food restaurants that were hoping to locate in the town. Moffat's cousin believes he has been murdered and persuades Lauren to look into the matter. There follows a spate of deaths made to look like accidents; Lauren suspects the murderous hands of a serial killer are responsible.

3003. Scott, Cyril Kay. *Sinbad*; a romance. New York: T. Seltzer, 1923. 282p.

"Mr. Scott … sees Greenwich Village through the eyes of intense bitterness more as a menace than an object of amusement. And indeed, the bohemian of this novel is an unhealthy community, a turgid welter of emotions, of unsatisfied restlessness and banal cynicism. … The story deals with the love life of a woman, Emily Tyler, who yearns for suffering because life seems so much more real when she is on the rack. Her first lover is a famous scientist, an idealist, and she is miserable with him because he tries to make her happy; in spite of her efforts, they do not quarrel enough, so she leaves him for an artist who is a rather complete cad. After a satisfactory unhealthy time with him, she becomes jealous and returns to her first lover, whom she eventually deserts a second time. Emily typifies the sincerely morbid pseudo-artist, her self-analysis and self-torture are painful, and her associates in the Village are even less attractive. They all seem to be suffering from a type of hysteria"— Boston transcript.

Scott, Dana, pseud. See: Robertson, Constance Noyes, 1896 or 7-1985.

3004. Scott, Denis, pseud. *Murder makes a villain*. Indianapolis: Bobbs-Merrill, 1944. 297p.

The beautiful actress, Sylvia Kent, formerly the second wife of art collector Philip Carstairs, had also been the wife of Philip's son Robert. The latter divorced Sylvia and married Jacqueline Van Arsdale. The unfortunate Sylvia becomes the victim of a killer while on Long Island and Detective Mike James and his sidekick, David Haxton of Army Intelligence, come forward to research the case. Another element in the plot is the disappearance of a valuable manuscript owned by Victor Collingwood, which Sally Oakes had borrowed during her vacation.

3005. Scott, George, b. 1838. *Tamarack Farm*; the story of Rube Wolcott and his Gettysburg girl. New York: Grafton Press, 1903. 236p.

Rube Wolcott's boyhood is spent in Upstate New York; the Adirondacks play a role in his youth, for he hunts in their forests and bewails the fate of deer that are 'victims of cruel sport'. Rube is drawn into the Civil War and soldiers quite effectively and even pitilessly. When the war is over he returns to his New York State home and is married to his 'Gettysburg girl.'

3006. Scott, Joanna, 1960- . *The Manikin*; a novel. New York: Holt, 1995. 276p.

Harold Craxton made a lot of money as a taxidermist and he used some of it to form the estate with the imposing house dubbed The Manikin. It stood in the secluded countryside of Upstate New York and here the story begins in 1927. Incidentally 'manikin' is a term used in taxidermy for 'the durable frame used to replace the animal's skeleton.' Among those ensconced in the mansion are Mrs. Craxton, the irritable widow of Harold, and a dedicated if overworked and underpaid body of black and white servants. On this stage various

768

characters play their roles, air their antagonisms, and see romantic hopes consummated or frustrated. On Christmas Day, 1927, a blizzard sets off events that change the course of several lives. The region's 'irascible climate', its flora and fauna, are described in loving detail.

3007. **Scott, Justin, 1944- .** *Treasure Island*; **a modern novel. New York: St. Martin's Press, 1994. 234p.**

An amusing modernization of Robert Louis Stevenson's classic with Long Island in the 1950s as the scene of this version. The 'Hispaniola' is now a war-surplus salvage tugboat; Dr. Livesey is a sexy lady who indulges in an affair with Senator (formerly 'Squire') Trelawney; Captain Smollett and Ben Gunn are present, notable for their partiality to fig newtons.

3008. **Scott, Leroy, 1875-1929.** *Children of the whirlwind.* **Boston: Houghton, Mifflin, 1921. 314p.**

After his release from Sing Sing Prison Larry Brainard resolves to stay away from any future illegal activities (the kind he practiced as a member of New York's underworld) and to convince Maggie Carlisle, his girlfriend, who still has a felonious bent, to do the same. Maggie refuses to reform, joining up with those who are trying to bring Larry back to his former criminal life. The police suggest to Larry that he act as a stoolpigeon; when he rejects their offer, he kindles their malevolence also. Over the long haul, however, Larry plays it straight with the timely assistance of influential friends and ultimately pulls Maggie into his circle.

3009. ————. *Cordelia the magnificent.* **New York: H. Holt, 1923. 395p.**

"A member of one of New York's first families, Cordelia Marlow, is the unacknowledged leader of the younger set. When misfortune overtakes the dwindling fortunes of the Marlowes, Cordelia takes stock of her own resources and advertises them in a daily paper, calling for a bidder. The novel advertisement comes to the attention of Franklin, an unscrupulous and grasping lawyer with social ambitions far in advance of his earnings. Deceived by his appearance, she is engaged as an investigator at a fabulous salary; the real purpose of her work is to ferret out the secrets of her rich friends so that Franklin may use them for his own evil purposes. Cordelia on her wedding day is exposed to society as a scheming spy and adventuress who blackmailed her friends to support herself in luxury. Mitchell, a butler who becomes a business man, finally discloses the true nature of Franklin, clears the name of Cordelia and ends by marrying her"—Springfield Republican.

3010. ————. *A daughter of two worlds*; **a novel of New York life. Boston: Houghton, Mifflin, 1919. viii, 458p.**

Jennie Malone makes the transition from New York's underworld to the upper ranks of the city's society. However, her marriage to an aristocratic husband ends in disaster when she takes the blame for his illegal activities, whereupon

Jennie returns briefly to her old lower level friends and then marries a man who was her first love.

3011. ————. *Folly's gold.* **Boston: Houghton, Mifflin, 1926. vi, 291p.**
"In this sequel to 'Mary Regan' [q.v.] the three principal figures in that story are re-introduced: Clifford, a private detective, his enemy, Bradley, the crooked ex-chief of a [New York City] detective bureau, and Mary Regan, the girl they both love. Immediately after her secret marriage to Clifford, Mary left him, and in the present story she appears as Bradley's accomplice in his schemes of extortion and blackmail. Clifford spoils one after another of his enemy's pretty plans, but cannot get evidence to convict him. In the final exploit Mary's part in these plans is satisfactorily explained and the lovers are reunited, but the wily Bradley still escapes conviction"—Book review digest. "The Long Island atmosphere is rather better than the conventional sort"— Boston transcript.

3012. ————. *The heart of Katie O'Doone.* **Boston: Houghton, Mifflin, 1925. 385p.**
The progress of Katie O'Doone from the rough and tumble world of the slums to the possibility of 'making it' in the theaters of the Broad White Way is 'documented'. At the age of twelve, after her mother passed away, Katie escaped the tenement that housed her and an alcoholic father and eluded the truant officer who would send her back to school. Irish Katie used her charm and spunk and the interest in her of a number of friendly and even antagonistic people to gain a foothold on the Broadway stage. When she finally reached stardom, Katie took her father back, but sacrificed a chance at real love.

3013. ————. *The living dead man.* **New York: Ives Washburn, 1929. 293p.**
This murder mystery takes place in a Long Island setting and follows the 'fortunes' of Peter Buchanan who is an accident victim and is paralyzed. Nevertheless he is a suspect when two people are murdered; his girlfriend also falls into the category of suspects. It takes a lot of effort on Peter's part to work toward his own recovery, avoid arrest and point out the individual who committed the homicides, incidentally clearing the name of the girl he is in love with.

3014. ————. *Mary Regan.* **Boston: Houghton, Mifflin, 1918. v, 384p.**
A private detective, Bob Clifford, falls in love with Mary Regan, a striking young woman who chooses to associate with the kingpins of New York City's underworld. Clifford's efforts to turn Mary's life around meet with resistance; she opts for a luxurious life style, marrying Jack Morton, but then locking herself into situations she cannot control. Loveman and Bradley, two unsavory characters, try to use Mary and Jack for their own purposes. Clifford stands in their way; Mary at last shakes off her past and is prepared to fit into Clifford's world.

3015. ———. *No. 13 Washington Square*. **With illus. by Irma Deremeaux. Boston: Houghton, Mifflin, 1914. 280p.**

"The great Mrs. DePeyster, an envied social leader of New York, is on the point of departure for Europe when she suffers a series of shocks culminating in the announcement that the railroads providing her income have decided to … [forego] dividends for the quarter. She ingeniously hits upon the scheme of remaining in her boarded-up home with only a faithful servant aware of her presence. Her son, whom she disinherits because he wanted to give up the life of an idler and become a civil engineer and, too, because he insists upon marrying the girl of his choice rather than one of his mother's, falls upon the same plan, also for financial reason, of living behind the shutters with his bride for the summer while he … [plugs] away at his engineering work at Columbia. Complications, funny and exciting, follow in quick succession, which serve to make the scales fall from the eyes of the proud, dignified, blue-blooded Mrs. DePeyster"—Book review digest.

3016. ———. *Partners of the night*. **Illustrated by Dalton Stevens. New York: Century Co., 1916. 361p.**

A recent graduate of Yale, Bob Clifford, has joined the detective force of the New York City Police; his superior, Chief Bradley, may very well be guilty of taking bribes and graft, and Clifford is determined to prove it. Bradley becomes aware of Clifford's posture and the two become antagonists lining up their adherents for a showdown. The young detective's love affair with Mary Regan is complicated when she is uncertain which side of the face-off she should support.

3017. ———. *To him that hath*. **Illustrated from paintings by Sigurd Schou. New York: Doubleday, Page, 1907. 401p.**

The novel, with its major scenes taking place in New York City, tells the story of David Aldrich and the sacrifices he made for his best friend, the Rev. Philip Morton. Morton had been blackmailed out of trust funds by a deceiving woman, had sickened and died. To keep his friend's name from dishonor and continue Morton's missionary work Aldrich takes the blame for the loss of the trust funds and is sentenced to four years in prison. There he has a clear view of prison discipline and reform. When David Aldrich is released he finds out just how difficult it is for a convicted felon to be accepted back into society and make a living. The author is much disturbed by the avarice of men of means and yet has hope that the majority of the citizenry can, by concerted efforts, be raised to a state of physical, moral and mental health.

3018. ———. *The walking delegate*. **New York: Doubleday, Page, 1905. 372p.**

"The rather touching story of Tom Keating, a skilled [New York City] construction worker (in the days when they earned three dollars a day), who learns trade unionism through painful experience. Tom opposes the corrupt walking delegate, Buck Foley, who has used his position in the union to line his own pockets. Tom's pathetic love affair with a sympathetic secretary and his tremendous struggle to retain integrity in the midst of graft and corruption are honestly, if somewhat sentimentally, portrayed. Although overdrawn, the novel is an early example of realism in the labor novel. Union meetings, the life of the walking delegate, struggles to make unions democratic, and behind-the-scenes strike negotiations are well reported, although Scott's style is undistinguished and his plot overcomplicated"—Blake, F.M. *The strike in the American novel.*

3019. **Scott, Milton Robinson, 1841-1921. *Henry Elwood*; a theological novel. Newark, Ohio: Newark American Print, 1892. 324p.**

The hopes of his mother and mentors were fulfilled when Henry Elwood spent three years at New York's Union Theological seminary. He wrote to his mother (his correspondence with her appears frequently throughout the novel) that he had seen much of the dark side of this great city, appreciative though he was of the metropolis' cultural life. At the seminary his friend Homer Vernon (later a physician in 'Excelsior') tells Henry that his doubts cancel out the ministry as a profession for him. Henry goes back to Arcadia (in the State of X——) and occupies a Presbyterian pulpit. After three years there he moves on to the First Presbyterian Church in Excelsior, a large city in some ways comparable to New York. Assailed by his own questioning of the Confession of Faith, Henry consults his parishioners who stand by him. Meanwhile he has married Alice Carroll, continues his friendship with Dr. Homer Vernon and discusses the doctrines and dogmas of the church with Prof. Humboldt of the State University at Excelsior. After delivering a charge to the new pastor at Geneva, Henry and Alice are involved in a railroad accident. Alice dies from injuries received therefrom. Before death Alice, leaving behind Henry and their two children, implores Henry to continue his ministry.

3020. **Scoville, Joseph Alfred, 1815-1864. *Clarence Bolton*; or, *A New York story*, with city society in all its phases. New York: Garrett, 1852. 104p.**

Clarence Bolton, son of a journeyman carpenter and a Creole mother, attends Columbia College after his father's accidental death and benefits from an acquaintanceship with Colonel Vanderhoost, the uncle of Fanny Gould, a young woman he had saved from drowning. A romance develops between Fanny and Clarence but the years pass and Clarence graduates from Columbia and becomes a businessman. He and a partner establish the firm of Lee & Bolton that has its successes and failures. Meanwhile Fanny has married unstable Fred Dresser and stays with him despite his wayward behavior. Clarence wins a seat in the New York State Legislature and is eventually elected to Congress. Fred Dresser drowns himself and Fanny's father deteriorates mentally, still clinging to a rapidly diminishing fortune. Fanny slips into death and Clarence marries Mary Lee, his business partner's sister.

3021. **————. *Vigor*; a novel, by Walter Barrett, clerk [pseud]. New York: Carleton, 1864. 428p.**

Presents a picture of a roiling New York City in the 1830s and 1840s. The novel is somewhat episodic with the hero, Marion Monck, a South Carolinian in New York seeking his fortune. He interacts with a bewildering array of characters: down-and-out Count Falsechinski; Clara Norris, mistress of Mr. Nordheim, one of his employers—she is destined to be New York's most famous courtesan; the wrangling Granvilles; confidence man John O'Doemall; the gallant but improvident Colonel MacNeill; seducer-rapist Frank Gaillard; a bevy of just-beyond-puberty young women, some to be married, others to be street or brothel prostitutes; et al. The position Marion fills in the firm of Granville and Nordheim doesn't last very long; Pitt Granville fires him. Marion is a failure as an entrepreneur/merchant, so he tries writing for a living; the noted editor, James Gordon Bennett, steers him into journalism.

3022. Scudder, Sam. *A counterfeit citizen.* **New York: Broadway Pub. Co., 1908. 346p.**

Two recent arrivals in New York City's 'Little Italy' are: a priest with false documents that present him as an American citizen returning to his home, and an Italian army deserter. The novel devolves into one that describes graphically corruption in voting and brutal murder and the relationship of the two newcomers to these incidents.

Sealsfield, Charles, 1793-1864. *Die deutsch-americanischen.* **Wahlverschaften. For the English translation of this work see Item #3023.**

———. *Flirtations in America.* **See note under Item #3023.**

3023. ———. *Rambleton*; **a romance of fashionable life in New York during the Great Speculation of 1836. Translated from the German. New York: J. Winchester, New World Press, 1844. 285p.**

Republished in 1846 under the title: Flirtations in America. Translation of Die deutsch-amerikanischen Wahlverwandtschaften. The financier Ramble lives in New York City with his daughter Dougaldine, while his nephew, the corrupt, sophisticated Erwin Dish, hovers in the background. "Acreshouse in Upstate New York, the home of the conservative Rambleton family, forms a natural contrast to the degenerate life in the city. The Rambletons … stress the significance of agriculture and of rural life in general and refuse to enter into reckless and uncertain financial speculation" (Grundzweig, W. Charles Sealsfield). The Rambleton son, Harry, falls in love with Dougaldine, but she refuses to marry him when he uses trickery to conceal his rural origin. When Mr. Ramble demands that Dougaldine marry Erwin Dish, she flees to the Rambletons. The economic troubles of the time bankrupt Mr. Ramble. The novel ends in an aura of uncertainty, although there are hints that Dougaldine has a new romantic attachment, this time to a German nobleman.

3024. *Searching for the white elephant in New York*; **a humorous record of many**

adventures. New York: Office of 'Wild Oats', 1872. 47p. (in double columns).
Country-bred, wealthy young Harry Queer heads happily for the big city to experience the nuances of metropolitan life (i.e., seeing the 'white elephant'). Harry falls prey to a number of confidence men and women, chief among which is Tom Lanky, a friendly new acquaintance. They go about stripping Harry of his money—Harry has a special affinity for pretty young women, falling in love with several unworthy specimens. As Harry begins to catch on to what is happening around him, he hires Detective Vaun; together they set traps for Harry's erstwhile 'friends'. In the end Harry himself is not above initiating a scam and he has now become a man-about-town who still clings to his bachelorhood.

3025.   **Searing, Annie Eliza Pidgeon, 1857-1942.** *A social experiment.* **New York: G.P. Putnam, 1885. 182p.**
"The social experiment consists in the transplanting of a pretty and intelligent village girl to a home of wealth [Mrs. Chauncey's] in New York City, where with native intuition she soon adapts herself to her new surroundings and becomes a social success. 'She had a way of pushing unwelcome thoughts behind her at all times, and without distinctly planning to be selfish, took the goods the gods provide, nor asked the reason why.' How the ties of her early years tightened when she thought them severed forever, how at length she hears the message that no real happiness can come to her unless she takes up her burden and by self-sacrifice makes reparation for her selfish neglect of duty; and how she returns to the crude, hard conditions of her girlhood to work out that self-sacrifice, and how at last she finds peace—this the author relates with sincerity and enthusiasm"—Literary world (Boston).

3026.   **Sears, Mary Hun.** *Hudson cross-roads*; **a documentary narrative of three centuries in Upper New York State. New York: Exposition Press, 1955 [c1954]. 568p.**
The author uses four fictional characters of Dutch origin or ancestry: Harmen Thomase; his son Thomas Harmense; his grandson Johannis Harmense; and Leonard Gansevoort—all of whom are participants in and narrators of significant events in the history of Albany and the Hudson and Mohawk Valleys from 1642 to 1781 (140 years, hardly 'three centuries' as stated in the subtitle). A rather extensive bibliography of primary and secondary sources is indicative of the author's intention to establish the factual bases of her narrative.

3027.   **Seaton, Walter.** *A man in search of a wife*; **or,** *The adventures of a bachelor in* **New York. New York: De Witt & Davenport, 1853. 100p.**
At 49, Jonathan Oldbuck, a native of New Bedford, Mass. (but for several years a man who enjoys the variety of New York City, its theaters and restaurants), contemplates ending his bachelor existence. Unfortunately he is quite unhandsome and exists on an income perhaps inadequate to support a family of any size. These factors operate against any success in obtaining the

consent to marriage of several young women he finds appealing. In part, at the urging of his mother, he suddenly marries the awkward Catherine (Kitty) Spicer; to his dismay she soon proves to be a shrew who compounds his misery. They separate; Jonathan learns the truth of the adage: 'Marry in haste, repent at leisure.'

3028. **Seaver, Edwin, 1900- .** *The company.* **New York: Macmillan, 1930. ix, 209p.**

The novel presents the author's conception of a typical corporate headquarters in New York City and its personnel just before the onset of the Depression of the 1930s. Among the people who devote themselves to the company (a dominating force in most of their lives) are: Miss Grim, the spinsterish, often giggly secretary; Miss Croker, more attractive than her colleague and quick with off-color stories; a young married couple, 'Mr. Young and Miss Childs', who earn just enough to rent an apartment kept tidy by a cleaning woman; Mr. Nash, the office's practical joker; Mr. Mold and Mr. Reynolds, executive types whose wives are a source of constant worry; and Mr. Aarons, the embittered but capable Jew who feels that his talents are purposely overlooked.

3029. **Seawell, Molly Elliot, 1860-1916.** *Midshipman Paulding.* **New York: D. Appleton, 1895. 133p.**

A fictionalized account of youthful Hiram Paulding's service as a naval officer in the War of 1812. The energetic midshipman marched his contingent through the Upstate New York wilderness on two occasions, the second time from Sackett's Harbor to Plattsburgh to join Thomas Macdonough's fleet on Lake Champlain. A leading character in the story is the loquacious boatswain's mate Danny Dixon, a veteran who served under John Paul Jones. Paulding pilots a gunboat past the waiting British and, under Captain Stephen Cassin, participates bravely in the Battle of Lake Champlain, a victory for American naval forces. Hiram Paulding in later years had a distinguished naval career up to and including the American Civil War.

Second, Henry, pseud. See: Harrison, Henry Sydnor, 1880-1930.

Sedgwick, Alexander Cameron, 1901- . See: Sedgwick, Shan, 1901- .

3030. **[Sedgwick, Catharine Maria] 1782-1867.** *Clarence*; or, *A tale of our times*, **by the author of Hope Leslie, & c., & c. Philadelphia: Carey & Lea, 1830. 2v.**

Mr. Clarence of New York City moves to the country after he inherits a fortune from his father, taking his daughter Gertrude with him. There the two will not be subjected to the artificialities of fashionable New York. One of their acquaintances in 'Clarenceville' is a Mrs. Layton who has social ambitions and a predilection for the big city. When Mrs. Layton offers her daughter Emilie to the rich, corrupt Spaniard, Pedrillo, the toast of New York society, shrewd, practical, well-read Gertrude rescues Emilie. The two women eventually marry men they really love and respect. Gertrude's choice is the poor but proud Gerald Roscoe; she rejects the suit proffered by the artist Louis Seton. Trenton Falls, New York is one of the places visited by Mr. Clarence and Gertrude in their travels.

3031. ————. *The Linwoods*; or, *'Sixty years since' in America*. **By the author of** *Hope Leslie, Redwood, & c.* **New York: Harper, 1835. 2v.**

The Linwoods of New York City are of the Tory persuasion but when Herbert Linwood boards in the New England home of the Lees while attending school, he embraces the patriots' cause and joins the rebel army. Mr. Linwood disowns Herbert. Bessie Lee, attending school in New York City, falls in love with Jasper Meredith, a Tory, who fixes his attention on Isabella Linwood, presumably the heir to the family fortune. Bessie's brother, Eliot Lee, a soldier in Washington's army, meets Isabella when he finds himself in New York, now occupied by the British. Bessie, recovering from a nervous breakdown, decides to stay single despite a marriage proposal from Herbert Linwood. When the war ends Eliot Lee and Isabella Linwood are married.

3032. ————. *Married or single?* **By the author of** *Hope Leslie, Redwood …* **New York: Harper, 1857. 2v.**

Sedgwick chooses as the locales of her novel New York City and the Hudson Highlands. The story opens with a look at the unhappy marriages that afflicted the parents and relatives of Grace and Elinor Herbert. Elinor marries the clergyman Frank Everly and the union is a conventionally happy one. Grace, much more forthright than her sister, sets her own agenda. When Grace does agree to wed Horace Copley, she changes her mind after learning about Copley's dalliance with various women. Seemingly resigned to spinsterhood, Grace joins Elinor's household; before the novel ends, however, Grace finds a suitable mate. Sedgwick implies that the single state is preferable to an uncomfortable marriage.

3033. ————. *The poor rich man and the rich poor man*. **By the author of** *Hope Leslie, The Linwoods, & c.* **New York: Harper, 1836. 186p.**

The first third of the novel takes place in the 'little village of Essex, in New England.' The last two thirds of the novel has New York City as its locale. The May family includes the improvident 'Uncle Phil', the father, and two daughters, Susan and Charlotte (the latter incurably ill). They leave Essex when Henry Aikin marries Susan and take up residence in New York City. However, they carry their New England virtues with them and find numerous occasions to practice them in the teeming city. The author contrasts the poor but proud (and charitable) Mays-Aikins (the rich poor) and the harsh, selfish behavior of some New York businessmen (the poor rich).

3034. **Sedgwick, Shan, 1901- .** *Wind without rain*. **New York: Scribner, 1930. 396p.**
"Big Wall Street captains of finance, their pretty stenographer-playmates, their debutante daughters who are expected to make successful marriages, and their noisy but futile efforts to have a good time behind the shelter of their

costly and fashionable park residences, are satirized in this story of upper-class American life"—Book review digest.

3035. **Seeley, Clinton, 1921- .** *Storm fear*; **a novel. New York: Holt, 1954. 214p.**
The novel's hero and narrator is a twelve-year-old lad, David, who lives on an isolated Upstate New York farm. To the farm come three bank robbers, one of whom is brother to the farm's owner. They are, of course, fugitives from pursuing lawmen; their presence portends an atmosphere of sheer terror and murder.

3036. **Seelig, Rayner.** *The eternal huntress.* **New York: Knopf, 1924. 229p.**
Several New Yorkers, especially those of the younger, sophisticated, marriageable set, are the author's center of attention. "The 'eternal huntress' is woman in her quest for a mate. Isabel Rayburn is madly in love with Richard Du Maurier, but he does not reciprocate her affection. Her father, Captain Rayburn, who had been horribly maimed years before while hunting big game, now spends his days in retirement in their Washington Square apartment drinking whiskey and making sardonic remarks. It is he who foresees that there is no escape for Richard Du Maurier. For a time a Titian-haired friend of Isabel's holds Du Maurier's attention, but eventually he marries Isabel as her father predicted"—Book review digest.

3037. **Sellingham, Ella J.H.** *The hero of Carillon*; **or,** *Fort Ticonderoga in 1777.* **Ticonderoga, N.Y.: W.T. Bryan, 1897. 171p.**
On his deathbed patriot Richard Carlyon exacts a promise from his daughter Marguerite that she will become the wife of his nephew Pierre, recently arrived from England to the Carlyon manor near Fort Ticonderoga. The two young people marry, but it is an unconsummated one. Pierre has Tory sympathies yet remains neutral as the Revolution rages around him. Marguerite, falling in love with her standoffish husband, is hurt by his supposed attentions to a guest, an old flame, Isabel Beaufort. Slowly Pierre is converted to the patriot cause and finally joins the Continental Army and participates in several battles, notably the Battle of Hubbardston where he is wounded. Marguerite comes to him and he recovers in a settler's cabin; their marriage is consummated. At the war's end Marguerite and Pierre, now the Earl of Carlyon, are in England, which becomes their permanent home. Their Ticonderoga mansion was destroyed by Burgoyne's forces before the British surrendered at Saratoga. The author's Marguerite is an insufferably virtuous woman and Pierre must be commended for his tolerance of her moods.

3038. **Seredy, Kate, 1896-1975.** *Listening.* **Written and illustrated by Kate Seredy. New York: Viking Press, 1936. 157p.**
The scene of this short novel is an ancient colonial house of Dutch ancestry in the Ramapo Mountains of southeastern New York and northeastern New Jersey. Gail, a young visitor, listens while her uncle relates the history of the

house and the additions to it constructed by succeeding generations. She also finds time to get acquainted with her cousins and their animal friends.

3039. **Serrian, Michael. *Captured*. New York: Critic's Choice/Lorevan, 1987. 272p.**
The quiet life beckons Jeff Mitchum, former policeman, who is a winner in the New York State Lottery; he takes a job as manager of a video store on Long Island. Then one morning he comes out of a deep sleep to find a dead woman in his bed. He has to prove that he had nothing to do with her demise and his investigations draw him into confrontations with video pirates. Arson demolishes his store and several lady friends are stabbed with ice picks. An ex-police partner comes to his aid and Jeff tries to dispel horrible memories as he comes closer to identifying the killer or killers.

3040. **Servos, Launcelot Cressy. *Frontenac and the Maid of the Mist*; a romance of Theala and Frontenac at the time when Frontenac ruled Canada and Ourouehati dominated over what is now New York State. Toronto: H. De Gruchy Co., 1927. 310p.**
The author's fertile imagination has conceived a tale in which Count Frontenac, Governor of New France during the latter years of the 17th century, negotiates with the hostile Iroquois, temporarily detaining the Onondaga Big Mouth (Ourouehati), spokesman for the Iroquois Confederacy, and Theala, a Missisauga woman. Theala's beauty arouses the passion of Chevalier de La Salle, the great explorer, but she resists his advances. However, there arises a mutual love between Frontenac and Theala which can never be consummated, for Theala, selected by the Iroquois to be the Maid of the Mist, goes willingly to her death over Niagara Falls as a sacrifice to the Great Manitou who dwells in the Cataract of Niagara; Frontenac looks helplessly on. Big Mouth is an authentic historical personage; Theala is very likely Servos's creation.

3041. **Seton, Anya, 1916-1990. *Dragonwyck*. Boston: Houghton, Mifflin, 1944. 336p.**
The primary scene of the novel is the Hudson Valley, particularly the country near Kinderhook and vicinity. The time is the 1840s when the patroons lived on great estates that were financed largely by their real estate holdings in New York City. Nicholas Van Ryn maintains the imposing manor, Dragonwyck, and to it comes Miranda Wells to serve as companion to the small daughter of Nicholas and his corpulent wife Johanna. Nicholas with his dark, good looks fascinates Miranda, but she has a sense of foreboding evil wrapping itself around Dragonwyck. Van Ryn's tenants are beginning to voice their discontents and have an ally in Jeff Turner, a young physician. The latter has his suspicions aroused when Johanna Van Ryn dies suddenly and Nicholas marries Miranda. The object of Nicholas's abrupt outbursts of cruelty, Miranda discovers dark secrets in her husband's past and the weakness that lies behind his arrogant facade. The tenants' anger boils over and a turbulent climax ensues.

3042. Seton, Ernest Thompson, 1868-1946. *Rolf in the woods*; the adventures of a boy scout with Indian Quonab and little dog Skookum. Written & illustrated by Ernest Thompson Seton. Garden City, N.Y.: Doubleday, Page, 1911. xv, 437p.

About 1810 the orphan Rolf Kettering is taken in by his uncle, Michael (Mike) Kettering, a bullying, mean-spirited Connecticut farmer. Rolf finds a friend in the Indian Quonab. Together they leave Connecticut for the forests of the Adirondacks. Quonab acts as Rolf's mentor and the lad learns much about the fauna of this Upstate New York region. They build a cabin, hunt, fish and trap, and take their furs to traders in the settlements. Rolf occasionally hires out to farmers and merchants; an Albany venture brings Rolf in touch with Henry Van Cortlandt, the governor's son, and he and Quonab are 'commissioned' to take the young man in hand and restore him to good health by way of an 'Adirondack education.' During the War of 1812 Rolf and Quonab act as scouts for the American armed forces in northern New York. Rolf is wounded, recovers, and the novel concludes with a glimpse of his future prosperity in business and politics, and marriage to Annette Van Trumper, a farmer's daughter. He does not forget Quonab, but the latter chooses to live alone, mourning the passing of the old native and woodsman way of life.

3043. Seton, Julia, b. 1862. *Destiny*; a New Thought novel. New York: Clode, 1917. vii, 324p.

"The heroine [Audrienne Lebaron] is a young girl who is keen scented for a life of adventure. She grows irritable among the commonplaces of life with her country foster parents and her country lover. She longs for the world. Her opportunity comes, and with it encouragement to delve deep into all 'sciences, psychologies, philosophies, and religions' [when she comes to New York]. With the husband of her friend [Lolone, Dr. St. Elmo], who had opened the door to her new life, she enters the world beyond and 'sees at work the laws of the inner relationship of spheres and consciousness.' Here the lay reader loses her, but soon finds her again as she emerges to the discovery that she is the soul mate of her friend's husband. The reader is led to believe that the events swiftly following this development, the resistance, and final conquest, are wholly in keeping with the teachings of New Thought"—Book review digest.

3044. Sewell, Cornelius Van Vorst, d. 1927. *A gentleman in waiting*; a story of New York society. New York, Chicago: F.T. Neely [c1889]. 291p.

"The story of a married couple reduced a few weeks after the wedding to comparative poverty. Their only possession is Grassmere Farm near New York City, a heavily mortgaged estate given to the bride by her father, supposed to be a millionaire. His failure deprives them of all help, and the bride raises money on a note and plans to open a millinery shop in New York. Her ignorance of business methods involves her in the toils of an unprincipled man. But her troubles all come to an end finally like a fairy tale"—Annual American catalogue.

3045. Shackelton, Robert, 1860-1923. *Many waters*; a story of New York. New York: Appleton, 1902. vii, 372p.

The scene is set in New York City at the turn of the century (ca. 1900)—Wall Street complots, the crowded goings-on in the plush hotels, newspaper reporters grinding out sensational stories, other segments of metropolitan activity. A major proportion of the 'actors' are newspapermen (the novel offers a knowledgeable smattering of the journalist's life). Romantic episodes are inserted amidst the hubbub there with their counterpoint—the ruin of a husband's sought-for peace by a demanding, uncongenial wife.

3046. ————. *Toomey and others.* New York: C. Scribner, 1900. 254p.

A collection of short stories with New York City—the Lower East Side, Blackwell's Island, Cherry Hill—as the foci, and with a varied list of characters: a Civil War veteran, several Irish-Americans, German-Americans, Jews, et al. Contents: How Toomey willed his government job.—A burial by friendless post.—Over the river from Blackwell's.—A police court episode.— The experiment of Frederica.—The misery in Mis' Randolph's knee.—Before the Archbishop.—The promotion of Berkwater.—On Cherry Hill.—A proposal during shiva.

3047. Shafer, Donald Cameron, b. 1881. *Barent Creighton*; a romance. New York: A.A. Knopf, 1920. 327p.

A novel of adventure and love with New York State and the trouble-filled period of the 1840s as background. "When the hero's fortunes are at their lowest, an old aunt leaves him a legacy of four old keys, a box full of small figures of Inca gods, an undecipherable manuscript and the family estate with 5,000 acres to hold in trust for his wife to be. The first three items point to family secrets, all of which develop and unravel in the course of the story in quaintly romantic fashion with underground passages and chambers and hidden treasures. Of immediate interest to Barent, however, is to find a wife to save him from a debtor's prison. How a wealthy, land-greedy neighbor of the Creighton estate offers his daughter to fill the place; how Barent tears up the contract when he finds he loves her and faces a variety of troubles instead; how the tables turn and how Ronella comes to require Barent's help; and how the two really love each other more than gold and acres, makes a fascinating tale"—Book review digest.

3048. ————. *Smokefires in Schoharie.* New York: Longmans, Green, 1938. 357p.

The story follows the fortunes of three generations of Palatine Germans who first settled in the Schoharie Valley in 1713. Because these new colonists had good relations with the Mohawks and other Iroquois (in fact they were on land promised to them by a Mohawk chief) they were unprepared for the hatreds released by the American Revolution. Many perished in the Cherry Valley

Massacre and other Tory/Indian raids. By 1782, when the novel comes to an end, there were no more Indians in New York's Schoharie Valley.

Shane, Susannah, pseud. See: Ashbrook, Harriette, 1898-1946.

3049. **Shannon, Robert Terry. *Forbidden lips*. New York: Clode, 1929. 285p.**
After three years of voice training in Chicago Jacqueline Kay hopes to impress blasé New Yorkers with her talent. With her funds at low ebb she is hired as a songstress at the Sea Shell, a Manhattan nightclub, by the owner, Julius Lupino, an imposing, heavyset man with an air of the sinister about him. Lupino is fascinated by his beautiful employee; Jacqueline finds him alternately attractive and repulsive. When Lupino declares he is in love with her and will not allow any man to come between them, the frightened Jacqueline seeks help from Tom Ware, a broker and frequent visitor to the Sea Shell. She and Ware fall in love and quickly marry, but, cognizant of Lupino's threats, Jacqueline tears herself away from her husband, hoping Lupino will leave him alone. Lupino and Ware have inevitable confrontations, but it is one of Lupino's lieutenants (the so-called 'Spook') who kills his boss—past injuries and indignities visited upon the Spook have long festered in his memory.

3050. **Shaw, Edward Richard, 1855-1903. *Legends of Fire Island Beach and the South Side*. New York: Lovell, Coryell, 1895. 212p.**
Seven stories embodying some of the folklore and tradition that pertains to Long Island's Great South Bay. "Fact, imagination and superstition—each contributed its part. In the tavern, among groups of men who collected on shore from wind-blown vessels, at gatherings around the campfire, and in those small craft that were constantly going from one part of the bay to another, not only these tales, but others, irrevocably lost, were elaborated and made current in days homely and toilsome, yet invested with an atmosphere of romance"—Preface. Contents: The pot of gold.—The bogy of the beach.—The mower's phantom.—Enchanted treasure.—The money ship.—Widow Molly.—The mineral-rod.

3051. ————*The pot of gold*; a story of Fire Island Beach. Illustrated by **Hatheway and Graves. Chicago & New York: Belford, Clarke, 1888. 162p.**
The 'pot of gold' is a resin-sealed jar full of gold coins found by 'the Captain' who patrols Fire Island Beach. The story backtracks and we are introduced to sedge mowers, old natives of the area, John and Jess, two boys (ages 7 and 12), et al., who espy phantom vessels on the Great South Bay and observe the movements of buccaneers (e.g., Tom Knight and Jack Sloane) as the latter go about hiding their ill-gotten loot in the beach sands. A second story, 'Widow Molly', takes place ca. 1788. The Widow keeps an inn off the Bay and safekeeps a splendid hunting gun for a young squire. Pirates invade the inn, rob the Widow and walk away with the prized weapon. Pursued by a posse of aroused natives the outlaws are subdued and the gun returned to Molly. She

cleans and polishes it; when the squire comes to the inn he takes the gun and Molly, no longer a widow, to his home.

3052. **Shay, Frank, 1888-1954.** *The Charming murder.* **New York: Macaulay, 1930. 255p.**

Dr. Charming has entertained seven people with an evening at the theater; upon their return to his home on East Fifty-third Street they are lounging about drinking when the temporarily absent doctor turns up—as a corpse, obviously a murder victim.

3053. **[Shebbeare, John] 1709-1788.** *Lydia*; or, *Filial piety.* **A novel. By the author of** *The marriage-act,* **a novel, and** *Letters on the English nation.* **London: Printed for J. Scott, 1755. 4v.**

The reason for including this work in a New York State annotated bibliography is that it is one of the earliest pieces of fiction to go beyond mere mention of the region, however briefly. The first 40 or so pages describe the Onondagas and Cayugas and their two leading chiefs—Cannassatego, the Onondagan, and Decanessora, the Cayugan. Cannassatego decides to go to England to improve relations with the English nation. He rescues the heroine, Lydia Fairchild, from ravishment by the ship's captain. The novel then proceeds to England, the scene of the rest of the story.

3054. **[Shecut, John Linnaeus Edward Whitridge] 1770-1836.** *Ish-Noo-Ju-Lut-Sche*; or, *The Eagle of the Mohawks.* **A tale of the seventeenth century. New York: P. Price, 1841. 2v.**

The Dutch are still a major factor in the Mohawk Valley, especially in the settlement of Schenectady, when the hero, Conrade Weisser (a.k.a. Weisse or White?) joins his Mohawk friends and allies in an effort to end French and Indian depredations. The author relies on historian Cadwallader Colden's writings to buttress his account of the conflict in Upper New York State and Lower Canada in the latter part of the 17th century. When Schenectady is sacked in 1690 by a party of French and Canadian Indians, Wilhelmina Kreift, the heroine and Conrade's sweetheart, is taken prisoner. Conrade comes to her rescue and the novel ends with English influence increasing in the affairs of the former Dutch colony. The title refers to a Mohawk sachem who really has little to do with the events depicted in the story.

3055. ————. *The scout*; or, *The fast of St. Nicholas.* **A tale of the seventeenth century. By the author of** *The Eagle of the Mohawks.* **New York: C.L. Stickney, 1844. 312p.**

A sequel to *Ish-Noo-Ju-Lut-Sche*; or, *The Eagle of the Mohawks* (q.v.). The story continues its earlier account of Mohawk-French relations and hostilities, with British and colonial forces making their presence felt. Chief characters are: the daughter, Clara, of Conrade and Wilhelmina Weisser; their sons Edward William and Frederick and a cousin, Gustavus Adolphus; two former New Englanders, Caleb Frizzle, a schoolteacher, and Aminadab Wilding, a trader, also have prominent roles. The young men and Clara are sorely tested by their French and Indian enemies before peace returns and Clara and Gustavus Adolphus renew their love affair.

3056. Sheed, Wilfrid, 1930- . *The boys of winter*; **a novel. New York: Knopf, 1987. 280p.**

The author assembles a group of writers and editors, year-round residents of Long Island's Hamptons, who look down on the 'summer people' and in turn are barely tolerated by the 'natives.' Jonathan Oglethorpe is a publisher rather disgusted with some writers but a would-be novelist himself; overly masculine Waldo Spinks cranks out trashy fiction; Billy Van Dyne writes superlatively and has a luscious, lust-inspiring wife; Ferris Fender is a Civil War novelist with genteel Southern airs; and Cecily Woodward documents the 'heart-rending' lives of Park Avenue wives. They are all melded after a hard winter into a softball team that will lock horns with a bunch of visitors from Hollywood.

3057. Sheffer, Roger. *Lost River.* **Boonville, N.Y.: Night Tree Press, 1988. 133p.**

A collection of short stories that brings the fictional Adirondack township of 'Lost River' into focus. Lost River is economically played out. Welfare is the recourse of most of the long-time inhabitants for there is hardly any industry in the region; the only jobs available are those in diners, gas stations and other services. In the summer several camps hire people to look after the needs of visitors. Despite all that the people of Lost River have not lost all their resiliency or self-respect. Contents: Deer flies.—The skill of silence.—Ancient history.—Feeding on words.—The blue trail.—Delivering bread.—Amazing grace.—Heat and hot water.—Olympic.—Three windows.—Hemlocks.—Covered bridge.—Hamilton Lake.—Lost River.

3058. Sheldon, Alethia. *The butterfly net.* **New York: Coward-McCann, 1957. 251p.**

"The action of Miss Sheldon's sophisticated and intricately plotted story covers the space of a single June day on the vast Stanton estate in Westchester—a day in which Schuyler Stanton's heirs find, each in his or her own peculiar way, some resolution of their problems"—Publisher's note. One of them, Will Stanton, adds to the stress by bringing his mistress with him to the Stanton 'compound.'

Sheldon, Mrs. Georgia b. 1843. See: Downs, Sarah Elizabeth Forbush, b. 1843.

3059. [Shepherd, Daniel]. *Saratoga*; **a story of 1787. New York: W.P. Fetridge, 1856. 400p.**

Arthur Walcott, fiancé of Marion, the daughter of Colonel Belden, exercises a mysterious power over the mad Wild Jacob Whittaker who prowls the forests and glens near Ballston Spa and Saratoga. However, that does not prevent the madman from inflicting harm on the Colonel and kidnapping Lucile Valcour,

Marion's friend. Arthur, Catfoot (a Mohawk), the woodsman Sandy Brigham, the half-breed Indian Joe and Jim McCarty, the Colonel's handyman, spend much of the novel tracking down Whittaker and rescuing Lucile, although the lunatic manages to escape his trackers time and again. Whittaker is finally shot by Indian Joe when he attacks Arthur Walcott and Lucile who have declared their love for one another. Marion, formerly Arthur's fiancée, is content to commit herself to the arms of Major Richard Floyd, an American army officer. The author's interest in the locale of the story is evinced by his colorful descriptions of its forests and waters.

3060.   **Sheppard, William Henry Crispin, b. 1871.** *The Rambler Club's house-boat.*
Illustrated by the author. Philadelphia: Penn Pub. Co., 1912. 120p.
Bob Somers and several other members of the Rambler Club take a houseboat northward up the Hudson River. The trip provides some unusual experiences, especially when they put in at the towns and villages lining both sides of the Hudson.

3061.   **Sherburne, James, 1925- .** *Death's pale horse*; **a novel of murder in Saratoga in the 1880s. Based on research by Betty Borries. Boston: Houghton, Mifflin, 1980. vii, 194p.**
The racing season at Saratoga in the late 1800s is the scene of this mystery. A newspaper reporter comes into the resort town to dig up a story for his demanding editor and encounters a medley of crooked gamblers, swindlers, fake clairvoyants and other scoundrels. His chief focus is trying to determine the connection, if any, between the intense competition of two race-horse owners, their horses, and their jockeys, and the murder of a man whose nude body has been wedged into a local hotel's dumbwaiter.

3062.   **[Sheridan, Eugene].** *A false couple*; **a novelization of the drama, 'A false couple.' New York: Exchange Pub. Co., 1889. 227p.**
Two young men-about-town (New York City), Edward Morton and George Allison, fall in love with the same girl, Ellen Van Courtlandt. Wealthy and upright George Allison is Ellen's fiancé, meeting with the approval of Ellen's parents. The duplicitous Edward's affection for Ellen is matched by his desire for the money a marriage with her should bring him. He convinces Ellen that George has been unfaithful and is known as a gambler; Ellen elopes with Edward. Enraged by the betrayal George vows to make both of them pay dearly. He relents when he faces them on a Long Island beach. The years go by and Edward, unable to touch the money left in trust to Ellen by her late father, reverts to his idle, dissipated ways. George keeps his eye on the situation. Half-drunk Edward attacks Ellen, stumbles, and strikes his head on an iron grate. George and Ellen hear the dying Edward ask their forgiveness for his transgressions.

3063.   **Sherlock, Charles Reginald, b. 1857.** *Your Uncle Lew*, **a natural born American; a novel. With a front. by B. West Clinedinst. New York: F.A.**

Stokes, 1901. 305p.

Uncle Lew is proprietor of a railroad restaurant in central New York State; he is also a horse-trader and the leading light of a club of 'good old boys' that meets on various nights at the town's best hostelry. Woven into the novel is an account of the Cardiff Giant and how it eluded exposure when first exhibited.

3064. **Sherman, Ray Wesley, 1884-1971.** *The other Mahoney*; **a novel. New York: Ives Washburn, 1944. 343p.**

The 'saga' of Peter Mahoney, an Irishman who comes to an Upstate New York city with his parents while only eight years of age. His father came with high hopes, but ended up as an embittered tenant farmer. Peter leaves home at fifteen. Friends along the way include: Tony Kowicz who says, 'Get a soft job and hang on to it'; Pinto, a girl who tells Peter to trust his own talents; Bill Gaggen, a carpenter and a strong union man. Eventually Peter becomes owner of the Spargo Electric Company and nurses it through good times and bad. He is an employer who cares for the people who work with and for him, although he has to face sporadic economic downturns and unions run by racketeers.

3065. **Sherwen, Grayson N., pseud.** *The romance of St. Sacrement*; **a story of New France and the Iroquois. Burlington, Vt.: Free Press Print. Co., 1912. 197p.**

Sherwen states in Chapter I that his tale is based on a manuscript written in 1726 by a Jesuit missionary which purports to be the memoirs of an Iroquois chieftain, Lenori. The latter, also known by the name Atotarho, was an Onondagan, the would-be lover of Félecie de Válerie, an orphan captured and adopted by the Mohawks. Her captors called Félecie Flying Star; she soon accepted the Indian way of life and only near the story's conclusion had her memory reawakened to her earliest years as 'Pierre Gavard's child.' Gavard was an old soldier who took care of Félecie after her mother perished at sea. He had to leave her when his company was recalled from New France to the mother country. Snatched from a French garrison at the head of Lake Champlain Félecie was taken by the Mohawks to St. Sacrement country (the Lake George region) and held in awe by them (she wore around her neck a protective totem given her by Gavard by way of an Iroquois chief. Atotarho helps Félecie and a young French officer find their way back to New France, risking the wrath of the Mohawks who were once again at war with French Canada.

3066. **Sherwood, Mary Elizabeth Wilson, 1826-1903.** *Sweet-brier*. **Pictures by W.L. Taylor. Boston: D. Lothrop, 1889. 262p.**

There is no lack of stories about innocent but forthright girls with rural upbringing whose openness and honesty shames their snobbishly sophisticated urban cousins. But in the novel at hand the heroine, a country girl, is so disregardful of the civilities of Saratoga society, which she enters under the auspices of wealthy relatives, that her conduct verges on boorishness. She not only makes things unpleasant for herself but also embarrasses her friends.

However, she finally realizes how abrasive she has been; her beauty and usually sunny disposition are most helpful in bringing about changes in her attitude toward the social milieu she has joined.

3067. ————. *A transplanted rose*; a story of New York society. New York: Harper, 1882. 307p.

A Western heiress, Rose Chadwick, is eighteen and unsophisticated when sent by her father, Pascal, to New York City for her introduction to the upper ranks of society. She is a quick learner; her naturalness and attractiveness draw the attention of several men, among them the so-called 'lady-killer', handsome Jack Townley, Hawthorne Mack, a devious character, and Lord Lytton of Leycester. The latter two are well acquainted with Rose's father; Pascal Chadwick is much admired by Leycester, while Mack seems intent on ruining him and acquiring his mines and other properties. Rose rejects Hawthorne Mack's proposal of marriage; Jack Townley had once thought of asking for Rose's hand but backed off; Leycester wins Rose and after her father's tragic death they depart for England.

3068. Sholl, Anna McClure. *Blue blood and red*, by Geoffrey Corson [pseud.]. New York: Holt, 1915. 395p.

Although Neal Carmichael and Patricia McCoy were playmates as children, class barriers inhibit a closer association in adulthood. Neal is from the upper class while Patricia lives on Staten Island's waterfront with her lower class parents. The marriage of Neal Carmichael and Ada Fleming, a member of his social class, would seem to be in the natural order of things. But Ada is a selfish, uncaring woman of whom Neal soon tires. He knows now that Patricia, a nurse, is his true love. Her love for Neal breaks through Patricia's own scruples. She leaves the New York area; Neal divorces Ada and begins his search for Patricia.

3069. ————. *The law of life*. New York: Appleton, 1903. 572p.

In his *A Mirror for the Nation* (New York: Garland, 1985) Archibald Hanna suggests that this novel deals with "life in a large university, possibly modeled after Cornell." An immature girl is married to a middle-aged professor who is too immersed in his scholarship to pay much attention to his young spouse. The reader is introduced to the social circles of academia and to the professional activities of the faculty. All the while the young wife is understandably restless and dissatisfied. The question that seems to be posed is whether allegiance to one's marriage vows is 'the law of life' and supersedes the strong pull of other considerations.

3070. Shortfellow, Tom, pseud. *Mary Kale*; or, *Big Thunder! chief of the anti-renters*. Boston: F. Gleason, 1845. 56p.

The story is built around the revolt of leasers or tenant farmers in eastern and central New York State in the early 1840s against the wealthy landowners. John Kale, Mary's father, is in sympathy with the anti-renters and dislikes his daughter's preference for George Arlin, a rich landowner, over Jerry Huss, who leads a group of protestors disguised as Indians. Huss (Big Thunder) murders the Squire Van Alstine, a friend of George Arlin. The latter assaults Huss and receives a sword thrust from one of Huss's men. There is a presumption that Arlin has been killed and John Kale, known for his dislike of Arlin, is accused and convicted of Arlin's 'murder.' As Kale mounts the gallows George Arlin suddenly appears. Kale is cleared, Deputy Sheriff Thomas Loper arrests Huss, and John Kale finally gives his consent to the marriage of his daughter and George Arlin.

3071. Shostac, Percy. *14th Street*; **a novel in verse. Illustrated by Kurt Wiese. New York: Simon and Schuster, 1930. 363p.**

"Tells the simple story of a Jewish boy, a dweller in New York's Bohemia, who loved a married lady and lost her to her husband. Deserted by her, he cannot understand why she has left him and cannot forget her. He tells, first, the history of their love affair, and then analyzes the reasons for its ending in terms of his knowledge of life, especially sex-life, work and his race"— Outlook.

3072. Shreve, Anita, 1947- . *Eden Close*. **San Diego: Harcourt Brace Jovanovich, 1989. 265p.**

Andrew, a New York City advertising executive, goes back to his hometown in Upstate New York to make arrangements for his mother's burial. He is in his thirties and has recently divorced his wife. Eden Close and her mother Edith live in a run-down house next to his mother's. In a dream Andrew recalls the night Mr. Close was murdered and Eden raped. Eden also suffered blindness that night from the gun used on her father. Since then she has lived in isolation, closely watched over by her mother. Andrew is anxious to resume his acquaintance with Eden, a friend of his youth. The story's climax discloses the secret of Eden and her mother.

3073. Shriber, Ione Sandberg, 1911-1987. *The dark arbor*. **New York: Farrar and Rinehart, 1940. 307p.**

Terry Jamison comes back to Troy, New York at the urging of her brother Steve. She had fled her hometown two years before after a wedding that never came off and now she is catapulted into the middle of the murders of Grey Halliday and another victim. Detective Lieutenant Grady takes charge of the situation, proclaiming the killer the cleverest in his experience. Terry is one of several suspects.

3074. ————. *Family affair*. **New York: Farrar & Rinehart, 1941. 305p.**

"Polly Drake, young secretary who tells the story, carries a mystery message to 'Beacon Hill' near Troy [New York] to old Godfrey Beacon, pacifist and president of a machine tool company, then gets well-mixed up with family affairs, murder and a problem of no mean social significance. She is properly scared, too, by low moans of scarcely human quality, and you may keep guessing which of the old man's two grandsons she'll wed, Randy or Clay"—New York herald tribune books.

3075. ———. *Head over heels in murder.* **New York: Farrar & Rinehart, 1940. 335p.**

"Deborah Laurance, who tells all, lives with her Aunt Emily (weak) [at suburban New York Hilltop House] on money rather ungraciously provided by horrible Dana Laurance, widow of Deb's brother, and … [Deb's] suspected when … [Dana] is found 'with one side of her lovely head bashed in.' Deeply involved, too, is Jeff Leighton, beloved by Deb and also by Miser, her black Scotty. The final chapter teems with turnovers, upsets and surprises, among the most startled … being Lieutenant Grady, the sleuth"—New York herald tribune books.

3076. **Shurts, Jacob Van der Veer, b. 1849.** *Kedar Kross*; **a tale of the North Country. Boston: R.G. Badger, 1907 [i.e. 1908?]. 430p.**

The master of a stately home in the Adirondacks known as Kedar Kross is bereaved when in 1837 his small son is abducted and when, a few years later his wife, suffering from a mental breakdown, wanders off. The husband/father pours most of his resources into the search for his wife and son; twenty years of despondency and unfulfilled expectations go by before the three are reunited.

3077. **Sidney, Margaret, 1844-1924.** *An Adirondack cabin*; **a family story, telling of journeying by lake and mountain, and idyllic days in the heart of the wilderness. Boston: D. Lothrop, 1890. 432p.**

The motherless Dodge family of 'Buxton', N.Y.—their father is away on business—is homeless after their mansion burns down. Their recourse is to call for assistance from Uncle Joe Dodge in New York City. He makes arrangements for the Dodge children—Travers, Cicely and Marmaduke (Duke)—and their cook, Maum Silvy and her child Biny, and Aunt Sarah Brett—to join him at a cabin in the Adirondacks that will be their home for the summer. Thus begins the family's opportunity to camp out, to visit many of the famous spots in the Adirondacks and to mix with other people who are vacationing there. By the time their stay is over Uncle Joe has won the hand of Aunt Sarah Brett, Cicely is somewhat romantically involved and the family is looking forward to a new home in New York City.

Siller, Van, pseud. See: Van Siller, Hilda.

3078. **Silman, Roberta, 1934- .** *The dream dredger*; **a novel. New York: Persea Books, 1986. 223p.**

The Branson family—Lise, housewife and mother; Murray, husband and scientist; and the two children, Gil and Diny—owned a home on the shores of the Hudson River in the post-World War II years. Diny, the story's narrator, from the vantage point of 1980, recalls her mother's suicide by drowning while Diny was quite young. Diny traces Lise's escape from Austria in the 1930s, her childhood in 'Honeywell', N.Y., her marriage and gradual mental breakdown intensified by the death from polio of her eldest son and the need to hide her psychological struggles from her children.

3079. Silsbee, Peter. *Love among the hiccups.* **New York: Bradbury Press, 1987. 213p.**

Palmer, a teenager in an Upstate New York town, falls for a girl, Liana, guest at a resort in the Thousand Islands, who warily accepts his attentions. Palmer's ancestral home is the Swain Mansion, presently in possession of two peculiar old sisters who are debating whether to award the mansion to Palmer or to Liana. With little warning several very strange events intrude on the lives of the principal actors in the story. Liana, even though she is unaware of it, is the repository of a buried, ominous secret. It doesn't seem out of place that a Boy Scout handbook should be the key to some of the questions posed in the story.

3080. Silver, Alfred, 1951- . *Keepers of the dawn.* **New York: Ballantine Books,1995. 468p.**

A fictional account of the lives of Joseph Brant and his sister Molly, members of the Mohawk nation (the book is quite informative of its customs and traditions). Molly takes center stage for much of the novel; as mistress of Sir William Johnson she joined him in his pursuit of a just and harmonious union of British and Native American interests. Joseph's military career stretched from the French and Indian War to his cooperation with British forces in the Mohawk Valley during the American Revolution.

3081. Simon, Robert Alfred, 1897?-1981. *"Our little girl."* **New York: Boni and Liveright, 1923. 328p.**

"It was a foregone conclusion with Dorothy's mother that 'our little girl' was unusual. Soon it is discovered that she has a wonderful ear and musical talent. Her mother pets her, shields her from all contact with real life and maps out a musical career for her. After her first song recital, with its much-forced publicity, [Dorothy] feels herself every inch a prima donna and acts it towards all her friends and relatives, including the nice boy she has married. Then after her second large concert at Carnegie Hall, arranged for and boosted inordinately by a rich and doting uncle, comes this shattering truth from the press; that the much advertised Dorothy Reitz is a good-looking mediocrity, an ambitious priestess of the commonplace, a singer of pretension but no great talent, who has not improved materially in anything except advertising matter since her debut"—Book review digest.

Sinclair, Grant, pseud. See: Drago, Harry Sinclair, 1888-1979.

3082. Sinclair, Robert B., 1905- . *It couldn't be murder.* **New York: M.S. Mill Co.,**

1954. 213p.

The unpopular chief of an advertising agency invites a number of his employees to spend a weekend on his Long Island estate. Included in the group are two young people who, when their host falls from his horse and is killed, do some amateur detecting and fall in love; and a murderer who, when accused, stays cool and doesn't confess. The motivation for the murder (it is no accident) is the old bugaboo, money; it seems $300,000 is a trifling sum in this circle.

3083. Sinclair, Upton, 1878-1968. *The metropolis.* **New York: Moffat, Yard, c1908. 376p.**

Allan Montague, a young Southern lawyer, is perturbed by the concentration of wealth in New York's 'high society' and the use of that wealth for luxurious styles of living. His brother Oliver is a part of that society and he tries to bring Allan into it. Allan removes himself and proceeds to denounce the demagoguery and extravagance he sees all about him as disruptive of the political, moral and social order.

3084. ————. *The money changers.* **New York: B.W. Dodge, 1908. 316p.**

Allan Montague, protagonist of Sinclair's *The Metropolis*, reappears in this novel. Montague is appointed president of a railroad that is managed by a trust. A female cousin comes to New York with a fortune in the millions and loses it all in circumstances that point to misuse of the trust's methods. A newspaper reporter writes that the Panic of 1907, described by the author, is part of a plan by New York's moneyed interests to forestall the president's measures against the trusts. Muckraker Sinclair is of course intent on exposing the essential wastefulness of Wall Street's high finance.

3085. ————. *Prince Hagen*; **a phantasy. Boston: L.C. Page, 1903. 249p.**

"The novel tells the story of a gold-seeking Nibelung [from Germany] who amazingly turns up in America and successively becomes a Tammany organizer, a Republican orator and finally an unscrupulous Wall Street financier. Fortunately Hagen dies while exercising two new Arabian horses on the day he is scheduled to marry into a prominent New York City family"— Bloodworth, W.A. Upton Sinclair. The work is a muckraking, satirical exposé of New York City politics and Tammany Hall and an indictment of so-called 'society' and the ethics of journalism.

3086(1). ————. **[West Point novels].**

The five juvenile stories listed below are probably an offshoot of weekly tales about a West Point cadet that Sinclair wrote in installments for the publishing house of Street & Smith in the latter years of the 1890s:
A cadet's honor; or, *Mark Mallory's heroism,* by Lieut. Frederick Garrison [pseud.]. New York: Street & Smith, 1903. 274p.
Off for West Point; or, *Mark Mallory's struggle,* by Lieut. Frederick Garrison [pseud.]. New York: Street & Smith, 1903. 251p.

3086(2). *On guard*; or, *Mark Mallory's celebration*, by Lieut. Frederick Garrison [pseud.]. New York: Street & Smith, 1903. 283p.
The West Point rivals; or, *Mark Mallory's stratagem*, by Frederick Garrison [pseud.]. New York: Street & Smith, 1903. 277p.
A West Point treasure; or, *Mark Mallory's strange find*, by Frederick Garrison [pseud.]. New York: Street & Smith, 1903. 285p.

3087. Singer, Loren. *That's the house there.* Garden City, N.Y.: Doubleday, 1973. 199p.

Sergeant Baird is investigating the probable murder of a woman in a small Upstate New York town (close by the Hudson River). The missing woman's kitchen is splattered with blood, and foul play is suspected of her husband who has been consorting with other females. The story is told through interior dialogues stated by Baird as he lays bare the actualities of the case and incidentally discovers some truths about himself.

3088. Singleton, Esther, 1865-1930. *A daughter of the Revolution.* New York: Moffat, Yard, 1915. 309p.

In the early years of the present century Mildred Ashton is left without means of support other than a family estate, Wild Acres, on Long Island. She does not earn sufficient income from her writings and is forced to put Wild Acres on the market. After a stay in a New York boarding house where she ingratiates herself with follow boarders, Mildred makes a trip back to Wild Acres. In the attic of the main house she finds the diary of her great-grandmother, Dolly Aston (*A daughter of the Revolution*) and most fascinating reading it is. Mildred's own life deepens; she receives proposals of marriage from two suitors, neither of whom she particularly cares for, and then Gilbert Greene comes along.

3089. Singmaster, Elsie, 1879-1958. *A little money ahead.* Boston: Houghton, Mifflin, 1930. 194p.

The young heroine, supporting herself in New York City, is quite alone in the world; her chief problem is trying to find a way to put 'a little money ahead' in case of dire need. There is a mystery involving real and false pearls, a little romance, and the coming onto the scene of two elderly, humorous characters.

3090. ————. *The long journey.* Boston: Houghton, Mifflin, 1917. 190p.

A large portion of this story is devoted to the epic journey of John Conrad Weiser and his children from southern Germany to the Mohawk Valley during the reign of Queen Anne of England. Young Conrad Weiser is only 13 years old; he has seen Indians in the streets of London and is able to endure the hardships that accompany the Weisers' trek from Europe to America and finally the wilderness of the Mohawk Valley.

3091. Skeel, Adelaide, 1852-1928. *King Washington*; a romance of the Hudson

Highlands, by Adelaide Skeel and William H. Brearley. Philadelphia: Lippincott, 1898. 307p.

General George Washington's headquarters in Newburgh, N.Y. and the nearby village of New Windsor provide the settings for a hypothetical (?) tale that hinges on a British plot to kidnap Washington; the time is 1782 shortly after Yorktown and during peace negotiations. The chief plotter is Louis Paschal, Major-General Robert Prescott's servant and confidante. Paschal comes to Newburgh and gains a small measure of Washington's trust. His co-conspirators include Tories in the area (Thomas Ettrick, Richard Colden, Mr. Jansen), several Indians, et al. The kidnapping plot ends in disaster chiefly because of the patriot-leaning loyalty of Margaret, daughter of Thomas Ettrick, Washington's own wariness, and the suspicions of the young American, Captain Jonathan Ford, would-be lover of Margaret. Crushed by his failure Paschal dies by his own hand, revealing to Margaret before expiring that 'he' is actually a woman, Louise Paschal, the paramour of Prescott. The title refers to the attempt by Colonel Lewis Nicola and others to persuade the adamantly opposed Washington to become monarch of the new nation.

Skidmore, Adam, pseud. See: Otis, James, 1848-1912.

3092. **Slade, Caroline Beach, 1886-1975.** *Job's house.* **New York: Vanguard Press, 1941. 318p.**

During the Depression years (the 1930s) it had become increasingly difficult for Jobie Mann to find a job; he and his wife Katie had never appealed for help from anyone, but the relief and welfare services in the Upstate New York town where they lived were available to them. Contacts with social workers and various administrators, the questions they asked and the forms they required only stiffened Jobie's resolve to bypass them; he and Katie sell the house into which they had sunk 40 years of toil and move to a tenement. They find many positives in new surroundings, improving their own lot as well as that of their neighbors.

3093. ———. *The triumph of Willie Pond.* **New York: Vanguard Press, 1940. 370p.**

"Story of Willie Pond, his wife Sarah, and their numerous children [in an Upstate New York town]—decent, self-respecting Americans until the Depression [of the 1930s] hit them. First Willie lost his good job; then he struggled to make a living at any kind of work, including a WPA job. Stricken with TB Willie is sent to a sanatorium while the family settles down to despair and welfare organizations. Just as they have found help from an understanding welfare worker and have pulled themselves out of their morass, Willie is pronounced out of danger. When he finds that his recovery means the end of Sarah's 'pension' and all security, Willie sees only one way out of the problem and he takes it"—Book review digest.

3094. Slater, Charles William. *A modern Babylon*; a tale of the metropolis. **Poughkeepsie, N.Y.: Queen City Pub. Co., 1897. 189p.**

The modern Babylon is New York City, whose institutions and so-called reformers are the butt of the author's comments. Walter Everett, a model young man from St. Lawrence County in Upstate New York, comes to New York to fill the position of secretary to the banker Jarvis Edgerly. Walter is in love with Agnes Cornwell, a convent-educated girl whom he met on the boat from Albany. In the course of the novel Walter rescues Agnes twice from perilous situations: first, from the hands of a vicious clergyman, Rev. Jonas Judkins, who poses as the avowed enemy of dens of vice; second, from the murderous intent of Lucia Edgerly, the banker's insanely jealous daughter, passionately in love with Walter. Agnes is shocked to discover when her mother, Madam Clarke, exposed as the owner of a house of prostitution, and she, Agnes, is the offspring of a youthful, short-lived marriage between Jarvis Edgerly and her mother. The dying, repentant Edgerly explains everything in a letter attached to his will which names Agnes as his legitimate daughter and leaves most of his property to her.

3095. Slaughter, Frank, 1908- . *A savage place*; a novel. Garden City, N.Y.: **Doubleday, 1964. 248p.**

A graduate of Cornell and Stanford, Michael Constant, with a solid reputation as a surgeon, comes back to his Hudson River hometown of 'New Salem' to help boost New Salem Memorial towards accreditation. He looks up his former girlfriend, Sandra West, who is still carrying a torch for the egotistical, selfish, half-deranged Paul Van Ryn, the artist son of Marcella Van Ryn, the 'Duchess of Rynhook', the great patroon castle on a hill overlooking the town. Michael faces hostility from part of the profit-oriented medical staff at the hospital and must sort out his relationships with Paul Van Ryn, Sandra, the industrialist Aaron Zeagler (who wants to acquire the decaying Van Ryn property), the matriarch, Marcella Van Ryn, and Anna Zeagler, Aaron's daughter and the wife of Paul Van Ryn.

3096. Sleight, Mary Breck, d. 1928. *At the manor*; when the British held the **Hudson. New York: R.F. Fenno, 1912. 289p.**

Followed are the fortunes of a young heroine, Virginia Theodosia Culpepper Sprague, as the American Revolution begins. While her father, Major Sprague, and her brother, Harold, are in the patriot army, Virginia leaves 'her family home', Oak Glade Manor on the Hudson, to stay with her Aunt Vanderbeek in New York City. There she and her cousin Catalyntie Vanderbeek, are witnesses to and even participants very briefly in the early struggle for New York City and the surrounding countryside. The fortunes of war necessitate the removal of Virginia, Catalyntie and Mrs. Vanderbeek to Philadelphia and then to Culpepper Hall in Virginia. They return to New York as the Revolution winds down. Virginia and Catalyntie have matured to young womanhood and are ready for romantic attachments and marriage.

3097. ———. *The flag on the mill.* New York: Funk & Wagnalls, 1887. 455p.

"It was a time-honored custom in 'Port Sagg' to hoist a flag on the old windmill every time a ship was sighted in the bay. This ensign also heralds the chief events of the story, and generally signals that the vessel in port is the Bermuda [presumed lost] whose captain [Stephen Roy] has a prominent part in the book; the scene is a quaint old seaport town [on Long Island]"—Annual American catalogue. The heroine is Barbara Raynor whose magnificent singing voice is discovered and trained by Prof. Enos Dhall. Stephen's return from a supposed watery grave and the pledge of love and marriage between him and Barbara concludes the novel. Prof. Dhall has meanwhile died and left the two much of his property; Barbara continues to utilize her talent in concert halls, churches, and especially in her Long Island surroundings.

3098. ———. *An island heroine*; the story of a daughter of the Revolution. **Illustrated by George Foster Barnes. Boston: Lothrop Pub. Co., 1898. 432p.**

An historical novel centering on the role of Long Island patriots in the Revolutionary War, with East Hampton as a primary locale. The heroine is Margaret Thurston, granddaughter of a famous Quaker; her courtship by Lodowick Brewster is one that is filled with events that take the reader from Long Island to New York City, Philadelphia and Boston shortly before the Declaration of Independence. Included in the book are muster rolls of regiments from Long Island that fought on the American side.

3099. Sloane, Robert C. *A nice place to visit*; a novel. New York: Crown Publishers, **1981. 278p.**

An unbridled imagination has produced this overwrought tale of mythical or alien beings entering the lives of a modern family in a new home on Long Island. Nick and Christine Marino are frightened by the decapitation of their son Joey's dog and the murder of two teenagers not far from their house. Nick begins to spend time away from home with Karla Anderson, a nubile neighbor. A local academician theorizes that supernatural beings hostile to humans—trolls—are in the neighborhood, and that Karla's father, a troll himself, is using his daughter to lure Nick into his fold.

3100. Sloane, William Milligan, 1906-1974. *To walk the night*; a novel. New York: **Farrar and Rinehart, 1937. 307p.**

Detective Berkeley Jones, the story's narrator, investigates a double death on Long Island: Prof. LeNormand, a mathematician, burned to death in his laboratory; and Jerry Lister (son of Dr. Lister), who took his own life following revelation of secrets about his beautiful yet sinister wife, Selena. Jones and Dr. Lister have a long session concerning the two deaths and the scientific data (time-space relationships) that flow through the novel. Of course, Jones ultimately comes up with the correct explanation of what has been transpiring and why.

3101. Slote, Alfred, 1926- . *Denham Proper.* New York: G.P. Putnam, 1953. 313p.

Robert Denham Manning is heir to the Denham family fortunes and traditions (his mother was a Denham) and thus was presumably forever tied to the Westchester community ('Denham Proper') where the Denhams had long resided. His wife and two teenage daughters were a satisfying responsibility, to be sure, but the pull of an old love far removed from his home base was strong—should he break the mold and leave Denham Proper as had Uncle Will (although the latter did eventually return to the family business)?

3102. **Slouka, Mark.** *Lost Lake*; **stories. New York: Knopf, 1998. vii, 177p.**
The son of Czech immigrants by the name of Mostovsky is the narrator of twelve interwoven short stories that are based around Lost Lake ('A particular forty acres of water'), a manmade body of water outside New York City. The tales dwell not only on his experiences in the countryside and on the lake, but also on the inhabitants and natural beauty of the region.

Small, George G., fl. 1871-1894. See under his pseudonym: Bricktop.

3103. **Smith, Arthur Douglas Howden, 1887-1945.** *Beyond the sunset.* **New York: Brentano's 1923. 291p.**
"A story of adventure among the North American Indians, mid-18th century. Scarcely historical in any full sense, but gives a picture of New York [State], etc. at the time when Canada was under French rule"—Nield, J. Guide to the best historical novels. "Records how Henry Ormond accompanies Tawannears, the Seneca 'Warden of the Western Door of the Long House', and fat Peter Oorlaer on a remarkable journey, seeking forgetfulness of the loss of Marjory, his wife. Tawannears, having lost Gehano, his sweetheart, seeks the Land of the Lost Souls, which supposedly lies beyond the setting sun, in order that he may find and recover her. Their journey is a long one and their adventures absorbingly interesting"—Greensboro (NC) daily news.

3104. ————. *The doom trail.* **New York: Brentano's 1922. viii, 312p.**
A novel about the fur trade in 17th century New York State and Canada and the rivalry between Great Britain and France to control it. Andrew Murray, proprietor of the Provincial Fur Company, is well on his way to monopolizing the trade when he meets resistance from independents like Robert Juggins and Harry Ormerod, recent arrivals in New York. Ormerod has the temerity to fall in love with Murray's daughter Marjory, which, of course only aggravates an already tense situation.

3105. **Smith, Chard Powers, 1894-1977.** *Artillery of time.* **New York: Scribner, 1939. 853p.**
The Lathrops of 'Byzantium', a town in Upstate New York near Lake Ontario, have long been tied to the land with a prosperous farm in 'Lathrop Hollow.' Circa 1850 John, mercurial, intelligent, and Isaac (Ike), a shrewd Yankee, are at the head of the family. The two women they love are Octavia Samson, a college graduate and feminist, and Prudence Stark, a beauty and a schemer.

The outbreak of the Civil War finds John and Ike taking different paths. John serves in the Union Army and is wounded; Ike stays home and begins manufacturing guns (some of them are of poor quality) and prospers. John, like his father, is a champion of the old order of things, but Ike senses the Lathrop's are headed for failure unless they make use of the new gospel of wealth and travel new avenues for the creation of capital. The town of Byzantium is a rich creation of the author's imagination with its gallery of tradesmen, minor scale 'robber barons', reformers, saloon keepers, bankers, bunco artists, et al.

3106. ————. *Ladies Day*. **New York: Scribner, 1941. 491p.**
"A sociological novel based on the life in an Upstate New York town, in the period from 1884 to 1900. The Blaine-Cleveland campaign, the railroad strike, the panic of 1893, are included in this story of the days when the men were supposed to make money and 'the ladies' upheld the morals of their families and towns. Pretty Sally Lathrop took her duties in that line seriously, and so came into conflict with Race Kirkwood, a rising young businessman with a questionable reputation. The struggle between these two, and Sally's repeated denial of her love for Race is the central theme of the book"– Book review digest.

3107. **[Smith, Charles Hatch]. *George Melville*; an American novel. New York: W.R.C. Clark, 1858. 386p.**
George Melville and his best friend, Thomas Griswold, are students at Hamilton College, Clinton, N.Y. when the story opens. The two women in their lives are Bell Mortimer and Clara Edgemonte. James Mordaunt, a lawyer from New York City, is urged by his aunt, Mrs. Tryon, to seek Bell's hand in marriage, for Bell's father, Benjamin F. Mortimer, represents both wealth and political influence. In Mordaunt's way are Melville and Griswold, so he spins various plans with the assistance of criminals, to get rid of them. Melville suffers the most, spending two years in Auburn State Prison after conviction for forgery (the real culprit is a Mordaunt accomplice). Thomas Griswold's father, James, is ruined financially via a Mordaunt scheme, but he rebounds when his son secures aid from friends in business. Crimes past and present finally catch up with Mordaunt and his aunt when Mordaunt's secret wife Mary and another woman he was involved with testify against him. Mordaunt, somewhat remorseful, dies of typhus in prison; Mrs. Tryon follows him in death. A large part of the novel is based in Upstate New York (Aurora, Utica, Auburn, Cayuga Lake, etc.).

3108. **Smith, Dinitia, 1945- . *The illusionist*; a novel. New York: Scribner, 1997. 253p.**
Androgynous Dean Lily has ambitions to become professionally adept in the magic arts. He shows up at the Wooden Nickel Bar in Sparta, New York, wins at cards and gains the rapt notice of all the females in the dive and starts on a

flurry of seductive affairs. But his feminine characteristics cannot be masked for long and the townspeople react savagely.

3109. Smith, Edgar Maurice. *A daughter of humanity*; **a novel. Boston: Arena Pub. Co., 1895. 317p.**

"Helen Richmond, a Boston heiress, becoming interested in the life of the saleswoman in the large dry goods establishments of New York, obtains a situation under a feigned name in a large store, where she remains for seven months, living the life of a working girl, forming friendships with other girls, winning their confidence, and learning at first hand the terrible evils and temptations of their lot. The tragical fate of several girls, working at starvation wages, is told. Miss Richmond relates her experiences finally from the lecture platform"—Annual American catalogue.

Smith, Elizabeth Oakes, 1806-1893. *Hugo.* **See note under Item #3111.**

3110. [Smith, Elizabeth Oakes] 1806-1893. *The newsboy.* **New York: J.C. Derby, 1854. 527p.**

Smith paints an appalling picture of the conditions under which newsboys in New York City lived, many of them orphans who were hard-pressed to find shelter at night. Bob, the hero, rises from poverty to relative prosperity through his own determination and his assistance in finding the abducted child of a wealthy New York businessman. He performs other acts of kindness—e.g., caring for the child Minnie (her mother had drowned herself) in the abandoned railway car in which he lives. By portraying the poor and lowly, the discards of society, Smith created public interest and concern for their situations.

3111. ————. *The salamander*; **a legend of Christmas. Found amongst the papers of the late Ernest Helfenstein. Edited by Elizabeth Oakes Smith. New York: G.P. Putnam, 1848. 149p.**

Also published under the titles: Hugo (New York, Putnam, 1851) and Mary and Hugo (New York, Derby and Jackson, 1856), "The scene of the story is the Ramapo Valley, Rockland County [New York] on the lower west side of the Hudson [River] … he [Indian] natives of the Ramapo Valley were supplanted by a colony of iron-workers of French, German and Dutch extraction, led by a man of strong will and pride—Hugo. … Hugo refuses to take heed of a tradition which says that unless the fires in blasting furnaces were put out once in seven years, there would emerge at the end of that time a flaming creature causing death and destruction. Hugo maintains the fires and to be sure there gradually appears in the furnace a fiery shape … [which is essentially embodied in the iron-master's newborn son]. … The boy appears and disappears magically at various intervals during the twenty years or more covered by the tale. At the end of the story he explains his existence as 'that of a lost angel shut out of heaven through pride of power'"—Wyman, M.A. *Two American pioneers.*

3112. Smith, Francis Hopkinson, 1838-1915. *Colonel Carter of Cartersville.* **With illus. by E.W. Kemble and the author. Boston: Houghton, Mifflin, 1891. x, 208p.**

"A typical Southern gentleman, a Virginian whose best days dated before the [Civil] War, is personified in 'Colonel Carter.' Living in New York with his faithful servant and former slave, 'Chad', he remains in spite of contact with that progressive, bustling city, a 'reb', a believer in slavery, whom nothing short of death can reconstruct. He and his friends are delightfully described. His poverty and lavish hospitality, his debts and high sense of honor are most amusingly contrasted. He has many visionary schemes for growing rich, and the reader is entirely in sympathy with him when coal is found in Cartersville, and through an English syndicate he is a wealthy man"—Annual American catalogue.

3113. ————. *Enoch Crane*; **a novel planned and begun by F. Hopkinson Smith and completed by F. Berkeley Smith. Illustrated by Alonzo Kimball. New York: Scribner, 1916. vi, 337p.**

Enoch Crane lives on the top floor of a house on Waverly Place, Greenwich Village; he is the owner and rents out the rooms on the floors below. He has an unwarranted reputation as an irascible old codger, for Enoch is keenly interested in the welfare of his tenants. It is Enoch who saves Sue Preston (a young Southern woman living on the second floor with her mother and stepfather) from the grasp of an unprincipled suitor and points her in the direction of the smitten Joe Grimsby, architect and third floor tenant. Neither Joe nor Sue realizes how large a role Enoch has played in their eventual engagement.

3114. ————. *Felix O'Day.* **Illustrated by George Wright. New York: Scribner, 1915. 370p.**

"Mr. Smith, like his Irish hero, had discovered that the great middle class is the backbone of New York, and that the self-restraint, sanity, and cleanliness of this class marks the normal in the time-gauge of the city's activities, 'the hysteria of the rich and the despair of the poor' being the two extremes. He found his large-hearted, Dickensy type of this class in 'The Avenue', as its denizens used to call Fourth Avenue between Madison Square Garden and the tunnel, in the days when that section was a little city in itself. ... It is in this wholesome environment that Sir Felix O'Day, reduced to poverty and seeking his erring young wife, who had run off to America with the man who ruined them, finds help and peace. ... Mr. Smith was too genuine an artist to make a picture of life out of sunshine alone, with no shadows. The shadows are present ... and are dark enough in the sufferings of the wayward wife and the brutality of the man who has her in his power"—Book review digest.

3115. ————. *The fortunes of Oliver Horn.* **Illustrated by Walter Appleton Clark. New York: Scribner, 1902. vii, 551p.**

Shortly before the Civil War began Oliver Horn left his Virginia home and its social scene to take his chances in New York City. After several missteps he becomes an art student and eventually builds up an excellent reputation as a professional artist. The author portrays with humor and with guarded emotion the bohemianism of the young, taste-conscious set in a period when New York's social boundaries did not continue much beyond Union Square.

3116.   ————. *Peter*; a novel of which he is not the hero. Illustrated by A.I. Keller. New York: Scribner, 1907. 482p.

"Peter, gentle and manly, shrewd and ingenious, young and sixty, gives unstintingly of his time, his service and his love to young Jack, the hero, an impulsive Southern lad who cares more for honor, independence, and friendship, than for the profit to be derived from his uncle's Wall Street office. Peter, as Jack's Prospero, provides him with adventure and opportunities for heroism as the confidential clerk to a contracting engineer; nor is the magic wand laid aside until Jack has come into his fortune and has brought to a successful issue a diffident courtship of his employer's daughter"—Book review digest.

3117.   ————. *Tom Grogan*. With illus. by Charles S. Reinhart. Boston: Houghton, Mifflin, 1896. 246p.

'Tom' is a robust woman who manages a Staten Island hauling business; she is also a frequent visitor to the wives of workers who live on the Lower East Side of New York City. Tom raises two children of her own in the absence (or death?) of her husband. She is respected by many with the exception of certain elements of the union—Tom herself has little use for labor unions; she has had to expend time and energy defeating a corrupt union man's plans to steal her city contract and even her life.

Smith, Frank Berkeley, b. 1868 or 9, joint author. *Enoch Crane*. See Item #3113.

3118.   Smith, Frank Berkeley, b. 1868 or 9. *The lady of Big Shanty*. New York: Doubleday, Page, 1909. 323p.

"A story of the Adirondacks in which a New York banker, worn out with artificial society and alarmed over the peril of inconstancy threatening his wife, prepares a wilderness habitation as sumptuous as money and skill can make it, and, with authority that precludes opposition, sets down in the midst of it a rebellious wife and a delightful daughter. The story concerns itself chiefly with the lady of Big Shanty's awakening in this primeval environment, to the real and fundamental facts of life"—Book review digest.

3119.   Smith, I. Anderson. *Blanche Vernon, the actress*; a romance of the metropolis. New York: For sale by all the principal booksellers throughout the United States, 1846. 56p.

A native of 'Daisy Hill', a hamlet in Upstate New York, Charles Maitland, is employed in New York City by the merchant Alfred Graves. A casual stroll on the streets of the city brings Charles in touch with Benny Warren, a comb salesman and sole support of his mother and two sisters, Jane and Julia. Charles and an actress, Blanche Vernon, 'adopt' the Warrens. The true character of Alfred Graves is exposed. Unsuccessful in his attempt to seduce Charles's sister 'Bella', Graves hires a Mrs. Critch to poison Julia Warren and trumps up a charge of forgery against Charles. The confessions of the people Graves hired to carry out his crimes and the evidence Blanche Vernon presents of Graves as the seducer and deserter of Julia Warren are enough to send the perpetrator to prison. After Benny Warren dies, Charles and Blanche, now married, take care of Jane, the surviving Warren.

Smith, Jerushy, of Smithville. See Item #669.

3120.   **Smith, John Talbot, 1855-1923.** *The art of disappearing.* **New York: W.H. Young, 1902. iv, 367p.**

"A young blue-blood from Boston, Horace Endicott, finding his wife faithless, instead of divorcing her, resolves to punish her by disappearing, after having disposed of all his property. Acting on a suggestion from a Catholic priest, and through his co-operation, Horace Endicott turns up in New York as Arthur Dillon, the long-absent son of a worthy Irishwoman. He soon finds himself launched into 'politics' under the auspices of Tammany Hall. Arthur's gradual change under his new environment; his successful efforts to elude his wife and her detectives; the intrigues of anti-Catholic bigots; some municipal and a little national politics; the versatilities of a lady who simultaneously plays the role of a ballet dancer; a detective's wife; an escaped nun lecturing on the public platform; and a sick sister from the West enjoying the hospitality of a local convent, are woven … into … [the] story. … When the hero, whose wife still lives, falls in love with a Catholic girl, the author presses into his service the Pauline privilege in order to give the story a satisfactory ending"—Catholic world.

3121.   ————. *The boy who looked ahead.* **New York: Blace Benziger, 1920. 188p.**
'The boy who looked ahead' is Eddie Travers, an orphan taken in by the widow. Mrs. Radkey of 'Fallville' on the Mohawk River. Mrs. Radkey's son Vincent and her nephew Harold Sullivan are Eddie's closest companions. Eddie is president of the Lookahead Club whose members are fun-loving but also serious boys guided in large part by a kindly priest, Father Thomas Fleming. Eddie is an Alger-like creation, a paragon of honesty and industry, who on more than one occasion rescues the prideful and careless Vincent Radkey and Harold Sullivan from their follies. The latter two, after having lost their jobs in Fallville, run off to central and western New York, have several harrowing misadventures and are finally tracked down by Eddie and former detective McGinnis. Eddie himself survives a conspiracy by the nephew of his

employer, Mr. Hurley the grocer, and eventually becomes a wealthy, philanthropic figure, the first citizen of Fallville.

3122. ⸻. *Saranac; a story of Lake Champlain.* **New York: Catholic School Book Co., 1892. ii, 280p.**

The subtitle is misleading; most of the story takes place in Saranac, Clinton County. Chief characters are: Capt. Hugh Sullivan, commander of a Lake Champlain vessel; John Winthrop, lawyer and Sullivan's close friend; Amedée LaRoche, a lake pilot's son; Harold DeLaunay, richest man in town; his daughter Regina and his wife. The plot hinges on the theft of $3,000, of which Amedée, in the wrong place at the wrong time, is accused. The real thief is DeLaunay, but 15 years pass before that is known. Capt. Sullivan tries to protect all parties involved. Amedée, suffering from consumption, comes back to Saranac from his refuge in Texas, but lives only a few more months. His pregnant widow is left with a relatively prosperous clothing store. John Winthrop's love for Regina DeLaunay is not reciprocated, especially after he confesses to a 'betrayal' of his friend Hugh Sullivan. John leaves Saranac, a broken-hearted man, whose fate is an accidental drowning. Hugh and Regina marry. The somewhat repentant Howard DeLaunay is now completely subservient to his wife who has a large part in repairing the damage from the Amedée LaRoche affair.

Smith, Johnston, pseud. See: Crane, Stephen, 1871-1900.

3123. **Smith, Laurence Dwight.** *Adirondack adventure.* **Illus. by Gwen B. Johnson. New York: S. Curl, 1945. 286p.**

Three boys from the city (New York)—Wendell (Wen) Marriott, Vincent Ten Eyck ('Cookypuss') and Bud Moriarty—go by car and trailer to 'Green Lake' deep in the Adirondacks. Shortly after they set up camp on its shores (the lake is owned by Cooky's uncle) they find a note warning them to get out of the region. Befriended by a forest ranger, 'Owlface' Nelson, the boys encounter a gang of counterfeiters to add to their difficulties with the weather and their natural surroundings. Prominent in the story are Fingal's Folly, a castle built by an eccentric millionaire, and 'Gashouse' Monk, a counterfeiter and murderer wanted by the Federal Government. The lads and Owlface assist State troopers in the final roundup of the counterfeiters.

3124. ⸻. *Death is thy neighbor.* **Philadelphia: Lippincott, 1938. 313p.**

"Long Island beach outage [is the] scene of two unsavory killings, considerable intrigue and subtle sleuthing by a young lawyer. Humorous interludes by [an] ex-strip-tease dancer are slightly overdone [but] otherwise [this is] a logically worked out and entertaining yarn"—Saturday review of literature.

Smith, Lydia Annie Jocelyn, b. 1836. See: Jocelyn, Lydia A., b. 1836.

3125. [Smith, Miss M.E.]. *Emma Parker*; or, *Scenes in the homes of the city poor*. By the author of *Witnessing for Jesus*. New York: A.D.F. Randolph, 1871. 408p.

A story in which the crusading author vilifies absentee landlords who provide few repairs to the tenements that house the poor of New York City and who hire as their rent collectors grasping, unsympathetic men not hesitant about evicting families unable to make payments on time. Little Emma Parker is the catalyst; abetted by her mission/Sunday School teacher, Mary Ellis, she awakens the conscience of certain individuals, especially the young gentleman, Harry Lewis, and his sisters, Fanny and Martha. Emma and her care-worn mother are granted the luxury of a sojourn in the country with the Lewises. Harry Lewis plans to devote his energies to the improvement of the living conditions of the poverty-stricken dwellers in Manhattan's Forties. One of the more discerning, intelligent tenement women, Mrs. Linders, says to Lewis: 'Give our homes Christian landlords and all the rest will come right.'

Smith, Seba, 1792-1868. *Jack Downing's letters*. **See note under Item #3126.**

3126. [Smith, Seba] 1792-1868. *May-Day in New York*; or, *House hunting and moving*. **Illustrated and explained in letters to Aunt Keziah. By Major Jack Downing [pseud.]. New York: Burgess, Stringer, 1845. 120p.**

Also published under the title: Jack Downing's letters, by Major Jack Downing [pseud.]. (Philadelphia, 1845). Includes: Smith's Christopher Crotchet, the singing-master; Polly Gray and the doctors; and Sketches from life. Jack Downing in three letters to Aunt Keziah tells of the difficulties he faced when moving on the 1st of May in New York City, dealing with recalcitrant landlords, etc. After much footwork and negotiating he finally takes a lease for a year at $75 on four rooms in Greenwich Village. Downing states: "There is no day in this world, Aunt Keziah, like May-Day in New York, you may depend on it."

3127. Smith, Warren Hunting, 1905-1998. *The Misses Elliot of Geneva*. **Illustrated by Esta and John O'Hara Cosgrave II. New York: Farrar & Rinehart, 1939. 186p.**

"The Elliot girls had their coming out parties in the 1860s and were swept away in a flood of gaiety. For years they traveled everywhere and took Geneva [New York] with them. Spinsters, Candia and Primrose never missed their work. They saw the architect's plans for the new city hall and fought against 'that municipal chicken coop.' They suspected the postman of stealing their letters, so they took their mail 'downstreet' to the post office. They had close friends and even closer enemies. They owned a huge swamp, which brought them no income. They had railroad stocks, which brought them no dividends, but they managed to live—in Geneva money didn't matter. They were dyed-in-the-satin-brocade Republicans. 'Just as Crusaders in olden days set out to rescue the Holy City from the infidels, so did the Elliot sisters intend to do their part in rescuing America from foreigners, Democrats, high churchmen, and companies that didn't pay dividends'"—New York herald tribune books.

3128. **Smith, Willard K.** *Bowery murder*. **Garden City, N.Y.: Published for the Crime Club by Doubleday, Doran, 1929. vii, 325p.**

A mystery story told through newspaper reports of the murder of a 'big wheel' in New York City politics and finance; the crime occurs in the Bowery Bar and some of the people who are involved include: the communist Max Ratkowsky; Rose, the 'Belle of Broadway'; another Broadwayite, Peggy Carroll, beauteous blonde; the movie star Irene Morins; Dixie Blake, who has no permanent address or occupation; Chinese Charlie Whango, a mobster; and a mysterious old man who has been charted off to Bellevue for observation. New twists and turns and additional murders follow as the police come forward to figure it all out.

Smith, Winchell, 1871-1933. *Turn to the right.* **See Item #2457.**

Smithies, Richard H. R., 1936- . *Death takes a gamble.* **See note under Item #3129.**

3129. **Smithies, Richard H. R., 1936- .** *Disposing mind.* **New York: Horizon Press, 1966. 225p.**

Also published under the title: *Death takes a gamble* (New York: Signet, 1968). The scene of the action is a house on Long Island Sound inhabited by somber people: a father and mother who rule with hands of iron, their children who lack a decent allowance despite the wealth of their parents, and two Irish servant-girls. Murder visits this dysfunctional household: the mother dies after swallowing a capsule that someone has meddled with; the father drinks tea laced with poison; and a daughter suffers convulsions and death after eating chocolates. One of the sons is a horse fancier; another is a student of Freud's writings. Possible suspects include the above two sons-in-law, and the murdered man's secretary. In steps the old man's law partner and the latter's clerk to attempt to clarify the situation.

3130. **Sousa, John Philip, 1854-1932.** *The fifth string.* **Illus. by Howard Chandler Christy. Indianapolis: Bowen-Merrill, 1902. 124p.**

Engaged for a series of concerts in New York City, the celebrated violinist, Angelo Diotti, meets and falls in love with the austere Mildred Wallace, daughter of a prominent New York banker. His playing evokes little response from Mildred, so Angelo makes a pact with Satan who gives him a superb instrument whose only 'flaw' is a fifth string which is deadly if bowed. Diotti wins over Mildred, but her brother objects to the match. Mr. Wallace's associate, 'old' Sanders, while trying to break up the couple, has the misfortune of 'borrowing' the violin and touching the forbidden string. Following Sander's death Mildred importunes Angelo in his latest concert to bow the fifth string as a sign of his deep love for her. He tries to dissuade her, but... .

3131. **Sparkle, Sophie, pseud.** *Sparkles from Saratoga*. **New York: American News Co., 1873. 340p.**

The "I" narrator persuades 'Papa' to let her and 'Madge' spend a season at Saratoga, "that Mecca of fashionable pilgrims". The observant "I" carefully takes note of life in the resort, which includes: the search by unattached females for suitable husbands (preferably wealthy), the presence of fortune hunters, worldly bachelors, young belles and accompanying flirtations. When Saratoga palls, excursions to the Adirondacks, Lake George, Fort Ticonderoga, Niagara Falls and West Point are welcome diversions. Madge proves to be unmanageable, especially when she circulates among the Saratoga male contingent, to the consternation of the young ladies' chaperon, Aunt Prim.

3132. **Sparks, Alice Wilkinson.** *My wife's husband*; **a touch of nature. Chicago: Laird & Lee, 1897. 303p.**

Elias Chatterton of 'Lynxville', New York, tells amusingly in a gathering of sketches of his unusual encounters and his impressions of a number of people and things—preachers, how to conduct oneself while riding on streetcars, the mysteries of typewriters, the use of the bicycle, etc.

3133. **Spear, John W.** *Peg Bunson*; **a domestic story. New York: G.W. Dillingham, 1897. 271p.**

Ralph Hammersley, a lawyer, comes to Rochester, New York where an accident lands him in the farm home of the Bunsons. There he meets the daughter of the house, 'Peg', almost a teenager. She has an uncouth, unattractive appearance and makes no effort to change her slovenly ways until Ralph takes her in hand. Her transformation is startling—guided in her education by the lawyer she releases talents as a painter and a singer; the finale is her introduction to society as a lady of charm and beauty.

3134. **Speare, Dorothy, 1898-1951.** *The gay year*. **New York: Doran, 1923. 314p.**

"Presents the life of reckless gaiety of the young married set [in the suburbs of New York City] with their endless craving for excitement. Jerry Lancaster solves her own problem through constructive work and love for her husband. A crisis arrives when the more conservative members of the community ostracize the younger set. The latter come to a more sober realization of life, and agree to limit their social activities to less objectionable pastimes"—Book review digest.

3135. ————. *The girl who cast out fear*. **New York: G.H. Doran, 1925. 324p.**

The young heroine comes to New York City with the notion of carving out a career for herself as a painter, actress, writer or some other artistic niche. The people she meets—an actress, an artist, a playwright, a vaudeville tumbler, a literary poseur, etc.—make varying contributions to her advancement in the big town. When the prospect of marriage looms, she has some difficulty dealing with it, but relies on past and present experiences to carry her through.

3136. Spearman, Frank Hamilton, 1859-1937. *Merrilie Dawes.* **Illustrated by Arthur E. Becher. New York: Scribner, 1913. 382p.**

"A novel in which the characters are a group of financiers who buy and sell railroads with the celerity and nonchalance with which lesser men might acquire and dispense of so much kindling wood. Merrilie Dawes, the heroine, is a very rich young woman who says she is tired of being looked upon as 'an estate.' She cannot escape her destiny, however; the wealth is hers, and through the possession of it she finds herself involved in the financial ventures that threaten to overwhelm her friend, John Adrane. She meets Adrane only after he has become engaged to Annie Whitney, but in the [Wall Street] panic which bankrupts John, this inconvenient engagement is dissolved and he is free to become something more than a friend to Merrilie"—Book review digest.

3137. Spewack, Samuel, 1899-1971. *The skyscraper murder.* **New York: Macaulay, 1928. 279p.**

A sophisticated New Yorker, a man-of-the-world, Oliver Sewell, has interfered once too often in the lives of others. He was a co-respondent in the divorce case of the Edisons, e.g., and to no one's surprise he turns up a murder victim in his own apartment. Of course, the Edisons, ex-husband, ex-wife, are questioned as are the many women Sewell played around with—the woman in blue, the woman in red, et al. There seems to be a close connection between Sewell's murder and the theft (by Sewell) of a Romanov diamond as well as ongoing revolutionary plots. A clue picked up by an amateur detective leads him to Paris and the arrest of the murderer.

3138. Spicer, Bart, 1918- . *Brother to the enemy.* **New York: Dodd, Mead, 1958. 308p.**

A novel about an attempt by patriots to pierce the British lines and capture the traitor Benedict Arnold from occupied New York City. "Protagonist is John Champion, an able and ambitious young sergeant-major in [Light-Horse Harry] Lee's Legion who accepts the dangerous assignment ... Though Champion's mission to take Arnold fails at the final moment, he gains from it an understanding of treason and a clear understanding of his own future path"—Booklist. The author's note explains that the character John Champion is based on Lee's historical Sergeant-Major John Champe.

3139. Spiegelman, Katia, 1959- . *Soul catcher.* **New York: Marion Boyars, 1990. 207p.**

Kate Steiner, 15, is placed in a Long Island boarding school for children with emotional problems, put there by her unhappy Westchester parents, both lawyers. It is the 1970s and Kate struggles to be accepted by and to relate to her peers on various levels. One student who draws her interest is Patrick, an up-and-down druggie, whose habit ultimately kills him. Kate's parents split and choose other lovers, adding to Kate's emotional problems.

Spielhagen, Friedrich, 1829-1911. *Deutsche Pioniere.* **For the English translation of this work see Item #3140.**

3140. **Spielhagen, Friedrich, 1829-1911.** *The German pioneers*; **a tale of the Mohawk. Translated from the German by Levi Sternberg. Chicago: Donohue, Henneberry, 1891. 250p.**

Translation of Deutsche Pioniere. In 1758 Lambert Sternberg, on business in New York City, buys the services of a beautiful girl, Catherine Weise, an orphan whose clergyman father had died at sea on the passage from Europe to America. Ostensibly Catherine is to be the maidservant of the Sternberg family, but when she and Lambert reach his Mohawk Valley home she discovers that the only other occupant is Conrad, Lambert's brother. There ensues a bitter rivalry between the brothers for the love of Catherine; when she makes known her choice—Lambert—Conrad stalks off angrily vowing never again to cross their threshold. Then the French and Indians attack the Sternberg Farm and Conrad comes back to join Lambert and several friends in its defense. Conrad dies heroically just before a unit of Nicholas Herkimer's mounted troops relieves the defenders. The novel concludes a few years later with Catherine, Lambert and their children enjoying the peace that has settled over the valley.

3141. **Spiezia, Anthony.** *The lioness and the lambs.* **New York: Pageant Press, 1956. 235p.**

With the Civil War receding into the past and her husband dead, a widow faces the problem of supporting herself; the shipyards and shipping ventures in the Hudson River that her late husband had charge of become the focus of her managerial endeavors.

3142. **Spinell, Ruby, 1937- .** *Dies irae.* **Sag Harbor, N.Y.: Permanent Press, 1990. 208p.**

Set in a Catholic monastery outside of New York City. Sister Damian picks up the mail one day; included in it are three detached hands and feet. Jewish detective Eli Janah is called in to investigate the grisly situation. Eli has problems of his own, however; Mir, his Catholic wife, whom he deeply loves, leaps for her freedom to concentrate on her writing career and incidentally carries on an affair with Bishop Danley. Eli takes out his frustration on a woman who falls into his hands as he digs deeper into the case.

3143. **Spitzer, Marian.** *Who would be free.* **New York: Boni and Liveright, 1924. 319p.**

The heroine, Eleanor Hoffman, daughter of German-Jewish parents who cling to their privileged life in the Upper West Side of New York, is certain that her freedom is of prime importance. She cuts loose from the strictures of her traditional Jewish family-oriented mother and father and establishes her own artist's studio. The man whom first she loves dies in World War I; a new lover, Steve Sayre, enters the picture, but Eleanor decides against marrying him, prizing her independence above all.

3144. **Spivey, Thomas Sawyer, 1856-1938.** *Dr. Paul McKim.* **Illustrated by Glen Tracy. Washington, D.C.: Neale Pub. Co., 1908. 401p.**

Dr. Paul McKim is a physician in New York City who is suddenly informed that he is claimant to an English estate and title (duke). However, McKim has a double, a look-alike, who also puts in his claim for the property. Before the dilemma is solved, several female characters play their parts in the story and two romantic affairs are brought to promising conclusions.

3145. ———. *The Hoosier widow.* **Illustrated by Glen Tracy. Washington, D.C.: Neale Pub. Co., 1908. 294p.**

A lawyer prominent in the New York social scene has difficulties with a wife who refuses to break off some dubious relationships. She walks out on him and goes back to her mother. It is then that the lawyer takes on a new client, an Indiana woman who has recently arrived in New York. She had married a dying man and became a widow before any consummation took place. The two are drawn to one another and the novel tells how their love cuts through the thicket in which the lawyer has become entangled.

3146. **Spofford, Harriet Elizabeth Prescott, 1835-1921.** *The making of a fortune*; a **romance. With illus. by Alice Barber Stephens. New York: Harper, 1911. 113p.**

The wealthy Wall Street 'player', John Aversleigh, faces two perplexities. Firstly he wonders whether his young wife really loves him or whether she is clinging to him because of the costly presents with which he showers her. Secondly he is in a real financial bind; to get the money to tide him over he must steal his wife's rubies, worth a quarter of a million dollars. Fortunately Aversleigh's luck holds up and with the money realized from the sale of the gems he wins a fortune larger than that he earlier possessed. Ironically he discovers that his wife really loves him and that she was more than willing to give over all her possessions to help her husband through his crises.

3147. **Sprague, Gretchen, 1926- .** *Signpost to terror.* **New York: Dodd, Mead, 1967. 217p.**

Gail, a teenage girl hiking alone in the Adirondacks as a means of quelling her inner turmoil caused by a quarreling family, comes upon a fellow hiker, a young man named Lew. However, it is not too long before Gail is aware that Lew is no ordinary outdoorsman; as tension builds up between the two we are apprised that Lew is on the run following a bank robbery.

3148. **Springer, Mary Elizabeth.** *Elizabeth Schuyler*; a story of old New York.

New York: Press of L.H. Blanchard Co., 1903. 256p.

Despite the book's title Elizabeth, daughter of General Philip Schuyler and wife of Alexander Hamilton, is a less important character in this historical novel than her husband. Moreover the married life of Alexander Hamilton and Elizabeth Schuyler is covered with relative brevity. Actually the author seems more interested in following the course of the American Revolution and its aftermath, the career of Alexander Hamilton, and also introducing many secondary historical characters, men and women, who persevered in their quest for freedom from English rule.

3149.   *The Spuytenduyvel chronicle.* **New York: Livermore & Rudd, 1856. 318p.**

This novel follows the fortunes of the late Silas Page's family of New York City and Aiglemont, their country estate in Westchester County. The widow Maria Spuytenduyvel Page is determined that her three daughters and one son will be outstanding members of polite society, but they, in one way or another, undercut her wish. Dubious suitors besiege the daughters and Samuel Hyson, Mrs. Page's financial advisor, loses heavily in commercial ventures with the result that the Page income is greatly diminished. That fact leads to Mrs. Page becoming much less snobbish and accepting a farmer and a physician as future husbands for two of her daughters while the third is ready to 'come out' in society. The son, once a wastrel and a gambler, accepts employment with a transit company in Panama.

3150.   **Spyker, John Howland, pseud.** *Little lives.* **New York: Grosset & Dunlap, 1978. 215p.**

In a series of vignettes consisting anywhere from a few lines to five pages the author limns a large number of fictional characters who live (or lived) in a township of Upstate New York. To Spyker they are representative of 'the human condition north of Albany', with their idiosyncrasies, their aphorisms, vital statistics, sex habits, etc. "He has fine insight into the nature and behavior of the people" Library journal.

Squire, Frances, pseud. See: Potter, Frances Boardman Squire, 1867-1914.

3151.   **St. Clar, Robert.** *The metropolites*; or, *Know thy neighbor.* **A novel. New York: American News Co., 1864. 575p.**

A long, drawn-out piece of fiction whose hero, Nathan Trenk, of uncertain origin, is followed from his youth to early adulthood. Supplied by nebulous benefactors with adequate financial resources Nathan graduates from college and enters the law profession in New York City. He is drawn into fashionable social circles there, forming friendships with a coterie of gentlemen and young ladies. The story veers near mid-point to the American tropics in order to give background of the villainous Nicolas Sabina, one of Trenk's gentlemanly acquaintances. Back in New York Trenk's law practice is quite successful, yet poor investments endanger his livelihood. In the novel's closing pages Nathan Trenk is finally informed that he is actually the son of Lionel Gray who had died penniless and in disgrace. The elderly 'Lady Dowager', a towering figure in New York society, whom Lionel Gray had grievously wronged, makes Nathan her principal and residuary legatee.

3152. *St. George De Lisle*; or, *The serpent's sting*. A tale of woman's devotion & self-sacrifice. A true and thrilling narrative of crime in high life in the City of New York. Philadelphia: Barclay, 1858. 34p.

The year is 1856 and Adelaide De Lisle basks haughtily in the wake of her husband St. George De Lisle's supposedly strong financial and social position in New York City. However, De Lisle, a Wall Street figure, uses forgery to extricate himself from tremendous losses. He breaks down and tells Adelaide of his critical financial condition. She immediately takes charge and goes to Hudson, N.Y. to seek the help of her husband's two brothers and father. They pay off St. George's debts, but old Mr. De Lisle disowns St. George, and the latter's family sinks into poverty. George makes a trip back to Hudson, scene of his youth, and dies at his mother's gravesite when struck by a lightning bolt. The tale closes with Adelaide De Lisle barely holding her family together with the wages she earns from sewing.

3153. St. John, Robert Porter, b. 1869. *Jerusalem the Golden*; an historical novel of the Finger Lake country of New York. New York: P.H. Hitchcock, 1926. vi, 316p.

John Spaulding, the novel's narrator, is only 16 when he leaves behind in New Milford, Conn., the pretty young 'Jerie' Wilkinson, joins Morgan's Riflemen and takes part in General Sullivan's sweep through Iroquois country. Captured by Loyalist forces he escapes after several years to the border. John is studying law when he again meets Jerie who has metamorphosed into Jemima Wilkinson, the 'Public Universal Friend', a woman with a determination to establish a religious community in central New York State that is an odd combination of Shakerism and Quakerism. Spaulding helps Jemima settle in the Seneca-Keuka Lake region and tries in vain to convince her to marry him. The novel shifts to an account of Iroquois-American negotiations to fix the permanent status of western New York. In the end John and Jemima go their separate ways—he to leave the practice of law and return to New Milford and Jemima to develop an exceedingly small circle of religionists.

3154. St. Remy, Dirck. *Stories of the Hudson River counties*. New York: For the author [by] G.P. Putnam, c1871. 174p.

An expanded edition of the author's *Seven stories of the river counties* (Saratoga Springs: A.S. Baker, 1868). Contents: Polipel's Island.—Last of a generation.—The mystery of Danskammer.—A waif of the war.—Almost married.—Warden of Mahopac.—St. Antony's nose.—Gold underground.—The magician's daughter.

3154a. Staffel, Megan, 1952- . *The notebook of lost things*; a novel. New York: Soho

Press, 1999. 240p.

Helene Hugel had been brought to 'Paris', N.Y. by her now deceased mother Uta, a survivor of the bombing of Dresden in World War II. William Strick had sponsored them and Uta had become his lover. Helene is searching for stability in her life with a boyfriend, Harry, tagging along. She uncovers a journal that helps her sort out her mother's Dresden memories. A subplot deals with Stella Doyle, a young Mexican-American saddled with an obese, drunken mother.

3155. **Stagg, Clinton Holland, 1890-1916.** *Silver Sandals.* **Illus. by Will Foster. New York: W.J. Watt, 1916. 305p.**

An elderly gentleman accompanied by an equally aged old woman wearing silver sandals patronizes the Beaumonde, New York City's most expensive restaurant. In short order (no pun intended) it is discovered that the man, John Neilton, is dead, murdered actually (but perhaps with his own consent). Enter the blind sleuth Thornby Colton with his secretary Sydney Thames. Before Colton unmasks the murderer the story has encompassed several areas of the city, and the dead man's daughter, Ruth, her lover Philip Bracken, Manager Carl of the Beaumonde, 'Silver Sandals' (the name given to the woman with that footwear), et al., have to explain their involvement with the strange John Neilton. The latter kept a cryptogram (or map, according to Colton) that was the key to a treasure Neilton intended his daughter should have.

3156. **Stanley, Edward, 1903- .** *Thomas Forty*; **a novel. New York: Duell, Sloan & Pearce, 1947. 307p.**

"Historical novel about Westchester County during the Revolution. Thomas Forty, an ex-bound boy, is at first undecided about his side in the struggle, but an encounter in a New York tavern decided him—he is with the colonies. He becomes a lieutenant in Armand's Partizan Legion, and plays an important role in the Westchester part of the struggle to the end of the war"—Book review digest.

3157. **Stanley, Hiram Alonzo, b. 1859.** *The backwoodsman*; **the autobiography of a Continental on the New York frontier during the Revolution. New York: Doubleday, Page, 1904. viii, 371p.**

A novel of precarious existence in the Mohawk Valley as British, Tories, Indians and rebels contested control of the region, and especially of the formation of Sullivan's punitive expedition against the Iroquois villages of central New York. The hero, a backwoodsman, not unlike Robert W. Chambers' protagonist, Cardigan, in his book with that title (q.v.), serves as a scout for Sullivan's forces. Familiar historical figures who are prominent in the story are: Walter Butler (as usual, the primary villain), members of the Sir William Johnson family, Joseph Brant, and, of course, General John Sullivan.

3158. **Stanley, John Berchman, 1910- .** *Cadet Derby, West Pointer.* **New York: Dodd, Mead, 1950. viii, 276p.**

Cadet Derby evinces a measure of antagonism toward the (to him) rigid training required by the Military Academy; however, as the years pass, he begins to change his mind and contributes to the spirit of West Point by rising to the challenge of football stardom.

3159. **Stanley, Martha Melean Burgess, b. 1872.** *The souls of men.* **Illus. by Joseph Cummings Chase. New York: Dillingham, 1913. 353p.**
Dissatisfied with her life in Cuba's tobacco outback Beth Mannering leaves her husband Bob and goes to New York at the urging of a visiting gentleman from that city who is intrigued by Beth's remarkable voice. With his influence he gains entry for Beth to the New York stage; she achieves almost instant success. However, her benefactor demands his reward for all he has done for her, a price Beth is unwilling to pay. Fortuitously Beth worms her way out of the 'obligation' and returns to her husband's protective arms and ultimate contentment.

Stanton, Mary, 1947- . See under her pseudonym: Bishop, Claudia, 1947- .

Stark, Cordelia, supposed author. *The female wanderer.* **See note under Item #1109.**

3160. **Stark, Harriet.** *The bacillus of beauty.* **New York: F.A. Stokes, 1900. 340p.**
Entering Barnard College in New York City for the graduate study of biology, Helen Winship, an unprepossessing Midwesterner, is transformed into a striking young woman by Professor Darnstetter, discoverer of a bacillus that has physical beauty-creating properties. She becomes the center of attraction for a multitude of suitors, newspapers and magazines. The professor himself falls in love with Helen and is struck by a fatal heart attack when he attempts to lay hands on her. Helen soon wearies of all the attention, and in despair as her situation deteriorates, takes her own life.

Stark, Richard, pseud. See: Westlake, Donald E., 1933-

3161. **Starr, Jonathan.** *Grapevine.* **New York: Liveright, 1930. 169p.**
"The story of a crook and his pals, told in the vernacular of the New York underworld. The Kid's best friend is Harry the Dope, a White guy. They both work for the Boss. The Boss double-crosses Harry. But the 'grapevine', or chain of crooks, gunmen and police operates to save the Kid when he wreaks vengeance on the Boss"—Book review digest. The New York Times book review of June 29, 1930 states that the novel "gives a deft thumbnail sketch here and there of political corruption, law fixing and the machinations of a municipal underworld."

3161a. **Staub, Wendy Corsi, 1964- .** *All the way home.* **New York: Kensington Pub. Corp., 1999. 412p.**

Ten years before Rory Connolly returned (after her father's death) to her hometown, 'Lake Charlotte', N.Y., four girls had disappeared from that town. Rory is now taking care of her sister Molly and their mentally ill mother, but memories of the past persist. Emily Anghardt, Rory's best friend, and Carleen, Rory's older sister, had been among those vanished girls. Pregnant Michelle Randall currently occupies the Anghardt home. Molly is baby-sitting for Michelle's youngster Ozzie when Molly's friend Rebecca disappears, calling attention of startled Lake Charlotte residents to the old Anghardt house.

3162. **Steel, Kurt.** *Crooked shadow.* **Boston: Little, Brown, 1939. 311p.**
"Hank Hyers, the hard-boiled detective … [looks into] subversive activities and other high crimes and misdemeanors in Eckhart Zimmer's Americanische Bruderschaft, an organization operating out in 'Shelburne Township', L.I. The corpse is John Thompson, newspaper publisher and mayor of Shelburne, who had called the Bruders a bunch of gangsters and worse in 'The Clarion.' Oddly enough the Long Island authorities jail Orson Quick, Hank's redheaded chauffeur-factotum, who had been beaten by Green Shirts in Yorkville (Orson loves pretty Brook Lanson, niece of the deceased). It all makes a vigorous and timely yarn with quantities of dash and picturesque people—Willy Kunkelblutzen and others with suspicious names and origin"—New York herald tribune books.

3163. **Steere, Charles Allen, b. 1860.** *When things were doing.* **Chicago: C.H. Kerr, 1908. 282p.**
Former New York State Assemblyman Bill Tempest had a brief stay in Albany, for he was too upright to go along with some of the questionable, borderline ethical tactics indulged in by his colleagues. Back home in New York City a renowned socialist notifies him that he has been chosen president of the Socialist Strategy Board. Without further ado the socialists take over New York City and exert their power throughout the civilized world. Tempest has a startling vision of being near death in a railroad accident when he suddenly wakes up in his own bed and discovers that he has been dreaming.

Stein, Aaron Marc, 1906-1985. See under his pseudonym: Stone, Hampton.

3164. **Stein, David Lewis, 1937- .** *The Golden Age hotel*; **a novel. Toronto: Macmillan of Canada, 1985. 237p.**
After losing most of their money in a bad business deal promoted by Stan's son, Lilly and Stan Monteith open a residential inn for senior citizens on Long Island and call it the Golden Age Hotel. Among their guests are some rather odd residents: Faygie, an old tart estranged from her daughter; the 'Dutchess', a psychologist who failed in understanding her own husband; Sally, the object of Nate's affection despite drifting into sloughs of mental depression; Benny Longo who is traumatized after a heart attack.

3165. **Stein, Sol, 1926- .** *The childkeeper.* **New York: Harcourt Brace Jovanovich, 1975. 211p.**

After a promotion at his bank Roger Maxwell moves out of New York City to the suburbs with his wife and four children. During a long weekend at his new home Roger discovers some unpleasant truths about his offspring. If it had not been obvious before, Roger is now aware that his children are self-centered, mean, sadistic and scheming. They have invited a number of their peers to the suburban house, among them a 19-year-old Black fellow who deals in drugs and carries a switchblade. Roger is suddenly placed in confrontation with the drug dealer and is compelled to take extreme measures in self-defense.

3166. **————.** *The magician*; a novel. **New York: Delacorte Press, 1971. 258p.**

Ed Japhet, 16, of Ossining, New York, prides himself on his accomplishments as an amateur magician, but for some reason a classmate named Urek batters him and Ed is hospitalized. Urek walks into the hospital and tries to kill Ed. A smart criminal lawyer, Thomasay, gains acquittal for Urek who then proceeds to assault Ed once more; the latter uses his beginner's knowledge of karate and kills his assailant. The police arrive on the scene along with Ed's father who immediately contacts Thomasay to defend his son.

3167. **Stein, Toby, 1935- .** *Only the best*; a novel. **New York: Arbor House, 1984. 383p.**

Charlotte Hudson is almost 40; she has had a relatively trouble-free existence in the affluent 'Five Towns' of Long Island. However, several problems are beginning to mar her tranquility—her husband is carrying-on with another woman; her son has been hit by the odd-ball religion bug; Charlotte has to confront the vexatious enigmas of her first marriage and the sudden awakening of her own passions.

3168. **Steiner, Edward Alfred, 1866-1956.** *The mediator*; a tale of the Old World and the New. **New York, Chicago: F.H. Revell, 1907. 356p.**

The hero, Samuel Cohen, is a Jewish boy who converts to Catholicism in the Old World, but then abandons it after witnessing a pogrom committed by Russian Christians. He comes to America and preaches Christ's love to Jew and Gentile on New York's Lower East Side. He has allies in the philanthropists Mr. and Mrs. Bruce. There is disagreement over the Bruces' insistence on 'Christianizing' their audience, but by the novel's conclusion Samuel marries the Bruces' daughter and is the mediating influence between the different cultures and religions.

3169. **Stephens, Ann Sophia, 1813-1886.** *Fashion and famine.* **New York: Bunce & Brother, 1854. 420p.**

Mid-19th century New York City, with its contrast of the desperately poor and the fashionable rich, is the scene of Mrs. Stephens' rather sensational and ultimately sentimental tale whose prime movers are the vicious William Leicester and his estranged wife Ada. Mr. Leicester, a forger and bigamist at the least, is a charmer and manipulator who comes to an untimely and mysterious end (was his stabbing death accidental or self-inflicted, or was it murder?). However, Ada Leicester, torn between hate and love for the man she fled from years ago, is finally able to piece together the fragments of her selfish, disrupted life, to reunite with her parents (under tragic circumstances) and with a deserted daughter.

3170. ————. *Henry Longford*; or, *The forged will*. **A tale of New York City. Boston: F. Gleason at the Flag of Our Union Office, 1847. 50p.**

The prominent New York lawyer James J. Woodville owes his position in large part to the money he received from a will he forged with the complicity of Doctor Elijah Smith and the pawnbroker Elmendorf. The client, whose family Woodville cheated out of their rightful inheritance, was Henry Longford, Sr. The latter's son, Henry Junior, given employment in Woodville's office, is fired on trumped-up charges by the lawyer when Mary Woodville, his daughter, refuses to accept her father's choice for her fiancé, and declares her preference for Henry Longford. Languishing in poverty Henry is revivified by Mr. Montague, an acquaintance of his father who has obtained a confession from Doctor Smith of his and Woodville's perfidy. Woodville tells Mary of his misdeed and flees the country. Henry Longford and other members of his family finally receive their rightful inheritance and Henry marries the lawyer's innocent daughter.

3171. ————. *High life in New York*, **by Jonathan Slick, Esq. [pseud.] of Weathersfield, Connecticut. A series of letters to Mr. Zephariah Slick, Justice of the Peace, and deacon of the church over to Weathersfield, in the State of Connecticut. Philadelphia: Peterson, 1854. 299p.**

Jonathan, a bachelor onion farmer, comes to New York to seek a market for his produce. He hits upon the device of getting a letter to his father published in the New York Express, saving postage and acquiring some notoriety thereby. Urged to submit more letters to the paper, he complies and becomes a personality much in demand by the social arbiters of the city. Jonathan describes in his own dialect his journey from total naiveté to an acceptable level of sophistication. The people he meets do little to change Jonathan's opinion about the pretensions and hypocrisies that riddle the New York social scene. In the end Jonathan exits from New York after a woman he is attracted to and her 'brother' (actually her husband) strip him of his money and property. Captain Doolittle, a friend from Connecticut, helps Jonathan recover most of his losses. A 2-volume edition appeared in London (Printed for J. How) in 1844. Abbreviated editions appeared in New York in 1843 and 1845.

3172. ————. *The Indian queen*. **New York: Beadle and Adams, 1864. 112p. (Beadle's new dime novels. Old series, no. 507).**

A romance of life among the Seneca Indians of New York State. An earlier work by Stephens published under the title: The Indian princess in 1863

(100p. Beadle's new dime novels, 194) which the compiler has not seen, may be a separate work or the same as the above with a slight change in title.

3173. ————. *Mabel's mistake.* **Philadelphia: T.B. Peterson, 1868. 431p.**

Much of this moody, semi-gothic tale takes place in a mansion not far from New York City. The Hudson River plays a role at the beginning and end of the story. Zillah, a servant of mixed white and Negro blood, who had been the General's mistress and borne him a child, vehemently hates General Harrington's second wife, Mabel Crawford Harrington. Ralph Harrington, Mabel's son by the General, loves Lina French, adopted daughter of Mabel and the General. Lina's tutor, Agnes Barker, is in love with Ralph and seeks ways to win him for a husband. James Harrington, the elder son of the General by his first wife, is secretly in love with his father's second wife. Zillah falsely claims Lina as the daughter she bore the general. Bin Benson, an elderly Hudson riverman, proves Lina to be his deceased sister's child. In her jealously Zillah accidentally murders the General, sinks into madness and is confined to a lunatic asylum on Blackwell's Island, New York City. After further surprising revelations the novel concludes happily for the remaining chief characters.

3174. ————. *Malaeska, the Indian wife of the White Hunter.* **New York: Beadle, 1863. 126p.**

The hunter William Danforth is killed in a war between Indians and settlers in the Catskills fomented by Danforth's slaying of an Indian in self-defense. He leaves behind a widow, Malaeska, daughter of an Iroquois chief, and an infant son. Before he dies Danforth enjoins Malaeska to go to his people rather than her own. She takes her son to the home of William's father, John Danforth, in New York City. Malaeska is relegated to a subordinate, servant-like place in the household; her son is reared as one of their own by the Danforths. John Danforth never tells William, Jr. that Malaeska is his mother; William is taught to despise Indians. An attempt by Malaeska to take her son to Upstate New York is intercepted by Danforth. Sarah Jones, daughter of an old friend of the deceased hunter, befriends Malaeska, the latter now living in the forest near the Jones residence. Some years later while going to school in New York, Sarah falls in love with William. Bringing him to her family Sarah urges William to meet Malaeska. The revelation by Malaeska of her motherhood is a devastating blow to William. This novel was ostensibly the first of the dime novels in the Beadle Library. It was reprinted in 1929 by John Day Co., New York (xvi, 254p.).

3175. ————. *The old homestead.* **New York: Bunce, 1855. 435p.**

The first part of this novel is an indictment of New York City's social conditions, its disregard for the poor, yet hard-working occupants of its tenements. Mary Fuller's father dies and her drunken mother ends up in prison. The policeman, John Chester, and his wife take Mary into their home, but both of the Chesters die tragically. The widow of the mayor of New York

City brings their children to the countryside. Mary lodges with a poor farmer and his sister. The second part of the story focuses on rural life, which, hard as it is, offers more hope than the beckoning city.

3176. **Stephens, Robert Neilson, 1867-1906.** *The continental dragoon*; a love-story of Philipse Manor-House in 1778. **Illustrated by H.C. Edwards. Boston: L.C. Page, 1898. 299p.**

New York State in the American Revolution is the scene of this historical novel, with particular reference to the famous Philipse Manor House in Yonkers. It is there that Elizabeth Philipse meets Henry Peyton, officer and standard-bearer of the First Continental Dragoons. The soldier, in between his military responsibilities, woos Elizabeth, a Tory like her father. The novel's characters are chiefly actual historical figures prominent in Westchester County, e.g., the Delanceys, Van Courtlandts, Philipses, et al.

3177. ⸻. *The mystery of Murray Davenport*; a story of New York at the present day. **Illustrated by H.C. Edwards. Boston: L.C. Page, 1903. 312p.**

The protagonist is Murray Davenport, a playwright and book illustrator, and a person of undoubted talent who has been the victim of ill fortune. The plot hinges upon Davenport's resolve to turn his life around by changing his identity and correcting, regardless of legalities, an injustice foisted upon him. The Saturday review of books and art of the New York Times of May 9, 1903 has this to say about the author's use of New York City as the scene of his novel: "Mr. Stephens is particular to seek verisimilitude in careful descriptions of familiar neighborhoods. He aims to reproduce the bustle and excitement of New York, its architecture, its manners, and its customs. The well-appointed flat, the boarding house, the hotel, the pseudo-Bohemian café, the chophouse, the waterside neighborhood are all recognizable."

3178. ⸻. *Philip Winwood*. **Illustrated by E.W.D. Hamilton. Boston: L.C. Page, 1900. 412p.**

The novel's subtitle is: 'A sketch of the domestic history of an American captain in the War of Independence: embracing events that occurred between and during the years 1763 and 1786 in New York and London; written by his enemy in war, Herbert Russell, lieutenant in the Loyalist forces, and told anew by Robert N. Stephens'. "The wife of a patriot is courted by a British officer and takes the Loyalist side, while he fights for the Americans. The British occupation of New York, warfare in the Mohawk Valley, and the fate of the Loyalists after Yorktown figure in the story"—Klein, M.M. *New York in the American Revolution.*

3179. **Stephenson, Henry Thew, 1870-1957.** *Patroon Van Volkenberg*; a tale of old Manhattan in the year sixteen hundred & ninety-nine. **Illustrated by C.M. Relyea. Indianapolis: Bowen-Merrill Co., 1900. 360p.**

There seems to be little hope of a meeting of minds between the Governor, the Earl of Bellamont (or Bellomont) and Van Volkenberg, spokesman for the commercial interests of the city and colony. The latter are for unrestricted wide-open trade in all its manifestations and that includes making deals with the pirates who comb the Atlantic for prizes. Bellamont has a lot of support from the general public when he closes the New York ports to entry by the ships of the buccaneers. The fact is that a number of businessmen put money into ships manned by questionable seamen (freebooters, to be sure). Under these circumstances was a satisfactory resolution possible?

3180. **Sterling, Charles F.** *Buff and blue*; or, *The privateers of the revolution*. **A tale tale of Long Island Sound. New York: W.H. Graham, 1847. 128p.**

Ned Wilton and Melville (a.k.a. Jack) Marlow are American privateers who harass British shipping on Long Island Sound during the American Revolution; they must also deal harshly with pirates who attack both British and American vessels. The heroines, Katrina Vandeveer and her cousin Ethel Grosvenor, are patriots, even though Katrina's father, professing neutrality, supplies the British with victuals. Ned and Jack upset the plans of devious Mr. Colby to marry off his ward, Ethel, to British Major Lipscombe to whom he owes a large sum of money. Even in 19th century potboilers villains of the caliber of Mr. Colby do not invariably get their just desserts. After the war's end Colby becomes a prominent politician in New York City.

3181. **Stern, Edith Mendel, 1901-1975.** *Purse strings*. **New York: Boni & Liveright, 1927. 285p.**

"Draws the life of a certain section of New York society … with an incisive stroke. Stanley Jackson, a young man of lively intelligence and sensitive tastes but rather dissolute habits, marries the daughter of a wealthy but offensively bourgeois family. Being unequipped to earn money himself, he is forced by his father's action in disinheriting him to accept aid from his wife's family and to endure their criticism and disapproval. All his own plans for solving his financial difficulties fail miserably. He endures bitter years of the scorn of persons whom he feels to be his cultural inferiors, forced, at the same time, to accept their grudging assistance. He is finally rescued by an ample legacy from his father, which restores to him everything except his youth and happiness"—New York herald tribune books.

Stern, Elizabeth Gertrude Levin, 1889 or 90-1954, joint author. *A friend at court*. **See Item #3182.**

3182. **Stern, Leon Thomas, b. 1887.** *A friend at court*, **by Leo Stern and Elizabeth Gertrude Stern. New York: Macmillan, 1923. x, 335p.**

The authors have fictionalized in twenty short stories cases involving domestic relations primarily that were presented before the New York City courts. Mary Ellen Wright is a probation officer, the 'friend at court', i.e. she has heard both sides of the dispute and undertakes to negotiate between the disputants and hopefully get them to come to a settlement out of court. While she is performing her duties in this area, Mary is also having a romantic affair of her own to settle.

3183. Stern, Philip Van Doren, 1900-1984. *The thing in the brook*, **by Peter Storme [pseud.]. New York: Simon and Schuster, 1937. viii, 309p.**

When the State Police fail in their investigation of the murder of a local farmer, James Whitby, assistant professor of biology at State University (located at some distance form New York City) asks his friend, amateur sleuth Henry Hale, to work with him on the case. These two nonprofessional 'detectives' are up to the task (despite police discomfort at their 'interference'), but not before two other local figures have their lives terminated by the murderer.

3184. Stern, Richard Martin, 1915- . *Cry havoc.* **New York: Scribner, 1963. 184p.**

"A small community ['Rockville' in Upstate New York is] beset by fear after the wife of a prominent lawyer is criminally attacked in her home by an unknown man. The community would look no further for the rapist than a nearby and resented [Nike] installation. But a sane police captain [Sam Walter] and an equally intelligent military commander do not permit panic to erupt. Nor does Mr. Stern permit any artificial plot manipulations to sully his absorbing story"—New York herald tribune books.

3185. ⸺. *These unlucky deeds.* **New York: Scribner, 1961 [c1960]. 248p.**

A Hudson River village in 'Quidnunc' County numbers among its residents a large number of commuters to New York City who are inclined to lord it over the long-term inhabitants of the community. Roz Warren, a scheming, power-seeking individual, is a leading figure in the village; when she is suddenly 'done in', some would suggest that she was asking for it.

3186. Sterner, Lawrence. *The un-Christian Jew.* **New York: Neale Pub. Co., 1917. 307p.**

Simeon Sachs, managing director of Cosmopolitan Bargaining Stores and president of the Orthodox Jewish Temple B'Nai-Israel in New York, is shocked by young Rabbi Cordova's mention of Jesus Christ in a sermon and his condemnation of the poverty-level wages offered by too many Jewish and Christian businessmen. Ejected from the Temple, Cordova establishes a Utopian community, 'Quality Town' in or near the Catskills where fair treatment of workers is the standard and where traditional Judaism and Christianity are set aside in favor of what Cordova interprets as Christ's true teachings. Sachs is horrified when his beloved daughter Rachel joins Cordova. Fragile Margaret Olsen dies from overwork in Sachs's store. Her brother Tom, seeking revenge, lures Rachel, who has fallen in love with him, to Russia and demeaning labor in a sweatshop. Rachel's patience shames Tom. After he dies Rachel slips away from Russia, returns to New York, and then to Quality Town, now a smoldering ruin after being firebombed by hirelings of vicious Christian businessmen. Rachel and Cordova visualize the rebuilding of Quality Town.

3187.   **Stevens, Isaac Newton, 1858-1920.** *An American suffragette*; a novel. New York: W. Rickey, 1911. 248p.

Dr. John Earl, famous physician and experimenter with 'mental therapeutics', returns to New York City from India to marry socialite Leonora Kimball. But he finds himself drawn inexorably to feminist Silvia Holland, lawyer and militant suffragette. Earl and Ms. Holland collaborate in caring for Mrs. Bell's injured daughter; their frequent meetings on the girl's behalf arouses the jealousy of Dr. Orrin Morris, an ambitious surgeon who hopes to win Silvia's hand. When Mrs. Bell is murdered, circumstantial evidence points to Dr. Earl as the culprit—rumor has it that Earl and Mrs. Bell may have been lovers. Earl is cleared when an accusatory letter Mrs. Bell had addressed to Silvia Holland, but never mailed, is found in a coat pocket. The letter, implicating Orrin Morris as Mrs. Bell's former lover, is read at Earl's trial (Silvia is his defense attorney) and Earl is released. Leonora Kimball goes her own way and a closer union between John Earl and Silvia Holland is a certainty.

3188.   **Stevenson, Burton Egbert, 1872-1962.** *The girl with the blue sailor.* New York: Dodd, Mead, 1906. 310p.

Jack Sheldon, a bachelor and journalist based in New York City, takes a long vacation at a Catskill resort where he meets an old, just-married friend, Harry Agens, and the four daughters of a vacationing couple, the Roberts. He recalls 'the girl with the blue sailor' whom he saw on the train and is pleasantly surprised when she, Dorothy Merton, turns up at the resort as a guest of the Roberts. Although Sheldon had been spending many agreeable hours with Cecil Roberts, oldest of the four daughters, he is now more frequently in the company of Miss Merton. A budding romance between these two does not progress very far, for Sheldon is called upon to serve as foreign correspondent during the Boer War. Upon his return to New York Sheldon makes a declaration of love—not to the girl in the blue sailor but to….

3189.   ————. *The gloved hand*; a detective story. With illus. by Thomas Fogarty. New York: Dodd, Mead, 1913. 343p.

Godfrey, the reporter, formerly a detective in the New York City Police Department, again teams up with his friend Lester, the lawyer, to investigate the mysterious murder of Worthington Vaughan in his Bronx home. Vaughan's interest in Eastern religions had led him to shelter a yogi and his servant who are endeavoring to take control of Vaughan's daughter. Godfrey and Lester are especially interested in this case because their good friend, Fred Swain, has been accused of murdering Vaughan. This story was first published serially in Popular Magazine under the title: The mind master.

3190.   ————. *The house next door*; a detective story. New York: Dodd, Mead, 1932. 313p.

"Phillip Verity, formerly professor of Oriental philosophy at Columbia, is found dead in his home at Mount Vernon [New York] with a fracture of the odontoid process of the axis (neck broken) just as he was about to change the old will that left everything to his daughter Janet (Barnard). One of his neighbors is Emilio Carnevali, an antique dealer 'with the look of plumpness so many middle-aged Italians have' and maybe a seducer of the worst type. Another is Mr. Chunder, a connoisseur of Hindu objets d'art and a religious leader who probably possesses idols and goodness knows what. So, naturally, Janet is abducted and it is up to Walter Challis, her fiancé, to get her back. Meanwhile, our lawyer-narrator, Sleuth Simmonds, Chief Jenkins, Coroner Bernstein, and Godfrey of the 'Record' search for the stolen document, find the hairpin and otherwise disport themselves among some not very keen suspects"—New York herald tribune books.

3191. ————. *The Marathon mystery*; a story of Manhattan. With five scenes in color by Eliot Keen. New York: H. Holt, 1904. vi, 323p.

Murder is committed in the 'Marathon', an apartment house in New York City, and circumstantial evidence points to a well-bred young woman as the culprit. While the police are searching for more clues, another homicide occurs and this time the young woman's boy friend is implicated. Among the cast of characters in the apartment is one person suspected of vampire proclivities.

3192. ————. *The mystery of the Boule cabinet*; a detective story. With illus. by Thomas Fogarty. New York: Dodd, Mead, 1912. 362p.

"A lively mystery story in which a New York detective and an invincible French criminal of the Arsène Lupin type match imagination and resourcefulness. A Louis Fourteenth cabinet is bought by a New York connoisseur [Philip Valentine] with tragic results. Three individuals including the buyer himself are one after another unaccountably stricken before it, each revealing upon examination two tiny incisions on the back of the right hand with evidence of bitter almond poisoning. The contents of the cabinet, the deadly contrivance that had been set to guard its secrets, and the clever brain that lay back of the device, furnish the strategical points that are attacked in the course of the attempt—for it proved only an attempt—to outwit 'Crochard L'Invincible'"—Book review digest. Geoffrey a reporter, and Lester, a lawyer, are instrumental in the mystery's solution.

3193. Stevenson, James, 1929- . *Do yourself a favor, kid*. New York: Macmillan, 1962. 115p.

Young journalist Tim Kirk is in the Catskills on a four-day assignment to get a story on a shy, star Black basketball player, Beanpole Baker, seven and a half feet tall. Tim ends up at Manny's Country Club, a resort that employs Beanpole as a bellhop. The novella aptly describes the fast-paced activity that typifies a large Catskill haven for vacationers.

3194. Stevenson, Richard, 1938- . *Ice blues.* **New York: St. Martin's Press, 1986. 212p.**

Jack Lenihan had left a letter for the Albany-based gay private detective, Don Strachey, asking him to deliver a large sum of money to Albany's Reform Party. Lenihan's corpse was in Strachey's car and the laundered cash had disappeared. To recover the stolen funds the detective flies to the West Coast for needed information and returns to Albany in time to snatch the money back. Meanwhile the killer thieves had taken Timothy Callahan, Jack's live-in companion for ransom. Jack is forced into reckless, desperate actions to turn the situation around in his favor.

3195. ————. *On the other hand, death;* **a Donald Strachey murder mystery. New York: St. Martin's Press, 1984. 216p.**

Albany, N.Y.'s, gay shamus, Donald Strachey, doesn't like the employer—but he likes the assignment—when he's hired to look into vandalistic death threats against grandmotherly lesbian activist Dorothy Fisher. The employer? Millpond Plaza Associates, a small building company which has been pressuring Mrs. Fisher to sell them her property. Is Millpond behind the harassment? Apparently not. So Strachey talks to a couple of Dorothy's neighbors—who will benefit financially if she sells up. Then the case gets even nastier: gay poet Peter Greco, one of Dorothy's houseguests, is kidnapped, with a $100,000 ransom demanded. And, after some tedious kidnap negotiation filler, he'll turn up dead—just as gay activist Fenton McWhirter (Greco's lover and another houseguest) is likewise kidnapped. … [There are] neat glimpses of Albany offered [by the author]"—Kirkus reviews.

3196. ————. *Shock to the system;* **a Donald Strachey mystery. New York: St. Martin's Press, 1995. 183p.**

An Albany, New York psychologist, Dr. Crockwell, asserts it is his duty to restore to 'normalcy' those homosexuals who want to change their sexual orientation. Donald Strachey, a gay private investigator, confronts Crockwell especially after one of Crockwell's patients, Paul Haig, dies. Haig's ex-boyfriend, Larry, could be a very likely suspect if Haig's death was a homicide and not a suicide (the police theory). Haig's alcoholic mother would like to pin the killing on Larry. Strachey gets contradictory pleas from all parties involved to disentangle the confusion or to mind his own business.

3197. ————. *Third man out.* **New York: St. Martin's Press, 1992. 216p.**

Gay private investigator of Albany, N.Y., Donald Strachey, is dubious about the fears of his client John Rutka, who specializes in forcing establishment figures to 'come out of the closet' and announce their homosexuality. Rutka has insisted that his life is in danger and he does end up a murder victim. Strachey begins to realize that there is a long list of potential killers. He combs Rutka's files and finds data that singles out one especially malevolent homosexual whom Rutka has not brought out into the open.

3198. **Stewart, Donald, 1932- .** *Crow*; **a novel. Garden City, N.Y.: Doubleday, 1959. 286p.**

Thrown together on an unproductive parcel of Upstate New York land, farmer Myron Greenhalgh and his wife; a lonely boy from the city; and John Dietche, a parolee on the run, are victims of their own selfishness, fear, egotism and folly.

3199. **Stiles, Pauline.** *Cloud by day.* **Garden City, N.Y.: Doubleday, Doran, 1929. 284p.**

"Stephen was a gifted youth of American birth and continental upbringing. When he married Jeanne, who had been engaged to George Manton before Stephen came into her life, he had prospects of a substantial fortune. But two years later, penniless, the young couple arrived in New York. Stephen's pride prevented his asking George for help. Unequipped for the struggle by birth or training, the two young people begin their battle for existence in an indifferent, unfriendly New York till chance brings George into their lives again"—Book review digest.

3200. **Stimson, Alexander Lovett, b. 1816.** *A tale of Easy Nat*; **or,** *The three apprentices.* **A tale of life in New York and Boston, but 'adapted to any meridian.' With original drawings by McLenan, engraved by N. Orr. New York: J.C. Derby, 1854. 465p.**

"In the three printer's apprentices, Edwin Fairbanks, Nathan Mudge and Thomas Braxton, the author has portrayed three kinds of youth—the first, a lad of 'correct' principles, industrious habits and ambition to excel as a good citizen—the second, 'a real good-hearted boy', but full of fun and conviviality, and easily led astray by his fellow apprentice, Thomas Braxton, whose precocity is vice and low indulgences we see paralleled daily in the conduct of numerous half-grown men about town"—Preface. John Hard, a Massachusetts farmer, plays a leading role as he strives to save Nathan ('Easy Nat') from the gallows for a crime actually committed by Braxton. Easy Nat is saved at the last minute and reunited with his wife Kate. New York City's Five Points plays an important role in the novel when various good people rescue several of its denizens from the grinding poverty of the area.

3201. **Stimson, Frederic Jesup, 1855-1943.** *The crime of Henry Vane*; **a study with a moral. New York: Scribner, 1884. 206p.**

Henry Vane is smitten by Miss Baby Thomas, a New York social butterfly, and he anxiously awaits her assent to his proposal of a binding commitment. When she summarily rebuffs him, Henry suffers severe depression and finally commits suicide—and that is 'the crime of Henry Vane.' The author treats New York society satirically.

3202. ———. *First harvests*; **an episode in the life of Mrs. Levison Gower. A satire without a moral. By F.J. Stimson (J.S. of Dale). New York: Scribner,**

1888. ix, 468p.

"The author describes the present conditions of American business social and business life as the 'first harvests' of the virgin soil of American freedom. ... The picture drawn of the leaders of society, their aims and ambitions, their ingrained selfishness and self-indulgence of businessmen and their methods, of workingmen, their wrongs and dangerous ignorance, is a scathing arraignment of society as it exists today, notably in New York City. The lawyer's training shows in the nice choice of words to convey fine shades of irony and wit. There is an overtone of hope and faith"—Annual American catalogue.

3203. ————. *My story*; **being the memoirs of Benedict Arnold, late major general in the Continental Army and brigadier-general in that of His Britannic Majesty, by F.J. Stimson (J.S. of Dale). New York: Scribner, 1917. viii, 622p.**

A novel that "purports to be the life story of Benedict Arnold, written by his own hand, with the purpose of justifying his career to the eyes of the British King. Events of his public and private life are closely followed. He is represented as a Tory by nature, an aristocrat with no understanding of the more democratic aims of the Revolution. To see the colonies self-governing under the British King was from the beginning his ideal, and the alliance with the British which has branded him as traitor appears to have been partly motivated by a desire to bring about this end"—Book review digest. The first half of the book takes Arnold (after a few pages on his birth and New England childhood) to the beginning of the Revolution and his participation from Ticonderoga to the Canadian campaign and Saratoga. About 70 pages are devoted to the West Point affair. The concluding sections of the novel find Arnold in British service in Philadelphia, New York City, etc., to his last years in London and death in 1801.

3204. **Stockenberg, Antoinette. *Dream a little dream*. New York: St. Martin's Press, 1997. 354p.**

An Upstate New York town contains a showplace called Fair Castle that has been the home for three generations of MacLeishes. From England appears William Braddock, Lord Norwood, to purchase the Castle for removal to England; after all he was its former owner. Elinor MacLeish proudly refuses to sell Fair Castle. Various weird manifestations occur and Tucker O'Tool, an historian, starts digging into William Braddock's family secrets. Evidently Tucker is intent on ruining William, although Elinor cannot discern why.

3205. **Stockton, Frank Richard, 1834-1902. *The associate hermits*. With illus. by A.B. Frost. New York: Harper, 1899. 257p.**

"The novel deals with the adventures of a middle-aged gentleman and his wife, who take their daughter's wedding journey by proxy, in order to permit the newly married couple to enjoy all the comforts of home during their honeymoon. Their trip lands them in an Adirondack camp, where they find

823

themselves entrusted with the care of a young maiden, the daughter of a friend, whose attractions are such that all the young unmarried men in the vicinity fall in love with her. As a possible relief from the rigors of the situation, they welcome an idea of a sister of one of the numerous lovers, and at her instigation they form an association of hermits, all dwelling together, but each working out in his own way his own individual inclinations"—Annual American catalogue.

3206. ————. *The hundredth man.* **New York: Century Co., 1887. 432p.**
The scene shifts between a country farm and a New York restaurant managed by a proprietor who aims to keep himself incognito. "It had come to Horace Stratford that in every hundred books on a kindred subject, in every hundred events of a like nature, and in every hundred men who may come within one's cognizance, there is one book, crime, circumstance, or man which stands above and distinct from the rest, preeminent in the fact that no one of the others is or could have been like it. Horace Stratford's immediate occupation was the discovery of a hundredth man among his present friends and associates. ... The heroine has profited by the higher education of women. Unselfishness is the distinguishing characteristic of the hundredth man. Mr. Stratford discovers him nearer home than he had looked for him"—Annual American catalogue.

3207. **Stockton, John P.** *Zaphra*; **a story of to-day. Boston: Arena Pub. Co., 1894. 95p.**
Zaphra Offerman, a daughter of privilege, is disturbed by the abject poverty she sees on New York City's East Side. Brother Joseph (an Anglican priest?) finds her sharing the life of the poor; but she is ailing and has been placed in a home for the destitute. His plea to mercenary Dr. Moneybones to tend her goes unheeded. Some time later, after Zaphra has returned to her parents' residence, Mr. Offerman gives a dinner at which the doctor, Brother Joseph, Zaphra and distinguished guests are present. Dr. Moneybones, confronted by Zaphra and Brother Joseph, confesses to his uncharitable acts, but attributes them to the baleful influence of an evil alter ego. Zaphra, with the help of her father, Brother Joseph, et al. founds a 'society for ameliorating the condition of the laboring classes.' Dr. Moneybones gives up his lucrative practice and devotes himself to the medical needs of the society. Zaphra's 'Bible' is Jacob Riis's 'How the Other Half Lives.' Psychic phenomena make their impress on the leading personages in the tale.

3208. **Stoddard, William Osborn, 1835-1925.** *The battle of New York*; **a story for all young people. New York: Appleton, 1892. 248p.**
"The Draft Riots, which occurred in New York City, July, 1863, are the culminating scenes in a story of a most exciting period. The young heroes are a Southern boy, who is playing the spy between General Lee and traitors in New York City who only wait an opportunity to betray the government, and a Northern boy who is selling newspapers to help his mother while his father is

at the front. The boys fraternize during the days New York City is in the hands of a mob … The Southern boy's experience at Gettysburg is a vivid piece of description—Annual American catalogue.

3209. ————. *The captain's boat.* **New York: Merriam Co., 1894. 272p.**
The protagonists of the story are two boys who live in a small town on Long Island. They become fast friends, fishing and sailing the waters off Long Island, and joining in a couple of rescue efforts that bring gratifying diversity into their lives. One of their acquaintances is Captain Vrooman, proprietor of a museum whose chief display item is the 'captain's boat', actually a lifeboat with a fascinating story behind it.

3210. ————. *Chris the model-maker*; **a story of New York. With illus. by B. West Clinedinst. New York: Appleton, 1894. iii, 287p.**
"Chris Huyler is a lame boy full of talent; the story of his career, with that of his friends, is rich in suggestion and inspiration. The story takes place in a house in one of the old streets in the lower part of New York City. Mr. Gerichten, who owns the shop in which Chris works, was once an officer in a Polish regiment; his daughter, the heroine, is passionately fond of music and yearns for culture"—Annual American catalogue.

3211. ————. *Chuck Purdy*; **the story of a New York boy. Boston: D. Lothrop Co., 1890. 318p.**
"Presents an almost photographic reproduction of the New York boy of today—not the impossible creation of romance, but a real, live, active, inquiring, go-ahead New York boy, who goes to school and helps in his father's grocery-store, and goes crabbing in the Harlem [River], and sees and studies and stores his mind with practical, helpful, odd and entertaining studies of life in the great metropolis that make a boy of him and will surely make a man of him"—Annual American catalogue.

3212. ————. *Crowded out o' Crofield*; **or, *The boy who made his way.* New York: Appleton, 1890. 261p.**
'Crofield', New York, the hometown of Jack Ogden, the 15-year-old son of a blacksmith, offered little in the way of variety or employment, so Jack made up his mind to put the village behind him. On the way to New York City he fell into a number of adventures that continued when he finally landed in the big city. It was a learning experience for the boy from lethargic Crofield.

3213. ————. *Dab Kinzer*; **story of a growing boy. New York: Scribner, 1881. vi, 321p.**
Dabney ('Dab') Kinzer lives with his widowed mother and four sisters on a farm a half-mile from the Great South Bay of Long Island. Although only fifteen Dab exhibits talents and qualities that indicate he can serve as a role model for the recently arrived 'city' boy, Ford Foster, and Dick Lee, a bright Black lad, whose family descended from slaves held by the early Dutch

settlers of Long Island. Dab leads the other boys on fishing and crabbing sorties, brings them home safely after battling the elements while yachting in dangerous Long Island waters, and rescues Ford's sister Annie from an attack by a thieving tramp. After several other adventures the story concludes with the boys at Grantley Academy in New England, Dick Lee among them, for Dab, his peers and their families ignore the color bar that was still so prevalent in the America of the late 1800s.

3214. ————. *The fight for the valley*; a story of the siege of Fort Schuyler and the Battle of Oriskany in the Burgoyne campaign of 1777. New York: D. Appleton, 1904. vi, 250p.

Through the adventures of the fictional Brom Roosevelt, a patriotic lad who serves as courier between the American forces in Fort Schuyler (better known as Fort Stanwix)—besieged by St. Leger and his British regulars, Tories and Indians—the militia under General Herkimer, and the troops of General Philip Schuyler (poised to block Burgoyne's army), the author yields a quite comprehensive account of the events mentioned in the book's subtitle. Stoddard purports to have interpreted and translated a number of Dutch sources in order to achieve a degree of historical accuracy in his novel. Presumably intended for a young audience the story is worthy of adult perusal. A large proportion of the characters are historical figures: e.g., Herkimer and Schuyler, Benedict Arnold, Marinus Willett, Barry St. Leger, Joseph Brant, Peter Gansevoort, et al.

3215. ————. *Guert Ten Eyck*; a hero story. Illus. by F.T. Merrill. Boston: D. Lothrop, 1893. 258p.

Fourteen-year-old Guert Ten Eyck is one of the participants when a group of disgruntled Americans dump the tea in the hold of the ship 'London' into New York Harbor. When the Revolution breaks out in full force Guert finds fruitful ground for further patriotic activity. Among the historical figures that pass in review in the story are: Aaron Burr, Alexander Hamilton, Paul Revere and General Washington. The story's climax is the capture by the British of the spy, Nathan Hale, and his execution.

3216. ————. *Montanye*; or, *The slavers of old New York*. Philadelphia: H. Altemus, 1901. 356p.

In 1783 the American Revolution had been over for two years and the problems of the new nation were many. At this time in New York City the Montanye (a variation of 'Montaigne') family were clinging to land granted them (land that is now a part of Central Park) and to their precarious position in a fluid city.

3217. ————. *On the old frontier*; or, *The last raid of the Iroquois*. With illus. by H.D. Murphy. New York: Appleton, 1893. iv, 340p.

The frontier settlements of New York under siege and attack by the hostile Iroquois in the later years of the eighteenth century are the setting for this story of a lad who undergoes the rough, dangerous life in and around 'Plum Hollow Fort.' The Iroquois themselves, with their meetings in the Great Council House and their climactic final raid, are an integral part of the story.

3218. ————. *Success against odds*; or, *How a boy made his way*. **Illustrated by B. West Clinedinst. New York: Appleton, 1898. 273p.**

"Owing to his ability to swim and manage boats the young hero succeeds in rescuing a party of six girls from drowning, from which circumstance dates his steady advancement from pinching poverty and drudgery [in a Long Island seashore town] to a successful career on the bench. While perhaps real life offers few counterparts to this biography, such sterling qualities as the young man possessed never go wholly unrewarded"—The Chautauquan.

3219. ————. *Tom and the Money King*. **Illustrated by Charles Edward Boutwood. St. Paul, Minn.: Price-McGill, 1893. 269p.**

New York City is the scene of much of the story, although later on a sea voyage is described. Tom Tracy, son of the custodian of an office building in downtown Manhattan, performs services for the physician, Dr. Harbeck, and Angus, the Money King. They mark the beginning of Tom's career—the Money King uses Tom's services further and from thereon Tom has numerous opportunities to prove his worth.

3220. ————. *Walled in*; a true story of Randall's Island. **New York, Chicago: F.H. Revell, 1897. 134p.**

A lad has been falsely convicted of thievery and placed in the House of Refuge on Randall's Island. He and four other young prisoners plan and successfully carry out an escape from the New York City Island.

3221. ————. *The young financier*. **Illustrated by J.H. Betts. Philadelphia: Penn Pub. Co., 1900. 209p.**

The story is in the typical Horatio Alger mode wherein the hero's first job is that of a messenger in a New York City brokerage house; through industry, close, studied observation and perhaps some element of luck, he rises to a prestigious position in New York financial circles.

3222. **Stoddard, William Osborn, b. 1873.** *The farm that Jack built*; making good on the farm. **Illustrated by George Varian. New York: Appleton, 1916. 311p.**

"Even while Jack was pitching for the winning team in school, his thoughts were centered on the course in the agricultural college [at Cornell University] and the farm that would subsequently be his. When the practical test came, his neighbors in the country scoffed loudly at his scientific methods—loudly, but not long. He soon proved their efficacy, won several of the prizes offered by the Department of Agriculture, and even inspired his fellow farmers with the desire to know how it was done"—Boston transcript.

3223. **Stoehr, Shelley.** *Tomorrow Wendy*; a love story. **New York: Delacorte Press,**

1998. 166p.

A novel about privileged high school students on Long Island with their cliques and their chaotic life-styles. The heroine, Cary, tries to muffle her strong feelings for dangerously insouciant Wendy by having sex and drug sessions with Wendy's twin brother. As Cary becomes increasingly depressed and distant from family and friends, a new girl in school, Raven, a lesbian, takes her in hand and tells her to face up to her problems and inclinations.

3224. **Stokes, Manning Lee.** *The dying room.* **New York: Phoenix Press, 1947. 256p.**

The larger part of the events in this mystery occurs on the Bates family's Long Island estate. Young Carol Bates vanished a couple of years ago and it has been presumed that she drowned while swimming, but her body has never turned up. The connection of the above with Thomas Fain, fugitive from a military hospital where he was to have an operation, is this: after a fight with the military police, Fain meets a girl with the name Carol Bates on a plane. Is she the Long Island Carol Bates, heiress to fifty million dollars, or is she a fraud? If she is an impostor, she seems to be fooling the Bates's family lawyer and those who had known her for quite a few years.

3225. **Stone, Eugenia, 1879-1971.** *Free men shall stand.* **Illustrated by George Avison. New York: Nelson, 1944. vii, 264p.**

In this historical novel John Peter Zenger stands up for freedom of the press in colonial New York in the 1730s. Sharing his concerns about the abuses of the province's governor and the injustices visited upon new arrivals in America is Zenger's youthful apprentice, Matthew Ferris. When the printer and journalist Zenger is arrested for libel against the authorities, Matthew hastens to find the brilliant lawyer, Andrew Hamilton, and persuades him to defend Zenger.

3226. **Stone, Grace Zaring, 1896-1991.** *Dear deadly Cara.* **New York: Random House, 1968. 215p.**

'Cold Harbor' is a serene community on Long Island Sound which is subject to disquieting influences emanating from two women (Cara is one of them) that may well dissolve the social glue that holds the village together.

3227. **Stone, Hampton, pseud.** *The strangler who couldn't let go.* **New York: Simon & Schuster, 1956. 275p.**

"The account of one fiercely busy night somewhere on respectable Long Island where the oystermen and duckmen are quarreling. [Manhattan D.A. Gibson and pal Mac are vacationing on Long Island when] Mac reports this account of a complex encounter with a fierce young man who has a dislike for the local law and draws both Mac and Gibby into indiscretions they worry about conscientiously in spite of the … preoccupations lent them by circumstances and the condition of local law"—New York herald tribune books. The local population is highly resentful of the intrusions of the two New Yorkers.

3228. Stone, Jane, pseud. *The new man.* **New York: Crowell, 1913. 123p.**

John Ridgeway is a wealthy New Yorker who is disturbed by the enormous amount of attention his fiancée, Mollie Preston, devotes to the dangers faced by young women from white slavers in the metropolis. Then Frances Stevens, daughter of a Western senator, is abducted while strolling in Central Park. The possibility of Miss Stevens being sold into prostitution awakens Ridgeway and he realizes that Mollie had good reason for her concern.

3228a. Stone, Jonathan. *The cold truth.* **New York: St. Martin's Press, 1999. 276p.**

'Canaanville' in Upstate New York is territory covered by Sheriff Winston ('Bear') Edwards for the past 30 years. It has been quiet murder-wise for that stretch until the body of a local waitress turns up. The sheriff embarks on the case accompanied by Julian Palmer, a police academy graduate, who, to his dismay, is a she. Their collaboration is an uneasy one and it is not furthered by the presence of the sheriff's suspicious wife, a peculiar clairvoyant, and the harsh winter of Upstate New York.

3229. Stone, Katherine, 1949- . *Love songs.* **New York: Zebra Kensington, 1991. 480p.**

Southampton, Long Island has a population of 'successful', handsome people who seem to have everything 'going' for them. But, of course, there exist undercurrents—clandestine facts, falsifications, etc.—that get in the way of 'perfection' in love and life. Some of the individuals whom we meet with the author's permission are: Jeffrey, a TV news anchorman, presumably unable to impregnate a woman, suspects his wife must have had a lover in order to bear Merry, their only child; brilliant Diana, creator of an artificial heart, is on the verge of a divorce because she will not allow Chase, her husband, to know that the stunning loss of a daughter early on has led to her determination not to have any more children; Casey, a rising star in the legal profession, is worried about her lack of knowledge of her lover Patrick's past even though he has been dropping hints about it all along.

3230. *Stories of New York.* **New York: Scribner, 1893, 214p.**

A collection of four short stories and a one-act play reprinted from Scribner's magazine, noteworthy for containing Edith Wharton's first published piece of fiction. The 'New Yorkers' portrayed include: an 'amateur' writer and would-be author, a successful but almost friendless lawyer, a sophisticated, 'unemployed' gentleman on-the-town (who falls hopelessly in love with the 'Puritan ingénue' whose New England upbringing gets in the way of her pursuing an artistic career), and a lonely impoverished widow whose greatest pleasure is observing life outside her apartment window. Contents: From four to six; a comedietta ... by Annie Eliot.—The commonest possible story, by Bliss Perry.—The end of the beginning, by George A. Hibbard.—A Puritan ingénue, by John S. Wood.—Mrs. Manstey's view, by Edith Wharton.

Storme, Peter, pseud. See: Stern, Philip Van Doren, 1900-1984.

3231. **Story, James P.** *Choisy*; a novel. **Boston: J.R. Osgood, 1872. 131p.**

"Charley Wales, a young man with 'big brown lion's eyes with baby lashes', is the son of a wealthy New York banker and the friend of Dick Huntley, well known for his 'spotless Italian skin, blazing black eyes, and famous long moustaches which were the envy of masculine New York'"— The nation). Charley is ruined when Huntley, a runner for gambling-houses, beguiles him to a fashionable gambling 'hell' where he loses very heavily. Off he goes to Europe, leaving behind a cousin he loves. In Europe Charley bounces around with a French baroness until he finally recovers his moral sense, ditches her and returns to New York to marry his cousin. Huntley, ostensibly a rising young star on the banking scene, is unveiled for the cad he is and is driven out of the country.

3232. **Stout, David, 1942- .** *The dog hermit*. **New York: Mysterious Press, 1993. 311p.**

In the course of Upstate New York editor Will Schaefer's efforts to locate a kidnapped 5-year-old, Jamie, he loses an ally and friend, Fran Spicer, when the latter's car fails to stay on the snow-covered road; alcoholic abuse is a contributing cause in his death, the authorities say. After a ransom is paid for the boy's release and he still fails to appear, law enforcement officials (including the FBI) gather in 'Hill County.' An emotionally tormented recluse is drawn into the situation when he hears a child's voice in the thick, dark forests he inhabits. Will Schaefer goes about his job in an Upstate New York town that has never really accepted him (although he does fall in love with a local woman), endeavoring to prove that Fran Spicer's death was not Spicer's fault.

3233. ————. *Night of the ice storm*. **New York: Mysterious Press, 1991. 362p.**

"In a decaying Upstate New York town, on a night when freak weather drives most of the inhabitants into darkened houses, one young man goes out for a drink, meets a priest, spurns a sexual advance, and kills with ferocious brutality. A few nights later he attends a going-away party for a worker at the local paper and a few things best left unsaid are mumbled in a wash of hashish and booze. The crime, however, remains undetected because of police incompetence and/or official pressure. Twenty years later on the eve of the newspaper's fancy reunion party, one liquor-riddled police reporter remembers the party conversation and promptly dies. With his secret lurking close to the surface the killer is desperate. Stout … eventually delivers a solution and a killer … but not before exploring the troubled lives of several newspaper employees … [and delivering] a dizzying montage of background detail, socioeconomic observation (most about the death throes of an [Upstate New York] industrial town"—Booklist.

3234. **Stout, Rex, 1886-1975.** *Double for death*. **New York: Farrar & Rinehart,**

1939. 284p.

Another Rex Stout creation—Tecumseh Fox, a gentleman farmer—is the investigator when Ridley Thorpe, the millionaire, is a probable homicide victim; his body is discovered in a Westchester bungalow Thorpe had used as a refuge/hideaway from a too curious world.

3235. ————. *Some buried Caesar.* **New York: Farrar & Rinehart, 1939. 296p.**

Nero Wolfe, accompanied by his constant companion, Archie Goodwin has come to 'Crowfield' in Upstate New York to exhibit his albino orchids at the 'North Atlantic Exposition.' His services are called upon when Mr. Clyde Osgood is found gored to death and the suspect is Hickory Caesar Grindon, the prize bull of Thomas Platt. Besides Platt, Nero focuses upon Monte McMillan, former owner of Caesar, and Lew Bennett, secretary of the National Guernsey League.

3236. Stowe, Harriet Beecher, 1811-1896. *My wife and I*; or, *Harry Henderson's history.* **New York: J.H. Ford, 1871. viii, 474p.**

"A young country-bred college graduate [Henry Henderson], who goes to New York and lives by literature, marries … a young girl of wealth and fashion, and they set up housekeeping on one of the [city's] back streets; and in a little house which the artistic feeling and domestic genius of the wife have made beautiful, they live happily upon a pittance of $7,000 a year"—Literary world (Boston). The two experience 'fashionable' life in New York and through Henry, now a 'newspaper man', we get a glimpse of big-city journalism.

3237. Stowell, William Averill, 1882-1950. *The Marston murder case.* **New York: Appleton, 1930. 289p.**

"William R. Marston, a lewd Wall Street banker, is found dead in his study, beside him his beautiful female secretary and her brother (with a clot in his Broca's convolution), so it looks like a case of you know what. In fact, the financier had willed the girl a fourth of his vast fortune, but he was also keeping an apartment for a musical comedy actress whose husband was in Atlanta. 'It's the damndest case I ever had anything to do with', growled Dr. Dinsmore when he heard of the secret code, the poison pill, the golf score belonging to Aubrey Walton and what not. Complete with suicide, confession, scandal and sleuthing by Chief Inspector Burke and the narrator, a handwriting expert"—New York herald tribune books.

3238. Strange, John Stephen, b. 1896. *The man who killed Fortescue.* **Garden City, N.Y.: Published for the Crime Club by Doubleday, Doran, 1928. 310p.**

"The man who killed Fortescue was never discovered—a young woman was tried for the murder and acquitted, and the case remained a mystery. A year later a writer of detective stories who is near a solution of the Fortescue case is killed on a Fifth Avenue bus in New York. Joan Archer, the girl of the previous trial, is implicated in the second tragedy. But Detective Ormsby believes in her innocence and does not give up until he finds the double murderer"—Book review digest.

3239. ————. *A picture of the victim*. **Garden City, N.Y.: Published for the Crime Club by Doubleday, Doran, 1940. 268p.**

"Barney Gantt, news photographer, merely wants a shot of Jesse Jordan, publicity-shy millionaire, when he finds a way to enter the Jordan estate on Long Island. He gets the picture, but it is a picture of a dead man"—New Yorker. Three more die before final exposure of the murderer.

3240. **Stratemeyer, Edward, 1862-1930.** *Richard Dare's venture*; or, *Striking out for himself*. **New York: Merriam Co., 1894. 248p.**

"When the story opens Richard Dare's father, a journeyman painter, is killed by a fall from a scaffolding. The sixteen-year-old son, left the head of the family, leaves his village home for New York, where he hopes to make a living and find a missing witness to his father's pension papers. A railway accident makes him some useful friends, and after varied experiences as stock clerk in a large book and stationery store, the missing witness is found, the pension secured, and Richard, in partnership with a friend, is launched in a promising, independent book business"—Annual American catalogue.

3241. ————. *Shorthand Tom*; or, *The exploits of a young reporter*. **New York: W.I. Allison, 1897. 259p.**

The hero has a name famous in boy's fiction—Tom Swift. Tom is well versed in shorthand and works in the office of a lawyer who turns out to be a rogue anxious to push Tom out of New York City and swindle Tom and his sister out of property bequeathed to them. Tom is lucky; the editor of a newspaper hires him as a reporter. His new duties take him to unusual sites and once again Tom is brought in touch with several scoundrels with robbery on their minds.

3242. **Straub, Peter, 1943- .** *Ghost story*. **New York: Coward, McCann & Geoghegan, 1979. 483p.**

The setting is a snow-bound village in Upstate New York that is threatened by a supernatural, alien form that deprives humans of their memories and eventually of their vital body fluids. Opposed to this 'thing' are a novelist, two old lawyers and a teenager. The 'alien' is able to change itself at will into whatever shape or form a villager might imagine. No matter how often the alien is frustrated by those aware of its presence, it will continue to keep coming back to inflict harm on the hated humans.

3243. **Stream, Arnold C.** *The third bullet*. **New York: Stein and Day, 1986. 219p.**

Mike Monett, a saloon keeper in the Upstate New York town of 'Dentonville', kills James Franklin, a young black man, during a brawl. Monett says it was self-defense, but the police, with an eye on black resentment, charge Monett with premeditated murder. Abel Creighton takes Monett's case; he and his assistant, Jennifer Rand, utilize all their technical skills and a bit of luck defending their client. Nevertheless the two are never completely comfortable with Monett's account of the brawl and they learn the real reasons for the killing only months after the trial's end.

3244. Street, Alfred B., 1811-1881. *Frontenac*; or, *The Atotarho of the Iroquois, a metrical romance.* **New York: Baker and Scribner, 1849. xii, 324p.**

A narrative poem that consists of 7,000 octosyllabic lines and is based upon the expedition undertaken in 1696 by Count Frontenac, Governor-general of Canada, against the powerful confederacy of the Iroquois. The Indians are shown on their native grounds in Upstate New York. Thurenserah, the 'Dawn of the Day', an Onondagan, is called the Atotarho (after the Onondagan chief who became the first ruler of the Iroquois). The Atotarho is captured in battle and led to the stake whereupon a traitorous chief reveals 'him' as Lucille, daughter of Frontenac's Indian wife, Sa-ha-wee (he had married her 24 years before and she and the kidnapped Lucille had returned to their people) who had been presumed dead. The horrified Count Frontenac is witness to the death of both Lucille and her mother. The author takes particular pains to describe the scenery of northern New York in its wildest state.

3245. Street, Julian Leonard, 1879-1947. *Rita Coventry.* **Garden City, N.Y.: Doubleday, Page, 1922. 306p.**

Richard Parrish, thirty-five, a Southerner, has been very successful at moneymaking in Wall Street. He takes a languid interest in Alice Meldrum, a nice, intelligent young woman. When Richard encounters Rita Conventry, opera singer, beautiful, haughty, however, he falls hard for her. Rita dangles Richard on a string; he is only one of her many conquests. She tells him, "You lack the light touch," and cuts him loose. The shock to Richard's vanity has one good result—he goes back to sensible Alice and marries her despite his long commitment to bachelordom.

3246. Strieber, Whitney, 1945- . *The forbidden zone.* **New York: Dutton, 1993. 309p.**

A horror story that uses an Upstate New York town and its inhabitants as the focus of its terrifying narrative. Nothing is safe from the tentacled, odoriferous, alien being that has suddenly appeared in the village—humans, animals or plants. Brian Kelly, a physicist, and his pregnant Vietnamese wife, Loi, had been the first to hear human cries issuing from a mound of dirt. Not only the above-mentioned entity but also waspish fireflies are a very present danger to the unprotected people. Brian and several associates are battling these strange creatures and simultaneously trying to surmise their origin.

3247. Stringer, Arthur John Arbuthnott, 1874-1950. *The city of peril.* **New York: Knopf, 1923. 317p.**

"Woodruff, a man of means fond of nothing but amusement, is suddenly stirred to action and hard work when Marvin Stillwell receives the fatal scrap of paper signed 'The Hammer of God.' He determines to unearth the villains.

In the solving of the mystery there are many adventures, with New York [City] for their background. The scenes change quickly from the Stock Exchange to a second-hand bookshop on the East River and end up with a fight on a tenement roof. A beautiful girl who seems the very contradiction of her sordid surroundings adds the flavor of romance to the tale"—Book review digest.

3248. ————. *The silver poppy*; a novel. New York: D. Appleton, 1903. vi, 291p.
Cordelia Vaughan comes out of the West to 'conquer' New York. *The silver poppy* is the title of a novel that she hopes will receive favorable notice and give her a lead into the ranks of high society. Cordelia is clever and not averse to using all her feminine wiles to get what she wants. On the other hand the hero of the story, John Hartley, an Oxfordian who has drifted into New York journalism, is a man of integrity who finally sees through Cordelia and walks away from her, leaving her in tears. The two other chief characters are Repellier, an honest old artist, and the tragically silly Mrs. Sawyer—Cordelia is her 'protégé.' New York's 'upper' Bohemia and the vitality of the city's day and night are drawn by an author familiar with them.

3249. ————. *The under groove*; a novel. New York: McClure Co., 1908. 335p.
"In a series of seven short stories an old offender against the law tells in the first person his experiences in New York while assuming the rather novel role of detective. With a facility born of long experience in practical criminality he makes use of the usual methods of perpetrating crime in order to ferret it out for his own private ends. The mental processes of the scientific burglar are analyzed, so that the book is at once a thrilling story of adventure and a study of criminology"—Book review digest.

3250. ————. *The wine of life*. New York: Knopf, 1921. 389p.
"Owen Storrow, a young Western artist, fresh from four months of North Woods life, comes to New York. He finds the city too busy to pay much attention to his trunkful of clay modelings, but Torrie Throssel, an actress whom he first sees as she sits drying her hair on the fire-escape of a third-rate Tenderloin hotel, for a time supplies the 'wine of life' for him, and he becomes indifferent to everything else. Marriage follows and disillusion. The life into which she drags him becomes distasteful and finally impossible. After repeated failures to get his old grip on life, he gives Torrie her freedom and goes back to his Canada woods"—Book review digest.

3251. ————. *The wire tappers.* Illustrated by Arthur W. Brown. Boston: Little, Brown, 1906. 324p.
The two main characters are an electrical wizard and the girl he loves, a beautiful Englishwoman. They inadvertently become embroiled with a book-maker who has in mind employing the electrical knowledge of the hero to wiretap the gambling operation based in a New York poolroom. The heroine

exercises all her ingenuity to deliver herself and her lover from their association with some very shady characters.

3252. ————. *The wolf woman*; a novel. Indianapolis: Bobbs-Merrill, 1928. 331p.
Aurora (Rorie) Mary Moyne is a backwoods girl who manages John Cave's Trail-End Camp in Ontario, saves him from drowning and delivers the illegitimate baby of his daughter Joan. Cave takes Rorie to his Long Island home. She is to be known to the servants as Mrs. Moyne, 'mother' of the child that Joan carried. Joan flinches when her father considers adopting Rorie and is resentful when her fiancé, Arthur Somer, is attentive to Rorie. The baby, a bone of contention between Rorie and Joan, dies; Arthur Somer discovers the truth, ends his engagement to Joan and has a rough and tumble fight with Rorie. Rorie has picked up some of the more pleasant aspects of life in New York City and Long Island, yet opts to return to the Trail-End Camp that Arthur now owns. He goes to the camp and once again Rorie performs her rescue act, pulling Arthur from a burning boat and a near drowning. The two then realize how much in love they are.

3253. Strobel, Marion, b. 1895. *Kiss and kill*. New York: Scribner, 1946. 213p.
Nina Alexander, college sophomore, has $20 stolen from her while staying at an Adirondack resort. Despite having a waiting fiancé, Nina has compromised herself with J. Anthony Niles, former Olympic champion and a prime murder suspect. She also comes across the body of Gwethalyn, Anthony's first wife. Caroline Earlings, an heiress, fortuitously snapped photographs that might be of help to detective A. Lincoln Lacy (on vacation) as he seeks answers to several murders.

3254. Strong, Paschal Neilson, 1901- . *Three plebes at West Point*. With illus. by Walter J. Heffron. Boston: Little, Brown, 1935. viii, 248p.
The three plebes are: Walter, a Southerner from a family of little means; Hale, a Westerner fresh from a ranch in Colorado; and Cortlandt, the pride of an aristocratic well-to-do Albany dynasty. West Point brings them together and friendships are formed in their first year at the United States Military Academy.

3255. ————. *West Point wins*. With illus. by George Avison. Boston: Little, Brown, 1930. vi, 267p.
Cadet Leslie, a country boy from North Carolina, undergoes the trials of West Point life. Football and student pranks, a tour of the grounds of the Academy and the student code of honor are important elements of the story.

3256. Strunsky, Simeon, 1879-1948. *Belshazzar Court*; or, *Village life in New York City*. New York: Holt, 1914. 190p.
"Account of family affairs and certain other intimate concerns of a young married couple and their two children in their life on the third floor of a mammoth apartment house in the far up-town regions of New York. … It is

the young head of the family who acts as scribe, and who realistically pictures the pleasures and a few of the vexations of domestic life in a household just a little less prosperous … than its tastes, its refinement, its ideals might have rendered desirable. … What the humorously communicative young father has to say about his irrepressible son Harold and the latter's baby sister, about his wife Emmeline, and, not least of all, about himself, his interests and diversions, his views of things metropolitan and cosmopolitan and miscellaneous will be found entertainingly set forth in the eight discursive chapters of the book"—The dial. "With shrewd discernment it takes up the trivialities of life, the life of the apartment house, of the city streets, of the toiling factories, of the city's playtime, at the ball game, the opera. … One realizes that it is the trivialities, which really make up the big moments of life"—Bookman.

3257. **Stuart, Eleanor, b. 1876.** *Averages*; **a story of New York. New York: Appleton, 1899. 410p.**

"It is a far call from the female barber of a mining town who was the heroine of 'Stonepastures', to the brilliant New York society woman who is the chief influence in the destiny of her friends. Among these a doctor and his wife devoted to amateur philanthropy, a former dancer (crippled, and full of all her old vanities and frivolities), an adventurer (playing at social reform), and her husband (rich, idle, devoted to dress and visiting notabilities), play leading parts. The object of the story seems to be to show that when all social conditions are realized there remains a general average of happiness and sorrow"—Annual American catalogue.

3257a. **Sturges, Karen.** *Death of a baritone*. **New York: Bantam Books, 1999. 304p.**

Deaths in the upscale Hamptons of Long Island—namely that of allergic Frank Palermo, leading baritone of the Varovna Vocal Colony and Opera Workshop, from a dose of penicillin, and the murder of the Colony's cook—lead the chief investigator to ask Phoebe Mullins, 50, a widow and recent employee of the Colony, to keep her eyes and ears open.

3258. **Stuyvesant, Peter.** *The great adventure*. **Cincinnati: Standard Pub. Co., 1918. 340p.**

Dutch customs and traditions in the 17th century are scrutinized in this novel whose hero, Will Gerrits, the aimless son of a carpenter, migrates to America and New Amsterdam. He sets out to make a name for himself, to establish himself as a solid citizen; he succeeds to the extent that he is accepted as the son-in-law of the governor of the colony.

3259. **Sugden, Herbert John, 1914- .** *Siege of the St. Lawrence*. **Boston: Christopher Pub. House, 1948. 291p.**

The historical background for the novel is the French and Indian War (1754-1763). Tolerant Father François Piquet accompanied by Cerise François (who serves him to avoid marriage to a colonist), helps establish and fortify La

Galette (Later Oswegatchie) from whence he shall attempt to Christianize the fierce Iroquois. Another Frenchman, Pierre Vergennes, is the partner of the former adventurer/pirate, William Tyson, now engaged in the fur trade from his headquarters near Albany. Pierre, an ally of the English, comes to La Galette on business; he and Cerise fall in love. The war separates them for a while; Pierre is captured and tortured by the Iroquois, is released and returns to La Galette. He marries Cerise and joins the English forces, ultimately acquiring a colonelcy. With the war's end Pierre rejoins his wife and son at La Galette; the end of French hegemony in North America pulls Father Piquet back to France and retirement from worldly concerns.

3260. **Suhr, Elmer George, 1902-1976.** *The magic mirror.* **New York: Helios Books, c1965. 311p.**

The emotional life of a young man with tuberculosis who enters a sanatorium in Upstate New York in the 1930s—with minor echoes of Thomas Mann's *The magic mountain.*

3261. **Sullivan, Francis William b. 1887.** *Alloy of gold.* **New York: R.M. McBride, 1915. 336p.**

Educated abroad Worth Pryce comes home to participate in New York City's social swim; he easily wins friends and has the notion that human beings generally can be trusted to 'do the right thing.' But after six months Worth suffers some keen disappointments. The father he had idealized falls from the pedestal on which Worth had placed him; his best friend stumbles badly; he is disillusioned with the girl he is engaged to. Then Ruth Barrett, a friend of his childhood, comes back into his life. She possesses patience, tranquility and practical wisdom and is the greatest influence in Worth's renewed efforts to reclaim his former idealism and optimism.

3262. **Sullivan, James William, 1848-1938.** *Tenement tales of New York.* **New York: H. Holt, 1895. v, 233p.**

Stories dealing with well-known types of cosmopolitan life in which the street Arab plays a prominent part. Sullivan, a journalist, gathered much of his material through observation; he wrote a column for the New York Times in the 1880s and saw what was happening to workers in the sweatshops and factories of New York City. Contents: Slob Murphy.—Minnie Kelsey's wedding.—Cohen's figure.—Threw himself away.—Luigi Beriberi. Leather's banishment.—Not yet.—A young desperado.

3263. **Sullivan, Thomas Russell, 1849-1916.** *The courage of conviction*; a novel. **New York: Scribner, 1902. 257p.**

"A novel of New York life. It is based on familiar themes—the woman who marries without love and the man who is tempted by material rewards to forsake the higher calling which nature has planned for him. Both come to grief, as is just, and afterwards contrive to patch up, after a fashion, the lives that their mistaken choices have marred"—The dial.

3264. **Summers, E.W.** *This never happened*; a novel. **New York: Random House, 1997. 273p.**

Richard Hayes, a New York City accountant, investigates the ghosts of his family's past in the Upstate New York town of 'Waterton', for his sister Claire, an artist, has just killed her bullying husband, imagining he was her father. Richard confronts sickening facts about his and Claire's parents—the elder Mr. Hayes was an esteemed obstetrician to the outer world but a demon in the treatment of his children; his wife, an alcoholic, was a cold and uncaring mother. Richard himself has some unpleasant characteristics; it is Claire who wins the reader's sympathy as the horrors of the siblings' past unfolds.

3265. **Sutherland, Joan, b. 1890.** *Unquenchable fire.* **New York: Harper, 1927 [c1926] 294p.**

The central figure in the novel is based on an actor (John Barrymore?) who has the New York theatrical world in thrall. However, John Ingram, in love with Paula Hill, is tied to an incurably mentally ill wife. Paula offers him her steadfast devotion while John's conscience erects a barrier between them. But in a melodramatic fashion the lovers do find a way out of their dilemma.

3266. **Sutphen, William Gilbert Van Tassel, 1861-1945.** *The Doomsman.* **New York: Harper, 1906. iii, 294p.**

A fictional look into a frightening future with the former city of New York known as Doom and inhabited by a gang of criminals, the Doomsmen, but otherwise deserted. It is 2015 A. D., 90 years after a plague (the 'Terror') had decimated the earth's human population. Those who survived, other than the Doomsmen, were thrust back into a pristine condition with miniscule knowledge of the arts and sciences. However, electricity and other technologies are recovered and there is room in the author's imagination for a love story to develop.

3267. —————. *The gates of chance.* **New York: Harper, 1904. v, 301p.**

Two male companions are footloose in New York: Esper Indiman is an energetic young man with bohemian and mystical tendencies; Winston Thorp is a rich man's son who has no idea of what he wants to do with his life. They jointly experience a series of odd adventures and finally join a club whose qualification for membership they fit: lack of success at any endeavor. Already on the club's rolls are a failed author and playwright, a bankrupt businessman, a floundering artist, and a bank clerk with a short memory accused of stealing $50,000 who forgot that he had put the money in his employer's safe deposit vault.

3268. **Sutro-Schücking, Kathinka, b. 1835.** *Doctor Zernowitz.* **Willa Montrose. Chicago: Laird & Lee, 1894. 194p.**

Doctor Zernowitz, a famous New York physician, is surprised when a coachman in his employ informs him that he has acquired a good knowledge of Latin. The doctor asks him to relate the story of his life. What follows is presumably based on fact. 'Willa Montrose' is about a civil engineer whose love for a woman is so intense and perhaps even slightly deranged that he commits suicide by her grave.

3269. **Sutton, Margaret, 1903- .** *The ghost parade.* **Illustrated by Pelagie Doane. New York: Grosset & Dunlap, 1933. vi, 217p.**

A summer camp in the Thousand Islands of the Saint Lawrence River is the scene of several bizarre and perplexing adventures experienced by a group of girls with their leader, Judy Bolton.

3270. **Swift, Hildegarde Hoyt, 1890?-1977.** *House by the sea.* **Illustrated by Lynd Ward. New York: Harcourt, 1938. 245p.**

"A house built 300 years ago, overlooking Long Island Sound, is the continuing character of the tale. The old house does not directly speak and its thoughts, which are many, are told by indirection. They are concerned with such a mystery as makes a well-knit story. It must indeed be knitted well to hold together over the gaps so long a history makes necessary, for unlike 'Hitty', who went into camphor between appearances in the world, the house goes into recurring periods of neglect when nobody lives there at all. Through everything the memory of a lost ring, a waiting treasure, keeps its mind clear. Freebooters, quarreling Indians, Redcoats sweep through its rooms. It is confiscated as 'the property of a notorious Tory'; more than once destruction almost catches up with it. But in the last chapter, with foundations deep in the past, its windows look into the future"—New York herald tribune books

3271. **Swiggett, Howard, 1891-1957.** *The corpse in the derby hat.* **Boston: Little, Brown, 1937. 294p.**

Long Island and New York City are the two locations in which the story takes place. Craven Embree, an unpleasant alcoholic, tries to blackmail Steve Dongan and is subsequently murdered. Steve happens to be in love with Linnet, the murdered man's wife, so he is a prime suspect. Detective Garrett Maynard appears, fills in the blanks and nabs the murderer.

3272. **Tabak, Mary Natalie.** *But not for love*; **a novel. New York: Horizon Press, 1960. 255p.**

The art colonies of Long Island, centered around East Hampton, are the scene of the novel. The several couples the reader gets to know are presumably engaged in various intellectual pursuits, but they have their common needs— love, group recognition (e.g., not being invited to some party or other is depressing), the hoped-for discovery of a meaningful artistic itinerary.

3273. **Taber, Susan.** *Unexpected affinities*; **a serio-comedy. New York: Duffield, 1913. 397p.**

Two New York City families provide the chief characters for the novel. Rosalie and Alice Harvey, the two daughters of one of the families, are a study in contrasts: frivolous, coquettish Rosalie is married to one of the members of the other family, Peter St. Clair, an artist; idealistic, serious Alice draws the impassioned attention of St. Clair's cousin, Herbert Norton, a millionaire, who had a brief flirtation with Rosalie. Herbert goes through a period of bored selfishness and then develops an interest in ideas of social improvement; he even puts some of the theories of societal betterment into practice and recognizes that he has come upon 'unexpected affinities.'

3274. **Taggart, Marion Ames, 1866-1945. *Beth's wonderful winter*; a story. Illustrated by William F. Stecher. Boston: W.A. Wilde, 1914. 349p.**

Great-aunt Rebecca had reared Beth in Massachusetts with a firm hand and attention to the development of the girls' moral character. When Beth goes to New York to stay in her uncle's fashionable Fifth Avenue home for several weeks, one wonders what effect it might have on her. Beth does not change however; wholesomeness, helpfulness and enthusiasm meld well with her uncle's family, and she wins admiration and love from her sophisticated relatives. She returns to Aunt Rebecca with a broadened view of life, but retaining the same sterling qualities she always had.

3275. **————. *Loyal blue and royal scarlet*; a story of '76. New York: Benziger Bros., 1899. 233p.**

Actually this novel covers the years 1775 to 1781 with most of the scenes laid in New York City. Royalist Governor William Tryon's plot to kidnap (or even assassinate?) General George Washington and Benedict Arnold's treason are features of the story along with a slight romance.

3276. **————. *Six girls and the room*; a story. Sequel to *Six girls and Bob*. Illustrated by William F. Stecher. Boston: W.A. Wilde, 1907. 319p.**

The six Scollard girls confront the family's lack of money by returning to New York City after a relaxing summer at Aunt Kerrenhappuch's farm and opening a tearoom and circulating library in one of the city's shopping areas. By virtue of hard work and a dab of good luck the girls turn their venture into a profitable one. The family's fortunes take an upward turn.

3277. **————. *Three girls and especially one*. New York: Benziger Bros., 1897. 150p.**

The lives of the Merricks—a Catholic family set firmly in New York City—are changed when the oldest child, Marcy, is made an invalid by a nasty fall. Thereafter the other members place talented Marcy at the center of their actions, with a consequent alteration in Marcy's character. When a cousin from Kansas comes to visit, the Merrick children are inclined to smile at her country ways as contrasted to their urban 'sophistication', but they soon learn to value her as a loveable person.

3278. Tallman, Mariana M. Bisbee. *Tent V, Chautauqua.* **Boston: D. Lothrop, 1885. 339p.**

"Molly, Marjorie and Frank Van Amringes take a great fancy to spending a summer at Chautauqua through reading 'Pansy's' Hall in the Grove. Their mother is finally infected with their enthusiasm, and it is decided the family shall summer there in place of Saratoga or Newport. The father's illness at the last moment prevents the mother going, and the children are permitted to travel to Chautauqua alone in charge of Molly, the eldest. They take a trip first to Niagara and have some amusing adventures. Their experience of Chautauqua in Tent 'V' is quite entertaining. The everyday life of the place with its attractions and advantages is well described"—Annual American catalogue.

Tainter, Helen Davies. See: Davies, Helen.

3279. Tamar, Erika, 1934- . *Fair game.* **San Diego: Harcourt Brace, 1993. 293p.**

The story is taken from news stories of the time which frequently reported incidents of juveniles, athletes especially, involved in rape and sexual abuse. In this novel a Long Island town has to deal with the distasteful fact that several of its role-model, bright young male athletes have participated in the rape of Cara Snowden, a slow-thinking, special education student anxious to join the 'in' crowd. The incident is reported on three levels by: Cara herself; Laura Jean Kettering, girlfriend of one of the boys who took part in the crime, reluctant to believe the truth; and athlete Julio ('Joe') Lopez who declined to participate in the gang rape.

Tanner, Edward Everett, 1921-1976. See under his pseudonym: Rowans, Virginia.

3280. Tapp, Sidney Calhoun, b. 1870 or 2. *The struggle.* **New York: A. Wessels Co., 1906. 124p.**

The author uses the novel as a device to accuse the trusts and great wealth of a few of corrupting America and creating conditions that inspire a worker's revolt against the moneyed titans. Four daughters of a wealthy Kentucky family marry men whose livelihoods depend, respectively, on sugar, tobacco and cotton growing and on New York mercantile life. The machinations of Wall Street insiders and their penchant for stock manipulation have a destructive effect on those directly concerned and those innocent of involvement in these 'games.'

3281. Tarr, Herbert, 1929- . *Heaven help us!* **New York: Random House, 1968. 277p.**

"Rabbi Gideon Abel (25—and still unmarried) comes to Hillendale [a New York City suburb] determined to show his congregation the way to religion. But they ... are more concerned with fashion shows, the temple musical comedy (My Fair Sadie), and fund-raising for a brand-new kitchen. So the battle lines are drawn between Gideon and his people"—Publisher's note.

3282. **Taylor, Bayard, 1825-1878.** *Hannah Thurston*; **a story of American life. New York: G.P. Putnam, 1863. 464p.**

'Ptolemy', New York in 1852 is the opening scene of the novel, although it would seem to be a disguise for Kennett Square, Pennsylvania, Taylor's birthplace. Hannah Thurston, a Quaker and an abolitionist, is a firm believer in the rights of women and as such dismays rich Maxwell Woodbury who is strongly attracted to her. Nevertheless Woodbury woos and wins Hannah for his wife. In her new situation Hannah defers increasingly to her husband's views on the 'true' place of women, eventually losing all semblance of her former strong-willed feminism.

3283. ————. *John Godfrey's fortunes*: **related by himself. A story of American life. New York: G.P. Putnam, 1865. viii, 511p.**

After childhood and youth in Pennsylvania John Godfrey sets out for New York City and a hoped-for literary life; he gravitates towards journalism, however, and even helps plan a magazine, the Oracle, whose forte is literary scandal. Cynicism grips Godfrey when he meets with a rebuff from Isabel Haworth, a wealthy young lady, after she hears of his efforts to help a prostitute, Jane Perry, in Washington Square. Godfrey starts drinking heavily following the failure of the Oracle. An old friend, Bob Simmons, rescues him. As his fortunes take a gradual upswing Godfrey becomes engaged to and marries Isabel and also realizes a tidy sum from his Uncle Woolly's successful speculations. The novel offers a fairly plausible picture of New York literary circles in the 1850s.

3284. **Taylor, David, 1900-1965.** *Storm the last rampart.* **Philadelphia: Lippincott, 1960. 384p.**

The two main characters in the novel are a captain in General Washington's Secret Service and a waitress in a tavern who is also a spy for the Americans. Much of the action takes place in and around Tarrytown, N.Y. in 1780 and 1781 with the capture of Major John André and the exposure of Benedict Arnold's treason and its aftermath as key events.

3285. **Taylor, Elizabeth Atwood, 1936- .** *Murder at Vassar.* **New York: St. Martin's Press, 1987. 257p.**

Private detective Maggie Elliott investigates the sudden deaths of two women at a Vassar College reunion—Chloe Warren, a wealthy old alumna of the College, and Deborah Marten, a scholarship student. Pudgie Brown, number one heir to the Warren fortune, is fingered by the police as a very probable homicide suspect, but Maggie finds there are other relatives who could profit from Chloe Warren's demise. One of them is Peter Warren and Maggie perhaps foolishly falls into his arms and bed. Before the case is closed Maggie is in harm's way on several occasions.

3286. **Taylor, Florance Walton.** *Towpath Andy*. **Illus. by Lillian Wuerfel. Chicago: A. Whitman, 1938. 249p.**

It is the 1850s in Erie Canal country and Andy—his mother has recently died and his father has been missing for a number of years—fearful of being sent to a workhouse, takes a job as a towpath boy. Andy's adventures as a canal worker include an incident with a gang of horse thieves and a reunion with his long-lost father. At the close of the story Andy is a freshman at Wabash College in Indiana.

3287. **Taylor, Robert Lewis, 1912- .** *Niagara*. **New York: Putnam, 1980. 500p.**

In the 1850s James Gordon Bennett of the sensation-mongering New York Herald sends a well-heeled 21-year-old, William Morrison III, to Niagara Falls. Mr. Morrison (Bill) is to report on any unusual or scandalous occurrences in the fast-growing resort town. When he takes rooms in the upscale Cataract House, Bill is promptly seduced by a mature English lady, Frances, nine years older than he, is entranced by Samantha, a Southern belle, and, after too much liquor, is put to bed by Betsy, a chambermaid. Bill looks on as dim-witted sensation-seekers go over the Falls in metal barrels and tightrope walkers cross above the roiling waters. Samantha perishes in the Falls despite the efforts of Bill and Betsy to save her. Betsy's father, a scientist, induces Bill to travel to France to study winemaking. On his return he marries Betsy and becomes the initial Niagara wine producer.

3288. **Teal, Cornelia Adele.** *Counting the cost*; **or,** *A summer at Chautauqua*. **Introd. by Frank Russell. New York: Hunt & Eaton, 1889. 316p.**

"In the form of a story, and with a number of characters, [the author] pictures vividly the life at Chautauqua during one summer. She also gives in the course of the story an explicit account of the object and methods of the C[hautauqua] L[iterary and] S[cientific] C[ircles], the cost of living there, the courses of studies, etc., etc."—Annual American catalogue.

3289. **Tebbel, John William, 1912- .** *The conqueror*; **a novel. New York: Dutton, 1951. 352p.**

Just about all the personages mentioned on the pages of this historical novel based on the life of Sir William Johnson, British Superintendent-General of Indian Affairs in North America, actually participated in the events of their time in history. However, the author has set up a fictional rival of Johnson, Harry Percival; the latter, an Englishman, is disdainful of Johnson's Irish ancestry and later in the novel he contends with Johnson for primacy in the Mohawk Valley. The story opens with Johnson's arrival in New York City in 1738; he takes charge of his uncle Sir Peter Warren's estates along the Mohawk River and gradually acquires lands of his own as he cements good relationships with the Iroquois. Johnson's marriages and his brief but notable military career are covered in more detail. By the end of the novel Johnson has successfully ousted the French from Fort Niagara (1759) and has killed his enemy, Harry Percival, in hand-to-hand combat when the latter attacks Mount (Fort) Johnson.

3290. **Tennenbaum, Silvia, 1928- .** *Rachel, the rabbi's wife.* **New York: Morrow, 1978. 395p.**

This "novel encompasses a year in the life of Rachel Sonnshein, the wife of a rabbi serving a suburban congregation in 'Gateshead', Long Island. In the course of the year ... the rabbi fights for renewal of his contract. He becomes involved with the wife of a rich congregant. Rachel, who is a painter, tries to get her own studio. Her son shares a secret with her while the two of them do together one of the things they most love: watch the Mets play baseball. Rachel meets an old lover in New York City, the land of her dreams"—Publisher's note.

3291. **Terhune, Albert Payson, 1872-1942.** *The amateur inn.* **New York: G.H. Doran, 1923. 287p.**

"Because of a certain clause in his great-uncle's will Thaxton Vail finds that part of his newly-inherited [New York] home is to be set aside, if necessary, for wayfarers' accommodations. Osmun Creede, one of the few who know this fact, dislikes him for reasons of his own, and advertises this provision of the will. Immediately guests appear and soon after strange robberies and a murder take place. Circumstantial evidence undoubtedly points to young Vail. A man frozen to death on a hot summer day furnishes the clue that leads to amazing discoveries and unraveling of the mysteries"—Book review digest.

3292. ————. *Columbia stories.* **Illustrated by F. Thornburgh. New York: G.W. Dillingham, 1897. 214p.**

Undergraduate life at Columbia University as portrayed by a former student. Contents: A tale of two cards.—His right hand neighbor.—The fall of the fountain.—The basket of Alnaschar.—One joke and another.—A fin de siécle Punchinello.—The metamorphosis of John Lee, freshman.—A poetess of passion.—Misspent.—The '9-"Lit."—A baffled Puritan.

3293. ————. *Fortune.* **Illustrated by W. Clinton Pette. Garden City, N.Y.: Doubleday, Page, 1918. vii, 360p.**

"Eve Gourlay, the heiress, marries Brant Errol, a thirty-five dollars a week reporter on a New York newspaper. A complete break with her family follows, and since her brother, Peter Gourlay, controls her fortune, she is cut off without a cent and is forced to live within her husband's income. This is the story of the life lived in the modest little uptown apartment. It is all a new world to Eve, and because she sees it with new eyes, she is able to write a book about it, about the strange New York above 72nd Street, where Broadway ceases to be Broadway and becomes Main Street. Later her inheritance is restored to her, and when she finds that it is making difficulties, she chooses an ingenious way of getting rid of it"—Book review digest.

3294. Terreve, Retsel, pseud. *A man without principle?* **Baltimore: Hocking Pub. Co., 1908. 345p.**

The rise and fall and rebirth of Anson Van Anholt—his boyhood was turbulent; he amassed a fortune and lost it on Wall Street; in poverty he commits a crime to help secure food and medicine for his wife. Sent to prison he is paroled and gains admittance into the Young Men's Christian League of New York. And thus begins Van Anholt's reformation and new start in life. The author uses his novel as a sounding board for his views on questions of the day.

3295. Terrill, Haidee, 1910- . *The Square.* **New York: Macmillan, 1949. 302p.**

Covenant Square, an upscale neighborhood in a New York State town in the earliest years of the 20th century, was the home of people who clung to custom and refused to take notice of uncomfortable facts. Lucee Landry, who came to the Square as a visitor, ended up as the wife of one of its most eligible bachelors. She assumed social leadership in the community until the 1920s when its character began to change. The imposing old houses were increasingly turned into apartments or stores and the up and coming young people left the Square. However, even when Lucee herself moved to Washington, D.C. with her politically ambitious husband, she often harked back to her gracious days in Covenant Square.

3296. Thayer, Lee, 1874-1973. *Alias Dr. Ely*; Peter Clancy's new impersonation. **Garden City, N.Y.: Doubleday, Page, 1927. viii, 320p.**

"Who (a) drove the steel gadget into the medulla oblongata of Warren Heywood, the Long Island millionaire and later (b) threw the corpse out of the upstairs window? Among the suspects are the victim's son, bedridden with the willies; the son's nurse, who has done time; the old artist in love with the Florentine bust; and 'They' (a variant of the more usual 'It'). The solution, arrived at by accident after the case has collapsed, is in the hands of a detective who disguises himself as a psycho-analyst so that nothing he may say or do will seem foolish"—New York herald tribune books.

3297. ————. *A man's enemies.* **New York: Dodd, Mead, 1937. 279p.**

Peter Clancy, redheaded private investigator, "dashes about Long Island seeking the killer of Nolan Whittlesey, millionaire, strangled (and maybe jabbed with something, too) at Graytowers, near Huntington. Indeed he outdoes himself as does Wiggar, his valet, in handling the footprints in the shrubbery, the green back numbered H76394129A, and the scrap of paper reading: '5,000 dollars in hundreds. Have it ready night of October 28. Failure means Sudden Death. You know me.' Keep your eye on Top Hat Rafferty, seen climbing the balcony on the night of the crime; Faulkner Terrell, an experimental chemist (always a bad sign), and Kilroy, the butler"—New York herald tribune books.

3298. ————. *The mystery of the thirteenth floor.* **New York: Century Co., 1919.**

396p.

When brilliant but ruthless lawyer James Randolph Stone is murdered in his place of business on the 13th floor of a New York office building, he has few mourners. His nephew of the same name, very much in love with Phyllis Calvert, daughter of a man ruined by the elder Stone's financial chicanery, is the prime suspect. It is he and the secretary, Estelle Daudray, who had witnessed Stone's will just before the latter was found with a dagger through his heart. Fortunately for Jimmy he has fast friends in Philip Gregory, an associate of Jimmy's uncle, in Pete, the office boy, and others, although not in his cousin, Chester Morgan. The confession of the real murderer is read at the last minutes of Jimmy's trial; he is exonerated and reunited with Phyllis.

3299. ————. *Persons unknown.* New York: Dodd, Mead, 1941. 263p.

"Harvey Graydon disappeared after receiving this final warning: 'Leave the $10,000 in small, unmarked bills under the oar box at the end of the old dock one week from tonight—or else!' Peter Clancy, private detective, came to attention, then fairly burned up the roads to and from New Canaan, White Plains, Manhattan and Shinnecock Hills, where a grisly state of affairs came to light. 'I'm the divil for putting two and two together', says he. Herewith you get poison, painting, amour, a mixed collection of suspects, weekend chatter, voices from the past, and a solution you can easily swallow. Yes, Wiggar, the valet, is present with his line of sapient remarks"—New York hearld tribune books.

3300. ————. *Stark murder.* New York: Dodd, Mead, 1939. 268p.

An unoccupied hotel in the wintry Adirondacks gives up a frozen corpse. Peter Clancy just happens to be in the neighborhood; he avails himself of the opportunity to utilize his powers of detection.

3301. ————. *The unlatched door.* New York: Century Co., 1920. 317p.

"The hero of this mystery tale, after a night with Bacchus, misses his own doorway and steps through the unlatched door of his next door neighbor in the brownstone block [in Manhattan] in which his house is situated. But in a few moments he emerges, thoroughly sobered, for just within the door lay the dead body of a beautiful woman. She has been murdered of course, and the young man instinctively decides that he will be wise to maintain ignorance. The next day, however, he is drawn in when the servants next door summon him. Unfortunately he has accidentally left evidence of his visit, and when the police take charge he becomes one of the suspects. A considerable group is involved, and characteristically in stories of this type, each one suspects the other. When guilt is fixed, the one least suspected proves to be the murderer"—Springfield Republican.

3302. **Thayer, Stephen Henry, 1839-1919.** *Daughters of the Revolution.* **New York: Abbey Press, 1901. 244p.**

The novel's primary hero is Richard Andros, a recent arrival in New York from England, who coolly observes the widening breach between the colonies and the Mother Country, and decides to cast his lot with the 'Sons of Liberty.' However, he has fallen in love with Charlotte Carroll, daughter of a Loyalist. In view of their political differences Charlotte deems it best that they part, at least temporarily. The Revolution begins and Andros serves as an officer in the American army along with his friends James Monroe (later the president of the United States) and John Fairfax, taking part in the Long Island and New York City battles and the Ticonderoga campaigns. Both Andros and Fairfax are wounded, the former dangerously, and are taken prisoners by Burgoyne's troops. Charlotte travels up the Hudson River and Valley to attend to the stricken Andros, while Fairfax is nursed by and falls in love with Grace Montreau, daughter of a clergyman. Andros dies and the two women, 'Daughters of the Revolution', continue to nurse the war's casualties. With the end of the Revolution Fairfax marries Grace. Charlotte never marries despite a proposal by James Monroe.

3303.   **Thébaud, Augustus J., 1807-1885.** *Louisa Kirkbride*; a tale of New York. **New York: P.F. Collier, 1879. 528p.**
The author says "his great object was to describe life in New York and to warn the people of this country against some social dangers, which all must admit are only too real" (Preface). Louisa, aristocratic and open-minded wife of merchant Ralph Kirkbride, takes more than a passing interest in the two O'Byrne siblings, Cornelius ('Con') and Julia. Con is a detective with the New York Police. Julia, of inestimable help and comfort to Louisa, is 'adopted' as her daughter after Mrs. O'Byrne's death. Frederick, the son of Louisa and Ralph Kirkbride, invests unwisely in the stock market in spite of his father's caveat. Mr. Kirkbride passes away suddenly and Frederick, his chief heir, loses most of the Kirkbride fortune when he attempts to corner the gold market (on Black Friday, September 24, 1869). Her son dies and Louisa is in much reduced circumstances. Fortunately Con O'Byrne, now a lawyer, and the Kirkbride attorney discover valuable real estate Mr. Kirkbride purchased just before his death. They force a crooked lawyer involved in the transaction to disgorge the pertinent papers he has been concealing. Louisa, a recent convert to Catholicism, is able to live comfortably again; she is most generous with her funds to friends and neighbors.

3304.   **Theiss, Lewis Edwin, 1878-1963.** *With young Bruce on the Indian frontier*; a story of General Sullivan's expedition. **Illustrated by Michael Barker. Boston: Wilde, 1952. 347p.**
When Bruce is left an orphan by the death of his parents in a surprise Indian attack in Upstate New York during the American Revolution, he eventually accompanies the expedition of General Sullivan whose purpose is to punish the Iroquois for their depredations.

3305.   **Thiusen, Ismar, pseud.** *The Diothas*; or, *A far look ahead*. **New York: G.P.**

Putnam, 1883. iv, 358p.

A futuristic novel that takes New York City to the 90th century with advances in transportation enabling people to live 50 miles from their places of business. New inventions are discussed—malleable glass, steel with the look of silver, elevators run by force derived from the rise and fall of ocean tides. Brooklyn is a university town of coeducation, women are released from arduous housekeeping and occupy themselves with the arts and sciences; thievery and the profession of law are things of the past. Also published later (1890) under the title: *A far look ahead; or, The Diothas.*

Thiusen, Ismar, pseud. *A far look ahead; or, The Diothas.* **See note under Item #3305.**

3306. **Thomas, Albert Ellsworth, 1872-1947.** *The double cross.* **New York: Dodd, Mead, 1924. 284p.**

"In 'The double cross', a new love and mystery story of New York, we find Jim Stanley and Rollin Waterman in love with the same girl. These two young men have been the Damon and Pythias of Wall Street. The heart complication spells trouble—[it] accounts for much of the stir and trouble in Mr. Thomas' book. The tale is one of betrayal, revenge, maneuvers of 'The Street' and all sorts of rapid life in the big city"—New York world.

Thomas, Curtis. See under his pseudonym: Kinney, Thomas.

3307. **Thomas, Eugene, b. 1893 or 4.** *The intimate stranger.* **New York: Sears, 1932. 272p.**

"In which Norry Parker, an upstanding young under gardener, horsewhipped and driven from Sea Cliff [the Van Tuysdale estate on Long Island] twelve years ago for daring to love the unbelievably aristocratic Cadence (really!) Van Tuysdale comes back with money and turns the tables. Says he: 'Mrs. Van Tuysdale, what new clothes you need in the future you will make yourself. If you don't, you won't get them. ... And that goes for you also, Miss Van Tuysdale.' [This is complemented] with a stolen bracelet, a rajah, a shooting and international intrigue"—New York herald tribune book review.

3308. **Thomas, Frederick William, 1806-1866.** *Clinton Bradshaw; or, The adventures of a lawyer.* **Philadelphia: Carey, Lea & Blanchard, 1835. 2v.**

"Clinton Bradshaw ... is another farmer boy who strives for success in a large city, presumably New York. He is a law student and distinguished among his fellows for skill in the debating society which meets to discuss such serious problems as 'Whether woman was equal to man in intellect.' Like his companions he was fond of spending pleasant hours at one of the city's many oyster saloons, but afterwards in his own room, no matter how late, [he would read] the life of Caesar, Themistocles, Napoleon or Chatham, or study a chapter on executory devises, and then read from a fashionable novel before going to sleep. A young man endowed with such powers of endurance and in addition, equipped with the natural gifts of an orator, was certain of success. ... Bradshaw did not fear to explore the unsavory sections of the city, and ... he aided in the rescue of an innocent young woman imprisoned there. His law practice indeed was largely built upon his wide acquaintance with criminals whom he did not hesitate to accept as clients"—Dunlap, G.A. *The city in the American novel, 1783-1900*.

3309. **Thomas, Henry Wilton, b. 1867. *The last lady of Mulberry*; a story of Italian New York. Illustrated by Emil Pollak. New York: D. Appleton, 1900. vii, 330p.**

Bertino Manconi and his uncle, Giorgio DiBello, a prosperous grocer in the 'Little Italy' of Mulberry Street, fall in love with the entertainer 'Juno the Superb' (Juno Castagna). Bertino's friend, Armando Corrini, a sculptor, waits in Italy for Bertino to send him a photograph of the American president's wife from which he will sculpt a likeness that will assure his fame. Juno, quickly married to Bertino, substitutes her portrait for that of the president's wife in the packet Bertino sends to Armando. When Di Bello unaware that Juno is married to Bertino, proposes to Juno, she tries to rid herself of the less than prosperous Bertino, telling her husband that his uncle, DiBello, is dead, and that he, Bertino is suspected of murdering him. The completed bust, shipped to New York, has the features of Juno. Bertino comes out of hiding; Armando Corrini turns up in New York to bask in fame. Juno smashes the bust and vanishes. The chagrined DiBello remains a bachelor and Armando and Bertino go back to Italy.

3310. **Thomas, Howard, 1898-1969. *The road to sixty*. Prospect, N.Y.: Prospect Books, 1966. viii, 336p.**

A novel about Welsh-American life in the Steuben Hills, N.Y. north of Utica, covering the years 1844 to ca. 1894. Two brothers, Jonathan and David Davies, fall in love with Gwen Rowlands. David stays on the family farm; Jonathan leaves temporarily for the Mexican War and the California goldfields. David is a stern Baptist, Gwen a Wesleyan Methodist; Jonathan belongs to no church. The crux of the story lies in Gwen's difficulty in choosing between the brothers and dealing with religious constraints, for Gwen tries to sway the brothers to adopt Methodism. The Adirondacks are in the background when Gwen, in her latter years, sits alone with her memories.

3311. **————. *The singing hills*. Prospect, N.Y.: Prospect Books, 1964. viii, 336p.**

"A novel about Welsh settlers in the Steuben Hills in the 1840s. In this and a second novel, *The road to sixty* [q.v.], Thomas drew memorable pictures of Welsh-American customs and traditional ceremonies that had found their way from ancient Wales to the rolling hills of Oneida County"—O'Donnell, Thomas F., Oneida County: literary highlights (In *Upstate literature*. Syracuse University Press, 1985).

3312. **Thompson, Charles, 1930- . *Halfway down the stairs*. New York: Harper,**

1957. 277p.

One third of the novel takes place at Cornell University where Dave Pope is a student; his Ithaca sojourn is marked by wild parties and sexual encounters and his continued involvement with Ann Carlin, a relentless man hunter. After graduation Dave takes the business route in New York City; as he looks back at his life, he sees that those early years had been a waste.

3313. Thompson, George, fl. 1848-1858. *The brazen star*; or, *The adventures of a New York M.P.* **A true tale of the times we live in. New York: G.W. Hill, 1853. 59p.**

'Nativism' (the promotion of the interests of natives or citizens against those of immigrants) is the theme that propels the plot of this story. Maxwell and Carlton are two corrupt policemen who have taken to counterfeiting. When caught in the act by Dennis Finnegan, a recent immigrant from County Cork and also a policeman (although a dishonest one), Maxwell states his preference to be arrested by his co-conspirator Carlton. The latter draws Finnegan to a counterfeiting gang hideout where he is tormented and finally hung. Since the only witness to his crime is now dead, Maxwell goes free.

3314. ————. *City crimes*; or, *Life in New York and Boston*. **A volume for everybody: being a mirror of fashion, a picture of poverty, and a startling revelation of the secret crimes of the great cities. By Greenhorn [pseud.]. Boston: W. Berry, 1849. 192p. (in double columns).**

Frank Sydney marries Julia Fairchild, unaware of her nymphomania. Being wealthy and tenderhearted he takes a special interest in helping the troubled, in particular a young prostitute, Maria Archer. Unfortunately he happens to be present when Maria's pimping husband, Fred, kills her and flees the scene. Frank is charged with murder. Just before Frank is to be hanged, the dying Fred Archer confesses. After he separates from the unfaithful Julia, Frank falls into the hands of the mysterious 'Dead Man' and his cronies. Another mysterious individual, the 'Doctor', rescues Frank. Meanwhile bigamous Julia has married a Mr. Hedge and murders him when she is consumed with passion for a young Italian (Frank in disguise). Julia commits suicide and Frank finally finds love and peace with the virginal Sophia Franklin. The Doctor puts an end to the criminal activities of the Dead Man.

3315. ————. *The gay girls of New York*; or, *Life on Broadway*. **Being a mirror of the fashions, follies and crimes of a great city, by George Thompson, 'Greenhorn.' New York: 1858. 118p.**

A grisly fictional account of the sad lives of the 'gay girls' (the prostitutes) in the brothels or on the streets of New York. The most depressing of the story's several plots is that which concerns Hannah Sherwood, one of brothel madam Estelle Bishop's 'girls' who tries to rescue an innocent sewing-girl, Lucy Pembroke, from ravishment by Arthur Wallingford, one of New York's 'solid citizens'. For her pains Hannah is thrown out of the brothel and joins her lover, Frank Rattleton in several wild escapades. Hannah gets into a vicious fight with her former employer, Estelle Bishop, the upshot of which is Hannah's horrible disfigurement and blinding when Estelle throws a vial of vitriol in her face. Hannah is abandoned by Rattleton, ends up in a freak show and dies in the stews of the city's 'Five Points'. The author writes of other young women dragged into the 'world's oldest profession', some of whom choose suicide when they see no way out of their grim life or who murder their persecutors.

3316.   ————. *The house breaker*; or, *The mysteries of crime*, by Greenhorn [pseud.] Boston: W.L. Bradbury, 1848. 48p. (in double columns).

New York City's infamous 'Five Points', an area of slums and criminal activity, is the locale of much of the story. The 'Captain' (Henry Stuart) has been driven to thievery and housebreaking by the manipulations of a shyster lawyer, William Roberts, who stripped him of his inheritance. Stuart is arrested and sent to the Tombs. At his trial documents are produced that yield proof of Robert's infamy. Stuart is released and Roberts takes his place in prison. Two thugs from Five Points, Flash Bill and Guinea Bill, murder Stuart's sister—earlier in the story Stuart had prevented Guinea Bill from raping poor Jane Carr, innocent daughter of a vicious, drunken cripple. Stuart kills the two Bills and marries Jane Carr. Discharged from prison, Roberts is also killed in self-defense by Stuart.

3317.   ————. *The locket*; a romance of New York. P.F. Harris, 1855. 89p.

'Smutty Tom', a chimney sweep, is the secondary hero of this tale of the big city, for he is the one who apprises the primary hero, Walter De Lacy, of the existence of De Lacy's beauteous next-door tenant, Edith Hargrave, and the under-handed activities of De Lacy's servant Jowls and De Lacy's agent Snarley. De Lacy secretly places a locket with his portrait in Edith's chamber and she immediately falls in love with his image. When Edith and her mother (left penniless when their trust fund is plundered by an absconding Wall Street banker) are unable to pay the rent, Snarley, a rejected suitor for Edith's hand, evicts them. De Lacy comes to their rescue; he terminates his employ of Snarley and Jowls. The two villains pay further for their transgressions— Jowls is incarcerated and Snarley's female retainer, old Muff, poisons him. Of course, Tom is properly rewarded and the bachelor De Lacy takes Edith for his bride.

3318.   **Thompson, Joyce.** *Hothouse.* **New York: Avon Books, 1981. 430p.**

An Ivy League university in Upstate New York (could it possibly be Cornell University?) is the focus of the author's dissection of the Class of 1970, a batch of professors and an Irish priest active in the anti-war movement. Along the way McCarthyism, pot (marijuana), and virginity and its loss attract attention.

3319.   **Thompson, Ray.** *A respectable family.* **Chicago: Donelley, Gasette & Loyd, 1880. 552p.**

'Arlington', a town in Upstate New York 50 miles from New York City, has illusions of economic grandeur, but it has just lost a large manufacturing plant to a neighboring city, 'W———'. The town takes note when Richard Worth, son of a wealthy towner, falls in love with Sally Jones, daughter of an uneducated, shanty-dwelling odd-jobber, Bob Jones. Richard's father is certainly displeased. Richard quits college, takes lodgings in New York City and befriends philosopher/phrenologist Jerome Augustus 'Dillingham'. The two strike oil in 'Wolfton', Pennsylvania. Meanwhile Sally is receiving an education via benevolent Captain Jack Burton; the elder Worths and their daughter visit Sally and are quite impressed with her. To Arlington's surprise Bob Jones inherits a goodly sum of money from a brother in California who also happens to be Dillingham's brother. Dillingham/Jones, Sally's uncle, and Richard appear in Arlington and preparations are made for an old-fashioned country wedding joining Richard and Sally. The whole town is invited, including those who have been censorious of Sally.

3320. **Thompson, Vance, 1863-1925.** *Mr. Guelpa, the famous French detective, visits America, and finds the most baffling mystery of his career awaiting him.* **Indianapolis: Bobbs-Merrill, 1925. 339p.**

A curious murder and an insurance swindle interrupt the social visit to New York City of Mr. Guelpa, the French criminologist. Mr. Benton, the murder victim, left behind an insurance policy worth $50,000 that his widow comes to collect. She is recognized by a claims agent as the person who five years earlier had collected $10,000 in insurance money from another deceased husband. Is she a murderous lady who gets rid of spouses by devious means—poison, e.g.? But then she disappears from view and Guelpa comes upon a new set of fingerprints and another species of motive for Benton's murder. The actual murderer is of course an individual who is the least suspected.

3321. **Thomson, Mortimer, 1831-1875.** *Doesticks, what he says,* **by Q.K. Philander Doesticks, P.B. [pseud.]. New York: E. Livermore, 1855. 330p.**

Q[ueer] K[ritter] Philander Doesticks, P[erfect] B[rick], moves about New York City and several other American places (Niagara, e.g.) giving his informed opinions on such items as Barnum's Museum, city boarding-houses, fortune-tellers, charity balls, churchgoing, the Croton water supply, political patronage, escaping manure in the streets, fire companies battling one another on their way to fires, & c.

3322. **Thorp, Roderick, 1936- .** *Into the forest.* **New York: Random House, 1961. 336p.**

The undergraduates in this college novel are split into those who, though New York City natives, attend Cornell University and Cortland State, and others from Upstate New York who are enrolled at City College of New York and Hunter College. A CCNY student, Charlie Cumberland, contests Cornellian Cal Torrenson for the favors of Elaine Spelman, Jewish, and also a Cornell undergraduate. Charlie is the winner despite the qualms of Elaine's parents over the marriage of a Gentile with a Jew.

3323. *The Three widows*; or, *Various aspects of Gotham life.* **By a member of the New York Bar. New York: W.F. Burgess, 1849. 96p. (in double columns).**

The difficulties the three widows—Mrs. Blane (she has a comely daughter, Mary); Dorothy Hamilton, housekeeper for Colonel William Mansfield; and Rachel Seymour—have in finding husbands are compounded by the presence of other women who have had various connections to the most likely suitors in the past. Two succeed in the quest: the Widow Blane is 'won' by Captain Forrest after he had vainly pursued her daughter; and Rachel Seymour marries Colonel Mansfield who had avoided the traps set for him by his aggressive housekeeper, Dorothy Hamilton. Mrs. Hamilton drops out of contention and out of sight.

Thrice, Luke, pseud. See: Russell, John, 1885-1956.

3324. **Thurman, Wallace, 1902-1934.** *The blacker the berry*; **a novel of Negro life. New York: Macaulay, 1929. 262p.**

"Emma Lou [Morgan's] black skin was an embarrassment to her among her lighter-hued family and friends in Boise [Idaho] and again at college [in Los Angeles]. She thought in Harlem it might be different. But her experience there, at work, at play in the night clubs and in casual love relationships end in bitter disillusionment and flight"—Book review digest. Emma Lou's Harlem and New York City experiences take up more than two-thirds of the novel. She is 'used' by men who walk in and out of her life, but does finally exhibit some gumption at the story's conclusion when she walks away from dissolute Alva and his idiot child. Thurman's novel is important to one's understanding of Harlem and its people in the 1920s.

3325. **Thurston, Mabel Nelson, b. 1869.** *Sarah Ann.* **With illus. by E.C. Caswell. New York: Dodd, Mead, 1917. 230p.**

"Sarah Ann is a tenement child who has grown up in one of the most crowded sections of New York City, and who has succeeded quite thoroughly in evading education. ... The story pictures the efforts of this little tenement girl to keep house and care for Bobby and her baby sister. The crucial moment of existence comes when she first meets the 'Lady Cop' who takes an interest in the child and ... finally brings her to the point of wishing to go to school and of entrusting her adored baby sister to a day nursery"—Boston transcript.

3326. **Tibbitts, George Franklin, b. 1864.** *The mystery of Kun-ja-muck Cave.* **A strange mystery trailing through the beautiful mountain and lake country of the Adirondacks. New York: Brieger Press, 1924. 319p.**

Another edition appeared in 1928 (Cornwall, N.Y.: Cornwall Press). In order to rejuvenate his mental and physical well being after exhausting sessions on Wall Street Byron Gray comes to Adirondack Park. After slight hesitation

Byron immerses himself in the demanding outdoor life of the Adirondacks. He establishes a friendship with the guide Jack Black; together these two set out to contact the reclusive Louie Lamont. That French-Canadian had a reputation as a heedless destroyer of wildlife, but in recent months had changed into a caretaker of the fauna of the Adirondacks. The reason for this metamorphosis was determined to be the influence emanating from the stranger or strangers who presumably occupied the Kun-ja-muck Cave. After Louie's death Byron and Black unlock the mystery of the cave to the satisfaction of inquisitive natives and visitors.

Tierney, Christopher, joint author. *God is my broker.* **See Item #3423.**

Tierney, John Marion, joint author. *God is my broker.* **See Item #3423.**

Tillett, Dorothy Stockbridge, b. 1896. See under her pseudonym: Strange, John Stephen, b. 1896.

3327. **Tippetts, Katherine Bell, b. 1865.** *Princess Arengzeba*; a romance of Lake George, by Jerome Cable [pseud.]. *And Beautiful Lake George.* **Glens Falls, N.Y.: W.H. Tippetts, c1892. 154p.**
Without Clyde Ashurst's knowledge a friend, Robert Morrison, passes him off to the young women guests at Lake George as a prince from India, who is traveling under the alias of Clyde Ashurst. Morrison's ruse creates trouble for Clyde when he falls in love with Rita Lisle, a young lady who has promised her father she will marry only an American. Amidst description of jaunts around New York's Lake George region the quandary is resolved to the satisfaction of lovers and friends. *Beautiful Lake George*: p.124-154.

3328. **Tobenkin, Elias, 1882-1963.** *The house of Conrad.* **New York: Stokes, 1918. 375p.**
Gottfried Conradi (later Conrad), a follower of the socialist doctrines of Ferdinand Lassalle, comes to the New World in 1868 with the vision of founding a proletarian community/state there. He and his wife Anna settle in New York City; the only work he can find is as a cigar-maker; he defers his dream. Fred, their only surviving child, reaches adulthood, becomes a national organizer for the labor union movement and marries Elsie Whitney. Sent to prison on a false charge, Fred comes out a changed man, without purpose. Elsie dies; the Juvenile Society takes the children Ruth and Robert, from their father. The two young people have their share of travails in New York before Robert strikes out for California, purchases a homestead there and is reunited with his grandfather Gottfried and his sister Ruth—Fred Conrad dies a homeless man in San Francisco.

3329. **————.** *The road.* **New York: Harcourt, Brace, 1922. 316p.**
"Hilda Thorsen bears her illegitimate child alone and works in New York's garment industry to support herself and her son. She is gradually drawn into

union activity and a close friendship with socialist union organizer Frank Hellstrom. Hilda's sincerity, dedication and personal knowledge of the working class make her a top-flight union organizer whose life becomes absorbed in a series of strikes. Raymond Evert, the father of her son, turns up again years later, but by then Hilda realizes he is a weak and vacillating man. In 1921 Hilda joins Frank in the Soviet Union where he has become the superintendent of a Russian locomotive repair plant. Tobenkin's sympathetic portrayal of Hilda is heightened by a style which owes much to Hemingway"– Blake, F.M. *The strike in the American novel.*

3330. **Toland, Mary M.B.** *Onti-Ora*; **a metrical romance. With illus. from designs by W. L. Sheppard. Philadelphia: J.B. Lippincott, 1881 [c1880]. 117p.**

'Onti-Ora', according to the author, is the Indian name for the Catskill Mountains, the scene of most of this narrative poem's story. The lovers, Leon de Maury and Edith, daughter of Judge Lee Von Emich, are separated when Edith's Southern cousin, John Winstone, a rival for Edith's hand, is found shot to death in the Catskills, and Leon, a prime suspect in the killing, is forced to flee. The presumed Leon is arrested in New York City as he tries to board a ship for Europe. Edith visits 'Leon', now half-mad from his imprisonment, and Judge Von Emich promises to defend him. However, all turns out well for Edith and Leon. The prisoner 'Leon' is actually Louis de Maury, a look-a-like relative of Leon; Leon himself had made his way to France where he gained distinction as a soldier. And a gypsy, Sybil Metis, tells all concerned that John Winstone had been killed when he accidentally fell on his hunting rifle and it discharged. The gypsy had kept silent for fear that her people would be blamed for Winstone's death.

3331. **Tomerlin, John, 1930- .** *Prisoner of the Iroquois.* **New York: Dutton, 1965. 189p.**

Young Jed Horne's father seriously embarrassed the leader of the Onondaga Nation and in so doing was probably responsible in part for pushing that branch of the Iroquois into the arms of the British during the early stages of the Revolutionary War in the Mohawk Valley (German Flats in particular). Jed is taken prisoner by the Onondagas and he has to adjust to the Indian way of life until he grasps the opportunity to escape and return to his home.

3332. **Tomlinson, Everett Titsworth, 1859-1931.** *The boy soldiers of 1812.* **Boston: Lee and Shepard, 1895. 319p.**

Two sets of brothers, Andrew and David Field and Elijah and Henry Spicer, are the young lads offering their services to General Jacob Brown who commands American forces at Sackett's Harbor and later Ogdensburg. One companion in arms is Tom Garnet, a sailor serving under Commodore Isaac Chauncey; Chauncey is trying to establish American supremacy on Lakes Ontario and Erie. Another ally is Herman Jeduthun Chubb, a fellow who joins Elijah Spicer in flight after the Americans are routed at Queenston; several other engagements on the New York-Canadian border are described. Andrew

Field falls into British hands, is imprisoned at Brockville, Ontario, and is rescued by David and Elijah, members of a task force headed by Captain Forsyth. The novel is one of a series that Tomlinson wrote about the War of 1812.

3333. ————. *Camping on the St. Lawrence*; or, *On the trail of the early discoverers*. **Illustrated by A.B. Shute. Boston: Lee and Shepard, 1899. vi, 412p.**
Four college-age men—Robert (Bob) Darnell, Benjamin (Ben) Dallett, Josiah (Jock) Cope and Albert (Bert) Bliss—spend a summer camping on 'Pine Tree Island' on the St. Lawrence (not far from Goose Bay). With their guide, 'old Ethan', they fish, hunt, canoe, enter boat races, and listen to Ethan's tales about War of 1812 sites in the region and early French exploration. Alexandria Bay, Ogdensburg and Massena are among the towns on the New York side of the St. Lawrence they touch.

3334. ————. *Cruising on the St. Lawrence*; **a summer vacation in historic waters. Illustrated by A. B. Shute. Boston: Lee and Shepard, 1902. ix, 442p.**
In two earlier works—*Camping on the St. Lawrence* (1899) and *The houseboat on the St. Lawrence* (1900)—Tomlinson took Bob Darnell, Ben Dallett, Jock Cope and Bert Bliss to various historic sites along the famous river. In the present novel the four continue to explore places of interest in a sloop yacht, paying particular attention to Indian history, habits and customs.

3335. ————. *Elder Boise*; **a novel. New York: Doubleday, Page, 1901. vii, 403p.**
The story "sets forth the trials and triumphs of a young clergyman [in a small New York State town] of large soul and liberal views, whose first pastoral position places him over a narrow-minded, close-fisted, and generally ... [materialistic] congregation. The story is full of Yankee humor, shrewd saws, and tricksy bargainings, all of which the reader is sure to enjoy. It shows the typical village life of the Eastern States, and is racy of the soil"—Outlook.

3336. ————. *Exiled from two lands*. **Boston: Lee and Shepard, 1898. 119p.**
"The story of a French family who sought a home in Canada at the end of the last [18th] century. A series of misunderstandings between the young daughter and her father banishes the former to America [northern New York]. The tragedy of her life is told many years afterward near her grave in the Adirondacks, where a party of 'city folks' have made a camp"—Annual American catalogue.

3337. ————. *The fort in the forest*; **a story of the fall of Fort William Henry in 1757. Illus. by Chase Emerson. Boston: W.A. Wilde, 1904. 341p.**
The novel offers an animated picture of life on the New York frontier in the late colonial period including races by the protagonists over snow and ice and on snowshoes, a hazardous scouting trip, and reconnoitering by canoe along the shores of Lake Champlain—all culminating in the capture and sacking of Fort William Henry on Lake George by the French and Indians under

Montcalm. This work was reprinted in 1924 (New York: Appleton) under the title: *Scouting in the wilderness*; the fort in the forest.

3338.   ————. *The houseboat on the St. Lawrence.* **Illustrated by A.B. Shute. Boston: Lee and Shepard, 1900. vii, 402p.**

"Continues the story of the four friends of 'Camping on the St. Lawrence' [q.v.]. The author has placed them in this book on a houseboat on the same river and given them Frontenac instead of Cartier as the discoverer who affords them inspiration"—Annual American catalogue.

3339.   ————. *Marching against the Iroquois.* **Boston: Houghton, Mifflin, 1906. viii, 388p.**

The novel is intimately based on General John Sullivan's punitive expedition against the Iroquois in 1779. The Mohawk Valley and the Finger Lakes are the regions where the events narrated occur. Many of the characters who appeared in Tomlinson's *The Red Chief* (q.v.) are present in this story.

3340.   ————. *Old Fort Schuyler.* **Philadelphia: Griffith & Rowland Press, 1901. 296p.**

A fictional representation of the siege of Fort Stanwix (here called Fort Schuyler) on the Mohawk River by British forces under Colonel Barry St. Leger in 1777. The author's two heroes who stood with the successful American defendants under Colonel Peter Gansevoort are brothers of sixteen and eighteen years.

3341.   ————. *The Red Chief*; **a story of the massacre of Cherry Valley. Boston: Houghton, Mifflin, 1905. viii, 381p.**

After the defeat of Burgoyne at Saratoga the people scattered about New York's frontiers were still faced with the hostility of the Iroquois, led by Joseph Brant, the 'Red Chief'. The Indians in alliance with the Tories and a few British regulars continued to attack the outlying settlements. The novel is a fictionalized version of the tragic fate of Cherry Valley whose inhabitants were left largely to their own defenses.

3342.   ————. *The self-effacement of Malachi Joseph.* **Philadelphia: Griffith & Rowland Press, 1906. 235p.**

Malachi Joseph graduates from a theological seminary and on the advice of one of his teachers starts out on his ministry in a little town in the northern regions of New York State. The story relates how he reacts to the adversities that come his way and how he achieves some lasting successes.

————. *Scouting in the wilderness.* **See note under Item #3337.**

————. *Scouting on Lake Champlain*—**the young rangers. See note under Item #3350.**

————. *Scouting on the Mohawk*: **a soldier of the wilderness. See note under Item #3343.**

3343. ————. *A soldier of the wilderness*; **a story of Abercrombie's defeat and the fall of Fort Frontenac in 1758. With illus. by Chase Emerson. Boston: W.A. Wilde, 1905. 357p.**

Reissued in 1925 under the title: *Scouting on the Mohawk*: a soldier of the wilderness. "Mr. Tomlinson's third story in this 'Colonial series' is based on history centering about the French and Indian War—the fall of Fort Frontenac and the disaster under Abercrombie at Ticonderoga. The adventures introduce Abercrombie ('Old Nabby'), young Howe, Israel Putnam and Montcalm, a young hero, Peter Van de Bogert, besides hunters, rangers, and [other] men prominent in those times"—Book review digest.

3344. ————. *The spy of Saratoga*. **New York: Appleton, 1928. vii, 256p.**

"Joe Beattys was a real character and his name is still not unknown in the region of Saratoga"—Preface. The two fictional 'heroes' of the story are Young Gordon and Hans, a Dutchman and waiter at the Goode Vrouw Tavern (20 miles northeast of Albany). Beattys ('the spy of Saratoga') had fought heroically for the Americans at the naval encounter (Valcour Island, etc.) on Lake Champlain in 1776. However, when he was taken prisoner by the British and the Americans made no attempt to arrange an exchange for him, Beattys switched sides and began spying, raiding the settlements and taking Americans as prisoners to Montreal. He attempted to kidnap General Philip Schuyler but failed. Eventually Young Gordon, Hans and other patriots seized Beattys; he was taken to Albany, tried and hanged.

3345. ————. *Three colonial boys*; **a story of the times of '76. Illustrated by Charles Copeland. Boston: W.A. Wilde, 1895. 368p.**

Much of the novel is concerned with life in New York City as the American Revolution breaks out in full force. The 'boys' of the title are patriots who are ardent participants in the momentous events of the period. The author has an abiding interest in pointing out Whig and Tory differences, the resentment of the colonials as the British pursue their particular goals, and the behavior and thoughts of the ordinary soldier.

3346. ————. *The trail of the Mohawk chief*; **a story of Brant (Thayendanegea). Illustrated by Walt Louderback. New York: D. Appleton, 1916. viii, 313p.**

A fictional representation of Joseph Brant's life, including his association with Sir William Johnson, his visit to England, generalship at the Battle of Oriskany, and his forays against the Cherry Valley settlers and other New York villages.

3347. ————.*Two young patriots*; **or, *Boys of the frontier*. A story of Burgoyne's Invasion. Illustrated by Charles Copeland. Boston: W.A. Wilde, 1898. 366p.**

The work is a cross between fiction and a quite detailed history of Burgoyne's invasion and subsequent surrender at Saratoga. The 'two young patriots' are the fatherless Samuel and Jarius Goodwin who are almost drafted into British General Simon Fraser's forces, but manage to escape; they spend the balance of the story working their way back to the American lines with the help of several knowledgeable scouts and soldiers.

3348. ————. *With flintlock and fife*; a tale of the French and Indian War. With illus. by Frank O. Small. Boston: W.A. Wilde, 1903. 356p.

A tale of adventure covering the Battle of Lake George (1755), etc. Sir William Johnson appears here as General Johnson, shortly before he was knighted. This work was issued later under the title: Scouting on the old frontier: with flintlock and fife (1923).

3349. ————. *The young minute-man of 1812*. Boston: Houghton Mifflin, 1912. viii, 343p.

Luke Fox, 18, had grown up on the shores of Lake Ontario. When war broke out between the United States and England in 1812, Luke was able to offer his knowledge of the waterways to the American naval officers. Commodore Chauncey sent Luke from Sacketts Harbor down the St. Lawrence River to observe British operations. Eventually the young hero was on Lake Champlain when Macdonough's American naval forces shattered British hopes for control of that strategic body of water.

3350. ————. *The young rangers*; a story of the conquest of Canada. With illus. by Chase Emerson. New York: Appleton, 1906. 351p.

Reissued in 1925 under the title: Scouting on Lake Champlain—the young Rangers. Peter Van de Bogert and Sam, hunter and trapper turned farmer, and Sam's wife, Mary, are among the leading personages in the story which continues earlier works by the author about colonial New York State and the frontier during the French and Indian War. Peter and Sam join the English and provincial forces under General Amherst as the latter moves up the western shore of Lake Champlain to recapture Fort Ticonderoga and Crown Point. Major Robert Rogers' expedition against the Abenaki Indians and its cruel aftermath find Peter and Sam in the ranks. They are among the survivors who are able to celebrate the final victory. Sam returns to Mary, their young son and farm on the New York frontier.

3351. Tomlinson, Lena. *The triangle*; a story for girls. Boston: A.J. Bradley, 1899. 264p.

Three girls spend a summer in the Adirondacks. The author's description of their natural surroundings is colorful, detailed and accurate.

3352. Tompkins, Juliet Wilbor, 1871-1956. *The top of the morning*. New York: Baker and Taylor, 1910. 342p.

A novel portraying the struggles of six young people—three men and three women—in New York to make a living and gain recognition in art and literature. A driving force is a widow of 36 years. These talented, occasionally temperamental people adopt an expected, unconventional, Bohemian way of life, but readily take under their sheltering wings two boys who wander into their enclave.

3353. **Toohey, John Peter, 1880-1946.** *Fresh every hour*; **detailing the adventures, comic and pathetic, of one Jimmy Martin, purveyor of publicity, a young gentleman possessing sublime nerve ... New York: Boni and Liveright, 1922. 256p.**

"The hero is Jimmy Martin who blithely fills the position of press agent for shows ranging from 'Jollyland' at Coney Island to classical performances by a tragedienne. Some of his conceptions are employed to forward the dramatic success of Lolita Murphy of Cedar Rapids, Iowa. Jimmy fails to differentiate between the garish methods employed in advertising the Coney Island amusement park and the dignity surrounding the performances of a tragedy star. ...But setbacks or difficulties refuse to dampen his ardor for the spectacular. Generally he turns his difficulties to good account. After all his adventures and escapades Jimmy ends his career by marrying Lolita and taking over the management of a 'movie' house at Cedar Rapids"—Springfield Republican.

3354. **Tooker, Helen V.** *The 5:35*; **a novel of suburban life. Garden City, N.Y.: Doubleday, Doran, 1928. 332p.**

The Flemings are a suburban family whose daughter, Neil, worked in the city of New York, but returned home each evening. Mrs. Fleming is one of those women whose motherly instincts impel her to arrange the lives of her children 'for their own good.' Yet Neil has the presence of mind to give up her temporary infatuation with an undesirable man and to ameliorate her mother's opposition to the man she really loves. Neil's brother is not as fortunate; Mrs. Fleming's interference where he is concerned is disastrous.

3355. **Torbett, D., pseud.** *The schemers.* **New York: C.H. Doscher, 1908. 157p.**

The author satirizes the never-ending quest of New Yorkers for social status and the funds necessary for membership in the 'smart set.' Mrs. Van Agan, a widow, belongs to an old Knickerbocker family, but is anxiously searching for a wealthy second husband. Mr. Wentworth is rich, but he lacks polish and social position. Bringing these two together requires the proper strategy. Mrs. Van Agan's pretty daughter, to her mother's dismay, is enamored of an honorable but penniless young man.

3356. **Tourgée, Albion W., 1838-1905.** *Black ice.* **New York: Fords, Howard & Hulbert, 1888. 435p.**

"Tourgée begins the tale effectively by remaining close to actual experience. The village that is described is obviously Mayville, New York, where Tourgée himself had bought a home, 'Thoreim', in 1881...; the lake, covered by black ice, is Chautauqua. ... Tourgée draws the quiet picture of Upstate New York in a rather attractive, subdued manner. But he soon resorts to artificial and factitious narrative as he describes a faultless heroine, Helen Somers, tending wounded soldiers during the Civil War; various children engaged in dangerous escapades on the black ice; and a hero, Percival Reynolds, who saves the life of Helen Somers by climbing mountains to discover her mourning at the grave of her child"—Gross, T.L., Albion W. Tourgée.

3357. ————. *Button's Inn*. **Boston: Roberts Bros. 1887. x, 418p.**
"The locale of the story is Tourgée's surroundings in Upstate New York— Button's Inn had once been an actual inn northeast of Mayville—and ... the part of the novel describing the quiet life of his area is effective"—Gross, T. L. Albion W. Tourgée. The main character of the novel, Jack Button, kills in self-defense and comes back after many years to help the son of the man he murdered, and also converts to Mormonism.

3358. ————. *Hot plowshares*; **a novel. New York: Fords, Howard & Hulbert, 1883. 610p.**
"The novel dramatizes pre-war slavery complications in a New York factory town and a New England seminary village. Avowedly a novel of propagandism, Hot Plowshares shows the reaction of New York townspeople against what they considered the racial malpractices of southern plantation owners. In the course of a long-winded and didactic tale of mystery, adventure and intersectional hatred, one catches glimpses of the Paradise Valley town of 'Skendoah', eventually to become a mill center where as early as 1848 the contest between liberty and slavery took on a serious cast"—Herron, I.H. *The small town in American literature.* The heroine is Hilda Hargrove; she is rumored to have Negro blood via the marriage of Mervyn Hargrove's brother to a quadroon. Martin Kortright, the hero of the story, whose father, Harrison, is an abolitionist, springs to Hilda's side. But proof is forthcoming that Hilda is really the daughter of Mervyn, a liberal Southern gentleman—and the young people take their wedding vows.

3359. ————.*The man who outlived himself.* **New York: Fords, Howard & Hulbert, 1898. 215p.**
Contains three short novels: The man who outlived himself; Poor Joel Pike; and The grave of Tante Angelique. Our concern is with the first two only. In the first, Philip Devens, wiped out in Wall Street, dies, returns to life, determines that he has been affected by amnesia, settles once more in New York City and, largely due to his wife, finds himself once again in a comfortable financial position. In 'Poor Joel Pike' the peculiar old protagonist loves successively Susan Gidney Harrington and her daughter, Sadie, but is rebuffed by both. We learn that Joel has really been a most benign, congenial person who has been supporting Susan and Sadie since the death of the 'no-good' Mr. Harrington.

3360. ————. *The mortgage on the hip-roof house.* **Cincinnati: Curtis Jennings, 1896. 206p.**

"The central problem of the novel is the mortgage that must be paid; and, as might be expected, the young hero, an adopted grandson, helps his poverty-stricken grandfather with his debt and wins the admiration and eventual love of the granddaughter. The scene is once again Tourgée's neighborhood of Mayville [New York], near Lake Erie"—Gross, T.L., Albion W. Tourgée. All in all a sentimental tale with a nod to the Horatio Alger myth.

3361. Towne, Charles Hanson, 1877-1949. *The chain*; a novel. **New York: Putnam, 1922. vii, 364p.**

"A story of the youth of twenty years ago [ca. 1900], not quite so arrogant and self-assertive as the youth of today [ca. 1920], but just as eager and aspiring. John Darrow, a young poet from the country, comes to New York to make a literary career for himself. He is sensitive and idealistic, yet he has a curious belief in himself and his talents. Bound, as he realizes himself to be, in the chain of circumstances, he is not afraid of his destiny. Before long he has become the editor of a promising new magazine and an accepted member of the group of young literati. The story has a distinctive atmosphere, but little plot. From the first page John Darrow is a friend whose career and personality and love affairs it is pleasant to follow"—Book review digest. "A picture is drawn of editorial life in New York in the early years of this century that contains much verisimilitude"—Literary review of the New York evening post.

3362. ————. *The gay ones.* **New York: Century Co., 1924. 323p.**

In this novel of the Long Island 'smart set' "Roger Firth, a young engineer, marries a quite useless, pretty young woman who starts out to lead a gay life and succeeds. Gertrude Randall is not at all a society person, but she plays a very important part in the development of 'The gay ones.' Two more radically different types than Roger Firth's butterfly wife who refuses to be inconvenienced with a family, and Gertrude Randall, who devotes most of her youth to caring for her mother, and who loves Firth, it would be hard to find. The [First World] War affords an escape for these persons caught in a situation strained to the breaking point"—Springfield Republican.

3363. Townley, Houghton. *The scarlet feather.* **Illus. by Will Grefé. New York: W.J. Watt, 1909. 356p.**

Forgery is the ruse employed by Mrs. Swinton, the wife of a rector of a church on New York's East Side, when her father's stinginess and her own prodigality leave her with many debts. The forgery is attributed to Mrs. Swinton's son whose death in war has been announced almost simultaneously. Mrs. Swinton lets the accusation stand and persuades her husband to keep quiet. The unexpected return of their 'deceased' son and his ongoing love affair demand that the truth be told. Rev. Swinton breaks his silence and discloses the truth from the pulpit.

3364. **Townsend, Charles, b. 1857 (Oct. 7).** *The Mahoney million.* **Illustrated by Clare Angell. New York: Amsterdam Book Co., 1903. 215p.**

The Michael Mahoney family—father, mother and daughter Kitty—are now residents of the old Greenwich section of New York City's lower West Side. Michael's million derives from an oil strike on his land in Pennsylvania. Mrs. Mahoney, basking in her new-found wealth and leisure, is certain that she must establish a bridge to New York 'society' for herself and her daughter.

3365. **Townsend, Edward Waterman, 1855-1942.** *Chimmie Fadden and Mr. Paul.* **Illustrated by Albert Levering. New York: Century Co., 1902. 382p.**

The book consists of 27 pieces that relate various events in the lives of the Bowery newsboy, Chimmie Fadden, and Mr. Paul, who has become sentimentally involved with a Miss Fannie. Chimmie finds that the plans he has carefully nurtured are being upset by new characters, including Mr. Paul, that the author has introduced—the 'Duchess', Wily Widdy, the sturdy Mrs. Murphy, and the aforementioned Miss Fannie, et al.

3366. *Chimmie Fadden explains. Major Max expounds.* **New York: Lovell, Coryell, 1985. 266p.**

"Chimmie is still chasing after 'dat bull pup' and smuggling 'small buts' for Mr. Paul. But it is the presence of innate gentleness and chivalry in the rough-bred Bowery lad evoked by Miss Fannie which again touches us most deeply." There are several chapters about Major Max "in which we are regaled with his cynical wit and worldly wisdom tinged with bonhomie, and a few other stories eke out the book"—The Bookman.

3367. ————. *Chimmie Fadden, Major Max, and other stories.* **New York: Lovell, Coryell, 1895. 346p.**

" 'Chimmie Fadden' is a New York newsboy who enters the employment of a rich family as footman, as a reward for a service rendered the young lady of the house; he tells his experience, which is unique and amusing, in the slang of the Bowery in a succession of chapters entitled: Chimmie Fadden makes friends; Chimmie enters polite society; Meets the Dutchess; Observes club life; Mr. Fadden's political experience; Chimmie Fadden in court, etc. The 'Major Max' stories take the reader into a higher stratum of society"—Annual American catalogue.

3368. ————. *The climbing Courvatels.* **With eight full-page illus. in colour by J.V. McFall. New York: F.A. Stokes, 1909. vi, 290p.**

Dick and Betty Courtney, a young married couple with a stage name—the Courvatels—make enough money on the vaudeville circuit as jugglers to quit their occupation and contemplate entering a fairly high level of New York society. Their plans turn out well, although their theatrical origins are occasionally in danger of being revealed. One of their old stage associates is taken in by the Courtneys to assume the role of their butler.

3369. ————. *A daughter of the tenements*. New York: Lovell, Coryell, 1895. 301p.

Carminella, the child of Teresa Cesarotti, a dancer in the Arcadian Burlesque Company, is taken in hand by Maggie Lyons of the same company when Teresa is crippled for life following a theater accident. Maggie places Carminella with her uncle, Dan Lyons, and Carminella thenceforth is 'a daughter of the tenements.' Eleanor Hazelhurst, a wealthy aristocrat and teacher in a mission school, becomes Carminella's sponsor as the girl displays her talents and eventually rises to celebrity as a ballerina. The story effectively portrays a number of typical New York characters (especially those hanging out in the Bowery).

3370. ————. *Days like these*; a novel. New York: Harper, 1901. iv, 443p.

"Mr. Townsend's novel deals with the manners and morals of the New York of today, and, to a considerable degree, as they are affected by the conditions of industry and finance which have made Wall Street affairs more than usually sensational, and politically and socially important"—Bookman. The financier Martin Farnham leaves his fortune to Rose Cavendish, his sister Mary's daughter; Mary had married Jack Cavendish and had entered into a life of deprivation in a tenement on New York's East Side. Rose had been working as a model in an East Grand Street department store when she was suddenly propelled into New York society with her new-found wealth. She adapts well to her new position in the world and falls in love with the young lawyer, Horace Maxwell.

3371. ————. *Lees & leaven*; a New York story of today. New York: McClure, Phillips, 1903. vi, 299p.

"Mr. Townsend introduces his readers to a motley crowd of his country people, and these gathered from the accommodating West, are ultimately hurled into the maelstrom of New York financial and social life. … The story begins with a Western oil-dealer's effort to extend his negotiations, has plenty of incident and movement, but never once seems real until the characters are removed to New York. There the scandalous practice of a great newspaper rouses interest for a moment, but the introduction of several stupidly facetious and impossibly naïve characters wearies inexpressibly. From that time on sensationalism, without any real apology for being, stalks through the pages, for which the presses are waiting"—Overland monthly. Obviously Townsend's intention was to portray in vivid colors the exciting New York of his time with its newspapers, theaters, opera and restaurants, and a tincture of gratifying domestic scenes.

3372. ————. *Near a whole city full*. Illustrated by F.A. Nankivell. New York: G.W. Dillingham, 1897. 260p.

These stories embrace both the sentimental/tragic and the comic aspects of life in New York City's 'Bohemia.' Contents: Just across the square.—A rose of the Tenderloin.—Ann Eliza's triumph.—The man outside.—The dog on the roof.—Guardians of the law.—A dinner of regrets.—The night elevator man's story.—By whom the offence cometh.—The reward of merit.—The house of yellow brick.—The little life of Pietro.—When a man judges.—Polly Slangeur's trousseau.

3373. ————. *Reuben Larkmead*; a story of worldlings. **Illustrated by Wallace Morgan. New York: G.W. Dillingham, 1905. 205p.**

The unworldly and idealistic Reuben Larkmead, a millionaire by virtue of western beet sugar, is an easy mark for New York City's slippery businessmen who are adept at stripping those who are credulous enough to expect honesty in transactions with them. As Reuben relates his experiences in the city and learns the hard way more about the grafting rascals who are eager to separate him from his fortune, he begins to apply the common sense that is also part of his nature. He meets with little success in his excursions into society; but in the end he achieves a highly satisfactory marriage with the widowed mother of the girl he had wooed unsuccessfully.

3374. ————. *A summer in New York*; a love story told in letters. **New York: H. Holt, 1903. v, 196p.**

A latter-day Alice (in Wonderland), Miss Alice Wonderly, daughter of a millionaire in the Western town of Ironville, records for the benefit of a confidential friend, her impressions and experiences in the great metropolis of New York. She is accompanied by her cousin Will as she mixes with the 'smart set', a number of whom decide to stay in town rather than scamper off to various summer resorts. Alice, the Westerner, with her distinctive vocabulary, is clever enough to hold her own and take several matters, including romance, in stride.

3375. ————. *"Sure"*; new 'Chimmie Fadden' stories. **New York: Dodd, Mead, 1904. 188p.**

"The education of the 'Little Duke', James Napoleon Emmet Fadden, is one of the concerns of the volume, and the drama of the present, politics in New York, [the strangeness of women], and automobiles are among the many subjects that come under discussion"—The critic.

3376. ————. *The Yellow Kid in McFadden's Flats*. **Illustrated by R.F. Outcault. New York: G.W. Dillingham, 1897. 192p.**

The creator of the 'Chimmie Fadden' stories and other tales of the poor in New York City comes up with another unique character, Mickey Dugan, designated as 'the Yellow Kid', who too spends his early years in the slums of New York.

3377. **Townsend, Olga.** *Blueprint of a dream*. **New York: Whittlesey House, 1950.**

224p.

Hope Blair, having completed her first year at Barnard College in New York City, spends the summer with her father on a yacht in the Hudson River. She finds herself contemplating two future directions: the first is her burgeoning interest in her architect father's profession—the second is the possibility of tying the knot with a young doctor.

3378. **Trachtman, Paula.** *Disturb not the dream.* **New York: Crown Publishers, 1981. 310p.**

Mulberry House in the Long Island Hamptons was the center of a massacre that occurred during the Hurricane of 1938. Unaware of that fact Dr. Bertram Bradley leases the mansion and brings his family to it in the summer of 1976. Alice, his wife, Bertram and their 5-year-old, Lissie, once settled in the house, begin to have horrible dreams. The Bradley's teenage son and older daughter are compelled to commit incest by debauchees. Bertram has sex with the hired girl and his son rapes her at his sister's insistence. And while ghosts seem to be walking around the house, the Hurricane of 1938 is repeated.

3379. **Tracy, Louise, 1863-1928.** *One wonderful night*; **a romance of New York. New York: E.J. Clode, c1912. 369p.**

After a long absence John Curtis comes back to New York and takes a room in a restful hotel on 27th Street. The calm is shattered when John witnesses a murder outside his door. In the ensuing confusion Curtis discovers he is in possession of the murdered man's coat that contains a marriage license. When he contacts the woman listed on the license, he finds her to be an attractive young lady who had actually paid the victim to marry her so she could elude a tyrannical father and a persistent but disliked suitor. Curtis and she marry and are immediately thrown into a wild series of adventures.

3380. **Train, Arthur Cheney, 1875-1945.** *Ambition.* **New York: Scribner, 1928. 439p.**

Following schooling in New England (Boston primarily), western New York State and Harvard (A.B., A.M. and a law degree) Simon Kent takes root in New York City. The law firm that he begins to work for disturbs him with its penchant for narrowly unethical practices. He marries Clarice Hungerford (against a friend's advice); Clarice is already the mother of a son born out of wedlock. She has social ambitions and ultimately proves her deceitfulness despite a cloak of straightforwardness. Clarice divorces Simon and finds a mate who is better able and willing to fulfill her desires. Tired of his law firm's wily machinations Simon turns to teaching and takes a position with a more ethical law concern. He also finalizes plans to marry a young woman whom he had tutored when he was still in college.

3381. ⸺. *The blind goddess.* **New York: Scribner, 1926. 338p.**

"Hugh Dillon, a young idealist, is practicing criminal law to get a foothold [in his profession]. The heroine, Moira Devene, is the daughter of a very wealthy contractor and politician. Richard Devene, Moira's father, is murdered, and the story hinges on the conviction of the murderer. The officials concerned show greater anxiety to obtain favorable publicity for themselves and petty political advantages than to see that justice is done. A strong chain of circumstantial evidence tightens around an innocent victim. It culminates in a dramatically projected trial scene. It is an interesting story ... [which] has much of the atmosphere of the Criminal Courts Building and of Tombs Prison [in New York City]"—Cleveland public library staff notes.

3382. ————. *The butler's story*; being the reflections, observations and experiences of Mr. Peter Ridges of Wapping-on-Villy, Devon, sometime in the service of Samuel Carter, Esq, of New York. Written by himself and edited by Arthur Train. With illus. by F.C. Yohn. New York: Scribner, 1909. 242p.
Upstairs and downstairs in the home of a nouveau riche New York City family, the Carters. The butler, Peter Ridges, had earlier served aristocrats in England and is inclined to make invidious comparisons between duties in an English versus an American household.

3383. ————. *By advice of counsel*; being adventures of the celebrated firm of Tutt, Attorneys and Counsellors at Law. New York: Scribner, 1914. 312p.
Seven tales, five of which involve court trials. Mr. Tutt is again expertly defending, e.g., a poor lad accused of smashing windows, an old unlicensed horse expert trapped as he practices veterinary medicine, a socially prominent woman who refuses to testify although she has heard an accused murderer's confession. Murder in New York's Syrian community is the subject of 'The kid and the camel.' Contents: The shyster.—The kid and the camel.—Contempt of court.—By advice of counsel.—'That sort of woman.'—You're another!—Beyond a reasonable doubt. Train wrote at least nine other collections of stories about Ephraim Tutt, the Upstate New York lawyer whose home was 'Pottsville' (Geneseo?), although a number of his cases were tried in New York City and other places around the country: *Mr. Tutt comes home* (New York: Scribner, 1941. 341p.); *Mr. Tutt finds a way* (New York: Scribner, 1945); *Mr. Tutt takes the stand* (New York: Scribner, 1936. 290p.); *Old Man Tutt* (New York: Scribner, 1938. 336p.); *Page Mr. Tutt* (New York: Scribner, 1926. 323p.); *Tut, tut, Mr. Tutt* (New York: Scribner, 1923. 315p); *Tutt and Mr. Tutt* (New York: Scribner, c1919/20. 348p.); *Tutt for Tutt* (New York: Scribner, 1934. 323p.); *When Tutt meets Tutt* (New York: Scribner, 1927. 283p.).

3384. ————. *The confessions of Artemas Quibble*; being the ingenious and unvarnished history of Artemas Quibble, Esquire, one-time practitioner in the New York criminal courts, together with an account of the divers wiles, tricks, sophistries, technicalities and sundry artifices of himself and others commonly yclept 'shysters' or 'shysters lawyers.' New York: Scribner, 1911. 227p.

"The autobiography of a New York 'shyster' lawyer who, under the guidance of an abler and even more unscrupulous partner, steps beyond the line that separates chicanery from crime, and on the last page starts for Sing Sing as a convicted felon. No one acquainted with the recent history of New York courts will fail to recognize the fact that use has been made of the notorious deeds of certainly scoundrelly lawyers, but there is also a liberal seasoning of fiction"—Outlook.

3385. [————]. *The Goldfish*; being the confessions of a successful man. New York: Century Co., 1914. 340p.
"A successful man, who finds an income of seventy-five thousand a year inadequate for the current expenses of his family, whose wife and daughters move in the inner circles of New York society, whose son, although nominally a lawyer like his father, has a reputation as an amateur dancer, having arrived at the age of fifty, sits down to analyze his way of life, to sum up his assets and liabilities. The assets as it turns out, are practically negligible. This rich man, too, is one of those who, having gained the world, has suffered the corresponding loss. The confession is frank to a surprising degree, and the whole forms an honest criticism of contemporary tendencies—Book review digest.

3386. ————. *The hermit of Turkey Hollow*; the story of an alibi, being an exploit of Ephraim Tutt ... New York: Scribner, 1921. 207p.
This Upstate New York story finds Skinny the Tramp (James Hawkins) accused of killing the title character, a recluse who lives in a cabin 3 miles northeast of 'Pottsville.' Squire Hezekiah Mason is the prosecutor, a politically ambitious and not very likeable individual. Skinny's defender is the legendary Train creation, Mr. Ephraim Tutt. The novel contains a good measure of small town atmosphere and Mr. Tutt is of course, more than a match for the devious Squire Mason.

3387. ————. *High winds*. New York: Scribner, 1927. ix, 365p.
"One of the Weybridge sisters, Enid, marries an expert polo player but a bungling businessman. The marriage is successful enough at first, but Enid wants more than Charles can give her and presently moves for a Parisian divorce. The other sister, Ursula, is still unmarried at thirty-nine. She falls in love with Peter McKay, and though yielding to their mutual passion, refuses to marry him until their love has been tested. The test with the separation it necessitates is almost disastrous. At the conclusion of the story, which moves from New York to Paris and back again, both sisters are happily, and perhaps permanently settled"—Book review digest.

3388. ————. *His children's children*. New York: Scribner, 1923. vi, 391p.
"The House of Kaynes had been founded by Peter B. who began his career after the Civil War, carrying a pick and dinner-pail, and what with gold-mining and railroad grabbing in good old pirate fashion, retired from affairs as

one of New York's leading financiers. In contrast to him, his son Rufus was a gentleman ... president of the Utopia Trust Company, installed with his family in a house of vulgar grandeur on Fifth Avenue built by Peter B. The story follows the fortunes of the family, giving at the same time a cross-section of post-war high society which, having outgrown its brownstone Victorianism, is giddily and recklessly reaching out for new standards and—especially in the case of women—skirting perilously near to the edge of a precipice. To Rufus Kayne and his family of daughters financial ruin proves a blessing in disguise and the voice of the auctioneer in the hall of the grand house, while it is Peter B.'s death-knell, rings in a new era for the younger generation"—Book review digest.

3389. ————. *Illusion.* **New York: Scribner, 1929. 321p.**
"At a dinner party for the Queen of Dalmatia, Carlee Tharp, vaudeville entertainer [and circus magician], makes a great hit. This sudden social success leads him to desert his partner, Felicity, and their act. [Passing himself off on New York society as a member of an old, prominent family] he gets engaged to the daughter of a self-made man who is also a social climber, and things go well for a while, but Carlee comes to learn that for him happiness without Felicity is an illusion"—Book review digest.

3390. ————. *McAllister and his double.* **New York: Scribner, 1905. 341p.**
This work contains 11 short stories: the first seven deal with McAllister, the last four with John Dockbridge, an assistant district attorney and his cases in court. 'Chubby' McAllister, a wealthy New York clubman, is a rather unsympathetic character who believes 'our tenements are all right and so are our prisons.' 'Fatty' Welch, who physically resembles McAllister, was fired by his employer (McAllister) for dishonesty and has been a thief ever since. McAllister, nevertheless, has on several occasions been targeted as a suspect in several criminal activities. The author effectively describes New York City's police, its hospitals and prisons at the beginning of the 20th century.

3391. ————. *Paper profits*; **a novel of Wall Street. New York: Liveright, 1930. 347p.**
"The effects upon the life of a highly intelligent young married man, suddenly obsessed by stock plunging, are shown in full, disastrous detail over a period of three frenzied years. At the beginning, living happily and unpretentiously with his wife and two children, he seems safely aloof from the temptation to take the road to easy riches. Then he essays his first modest flyer with surprisingly fat returns, and is embarked upon a skyrocketing career in finance. The inevitable loss of [his] whole fortune follows, and bitterly, in weakened character and self-respect and estrangement from his wife, does this victim of reckless stupidity pay for his lesson"—Saturday review of literature.

3392. ————. *Yankee lawyer*; **the autobiography of Ephraim Tutt. New York: Scribner, 1943. xiii, 464p.**

Mr. Tutt is based in 'Pottsville' in Upstate New York, even though much of his activity does take place in New York City. The 'autobiography' of Train's fictional lawyer relates Tutt's life story with a good deal of emphasis on cases which he handled that are not included in the various collections of Tutt's activity published to date.

3393. Train, Elizabeth Phipps, b. 1856. *A marital liability.* **Illustrated by Violet Oakley. Philadelphia: J.B. Lippincott, 1897. 213p.**

Murray Van Vorst spent 10 years in prison for a felony he did not commit; he had occupied a high place in the upper levels of New York society, but had incurred the dislike of his father-in-law who was the primary instigator behind his arrest. The newly released Van Vorst gets acquainted with his daughter; she and Charlotte Poindexter help him prove that it was his wife who had committed the crime for which he served time. An even greater surprise awaits Van Vorst and company before the novel ends.

3394. _____. *A queen of hearts.* **Philadelphia: J.B. Lippincott, 1898. 280p.**

The chief character, Pauline Mavis (the 'queen of hearts') tells her life story when she is 37 and attending the wedding of her daughter Lisa. Pauline's father, a French actor, deserted his wife early in their marriage. She gave birth to Pauline in the house of James Mavis, a rigidly orthodox clergyman who abhorred worldly gaiety, and she passed away shortly thereafter. In her late teens Pauline married Rev. Mavis. Sent by her husband to New York to select a piano for the Woman's Relief Corps of 'Sheraton' (New York?) Pauline fell in with the Transcontinental Burlesque and Variety Company and was captivated by the big city. She left husband and baby behind and began a theatrical career as a dancer/singer in New York and Europe. In later years she took in hand the daughter she had left in Sheraton and brought her up to the point of marriage to the son of a wealthy New Yorker.

3395. _____. *A social highwayman.* **Philadelphia: J.B. Lippincott, 1896. 196p.**

"The hero is a handsome, fascinating, well-educated young man, who lives in artistic, luxurious apartments in New York City, and pays his way by robbing his fashionable friends of their jewels and other valuables. He has a valet, who is also a thief, and who develops for his master, who has stood by his friend when all the world was against him, a most devoted, self-sacrificing affection that makes him ready, in a crisis of the 'highwayman's' affairs, to assume the odium of his crimes"—Annual American catalogue.

3396. Train, Ethel Kissam, 1875-1923. *Bringing out Barbara.* **New York: Scribner, 1917. 232p.**

She has completed boarding (or finishing) school and Barbara West, 17, is ready to 'come out' in New York and Newport society. Barbara finds the round of formal teas and dinners too hollow and boring for her tastes; she has about her an air of naturalness and simplicity that contrasts sharply (and unfavorably) with the artificialities of 'polite society.' She escapes unscathed and with the help of a lady friend engages the 'real world' of useful employment—and solid John Randall is already there.

3397. Transue, Joan. *First vice-president*; **a novel. Garden City, N.Y.: Doubleday, 1953. 254p.**

> At 56, Norman Frume's ultimate goal, the presidency of the insurance company for which he has toiled many years, has eluded him. Nevertheless he still has pride of possession in a summer cottage at his beloved Montauk Point, Long Island. Frume and his wife Ida invite a number of guests to their cottage, including Wilson Gladstone, president of the insurance company, and his wife; son Richard Frume and his wife Henrietta; Dirk Wesley, a journalist; Arthur Gwenn, Ida Frume's brother; Eleanor, Norman and Ida's spinsterish daughter; et al. Norman's relations with his son Richard and daughter Eleanor, never affectionate, deteriorate further. As the week passes Norman's world crumbles and he lashes out at family, servants, guests; during a rather frantic skeet shoot he accidentally (?) wounds Eleanor. Alone in his room Norman reaches for the gun in the drawer of his bedside table …

Trask, Kate Nichols, 1853-1922. See: Trask, Katrina, 1853-1922.

3398. Trask, Katrina, 1853-1922. *The invisible balance sheet*. **New York: J. Lane, 1916. 375p.**

> John Wright's intended marriage to Marion Meredith did not take place, for Wright's uncle had bequeathed him a bundle of money with the proviso that he would lose all of it should he marry. No stranger to hard times, John Wright chooses riches over marital bliss. Off to New York he goes to spend his inheritance and acquire new well-wishers in the social world. However real happiness is elusive; John longs again for Marion, but he seems fated to lose her forever until a bullet from the gun of one who detested the super-rich brings Marion to his side.

3399. ————. *John Leighton, Jr.*; **a novel, by Katrina Trask. New York: Harper, 1898. [c1897]. 252p.**

> When John Leighton, Jr. declares his agnosticism to his strict Calvinistic father, the senior Leighton asks him to leave the house. John searches New York City for suitable employment, finally accepting a job as office boy in a large law firm. He is promoted to clerk, and then sets up his own tiny law office and through his acquaintance with important figures in New York society rises rapidly to prominence. Along the way he brushes off the seductive advances of Mrs. Stephanie Romaine, but falls in love with Mrs. Howland Gray whom he had known in childhood as Madelaine Myntern. Howland Gray, a portraitist, begins to drink heavily. Madelaine, now fully aware of her love for John, contemplates divorce but elects to stay by her husband. John's father, on his deathbed begs his son's forgiveness and bequeaths him his estate; John has put aside his agnosticism and considers himself a practicing Christian. Madelaine is stricken with a mortal illness and

expires with John and Howland by her side. It is implied that their mutual loss may bind John and Howland in friendship.

3400. ————. *White satin and homespun.* **New York: A.D.F. Randolph, 1896. 139p.**

"Morton Hunnewell, a New Yorker, awakened and aroused to an over-powering sense of the miseries of his fellowmen sold what he had and moved to Delancey Street into the house of a cabinet-maker. Miss Katharine Van Santlandt, reared in luxury, goes to hear Hunnewell lecture, disguised as a washerwoman, and little by little becomes his valuable assistant. After many of her outings 'in homespun' Katharine agrees to give up all and live with Hunnewell among the poor"—Annual American catalogue.

3401. **Travis, Elma Allen, 1861-1917.** *The cobbler.* **New York: Outing Pub. Co., 1908. x, 287p.**

Peter Caverly is a dreamer; his father is cobbler for the village on the Hudson where Peter spends his youth. Wealthy Judge Farrington takes Peter in hand and helps him acquire the polish offered by an advanced education. The judge's daughter and Peter fall in love and marry at an early age. Refusing to accept money from his well-off father-in-law, Peter goes his bohemian way—it is a patchwork quilt that needs constant repair that is provided by a practical wife. Finally, whatever cobbler heritage was passed from father to son is supplemented by a spark of real talent that allows Peter to earn a living with pen in hand.

3402. **Travis, Gretchen.** *The cottage.* **New York: Putnam, 1973. 221p.**

Phyllis is a widow who rents her cottage in a suburb of New York City to a schoolteacher, Bruce Conroy. She doesn't suspect it, but Conroy turns out to be a cad who sleeps with Phyllis's daughter, blackmails various women, and is responsible for the suicide (or murder) of one of them.

3403. **Treat, Lawrence, 1903- .** *B as in banshee.* **New York: Duell, Sloan and Pearce, 1940. viii, 295p.**

The insufferable owner of some Adirondack real estate in the vicinity of 'Murmur Lake' is shot and his body is burned. Two of his servants are also murder victims. A scholarly deputy sheriff deals with several bizarre characters and ultimately traps the homicidal individual.

3404. **Trepoff, Ivan, pseud.** *He that is without sin.* **New York: Cosmopolitan Press, 1911. 355p.**

A tale of moral regeneration with New York City politics in its seamiest and most corrupt aspects as the starting point. The hero is a part of that sordid world until he finally awakens to the possibilities of a more meaningful, ethical way of life and begins to put it into practice. Accompanying him is a woman who too has pulled herself out of a morass of moral turpitude.

3405. Trites, William Budd, b. 1872. *Barbara Gwynne (Life).* **New York: Duffield, 1913. 285p.**

The history of a girl who tires of the stares and whispers of gossipmongers in her hometown who unfairly stain her name. Barbara leaves for New York City and it is there that she attains a successful stage career. But back in the town she walked away from there abides Jerome, a man whose business ethics are very questionable, but whose love for Barbara is of the highest order. Barbara suffers the loss of her first love, a doctor who dies while carrying on dangerous experiments. Slowly but assuredly the lives of Barbara and Jerome converge. Published in England under the title: *Life.*

3406. Trombly, Della. *The Hermit of the Adirondacks.* **Boston: Sherman, French, 1915. 264p.**

The several 'Adirondack' characters who move through the story are a mixed bag. The Hermit, ostensibly a leading figure, faces the disasters that seem to search him out with resignation and stolidity. Sharky Dandy has been the source of grievous affliction for far too many of his acquaintants, but he gets his comeuppance from a young woman he has tried to victimize. But much of the story tells how Mabel Lestrange and Blanche Lathrop were at one time or another taken as wives by Leslie Lathrop.

3407. Trotta, Geraldine. *Dune House*; **a story of summer people in the Long Island Hamptons. New York: Farrar, Strauss and Cudahy, 1960. 249p.**

When New York City 'types'—male and female—professionals, including journalists, people from the world of fashion, commercial photographers, magazine editors, et al. come to the beaches of the Hamptons for much-needed rest, one would expect them to lay aside their hang-ups for a while. That is not the case; they continue to air their quandaries and sip their cocktails, and finally face a climactic hurricane and ocean waves that sweep away their dune house.

3408. Troubetzkoy, Pierre, 1864-1936. *The passerby*; **an episode. New York: Doubleday, Page, 1908. 330p.**

Loneliness is an affliction of the idle rich too, and Angela Moore, wife of a New York financier, suffers from it. Her husband is so caught up in his business affairs that he neglects his wife. She turns to two charming foreigners for comfort—an idealistic Russian who is prone to philosophize, and a materialistic Englishman who views her as sexual quarry. Mr. Moore, the archetypical American/New York businessman, quite critical of the artistic temperament, suddenly takes severe business losses. With the departure of his fortune he turns to his wife for sympathy and she grants it quickly and wholeheartedly.

3409. Trowbridge, John Townsend, 1827-1916. *Farnell's folly.* **Boston: Lee & Shepard, 1885. 409p.**

"The people of 'Waybrook', their environment and traditions, are all in keeping with a village of western New York. Ward Farnell, whose magnificent house was to have been his pride and became his folly, is a type of the successful American, led on to financial ruin by love of display; and some of the minor characters are excellent from the way in which the limitations of their birth and nurture are portrayed, while their real worth and honesty are not sunk out of sight"—Griswold, W.M. *Descriptive list of American, international, romantic and British novels.*

3410. ————. *Lucy Arlyn.* **Boston: Ticknor and Fields, 1866. 564p.**
Our heroine, a native of northern New York State, enters into a secret marriage with the son of a squire who is her father's enemy. The young husband tires of his bride and joins up with a group of spiritualists searching for buried treasure. Lucy, left alone, gives birth and endures the scorn of her neighbors; they are unaware of her married state. Tragedy follows—murder, sudden death.

3411. ————. *A question of damages.* **Boston: Lee and Shepard, 1897. 78p.**
After he is injured in a railway accident at 'Camp Creek Crossing', Mortimer Frank, an Albany broker, recovers under the nursing ministrations of Lucy Tilbury. Mortimer and Lucy become engaged. Frank leaves Camp Creek Crossing, pens a few letters to Lucy and is then no longer heard from. Through the lawyer Jay Bradwaite of Albany Lucy learns of Frank's marriage to Helen Wilde. With Frank's letters to Lucy in hand Bradwaite collects $15,000 from Frank for his breach of promise and gives it to the reluctant Lucy. Frank's effort to make the railroad pay handsomely for his injuries yields only $2,500. Mortimer's fortunes take a sharp decline. His wife Helen dies; she is survived by her husband and a son. Frank pleads with Lucy for reconciliation; she forgives him for past neglect, but goes no further. Jay Bradwaite marries Lucy; she has her husband turn the $15,000 over to Frank's son. Mortimer Frank is killed during the Civil War while on a sutler's wagon. The period covered by the story: 1857 to about 1862.

3412. ————. *A start in life*; a story of the Genesee country. **Boston: Lee and Shepard, 1889. 163p.**
Post-Revolutionary Genesee County, New York, with its early settlements and some of the activities common to the frontier—hunting for raccoons and bears and other wild mammals, tree cutting and clearing, gathering the fruits of the forest (berries, honey, etc.)—is the setting of this novel whose hero is a 17-year-old lad who tires of the bullying of an older brother and departs from his home to make his own way in a rough inhospitable world. He has moments of despondency but by dint of his own vigor, perseverance and scrupulousness establishes a proud place for himself in a frontier community.

3413. Truax, Rhoda. *Green is the golden tree*; a novel. **Indianapolis: Bobbs-Merrill, 1943. 306p.**

A few years after the Civil War a utopian community, Elysian Field, is formed in Upstate New York. The Field deemed competition immoral: "Only all classes working together could bring about a new social order to benefit them all" (p.43). Among the Field's leading members are Dr. Arthur Hoyt and his strong-willed daughter Polly. Polly and the orphan Johnny Holden find Dan Crowley, a laborer and crusader for workingmen's rights, half-dead by the roadside. The Social Progressive Community within the Elysian Field accepts Dan. He and Polly fall in love and are 'unofficially married' by the Rev. Everett Allen. When Dan unintentionally kills a detective who is searching for an escaped prisoner—Dan's friend, the labor organizer Fred Muhlenberg—Dan flees the Field, leaving behind a pregnant Polly. Polly now has to determine her own future. Her father begs her to remain with him in the Elysian Field. As the novel ends Polly is about to leave to join the fugitive Dan wherever he may be, and to join "the hard, cruel world, but a good world, too, for it was filled with people who, though they might never have heard the phrase, were willing to make sacrifices to bring about the Brotherhood of Man" (p. 305).

3414. **[Trumble, Alfred].** *The Mott Street Poker Club*; **the secretary's minutes. Illustrated by M. Woolf. New York: White & Allen, 1889. 50p.**

Mr. Hong-Lung is president of the Club that meets in the Chinese quarter of New York City to devote itself to 'polkel'. His colleagues include Mr. Hop-Sam, Mr. Gin-Sing and Mr. Lee-Tip as they play poker on the 'Melican' plan. Interruptions occur when fraudulent and corrupt 'Caucasians' exact fees for 'licenses', etc., and the colored Rev. Thankful Smith upbraids the 'idollyturs' who worship 'graven' images. The Club is finally disbanded when its members lose interest and pursue other activities.

3415. **————.** *Mysteries of New York*. **Boston: Published at the 'Yankee Office', 1845. 64p.**

Ellen Bruce is a student at the Quaker Nine Partners' Boarding School near Poughkeepsie when her mother suddenly takes her home to Hudson, N.Y., away from the young man Ellen loves, Alfred Forrester. The two lovers flee to Flushing and Long Island; Mrs. Bruce hires Monkton, a man with dubious, perhaps criminal connections, to separate the two. Ellen disappears and Alfred frantically searches New York and Long Island for her, interviewing several prostitutes for clues to her whereabouts. He finally finds her in a forest on Long Island where she had been living with her father whom Mrs. Bruce had deserted years ago. Ellen's father is the leader of a gang of robbers; he intercepts the villainous Monkton and kills him; Bruce in turn is slain by one of Monkton's henchmen. Through all her trials Ellen has remained constant to Alfred; they return to Hudson and marry. The duplicitous Mrs. Bruce, left penniless by the thieving Monkton, receives financial assistance from Ellen and Alfred.

3416. **Truscott, Lucian K., 1947- .** *Full dress gray*. **New York: W. Morrow, 1998.**

384p.

Women cadets at West Point are an issue in this story for Brigadier General Jack Gibson, commander of cadets, who cannot totally conceal his antipathy towards their presence. The new superintendent, Lieutenant General Rysam Slaight, is faced with the death of Cadet Dorothy Hamner during parade—by heat stroke they say. Slaight's daughter, Jacey, cadet commander of Dorothy's Company H-3, learns that Dorothy had been raped shortly before she passed away and had partied the night before with members of the Cadet Honor Committee. The Honor Committee's chair, Jerry Rose, is a slippery, unpleasant character, the quintessence of modern indifference to principle. Could it have been murder? Truscott has the necessary background to portray accurately the crises affecting military education, West Point in particular.

3417. **Tucker, J.N.T.** *Theresa*; or, *The Chief Hyadata's fall.* **A legendary romance of Onondaga Valley. Boston: Gleason's Pub. Hall, 1846. 50p.**

Two French families, the Dunmares and the La Fortes settle in central New York in the mid-18th century. They are decimated by an Indian attack—the only survivors are Theresa La Forte, her lover, Eugene Dunmare, and his brother Frederick. Theresa is taken prisoner by the Onondaga Chief Hyadata who wants her for his wife. Theresa, aided by Oneida, Hyadata's sister, resists. There ensues a series of escapades and recaptures until Eugene Dunmare rescues Theresa and kills Hyadata, with assistance from Frederick Dunmare and Oneida. Theresa and Eugene find a new home on the shores of Lake Ontario; Frederick and Oneida marry. "The two wards, by Mrs. M.G. Sleeper": p. [37]-50.

3418. ————. *The two brides*; or, Romance at Saratoga. **Boston: Cochran, Cole, 1846. 32p. (in double columns).**

A very short piece of fiction accompanied by other sketches. The mother of two young women—Clarinda and Clarissa—is with them in Saratoga seeking well-to-do husbands for her daughters. Clarinda favors hardworking Edwin Townsend despite her mother's objections. When Edwin does achieve a measure of success in Boston, he and Clarinda are married and reside there. Clarissa marries the fortune hunter Tom Ayrault (real name: Thomas French), gives him her small inheritance and moves to New York. After momentary success as a gambler Ayrault loses everything. Bailed out of debt by Edwin, Ayrault tries forgery, is discovered, returns to Saratoga, but is brought back to New York and prison where he commits suicide. Clarinda, Edwin and Clarissa are back in Saratoga (as vacationers) by the story's end.

3419. **Tuckerman, Arthur, 1896-1955.** *Galloping dawns.* **Garden City, N.Y.: Doubleday, Page, 1924. v, 271p.**

The novel is set for the most part in New York City (from the 1880s to the 1920s) but also has brief interludes in the south of France and Egypt. "'You're stupid, Lawrence, I meant people like our fathers and mothers and relations. The older and finer your family is, the more rules you've got. Now, Matthew, for instance, could marry anyone he wanted, because he's just a coachman.' The words are those of young Janet Craig. They furnish the motive for the book, because they are spoken to Lawrence Dulac, a son of 'The' Dulacs, and they express the principles of social exclusiveness under which Lawrence grows up and by which he stands on the strength of his own breeding up to the moment when he has to surrender to the insurgency of his own daughter, Beryl, the child of an age when barriers are falling down"—New York world.

3420. **Tupper, Edith Sessions, d. 1927.** *Hearts triumphant.* **New York: Appleton, 1906. 285p.**

"The historic Jumel mansion, which may yet be seen at Washington Heights, New York, forms the background of a story of colonial times. The central figure is the famous Madame Betty Jumel, a heartless coquette and somewhat of an adventuress. Aaron Burr, whom she married later, was her ardent admirer. But her fancy at this time had flown to a younger man, one of the Trumbulls of New York, who was in love with a charming young girl. Madame Betty resorted to daring intrigue to capture him, casting Burr aside. Her better nature came to her aid in the end, and she helped the young lovers, giving up her own design"—Annual American catalogue.

3421. **Tuttle, Margaretta Muhlenberg Perkins, 1880-1958.** *His worldly goods.* **With front. in color by Paul Meylan. Indianapolis: Bobbs-Merrill, 1912. 410p.**

Nadine Carson's husband, Colin, has made her life with him a living hell. When he goes into nervous shock Dr. Carleton Thorne comes to the Carson's Long Island farmhouse to stay with him. Dr. Thorne's brother, Wrexford, rector of a New York parish, meets Nadine and falls in love with her. Colin Carson sinks into madness and is confined; Nadine has the burdensome responsibility of handling her husband's great estate. Escape from the marriage is denied her when proof of Colin's earlier marriage (and no divorce) falls through. Carson escapes from the hospital and nearly murders Nadine. Evidence that she was never really bound legally to Colin is certified and Nadine and Wrexford Thorne find happiness together.

3422. *Two ways to wedlock.* **A novelette. New York: Rudd & Carleton, 1859. 253p.**

Two New York City families go through good times and bad—the Lyndsays, their daughters Julia and Matilda; and the Sumners, Dr. John and wife Amy, daughters Helen and Marion, a son Oscar in poor health, and two adopted daughters, Cornelia and Melicent Boylston. Mrs. Matilda Lyndsay is snobbish, working feverishly to secure good marriages for her daughters. The great New York City fire of 1835 and financial reverses force Mr. Lyndsay to remove his family to his farm in 'Montiluna' on the Hudson. When Dr. Sumner dies his wife and daughters cast about for ways of supporting themselves. Most of the young women mentioned above do find suitable life partners. Matilda Lyndsay, however, following the guidelines of her vain mother, marries the devious Baron Gaspard de Brie, he being unaware that the Lyndsays are no longer wealthy. Mr. Lyndsay, a failure at farming, dies and

Julia and Mrs. Lyndsay make their new home with Mrs. Sumner. Matilda Lyndsay comes to a tragic end, expiring after her worthless husband commits suicide to avoid the law. The novel is sometimes attributed to Sarah Stickney Ellis.

3423. **Ty, Brother.** *God is my broker*; **a monk-tycoon reveals the 7-1/2 laws of spiritual and financial growth. By Brother Ty with Christopher Buckley and John Tierney. New York: Random House, 1998. 197p.**

An Upstate New York Catholic monastery, teetering on the edge of insolvency, is saved by Brother Ty, a former Wall Streeter, who attributes to God his ability to play the market for profit. However his abbot is certain that Deepak Chopra and others of his kind are reliable guides and nearly cancels out Brother Ty's gains. The latter takes the order's few remaining dollars, invests them in pork belly futures and wins big. Brother Ty's market triumphs continue and the monastery is so taken with its new-found prosperity that it metamorphoses into a theme park for the tourist trade.

3424. **Tyler, Esther.** *Murder on the bluff.* **New York: Simon and Schuster, 1936. 310p.**

A weekend party and an isolating hurricane combine to present a scene of unexpected tragedy at Farrington Bluffs, a seacoast mansion on Long Island Sound. The family playing host is a bickering, dysfunctional one and a friend of the family who has his own unresolved personal problems solves the three murders that occur at the Bluffs.

3425. **Tyler, Randall Irving.** *The blind goddess*; **being a tale of today, showing some of the undercurrents of a big city. Illustrated by Kauffman. New York: Stuyvesant Pub. Co., 1899. 253p.**

The 'big city' is New York. The death from poison of financier Judson Brownell and his friend David West is attributed to Sanford Crane whose incriminating letter to Brownell is found at the scene of the murders. Crane, the adopted son of Isaac Harden, a former business partner of Brownell, blamed the latter for Harden's financial reverses. At Sanford Crane's murder trial his brother Theodore unveils the real killer, Harriet Baxter. Harriet, natural daughter of Judson Brownell and Nora Baxter, had fallen in love with David West, an unsuccessful suitor for the hand of Brownell's daughter Helen. Harriet Baxter, infuriated by West's failure to respond to her passion, sent the poison to her supposed rival, Helen. Obviously the poison had fallen into the wrong hands. In the courtroom Harriet shoots at Helen and misses; she then commits suicide. Cleared of all charges Sanford Crane seeks out Helen Brownell and claims her love.

3426. **Tyson, John Aubrey, 1870-1930.** *The rhododendron man.* **New York: Dutton, 1930. vi, 317p.**

The very socially restricted North Shore colony of Long Island was shaken by the murder of Lloyd Jasperson, one of its own. Evidently someone had fired the fatal shot from rhododendron bushes outside Jasperson's library window. Harold Braincroft, a newspaper reporter but also a member of that colony, is known for his detecting talents, and he enters the case primarily because he has a personal interest in Evelyn Islesworth. She is involved in the matter at hand and she also has run up unpaid gambling debts.

Ullman, Alice Woods, b. 1871. See: Woods, Alice, b. 1871.

3427. **Ulmann, Albert, 1861-1948.** *Frederick Struthers' romance.* **New York: Brentano's, 1889. 195p.**

"The characters in this story are an old German watchmaker and his two daughters living in the top of a tall business building below the City Hall, in New York City, and a young man who calls to have some watches mended and falls in love with one of the daughters. The young man is Frederick Struthers, who has been cast off by his family on account of his intemperate habits. He seems to bring unhappiness to all who come in contact with him, and soon succeeds in breaking up the old German's happy home. His own suicide ends a gloomy story"—Annual American catalogue.

Uncle Ben of Rouse's Point. See: White, Rhoda Elizabeth Waterman.

Uncle Lute, pseud. See: Lute, Uncle, pseud.

Underhill, Elise Morris, joint author. *The runaway place.* **See Item #983.**

3428. **Updegraff, Allan Eugene, 1883-1965.** *Strayed revellers*; **a novel of modernistic truth and intruding war. New York: Holt, 1918. 190p.**

"A village in the Catskills ['Woodbridge'] to which a group of artists and modern thinkers from New York's Bohemia have repaired, is the scene of the story. Clotilde Westbrook, who comes to join the colony, has just made the surprising discovery that she is an illegitimate child, the daughter of Henry Hooghtyling, an old Dutch farmer back on the mountain, and with all a modern young woman's frankness, she insists on making the fact public. In doing so she has to reckon with Ethel, Henry's strong-armed wife. There is considerable war talk [World War I] in the book and before the end most of the male characters have enlisted and Clotilde has agreed to a conventional old-fashioned marriage with Corporal Clement Towns"—Book review digest.

3429. **Urner, Nathan D.** *Naughty New York*; **or,** *The apron-strings relaxed.* **A novel of the period, being a truthful narrative of a week's jollification of three young Benedicts, together with a bachelor friend, while their better halves in the country imagined them to be drenched with the brain-sweat of mental hard work for the support of their families. An account of whitherward they wandered, whom and what they saw, the shady resorts they visited, the forbidden fruits they tasted, the adventures that befell them, and the dread reckoning that overtook them in their mad career. By O.N. Looker [pseudo.].**

New York: For sale by the American News Co., 1882. 192p.

Tom Mixer, Jacob (Jakey) Espion and Harry Whopper leave their wives—Celestine, Naomi and Rory—in the country and meet bachelor Dick Tryall in New York City, ostensibly for business reasons (or so their wives are led to believe), but they are actually about to kick up their heels and take on the big town. They whoop it up at Delmonico's, Koster and Bial's theater, the Alhambra, Joe Weil's, 'Thee' Allen's and Coney Island, Central Park, Manhattan Beach and Elm Park. After an alcoholic binge the three Benedicts are trapped during their last revel by their wives who have come to New York too, disguised, and who eventually call the revelers to account.

Vail, Philip, pseud. See: Gerson, Noel Bertram, 1914-1988.

3430. **Valentine, Ferdinand Charles, 1851-1910.** *Gotham and the Gothamites*, **by Heinrich Oscar von Karlstein [pseud.]. Translated by F.C. Valentine. Chicago: Laird & Lee, 1886. 179p.**

The author speculates on life in New York City with a mixture of wry comment and illustrative fictional sketches: its women, education, flirting, high society, beer and beer gardens, the press, theater, local politics, 'crazes' ('in' activities), and ends with a prediction of 'Gotham' in 1986.

Valentine, Jane, pseud. See: Meeker, Nellie J.

3431. **Valtorta, Laura P., 1958- .** *Family meal.* **Durham, N.C.: Carolina Wren Press, 1993. 127p.**

Sally Linden recounts her family's life in Upstate New York during the 1950s. Her father owns a construction firm and Sally is the first of the Linden children to work for it, although her brothers, Forde and Stanley Jr., are in line to take charge of the business eventually. Sally's boyfriend is Mario Conti whose boisterous family is more than a match for the slightly eccentric Lindens. Sally is consigned by her parents to a college for women and Mario matriculates at Syracuse University. She is now fully aware of the sexism that banishes her as a woman to the outer fringe of meaningful activities.

3432. **Van Arsdale, Wirt, 1905-1952.** *The professor knits a shroud.* **Garden City, N.Y.: Published for the Crime Club by Doubleday, 1951. 217p.**

"Henry Von Fliegel, a best-selling novelist, is shot dead while a guest at the Upstate New York farm owned by Niles Carter, his publisher. By a happy coincidence another guest at the Carter farm is Pedro José Mariá Guadaloupe O'Reilly Apodaca, a professor of archeology at a New York City university" —Kramer, J.E., Jr. College mystery novels. The professor is known for his sock-knitting hobby, yet he also has the time and talent to search out and identify Fliegel's murderer.

3433. **Van de Water, Frederic Franklyn, 1890-1968.** *The Eye of Lucifer.* **New York: Appleton, 1927. 258p.**

"The Eye of Lucifer is an emerald of international fame. A wealthy collector of Upstate New York about to buy the stone is murdered in his home. Trooper Cameron of the mounted police knew nothing of the stone and its evil history or of its significance to the young Russians Boris and Ana Lyoff. In the course of his investigations Ana and Esther Somers, her friend who lives in the neighborhood, are alternately a help and a hindrance. But Trooper Cameron perseveres until he meets with success in two fields—the official affair of the murder, and the personal one with Esther"—Book review digest.

3434. **Van de Water, Frederic Franklyn, 1890-1968.** *Horsemen of the law.* **New York: Appleton, 1926. 273p.**

The story's natural audience is the teenage boy interested in the operations of State Troopers. Sergeant Daniel Delaney of the New York State Troopers is the chief character, often leading his fellow troopers in facing down and arresting bootleggers, narcotics smugglers, reckless Indians and other flaunters of the laws of the State.

3435. —————. *Hurrying feet.* **New York: Appleton, 1928. 272p.**

Wade P. Debrett and a mysterious friend named Mirko go fishing in a remote corner of Debrett's newly reopened estate in Upstate New York and do not return to the main house at the expected time. Corporal John Scarlett of the New York State Troopers and his associates look into the disappearance. Debrett is found the following day, but Mirko, a foreigner and an extremely important personage in his own country, remains missing. Oddly, Debrett will not tell the troopers what country Mirko represents, but assures them Mirko must be found if Europe is to avoid another war. The story ends with a question: What has become of Mirko?

3436. —————. *Still waters.* **Garden City, N.Y.: Published for the Crime Club by Doubleday, Doran, 1929. 298p.**

"Richard York of 'Aristides' [New York] got drunk one night, became involved in a bootlegging war, and was accused of murdering his uncle. But Richard, while dodging the New York State troopers, tracks down the real criminal, and wins lovely Desire"—Book review digest.

3437. —————. *This day's madness.* **New York: I. Washburn, 1957. 278p.**

"'Parker's Falls' was all agog at the installation of the new head of the local Colonel Orme Academy. The [Upstate] New York town was decidedly under the leadership of Warburton Orme Tench, a descendant of Colonel Orme of Revolutionary fame, and architect Richard Clave was his henchman. When the new headmaster's wife proved to be an old flame of Clave's, the stage was set for a scandal and near tragedy, but these were narrowly avoided"—Book review digest.

3438. **Van de Water, Virginia Belle Terhune, 1865-1945.** *The two sisters.* **New York: Hearst's International Library Co., 1914. vii, 332p.**

The story of two sisters who find life with their stepmother stifling and choose New York City as their new home. Julia takes a job in a department store; she is the patient, persevering sort. The younger Caryl, flighty and foolish, looking only for a good time, becomes stenographer to the writer Kelley Delaine. The latter meets Julia and falls in love with her. Despite Kelley's efforts to protect Caryl from herself, she runs off with a married man (she didn't know that) and is eventually traced by Delaine to a hospital, close to death. Julia, now Mrs. Delaine, is by Caryl's side in her last moments.

3439. **Van Deusen, Delia.** *The garden club murders*. **Indianapolis: Bobbs-Merrill, 1941. 320p.**

"Several persons suspected nice Barbara Moffitt when a dead woman was found in the parish house the day of the Garden Club's annual show (old hellions like Mrs. Sluyter and Mrs. Buskirk for instance). But Sergeant Holson Gridley of the State cops, six-foot-two and a furtive lover of hollyhocks and delphiniums knew better; so he went right ahead and cornered the real killer after a pretty-how-d'ye do in the quiet village of 'Martin's Hook', up the Hudson. Chapters are rather cutely entitled: Death prunes the Garden Club; Murder in full bloom; Weeding and sorting; Plant-analysis; Cross-pollination or cross-purpose"—New York herald tribune books.

Van Deventer, Emma Murdoch. See under her pseudonym: Lynch, Lawrence L.

3440. **Van Dine, S.S., 1888-1939.** *The Benson murder case*; a Philo Vance story. **New York: Scribner, 1926. xii, 348p.**

"A new manner of detective is introduced here in [Philo] Vance, the psychological sleuth who works with the police in the case of the murder of Alvin Benson of New York, and makes nonchalant deductions from clues that apparently are not there at all. He irritates and confounds the police, but since the latter get all the credit in the case, there is every indication that Vance will be shortly called to work with them again"—Book review digest.

3441. ————. *The Bishop murder case*; a Philo Vance story. **New York: Scribner, 1929. viii, 349p.**

When Joseph Robin, playboy and talented archer, is murdered via an arrow through his heart while at a range in New York City, Philo Vance is called in to investigate. The murderer, a fancier of nursery rhymes, calls himself 'the Bishop.' Involved in Philo's quest are two professorial scientists, the semi-retired Bertrand Dillard, and his adopted son, Sigurd Arneson, mathematics teacher at Columbia University, who share a house with Dillard's daughter, Belle, on West 75th Street. Inevitably Vance comes upon secrets that the two professors had long kept sealed.

3442. ————. *The 'Canary' murder case*; a Philo Vance story. **New York: Scribner, 1927. x, 343p.**

Philo Vance "is invited to aid his friend Markham, the district attorney, and Sergeant Heath of the Homicide Bureau in their efforts to discover the murderer of the 'Canary', a noted Broadway blond who is found strangled in her apartment on West 71st Street. The only entrance to the apartment is through the main hall past the telephone operator's booth. Thus the number of suspects is narrowed down to four men known to have been enamored of the Canary. In his debonair fashion Vance applies psychology to the case and solves it"—Book review digest.

3443. ————. *The Greene murder case*; a Philo Vance story. New York: Scribner, 1928. x, 388p.

"The gloomy Greene mansion in New York is the scene of a double tragedy. The eldest [Greene] sister is shot and killed; the youngest, a sister by adoption, is wounded by an intruder. While Philo Vance and his friend Markham, the district attorney, are at work on the case, the two Greene brothers are killed. This leaves alive in the sinister household the mother who is a helpless invalid, Sibella, her [other] daughter, and Ada, the adopted sister. Philo Vance discovers the guilty person in time to save the last surviving member of the family"—Book review digest.

3444. ————. *The scarab murder case*; a Philo Vance story. New York: Scribner, 1930, c1929. xii, 328p.

Beside the corpse of Benjamin H. Kyle, philanthropist and patron of the arts, lying on the floor of the private museum in Gramercy Park of Egyptologist Dr. Bliss, is a rare blue Egyptian scarab. Philo Vance puzzles over a superabundance of clues; he has acquired a reading knowledge of Egyptian hieroglyphics and is, of course, a student of human nature. The scarab is a most important clue, however, and Hani, the mysterious Egyptian servant, could perhaps shed light on arcane aspects of the case.

3445. Van Doren, Dorothy Graffe, b. 1896. *Strangers*. New York: Doran, 1926. 275p.

"The protagonists of the piece are two married couples—Ann and William, Stephen and Ruth—and Emily, their friend, a prosperous unmarried businesswoman. They are cultured [New Yorkers], well-to-do people, and move in a literary and artistic milieu. Their long-standing friendship has developed on the part of Ann and Stephen into a new and urgent intimacy. William and Ruth, standing aside to watch the development, with what grace is given them, find brief comfort in each other. Running through the tale of these marital entanglements is the love story of Rachel, Ann's sister, and Paul, their courtship, their marriage, and its abrupt and tragic end. The title refers to the fact that however near to each other two people may come, fundamentally they remain strangers"—Book review digest.

3446. Van Duyn, Janet H. Dunning, 1910- . *I married them*; a novel. Illustrated by Garth Williams. New York: Howell, Soskin, 1945. 281p.

"Both subject matter and illustrations are farcical in this addition to the life-in-an-out-of-the-ordinary-family shelf, but this one is admittedly fictional. The girl who married a young doctor [Carrie and George MacLean] and was absorbed into the heterogeneous group of in-laws in the dilapidated Greek mansion in Upstate New York found herself in a bedlam which was kindly but uproarious. There is no plot; fortified by frequent drinks, the family proceeds from one extravaganza to another, social leadership and successful medical practice emanating from a household where individualism was a fetish"—Booklist.

3447. **Van Duzer, Winifred.** *The good bad girl.* **New York: Grosset & Dunlap, 1926. 243p.**

The story of a girl, Mimsi Marsh, 19, from 'Tranquillity', Connecticut, who comes to New York City to find a niche in the art world. A prominent painter, Winship White, finds her useful as a model; when White leaves for Europe, Mimsi, already introduced to reckless aspects of night life in Greenwich Village, is adrift and struggles to recover from illness. Willy Perry a playboy separated from his wife, offers Mimsi the use of his apartment while he is in California. Mimsi's former roommate, Trixie True, dies from a drug overdose; another friend, Nita Mori, is murdered by a blackmailing prowler. Although she feels indebted to Perry and almost succumbs to his charm, Mimsi is drawn to a landscapist, Merle Lengel. Mimsi begins to paint in earnest; in addition to some lucrative commercial art, she develops real talent with her drawings and an occasional oil. She attracts a patron, Eli Harbeck; he provides an apartment and a maid, no strings attached, and Mimsi finally has a successful showing of her work. Mimsi is at last on her own; Merle Lengel reenters her life and the two look forward to a bright future together.

3448. **Van Hoevenbergh, Henry, d. 1918.** *Told around the campfire.* **Edited and with biographical sketch by Maitland C. De Sormo. North Country Books, Inc., Utica, New York: 1967. xiii, 102p.**

A collection of short tales ('pure fiction') about the Adirondacks and its people that were told by Van Hoevenbergh around the log fire at Adirondack Lodge (which burned to the ground in 1903). One of the stories, 'The Legend of Indian Pass', is told in verse form.

3449. **Van Schaick, George Gray, 1861-1924.** *A top-floor idyll.* **Illustrated by Chase Emerson. Boston: Small, Maynard, 1917. 433p.**

The narrator of the story is David Cole, a shy, middle-aged bachelor and novelist, who lives in Mrs. Milliken's boarding house near Washington Square, New York City. He does have a friend in Frieda Long, an unmarried, plump, pleasant artist—she is no threat to his single status. Then a young widow, Frances Dupont, takes a room neighboring Cole's on the top floor of the house. Mrs. Dupont's husband, a Frenchman, was killed in the Battle of the Marne (1914), leaving her pregnant. The baby arrives and David's increasing interest in Frances and her infant son evolves into profound, heart-felt love.

3450. **Van Siller, Hilda.** *The watchers.* **Garden City, N.Y.: Published for the Crime Club by Doubleday, 1969. 192p.**

"A young woman struggles to prove her husband's sanity against seemingly overwhelming odds. The locale is New York [City, where most of the story takes place] and Connecticut"—American news of books.

3451. **————.** *The widower,* **by Van Siller [pseud.]. Garden City, N.Y.: Published for the Crime Club by Doubleday, 1958. 192p.**

"About malicious gossip in suburbia [of New York]. Louise Sargeant seems an unlikely suicide and a woman with all the perquisites of social success for all that the Sargeants' marriage has been a bumpy one. But even her numbed husband [Philip] cannot doubt evidence that satisfies the police. Then the rumors begin as 'Bishop's Corner' assembles tooth and fang"—New York herald tribune books. Louise's sister has unpleasant encounters with Mrs. Winters, an unconventional new arrival in the community, and Philip Sargeant defends Mrs. Winters while fending off suspicion that he himself was responsible for his wife's death.

3452. **Van Slyke, Lucille Baldwin, b. 1880.** *Eve's other children.* **With four illus. by Wladislaw T. Benda. New York: Stokes, 1912. v, 275p.**

Tales about the Syrian lace-makers of Brooklyn's poorer sections, displaying their strong emotions, poetic sensibilities, Old World ways of speaking, and efforts to adjust themselves to modern industrial America and a distinctly different mode of life. Contents: The tooth of Antar.—Rug of her fathers.—Eyes with sorrow.—Rodania the magic mare.—Dreams in lace.—Eve's other children.—Pieces of silver.—Gift of tongues.—Thing called play.—Camel of Bethlehem.—The housetop.

3453. **————.** *Little Miss By-the-Day.* **With a front. in color by Mabel Hatt. New York: F.A. Stokes, 1919. 304p.**

Brought up by her old-fashioned grandfather in a great house in Brooklyn, unworldly Felicia Day returned to it at the age of 27 and found the mansion for sale because of unpaid taxes. She sets about to restore the house to its former stateliness with the aid of friends, her own charm and talent for sewing and her vivid imagination. She makes her goal and also wins a happy future adorned with love.

3454. **————.** *Nora pays.* **New York: Stokes, 1925. 309p.**

"Nora Laurens [is] a successful businesswoman at the height of her career, the owner of a smart Fifth Avenue shop. Fifteen years before in a fit of exasperation she had abandoned her professor husband, her three young daughters and an over-bearing mother-in-law. With the passing of the years she was quite confident that she had overcome her desire for her children, but a note from Daphne, the youngest, sends her post-haste to the old house to make the acquaintance of her offspring. The story then concerns itself with Nora's problem—that of establishing motherly relations with her daughters, and to this difficult job she gives herself unstintingly. Of the three daughters only Daphne finds happiness; for Nora there is the sad realization of the price she paid for her freedom"—Book review digest.

3455. Van Vechten, Carl, 1880-1964. *The blind bow-boy.* **With a decoration by Robert E. Locher. New York: Knopf, 1923. 261p.**

"The situation around which the story revolves is that of a youth whose father is determined that his son shall have none of the disadvantages of education, and all the advantages of sophistication which he himself would like to have enjoyed. Consequently his son is entrusted to a tutor who must make of him an urbane and civilized fellow. To this end certain qualifications are required of the tutor; he must be 'of good character but no moral sense. ... It is absolutely essential that he should have been the central figure in some public scandal. Age not above thirty.' Equipped with unlimited funds, a tutor answering to these requirements, and an English valet of unusual talents, Harold Frewett is launched forth upon the gently swelling seas of New York life, whose waves are so beautifully navigated by Campaspe Lorillard, Paul Moody, the essential tutor, Zimbule O'Grady, Coney Island snake-charmer, the Duke of Middlebottom, and other representative citizens of this New York world. Harold serves as a foil for the virtuosity of his friends whose activities provide Mr. Van Vechten with his pictures of present-day New York"—The nation.

3456. ————. *Firecrackers*; a realistic novel. **New York: Knopf, 1925. 246p.**

"This is the story of a New York smart set in which several familiar characters reappear. Gunnar O'Grady is an unusual young man. There is about him a dynamic quality that stirs up new and sometimes-uncomfortable emotions in the people he meets. He is the fuse that sets them off. Paul Moody, Campaspe, and the child Consuelo each explodes in characteristic fashion. Lastly the young man blows himself up"—Book review digest. "Bright figures come trooping in from 'Peter Whiffle' and 'The tattooed countess' and go on talking to one another in the now unmistakable Van Vechten manner"—Donald Douglas in The nation.

3457. ————. *Nigger Heaven.* **New York: Knopf, 1926. 286p.**

"Tells the story of modern Negro life, in the greatest Negro city in the world, the district of Harlem in New York City. ... The characters who enter into the story are mostly Negroes of the wealthier and more educated class, the hero being a young graduate of the University of Pennsylvania, who comes to New York with ambitions to become a writer, but who has not displayed sufficient stamina to withstand the vices to which he is introduced. His character gives way under the strain and he loses all self-respect [and he is falsely accused of a murder]. In the course of his brief downward career, the abnormal conditions under which the Negro is living in New York, his intellectual strivings, his opinions on race questions, the pleasures and vices of night life, his whole social background, are shown in detail—Book review digest.

3458. ————. *Parties*; scenes from contemporary New York life. New York: Knopf, 1930. xiv, 260p.

"Wealthy, bored with life and each other, and perpetually in need of artificial stimulation, New York's younger generation (or certain members of it exploited in this novel) find release only in a constant round of cocktail parties. Among those present at these parties, in and out of Harlem, are David Westlake and his wife Rilda, who are so much in love with each other that they must find consolation in gin and the arms of others; Hamish, a faithful friend; Roy Fern, for whom gin is not enough, and death is better; the Gräfin, a good soul from Central Europe discovered by Roy; and Donald, an efficient bootlegger"—Book review digest.

3459. Van Vorst, Frederick B. *Without a compass*; a novel. New York: Appleton, 1885. 414p.

Social, political and financial life in New York City two or three years before the Civil War is an important aspect of the novel. The protagonist, Van Dorn, recoups the fortune he had lost in New York by going to California for 15 years and successfully investing there. He returns to New York and finds his sister married to Mr. Chisholm, a wealthy speculator. She sets about searching for a suitable wife for her bachelor brother. An intimate friend of Mrs. Chisholm, Agnes Elliott, is unhappily married to a Navy lieutenant and Van Dorn falls in love with her. Yet he surrenders to practicality and marries Laura Walker-Brice. Wall Street operations and maneuvers by Van Dorn and his peers now begin to take center stage.

3460. Van Vorst, Marie, 1867-1936. *Mary Moreland*; a novel. With front. by C.H. Taffs. Boston: Little, Brown, 1915. 359p.

"The heroine [Mary Moreland] is a businesswoman of high character, acting as private secretary to a Wall Street banker. Their relations have been wholly impersonal, and his confession of private unhappiness followed by a proposal that she go away with him, comes to her without warning. Fate takes the matter out of her control and saves her from the compromising step. She leaves his employ to become secretary to an English man of letters, but finds that their two lives are not so easily severed. She meets Thomas Maughm [again] under various circumstances [and] his respect and admiration for the girl grows … and in the end the death of his selfish and shallow-minded wife makes their marriage possible"—Book review digest.

3461. ————. *Philip Longstreth*; a novel. New York: Harper, 1902. 395p.

Philip Longstreth is something of an idealist who buys a two-thirds interest in a shoe factory in the Upstate New York town of 'Randall', although his millionaire father and Constance Throckmorton, a young society woman in love with Philip, frown upon his plans. Philip moves quickly, creating excellent employer-employee relations, bringing many benefits to the town and forging a close relationship with Amber Garland, a factory operative supporting her ill father. Shertzy, Philip's business partner, seeks sole ownership of the firm and forces Philip into bankruptcy. Joel Longstreth bails his son out and Shertzy dies in an accident. Philip's personal life is complicated by his love for both Constance Throckmorton and Amber Garland. His choice is a conventional one—Constance—despite his lingering concern for Amber who has left the man she loves to be a nurse in the American-occupied Philippines.

3462. ————. *The sentimental adventures of Jimmy Bulstrode.* **With illus. by Alonzo Kimball. New York: Scribner, 1908. vii, 374p.**

Bachelor Jimmy Bulstrode lives in Washington Square surrounded by all the luxuries and comforts that wealth can bring. He is generally admired for his childlike enthusiasms, unselfishness and originality, but there resides in his heart a deep, abiding love for a married woman whom he treats with chivalrous delicacy and propriety. Jimmy travels and has adventures in America and Europe, in thought and deed remaining faithful to his love, and that constancy is eventually rewarded.

3463. ————. *The sin of George Warrener.* **New York: Macmillan, 1906. 316p.**

George Warrener commutes to his job as a clerk in a successful New York brokerage firm from his suburban home in New Jersey. His wife begins to look upon their quiet, cozy existence as an impediment to her own desire for a more sophisticated one. She has an affair with a suave, insincere artist, piles up debts, and blithely ignores her husband's concerns. George speculates in stocks at the New York Exchange and comes out a loser. The Warreners' situation demands a retrenchment; they take the necessary, difficult steps; Mrs. Warrener gives up her gossamer dreams to return to the realities of a relatively good marriage.

3464. **Van Wormer, Laura, 1955- . *Just for the summer.* Don Mills, Ont.: MIRA Book, 1997. 380p.**

Mary Liz Scott, retired at the early age of 33 from investment brokering, has a secret yearning to be a detective. She gets an opportunity to do some sleuthing while she is a guest at the very comfortable digs of her godmother, Nancy Hoffman, in East Hampton, Long Island. It seems that Nancy's husband, film producer Alfred, met with a fatal accident, leaving behind financial entanglements. Mary suspects that Alfred's passing was not happenstance. In her pursuit of the true facts she has to confront sleaze—pornography, money laundering, child abuse, and her own parents' checkered past. Mary also falls for summer vacationer Sky Preston, a good-looking guy who may not be what he seems.

3465. **Van Zile, Edgar Sims, 1863-1931. *A duke and his double.* With front. by**

Florence Scovel Shinn. New York: H. Holt, 1903. vi, 187p.

'Flour Baron' John T. Flint of Chicago essays entry into New York society, relying on an English peer, the Duke of Hastings for help. When the Duke falters, Flint turns to his butler who is transformed into a duke and then actually turns out to be a legitimate nobleman. Millionaire Flint's two daughters are agreeable young women who are certainly no hindrance to the Flints' pursuit of social acceptance. Mr. Flint is, of course, the stereotypical American businessman, clear-headed but rather ruthless and conscienceless.

3466. —————. *The Manhattaneers*; **a story of the hour. New York: Lovell, Coryell, 1895. 257p.**

The cast of the novel is a mixed bag of journalists and habitués of New York social circles. Richard Stoughton, a young reporter seeking to make his mark, develops a Platonic friendship with Mrs. Percy Bartlett, one of high society's arbiters, while John Fenton, a seasoned journalist with an interest in the city's social dilemmas, has an affair with Gertrude Van Vleck, a beauty with all the proper connections.

3467. —————. *Wanted——a sensation*; **a Saratoga incident. New York: Cassell, 1886. 173p.**

"The scene is laid in Saratoga; the story hinges upon the rivalry of two leading New York journals and their specials, Badger and Slushington, whose duty it was to supply their respective papers with news of this famous summer resort. A demand made upon Slushington and a desire to get the better of Badger led him to drug a detective, interview a noted gambler, expose a celebrated clergyman and separate a betrothed couple before his ardor was rewarded and he scored one ahead of his enemy as well as supplied the 'sensation wanted' by the Morning Era"—Annual American catalogue.

3468. **Vanamee, Lida Ostrom.** *An Adirondack idyll.* **New York: C.T. Dillingham, 1893. 152p.**

Hilda Ward, 28, while camping in the Adirondacks with her friend Mary Bruce and Mary's two children, by chance meets George Scanning, a man she had known ten years before. Hilda is a writer and George spends much of his time in England; unmarried at 38, George falls in love with Hilda. His feelings are reciprocated and the path to engagement and marriage seems smooth until Hilda learns that George had made a commitment to marry his cousin, Gertrude Palmer. Heartbroken, Hilda leaves the Adirondacks and George, returning home to her father. George reappears and shows Hilda a letter in which Gertrude absolves him of any promise to marry her: Gertrude concludes that she would be happier in her unmarried state.

Vanamee, Mrs. William. See: Vanamee, Lida Ostrom.

3469. **Vance, Louis Joseph, 1879-1933.** *Baroque*; **a mystery. New York: Dutton, 1923. 204p.**

The Barocco brothers, Liborio and Aniello, have been brought up in the darker sections of New York City. Liborio has embarked upon a criminal career; Aniello has traveled in the opposite direction—his two children are twins: Francesca, a delightful young woman, and Angelo, the bad seed. Rodney Manship, a young lawyer, meets Francesca in an Italian antique shop and falls in love with her. He is drawn into the Camorra (a secret criminal society with bases in Naples and New York) and becomes aware of a superstition that states if one of the Barocco twins dies the other must follow soon after.

3470. ————.*The brass bowl*. **With illus. by Orson Lowell. Indianapolis: Bobbs-Merrill, 1907. 379p.**

The hero is a New Yorker, a wealthy young man-about-town and a bachelor, who unknowingly resembles a clever jewel thief; the heroine is a socially prominent girl who steals data from a safe to free her father from a lawsuit. Another character is a lawyer who gets a thrill out of giving useful tips to professional thieves. Action comes hard and fast as automobiles race and break down, high-rise buildings are 'invaded' and gunshots ring out. The function of 'the brass bowl' of the title is to cover the impression made by a woman's hand on a dust-covered table in the bachelor's apartment.

3471. ————. *The dark mirror.* **Illustrated by Rudolph Tandler. Garden City, N.Y.: Doubleday, Page, 1920. ix, 368p.**

"Priscilla Main, the heroine, is subject from childhood to strangely realistic dreams. She is a wealthy young society woman and artist [in New York City]; but in the dreams she assumes another personality and moves in an unfamiliar environment … [and] associates with denizens of the [New York] underworld in 'the street of strange faces' and is known as 'Red Carnahan's girl'. She is loved by Mario who belongs to another world, but dwells in the lawbreakers' region of the city, and who wants to remove her from those unwholesome surroundings. Priscilla grows to love this man of her dreams. The dreams become so vivid and distressing that the girl seeks the aid of a psychoanalyst [Philip Fosdick] who loves her, and who undertakes to solve the mystery of her wandering ego. The mental experimentalist gradually is able to harmonize dreams with reality and startling data from the realm of psychology are brought to light"—Springfield Republican.

3472. ————. *The day of days*; **an extravaganza. With illus. by Arthur William Brown. Boston: Little, Brown, 1913. 300p.**

New York City is witness to the sudden rise to 'heroic' stature of an obscure clerk, P., Sybarite. A well-to-do relative has 'tossed' Sybarite a few dollars with which the latter treats three of his boardinghouse friends to the play 'Kismet.' In the next twelve hours P. Sybarite gathers in a fistful of money at a gambling house, saves a wife from a murderous husband, cuts a dashing figure at a posh masquerade ball and 'stands tall' in one of New York's criminal-infested joints, and above all, rescues his wife-to-be, Molly Lessing, from the artifices of three rascals—Molly, you see, is really Marian Blessington, an heiress for whom there had been an extensive search.

3473. ——————. *Joan Thursday*; a novel. **With illus. by Oscar Cesare. Boston: Little, Brown, 1913. 385p.**

The story "of the rise of a young and attractive shop girl in the theatrical profession. Wearying of her sordid home conditions, Joan runs away, determined to succeed on the stage. She finds an opening on a 'four-a-day' vaudeville circuit, and after a variety of experiences finds herself established on Broadway—a success. Joan is a girl possessed in the beginning of the finer instincts, and it seems for a time that, under the influence of John Matthias, they are to triumph, but she weakens, and the end of the story is disappointing in that Joan's success is won only at the expense of her better nature"—Book review digest.

3474. ——————. *The Lone Wolf returns.* **New York: Dutton, 1923. 367p.**

Vance's famous creation, Michael Lanyard, the Lone Wolf, comes to New York on leave from the British Secret Service and is immediately drawn into a confrontation with the criminal Morphew, also known as the 'Sultan of Loot' and 'King of the Bootleggers.' Their first meeting is set up by Liane Delorme, a dangerous woman from the Parisian demi-monde. Morphew tries to interest Lanyard in a profitable but illegal venture; the Lone Wolf turns him down and earns Morphew's enmity. Several New York friends, including Detective Crane, are most useful in shielding Lanyard from Morphew's vengefulness.

3475. ——————. *Nobody.* **Illustrated by W.L. Jacobs. New York: Doran, 1915. 352p.**

"Nobody was Miss Sally Manvers, a [New York] shopgirl who found life joyless on a salary of seven dollars a week. At the moment the story opens, she has not even that amount to depend on: she has been 'laid off.' She is ready for almost any desperate deed, and fate plays into her hand. Caught on the roof by a sudden thunderstorm, she drops down through the wrong skylight, and her adventures begin. The house… she enters is empty, but its owner, a woman of Sally's own size and build, has left her wearing apparel behind and Sally cannot resist the luxury of a warm bath and a 'try on' of some of the beautiful garments. How this escapade leads to an engagement, as secretary to an eccentric woman of wealth, how she has a taste of high society and becomes involved in a mysterious burglary, and how finally an apartment on Riverside Drive is her reward, all this is told"—Book review digest.

3476. ——————. *They call it love*; a novel. **Philadelphia: Lippincott, 1927. 316p.**

"Lona is on her own in New York. A year after the death of her fiancé she becomes the mistress of her married employer. In the set Lona goes about with is Fay Lascelles, a Southern girl with a very different ideal of love. Out with the same crowd, attending the same parties, the two girls become friends, and for a time, intimates. Lona breaks up Fay's engagement and ruins her brother, but at the end of their long history, Fay's virtue is more or less rewarded"—Book review digest.

3477. Vanderbilt, Cornelius, 1898-1974. *Park Avenue.* **New York: Macaulay, 1930. 382p.**

The familiar plot of this overblown story is that of the rich boy, Schuyler Courtland, who falls in love with the poor girl, Violet, and marries her despite opposition from his aristocratic mother, the machinations of Gertrude James, and Violet's own feelings of her unsuitability. Other obstacles are cast in their way (e.g. a murder trial), but love conquers all.

3478. Veder, Bob, 1940- . *Playing with fire*; **a novel. New York: Linden Press/Simon & Schuster, 1980. 250p.**

'Fallsview', a resort town in the Catskills, is plagued by a succession of fires whose origin no one knows. The permanent residents of the town are a scurvy lot who have committed with seeming impunity most of the venial and even more serious sins. Is an arsonist paying them back? If so, who might he/she be? The postmaster who isn't above reading other people's mail? The grocer/preacher, Mr. Grey, who cheats his customers but whose Sunday sermons are full of hellfire and damnation? The businessman whose lumberyard is close to bankruptcy?

Venning, Michael, pseud. See: Rice, Craig, 1908-1957.

3479. Ventura, Luigi, Donato, 1845-1912. *Peppino.* **New York: W.R. Jenkins Co., 1913. 65p.**

Written in French by an Italian-American author. Peppino, a 12-year-old, lives at the corner of Prince Street in New York City and dreams of his native village in Italy. He shines shoes and he and his brothers are saving their money in the hope of returning to that village, Viggiano. Until that time, if ever it arrives, Peppino takes pride in his ability to earn a living and makes friends with the men whose shoes he shines. One of these friends is the author, Ventura, a struggling New York journalist whom Peppino and his brothers help when Ventura is unable to pay his rent.

3480. Verdendorp, Basil, pseud. *The Verdendorps*; **a novel. Chicago: C.M. Hertig, 1880. 376p.**

The New York financier, Mr. Verdendorp, has compiled a fortune through his control of political personages and railroads, but his eldest son, Richard, plots to take over the old man's holdings. Richard uses Mary Craven, a supposed divorcée, and her mother, persuading Mr. Verdendorp to marry the daughter. Then the schemer blackens his brother Basil's reputation before his father and more or less dismisses his sisters as significant heirs to the Verdendorp estate. The old man's will benefits Richard above all others. The sisters receive small legacies while Richard as trustee holds Basil's share. Basil and one of the sisters, Mrs. Latour, contest the will, but Richard wins. Basil shoots Richard, is tried for murder and gains acquittal. However, the Verdendorp property quickly loses its value and thus Basil too is a loser. The author of the novel, 'Basil' himself, gives no explanation for penning his 'memoirs.'

Versace, Marie Teresa Rios, 1917- . See: Rios, Teresa, 1917-

3481. **Veysey, Arthur Henry, b. 1869.** *Hats off!* **New York: G.W. Dillingham, 1899. 255p.**

A comedy of social life in New York City. "The Van Winkle Dames are represented as an organization of society women who revere the customs of European court life and … elect a queen [Belinda Van Winkle]. A congratulatory letter sent to her falls by mistake into the hands of the queen of a rival society [Angelica Saunders of the Dutch Fraus]. Following this incident are some grotesque scenes in an original plot. The novel is evidently a satire on a recent social agitation at the Society of Holland Dames" —Annual American catalogue.

3482. **Victor, Barbara, 1946- .** *Misplaced lives*; **a novel. New York: Harper & Row, 1990. 293p.**

Gabrielle Carlucci-Molloy returns to Long Island from Paris after her domineering husband, District Attorney Peter Molloy, dies suddenly. She takes a job as a photojournalist and tries to reconcile with her intractable daughter Dina, with little success. Then Gabrielle meets a decent man, Nick Tressa, a plain-speaking, unpolished contractor, who falls in love with her. The usual misunderstandings take their course before the programmed happy ending arrives.

3483. **Victor, Metta Victoria Fuller, 1831-1885.** *Abijah Beanpole in New York*; **the misfortunes and mishaps of a country storekeeper on a business visit to the great City of New York. By the author of** *A bad boy's diary*. **New York: G.W. Carleton, 1884. 202p.**

Young Abijah (he is not quite 21) leaves Beanville and his sweetheart, Kitty Caraway, for New York City where he intends to purchase goods for a store to be opened in Beanville under his proprietorship. His misadventures in the metropolis include the temporary loss of his seed money, a discomforting and almost disastrous outing at the opera, a timely escape from the marriage plans of the Widow Mousetrap and an unintentional bout of drunkenness at a Fifth Avenue party. Bijah returns to his hometown and is chagrined to learn that dear Kitty has married his rival, Reub Lummis. He sets up his store and concludes that plenty of 'gals' are available and eager to go into 'pardnership' with him. This work has been attributed by the American Catalogue and Allibone (Critical Dictionary of English Literature) to Walter T. Gray.

3484. **Victor, Ralph.** *Comrades in New York*; **or,** *Snaring the smugglers*. **Illustrated by S. Schneider. New York: Chatterton-Peck Co., 1908. 253p.**

Chot, Fleet and Tom are the three comrades in the novel. Mr. Ford, on whose farm they worked in the summer, invites them to his home in New York for the Christmas holidays. In getting to the city there is an accident on the railroad and they lose their luggage. In trying to regain it, the three lads are innocently involved in some criminal activities. Thus it is incumbent on them to offer their services to the authorities in the final track down of a gang of smugglers.

Vidal, Gore, 1925- . See under his pseudonym: Box, Edgar.

3485. **Viereck, George Sylvester, 1884-1962.** *The house of the vampire.* **New York: Moffat, Yard, 1907. 190p.**

Reginald Clark lives in an apartment overlooking Riverside Drive in New York City and is reputed to be a man of rare intellect; however, he is actually a literary vampire, picking the brains of close friends who have been published. These friends often share his apartment, but after he has drawn from their creative minds all he can use, Clark asks them to leave; by then they have been reduced to pale images of their former selves.

3486. **Vinton, Iris, 1905- .** *Flying Ebony.* **Illustrated by Marc Simont. New York: Dodd, Mead, 1947. xi, 289p.**

It had been the intention of Jonathan Feather, a lad of fourteen to leave home to go to sea, but instead he and his horse, Flying Ebony, were put to the task of patrolling the beaches of the South Shore of Long Island in the mid-19th century. If he sighted a ship in dire need of help, Jonathan would race to the nearest village where experienced men were available to man the lifeboats.

3487. **Virga, Vincent, 1942- .** *Gaywyck.* **New York: Avon Books, 1980. 375p.**

A modern 'gothic' wherein Robert, who is gay, takes a job cataloging a large book collection housed in the Long Island home ('Gaywick') of a bachelor who is very wealthy and is a well-known man-about-town in New York City. Of course, it is inevitable that Gaywyck will be the scene, among other things, of a romantic attachment between Robert and his employer.

Virginian, A. *The Kentuckian in New York.* **See Item #557.**

3488. **Vogel, Joseph, 1904- .** *Man's courage.* **New York: Knopf, 1938. 312p.**

Adam Wolak, a Polish immigrant living for 18 years in the city of 'Genesee' (i.e. Utica, N.Y.), is a simple but worthy man who welcomes the possibility of becoming an American citizen. But he is buffeted by the political and welfare systems, and in the end is killed by officers when he resists eviction of his family from their rented house.

3489. **———.** *The straw hat*; **a novel. New York: Modern Age Books, 1939. 288p.**

Vincent's Uncle Gus asks him to come up to the Upstate New York resort where Vincent assumes his uncle to be a person of some importance. Five days after his arrival Vincent has learned the truth about Gus, a crude, swaggering, woman-chasing bully. Rather than attempt to search for any redeeming qualities in his miserable uncle and depressed by the incessant rainfall at the resort, Vincent hitchhikes his way home.

3490. **Vonnegut, Kurt, 1922- .** *Player piano*. **New York: Delacorte Press, 1952. 295p.**
The scene is Upstate New York, the Albany-Troy-Schenectady (the 'Capital') area—the name of the town in which the plant Dr. Paul Proteus manages is located in 'Ilium' (assuredly Schenectady). Cornell University (which Vonnegut attended) is mentioned at several points in the novel. Vonnegut's futuristic tale pictures life in Ilium where electronic devices have replaced people as producers of all consumer products, leaving ordinary human beings a listless and useless clump, all of whose wants are taken care of by the managers and engineers who run the machines. A Luddite-like revolt is inevitable and is led by Dr. Paul Proteus and several colleagues with inconclusive results.

3491. **Vorse, Mary Marvin Heaton, 1874-1966.** *I've come to stay*; **a love comedy of Bohemia. New York: Century Co., 1918. 190p.**
"A story of New York's Bohemia and of the people who live around Washington Square. According to the author these are the 'children of the righteous' who come there 'to escape the cramping memories of a childhood.' Such a one is Camilla of the blue serge past. This is the love story of Camilla and Ambrose Ingraham, a story somewhat involved with that of Serge Askoff, on the one hand, and of Sonya Mucha, the little Italian dancer who adopts Ambrose, on the other"—Book review digest.

3492. **Vose, John Denison, 1828-1881.** *Fresh leaves from the diary of a Broadway dandy*. **Edited by John D. Vose. Rev., enl., and corr. by the author. New York: Bunnell & Price, 1852. vi, 123p.**
'Harry' is the young scapegrace who carefully records his various escapades, amusements, etc. as he tastes New York life, supplied with a handsome allowance by a doting father. When his funds shrink, an aunt in Virginia leaves Harry $60,000. Harry's father finally decides to disinherit his seemingly irredeemable son. But Harry comes out on top after all when he marries Elvirato Coddington, a girl from an undistinguished family—Elvirato's uncle, pleased by the union, provides Elivirato with a handsome dowry and endows the pair with valuable properties in New York City.

3493. **Vrooman, John J.** *Clarissa Putnam of Tribe's Hill*; **a romantic history of Sir William Johnson, his family and Mohawk Valley neighbors through the flaming years 1767-1780. Johnstown, N.Y.: Baronet Litho Co., 1950. 423p.**
A sweeping historical novel of the Mohawk Valley, its settlers and Indians in the years preceding the American Revolution and, briefly, Tory and Indian raids in the Valley (led by Sr. John Johnson and Joseph Brant), 1777-1780. Central characters are Sir John, William's son, and Clarissa (Clisty) Putnam

who bore him a son and a daughter; John, on the advice of his father, did not marry Clarissa, taking as a bride instead a young lady from the influential Watts/De Lancey families. Sir William Johnson is a domineering presence in the story until his death in 1774. At the novel's end Clarissa is a matron in a hospital for the war's wounded, surviving the bloody raids of Brant's Indians and Johnson's Tories.

3494. ———. *The massacre.* **Johnstown, N.Y.: Baronet Litho Co., 1954. 267p.**
The 'massacre' of the title occurred in 1690 when the village of Schenectady was sacked and burned by a force of French and Indians. It is described in detail in the concluding pages of the novel, which recounts the events leading up to that disaster. French, Indian, Dutch and British characters pass through the pages of the story with scenes set in the Mohawk Valley, Quebec and France. Two Indian women, Gahada and her daughter Georgette by the famous Count Frontenac assume the mantle of 'heroines.' Gahada is slain in a Mohawk raid on Lachine, Quebec and Georgette is carried off. She is bought from her Mohawk captors by a Schenectady innkeeper and is one of the 60 people killed in the Schenectady massacre.

Waddel, Charles Carey, 1868-1930. See: Waddell, Charles Carey, 1868-1930.

3495. **Waddell, Charles Carey, 1868-1930.** *The girl of the guard line.* **New York: Moffat, Yard, 1915. 292p.**
While on sentry duty at midnight, West Point cadet Burr Beverly confronts a beautiful and high-spirited girl. They meet again socially and the two begin to fall in love with one another. She is the daughter of the Aureatan ambassador to the United States and is a guest on a yacht lying off West Point. Certain people on the boat turn out to be engaged in a plot against the American government and Burr, with vital assistance from his girlfriend, is able to quash the conspiracy, winning a promotion as well as the girl.

3496. **Wade, Blanche Elizabeth, d. 1928.** *Anne, princess of everything.* **New York: Sully and Kleinteich, 1916. 207p.**
A 'modern' fairy tale in which Anne Lane, accompanied by her plain-spoken aunt, walks into a New York City shop that has real butterflies among its stock in trade. She is more than astonished when an obvious foreigner assumes she is the princess who had been abducted from her kingdom not too long ago. From that point on, extraordinary, magical things happen that may terminate in Anne actually becoming a real princess.

3497. **Walden, David.** *The season.* **New York: Greystone Press, 1942. 378p.**
"Summer in the Catskills is the theme. … It's a bad season, and Sam Barsky, proprietor of Pinecrest, isn't a very good businessman. To make matters worse, he has a new wife to cope with. The only way he can wrest a profit

from his hotel is to exploit his assorted 'helps', which he does unscrupulously"—The nation.

3498. **Walk, Charles Edmonds, b. 1875.** *The time lock.* **With illus. by Will Grefé. Chicago: McClurg, 1912. 419p.**

At an exclusive gentlemen's club in New York City two of the members, Rudolph Van Vechten and Tom Finney, are observers through the club windows of peculiar goings-on in the deserted mansion across the street. At various intervals they see four men and a young woman entering the house. They follow one of the men who leaves the mansion at approximately 1:30 P.M., only to watch as he falls dead a few blocks later. Van Vechten and Finney soon learn they have chanced upon a murder and they seek to identify the mysterious girl they had seen entering the house, for, as it turns out, she had been witness to a homicidal act. And then Van Vechten's fiancée is enmeshed in the strange affair. The climactic moment in the mystery arrives when New York's foremost financial tycoon hosts a banquet, which is intruded upon by the appearance of a coffin consigned to the tycoon.

3499. **[Walker, Ambrose].** *The highlands*; **a tale of the Hudson. Philadelphia: Printed for the author, 1826. 2v.**

The American Revolution and its unsettling aftermath lead Mr. Brownly to settle in the Hudson Highlands. Brownly had had Loyalist sentiments while his business partner, Theodore Standbury, had served as a colonel in the Continental Army. But when William Harrington, son of the forester neighbor of Mr. Brownly, kills Brownly's son, Alexander, in a quarrel brought on by the latter's resentment of Harrington's attentions to his sister, Harriet, Colonel Standbury and his son, Captain Standbury, come to the aid of the grieving father. They and the Mohawk, Buckfoot, track down the murderer in the forests of the Highlands. Harrington is shot and killed by Buckfoot when he attempts to escape from his temporary jail in the Brownly mansion by setting fire to the building. Harrington had at one time been a close friend of his victim, Alexander Brownly, and Harriet Brownly, already consumptive, is unable to withstand the double shock of her brother's and Harrington's demise.

3500. **[Walker, Jesse], 1810-1852.** *Fort Niagara*; **a tale of the Niagara frontier. Buffalo: Steele's Press, 1845. 156p. (***Tales of the Niagara frontier***, part II)**

A sequel to the author's *Queenston*; a tale of the Niagara frontier (q.v.) Harry West and Captain Gray travel on horseback to Lewiston and other points in northwestern New York and finally come to Fort Niagara. There the colonel in command meets them and tells the story of Fort Niagara from its beginnings. Evidently the Captain feels that Harry needs a short course in New York State history for he takes the opportunity to follow the colonel's discourse with one of his own, covering the Iroquois, Joseph Brant, the Tory Walter Butler and his role in the American Revolution.

3501. ———. *Queenston*; a tale of the Niagara Frontier. **Buffalo: Steele's Press, 1845. 151p. (*Tales of the Niagara Frontier, part I*)**

Captain Gray, residing in a small town in western New York with his two daughters and son Charles, relates to his visiting nephew, Harry West, his memories of the New York-Canadian confrontations in the War of 1812 in which the Captain was a full participant. Harry, Charles and the Captain then journey to scenes of battles and to a Tuscarora Indian village. Harry is introduced to survivors of those who lost their lives in the war while the Captain continues to expand Harry's knowledge of the conflict.

Wall Street man. See: Proudfit, David Law, 1842-1897.

3502. Wallace, Marilyn. *The seduction.* **New York: Doubleday, 1993. 209p.**

Lee Montara is visiting her sister, Rosie Cooper, in the latter's rural Upstate New York home where the two are receiving intimations that someone is waiting to do them harm. Lee, a New York City photo editor, is trying to avoid Stewart McClaren, an aggressive photographer. Paul Cooper, Rosie's husband, tells Sheriff Riley Hamm the sisters' qualms, but he is not too interested until a corpse is uncovered on a farm near the Cooper house. The stalker may be coming closer and the sisters and the sheriff are in a race to identify him before he acts again.

3503. ———. *So shall you reap.* **New York: Doubleday, 1992. 277p.**

Sara Hoving's mother-in-law talks her into playing a major role in the pageant celebrating the bicentennial of their native village, 'Taconic Hills' ('a tiny hamlet halfway between the Hudson River and New England'). Shortly thereafter several weird events occur, including a murder and the near-destruction of the Hoving farmhouse by a suspicious fire. It seems that 200 years ago events similar to these took place. Sara begins to dig into her own past—e.g., her mother deserted Sara when she was just four years of age. As further memories surface Sara comes to believe that Roy Stanton (her father), her mother-in-law, Ruth Hoving, and other people in Taconic Hills are concealing facts that are pertinent to her early years.

3504. Wallenrod, Reuben, 1899-1996. *Dusk in the Catskills.* **New York: Reconstructionist Press, 1957. 264p.**

Translation of: *Ki fanah yom.*

Leo Halper and his wife Lillian are proprietors of the Hotel Brookville in the Catskills; it caters to New Yorkers who leave the city in the summer to rest in the quiet, rejuvenating mountains. The Halpers are hard-pressed to keep up with payments to the bank, although they have a good friend in old Sam Douglas (the bank's semi-retired president) who is willing to carry them as long as he can control his son Bill, the bank's chief officer. Leo Halper reflects unhappily and with sharp twinges of conscience on the fate of his fellow Jews in Europe under Nazi persecution—the story takes place during World War II—while he and his guests enjoy the freedom of city and countryside. The summer visitors at the Hotel Brookville and the natives of the region share romance, tragedy, unfulfilled expectations, moments of high humor, most of the quandaries of the human condition.

Wallenrod, Reuben, 1899-1966. *Ki fanah yom.* **For the English translation of this work see Item #3504.**

3505. **Wallis, James Harold, 1885-1958.** *Cries in the night.* **New York: Dutton, 1933. 317p.**
> The snatching of wealthy sportsman Whitney Sinclair's dazzling wife from their yacht on Long Island Sound by modern buccaneers is only the first of a sequence of strange, terrifying occurrences. But real inquiries begin only after a second and similar vanishing ends in murder.

3506. **Walsh, Thomas, 1908-1984.** *The action of the tiger.* **New York: Simon and Schuster, 1968. 222p.**
> When he loses his beloved 16-year-old sister in a tragic incident in the Adirondacks that has the odor of a murder, detective John Dillon is frantic with grief and thoughts of revenge. He makes his way to 'Hazard Lake' and discusses the situation with the local police chief. As the weeks pass by and the main suspect seems to have an ironclad alibi, John suddenly grabs his weapons and returns to Hazard Lake to settle the matter once and for all.

3507. **Walter, Eugene, 1874-1941.** *The easiest way*; **a story of metropolitan life, by Eugene Walter and Arthur Hornblow. Illus. by Archie Gunn and Joseph Byron. New York: Dillingham, 1911. 347p.**
> Based on the play by Eugene Walter. Laura Murdock, 25, an actress of limited talent, has consistently supplemented her paychecks with money provided by male admirers. She bestowed her favors on several of them, most notably Willard Brockton, a New York broker and 'honest sensualist', who has enough influence in theatrical circles to get roles for those actresses he favors. While in Denver for the summer Laura meets and falls in love with John Madison, a newspaperman and sometime miner. When she returns to New York she vows to end her relationship with Brockton and live simply and honestly until Madison calls for her. Unable to find work in the theater and bereft of funds, Laura reverts to 'the easiest way', returning to Brockton and the luxuries he can offer her. When John Madison finally comes to New York intending to marry Laura, he becomes aware of Laura's basic dishonesty, her lack of moral fiber. He walks away from her; Laura has already made the final break with Brockton. As the story concludes she has only a rather grim, dissolute future before her.

3508. **Walworth, Dorothy, 1900- .** *They thought they could buy it.* **Garden City, N.Y.: Doubleday, Doran, 1930. 313p.**
> "Three social levels in suburban life are contrasted respectively in this novel through a study of three young married couples: Amelia and Joe Browning,

hard-working, virtuous, family-raising; Lydia and Seth Smith, a little higher in the financial scale, who give cocktail parties and imitate the New York intelligentsia in other ways; and Joyce and Clifford Millard, wealthy, and unhappily married. These people, in typical American fashion, measure happiness in terms of money. Joyce alone—when everything that money can buy has failed her—finds something that is much more essential to real living"—Book review digest.

3509. **Walworth, Jeannette Ritchie Hadermann, 1837-1918.** *An old fogy*. **New York: Merriam Co., 1895. 292p.**

"The 'old fogy' is Colonel Burnett, a Southerner of old family and strict honor, who is obliged to sacrifice his ancestral home to satisfy his creditors. With his wife, two daughters, and a son, all grown, he comes to New York City to seek employment under the auspices of his rather purse-proud, successful brother. The trials of the Colonel amid the excitement of New York life and the totally new code of morals of business life are told with some humor"—Annual American catalogue.

3510. ————. *Old Fulkerson's clerk*. **New York: Cassell, 1886. 171p.**

New York businessman, 'Old' Fulkerson, is duped by his clerk who flees to Canada with a tidy portion of Fulkerson's fortune. When the businessman's nephew, a well-to-do socialite physician who lives with his uncle, advertises for a nurse to provide care for the ill-humored, incapacitated old codger, the clerk's wife, still in the city, puts on a disguise and takes the job—she and her sister were without funds and were badly in need of any type of work. And thereby hangs the tale.

3511. **Walworth, Mansfield Tracy, 1830-1873.** *Hotspur*; **a tale of the old Dutch manor. New York: Carleton, 1864. 324p.**

The events of the novel take place within "the town of C——: the noble old State of New York boasts of no fairer garden spot within its limits" (p. [5]). Henry Lansing leaves town when he is accused of the murder of Benjamin Hartwell. Blonde Grayson, the woman he loves, investigates and finds clues that point to the true murderer. However no one seems willing to pursue the data and the years go by. A new doctor comes to C—— and successfully treats ill Blonde and Gurty Lansing, Henry's younger brother. The doctor removes his beard and other facial disguises—he is Henry Lansing! Blonde and Henry are married; the authorities take him into custody. At his trial Henry wins acquittal. Judge Peyton, in whom Blonde had always confided, tells the court he killed Hartwell for raping the judge's wife. Judge Payton's act is treated as justifiable homicide.

3512. ————. *Married in mask*; **a novel. New York: Street & Smith, 1890. 345p.**

Kidnapped by 'Red-Eyed Mag' at an early age, Bessie Truelove is separated from her angelic mother for many years. Sam, a young thief on the streets of New York, becomes Bessie's protector, wresting her forcibly from Mag's clutches until Bessie is again stolen, this time by 'Old Hawk', who 'sells' her to an elderly merchant, a Mr. Thorne, who wants to raise a daughter. Sam has meanwhile been adopted by the banker Nicholas Rudd and prospers. He confronts Old Hawk; the latter reveals Bessie's whereabouts and is present when Sam and Bessie are 'married in mask'. A detective who has spent years tracing Sam and Bessie, has Sam arrested for the murder of Red-Eyed Mag; Sam goes to trial and is acquitted. Revelations and reunions now come quickly: Sam is Nicholas Rudd's real (not adopted) son by an Italian lady who is the sister of Sam's friend, Dr. Ruffini, one-time street musician. Mrs. Truelove is the estranged sister of Rudd; she finds her long-lost daughter Bessie when she visits her brother for the first time in years.

3513. ————. *The mission of death*; a tale New York's penal laws. New York: D. & J. Sadlier, 1853. 281p.

A condemnatory portrayal of the persecution of Roman Catholics in New York Colony, 1739-1741. Mary Sidney, daughter of Colonel George Sidney of the New York General Assembly, sympathizes with Catholics Agnes and Harry Clarke; Harry's 'servant', Father Ury (under the name John Bowers), is arrested and jailed. Mary converts to Catholicism and her father vainly tries to reduce the bigotry of the Protestant clergy and civil authorities. Fire breaks out in New York City and Father Ury and several slaves are blamed. Even Colonel Sidney is briefly imprisoned. A number of slaves are burned at the stake and Father Ury is hanged. After Agnes Clarke dies of smallpox, Mary Sidney and Harry Clarke are married and continue in the Catholic faith.

3514. ————. *Stormcliff*. A tale of the Highlands. New York: Carleton, 1866. 387p.

A discouraged Clarence Holden contemplates suicide—he is uncertain of his origins and his guardian, the late Judge Holden, left Clarence nothing, for the judge believed that his true son had been switched at birth. Mrs. Nora Rudd talks Clarence out of self-destruction. He begins to practice law and becomes active in local politics. A widow, Grace Baltimore, comes back to the Hudson Highlands village of her youth and to the estate known as 'The Glen'. Clarence Holden, who has changed his surname to Rutherford, is her attorney. Daily contact between the two results in a bond of love. New characters and complex relationships are introduced. When clarity returns, Clarence Holden/Rutherford is proved to be the rightful Holden heir—he is the judge's son by his first wife, the daughter of Nora Rudd; separated from the judge she had died shortly after giving birth to Clarence and the judge's second wife had posed as Clarence's mother.

Wanneh, Gawaso, pseud. See: Parker, Arthur Caswell, 1881-1955.

3515. **Warfield, David, 1866-1951.** *Ghetto silhouettes*, **by David Warfield & Margherita Arlina Hamm. New York: J. Pott, 1902. viii, 189p.**

"The stories ... are based upon sketches made from the daily life of the famous East Side of New York City" (Preface). The people that move through the tales are, as one would probably expect, Jews, many of whom are recent immigrants seeking the freedom they were not allowed in the 'old country' (Europe). One wonders about the extent of the famous actor Warfield's contribution to the collection—whether Ms. Hamm was really the major writer here. Contents: The end of the dream.—The romance of a minder.—Revenge is mine.—The story of Philip.—The run of Jobbleousky's.—A bird of prey.—Solomon and Santa Claus.

3516. **Warner, Anna Bartlett, 1827-1915.** *My brother's keeper.* **New York: D. Appleton, 1855. 385p.**

"Set in New York back during the War of 1812 [the novel] tells how the heroine ... sacrifices love, health, and happiness to keep house for her brother and by her womanly presence and patience to save him from gambling and drinking. In view of the fact that New York City is under siege, the sister's devotion is utmost heroism. ... When her work is accomplished, [she] is free to marry her beloved, a Quaker of considerably greater moral firmness than ... [her] brother. ... [She] has earned the right to be taken care of the rest of her life"—Baym, N. *Woman's fiction.*

3517. ————. *West Point colors*; a novel. **New York, Chicago: Revell, 1903. 428p.**

"A story of West Point, tracing the experiences of a cadet from his nomination to the graduating parade. Miss Warner has had expert assistance in the matter of technicalities, but she declined the suggestion of her cadet friends to use a certain tactical officer as 'villain' and constructed a plot of her own. Almost every incident, however, happened to some cadet or other at some time or other"—The critic.

3518. **Warner, Charles Dudley, 1829-1900.** *The golden house*; a novel. **Illustrated by W.T. Smedley. New York: Harper, 1895. [i.e., 1894]. 346p.**

"A story of the very rich and the very poor of New York City. The characters are Jack Delaney and his wife, a young couple born to wealth and idleness; Mr. Henderson, a multi-millionaire; and Carmen, his second wife—heartless and unscrupulous; Father Damon and Ruth Leigh, workers among the East Side poor; and other types of the business and fashionable and other work-a-day world of the great metropolis. The temptations that come alike to the rich and the poor are strongly drawn, while the types presented offer many points of resemblance to noted New York people"—Annual American catalogue.

3519. ————. *A little journey in the world*; a novel. **New York: Harper, 1889. 396p.**

The theme of Warner's novel is the effect a rise to sudden wealth has on the nature of a heretofore sensitive and good-hearted young woman, Margaret Debree, who leaves provincial society in Connecticut to become the wife of an extremely rich New Yorker, Rodney Henderson. The fashionable and luxurious life of the upper class in New York City eats away at some of her finer qualities, although she retains a certain graciousness and outward kindness.

3520. ──────. *That fortune*; a novel. **New York: Harper, 1899. 393p.**

Philip Burnett makes the transition from life in rural Massachusetts to the big city, New York, where he starts out as a clerk in a law office with the real goal of entering the literary lists. He meets, quite casually, Evelyn Mavick, unspoiled heiress to the vast Henderson/Mavick fortune and immediately falls in love with her. However, Mrs. Mavick has plans to elevate her social position by marrying off Evelyn to Lord Montague. Evelyn stubbornly resists her mother's scheme; Philip attains entry into the literary world with his first novel, leaves the law office and gains employment with a New York publishing house. When disaster strikes Mr. Mavick's commercial ventures and that fortune disappears, Philip, who had hitherto been cut off from Evelyn by Mrs. Mavick, is given a fresh opportunity to win her love.

3521. **[Warner, Susan] 1819-1885.** *The hills of the Shatemuc.* **By the author of** *The wide, wide world.* **New York: D. Appleton, 1856. iv, 516p.**

"Nominally the setting [of the novel] is the Hudson and the hills around it, but descriptions are vague, with little sense of local customs and life. There are occasionally good descriptions of the poorer sections of New York [City] but nothing to match those in 'Queechy'—Foster, Edward M. Susan and Anna Warner. Orphah Landholm sees his farm foreclosed by Mr. Haye and goes west to start anew. His son Winthrop is admitted to the practice of law and is admired by Elizabeth Cadwallader, Haye's niece, who purchases the former Landholm farm. As its owner and mistress she lives on the farm with Rose Haye (whose father has died insolvent) and Winthrop Landholm is one of their visitors. Elizabeth, once a spoiled and altogether selfish young woman, transforms herself and thus becomes a worthy soul mate for the stiff righteous Winthrop.

3522. ──────. *The house in town.* **A sequel to** *Opportunities.* **By the author of** *The wide, wide world.* **New York: R. Carter, 1872. 424p.**

Matilda and her brother Norton, originally from Poughkeepsie, come to New York to live. Their half-Jewish cousins, Judith and David, are native New Yorkers. The story follows their progress in school and out. David's good qualities shine through, although at first he is not at all popular with his classmates. Judith will have little to do with Matilda or Norton and displays a streak of intolerance.

3523. ──────. *The letter of credit.* **By the author of** *The wide, wide world.* **New York: R. Carter, 1882. 733p.**

A stranger traveling to Rochester, N.Y. comes down with sickness, is taken to a farmhouse in Upstate New York, and nursed to recovery by the farmer and his wife. In gratitude he gives the two rural dwellers a letter of credit to a firm in New York City which they may make use of should they ever be in financial straits. When the farmer dies, the farm is disposed of, and the widow and her daughter, Rotha, leave for New York City to make their livelihood. Stalked by poverty the widow sends in the letter of credit. The results are propitious. The son of the man befriended by the farm couple comes forward to comfort the dying mother and to assume guardianship of her daughter.

3524. ————. *The little camp on Eagle Hill.* **Boston: Bradley & Woodruff, 1873. 429p.**

Led by their uncle, Mr. Eden Murray, the three Candlish children, Fenton, 13, Esther, 11, and Maggie, 7, their friend Josie McAllister, and Mr. Murray's sister, Mrs. Patty Ponsonby, set up camp on 'Eagle Hill', Orange County, N.Y. Not only does Mr. Murray introduce the young people to the pleasures and rigors of life in the outdoors, but also he misses no opportunity to explain the Christian message and to belabor the greed that is one of the causes of gross economic inequality and poverty. The novel is directed toward a juvenile audience; it is lengthy and ultimately dull reading.

3525. ————. *Pine needles.* **By the author of *The wide, wide world.* New York: R. Carter, 1877. 346p.**

Didactic novel with its setting on Constitution Island, the Hudson River island which was the home of Susan and Anna Warner for many years after 1842. "Mosswood is patterned after the Warners' home and the various places in which the picnics take place are recognizably locations on Constitution Island and along the banks of the [Hudson] River"—Foster, Edward; H. Susan and Anna Warner.

3526. ————. *Queechy.* **by Elizabeth Wetherell [pseud.]. New York: G.P. Putnam, 1852. 2v.**

"The action [of the novel] is divided largely between New York City and a country village, Queechy, which is clearly based on Canaan, New York" (Foster, Edward H. Susan and Anna Warner). Fleda Ringgan, an orphan, lives alternately in Queechy, France, New York City, and then back to Queechy with her aunt and uncle, the Rossiturs. The once wealthy and fashionable Rossiturs become dependent on Fleda to eke out a living on her grandfather's old farm in Queechy. Fleda's final destination is England where she joins her husband, Guy Carleton, a wealthy young Englishman who has intervened twice with financial aid to save the Ringgan farm.

3527. ————. *Trading*: **finishing the story of *The house in town*, etc. By the author of *The wide, wide world*, etc. New York: R. Carter, 1873. 437p.**

Matilda's piety and charitable instincts glow as she, her brother Norton and their half-cousins, David and Judith, continue their New York City experiences; she is the chief influence in David's conversion to Christianity. Judith refuses to countenance any efforts to change her character and clings to her Jewish roots.

904

3528. ————. *The wide, wide world.* **By Elizabeth Wetherell [pseud.]. New York: G.P. Putnam, 1851 [c1850]. 2v.**

"'The Wide, wide world' depends heavily for its sense of time and place on the author's knowledge of Yonkers and Upstate New York customs and dialect" (Foster, Edward H.; Susan and Anna Warner). The rural village of 'Thirlwall', although located in New York State (close by the Massachusetts border), and the setting for much of the novel, has characteristics generally associated with New England. The heroine is Ellen Montgomery, raised in New York City, but relegated to Thirlwall by her father. Ellen associates with both rustic types and the more cultivated people in Thirlwall, eventually settling down with the Humphreys. By the end of the novel Ellen is in Scotland with the prospect of returning to America and close ties with John Humphrey, a divinity student.

3529. Warren, Benjamin Clark, 1859?-1952. *In the Land of the Romburg*; **a society story. New York: Broadway Pub. Co., c 1906. 281p.**

"'Quindauoquah' is a prosperous city. Situated between New York and Albany, occupying the fairest position on the banks of America's noblest river, Nature has given it every possible advantage of climate, waterway and soil" (p.11). The city's chief industrial plant is 'the Romburg'. A leading character in the novel is the Reverend Dr. Edgerton Dare, a recent widower, whose leadership of the State Street Methodist Episcopal Church is on shaky ground, harassed as he is by David Romburg, owner of 'the Romburg', and various other parishioners. Dare marries one of his church's wealthy members and decides to leave Quindauoquah. Romburg, although married, is having an affair with Daisy Brown, one of his office employees. In order to break away from the persistent attentions of Romburg, Daisy marries the illegitimate son of a black lady and Mr. Hillyer, Romburg's cousin; this couple's future does not look too promising.

3530. Warren, Grenliffe. *The Flying Cloud*; **a romance of the Bay of New York. Boston: H.L. Williams, 1845. 82p. (in double columns).**

This melodramatic tale concerns two affluent Hudson Valley families—The Leffingwells of 'Monmouth Park' and the Sheridines of 'Laurel Park.' The hero, Charles Winder, is tutor to Frank and Clara, children of Dr. Sheridine. He is in love with Rosa, the daughter of General Leffingwell and one of two heroines—the other being Clara Sheridine. Edgar Sheridine, the doctor's older son, is enamored of Rosa Leffingwell and plots to kidnap her. Charles Winder and Edgar's sister, Clara, frustrate his plans. Clara escapes Edgar's murderous wrath and is taken aboard the Flying Cloud by Captain Fordwell, an acquaintance of Edgar's. Clara informs Fordwell of Edgar's criminal activity and Fordwell, quickly falling in love with her, turns Edgar over to the authorities for eventual execution, the General and the doctor consenting to this harsh extreme. Charles and Rosa and Fordwell and Clara match up.

3531. Warth, Julian. *Dorothy Thorn of Thornton.* **Boston: D. Lothrop [1887]. 276p.**

"The northern shore of Long Island is the scene. The characters are an unsuccessful, optimistic experimenter in chemistry; his young, beautiful, enthusiastic daughter; the rich young man of the place, who builds a factory for the sake of practicing his theories of the peaceful union of labor and capital; the clergyman; the woman he loves, who has a secret in her life; and her devoted attendant, the woman-preacher, Hannah"—Annual American catalogue.

3532. —————. *The full stature of a man*; **a life story. Boston: D. Lothrop, c1886. 300p.**

Also published under the title: *John Greenleaf, minister* (Boston: D. Lothrop, c1888). Milly Burton, orphaned niece of the Hampton, Long Island farmer Ben Burton, leaves her governess's job in New York City to keep house for her uncle. Joining the household is the clergyman John Greenleaf. There is a mutual attraction between Milly and John, but she decides to return to the city. The train carrying her and Uncle Ben is derailed. Mr. Burton is hurt badly and Milly finds herself taking care of a young girl whose mother asks Milly to stay with the girl's aunt and her son, the Ogdens, a wealthy patrician New York family, until recovery of Ben Burton and the orphaned girl (her mother died shortly after the train wreck). In due course young Sidney Ogden falls in love with Milly; she sadly rejects his marriage proposal, but does instill in him some of her ideas concerning the misdistribution of wealth and the betterment of the working class. Ben dies, Milly marries John Greenleaf, and the two return to Hampton eager to further the social gospel.

Warth, Julian. *John Greenleaf, minister.* **See note under Item #3532.**

3533. Warwick, Anne. *The unknown woman.* **With front. in color by Will Grefé. New York: J. Lane, 1912. 345p.**

"Maurice Maury, an American sculptor, has lived many years in Rome [as has his wife, Sandra, an Italian on her mother's side]. But at the opening of the story they have lately arrived for the first time in New York, and Maury, Sandra's brother Jim, and an old family friend, Herndon Kent, are renewing old memories. ... The theme of the book, stripped of surplusage, is the manner in which Sandra is awakened from her lethargy to a capability for renewed suffering, because it is the only way that she can also become capable of renewed happiness"—Book review digest. Much of the story has to do with sculptor Maury recovering his pride and sense of achievement after truckling for too long to a millionaire art patron's vanity.

3534. Washburn, William Tucker, 1841-1916. *The unknown city*; **a story of New York. New York: J. Haney, 1880. 448p.**

The chief character is Frank Hazlet, reporter for the New York 'Comet'; his millionaire father died penniless, but his name still 'rings a bell' in New York financial and social circles. Frank has several run-ins with 'the law' and meets a myriad of individuals who often relate the stories of their lives to him. The novel depicts burglars and others from the 'lower depths' of society as no worse than the corrupt lawyers, bankers, businessmen, et al. who sit at the head of the city's social scale. Our hero falls in love with two women: the married Jesse Decker and her cousin Rhoda, daughter of Judge Thorne. Unfortunately Jesse suffers from a hereditary streak of insanity; she divorces her husband, but neither she nor Rhoda is marriageable in Frank's eyes. He is satisfied, at age 25, to be a bachelor 'in perfect health and hard at work'. His cynical friend Jack Rutgers suggests to Frank that he write down the many stories and secrets he has gathered in his wanderings through the metropolis.

3535. **Watkins, Richard Howells.** *Half a clew.* **New York: E.J. Clode, 1927. 312p.**

An evil old man, Phineas Altamont, even at the point of his own death, is determined to top off his 'career' with one last diabolical deed. He wills a magnificent estate on Long Island's North Shore to Roger Turrentine, the son of a man he had bankrupted. Simultaneously Phineas drops a hint to Roger and to another man that a successful search on the estate will yield a valuable treasure. Of course, Phineas's aim is to pit the two men against one another with hoped-for resulting mayhem.

3536. **Watson, Augusta Campbell, 1862-1936.** *Beyond the city gates*; **a romance of old New York. New York: E.P. Dutton, 1897. iv, 324p.**

Freida Van Dycke has to make a choice between two men: Adriaen de Witte, nephew of a prominent patroon in New York's affairs (ca. 1700), and Morris Van Cortlandt, son of a tea merchant. Although Freida's father is a successful farmer, the patroon has plans to marry his nephew to a woman of higher social standing than Freida's. Actually, when Freida does show her preference for Adriaen her family protests. A factor in the situation is the revelation that Adriaen and his uncle have been communicating with the notorious Captain Kidd.

3537. **Watson, Clarissa.** *The bishop in the back seat.* **New York: Atheneum, 1980. 213p.**

The chic, snobbish, wealthy art collectors of an enclave on Long Island are inveigled into lending some of their treasures for a showing at the local museum. A probable but unproven Rembrandt is the star attraction. Strange, unsettling things begin to happen, among them murder, a kidnapping and the theft of the 'Rembrandt'. One of the socialites, a young woman painter, digs up data that questions the authenticity of the 'Rembrandt'; motivations for a number of odd things going on, she discovers, have a World War II origin.

3538. ————. *The fourth stage of Gainsborough Brown.* **New York: D. McKay, 1977. 204p.**

The Long Island estate of that patroness of art, Lydia Wentworth, is the setting of capricious, vain artist Gainsborough Brown's drowning in a swimming pool. Was it accidental? Mrs. Wentworth's niece, Persis Willum, an artist too, has the notion that Gains was a murder victim. A batch of questions is formulated by Persis: Was it logical to suspect that Gregor (who handled Gains' art work and ran a gallery that employed Persis) was a murderer? Why is Alida, the artist's French widow, avoiding everyone as she stays behind tightly closed doors? Where is Gains' first wife; what has she been doing these last few years? And why did Gains fill his latest compositions with uncharacteristic, ugly, macabre effigies?

3539. ————. *Somebody killed the messenger.* **A Persis Willum mystery. New York: Atheneum, 1988. 224p.**

"When Persis Willum and her boss, Gregor Olitsky, plan a benefit art show in their fashionable 'Gull Harbor' art gallery, they have no idea of the trouble they are courting. Seraphine Bracely, former Gull Harbor resident, phones from Europe insisting they must include one of her paintings in this exhibition. Persis and Gregor are apprehensive, because Seraphine has already caused plenty of controversy in the upper crust Long Island community, and their fears prove to be well founded. The painting, a nude study of Seraphine herself, opens a number of old wounds among the locals. Then the man entrusted to deliver the painting vanishes, and Seraphine's dead body is found covered with red roses. Persis vows to find the killer"—Booklist.

Watson, Lewis H. See under his pseudonym: Harrison, Lewis.

3540. **Watson, Richard A., 1931- .** *Niagara;* **a novel. Minneapolis: Coffee House Press, 1993. 178p.**

An unlikely duo, 'the Great Gravelet', a French high-wire performer, and Anna Taylor, a widowed ex-schoolteacher from Nebraska, meet in Niagara Falls, N.Y. and combine for derring-do—he pushes her across the Falls in a wheelbarrow balanced on a cable—the date is the Fourth of July, 1901. That the two share that aspect of their existence is noteworthy since Gravelet assumes he is God's gift to womankind and Anna is fat, addicted to cigars, a free spirit 15 years older than her partner. When Gravelet refuses to give her lessons on the high wire, Anna reaches for fame by surviving a trip over the Falls in a barrel. Twenty years later, in 1921, the two meet again by chance and quickly part.

3541. **Watts, Mary Stanbery, 1868-1958.** *The Boardman family.* **New York: Macmillan, 1918. 352p.**

Alexandra Boardman is almost reconciled to marriage with her small-town Ohioan, Sam Thatcher, when her independent spirit asserts itself and she flies off to New York City with the intention of furthering her dancing talents. She quickly strikes gold—billed as 'Sandra', the dancer, she commands a large salary and the love of her manager, Max Levison. The onset of World War I brings unanticipated changes in Alexandra's (Sandra's) life; one of them is marriage to her quondam lover, Sam Thatcher.

3542. ————. *The house of Rimmon.* **New York: Macmillan, 1922. 378p.**

"From his boyhood when he began to write secretly and hid his manuscripts from an unsympathetic family, Cleve Harrod had an irresistible urge to literature, and all the artist's hopeless belief in himself. His already low credit with his family was still further reduced by his failure, after his father's sudden death, to contribute his share to the family income, and pride stung him into taking a job in a bakery. This was the beginning of a succession of uncongenial employments, but all the while he was nursing his talent and quietly writing poetry and plays. Finally he attracted the interest of a successful author [in New York's literary and dramatic circles] who helped him to recognition and he suddenly found himself a rising dramatist [in New York] of whom much was expected. The test to which his ideals were put by a commercially-minded theatrical manager and under stress of financial need forms the developing interest of the story"—Book review digest.

3543. ————. *The rise of Jennie Cushing.* **New York: Macmillan, 1914. 487p.**

Jennie from the New York slums, a graduate of reform school, placed there for five years because society had no other place for her, retained her sympathetic qualities. She found work as a hairdresser, as a lady's maid, as personal aide to Donelson Meigs whose offer of marriage she rejected, as secretary to a British lady, and as a defender of civil rights. When she had reached a fairly secure financial station, she became an advocate for unloved children who came from the same environment she had known as a girl.

3544. Waugh, Hillary, 1920- . *Madam will not dine tonight.* **New York: Coward-McCann, 1947. 244p.**

Hostess Valerie King cannot meet her dinner guests on this particular night because her inert body is found in the woods near her Westchester home. Sheridan Wesley, a private detective, and his wife cooperate in the police investigation, nevertheless holding back several pieces of information from the lawmen. In the end Sheridan calls all the suspects together at the scene of the crime and pulls a few tricks that are instrumental in solving the crime.

3545. *Way-way-seek-a-hook-ah*; **a stilted story of '92. New York: Eagle Print. Co., 1893. 41p.**

This little op piece is presumably "intended as a political squib on civic elections of 1892 in New York City and the rivalries of the daily papers—especially *The World, The Sun, Advertiser* and *Mail and Express*"—Annual American catalogue.

3546. Wayne, Charles Stokes, b. 1858. *The city of encounters,* **by Horace Hazeltine [pseud.]. Illustrated by Harry Stacey Benton. New York: M. Kennerley, 1908. 384p.**

A young man from Hawaii is involved in a train wreck in Indiana while heading for the Boston residence of his rich uncle. Detoured to New York he takes a room in the Hotel Astor and opens the bag given him by a porter following the accident. It contains $300,000 in currency; naturally he must find out where this money came from. His inquiries put him in touch with reporters, the police, bank personnel, guests in the hotel, et al., and with two sisters who look pretty much alike and bring a romantic component to the story. *The city of encounters* quite obviously is New York.

3547. Weaver, John Van Alstyn, 1893-1938. *Her knight comes riding.* **New York: Knopf, 1928. 291p.**

The story of a lower middle class family in New York/Brooklyn. "To Fanny her father was the hero of all the knightly tales he wove for her. But to her mother Pa was no hero. He was a second-rate carpenter who had once been a sailor. Yet in spite of Ma's hard common sense, Fanny grew up with the hero idea firmly entrenched, and when her knight came riding, during the [First World] War, it was not surprising that he was a marine, much like Pa in spirit. For a time the little Brooklyn stenographer loved to the full her happiest romantic dream. It ended in heartbreak from which she was young enough to recover, and brought her finally to the sheltering domesticity Ma had always hoped for her"—Book review digest.

3548. Webb, Christopher. *Matt Tyler's chronicle.* **New York: Funk & Wagnalls, 1958. 216p.**

Matt Tyler, 16, is an active participant in the American struggle for independence from the mother country. He narrates his adventures—from the Battle of Long Island to capture and imprisonment by the British, and finally accompanying Washington's troops on the Delaware crossing.

3549. Webb, Jean Francis, 1910-1991. *From the Shamrock shore,* **by Ian Kavanaugh [pseud.]. New York: Dell/James A. Bryans, 1982. 319p.**

The potato famine of 1848 in Ireland motivates the musician (a fiddler) Liam O'Donnell to take passage to New York accompanied by his pregnant wife and his young brother Tom. Mrs. O'Donnell and her baby die at sea; the surviving Liam and Tom settle in the Hudson Valley. Liam becomes a contractor and remarries; his second wife bears him six children. The oldest son loses his life when he chooses to take the path of a fighter for Irish independence. The novel brings the rest of Liam's children and Tom's family to the turn of the century. Liam is now an old man pursuing the publication of a volume on Ireland's traditional music.

3550. ————. *No match for murder.* **New York: Macmillan, 1942. 296p.**

Polo is being played in the upscale Long Island colony of 'Farm Neck'. Unfortunately as the game progresses several of the polo players fall from their perches to their deaths and suspicion of murder surfaces. Former news reporter Ted Perry and detective Captain Cyryus Flexner and his sidekick Sergeant Tulpetaka enter the picture and do some heavy sleuthing. Among the personages they query are: millionairess Hester La Barr, Maxie Hymen (a Broadway showman), beautiful Lacy Burnell and the La Barr butler, Maunsi.

3551. Webb, L.J., pseud. *Walking the dusk.* **New York: Coward-McCann, 1932. 278p.**

In Long Island's society world a sterling member, Mabel Randolph, is poisoned—by whom? a love-obsessed married man, one of the sophisticated women who hovered around Mabel, Benson the butler, et al.? The narrator of the story, a pretty young woman, an amateur detective in her own right, makes the rounds of the parties while keeping her eyes and ears open for the unusual.

Webb, Richard Wilson, 1901 or 2- . See his shared pseudonym: Patrick, Q.

3552. Webb, Robert N. *We were there with Ethan Allen and the Green Mountain boys.* **Historical consultant: Chilton Williamson. Illustrated by Robert Pious. New York: Grosset & Dunlap, 1956. 182p.**

When Ethan Allen and his Green Mountain Boys made their move to capture Fort Ticonderoga and its stores from the small British garrison defending them, they were given useful information by the fictional Tom Botsford and his sister Lucy.

3553. Webster, Leigh. *Another girl's experience.* **Boston: Roberts Bros., 1894. 278p.**

The moral of this story is that money can often be more of a burden than the key to happiness and that one's station in life may be preferable to any number of alternatives. Frances Prescott has become wholly dissatisfied with the dull, penny-pinching routines of her impoverished clergyman father's household. She leaves the small town and takes a job in New York City as companion to a wealthy but sickly lady. And it is in this new home that Frances experiences the bickering and constant discord that was muted in her father's house.

3554. Wegman, Dorothy. *Glorified.* **New York: Brentano's, 1930. 299p.**

Molly Robbins decides that her personal beauty can be put to better use money-wise than merely modeling or sketching in New York City's garment district. She is accepted as a chorine in Ziegfeld's Follies; her paycheck exceeds what she had earned in earlier employment. Molly is a cheerful, large-hearted girl, not at all overconscious of her own good looks; there is nothing of the stereotypical tough, selfish, gold-digging chorus girl about her, but she does find love with a man of taste and wealth.

3555. Weikel, Anna Hamlin. *Betty Baird's golden year.* **Illustrated by Ethel Pennewill Brown. Boston: Little Brown, 1909. 306p.**

Betty Baird, of Scottish descent, has achieved a measure of success as an interior decorator in New York City. Lois, her best friend, becomes engaged and marries, and it isn't until the story is nearly concluded that Betty herself finds a life partner, a wealthy young man who is prepared to buy back the Baird family's ancestral home in Scotland.

3556. Weiman, Rita, 1889-1954. *Footlights.* New York: Dodd, Mead, 1923. x, 341p.

"A collection of stories from the world of shifting scenery, of hustling property men, frantic stage managers, husky last minute orders, dressing room shadows. The title story ... relates the career and romance of Lizzie Parsons, a Vermont country girl who dares to follow her ambition and become an actress. ... As Lisa Parsinova, 'the rare Russian genius' [she] dazzles the theatre public. Forthwith she leads a double life and suffers accordingly. When love comes to her, she is on the verge of tragedy, but it is only the 'Russian devil' who commits suicide, while a happy Lizzie Parsons survives. The other stories are: Madame Peacock.—Grease paint.—The back drop.—Two masters.—Up stage.—" Curtain!"—Book review digest.

3557. ————. *Playing the game*; the story of a society girl. New York: Cupples & Leon, 1910. 270p.

This story of New York society in its less palatable aspects is told by the heroine (Gypsy) who is pushed by her social-climbing mother to make a 'suitable' marriage. Gypsy is pursued by the Baron de Berenzig whom she discovers is married. The Baron divorces his wife and paves the way for marriage to Gypsy, but by now she is thoroughly disenchanted with the New York social scene, especially after one of her acquaintances, a 'kept woman', commits suicide. Gypsy no longer wishes to 'play the game' and finally finds surcease and happiness as the wife of Robert Stead, her brother Dick's friend.

3558. Weingarten, Violet, 1915-1976. *Mrs. Beneker*; a novel. New York: Simon & Schuster, 1968, c1967. 224p.

Mrs. Beneker, a Westchester matron and Jewish grandmother, studies comparative religion at Columbia, is suspicious of her husband (is he having an extra-marital affair?), is psychoanalyzed for two years, and provides abortion money for Carla, her son's girlfriend. She is a 'typical' (?) modern do-gooder who tries to be sympathetic and caring, but is an inhibiting force in the long run—as one character says: "You swallow people up with your understanding."

3559. Weinman, Irving, 1937- . *Hampton heat.* New York: Atheneum, 1988. 225p.

During a summer spent in Long Island's Hamptons Lenny Schwartz, a detective in New York City's Police Department, and his wife Karen, an art historian, hope they can patch up a faltering marriage. Lenny is drawn into a murder investigation—the victim has been researching the land rights of the Shinnecock Indians; Lenny questions the arrest of a retarded young man as chief suspect. An indication that a conspiratorial group is grabbing Indian lands brings Russian immigrants in the area into the picture and to the attention of both Lenny and his wife. The two narrowly escape death from ingesting poisoned mushrooms and have to ward off other attempts on their lives.

3560. Weisman, Paul, 1932- . *Lords of power.* New York: Morrow, 1972. 220p.

The governor of New York State, Alexander Christman, although quite wealthy, has an avid outside interest in American Nuclear, a group of companies seeking to control nuclear-generated energy. He is urged by his son and political advisors to seek his party's presidential nomination. Christman is extremely reluctant to do that—he believes the American president really commands little actual power. But he is propelled into the race and broadens his involvement.

3561. **Welch, Ronald, 1909- .** *Mohawk Valley*. **Illustrated by William Stobbs. New York: Criterion Books. 1958. 226p.**

"The story of a squire's son [Alan Carey] who is sent down from Cambridge [University] for dueling and on the advice of the elder Pitt goes to America [in 1755, settling in the Mohawk Valley region]. There he is captured by hostile Indians, but escapes to join Wolfe's forces in the battle for Quebec"—Manchester guardian. The story contains material that is quite pertinent to American colonial and New York State history.

3562. **Wellington, Courtney.** *Congressman Hardie, a born democrat.* **New York: G.W. Dillingham, 1900. 240p.**

"A political novel. The book opens with a political speech made by Hardie, then a candidate for Congress, at a country barbecue. A romantic adventure begins at the close of his speech, when Hardie discovers in a sad-eyed girl, a character which influences his whole life and career from that time. The life of this girl, Bena, after he is elected to Congress and she goes to New York to earn a living, contains some most original features, notably a speech she delivered before a ladies' club which made her famous in a night"—Annual American catalogue.

3563. **Wells, Amos Russel, 1862-1933.** *Tuxedo Avenue to Water Street*; **being the story of a transplanted church. Illustrated by Josephine Bruce. New York: Funk & Wagnalls, 1906. 259p.**

A New York City church with a fashionable clientele, presided over by an earnest, scholarly young minister, is removed from its comfortable quarters to Water Street, the abode of poor tenement dwellers. The minister realizes that the new parishioners would find his previous erudite sermons of little value, so he preaches in a simple, homely fashion to them. In the course of his new venture he embarks on a romance with a girl named Irene, 'the flower of his flock.'

3564. **Wells, Carolyn, 1869-1942.** *The affair at Flower Acres.* **New York: Doran, 1923. 284p.**

"The affair—the murder of Douglas Raynor in the sun-parlor of his Long Island estate, Flower Acres—was a complicated one. The persons and motives involved were many: there was a martyred wife whom Raynor had tricked into marrying him and whom he had goaded to despair by his treatment of her; a former lover of the wife, likewise in despair over the condition in which he finds his beloved; a devoted brother of Mrs. Raynor's, capable of any sacrifice to save his sister; a revengeful nurse, the victim of Raynor's former wrong-doing; a disinherited son by a former marriage, in possession of a first will and stealer of the second one; a black-mailing accomplice of Raynor's with secret information. The unique feature of the case is that with the many clues and the many serious suspects, there are almost as many volunteer confessors, willing to take the guilt upon themselves to shield another"—Book review digest.

3565. ————. *The bride of a moment.* **New York: G.H. Doran, 1916. 307p.**

After an opulent church wedding in an affluent community near New York City, the bride is the sudden victim of a gunshot wound that kills her. Strangely no one heard the gun being fired or caught sight of it. Two major suspects emerge: the bridegroom was 'forced' into the marriage because inheritance of his father's fortune was based on his being wed immediately—and he was already involved with another woman; the best man was in love with the bride but feared losing the money she had willed to him by her marriage. The detective Alan Ford is brought into the situation, despite the bridegroom's objections, at the request of the latter's girlfriend and her father. An important piece of evidence in the case is a note that was sent to the bride, which turns out to be a musical cipher.

3566. ————. *A chain of evidence.* **With illus. in color by Gayle Hoskins. Philadelphia: J.B. Lippincott, 1912. 324p.**

Young and beautiful Janet Pembroke lives in a New York City apartment with her money-grubbing uncle. In the opposite apartment are Otis Landon and his sister who have been in the city for only two weeks. Janet asks for their support and assistance when she finds her uncle dead in his bed. He did not, as at first supposed, die a natural death, for a long pin driven into his brain is discovered. Janet is, of course, the prime suspect, although a grandniece and nephew, sole heirs of the miser, are not to be overlooked. Detective Fleming Stone comes upon the scene after other investigators have failed and destroys the 'perfect' alibi of the actual murderer. Otis Landon and Janet are free to pursue their burgeoning romance.

3567. ————. *The clue of the eyelash*; a Fleming Stone detective story. **Philadelphia: Lippincott, 1933. 312p.**

"Rushing out to 'Golden Sands', L.I., for a holiday the diabolically clever sleuth [Fleming Stone] runs spang into as pretty a killing as you'll meet in a month of Sundays, ye corpse being Wiley Vance, master of Greencastle, a collector of old coins, rare books and antique curios—shot between 6:45 and 7:30 with a houseful of guests assembled for a Fourth of July dinner party. He's smart enough to notice a small hair on the dead man's cheek which leads to a liberal education in beauty secrets and a finish of the exciting type for which Miss Wells is justly famous. In the matter of guiding clews, our author has been especially generous; watch the documents, the imported and domestic eyelashes the photographs of a dazzling blonde inscribed: "To Wiley, his Booful." ... Oh yes, there's a second murder too"—New York herald tribune books.

3568. ————. *Crime incarnate*; a Fleming Stone detective novel. **Philadelphia: Lippincott, 1940. 314p.**

"The elegant first line for [the] new Fleming Stone thriller [is]: 'Take my things will you, Craig? I want to run quick and murder Uncle.' Speaker is Rosemary Marlowe, divinely beautiful but rather silly foster daughter of Jerome Marlowe, head of a strange family dwelling on the brink of 'Lake Curlew', in the Adirondacks. The way this girl carries on causes young Basil to mutter: 'If it was anybody but our Rosemary, I'd say she was off her rocker.' Oddly enough, she is the first to vanish, whether lured away by an Italian acrobat or tossed off the precipice, nobody knows. Whatever you may think of the Marlowes and their many troubles, you can't laugh off the meritorious deducing of the great Fleming Stone who adds action to the ruckus when he arrives at the halfway mark. Looks as though the disappearance, the suicide and the accident might turn out to be three diabolical murders"—New York herald tribune books.

3569. ————. *Crime tears on*; a Fleming Stone detective novel. **Philadelphia: Lippincott, 1939. 315p.**

Fleming Stone looks into "the killing of Harley Madison, an eccentric philanthropist of 'New Plymouth', L.I. [and his faithful housekeeper]. At the scene are certain irate town councilmen who opposed the corpse's improvement plans, a jealous woman, a nephew in love with Yvette Verne, fiancée of the dead man, and so forth. ... Fleming Stone makes sense of it somehow ... [despite] unexpected developments"—New York herald tribune books.

3570. ————. *The curved blades.* **With a front. in color by Gayle Hoskins. Philadelphia: Lippincott, 1916. 333p.**

The very wealthy and very quick-tempered Miss Carrington lives on a magnificent Long Island estate. Present in her house when she was foully struck down were: Pauline Stewart, her niece; Anita Frayne, her secretary; Gray Haviland, her cousin; and two guests Stephen Illsley and Count Henri Charlier. Miss Carrington was a tyrannical dowager and there would have been few regrets at her passing. Charlier's glove was found on the murdered woman's person, so much suspicion rests on him, but he is hardly alone. Detective Fleming Stone only complicates matters when he investigates and falls in love with one of the young women.

3571. ————. *The daughter of the house*; a Fleming Stone story. **Philadelphia: J.B. Lippincott, 1925. 317p.**

"The story is set in the Westchester home of a multi-millionaire. Mary Lang, the idolized daughter of the house, disappears with amazing completeness an hour before her marriage ceremony was to have taken place. As the family is in excited consultation the volatile best man arrives with the news that the bridegroom has also vanished, but an investigation of the clues seems to indicate that the two did not go together, nor even with a common purpose. The assembling wedding guests are kept waiting as long as possible ... [but] are necessarily dismissed with the mere notice that the wedding will not take place. A tumultuous day or so ensues ... and then one night comes an astounding murder, so cleverly contrived that it would not be pronounced murder except that the victim's healthy body could not have died in any other way. [Present] is the wily widow Giulia Castro ... a lady of mystery par excellence and there is yet unexplained the 'strange and terrible face' that Mary Lang had seen at one of her windows. Finally the inimitable Fleming Stone is asked to take the case in hand"—New York herald tribune books.

3572. —————. *The doomed five*; a Fleming Stone story. **Philadelphia: J.B. Lippincott, 1930. 295p.**

"A New York capitalist, Stephen Brandon, invests $10,000,000 in a city garden project detailed to the care of five people called the Garden Guardians—much to the ire of his sister, nephew and adopted daughter. Shortly thereafter Brandon dies of peritonitis. Then, one by one, four members of the garden committee succumb because of similar kinds of stomach trouble. The doctors are puzzled. So is Fleming Stone, detective, called in by Aunt Amanda to investigate the strange coincidences. Then the last member of the committee is stricken—but does not die; and the mystery is on the way to solution"—Book review digest.

3573. —————. *Doris of Dobbs Ferry*. **Illustrated by Frances Rogers. New York: Doran, 1917. 290p.**

Doris Ballard, heir to the family estate in Dobbs Ferry, N.Y., is intrigued by an account of a valuable pearl necklace that was hidden by a French officer in the house (which also served as the headquarters of Generals Washington and Rochambeau) during the American Revolution. Doris meets with some scary experiences, not the least of which is the loss of most of her money when her guardian makes bad investments. Compensation comes from a romantic affair, the laying to rest of ghostly vestiges and the retrieval of the necklace.

3574. —————. *Faulkner's Folly*. **New York: Doran, 1917. 294p.**

This mystery is set in Faulkner's Folly, the ostentatious Long Island home of prosperous portrait painter Eric Stannard and his wife. Mrs. Faulkner was a guest of the Stannards; it was she who came downstairs towards a darkened room and asked the footman to turn on the lights. Before her eyes was the artist seated in a chair dying, an etching needle in his body. Nearby were Mrs. Stannard and Natalie, one of Stannard's models. Prior to his demise Eric Stannard named Natalie as his murderer. Police detective Roberts seemed to be getting nowhere when Alan Ford was called in on the case. Despite a false trial suggested by a clairvoyant, it was Ford who came up with the right answers.

3575. —————. *Feathers left around.* **Philadelphia: J.B. Lippincott, 1923. 348p.**
"The death of Hugh Curran seems to be a complete mystery. Valentine Loft and his guests are dismayed by the discovery of his body the morning following a dinner party [at Loft's country house near New York] at which he appeared to be in perfect health. The doctor pronounced poison to be the cause and the police proceed to hunt for the culprit. Curran's watch, which had disappeared, is found in Pauline Fuller's room and her picture, taken some years before, is in the case. Pauline is engaged to Loft and he refuses to believe the evidence against her, though it is made stronger by her sudden disappearance from his house. Not satisfied with the results gained by the local police, Loft engages an expert detective [Fleming Stone] who fathoms the whereabouts of Pauline, and in a masterly way brings the evidence together which explains the manner of Curran's death"—Book review digest.

3576. —————. *For goodness' sake*; **a Fleming Stone detective novel. Philadelphia: Lippincott, 1935. 308p.**
"Henry Parsons, a mean millionaire, of 'South Neptune', L.I., succumbs to what appears to be mushroom poisoning, maybe administered while he was leaving the Polo Grounds. His last words were, "Something stung my leg. Not a mosquito—more like a wasp." Where is the poisonous needle? Watch Chester Gaylord, who had said to Parsons, "Sometime I'll give you what for if you continue this deplorable treatment of your niece." The niece is Diana Berre, in love with Guy Allen, and at one time they pull that double confession stunt to save each other. There's a second death, a novel turn to the love interest, and a scrap of paper reading, "hbjlveqyuspmGClorr." Fleming Stone lives up to his reputation as a surefire detective, forcing a confession from one of the most unexpected fiends of the year"—New York herald tribune books.

3577. —————. *The fourteenth key.* **New York: Putnam, 1924. 334p.**
Mark Winslow of 'Willowvale', N.Y., is a wealthy old man who decides to locate his grandchild. He had disinherited his only daughter when she married contrary to his wishes and she and her husband had subsequently died. They had a child, Joyce Gilray, gender unknown, and Winslow sends for this person. A telegram from San Francisco states that Joyce Gilray is on the way to Willowvale by train. The train is wrecked and several people die; the passenger list contains no Joyce Gilray. Two Gilrays appear in Willowvale, a young man and a young woman. Both wear an amethyst cross that belonged to Winslow's daughter, but only one has identifying documents. Then a woman is stabbed in front of the Winslow home and Mark Winslow is killed—possibly by a Professor Curran who has been in the house and has never left. Detective Lorimer Lane solves the puzzles without using the 'fourteenth key', which he eventually finds anyway.

3578. ————. *The ghosts' high noon*; a Fleming Stone story. Philadelphia: J.B. Lippincott, 1930. 296p.

"When Irma Steele's second husband died suddenly from poisoning after a supper party in their smart Westchester home, she was unceremoniously hauled off to jail. Her first husband had gone the same way. Fleming Stone reviews the facts. It comes out all right in the end, but Irma and Mark Stanholpe, who proposes to be the third husband, put in some very bad weeks while Stone is sorting the wheat from the chaff"—Bookman.

3579. ————. *Gilt-edged guilt*; a Fleming Stone detective novel. Philadelphia: Lippincott, 1938. 318p.

The author "eggs Fleming Stone on to solve the killing of Brice, a valet (stabbed with a big knife smelling of gardenias), and Larry Holden, his employer, at the Conifers, in deadly Long Island. At the same time the detective wants to save an inheritance for an infant whose wicked relatives are trying to get away, with kidnapping or worse. What are the secrets of the scarab and the ball of string? How guilty are Professor Alexander Watts, the beautiful daughter of the second corpse, and the rest?"—New York herald tribune books.

3580. ————. *In the onyx lobby*. New York: Doran, 1920. 288p.

A mystery story with the plot laid in New York City; Sir Herbert Binney of 'Binney's buns' was murdered while he, a notorious pursuer of chorus girls, was in the lobby of the Campanile Apartments late at night.

3581. ————. *The luminous face*. New York: G.H. Doran, 1921. 270p.

"The shooting of a wealthy Western man at his apartment in Washington Square, New York [City] is unsolved until Pennington Wise is called in, and his methods of investigation embody the later chapters of this book. Of course, the person seemingly the least likely to have done the deed, is proved to be the criminal"—Springfield Republican.

3582. ————. *The mark of Cain*. With a front. in color by Gayle Hoskins. Philadelphia: Lippincott, 1917. 307p.

"A millionaire is murdered in Van Cortlandt Park, New York [City], and circumstances seem to point to his nephew, Kane Landon, as the murderer. The fortune of the murdered man is left to his niece, Avice Trowbridge, on condition that she marry the millionaire's lawyer and trusted friend, Judge Hoyt. But Avice loves Landon and she only consents to marry Judge Hoyt on condition that he obtains the freedom of Landon, whether the latter is innocent or guilty. With the aid of the millionaire's office boy who had done some private detective work and as a consequence had been kidnapped and imprisoned in the home of the lawyer who is the real murderer, Fleming Stone convicts the lawyer of his guilt, aids thereto being the dirk cane and the shoes

worn at the time of the murder which he had left as evidence in the house"—
Book review digest.

3583. ———. *The missing link*; a Fleming Stone detective novel. Philadelphia:
Lippincott, 1938. 287p.
"Seems that Peter Tolman, a business man of dubious reputation, had a habit
of eating the kernels of peach stones ... although he had been warned that they
contain prussic acid in minute doses. When he turned up dead at the Van
Winkle Inn in Westchester, one of the physicians thought the peach pits
responsible, but the other did not, and who should be right on the spot but
Fleming Stone? ... What is more, Mrs. Isabel Murray, a friend of the corpse's
divorced wife, came down with a strange ailment—symptoms of poison ivy or
sunburn, only worse; which did not prevent her, however, from starting on a
yachting cruise with a party of suspects and commentators. Soon there's a
second death ... [perhaps] connected in a highly sinister way [to the first]"—
New York herald tribune books.

3584. ———. *More lives than one.* New York: Boni & Liveright, 1923. 241p.
"The beautiful society leader, Madeline Barham, was found murdered in an
artist's apartment in Washington Square, at the height of the gayety of a
masquerade party. When the police arrived, the artist, Locke, had disappeared
and so had his Chinese servant. No one present knew Mrs. Barham, nor who
had invited her to the party, and excitement reigned. The next morning the
Chinese servant reappeared, but he knew very little about the murder, except
that he had seen one of the guests, Pearl Jane Cutler, leaning over the body.
Suspicion had pointed to Pearl Jane who was known to be in love with Locke
and this statement helped. But Pearl was not guilty and Locke could not be
found, and the case languished until Lorimer Lane, a clever detective, was
finally summoned. In a few short weeks Lane had solved the problem"—
Book review digest.

3585. ———. *Murder at the casino*; a Fleming Stone mystery novel.
Philadelphia: Lippincott, 1941. 266p.
"Renny Loring was a beautiful young orphan though silly, and she didn't
know real love when she saw it. (Or, did she?). So she up and married wealthy
and unattractive Nicholas Talbot, all of forty years old, and her brother
exclaimed: 'Oddzooklums! Renny, you have struck it rich! You're a real
Cinderella!' Well, it just didn't seem to work out, for there was quarreling on
the Mexican honeymoon, and after the couple's return to 'Banbury Gardens',
Westchester, mostly jealousy on Nick's part. Then something fatal occurred at
a charity fiesta. ... [Fleming Stone is summoned]. Some of the clues are a
scarab ring, a chrysoberyl and a kitchen knife, but Stone picks a different one
altogether and finds out something pretty sinister in a chemical laboratory—
New York herald tribune books.

3586. ———. *Patty in the city.* New York: Dodd, Mead, 1905. ix, 274p.

"Patty Fairfield leaves her home in Vernondale, New Jersey in the beginning of the story, and comes with her father and Grandma Elliott to New York City for the winter. Her father desires that she shall go to school another year and also take up music. Mr. Fairfield rents a fine apartment facing Central Park and Patty's school days begin again. The story relates her experiences at a fashionable school and describes her schoolmates, and also pictures her ... Saturday afternoons at the circus, theatre, etc."—Annual American catalogue.

3587. ————. *Prilligirl*; A Fleming Stone story. Philadelphia: Lippincott, 1924. 332p.

"A general upheaval takes place in [New York's] theatrical circles when the news of the murder of Mallory Vane, a well-known manager, is made known. Bloody fingerprints are evident on the curious weapon with which Mallory was killed, and on a telephone book, while on the floor of the private telephone booth is found, unconscious, Prilligirl, the beautiful child-wife of Guy Thorndike, a prominent actor. The fingerprints are identified as those of Mrs. Guy Thorndike but what motive had she in killing Vane when he had just completed a play for her husband, one that promised great triumphs for both actor and manager? nd what was Thorndike's purpose in claiming to be the criminal? Into this perplexing maze steps Fleming Stone, master detective, and with the aid of radio traps the murderer"—Book review digest.

3588. ————. *The sixth commandment.* New York: G.H. Doran, 1927. 300p.

"Guy Mackenzie invites a group of college friends to his [Long Island] country home to celebrate his engagement to a beautiful girl whom he has 'discovered' outside his own social circle and whom he has preferred to his life-long friend Sylvia. The girl arrives, as beautiful as advertised, but her unconventional behavior displeases her fiancé's father. She seems, however, to be all innocence and charm, and her sudden death on the second night of the house party closely following the discovery of a jewel theft, is a shock to all the guests. Amateur as well as professional sleuths set to work on the case. As a result of their investigations Guy awakes from his dream to discover a reality"—Book review digest.

3589. ————. *Sleeping dogs.* Garden City, N.Y.: Published for the Crime Club by Doubleday, Doran, 1929. 300p.

"Who slipped the lethal drug to Eileen Abercrombie, a Long Island society queen? Suspicion points ... to Hugh Abercrombie, the widower, who is very fond of clam chowder and Lorna Garth; Maisie, the daughter, a modern girl, who, nevertheless, wears all-over lace pajamas; Murgatroyd Loring, a faintly obnoxious lawyer; and Percy Van Antwerp and Eric Redmayne, a couple of East Hampton cane carriers. There's poison all over the place, a most entertaining inquest, additional murder and some more than competent detectivism by Kenneth Carlisle, an ex-movie star, who catches miscreants by pure deductive genius, with or without clues"—New York herald tribune books.

3590. ————. *Triple murder*; a Fleming Stone story. **Philadelphia: Lippincott, 1929. 309p.**

"Maxwell Garnett's third wife is killed as mysteriously as the first two, causing unpleasant comment and police interference at a summer resort near New York [City]. At the request of Garnett and his brother, Fleming Stone, keen criminologist, is called and finds not only Jean Garnett's murder, but once and for all breaks the chain of misfortune that has entangled the unlucky husband since his first marriage"—Bookman.

3591. ————. *Two little women on a holiday*. **With front. by E.C. Caswell. New York: Dodd, Mead, 1917. 300p.**

Two girls, Dorothy and Dolly, go to New York City, bent on having a lighthearted good time. That all seems to disappear when one of them is suspected of having broken the law. Fortunately two Galahads offer Dorothy and Dolly timely assistance.

3592. ————. *The vanity case*. **New York: Putnam, 1926. vi, 333p.**

"There is no apparent reason why any of the four people assembled in the Heath bungalow [on Long Island] should commit murder. Yet that next morning Myra Heath is found dead, and garishly dead, for her pale, beautiful face, which in life she never doctored with make-up, has been transformed by an artist's hand. There are candles burning at head and foot of the corpse, but there is no reason so far as one knows why any of the three people who alone could have committed the murder should be deemed capable of a crime of passion"—Book review digest.

3593. ————. *Vicky Van*. **With a front. in color by Gayle Hoskins. Philadelphia: Lippincott, c1917/18. 304p.**

Two houses abutting one another—a mansion on Fifth Avenue and a much smaller dwelling on the corner—are the scenes of this mystery novel. Victoria Van Allen (Vicky Van), a vivacious party giver, lives with a servant in the small house. Chester Calhoun, junior partner in the law firm of Bradbury and Calhoun, is the story's narrator. Randolph Schuyler, the millionaire, under the alias R. Somers, drops in during one of Vicky's parties and promptly becomes a murder victim (stabbed with a kitchen knife). Carolyn Wells's well-known creation, the detective Fleming Stone and his young assistant, Terence McGuire ('Fibsy') are called upon to decide whether Vicky Van, as everyone supposes, is the culprit.

3594. ————. *The white alley*. **With a front. in color by Gayle Hoskins. Philadelphia: Lippincott, 1915. 300p.**

A house party at the 'White Birches', a handsome country estate just outside New York City owned by Justin Arnold, is interrupted by the discovery of Arnold's body in the mansion's cellar. Suspicion falls on beautiful Dorothy Duncan, fiancée of the middle-aged Arnold, in whose honor he was staging the party. Detective Fleming Stone doesn't buy into that, but it is obvious from what he has already learned that the guilty party is one of the guests.

3595. **Wells, Paul.** *The man with an honest face*; **being the personal experiences of a gentleman who signs the name of Howard Dana, at a critical time in his career. New York: Appleton, 1911. x, 322p.**

Haunted by the face of a beautiful young woman he has seen while strolling down Fifth Avenue in New York, a businessman, Howard Dana, must admit to himself that he has fallen in love with an unknown woman in the space of a few hours. That night he receives a package addressed to 'the man with an honest face'; an accompanying note solicits him to convey the mysterious parcel to a person who asks for it by intoning the phrase "Vive Olivia." The next morning a burly Irishman attempts to pull the package from Dana's hands. There follows a series of escapades and the intervention of powerful financial factions and the queen of a mythical European kingdom.

3596. **Wersba, Barbara, 1932.** *Whistle me home.* **New York: Holt, 1997. 108p.**

Noli is beginning her junior year in high school at Sag Harbor, Long Island, when she meets and is infatuated with T.J., a handsome, bright newcomer, who in turn accepts Noli as a close friend. Noli's unsettling discovery that T.J. is gay propels her into alcoholic binges, but she survives and develops an understanding of her own strength and individuality.

3597. **West, Mae, 1892 or 3-1980.** *Babe Gordon.* **New York: Macaulay, 1930. 313p.**

Reprinted in 1931 under the title: *The constant sinner.* "The story of an amoral lady of pleasure [Babe Gordon], whose career takes her from the dives of Harlem to the smart circles of New York and Paris. Convincing portrait of the seedy [New York] underworld of drugs, lust, prostitution and crime. [West's] gift for language is again displayed in her slang and dialect that evoke the Harlem night life of the [nineteen] twenties"—Ward, C. M. *Mae West.*

3598. **Westcott, Edward Noyes, 1846-1898.** *David Harum*; **a story of American life. New York: Appleton, 1898. viii, 392p.**

The Upstate New York rural banker, David Harum, is an unread but astute, and in his own way, benevolent fellow given to aphorisms and stories that sometimes arrive quickly but often slowly to the point. He is rarely outfoxed when it comes to a swap or a deal (horses and horse-trading are his specialties). When a young man from New York City comes to Harum's village (Homer, N.Y. is generally taken to be the model), having lost a fortune, Harum hires him as a bank cashier. Eventually the cashier falls in love with one of the local belles; this slight love story is, of course, secondary to the author's main theme—the sayings, stories and actions of David Harum.

3599. **Westcott, Frank Noyes.** *Hepsey Burke.* **Illustrated by Frederick R. Gruger. New York: H.K. Fly, 1915. 314p.**

"As the work of a brother of the author of 'David Harum', the novel invites comparison … but their only similarity lies in the fact that both deal with homely folk in homely situations [in the same type of an Upstate New York town]—the one with a shrewd but kindly man, the other with a charitably disposed and energetic widow [Hepsey Burke]. The latter becomes a voluntary assistant to a young Episcopal clergyman and his bride, who take a small parish and carry on their work under circumstances which but for Hepsey might have been disheartening"—The dial. Hepsey herself is the female portion of a middle-aged romance.

3600. Westerman, John, 1952- . *Exit wounds.* **New York: Soho Press, 1990. 273p.**
Corruption is rife in a law enforcement agency in suburban Long Island and Vietnam veteran Orin Boyd, an alcoholic, muddled cop, is in the midst of it. He has endured a crumbling marriage, has seen his best friend waste away with terminal cancer, and is asked to turn in his dishonest fellow cops. Boyd comes across a payoff system deeply implanted in the precinct to which he has been transferred and he has to choose whether to lay bare the dirty facts or take proffered money and run.

3601. —————. *High crimes.* **New York: Soho Press, 1988. 205p.**
Two young men, Tree Nelson and Jimmy Tebaldi, in the town of 'Seaport', Long Island, are undergoing their probationary period as street cops. Almost immediately they begin checking up on a high-up Jamaican drug dealer, Gladstone Lanier, while their superiors are also hectoring them. Jimmy is shot in an ambush, leaving Tree with the responsibility of putting the clamps on Lanier and convincing the 'brass' that both he and Jimmy are on the up-and up.

3602. —————. *The honor farm.* **New York: Pocket Books, 1996. 310p.**
Orin Boyd, a Vietnam veteran and a cop in Nassau County, Long Island, has been bypassed for promotion because of his disdain for his superiors. He gets into trouble when he hassles State Senator Tommy Cotton on grounds of assault. The crooked Cotton demands that Boyd be punished, but David Trimble, the police commissioner, mollifies Cotton by putting Boyd on the shelf (actually a six-month's 'rest' in the upscale county jail). Trimble will give Boyd a gold shield if he goes undercover in the jail to look into the apparent suicide of Trimble's son who had only one day left in his eighteen-month sentence. Another suicide occurs and Boyd becomes the target of a prisoner who is certain that Boyd has a cache of stolen money. Boyd and his wife are harassed, their savings account is diminished, their boat is sunk, someone sets fire to their house and a professional killer threatens Mrs. Boyd and her daughter.

3603. —————. *Ladies of the night.* **New York: Pocket Books, 1998. 323p.**
Politics and police work in Nassau County, N.Y., are featured in this novel. County Executive Martin Daly is hoping to be reelected; he has to contend

with an alcoholic wife, an incompetent, marijuana-smoking son, and the animus of his political boss. Then his deputy vanishes as does the chairperson of the Republican Women's Caucus and the police commissioner appoints two homicide cops—lesbian Maude Fleming and muscle man Rocky Blair—as the cases' investigators. The duo uncovers enough dirt to embarrass several politicos and eventually clear the air.

3604. ————. *Sweet deal*; a novel. **New York: Soho Press, 1992. 231p.**
Bored with public relations and desk work, policeman Jack Mills seeks more demanding duty as a homicide detective. Jack is 36, divorced and a former star athlete (lacrosse), something of a womanizer; he is assigned to a case involving the killing of two cops (Captains Artie Blackman and Richard Mazzarella) who were 'on the take' in Nassau County, Long Island. Jack's partner is Claire Williamson, a no-nonsense policewoman from Suffolk County. A successful conclusion to the investigation finds Jack a changed ('reformed') man with a romantic attachment to Claire.

3605. **Westlake, Donald E., 1933- .** *Backflash*, **by Richard Stark [pseud.]. New York: Mysterious Press, 1998. 292p.**
Professional crook Parker concocts a foolproof scheme for plundering a floating casino that plies the Hudson River between Albany and Poughkeepsie and gathers a crew to carry it out. Yet he seems unaware that other people know his plan and the consequence is a bloodstained collision.

3606. ————. *Bank shot.* **New York: Simon & Schuster, 1972. 224p.**
"Criminal mastermind Dortmunder returns to action with plans to rob a Long Island suburban bank by stealing the whole bank—a mobile trailer home being used temporarily while the new bank building is under construction. Dortmunder's cohorts include Victor, a former FBI agent, ousted because he thought the FBI ought to have a secret handshake; Herman X, a black militant lock expert; and a female cab driver who wears a neck brace while trying to collect a phony insurance claim. The Mack Sennett chase is on when the gang takes off with the mobile bank and tries to keep it hidden in plain view of the police"—Booklist.

3607. ————. *Drowned hopes.* **New York: Mysterious Press, 1990. 422p.**
Two recently released cellmates, John Dortmunder and Tom Jimson, head for Upstate New York where Jimson says $700,000 is buried—unfortunately the loot is under water for the original burial site was a town that had been inundated to form part of a reservoir serving New York City. Jimson wants to blow up the dam, but that would be catastrophic for several nearby villages. Dortmunder must convince the reckless Jimson that he can find a less drastic means of recovering the loot.

3608. ————. *The green eagle score*, **by Richard Stark [pseud.]. New York: Fawcett/Gold Medal, 1967. 173p.**

Parker is a proven expert at setting up big-time robberies and at this juncture he has his eyes on the half-million dollar payroll at an Air Force base in northern New York State near the Canadian border. Plans are laid, action begins and success seems almost assured, but a last-minute glitch is responsible for partial failure. Parker's only recourse is to flee to his well-appointed hideaway in Puerto Rico and his girl friend.

3609. ————. *Help, I am being held prisoner*. **New York: M. Evans, 1974. 275p.**

Addicted to practical jokes (his biggest caper leads to a 27-car accident) and a variety of criminal activities Harry Künst is fated to end up in a New York State penitentiary. He joins up with several convicts who have dug a tunnel that enables them to escape and commit robberies—then they return to their prison quarters with airtight alibis: they have been behind bars all the time, have they not? Eventually Harry sees the light and the possibility of going straight.

3610. ————. *Killing time*. **New York: Random House, 1961. 183p.**

"Tim Smith, confidential investigator for 'Winston City' in Upstate New York, is the bull's eye when he turns down 'Citizens for Clean Government' out to reform small towns. Admitting the fact that the town is not too upright, he is faced with several killings, fights the city fathers, evades death himself, and is the cause of a lethal community warfare"—Kirkus service.

3611. **Weston, George, 1880-1965.** *The horseshoe nails*. **New York: Dodd, Mead, 1927. 301p.**

Four young clerks in New York City seek a way out of their humdrum existence and decide to pool their resources. They raise capital in peculiar but successful ways: getting their hands on a valuable brooch via a pawn ticket and selling it for $2,500; using solid tips on horse races and winning $10,000; then, under the name of the H.S. Nails Company, purchasing unclaimed goods at the Appraiser's Store and selling them for a hundred percent profit. A venture into the stock market is rather disastrous, but the young capitalists use their experience and contacts to recover much of what they had lost. It isn't all business with the four; there is time set aside for affairs of the heart and they play the roles of lovelorn swains with verve.

Wetherell, Elizabeth, pseud. See: Warner, Susan, 1819-1885.

3612. **Wetmore, William, 1930- .** *House of flesh*; a novel. **Boston: Little, Brown, 1968. 374p.**

"The Townsends of 'Beekman County' [New York] were highborn ... with a name that stretched back as far as the county's history. They know their place in society—at the top—and their role. All but unaffected by the Crash of '29, they endured, became richer and more ingrown ... [and] they degenerated. This is the story of the Townsends, and, in particular, of Carter Townsend"—Publisher's note.

3613. **Whalen, William Wilfrid, b. 1886.** *The golden squaw*; being the story of Mary Jemison, the Irish girl stolen by the Indians from Buchanan Valley, Adams County, Pennsylvania, in 1758. A story too strange and grim not to be true, by Will W. Whalen. New York: Dorance, 1926. 228p.

An historical novel based on the life of Mary Jemison (1743-1833), the 'White Woman of the Genesee', who was taken from her Pennsylvania home by Seneca Indians in 1758 and adopted by them. She was successively the wife of a Delaware, Sheninjee, and the Seneca Chief, Hiokatoo. Mary was given the Indian name Deh-hewo-mis (or its variant Dickewamis); honored by the Indians, they gave her a large tract of land in the Genesee Valley in 1797. A kind, sweet-natured woman, Mary Jemison eventually wandered back to the white settlements and supported herself in part with the sale of her autobiography. She always looked upon her Indian captors with affection despite those early years with them when, among other tragedies, they killed her parents, three brothers and a sister.

3614. **Wharton, Edith, 1862-1937.** *The age of innocence.* New York: Appleton, 1920. 364p.

"The milieu of the story is New York 'society' in the early [eighteen] Seventies. It describes the old aristocracy who took life 'without effusion of blood', who 'dreaded scandal more than disease', who 'placed decency above courage' and who considered 'nothing more ill-bred than "scenes".'" Newland Archer was one of the few whose vision penetrated this crust of conventionality and he fell in love with the one off-color member of the tribe just as he had engaged himself to its most perfect product. Ellen Olenska, wife of a profligate European count, had left her husband and returned to America at this critical moment and Archer hastens his marriage to Mary Welland before he becomes too deeply involved with Ellen. Ellen's fine sense of honor and of human kindness, on the other hand, holds him to his compact, and puts the ocean between herself and Archer by returning to Europe. Almost thirty years later, Archer has the satisfaction of seeing his own children step out freely and joyously on the road that had been closed to him"—Book review digest.

3615. ————. *The custom of the country.* New York: Scribner, 1913. 594p.

The 'heroine', if the greedy, selfish, social climbing, ruthless and physically beautiful Undine Spragg can so be called, comes to New York with her parents after divorcing Elmer Moffatt in Midwestern 'Apex City.' She marries Ralph Marvell, son of an aristocratic, conservative New York family, uses her charms on wealthy, debauched Peter Van Degen, makes the European tour, comes back to New York, divorces Ralph in a Dakota court (but not before bearing a child, a son, Paul) and returns to Europe. Ralph, alone in New York, is in financial straits and unable to secure custody of Paul; he commits suicide. Undine, no longer of any interest to Van Degen, marries the nobleman Raymond de Chelles. The quiet life of the French aristocracy has little relevance to Undine's craving for the glittery social whirl and by the story's end Undine is back in New York giving lavish parties, again the wife of Elmer Moffatt who is now a multimillionaire.

3616.   ————. *False dawn* (The 'forties'). **Decorations by E.C. Caswell. New York: Appleton, 1924. 142p. (Old New York, v. 3)**

An ironic tale that opens in the 1840s on the eve of Lewis Raycie's tour of Europe, a chief purpose of which is to collect specific masters named by Lewis's father that will be brought back to New York City to grace 'Raycie Gallery'. But with a new sense of freedom from his tyrannical parent and with the advice of John Ruskin and other connoisseurs Lewis purchases Italian 'primitives', as yet unrecognized by the world at large. The outraged old Mr. Raycie virtually disinherits Lewis and Lewis's wife Treeshy. Lewis stubbornly sets up his own gallery that through the years sustains little interest. Many years later the pictures are found in the attic of Miss Alethea Raycie's house (she is the sole surviving Raycie) and they serve as the foundation of the substantial wealth of a distant relative, Netta Kent Cosby, and her husband.

3617.   ————. *The house of mirth*. **With illus. by A.B. Wenzell. New York: Scribner, 1905. 532p.**

"A [classic] novel tracing the career of Lily Bart, a beautiful, fascinating young woman, a conspicuous figure in the New York society of … [the turn of the century]. In an atmosphere of gossip and bridge, surrounded by a crowd of shallow, empty-headed people, whose only thought is the amusement of the moment, Lily is led into a succession of indiscretions to keep up her social position, which finally cause her to be thrown over by the selfish, heartless crowd with which she is identified. She sinks from one level to another until at last she is seen in a shabby boardinghouse, vainly striving to earn a living. In her distress she finds herself without a friend; even the men who had striven to win her turn away. Her character is most artistically developed, while the scenes of fashionable life, with their silly actors, are depicted with stinging satire"—Annual American catalogue. Lily's eventual suicide occurs almost simultaneously with the arrival of the man she loves who is ready with an offer of marriage.

3618.   ————. *Hudson River bracketed*. **New York: Scribner, 1929. 559p.**

Aspiring writer Vance Weston, lately ill with typhoid fever, leaves his culturally backward hometown, Euphoria, Illinois, for the seat of relatives, the Tracys, in the Hudson Valley (Dutchess County) known as The Willows. The Willows is a fine example of an American architectural style dubbed 'Hudson River Bracketed.' In the house's library Vance browses and fills in gaps in his education. He also meets Heloise (Halo) Spear who will be an increasingly important influence in his artistic life. Vance impulsively marries his beautiful cousin, Laura Lou Tracy, has his first novel published (a critical if not a commercial success). Now in New York City Vance and Laura Lou struggle with poverty, Vance is exploited and then fired by magazine editor Lewis Tarrant, the man Halo Spear has married. Laura Lou dies of tuberculosis, Halo is prepared to sever her ties to Tarrant and Vance and Halo, in love with one another, look forward to a new life together.

3619. ————. *The mother's recompense.* **New York: Appleton, 1924. 341p.**
Kate Clephane had left her husband and had lived in Europe for almost 20 years when her daughter Anne summoned her back to New York. Kate's husband had died and had left Anne his fortune. The city Kate returned to, especially Fifth Avenue, had undergone many changes, but Anne's house was the same one of which Kate had once been mistress. Anne and Kate establish an immediate intimacy and Kate is quite happy until she discovers that Anne's fiancé is Chris Fenno, a one-time lover of Kate's early in her European sojourn. Kate faces a dilemma—should she tell her daughter that Fenno is not a particularly worthy or reliable man, that he had deserted Kate. She decides, with the help of an Episcopal rector, that Anne's happiness may depend on marriage with Fenno and withdraws from the scene, leaving New York and rejoining her old, languid, bored Riviera companions.

3620. ————. *New Year's Day* **(The 'Seventies'). Decorations by E.C. Caswell. New York: Appleton, 1924. 159p. (*Old New York*, v. 2).**
"When Lizzie Hazeldean … is seen leaving the Fifth Avenue Hotel with Henry Prest, a society wolf with whom she is rumored to be having an affair, old New York cuts her dead and extends its sympathy to her invalid husband. Following Charles Hazeldean's death, Lizzie wounds her lover's vanity unforgivably by telling him she never loved him and that she became his mistress to pay the bills which would have destroyed the tranquility of her husband's last days. Although in the years that follow she remains faithful to her husband's memory, society never gets around to giving her credit for her heroism"—Nevius, B. *Edith Wharton* …

3621. ————. *The old maid* **(The 'Fifties') Decorations by E.C. Caswell. New York: Appleton, 1924. 190p. (*Old New York*, v. 1).**
"The old maid tells the story of Tina, Charlotte Lovell's illegitimate daughter, who is brought up by Charlotte's cousin Delia in ignorance of her parentage. As she grows up she regards Aunt Chatty as a typical old maid; her devotion is given to Delia. The situation is almost too much for Charlotte, but to save the girl's happiness she finally reconciles herself to it"—Benet's reader's encyclopedia of American literature.

Wharton, Edith, 1862-1937. *Old New York (1924)*. See her four short novels: *False dawn*; *New Year's Day*; *The old mail*; *The spark*.

3622. ————. *The spark* (*The sixties*). **Decorations by E.C. Caswell. New York: Appleton, 1924. 109p. (Old New York, v. 4).**

Hayley Delane moves in the trivial social circles of New York and bows to a fickle wife, but still recalls his contact with Walt Whitman who nursed him after Hayley was wounded at the Battle of Bull Run. Yet the spark of human sympathy that passed between them was countered by Hayley's dismissal of Whitman's poetry years later as unpalatable 'stuff.'

3622a. ————. *The touchstone* [a story]. **New York: C. Scribner, 1900. 156p.**

In order to obtain money for his marriage to Alexa, socially prominent but financially strapped New Yorker Glennard sells for publication passionate letters written to him by the late Margaret Aubyn before she achieved fame as a novelist. Eventually Glennard is made through repentance and penance a wiser and nobler individual. Wharton's short novel bespeaks the stern moral code of the upper echelons of society in old New York.

3623. ————. *Twilight sleep.* **New York: Appleton, 1927. 372p.**

"The scene of the story is present day New York and its characters are restless, dissatisfied men and women who, to escape from the fever or vacuity of their lives, lull themselves into a self-delusive twilight sleep. Their anodynes are various. The morning engagement list of Pauline Manford, society leader, is so closely divided into fifteen-minute periods of mental uplift, psychoanalysis, eurythmic exercises, facial massage, and committee meetings that she is unable to squeeze in an unappointed word with her daughter. The story, told more by implication than by direct statement, shows Pauline Manford's family riding straight to tragedy, yet after the blow has fallen, evading the issue in a pretence of concealment from each other and wrapping themselves in a false security"—Book review digest.

3624. Wharton, Thomas Isaac, 1859-1896. *Hannibal of New York*; some account of the financial loves of Hannibal St. Joseph and Paul Cradge. **New York: H. Holt, 1886. 326p.**

"Hannibal St. Joseph and Paul Cradge are two millionaires who have not scrupled at many crooked dealings to amass their fortunes. The wife of Hannibal St. Joseph is the leading character. Having deceived him concerning her past when he married her, he never lets her forget that he no longer trusts her; she is his slave and tool, and he is a most cruel taskmaster. He desires to conquer society, and her clever head is set to work; with unscrupulous impudence she routs her enemies and rivals, and soon takes a leading place in the fashionable world of New York and Newport. ... The book [is] a succession of scenes taken from social and business life, in which the worst traits of humanity are illustrated"—Annual American catalogue.

3625. Wheeler, Andrew Carpenter, 1835-1903. *A journey to nature*, by J.P. Mowbray [pseud.]. **New York: Doubleday, Page, 1901. 315p.**

The stress of business activity on Wall Street leads a broker, at the advice of his doctor, to seek renewal of his tired mind and body by taking up country living. His 8-year-old son Charlie joins him in the venture. As his enjoyment of nature and the natural surroundings increases, he interrupts his comparative solitude to become acquainted with a country girl and love soon follows.

3626. ————. *The primrose path of dalliance*; a story of the stage, by 'Nym Crinkle' (Andrew C. Wheeler). New York: L. Vanderpoole, 1892. 312p.
Marc Allen, a young New York journalist, falls into an ill-advised but passionate affair with an actress from the musical (opéra comique) stage. When she dismisses her ardent lover, Marc is left with a bitter memory. But he finds consolation in Mary Scranton who is a more likely choice for his affections. The novel paints some fascinating scenes of the bohemian way of life in New York City.

3627. ————. *The Toltec cup*; a romance of immediate life in New York City, by 'Nym Crinkle' [pseud.]. New York: Lew Vanderpoole Pub. Co., 1890. 333p.
A primary reason for perusing this novel is its detailed attention to aspects of life and places of interest in New York City in 1861-1863. Special attention is paid to the so-called lower classes of the metropolis ('O'Reardon's Terrace' and its shabby neighbors are presented in several chapters) and the Civil War Draft Riots of 1863 are described. The plot itself focuses on the disappearance of a valuable Toltec artifact, a handsomely designed cup. The reward for finding it entices a detective well acquainted with the city to search extensively in the course of which he encounters a small portion of romance.

Wheeler, Hugh Callingham, 1912-1987. See his shared pseudonym: Patrick Q.

3628. **Wheeler, Keith, 1911- . *Peaceable Lane*. New York: Simon and Schuster, 1960. 345p.**
"Describes the events that follow upon the decision of a rich Negro artist to move into a fairly exclusive [Westchester community]. The name of the street involved is Peaceable Lane, and the artist, Lamar Winter, takes possession of his house in a mood of angry anticipation as he imagines the uproar his arrival will cause among his white neighbors. These neighbors represent every degree of opinion from thoroughly bigoted to thoroughly non-bigoted, and they are united, at least for a time, in their fear that Winter's presence among them will cause the value of their properties to go down"—New Yorker. Lamar has a white friend in the community, but he is not very effective in stilling the concerns of his neighbors.

Wheeler, Mrs. Post, 1876-1956. See: Rives, Hallie Erminie, 1876-1956.

3629. **Wheelock, Dorothy. *Murder at Montauk*. New York: Phoenix Press, 1940. 255p.**
The Jessup family of Highway House (on an island off Montauk Point, Long Island) is dysfunctional; the widowed Lydia Jessup maintains a stranglehold

on her two children, Cassandra and Paul. The latter has just married Jill, daughter of Captain Howell, a native of the Montauk area. Paul had been institutionalized for mental aberrations and cannot seem to leave his mother and strike out on his own with Jill. The sudden death of Jim Milford, a Wall Street broker in big financial trouble and a friend of the Jessups, bears investigation by Kemp Hall, reporter from New York. Later, during an excursion to an old Revolutionary fort, Lydia Jessup is pushed from a high place to the rocks below as a violent storm hits the island. She survives but is in a coma, which may be terminal. To insure her silence the murderer completes the crime by stabbing her to death in her bed at Highway House, again as a storm rips through the area. Reporter Hall digs up incriminating and surprising material about the Jessups and their acquaintances, but the key to the two murders is old antagonisms between multi-generational inhabitants of Montauk and the Hamptons and the rather newly arrived Jessups and other New Yorkers.

3630. **Wheelock, Julia Flander.** *Annis Warden*; or, *A story of real life.* **Hamilton, N.Y.: Republican Print., 1889. 295p.**

Annis Warden (born 1855) is the child of John Warden and his wife Amelia (Ausman), the latter being the daughter of a wealthy Mohawk Valley farmer (whom the novel traces briefly from his humble start in 1813). The youthful Annis writes essays and poetry, keeps a journal and teaches in a rural school. The Wardens move from 'Cherry Grove' to 'Ricksport'; Annis furthers her education and religious interests. Merton Harwood, whom Annis had met earlier and who was quite taken with her, returns to New York State from a venture in raising livestock in Colorado. Annis is 21 when she and Merton are engaged; she has seen little of the world outside Upstate New York but takes the opportunity to attend the Philadelphia Exposition of 1876 and tour the Hudson River and Valley. 1887 is the date of the last entry in Annis's journal. By then she and Merton are the parents of two boys and two girls.

Whicher, Frances Miriam Berry, 1811-1852. See: Whitcher, Frances Miriam Berry, 1811-1852.

3631. **Whitcher, Frances Miriam Berry, 1811-1852.** *The Widow Bedott papers*, **by Frances M. Whicher. With an introd. by Alice B. Neal. New York: J.C. Derby, 1856. 403p.**

These sketches satirize the manners and morals of the Yankees of Upstate New York. The widow Priscilla Bedott is a 'hatchet-faced', talkative individual whose chief goal is latching on to a new husband. She does snare the Rev. Sniffles after a long pursuit of the widower Mr. Crane and proceeds to make herself quite obnoxious to all around her. In the dialect of Upstate New Yorkers Whitcher, especially in the person of Bedott's sister, Aunt Maguire, criticizes unsparingly the manners and morals of so-called genteel society in that area; in so doing the author stirred up resentment by a number of people who apparently recognized themselves in Whitcher's sketches.

Whitesboro and Elmira, N.Y. are quite likely the actual (though masked) scenes of the satires.

3632. ————. *Widow Spriggins, Mary Elmer, and other sketches.* **Edited, with a memoir, by Mrs. M.L. Ward Whitcher. New York: G.W. Carleton, 1867. 378p.**

Permilly Ruggles Spriggins is a ridiculously sentimental widow (who remarries) residing in Upstate New York who falls into situations to which she responds quite foolishly. She relates her story in words replete with malapropisms and misspellings. The Widow Spriggins is fixated on Regina Maria Roche's 'Children of the abbey', and attempts to imitate the heroine of that novel, Amanda, in language and action. 'Mary Elmer' is a short novel relating the trials and tribulations of a central New York family whose father has disappeared in California and is presumed dead. Mary Elmer, the child heroine, is ill-treated by the pretentious Mrs. J. Pixley Smith, to whom she has been farmed out. However, there are sympathetic souls in the village who try to help the poverty-stricken Elmers. Resolution of the Elmers' problems is fully achieved when the paterfamilias, George Elmer, returns to his wife and children, no longer suffering from amnesia. Contents: Widow Spriggins (p. c37,-140).—Mary Elmer; or, Trials and changes (p. c141,-123).—Letters from Timberville.—Aunt Maguire's account of the mission to Muffletegawny.—Going to see the President.

3633. **White, Grace Miller, 1868-1957. *A child of the slums*; a romantic story of New York life based upon Martin J. Dixon's play of the same name. New York: J.S. Ogilvie, 1904. 191p.**

Ruth Ferris still waits for Frank Wentworth although the latter, living in poverty and illness in the Bowery, is too ashamed to get in touch with her. Hilda Rhodes, on the other hand, marries Richard Gerson who had been Frank's roommate at Harvard. Just before she gives birth to a male child Hilda receives news of Gerson's death. A delirious young woman steals Hilda's baby. Hilda marries an Upstate New Yorker, Tom Brittle. Ruth and Hilda become acquainted and are soon inseparable friends. Richard Gerson, the story's villain, reenters. Believing Frank to be dead Gerson assumes his identity, hoping to come into a fortune that has been willed to Frank. Frank, aided by the special talents of Midge, a child of the slums, disrupts Gerson's scheme and is reunited with Ruth. The 'marriage' of Gerson and Hilda is disclosed to have been a mock one. It isn't difficult to figure out who Midge's mother is.

3634. ————. *Driven from home*; a romantic story. **Based on Hal Reid's famous, *Driven from home*. New York: J.S. Ogilvie, 1903. 180p.**

The opening scenes of the story take place in Fishkill, Dutchess County, N.Y. Margie Maynard, daughter of the prosperous but exceedingly strict farmer John Maynard, is accused by her father (despite the lack of any real proof) of yielding to the sexual advances of Hamilton Van Cruger, a philanderer from the city. Mrs. Maynard and Tom Anderson, the man Margie loves, go looking for Margie and her crippled brother David after Mr. Maynard has expelled Margie. Much of the action of the tale later moves to New York City. After several weeks of destitution and hunger, Tom Anderson rescues Margie and David; Mrs. Maynard, half-mad with anxiety, returns to normalcy. Van Cruger makes a last effort to persuade Margie to marry him, which of course fails. John Maynard finally sees the folly of his suspicions and all return to Fishkill, happy to leave a city that had been most unwelcoming.

3635. —————. *From the valley of the missing.* **Front. by Penrhyn Stanlaws. New York: W.J. Watt, 1911. 342p.**

The twins, Flea and Flukey, were assumed to be the children of widower Lon Cronk, bargeman and squatter of Ithaca and the Cayuga Lake area. Actually he had stolen them from the home of Syracuse attorney Floyd Vandecar when the latter refused to give jailed Cronk time off to see his ill wife. Contrarily the son of brutal Lem Crabbe and Scraggy Peterson was slipped to the wealthy Brimbecombes of Tarrytown by Scraggy to protect him from the rages of Lem. Renamed Everett the boy graduates from Cornell and practices law. Flea and Flukey run from Cronk and find refuge with Ann and Horace Shellington and are renamed Floyd and Fledra. Horace falls in love with Flea/Fledra; Everett Brimbecomb lays plans to seduce her despite his engagement to Ann Shellington. In a wild climax Floyd Vandecar rejoins his long-missing children; Lem Crabbe and his son, Everett, have a fatal encounter and Lon Cronk is apprised that he has a daughter, Katherine, whom the Vandecars had reared after Mrs. Cronk's death. On pages 59-72 the once famous Dryden Fair has a role in the story.

3636. —————. *The ghost of Glen Gorge.* **Front. by William Leipse. New York: Macaulay Co., 1925. 319p.**

The pious hypocrite Philander Johnson and his lawyer, Senator Pennypacker, are intent on clearing the shores of Cayuga Lake in Ithaca of the squatter fishermen who have lived there for many years, presently with the permission of Lucina Wiley. Johnson persuades his servant Lizzie Smith to steal deed and quitclaim from the Wiley home; they are the keys to his gaining possession of the squatter district. Standing in the villains' way is Peggy Pry, a squatter girl from the 'Silent City' (the squatter settlement). Peter Johnson, Philander's son, in love with Peggy, tries in vain to curb his father's vengeful actions. Peggy outsmarts Philander, Lizzie and Pennypacker and insures the survival of the Silent City and its poor but proud inhabitants.

3637. —————. *The House of Mystery*; a romantic story. **Founded upon the play of the same name. New York: J.S. Ogilvie, 1905. 186p.**

Naïve Bonny Colville, in New York City searching for the father who had deserted her and her mother, is lured into the House of Mystery by friendly Mr. Serapia. The house is really a brothel owned by the 'Black Five' (Serapia is one of them). Another young woman, Faith Worthing, just fired from her job at Robert Allison's department store, also finds herself in the infamous House, enticed there by Julian Hargraves. Out of the West comes Jim Denton; he recognizes Allison as a former colleague, Jeff Colville, in a mining operation. Allison/Colville is now an associate of Hargraves and Serapia in the Black Five. Denton tells him that Bonny, a girl Colville had planned to seduce, is his daughter. Denton and the police break up the cabal. Repentant Jeff Colville returns to his wife and daughter, selling off his New York holdings (the store, etc.) and sharing the proceeds with Denton.

3638. ————. *Judy of Rogue's Harbor.* **Front. by Howard Chandler Christy. New York: Fly, 1918. 357p.**

Sylph-like nature-lover Judy Ketchel believes herself to be an orphan; mean-spirited Grandfather Herman Ketchel has reared her. Ketchel is a German sympathizer mixed up (along with Peter Kingsland, Senator Kingsland's son) in a plot to blow up the Morse Chain plant in Ithaca, N.Y. (the United States has just declared war in 1917). Theodore Kingsland, grandson of Senator Roderick Kingsland, sees Judy near McKinney's Point on Cayuga Lake and detects a resemblance to Claudia Ricardo, widow of David Ricardo, whose funds the Senator had misappropriated. Claudia, Judy's 'Lady of Roses', owns a house not far from Herman Ketchel's run-down farm. Gradually various mysteries are unraveled. Upon his death Senator Kingsland turns over his estate to Judy and Claudia (Judy's mother). Ted Kingsland enlists in the army, assured of Judy's love; Peter Kingsland regrets his past actions; and Herman Ketchel, rejoining his daughter, Claudia, has cast off his surly nature.

3639. ————. *Rose O'Paradise.* **Illustrated by W.J. Shettsline. New York: H.K. Fly, 1915. 352p.**

"The scene of the story is that of the author's earlier novel, *Tess of the storm country*, the region around Lake Cayuga, New York. The heroine is a girl of great natural sweetness and charm who has grown up with little care or training. At eighteen she is to inherit a fortune, but in the meantime (she is fifteen when the story opens) her life is endangered by the evil designs of a villainous uncle. Her father's dying words bid her hide herself from this man until her inheritance is safely in her own hands. She finds shelter with a humble cobbler's family and makes their life hers. She has an untrained talent for the violin and a young millionaire interests himself in her and finally comes to love her. The uncle makes two attempts to abduct her, but fails. Her eighteenth birthday is reached in safety and the story ends happily"—Book review digest.

3640. ————. *The secret of the storm country.* **Illustrated by Lucius W. Hitchcock. New York: H.K. Fly, 1917. 352p.**

Sequel to *Tess of the storm country* (q.v.). Squatter Tessibel Skinner secretly marries the weak-willed Frederick Graves and incurs the almost unreasoning enmity of Ebenezer Waldstricker, Ithaca's wealthiest citizen and a hypocritical churchman, who believes Tess knows the whereabouts of the dwarf Andy Bishop, an escapee from Auburn Prison accused of murdering Ebenezer's father. Waldstricker is serious about flushing the squatters from their shanties on the shores of Cayuga Lake. Frederick Graves complies with his mother's wishes and bigamously marries Madelene Waldstricker. Persecuted by Ezenezer Waldstricker, Tess is drummed out of the church she attends; she has a baby boy and is protected by the lawyer Deforrest Young who is in love with her. Several years go by. Frederick Graves, still in love with Tess, dies; Tess loses her precious boy child but saves Waldstricker's girl Elsie from harm at the hands of the vengeful squatters. Waldstricker, now aware of all the tragedies Tess has suffered, repents. Tess and Deforrest Young face the future with hope.

3641. ————. *The shadow of the sheltering pines*; a new romance of the Storm Country. **New York: H.K. Fly, 1919. 314p.**

Ithaca, Cayuga Lake and environs are again the scene of the fourth of eight novels White wrote about this Finger Lakes area. Tonnibel ('Tony') Devon, reared by brutish, drunken Uriah Devon and his wife, Edith, is a poor, uneducated girl of high intelligence and pure good-heartedness. It is clear from the story's opening that Tony is the long-lost child of the widower Dr. Paul Pendlehaven, taken from her crib by Edith Devon, then a servant in the Pendlehaven household. Why, the reader may ask, isn't Tony's true identity apparent to Dr. Pendlehaven? A wealthy Salvation Army captain, Philip MacCauley, falls in love with Tony; she touches the heart of ill Paul Pendlehaven. The doctor's relatives disparage Tony before Paul and his brother. Their efforts miscarry, even though Tony places her future in jeopardy by taking the blame for a theft and a shooting that she feared Edith, the only mother she had ever known, was responsible for.

3642. ————. *Storm country Polly*. **With front. by Frank Tenney Johnson. Boston: Little, Brown, 1920. 309p.**

"The scene of the story is a squatter colony on the shores of Lake Cayuga. The colony is known as Silent City and Jeremiah Hopkins is its unofficial mayor. His daughter Polly is the story's heroine. Polly, the one person in Evelyn Robertson's confidence, knows the story of Evelyn's secret marriage to Oscar Bennett. Evelyn desires silence, for she is now in love with Marc MacKenzie, the man making war on the squatters, and Bennet will grant it only on condition that Polly agrees to marry him. And Evelyn, who might intercede with MacKenzie, promises to do so if Polly will pay the price, but Polly cannot, for she is in love with Robert Percival, Evelyn's cousin. Marc carries out his threats. Daddy Hopkins is sent to jail, wee Jerry is taken from Polly's arms, and her love is turned to hate. But not for long, and love triumphs all around in the end"—Book review digest.

3643. ————. *Susan of the storm*. **Front. by John Drew. New York: Macaulay, 1927. 320p.**

Despite the title this is not one of White's novels about the 'Storm country' around Cayuga Lake in the Finger Lakes region. Rather the scene is 'Evergreen Island' and the town of 'Bradmere' on Long Island Sound. Susan, daughter of Matilda Holiday, her father unknown (to Susan), has been raised by humble Dort and Abecena Pock on Evergreen Island. Susan is a bright girl whose paternity is known only too well to socially elite Willard Blackstone; he is able to wean her from the Pocks and place Susan with his sister Henriette—the latter treats Susan meanly. Meanwhile Judah Rixby, Willard's stepson (his mother is Blanche Rixby Blackstone) falls in love with Susan. The arrival in Bradmere of Andrew Atherton, brother-in-law of Agnes Blackstone Atherton and uncle of her snobbish daughter, Estelle, signals the disclosure of Susan's father. Susan's legitimacy is documented—the deceased Francis Atherton, Andrew's brother, is the key. Susan's Uncle Andrew Atherton makes arrangements for her future well-being.

3644. ————. *Tess of the storm country*. **Illustrated by Howard Chandler Christy. New York: W.J. Watt, 1909. 365p.**

The first and most successful commercially of the author's novels about the 'Storm Country', a region that embraces Ithaca, New York and other settled areas on the shores of Cayuga Lake. The heroine of the story, Tess Skinner, is the daughter of one of the squatters who live in poverty on the fringes of Cayuga Lake; they fish and hunt illegally, grub out an existence in any way they can, and are generally a thorn in the sides of the 'solid' citizens of Ithaca. Tess's father is reputed to have murdered a gamekeeper. The Rev. Elias Graves owns the land on which the Skinner shack stands and he has been trying to oust the Skinners for a long time. Tess is in love with the minister's son, and despite her ignorance is a committed Christian prepared to sacrifice everything for her lover and his sister. Students and teachers from Cornell University and Ithaca townspeople are woven into the novel.

White, Henry, b. 1876. See under his pseudonym: Oliver, Roland.

3645. **White, Lionel, 1905- . *Clean break*. New York: Dutton, 1955. 189p.**
After spending four years in Sing Sing, Johnny Clay has formulated plans to snatch the proceeds (ca. two million dollars) of Saturday's races at the Long Island track in Jamaica. The plot is most ingenious and success would have been his and his confederates had not a lady accomplice dispensed her favors too easily to the wrong party and unintentionally given away the whole enterprise.

3646. ————. *The house next door*. **New York: Dutton, 1956. 191p.**
Feckless Len Nielsen, under the influence of too much alcohol, stumbles onto murder at a Long Island suburban development; someone discovers another corpse, and Len finds himself accused of murder and in jail. The author throws in six other incidents relating to Len's situation and in the doing gives the reader a sharply etched picture of suburbia, Long Island style.

3647. ————. *Invitation to violence*. **New York: Dutton, 1958. 187p.**

"Gerald Hanna [of Long Island] is rudely jolted out of his humdrum existence as an insurance actuary—with a longstanding librarian fiancée—when a dying man with a big boodle in gems lands in his car. Disposing of the body, Hanna keeps the jewels and manages to get the best of both the cops [Detective Lieutenant Hopper] and the robbers who are on his tail"—Kirkus service.

3648. ————. *The time of terror*. **New York: Dutton, 1960. 191p.**

"Two and a half year-old Chris Dobie disappears in front of a Long Island supermarket … and it is the spontaneous, later regretted, action of Frank Mace, hard pressed—he is jobless and his wife and children have left him. He is about to return the child when an old associate, Barney, forces him to raise the ante, and before the case is closed, it extends its sphere of suffering and fatality"—Kirkus reviews.

3649. White, Matthew, 1857-1940. *The affair at Islington*. **New York: F.A. Munsey, 1897. 233p.**

From his residence in 'Islington' in Upstate New York Gilbert Dean entrains for Albany to meet clandestinely with the actress Marie Myrwin (born Estelle Goodwin). His wife Louise confronts the guilty pair in Albany and returns in high dudgeon to Islington. The following morning she is found dead with marks on her throat. Gilbert had followed Louise home, but in the night before her death, had again taken the Albany train, getting off at Schenectady. Arrested on suspicion of murder, tried and convicted, Gilbert is sent to death row in Auburn Prison. Estelle who had planned to perform in Islington is threatened by incensed citizens. When Gilbert is executed, she loses her mind. The novel concludes as the Islington paper prints a newly discovered note Louise had written just before she died. The note casts a startling light on the whole affair.

3650. ————. *A born aristocrat*; a story of the stage. **New York: F.A. Munsey, 1898. 228p.**

A formerly wealthy New York family, the Van Dykes, come upon hard times and it is incumbent upon the two daughters, Barbara and Freda, to find remunerative employment. Barbara has the good luck to be given a part in the chorus of a current stage piece; from there she graduates to a speaking/singing role in a musical comedy, 'The summer girl.' Differences with the stage manager cause Barbara to walk out on the part. A layoff of several months is followed by personal success in a new Broadway play. But Barbara's heart is not really in the theater. She is happy to cede her role in a drama written by Donald Farrington to Freda, Farrington's fiancée. Farrington's play, entitled 'A born aristocrat', attacks the pettiness of upper crust New York society and it is very successful. Barbara leaves the theater for marriage with Allan Thurwell, a young businessman. Implicit in the novel is the view that a theatrical career is not really a 'respectable' option for 'properly bred' young women.

3651. **[White, Rhoda Elizabeth Waterman].** *Jane Arlington*; or, *The defrauded heiress*. **A tale of Lake Champlain. By Uncle Ben [pseud.] of Rouse's Point. Rouse's Point [N.Y.]: D. Turner, Printer, 1853. 48p.**

Jane Arlington comes to a village on the western banks of Lake Champlain expecting a welcome from Mr. William Goodpy. There is no Goodpy. William Merton, brother of the man who adopted her, James Merton, has misled her. Jane seeks employment and finds friends in Kate Lawrence, a landlord's daughter, and George Barton, a store clerk who falls in love with her. Barton goes to 'Shell Harbor', N.Y. and discovers the plans of William Merton to steal Jane's inheritance from the deceased James Merton. A hateful stepmother has victimized Barton himself; his real name is George Sinclair. Fortuitously the father who had previously disowned George now welcomes him back.

3652. **White, Stewart Edward, 1873-1946.** *The sign at six*. **Illustrated by M. Leone Bracker. Indianapolis: Bobbs-Merrill, 1912. 264p.**

A half-mad scientist has decided that New York City must be freed from the clutches of a politico named McCarthy. The scientist has the wherewithal to shut off sound and light over large areas and he gives McCarthy a clue to his authority by cutting the electricity in the Atlas Building where McCarthy has an office. On the day following, all electric power in New York City is shut down for a while. The disruptions continue for several days, but the crazed eccentric meets his Waterloo when a young scientist, Percy Darrow, figures out where to find him.

White, Thom., pseud. See: Elliot, Charles Wyllys, 1817-1883.

Whitelock, Louise Clarkson, 1865-1928. See: Clarkson, L[ouise], 1865-1928.

3653. **Whitfield, Raoul, 1897-1945.** *The Virgin kills*. **New York: Knopf, 1932. 270p.**

Millionaire stock market gambler Eric Vennell has several guests on his yacht, the Virgin, as it sets out for the Poughkeepsie Regatta: a newspaper columnist, a sportswriter, a movie actress, an aviator, a gangster/bodyguard, et al. Two murders throw a veil of confusion and suspicion over the party. Detectives come on board to investigate, but it is a young woman with an apt idea who furnishes the key to the solution of the homicides.

3654. ————. *Green ice*. **New York: Knopf, 1930. 282p.**

Mal Ourney has just been released from Sing Sing after serving time for manslaughter. Actually Mal was innocent of the unlawful killing; he had 'taken the rap' for the real culprit, Dot Ellis. The latter awaits Mal at the prison gate, but he ignores her. Just a moment later Dot is killed. Mal rejects the notion that she is a suicide; he deems it murder and is more than ever determined to make the big crime lords in downstate New York pay for their misdeeds.

3655. **Whitman, Stephen French, b. 1880.** *Predestined;* **a novel of New York life. New York: Scribner, 1910. 464p.**

With the handicap of a morally degenerate inherited family background Felix Piers sets out on a career as a journalist, but has plans to enter the more demanding theater of literature. In his struggle to rise to literary fame Felix must array the better impulses of his nature against the unworthy inherited tendencies. He acquires many pleasant friendships and experiences, but is subject to all the temptations of New York City and to the four women who in one or another way are dominant forces in his life. He could lose his way, but then again he could emerge wiser and more humble.

3656. **Whitman, Walt, 1819-1892.** *Franklin Evans;* **or,** *The inebriate.* **A tale of the times, by Walter Whitman. With introd. by Emory Holloway. New York: Random House, 1929. xxiii, 248p.**

Franklin Evans is a lad from Long Island whose life in New York City is punctuated by overindulgence in hard drink. He gets married and is presumably on the road to reform but relapses into his old vice. After his wife's death from heartbreak Franklin joins a gang, is imprisoned and then rehabilitated. He takes the temperance pledge and travels to Virginia, marries a Creole girl and gets mixed up with an evil 'white' woman who drives his wife to suicide. Returning to Manhattan the morose sinner swears total abstinence and offers temperance advice to his young male readers. Originally issued in The New World (New York, 1842), extra series, no. 34, v. 2, no. 10.

3657. **Whitmire, Caroline Steward, b. 1869.** *Harmony Flats;* **the gifts of a tenement-house fairy, by C.S. Whitmore [sic], New York: Benziger Bros., 1907. 188, 14p.**

Under the guise of a game called 'Cleaning Up' the neglected children of a family in a New York tenement set an inspiring example for other residents and the building becomes a model of cleanliness. A leading figure behind the movement towards a sanitary atmosphere and a better life for the poor tenants is a gruff old gentleman who had been a figure of awe and apprehension for the young people.

Whitmore, Caroline Steward, b. 1869. See: Whitmire, Caroline Steward, b. 1869.

3658. **Whitney, Phyllis A., 1903- .** *The golden unicorn.* **Garden City, N.Y.: Doubleday, 1976. 279p.**

Whitney's novel is the familiar narrative of a girl searching for her biological parents; in this case the adopted Courtney Marsh picks up clues that guide her to the home of the Rhodes family at East Hampton, Long Island. The Rhodes are a quarrelsome, often violent clan that is obviously secretive of its guilty past. Courtney gets too close to various truths—she does find out the mystery behind her birth, but risks her own life when she comes upon a degrading, frightening scandal better left unknown.

3659. ————. *Mystery of the haunted pool.* **Illustrated by H. Tom Hall. Philadelphia: Westminster Press, 1960. 223p.**

"Susan Price has been sent ahead of her family to an aunt who has an antique shop in 'Highlands Landing', way up the Hudson. Susan and her aunt tuck themselves into Aunt Edith's crowded quarters while a search for a house for the family is on. And in the process the 12-year-old girl stumbles onto a mystery, does a great deal to bring a crippled boy out of a morbid sense of guilt, helps restore a neurotic spinster to a saner outlook on life, and unearths a treasure that seems not too unlikely a find"—Kirkus reviews.

3660. ————. *Rainsong.* **Garden City, N.Y.: Doubleday, c1984. 249p.**

Whitney describes quite effectively the Long Island scene in which the story takes place. Her heroine, Hollis Temple, is a widow (at 23) of pop artist Ricky Sands who from all indications committed suicide. Ricky's one-time girlfriend, Coral Caine, had taken her own life the year before. Hollis, a songwriter, tries to get away from bad memories by going to Cold Spring Harbor, the estate of elegant Geneva Ames, only to collide with a number of dangerous, life-threatening incidents.

3661. ————. *The stone bull.* **Garden City, N.Y.: Doubleday, 1977. 304p.**

When Jenny McClain follows her new husband to an inn located in the Catskills and owned by his family, she carries with her a sense of guilt for her sister Ariel's suicide. Jenny's sibling was a renowned ballerina and Jenny had always been merely identified as the dancer's sister. Now, on her own, she is enjoying her surroundings and the friendship of the sculptor, Magnus Devin. But Ariel will not go away; it seems that Ariel had been at the same inn, had an affair with Jenny's husband, and may have had something to do with the death of Magnus's wife. Jenny digs further into the past to set her mind at rest over Ariel's suicide, to discover the truth behind the so-called 'accidental' death of Mrs. Devin and absolve Ariel of any connection with it.

3662. ————. *Thunder Heights.* **New York: Appleton-Century-Crofts, 1960. 311p.**

Camilla King, formerly a governess in New York, leaves the city when summoned to her family's ancestral home (in the Hudson Valley), which her grandfather now rules. In that gothic mansion she finds mystery, suspense, love, and the causes of her mother's sudden death.

3663. **Whitson, John Harvey, 1854-1936. *The Castle of Doubt.* With a front. in color from a drawing by I.H. Caliga. Boston: Little, Brown, 1907. vi, 283p.**

"While enjoying a springtime stroll in Central Park [the hero] is suddenly confronted by an ... [automobile] containing two pretty women, one of whom declares she is his wife. Despite his remonstrances he is thrust into the [vehicle] and carried off to a luxurious house where he is told that he is Julian Randolph, a young millionaire whose sudden disappearance was a matter of national comment two years before. ... The concluding chapters, which establish the right of the hero to the love and position he has come to covet, are unusual, unexpected and well handled"—Book review digest.

Whittaker, James, B. 1891. See under his pseudonym: Barnes, Geoffrey, b. 1891.

3664. **Wick, Jean.** *The love quest.* **New York: A.L. Burt, 1929. 376p.**
A 16-year-old girl, Ada Brown, comes from 'Centreville' in Upstate New York to the big city to earn her living. An orphan with a strict moral code she is befriended by Hulda Jansen, an acquaintance of her deceased mother, who hires Ada as a helper in her beauty parlor. Ada 'graduates' to jobs as manicurist and clothes model, neither of which she keeps for long since she refuses to 'entertain' demanding male customers. A young Texan, Jim Randall, on business in New York, falls in love with Ada, but then suddenly goes back to Texas without making any commitment. Ada is next employed as companion to rich, demanding, and rather vulgar Amy Carstairs. The lady's nephew, Allan Carstairs, eyes Ada as a possible conquest. Ada resists his advances and Jim Randall, back in New York after selling the family store in Texas, manhandles Allan. Ada returns to Centreville and is followed by a repentant Allan Carstairs. Ada refuses Allan's marriage proposal; Jim Randall shows up and he and Ada wed and plan the opening of stores and beauty parlors in Texas.

Wickham, Martha, pseud. See: Huntington, Cornelia, b. 1803.

3665. **Widdemer, Mabel Cleland, 1902-1964.** *In the shadows of the skyscrapers.* **With illus. by George T. Tobin. New York: Harcourt, Brace, 1925. 268p.**
The novel relates various events in the lives of children from an American family and their counterparts from an Italian household who live side by side in an over-flowing tenement in New York City.

3666. ————. *The wishing star*; a mystery of old Tarrytown. **Drawings by Margaret Ayer. Indianapolis: Bobbs-Merrill, 1948. 230p.**
After surviving the Great Fire of 1835 in New York City a 15-year-old girl comes to Tarrytown in Westchester County. In her new life she develops several friendships, helps clear up an ongoing mystery and experiences the beginnings of a romantic involvement.

3667. **Widdemer, Margaret, 1890?-1978.** *Buckskin baronet.* **Garden City, N.Y.: Doubleday, 1960. 330p.**

Sir Lucian Tynedale is sent to America by Lord North in 1773 to observe and report on the temper of the Americans, especially those in the New York Colony. Lucian arrives in New York and immediately sets out for Albany and the Mohawk Valley. He meets his (presumed) mother, Rosamond Cantillon Tynedale (now Mrs. Ian Scott)—his father, Sir Geoffrey, had been slain by Indians when Lucian was a child of three and in the care of friendly Shawanese (Shawnee) Indians. Lucian is introduced to Sir William Johnson, Molly and Joseph Brant, and other members of Sir William's entourage. Lucian then travels through western New York to the Ohio country, home of the Shawanese, where he nearly loses his life before his Shawanese 'brother', Shamanth, rescues him. Lucian returns to the Mohawk Valley by way of Philadelphia and then goes east to survey conditions in Boston. At the novel's conclusion Lucian has returned to England, reported to Lord North, and learns of his true parentage; he marries Brigid Scott, daughter of Rosamond and Ian Scott, and is making plans to go back to the Mohawk Valley.

3668. ————. *Gallant lady.* **New York: Harcourt, Brace, 1926. 306p.**
"This is a story of youth and youth's way of meeting its problems today. Sibyl Burnham is happily married to Charles Logan and little Nonny is almost four years old. Charles in a moment of madness in [1st World] War days had married an army nurse. His feeling for her passes and he believed himself free of her when her name was found on the casualty list of a bombed hospital. Six years afterward she turns up, an adventuress determined to make trouble for her husband. Sibyl faces her trouble gallantly, determined that it shall not wreck her life or Nonny's. Most of the book is concerned with the new life she makes for herself and Nonny in New York, and the story ends on a note as happy as its beginning"—Book review digest.

3669. ————. *The golden wildcat.* **Garden City, N.Y.: Doubleday, 1954. 314p.**
The heroine of this historical novel is Mary Johnson, daughter of Sir William; she is 16 years old when the story opens (ca. 1760). Mary is affianced to a kinsman, Guy Johnson, whom Sir. William Johnson has called from Ireland to serve as his assistant in Indian affairs. Affronted by an engagement on which she was not consulted, Mary flees from the Mohawk Valley to Oswego. Seized by hostile Canadian Indians she is taken as his mistress by the half-breed De Castine. Escaping back to Oswego Mary faces her husband-to-be, Guy Johnson. De Castine is still around to stir up a lot of trouble and Guy must deal with his presence.

3670. ————. *Hand on her shoulder.* **New York: Farrar & Rinehart, 1938. 279p.**
Katherine had grown up elsewhere, but now she is headed for the countryside around Oriskany in the Mohawk Valley, the land of her ancestors. One of the latter, Catherine, of German extraction, had been very much in love with Sir Lucian who had come to Upstate New York 200 years ago, but she had been compelled to marry another man. Modern-day Katherine meets the young,

942

handsome Lucian, a descendant of Sir Lucian. The training of horses and horse racing play a prominent role in the story.

3671. ————. *Lady of the Mohawks*. **Garden City, N.Y.: Doubleday, 1951. 304p.**
An historical novel about Molly Brant, Joseph Brant's sister, who was loved by two men, Sir William Johnson (whose mistres.s she became) and François Joncaire. The French and Indian War (1754-1763) plays a significant role in the story.

3672. ————. *Let me have wings.* **New York: Farrar & Rinehart, 1941. 311p.**
Rosemary is one of those poor little rich girls who long for the freedom to make their own way in the world without interference from guardians or relatives. She lives on a Hudson River estate and her grandmother, a tyrannical personage, is determined to keep Rosemary penned in there. How Rosemary gains her independence is the nub of the story.

3673. ————. *Prince in buckskin*; **a story of Joseph Brant at Lake George. Illustrated by William Sharp. Philadelphia: Winston, 1952. 184p.**
A novel about the early life of Joseph Brant; it features his relationship with Sir William Johnson under whom he served when the British were trying to ensure their control of the Lake George area in 1755 and keep Crown Point from falling into French hands.

3674. ————. *The Red Castle women.* **Garden City, N.Y.: Doubleday, 1968. 273p.**
"The Red Castle, a form of wedding cake architecture which goes by the name of gothic, is on the Hudson in Upper New York State—circa 1840 where an old Indian curse has been visited on its inheritors. This is established early on in the 'dawning' here and without letting the cat out of the reticule; suffice it to say it's about Eugenia, who lives in the castle with her first cousin—Isabel—with a maimed face, and Mark Harradine, a major, who was to have married Eugenia but elopes with Perdita who tells the story, and about Mark's earlier involvement with one Drusilla ("Negroid!") and the Underground Railroad"—Kirkus service.

3675. ————. *Red cloak flying.* **Garden City, N.Y.: Doubleday, 1950. ix, 306p.**
From the border region of Scotland/England during the Jacobite Rebellion of 1745-1746 the novel swings to the Mohawk Valley, the domain of Sir William Johnson and his Iroquois allies. Married in an English debtor's prison, Rosamond Cantillon and Sir Geoffrey Tynsdale receive invaluable help from Sir William as they establish a manor in the wilderness. Rosamond, gifted with 'the sight' (psychic powers) is jealously watched by Sir Geoffrey, but she almost loses her life at the hands of several witch-haunted German settlers; Ian Craigvalloch, a Jacobite friend of Geoffrey saves her. Ian and Geoffrey quarrel, then Geoffrey finally comes to his senses. Ian is in love with Rosamond; she, however, turns to her first love, Geoffrey. Ian and Geoffrey

reconcile and Geoffrey states his intention of remaining in the new land, abandoning his earlier desire to return to England.

3676. ————. *Rhinestones*; a romance. New York: Harcourt, Brace 1929. 252p.
Janet Dorrance is lured by the bright lights of New York City and leaves behind her Ohio hometown and the man who loves her, Dr. David Hutchinson. Although she is not particularly intelligent Janet gets a job as secretary to the head of a lecture bureau and meets a millionaire when she helps out a friend at a large import business. The glittery rhinestones that she sees there impress Janet; the millionaire, bored but romantic, falls in love with Janet. However, she decides that she wants the 'real things' of life—he didn't know what they were and didn't want them anyway. So Janet eschews the sparkling, tinsely things she had previously coveted and returns to her hometown to the 'the shining things—that are true'.

3677. Wiechmann, Ferdinand Gerhard, 1858-1919. *Maid of Montauk*; [a story] by Forest Monroe [pseud.]. New York: W.R. Jenkins, 1902. ix, 164p.
The 'maid of Montauk' is a beautiful young Englishwoman (Sigrid Dare) cast upon the shore of eastern Long Island after the ship bringing her to the New World sinks. Sigrid is taken in and cared for by the Montauk Indians, allies of the English colonists of the Island. The scheming Dutchman, Van Doren, covets Sigrid and incites the Niantick Indians, a Narragansett tribe, to war on and decimate the Montauks. Held in captivity by hostile Indians and by Van Doren, Sigrid is rescued by her lover, Sir Harold Fenton (who had preceded her to America). In the preface the author states: "The story offers a picture of the habits and customs of those days gleaned from the records of old"—Long Island in then the mid-17th century when the Dutch and English shared it along with several Indian tribes.

3678. Wilcox, Constance Grenelle. *Such ways are dangerous*, by Constance Wilcox Pignatelli. New York: R.H. McBride, 1939. 273p.
"A quiet young woman from a little town in Vermont inherits a Sutton Place house and enormous wealth. Unused to the ways of the world, she is taken up by a set of New Yorkers and two impoverished members of the Italian nobility. Then she loses her money and returns thankfully to her quiet Vermont home"—Book review digest.

3679. Wilcox, Ella Wheeler, 1859-1919. *A double life*. New York: J.S. Ogilvie, 1891. 181p.
John Chester, a leading figure in 'Brandford' (New York?), falls from grace with the commission of a crime in that town. He leaves for New York City and over the years is successful in covering up his indiscretion while living under the sobriquet of John Walter, but he eventually has to pay for the misdemeanor. A secondary plot deals with the marital misstep of one Erastus Lounsbury.

3680. ———. *Sweet danger*. Chicago: F.T. Neely, 1892. 296p.

In a novel whose scenes shift between New York and Paris "Dolores King and Helena Moxon meet in a boarding school and become dear friends. Dolores has theories against marriage founded on a diary left by her mother, whose married life was a failure. Helena looks forward to a happy home with children to love and care for; such as she has always known her mother's to be. The 'sweet danger' comes to Dolores who, loving a man devotedly, consents to live with him, but not to marry him. The experiment ends after two years. Her old friend, Helena finds her home and happiness after Dolores has fallen a victim to impossible theories"—Annual American catalogue.

3681. Wilcox, Stephen F., 1951- . *The dry white tear*; a T.S.W. Sheridan mystery. New York: St. Martin's Press, 1989. 217p.

"When his Uncle Charlie is murdered, Manhattan journalist Timothy Sheridan inherits a rural New York cottage, several much sought after acres of land, and an unsolved murder. A wine grower and a property developer badly want Charlie's land and the neighboring property, which is owned by a possibly deranged fundamentalist widow. Murder quickly becomes a popular pastime in the tiny Finger Lakes community. Both prospective buyers expire as rumors of homosexuality and Mob connections drift to the surface, with Sheridan's street-smart journalistic savvy operating in overdrive and the author providing local color aplenty in the form of tough rednecks, good-time waitresses and lazy police officials"—Booklist.

3682. ———. *The green mosaic*. New York: St. Martin's Press, 1994. 280p.

Wilcox's T. (Timothy) S.W. Sheridan, crime writer and freelance sleuth, on a vacation in the Adirondacks (with his girlfriend) becomes interested in the case of environmentalist Glenny Oldham who died from a fall near her mountain cabin three years before. In the course of his inquiries he mixes it up with a local bully in a bar—said bully later turns up dead. Environmental terrorists, the area's law network, and timber tycoons also come under his scrutiny. Shredding the alibis of several suspects and bringing to light a murderer who frequented the Adirondack Park quite recently, Sheridan closes in on a solution to Glenny Oldham's sudden demise.

3683. ———. *The Nimby factor*; a Hackshaw mystery. New York: St. Martin's Press, 1992. 249p.

That Upstate New York journalist and part-time restorer of interesting old houses, Elias 'Hack' Hackshaw, acquires a beat-up Victorian mansion while his fellow townspeople are in the midst of a fight over a proposed landfill. Hack kicks in with an editorial in support of the landfill to the dismay of many and then stumbles upon the corpse of the anti-landfill leader in the vestibule of his dilapidated acquisition. The body vanishes and several more corpses appear. As a prime suspect Hack has to dodge the police. He also has to fend off Fawn, a sexy college student, as he trails a wealthy woman who is involved with a home preservation group.

3684. ———. *The painted lady*; a Hackshaw mystery. New York: St. Martin's Press, 1993. 297p.

Elias 'Hack' Hackshaw takes time out from his duties as publisher/editor of a weekly newspaper in western New York State to contemplate a new arrival in town, Hester DelGado who is not only beautiful but also in the process of making over a Victorian house that Hack had hoped to own. Hester shelters girls with pregnancy and other problems, although elements in the community are less than enthusiastic about her project. When one of Hester's girls is murdered there is no lack of possible suspects—even Hester with her penchant for mysticism cannot be dismissed.

3685. ———. *The St. Lawrence run*; a T.S.W. Sheridan mystery. New York: St. Martin's Press, 1990. 244p.

"Set in the Thousand Islands—the picturesque stretch of the St. Lawrence River that has long been a favorite haunt of fishermen, tourists, bootleggers, and fugitives, Castle House is a hulking mansion that dominates one of the islands off 'Widows Cape', New York. Fifty years ago it was the site of a sensational tragedy [when] … in the course of … [a] robbery, the mansion went up in flames. Today it is part of a new puzzle, when a professor at the local college, who has begun looking into the Castle House, is murdered. Curiosity—and a cryptic letter from the dead man—bring Sheridan to the village to pick up the inquiry. The Castle House affair, he finds, is far from over. It involves some of Widows Cape's most prominent citizens, and deadly secrets from both the present and the past"—Publisher's announcement.

3686. ———. *The twenty-acre plot*. New York: St. Martin's Press, 1991. 214p.

Elias Hackshaw, editor of a weekly in western New York, is very well-informed about the region he covers. He is somewhat addicted to playing cards and alcohol, but his two chief pursuits are womanizing and rummaging around 19th-century buildings. The sudden demise from a fall of an 80-year-old farmer from a hayloft piques Hackshaw's curiosity, for that farmer had a plastic hip joint that would have made a climb to the loft highly unlikely. Did a developer covet the farm? Did the farmer alter his will? Hackshaw's research touches several bases: the local real estate market, speculation, murder, Native Americans, and scandalmongering. He has a propensity for sticking his proboscis into other people's business and almost gets himself killed.

3687. Wilde, Percival, 1887-1953. *The devil's booth*; a novel. New York: Harcourt, Brace, 1930. viii, 368p.

"Molly May Millen, nineteen, stood watching the Easter parade on Fifth Avenue in 1889. She was a poor girl of Irish parentage with one consuming ambition: to be somebody, to ride one day, like Mrs. Stirling Severance, in a glistening victoria. Molly May, aware of her physical charms, knows one way only to elevate her station and takes it. She passes from one lover to another, each time increasing her price, till she becomes the mistress of a millionaire. Then having fallen ardently in love with young Brierly, an employee of the Severance Corporation, she later learns that he is the rich Brierly Severance. Through him Molly May attains her life ambition—all the money she wants, a purchased husband, a New England estate, and social leadership"—Book review digest.

3688. **Wiley, John Wilmot, 1899- .** *Queer Street*; **the story of some native New Yorkers. New York: Scribner, 1928. 283p.**

"The story of a family of native New Yorkers in its decadence. The gentle street, on which the Skeffingtons lived, with its respectable brownstone houses, was already beginning to get queer when the eldest daughter, Maria, secured her Italian prince at a price that depleted the Skeffington fortune. Geoffrey's affair with an actress was expensive. Faced with an immediate need for a husband, Louisa was forced to marry poor, faithful Mr. Potts, a lodger down the street. Anna, the youngest, married out of her class to renew the family fortune. But the Skeffingtons faced all these and other misfortunes with a suavity and pride which deceived themselves, if no one else"—Book review digest.

3689. **Wilford, Florence, b. 1836.** *Dominie Freylinghausen.* **London: Mozley and Smith, 1875. viii, 323p.**

Dominie (Pastor) Freylinghausen 'was hard and narrow and bigoted, and his mind was warped by the heretical teaching of his school [he was a strict Calvinist], but he was true to what he thought the truth; he was thoroughly, even fiercely in earnest' (p.209). He was, however, highly regarded by his Dutch flock in Albany, which included the heroine, Franzje Ryckman, his prize pupil. Most disturbing to the Dominie is Franzje's relationship to the worldly Lieutenant Russell Vyvian of the King's Army, who is billeted in Albany (in the 1750s during resumption of hostilities between the French and the British). The charming, persistent Vyvian falls for the beautiful Franzje and eventually proposes to the confused girl who has been warned by the Dominie and her father of the young officer's unsuitability. The Dominie, sensing that his influence over Franzje and his parishioners is waning, sets sail for Holland, but is drowned in passage. The guilt-laden Franzje, only briefly in love with Vyvian, decides to spend the remainder of her life in spinsterhood, performing good works (e.g., nursing) and abiding by the Christian ideals her mentor, the Dominie, had instilled in her.

3690. *Wilfred Montressor*; **or,** *The Secret Order of Seven.* **A romance. By the author of** *Abel Parsons* **... etc. New York: C.G. Graham, 1848. 408p.**

Wilfred Montressor's youthful love, Mary Cameron had, in deference to her dying mother's wishes, married an elderly businessman, Owen Tracey. In 1828, after years in the East, Wilfred comes back to New York accompanied by beautiful, faithful Zorah, a young Georgian (Caucasia) woman. An intruder kills Zorah and Wilfred vows to bring the murderer to justice. Owen Tracey's spendthrift brother, Alfred, seems a likely suspect. Montressor forms the Secret Order of Seven and questions his New York friends to learn more about the Traceys. Toward the novel's end Alfred, the confessed murderer, is slain by a former associate, the gambler/swindler John Harden. Owen Tracey falls prey to mental illness; Mary Cameron, his wife, devotes herself to caring for him, proof to Montressor that she is no mercenary individual, but a woman worthy of the greatest respect. She tells Wilfred she will always be his friend and urges him to use his "talents, education, wealth …to relieve the sufferings of the destitute and the oppressed, to encourage honest industry, and foster rising genius" (p. 402).

3691. **Wilhelm, Kate.** *Sweet, sweet poison.* **New York: St. Martin's Press, 1990. 262p.**

Al and Sylvie Zukal, natives of the Bronx, use lottery winnings to purchase a country estate in 'Spender's Ferry', New York. The deaths of the Zukal's watchdog Sadie and their young friend bring the detective duo of Charlie Meiklejohn and Constance Leidl to the scene. They tend to disagree with the local sheriff who counts these and further deaths (by poison, drugs, bee stings and gas) as accidents or suicides. Charlie and Constance take a hard look at a number of possible murderers; big wheel Warren Wollander, his immature daughter and the evangelist she adheres to, and a group of agricultural researchers (Wollander's wife is one of them).

3692. **Wilkins, W.A.** *The Cleverdale mystery*; or, *The machine and its wheels.* **A story of American life. New York: Fords, Howard & Hulbert, 1882. 287p.**

Darius Hamblin, a resident of 'Cleverdale' in Upstate New York (8,000 inhabitants—somewhere north of Albany?) is a financially strapped State senator who wants his daughter Belle to marry Walter Mannis, another ambitious politician. However, Belle is in love with a bank clerk, George Alden. When fire breaks out at the local woolen mill George rescues several people, but is badly injured. He and Belle are secretly married. Alden is falsely accused of mishandling bank funds; he leaves town. Mannis and a cohort dress the body of an Alden look-alike in the bank clerk's clothes so that it appears that 'Alden', with a gun at his side, has committed suicide. Just before Belle (believing her husband dead) is to take marriage vows with Mannis, George Alden appears—he had struck it rich in the silver mines of Colorado. Mannis learns that a farm-girl, Mary Harris, whose virtue he had sullied, has committed suicide. The girl's father shoots and kills Mannis. Senator Hamblin confesses his derelictions; George and Belle offer him forgiveness.

3693. **Wilkinson, Florence.** *The strength of the hills*; a novel. **New York: Harper, 1901. iii, 395p.**

The novel is laid in the Saranac region of the Adirondacks except for several chapters at the book's end that take one to New York City. The lumberman Enoch Holme is engaged in a logging operation near the village of 'Elk

Mountain' whose laconic inhabitants are descendants of the miners who worked in the area 30 years ago. Enoch quarrels with timber contractor Joe Hartl and becomes manager of the Hollister lumber business. Enoch is also an ordained Methodist minister whose interest in Alison Macdonald is qualified by her sophistication and lack of religious ties. He had heard that Alison might marry Dick Hollister and that is exactly what occurs with Enoch as the presiding clergyman. Crises and conflicts arise and the principal characters have to navigate their way through them. e.g., Sararose Holme, Enoch's sister, moves to New York City to study music and is drawn into the bohemian way of life. Worried about his sister and still curious about Alison, Enoch follows both to the city; however, the story glides back to the Adirondacks and concludes with a forest fire and Dick Hollister's death.

3694. **Willard, Joshua.** *The Thorne Theatre mystery*. **New York: Phoenix Press, 1937. 255p.**

The show must go on despite three murders during the company's rehearsals in an Upstate New York theater. Members of the troupe participate in the usual romantic dalliances and flirtations and investigator Doc Glover sifts through intrigues to pinpoint the efficient killer.

3695. **[Willet, W.N.]** *Charles Vincent*; or, *The two clerks*. **A tale of commercial life. New York: Harper, 1839. 2v.**

Charles Vincent, of uncertain origin, is reared by the Wilmots, given an excellent education and is deemed a sober, hard-working young man. He and Richard Brown, a nephew of the Wilmots, are clerks in the 'counting house of Messrs. Wilmot & Co. ... of the City of New York.' Brown is a dandy with a deep dislike for Charles, primarily because of the Wilmots' daughter Clara's partiality for Charles. Accused of forgery Charles Vincent leaves the company, despite Mr. Wilmot's belief in his innocence, and seeks employement elsewhere in the city. The 'forgery' imputation makes that exceedingly difficult. Suspecting that Richard Brown may be the cause of his troubles, Charles, with the help of friends and a strange woman, Judith, learns of Brown's connection with a trio of criminals. At the same time Judith informs Charles that he is the long missing son (kidnapped in infancy) of wealthy Edward Aubrey. There is little doubt that Brown will receive an overdue comeuppance (in fact a rather grim one) and that Charles Vincent/Aubrey will be restored to his father and the good graces of all the Wilmots.

3696. **Williams, David L., 1939- .** *Second sight.* **New York: Simon & Schuster, 1977. 221p.**

"When Jennie drags unfaithful hubby Michael from the city to a country house [in 'Chesapequa', which in its heyday was a little Saratoga—a lake, big old hotels, country roads, mineral waters] once owned by a turn-of-the-century artist, boorish Michael is bored and watches TV. But Jennie's not bored because she finds some old, old sketches of a girl-in-white in the attic and has a dress made to match the sketch. And ... when Jennie puts on that old-timey dress and wears her hair 'piled atop her head' … she … gets headaches, has visions, and … goes a-time-travelin', happy to be back in 1899 again. Back in 1899—away from her husband and her shrink … Jennie dallies passionately with the artist but is terrified because she knows he'll be murdered (perhaps because of her—she's the girl in the sketch!) unless she can change the past"—Kirkus reviews.

3697. **Williams, Emily Coddington, b. 1876.** *Quest for love.* **New York: Macaulay, 1920. 320p.**

Against the background of New York City from 1860 to Theodore Roosevelt's presidency is told the story of Claudia Honey's 'quest for love' that stretched from her childhood until she attained the age of fifty-two; it was then after a bad marriage and a suddenly terminated affair of the heart that she finally found true love and bliss.

3698. **Williams, Francis Churchill, 1869-1945.** *J. Devlin—Boss*; a romance of **American politics. Illustrated by Clifford Carlton. Boston: Lothrop Pub. Co., 1901. 520p.**

Jimmy Devlin quickly worked his way up—bribery and ballot box stuffing were tools. As political boss of New York City he had two 'partners' whom he quietly eased out. He took pride, however, in the fact that his word could be trusted, and he was basically big-hearted. In Devlin's pocket were the city council, the 'Water Trust' and a number of State officials all of whom followed his suggestions. The time span of the novel is 1855 to 1880.

3699. **Williams, Henry Llewellyn, b. 1842.** *Gay life in New York*; or, *Fast men and grass widows.* **By an old traveler. New York: R.M. De Witt, 1866. 100p.**

Three Ohioans—Henry Harry Callow, Frank Dutton and Charlie Ross—come to New York City to enjoy its sights and sounds. The three outlanders are easy prey for the thieves, gamblers and confidence men and women who immediately flock around them. Charlie Ross is especially susceptible to the charms of a lovely lady, Blanche Merideth, who bemoans her ties to a brutish husband. Mr. Merideth accuses Charlie of alienation of affections and demands a payment of $5,000. Fortunately the three young men have become acquainted with a guide, John Winstone who, unknown to them, is really a detective. It is Winstone who pulls them out of their predicaments (notably Charlie's) and advises them on the pitfalls of the metropolis. The author contends that he has 'written it [the story] with a good motive, and if those who read it profit by the lessons it is intended to teach, our object will be served.'

3700. **[Williams, Henry Llewellyn] b. 1842.** *Rip Van Winkle*; or, *The sleep of twenty years.* **A legend of the Kaatskills. By the author of** *The reef, L'Africaine* **and and** *The ticket-of-leave man.* **New York: R.M. De Witt, 1866. 100p.**

Includes 'Hugh the Rover' and several other short pieces. Rip Van Winkle is well known in his Dutch Catskill village for his excessive tippling, a fact that does not please his wife, Gretchen, and their daughter, Meenie. The wily Derrick Von Beeckman wants Rip's land and tries to trick Rip into signing a deed conveying the property to him. Rip does not sign but holds onto the document. When Gretchen forces Rip to leave their cottage, he goes into the mountains; there he runs into the demonic revels of Henrick Hudson and his crew. Falling into a deep sleep Rip awakens 20 years later, in 1665. He returns to his village and notices some startling changes. Gretchen, assuming Rip is dead, has married Derrick Von Beeckman, and Meenie is being proposed to by Beeckman's nephew, Cockles. Quite sober now, Rip reclaims his wife, daughter and property; Beeckman and Cockles leave the area empty-handed. Meenie is able to marry her true love, Hendrick Vedder. Willliams' version of the Rip Van Winkle legend is one of several, the most famous of course being that of Washington Irving.

3701. ————. *The steel safe*; or, *The stains and splendors of New York life*. **A story of our day and night. New York: DeWitt, 1868. 100p. (in double columns).**

Prosper Roadhouse, chief cashier in the New York banking firm of Andrew Van Kieft, is assumed to be the thief who took $100,000 from the bank's steel safe. However, there is little evidence to support that conjecture and the two detectives on the case, Jacob ('Coon') Hall and Charles Newlife (a.k.a. Jehiel Sharpson, Clayton Palmer, et al.—he is a master of disguise)—poke around the city for more information. The two villains, Colonel Girard Haviland and Burnett Clanmoran, are the thorns in Prosper Roadhouse's side; Haviland is determined to snatch Prosper's fiancée, Viandra Oestervelt, for himself, while Clanmoran tries to implicate Prosper in the robbery and also disrupts the married life of the Van Kiefts. By the tale's end Sharpson/Newlife has leveled the playing field (Haviland and Clanmoran are identified as the robbers), Prosper and Viandra are married, and Colonel Haviland meets with a fatal accident in a foundry. Sometime later Prosper and Viandra learn that the detective Jehiel Sharpson was killed in the Battle of Fair Oaks (May 31, 1862).

3702. **Williams, Henry Smith, 1863-1943.** *The witness of the sun*. **Front. by C. Lotave. Garden City, N.Y.: Doubleday, Page, 1920. vi, 305p.**

"When John Theobold is killed in his office, someone has to be found to fasten the murder to, as is usual in such cases. The guilty man seems to be Señor Cortez, a fiery Brazilian, jealous of Theobold's interest in his wife, with Frank Crosby, the murdered man's private secretary, as his accomplice. The case comes to trial and the counsel for the defense springs a surprise. With the aid of Jack Henley, a bright office boy with an interest in photography, he presents proof, substantiated by actual pictures taken on the spot, showing that Cortez and Crosby could not have committed the crime, and who did and why. But all the surprises are not yet over; the counsel for the defense learns that no amount of circumstantial evidence ever proves anything; it only shows that things might have happened in some other way, and in this case they did"—Book review digest.

3703. **Williams, Jesse Lynch, 1871-1929.** *She knew she was right.* **New York: Scribner, 1930. 345p.**

"The principal character [in this story with a New York City locale] is [Hilda], a beautiful woman, and in the eyes of all, including her own, one of exemplary virtue and integrity. She is a woman of large affairs and supposedly of great executive ability. The power of the family centers in her. She has married a young journalist professor and it is a long time before he realizes her real significance and the hollowness of her virtue. She never realizes it. In her self-righteous effort to throw him over for another man, she rationalizes every step, but she is caught in the ecclesiastical technicalities, and, unable to see the spirit, she is thwarted by the letter. In contrast to this lady is her extremely charming secretary, Connie, the true heroine of the book"—Publisher's note.

3704. **Williams, John Alfred, 1925- .** *The Junior Bachelor Society.* **Garden City, N.Y.: Doubleday, 1976. 247p.**

A member of black athletes (former members of the Junior Bachelor Society) gather 30 years after their high school days in the industrial town not far from New York City where they grew up. Their old football coach and mentor, Chappie Davis, is about to turn 70, and they wish to honor him on that occasion. It is a varied group of individuals. Some of them put their roots down in the town: e.g., Shurley, secretive owner of the restaurant where the group first meets; Snake, now in a responsible position in the town's government; Bubbles and several other blue collars who work in the local foundry. Those who come from a distance include a teacher, an editor, a playwright, a concert artist—and Moon, a pimp running from the law. The men unite for one last time when one of them is threatened by a cop (and a black one at that).

Williams, Nathan Winslow, 1860-1924. See under his pseudonym: Dallas, Richard.

3705. **Williams, Valentine, 1883-1946.** *The clue of the rising moon.* **Boston: Houghton, Mifflin, 1935. 268p.**

Trevor Dene, an English detective on vacation, is nearby when the body of Vic Haversley, the millionaire brewer, is found in a trapper's cabin on the Lumsden estate/camp in the Adirondacks. Dene suspects Haversley has been murdered and local Sheriff Wells lets him do the sleuthing. Peter Blakeney, a playwright living in a shack on the Lumsden property, relates how Dene solved the crime.

3706. ————. *Masks off at midnight.* **New York: Houghton Mifflin, 1934. 266p.**

The crème de la crème of Long Island society attends the masked ball hosted by the Waverleys and is suitably horrified by some frightening happenings during the evening. "The interest of the story consists not only of the unraveling of the mystery itself, but in the clear presentation of a variety of characters and in the subtle skill with which the whole social atmosphere in this Long Island town is conveyed to us"—Saturday review of literature.

3707. **Williams, Wilbur Herschel, 1874-1935.** *The Merrymakers in New York*; the lively adventures of four young people. **Illustrated by John Goss. Boston: Page Co., 1919. 321p.**

> The title would suggest that this novel is about young people looking for a good time in the Big Apple. Actually it is a piece for a teenage audience that relates the experiences of the four youthful Merrymakers (the family name!) during the Christmas season in post-World War I New York. The four are orphans visiting an older brother, Ned, a reporter for one of the city's dailies. The significance of the book lies in its descriptions of various New York City landmarks of the period and boarding-house 'culture', a way of life that has long since faded away.

3708. **[Willis, John R.]** *Carleton*; a tale of seventeen hundred and seventy-six. **Philadelphia: Lea & Blanchard, 1841. 2v.**

> When the novel opens Lord Howe is poised on Long Island, preparing to invest New York City. Henry Carleton's sympathies are with the Americans; his stance incurs the displeasure of both his father and Hugh Stafford, father of the woman he loves, Alice Stafford. Carleton participates in a couple of patriot military actions, but does not join Washington's troops until his best friend, Captain H— (assuredly Nathan Hale) is sent to the gallows for spying on the British. Among the characters Henry Carleton has dealings with are: Richard Crawford, somewhat of a freebooter who is eventually revealed as Henry's uncle; the fiery patriot Captain Marriner; Julian Melville, a Tory and Henry's rival for Alice's hand; the comical Parson Peleg Strong; and the aforementioned Captain H—. Henry takes part as an American officer in the Battle of White Plains, is captured and escapes to the American lines. At the war's end he is reconciled with his father and Mr. Stafford accepts the inevitable—the marriage of Alice to Henry.

Willis, Kate, pseud. See: Coolidge, Sarah E.

3709. **Willmott, Nellie Lowe.** *A dash of red paint.* **New Haven: Press of the E.B. Sheldon Co., 1894. 86p.**

> The opening scenes take place in a quiet little town in Upstate New York, 'Lisle' (not to be confused with the actual village of Lisle in Broome County). George Ellsworth, a medical student and the only son of Major Ellsworth who has selected Lisle for his retirement, is attracted to Hetty Head, a farmer's daughter. Following a lawn party George has Hetty and her little brother Jamie in his carriage when the horses suddenly rear, the carriage tips over,

Jamie is killed, George and Hetty survive. Not long thereafter, Hetty leaves Lisle for Albany where her aunt pays Hetty's tuition at the Elmwood School. Several years go by; Hetty is in Lisle attending her mother's funeral; George, on the verge of proposing to her, is suddenly called away. It is only after Hetty is serving as a nurse in a disease-stricken foreign city that George finds her and their lives merge.

3710. **Willoughby, John.** *Crimsoned millions.* **New York: E.J. Clode, 1927. 319p.**
"Two murders, first that of a young millionairess [Helen Bogart], then that of her friend and physician, occurring in peaceful Captain's Haven, Long Island arouse the police of the district. … A Secret Service man, working as a spy against a dangerous gang of bootleggers, is falsely accused of the crimes, and escapes arrest by fleeing to New York. Here he secures the aid of Detective-Captain Viggiano, who, going at once to the scene of the homicides, takes charge of the investigation. … The plot from that point on is most elaborately constructed, its main factors being an eminent explorer, a retired district attorney, underworld thugs, forged wills, and a third murder"—Saturday review of literature.

3711. **Willson, Thomas Edgar, 1846-1901.** *It is the law*; **a story of marriage and divorce in New York. New York, Chicago: Belford, Clarke, 1887. 218p.**
The novel takes a rather detailed look at the laws of New York State governing marriage and divorce. Chief characters in the story are Mrs. Mabelle Smith, Dick Jones, her would-be lover, Nellie Carter, Dick's 27-year-old aunt, and William Smith, Mabelle's lawyer-husband. Dick suggests to Mabelle that they go to Illinois where she has obtained a divorce from her husband; there Dick and Mabelle can be married legally although the union will not be recognized in New York State. William Smith had been previously married to Jane Smith, but she disappeared for several years and he was granted the right to marry Mabelle—it is the law. Jane Smith reappears and creates mischief for the distressed William who is very much in love with Mabelle. The latter has studied the marriage and divorce laws of New York and, surpassing her husband in such knowledge, pulls him out of his quandary. Mabelle and William renew their marriage bond. Dick Jones, no longer of romantic interest to Mabelle, turns to Nellie, for Mabelle convinces him that his aunt is Dick's true love.

3712. **Wilson, David, 1818-1887.** *Life in Whitehall during the ship-fever times.* **Whitehall, N.Y.: Inglee & Tefft, 1900. 76p. (in double columns).**
Charles O'Leary, proprietor of the Shamrock Tavern, and his gang prey upon emigrants from Ireland who land in Whitehall. The emigrants' defender is Tom Bovee who thrashes the villains on several occasions. Young Englishman Richard Florence, a close relation of Philip Skeene (the Tory founder of Skeenesborough—later Whitehall) becomes aware of Bovee and falls in love with Kathleen O'Cormick, an emigrant. Kathleen's mother shows Florence a document signed by Kathleen's grandfather, a soldier in

Burgoyne's army that describes £1000 buried in the vicinity of Skeenesborough. Richard Florence and Barney O'Riley, a friend of Tom Bovee, unearth the treasure. Charles O'Leary, after a life of thievery and murder, sickens and dies. Tom is killed at Chapultepec during the Mexican War and his remains are transported to England where Richard and his wife Kathleen erect a monument to him.

3713. Wilson, Edmund, 1895-1972. *I thought of Daisy.* **New York: Scribner, 1929. 311p.**

"The reactions of a young man who comes to New York just after the [1st World] War and meets [bohemian] life, especially as typified by two girls: Daisy, a chorus girl, and Rita, a young poet. In some of the main characters may be seen likenesses to well-known members of New York's bohemian circles"—Book review digest. "The author moves easily from one atmosphere to another, relating Professor Grosbeak's abstractions, the sufferings of Dostoevsky, Daisy's wisecracks, Rita's poems, Hugo Bamman's dislike of almost everything and translating one into the terms of the others"—New York herald tribune books.

3714. Wilson, Grove, 1883-1954. *The monster of Snowden Hall.* **New York: Ives Washburn, 1932. 352p.**

Walter Neubahr, foster father of wealthy bachelor Roark Snowden, is found murdered near the entrance to Snowden Hall in Westchester County. There is no lack of strange suspects. Toad Zaisan, the monster of the title, is an 'ape-man', origin unknown. The housekeeper, Martha dies, and her husband Horace, the butler, disappears. Sigurd Bland, an anthropologist, snoops around. Chester Pagl, alias Cherna Pagerave, a psychopathic Slav, and a tyrannical woman named Cynthia play prominent roles. Before the story is over there are at least four bodies lying around and a plethora of terrifying events.

3715. ⸺. *Sport of the gods*; **a novel. New York: Frank-Maurice, 1926. 291p.**

"Jean Poussin is an impecunious doctor of uncertain origin. His wealthy and not over scrupulous rival for the hand of the fair Clarabel is Justin Carter. The plot plays battledore and shuttlecock between upper Fifth Avenue and Greenwich Village with Jean's star gradually but firmly in the ascendant. The rich villain passes out of the picture and the scene closes as the doctor, with the blot removed from his scutcheon, clasps the willing Clarabel to his heart"—Book review digest.

3716. Wilson, Sloan, 1920- . *Small town.* **New York: Arbor House, 1978. 514p.**

Ben Winslow fails to persuade his 17-year-old son Ebon to return to California with him, so he decides to stay in the Adirondack town of his birth, at least for a while. Ben is 45, a former photographer and reporter; this background comes in handy when he starts up a newspaper for the small community. A growing attraction to Rose, sister of his son's girlfriend (Ann) leads to the altar; tragedy intervenes when Rose's heart stops beating on her wedding day. Then Ben finds himself drawing ever closer to Ann, but he succeeds in mastering his passion. "A simple story, memorable chiefly for its lovingly detailed descriptions of the Adirondack countryside (Library journal).

3717. **Winslow, Pauline Glen.** *A cry in the city*. **New York: St. Martin's Press/ Dunne, 1990. 216p.**

A 36-year-old widow, Mary Christopher, departs her husband's Upstate family home in 'Burgoyne', New York for her apartment in Greenwich Village, presumably leaving her children in the care of Alice Christopher, her mother-in-law. When the latter fails to find the children in the expected place, she assumes they have accompanied Mary to New York City. The bodies of the children turn up a few weeks later, and bewildered, despairing Mary is blamed by the closed community of Burgoyne which has always looked upon her as an 'outsider.' Alice, victim of a stroke, is taken into the home of Boy Burgoyne, the town's social leader and his malevolent sister. Chief investigator Danny Valenti is certain of Mary's innocence and gets help from an unexpected source.

3718. **Winsor, Roy, 1912-1987.** *Three motives for murder*. **Greenwich, Conn.: Fawcett, 1976. 176p.**

Steve Barnes, a professor at Columbia University, comes across the corpse of his fiancée's brother Ned in her family's Westchester home, Pelham Manor. Ned was a scoundrel and there was no shortage of people (even his own mother) with motives for doing him in—permanently. Blackmail and a vendetta are mixed into the plot; however the author fails to elicit much interest in the story he tells, in part because of his maladroit writing.

3719. **Winthrop, Theodore, 1828-1861.** *Cecil Dreeme*. **Boston: Ticknor and Fields, 1861. 360p.**

The novel is set in New York City with places like 'Chuzzlewit Hotel' and 'Chrysalis College' masking real locales in the city (Washington Square, e.g.). Cecil Dreeme is an artist with whom Robert Byng, the hero, becomes friendly. Byng also keeps running into a man named Densdeth, a villain who exerts influence over Emma Denman, the woman Byng loves. In quick succession Densdeth kidnaps Dreeme, Emma commits suicide and a former cohort murders Densdeth. Dreeme is rescued from the asylum in which Densdeth placed him. But Dreeme, it turns out, is no man, but rather Clara Denman, Emma's sister. There is a cogent explanation for her disguise and her future with Byng.

3720. ————. *Edwin Brothertoft*. **Boston: Ticknor and Fields, 1862. 369p.**

Brothertoft Manor in the Hudson Highlands is the scene of most of the action in this novel of colonial and Revolutionary New York State. Mild, honorable Edwin Brothertoft marries the ambitious, unscrupulous Jane Billop, daughter of the man who had sealed the fiscal doom of the ancient Brothertoft family. Their differences lead to separation; under a pseudonym Edwin joins the American army while wife Jane retains the manor and entertains British officers. Lucy, daughter of Edwin and Jane, is forced by her mother to contemplate marriage to the bilious British Major Kerr. Peter Skerett, aide-de-camp of General George Washington, heads a plan to capture Major Kerr and incidentally reunite Lucy with her father. The carrying out of this mission results in tragic consequences for Jane Brothertoft and Brothertoft Manor. Historical characters who appear in the novel include: Washington, Israel Putnam, Major John André, William Lord Howe, Colonel Andreas von Emmerich, et al. The British campaign in the Hudson Highlands in 1777 and the failed American response are described (all preliminary to Burgoyne's invasion).

3721. **Wister, Owen, 1860-1938.** *Mother.* **Illus. and decorations by John Rae. New York: Dodd, Mead, 1907. 95p.**

Richard Field is a '600 dollar clerk' when he falls in love with Ethel Lansing, daughter of a wealthy man. When he inherits a fortune from a relative, Richard decides to increase it by investing in the stock market, thereby impressing his fiancée. He falls into the hands of a shifty Wall Street broker, Mr. Beverly, who persuades Richard to put more and more money into stocks that Beverly claims he has put his mother onto. Ethel cautions Richard to be more circumspect, but Richard is unheedful and ultimately loses a major portion of his inheritance. Ethel and Richard learn that Beverly's mother has been dead for 15 years. Later Ethel sells some land in Michigan to Beverly for $700,000. The copper on that land that drew Beverly to make the purchase turns out to be worth much less than his purchase price.

3722. *The witch-woman's revenge*; or, *The golden secret of the 'Oswego'.* **By J. McOswego, N.Y.: R.J. Oliphant, Book & Job Printer, 1882. 16p.**

Annawau, the Onondagan witch-woman, mother of Winona, seeks revenge for the slaying of her husband Kaleh by Monada, chief of the Swa-geh. The latter is father of Winona's lover, Wanketo. Casting her spell Annawau gleefully watches as the Swa-geh are decimated by disease (actually malaria). A bolt of lightning kills the witch-woman; Winona, possessing knowledge of medicinal herbs, brews a liquid that terminates the epidemic. She and Wanketo are married. Years later, according to this peculiar little piece, the herbs that Winona gathered on the banks of the Oswego River are the basis of Austen's Swa-geh Remedy and Cure-All.

Witt, Julia A. Woodhull de, d.1906. See: De Witt, Julia A. Woodhull, d.1906.

3723. **Witten, Barbara Yager.** *The Isle of Fire murder.* **New York: Walker, 1987. 204p.**

Lily Lambert, a widow, has time on her hands and investigative talents that she puts to good use when a popular swimming coach in a Fire Island colony of twenty-two families is murdered. Why that particular individual has been struck down is the puzzle that Lily must solve, and Fair Harbor is one of the communities that bears looking into.

3723a. Witten, Matthew. *Grand illusion.* **New York: NAL Books, 1999. 256p.**
Jake Burns, a resident of Saratoga Springs, N.Y., has recently won a million dollars for a screenplay, but his chief concern for the nonce is the influx of drug dealers into his neighborhood. Any improvement in the situation is inhibited by corruption in the local police force. The shooting of Pop Doyle, one of the crooked cops, is attributed to Jake; after his release on bond Jake digs around, hampered though he may be by politicians and 'on-the-take' officials.

3724. Witwer, Harry Charles, 1890-1929. *Alex the Great.* **Illustrated by Arthur William Brown. Boston: Small, Maynard, 1919. 313p.**
Country bumpkin Alexander Hanley leaves a Vermont farm to make his mark in New York City. With luck and brash self-confidence Alex achieves, among other things, a fairly good job, rewarding acquaintances with a millionaire and a famous film star and marriage to a beautiful young woman. He also helps several failures find success. His cousin's husband, Joe, relates the humorous tale.

3725. ————. *Bill Grimm's progress.* **New York: Putnam, 1926. v, 336p.**
"Bill Grimm's progress was from taxi-driving in 'Fairfax Falls', N.Y., to taxi-driving in New York City. From this to the prize fighting ring as a contender for the championship was the next step, and into the moving pictures was for Bill only a short distance further. All the way along he was helped by Barbara Baxter, his winsome revenue agent ladylove, and hampered by Jack Fairfax, a villain of old-time thoroughness. Bill tells his own story with the customary Witwer gusto and humor"—Book review digest.

3726. ————. *There's no base like home.* **Illustrated by Arthur William Brown. Garden City, N.Y.: Doubleday, Page, 1920. 284p.**
"A combination of baseball and the movies. Ed Harmon, 'the undisputed monarch of the diamon', continues the series of letters to his friend Joe, and tells what happened after he brought his French wife, Jeanne, to New York. Jeanne not only learns English; she [also] undertakes to teach that language to her husband. She … goes into the movies and drags her reluctant husband with her. Jeanne's relatives come from France to pay a surprise visit, but as suddenly return, inspiring their son-in-law to give three cheers for prohibition"—Book review digest.

3727. Wodehouse, Pelham Grenville, 1881-1975. *Piccadilly Jim.* **Illus. by May Wilson Preston. New York: Dodd, Mead, 1917. 363p.**
James (Jimmy) Crocker had been a hard-working reporter for the New York Chronicle when he was yanked off to London by his wealthy stepmother.

There he had a leisurely existence until he got into a fistfight with Lord Percy Whipple and decided to go back to New York. Crocker's New York roots are reestablished, but he begins to fall for Ann Chester, niece of Peter Pett who had married Crocker's stepmother's sister. It was Ann who had described Jimmy Crocker as 'a perfect, utter, hopeless worm.' Ann herself is described as a girl who 'combined every charm of mind and body with a resolute determination to raise Cain at the slightest provocation', and therefore an ideal partner for Jimmy.

3728. —————. *Psmith, journalist.* **Containing twelve full-page illus. from drawings by T.M.R. Whitwell. London: A. & C. Black, 1915. viii, 247p.**

"Psmith, tired of the monotony of a student's life at Cambridge [England], spends his long vacation by coming to New York. He hopes to find adventure, and when he meets Billy Windsor of Wyoming, acting editor of Cozy Moments, he is on the trail. Psmith sees a group of crowded, filthy tenements and suggests that Windsor change the policy of his paper while the boss is away, and get after the owner of the property. The suggestion is adopted and its carrying out leads to about 100 pages of ambushes and hairbreadth escapes, at the end of which the owner of the tenements pays Psmith $5,000 with which to remodel them, and Psmith, who in the meantime has bought Cozy Moments, restores it to its pristine cosiness. At the end of the book he is dozing in his room at Cambridge"—Springfield Republican.

3729. —————. *The small bachelor.* **New York: Doran, 1927. 317p.**

"George Finch was a [New York] bachelor very well-fixed and comfortably aware of it until he met Molly Waddington in the street one day and promptly lost his head and heart and no time in getting acquainted. Molly had no objections to George—on the contrary—but her mother hoped for a lord at least, as her future son-in-law. George was not to be outdone by a lord. The author provides for him in his wooing of Molly a full program of diverting complications"—Book review digest.

3730. **Wohlforth, Robert, 1904- .** *Tin soldiers*; **a novel. New York: A.H. King, 1934. 346p.**

An 'informative study', although a fictional one, of how several young men fare as cadets at the United States Military Academy (West Point). John Alvin, fresh from Princeton, is perhaps a good example of the 'norm'; Art Banks is an imaginative intellectual who wanders off limits by falling in love with an officer's wife; Cedric Bradley, heir of a military tradition, lacks backbone, the 'right stuff'. Dok Cipriano is the odd man out—he comes from the coal region of Altoona, Pennsylvania, his family recent immigrants, and he has dug coal himself; Cipriano adapts easily and most successfully to the demands of the Academy.

3731. **Wolfert, Jerry.** *Brother of the wind*; **a story of the Niagara frontier. New York: John Day Co., 1960. 253p.**

The adolescent Oliver is homeless and he and a companion traverse the Niagara frontier; the latter is killed when their boat is wrecked on Goat Island in the Niagara River. It is the period when the Erie Canal was under construction and Oliver must now find employment—which he does as a keelboat man on the river and canal.

3732. Wolff, Geoffrey, 1937- . *The age of consent.* **New York: Knopf; distributed by Random House, 1994. 226p.**

'Doc' Halliday founded Blackberry Mountain in the Adirondacks in the 1960s as a place for young people fleeing from materialism and conservatism of their elders and American society in general. Ann and Jinx Jenks and their children, Maisie and Ted, are devoted followers of the magnetic Doc until Maisie, only 15, leaps to her death one July 4th; the Jenks's idyll is shattered by the suicide and even further impaired by the revelation that self-centered Doc has violated a number of young women and girls, Maisie among them. The long-term residents, the 'natives' of the area probably felt confirmed in their low opinion of Blackberry Mountain and its inhabitants.

3733. Wolff, William Almon, 1885-1933. *Manhattan night.* **New York: Minton, Balch, 1930. 252p.**

"All about the shooting of Tack Thayer, a dipsomaniacal Yale man, and the subsequent activities of the New York police and Peter Wrayne, a friend of … [Thayer's] widow, in unraveling a trying coil of ups, downs and sideways. The tale is marred by the peculiarities of the leading personae, probably members of the upper bourgeoisie, especially Dr. Meyer Zahn, a psychoanalyst who seems to have lost his mind since studying with Freud. Among the ingredients stirred and served with a decidedly amateur touch are roughneck cops, a night club and a few underworld characters"—New York herald tribune books.

3734. Wolfson, Victor, 1910-1990. *The eagle on the plain*; a novel. **New York: Simon and Schuster, 1947. 248p.**

'Plutarchus' is a small village in the Catskills that flounders further into decline when a modern concrete highway bypasses it. Poggi Brenero is the one person in Plutarchus who asserts his individuality and tries to counter the village's hopelessness, but his efforts are dampened when he and his father are charged with operating an illegal whiskey still. However, he has given the villagers a dash of spirit and vitality.

3735. Wonderly, William Carey, b. 1885 or 90. *The world to live in.* **New York: Moffat, Yard, 1919. 361p.**

Rita is a stenographer by day who boards at a house on New York's 23rd Street, and at night is attractive enough to find dining-out partners among well-to-do and socially prominent men. Her goal, of course, is to marry one of them, it doesn't matter which one, and partake of a carefree if entirely selfish existence. A young clergyman waiting patiently in the wings brings about Rita's conversion to responsibility and true love.

3736. **Wood, Bari, 1936- .** *Doll's eyes.* **New York: Morrow, 1993. 303p.**

Eve Klein is separated from her husband who is weary of her too frequent use of psychic powers that enable her to see into the future of those people she touches. Hoping for a compromise and reunion Eve traces her husband to a cottage on an Adirondack lake. The dwelling has a dark past; it is where a young boy was tortured and cast aside several decades ago. Eve begins picturing in her mind's eye this youth, now grown to adulthood and a sadistic serial killer of women. The local police involve her further in their pursuit of the murderer and she is soon aware that he intends to slay her.

Wood, Charlotte Dunning, b. 1858. See under her pseudonym: Dunning, Charlotte, b. 1858.

3737. **Wood, Clement, 1888-1950.** *Other men's wives,* **by Alan Dubois [pseud.]. New York: W. Godwin, 1933. 272p.**

Two aspects of marriage, faithfulness and infidelity, are explored in this novel laid in a Westchester County village, 'Woods Ferry.' Larry Dorsey has a nervous breakdown and is ordered by his doctor to 'retire, live naturally in the country' with his wife Madeline and their two children, Bets and Paul. After 15 years of almost complete fidelity Larry suddenly awakens to the desirability of several neglected wives in his new community. Once he starts on these sexual encounters he cannot stop until his faithful wife confronts him with proof of his philandering. Larry's denials are useless and he finally realizes that Madeline and the children are of overriding importance to him and that he must relinquish his amorous adventuring to regain their love.

3738. —————. *The tabloid murders*; **mystery story in startling new technique. New York: Macaulay Co., 1930. 286p.**

Millionaire Eric Vant and his wife and son are victims of a murderer who entered their Westchester home to commit his gruesome deed. A short while later, Olga Bearn, a beauty contest winner (Eric Vant had been one of the judges) is also slain. The author tells the story as if he were covering it for tabloids.

3739. **Wood, Clement Biddle, 1925-1994.** *Ocean vu, jog to beach*; **a novel. New York: St. Martin's Press, 1988. ix, 308p.**

Vladimer Ouspenskiy, Russian émigré poet and amateur sociologist, reports the activities of 'yuppie' acquaintances who rent a house for the summer on Long Island. Among them are: Clive Wheelwright, a Wall Street lawyer and his fiancée, Moira Fairchild; Dreda Scott, an Afro-American with commodity market talents; Stu Stuart, a Sports Illustrated reporter; and Catherine, Moira's sister, novelist in the making who drags along a couple of ex-footballers. Although these summer visitors, away from their usual metropolitan surroundings, behave rather strangely in Ouspenskiy's eyes, he does find grounds for sympathizing with and caring about them, all stereotypes aside.

3740. **Wood, John Seymour, 1853-1935.** *Gramercy Park*; **a story of New York. New York: Appleton, 1892. 218p.**

"A story of the life of a young Wall Street broker whose wife is ordered to the mountains in summer and to Florida in the winter; the wife's father and mother, old-fashioned residents of Gramercy Park, represent the real, honest life that built up American cities, the younger generation the weak imitation of foreign customs that is sapping the strength and morality of modern home life"—Annual American catalogue.

3741. **Woodrow, Nancy Mann Waddel, 1875?-1935.** *The beauty.* **With illus. by Will Grefé. Indianapolis: Bobbs-Merrill, 1910. 322p.**

Story of a New York couple whose marriage teeters on the brink because the husband fails to appreciate his wife's true value and capabilities. She is a beautiful and rather lonely Southern girl of meager means; he is a wealthy bachelor who plies her with luxuries before and after they wed, but they are of little interest to her. The two separate amicably and she startles the New York social circle she belonged to by virtue of her marriage by becoming a clothing designer. Her success wins the respect of her husband who now looks beyond her personal beauty to her intelligence and very human qualities.

3742. ————. *Swallowed up.* **New York: Brentano's, 1922. 320p.**

Hope Ranger is the fetching, beautiful daughter of wealthy parents meeting friends for luncheon at the Plaza Hotel in New York City; as she steps out on Fifth Avenue she does a disappearing act. In reality she has been kidnapped by a master criminal, the leader of a 'combine', and taken to an institution that treats people with moderate mental problems. The story focuses on her ordeal and on the plans of the criminal conspiracy to divest Hope's father of his fortune.

Woodrow, Mrs. Wilson, 1875?-1935. See: Woodrow, Nancy Mann Waddel, 1875?-1935.

3743. **Woods, Alice, b. 1871.** *A gingham rose.* **With a front. by the author. Indianapolis: Bobbs-Merrill, 1904. 381p.**

The heroine, Anne, is attending the New York Art School together with two young men, John Warren who is attracted to her, and Victor Stetson who is in love with her. After art school Anne has to earn a living and turns to the writing of short stories that are not a huge success. Victor becomes an art editor of a Chicago paper while John caters to popular tastes with fanciful drawings of the occult. When Victor contracts tuberculosis compassionate Anne agrees to marry him; John meanwhile has married a wealthy but dull young woman. Then John discovers he really loves Anne and the author has to untangle the complications that ensue in order to provide the expected happy ending.

3744. **Woolley, Edward Mott, 1867-1947.** *The cub reporter.* **With illus. by Arthur Hutchins. New York: Stokes, 1913. vii, 255p.**

"A stirring newspaper story in which fires, riots and other exciting incidents figure. Dent Lockwood's struggle to make good on the New York Morning Sentinel is an uphill one. Inexperience and some pretty bad luck succeed in defeating him, but pluck and perseverance triumph in the end, and after some severe rebuffs we leave him graduated from a 'cub' to a member of the regular staff"—Boston transcript.

3745. **————.** *Donald Kirk, the Morning Record copy boy.* **With illus. by George Varian. Boston: Little, Brown, 1912. 273p.**

A book aimed at teen-age readers but one that provides a good description of life in a New York City newspaper room and the reporters' beats round and about the metropolis. Donald Kirk is just starting his job as a copy boy (he carries the reporters' copy and runs errands for them) and is quickly taken under the wing of reporter Ordway. His progress is impeded by another copy boy, Felix Grompe, who, together with an irresponsible newsman, Duff, is able to pin the blame on Donald for leaking a prime story to a rival newspaper. Discharged, Donald finds employment in a railroad office and moves back into favor on the Morning Record by chronicling the events around a flood that engulfs the city of 'Parkstown.' An earlier assignment had Donald accompanying Ordway to Tuxedo [Park] from which point Donald made a heroic dash to the telegraph office in Ramapo with copy given him by Ordway.

3746. **Woolley, Lazelle Thayer, b. 1872.** *Faith Palmer in New York.* **Illustrated by Paula B. Himmelsbach. Philadelphia: Penn Pub. Co., 1914. 335p.**

Completing a year in an upscale boarding school Faith Palmer goes to New York City with her elderly aunts. They rent an apartment; the country-bred aunts are introduced to the bustle of urban life while Faith studies home economics. The aunts are stoic in their confrontation with the metropolis and Faith has enough time on her hands to form friendships—notably with a girl who lives in the same apartment house, another with a salesgirl in the glove department of a huge store.

3747. **Woolrich, Cornell, 1903-1968.** *Cover charge.* **New York: Boni & Liveright, 1926, 286p.**

"Alan Walker, lounge lizard from Park Avenue, is tired of the old ties and he flees from the monotony of the drawing rooms to the variety of a noisy dance floor. He becomes a gigolo, a paid dancing partner. Veronica, out of a Ninth Avenue flat, is also bored. She runs away, is seduced, browbeaten, cast away. She comes back. Armistice Day on 34th Street, Alan and Veronica. Alan Walker and 'Vera' Daugherty, dancers. Fame and money. South America.

Georgine. Alan and Georgine. Back to New York. Alan, Georgine, Vera, triangle. A wild, wild auto ride and debacle"—New York world.

3748. ————. *Times Square*. **New York: Liveright, 1929. 274p.**

"Concerning the life and frequent loves of a boy and girl on Broadway. The girl is a dance hall hostess. The boy falls in love with her when she is injured in the dance hall, and he takes her home and looks after her. They take an apartment together, but she leaves him to become the mistress of a rich man, and he marries another girl. The Times Square section in which they live and love is as much a part of their story as the events which take place in it"— Book review digest.

Worth, Ellis, pseud. See: Ellsworth, Louise C.

3749. **Worth, Marc, pseud.** *Walls of fire.* **New York: Cosmopolitan Pub. Co., 1925. 272p.**

The novel presents the contrasting and sometimes conflicting worlds of Jews and gentiles in New York City. The Jew Daniel Lawrence is an individual who has been greatly influenced by heredity and environment but has fashioned his own strong personal characteristics. Some of the author's minor characters are especially memorable and his portrayal of New York ghetto life rings true.

3750. **Worthington, Marjorie Muir, 1898 or 1900-1976. New York: J. Cape & H. Smith, 1930. 263p.**

"Hedwig Mendelsohn, shrewd, tyrannical and gluttonous, has built up her own millinery business in New York. But her sons turn out to be untrustworthy weaklings, and her unattractive daughter Dora marries Max Bikof who had wanted to be a doctor and failed. Hedwig tries to mold him to her business when she is stricken bedfast with a lingering heart disease. Max, nagged on by Dora and his malicious mother-in-law, makes a surprising success of the business in which he is by nature a misfit. Hedwig, intolerant and despising her weak, grasping children, dominates their lives up to her death. Only Miriam, Bikof's youngest daughter, saves her soul from the wreckage"—Book review digest.

3751. **Worts, George Frank, b. 1892.** *The blue lacquered box.* **New York: H.C. Kinsey, 1939. 309p.**

"William Boone, [the] mystery man at [the] Manhasset [Long Island] mansion [owned by Rodney Barnett, is] accused of killing his valet. [A] blackmailing maid [is] later slain, making [the whole thing just that much more puzzling. This is a] society melodrama with romantic trimmings, wrongful and rightful heirs, glamorous background, [a] plainly visible criminal and virtue triumphant"—Saturday review of literature.

3752. **Wright, H.W.** *Running for the exit.* **San Francisco: Strawberry Hill Press;**

Harrisburg, Pa.: Distributed by Stackpole Books, 1979. 152p.

The Oliphants have been accustomed to spending part of their summers at the Scotch Lake Hotel in the Adirondacks. Their son Ned is 10 years old in 1922 and it is through his observations that the other summer visitors and the authoritative Mrs. Hatch, the hotel's owner, come to life. When Mrs. Oliphant mentions bypassing Scotch Lake the following summer and going to Europe, Ned is disconsolate. Unfortunately the hotel burns down in the spring of 1923. Twenty-seven years later Ned takes a trip to the site of the Scotch Lake Hotel; there are few evidences that a huge building once stood there, but Ned's memory recalls graphic events of those long-ago summers.

3753. **Wright, Julia McNair, 1840-1903.** *The corner stall*; a New York story. **Boston: H. Hoyt [1868]. 257p.**

As a novelist Wright is really a propagandist for Christianity and temperance. Her heroes and heroines are invariably imbued with the Christian gospel and seek to lighten the burdens of the underclass. In this novel Wright's chief character is Thomas Twigg, a humble 'pieman' and proprietor of a corner food stall on Union Square. Twigg's mentor is the Rev. Mr. Allston who is presently tutoring the almost illiterate shopkeeper. As Twigg absorbs the words of the Gospel he begins to apply their lessons to the slum dwellers around him. Among those he nurtures are: Maggie Dodd, a child of six forced to sell little picks on the street; her drunken father George Dodd; Jerry Hockney ('Ratty') who prowls the wharves in search of sustenance; Paddy McClure, a brawling Irishman from a particularly offensive slum, Joy Alley; and Twigg's 'business partner', the skeptical Becky Killigan. When a priest attempts to bring Becky back to her earlier Catholic roots, she rejects him and finally accepts Thomas Twigg's simple Christian precepts. The Rev. Mr. Allston and several of his upper class parishioners play a smaller role in bettering the lives of the poor.

3754. ————. *Firebrands*; a temperance tale. **New York: National Temperance Society and Pub. House, 1879. 357p.**

The novel is set in western New York State. The protagonist is a young man who strays from the path of righteousness and ends up another victim of the intemperate use of alcoholic drink.

Wright, Julia MacNair, 1840-1903. *The making of a man.* **See note under Item #3760.**

3755. ————. *Mr. Grosvenor's daughter.* A story of city life. **New York: American Tract Society, 1893. 384p.**

"After experiencing a life of luxury with the many favorable conditions which attend great wealth, Deborah Grosvenor is compelled by reverses to exchange 'the pomp of Dives for the poverty of Lazarus'—in brief to experience the life of a working girl in a great city [New York is the model]. Her way of adapting herself to her changed circumstances is the theme of the story"—Annual

American catalogue. Actually living in the slums moves Deborah to works of Christian charity; the story concludes with the restoration of her presumably 'lost' fortune.

3756. ————. *A new samaritan.* **The story of an heiress. New York: American Tract Society, 1985. 317p.**

"Describes ... a scheme of Persis Thrale, the heiress, for bettering the condition of the poor. Her plan includes aid to men, women and children, and finds full illustration in a story which presents several phases of life in a large city [of the New York type]"—Annual American catalogue.

3757. ————. *The New Yorkbible-woman.* **Philadelphia: Presbyterian Publication Committee; New York: A.D.F. Randolph, 1869. 279p.**

In the neighborhood of Broome and Sullivan Streets in New York City two seamstresses, Mary Ware (a widow) and Prussia (Prussy) Wiggins share living quarters. Mary, filled with Christian charity, is ever attentive to needs of her neighbors, in particular Margaret Wishalow and her five children. The rather helpless (and useless) Mrs. Wishalow has just suffered the loss of her husband Patrick by drowning. Well-to-do Agnes Warren looks in on the Wishalows (Margaret had served her mother) and is appalled by their circumstances, but she also has the opportunity to observe the good works of Mary Ware. Mrs. Warren provides financial support for Mary to carry on a full-time mission to the poor of New York City, always with her Bible in hand. Late in the novel we meet Mary's alcohol-sodden son, Richard. He finally takes 'the pledge' after attending an inspiring temperance lecture. Patronized by Judge Warren, Richard wins a policeman's badge. Other contributors assure the continuance of Mary's calling; her son is now a very present comfort and ally.

3758. ————. *The New York needle-woman*; or, *Elsie's stars.* **By the author of** *The shoe binders of New York* **... & c., & c. Philadelphia: Presbyterian Board of Publication, 1868. 254p.**

Hard-working Dan'el Hart, his alcoholic, abusive wife and their four children, Rhoda, Jane, Matthew and baby Jack live in an abysmal attic room on Cherry Street. Also sharing that room are the criminal Michael Hoffer and his slovenly daughter Charlotte. The 'needlewoman', Elsie Ray, despite her limited resources, decides she must help the Hart family. With the timely assistance of Sophie Randall, a young lady of means, Elsie feeds the bodies and especially the souls of the Harts. The task is made easier when the habitually drunken Abigail Hart, mother of the brood, dies after she falls down the stairs; Baby Jack dies in the same accident. As the years go by the Hart children enjoy varying degrees of success. However, perhaps Elsie Ray's greatest achievement is her conversion of the hitherto 'lost' Charlotte Hoffer into a productive, caring Christian young woman who keeps long watch over the dying father who had been so cruel in her early years.

3759. —————. *The shoe binders of New York*; or, *The fields white to the harvest.* **Philadelphia: Presbyterian Publication Committee; New York: S.D.F. Randolph, 1867. 237p.**

> Several years prior to the Civil War "in the sinks and dens of the city [of New York] with its misery and vice May comes hot-breathed and enervating, raising hot garrets to a fever-heat and making dismal cellars more odious with suffocating smells" (p.[7]-8). Into that environment comes well-off Miriam Elliott with a helping hand for two sisters, Ruth and Lettie; their father is in prison. The girls live in a squalid room with their often-inebriated Aunt Nab Wool. Ruth and Aunt Nab earn a pittance by 'binding' shoes (sewing uppers to the soles?); deaf and dumb Lettie peddles odd items on the street. Miriam introduces Ruth and Lettie to mission Sunday-School and enlists her dressmaker, Cousin Becky, in the Christian effort. One day Ruth runs off to take care of her father, a prison escapee. She leaves Lettie in Miriam's hands. Eventually Ruth and her dying father return to the city from their country hiding-places. He expires and is buried in Potter's Field. Ruth is forgiven for her absence. The Civil War comes and goes and Ruth takes up dressmaking under the tutelage of Cousin Becky. Ben Wool, a war veteran, appears, searching for his long-lost wife, Nab. At the novel's conclusion Ruth, Lettie, Aunt Nab and Ben are "dwelling together in the fear of God, working honestly for daily bread and clothing" (p.236).

3760. —————. *The story of Rasmus*; or, *The making of a man.* **New York: National Temperance Society and Pub. House, 1886. 326p.**

> A child of the slums of New York, Rasmus witnessed the slide of his father, a stonemason, into debilitating alcoholism; the demise of both parents (his grief-stricken mother followed her husband to an early grave) left Rasmus responsible for the nurture of Robin, his younger brother. When Robin is hospitalized after an accident, Rasmus loses touch with him; a long, wearisome but determined search is rewarded with the recovery of his missing sibling. Also published under the title: *The making of a man*; the story of Rasmus.

3761. Wright, Mabel Osgood, 1859-1934. *Aunt Jimmy's will.* **Illustrated by Florence Scovell Shinn. New York: Macmillan, 1903. ix, 272p.**

> Orphaned by the death of her artist father who had lived with her in a rural setting, Bird O'More is taken by her father's half-brother to New York City and placed with unsympathetic people. Bird does derive some pleasure from an association with a young cripple. She escapes from the relatively unfriendly urban environment by virtue of her Aunt Jimmy's will and an intriguing pewter teapot and its contents. Back to the countryside and to her friends there goes Bird possessing certain skills in drawing that she expects to improve upon.

3762. —————. *People of the whirlpool from the experience book of a commuter's wife.* **New York: Macmillan, 1903. ix, 365p.**

"The title ... alludes to a colony of New York society people who built suburban residences somewhere in sight from 'the garden of the commuter's wife.' And thus they brought the evidences of the wicked world and of their own foolish ambitions under the observations of a lady who had already practiced keeping a diary of her own and now kept one in which she recorded the shortcomings of her rich neighbors. ... According to the 'commuter's wife' these people of the whirlpool, with the energy of selfishness, become a distinctly new kind of vandal, unspiritually and practically bent upon their own pleasure at the expense of nature and righteousness. ... They are spiritually decadent, just as the poor are physically decadent. ... We catch a fragrant breath from her garden when she [the 'commuter's wife'] opens the attic window to observe the wicked extravagances of her wealthy neighbor"— The independent.

3763. **Wright, Mason, b. 1895. *Murder on Polopel*, by Mason Wright and William R. Kane. Garden City, N.Y.: Published for the Crime Club by Doubleday, Doran, 1929. 287p.**
Quimper, the detective, delves into a 10-year-old mystery, the disappearance of Nora Fane, a New York debutante; the scene of his investigation is a millionaire's castle on an island, 'Polopel', in the Hudson River.

3764. **Wright, T. J., 1947- . *The island*. New York: TOR, 1988. 278p.**
'Many Pines' is a run-down resort in the Adirondacks and the people associated with it are haunted by the undead souls trapped at the bottom of a nearby lake for 10 years. The widowed owner of Many Pines, Arnaut Berge, is a good-natured man whose wife had drowned in that lake several years ago; Lynnette Meyer's husband had met the same fate. These two lonely people and other characters in the novel drift aimlessly and become prime candidates for the summons to extinction given by the lake bottom's half-dead beings.

3765. **————. *The school*. New York: Tom Doherty Associates, 1990. 245p.**
Following the accidental death of their son Joey, Frank and Allison Hitchcock purchase an old schoolhouse in the Finger Lakes region of Upstate New York. They move into the building with plans for its renovation but learn that a teacher and four children who died of food poisoning are haunting presences in it. Frank and Allison experience visions of Joey and the recollections of their own youthful school days. Ominous things happen to the structure— windows break, foundations crack, and evidences of vandalism multiply. There is no cessation in the appearance of ghostly figures. The story includes extracts from Allison's own novel about people visited by ghosts of their former selves.

3766. **————. *Strange seed*; a novel. New York: Everest House, 1978. 236p.**
In this horror tale Rachel and Paul Griffin leave noisome New York City for the comparative isolation of the countryside in southeastern New York State. A secluded neighbor, Lumas, who later dies mysteriously, abets their

adaptation to rural life. Then the Griffins' solitude is broken by the appearance of several naked, wild, child-like beings from the nearby forest. The Griffins try to domesticate one of them, a boy, whom another neighbor, Hank, tries to strangle; Hank himself meets death. When the Griffins decide it is best to leave the area, they do not go far. A portentous fate awaits them as they return to the country house.

Wright, Willard Huntington, 1888-1939. See under his pseudonym: Van Dine, S.S., 1888-1939.

3767. **Wylie, Philip, 1902-1971.** *Babes and sucklings.* **New York: Knopf, 1929. 300p.**
The author peoples his novel with several New Yorkers, primarily denizens of Greenwich Village; among them are: Michael, an artistic loner with an imposing physique who died before he could achieve anything noteworthy; Thornton, contemptuous of the everyday world; Cynthia, fleeing from California and a husband, a statuesque and level-headed lady who takes Thornton as her lover; Gerry, sexually alluring but cold; Nadine, outgoing, passionate yet resigned to whatever fate offers her; and Aurelius, spinner of tales of exaggerated adventures, but with the heart of an angel.

3768. —————. *Corpses at Indian Stones.* **New York: Farrar & Rinehart, 1943. 282p.**
Nearby a country estate in Upstate New York two murders occur. Archaeologist Agamemnon Telemachus Plum adopts the stance of investigator and eventually arrives at the solution of the crimes. Meanwhile his Aunts Sarah and Aggie are acting as matchmakers, pushing Agamemnon in the path of Beth Calder; Danielle Davis, a woman of mystery, also arouses his interest.

3769. **[Yardley, Jane Woolsey].** *A superior woman.* **Boston: Roberts Bros., 1888. 348p.**
"The scene is laid in the City of New York and its environs, and the fact that there is no exhaustive study of the fashionable life of that city is one which calls for grateful praise" (Griswold, W.M. *Descriptive lists of American, international, romantic and British novels*). Rosamond Leigh, cousin of Richard Thorne, loses her patrimony because of bad investments by her broker and supports herself as a governess and teacher. Richard, a bachelor who worshiped his recently deceased mother, would marry if only he could find 'a superior woman,' one almost the equal of his mother. Rosamond accepts spinsterhood as time passes in the countryside and in New York City (which she finds rather stifling after a while). It only remains for Richard and Rosamond to rediscover one another—for Richard to realize that Rosamond is the superior (or even 'supreme') woman for whom he has been searching. The novel itself may be considered a 'superior' portrait of bourgeois New York life.

3770. **Yates, Richard, 1926- . *Cold Spring Harbor*. New York: Dalacorte Press, S. Lawrence, 1986. 182p.**

The author has chosen Cold Spring Harbor, a town on the North Shore of Long Island, as the scene of his story. The period is the time just before and after Pearl Harbor. His characters are not tourists and summer people, but rather permanent residents who are an unhappy lot. Their lives are dull, trite, angrily disappointing, although not entirely inconsequential. Retired Army officer Charles Shepard has a small pension and an alcoholic wife. Their divorced son Evan, a machinist, skips college and marries Rachel Drake, daughter of a loquacious, socially pretentious woman. Evan is rejected on physical grounds for military service; he and Rachel go to live with her mother, unhappily so it turns out. And so Evan drifts into an affair with his first wife. Rachel's brother Phil is sixteen and attends prep school; he is one of the few persons in the story who shows promise.

3771. **Yechton, Barbara, b. 1864. *Derick*. With illus. by Minna Brown. New York: Dodd, Mead, 1897. viii, 370p.**

"A story of New York and of the family of the Waldrons, the father being a teacher of music and an organist. The four young Waldrons are strongly individualized, and are most interesting. The fifth member of the family is little Derick, or Roderick Mackenzie, to whom the Waldrons have given a home since the death of his parents. He is a lovable little fellow, and it almost breaks their hearts when Mrs. Lovell, a rich society woman, offers to adopt him. He makes her a trial visit of six months, his high spirits leading him into constant mischief. He finds an uncle with money, and the test comes to him as to which of the two homes offered him he shall accept"—Annual American catalogue.

3772. **————. *A little turning aside*. With illus. by Wilhelmina and Jessie B. Walker. Philadelphia: G.W. Jacobs, 1898. 224p.**

"The story of a young girl who is an art student in New York City. She leaves her country home to study art against the wishes of her aunt, who believes herself dying. Just as the young girl is apparently about to take the prize for a five years' course in Paris she becomes blind. The divisions of the work indicate the story—Work, Strife and Victory"—Annual American catalogue.

3773. **————. *We ten*; or, *The story of the Roses*. With illus. by Minna Brown. New York: Dodd, Mead, 1896. 383p.**

The 'ten' are the Rose children who live in New York City with their father (their mother has passed away). Mr. Rose is more interested in writing ancient history than he is in his children. They are pretty much on their own despite the presence of a governess, and their experiences, in the absence of a neglectful father, range form the gently humorous to the heart-rending.

3774. **Yenni, Julia Truitt, 1913- . *The spellbound village*; a novel. New York: Harcourt, Brace, 1951. 221p.**

"Faith Goodbind, seeking a home as compensation for her youthful years of wandering with her sinister father, chooses a little New York State village. She knows very few of its inhabitants until her book is published. Although written before she came to 'Two River Junction', strangely enough the book explores secrets better kept hidden and the village is up in arms over its fancied wrongs. The repercussions produced by the book provide the plot of this story"—Book review digest.

3775. Yezierska, Anzia, 1885-1970. *Arrogant beggar.* **Garden City, N.Y.: Doubleday, 1927. 279p.**

The heroine, Adele Lindner, is a girl from the tenements of New York City who has a strong imagination and a rebellious turn of mind. Circumstances impel her to become a domestic in the household of a hypocritical woman philanthropist and spend some time in Mrs. Hellman's Home for Working Girls. Organized charity does little to help Adele improve her situation so she uses what she has learned the hard way and applies it to her own search for self-support and a better way of life.

3776. ————. *Bread givers***; a novel. A struggle between a father of the Old World and a daughter of the New. Garden City, N.Y.: Doubleday, Page, 1925. viii, 297.**

Sara Smolinsky wages war against the stifling poverty of the New York ghetto and the despotic tirades of her father (who has already tyrannized her sisters) and pulls herself out of the depressing Hester Street environment by attending night school, college, and finally reaching her goal—that of teaching. Her story is told in Sara's own words.

3777. ————. *Children of loneliness***; stories of immigrant life in America. New York: Funk & Wagnalls, 1923. 270p.**

A collection of short stories and sketches about Russian Jewish immigrants in New York City and their attempts to adopt (or distance themselves from) the new ways. e.g., "Rachel in the story, 'The Lord giveth' ... is already a student of the language, which enables her to write letters for everybody on the block. Rachel's desire for the learning that will usher in her assimilation helps her break out of the self-imposed separateness of her impoverished orthodox parents whose pious Old World scorn for the material has unfitted them for the New World. ... A grown-up Rachel earns college money by tutoring pious immigrants more recent than herself, proof, at least to her, that Jewish wisdom needs the help of American knowledge"—Hapke, L. Tales of the working girl. Contents: Mostly about myself.—America and I.—An immigrant among the editors.—To the stars.—Children of loneliness.—Brothers.—A bed for the night.—Dreams and dollars.—The Lord giveth.—The song triumphant.—An interview with Anzia Yezierska ... by R. Duffy.

3778. ————. *Hungry hearts.* **Boston: Houghton Mifflin, 1920. 297p.**

"The Russian [-Jewish] immigrant in the [New York] ghetto, reaching out with hungry heart to higher things, is the subject of this collection of sketches. There is something fierce and savage, and to our sober self-control, almost unreasonable in this cry for beauty, life and freedom that rings down from the heart of this oppressed race in the voice of one of their number"—Book review digest. Contents: Wings.—Hunger.—The lost 'beautifulness.'—The free vacation house.—The miracle.—Where lovers dream.—Soap and water.—'The fat of the land.'—My own people.—How I found America.

3779. ———. Sa*lome of the tenements*. New York: Boni & Liveright, 1922. 290p.

"The moment John Manning, the millionaire-philanthropist, crossed the path of Sonya Vrunsky, the ghetto girl, the emotional Jewess was all aflame with ambition and passion to 'marry herself to him.' Did he not hold within himself the promise of everything she craved in the way of beauty and luxury and distinction? With ruthless ingenuity she sets about to gain her point and she becomes Mrs. Manning. Then in the ancestral Manning mansion, with a houseful of servants, among straight-laced relatives, comes the awakening. Sonya's wildness will not be cramped into such an environment and with the same passion with which she flung herself into Manning's arms she now flings away from him. She discovers that she has a talent and a zest for designing dresses and as a designer she is rediscovered by an old admirer, the costume artist of Fifth Avenue"—Book review digest.

3780. Yorke, Anthony, 1865-1930. *Passing shadows*; a novel. New York, Cincinnati: Benziger Bros., 1897. 301p.

The Crystal family of Eldridge Street shares experiences in New York City at the end of the 19th century. Two daughters, Agnes and Gabrielle, travel quite different paths. Agnes opts for the religious life of a nun; Gabrielle finds herself involved in a heated love affair.

3781. Youmans, N.O., pseud. *Best seller*; the story of a young man who came to New York to write a novel about a young man who came to New York to write a novel. Indianapolis: Bobbs-Merrill, 1930. 314p.

Jasper Watts escapes from his father's bathroom accessories business in the Midwest and attempts to conquer New York with his literary talent. He finds employment as assistant to the advertising chief of a successful New York publishing firm; in his free time he starts to write a novel which, lo and behold, becomes a best seller. With success comes Jasper's leap into amorous dalliances and the 'good life.' The president of the publishing company pursues chorus girls while the chief editor is an unimaginative bungler. The sales, publicity and advertising staffs are portrayed as crude and ignorant of the literary worth of the firm's products. Obviously the pseudonymous author is disgusted with what he believes is the publishing 'racket' in New York.

3782. Young, Albert A. *Stories from the Adirondacks*, by Albert A. Young, 'Adirondack Al.' New York, Chicago: F. Tennyson Neely, c1899. 126p.

The author spins tales about some people and animals who are native to the forests and settlements of the region, and about other persons who wander into the Adirondacks searching for something or someone. Are these tales embellished fact or chiefly fiction based on fact? Contents: The mysterious lake; or, The hermit of Blue Ridge.—Adventures of camp life.—The Club of Mysterious Characters.—The hero of Topham's Camp.—Bear stories.

3783. **Young, Julia Evelyn Ditto, 1857-1915.** *Adrift*; **a story of Niagara. Philadelphia: J.B. Lippincott, 1889. 275p.**

Bella Forrester, a woman with literary and artistic tastes, tells her rather smug, pragmatic, banker/broker husband, John, that she wishes to visit her cousin, Diana, in Niagara Falls. Actually she wants a change of scene badly, finding her Buffalo home stifling. Diana Forrester is a lady of 30 with a strong commitment to spinsterhood. Bella arrives in Niagara Falls, stays with Diana and meets two young men from New York City: Stephen Brooks and his adopted brother, Jerome Harvey. Brooks is attracted to Bella, Jerome to Diana. Bella extends her stay far beyond the few weeks originally contemplated and draws increasing attention from Stephen Brooks. She tries in vain to divert his affirmation of love, becomes very ill and dies. Diana in turn refuses to marry Jerome. The two crestfallen men go boating on the dangerous Niagara River; the boat overturns and both are presumed drowned. Brooks' body is found, but Jerome, with a broken arm, reappears. Again he presses Diana who seems to be wavering, but the novel concludes with her words: "This contest troubles me; it tires me; and so—oh please promise never to ask me again!"

3784. **Young, Rose Emmet, 1869-1941.** *Murder at Manson's.* **New York: John Day Co., 1927. 267p.**

"Gathered at Manson's boarding house in the West Fifties is a motley crew of stage folk. The latest arrival is a young aspirant [a young woman from Kansas] whom Manson himself has made his protégée and whom he is trying to coach. Late at night after one of these rehearsals Manson is found dead, poisoned. He has made the girl from Kansas his heir. The suspicious actions of certain of the boarders complicates the solution of the mystery, but Inspector Conrad finds the right trail"—Book review digest.

3785. **Young, Stark, 1881-1963.** *The torches flare.* **New York: Scribner, 1928. 381p.**

The first half of the novel takes the reader into the New York theatrical scene of the 1920s (critic Young's forte) and the sophisticated world of Greenwich Village. The narrator is Henry (Hal or Lafe) Boardman who teaches at Columbia University and is a relative and close friend of Eleanor (Lena) Boardman, a Mississippian and recent arrival in the city. Lena's beauty and striking presence win her a leading role in a new play in which she becomes a huge success. Lena begins a torrid love affair with Arthur Lane, poet and occasional instructor at Columbia. Illness in her family takes Lena back to Mississippi. Arthur follows and his relationship with Lena cools, especially when she learns he had been previously married and had just received his divorce. Arthur elects to stay in Mississippi and join the faculty of Clearwater University. Lena is offered a role in a play in Chicago prior to its New York opening.

3786. **Zagst, Michael, 1950- . *The greening of Thurmond Leaner*; a novel. New York: D.T. Fine, 1986. 269p.**

A contractor from Houston, Texas by the name of Thurmond Leaner, enters his first professional golf tournament, the Max Catalina invitational, in New York State's Catskills. Leaner is talented and smart, but he is not fully prepared for the preconditions of entry—participating in a canoe race and playing Scrabble. Yet Leaner takes an early lead in the tournament and maintains it until the last round when he is locked into a sudden death situation with an old pro. Leaner's offbeat personality assures him a future in golf and endorsements for advertisers, let alone the attention of certain attractive females.

3787. **Zeman, Josephine. *The victim's triumph*; a panorama of modern society. New York: G.W. Dillingham, 1903. 244p.**

Bob Armstrong, a retired banker and broker; Chauncey Lamont, son of a wealthy merchant; Lord Oliver Brighton, a rich Englishman—these three are in the upper echelons of New York City's social world. Count Nicholas Ivanovitch and his sister, the Countess Ravenna, gain entry into the magic circle. Lord Brighton marries the beautiful Ravenna. Bob Armstrong sees a striking resemblance between Nicholas and a 'Herbert Stanley' who had ruined Bob's sister and had been incarcerated in Sing Sing. As evidence mounts of the Count's criminal past (and present), Lord Brighton wonders if his wife is an adventuress in close league with her brother. Fanny Chase, a friend of Bob Armstrong, assures Lord Brighton that Ravenna is essentially a good woman who has long been abused by her brother. Nicholas, cornered by the police, takes poison rather than return to prison.

Zimm, Mrs. Bruno Lewis, b. 1883. See: Hasbrouck, Louise Seymoure, b. 1883.

3788. **Zindel, Paul, 1936- . *The amazing and death-defying diary of Eugene Dingman*. New York: Harper & Row, 1987. 186p.**

Eugene Dingman's diary tells of the young man's experiences as a waiter at the Lake Henry Hotel, a summer resort for the affluent in the Adirondacks. Eugene is the youngest waiter; he suffers the displeasure of the hotel chef and is infatuated with Della, a waitress who loves things French and leads Eugene to Flaubert's Madame Bovary. The negatives in Eugene's existence far outweigh the positives—Della does not reciprocate his love; his mother is seeing an ex-Mafioso; the father he has not seen for a long time does not answer his letters. As his job winds down Eugene takes steps to prop up his self-esteem.

Zubof, Roman Ivanovich, b. 1866. See: Appleton, Robert, pseud.

3789. **Zugsmith, Leane, 1903-1969.** *All victories are alike.* **New York: Payson & Clarke, 1929. 251p.**

"Once Page Trent had had a sense of wonder. But years of clever clowning in a [New York] newspaper column, of posing among other poseurs, had destroyed it, had all but destroyed him. Then he married Lucy—for no particular reason but that she was small and lonely and 'wanted to give him something.' What she gave him, finally, after he had tired of her, was knowledge of himself. But that his final conversion was really final, we doubt"—Outlook.

PLACE INDEX

New York City (cont.)

1390, 1392-1393, 1395-1401,
1404-1406, 1409, 1412, 1414,
1418-1421, 1425-1426, 1428-
1431, 1435-1437, 1439-1440,
1446-1449, 1454, 1457, 1459,
1466- 1467, 1470-1474, 1478-
1479, 1481, 1485-1486, 1488,
1491-1495, 1497, 1499-1500,
1502, 1506-1515, 1517-1518,
1520, 1524, 1527, 1530, 1536-
1541, 1543-1546, 1548, 1550,
1552, 1560, 1562- 1564, 1566-
1568, 1570, 1573-1576, 1578-
1579, 1581, 1585-1586, 1588-
1589, 1592, 1594, 1607- 1609,
1617, 1620, 1622-1624, 1626,
1630, 1637, 1646-1649, 1655-
1656, 1662, 1667, 1669-1671,
1673-1674, 1677, 1679-1681,
1683-1691, 1693-1694, 1696-
1712, 1717-1718, 1722, 1724-
1730, 1732-1743, 1745-1746,
1749-1756, 1758-1760, 1763-
1764, 1766, 1769-1772, 1774-
1775, 1779- 1783, 1789-1790,
1792, 1797-1798, 1801-1803,
1805-1806, 1811, 1814-1816,
1818-1821, 1823, 1825-1831,
1837, 1841-1842, 1849-1851,
1854, 1859, 1864, 1866, 1869-
1873, 1875-1879, 1881, 1883,
1885-1886, 1891, 1894-1895,
1901, 1903, 1905-1908, 1911,
1913-1915, 1917, 1927, 1930,
1935-1938, 1942-1954, 1956-
1957, 1959, 1966-1974, 1976-
1979, 1985-1989, 1991, 1996,
2002, 2006, 2012, 2015-2016,
2022-2026, 2030, 2032, 2038,
2040-2042, 2044, 2051-2054,
2057-2061, 2064-2065, 2068,
2072, 2076, 2079-2082, 2084,
2090-2092, 2096, 2099-2103,
2106-2107, 2110- 2112, 2114-
2116, 2118, 2122-2124, 2144-
2145, 2149, 2156, 2158-2161,
2163-2166, 2168, 2170, 2175-
2176, 2178, 2182-2184, 2186,
2188-2189, 2192, 2194-2195,
2198-2199, 2207-2213, 2220-
2221, 2229-2230, 2232, 2234,
2236-2238, 2241, 2244-2254,
2256-2265, 2269-2277, 2280-
2287, 2289, 2291-2294, 2297-
2299, 2304-2306, 2308, 2310-
2311, 2313-2315, 2317, 2323-
2332, 2334- 2335, 2337, 2341-
2342, 2348, 2350, 2357, 2359,
2361-2364, 2366, 2370-2373,
2375-2377, 2379- 2380, 2383,
2387-2391, 2393-2400, 2409,
2413, 2416, 2418, 2420-2424,
2426, 2431, 2436-2438, 2443,
2445-2447, 2450, 2456, 2458,
2460, 2469- 2470, 2474-2476,
2478-2479, 2482-2484, 2487-
2489, 2492-2493, 2495-2498,
2500-2501, 2503- 2504, 2507,
2509, 2534, 2537-2544, 2546-
2547, 2549-2551, 2554-2559,
2561, 2563-2564, 2572- 2574,
2576-2577, 2579, 2581, 2583-
2586, 2588, 2590, 2592-2600,
2602-2610, 2612, 2614, 2616-
2625, 2627-2628, 2636, 2641,
2650, 2657, 2663- 2666, 2668-
2671, 2673, 2679-2680, 2682,
2686, 2689, 2700, 2702, 2704-
2713, 2717-2718, 2721- 2722,
2724-2725, 2728-2729, 2732-
2738, 2742-2748, 2751-2752,
2755-2759, 2765, 2768-2769,
2773, 2776, 2778, 2780, 2784-
2785, 2789-2791, 2798, 2802-
2804, 2806, 2808-2812, 2814,
2821- 2822, 2828-2831, 2835,
2837, 2841-2844, 2847, 2850-
2851, 2854, 2868-2871, 2873-
2878, 2881- 2884, 2892-2895,
2897, 2901, 2908, 2914, 2918,
2926, 2928-2929, 2933-2935,

New York City (cont.)
2938, 2945-2948, 2950-2952,
2954-2964, 2966, 2970, 2975-
2982, 2984-2987, 2990-2991,
2993, 2995-2996, 3003, 3008-
3012, 3014-3025, 3027-3028,
3031-3034, 3036, 3043-3046,
3049, 3052, 3062, 3067-3068,
3071, 3083, 3085, 3089, 3094,
3097, 3109-3110, 3112-3117,
3119-3120, 3125-3126, 3128,
3130, 3135-3138, 3143-3146,
3149, 3151-3152, 3155, 3159-
3161, 3163, 3166, 3168-3171,
3175, 3177- 3179, 3181-3182,
3186-3187, 3189, 3191-3192,
3199-3202, 3206-3208, 3210-
3212, 3215-3216, 3219-3221,
3225, 3228, 3230-3231, 3236-
3238, 3240-3241, 3245-3251,
3256-3258, 3261-3263, 3265-
3268, 3271, 3273-3277, 3280,
3283, 3291-3294, 3298, 3301-
3303, 3305-3306, 3308-3309,
3313-3317, 3320-3325, 3328-
3329, 3345, 3352-3355, 3361,
3363-3376, 3379-3385, 3387-
3396, 3398-3400, 3402, 3404-
3408, 3414-3415, 3419-3420,
3422, 3425, 3427, 3429-3430,
3438, 3441-3445, 3447, 3449-
3450, 3452-3460, 3462-3463,
3465-3466, 3469-3477, 3479-
3481, 3483-3485, 3491-3492,
3496-3498, 3507-3510, 3512-
3513, 3515-3516, 3518-3520,
3522-3523, 3526-3527, 3533-
3534, 3536, 3541-3543, 3545-
3547, 3553-3556, 3562-3563,
3566, 3572, 3580-3582, 3584,
3586-3587, 3591, 3593, 3595,
3597, 3611, 3614- 3617, 3619-
3627, 3633-3634, 3637, 3650,
3652, 3655-3657, 3663-3665,
3668, 3676, 3678-3680,
3687-3688, 3690, 3695, 3697-
3699, 3701-3703, 3707-3708,
3713, 3715, 3719, 3721, 3724-
3729, 3733, 3735, 3740-3751,
3753, 3755-3762, 3767, 3769,
3771-3773, 3775-3782, 3784-
3785, 3787,
**See also boroughs and districts
of the City: Bowery; Bronx;
Brooklyn; Central Park;
East Side; Harlem; etc.**
Newark 1787
Newburgh 3091
Niagara Falls 256a, 402, 502,
556, 1006, 2988, 3040, 3287,
3540
Niagara Falls (City) 1006,
1046-1047, 1992, 3287, 3540
Niagara Frontier 2, 7, 316,
402, 502, 556, 1006, 1046-1047,
1678, 1992, 2565, 2988, 3040,
3287, 3500-3501, 3540, 3731,
3783
Niskayuna 2074
**'North Country'. See:
Northern New York State
('North Country') Northern
New York State ('North
Country')** 135, 147-150, 152,
154-155, 158, 178, 283, 428,
595, 671, 990, 1236, 1748, 2214,
3244, 3332, 3336, 3342, 3410,
3608.
**See also: Adirondacks; St.
Lawrence County; etc.**
Nyack 13

Odgensburg 318, 1083, 1910
Oneida County 797-798, 1574,
2486, 3000, 3310-3311
Onondaga County and Valley
2833, 3417
Orange County 1411, 3524
Orient Point 2067
Oriskany 3670
Oriskany Falls 2826

Ossining 1897, 2419-2420, 3166
Oswegatchie 3529
Oswego 240a
Otego 1934
Otsego Lake 692, 696
Oyster Bay 2318, 2381

Palisades 303, 1199, 2078
Palmyra 20
Patchogue 408, 2321
Peekskill 2654
Phelps 2647
Plattsburgh 186, 766, 2719
Pleasantville 163
Plum Island 874
Port Jervis 730
Poughkeepsie 247, 390, 2448, 2939
Putnam County 2128, 2130, 2138-2140

Ramapos 1411, 1832, 3038, 3111
Randall's Island (New York City) 3220
Rensselaer 255
Rhinebeck 1813, 1982
Richmond (New York City) 2549
Rochester 624, 646, 846, 985, 1654, 1834, 2231, 2352, 2473, 2524-2527, 3133
Rockaway Beach 2074
Rockland County 1832, 3111
Rosendale 2611

Sacandaga 1109
Sacketts Harbor 2180
Sag Harbor 1845, 3596
Saranac (Clinton County) 3122
Saranac Lake 1460, 2154, 3693
Saratoga Lake 644

Saratoga Springs 666, 668, 902-910, 943, 970, 972, 1117, 1166, 1255, 1487, 1554, 1638, 1672, 1675, 2276, 2471, 2685, 2697, 2880, 3059, 3061, 3066, 3131, 3418, 3467, 3723a
Scarsdale 919, 1643, 1810
Schenectady 106, 1288, 1415, 2162, 3054, 3490, 3494
Schoharie 877, 2928a, 3048
Schonowe 255
Seneca Falls 864, 2223, 2403-2406
Seneca Lake 2384, 3153
Seneca River 2019
Setauket 1715
Sharon Springs 2694
Shelter Island 1107
Sherwood 2458a
Shinnecock Hills 611, 2144a, 2440
Shoreham 1777
Skenesborough. See: Whitehall
Smithtown 1939
Snake Hill 644
Southhampton 381, 2451, 2823, 3229
Southhold 677
Sparta 3108
St. Lawrence County 149-150, 3259
St. Lawrence River 179, 773, 1748, 3333-3334, 3338
St. Lawrence Valley 613, 1526, 2805
Staten Island 1198, 1314, 1626, 3068, 3117
Stony Point (Rockland County) 1892
Suffolk County 253
Sullivan County 728-729
Syracuse 323-326, 895, 1160, 1167, 1274, 1461, 1668, 1904, 2073, 2473, 2855

SUBJECT INDEX

Abduction. See:
Kidnapping
Abercromby, James (1706-
1781) 629
Abolitionists. See: Slavery.
Actors and actresses. See:
Motions pictures; Theater.
African Americans 168,
332, 528, 533, 647, 835, 876,
1075-1076, 1145, 1164, 1354,
2032, 2155, 2236, 2329, 2362,
2369, 2458a, 2477, 2511,
2690-2691, 2724, 2730, 2741,
2973, 2992, 3165, 3173, 3193,
3213, 3243, 3324, 3358, 3457,
3628, 3704
Afro-Americans. See:
African Americans.
Agriculture. See: Farmers
and farming.
Airplanes and air pilots
686, 725, 946, 1126, 1443,
1592, 2988, 3608
Alcoholism and temperance
181, 308, 334, 411, 438, 536,
689, 726, 962, 1091, 1319,
1414, 1640, 1728, 1923, 1947,
2165, 2263, 2294, 2296, 2304,
2332, 2355, 2403, 2417, 2492,
2851, 3264, 3271, 3427, 3436,
3458, 3516, 3596, 3656, 3734,
3754, 3757, 3759-3760
Aliens from outer space.
See: Life on other planets.
Allen, Ethan (1738-1789)
2787, 3552
American Loyalists 394,
396, 441, 595, 601, 630, 644,
699, 701, 761, 764-765, 769,
771, 859, 890, 977, 1004,
1031, 1239, 1333, 1411, 1489,
1664, 1756, 1832, 1854, 2008,

2083, 2228, 2385, 2459, 2539,
2611, 2654, 3001, 3031, 3176,
3178, 3302, 3708
American Revolution (1775-
1781) 17, 86, 95, 127, 159,
169, 175, 205, 213, 221, 266-
267, 278, 317, 353, 391-392,
394, 396-398, 439, 441, 470,
529-530, 555, 584, 595-597,
600-601, 626-627, 630, 644,
699, 601, 715, 757-758, 761-
762, 764-765, 768-769, 771,
777, 824, 859, 881-882, 890,
977, 994, 1004, 1031-1032,
1042, 1072, 1169-1170, 1202,
1209, 1233, 1239, 1289, 1291,
1333, 1367, 1377, 1411, 1424,
1489, 1498a, 1502, 1593,
1613, 1649, 1652-1653, 1660-
1661, 1663-1665, 1681, 1745,
1750, 1756-1757, 1795, 1812,
1832, 1854, 1892, 1934, 2008,
2013-2014, 2020, 2077, 2083,
2107, 2151, 2183, 2228-2229,
2318, 2367, 2385, 2449, 2459,
2469, 2490, 2494, 2507, 2539,
2585-2586, 2589-2591, 2599,
2601, 2606, 2611, 2645, 2654,
2661, 2697, 2731, 2770, 2787,
2807, 2827, 2853, 2864, 2890,
2926, 2953, 3001, 3031, 3037,
3048, 3096, 3098, 3138, 3148,
3153, 3156-3157, 3176, 3178,
3180, 3203, 3214-3215, 3217,
3275, 3284, 3302, 3304, 3331,
American Revolution (cont.)
3339-3341, 3344-3347, 3493,
3500, 3548, 3552, 3708, 3720
Amnesia 1868, 2170, 2407,
2474, 2633
Anarchism and anarchists
1005, 2955

André, John (1751-1780)
169, 266, 600, 1042, 1498a,
1757, 2014, 2661, 2731, 3284
Anglicans (U.S.) See:
Episcopalians.
Anthony, Susan Brownell
(1820-1906) 2458a
Antirent Wars. See:
Patroons.
Architects 231, 342, 1299,
1779, 1838-1840, 1947, 2247,
2752, 2985
Arnold, Benedict (1741-
1780) 169, 266-267, 1042,
1289, 1291, 1498a, 1652,
1665, 1757, 2151, 2184, 2490,
2606, 2645, 2675, 2697, 2731,
2853, 3138, 3203, 3275, 3284
Art and artists 81, 104, 254,
259, 296, 298, 315, 354, 425,
452, 459, 491, 518, 521, 585,
593, 611, 658, 670, 678, 683,
703, 709, 729, 731, 807, 834,
865, 892, 934, 940, 945, 1054,
1058, 1062, 1065, 1139, 1253,
1297, 1318, 1329, 1412, 1420,
1428, 1480a, 1525, 1535-
1536, 1570, 1604, 1609, 1622,
1671, 1717, 1730, 1733, 1803,
1814, 1820, 1831, 1909, 1959,
2258, 2276, 2284, 2359, 2363,
2475, 2488, 2495, 2504, 2509,
2537, 2679, 2694, 2783, 2851,
2910, 2917, 2928, 3115, 3133,
3143, 3272, 3352, 3428, 3447,
3537-3539, 3616, 3628, 3743,
3772
Astor Place Riot (New York
City, May 10, 1849) 463
Auctioneers 2185
Austrians 2373, 2910
Authors 81, 84, 363, 380,
425, 438, 507, 548, 599, 678-
679, 682-683, 735, 804, 809,
1065, 1078, 1137, 1171, 1200,
1204, 1214, 1321, 1346, 1349,

1360, 1475, 1483, 1492, 1500,
1504, 1529, 1540, 1566, 1568,
1580, 1607, 1645a, 1677,
1866, 1889, 1897, 1908, 1973,
2089, 2099, 2148, 2219, 2281,
2293, 2346, 2359, 2366, 2398,
2426, 2542, 2550, 2554, 2669,
2694, 2703, 2796, 2804, 2815,
2835, 2852, 2857, 2907, 2918,
2964, 3056, 3248, 3283, 3352,
3361, 3401, 3485, 3520, 3542,
3618, 3655, 3713, 3743, 3774,
3781.
See also Journalism and
journalists.
Automobiles 2647, 2822

Bachelors. See: Single men.
Banks and bankers. 118,
134, 237, 308a, 851, 917,
1023, 1048, 1185, 1210, 1252,
1277, 1398, 1541, 1550, 1691,
1903, 1943, 1948, 2033-2034,
2056-2057, 2207, 2217, 2813,
2981, 3118, 3231, 3598, 3606,
3701
Barnard College (New York
City) 1585, 3160
Baseball 174, 423, 795, 1142,
2026, 2818-2819, 3726
Baseball Hall of Fame
(Cooperstown) 795
Basketball 1043-1044, 1107,
1134, 2031, 3193
Beauty shops 22, 800, 842,
3664
Beekeeping 1376a
Belmont Park 1059
Birth control 2497
Black Americans. See:
African Americans.
Black Friday (Sept. 24,
1869) 1488, 1780, 3303
Blind 1039, 1386, 1919,
2097, 2102, 2277, 2759, 2804,
2809, 3072, 3155, 3772

Boarding houses 4, 24, 50, 58, 687, 823, 967, 1359, 1404-1405, 1414, 1465, 1610, 2247, 2429, 2592, 2758, 3449, 3707, 3784

Bond servants 335, 1288, 2811, 3140

Books and book trade 1108, 1126, 1478, 2304, 2376, 2416, 2418, 2509, 2686, 2828, 3240, 3276, 3487, 3781

Bowen, Betty (1775?-1865) See: Jumel, Eliza Bowen (1775?-1865)

Boxing 1564, 2236, 2841, 3725

Boy Scouts 1153, 1632, 1811, 2667

Brant, Joseph (1742-1807) 48, 392, 470, 571, 1596, 1928, 3080, 3157, 3341, 3346, 3671, 3673

Brant, Molly (1736-1796) 3080, 3671

Bridge (Game) See: Card games.

Burgoyne, John (1722-1792) 777

Burgoyne's Invasion (1777) 95, 127, 159, 596, 644, 715, 757, 771, 777, 1377, 1593, 2013, 2151, 2827, 2853, 3302, 3347

Buried treasure 1902, 1989, 2145, 2285, 2442, 3051, 3410, 3535, 3607, 3712

Business and business people 13-15, 76, 118, 151, 160, 184, 197, 211, 217, 229, 239, 301, 307, 318, 339, 357, 362, 378-379, 388, 404, 408, 421, 512-514, 579, 594, 609, 617, 641, 646, 704, 733, 735, 746, 805, 810, 816, 861, 879, 886, 899, 925, 934, 950, 952, 1091, 1095, 1115-1116, 1208, 1228, 1235, 1240, 1265, 1277, 1279, 1322-1324, 1326, 1328, 1338, 1348, 1365 1408-1409, 1421, 1448, 1461, 1488, 1506, 1517, 1544, 1680, 1686, 1727, 1780, 1789, 1825-1826, 1841, 1943-1946, 1952, 1976, 1978, 1986, 2037, 2043-2044, 2057-2061, 2064, 2084-2085, 2156, 2168, 2175, 2215, 2251, 2256, 2282-2283, 3208, 2364, 2393, 2395, 2422, 2447, 2471, 2496, 2570, 2573, 2643, 2657, 2666, 2689, 2704-2705, 2709, 2727, 2737, 2751, 2769, 2837, 2874, 2881-2882, 2884, 2891, 2895, 2938, 2958, 2984, 3020, 3023, 3034, 3064, 3084, 3117, 3136, 3141, 3146, 3221, 3245, 3280, 3373, 3388, 3397, 3408, 3454, 3560, 3465, 3480, 3483, 3611, 3624-3625. **See also: Wall Street (New York City)**

Butler, Walter (d. 1781) 394, 396, 630, 1031, 2385, 3157

Canoes and canoeing 1211

Capitalists and financiers. See: Business and business people.

Card games 1616, 3414

Cardiff Giant 1793, 1904, 1941, 3063

Catholics 106, 275, 463, 514, 547, 639, 702, 921-923, 927, 1012, 1014-1016, 1303, 1376, 1450, 1482, 1507, 1679, 1730-1732, 1735, 1921, 1930, 1935, 1992, 2022, 2048, 2213, 2215-2216, 2551, 2655, 2951-2952, 3120, 3142, 3259, 3277, 3423, 3513, 3780

Cayuga Indians 539, 3053

Challenger (Space shuttle) 1122

Chautauqua Institution   42-
44, 1445, 1522, 1587, 2410,
3278, 3288
Chess   209
Chinese   10, 1061, 1810,
2930, 3414
Christian life   100, 620, 820,
830, 1313, 1426, 1482, 1648,
1858, 2075, 2108, 2358, 2458,
2493, 2814, 2868, 2886, 2888,
3527, 3532, 3753, 3755-3759
Christian Science   942
Christmas   2381, 2775, 2843,
3006
Circus   993, 1666, 2794,
2800, 2943
Civil War (1861-1865)   399,
567, 580, 864, 978, 1060,
1241, 1317, 1408, 1422, 1517,
1943, 1987, 2246, 2291,
2403a, 2414, 2458a, 2860,
2892, 2983, 3005, 3105, 3141,
3208, 3356, 3411, 3627
Clairvoyance.   See:
Parapsychology.
Clergy   16, 49, 201, 204, 338,
453, 620, 663, 689, 830-831,
898, 927, 1005, 1012-1013,
1237, 1320, 1643, 1933, 1935,
1951, 2046, 2048, 2108, 2119,
2165, 2201, 2260, 2278, 2324,
2358, 2438, 2533, 2551, 2640,
2717, 2729, 2746, 2883, 2900,
2962, 2975, 3019, 3094, 3259,
3335, 3342, 3363, 3394, 3421,
3529, 3531-3532, 3563, 3599,
3689, 3693, 3735, 3753
Cleveland, Grover (1837-
1908)   1148
Clothing and fashion   1115-
1116, 1234, 1251, 1319, 1322-
1324, 1419, 1705, 1883, 1957,
2161, 2245, 2557, 2828, 3044,
3329, 3741, 3750, 3779

Colleges and universities.
See: Universities and
colleges.
Columbia University (New
York City)   1144, 1811,
2841, 2861, 3020, 3292
Communism   586, 1556,
1692, 2480   See also:
Socialists.
Computers   1784
Cooper Union (New York
City)   2917
Cornell University (Ithaca)
300, 358, 1066, 1433, 1444,
1762, 2902, 2931, 2969,
2977a, 3069, 3312, 3318, 3322
Crime and criminals   96,
103, 206, 233, 308a, 309, 330,
424, 435, 443, 451, 465, 467-
469, 471-472, 474-475, 478,
527, 622, 624-625, 636, 638,
650, 767, 815, 827, 848, 862a,
873, 880, 885, 911, 915, 984,
1023, 1045, 1048, 1050, 1052,
1173-1175, 1214-1215, 1220-
1221, 1273, 1284, 1335-1336,
1361, 1369, 1402-1403, 1442,
1496, 1541-1542, 1550, 1656,
1694, 1749, 1755, 1782, 1801,
1897, 1912, 1924, 1985, 2001,
2006, 2030, 2072, 2079, 2190,
2198, 2227, 2289, 2322, 2328,
2373, 2406, 2413, 2470, 2482,
2546, 2571, 2581-2583, 2607-
2608, 2616-2622, 2696, 2729,
2768, 2785, 2813, 2850, 2871,
2876, 2930, 2944, 2984, 3008,
3010-3011, 3014, 3035, 3049,
3123, 3147, 3152, 3161, 3249,
3266, 3313-3314, 3316, 3395,
3434, 3469-3471, 3474, 3524,
3597, 3605-3609, 3645, 3712,
3723a, 3787
Cults   2003, 2452
Czechs   1159, 3102

Dairying. See: Farmers and farming.
Delaware Indians 692
Department stores 954, 1378, 1702-1703, 1977, 2756, 3109, 3637
Depression (1929-1939) See: Great Depression (1929-1939)
Detectives 35, 38, 77-79, 114, 116, 121, 125-126, 183, 190, 320, 323-326, 341, 352, 384, 451, 484, 516, 619, 638, 755, 772, 786, 788-789, 793-795, 839, 842-843, 845, 849, 853, 855, 867-868, 874, 880, 902-910, 915, 929, 957, 971-972, 975-976, 1046, 1050-1051, 1062, 1110-1111, 1133, 1135-1136, 1146-1147, 1155-1158, 1168, 1174-1175, 1249-1250, 1257, 1278, 1332, 1334-1335, 1342-1343, 1363, 1382, 1384, 1386-1387, 1390-1391, 1395-1397, 1399, 1401, 1474, 1497, 1504, 1508, 1523, 1537-1538, 1541, 1544, 1546, 1555-1557, 1580, 1601, 1642, 1651, 1678, 1687-1688, 1761, 1775, 1777, 1788, 1800, 1808-1809, 1829, 1833, 1836-1840, 1857, 1888-1889, 1893, 1919, 1929, 1961, 1982, 2010, 2015, 2028, 2033-2034, 2036, 2043, 2081, 2104-2105, 2121, 2125-2143, 2183, 2239, 2257, 2262, 2279, 2307, 2322, 2325, 2341, 2343, 2476, 2524, 2526-2527, 2529-2530, 2536, 2541, 2562, 2576, 2579-2583, 2609, 2631, 2652, 2656, 2683, 2723, 2765, 2769, 2775-2778, 2794, 2820-2825, 2832, 2928a, 2943, 2949, 3002, 3004, 3011, 3014, 3016, 3024, 3039, 3073, 3075, 3087, 3100, 3137, 3142, 3155, 3162,
3183, 3189-3190, 3192, 3194-3197, 3234-3235, 3237-3238, 3249, 3253, 3271, 3285, 3296-3297, 3299-3300, 3320, 3403, 3433, 3439-3444, 3464, 3474, 3512, 3544, 3550-3551, 3559, 3565-3572, 3574-3579, 3581-3585, 3587-3590, 3593-3594, 3681-3682, 3699, 3701, 3705, 3710, 3717, 3763, 3784
Diamond, Jack 'Legs' (1896-1931) 1924
Doctors (Medicine) See: Physicians.
Draft Riots (New York City, 1863) 1392, 1987, 3208, 3627
Dramatists. See: Authors; Theater.
Drugs 186, 536, 884, 925, 1490, 1542, 1557, 1743, 2011, 2031, 2263, 2294, 2690, 2711, 2894, 3135, 3165, 3601, 3723a
Dryden Fair 3635
Dutch 213, 216, 219, 222, 229, 255, 269, 314, 360, 403, 503, 631, 710, 1164, 1266, 1292, 1877, 1903, 1965, 1986, 1988, 2151, 2162, 2230, 2449, 2460, 2463, 2502, 2603, 2636, 2659-2660, 2702, 2791, 2807, 2810-2811, 2951, 3026, 3038, 3054, 3179, 3258, 3494, 3536, 3689, 3700

East Indians 503
Economic Depression (1929-1939) See: Great Depression (1929-1939)
Educators 198-199, 377, 524-525, 532, 537-538, 545, 568, 663, 808, 857, 862a, 998, 1226, 1290, 1342, 2022, 2458a, 2465, 2553, 3630
Episcopalians 100, 1935, 2046, 2637, 2962

See also: Iroquois Indians and various tribes.

Inns. See: Hotels and motels.

Irish 275, 291, 344, 570, 639, 880, 921-923, 1013, 1329, 1352, 1499, 1501, 1700, 1732, 1746, 1898, 1921, 2080-2081, 2181, 2451, 2484, 2703, 2795, 3549, 3712

Iroquois Indians 48, 135, 371, 373-374, 391-392, 398, 470, 517, 529-530, 559, 571, 592, 595, 630, 701, 763, 918, 1030-1032, 1034, 1164, 1169, 1224, 1248, 1266, 1288, 1415-1416, 1424, 1659, 1796, 2008, 2020, 2049, 2068, 2077, 2098, 2339, 2384, 2403, 2433-2435, 2449, 2459, 2565-2566, 2635, 2655, 2838-2840, 3040, 3048, 3053-3055, 3059, 3065, 3080, 3103, 3153, 3157, 3172, 3174, 3217, 3244, 3259, 3289, 3304, 3331, 3339, 3341, 3346, 3417, 3613, 3671, 3673, 3722

See also specific tribes: Cayuga Indians; Mohawk Indians; Onondaga Indians; etc.

Italians 184, 211, 376, 553, 565, 625, 636, 1013, 1036, 1198-1199, 1910, 2070, 2231, 2350, 2352, 2467, 3022, 3309, 3469, 3479, 3613

Japanese 1050a

Jemison, Mary (1743-1833) 3613

Jews and Judaism 11, 124, 227, 240a, 248, 253, 276, 279, 434, 450, 497, 507-511, 651, 894, 1118, 1138, 1231, 1311, 1322-1328, 1340, 1347, 1375, 1376a, 1430-1431, 1452, 1491-1495, 1575, 1606,

1611a, 1711, 1738, 1783, 1794, 1810, 1896, 1957, 2005-2006, 2040, 2066, 2076, 2088, 2095, 2291, 2403, 2484, 2522, 2555, 2559, 2563, 2670-2671, 2725, 2825, 2828, 2895, 2906, 2913, 2935, 2948, 3071, 3143, 3168, 3186, 3281, 3290, 3322, 3504, 3515, 3522, 3527, 3558, 3749, 3776-3779

Johnson, Guy (1740-1788) 3669

Johnson, Sir John (1742-1830) 3493

Johnson, Mary (b. 1744) 3669

Johnson, Sir William (1715-1774) 742, 769, 1613, 2433-2434, 2660, 3289, 3493, 3671, 3673, 3675

Jordanians 12

Journalism and journalists 30, 131, 216, 304, 423, 438, 573, 672, 782, 817, 883, 900, 955, 962, 1018, 1114, 1181, 1187, 1201, 1222, 1242, 1273, 1278, 1301, 1318, 1321, 1335, 1357, 1520, 1548, 1607, 1627-1628, 1673, 1684, 1711, 1718, 1783, 1866, 1871, 1885-1886, 1899, 1920, 1922, 1975, 2003, 2064, 2158, 2194, 2204, 2217, 2250, 2353, 2361, 2377, 2445, 2504, 2524-2527, 2624, 2641, 2668, 2698, 2708, 2713, 3021, 3045, 3188, 3193, 3226, 3232-3233, 3236, 3241, 3248, 3283, 3293, 3466-3467, 3479, 3534, 3545, 3629, 3655, 3681, 3683,

Journalism and journalists (cont.)
3684, 3686, 3716, 3728, 3744-3745, 3789

See also: Authors.

Judaism. See: Jews and Judaism.

Mohican Indians 694, 970
Mohonk Mountain House (Ulster County) 656
Morgan's Rifles 397, 592, 2827, 3153
Moslems See: Muslims.
Motion pictures 1046, 1549, 1706, 1778, 2139, 2179, 2531, 2554, 2820, 2854, 2873, 3725-3726
Moving pictures. See: Motion pictures.
Murder. See: Homicide.
Murphy, Timothy (1751-1818) 397
Museums 496, 2327, 2821
Music and musicians 238, 258-259, 274, 315, 687, 808, 822, 857, 947, 1036, 1073, 1093, 1214, 1418, 1425, 1491, 1539, 1563, 1581, 1654, 1701, 1710, 1717, 1733, 1747, 1942, 2093a, 2123, 2145, 2165, 2211, 2244, 2254, 2272, 2396, 2710, 2738, 2803-2804, 2878, 2936, 2995, 3049, 3081, 3130, 3133, 3159, 3245, 3257a, 3660
Muslims 12, 452

Negroes, American. See: African Americans.
New Thought 3043
Newsboys 55, 64-65, 74, 83, 702, 1028, 1189, 2116, 2447, 2592, 2598, 2604-2605, 3110, 3365-3367, 2275
Norwegians 776
Nurses 2477, 2482, 2963, 3510
Nursing homes 224

Occultism 618, 796, 838, 989, 1491, 1518, 1847, 1879, 2158, 2267-2268, 2290, 2301, 2338, 2348, 2443, 2506, 2512,

2613, 2677, 2739, 2760, 2789, 2797, 2826, 2931, 3099, 3111, 3573, 3696,
See also: Parapsychology.
Oneida Community 1021, 1558
Oneida Indians 630, 1797, 2020, 2049, 2459, 2838, 2840
Onondaga Indians 361, 1266, 3040, 3053, 3244, 3331, 3417, 3722
Oriskany, Battle of (1777) 1239, 1795, 2008
Orphans 50, 75, 91, 107, 139, 287, 348, 448, 531, 562, 564, 587, 632, 645, 776, 940, 1028, 1035, 1037, 1088, 1168, 1210, 1372, 1438, 1438, 1494, 1590, 1622, 1760, 1823, 1986, 2118, 2146, 2213, 2246, 2263, 2344, 2421, 2489, 2546, 2665, 2681, 2759, 2857, 2950, 2970, 2977, 2979, 3121, 3140, 3526, 3532, 3664, 3761
Oswegatchie Indians. See: Oneida Indians.

Painters. See: Art and artists.
Parapsychology 349, 581, 605, 621, 796, 1485, 1523,
Parapsychology (cont.) 1861, 2512, 2613, 3043, 3675, 3736
See also: Occultism
Patroons. 540, 542, 697, 1464, 2151, 2218, 2463, 2762, 3041, 3070
Paulding, Hiram (1797-1878) 3029
Pedophiles 1642
Physicians 204, 208, 210, 215, 276, 365, 481, 500, 621, 640, 652, 674, 944, 1038, 1091, 1097, 1127, 1146, 1436,

1452, 1476, 1518, 1600, 1747,
1816, 1874, 1927, 1958, 2007,
2017, 2035, 2053, 2065, 2088,
2277, 2301, 2373, 2403, 2450,
2456, 2503, 2555, 2559, 2608,
2919, 2985, 3095, 3144, 3187,
3207, 3264, 3268, 3446, 3511,
3641, 3715
Pirates 403, 464, 549, 690,
1367, 1528, 1751-1752, 1877,
2221, 2442, 2850, 3007, 3051,
3179-3180, 3505
**Plattsburgh, Battle of (1814)
See: Lake Champlain, Battle
of (1814)**
Poles 1595, 1710, 3488
Police See: Detectives.
Politics and politicians 188,
198, 232, 256a, 358, 379, 393,
417, 507, 560, 566, 619, 664,
746, 753, 924, 1056, 1095,
1148, 1165, 1182, 1186, 1242,
1280, 1286, 1341, 1373, 1376,
1407, 1438, 1449, 1473, 1520,
1543, 1640, 1712, 1819, 1822,
1890, 1895, 1920, 1938, 1975,
2064, 2080-2081, 2177-2178,
2189, 2196, 2261, 2270-2271,
2332, 2353, 2372, 2450, 2520,
2572, 2615, 2649, 2664, 2704,
2979, 3085, 3120, 3163, 3381,
3404, 3545, 3560, 3562, 3603,
3610, 3652, 3698
Poor 55, 58, 62, 66, 68-69,
71-73, 83, 124, 176, 200, 281,
450, 465, 477, 480-481, 487,
562, 568, 654, 726-727, 744,
837, 878, 891, 960, 967, 1010,
1017, 1025, 1053, 1073, 1084,
1186, 1380, 1428, 1466, 1485,
1579, 1630, 1655, 1755, 1915,
1937, 2082, 2114, 2249, 2253,
2305, 2383, 2400, 2479, 2492-
2493, 2563, 2593-2595, 2671,
2742-2743, 2746, 2759, 2809,
2842-2844, 2869, 2897, 2950,

2976, 2993, 3092-3093, 3110,
3119, 3125, 3152, 3175, 3199-
3200, 3207, 3325, 3376, 3400,
3452, 3518, 3543, 3633, 3636,
3657, 3753
**Pratt Institute (New York
City)** 1472
Presbyterians 8, 100, 2307,
2637, 2900, 3019
**Private investigators. See:
Detectives.**
Private schools 382-383,
956, 976, 998, 1226, 1410,
1791, 1956, 2153, 2323, 2417,
2773, 2829, 2848, 2928,
2938a, 3437, 3586
Prohibition 2294 **See also:
Alcoholism and temperance.**
Prostitution 97, 365-366,
369-370, 461, 465, 467-468,
471, 727, 1007-1009, 1229,
1315, 1574, 1753, 1806, 1891,
2111, 2711, 3094, 3228, 3314-
3315, 3637
**Psychic phenomena See:
Parapsychology.**
Publicity 410, 2665, 3353
Puerto Ricans 2848
**Putnam, Clarissa (1751-
1833)** 3493

**Quakers See: Society of
Friends.**

Radio 2428, 2877
Railroads 151, 357, 402,
1117, 1713, 2204, 2216, 2560,
3084, 3136, 3411
Red Jacket (1758?-1830)
1032
**Religious life (Christian)
See: Christian life.**
Restaurants, tea rooms, etc.
161, 1545, 1696, 1810, 1827,
2012a, 3063, 3155, 3206, 3276

1631, 1800, 1900, 1992, 2009,
2031, 2035, 2157, 2174, 2340,
2368, 2374, 2465, 2518, 2841,
2861, 2905, 2917, 2931, 2995,
2998-2999, 3069, 3160, 3292,
3312, 3318, 3322

Upper class 85, 108, 110,
119, 165-166, 168, 178, 183,
189, 228, 231, 256-257, 261,
263, 270-271, 275, 277, 295,
301, 356, 359, 381-381a, 407,
419, 444-445, 505, 520, 546,
552, 587-588, 604, 608, 623,
680, 707, 713, 732, 734, 736,
740, 750, 759-760, 778, 781,
805, 825-826, 835, 873, 889,
914, 952, 1020, 1058a, 1060,
1077-1079, 1082, 1086, 1088,
1090-1091, 1094, 1098, 1101-
1102, 1104-1105, 1124-1125,
1308, 1321, 1357, 1369-1370,
1507, 1509-1514, 1519, 1530,
1560, 1670, 1674, 1683,1707,
1726, 1734, 1780, 1792, 1806,
1818, 1837, 1870, 1881, 1906,
1949, 1967, 1971, 2068, 2097,
2124, 2149, 2160, 2212, 2234,
2245-2246, 2251, 2256, 2273,
2280, 2292-2293, 2304, 2308,
2311, 2316, 2342, 2360, 2362,
2380, 2383, 2393, 2436, 2439,
2443, 2549, 2657, 2681, 2687,
2697, 2700, 2744-2745, 2773,
2789, 2803, 2814, 2847, 2851,
2872, 2876, 2880, 2934, 2938,
2958-2959, 2963, 2990, 3009-
3010, 3015, 3025, 3034, 3067-
3068, 3083, 3149, 3151-3152,
3169, 3201-3202, 3252, 3257,
3295, 3303, 3307, 3355, 3374,
3382, 3396, 3398-3399, 3419,
3422, 3466, 3477, 3481, 3518-
3520, 3530, 3557, 3612, 3614-
3617, 3623-3624, 3706, 3751,
3762, 3787

**Vassar College
(Poughkeepsie)** 1263, 2374,
2998-2999, 3285
Veterinarians 1863
**Vietnamese Conflict (1961-
1975)** 1876, 2552

**Waldorf-Astoria Hotel (New
York City)** 2812
Wall Street (New York City)
15, 122, 197, 217, 237, 356,
579, 641, 746, 805, 879, 934,
1421, 1448, 1488, 1686, 1825,
1945, 1976, 2059-2061, 2447,
2704-2705, 2737, 2837, 3034,
3084-3085, 3245, 3280, 3294,
3306, 3391, 3423, 3459, 3463,
3721 **See also:
Business and business
people.**
War of 1812 7, 148, 309,
316, 690, 766, 854, 1682,
2180, 2441, 2532, 3029, 3042,
3332, 3349, 3501, 3516
**Washington, George (1732-
1799)** 1072, 3091, 3275
Weiser, Conrad (1696-1760)
2435, 3090
Welsh 3310-3311
West Point 111, 169, 266,
488-489, 567, 719, 1042-1043,
1140, 1184, 1422, 1469, 1480,
1824, 1955, 2113, 2224-2226,
2816-2819, 2932, 2936-2937,
West Point (cont.)
3086, 3158, 3254-3255, 3416,
3495, 3517, 3730
Whitman, Walt (1819-1892)
3622
Wildlife conservation 2349
**Wilkinson, Jemima (1758-
1819)** 3153
Wine and wine making 346,
2181, 3287

Women's rights See:
Feminism, women's rights.
Working class 23, 31-32, 55,
57-58, 61-62, 64-70, 74, 76,
112, 123, 177, 181, 217, 249-
250, 254, 312, 344, 409, 436,
450, 477, 509-511, 522, 541,
553, 568, 651, 675, 726, 869-
871, 928, 967, 1013, 1029,
1033, 1035, 1053, 1084, 1193,
1197-1198, 1216, 1229, 1240,
1306, 1340, 1364, 1378, 1501,
1568, 1702-1703, 1739, 1891,
1899, 1936, 1957, 1974, 2054,
2075, 2084, 2090-2091, 2097,
2109, 2115, 2144, 2163, 2176,
2192, 2214-2215, 2220, 2251,
2259, 2297, 2299, 2352, 2370,
2422, 2456, 2458, 2479, 2557-
2558, 2588, 2593-2595, 2597,
2628, 2644, 2673, 2733, 2741,
2756, 2758, 2790, 2869, 2894,
2914, 2940-2942, 2955, 2978,
2996, 3018, 3028, 3057, 3092-
3093, 3109, 3119, 3186, 3200,
3202, 3207, 3219, 3262, 3328-
3329, 3401, 3413, 3438, 3461,
3475, 3479, 3490, 3508, 3543,
3627, 3735, 3775-3777

World War (1914-1918)
238, 240a, 894, 951, 961,
1443, 1737, 1849, 1907, 1947,
2179, 2189, 2314, 2416, 2719,
2725, 2734, 2772, 2924, 3143,
3154a, 3362, 3428, 3541,
3547, 3638, 3668

World War (1939-1945)
739, 1413, 1606, 1650, 2553,
2740, 2866, 2910, 2972, 3770

Wright, Silas (1795-1847)
154

Writers. See: Authors;
Journalism and journalists.

**Zenger, John Peter (1697-
1746)** 3225

TITLE INDEX

Beyond the shining river   626
Beyond the sunset   3103
B'hoys of New York, The   461
Big Abel and the Little Manhattan   2269
Big barn, The   991
Big dig, The   2322
Big Eyes   136
Big freeze   2646
Big town, The   2025
Big town round-up, The   2785
Bildad Road   2920
Bill Grimm's progress   3725
Billtry   785
Billy Duane   2271
Billy Phelan's greatest game   1920
Billy's mother   1038
Birds of prey   1667
Bishop in the back seat, The   3537
Bishop murder case, The   3441
Bits of broken china   1061
Bitterwood   1408
Black Adonis, A   2907
Black Cross Clove, The   2164
Black Eagle, The.   See note under
     Item #1796
Black Eagle mystery, The   339
Black Friday   1780
Black gown, The   1463
Black ice   3356
Black lamb, The   424
Black light   1480a
Black oxen   130
Black-plumed riflemen, The   762
Black Sadie   528
Black sheep   2665
Black stream   652
Black summer   1455
Black sun   1885
Black, the grey and the gold, The
     1184
Blacker the berry, The   3324
Blackwater spirits   2403
Blades   2309
Blanche Vernon   3119
Bleeding scissors, The   1132
Blind alleys   1018

Blind bow-boy, The   3455
Blind fury   1334
Blind girl, The.   See note under
     Item #1037
Blind goddess, The (Train)   3381
Blind goddess, The (Tyler)   3425
Blind lead, A   2182
Blind road, The   1354
Blindfold   1821
Blonde is dead, The.   See note under
Item #841
Blondes and brunettes   1730
Blood money   2813
Blood solstice   2003
Blood sugar   862
Bloodied Ivy, The   1342
Blow at the heart, The   1329
Blue blood   1825
Blue blood and red   3068
Blue lacquered box, The   3751
Blue scarab, The   35
Blueprint of a dream   3377
Blythe girls, The   1647
Boardman family, The   3541
Bobbed hair   329
Bodkin   2369
Bohemia invaded   1178
Bohemian, The   833
Bolted door, The   1293
Bond, The   354
Book of Evelyn, The   340
Book of knowledge, The   1433
Book of St. Nicholas, The   2659
Bootmaker of Fifth Avenue, The
     2718
Border iron   287
Borgia blade, The   2944
Born aristocrat, A   3650
Born of flame   2677
Boss and how he came to rule New
     York, The   2080
Both were mistaken   801
Bounder, The   1607
Bow of orange ribbon, The   213
Bowery murder   3128
Bowl of night, The   989

Boxwood maze, The 2726
Boy broker, The 2447
Boy crazy 2687
Boy in the sun, The 2906
Boy Scouts of Snow-Shoe Lodge,
    The 1632
Boy Scouts of the Eagle Patrol, The
    2667
Boy soldiers of 1812, The 3332
Boy spies of old New York, The
    2586
Boy who looked ahead, The 3121
Boyds of Black River, The 992
Boys in the block, The 1013
Boys of Fort Schuyler, The 2587
Boys of winter, The 3056
Boys' revolt, The 2588
Bracknell's law 1584
Brake up 2560
Bramble bush, The 1253
Brass bowl, The 3470
Brave and bold 54
Brave Tom 1028
Brazen calf, The 1179
Brazen star, The 3313
Bread givers 3776
Bread line, The 2624
Breaking the ring 1748
Brennan's Point 2181
Brewster's millions 2310
Brian Blonday. See note under Item
    #764
Briarcliff Manor 2965
Bride dined alone, The 1916
Bride laughed once, The 2968
Bride of a moment, The 3565
Bride of Fort Edward, The 159
Bride of the northern wilds, The
    763
Bridget 344
Brigantine, The 403
Bright battalions, The 389
Bright intervals 1680
Bright tiger 1317
Brilliant kids 1616
Bringing out Barbara 3396

Britz, of Headquarters 190
Broadway; a novel 969
Broadway butterfly murders, The
    320
Broadway interlude 9
Broadway Jones 2248
Broadway melody, The 2012
Broadway murders, The 915
Broke heart blues 2512a
Broken snare, The 2086
Bronze Buddha, The 796
Brook Farm 413
Brooklyn bachelor, A 2051
Brother Jonathan 2469
Brother of the wind 3731
Brother Owl 1596
Brother to the enemy 3138
Brotherly Love Unlimited 1692
Brown-Laurel marriage, The 144
Brown moth, The 1364
Brown stone front, A (Fulton)
    1255
Brown studies 1571
Brownstone front (Gabriel) 1260
Brute, The 2002
Buccaneers, The 1877
Buchanan's wife 1203
Buckskin baronet 3667
Buff and blue 3180
Bugles in the night 264
Bullet proof 841
Bungalow Nine 2522
'Burkeses Army' 2114
Burning spring, The 2924
Burning witches 836
Burnt offering (Lockridge) 2128
Burnt offerings (Marasco) 2235
Burton 1750
Bury the hatchet 2147
Business of life, The 583
But not for love 3272
Butler's story, The 3382
Butterfly net, The 3058
Buttes Landing 2845
Button, Button 927
Button's Inn 3357

Cousins, The 2323
Cover charge 3747
Covered bridge, The 2695
Cow Neck rebels, The 1202
Cowardice Court 2312
Cowboy of the Ramapos 1411
Cowkind 2699
Crazy Luce 737
Crazy man 330
Creeping tides, The 1873
Crescendo 259
Cries in the night 3505
Crime in Car 13, The 572
Crime incarnate 3568
Crime of Henry Vane, The 3201
Crime of the century, The 2607
Crime tears out 3560
Crimson goddess, The 546
Crimson thread, The 2039
Crimson tide, The 586
Crimsoned millions 3710
Crisis in the Catskills 333
Crooked 1216
Crooked Elm, The 1583
Crooked mile, The 1059
Crooked shadow 3162
Cross currents 2742
Cross of heart's desire, The 2623
Croton waters 1451
Crow; a novel 3198
Crow-Step 1233
Crowded out o' Crofield 3212
Crucible, The 2176
Cruise of the 'Ghost' 45
Cruising on the St. Lawrence 3334
Crum Elbow folks 207
Cry havoc 3184
Cry in the city, A 3717
Cry in the night 2779
Cub reporter, The 3744
Cubical city, The 1161
Curious case of Marie Dupont, The
    2170
Curved blades, The 3570
Custom of the country, The 3615
Cut; a story of West Point 567

Cynthia Codentry 2651
Cynthia Wakeham's money 1383

Dab Kinzer 3213
Daddy's widow 2763
Dalzells of Daisydown, The 311
Dame Fortune smiled 208
Damnation of Theron Ware, The
    1237
Damned; the intimate story of a
    girl 792
Dan the detective 55
Dance magic 1901
Dancehall 673
Dancing Feather, The 1752
Danger mark, The 587
Daphne decisions, The 2524
Dark arbor, The 3073
Dark beneath the pines, The 1022
Dark destination. See note under
    Item #2754
Dark Eagke 1498a
Dark Hollow 1384
Dark mirror, The 3471
Dark mother, The 1228
Dark places 88
Darkness and dawn 1049
Darrel of the Blessed Isles 147
Dash of red paint, A 3709
Daughter of Adam, A 1500
Daughter of Eve, A 1968
Daughter of humanity, A 3109
Daughter of Judas, A 2980
Daughter of silence, A 1081
Daughter of the house, The 3571
Daughter of the Huguenots, A 610
Daughter of the philistines, A 356
Daughter of the Revolution, A 3088
Daughter of the tenements, A 3369
Daughter of Thespis, A 234
Daughter of two worlds, A 3010
Daughters of the Revolution 3302
Dave Morell's battery 1338
Dave's daughter 655
David Harum 3598
Dawn at Shanty Bay, The 1990

Ghosts' high noon, The   3578

Ghosts of their ancestors, The
2389

Giant Jack …   See note under Item
#767

Giant's house, The   2755

Gift horse murders, The   1839

Gilded Fly, The   2664

Gilded rose, The   622

Gilded way, The   2234

Gilt-edged guilt   3579

Gin Lane   381

Gingham rose, A   3743

Girl for Danny, A   112

Girl from Arizona, The   2829

Girl from Sunset Ranch, The   2245

Girl I left behind me, The   2390

Girl in golden rags, The   591

Girl in his house, The   2195

Girl in the death seat, The.   See note
under Item #2485

Girl in the mirror, The   1864

Girl of the guard line, The   3496

Girl on the best seller list, The   2346

Girl Scouts in the Adirondacks
2927

Girl who cast out fear, The   3135

Girl who had to die, The   1619

Girl who trod on a loaf, The   822

Girl who wrote, A   782

Girl with the blue sailor, The   3188

Girls of a feather   215

Girl's ordeal, A   2101

Girls together   315

Glanmore   644

Glenelvan   2392

Gloria victis   2394

Glorified   3554

Glorious hope, The   491

Glory of Peggy Harrison, The   2756

Gloved hand, The   3189

Gloyne murder, The   638

Go and catch a falling star   2857

Go forth and find   2397

God and the others   707

God bless the child   1108

God is my broker   3423

God of Gotham, A   240

Goddess girl, The   973

God's puppets   631

Going for the gold   2034

Going to Patchogue   2321

Gold; a novel   780

Gold by Gold   1360

Gold Coast, The   873

Gold-Killer   2768

Gold-laced coat, The   2565

Gold must be tried by fire   2214

Gold of the gods   2821

Golden Age Hotel, The   3164

Golden calf, The   357

Golden Feather   1367

Golden flood, The   2056

Golden house, The   3518

Golden ladder, The (Hughes)   1698

Golden ladder, The (Potter)   2751

Golden season, The   137

Golden slipper and other problems
for Violet Strange, The   1387

Golden squaw, The   3613

Golden unicorn, The   3658

Golden wildcat, The   3669

'Goldfish, The'   3385

Gone tomorrow   922

Gonna take a homicidal journey   3002

Good Americans   1512

Good bad girl, The   3447

Good of the wicked, The   1936

Goodbye Rosie   2340

Gotham and the Gothamites   3430

Grace Dudley   2697

Grail brothers, The   1262

Grain of dust, The   2707

Gramercy Park; a story …   3740

Grand illusion   3723a

Grandfather stories   26

Grandison Mather   1492

Grandma   1362

Grapevine   3161

Grass on the mountain   2097

Grass roots   232

Grave undertaking   2295

Mahoney million, The   3364
Maid and wife   250
Maid-at-arms, The   597
Maid of Maiden Lane, The   218
Maid of Montauk   3677
Maid of old Manhattan, A   1988
Maid of old New York, A   219
Maid of the Mohawk   2807
Maid of the Saranac, The   766
Main stream, The   2427
Mainspring, The   2204
Maison De Shine, The   1405
Major André   169
Make way for romance   1716
Making money   1826
Making of a fortune, The   3146
Making of a man, The.   See note
    under Item #3760
Making of a stockbroker, The
    2058
Making of George Groton   239
Making of Jane, The   1027
Malaeska   3174
Mammon of unrighteousness, The
    358
"Mammy Rosie"   168
Mam'zelle Beauty   736
Man and his money, A   1781
Man behind the door, The   1439
Man can build a house, A   653
Man crazy   2516
Man from the West, The   2769
Man in Lonely Land, The   345
Man in search of a wife, A   3027
Man in the jury box, The   2580
Man in the shadows   721
Man nobody knows, The   1461
Man of two minds, A   446
Man they hanged, The   598
Man who convicted himself, The
    2581
Man who killed Fortescue, The
    3238
Man who never blundered, The
    1335
Man who outlived himself, The

3359
Man who slept all day, The   2832
Man with a thumb, The   1688
Man with an honest face, The   3595
Man without principle, A   3294
Manchester boys   412
Mandarin's sapphire, The   2239
Manhattan cocktail   1646
Manhattan fever   414
Manhattan night   3733
Manhattan transfer   936
Manhattaneers, The   3466
Manikin, The   3006
Manitou's daughter   2049
Mannequin   1741
Manowen   348
Man's calling, A   1292
Man's courage   3488
Man's enemies, A   3297
Man's hearth, A   1758
Man's will, A   1091
Man's world, A   451
Manville murders, The   1156
Many are the travelers   2354
Many mansions   2188
Many waters   3045
Marathon mystery, The   3191
Marching against the Iroquois   3339
Marcia   1970
Marco Polo's travels … On the Erie
    Canal   1
Marguerite's mistake   917
Mariette in ecstasy   1482
Marion Darche   733
Marionettes   1356
Marital liability, A   3393
Marjorie Huntingdon   261
Mark of Cain, The (Comstock)   671
Mark of Cain, The (Wells)   3582
Mark of Seneca Basin   2019
Marked "personal"   1392
Marriage bed, The   632
Marriage guest, The   274
Married above her   2246
Married in mask   3512
Married money   2757

Married or single? 3032

Marsena 1241

Marsh lights 1727

Marston murder case, The 3237

Martha by-the-day 2115

Martha's mistake 375

Martin Brook 241

Mary Allen 2258

Mary and Hugo. See note under
    Item #3111

Mary Beach 2259

Mary Elmer 3631

Mary Kale 3070

Mary Moreland 3460

Mary Regan 3014

Mary Tracy's fortune 2950

Mask, The 1768

Masked longing 2877

Masks off at midnight 3706

Mason and his rangers 1416

Massacre, The 3494

Master hand, A 786

Master influence, The 2330

Master of life, The 2098

Master of mysteries, The 484

Master of silence, The 155

Masters of the peaks, The 91

Mastery, The 2178

Matricide's daughter, The 767

Matt Tyler's chronicle 3548

Matter of millions, A 1393

Maude Baxter 1667

Max Fargus 1827

May-Day in New York 3126

May Iverson's career 1866

Mayor of New York, The 1376

McAllister and his double 3390

Me and Kev 308

Me and thee 2308

Mediator, The 3168

Medusa's head 162

Meeting Luciano 1050a

Meladore 175

Member guest, The 2862

Memoirs of a water-drinker. See
    note under Item #965

Men are strange lovers 2923

Men atwhiles are sober 2798

Men call it love 2946

Men of Morgan 2827

Mercy of fate, The 2331

Mere adventurer, A 1548

Merrilie Dawes 3136

Merry hearts 81

Merrymakers in New York, The
    3707

Metropolis, The 3083

Metropolitans, The 947

Metropolites, The 3151

Mickey Finn idyls 1804

Midge, The 456

Midnight Cry, The 2638

Midnight passenger, The 2984

Midnight patriot 2654

Midnight Queen, The 2111

Midshipman Paulding 3029

Mike's island 364

Mild barbarian, A 1092

Mildred's cadet 1469

Millbrook romance, A 916

Millionaire baby, The 1394

Millionairess, The 2789

Millions 2736

Mimosa smokers, The 1813

Minerva's maneuvoers 2155

Minglestreams 6

Minisink 2083

Minister of the world, A 2260

Minister's wife, The 2640

Minute boys of Long Island, The
    2599

Minute boys of New York City, The
    2600

Minute boys of the Mohawk Valley,
    The 2601

Miracle in the wilderness 1264

Miriam Balestier 1093

Mis MacRae 1593

Miseries of New York, The 1755

Miser's heir, The 2462

Misplaced lives 3482

Miss 318 1702

Miss 318 and Mr. 37 1703
Miss Bagg's secretary 488
Miss Betty of New York 863
Miss Blake's husband 1867
Miss Dulcie from Dixie 2784
Miss Emily 2458a
Miss Fizzlebury's new girl 832
Miss Frances Baird, detective 1893
Miss Frances Merley 754
Miss Gwynne, bachelor 1820
Miss Janet's old house 2492
Miss Jerry 304
Miss Livingston's companion 893
Miss Matilda Archambeau Van Dorn
    749
Miss Melinda's opportunity 522
Miss Nobody from Nowhere 1868
Miss Richard's boy 1633
Miss Sylvester's marriage 614
Miss Varian of New York 781
Miss Withers regrets 2631
Miss Worden's hero 2955
Misses Elliot of Geneva, The 3127
Missing link, The 3583
Missing sisters 2213
Mission of death, The 3513
Mission of Victoria Wilhelmina, The
    2209
Misteri di Mulberry, I 625
Model wife, A 568
Modern Babylon, A 3094
Modern marriage, A 2024
Modern Othello, The 372
Modern pharisee, A 831
Modern wizard, A 2608
Moderns, The 807
Mohawk 2940
Mohawk Valley 3561
Mohawk woman 2839
Molly, bless her 2240
Mona in the promised land 1810
Money changers, The 3084
Money for love 1573
Money makers, The (Keenan) 1899
Money makers, The (Klein) 1978
Monique 959

Monkey's tail, The 2991
Monster of Snowden Hall, The
    3714
Montanye 3216
Montgomery's children 2690
Moon Harvest 565
Moon lady, The 1728
Mooncalf murders, The 554
Mooney 2355
Moral pirates, The 46
More lives than one 3584
More miles 1917
More than welcome 355
Morgan rifleman, A 2490
Morning's mail, A 679
Mortgage on the hip-roof house,
    The 3360
Moosefoot, the brave 630
Mostly canallers 997
Mother (Wister) 3721
Mother, The (Asch) 124
Mother; a story (Norris) 2500
Mothers cry 534
Mother's recompense, The 3619
Mother's son 896
Mott Street Poker Club, The 3414
Motto for murder 2193
Mount Allegro 2231
Mr. Arnold 2184
Mr. Benedict's lion 998
Mr. Billy Buttons 2047
Mr. Grosvenor's daughter 3755
Mr. Guelpa … 3320
Mr. Incoul's misadventure 2958
Mr. Jackson 1406
Mr. Oldmixon 1477
Mr. Splitfoot 2301
Mr. Teach goes to war 690
Mr. Trumper Bromleigh presents No
    ugly duckling 576
Mr. Winkfield 2438
Mrs. Balfame 131
Mrs. Beneker 3558
Mrs. Clift-Crosby's niece 1734
Mrs. Harold Stagg 1372
Mrs. Herndon's income 523